ALAN ROGERS'
GOOD CAMPS GUIDE

EUROPE
1999

Quality Camping and Caravanning Sites

Compiled by: Deneway Guides & Travel Ltd
Cover design: Design Section, Frome
Cover photography: Ésterel Corniche (Var), Côte d'Azur, France
by Michael Busselle

Clive Edwards, Lois Edwards & Sue Smart have asserted
their rights to be identified as the authors of this work.

First published in this format 1998

© Haynes Publishing & Deneway Guides & Travel Ltd 1998

Published by: Haynes Publishing, Sparkford, Nr Yeovil, Somerset BA22 7JJ
in association with
Deneway Guides & Travel Ltd, West Bexington, Dorchester, Dorset DT2 9DG

British Library Cataloguing-in-Publication Data:
A catalogue record for this book is available from the British Library.

ISBN: 0 901586 95 1

Printed in Great Britain by J H Haynes & Co Ltd

Contents

EASTERN EUROPE
We have inspected a number of campsites in the Czech and Slovak
Republics, Slovenia and Poland, but lack of space and limited
demand precludes us from featuring these in this edition of our
guide. We are, however, pleased to provide reports on these sites to
anyone interested, on receipt of a large (A4) SAE and a cheque or
PO for £2.00 to cover our production costs.

Foreword

"Each report comprises not only an honest appraisal of the site in question, but also lists all the vital details" - so said Motor Caravan Magazine when they reviewed our Guides in their publication and these few words sum up almost precisely our philosophy over more than 30 years.

The Europe guide features reports on all the main countries (17) in Western Europe. Readers should note that lack of space means that we can only include a fairly limited selection of sites in Britain and France in this guide. A much larger selection of sites in Britain, Ireland and France can be found in our specialist guides for **Britain and Ireland** and **France** respectively. During '98 we also launched a completely new guide, the **'Alan Rogers Guide to Rented Accommodation on Quality Sites in France,'** which is proving very popular with those who don't own their own caravan, motorcaravan or tent, and with campers or caravanners who have friends or relatives who would like to go on holiday with them but have no accommodation of their own This new guide is available from book shops or direct from Haynes Publishing (01963 440635, price £7.99, ISBN no. 0901 586 617).

The introduction of our **Discount Voucher Scheme** in '96 proved to be very successful and it was extended in '97 and '98. For 1999 we are pleased to have been able to negotiate an even wider range of discounts for readers, and now include a seven-part discount voucher in every guide which gives readers opportunities to enjoy substantial savings on travel, breakdown, caravan or motorcaravan insurance, on site fees at certain sites, and on travel arrangements when booked through Sites Abroad or the Caravan & Camping Service (whereby they can recover the full cost of the guide). Full details of the 1999 Discount Vouchers are on the vouchers themselves. We would remind readers that the vouchers in this edition are valid only for use during the period 1 Jan - 31 Dec '99.

We hope that the innovations and 'added value' arrangements we have introduced over the past few years will make the 1999 edition of our Europe Guide even more useful, informative and even better value than previously, and we wish all our readers a very happy and enjoyable camping or caravanning season favoured by good weather!

Lois Edwards Cert.Ed, MA, FTS
Clive Edwards BEd, FTS
Sue Smart   Directors

The Guide's Aims and Principles

In producing all our Guides we have a number of aims and objectives designed to:

- Provide readers with details of well maintained, good quality sites, selected after inspection on merit alone. Sites are not charged for their entry in our guides. We aim to give a straightforward, honest report on which our reputation rests.

- Provide readers with the sort of factual information which, from our own experiences, we would wish to know ourselves; for example, most of us want to know if the sanitary facilities are sufficient and regularly cleaned, if electrical connections are available, what sort of shopping, catering and leisure facilities are provided, and when these facilities are open.

- Provide some 'insight' into what a site is like - to try to convey a picture in words that will give the reader an impression of the kind of atmosphere or ambience they can expect. This aspect of our reporting is the most difficult to achieve because what appeals to one person may have exactly the opposite affect on another, but the large number of readers' reports and comments we receive each year is reassuring. We make no claims to infallibility, but this feedback from readers suggests that we get it right most of the time.

- To present the factual information and our assessment of a site in a form that is easily understood, without the use of symbols. Many guides seem to rely on masses of symbols and require their readers to be expert code-breakers. Our Guides have no symbols, and therefore no 'key'.

- To provide basic information concerning tourism, particularly camping and caravanning, in each of the countries featured in the Guide and tourist attractions to visit near the sites themselves.

- To report on our own experiences in respect of ferry services.

- To provide general information on Camping and Caravanning in Europe, the legal requirements and necessary formalities. This is particularly aimed at those who have never camped abroad before but, as the information is regularly up-dated, it should also provide a useful 'aide-memoire' for the more experienced.

- To provide readers with the opportunity to benefit from a range of discounts through our new **Discount Voucher Scheme,** as detailed above and on the attached vouchers.

Quality Assurance

Having stated our objectives concerning the provision of both factual information and the more subjective aspect of 'insight', readers may be interested to know how we set about this. Firstly, we are a small organisation with only four full-time staff and a small team of part-time Site Assessors. The majority of the sites featured in our Guides have been recommended by readers initially, after which they are visited by one of our Site Assessors *before* they are featured in the Guides.

All our 1,500 or more sites are inspected regularly every one or two years (occasionally every three years for the more inaccessible ones) to monitor standards and changes, and our reports are updated accordingly. Sites are also required to return a detailed questionnaire which is used to up-date factual information concerning prices, opening dates, etc. To ensure that our reports are consistent, we also undertake a programme of site visits each year designed to monitor the situation as a whole and to make sure that there is a high degree of uniformity in terms of our assessment and reporting procedures.

Currently, our small team of dedicated part-time Site Assessors, all experienced campers or caravanners, specialising in particular countries and/or areas comprises:

Rosemary & George Boyce	Netherlands, Finland	Gerry Ovenden	Switzerland, Austria, Italy
Gordon & Joyce Pearce	Scandinavia, Belgium	Keith Smart	Germany
	Luxembourg	Kate Sutton	Spain
Colin & Maggie Samms	Spain, Portugal	Tibor Toka	Hungary

Our thanks are due to them for the many miles they have travelled, their patience with our detailed site reports and their commitment to the philosophy of the guides.

We must also thank our readers for their reports and recommendations, particularly in terms of identifying potential new sites. The other points you raise all receive individual attention, although we cannot always respond as quickly as we would wish, particularly in the summer when are away on site visits and in the autumn when we are literally working eighteen hours a day putting the following year's Guides together. We do follow them up and do try to let you know the outcome.

On the subject of complaints about any of our featured sites, please bear in mind the following - we are the authors of the Guide, and we have no contractual arrangements with any of our featured sites, so we cannot actually intervene in any dispute between our readers and any featured site(s). In the event of you having a complaint about a site, ideally this should be addressed to the *campsite owner in person, at the time* - that way you stand the best chance of getting any problem resolved quickly. Of course we are always interested to know about any serious problems encountered by our readers in respect of a particular campsite, as they may well influence our choice of sites for the following year.

How to Use the Guide

The Guide is divided firstly by **country**, subsequently (in the case of larger countries) by region. These are both indicated by the page title lines which should help readers locate their area of interest fairly quickly, although for a particular area the town index provides more direct access. Regions appearing in the title lines are either defined political entities, for example the Départements in France, or more familiar tourist regions such as the Costas in Spain.

The **Index** provides an invaluable source of reference, particularly when used in conjunction with the **site number, grid reference** and appropriate **map**. These maps are necessarily diagrammatic, showing the various countries and regions within them, and the approximate location of each site by reference to its site number. Their use is facilitated by dividing each map into 'grid squares', each of which is referenced by two co-ordinates in the form of letters of the alphabet (top line first). These co-ordinate letters are reproduced alongside the site name in the main index. We emphasise however that our maps are intended as a quick reference to the approximate position of sites, and not as basis for navigation.

The **Title Line** for each site seeks to provide the reader with a reasonably accurate idea of the campsite location on a medium-scale map, such as the Michelin Atlas. More precise details can be found in the 'How to find it' section below the individual site reviews.

Notes on information provided in the site reviews

'Site' and 'Pitch' - the word 'site' is used to describe the campsite itself (in Britain more commonly referred to as 'parks), and the word 'pitch' is used to define individual places on the campsite.

Distances - these are quoted in kilometres and metres.

Opening Dates - we give the dates when the site should be open - if we know that facilities on the site (such as restaurants) are open for a shorter period, this is mentioned. However, in some countries (Spain is a frequent culprit), site operators tend to close facilities almost at random. It is a good idea to check with the site first if you are concerned as to whether a certain facility (or even the site!) will be open.

Sanitary Facilities - in years past continental sanitary facilities were by far the biggest cause of complaint from British visitors, but in recent years facilities in most European countries have improved enormously and, in many cases, are superior to those in the UK. We have tried to give brief details without expanding into a detailed survey. When describing WCs the word `British' denotes the normal (pedestal) type of WC found in the UK - it may or may not have a lifting seat. Some European sites have toilets of the squatting type with a hole at ground level - nowadays these are usually known as `Turkish' style lavatories. So far as personal washing facilities are concerned, on the plus side we normally say if washbasins are in private cabins, whereas on the minus side we say if only cold water is provided. Virtually all sites in this guide have good hot showers, sinks for washing dishes and clothes (cold/hot water). Many sites have washing machines, dryers, etc, and mention is made of these where they exist.

Charges - Some sites have fixed their prices for the following year when our Guides go to print in November, but many have not. We state which year prices refer to, except in those cases when we only have, and can thus only provide, an indication or guide to charges. Some sites accept payment by credit card, which we indicate. In general (not just at campsites) it is wise to check acceptability first, as some of these magnetic type cards are incompatible with European electronic readers.

Self-catering accommodation - e.g. mobile homes, static caravans, chalets, bungalows, apartments, hotel rooms, gites, etc. - in short any accommodation provided by the site which is available for rent. The range of accommodation and prices is far too extensive for us to describe in our individual site reviews, but we do try to mention if such accommodation is available, firstly because some readers may be interested to rent this type of accommodation, and secondly because other readers prefer sites which cater exclusively, or mainly, for campers or caravanners with their own tent or caravan.

Reservations - This is an important subject, but it is difficult to describe comprehensively the various systems operated by all the individual sites. We therefore indicate in our reports whether a site accepts advance bookings or not and, if so, the most important special features of their system. It is important to distinguish between a `booking fee' and a `deposit'. The former is a fee payable by you to the site in addition to the cost of staying on the site and will always be forfeited if you cancel. A deposit, on the other hand, is a payment in advance to be deducted from your final bill. Whether or not a deposit will be refundable if you cancel is dependent on several factors and cancellation insurance is a wise precaution. In general it is best not to send money in the first instance, but rather to write to the site asking for a reservation. If they can offer what you want they will normally write asking for a deposit and/or booking fee to confirm the booking. Most sites will now accept a Eurocheque, obtainable from your bank. Several organisations, including of course the camping tour operators, such as Eurocamp Independent, the Caravan and Camping Service and Select Site Reservations operate systems whereby you can book sites abroad from the UK and details are given in their respective advertisements.

In co-operation with Eurocamp Independent we are planning to launch the Eurocamp/Alan Rogers **Campsite Internet Reservation Service** during 1999 which will enable you to book many of the sites featured in our Guides direct from your computer terminal.

As to the question of when it is necessary to make a reservation, the peak season in Europe generally runs from about 10 July to 20 August, with some variations between individual countries. Outside of that peak period you stand a good chance of finding space without having booked in advance, except in some particularly popular areas. Occasionally we get complaints from readers who have booked (and sometimes also paid) in advance at a particular site, but after being there for a day or two decide to leave, sometimes because of bad weather, but then have difficulty in recovering their advance payment. The only advice that we can offer in this respect is to consider very carefully the wisdom of parting with a substantial amount of money in advance unless you know the site personally and are prepared to stay for the whole of the period you have booked irrespective of the weather. Frankly the chances of a refund if you book for two weeks but leave after two days are remote and certainly there is no mechanism by which we can assist in such cases.

Telephone numbers The numbers quoted assume you are actually IN the country concerned, and are normally nine or ten digit numbers beginning with an `0' (or in Spain, `9'). For most European countries, if you are 'phoning from the UK, this `0' should be disregarded and replaced by the appropriate Country Code - for details refer to your telephone directory. **However**, during '98, changes were made in respect of dialling codes for **Italy** and **Spain**. To call from the UK it is now necessary to dial the relevant International code (00 39 for Italy and 00 34 for Spain, followed by the local Area code IN FULL, then the number of the person being called.

Time: Apart from a period of about three weeks during October, the clocks in most European countries are one hour ahead of those in Britain.

Camping and Caravanning in Europe

When visiting sites featured in this Guide you should not encounter any particular problems and the formalities now required for visiting countries in Western Europe are few. The following information may however be useful, particularly for those who do not take their cars abroad all that often.

Sites in Europe - Whether you have a caravan, tent, trailer tent or motorcaravan you will seldom encounter any difficulty with admission to a particular site, with the possible exception of some sites where the terrain is unsuitable for certain vehicles, such as large motorhomes of the American type or occasionally twin axle caravans.

Essential Documents and Equipment - The documentation required to take a vehicle abroad is now minimal, and the following list covers both the essential and the advisable items:

- [ ] **Passport:** a valid full Passport is essential - details from the Passport Office or main post offices.

- [ ] **Motor Insurance:** a Green Card is no longer compulsory for countries within the EC but it is strongly recommended, and is actually a requirement for some non-EC countries. Your insurance company or broker will advise. Similarly a Bail-Bond is still recommended for Spain

- [ ] **Driving Licence:** a full (not provisional) British licence of the new type (pink and green) is sufficient in most countries, but the old-style British licence is no longer acceptable in several countries, including Spain, Italy, and Austria, without a translation in the local language. The alternative and essential for most East European countries is an International Driving Permit (IDP) - obtainable from the AA or RAC.

- [ ] **Car Registration Document** (log book).

- [ ] Letter granting **authority to drive if** the vehicle is not your own.

- [ ] **GB sign** on rear of vehicle and on rear of caravan or trailer.

- [ ] **Red Warning Triangle** - from motor accessory shops.

- [ ] **First-Aid kit.**

- [ ] **Spare set of vehicle light bulbs.**

- [ ] **Form E1-11:** this form, obtainable from main Post Offices, extends National Health Insurance to the continent, although it may provide for recovery of only about 80% of any medical expenses, so independent medical expenses insurance cover is a wise precaution - see below.

- [ ] **Travel/Breakdown Insurance:** not absolutely essential, but strongly recommended - we have negotiated terms for readers with Heritage European Rescueline, one of the most reputable (and competitive) insurers for this type of policy; see details between pages 224/5. The cover can be arranged to include breakdown insurance, personal accident insurance, cancellation insurance and medical expenses cover.

- [ ] **Camping Carnet:** useful (but by no means essential) if you dislike having to lodge your passport with campsite receptions. They can be obtained from various motoring organisations.

EUROPE 1999 - DISCOUNT VOUCHERS

Inside this Guide you will find several different Discount Vouchers which will provide you with potential savings of much more than the cost of the Guide itself!

Voucher A Alan Rogers' Exclusive Offer
At sites in this Guide which have a small Alan Rogers' logo beneath the Site Report, alongside which you will find details of the offer applying to that particular site.

Voucher B Heritage Breakdown and Personal Travel Insurance Discount *(pages 224/5)*

Voucher C Bakers Insurance for Caravan or Motorcaravan Insurance
Write to Bakers at Freepost GR1604, The Quadrangle, Imperial Square, Cheltenham GL50 1BR enclosing the discount voucher.

Voucher D Caravan & Camping Service *(see advertisement on page 377)*

Voucher E Sites Abroad Holidays *(see page 212)*

Voucher F Free copy of the Camping Cheque Catalogue
Send the completed voucher to Camping Cheques, Hartford Manor, Greenbank Lane, Northwich, Cheshire CW8 1HW

Voucher G Chantilly Museums
This voucher entitles the holder to discounts at three museums in France - Musée Condé, Musée Vivant du Cheval and the Aérophile Balloon *(see voucher)*

For full details, see the vouchers and/or the page references above

CAR FERRY INFORMATION

Many operators had not finalised their schedules or fares when we went to press in Nov '98. The following, therefore, is a preliminary list of services for 1999 based on the latest information available. Readers are advised to contact the operators direct (or their local travel agent) in the New Year for definitive details of services to be operated in 1999.

Destination	Ferry Company	Routes	Time
FRANCE	Brittany Ferries	Plymouth-Roscoff	6-8 hrs
		Portsmouth-St Malo	9-11 hrs
		Portsmouth-Caen	7-8 hrs
		Poole-Cherbourg	4-7 hrs
		Cork-Roscoff/St Malo	13 hrs
	Hoverspeed	Dover-Calais	35 mins
		Folkestone-Boulogne	55 mins
	P&O European Ferries	Portsmouth-Le Havre	5¾ hrs
		Portsmouth-Cherbourg - Ferry	5-9 hrs
		Fast craft (May-Oct)	2¾ hrs
	P&O Stena Line	Dover-Calais	45-90 mins
		Newhaven-Dieppe	2-4 hrs
	Condor Ferries	Weymouth-St Malo	2½ hrs
	Irish Ferries	Rosslare-Cherbourg	18 hrs
		Rosslare-Le Havre	5¾ hrs
		Cork-Cherbourg/Le Havre	18-22 hrs
	Eurotunnel	Folkestone-Calais	35/45 mins
BELGIUM	P&O North Sea Ferries	Hull-Zeebrugge	14 hrs
	Hoverspeed	Ramsgate-Ostend	110 mins
NETHERLANDS	P&O North Sea Ferries	Hull-Rotterdam	14 hrs
	P&O Stena Line	Harwich-Hook (ferry)	6-8 hrs
GERMANY	Scandinavian Seaways	Harwich/Newcastle-Hamburg	20-23 hrs
SPAIN	Brittany Ferries	Plymouth-Santander	24 hrs
	P&O European Ferries	Portsmouth-Bilbao	28½ hrs
DENMARK	Scandinavian Seaways	Harwich-Esbjerg	20 hrs
NORWAY	Color Line	Newcastle-Stavanger/Bergen	c. 24 hrs
SWEDEN	Scandinavian Seaways	Harwich/Newcastle-Gothenburg	c. 24 hrs

Ferry Reports

As our France Guide features reports on many of the services to France, we have included in this Guide only those services we have used in the last year to destinations other than France.

Brittany Ferries - Plymouth/Santander

This service is operated by Brittany Ferries flagship, the 'Val de Loire'. Although this is a long crossing, which on the face of it appears relatively expensive, if you are travelling to Spain, Portugal or even the Basque area of France, the higher ferry cost may well be offset by the saving in fuel, autoroute tolls or overnight accommodation en route, so it's well worth making a comparative calculation of the **total** cost of your journey! Facilities on the Val de Loire are almost up to cruise liner standards, and the 24 hour voyage itself can be very enjoyable indeed, with plenty to keep you occupied or pleasantly relaxed - a good choice of restaurants, cinema, sun-decks, etc. all add to the 'cruising' atmosphere.

P&O North Sea Ferries - Hull/Rotterdam and Hull/Zeebrugge

We have used these services on several occasions during the last two or three years, and our opinion is generally favourable. The two ferries on which we have travelled recently (the 'Norstar' and 'Norsea') are designed as a 'floating hotels', with first class facilities, plenty of space and ample entertainment; unfortunately the ticket price no longer includes a five-course evening meal and full English breakfast! The cabins are situated towards the forward end of the ship, away from the public rooms, providing the opportunity of an undisturbed night's sleep. The decor is above average, and there are private facilities; a nice touch was early morning tea served in your cabin, which helps soften the blow of an early start!

Overall, North Sea Ferries provide an excellent service, neatly illustrated by their getting us and our car on-board at Europort (Rotterdam) even though we arrived at the terminal at the precise time that the vessel was due to sail! This route must be a particularly attractive proposition for those living in the north or in Scotland.

Stena Line HSS - Harwich/Hook of Holland - Holyhead/Dun Laoghaire- Stranraer/Belfast

Being frequent travellers on the Stena Line HSS between Ireland and mainland Britain we had no hesitation in using the fast ferry service when introduced on the Harwich/Hook of Holland route. Getting to Holland in 3 hrs 40 mins, the HSS offers an amazing saving of time. This modern efficent service boasts a turn-round time of 30 minutes, precision docking and fast check-in time, also a comfortable, spacious and airy atmosphere on board. Most important to the traveller, it means that final destination may be reached within hours, rather than the next day. The range of facilities on board includes a selection of snack bars and restaurants, lounge bars, business class lounge, Stena shopping and duty free, video lounge, viewing gallery, playroom for children and possibly more, depending on the ship. It goes without saying - the HSS has revolutionized ferry crossings to Holland and Ireland. RB

Color Line - Newcastle/Bergen

Having never previously travelled to Scandinavia by sea, we were quite excited at the prospect of this crossing, and we weren't disappointed, despite the irritation of a two hour check-in time. In fact the two hours are necessary, as vehicles have to be loaded according to their port of disembarkation, because, unlike most ferries, this service calls at several ports. Finally arriving on board, we wished we'd booked a better cabin - the standard inside cabins are pretty small and somewhat claustrophobic, so next time we'll opt for one of the much nicer (but somewhat more expensive) outside cabins. The views, despite some very indifferent weather, as the vessel nosed her way into Bergen were rather spectacular, and we regretted having to disembark at the first port of call instead of being able to enjoy the views as the voyage continued down the coast. All in all a thoroughly enjoyable way to get to Norway. We used the `Venus' which operates the thrice weekly service on this route - although built in 1975, this vessel has been extensively and continuously upgraded and now provides a modern smart and comfortable service in keeping with the length of the crossing. Catering is now of a very high standard; particularly impressive are the good-value Norwegian breakfasts. The whole operation gives the impression of a well-run company. The decor and overall design on board is distinctly different from the cross-channel ferries, so we spent quite a lot of time exploring the ship, sampling the restaurants, etc, hence the time passed all too quickly. We were generally very impressed with everything about this service (even the briefing about disembarkation was presented in a quite amusing fashion!) At first sight the fares might seem rather high, but it must be remembered that this is a crossing that takes the best part of 24 hours, and saves a drive of some 2,000 km. Color's policy is, therefore, to offer a service which is equivalent to a holiday cruise rather than a ferry; reference to the cabin accommodation has already been made, but to be fair there is actually a wide range of overnight accommodation on offer, including four different grades of cabin, bunk-type couchettes, and airline-type reclining seats.

Scandinavian Seaways - Newcastle/Gothenburg - Harwich/Gothenburg

Travelling with Scandinavian Seaways from Newcastle to Gothenburg on the `Princess of Scandinavia' line added 22 hrs cruising time to our journey. This leisurely crossing provided the perfect opportunity to relax and unwind after a hectic, pre-travel rush. Once on board, we found all services to be efficiently run by a friendly crew. Our twin berth outside cabin with en-suite facilities was comfortable, airy and spacious. Catering facilities included an à la carte restaurant offering Scandinavian and German cuisine, the popular Smörgasbord/carvery, a traditional Scandinavian feast, or the cafeteria and bistro is another option. Discounts for children are a plus, with under-4s eating free and under-12s getting 50% discount on buffet meals. The list of on board activities is also extensive with live entertainment, disco, casino, cinema, sauna, solarium, swimming pool, etc. There are shops and a bureau de change; vouchers, received with our travel documents, meant discount on certain duty free items. A most important factor on any journey is the cost, but with fare structuring and book in advance deals, we believe Scandinavian Seaways offers excellent value for money. Arriving in Gothenburg thoroughly refreshed, we also had to agree that the top AA rating awarded to the Princess of Scandinavia is well deserved.

The Channel Tunnel - "Le Shuttle"

Eurotunnel is now firmly established as an alternative to the conventional ferries adding choice between ships, catamaran and hovercraft to those wishing to travel to the continent. In terms of time taken, although the actual crossing time is 35 minutes which, in our experience is always the time taken from when the wheels begin to turn at Folkestone and stop at Calais, if one wishes to take advantage of duty free sales, a coffee or a meal, the real time taken is about the same as travelling on the surface. It is a very smooth operation, the height of the carriages which transport vehicles and the good lighting, soon dispel any fears of claustrophobia which some travellers may have expected. Although it is possible to 'turn up and go', booking at least 48 hours in advance is recommended. Arriving 'on spec' may result in higher fares and delay, particularly at peak times, and missing out on cheaper promotional fares. This is particularly the case with those towing caravans or using larger motorhomes when space is scarce.

AUSTRIA

Centrally situated in Europe, Austria is primarily known for two contrasting attractions - its capital Vienna with its fading Imperial glories, and the variety of its Alpine hinterland. Ideally suitable for all year round visiting, either viewing the spectacular scenery and enjoying the various opportunities for winter sports or visiting the historical sites and sampling the cultural attractions. For further information about Austria contact:

Austrian National Tourist Office, 30 Saint George Street, London W1R 0AL.

Tel: 0171 629 0461. Fax: 0171 499 6038.

Population
7,915,000 (1993), density 94.2 per sq. km.

Capital
Vienna (Wien).

Climate
Austria has a moderate Central European climate. The winter season is from December to March (in higher regions the end of May) and warm clothing, including waterproof shoes or boots, is a necessity. Even in summer the evenings in mountain resorts can be quite cool.

Language
German is the usual language but English is widely spoken and understood.

Currency
The unit of currency is the Austrian Schilling which is divided into 100 Groschen. There are bank notes to the value of 5,000, 1,000, 500, 100, 50 and 20 schillings, coins of 20, 10, 5 and 1 schillings and 50 and 10 groschen.

Banks
Banking hours are mainly 08.00 - 12.30 hrs and 13.30 - 15.00 hrs on Mon, Tues, Wed and Fri. Thurs hours are 08.00 - 12.30 and 13.30 - 17.30.
Credit Cards: Most major credit cards are accepted in the larger cities and tourist areas. Travellers cheques and Eurocheques are widely accepted.

Post Offices
Offices are open Monday to Friday 08.00 -12.00 hrs and 14.00 - 18.00 hrs.

Time
GMT plus 1 (summer BST plus 1).

Telephone
To Austria from the UK the code is 0043, ignoring the '0' at the start of the area code. For calls from Austria to the UK the code is 0044.

Public Holidays
New Year; Epiphany; Easter Mon; Labour Day; Ascension; Whit Mon; Corpus Christi; Assumption, 15 Aug; National Day, 26 Oct; All Saints, 1 Nov; Immaculate Conception, 8 Dec; Christmas, 25, 26 Dec.

Shops
Shops open 08.00-18.30 hrs but many close for 2 hours at lunch and 13.00 on Sats except first Sat in every month, when they open to 17.00.

Motoring
Tolls: It is now (from 1 Jan 97) compulsory to purchase a motorway disc. For visiting cars, motorhomes and towed caravans with a combined weight under 3.5 tons a 'weekly' disc costing 70 schillings (valid up to 10 days Thurs midnight to midnight 2 Sundays later) or 'monthly' (valid for 2 consecutive months) at 150 schillings is available. Motorbikes can only purchase a 'monthly' at 80 schillings. They are available at major border crossings, petrol stations and post offices at present and for cash only. Fines for non-compliance are heavy. Previously levied road and tunnel tolls still apply, but a discount of 15% applies to discholders on the S16 Arlberg Tunnel, A13 Brenner - A9 Pyhon and A10 Tauern motorways.

Speed limits: For caravans and motorhomes (3.5t): 31 mph (50 kph) in built up areas, 62 mph (100 kph) other roads (including motor- ways for caravans) and 81 mph (130 kph) for motorhomes on motorways. There is a lower limit of 68 mph (110 kph) between 2200 - 0500 on the A8, A9, A10, A12, A13 and A14. A min. speed of 37 mph (60 kph) applies on roads with a rectangular blue sign showing a white car.

Towing Restrictions: The maximum overall length for car and caravan is restricted to 12 metres. It is also important that your caravan or motorhome is not overloaded.

Parking: Limited parking (blue zones) with max. parking time of 1.5-3 hrs. Parking clocks can be obtained free of charge from tobacconists (Tabak-Trafik), shops or local police stations. However in Vienna, Graz, Linz, Klagenfurt, Salzburg, Innsbruck and a few other cities there is a charge for parking vouchers which can be obtained in banks, some petrol stations and from tobacconists. They must be clearly displayed on the inside of the windscreen.

Overnighting
It is possible to park outside campsites provided permission has been obtained beforehand from the landowner. Except in Vienna and protected rural areas visitors are permitted to sleep in the camping vehicle but local restrictions can apply and campers are not allowed to set up camping equipment beside their vehicle.

Useful addresses

OCC (Osterreichischer Camping Club), Schubertring 1-3, 1010 Wien.
Tel: 01 771 99/1272. Fax: 01 711 99/1498.
OAMTC (Osterreichischer Automobil-Motorradund Touring Club), Schubertring 1-3, 1010 Wien.
Tel: 01/72990.

Tirol and the West

This is the best known area of Austria as far as British visitors are concerned and the most easily accessible part of the country. It has considerable charm and a wealth of scenic, sporting and historical interest as a centre for both winter and summer tourism. Folk-lore entertainment (Tirolerabend) is on offer outdoors in summer and in Gasthof bars and Hotels in winter. Mountain paths are well marked and maintained and local authorities provide information centres in towns and lay-bys. Innsbruck is the famous capital of the region, good camp sites abound and there are many pleasant valleys to explore.

023 Camping Waldcamping, Feldkirch

Good municipal site on edge of town near borders.

Feldkirch lies near the borders with Germany, Switzerland and Liechtenstein and Waldcamping is part of the Gisingen sports stadium on the edge of the town. The Vorarlberg mountains and Bodensee (Lake Constance) are nearby and there are good sporting facilities, including a large outdoor pool with water slides, at the stadium next to the site. Set in a quiet residential suburb, about 4 km from the centre, tall trees surround the site. The 170 tourist pitches are on flat grass, either in the centre, or to the side of the hard road which runs round the camping area. In high season an overflow area may be brought into use (without electricity). There are two well constructed sanitary blocks near the entrance, one of which is open and heated in winter plus an older block at the back of the site. British type WCs. A neat, tidy site which caters for winter skiing and summer touring guests.

How to find it: Follow signs from the centre of town for Gisingen Stadium (4 km.).

General Details: Open all year. 40,000 sq.m. Electricity connections (6A). Shop (May - Sept). Large, heated swimming pool (free for campers). Children's pool and playground. Tennis. Football. Fishing 4 km. Bicycle hire 4 km. Club room. Bar/restaurant 1 km. Washing machines and dryers. Chemical disposal. Motorcaravan services.

Charges 1998: Per person sch. 50 - 61; child (6-14 yrs) 23 - 34; local tax 10, young person 5, child free; caravan 42 - 56, over 6 m. 56 - 70; tent 46 - 56, small tent 29 - 37; motorcaravan 66 - 84; car 33 - 46; m/cycle 25 - 33; electricity 25 (plus 4 per kw. in winter). Credit cards accepted.

Reservations: Write to site. Address: Postfach 564, 6803 Feldkirch. Tel: 05522/74308 (or mobile 0664/4321372). FAX: as phone. E-mail: fbg@montforthaus.felkirch.com.

015 Camping Riffler, Landeck

Small, compact site with good facilities.

This small, pretty site is almost in the centre of the small town of Landeck and, being on the main through route from the Vorarlberg to the Tirol, would serve as a good overnight stop. Square in shape, it has just 45 pitches on either side of hard access roads on level grass, with the main road on one side and the fast flowing river on the other edge. Trees and flowers adorn the site giving good shade. The site is open all year except for May, but static caravans are only allowed to stay in winter. One small section is kept for groups with tents. The single toilet block has been rebuilt to an excellent standard and has British WCs and hot water in washbasins, showers and sinks. There are few other amenities on the site but there is a supermarket just outside the gate and other shops and restaurants about 100 m. away.

How to find it: Site is at the western end of Landeck on the main no. 316 road.

General Details: Open all year except May. 3,000 sq.m. Electricity to all pitches (10A). Small general room. Restaurants and shops 100 m. in village. Children's play area. Table tennis. Fishing. Bicycle hire 500 m. Riding 1 km. Washing machine and dryer. Chemical disposal. Motorcaravan service point.

Charges 1999: Per person sch. 55 - 70; child (5-14 yrs) 50 - 55; car on pitch 30; caravan or motorcaravan 90 - 105; tent 55 - 90; electricity 30; trailer 50; local taxes 16. Less 5% for over 10 days. Winter prices more. No credit cards.

Reservations: Contact site. Address: Bruggenfeldstr. 2, 6500 Landeck. Tel: 05442/624774. FAX: 05442/624775.

022 Ötztal Arena Camp Krismer, Umhausen

Good site in quiet valley, with excellent toilet facilities.

This is a delightful site in the beautiful Ötz valley, on the edge of the village of Umhausen. Situated on a gentle slope in an open valley, it has an air of peace and tranquillity and makes an excellent base for mountain walking, particularly in spring and autumn, skiing in winter or a relaxing holiday. The 98 pitches are all marked and numbered and have electrical connections; charges relate to the area available. The single, new reception building houses an attractive bar/restaurant, a TV room (with Sky) and the sanitary facilities. These are of exceptional quality with under-floor heating, British style WCs and free hot water in the washbasins (private cabins) and sinks and on payment in the showers. Special baby room with bath and changing area. A small toilet/wash block at the far end of the site has been refurbished for summer use. Good children's playground at 300 m. The young, enthusiastic man and wife management team speak good English.

How to find it: Take the Ötztal Valley exit from the Imst - Innsbruck motorway, and Umhausen is 13 km. towards Solden; well signed in village.

continued overleaf

AUSTRIA - Tirol and the West

022 Ötztal Arena Camp Krismer (continued)

General Details: Open all year. 6,800 sq.m. Electricity connections (12/16A). Bar/restaurant (all year). Shops in village (bread can be ordered). Children's play area. TV room with satellite. Ski room. Fishing. Bicycle hire. Swimming pool, tennis and table tennis 100 m. Para-gliding, mountain walks and Stuiben waterfall nearby. Washing machine and dryer, iron from reception, drying room. Chemical disposal. Motorcaravan services. Caravan to rent.

Charges 1999: Per pitch sch.1 per sq.m. (65 - 85 in winter); person 70; child 50; dog 35; electricity 35 plus 10 per kw; local tax 10. No credit cards.

Reservations: With sch. 500 deposit. Address: 6441 Umhausen 387. Tel: 05255/5390 or 8196. FAX: 05255/5390. Internet: www.tiscover.com.oetztal-arena-camp-krismer.

AR Discount
Less 20%
excl. July/Aug.

020 Sport Camp Tirol, Landeck

Well run site with good facilities and opportunity for white water boating.

There are several medium sized sites in this area bordering the Vorarlberg and Tirol, of which this and Camping Riffler are good examples. The district is popular for winter skiing and summer watersports and mountain walking. White water sports are organised on the River Sanna which runs alongside (with access) and the River Inn. On the other side of the narrow site are fir clad mountains which, with many trees on the site, make it a very pleasant place to stop, either for one night whilst passing through, or for longer stays to explore the region. The 100 pitches, all with electricity and 70-100 sq.m, are on either side of gravel roads which run from the hard central road. The pitches are not marked, but visitors are shown where to go. There is space for about 20 tents at the far end of the site. As with most Austrian sites which remain open all year, the sanitary facilities are of a good standard. The block for ladies is central, with the men's block behind reception. There is hot water (pre-set) in the showers and sinks and about half the washbasins, British style WCs, facilities for disabled people and a children's washroom. The reception block also has a pizzeria/café and, just outside the entrance, is a shop and restaurant. Children's playground on sand base. Good English is spoken by the enthusiastic couple who run the site.

How to find it: Site is on the main Vorarlberg - Tirol road by the river bridge, 1 km. west of Landeck. Signed Camping Huber and/or Sport Camp Tirol.

General Details: Open all year. 11,000 sq.m. Restaurant. Pizzeria/café. Shop. Table tennis. Children's playground. Volleyball. Programme of watersports, canyoning, rafting, kayak, etc. organised. Roller skating rink. Bicycle hire and mountain biking. Fishing. Swimming pool 1 km. Riding 15 km. Washing machine and dryer. Motorcaravan service point. Bungalows and studio to let.

Charges 1999: Per adult sch. 62; child (5-15 yrs) 42; local tax (adults) 6; car 40; m/cycle 30; caravan 95; motorcaravan 115; 1 man tent 40, 2 man tent 68, family tent 95; electricity 28. Special winter rates. No credit cards.

Reservations: Made without deposit. Address: Mühlkanal 1, 6500 Landeck. Tel: 05442/64636. FAX: 05442/64037. E-mail: sportcamptirol@msg.at. Internet: http://tiscover.com/sportcamptirol.

AR Discount
Less for stays over 14 days

010 Camping Seeblick Toni-Brantlhof, Kramsach, nr Rattenburg

Excellent, quiet site by Tirolean lake not far from Inn Valley autobahn.

Austria has some of the finest sites in Europe and Seeblick Toni-Brantlhof is one of the best. In a quiet, rural situation on the edge of the small Reintalersee lake, it is well worth considering for holidays in the Tirol with so many varied excursion possibilities nearby. Kramsach, a pleasant, busy tourist resort is some 3 km. from the site. The mountains which surround the site give scenic views and the camp has a neat and tidy appearance. The 250 level pitches (220 for tourists) are in regular rows from hard access roads and are of good size with grass and hardstandings, electricity (10A), TV connections, with 40 having telephone points also. The two sanitary blocks are of quite outstanding quality with free hot water in all basins (some in cabins), sinks and good showers. The main one, part of the reception, restaurant and shop building has been extended and now includes en-suite toilet/basin/shower rooms (free) and the second one, on the opposite side of the camping areaakso has bathrooms to let. Both blocks are heated in cool weather and have baby rooms, facilities for disabled people and drying rooms. The large restaurant has a roof-top terrace where one can enjoy a meal and admire the lovely scenery. Path to lake for swimming, boating and sunbathing meadow. With a good solarium, sauna and fitness centre, children's playground and a kindergarten in high season, this makes for an excellent summer holiday and, with ski areas near, an excellent winter holiday also. Family run, good English is spoken.

How to find it: Take exit for Kramsach from A12 autobahn and follow signs `Zu den Seen' in village. After 3 km. turn right at camp sign. Note: there are two sites at the lake - ignore the first and continue through to Seeblick Toni.

General Details: Open all year. 40,000 sq.m. Electricity on all pitches. Cable TV. Restaurant. Bar. Snack kiosk. Shop. Fitness centre. Children's playground. Fishing. Bicycle hire. Riding. Golf 2 km. Kindergarten in high season. Tepi club and organised activities for children in high season. Washing machines and dryers. Chemical disposal.

Charges 1998/9: Per pitch sch. 97 - 140; person 72 - 89 + local tax 8; child (under 14 yrs) 56 - 64; dog 57 - 70; electricity 43. Credit cards accepted. **Euro:** Per pitch € 6.98 - 10.07; person 5.18 - 6.40 + local tax 0.58; child (under 14 yrs) 4.03 - 4.60; dog 4.10 - 5.04; electricity 3.09.

Reservations: made for min. 1 week with deposit. Address: Reintaler See, 6233 Kramsach (Tirol). Tel: 05337/63544. FAX: 05337/63544-305.

017 Camping Innsbruck-Kranebitten, Innsbruck

Site with good facilities, just outside Innsbruck.

This site is on a sloping meadow with good shade cover, in a pleasant situation. The 120 pitches are numbered, but not marked out and there are three separate terraces for caravans and motorcaravans. All pitches have electricity available, though long leads are necessary in parts. By the side of the site, with access to it, is a large open field with a good children's playground and plenty of space for ball games. Being so near to the attractive town of Innsbruck, it makes an excellent base from which to visit the ancient city and also to explore the many attractions nearby. The bar/restaurant also has an attractive terrace and there is a shop for basic supplies. The large, toilet block, although showing signs of age, has acceptable British WCs, free hot water in washbasins (some in private cabins), pre-set showers and sinks. The 'Innsbruck-Card', available from the site, gives various discounts for attractions in the city, plus free travel on public transport (park-and-ride from the site, even if you do not stay overnight).

How to find it: From the A12 Innsbruck - Arlberg motorway, take the Innsbruck - Kranebitten exit from where the site is well signed.

General Details: Open all year. 30,000 sq.m. Electrical connections (6A, 2 and 3 pin). Restaurant. Shop. Bicycle hire. Swimming pool 2 km. Large play field adjoining. Games for children and barbecues in summer. Riding 5 km. Golf 10 km. Washing machines and dryers. Chemical disposal. Motorcaravan services. Tents or caravans to rent.

Charges 1999: Per person sch. 7; plus local tax 7; car 40; tent 40; caravan 45; motorcaravan 60; m/cycle 25; electricity 30. Less 10% for stays over 10 days. No credit cards.

Reservations: Contact site. Address: Kranebitter Allee 214, 6020 Innsbruck (Tirol). Tel: 0512/284180. FAX: as phone. E-mail: campinnsbruck@holmail.com. Internet: www.cda.at/tourismus/campibk/html.

AR Discount
Less 5% for
over 3 days

Your holiday - our Camping Innsbruck-Kranebitten

5 km from Innsbruck-Altstadt with a splendid view on the mountains lies the terraced camping Innsbruck-Kranebitten, where a young and flexible team is waiting to welcome you on one of your journeys. On demand we create a personal programme such as town visits, mountain walks, mountainbike- and bicycle excursions, rafting, culture programmes or Tyrolean evenings, or enjoy the family-like atmosphere on the campsite and enjoy our restaurant. Direct bus to the downtown of Innsbruck. Starting point for different excursions - Magdeburger Hütte, Rauschbrunnen. On the camsite you can buy phone cards, bus tickets and the INNSBRUCK-card, with which you can use busses, trams of Innsbruck and visit the musees and other couriosities of the town and the outskirts.

Hotel Route System Innsbruck, follow the red arrow.

Camping Innsbruck-Kranebitten • Kranebitter Allee 214
A-6020 Innsbruck/Tirol • tel./fax 0043-512-28 41 80
http://www.cda.at/at/tourismus/campibk.html

Camping/caravanclubs welcome

025 Alpencamping, Weer, nr Schwaz

Pleasant Tirol site with outdoor activity programme and a friendly welcome.

This is a good family site run by a family who provide not only a neat, friendly site, but also a variety of outdoor activities. Formerly a farm, they now breed horses, encourage children to take an interest in these and give a free ride each day to youngsters. For children and adults, Herr Mark junior (a certified alpine ski guide and ski instructor) runs courses for individuals or groups in climbing (there is a practise climbing wall on site), rafting, mountain bike riding, tracking, hiking, etc. Guided alpine tours can be arranged and there are pleasant walks up the lower slopes of the mountains directly from the site. Set in the Inn valley, between mountain ranges, the site has 96 flat, grass pitches either side of gravel roads. Trees provide shade in some parts. The old farm buildings house a small, cheerful bar/restaurant, good sanitary facilities (recently refurbished with hot showers and British style WCs) and a room for washing dishes and clothes and there is an attractive wooden chalet where reception and the activities are administered. It could be used for a night stop when passing through from Innsbruck to Salzburg, but is even better for a longer stay for adventurous youngsters or for a holiday in the Tirol area. The Mark family would very much welcome visits by rallies in the Spring season and are happy to arrange programmes of entertainment and excursions. Good English is spoken.

How to find it: Site is 200 m. east of the village of Weer on the Wattens - Schwaz road no. B171.

General Details: Open 1 April - 31 Oct. 20,000 sq.m. Electricity connections (6/10A). Restaurant, shop (1/5-30/9). Small heated swimming pool. Activity programme with instruction. Bicycle hire. Riding. Glacier tours. Table tennis. Large children's play area with good equipment. Fishing 3 km. Golf 20 km. Freezer. Washing machines and dryer. Chemical disposal. Motorcaravan services. Cabin and caravans can be hired (site arranges with local dealer.)

Charges 1998: Per person sch. 60; child (1-13 yrs) 40; pitch for car/caravan or motorcaravan 65; small tent 25; electricity 25; dog 15; local tax 6. Reductions for stays over 14 nights.

Reservations: Necessary for 1/7-15/8 and made without deposit. Address: Maholmhof, 6114 Weer bei Schwaz (Tirol). Tel: 05224/68146. FAX: 05224/681466.

13

005 Camping Kröll, Laubühel, nr Mayrhofen

Good site in the Zillertal valley.

The pretty Zillertal valley runs south from the A12 Innsbruck-Worgl autobahn and then east over the Gerlos Pass. The picturesque red narrow gauge Zillertalbahn runs along the valley following the River Ziller. Camping Kroll stands back from the main B169 road at the foot of the mountains which are on either side of the valley. Of the 200 pitches, 120 are for tourists, and they are reasonably level with grass on gravel and all have electricity. Although there are a few trees, there is little shade but pleasant views. At the time of our visit a new building was almost complete which will house reception and shop and a small heated pool which will extend outside. The good quality heated sanitary block has British style WCs and free hot water. An extension has a sauna, solarium, games, TV and a children's room.

How to find it: Site is on the northern side of Mayrhofen and signed from the B169 road.

General Details: Open all year. 20,000 sq.m. Electricity connections (6A). Shop. Restaurant/bar. Children's playground. Small swimming pool. Washing machine and dryer. Rooms to let in Gasthof on site.

Charges 1998: Per person sch 60; local tax 9 - 12; child (under 14) 40; car 30; tent or caravan 30; motorcaravan 60; m/cycle 20; dog 20; electricity on meter.

Reservations: are made to guarantee admission (no deposit). Address: 6290 Mayrhofen, Laubichl 127, Zillertal. Tel: 05285/62580. FAX: 05285/64877.

007 Camping Hofer, Zell am Ziller, nr Mayrhofen

Small, family run site near village and sports opportunities.

Zell am Ziller is in the heart of the Zillertal valley nestling around the unusual 18C church noted for its paintings. Camping Hofer, owned by the same family for 50 years, is on the edge of the village just 5 minutes walk from the centre on a quiet side road. The 100 pitches, all with electricity, are on grass on gravel. The good heated sanitary provision is on the ground floor of the apartment building and has British style WCs and free hot water in basins (some cabins), showers and sinks. A pleasant new development has a bar/restaurant, games and TV room and a small heated pool which can be covered. A mini-market is opposite site entrance. Once a week in summer the owner takes those who wish to rise at 4 am. to a nearby mountain to watch the sun rise. A little road train gives a free service round the village. The pleasant owner, who speaks good English provides a friendly, family atmosphere.

How to find it: Site is well signed from the main B169 road at Zell am Ziller.

General Details: Open all year except Nov. and April. 15,000 sq.m. Electricity connections (6/10A). Grill room with bar (1/6-31/10 and 15/12-30/4). Shop opposite. Bicycle hire. Swimming pool (1/4-30/10). Organised entertainment and activities in high season. Guided walks, cycle tours, barbecues, biking, skiing. Ski room. Riding 4 km. Fishing 8 km. Baby room. Youth room. Washing machines, dryers and irons. Chemical disposal.

Charges 1998: Per person sch 50 - 55; local tax (over 15 yrs) 9 - 12; child (under 14) 40 - 50; pitch 65 - 85; electricity 7 + meter. Special winter packages. No credit cards.

Reservations: Necessary for July/Aug and Christmas; any length with deposit. Address: Gerlossastr. 33, 6280 Zell am Ziller (Tirol). Tel: 05282/2248. FAX: 05282/2248-8.

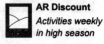

AR Discount
Activities weekly in high season

012 Komfort Camping Aufenfeld, Aschau, nr Mayrhofen

Pleasantly situated site for summer or winter with good toilet block and indoor pool.

This site is attractively situated in a mountain region with fine views. The main area of the site itself is flat with pitches of 100 sq.m. on grass between made-up access roads and further pitches on terraces at the rear. Following the addition of more pitches for '99, there will be 200 pitches (160 for touring units). The well kept toilet block in the main building is of excellent quality and size with British style WCs, washbasins well spaced out with free hot water, several in private cabins for each sex, one with baby bath and one with full bath for ladies and good fully controllable free hot showers; also a dog shower. Additional units, some new, provide private cabins and family rooms. The site can become full mid-July - mid-Aug. and at Christmas, but usually has space at other times. Ski lifts are nearby, one for beginners particularly close. A splendid, indoor swimming pool with whirl pool, sauna and sun-beds, has been added and there is a heated outdoor pool, paddling pool, and tennis court for summer use. Most facilities are now housed in the new main building. A lake and leisure area has been created alongside the site.

How to find it: From the Inntal motorway, take the Zillertal exit, 32 km. northeast of Innsbruck. Follow road no. 169 to the village of Aschau from which the site is well signed.

General Details: Open all year except 7-30 Nov. Electricity connections (6A). TV. Small shop. Self-service restaurant. General room. Indoor pool, sauna and sun-beds. Outdoor pool. Football field. Children's playground and Western fort. Beach volleyball and 'fun court'. Tennis. Riding. Fishing. Bicycle hire. Golf 500 m. Washing machines, dryers. Chemical disposal. Motorcaravan service point. Chalets and caravans for hire.

Charges 1998: Per person sch. 55 - 90, local tax 8; child (under 13 yrs) 35 - 60; caravan or tent with car 80 - 110; motorcaravan 80 - 110; m/cycle and tent 35 - 48; pitch with water and drainage 100 - 135; electricity 25 - 48; higher prices are for winter. No credit cards.

Reservations: made with deposit and fee for min. 1 week. Address: Distelberg 1, 6274 Aschau (Tirol). Tel: 05282/29160. FAX: 05282/291611. E-mail: camping.fiegl@tirol.com.

AR Discount
Low season offers

008 Schloss-Camping, Volders, nr Innsbruck

See colour advert between pages 16/17

Pleasant Tirolean site with heated pool near Innsbruck.

The Inn valley is not only central to the Tirol, but is a very beautiful and popular part of Austria. Volders, some 15 km. from Innsbruck, is one of the little villages on the banks of the Inn and is perhaps best known for the 17C Baroque Servite Church and monastery. Conveniently situated here is the very pleasant Schloss-Camp which is dominated by the castle from which it gets its name which towers at the back of the site with mountains beyond. The 160 pitches, all with electricity, are on level or slightly sloping ground. The sanitary block near the entrance has British style WCs and free hot water in all washbasins (some cabins), showers and sinks. Near the entrance is a nice bar/restaurant and shop with basic supplies. An animator provides games and entertainment for children in high season, when there is also a tent for groups of 30 persons. The well situated swimming pool is heated and there is a children's play area. The well laid out camping area is closely mown making this a most attractive site and the English speaking Baron who owns and runs the site gives a most friendly welcome.

How to find it: From A12 motorway, travelling east, leave at exit for Hall, going westwards, take exit for Wattens and follow signs for Volders where site is signed.

General Details: Open 15 April – 15 October. 25,000 sq.m. Electricity connections (16A). Bar/restaurant. Shop for basics, supermarket 400 m. Snack bar with terrace. Heated swimming pool. Minigolf, Children's playground. Activity programme for children in high season. Rooms to let in the castle.

Charges 1998: Per person sch. 65; child (3-14 yrs) 42; car 40; m/cycle 15; caravan or tent 40; motorcaravan 80; electricity 25; dog 15; local tax 15.

Reservations: Any length of stay with deposit and small fee. Address: 6111 Volders (Tirol). Tel: 05224/523333.

004 Tiroler Zugspitzcamping, Ehrwald

Excellent mountain site with fine views and superb facilities.

Although Ehrwald is in Austria, it is from the entrance of Zugspitzcamping that the cable car runs to the summit of Germany's highest mountain. Standing at 1,200 feet above sea level at the foot of the mountain, the 200 pitches (120 available for tourists), mainly of grass over stones, are on flat terraces with fine panoramic views in parts and all have electricity connections. A modern building at the entrance houses reception, shop, café and a fine restaurant with terrace which is open to those using the cable car, as well as those on the site. There is also a hotel 100 m. away. A large modern building which is heated in cool weather has an indoor pool with sauna, whirlpool and fitness centre, as well as an outdoor pool and children's pool with slide. The two excellent sanitary facilities are also here with British style WCs and free hot water in washbasins (some in cabins), showers and sinks. There are 20 private bathrooms for hire and a baby room. As well as providing a base from which to explore this interesting part of Austria and Bavaria by car or on foot, various activities are organised in high season.

How to find it: Follow signs in Ehrwald to Tiroler Zugspitzbahn and then signs to camp.

General Details: Open all year. 30,000 sq.m. Shop. Bar. Restaurant. Hotel. Cable-car to mountain summit. Swimming pools. Fitness centre. Table tennis. Children's play area. Washing machines and dryers. Apartments to let.

Charges 1998: Per person sch. 137 - 157; child (4-14 yrs) 99 - 112; pitch 75 - 103; electricity 10 per kw; local tax 9.50 - 12.50; dog 28; private bathroom 75 - 80. Special seasonal weekly offers.

Reservations: Made with 1,000 sch. deposit. Address: 6632 Ehrwald. Tel: 05673/2745. FAX: 05673/230951.

011 Tirol Camp, Fieberbrunn, St Johann, nr Kitzbühel

Site in mountain region for summer or winter camping, with good installations.

This is one of many Tirol camps which cater equally for summer and winter (here seemingly more for winter, when reservation is essential and prices 50% higher). In a quiet and attractive mountain situation it has 307 pitches on wide flat terraces, set on a gentle slope (200 for tourers). Marked out mainly by electricity boxes, they are 80-100 sq.m. and all have electricity, gas, water/drainage, TV and telephone connections. The excellent toilet block in the main building has British style WCs, washbasins with free hot water (a few in cabins), good, controllable showers and bathrooms on payment. A further splendid heated block at the top end of the site has washbasins in cabins and showers. Small, unheated swimming pool (12 x 8 m.) open June - Sept, with paddling pool. For winter stays, the site is very close to a ski lift centre and a 'langlauf' piste. Lake for fishing and playground and small zoo for children.

How to find it: Site is on the east side of Fieberbrunn, which is on the St Johann-Saalfelden road.

General Details: Open all year. Electricity connections (6A). Self-service shop and snacks. Restaurant (closed Oct, Nov and May). Separate general room. Tennis. Fishing in lake. Riding. Bicycle hire. Outdoor chess. Children's playground and zoo. Washing machines, dryers and drying room. Chemical disposal. Motorcaravan service point. Entertainment and activity programmes for adults and children (July/August) with Tepi club. Apartments to rent.

Charges 1998/9: Winter charges higher. Per pitch sch. 55 - 142; adult 50 - 100; child (4-15 yrs) 25 - 60; local taxes 18; dog 40 - 55; electricity connection (once only) 25 - 60 + meter; gas 120 + meter; TV/radio 60. Special weekly package deals with half-board offered in summer. Credit cards accepted.

Reservations: made for any length (with deposit in winter only). Address: Lindau 20, 6391 Fieberbrunn (Tirol). Tel: 05354/56666. FAX: 05354/52516. E-mail: tirol-camp@magnet.at. Internet: www.fieberbrunn.at/tirol-camp.

AUSTRIA - Tirol and the West

006 Terrassencamping Natterer See, Natters, nr Innsbruck

See colour advert opposite

Excellent site in quiet lakeside situation above Innsbruck amid fine scenery.

Above Innsbruck, 7 km. southwest of the town, this site is in a quiet and isolated location around two small lakes. One of these is for bathing with a long 67 m. slide (free to campers, on payment to day visitors), while boats such as inflatables can be put on either lake. There are many fine mountain views and a wide variety of scenic excursions. For the more active, signed walks start from the site. The site offers about 200 individual pitches of varying, but adequate size, some on flat ground by the lake, others on higher, level, terraces. Electrical connections are available, with 28 pitches also having water, drain and telephone connections and 42 with drain and telephone. Many are reinforced by gravel (possibly tricky for tents). There are two sanitary blocks of excellent standard with under-floor heating, British type WCs, free hot water in washbasins (some in private cabins) and showers, baby baths and facilities for disabled people. For winter camping the site offers ski and drying room and a free ski-bus service. There is a toboggan run and langlauf developed on site and ice skating, ice hockey and curling on the lake. During high season there is an extensive daily entertainment programme for children and adults offering different sports, competitions, amusement and excursions. Occasional services are held in the small chapel. The excellent restaurant with bar and large terrace overlooking the lake has a good menu and takeaway service. Used by tour operators (50 pitches). Well appointed apartments and rooms to let. Very good English is spoken. This family run camp must rate as one of the best in Austria.

How to find it: From the Inntal autobahn (A12) take the Brenner autobahn (A13) as far as the Innsbruck-sud/Natters exit (no. 3) without payment. From Italy, take exit for Innsbruck-Sud/Natters. Site is signed from the exit (4 km).

General Details: Open all year except 1/10-15/12. Limited shade. Excellent bar/restaurant (20/12-10/01 and 1/03 -30/09). Good shop (15/03 - 30/9). Three children's playgrounds. Sports field. Basketball, beach volleyball and 'waterball'. Table tennis. Bicycle hire. Youth room with games, pool and billiards. TV room with Sky programmes. Electric 'bumper' boats and mountain bikes for hire. Animation programmes, child minding (day nursery) in high season. Indian 'tipi' tents. Aqua jump (water trampoline), surf-bikes and wind-glider. Canoes for rent. Tennis, minigolf nearby. Riding 6 km. Golf 12 km. Laundry facilities. Chemical disposal. Motorcaravan service point and car wash. Apartments and rooms to let.

Charges 1998/9: Per person sch. 72 - 93; child (under 14 yrs) 54 - 64; pitch 98 - 125; electricity (6A) 43 - 45; local tax (adults) 6. Special weekly, winter, summer or Christmas packages. No credit cards.

Reservations: made for min. 7 days with deposit (sch. 500). Address: 6161 Natters bei Innsbruck (Tirol). Tel: 0512/546732. FAX: 0512/546695. E-mail: natterer.see@netway.at. Internet: http://www.tiscover.com/natterer.see.

AR Discount
Free bottle of wine

014 Euro Camping 'Wilder Kaiser', Kössen, nr Kufstein

See colour advert in section opposite

Well designed site with superb facilities for summer and winter visits.

The village of Kössen lies to the south of the A8 Munich - Salzburg autobahn and east of the A12 motorway near Kufstein. It is, therefore, well situated for overnight stops but even more for longer stays. 'Wilder Kaiser' is located at the foot of the Unterberg with views of the Kaisergebirge (the Emperor's mountains) and surrounded by forests. Being about 2 km. north of the village, it is a quiet place away from main roads. The well constructed main building at the entrance houses reception, a restaurant, shop and sanitary facilities. About 150 of the 250 pitches (grass over gravel) are available for tourists with electricity (6/10A), water, drainage, TV and gas points. They are of good size on either side of decorative brick paved roads. Some have shade from the attractive trees and all have good views. The heated central sanitary block is of excellent quality with British style WCs and free hot water in washbasins, generously sized showers and sinks. Very nicely tiled, it is kept exceptionally clean. There is also a baby room. The well stocked shop and very fine restaurant with terrace are open all year and in high season there is a snack bar. A large, imaginative children's playground is by the entrance and there is also a café here. In front of the restaurant is a heated swimming pool with children's pool. In high season, special staff run a Tepi club and other activities for adults and children. A weekly programme is displayed on notice boards. One of the top 10 best camps in Austria, it can be recommended without reservation.

How to find it: From the A8 autobahn (München - Salzburg), take the Grabenstatt exit and go south on B307/B176 to Kössen where site is signed. From the south go north on B176. From A93 (Rosenheim - Kufstein) autobahn take Oberaudorf exit and go east on B172 to Walchsee and Kössen.

General Details: Open all year. 52,000 sq.m. Shop. Large restaurant. Snack bar (high season). Club room with TV. Youth room. Sauna and solarium. Tennis. Large adventure playground with café. Entertainment programme (more comprehensive in high season). Washing machines and dryers. Motorcaravan service point.

Charges 1998: Per person sch. 58 - 74; local tax (over 14 yrs) 9; child (under 14) 35 - 45; pitch with electricity and TV 63 - 89; with all services 73 - 104; dog 37 - 47; electricity 27 - 32; gas connection 49; TV connection 55. Reductions for long off-season stays.

Reservations: made with deposit and fee for exact dates in high season; no minimum stay except at Christmas (3 weeks). Address: 6345 Kössen (Tirol). Tel: 05375/6444. FAX: 05375/2113.

Your ★★★★★ Holiday Paradise in the Tirol Alps near Innsbruck...

full of life

Natterer See

8 convincing reasons for you to spend your holiday with us:

- the **unique scenic location** in the middle of unspoilt nature
- the **well-placed situation** - also perfect when en route to the South
- the **thrilling water experience** of our own swimming lake (average 22°C)
- the **guarantee of sport, amusement, fun, animation** - ideal for all the family
- the **weekly discounted prices for senior citizens** and bargain hunters
- the comfortable **apartments and guest rooms** for friends and relatives
- the central position in the „**Olympia" ski region** Innsbruck/Seefeld/Stubaital
- the **high praise from ADAC** for the facilities at our site

Facilities•**individual terraced pitches** with water, drainage, electricity and telephone hook-up • motorhome service station • top quality sanitation facilities • mini-market • restaurant with lake terrace • **comfortable guest rooms** • **holiday apartments** • mini-club • pool room • youth room • sport & games areas • streetball • beach volleyball • swimming lake with 66m giant waterslide • bumper boats • children's swimming bay • archery • mountainbike and cycle hire • indian camp • table-tennis • open-air chess • **top animation programme** • attractive walks

• ski and drying room • ice skating • ice hockey • curling and tobogganing on-site • cross country skiing • "Olympia"ski region • ski bus

ADAC '98 Superplatz

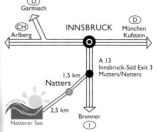

We will be pleased to send you our detailed brochure.

Ⓓ Garmisch

ⒸⒽ Arlberg

INNSBRUCK

Ⓓ München Kufstein

A 13 Innsbruck-Süd Exit 3 Mutters/Natters

1,5 km

Natters

2,5 km

Natterer See

Brenner Ⓘ

Terrassencamping Natterer See
A-6161 Natters/Tirol/Austria

Tel. ++43(0)512/546732...
Fax ++43(0)512/546695...

email: natterer.see@net4you.co.at
http://www.tis.co.at/natterer.see

Servus in Österreich

TOP CAMPING AUSTRIA

Tirol

Spend more time on the Continent and less time getting there

Travel with Eurotunnel to the Continent, the vehicle carrying service running from Folkestone to Calais/Coquelles via the Channel Tunnel. With a journey time platform to platform of 35 minutes* and up to 4 departures an hour during peak periods we get your holiday off to the right start. Our bright, spacious air-conditioned shuttle carriages whisk you to the Continent unaffected by adverse sea conditions.

*45 minutes at night

For details on price and booking information call

0990 35 35 35

or see your Travel Agent

Folkestone to Calais/Coquelles in 35 minutes, up to 4 times an hour, 24 hours a day

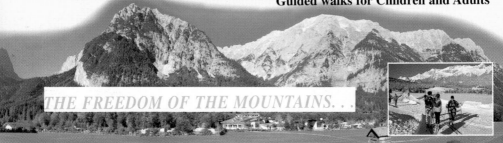

018 Sport Camp Woferlgut, Bruck a.d. Grossglocknerstrasse, nr Zell am See

Good, attractive, well equipped site in mountain region for summer and winter camping.

The village of Bruck lies at the junction of the B311 and the Grossglocknerstrasse in the Hohe Tauern National Park, with Salzburg to the north and Innsbruck to the northwest. Sport Camp Woferlgut, a family run site, was opened in 1983 and has been progressively developed and improved to make it one of the best in Austria. Although surrounded by mountains, the site is quite flat with pleasant views. The 250 level pitches on grass are of generous size and marked out by shrubs (200 for touring units) and each has electricity connection, water, drainage, cable TV socket and gas point. Three modern sanitary blocks with under-floor heating and music, have excellent facilities with British type WCs, hot showers (now free) and facilities for disabled people. A new block will be ready for '99. The fitness centre has a fully equipped gym, a small heated pool with `jet-stream', sauna, Turkish steam bath, solarium, cold spa-baths, exercise and massage rooms, and a bar. In summer there is a free activity programme, evenings with live music, club for children, weekly barbecues and guided cycle and mountain tours. The site's own lake is used for swimming and fishing, surrounded by a landscaped sunbathing area. In winter a cross-country skiing trail and toboggan run lead from the site and a free bus service is provided to nearby skiing facilities. A new restaurant has been built. The management is pleased to advise on local attractions and tours, making this a splendid base for a family holiday.

How to find it: Site is southwest of Bruck. From road B311, Bruck by-pass, take southern exit (Grossglockner) and site is well signed.

General Details: Open all year. 160,000 sq.m. Electricity connections (16A). Shop, restaurant (both 18/12-15/4 and 15/5-30/10). Swimming pool (15/5-30/9). Fitness centre. Two children's playgrounds. Tennis courts. Volleyball. Football area. Bicycle hire. Hobby room equipped with billiards, table tennis and TV. Fishing. Watersports and swimming at local lake. Riding 2 km. Golf 3.5 km. Hiking and skiing (all year round) nearby. Free programme of activities throughout the year for adults and children (Topi club) with three special staff during the summer. Collection of small animals with pony rides for young children. General room. Cooking facilities. Washing machines and dryers. Chemical disposal. Motorcaravan service point. Apartments, rooms and caravans to let.

Charges 1999: Per person sch. 54 - 70, plus local tax 10; child (under 10) 44 - 60; car 48 - 64; tent 58 - 74; caravan 64 - 74; motorcaravan 85 - 138; m/cycle 38 - 54; cable TV (once) 100; electricity and gas on meter. Special prices for senior citizens and families. Credit cards accepted.

Reservations: Contact site. Address: 5671 Bruck a.d. Glocknerstrasse. Tel: 06545/73030. FAX: 06545/73033. E-mail: info@sportcamp.at. Internet: www.sportcamp.at.

See colour advert opposite

This site appears out of order - it should appear on page 19

See colour advert opposite

003 Holiday Camping, Leutasch, nr Seefeld

Well developed site in mountain setting north of Seefeld.

Being away from main routes (particularly for caravans), this site is not for single night stops but is well suited for those who want to spend a few days, or longer, in a mountain area in a quiet setting with opportunities for walking, climbing or touring. Although there are mountains on either side, the site itself is level and offers fine views. Additionally there is an excellent indoor heated swimming pool with sauna, steam bath, whirlpool and sun beds. Trees decorate the site (but not much shade) and it has a pleasant appearance with plants and shrubs. There are 150 level, numbered pitches of grass on stones, all with electricity, water, drainage and TV sockets. Two modern, heated sanitary blocks have British style WCs and free hot water in all basins (mainly in cabins), showers and sinks with two well equipped baby rooms and one for disabled visitors. The site works closely with the local tourist board to offer a variety of excursions, walking, mountain biking and games for children. A baby sitting service is available. Games room with pool, table tennis, etc. `Wildmoos' golf course 15 km. Good English is spoken by the friendly owners.

How to find it: Site is 4 km north of Leutasch; caravans should approach either from Seefeld from the north or via Telfs - Mosern - Seefeld from the south as Littenwald - Leutasch and Zirlerberg on the Innsbruck to Seefeld road are banned to trailers.

General Details: Open all year except Nov. 26,000 sq.m. Electricity connections (6/12A). Mini-market. Good restaurant with music twice weekly in high season. Children's playground. Bicycle hire. Fishing. Tennis. Activities and excursions. Golf 15 km. Riding 3 km. Washing machines, dryers, irons. Exchange facilities. Motorcaravan service point.

Charges 1999: Per unit incl. 2 persons, electricity, TV, water and drainage sch. 210 - 280 (winter 210 - 320); tent pitch 40; extra adult 85; child 12-18 yrs 60, 2-12 yrs 40; local tax 12-13; electricity 8 per kw/h. No credit cards.
Euro: Per unit incl. 2 persons, electricity, TV, water and drainage 15.00 - 19.50 (winter 15.00 - 22.50); tent pitch 2.90; extra adult 6.20; child 12-18 yrs 4.40, 2-12 yrs 2.90; local tax 0.90 - 0.95; electricity 0.60 per kw/h.

Reservations: made for any length with deposit. Address: 6105 Leutasch. Tel: 05214/65700. FAX: 05214/657030. Internet: www.tis.co.at./holiday-camping.

AR Discount
Welcome drink; Free tennis

AUSTRIA - Tirol and the West

009 Camping Zillertal-Hell, Fügen, nr Schwaz

Small attractive site with excellent facilities.

The village of Fügen lies about 7 km. from the A12 autobahn at the start of the Zillertal, so is well placed for exploring the valley and the area around Schwaz. Camping Zillertal-Hell is easy to reach and has 127 marked pitches on flat grass, all with electricity (6/10A) and nine with water and drainage also. There are also hardstandings for motorcaravans. The modern heated sanitary block is of top quality with British style WCs, free hot water in washbasins (some in cabins), showers and sinks and a children's wash room. There is an attractive bar with terrace. Basic food supplies kept with shops and restaurants in the village (800 m). Pleasantly landscaped, heated swimming pool with sunbathing area. Programme of games for children during summer, at Christmas and at Easter with bicycle trips and hiking for adults. A good overnight stop or for a longer stay but, being on a main road, there is some road noise.

How to find it: Site is beside the no. 169 road, 7 km. south of the exit for Gagering (also signed Zillertal) from the A12 Innsbruck - Worgl motorway.

General Details: Open all year. Bar and small restaurant. Shop (1/5-1/11, 20/12-15/4). Swimming pool (20 x 10 m, 1/5-15/10). Children's playground. Games, activities and entertainment. Bicycle hire. Fishing 500 m. Riding 2 km. Golf 15 km. Washing machine, dryer, iron and drying room. Car wash. Chemical disposal. Motorcaravan services.

Charges 1998/9: Per person sch. 50 - 75, plus local tax 7; child (under 14 yrs) 35 - 55; pitch 60 - 90; electricity 30 - 35; water and drainage 20. Less 10% for stays over 8 days. No credit cards.

Reservations: accepted for min. 7 days, 10 days at Christmas. Address: 6263 Fügen/Zillertal (Tirol). Tel: 05288/62203. FAX: 05288/64615.

013 Terrassencamping Schlossberg Itter, Hopfgarten, nr Kitzbühel

Site with good facilities west of Kitzbühel.

With some 200 pitches, this well kept site is suitable both as a base for longer stays and also for overnight stops, as it lies right by a main road. It is on a slight slope but most of the 200 numbered pitches are on levelled terraces. All have electricity and cable TV connections, 150 have water and drainage and 25 have telephone sockets also. Space is said to be usually available. The site has two remarkable features - the large children's playground has a huge collection of ingenious fixed apparatus, and secondly, the sanitary facilities which have been added on the floor above the older provision. Both sanitary facilities are of a very high standard. The new section has a large room in which private cubicles have been placed round the walls and as free standing units. Some of these have washbasins with others having baths, one a massage type, or showers, with two slightly larger units for families, baby baths and footbaths. British style WCs; facilities for disabled visitors. Artificial flowers complete the hotel-like atmosphere of `Washland', all hot water is free and the facilities are heated in cool weather. The site has a pleasant open-air, solar heated swimming pool (16 x 8 m.) and children's paddling pool. Good walks and a wealth of excursions by car are near. Free ski-lift from site in winter, especially suitable for beginners and children; also own toboggan run. Some road and rail noise.

How to find it: Site is 2 km. northwest of Hopfgarten on B170 road to Worgl (not up by Schloss Itter). The entrance is on a bend opposite a garage and as much of the site is hidden from the road by trees, care is needed to spot it.

General Details: Open all year. 40,000 sq.m. Small shop, bar/restaurant (both closed Nov). Swimming pool (1/5-1/10). Sauna and solarium. Excellent children's playground. Tennis, fishing, riding, bicycle hire within 2 km; golf 10 km. Winter facilities see report. Refrigerator boxes for hire. Youth room. Washing machine and dryer. Cooking facilities. Chemical disposal. Motorcaravan service point.

Charges 1998/9: Summer: per person sch. 68; child (under 14 yrs) 44; car 45; tent or caravan 45; motorcaravan 75 - 90; m/cycle 30; dog 40; electricity 35; cable TV 48 plus 8 per night; local tax (over 14 yrs) 8. Prices higher for winter. Less 50% on pitch fee in mid-seasons. No credit cards.

Reservations: made with deposit and fee; usually min. 1 week (2 weeks at Christmas). Address: Itter, 6361 Hopfgarten. Tel: 05335/2181. FAX: 05335/2182.

018 Sport Camp Woferlgut This site appears on page 17, opposite its advertisement.

Salzburg and the Centre

There is more to Salzburg than 'The Sound of Music' and Mozart, although memorabilia of its most famous composer dominate from confectionery to souvenirs. Pasture-land, curative spas and interesting castles and monasteries abound. The Lake District, set amidst rolling hills, is near, along with salt mines to visit and music, art and drama festivals to enjoy. Salzburg has splendid gardens and ancient castles.

016 Seecamp, Zell-am-See

Excellent lakeside site for summer and winter camping.

Zellersee, delightfully situated in the south of Salzburg province near the start of the Grossglockner-strasse, is ideally placed for enjoying the splendid southern Austria countryside. Seecamp is right by the water about 2 km. from the town of Zell with fine views to the south end of the lake. On entering, one is immediately struck by the order and appearance, with good level, mainly grass/gravel pitches of above average size. All have electricity and about half have water, drainage and TV sockets. A large, modern building in the centre, houses reception, shop, restaurant (with terrace) and excellent sanitary facilities with British style WCs, a baby room and one for disabled visitors. The lake is used for boating and watersports. Children's entertainment in summer and programme for adults including rafting, canoeing, mountain biking, water ski-ing, hiking and coach excursions. Glacier ski-ing is possible in summer.

How to find it: Follow signs for Thumersbach where site is signed.

General Details: Open all year. 28,000 sq.m. Electricity connections (10/16A). Restaurant (closed Nov). Shop (June-Aug. and Dec). Activity programmes (see text). Beach volleyball. Fishing. Bicycle hire. Children's play area. Winter ski packages with ski passes, etc. Laundry facilities. Chemical disposal. Motorcaravan services.

Charges 1998: Per comfort pitch sch. 120, simple pitch 100 or tent pitch 50, all less 25-50% in low seasons; adult 85; child (2-15 yrs) 45; dog 45; electricity, gas. TV 30 (once only) plus meters; local tax 7. Winter package prices.

Reservations: Write to site for application form. Address: Thumersbacherstrasse 34, 5700 Zell-am-See. Tel: 06542/72115. FAX: 06542/7211515.

019 Kur-Camping Erlengrund, Badgastein

Mountain site catering for summer and winter.

Although in a fairly remote area, Badgastein became popular in the last century with those 'taking cures' in the waters from the hot natural springs which still fill the unique indoor swimming pool. The town is on a steep slope with the River Ache cascading down into the centre and under the main street. It also lies on the route to the south using the Tauern rail tunnel (which will take caravans) to travel between the Tirol and Carinthia. Erlungrund is on flat ground just south of the town, surrounded by wooded mountains. The 112 pitches, most with handstanding under grass, surround the main apartment building which houses the good, heated, sanitary facilities. These have British style WCs and free hot water to washbasins, showers and sinks. Family bathrooms for hire. All pitches have electricity and 60 are serviced with water, drainage and gas points as well. Basic food supplies are kept with a restaurant just outside the entrance. The site belongs to the Hotel Europaischer Hof, campers may take advantage of the hotel's recreational facilities. Small heated pool and Tepi club is for children in high season.

How to find it: Turn off the B167 road at sign 1 km before Badgastein.

General Details: Open all year. 45,000 sq. m. Electricity connections (16A). Small shop. TV room. Table tennis. Football ground. Children's playground. Washing machine and drying room.

Charges 1998: Per person sch. 61 - 68; local tax (over 15 yrs) 15; child (1-12 yrs) 47 - 52; pitch 66 - 88; small tent pitch 35 - 40; m/cycle 25; extra car 25; electricity and gas on meter; TV connection 10.

Reservations: min 1 week with deposit. Address: Erlengrund Str. 6, 5640 Badgastein. Tel/Fax: 06434/2790.

021 Camping Nord-Sam, Salzburg

Neat little site in suburbs near town and autobahn.

Nord-Sam is very close to the 'Salzburg-Nord' autobahn exit, and so makes a convenient stopover for those travelling through. It is also acceptable for a longer stay, being on the edge of the town and with its own small swimming pool (14 x 7 m.). The terrain is divided into about 90 marked pitches, which are not very large but are separated from each other by hedges, etc. which offer some privacy and are also attractive to wild life (including red squirrels). Pitches are quite well shaded and there are about 60 have electricity. The site is well tended, with flowers and shrubs. You should find space if you arrive fairly early. The small, heated sanitary block, below the house, is good with British toilets, individual basins with hot water, some in cabins, free hot water in showers and washing-up sinks. Salzburg is a major railway junction so you should expect some train noise at night. Cycle path directly to the centre.

How to find it: Site is signed from the 'Salzburg-Nord' autobahn exit and city centre; follow signs carefully.

General Details: Open 1 May - 30 Sept. 13,000 sq.m. Electricity connections (6A). Small shop. Room for general use where drinks served. Swimming pool (can be heated). Meals in high season. Unusual small children's play area. Bicycle hire. Washing machine and dryer. Chemical disposal. Motorcaravan service point. Bus service to city.

Charges 1998: Per person sch. 50 - 60; child (2-14 yrs) 27 - 40; pitch 79 - 99; dog 15 - 20; electricity 25.

Reservations: Are made - contact site. Address: Samstrasse 22a, 5023 Salzburg. Tel: 0662/660494.

AUSTRIA - Salzburg and the Centre

026 Camping Hirschenwirt, St Johann im Pongau

Small, pleasant site with first class sanitary facilities.

This small, but very pleasant site is ideally placed for a night stop when travelling on the Salzburg - Badgastein road, but could also make an excellent base for seeing this interesting area of mountains, lakes, salt mines, ice caves and famous towns. The flat, open site lies behind the Gasthof Hirschenwirt, with 40 tourist pitches on grass on either side of gravel roads. All pitches have electricity and sockets for satellite TV. Excellent sanitary arrangements are in the basement of the Gasthof. They have under floor heating, British style WCs, a baby room and some private bathrooms for hire. The sauna and solarium are also here. Small pool for summer use. Being on a major road route there is traffic noise.

How to find it: Site is behind the Gasthof Hirschenwirt at St Johann im Pongau on the main Salzburg - Badgastein road no. B311.

General Details: Open all year except Nov. 8,000 sq.m. Electricity (16A) and TV points. Bar/restaurant. Sauna and solarium. Swimming pool (June - Sept). Bicycle hire. Children's playground. Music (in restaurant) at weekends. Fishing 2 km. Riding 4 km. Golf 15 km. Washing machine, dryer and drying room. Chemical disposal.

Charges 1998: Winter prices in brackets. Per person sch. 50 (70); child (under 14 yrs) 20 (30); pitch 80 (100); electricity 6 per kw.

Reservations: Write to site. Address: 5600 St Johann im Pongau. Tel: 06412/6012. FAX: 06412/6012-8. E-mail: hirschenwirt@aon.com. Internet: www.telecom.at/gastroguide.

 AR Discount *Less 10%*

024 Camping Appesbach, St Wolfgang, nr Salzburg

Lakeside site in an attractive region for excursions.

The situation of this site is one of its main assets, being right by the lakeside with a reasonable frontage and with a very pleasant outlook to the high hills on the opposite side. The lake can be used for all types of sailing and sail-boarding; it is possible to leave small boats by the beach and there are also some for hire. Motor boats may be used, but for restricted hours, and bathing is possible if not too cool. The site is 1 km. from the village of St Wolfgang and the many excursions possible in the area include Salzburg some 50 km. away. The site has room for about 50 permanent caravans and 150 tourists, but the pitches are not numbered or marked out. Units go on large meadows in rows and could become crowded in the main season. It can be full for July and most of August if the weather is good. There are electrical connections in most parts The two toilet blocks have British WCs, a good supply of washbasins and free hot water, but less numerous free hot showers which in one block require external undressing.

How to find it: Approaching along the no. 158 road from west, turn left at camp sign just past Ströbl and continue round lake to camp which is 1 km. before St. Wolfgang.

General Details: Open Easter - 31 Oct. Electricity connections (10A). Shop. Pleasant restaurant/bar with good food, which also serves as general room with TV. Snack bar with terrace. Small children's playground. Table tennis. Tennis nearby. Motorcaravan service point.

Charges 1998: Per person sch. 56 - 63; child 33.50 - 39; pitch 40 - 130 acc. to position and size of unit; electricity 30 + meter; dog 20; boat 30; local tax: adult 9 - 12, child 4.50 - 6. Some reductions longer stays off season. Weekly inclusive package deals.

Reservations: made for min. 1 week with deposit. Address: Au 99, 5360 St. Wolfgang (Salzkammergut). Tel: 06138/2206. FAX: 06138/220633. E-mail: appesbach@aon.at

027 Seecamp-Neumarkt, Neumarkt am Wallersee

Lakeside site north of Salzburg with good facilities.

Surrounded by gentle hills and adorned with trees and flowers, Seecamp is separated from the lake by a narrow public road, although there is access to the water through the municipal bathing area. When seen in mid-week it was very quiet, but one would imagine that it is more lively during weekends in high season. The 170 grass pitches (100 for tourists, the remainder for long stay units) are on either side of gravel roads on a very gentle slope. They are not marked out or numbered but the position of electricity boxes allows sufficient space. All pitches have electricity and connections are available for TV/radio, water and drainage. Reception, a restaurant with terrace, very good sanitary facilities, heated in winter (with British type WCs, free hot water and baby room) and a first aid room are housed together in a modern, underground block near the lake. There are ramps by the steps to the toilets for disabled visitors but these are rather steep. Some facilities are used by non-camping members of the public.

How to find it: Approx. 26 km. from Salzburg, on B1/A1 Salzburg - Linz road, take turning for Neumarkt. Follow signs for Strandcamping just before the small town itself. If using motorway use Wallersee Ost exit.

General Details: Open Easter - 31 Oct. 37,000 sq.m. Electricity connections (6A). Restaurant with terrace. Shop. Minigolf. Volleyball. Children's playground. General room with TV. Bathing at lake station. Fishing. Riding 2 km. Bicycle hire 1 km. Medical/treatment room. Chemical disposal.

Charges 1999: Per pitch sch. 65 - 95; adult 65; child (2-15 yrs) 35; local tax 7; electricity 25 plus 8 per kw; TV/radio connection 60. No credit cards.

Reservations: Write to site. Address: Uferstr. 3, 5202 Neumarkt (Salzburg). Tel: 06216/4400. FAX: 06216/44004.

Vienna and the East

Although Vienna (Wien) is a vibrant centre for culture today, with museums, opera, famous choirs, the Spanish Riding School, well known cafés and the Danube, its glories lie in its illustrious past and the giants of music, architecture and psychology who lived and worked in the Austrian capital during its heyday. This, coupled with its Imperial history, make it a gracious and interesting city to visit. The provinces of Lower Austria, Burgenland and Styria, land of vineyards, mountains and farmland, are off the beaten tourist route, although walkers are attracted to the densely forested hills where hiking paths meander for hundreds of miles over hill and dale. There are less camp sites than in other parts of the country, but enough to provide bases from which to visit Vienna (use public transport) and other places.

029 Donaupark Camping, Tulln a.d. Donau, nr Vienna

Good, pleasant site in quiet situation near the River Danube.

The ancient town of Tulln (the 'city of roses') lies on the southern bank of the River Danube, about 20 miles northwest of Vienna. One can sail on the river through the Wachau vineyards, orchards and charming villages viewing the ruined castles and church belfries. There are interesting old buildings in the town and music concerts are held on the promenade of the river. Donaupark Camping, owned and run by the Austrian Motor Club, is imaginatively laid out 'village style' with grass pitches, grouped around six circular gravel areas which have a covered water point and drain in the centre. There are other pitches to the side of the hard road which links the circles and these include some with grill facilities for tents. 100 of the 130 tourist pitches have electricity and cable TV sockets. Tall trees surrounding the site offer shade in parts. The 140 long-stay caravans are tucked neatly away from the tourist area at the back of the site. There are three identical, modern, octagonal sanitary blocks, one at reception and the other two which are linked by a cover, at the far end. These are heated, with British style WCs and free hot water in all basins, showers and sinks. Two blocks have facilities for disabled visitors. Three play areas, two for younger children and a larger one with room for ball games. The Tipi club is held here. Entry is free for campers into the park with bathing lake next to the site. A range of activities is organised in high season for both children (including a room over reception for wet weather) and adults with guided tours around Tulln on foot, by bike and on the river by canoe (hired from site). There is a half-hourly train service to the Austrian Capital and a bus service there three times each week from the camp. The restaurant with terrace also includes the bar and keeps open quite late. This quiet location some 100 m. from the Danube makes an excellent venue for families visiting this part of Austria. The receptionist/manager speaks good English and is pleased to advise on tourist matters.

How to find it: From Vienna follow south bank of the Danube on B14; from the west, leave A1 autobahn at either St Christophen or Altenbach exits and go north on B19 to Tulln. Site is on the east side of Tulln and well signed.

General Details: Open 1 May - 30 Sept. 100,000 sq.m. Electricity connections (6A). Shop for basic supplies. Restaurant. Children's play areas. Tennis. Bicycle and canoe hire. Excursion programme, activities for children. Washing machines and dryers. Cooking rings. Chemical disposal point. Lake for swimming in park next to camp.

Charges 1998: Per person 60 sch; child (5-14 yrs) 40; pitch for caravan, motorcaravan or trailer tent 110 - 130; tent with car or m/cycle 40 - 50, bicycle 20 - 30; extra car or tent 40; electricity 20; cable-TV 20.

Reservations: Contact site. Address: Donaulande, 3430 Tulln a.d. Donau. Tel: 02272/65200. FAX: 02272/65201.

032 Donaupark Camping, Klosterneuburg, nr Vienna

Family site convenient for visiting Vienna.

Klosterneuburg lies just to the north of Vienna on the Danube, outside the city boundary away from the noise and bustle of the famous city but only minutes away by train. Donaupark Camping is only a few hundred metres from the river, a walk away from Klosterneuburg and its well known Baroque Abbey and the Wienerwald. The site is also owned and run by the Austrian Motor Club and is in a park-like situation, surrounded by trees but with little shade. The 140 pitches of varying size (some small) are on grass or hardstanding, accessed from hard roads and all with electricity. Two modern sanitary facilities, one at reception and the other by the pitches, have British style WCs, free hot water to washbasins, showers and sinks and a unit for disabled people. Shop for basic supplies and a snack bar/restaurant (both May - Sept) with others a short walk away in the town. Just inside the camp is an old Vienna tram car where money can be changed. There is a small children's play area but alongside the site is 'Happyland', an entertainment and amusement park which also has a large swimming pool (discounts for campers). The site organises excursions with bikes and guided sightseeing tours of Vienna. A good spot for families with the glories of historic Vienna easily reached and Happyland for the children.

How to find it: Leave Vienna on the west bank of the Danube following signs for Klosterneuburg, site is signed in the town from the main road B14 and is 400 m. behind the railway station.

General Details: Open Easter - end November. 22,500 sq.m. Electricity connections (6A). Small shop in restaurant/snack bar. Happyland. Washing machines and dryer. Chemical disposal. Good English spoken.

Charges 1998: Per person sch. 60; child (5-15 yrs) 40; pitch 110 - 140, small tent with car or m/cycle 40 - 60, bicycle 20 - 30; electricity 20; cable-TV 20; extra car or tent 40.

Reservations: Write to camp, Address: In der Au, 3402 Klosterneuburg. Tel: 02243/25877. FAX 02243/25878.

AUSTRIA - Vienna and the East

028 Camping Stumpfer, Schönbühel

Small, well appointed site between Salzburg and Vienna.

This small site with 60 pitches is directly on the River Danube, near the small town of Schönbühel, and could make a convenient night stop being near the Salzburg - Vienna autobahn. The sanitary block is part of the main building which also houses a Gasthof, with bar/restaurant of the same name, which can be used by campers. There is shade in most parts and a landing stage for boat trips on the Danube. The facilities are of good quality with British style WCs, washbasins and showers, both with hot water on payment. Facilities for disabled visitors include ramps up to the washing block. Small shop with basic supplies. The 50 pitches for touring units are on flat grass, unmarked, with electricity in all parts. This is very much a family run site with apartments for hire being added to the main building.

How to find it: Leave Salzburg - Vienna autobahn at Melk exit. Drive towards Melk, but continue towards Melk Nord. Just before bridge turn right (signed Schönbühel and St Polten), at T-junction turn right again and continue down hill. Turn right just before BP filling station (signed Schönbühel) and site is 3 km. on left with narrow entrance.

General Details: Open Easter - 31 Oct. 7,000 sq.m. Electricity connections (16A). Restaurant. Small shop. Children's playground. Swimming pool, fishing, bicycle hire, riding within 5 km. Chemical disposal.

Charges 1998: Per person sch. 45; child (6-14 yrs) 25; tent 30 - 50; caravan or motorcaravan 50 - 70; electricity 30; local tax (over 16 yrs) 10.50. Less 5% for stays over 7 nights. Eurocheques accepted but not credit cards.

AR Discount
Less 5%
after 7 days

Reservations: Write to site. Address: 3392 Schönbühel 7. Tel/Fax: 02752/8510.

030 Camping Rodaun, Wien-Sud/Vienna

Convenient city site for visiting Vienna.

This good quality site is within the city boundary and is an excellent base for visiting this old, interesting and world famous city. Just 9 km. from the centre of Vienna, there is an excellent public transport system for viewing the sights as car parking is almost impossible in the city. This is also a very pleasant camp in its own right with an excellent sanitary block (British type WCs). The site is situated in a southern suburb with a supermarket and a restaurant within 250 m. and a swimming pool, 2 km. It has space for about 100 units on flat grass pitches, neither numbered nor marked, either in the centre or outside the circular tarmac road running round the camping area. There is also a hardstanding area for motorcaravans (but no space for awnings).

How to find it: Take Pressbaum exit from Westautobahn or Vosendorf exit from Sudautobahn and follow signs. It is worth writing to the camp requesting a brochure which gives a good sketch map showing how to find the site.

General Details: Open 25 March - 15 Nov. 10,000 sq.m. Bar. Electricity connections (6A). Little shade. Washing machines, dryers and irons.

Charges 1998: Per person sch. 65; child (3-13 yrs) 45; caravan 50 - 60; tent 50; motorcaravan 60; car 12; m/cycle 15; electricity 24 + meter; dog 15.

Reservations: are advised - write to site. Address: 1236 Wien-Rodaun, An der Au 2. Tel: 0222/884154.

031 Schlosscamping Laxenburg, Laxenburg, nr Wien/Vienna

Site with good facilities, next to swimming pool, near Vienna.

Although this campsite is a little further out (15 km.) than some of the others, it has better facilities, is in a quieter location, is easier to find - particularly if towing a caravan - and has a bus service from outside the entrance to the city. Close to the historic castle of Laxenburg, it is on the edge of the castle grounds where campers can walk in the extensive park. Adjacent to the site is a pool complex and excellent restaurant with terrace, minigolf, and children's play area. The site has a number of permanent caravans but these are in a separate place on the edge of the tourist area. The seasonal camping part has room for 320 units, all with electricity. Pitches are not defined, but large flat meadows with a circular tarmac road encircling the main part and units go on each side of this road. Siting can, therefore, be a bit haphazard with a risk of crowding in high season, so arrive early. The large sanitary block is of a good standard, kept clean with British WCs and hot water in basins (some in cabins), showers and sinks. It is heated in cool weather. With an excursion programme available, this is an excellent base from which to visit the famous city. Parking in Vienna is no easier than any other capital so it makes sense to make use of public transport. Bus service to the city from outside the entrance (last return from Vienna is 9 pm) or from autobahn exit 'Vosendorf' and B17 to Liesing for P&R car park for the metro line which runs late.

How to find it: Laxenburg is south of Vienna, take autobahn exit 'Wiener-Neudorf' to Laxenburg village. Turn right at lights in village centre and site is on left beyond village. Site signed on motorway exit board through to site.

General Details: Open 30 March - 31 Oct. 50,000 sq. m. Electricity connections (4A, long leads in places). Shop (1/5-15/9).Restaurant adjacent. Swimming pool (charge for adults). Playgrounds. Minigolf. Riding 3 km. Golf 5 km. Excursions to Vienna and Budapest (2 days) with German speaking guides. Washing machines. Chemical disposal.

Charges 1998: Per person sch. 67 - 73; child (4-15 yrs) 38; pitch 62 - 69; tent 37 – 42; electricity 40; local tax 7. Credit cards accepted.

Reservations: Contact site. Address: Munchendorfer Strasse, 2361 Laxenburg. Tel: 02236/71333. FAX: 02236/713344.

050 Camping Fürstenfeld, Fürstenfeld, Styria

Pleasant, small site with basic facilities, near Hungarian border.

Fürstenfeld is the last village on the main route from Graz to Hungary and this site, although small with basic facilities, makes a good staging post when entering (or returning from) Lake Balaton and Budapest. The site is quietly situated on the edge of the village next to a large, well mown, play area with children's playground, space for all types of ball games and a really huge open-air swimming pool complex. This is the size of a football pitch, has a shallow end for paddling, a larger part for general swimming or pool games, an Olympic size racing pool and a diving pool with a 10 m. diving board. There are kiosks for drinks and ice creams, a cafe and changing rooms. The 50 pitches on the site are on terraces on either side of hard access roads, under a covering of trees, with electrical connections available. The single toilet block has British WCs and hot water in washbasins, showers and sinks. The provision is rather cramped and not as good as on most Austrian sites but is clean and acceptable. There is a small bar with TV, but no other facilities on site, but the village shops and restaurants are 2.5 km.

How to find it: From Graz - Vienna motorway, take exit for Fürstenfeld. Site is at western end of village, signed.

General Details: Open 15 April - 15 Oct. 3,000 sq.m. Good shade. Electricity in all areas (10A). Bar. Shops and restaurants 2.5 km. Large sports park adjacent. Washing machines and dryers. Baby room.

Charges 1998: Per pitch 30 - 50; person 40 - 50; child (2-14 yrs) 15 - 20; dog 10; electricity 20. Weekly package, pitch, 2 persons, electricity 600.

Reservations: Write to site. Address: Campingweg 1, 8280 Fürstenfeld. Tel: 03382/54940. FAX: 03382/51671.

Carinthia and the South

This gentle, tranquil land of some 200 lakes and mountain scenery deserves to be better known than just as a through route from Salzburg to Italy. The beautiful scenery and rural way of life make it an attractive holiday destination to those who know it. Unfortunately, few British have yet discovered its charms and those who have probably wish to keep the secret to themselves. There are few large towns, but many pleasant villages, good, often uncrowded roads and excellent sites.

048 Komfort-Campingpark Burgstaller, Döbriach, Millstättersee

Excellent large site close to the Millstättersee lake.

This part of Austria deserves to be better known as it is a most attractive region and has some excellent camp sites. Burgstaller is the largest of these and makes a peaceful base from which to explore Carinthia, northeast Italy and Slovenia. The site entrance is directly opposite the lawns leading to the bathing lido, to which campers have free access. There is also a heated swimming pool. The 450 pitches are on flat, well drained grass, backing onto hedges and marked out, on either side of gravel access roads. These vary in size (65-120 sq.m.), all with electricity, water and drainage and there are special pitches for motorcaravans. There are two very good quality sanitary blocks, the larger of which is part of the central complex. It has some basins in private cabins and special facilities for children and the disabled. Both have under floor heating for cool weather. A torch may be useful as site lighting is switched off late evening. There is a large, good quality restaurant with terrace, two children's play areas (one for under 6s, the other for 6-12 yrs). The games room with 3-lane bowling alley and mini bar leads off the restaurant. There is a secluded roof terrace for nude sunbathing. A covered stage and an outdoor arena provide for church services (Protestant and Catholic, in German) and folk and modern music concerts. Much activity is organised here, including games and competitions for children in summer with a winter programme of skiing, curling and skating. At Christmas, trees are gathered from the forest and there are special Easter and autumn events. This is an excellent family site for winter and summer camping with a very friendly atmosphere, particularly in the restaurant in the evenings.

How to find it: Site is well signed from around Döbriach.

General Details: Open all year. 56,000 sq.m. Electricity connections (6A). Restaurant, shop (May - Oct). Bowling alley. Disco (July/Aug). TV room. Sauna and solarium. Naturist terrace. Children's playgrounds. Beach volleyball. Basketball. Bathing and boating in lake. Fishing. Bicycle hire. Mountain bike area. Horse and pony riding. Golf 8 km. Special entrance rate for lake attractions. Comprehensive entertainment programmes. Chemical disposal. Motorcaravan service point.

Charges 1998: Per person sch. 65 - 88; child 40 - 78, under 4 free; local tax (over 18s) 17.50 - 18.50; pitch 80 - 120. Discounts for retired people. No credit cards.

Reservations: Write to site. Address: 9873 Döbriach (Kärnten). Tel: 04246/7774. FAX: 04246/77744. E-mail: dieter-burgstaller@campingpark.telecom.at. Internet: http://www.burgstaller.co.at/burgstaller.

AR Discount
Less 10% on
p/person fee

AUSTRIA - Carinthia and the South

033 Camping Central, Graz

Satisfactory site on outskirts of town with large swimming pool adjoining.

This appears to be the most sensible of the sites around Graz to use. It is of quite satisfactory quality and next door, with free direct access for those staying at the site, is an enormous swimming pool (120 x 90 m.) with sunbathing areas. Half of the 90 tourist pitches are individual, numbered ones on grassy strips between hedges and access roads; the other half are on a general meadow and not marked out. All have electrical connections. Four toilet blocks contain a good supply of washbasins (with hot water) and fewer toilets and rather unexciting, free hot showers. The city centre is about 5 km. and there is a regular bus service from nearby. Plans are in hand to build a new modern sanitary block and keep site open all year. If intending to visit outside opening dates given below, check with site beforehand.

How to find it: Site is just outside town to southwest. From west take `Graz W' autobahn exit and B70 from Klagenfurt. From Salzburg autobahn exit 'Graz-Sud'. Follow signs to Central and Strassgang.

General Details: Open 1 April - 31 Oct. 30,000 sq.m. Electricity connections (10A). In main months restaurant, also serving the swimming pool and keeping some basic provisions. Tennis. Table tennis. Children's playground. Jogging track. Minigolf. Excursions organised. Riding near. Washing machines. Caravans for hire.

Charges 1998: Per unit incl. 2 persons and electricity sch. 240; 2 persons and tent 220; extra person 60; local tax 5.

Reservations: probably unnecessary but will be made if you write. Address: Martinhofstr. 3, 8054 Graz. Tel: 0316/281831. FAX: 0316/28183183.

N036 Rutar Lido FKK-See-Camping, Eberndorf

Secluded naturist site with indoor and outdoor pools.

This is a large (150,000 sq.m.) and very well appointed site for naturist camping and it is a member of the International Naturist Federation (FKK). Situated in the heart of the countryside and surrounded by woodland, the main feature of the site is the provision of no less than six swimming pools (four outdoor and two indoor heated ones). As if this is not enough there is also a small lake for swimming. The 365 pitches, all with electrical connections and some with water and drainage also, are on flat grass marked out by hedges with a special area for campers with dogs. Four sanitary blocks are of good quality with British type WCs, some private washcabins and free hot water to the basins and showers and a special block for disabled visitors. There is a lake for fishing, a small chapel, table tennis, and dances are held in season. Well stocked supermarket, two bar/restaurants and two saunas adjacent to the indoor pools. The village is some distance away. Membership of the FKK or other naturist association is not obligatory but visitors are expected to comply with their rules and ideals.

How to find it: From Graz - Klagenfurt A2 road, take B82 south at Volkermarkt to roundabout at Ebendorf and follow signs to site.

General Details: Open all year. Some shade. Electrical connections (10/15A). Supermarket (April - Sept). Two bar/restaurants (all year). Swimming pools. Children's play area. Disco room. Bowling alley. Fishing. Bicycle hire 2 km. Riding 5 km. Golf 5 km. Laundry facilities. Chemical disposal.

Charges 1998: Per large pitch (100 sq.m. with electricity) 80 - 140 sch; small pitch (70 sq.m.) 80 - 100; adult 55 - 80; child (3-12 yrs) 40 - 60; tax 12; pitch with water/drainage 10 - 20 extra; No credit cards.

Reservations: Write with sch. 700 deposit. Address: Rutar Lido, 9141 Eberndorf (Carinthia). Tel: 04236/22620. FAX: 04236/2220. E-mail: eberndorf.tv@carinthia.com.

AR Discount.
Less 3% for organisations

049 Terrassencamping Maltatal, Maltatal

Site with pool and mountain view, 6 km. from autobahn, 15 from Millstättersee.

This site is good for an overnight stop but its pleasant situation and the good sized swimming pool on site encourage many to stay longer. The pool is over 300 sq.m. with a grassy lying out area and is open to all (free for campers). Many walks and excursions are available. There are 200 grassy pitches on shallow terraces (70-100 sq.m.) and mostly in rows on either side of access roads. Numbered and marked, but not separated, all have electricity and 20 also have water and drainage connections. The two toilet blocks, one with under floor heating, have British style WCs and free hot water in the washbasins (with shelf and mirror and about half in private cabins) and in the controllable showers and sinks. Six family washcabins. They should be a good supply and there are new facilities for babies and children.

How to find it: Site is 6 km. up a mountain valley from an exit at the southern end of the A10 Salzburg - Carinthia autobahn. Take autobahn exit for Gmund and Maltatal and proceed up Maltatal 6 km. to camp.

General Details: Open 8 April - 31 Oct. Electricity connections (6/10A). Only basic provisions kept (village 500 m.). Restaurant (all season). Swimming pool (20/5-15/9). Sauna. Entertainment programme for adults and children. Children's playground. Bicycle hire. Riding. Washing machines, dryers and irons. Chemical disposal. Motorcaravan services. Available from site: the Kärnten-card costing sch. 265 per adult (child 6-14 yrs sch. 130) which gives free travel on public transport and free entry to various attractions.

Charges 1999: Per person sch. 69 - 89; child (3-14) 44 - 54; local tax (over 18) 15.50; pitch 88 - 138, acc. to season and services; electricty incl. Less 5% for stays of over 11 days, 10% for 21 days. No credit cards.

Reservations: Made with deposit - contact site for details. Address: 9854 Malta 6. Tel: 04733/234. FAX: 04733/23416. E-mail: pirker-touristik@lieser-maltatal.or.at. Internet: http://www.lieser-maltatal.or.at/pirker.

044 Schluga Camping, Hermagor, nr Villach

Attractive site with swimming pool and excellent facilities in rural location.

Schluga Camping, under the same ownership as Schluga Seecamping, is some 4 km. to the west of that site in a flat valley with views of the surrounding mountains. The 300 tourist pitches are of varying size, all with electrical connections and some with water and satellite TV connections. Mainly on grass covered gravel on either side of the hard surfaced access road, they are divided by shrubs and hedges. Four sanitary blocks (one splendid new one, three good older ones) are well constructed and heated in cold weather. They have British WCs, controllable free hot water to basins (some cabins) and showers (small dressing space). Some family washrooms are for rent. There is a heated swimming pool (12 x 7 m), fitness centre and a sauna. Entertainment in high season includes a disco and cinema. A weekly programme sheet details events at both Schluga sites and nearby. The site is open all year, to include the winter sports season, and has a well kept tidy appearance, although it may be busy in high seasons.

How to find it: Site is on B111 Villach-Hermagor road just east of Hermagor town.

General Details: Open all year. 50,000 sq.m. Electricity connections (6+A). Shop (1/5-30/9). Bar/restaurant with terrace (closed Nov). Kiosk for snacks/ice creams. Children's playground. Games room. Bicycle hire. Sauna. Fitness centre. Swimming pool (1/5-30/9). TV room. Badminton. Tennis near. Fishing 4 km. Riding 10 km. Washing machines and dryers. Chemical disposal. Motorcaravan services. Mobile homes to rent. English spoken.

Charges 1999: Per person sch. 41.50 - 83; child 5-14 yrs 30 - 60, under 5 yrs free; pitch 47.50 - 95, with electricity 76.50 - 124; supplement for water, drainage, TV connection 20 - 35; local tax (over 18) 12 - 14; dog 15 - 55. Special weekly rates for families and senior citizens. No credit cards.

Reservations: Contact site. Address: Obervellach 15, 9620 Hermagor-Presseggersee. Tel: 04282/2051 or 2760. FAX: 04282/288120. E-mail: schluga.scampingwelt@carnica.ar. Internet: http://carnica.at/schlugas-campingwelt.

AR Discount
Less 10% on per person fee after 16 days

045 Schluga Seecamping, Hermagor, nr Villach

Pleasant site in attractive out-of-the-way part of Carinthia.

This site is pleasantly situated on natural wooded hillside. Pitches are individual levelled ones, many with light shade. It is about 300 m. from a small lake with clean water, where the site has a beach of coarse sand and a large grassy meadow where inflatable boats can be kept; also a sunbathing area for naturists. Many walks and attractive car drives are available in the area. This part of Carinthia is a little off the beaten track but it still becomes full in season. Sanitary blocks are modern and well constructed, they are of good size with British style toilets and individual washbasins, some in cabins. There are family washrooms for rent. Close by is Schluga Camping, under the same ownership (no. 044).

How to find it: Site is on the B111 road (Villach-Hermagor) 6 km. east of Hermagor town.

General Details: Open 20 May - 20 Sept. 70,000 sq.m. Shade in parts. Many electrical connections (6A). Shop (25/5-12/9). Restaurant/bar by entrance where drinks or meals are served; also takeaway (all 25/5-12/9). Room for young people and children. Kiosk at beach. Surf school. Pony rides. Bicycle hire. Children's playground. Badminton and volleyball court. Fishing. Tennis (indoor and outdoor) near. Weekly activity programme with mountain walks and climbs. Washing machines and dryer. Chemical disposal. Motorcaravan service point. English is spoken.

Charges 1999: Per person sch. 41.50 - 83; child 5-14 yrs 30 - 60, under 5 yrs free; pitch 47.50 - 95, with electricity 76.50 - 124; supplement for water, drainage, TV connection 20 - 35; local tax (over 18) 12 - 14; dog 15 - 55. Special weekly rates for families and senior citizens. No credit cards.

Reservations: Contact site. Address: 9620 Hermagor-Presseggersee (Kärnten). Tel: 04282/2051 or 2760. FAX: 04282/288120. E-mail: schluga.scampingwelt@carnica.ar. Internet: http://carnica.at/schlugas-campingwelt.

047 Camping Mössler, Döbriach, nr Spittal

Friendly family site with heated swimming pool, near a Carinthian lake.

A fairly small, flat, grassy site set in very pleasant surroundings with mountain views, Mössler is close to, but not right on, the Millstättersee, a reputedly warm lake (a 600 m. stroll). The site also has a free, well heated swimming pool of 200 sq.m. It is an excellent touring area with mountain lifts and many possible excursions to lakes and mountains near at hand. The site has about 200 pitches of two sizes but both adequate, on flat ground with connections for electricity, water, TV, telephone, gas and drainage. In high season cars stand on separate places in front of pitches. The two modern toilet blocks are of exceptional standard and quite luxurious, including under-floor heating. British type WCs. Washbasins in cabins and good, free showers with full controls for hot water. Full facilities for disabled visitors and private bathrooms (with bath, shower, basin and WC) usually let by the week.

How to find it: Go to Döbriach, at east end of Millstättersee, and camp is signed.

General Details: Open 1 April - 31 Oct. 30,000 sq.m. Electricity connections (12A). Shop and restaurant (both 20/5-30/9). TV facilities. Swimming pools and children's pool. Children's playground. Sauna. Washing machine. Motorcaravan service point. Caravans for hire.

Charges 1998: Per pitch sch. 85 - 160, acc. to type of unit and size of pitch; adult 71 - 91; child (6-14 yrs) 49 - 66; local tax (over 18s) 18.50. Reductions in low seasons for longer stays.

Reservations: can be made Sat. - Sat., with deposit. Address: 9873 Döbriach am Millstättersee (Kärnten). Tel: 04246/7735. FAX: 04246/773513 (summer) or 721313 (winter).

AUSTRIA - Carinthia and the South

040 Camping Arneitz, Faakersee, nr Villach

Site with excellent and comprehensive facilities by a Carinthian lake.

Camping Arneitz, directly on Faakersee is one of the best in this area, central for the attractions of the region, watersports and walking. Family run, Arneitz led the way with good quality sanitary facilities. Others have caught up but Arneitz have now gone one further by adding a splendid family washroom. This large, airy room has family cubicles around the walls and in the centre, washbasins at child height in a circle with a working carousel in the middle. British style WCs. There is also a hair washing salon with special basins and hairdryers. This building also houses the children's cinema. There is also a small toilet block nearer the lake. A newly built reception building at the entrance reflects the quality of the site and, apart from booking-in facilities, has a good collection of tourist literature and three desks with telephones for use by guests. Level marked pitches, mainly of gravel, are off hard roads, with electricity connections available and some having good shade from mature trees. Grass pitches are available for tents. The well stocked supermarket offers food items, wine, beer, clothes, camping and general articles. This is at the entrance of the site and includes a delightfully appointed restaurant where there is entertainment in high season. On the opposite side of the entrance road is a very well equipped children's playground with fixed climbing frames, go carts and small electric powered boats (on payment) with a large trampoline (small fee). Day trips can be made to Venice and the Postojna Caves and many other parts of northern Italy and the surrounding countryside.

How to find it: Site is southeast of Villach, southwest of Veldon. Follow signs for Faakersee and Egg rather than for Faak village.

General Details: Open 28 April - 30 Sept. 45,000 sq. m. Shade in part. Electricity connection included in price. Supermarket. Self-service restaurant, bar and terrace. General room with TV. Small cinema for children's films. Beauty salon. Sauna/solarium. Minigolf. Children's playground. Football field. Fishing. Bicycle hire. Golf 10 km. Exchange facilities. Doctor visits. Washing machines, spin dryer, irons. Chemical disposal. Motorcaravan services.

Charges 1998: Per person sch. 88 - 96; child (under 10 yrs) 83 - 91; pitch incl. electricity 120 - 150; plus local tax. No credit cards.

Reservations: only made outside main season. Address: 9583 Faak am See (Kärnten). Tel: 04254/2137. FAX: 04254/3044 or 24535. E-mail: camping@arneitz.at.

046 Terrassen Camping Ossiachersee, Ossiach, nr Villach

Popular site of excellent quality on Lake Ossiach.

As its name implies, this modern site has been constructed with terraces, on ground which slopes gently down to the lake shore. Because of the thick growth of reeds at the water's edge, there is limited access to the lake via two small clearings. One of these has a beach for bathing and a jetty, and boats may be launched from the other. The site is protected by rising hills and enjoys views across the lake to the mountains beyond. Trees, flowers, hedges and bushes abound adding atmosphere to this neat, tidy site. The 550 pitches (485 for touring units) are in rows on level grass terraces, separated by hard roads and marked by hedges, with electricity available. The site does become full in high season and although there is sufficient room on pitches, it gives the impression, on first sight, that it is overcrowded. Environmental protection is emphasised in this part of Austria and visitors are asked to follow instructions regarding disposal of various forms of waste. A large complex at the entrance includes a good self-service restaurant and well stocked supermarket. In high season a daily 'animation' programme is organised for both children and adults, giving a wide range of sports and activities. Young people are well catered for, with their own playgrounds, games rooms and disco dancing courtyard as well as many sports facilities. The lake is available for all forms of water sports including water-skiing and windsurfing schools and there are boats for hire. Although the facilities in the five sanitary blocks vary, they are all of good quality, heated in cool weather, with British WCs and free hot water in the washbasins (some in private cabins), showers and sinks. The newest block has family washrooms. A friendly, lively site where all ages and sports inclinations are catered for in a scenic location in a very beautiful part of Austria.

How to find it: Directly on the lake shore just south of Ossiach village. Leave the A10 autobahn at exit for Ossiachersee, turn left onto road 94 towards Feldkirchen and then right at Steindorf for Ossiach.

General Details: Open 1 May - 30 Sept. 100,000 sq.m. Shade in parts. Electricity connections (4A). Restaurant (15/5-15/9). Supermarket. Children's playgrounds. Tennis, volleyball and badminton courts. Football field. Sports area. Organised entertainment. Bicycle and moped hire. Fishing. Riding. Bank. Doctor calls. Washing machines, dryers and irons. Chemical disposal. Motorcaravan service point. Car wash.

Charges 1998: Per person sch. 59 - 89; child (2-9 yrs) 40 - 59; pitch 93 - 128, acc. to location and size; small tent pitch 50 - 72; tax 12.50 - 14.50; min. charge (summer) 247 - 284. No credit cards.

Reservations: Write with deposit (3,000 sch) and fee (100). Address: 9570 Ossiach (Kärnten). Tel: 04243/436. FAX: 04243/8171. E-mail: martinz.camping@kaernten.camping.at.

BELGIUM

Belgium is a small and densely populated country divided on a federal basis into the Flemish north, Walloon south and Brussels the capital, a culturally varied city. Despite being heavily industrialised Belgium possesses some beautiful scenery, notably the great forest of the Ardennes with its rivers and gorges contrasting with the rolling plains and historic cities of Bruges and Ghent with their Flemish art and architecture and the 40 miles of coastline with safe sandy beaches. For further information contact:

Belgian National Tourist Office, 29 Princes Street, London W1R 7RG Tel: 0891 887799.

Population
10,040,000 (1993), density 329 per sq km.

Capital
Brussels (Bruxelles).

Climate
Belgium's temperate climate is similar to Britain but the variation between summer and winter is lessened by the effects of the Gulf Stream.

Language
There are two official languages in Belgium. French is spoken in the south and Flemish in the north; however, in the eastern provinces, German is the predominant language. Brussels is officially bi-lingual. Road signs and place names maybe written in either language or in some cases both.

Currency
The currency is the franc which is divided into 100 centimes. Notes are 100, 500, 1000 and 5000 francs, coins 0.5, 1, 5, 20 and 50 francs. Note: The Luxembourg currency is interchangeable with the same exchange rate.

Banks
Banking hours are Mon-Fri 09.00-15.30. Some banks open on Saturday mornings.

Credit Cards: Major credit cards are all widely accepted, as are travellers cheques and Eurocheques.

Post Offices
Open Mon-Fri 09.00-12.00 and 14.00-17.00, some opening on Saturday mornings.

Time
GMT plus 1 (in summer BST plus 1).

Public Holidays
New Year; Easter Mon; Labour Day; Ascension; Whit Mon; Flemish National Day, 21 July; Assumption, 15 Aug; All Saints, 1 Nov; Armistice Day, 11 Nov; Christmas, 25 Dec.

Telephone
From the UK the code is 00 32. For calls within Belgium use the local code followed by the number. For calls to the UK the code is 0044 followed by the local STD code omitting initial 0. Telephone cards available from newsagents, post offices and train stations for Fr. 100 or Fr. 500.

Shops
Shops open from 09.00-17.30/18.00 hrs - later on Thursday and Friday evenings but a little earlier on Saturdays. Some close for two hours at midday.

Motoring
For cars with a caravan or trailer: motorways are toll free except for the Liefenshoek Tunnel in Antwerp. The maximum permitted overall length of vehicle/trailer or caravan combination is 18 m.

Speed Limits: Caravans and motorhomes (7.5 tons): 31 mph (50 kph) in built up areas, 56 mph (90 kph) on other roads and 75 mph (120 kph) 4 lane roads and motorways. Minimum speed on motorways on straight level stretches is 43 mph (70 kph).

Parking: Blue Zone parking areas exist in Brussels, Ostend, Bruges, Liège, Antwerp and Gent. Parking discs can be obtained from police stations, garages, some shops and offices of the RACB - Royal Automobile Club de Belgique.

Overnighting

055 IC-Camping, Nieuwpoort, nr Ostend/Oostende

Large holiday site 4 km. from beach with many on-site amenities.

This large site with 887 pitches caters particularly for families. On site is a heated pool complex with two pools, children's pool and a waterslide, many sporting activities, restaurants, takeaway, supermarket, children's farm and playground. The numbered pitches, all with electricity, are in regular rows on flat grass and, with 400 seasonal units, the site becomes full in July/Aug. A network of footpaths links all areas of the site and gates to the rear lead to a reservoir reserved for sailing and windsurfing (boards for hire) during certain hours only. The site is well fenced, with card operated barrier and a night guard. The seven functional sanitary units are clean and well maintained, providing British WCs, washbasins in cubicles, showers with dividers, dishwashing and laundry facilities. Hot water is free throughout and the units are accessible to disabled people. The nearest village is 2 km.

How to find it: From E40 take exit 4 (Middelkerke-Diksmuide). Turn towards Diksmuide following signs to Nieuwport. Pass through Sint-Joris and IC-Camping is on the right.

General Details: Open Easter - 14 Nov. Supermarket. Restaurant. Cafe/bar (weekends and BHs outside July/Aug). Swimming pools (two of 25 x 12.5 m, one 9 x 6 m).with waterslide and pool games (1/5-12/9). Laundry. Tennis. Football. Adventure playground. Minigolf. Fishing and bicycle hire within 500 m. Riding 3 km. Sports and show hall (volleyball, table tennis, stage shows, films). Entertainment programme July/Aug. TV. Chemical disposal. Motorcaravan services (for '99).

Charges 1998: Per family unit (max. 6 persons) Bfr. 975 in July/Aug. and B.H.s, otherwise 695; electricity 50. Largest unit accepted 2½ x 8 m. Less 10% with camping carnet. No credit cards.

Reservations: made with deposit (Bfr 3,000). Address: Brugsesteenweg 49, 8620 Nieuwpoort. Tel: 058/23 60 37. FAX: 058/23 26 82. E-mail: nieuwport@ic-camping.be. Internet: www.ic-camping.be.

BELGIUM

056 Camping De Lombarde, Middelkerke-Lombardsijde

Modern, spacious, good value holiday site, 400 m. from sea in popular resort.

Located between Lombardsijde and the coast, this site has a pleasant atmosphere and modern buildings. The 360 pitches are set out in level, grassy bays surrounded by shrubs, all with electricity (16A, long leads may be needed). Vehicles are parked in separate car parks. There are around 160 seasonal units and 20 holiday homes to rent, leaving 200 tourist pitches. The three modern sanitary units are clean and of an acceptable standard, with British style WCs, washbasins (some in cubicles), showers with hooks, dividers or curtains, facilities for disabled people, dishwashing and laundry sinks. Hot water is free throughout. Other facilities include a restaurant/bar and takeaway, shop and a laundry. The children's adventure playground is in the centre of the site. Other activities are listed below and there is an entertainment programme in season. Torch useful. A popular holiday area, the site becomes full at peak times. A pleasant stroll takes you into Lombardsijde or you can catch the tram to the town or beach.

How to find it: From traffic lights in Lombarsijde, fork left (towards sea) at next junction, follow tram-lines left into Zeelaan. Continue following tram-lines until crossroads and tram stop, turn right into Elisabethlaan. Site is on right after 200 m.

General Details: Open all year. Shop, restaurant/bar and takeaway (July/Aug plus w/ends, holidays 21/3-11/11). Laundry. Tennis. Table tennis. Basketball. Boules. Fishing. Bicycle hire 1.5 km. Riding and golf 500 m. TV lounge. Children's playground. Entertainment in season. Chemical disposal. Motorcaravan service point. Bungalows to rent.

Charges 1998: Per unit including electricity BFr. 475 - 795.

Reservations: Write or fax for details. Address: Elisabethlaan 4, 8434 Middelkerke-Lombardsijde. Tel: 058/23 68 39. FAX: 058/23 99 08. E-mail: de-lombarde@flanderscoast.be.

058 Camping Memling, Sint-Kruis, Brugge

Traditional site, ideal for visiting Brugge, conveniently located in town suburbs.

Located behind a bistro in a quiet suburb, this site is within walking distance of local shops and supermarkets. The 80 unmarked pitches (50 for tourists) are on slightly undulating grass, with gravel roads, a few trees and hedgerows providing some shade, and electricity available to 45 pitches. There is a separate field for tents. The sanitary facilities are in older style but are clean and tidy, with British style WCs and washbasins. The refurbished hot showers are on payment (Bfr 20). Dishwashing sinks (H&C), a laundry and a freezer. The bistro has a terrace and offers takeaway meals at reasonable prices, but there is no shop (supermarket 250 m). There is a tiny playground. The municipal swimming pool and a park are nearby. The Maldegem Steam Centre and narrow gauge railway are 12 km. Brugge itself has a network of cycleways and for those on foot a bus runs into the centre from nearby.

How to find it: From R30 Brugge ring road take exit 6 onto N9 towards Maldegem. At Sint-Kruis turn right at traffic lights, where site signed (close to garage and supermarket).

General Details: Open all year. Electricity connections (5A). Bistro/grill and takeaway (1/4-31/10). Children's playground. Bicycle hire. Fishing 2 km. Autobank exchange machine. Chemical disposal. Bungalows to rent.

Charges 1999: Per adult BFr. 105, plus local tax; child (under 12) 65; car 130; caravan 130; motorcaravan 200; small tent 100; electricity 70. No credit cards.

Reservations: Write or fax for details. Address: Veltemweg 109, 8310 Sint Kruis, Brugge. Tel: 050/35 58 45 FAX: 050/35 58 45. E-mail: memling@club.innet.be.

057 Camping Jeugstadion, Ieper (Ypres)

Small municipal site close to historic old town.

This is a developing site for tourists with only 21 pitches at present, some on hardstandings, all with electricity, plus a separate area for tents. The barrier key also operates the lock for the modern, heated but fairly basic sanitary unit. This provides British style WCs, washbasins (cold water only) and hot showers on payment. Outside are three sinks for dishwashing with hot and cold water plus a chemical disposal point. The adjacent sports complex has courts for volleyball and squash, whilst indoor and outdoor swimming pools are only 500 m, and there is a very large comprehensive children's playground. At the end of Leopold III Laan is the 'Menin Gate' built in 1927, which bears the names of British and Commonwealth soldiers who lost their lives between 1914-1918. The last post is sounded beneath the gate at 8 pm. every evening in their honour. The new interactive museum, 'The Flanders Experience' in the Cloth Hall is a moving experience. The Commonwealth War Graves Commission is a little further away in Elverdingestraat. In mid August there is a festival for young people in the town, when the site is usually fully booked. During school holidays the complex is extensively used by local children and can therefore be fairly busy and lively.

How to find it: Approaching the city from Lille turn right at roundabout in front of Lille Gate, then take second left, then left again into site access lane where site is signed. Park by barrier and walk through campsite to reception office at the 'Kantine', where they will issue a barrier key.

General Details: Open 16 March - 31 October. Electricity connections (16A). Bicycle hire.

Charges 1998: Per caravan BFr. 150; tent 50; adult 75; child (under 6-12 yrs) 25. Barrier deposit BFr 1000 or £20.

Reservations: Write for details. Address: Leopold III Laan 16, 8900 Ieper. Tel: 057/21 72 82. FAX: 057/21 61 21.

060 Camping Groeneveld, Bachte-Maria-Leerne, Deinze, nr Gent (Gand)

Traditional, quiet site, in a small village, within easy reach of Gent.

Although this site has 115 pitches, there are a fair number of seasonal units, leaving around 50 large tourist pitches with electricity (8A), most on an open grassy area with gravel access roads, plus an area for tents. The site has a friendly atmosphere, is quietly located and is also open over a long season. There are two clean sanitary units of differing age and design, which provide British style WCs, washbasins (cold water in one unit, H&C in the other), and free hot showers. The reception office is adjacent to a cafe/bar (open all day in July/Aug, weekends only off season) with a good range of snacks, and a comprehensive range of speciality and local beers. Also on site is a small coarse fishing lake (not fully fenced), a 3 lane floodlit petanque court (both free for campers), plus an adventure style children's play area. The range of family entertainment and activities organised in high season includes themed, musical or karaoke evenings, barbecues, petanque matches, etc. The village of Bachte-Maria-Leerne has a butcher, general store, café and bar, chemist, two restaurants, baker, plus a newsagent and tabac. The site has produced a location map of these for guests. The city of Gent is just 15 km. north of the site and 5 km. to the south is the pleasant town of Deinze.

How to find it: Deinze is southwest of Gent, between the E40 and E17. The village of Bachte-Maria-Leerne is 5 km. northeast of Deinze towards Gent via the N466 and the site is signed and accessed directly off this road.

General Details: Open 26 March - 12 November. Shops and restaurants nearby. Trekkers huts for rent. Motorcaravan service point.

Charges 1999: Per unit incl. electricity BFr. 515 - 595 acc. to season.

Reservations: Write to site for details. Address: Groenevelddreeef, 9800 Deinze (Bachte-Maria-Leerne). Tel: 09/380 1014. FAX: 09/380 1760.

061 Camping Blaarmeersen, Gent (Ghent/Gand)

Comfortable, well managed site on west side of city.

This relaxed municipal site adjoins a sports complex and a fair-sized lake which provide facilities for a variety of watersports, tennis, squash, minigolf, football, athletics track, roller skating and a playground. The 224 individual, flat, grassy pitches are separated by tall hedges and mostly arranged in circular groups; with electricity to all, 19 hardstandings for motorcaravans, plus a separate area for tents with barbecue facility. There could be some road noise as the the city's ring road is close. The four sanitary units vary in size but are of a decent standard, now with hot water to all washbasins. Most of the 20 free hot showers are in one block and there are showers and toilets for disabled people. The café/bar which serves a good range of snacks and meals is open from 10 am. and the shop from 8 am. - both daily March - Oct. In Gent, tour the markets, free of charge, with the Town Crier (May-Sept, Sunday 10.30). Central Gent is 3 km, the nearest bus stop is 500 m. and buses run every 20 minutes to the city centre. There are also good networks of paths and cycle routes around the city.

How to find it: From the E40/A10 exit 13, turn towards Gent-West, follow dual carriageway for 5 km. Look for Blaarmeersen sign, turning sharp right and following signs to leisure complex. In city avoid overpasses - most signs are on the lower levels.

General Details: Open 1 March - 15 Oct. Electricity connections (10A). Shop. Café/bar. Takeaway. Sports facilities. Sauna. Laundry. Playground. Minigolf. Fishing. Bicycle hire 1.5 km. Riding and golf 5 km. Bottle bank. Chemical disposal. Motorcaravan service point.

Charges 1999: Per person Bfr. 110 - 120; child (5-12 yrs) 55 - 60, under 5 free; car 60 - 65; caravan or tent 120 - 130; motorcaravan 165 - 180; electricity 30. Payment in Belgian francs, by credit card or by Eurocheque only.

Reservations: most advisable in main season; made for any period (no deposit) and kept until 5 pm. Address: Zuiderlaan 12, 9000 Gent. Tel: 09/221.53.99. FAX: 09/222.41.84.

063 Camping Grimbergen, Grimbergen, nr Brussels

Useful base from which to visit the city.

This popular little municipal site has a friendly atmosphere with 100 pitches on fairly level grass, of which around 50 have electricity. Sanitary facilities are in the older style, acceptable but not luxurious, and cleaning can be variable at times. The unit can be heated in colder months, and provides British style WCs, open washbasins, and basic showers, with free hot water throughout. In addition there are three sinks under cover outside for dishwashing and separate facilities for disabled people have now been installed. The site is well placed for visiting Brussels. The bus station is by the traffic lights at the junction of N202 and N211 and buses run into the city centre every 15 minutes. In Grimbergen itself visit Norbertine Abbey, St Servaas church, and the Sunday morning market. Also worth a visit are the nearby towns of Lier and Mechelen, and the botanical gardens at Meise.

How to find it: From Brussels ring road take exit 7 (N202) to Grimbergen, turn right at traffic lights on to N211 towards Vilvoorde (site is signed), then left by church (slightly oblique turn).

General Details: Open 1 April - 31 October. Electricity connections (10A).

Charges 1998: Per adult BFr. 100; child 40; caravan 100; car 50; motorcaravan 150; electricity 50, local tax 25.

Reservations: Write to site for details. Address: Veldkantstraat 64, 1850 Grimbergen. Tel: 02 270 2597.

Belgium

053 Camping du Waux-Hall, Mons (Bergen)

See colour advert opposite page 33

Convenient, well laid out municipal site, close to town centre and E42 motorway.

This is a useful site for a longer look at historic Mons and the surrounding area. The 75 pitches, all with electricity (10A), are arranged on either side of an oval roadway, on grass and divided by beds of small shrubs; the landscape maintenance is excellent. The single, central sanitary unit is in older style, basic but clean, with British WCs, washbasins with H&C (most in cubicles for ladies) and free hot showers with dividers and hooks. Dishwashing and laundry sinks (H&C) are outside but under cover. There is no shop on site, only a soft drinks machine, ice creams and free tourist information available. Restaurants and shops are within easy walking distance. A large public park with refreshment bar, tennis, children's playground and lake is adjacent, with direct access from the site. Places to visit include the house of Van Gogh, the Fine Art Museum, Decorative Arts, Prehistory and Stamp Museums.

How to find it: From Mons inner ring road, follow signs for Charleroi, La Louviere, Binche, Beaumont. When turning off ring road, keep to right hand lane, turn for site is immediately first right (signed Waux-Hall and camping).

General Details: Open all year. Public park adjacent. Shops and restaurants near. Fishing 300 m. Riding 2 km. Golf 4 km. Public telephone. Bottle bank. Chemical disposal.

Charges 1999: Per pitch for tent/caravan and car plus 1 adult BFr. 245; motorhome plus 1 adult 225; pitch for tent and m/cycle plus 1 adult 235; extra adult 135; child (under 12) 85; electricity more than 2 nights (10A) 6 p/kw. No credit cards.

Reservations: Write or phone for details. Address: Avenue Saint-Pierre 17, 7000 Mons (Bergen). Tel: 65/33 79 23.

AR Discount
Less 5%

054 Camping de L'Orient, Tournai (Doornik)

Attractive site in quiet green location, close to historic town, convenient for E42.

An excellent, quality municipal site, L'Orient is immaculately kept by the manager and his wife. The 51 level, grassy, individual pitches (all for tourists) are separated by laurel hedges and have shade in some parts and electricity. Two modern sanitary units are of high quality, spotlessly clean and heated in cool weather. They have British WCs, washbasins (some in cubicles) and roomy hot showers with curtains (on payment). Facilities for laundry, dishwashing and the disabled. Adjoining the site is an attractive restaurant and bar (10 am.- 10 pm. in season) with a superb terrace overlooking the lake where you can fish and hire pedaloes. Beside the lake are picnic and barbecue areas, a lakeside walk and a children's playground. There is also a new, high quality swimming pool complex (50% discount for campers) with cafeteria, indoor pool and outdoor pool with waterslide. Basic provisions are kept at reception. Tournai has the oldest belfry in Europe and you can also see the cathedral and museums dedicated to decorative arts, folklore, tapestry and military history. Good network of cycleways and footpaths around the town.

How to find it: Site is well signed from Tournai inner ring road. At exit 32 turn onto N48 Brussels road then turn almost immediately first right, site is signed at junction.

General Details: Open all year. Electricity connections (16A). Cafeteria. Bar. Laundry. Swimming pool and waterslide complex. Lake with barbecues, fishing, pedaloes for hire and children's playground.

Charges 1998: Per adult BFr 85; child (6-12 yrs) 65; caravan 100; car 80; motorcaravan 180; electricity 8 p/kw.

Reservations: Write or phone for details. Address: Vieux Chemin de Mons, 7500 Tournai. Tel: 069/22 26 35.

059 Provincial Domein De Gavers, Geraardsbergen

Modern, organised holiday site, in a peaceful location, with a large sports complex.

Adjacent to a large sports complex, with good security and a card operated barrier, located about 5 km. outside Geraardsbergen, this can be a busy site in season. There are 450 grassy, level pitches, many taken by seasonal units but with 80 left for tourists. Arranged on either side of surfaced access roads with some hedges and few trees to provide shade in parts, electricity (5/10A) is available to most. The five sanitary buildings are modern and well equipped, providing British style WCs, hot showers with dividers and seats (on payment), and washbasins (H&C). Facilities also include a modern laundry and rooms for disabled people and babies. Within the complex there is also a shop, cafeteria, restaurant, takeaway and bars. The site offers an extensive range of sporting activities (see below), an excellent children's playground and a full entertainment programme over a long season.

How to find it: From E429/A8 exit 26 towards Edingen, take N255 and N495 to Geraardsbergen. Down a steep hill, then left at camp sign towards Onkerzele, through village and turn north to site.

General Details: Open all year. Shop (July/Aug). Restaurant, bar and takeaway (daily April - Sept, otherwise weekends). Tennis. Volleyball. Basketball. Mini-football. Boules. 'Midget' golf. Fishing. Canoes, windsurfers, pedaloes, yachts and row boats for hire. Bicycle hire. Tourist train. Swimming and beach area. Climbing. Entertainment in season. Launderette. Chemical disposal.

Charges 1998: Per unit BFr. 380 - 490. Credit cards accepted.

Reservations: Write or fax for details. Address: Onkerzelestraat 280, 9500 Geraardsbergen. Tel: 054/416324. FAX: 054/410388. E-mail: gavers@oost-vlaanderen.be. Internet: http://home.virtual-pc.com/althea/gavers.

AR Discount
Less 5-30% for longer stays

066 Camping Baalse Hei, Turnhout

Friendly forest site peacefully situated close to city.

The 'Campine' is an area covering three-quarters of the Province of Antwerp, noted for its nature reserves, pine forests, meadows and streams and is ideal for walking and cycling, while Turnhout itself is an interesting old town. Baalse Hei is a long-established site and has recently added a separate touring area of 55 large pitches (all with 16A electricity and TV connections and shared water point) on a large grass field which has been thoughtfully developed with young trees and bushes planted. Cars are parked away from the pitches. New covered dishwashing facilities (hot water Bfr. 5), a small number of WCs, chemical disposal point and waste bins are close to the pitches beside the hard access road, but the main modern, heated sanitary building is a 100 m. walk from the tourist pitches. This provides hot showers (Bfr 20), some washbasins in cabins, further British style WCs (no paper) and facilities for disabled people. Upstairs is a club/TV room. Close to reception is a café/ restaurant with bar (July-Sept, then weekends, closed mid Nov-end Jan). A shop is planned for '99. Small lake for swimming (lifeguard) with beach, boating lake, large fishing lake (on payment), an adventure play area for children on sand and other activities listed below. Entertainment and activities are organised July/Aug. Walk in the woods and you will undoubtedly come across some of the many red squirrels. Pleasant 1.5 km. riverside walk to Ravels, the next village. A good cycle path (3 km. long) takes you direct to Turnhout.

How to find it: Site is northeast of Turnhout off N119. Approaching from Antwerp on E34/A21 go on to Turnhout ring road to the end (not a complete ring) and turn right. Small site sign to right in 1.5 km. then country lane.

General Details: Open all year. Arrival after 4 pm. departure by 10 am. Café/restaurant (daily July - Sept, closed Nov - Jan, weekends at other times). Lake swimming. Fishing. Bicycle hire. Tennis. Table tennis. Boules. Volleyball. Basketball. Football. Children's play equipment. Entertainment. Riding 1 km. Golf 20 km. Launderette. Chemical disposal. Motorcaravan service point. Hikers' cabins to rent.

Charges 1999: Per unit all incl. Bfr. 490 - 650; electricity 30. No credit cards.

Reservations: Contact site. Address: Roodhuisstraat 10, 2300 Turnhout. Tel: 014/421931. FAX: 014/420853.

AR Discount
Less 10% on daily tariff

Baalse Hei
't Groene Caravanpark

Baalse Hei offers a calm and quiet environment, boarding a nature reserve north of Turnhout. There are several lakes used for swimming, fishing and rowing, a large football field, volley- bas- ket- and tennis facilities. There are a lot of cycling routes in the area of which maps are available. A pleasant riverside walk brings you to a small vilage or to the interesting town of Turnhout. Baalse Hei is a perfect location from which you can visit the art city of Antwerp. Caravans, Hikers' cabins and bicycle hire. Via E34/A12 Eindhoven-Antwerpen, exit n° 24 direction Turnhout/Breda.

Roodhuisstraat 10 - 2300 Turnhout (Belgium)
Tel. 0032 (0)14 42 19 31 - Fax 0032 (0)14 42 08 53

065 Camping Floréal Club Het Veen, Sint Job In't Goor, nr Antwerpen

Top quality, good value site with many sports facilities, in woodland area.

A modern site with good security and efficient reception, the 319 marked pitches (60 for tourists) are on level grass, most with some shade and electricity (10A, long leads in some places). There are also 7 hardstandings for motorcaravans. The four sanitary units are modern and spacious, with free hot water, British style WCs, washbasins (a few in cubicles) with mixer taps set in marbled surfaces, and roomy hot showers (Bfr 20 payment). Well equipped facilities for disabled people. Dishwashing and laundry facilities complete the installations. The restaurant and bar opens both day and evening during July/Aug. (weekends only other times). A well stocked shop and takeaway open daily in high season, at weekends in low seasons. There is an indoor sports hall (charged Bfr 200 per hour) and courts for tennis (150 per hour), football, basketball and softball are outside. Children's entertainment in season, plus good, safe and exciting playgrounds. Antwerp is only 20 km. and there is good cycling and walking available in the area.

How to find it: From Brecht (exit 4 from E19/A1) follow road to St Job In't Goor, straight on at traffic lights and immediately after canal bridge turn left at campsite sign. Continue straight on for about 1.5 km.

General Details: Open Easter - 30 Sept. Shop. Restaurant, bar, café and takeaway (daily July/Aug. weekends only at other times). Tennis. Badminton. Volleyball. Softball. Basketball. Football. Table tennis. Boules. Fishing. Canoeing. Bicycle hire. Children's playground. Entertainment in season. First aid post. Laundry. Chemical disposal. Motorcaravan services. English spoken.

Charges 1998: Per pitch incl. electricity BFr. 260; person 100; child (3-11) 70; tent + m/cycle 160.

Reservations: Write or fax site. Address: Eekhoornlaan 1, 2960 Sint Job In't Goor. Tel: 03/636 13 27. FAX: 03/636 20 30.

Belgium

067 Parc La Clusure, Bure-Tellin, nr Rochefort

Agreeable site in the popular Lhomme Valley touring area, with swimming pool.

Set in a river valley in the lovely wooded uplands of the Ardennes, this site is close to the area's best tourist attractions. The 425 marked, grassy pitches have access to electricity (16A), cable TV and water taps and are mostly in avenues off a central, tarmac road. The three sanitary units (one heated in winter) have free hot water and provide British WCs, washbasins (some in cubicles), showers with dividers/hooks, and facilities for babies. Dishwashing and laundry facilities may be stretched at times. There is a very pleasant, well lit, riverside walk, a heated swimming pool and children's pool with pool-side bar/terrace plus a well stocked shop, snack-bar, tennis courts, restaurant and takeaway. An organised activity programme includes courses in canoeing, mountain biking and climbing. The nearby main Brussels - Luxembourg railway line, though not visually intrusive, can be noisy.

How to find it: Site is signed north off the N803 Rochefort - St. Hubert road at Bure, 8 km. southeast of Rochefort with a steepish, winding descent to site.

General Details: Open all year. Shop. Restaurant. Bars. Snack bar. Takeaway. Laundry. Tennis. Badminton. Volleyball. Swimming pools (open 1/5-15/9). Playgrounds. Motorcaravan service station. Activity programme (July/Aug). Fishing and riding nearby. Bungalows for hire. Bicycle hire. Barrier card deposit 500.

Charges 1998: Per pitch incl. up to 4 persons Bfr. 860 in July/Aug. otherwise incl. 2 persons 490; extra person 140 (90); electricity (16A) 80.

Reservations: Advisable for Easter, Whitsun and for July - mid-Aug. Made with deposit and fee (Bfr. 500). Address: Chemin de la Clusure 30, 6927 Bure-Tellin. Tel: 084/36 60 80. FAX: 084/36 67 77.

072 Camping Tonny, Amberloup (Ste Ode)

Family campsite with friendly atmosphere, in pleasant valley by the River Ourthe.

An attractive small site with 75 grassy touring pitches, the wooden chalet buildings here give a Tyrolean feel. The pitches (80-100 sq.m.) are separated by small shrubs and fir trees and electricity (4 or 6A) is available. Cars are parked away from the units and there is a separate meadow for tents. Surrounded by woodland, Camping Tonny is an ideal base for walking, cycling, fishing, canoeing and, in winter, cross-country ski-ing. The main chalet has a cafe/bar and open fireplace, small shop, TV lounge/library with a nice shady terrace for relaxing outside and is open all year (acc. to demand). There are two sanitary units (both can be heated in cool weather). These provide British style WCs, washbasins and showers with curtains, dishwashing and laundry sinks (all hot water on payment), freezer for campers use, laundry and a baby changing area. Nearby St Hubert has a Basilica, the St Michel Furnace Industrial Museum and a wildlife park, with wild boar, deer and other native species - all worth a visit.

How to find it: From N4 take exit for Libramont (N826), then to Amberloup (4 km.) where site is signed.

General Details: Open all year. Shop. Cafe/bar. TV lounge and library. Sports field. Boules. Games room. Children's playgrounds. Skittle alley. Bicycle hire. Fishing. Canoeing. Cross country skiing. Laundry. Chemical disposal. Six mobile homes and two chalets for rent.

Charges 1998: Pitch with electricity BFr. 300; without electricity 250; adult 80; electricity (6A) 6.00 p/kw. Off season discounts for over 55's and longer stays.

Reservations: Essential for high season. Write to or phone site for details. Address: Tonny 35, 6680 Amberloup (St Ode). Tel: 061/688285. FAX: as phone.

074 Domaine de L'Eau Rouge, Stavelot

Attractively located, lively site close to Spa and Grand Prix circuit.

In a sheltered valley location, this popular site has a fair number of permanent units but there is usually space for tourists. The main building houses the busy reception, shop, café, bar and the main sanitary facilities. A smaller sanitary unit serves the touring area. These provide good numbers of British WCs, mostly open washbasins, but rather fewer hot showers on payment - which could be stretched at times. However, some additional facilities should be available in the near future. Hot water is also on payment for dishwashing and laundry. There are 140 grassy pitches of 110 sq.m. on sloping ground either side of a central road with speed bumps. Baker calls 9.30 am. daily in season. There are plenty of sporting activities available in the area including skiing and luge in winter, and free archery lessons on site 10 am. daily in high season. The site is close to the motor race circuit at Spa Francorchamps and is within walking distance for the fit. The site's new Dutch family owners are not only embarking on a 3-5 year programme upgrading the infrastructure, but also have other ideas in the pipeline. So, for those who regularly visit this site at Grand Prix time, things can only get better.

How to find it: From A640 Francorchamps - Stavelot road, site is signed (3 km. from Stavelot, 5 km. from Francorchamps).

General Details: Open all year except 10 Dec - 31 Jan. Shop. Café. Bar. Football. Boules. Table tennis. Archery. Barbecues. Children's playground. Entertainment in season.

Charges 1998: Per unit BFr. 320-400; adult 42; child 32; electricity (10A) 80. Discounts with Carnet.

Reservations: Write to site. Address: Cheneux 25, 4970 Stavelot. Tel: 080/86 30 75. FAX: as phone.

Lakeland's Premier Camping & Touring Centre

- **Award Winning range of Family Facilities**

- **Spectacular 'Tranquil Valley' Location**

- **Touring Pitches - short stay & full season**

- **'State of the art' Holiday Caravans for hire**

- **Luxurious Holiday Homes for sale**

- **Only Ten minutes from Lake Windermere**

For a full colour brochure or to make a booking please ring (015394)32300 quoting '149' for entry into the 'Tranquil Valley' holiday draw!

Limefitt 🌲 Park

Windermere   The Lake District   Cumbria LA23 1PA

Looe Valley
TOURING PARK

Looe Valley, formerly Treble B,
is set in glorious countryside and is ideally situated
for touring beautiful South East Cornwall.
Close to beautiful, safe, sandy beaches, secluded coves
and picturesque villages.

- Under New management for '99
- **NEW** & refurbished toilet & shower blocks
- **NEW** Eurotents for '99
- 4 large utility blocks with Free hot water
- Level well drained pitches with electric hook-ups
- **FREE** heated swimming pool
- Licensed club
- **FREE** entertainment & children's club
- TV & Games rooms
- Shop, Restaurant, Takeaway & Launderette
- Holiday homes & apartments available
- Rallies welcome
- Semi seasonal pitches & winter storage available

Looe Valley Touring Park, Polperro Road, Looe PL13 2JS

AA ▶▶▶ **01503 262425**

QUOTE CODE: R1

073 Camping Moulin de Malempré, Manhay

Attractive site with swimming pools, very close to the E25.

This pleasant countryside site is well worth a visit and the Dutch owners will make you very welcome. The reception building houses the office and a small shop (basic provisions only), above which is an attractive restaurant and bar. The 120 marked tourist pitches are separated by small shrubs and gravel roads on sloping terrain. All have electricity (6/10A), forty have water and waste-water as well and the site is well lit. The stars of this site are the sanitary units - the existing ultra modern, two storey Scandinavian style unit is now joined by a new unisex unit which also boasts a family shower room among its warm and comfortable facilities. There are British style WCs, washbasins (some in cubicles), large pre-set showers, family bathrooms on payment, a unit for disabled people with automatic taps, hoists and rails, a baby room, dishwashing sinks and laundry. Other amenities include the recently refurbished heated swimming pool, children's pools (with mushroom fountain), a terrace for sunbathing, children's playground and trampoline. There is a little traffic noise from the adjacent E25 (not too intrusive). Nearby are the Hotton Grottoes, one of the prettiest Belgian caves (open daily Apr-Oct).

How to find it: From exit 49 off the E25/A26 (Liege-Bastogne), turn towards Lierneux on the N822, follow signs to Malempré and site.

General Details: Open Easter - 31 October. Shop (1/7-31/8). Restaurant (1/7-31/8). Bar (1/7-31/8 and weekends). Laundry. Swimming pools (1/6-31/8). TV. Table tennis. Pool table. Boules. Children's playground. English spoken.

Charges 1999: Per unit incl. 2 adults BFr. 650 - 750, acc. to size; extra adult 140; child (3-11 yrs) 100; electricity 90; family bathroom 250 per hour. Less in low seasons.

Reservations: Made with deposit (BFr. 500) - write or fax for details. Address: 1 Malempré, 6960 Manhay. Tel: 086/455504 or 455384. FAX: 086/455674.

BRITISH ISLES

The British Isles (England, Scotland, Wales, Northern Ireland and the Channel Islands) offer the camper or caravanner a choice of just about everything you could imagine in terms of scenery, campsites and weather! Whether you choose to visit the Highlands of Scotland, the English Lake District, Snowdonia in Wales, the Norfolk Broads, England's West Country, the unspoiled beauty of Northern Ireland or the Channel Islands, you are sure to find attractive countryside and/or much of historic interest. Visitors to the British Isles should not encounter any significant problems, other than driving on the left, and the fact that few Britons are proficient in any language other than English

Population
57,970,200 (93), density 239 per sq.km.

Capitals
London, Edinburgh, Cardiff and Belfast.

Language
Predominantly English, although Welsh also is spoken in many parts of Wales and Gaelic in parts of Scotland and Ireland.

Climate
Changeable and unpredictable - temperatures are generally a little higher in the south and southwest, and rather cooler and wetter in the mountainous regions of Scotland, Wales and the Lake District.

Currency
The Pound Sterling (£) divided into 100 pence.

Banks
Open at least Mon-Fri 09.30-15.30 hrs, except on Public Holidays.

Time
Late October - late March is Greenwich Mean Time (GMT); during the summer (late March - late Oct) clocks are put forward one hour to British Summer Time (BST). For most of the year (11 months) British time is 1 hour behind the time in other EC countries.

Post Offices
Mainly open Mon-Fri at least 09.30-16.30.

Public Telephones
Two main types of public telephone boxes, coin operated and 'phone card operated - cards can be purchased from Post Offices, newsagents, etc.

Public Holidays
New Year; Good Fri, Easter Mon; 1st Mon in May; last Mon in May; last Mon in Aug; Christmas, 25,26 Dec.

Shops
Most shops open at least 09.00-17.30 Monday - Saturday, but some still operate a half day (known as early closing day).

Motoring
In Britain one drives on the left-hand side of the road, and you go round roundabouts clockwise. The overall maximum speed limits are 70 mph (112 kph) on motorways, and 60 mph (96 kph) on other roads, except where a lower limit is indicated by signs. Overall limits are reduced to 60 mph and 50 mph respectively for vehicles towing trailers or caravans. Parking restrictions apply in most towns, and many villages, indicated by yellow lines on the roadside.

B020 Newquay Holiday Park, Newquay

Well run park with swimming pools and other amenities near town.

This park lies peacefully on a terraced hillside only just outside the town, 2 miles from the beaches and town centre. The main feature of the park is an attractively laid out group of three heated swimming pools with giant water slide (lifeguards in attendance) and surrounding 'green' sunbathing areas. Mainly a touring park, it has 350 marked pitches for any type of unit in a series of hedged fields, some sloping, with some fields just for caravans and some for tents, plus 137 caravan holiday homes which are let. Most pitches are individual ones marked out by lines on ground but with nothing between them. Electricity points (16A) are provided for caravans and tents, plus 10 special 'star' pitches with hardstanding, water and drainage. The sanitary installations include two good sized, modern blocks with washbasins set in flat surfaces with free hot water and fairly basic free hot showers with pre-mixed hot water which runs for four minutes and stops, with an extra block for the main season when they may be under pressure. There is a baby bath, covered external washing-up sinks with hot water and chemical disposal points. Entertainment each night with live music, discos etc. is provided in the site's Fiesta Club which also has a bar, TV lounge and games room with pool and snooker tables (all open when the site is open). Amusement arcade. Well stocked self-service shop and takeaway food bar (both all season, and good value). Full launderette with free ironing facilities. Pitch and putt course and crazy golf. Good children's playground, children's club and recreation field for football and volleyball. Fishing and bicycle hire 2 miles, golf 200 yds. Bus service to Newquay from site. No dogs or pets are taken.

Directions: Park is east of Newquay on A3059 road 1 mile east of junction with A3058. O.S.GR: SW853626.

Charges 1999: Per adult £3.20 - £5.75; child (3-15 yrs) free - £3.60; vehicle 85p; electricity (16A) free - £2.55; star pitch supplement £3.60. Min. charge per night in high season £12.35. Many special offers. VAT included. Credit cards accepted.

Open: Mid May - mid September.

Reservations: Recommended for peak season; made with £18 deposit per week plus £8 cancellation insurance (peak weeks Sat. - Sat. only). Address: Newquay, Cornwall TR8 4HS. Tel: (01637) 871111. FAX: (01637) 850818. E-mail: bookings@newquay-hol-park.demon.co.uk. Internet: www.newquay-holiday-parks.co.uk.

Looe Valley Holiday Park (Weststar Holidays, formerly Treble B).
This park is under new management and is currently being refurbished. It will be inspected with a view to a fully detailed report in our next edition.

See colour advert between pages 32/33

B022 Trevornick Holiday Park, Holywell Bay, Newquay

Large, busy, modern, family complex for all units near sandy beach, with wide-ranging amenities.

Trevornick has been converted from a working farm and has grown to provide caravanners and campers (no holiday caravans) with 450 grass pitches (386 with electricity) in five level fields and two terraced areas (few trees, but some good views), providing `all singing, all dancing' facilities for family holidays. The five toilet blocks of a standard modern design provide washbasins in vanity style, toilets, coin operated showers including a family shower room, baby bath, dishwashing and laundry facilities, and chemical disposal. The farm buildings now provide the setting for the farm club (recently refurbished) with licensed facilities and food, children's rooms, games room, cafeteria, chip bar and takeaway, plus much entertainment in season. The Trawlers' Bar serves meals and drinks for families (with TV). Activities include a good sized pool (all season) with slide, sauna, tennis, an adventure playground, crazy golf and indoor adventure play area (supervised for 2-8 yr olds at a small charge). Dogs are accepted in one field only with a walk provided. A good sized farm shop reminds one of the park's background. The rest of the development has provided an 18 hole golf course, pitch and putt, a small, quiet club with bar meals and lovely views out to sea, Holywell leisure `fun' park next door (site fun pass gives reduced rates) and recently much improved coarse fishing with three lakes. The sandy beach is 5 minutes by car or 20 minutes walk through the sand dunes past the Holywell. Bicycle hire and boat launching 4 miles, riding within 1 mile. The park has 60 `Eurotents' to hire (pre-erected, fully equipped tents sleeping 6; cot and TV hire available).

Directions: From A3075 approach to Newquay - Perranporth road, turn towards Cubert and Holywell Bay. Continue through Cubert to park on the right. O.S.GR: SW776586.

Charges 1998: Per adult £2.85 - £5.30; child (4-16 yrs) free - £3.50; car 80p; electricity £2.75 - £3.00; dog £1.75. Families and couples only. VAT included. Credit cards accepted.

Open: Easter -mid September.

Reservations: Made with £20 deposit per week (Sat. to Sat. only July/Aug). Address: Holywell Bay, Newquay, Cornwall TR8 5PW. Tel: (01637) 830531.

Tourist information

English Tourist Board, Thames Tower, Blacks Road, Hammersmith, London W6 9EL. 0181 846 9000.
Scottish Tourist Board, 22 Ravelston Terrace, Edinburgh EH14 2EU. 0131 332 2433.
Wales Tourist Board, Brunel House, 2, Fitzalan Road, Cardiff CF2 1UY. 01222 499909.
Northern Ireland Tourist Board, 59 North Street, Belfast BT1 1NB. 01232 231221.

BRITISH ISLES - England

B023 Glenmorris Park, St Mabyn

Family run, quiet park in north Cornwall.

The beaches of north Cornwall and the wilds of Bodmin Moor are all an easy drive away from Glenmorris Park and the Camel Trail for either cycling or walking all the way to Bodmin, Wadebridge or Padstow is only 2 miles. The amenities at the park include a heated, outdoor swimming pool and paddling pool (late May - early Sept), surrounded by sheltered, paved and grass sunbathing areas. Alongside is an excellent adventure playground which is fenced, with a bark safety base. Reception includes a small shop which caters for basic needs and, in the same building, is a games room for teenagers. Bodmin and Wadebridge are only 5 or 6 miles for supermarket shopping. There is no bar but the local village inn has a good reputation for food. A quiet, family run park, Glenmorris has fairly modern sanitary facilities which are clean and well maintained. Washbasins are in vanity style units with hairdryers, all hot water is free and showers are pre-set. They do feel a little cramped, but planned improvements should rectify that. Dishwashing sinks. Laundry with washing machine, dryer and iron. Chemical disposal. Of the 80 pitches, 52 have 16A electricity and all are reasonably level and well drained on well mown grass. Dogs allowed on leads with a good dog walk (a large, well mown field). Fishing, riding or golf 2 miles, bicycle hire 5 miles. Caravan storage available. All in all, this is a pleasant park in which to relax or to use as a base to explore the towns and beaches of Cornwall.

> **Directions:** From Bodmin or Wadebridge on the A389, take the B3266 north signed Camelford. At village of Longstone turn left signed St Mabyn and brown camping sign. Site is 400 yds. on right. Ignore all other signs to St Mabyn. O.S.GR: SX053735.
>
> **Charges 1998:** Per unit incl. 2 adults and awning £5.00 - £7.50; extra adult £1.00 - £1.75; child (2-15 yrs) 50p - £1.25; extra vehicle or pup tent free - £1.00; electricity (16A) £2.00; hiker or cyclist's tent (2 adults, no car) £5.00 - £6.50. Weekly rate available. Credit cards accepted (surcharge).
>
> **Open:** Easter - 31 October.
>
> **Reservations:** Made with £15 deposit - contact park for details. Address: Longstone Road, St Mabyn, Cornwall PL30 3BY. Tel: (01208) 841677. FAX: as phone. E-mail: gmpark@dircon.co.uk.

B035 Whitsand Bay Holiday Park, Millbrook, nr Torpoint

Self-contained, family holiday park with magnificent views, for all units.

The Rame peninsula, or 'Cornwall's forgotten corner', provides a unique setting for this unusual park, which was converted from a gun battery built in 1890 for defence from the sea - hence the marvellous views. Approaching the park along the cliff tops is deceiving, as the moatway and gun emplacements completely hide what is, in essence, a self-contained village, with even a chapel/reading room and owner's home. Holiday homes and chalets to let (beginning to look a little dated) blend into the fort's structure. The 120 marked grass touring pitches are terraced and tiered (quite steeply in places) into four areas and a rally field to give views landwards across to Plymouth, the Tamar estuary, Dartmoor and Exmoor. With tarmac access roads, they vary in size and 60 have electricity (16A). Several are taken by seasonal units. Two toilet blocks, placed between the fields, are acceptable and provide large, metered showers (no dividers), vanity style washbasins, razor points and hairdryers. Ramps allow use by disabled people. One washing up sink (H&C) under cover at each block and chemical disposal points. The facilities could be under pressure in high season and generally some 'TLC' would help. The laundry room is part of the Quartermaster's store, the rest of which has been used to develop the Battery Club (a 'real' pub), providing a cosy bar open to the public with family area, evening bar food and dance hall with entertainment in high season. Opposite, beside the well stocked shop, is the pool area, which is walled and paved. It is overlooked by the 'Café Bar', open all day in season, with dining area. Activities include a sauna and sun bed, games room with TV, crazy golf and a children's play area (never mind the tunnels linking the gun batteries!). An indoor pool is planned. All facilities are open in the main season - outside this opening is flexible. Torch useful. A steep 200 ft. cliff path provides access to Whitsand Bay (10 mins down, 20 mins up; unsuitable for small children or the infirm - other beaches are near) and the 'Whitsand Walk', a natural environment from which to enjoy the view at the edge of the park. Fishing ½ mile, boat slipway 2 miles, golf 2 miles. The Battery is a designated ancient monument and the area is one of 'outstanding natural beauty', ideal for fishing and walking, yet only 8 miles from Plymouth. Dogs accepted by prior arrangement.

> **Directions:** Using the Torpoint ferry, follow A374 Liskeard road and signs for Antony on disembarking (3 miles). Take left fork marked Millbrook (B3247) and continue for 2 miles to T-junction. Turn left for Whitsand Bay, then after less than 400 yds turn right and follow narrow road overlooking the bay for 2 miles. Signs for park on left. O.S.GR: SX417506.
>
> **Charges 1998:** Per pitch £7.00 - £14.00; electricity (16A) £2.00; small pitch for cyclist or walker less 50%. Club membership £1 per adult for entire stay. VAT included. Credit cards accepted.
>
> **Open:** All year.
>
> **Reservations:** Made with £10 deposit per week. Address: Millbrook, Torpoint, Cornwall PL10 1JZ. Tel: (01752) 822597. FAX: (01752) 823444.

Glenmorris Park

St. Mabyn, BODMIN, Cornwall PL30 3BY

Family Run, Tranquil, Picturesque, 10 Acre Level Park

Set between the Moors & the Shores

Heated Pool, Shop with Off Licence, Children's Play Area, Games room

80 Pitches ½ with EHUs, free hot water

Situated off the B3266 5½m North of Bodmin, 6½m South of Camelford

Telephone 01208-841677

Email gmpark@dircon.co.uk
Web Page www.gmpark.dircon.co.uk

B038 Wooda Farm Park, Bude

Spacious, relaxed, family run farm park with views of sea and countryside.

This well organised and cared for park with some nice touches is part of a working farm, 1¾ miles from the sandy, surfing beaches of Bude, in peaceful farmland with plenty of open spaces (and some up and down walking). The 200 pitches, spread over four meadows, are on level or gently sloping grass, 122 with electricity connections (10A), 21 with hardstanding and 21 grass, hedged 'premium' pitches (electricity, water, waste water). There are some holiday letting units situated beside the shop and reception at the entrance. Three well maintained toilet blocks with free hot water have fully tiled showers with seat and hooks, washbasins in vanity style with shelf and hand dryer, six washing up sinks (H&C) under cover, a unit suitable for the disabled and a baby room with small bath. Laundry with two washing machines, two tumble dryers, sinks with hot water and iron and board. A comprehensive range of facilities is provided Spr. B.H - Sept. These include a self-service shop with off-licence (8.30 - 8.30 in main season), a licensed courtyard bar with bar meals and a pleasant restaurant, Linney's Larder, with home cooking (closed Mon. and Sat. outside main season). A children's play area is in a separate field on grass, with plenty of room for ball games, a 9 hole 'fun' golf course (golf clubs provided), plus a woodland walk (where the pixies can be found) and an orchard walk. There is a small farm museum and friendly farm animals - children (and adults) can assist at feeding time! Tractor and trailer rides, pony riding and trekking, archery and clay pigeon shooting with tuition are provided according to season and demand, likewise barn dances. Games room with TV, table tennis and pool. Coarse fishing is available in a 1½ acre lake (permits from reception, £1.50 per half day, £2.50 per day). Dogs are accepted (not certain breeds) with a large exercise field. Public phone. Caravan storage available. The local village inn is five minutes walk. There is much to do in the area - the Leisure Centre and Splash Pool in Bude itself, sandy beaches with coastal walks, and Tintagel with King Arthur's Castle and Clovelly nearby.

Directions: Park is north of Bude at Poughill; turn off A39 on north side of Stratton on minor road for Coombe Valley, following camp signs at junctions. O.S.GR: SS225080.

Charges 1998: Per unit incl. 2 persons £6.50 - £10.00; extra adult £1.50 - £2.50; child (3-15 yrs) £1.00 - £1.50; awning/pup tent £1.00 - £1.30; dog 50p - £1.30; electricity (10A) £1.90; fully serviced pitch (incl. electricity) plus £3.50 - £4.50. VAT included. Credit cards accepted.

Open: Easter/1 April - October.

Reservations: Made with £20 p/week deposit. Address: Poughill, Bude, Cornwall EX23 9HJ. Tel: (01288) 352069. FAX: (01288) 355258.

BUDE - CORNWALL
Luxury Holiday Homes,
Excellent facilities for Camping and Touring
Tel: 01288 352069 Fax: 01288 355258

ANWB
BH&HPA

★ Set in 12 acre landscaped parkland overlooking Bude Bay
★ Beaches 1½ miles
★ 'Splash' indoor pool nearby   ★ Woodland walks
★ Restaurant and bar   ★ Children's play area
★ Own coarse fishing   ★ Fun golf course
★ Games room   ★ Laundry
★ Shop   ★ Free showers

MAIN SEASON

★ Clay pigeon shooting   ★ Archery
★ Pony trekking rides   ★ Tractor & trailer rides

For brochure please write, phone or fax to: Mrs A R Colwill
Wooda Farm, Poughill, Bude, Cornwall EX23 9HJ

B073 Twitchen Park, Mortehoe, nr Woolacombe

Holiday park with areas for tourers and tents, with family entertainment and close to superb beaches.

Set in the grounds of an attractive Edwardian country house, Twitchen Park's main concern lies in holiday caravans and flats. However, it also provides 90 marked pitches for tourers at the top of the park, with some views over the rolling hills to the sea. Of these, 50 have hardstanding and electricity, and are arranged around an oval access road in a hedged area. Behind are two open, unmarked sloping fields (blocks provided), with 90 electrical connections (16A). Two good sanitary blocks are on the sloping field, the larger of an unusual design with different levels and rather narrow corridors. Both have free, pre-set, hot showers (rather small), washbasins in rows and WCs. Dishwashing is under cover outside with laundry facilities in each block, plus a good launderette at the central complex. The touring areas are cared for by wardens who live on site. A smart, modern entertainment complex incorporates a licensed club and family lounge with snacks, restaurant, adults only bar, disco room, and cartoon lounge, with games rooms for table tennis, pool, snooker and arcade games, and entertainment day and evening. Shop and takeaway. Outside is a swimming pool (heated mid-May - mid-Sept) and paddling pool with free lessons in high season. Excellent indoor pool with sauna, paddling pool with fountain and viewing area. A super children's adventure play area (on bark), putting green and games field complete the facilities, which make Twitchen very popular for families with children. American motorhomes accepted (up to 30 ft.) by arrangement. No dogs permitted. Part of the Hoburne group.

Directions: From Barnstaple take A361 towards Ilfracombe and through Braunton. Turn left at Mullacott Cross roundabout towards Woolacombe, then right towards Mortehoe. Park on left before village. O.S.GR: SS466456.

Charges 1998: Per touring pitch, incl. electricity, awning and up to 6 persons £7.50 - £21.00; tent pitch (no electricity available) £5.50 - £18.00, all acc. to season; extra person 50p. VAT included. Credit cards accepted.

Open: 1 April/Easter - end October.

Reservations: Made with £50 deposit for tourers, payment in full for tent pitches. Min. period at Easter, May Day B.H. is 4 days, Spr. B.H. 7 days and mid July and Aug, 7 days from Sat. to Sat. Address: Mortehoe, Woolacombe, N. Devon EX34 7ES. Tel: (01271) 870476. FAX: (01271) 870498.

B138 Blue Anchor Park, Blue Anchor, nr Minehead

Beach-side site, for caravans and motorcaravans only, with views across the Bristol Channel.

Although mainly a holiday park, with 300 caravan holiday homes, Blue Anchor also offers good facilities for tourers (trailer tents accepted but not other tents), providing 103 pitches with hardstanding. All have 16A electricity and are virtually in a separate touring area. Facilities include a good size, irregularly shaped indoor swimming pool with an area for small children, complete with mushroom fountain. With views of the sea from the pool, it is heated and supervised, with a coffee shop. Crazy golf and an excellent children's play area in the wood. Small supermarket/shop (8 am - 9 pm in high season, less at other times). Sanitary facilities include large, free hot showers with push-button, vanity style washbasins, a launderette and chemical disposal, in a single, modern block serving just the touring area. Restaurants and takeaway food facilities are within walking distance. Riding 5 miles, golf 4½ miles. The park's situation, directly across the small road from the beach, is unusual and gives beautiful views across the Bristol Channel to South Wales. Dunster Castle, Exmoor, the Quantocks and Minehead are close and the West Somerset Steam Railway runs along one side of the park. No dogs accepted. American motorhomes accepted (max. 36 ft). Part of the Hoburne Group.

Directions: From M5 junction 25, take A358 signed Minehead. After 12 miles turn left onto A39 at Williton. After 4 miles turn right onto B3191 at Carhampton signed Blue Anchor. Park is 1½ miles on right. O.S.GR: ST025434.

Charges 1998: Per unit, incl. up to 6 persons, electricity and awning £5.50 - £15.00; extra pup tent £3.00. VAT included. Credit cards accepted.

Open: 1 March - 31 October.

Reservations: For stays of 1-6 days, payment required in full at time of booking; for 7 nights or more £50 deposit. Address: nr Minehead, Somerset TA24 6JT. Tel: (01643) 821360. FAX: (01643) 821572.

TWITCHEN PARK

Award Winning Holiday Park

HOLIDAY CARAVANS • TOURING & CAMPING PITCHES • FLATS

Popular family holiday Park close to the glorious sandy beach at Woolacombe and rugged coastal walks. New indoor pool. For FREE colour brochure or credit card bookings please contact:

TWITCHEN PARK, AR1, Mortehoe, Woolacombe, North Devon EX34 7ES

Telephone: 01271 870476

B089 Grange Court Holiday Centre, Paignton

Busy holiday park with excellent entertainment and recreation; touring sections for caravans only.

Situated to the south of central Paignton, with a short, signposted walk to the sea and some views of Torbay, Grange Court's major interest is the complex of 513 holiday homes (with letting service) which totally dominate the higher of the two touring sites. However there are 157 touring pitches (no tents) in two sections, each with its own resident wardens. One, probably the quieter of the two, is on flat grass by the entrance, with two modern toilet blocks (washbasins with free hot water, shelf and mirror, and free pre-set hot showers with push- button). The other is on higher ground, through the holiday homes at the top of the park with the site shops close by. It is on a gentle slope with some views, and has a larger, but older, tiled block. Individual pitches are of reasonable size, though with some variation, and all have electricity. The park can become full for most of July/Aug. and B.Hs. For those who like entertainment, the central complex is the park's best feature, with a good sized free outdoor, heated swimming pool (80 x 40 ft. open May - Sept). A super new indoor pool complex with views across the bay and over the outdoor pool is complete with flume, spa bath, sauna, steam room (all free for campers), plus a sun-bed. The clubhouse has a large bar lounge and separate room with dance floor - entertainment is organised almost nightly from Spr. B.H. to end Sept. and at Easter. Supermarket and other shops, takeaway for fish/chips, etc. and fast food bar (all 1 March - 31 Oct). Games rooms with two pool tables and one full size snooker table, and an amusement arcade, playground and large adventure play area (on bark). Large launderette, a range of recycling bins and chemical disposal. Up to 30 American motorhomes accepted (30 ft. max). No dogs or pets are accepted. Fishing and boat slipway 3 miles, golf 7 miles. Reception is busy, but efficient. Part of the Hoburne group.

Directions: Park is signed (not the normal camp site signs) from outer Paignton ring road. Turn off Goodrington Road into Grange Road. 150 yds from A379 coast road at signs for camp and Marine Park. O.S.GR: SX890585.

Charges 1998: Per unit £8.00 - £21.00, incl. electricity and awning, acc. to season (no tents, trailer tents or pup tents allowed). VAT included. Credit cards accepted.

Open: All year except 15/1-15/2.

Reservations: For 1-6 nights, full payment in advance required; for 7 nights and over £50 deposit per week (min. 7 days in Jul/Aug and B.H. weeks). Address: Goodrington, Paignton, Devon TQ4 7JP. Tel: (01803) 558010. FAX: (01803) 663336.

GRANGE COURT

Award Winning Holiday Park

HOLIDAY CARAVANS • TOURING PITCHES

Exciting indoor leisure complex compliments this already striking family Park in the heart of the English Riviera overlooking Torbay. Close to sandy beaches and Dartmoor.

For FREE colour brochure or credit card bookings please contact:

GRANGE COURT HOLIDAY CENTRE, AR1, Grange Road, Goodrington Paignton, Devon TQ4 7JP.

Telephone: 01803 558010

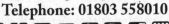

B079 Harford Bridge Park, Peter Tavy, nr Tavistock

Attractive, mature park on west Dartmoor bordering the delightful River Tavy.

Harford Bridge has an interesting history - originally the Wheal Union tin mine until 1850, then used as a farm campsite from 1930 and taken over by the Royal Engineers in 1939, it is now a quiet, rural park inside the Dartmoor National Park. It is bounded by the River Tavy on one side and the lane from the main road to the village of Peter Tavy on the other, with Harford Bridge, a classic granite moorland bridge, at the corner. With 16½ acres, the park provides 120 touring pitches well spaced on a level grassy meadow with some shade from mature trees and others recently planted; 40 pitches have electrical hook-ups and 8 have 'multi services'. Out of season or by booking in advance you may get one of the delightful spots bordering the river (these are without hook-up facilities). Holiday caravans and chalets are also available for hire, neatly landscaped in their own discrete area. The single toilet block is older in style but has been recently refurbished, It is kept perfectly clean, well decorated and properly maintained, and hot water is free throughout. The facilities include hand and hair dryers (free), baby bathroom, washing up sinks, a good launderette and drying room, freezer pack facility and chemical disposal point. At the entrance to the park a central grassy area is left free for games, which is also used by the town band, village fete, etc. It is overlooked by the site shop which is well stocked and reasonably priced. While the river will inevitably mesmerise the youngsters and the ducks and chickens attract their interest, a super central adventure play area on a hilly tree knoll will claim them. Two restored Wickstead stainless steel slides, a 45 year old carnival carousel roundabout, tunnels and model chimney like the original are just part of a well presented, safe and marvellous provision. Games room with additional campers' information, table tennis and separate TV room. Tennis court (free). Fishing (by licence, £2.80 p/day, £10 p/week). Communal barbecue areas. Well behaved dogs are accepted and a 4 acre exercise field is provided. With its own and the local history, plus its situation, this is a super place to stay.

Directions: Turn off A386 just south of Mary Tavy village, 2 miles north of Tavistock, towards Harford Bridge. O.S.GR: SX504768.

Charges 1998: Per unit, incl. 2 persons £6.00 - £9.00; extra adult £2.00 - £2.50; child £1.00 - £1.50; dog 90p; electricity £2.00; awning £1.00; extra car 50p. Less 10% for stays over 7 days (not electricity or fishing). Credit cards accepted. VAT included.

Open: Late March - early November.

Reservations: Made for any length with first night's fees. Address: Peter Tavy, Tavistock, Devon PL19 9LS. Tel: (01822) 810349. FAX: (01822) 810028.

B080 Higher Longford Farm, Moorshop, nr Tavistock

Quiet, small, family run park, ideal for staying on lower levels of Dartmoor.

Situated within the National Park boundaries, this small park has views up to the higher slopes of the moor. The site has a sheltered touring field where 40 level pitches are arranged on each side of a circular access road, two smaller touring areas for 12 units and a seasonal camping field for a further 80. Facilities include 49 electrical hook-ups and an area of hardstanding for poor weather. Residential caravans and chalets for hire are in a separate area adjacent and some attractive converted cottages also for hire form a courtyard area with the farmhouse, reception and bar. The main toilet block is alongside the touring field providing roomy showers, smallish washbasins and one en-suite cabin for ladies, hand and hair dryers and dishwashing, all with plentiful, free hot water. This is supplemented by extra heated facilities in the courtyard, which include showers with a communal dressing area. Extra smart chemical disposal (like a wishing well), full laundry facilities and a washing line, motorcaravan service point. Within the 14th century farmhouse is a small shop, open on demand, with some fresh farm produce. It adjoins a pleasant, cosy bar and restaurant with open fire and TV, where takeaway or full meals are offered (all April-Nov), and a spacious conservatory, useful in poor weather. Tourist information. Public phone. Dogs are welcome but must be kept under strict control (exercise field provided). This enables the site to keep small animals and lambs (in season) - an unending delight to youngsters. Higher Longford is an ideal centre for touring Dartmoor, either by car, on foot, or astride a local pony (riding stables nearby). The site is sometimes used as a base by groups of youngsters for trips onto the moor. Game or coarse fishing 3 miles, Tavistock golf course 1½ miles, bicycle hire or riding 3 miles. Caravan storage available.

Directions: Park is clearly signed from the B3357, 2 miles from Tavistock. O.S.GR: SX520747.

Charges 1998: Per unit incl. 1 person £6.50 - £7.50, 2 persons £7.50 - £8.50, family (2 adults, 2 children) £8.00 - £9.00; electricity £2.00; extra adult £1.00 - £1.50; extra child (over 3 yrs) 50p - 75p; extra car 75p; hiker/cyclist and tent £5.00 - £6.00, 2 persons £6.00 - £7.00. Less 50p per night for booked stays. No credit cards. VAT included.

Open: All year.

Reservations: Made with £5 deposit. Address: Moorshop, Tavistock, Devon PL19 9JU. Tel: (01822) 613360. FAX: (01822) 618722.

B090 Widdicombe Farm Tourist Park, Paignton

Well situated park on fringes of Torquay, yet with rural outlook.

Widdicombe Farm, just 3 miles from Torquay with easy access from the A380, offers 200 numbered pitches, 137 of which have electrical connections (10A) and 10 are fully serviced. Surrounded by farmland, the pitches are on gently sloping grass terraces giving a very rural feel. Many new trees and shrubs have been planted and there are tarmac access roads. A few pitches are fairly close to the A380 and there may be some traffic noise. Touring areas are separated into sections for families, couples or tents and some hardstandings are available. On site facilities include reception, shop, the 'Poppy' restaurant which provides evening meals, breakfasts and cream teas (takeaway also available). A large comfortable bar offers family entertainment and opposite the bar is a 'do it yourself' barbecue area with large gas barbecues, patio area and seating (£2 per session). Other amenities include a games room with video games and pool tables, children's play area and a recreation field for ball games. There are three sanitary blocks, one of older construction near the main reception/shop and two newer blocks, one at the top of the site, with provision for the disabled and the other in the new lower section. All have good facilities. Baby room, dishwashing under cover and a small laundry with two machines and dryers. A warden lives on site. Three caravan holiday homes for hire. Dogs permitted (but no dangerous breeds).

Directions: From Newton Abbot take the A380 south for approx. 5 miles; site is well signed off this road. O.S.GR: SX874641.

Charges 1998: Per unit incl. 2 persons £6.00 - £10.00; extra adult £2.00 - £2.50; child (3-16 yrs) £1.00 - £1.50; awning, extra car or dog £1.00 - £1.50; electricity (10A) £1.80. Bargain breaks available - contact park.

Open: March - November.

Reservations: Recommended for July/Aug. (min. 7 days, 4 days at other times) and made with deposit (£20 per week) and fee (£2). Address: The Ring Road, Compton, Paignton, Devon TQ3 1ST. Tel: (01803) 558325. FAX: (01803) 559426.

B091 Ross Park, Ipplepen, nr Newton Abbot

Excellent, friendly, relaxed park in attractive landscaped surroundings.

Ross Park has to be seen to appreciate its amazing floral displays with their dramatic colours, which are a feature of the park. These are complemented by the use of a wide variety of shrubs which form hedging for most of the pitches providing your own special plot, very much as on the continent. For those who prefer the more open style, one small area has been left unhedged. There are views over the surrounding countryside but as the foliage has developed these are not quite as extensive but there is more protection on a windy day. The owners, Mark and Helen Lowe, are constantly striving to provide quality facilities, re-tiling and re-fitting sanitary facilities to high standards but including nice personal touches as seen in the utility room with the beautiful photographs of the countryside and suggestions for visits. Also giving an individual touch is the impressive, heated conservatory with yet more named exotic and colourful plants. Seating is provided here as it is directly linked to the 'New Barn' which provides a comfortable lounge, mezzanine bar and restaurant with a la carte menu or bar snacks (all limited hours out of main season). The touring area is divided into bays or groups by the hedging and shrubs and provides 110 pitches all with electricity (10/16A), 82 of which have a hardened surface and some made larger with an increased gravel area. The main toilet facilities next to the New Barn open from under a veranda style roof, colourful with hanging baskets. They comprise six nicely equipped en-suite units, one with baby changing facilities, one suitable for disabled people. At the rear are further separate shower, washbasin and toilet facilities, all well equipped. Below the New Barn are further toilets and washbasins in a new well kept 'portacabin' style unit. Hot water is free and shaver points and hairdryers are provided. A separate new laundry room is fully equipped and a utility room provides dishwashing sinks, freezer and battery charging facilities. Chemical disposal facilities. Games room and billiards room. Comfortable reception with shop area alongside, fresh bread, etc. according to season. Tourist information chalet with herbs for your barbecues nearby. A 4 acre park area is for recreation with bowling and croquet greens and a large well equipped adventure play ground for older children. A conservation area with information on wild flowers and butterflies and extended views completes these environmentally considered amenities. Dogs are welcome with a variety of walks in fields and orchards and they are even provided with their own shower and grooming facilities, hot water included! Barn dances with barbecue are organised on Sundays in high season. Dainton Park 18 hole golf course is adjacent and fishing is 3 miles. A park well worth consideration, open all year.

Directions: From A381 Newton Abbot - Totnes road, park is signed towards Woodland at Park Hill crossroads and Jet filling station. O.S.GR: SX845671.

Charges 1998: Per unit incl. 2 persons £6.80 - £10.90; extra adult £3.00 - £3.50; child (3-16 yrs) £1.50 - £1.75; electricity (16A) £1.80 - £2.20. Christmas packages available. VAT included.

Open: All year.

Reservations: Made with £20 deposit. Address: Park Hill Farm, Ipplepen, Newton Abbot, Devon TQ12 5TT. Tel: (01803) 812983. FAX: as phone.

B104 Old Cotmore Farm, Stokenham, nr Kingsbridge

Charming, small and secluded park two miles from Start Point.

Sue and John Bradney recently acquired Old Cotmore Farm - that is the farmhouse, two cottages and a small touring site. The only livestock to be seen now are a few chickens and ducks, including a curious pair of black pilot ducks who patrol the site, and maybe some horses. They have worked hard to improve the facilities and now provide 30 pitches, all with electric hook-up, on neatly cut grass. Partly in an orchard situation with some pitches sloping, and partly on a level field with children's play equipment in the centre, so it tends to be used more for families with children. A small stream runs along one side with a pretty pond area and bridge near the entrance. Reception is past the pitches towards the farmhouse and adjoining the toilet block which has been converted from original buildings. The blocks have been refurbished with a degree of individuality to provide modern vanity style washbasins (H&C) and pre-set hot showers with stools, no dividers and non slip floor. A washbasin and changing area for babies is in the ladies' along with tourist information. Covered dish washing sinks (H&C). Telephone and small laundry room with three washing machines and two dryers. Chemical toilet and waste water disposal tucked away behind reception. A separate field with a 28 day licence has water points, an extra sink and a toilet, but it may put pressure on the main block when in use. Mountain bike hire and table tennis. Mrs Bradney holds a children's club once a week in high season. Reception stocks basic necessities - warm baguettes can be ordered and helpful wardens will help you pitch. The site is actually in an area of Outstanding Natural Coastal Beauty, with Slapton Sands, Salcombe and Kingsbridge near and Dartmouth just a little further. It is an ideal area for walking, boating, diving, windsurfing and safe bathing Two pubs are within one mile either way. Three cottages to let.

Directions: From Kingsbridge on A379 Dartmouth road, go through Frogmore and Chillington until you reach Carehouse Cross mini-roundabout at Stokenham. Turn right towards Beesands and follow camp signs for one mile. Site signed on left with tarmac entrance drive. Roads a little narrow in places. O.S.GR: SX804417.

Charges 1998: Per unit incl. 2 persons £8.50; tent incl. 2 persons £5.00; extra adult £1.50; child (up to 12 yrs) £1.00; car, dog or boat £1.00; electricity £2.00. Less £1.00 per pitch in low seasons. Credit cards accepted

Open: 14 March - 14 November.

Reservations: Made with 25% deposit; contact park. Address: Stokenham, nr Kingsbridge, South Devon TQ7 2LR. Tel: (01548) 580240.

B207 The Inside Park Touring Caravan & Camping Park, nr Blandford Forum

Small, family run, rural park ideal for touring Dorset.

The Inside Park is set in the grounds of an 18th century country house which burned down in 1941. Family owned and carefully managed alongside a dairy and arable farm, it is a must for those interested in local history or arboriculture and is a haven for wild life and birds. The reception/toilet block and games room block are respectively the coach house and stables of the old house. The 9-acre camping field, a little distant, lies in a sheltered, gently sloping dry valley containing superb tree specimens - notably cedars, with walnuts in one part - and a dog graveyard dating back to the early 1700s under a large Cedar of Lebanon. In total there are 125 spacious pitches, 90 with electricity (10A). The six acres adjoining are the old pleasure gardens of the house where campers can walk and exercise dogs in the former garden, now mostly overgrown and providing what must be one of the largest children's campsite adventure-lands in the UK. The toilet block, recently extended, houses comfortably sized showers (pre-set, push button type with curtain splash back), washbasins (some cubicles in ladies) and toilets, all with free hot water and non-slip tiled floors. A room for use by the disabled and mothers and babies has been added, plus new dishwashing sinks. A laundry room is in the same block. Chemical toilet disposal and recycling bins are provided. Spacious games room with video games, etc. and an information section. Safe based children's adventure play area with trampolines and organised farm tours, especially at milking time. Shop with basics (farm milk available) and camping provisions (open limited periods out of main season). Public telephone. No vehicle access to the park allowed after 10.30 pm. (separate late arrivals area and car park). Day kennelling facilities for dogs. Winter caravan storage available. The market town of Blandford with its leisure and swimming centre (free temporary membership for Inside Park guests) is 2 miles and the area is excellent for walking and cycling. Fishing and riding 2 miles, golf 3 miles. Extensive walking routes are marked through the farm and woodland, with a guide showing points of interest available in the shop.

Directions: Park is about 1½ miles southwest of Blandford and is signed from the roundabout at the junction of the A354 and A350 roads. If approaching from the Shaftesbury direction, do not go into Blandford but follow the bypass to the last roundabout and follow camp signs. O.S.GR: ST864045.

Charges 1998: Per pitch £2.95 - £4.30; adult £2.25 - £2.95; child (5-16 yrs) free - £1.00; dog 50p - 80p; electricity £2.00; tent light free - £1.00. VAT included. Credit cards accepted.

Open: 1 April - 31 October.

Reservations: Made with £10 deposit (min. 4 nights 13/7-1/9). Address: Blandford Forum, Dorset DT11 9AD. Tel: (01258) 453719. FAX: (01258) 459921. E-mail: inspark@aol.com. Internet: http://members@aol/inspark/ inspark.

B212 Hoburne Park, Christchurch

Well kept holiday home and touring site with many amenities; for caravans and motorcaravans only.

This well kept and tidy park, with a range of good quality amenities, is convenient for Bournemouth or the New Forest. There are 285 level, grass touring pitches (for caravans or motorcaravans only), all with 16A electricity and some with individual water supply and hardstanding, in three separated hedged, neatly grassed areas. The park also caters for 305 caravan holiday homes for hire. The amenities include an outdoor pool, with both paved and grass sunbathing areas, children's pool and an attractive indoor leisure pool with sauna, spa bath, solarium and steam rooms. We continue to be impressed with the number of lifeguards on duty and the attendance to safety here and at other Hoburne parks. A large reception area, restaurant, snack bar, takeaway, well furnished bar with terrace, video games room and snooker room form part of the indoor complex area. A large adventure play area with play castle is near this main complex together with hard court tennis, crazy golf and a field area with goal posts. There is an organised programme of entertainment for adults and children in the season. A well stocked shop and launderette complete the facilities. The sanitary facilities are modern and include free hot showers in blocks central to each field area, with additional facilities attached to the main building. A mother and baby room with bath are in one block and nappy changing units in all blocks. Free hairdryers. Chemical disposal. Many large sites have a somewhat frenzied atmosphere in the high season. This one can be busy but the atmosphere is pleasantly quiet and relaxed. No tents, trailer tents or pup tents are permitted. Dogs and pets not accepted. American motorhomes accepted in limited numbers up to 30 ft. Fishing or golf 3 miles, bicycle hire or boat slipway 2 miles, riding 6 miles. A well managed park, the flag flier of the Hoburne group.

Directions: Park is signed (left) from the roundabout about 2 miles east of Christchurch on the A337. From Lyndhurst, travel south on A35 to the junction with A337 - turn left onto A337 then left again at the first roundabout. O.S.GR: SZ169928.

Charges 1998: Per unit, incl. electricity and awning (up to 3 x 9m.) £9.00 - £23.00. Weekly rates and special weekend breaks. VAT included. Credit cards accepted.

Open: March - October.

Reservations: Made with payment in full (6 days or less) or £50 deposit; min. periods 4 nights for B.Hs, 7 nights mid July - end Aug. Address: Hoburne Lane, Christchurch, Dorset BH23 4HU. Tel: (01425) 273379. FAX: (01425) 270705.

B210 Sandford Holiday Park, Holton Heath, nr Poole

See colour advert
between pages 32/33

Pleasant, well run holiday park with first-class amenities; large touring section.

Sandford Park has a large permanent section with 248 holiday homes and lodges. However, the touring sections takes 460 units of any type, mainly on individual pitches, on level grass with mature hedging in the main area. All have 10A electricity. The main toilet block in the touring area provides facilities for disabled visitors and a baby room. It is supplemented by the former main block and `portacabin' style units in the touring and static areas (one a bath block). Free hot water in washbasins and pre-set showers (under pressure at peak times). Dogs accepted from 5 Sept. onwards. Sandford is a large, very busy holiday park with a wide range of entertainment. The spacious clubhouse (membership free) has a dance floor and bar. There is also a large air conditioned ballroom for entertainment and dancing. Both open over a long season. A variety of bars, restaurants (book in busy periods) and simple hot meals and takeaway elsewhere in peak season. The outdoor pool (25 m, open May-Oct. and supervised) and a very large play pool (0-2 ft.) with a sandy beach, are attractively situated with a snack bar and terrace. An impressive indoor pool is a nice addition, also a separate soft indoor play area for children (April - Oct and Christmas, also supervised). Large supermarket and other shops (all peak season only). Launderette. Ladies' hairdresser. TV lounges. Children's playground, tennis courts, mountain bike hire, table tennis, short mat bowling greens (outdoor) and crazy golf. Public phones. Riding and fishing (9 miles).

Directions: Park is just west off the A351 (Wareham - Poole) road at Holton Heath. O.S.GR: SY940913.

Charges 1998: Per pitch free - £5.75, acc. to season; adult £2.25; child (3-13 yrs) £1.50 - £2.50; extra car free - £1.50; awning free; electricity £2.50; `super hook-up (electricity, TV, water) £4.50; dog (1 only, after 4 Sept) £2.50; boat and trailer £1.50 - £2.00; visitor £3.95, child £1.75). VAT included. Credit cards accepted.

Open: Easter - January incl.

Reservations: Early booking advisable (min. 3 days) - write to park. Address: Holton Heath, nr Poole, Dorset BH16 6JZ. Tel: (01202) 631600.

B225 Bashley Park, New Milton

Pleasant park with large section for caravans or motorcaravans, with pools and entertainment.

A well run park with 380 holiday homes (40 for hire), Bashley Park also has a very sizeable tourist section taking 420 units (tents, trailer tents and pup tents not accepted). Spread over three flat meadows plus a woodland area, pitches are individual with electricity, marked but not separated. Groundsheets must be lifted daily. The four toilet blocks, one central to each area, are well constructed, fully tiled with free hot water, vanity style washbasins and push-button, pre-set showers (no divider, but shower heads set fairly low). In pleasant park-like surroundings not far from beaches, Bournemouth and the New Forest, the site has a good clubhouse with excellent facilities overlooking an 18 m. circular outdoor pool (heated mid-May - mid-Sept) and 18 m. paddling pool, a sensible size and fun with its geysers and beach effect. An indoor pool complex houses a water flume, sauna, spa bath and steam room. Evening entertainment (also for children) in the club with music Spring B.H. to mid-Sept; ballroom, large lounges and bars, restaurant, simple hot food takeaway all day, TV room. Video arcade and games room with snooker and pool tables spread among other rooms. Very well equipped children's play area, crazy golf, nine hole, `par 3' golf course on site, bicycle hire and three tennis courts. Fishing or riding 1 mile. Shop (mid-May to end Sept). Launderette. Up to 6 American motorhomes accepted (40 ft. max). One dog or pet is allowed per unit. A popular park with lots going on, part of the Hoburne group.

Directions: Park is on B3055 ¼ mile east of crossroads with the B3058 in Bashley village. O.S.GR: SZ246969.

Charges 1998: Per unit incl. all persons and electricity £9.00 - £23.00; multi service pitch £10.50 - £26.50; pet (1 only) £2.00. Weekly rates available. VAT included. Credit cards accepted.

Open: 28 February - 31 October.

Reservations: Necessary for peak season and made for any length: 1-6 nights with payment in full at booking; 7+ nights, £50 p/w. deposit, balance 3 weeks before arrival. Address: Sway Road, New Milton, Hants BH25 5QR. Tel: (01425) 612340. FAX: (01425) 612602.

B203 Wareham Forest Tourist Park, nr Wareham

Well run park in forest setting with swimming pool.

A tranquil, spacious park in an unspoilt corner of Dorset, this site has been developed to high standards, providing formal pitching, with or without hardstanding, for caravans or natural pitches for tents in pine wood or open field. Drainage should be good. The setting in Wareham Forest is attractive offering space for over 220 units, 102 with hardstanding and 180 with electricity. Also 8 luxury pitches on hardstanding with water, drainage, TV aerial, bin and light. A café for breakfasts, etc. (main season) looks out over a terrace onto the free, open-air pool, which can be heated (60 x 20 ft), with grass sunbathing area. Small shop with off-licence (limited hours) and busy games room with amusement machines next door. Two good, well maintained toilet blocks have some washbasins in cabins for ladies (adjustable showers on payment). Facilities for disabled people. Chemical disposal, motorcaravan services. Children's play area. Forest walks. Fishing 5 miles, bicycle hire or golf 3 miles. Well situated to explore the Dorset coast and Thomas Hardy country. Caravan storage. Resident wardens.

Directions: Park is north of Wareham between Wareham and Bere Regis, off the A35 road. O.S.GR: SY899903.

Charges 1998: Per pitch: standard £3.50 - £5.50, serviced £5.50 - £7.50; adult £1.80 - £3.00; child (2-14 yrs) £1.00 - £2.00; dog £1.50; electricity £2.00. Discount for OAPs in low season. VAT included. Credit cards accepted.

Open: All year.

Reservations: Made with £25 deposit and £2 fee, balance 28 days before arrival. High season min. 7 days for serviced pitch, 3 days others. Address: North Trigon, Wareham, Dorset BH20 7NZ. Tel/Fax: (01929) 551393.

B303 Tanner Farm Touring Caravan and Camping Park, Marden

Quality park in quiet, spacious, rural setting.

Developed as part of a family working farm, Tanner Farm has rapidly received recognition as a top class park. This is the heart of the Weald of Kent with orchards, hop gardens, lovely countryside and delightful small villages. The owners are concerned with conserving the natural beauty of the environment and visitors may walk around the farm and see the Shire horses at work. The park extends over 15 acres, part of which is level and part a gentle slope. The grass meadowland has been semi landscaped by planting saplings, etc. which units back onto as the owners do not wish to regiment pitches. Places are numbered but not marked, allowing plenty of space between units which, with large open areas, gives a pleasant, comfortable atmosphere. There are 100 pitches, all with electricity, 13 with hardstanding, 4 with water tap and 1 with waste water point. A member of the Caravan Club's 'managed under contract' scheme, non-members are also welcome. The farm drive links the park with the B2079 and a group of refurbished oast houses (listed heritage buildings) with a duck pond in front, along with rare pigs, pygmy goats, lambs, etc. make a focal point. The traditional farm building at the entrance houses a small shop (limited stock and opening hours in winter) and reception. The two sanitary blocks are centrally heated, tiled and with flower arrangements and flower beds. Free hot water in washbasins (private cabins in both blocks), showers and washing up sinks. Facilities for disabled visitors, small launderette, chemical disposal and motorcaravan services. A bathroom and baby facilities have been added in the newer block (not open Nov - Easter). Small children's play area and fishing on site. Good night lighting, but a torch may be advisable. The friendly management advise on local attractions, shops and pubs. There is a high concentration of National Trust attractions in the area, riding and golf within 6 miles, leisure centres and sailing facilities near. Caravan storage. Note: only one car per pitch permitted.

Directions: Park is 2½ miles south of Marden on B2079 towards Goudhurst. O.S.GR: TQ732417.

Charges 1998: Per pitch £3.00; adult £2.60 - £3.90; child £1.10 - £1.20; 2-man tent plus car (all incl.) £7.50 - £8.00, plus bicycles £5.00 - £5.50; electricity £1.45 - £2.20; all service pitch +£2.00. Credit cards accepted.

Open: All year.

Reservations: Essential for high season and B.H. Made with deposit (£5 for 1-3 nights; £10 over 3 nights and B.Hs). Address: Goudhurst Road, Marden, Kent TN12 9ND. Tel: (01622) 832399. FAX: (01622) 832472.

BRITISH ISLES - England

B321 Lee Valley Caravan Park, Dobbs Weir, Hoddesdon

Pleasant park north of London in Lee Valley Park.

Stretching for 23 miles along the Lee Valley and covering 10,000 acres from Ware to the east end of London, Lee Valley park is administered by the Lee Valley Regional Park Authority. Extensive development of the Park into a leisure area now means it offers a wide variety of outdoor and sporting pursuits, including riding, watersports, golf, cycle tracks and places of interest. Set between Hoddesdon, Broxbourne and Nazeing, and under the same management as Lee Valley Campsite (no. 325), this park is situated in the far north of the complex. The touring section, a large, open, well mown meadow with space for 100 units, 36 with electricity (10A), is quite separate from 100 caravan holiday homes. There is no shade, but tall trees surrounding the site offer adequate shelter, and it has a neat, tidy and well cared for appearance. A single, heated sanitary block (access by key) is of good quality with free hot water to washbasins, showers and sinks. Baby room, laundry and facilities for disabled people. No shop, but free bus service to a nearby superstore three times a week, and there is a bar/restaurant just 100 yds from the entrance. Some fishing is possible from the canal towpath that runs past the site, with further opportunities nearby and a swimming pool is 2 miles away. Trains run from Broxbourne (about 2 miles) to London, with he journey taking 30 minutes. Dobbs Weir industrial estate and garden centres are near, but surrounding trees screen out noise and create some privacy. Caravan storage.

Directions: Take exit 25 from M25 and then north on A10 for 4 miles; take the Hoddesdon exit, turn left at second roundabout following signs for Dobbs Weir and park is on the right within 1 mile. O.S.GR: TL383082.

Charges 1998: Per adult £4.60; child (under 16 yrs) £1.90; electricity £1.70. Min. charge £6.50 (but not backpackers). VAT included. Credit cards accepted. Checking out time 5 pm.

Open: Weekend before Easter - 31 October.

Reservations: Made with £5 deposit - write to park for reservation form. Address: Charlton Meadows, Essex Road, Dobbs Weir, Hoddesdon, Hertfordshire EN11 0AS. Tel: (01992) 462090. FAX: 01992) 462090. Internet: www.leevalleypark.org.uk. (For information contact PO Box 88, Enfield, Middlesex; tel: 01992 700766).

B325 Lee Valley Campsite, Chingford, North London

Friendly and well run park, conveniently placed for visits to the London area.

This site provides an excellent base for visits to the capital, having both easy access to the M25 and excellent public transport links into the centre of London. Closely situated to Epping Forest and in the heart of the Lee Valley, there is much to enjoy in the surrounding area, from walking and cycling, to golf, fishing and riding. Taking 200 units, the site is mostly level, with several bush sheltered avenues and plenty of trees. There are 20 pitches with hardstanding and 100 with electricity (10A). Three good toilet blocks, one heated, are more than adequate with free hot water to washbasins and controllable showers, and a few washing up sinks. Laundry room and shop. Children's playground. No other on-site amenities, but those staying are often out visiting London. A local bus stops by the site fairly frequently in season, with another equally good service, every 20 minutes to Walthamstow underground station just 500 yds away. Alternatively you can park at South Woodford or Chingford stations and go by train.

Directions: From M25 exit 26 (Waltham Abbey) from where site is signed; take A112 road towards Chingford and site is 3 miles on right. It can also be approached on A112 from the North Circular Road. O.S.GR: TQ378970.

Charges 1998: Per adult £5.00; child (under 16 yrs) £2.20; electricity £2.25. Min. charge £7.10 per unit/night. VAT included. Credit cards accepted.

Open: 25 March - 31 October.

Reservations: Any length up to 14 days with £5 depositAddress: Sewardstone Road, Chingford, London E4 7RA. Tel: 0181 529 5689. FAX: 0181 559 4070.

B347 Breckland Meadows Touring Park, Swaffham

Small touring park within walking distance of historic market town.

This is a pleasant little park which would make a good base to explore the local area. The 40 pitches are on fairly level grass, all with electricity (16A). There may be some road noise at times but newly planted trees should reduce this as they mature. Adjacent to the site is the Swaefas Way, a seven mile circular walk which links to the more well known Peddars Way. The recently redecorated, small sanitary unit is bright, clean and provides the usual facilities including showers. The new owners (Feb '98) are planning a brand new building to replace the current unit, which they hope will be ready for '99. Local attractions include Cockley Cley Medieval Iceni Village and Saxon Church (3½ miles), Castle Acre Priory (3 miles), and Oxburgh Hall. Swaffham (½ mile) is a historic market town with a popular Saturday market.

Directions: Park is just west of Swaffham on the old A47, approx. ½ mile from village centre. O.S.GR: TF820080.

Charges 1998: Per unit incl. 2 adults £6.00 - £8.00; extra adult £1.00; child (5-15 yrs) 50p; small tent £4.00 - £5.00; awning £1.00; electricity £1.80 - £2.00. VAT included. Credit cards accepted.

Open: 20 March - 31 October.

Reservations: Essential for B.Hs and advised for peak season; made with non-refundable deposit (£5 for 1 night, £10 for 2+ nights). Address: Lynn Road, Swaffham, Norfolk. Tel: (01760) 721246.

THE BEST OF

BOTH WORLDS

Countryside settings with London on the doorstep

The Lee Valley Regional Park stretches from the edge of London's Docklands up to rural Hertfordshire and Essex. It boasts five camping and caravan sites for you to choose from, all with modern facilities, all in pleasant surroundings and all with their own local leisure attractions. Yet, each is within easy reach of Central London by public transport. So you can sleep under the stars and still enjoy the thrills of the West End.

Roydon Mill Leisure Park, Roydon, Essex: Children's adventure playground. Riverside Club with regular entertainment, 40-acre lake for water-based activities. Fast train service to London. Tel: 01279 792777.

Lee Valley Caravan Park, Hoddesdon, Herts: Delightful riverside site with good fishing, walking and boating nearby. Fast train service to London. Tel: 01992 462090.

Lee Valley Campsite, Chingford, Essex: On the edge of Epping Forest, close to the River Lee Country Park, easy access from the M25. Bus and tube to London. Tel: 0181 529 5689.

Lee Valley Leisure Complex, Edmonton, N. London: Large leisure centre, 18-hole golf course, 12-screen UCI cinema. Bus and tube to London. Tel: 0181 803 6900

Lee Valley Cycle Circuit, Leyton, E. London: Small site in 40 acres of open parkland, yet only 4 miles from the Tower of London. Adjacent to Lee Valley Sports Centre and off-road Cycle Circuit. Bus and tube to the West End. Tel: 0181 534 6085.

Lee Valley Park

BRITISH ISLES - England

B339 The Dower House Touring Park, Thetford Forest

Peaceful park in a woodland setting.

The Dower House is situated in 20 acres of Britain's largest woodland forest on the Suffolk and Norfolk borders, it provides quiet woodland walks and cycle ways, with an abundance of wildlife. It is also an ideal centre from which to explore Breckland. The owners acquired the park some years ago and have worked hard to upgrade the facilities. There is provision for 60 tents and 100 vans on unmarked, fairly level, open grass with some mature oaks, in four field areas surrounded by the forest, with the Dower House in the centre. Electrical hook-ups (10-16A) are available on three fields with wheel hardstandings on one. A smallish swimming pool (only 1.1 m. deep, from late May), with a paddling pool alongside, is attractively situated in front of the house. The Dower House, as well as being the home of the owners, houses a pleasant bar which provides the history of the house and also serves basic bar food (only selected nights in low season), TV and quiet rooms, and a takeaway. No games machines. A patio area is used for special feature weekends (eg. Morris dancing, Swinging 60s). A licensed shop doubles as reception and opens daily in the season, on request at other times. There are two toilet blocks - a small, refurbished one near the entrance, and a larger one with free hot water in the row of washbasins and a baby room. The showers (20p for 4 mins with meter outside door) are in a separate building which also houses a unit for disabled people. Dishwashing room, including a lower sink for children or disabled visitors. Laundry room. Chemical disposal. Public phone. Information room. Torch useful. Fishing 1½ miles. Very large, open air market at Snetterton motor racing circuit (2-3 miles) on Sundays.

Directions: From A11 (Thetford-Norwich) road follow signs to East Harling and park is signed. Turn right at the church and right at T junction; park is on right. From A1066 Thetford-Garboldisham road follow signs for East Harling and park is on left after passing Forestry Commission site. Follow unmade road for approx. 1 mile driving slowly past the Gamekeepers cottage. O.S.GR: TL969853.

Charges 1998: Per unit incl. 2 persons £6.95 - £9.15; extra adult 50p - £1.50; extra child (4-17 yrs) 40p - 85p; hikers or cyclists (2 persons) £4.85 - £6.50; electricity £2.00 - £2.25. VAT included. Credit cards accepted.

Open: 20 March - 31 October.

Reservations: Accepted by phone; deposit of £10 required for electricity. Address: Thetford Forest, East Harling, Norfolk NR16 2SE. Tel: (01953) 717314. FAX: (01953) 717843.

the Dower house the touring park in the heart of the forest

GRADED HOLIDAY PARKS BRITISH Very good

Caravan TOP 100 FAMILY PARKS 1998

1997 SILVER

Enquiries to David or Karin
**The Dower House
Touring Park**
Thetford Forest
East Harling
Norfolk
NR16 2SE
(01953) 717314
www.dowerhse.dircon.co.uk/

B407 Somers Wood Caravan and Camping Park, Meriden

New, purpose built park in light pine woods near the National Exhibition Centre.

Use of natural materials and thoughtful design by Mark and Angela Fowler have combined to provide a new, modern park which blends comfortably into its surroundings. Log buildings have been used for reception, the owners' home at the entrance and for the sanitary facilities. An oval, gravel road provides access to 48 large pitches, 42 with 10A electricity. There are many hardstandings with pines, silver birch, foxgloves and natural grass providing pleasant surroundings with glimpses of the fishing lake, which adjoins the site, along with an 18 hole golf course. The centrally situated sanitary facilities can be heated and provide free, hot showers and vanity style washbasins, all neat and clean. Two dishwashing sinks with hot water are on the veranda (no laundry sinks). Simple chemical disposal point. Pigmy goats, hens and ducks provide entertainment. Tourist information and public phone in reception. A very useful park for visiting the NEC. Gas barbecues only. Riding 4 miles. Shops and a restaurant are less than 1 mile and visitors are also welcome to use the bar and restaurant at the golf club.

Directions: From M42 junction 6 (NEC) take A45 towards Coventry. Almost immediately take A452 signed Leamington. Turn right at roundabout on A452 then turn left into Hampton Lane at the next roundabout, signed Stonesbridge Golf Centre and site is signed with golf and fishing centres on the left. O.S.GR: SP228819.

Charges 1998: Per pitch incl. 2 persons £9.00; 1-man tent £6.00; extra adult £1.00; extra child (5-15 yrs) 50p; awning or extra car £1.00; electricity £2.50 (Apr-Sept) - £3.00 (Oct-March). No credit cards.

Open: All year.

Reservations: Recommended for B.Hs and certain NEC exhibitions; made with deposit of £3 per night booked. Address: Somers Road, Meriden, N. Warwickshire CV7 7PL. Tel: (01676) 522978.

B393 Sherwood Forest Caravan Park, Old Clipstone, nr Mansfield

Country park of 22 acres between the M1 and A1 roads.

A quiet country park, taking all types of unit, this is attractively landscaped in pleasant surroundings, and is close to many places of interest. Owned by the Civil Service Motoring Association, non-members are also welcome. The touring areas stretch alongside the River Maun, each offering a slightly different aspect, some set aside for dog owners, others overlooking the water. Trees and shrubs enhance the rural atmosphere and wild life abounds (the park is popular with bird watchers). One small lake is especially for inflatables and canoes, the other for fishing (coarse fishing on permit). There are 180 numbered pitches in total on level grass, 123 with electrical connections (presently 10A). The four toilet blocks, refurbished recently, have good, well maintained facilities, with free hot water throughout. Other facilities include covered dishwashing sinks, a laundry, chemical disposal and facilities for visitors with disabilities. Reception and the licensed shop, with souvenirs and caravan accessories, are central (one-way system in operation) and behind is the barn which provides a TV room and a large room for special events. Attractive children's play areas are located around the park, but perhaps feeding the ducks is more enjoyable. There are barbecue areas, a small wooden kiosk provides visitor information and there are resident wardens on site. Fishing near, bicycle hire close (½ mile). The Sherwood Forest Visitor Centre is 5 minutes away by car, and a Sherwood Forest Farm Park (rare breeds) is close by. The village is 1½ miles (no public transport) and there are walks from the site.

Directions: Best approach is via the Ollerton - Mansfield road A6075; turn south towards Old Clipstone opposite turning to Warsop and ½ mile to site. Follow signs to Sherwood Forest Farm Park. From M1 take exit 27 from south and 30 from north. O.S.GR: SK594650.

Charges 1998: Per family £7.00 - £9.95; per couple £6.15 - £8.45; single person £4.20 - £5.80; extra person £0.85 - £1.50; pitch £3.00; electricity £1.50 - £2.00; dogs and pup tents free. Min. stay 3 nights at B.Hs VAT included. Credit cards accepted.

Open: March - 2 November.

Reservations: Made with £5 deposit. Address: Nr. Edwinstowe, Mansfield, Nottinghamshire NG21 9HW. Tel: (01623) 823132.. FAX: (01623) 824637.

B385 Rivendale Caravan and Leisure Park, Alsop-en-le-Dale, nr Ashbourne

Brand new park in course of development in the Peak National Park

When we visited this new park at the invitation of the owners we were immediately struck by the size of the project they had taken on. The reception and shop building you first see on arrival has been carefully renovated and in due course there will be a small cafe/bar within this building (some time off yet, although we were shown the splendid floor tiles). Moving into the park proper which is situated in an old quarry, we were overwhelmed by the effort (and expense) which has been incurred to get everything as far as it is. There are 80 pitches completed, all with hardstanding and 16A electrical hook up. Set out in small groups with names such as `Little Delving' or `Crickhollow', each pitch is separated from its neighbour and each has a grass area. Sanitary facilities are first rate with under-floor central heating, excellent free showers, washbasins (with cubicles for ladies) and an excellent shower room for disabled visitors. The touring park will eventually take up about 11 acres of the total land space of 37. The park is situated almost on The Tissington Trail offering superb walks and off road cycling and, with the Peak National Park on hand and towns such Ashbourne, Bakewell and even Buxton nearby, there is lots to do and see here. The important thing to remember about this park is that it is brand new, with a large area still to be developed and that which is finished needs to mature. On the other hand the owners are only too pleased to hear suggestions from their customers as to what they should or should not do, so take the opportunity to make your thoughts about caravan park design known!

Directions: Park is on the A515 Buxton - Ashbourne road at Alsop-en-le-Dale, about 7 miles north of Ashbourne. O.S.GR: SK161566.

Charges 1998: Per pitch incl. 2 adults £5.00 - £7.00; extra adult £1.00; child (4-15 yrs) 50p; awning £1.50; extra car £1.00; dog 50p; electricity £2.20. Credit cards accepted. VAT included.

Open: All year exc. February.

Reservations: Made with £10 deposit; contact park. Address: Buxton Road, Alsop-en-le-Dale, Ashbourne, Derbyshire DE6 1QU. Tel: (01332) 843000. FAX: (01332) 842311.

B431 Luck's All Caravan and Camping Park, Mordiford, Hereford

Spacious site beside the River Wye, with good countryside views, canoeing and fishing.

Set in around 9½ acres on the bank of the river Wye, Luck's All has 80 large, well spaced and level touring pitches, of which 41 have electricity (10/16A). A small, unfenced playground and a large grassy area for children's games are provided. The river is open to the site but lifebelts and safety messages are in evidence. Canoes are available for hire - or bring your own - and fishing permits are obtainable from the local tackle shop. The site shop has basic supplies plus home-made cakes, and there is a mini-market within 1½ miles. The main sanitary facilities are housed in a new building which provides WCs, open washbasins, showers with curtains (20p payment), and a separate unit for disabled visitors with ramped entrance, WC, basin, shower and hand-dryer. In addition there are dishwashing sinks and a chemical disposal point. A smaller, older unit near the entrance to the site provides extra facilities for peak periods, also a laundry room with sink, washing machine, dryer and ironing facilities. Amongst the local places worthy of a visit are the Cider Museum and King Offa Distillery in Hereford, Belmont Abbey and Queenswood Country Park. The site is also a good base for touring the Wye Valley. Golf 5 miles.

Directions: Between Mordiford and Fownhope, 5 miles southeast of Hereford on the B4224, the site is well signed. O.S.GR: SO571355.

Charges 1998: Per unit incl. 2 adults £7.00 - £7.50; small 2-man tent £6.00 - £6.50; extra person over 5 yrs £1.00; extra car £1.00; dog 75p; awning with groundsheet £1.00, without 75p; pup tent on same pitch £2.00; porch awning 50p; electricity £1.75. Credit cards accepted. VAT included.

Open: Easter/1 April - 31 October.

Reservations: Essential for B.Hs. and peak season and made with £15 deposit; contact park. Address: Luck's All, Mordiford, Hereford HR1 4LP. Tel: (01432) 870213.

B410 Cotswold Hoburne, South Cerney, Cirencester

Good touring park with holiday caravans and a variety of watersports amenities close.

Since the park is adjacent to the Cotswold Water Park, those staying will have easy access to the varied watersports there which include sailboarding and water ski-ing. On the park itself there is a lake with pedaloes and canoes for hire. Its wide range of amenities includes an outdoor pool open from Easter (heated from May) and an impressive, large indoor leisure complex including pool with flume, spa bath, sauna, steam room (all free) and sun bed. There are 300 well marked touring pitches for any type of unit, all with hardstanding (only fairly level) and grass surround for awning or tent. Of good size but with nothing between them, all have electricity (some need long leads). Also 150 holiday units, mainly for letting. Six toilet blocks are quite small and maintenance can be variable. Hot water is free in the washbasins and pre-set showers. Basic facilities for disabled visitors are in the clubhouse, but are locked at night. The site has heavy weekend trade. The large clubhouse has a big general lounge with giant TV screen, entertainment at times, food service (or food bar in lounge), big games room and a lounge bar which overlooks the outdoor pool and lake with a patio. Supermarket. Launderette. Activities include a football field, tennis courts, a good quality adventure playground with bark base and crazy golf. Fishing lake (permits from reception). No dogs or pets are accepted. Part of the Hoburne group.

Directions: Three miles from Cirencester on A419, turn right towards Cotswold Water Park at new roundabout on bypass onto B4696. Take second right and follow signs. O.S.GR: SU055957.

Charges 1998: Per touring pitch incl. electricity £8.00 - £21.00; pup tent £2.00. Weekly rates and weekend breaks available. VAT included. Credit cards accepted.

Open: March - 31 October.

Reservations: Tents: 1-6 nights payable in full at time of booking; caravans with £50 deposit for min 4 days at B.Hs (3 days for May B.H). Address: Broadway Lane, South Cerney, Cirencester, Glos. GL7 5UQ. Tel: (01285) 860216. FAX: (01285) 862106.

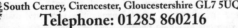

B571 Doe Park Touring Caravan Park, Cotherstone, nr Barnard Castle

Peaceful site in the old mould with character, ideal for couples (caravans and motorhomes only).

This is Hannah Hauxwell country and the Dales, less frequented than other upland areas, provide wonderful walking country; indeed part of the Pennine Way runs near the site. The farm and park are close to where the River Balder joins the Tees at Cotherstone and the ancient oak wood beside the river is a Site of Special Scientific Interest for its insects and flowers, but is also a haven for bird-watchers. Reception is in the farmhouse, formerly Leadgard Hall, a mellow three storey, Grade II listed building. Mr and Mrs Lamb make you very welcome and personally take you to your pitch. Visitors are welcome at the traditional Dales livestock farm. The camping fields with a lovely open aspect are of natural grass, neatly kept and the 52 pitches are spacious (all with 10A electricity, 20 with hardstanding). The newer ones have open fields in front, ideal for children. Two toilet areas, one part of the farmhouse, the other built in natural stone, provide en-suite toilets and washbasins and metered showers with curtain. Dishwashing and small laundry in the farmhouse. Chemical disposal. A new block is to be added for '99 with further WCs and washbasins and a large unisex unit for disabled visitors. Eggs and milk can be ordered. A regular bus service passes from Barnard Castle to Middleton. Cotherstone village is ½ mile with post office and a restaurant with bar meals, a pleasant walk by road or river bank. River fishing on site, reservoirs 3 miles, bicycle hire or golf 4 miles, riding 2 miles. Dogs accepted by arrangement.

Directions: Follow B6277 from Barnard Castle in direction of Middleton in Teesdale. The farm is signed on the left just after Cotherstone village (there is no need to go into Barnard Castle). O.S.GR: NZ005204.

Charges 1998: Per car and caravan incl. 2 persons £5.70 - £6.20; motorcaravan £5.25 - £5.75; extra person (over 7 yrs) 60p; full awning £1.00; electricity £1.70.

Open: 1 March - 31 October.

Reservations: Made with £5 deposit (send SAE); min. 3 days at B.Hs. Address: Cotherstone, Barnard Castle, Co. Durham DL12 9UQ. Tel: (01833) 650302. FAX: as phone.

BRITISH ISLES - England

B554 Fallbarrow Park, Bowness, Windermere

Quality park with Lake Windermere frontage, for caravans and motorcaravans only.

Fallbarrow Park is most attractively situated alongside Lake Windermere with a lake frontage of about 600 m; one can stroll among the lawns and gardens near the lake. Founded in the mid-fifties by the Whiteley family, Fallbarrow is still owned and managed by them. Over the years improvements have been made, and each year finds new projects - at present, `green' issues, for example, recycling, bio-degradable products, nest boxes, etc. The major part of the park is occupied by seasonal holiday homes - about 70 for letting and 180 private ones. There are also 72 level touring pitches in two areas. The `Glade' area amongst tall trees has pitches all with hardstanding and electric hook-up (10/16A), the `Lake' area (not actually by the lake, but some pitches have lake views) with 38 fenced or hedged, fully serviced pitches including TV aerial connections. The park is very popular and reservations are essential for June - Sept. and B.Hs. American motorhomes are accepted by prior arrangement. There is a motorcaravan service point and the site is well lit. Two excellent toilet blocks serve the touring sections (access by combination locks). With top quality fittings and heating when required, they provide vanity style washbasins, free controllable showers, make up and hairdressing areas and a baby room. There are dishwashing sinks and a well equipped laundry which also houses a freezer. The `Boathouse' pub has a spacious and comfortable lounge with bar meals and snacks, and an attractive outdoor terrace. There is also a TV lounge with occasional entertainment and a large games room with pool table and games machines. Very well stocked supermarket. Public phones. Dogs are accepted (one per booking) with an exercise area provided. Reception is smart and comfortable, with lots of tourist information. The site has a boat park with winter storage and two launching ramps and three jetties can cater for craft up to 18 ft in length. Fishing on site. Bicycle hire 1 mile, riding 2 miles, golf 3 miles. Bowness centre is only a short walk and facilities for pony trekking and numerous visitor attractions are close.

Directions: Park is beside the A592 road just north of Bowness town centre. O.S.GR: SD401971.

Charges 1999: Per unit inclusive: Glade pitch £11.35 - £15.95, Lake pitch £13.00 - £18.30; awning £2.95 - £4.00; boat (max 18 ft.) £10.00; car-top dinghy £5.00; sailboard or canoe £2.00. VAT included. Credit cards accepted.

Open: 13 March - 6 November.

Reservations: Made for 3 nights min. (7 at Spring B.H.). Payment in full at time of booking. Address: Rayrigg Road, Windermere, Cumbria LA23 3DL. Tel: (015394) 44428. FAX: (015394) 88736.

B555 Limefitt Park, Windermere

See colour advert between pages 32/33

Well managed and popular Lake District park.

Limefitt Park is owned and run by the Whiteley family who also own Fallbarrow Park and is centrally situated for the southern lakes. It has fine views and walks, with the beck running alongside. With various active pursuits nearby and some evening entertainment, it is very well managed and is for families or couples (no organised groups of young people). The 145 pitches for touring caravans are good and flat, with hardstanding, electricity (10A) and water, with cars parked at an angle on further hardstanding in front. The remainder of the park is on flat or slightly sloping grass with some terracing and shade provided by trees with numbered pitches for tents or more caravans or motorcaravans. The ground by the beck has been developed for 45 log cabins (for private sale) and there are 20 caravan holiday homes (7 for hire), plus another field for 20 long stay caravans. Sanitary facilities consist of one large, central block for the tent area and a smaller block for the caravan area, accessed by combination locks. Both are excellent, amongst the best we have seen and are well maintained and fully tiled with free hot water and modern fittings including oval washbasins, with mixer taps, flat surfaces, mirrors and side lighting. Toddlers' rooms with half-size bath and changing facilities, covered washing-up sinks and chemical disposal. Well stocked supermarket and licensed bar lounge with real ales, bar meals and weekly entertainment, both open all season, and takeaway. This should give good coverage all season. Campers' kitchen, launderette and motorcaravan service point. Activities include walking and fishing, and local facilities, including bicycle hire, can be booked from the park. Riding 3 miles, golf 5 miles. Games room with machines. Play field and adventure playground on grass by the river and small beach area with picnic tables. American motorhomes, dogs or boats are **not** accepted. No single persons, no groups and no rallies are accepted; to quote, "in order to preserve Limefitt's unique atmosphere and provide restful nights ... we accept families only (with a maximum of two families per caravan and one family per tent)." The park is full and very popular for a long season, reservation is advisable.

Directions: Limefitt Park lies 2½ miles north up the A592 from its junction with the A591 north of Windermere. O.S.GR: NY416030.

Charges 1999: Per unit incl. 2 persons, electricity and TV hook-up £9.50 - £13.00; tent £9.00 - £12.50; extra adult £2.00 - £2.50; child (2-14 yrs) £1.00 - £1.25; awning, pup tent, trailer or 2nd car £2.00 - £2.50. Max. charge 1 family per pitch £11.50 - £15.50 (excl. supplements). Prices are higher for stays not booked in advance. VAT included. Credit cards accepted.

Open: 26 March - 30 October.

Reservations: Made with full payment at time of booking; cancellation insurance available. Address: Windermere, Cumbria LA23 1PA. Tel: (015394) 32300. FAX: (015394) 32848. Internet: www.limefitt.co.uk.

B557 Wild Rose Park, Appleby-in-Westmorland

Well organised, neat family park in the Eden Valley with excellent facilities and holiday homes.

The entrance to Wild Rose is very inviting with its well mown grass, trim borders and colourful flowers. First impressions are of well maintained facilities and the feeling that nothing but the best will do, and this is reflected throughout the park. There are three touring areas - the top areas provide neat, level, fully serviced pitches separated by new hedges (and a small fence until the hedge grows), many with views. The lower, slightly sloping touring area caters for both tents and caravans. Next to this are six 'super' pitches, fenced or hedged with full services, some including patio, barbecue, picnic table, grass area and satellite TV connections. Caravan holiday homes have their own areas and do not intrude. The final field is for 60 tents, gently sloping with an oval roadway. Three toilet blocks (two heated) are of excellent quality, well maintained and spotlessly clean. Washbasins are mainly in cubicles, showers are free and there are hair washing basins, hairdryers, baby baths and bottle warmers, soap and hand dryers plus full facilities for disabled visitors, laundry and chemical disposal. The swimming pool (heated mid-May - mid-Sept) has a landscaped sunbathing area on grass and flagstones. Very well stocked shop (March - Nov). Licensed restaurant with takeaway and coffee lounge. Fenced play area with safety bases, indoor playroom for under-5s, games room and two TV rooms, one with cinema style screen. Bicycle hire, BMX track, half court tennis and a field for ball games. Fishing within a mile, golf, riding and tennis a little further. Dogs accepted (not dangerous breeds) with a small dog walk. Motorcaravan services. Wild Rose has a fully deserved, excellent reputation. Member of the Best of British group.

Directions: Park is signed south off B6260 road 1½ miles southwest of Appleby. Follow signs to park, in the direction of Ormside. O.S.GR: NY697165.

Charges 1998: Per unit incl. 2 persons £7.20 - £11.80; super pitch £12.50 - £25.00; walker or cyclist £3.00; extra person (over 4) £1.50; electricity £2.00 - £2.50; dog 50p. VAT included. Credit cards accepted.

Open: All year.

Reservations: Essential for B.Hs and July/Aug; made with deposit of £5 per night + £2 fee, remainder on arrival. Min. 3 nights at B.Hs. Address: Ormside, Appleby-in-Westmorland, Cumbria CA16 6EJ. Tel: (017683) 51077. FAX: (017683) 52551. E-mail: mail@wildrose.co.uk. Internet: www.wildrose.co.uk.

Excellence in Eden

Friendly family park in the beautiful EDEN VALLEY, between the LAKE DISTRICT and YORKSHIRE DALES.

Superb facilities for tourers and tents. Keep the whole family entertained with heated outdoor swimming pools, play areas, indoor games and TV rooms.

Well-stocked mini-market and licensed restaurant with take-away.

Seasonal and monthly rates for tourers, also Luxury Holiday Homes for sale - seasonal or all year use. **Sorry No Letting, No Bar, No Club**

Brochure with pleasure - Telephone 017683 51077

Email: mail@wildrose.co.uk

Ormside,
Appleby-in-Westmorland,
Cumbria
CA16 6EJ

AA ►►►

B668 James' Caravan Park, Ruabon, nr Wrexham

All year site, easily accessible and with good facilities.

This park has a new heated toilet block and attractive, park-like surroundings with mature trees and neat grass. Old farm buildings and a collection of original farm machinery, carefully restored, add interest. The toilet block offers roomy showers (20p) with useful rail to help those of advancing age with feet washing, curtain and shelf, vanity style washbasins with good mirrors and a hairdryer for ladies (20p). En-suite facilities for visitors with disabilities have a special 'clos o mat' toilet! The park has over 40 pitches, some level and some on a slope, with informal siting giving either a view or shade. Electricity (6A) is available (long leads may be useful). Tourist information, free freezer for ice packs and a telephone are in the foyer of the toilet block. Chemical disposal and motorcaravan services. The village is 10 minutes walk with a Spar shop, fish and chips, a launderette and four pubs. Golf 3 miles. A useful park with easy access from the A483 Wrexham - Oswestry road (possibly some road noise).

Directions: At junction of A483/A539 Llangollen road, accessible from west-bound A539. O.S.GR: SJ302434.

Charges 1999: Per unit incl. 2 persons £7.00; extra person £1.00; awning £2.00; dog 50p; electricity £2.00.

Open: All year.

Reservations: Contact park for details. Address: Ruabon, Wrexham LL14 6DW. Tel: (01978) 820148. FAX: as phone. E-mail: ray@carastay.demon.co.uk.

B595 Parciau Bach Caravan Park, St Clears, nr Carmarthen

Small park in a peaceful, rural setting, personally run by new owners.

There are some narrow lanes to be negotiated to get to Parciau Bach but it is worth it to enjoy the quality and peaceful setting of this park. The 24 privately owned caravan holiday homes (and 2 for letting) are hidden in the wooded slopes at the back of the park - a haven for wild flowers and squirrels. The open field for tents is sloping, but has individual terraced places with dividing hedges (10 pitches) and a lower level, part terraced for 25 caravans, all with electricity (16A), 9 with hardstanding, water and TV connections. All are on neatly cut grass with views across the valley. A wooded stream area unfortunately does not belong to the park but further up on the park is a small wildlife pond. The owner's pine chalet home, on the slope between the touring field and the wooded area houses reception, a tourist information room and two small toilet units for both sexes with separate showers, toilets and washbasins for each. The other toilet block, open in high season only, is in the wooded area reached by a steepish, hard-core path and steps through the trees, lit at night. Hot water is free and showers have the necessary seat, hook and curtain - not luxurious, but well maintained and clean. Laundry room, two washing up sinks, one beside reception, one near the tent area, and chemical disposal. Adventure play unit. Shop at reception. Bar snacks and evening meals are available at the Parciau Bach Inn (separate ownership) above the site. Tenby is 18 miles, with the 7 mile long Pendine sands 6 miles, or to the north, the Preseli mountains. Fishing 1 mile, golf 3 miles. Birdwatching opportunities abound.

Directions: From St Clears traffic lights, take the road to Llanboidy forking right after 100 yds. Follow road for 2 miles and turn right. After less than a mile turn right at small crossroads and park is on left. O.S.GR: SN298184.

Charges 1998: Per unit £6.50 - £8.50; 2 person tent £5.00 - £6.00, 3 person tent £6.00 - £7.00; electricity £1.50; TV connection 50p; extra car (per person) £1.00; awning free (only breathable groundsheets allowed).

Open: All year except 9 Jan. - 1 March.

Reservations: May be advisable for B.Hs; contact park for details. Address: St. Clears, Carmarthenshire SA33 4LG. Tel: (01994) 230647.

B635 Barcdy Caravan and Camping Park, Talsarnau, nr Harlech

Rurally situated park with good facilities and marvellous views.

Barcdy is partly in a sheltered vale, partly on a plateau top and partly in open fields edged by woods, with fells to the rear and views across the Lleyn peninsula in one direction and towards the Snowdon range in another. The park provides for all tastes with level or sloping grass pitches, either secluded in the valley or enjoying the view from the plateau or the lower field. There are 38 pitches for touring vans and 40 for tents, with or without 10A electricity (44 electricity points), with 30 caravan holiday homes also (3 for hire). There are two toilet blocks, the one at the top of the valley open in high season only. Facilities include large, comfortable, tiled showers, which open direct to the outside except for one in each male and female sections. Hot water is free to washbasins and metered to showers (25p) and washing up sinks (10p). Excellent chemical disposal and motorcaravan emptying point. All are nicely built in the local stone, as are the walls around the site. Shop (Spr. B.H - end Aug) for essentials with gas. The grounds of the farm include 28 acres of fields and oak woods (a haven for children) and further up the hills are the two Tecwyn lakes for fishing or just to relax and enjoy the views. Riding 4 miles, golf 4 or 6 miles. Harlech beach and castle are 4 miles. The Italianate village of Portmeirion is nearby and Snowdonia is on your doorstep. No dogs accepted.

Directions: Park is just off the A496 between villages of Llandecwyn and Talsarnau, 4 miles north of Harlech. O.S.GR: SH622371.

Charges 1999: Per unit incl. 2 persons £7.50 - £9.00; extra adult £3.00; child (up to 16 yrs) £1.50; awning free - £1.00; electricity (10A) £1.95. Credit cards accepted.

Open: Easter - 31 October.

Reservations: Contact park. Address: Talsarnau, nr Harlech, Gwynedd LL47 6YG. Tel: (01766) 770736.

B699 Mortonhall Caravan Park, Edinburgh

Attractive, large touring park in the mature grounds of Mortonhall mansion.

The Mortonhall park makes a good base to see the historic city of Edinburgh and buses to the City leave from the park entrance every ten minutes (parking in Edinburgh is not easy). Although only 4 miles from the city centre, Mortonhall is in quiet mature parkland, easy to find with access off the ring road. The park can accommodate 250 units mostly on numbered pitches on a slight slope with nothing to separate them but marked by jockey wheel points. There are over 170 places with electricity (10A), 16 with hardstanding, water and drainage as well, and many places for tents. Holiday caravans to let. The park is very popular but only part is reserved and tourists arriving early may find space. Two modern toilet blocks have free hot water in individual washbasins, showers and outside, uncovered dishwashing sinks. A third excellent, new facility at the top of the park has eight unisex units incorporating shower, washbasin and WC, with covered dishwashing sinks. The courtyard area provides further standard facilities and 'portacabin' type units are added for the high season to serve the large number of tents. There are facilities for the disabled, water points around site and chemical disposal units, plus a laundry room with washing machines and dryer. Self-service shop. An attractive courtyard development houses a lounge bar and restaurant, open to all, with good value meals in pleasant surroundings. Games room. TV room. Table tennis, children's play area on sand. Late arrivals area with hook-ups. Torches useful in early and late season. Golf courses and driving range very near.

> **Directions:** Park is well signed south of the city, 5 minutes from A720 city by-pass. Take Mortonhall exit from Straiton junction and follow camping signs. Entrance is alongside Klondyke Garden Centre. O.S.GR: NT262686.
>
> **Charges 1998:** Per unit incl. 2 persons £8.00 - £12.50; extra person (5 yrs and over) £1.00; serviced pitch + £4.00; electricity £3.00; awning £2.50 - £5.00; porch awning £2.50; dog £1.00. Credit cards accepted. VAT included.
>
> **Open:** 14 March - 31 October.
>
> **Reservations:** Made with 1 night's charge plus £1.50 fee. Address: 38 Mortonhall Gate, Frogston Road East, Edinburgh, East Lothian EH16 6TJ. Tel: 0131 664 1533. FAX: 0131 664 5387.

Mortonhall Caravan Park, Edinburgh

Country estate situated just 15 minutes from city centre and 5 minutes from the bypass.

Parkland estate hosts premiere graded park. Luxury holiday homes (Thistle Award), touring and tenting pitches. Excellent amenities - modern toilet and shower block, restaurant and bar, shop, games room, TV room and laundry. An ideal base to see Edinburgh and Southern Scotland. Free colour brochure and tariff.

Mortonhall Caravan Park, Frogston Road East, Edinburgh EH16 6TL   Tel: 0131-664 1533 Fax: 0131-664 5387

B723 Trossachs Holiday Park, Aberfoyle

Well run, friendly family park, ideal for exploring the Trossachs and Loch Lomond.

Nestling on the side of a hill 3 miles south of Aberfoyle, this is an excellent base for touring this famously beautiful area. Lochs Lomond, Ard, Venachar and others are within easy reach, as are the Queen Elizabeth Forest Park and, of course, the Trossachs. The park specialises in sales and hire of top class mountain bikes. A very neat and tidy park, there are 45 well laid out and marked pitches arranged on terraces with hardstanding. All have electricity and TV connections, most water and drainage also. There are trees between the terraces and lovely views across the valley. A modern wooden building houses the sanitary facilities which offer a satisfactory supply of toilets, showers and washbasins, the ladies' area being rather larger, with two cabins. The building also contains a laundry room and a large games room with TV and lots of seating. Several items of play equipment on gravel. The park purchased the adjoining woods in '97. A local leisure centre (10 miles) provides swimming, sauna, solarium, badminton, tennis, windsurfing, etc. Nearby are opportunities for golfing, boat launching and fishing (3 miles). Well stocked shop (all season) and bike shop are either side of reception, where you will receive a warm welcome from Joe and Hazel Norman. Luxury caravans (12) for hire in separate section.

> **Directions:** Park is 3 miles south of Aberfoyle on the A81 road, well signed. O.S.GR: NS544976.
>
> **Charges 1998:** Per unit incl. 2 persons £8.50 - £10.50; electricity and TV connection £2.00; all services £3.00; porch awning, extra car £1.00; full awning, small extra tent £1.50; extra adult £2.00; child (2-14 yrs) £1.25. Less 10% for weekly stays. VAT included. Credit cards accepted.
>
> **Open:** 1 March - 31 October.
>
> **Reservations:** Advisable and made for min. 3 days with £15 deposit. Address: Aberfoyle, Stirling FK8 3SA. Tel: (01877) 382614 (24 hr). FAX: (01877) 382732. E-mail: thp@scotland.force9.net.

B834 Drumaheglis Marina and Caravan Park, Ballymoney

Well kept site on the banks of the River Bann, convenient for the Causeway coast.

A caravan park which continually maintains a high standard, Drumaheglis is popular throughout the season. Situated on the banks of the lower Bann, approximately 4 miles from the town of Ballymoney, it appeals to watersports enthusiasts or makes an ideal base for exploring this scenic corner of Northern Ireland. The marina offers superb facilities for boat launching, water-skiing, cruising, canoeing or fishing, whilst getting out and about can take you to the Giant's Causeway, seaside resorts such as Portrush or Portstewart, the sands of Whitepark Bay, the Glens of Antrim or the picturesque villages of the Antrim coast road. For tourers only, this site instantly appeals, for it is well laid out with trees, shrubs, flower beds and tarmac roads. Electricity (5A) and water points are available on 52 pitches, of which 47 have hardstanding. The toilet blocks are modern and were spotlessly clean when we visited. They house showers which are free, individual wash cubicles, toilets and facilities for disabled visitors, plus four new family shower rooms. There are razor points, hand dryers, dishwashing sinks, washing machine and dryer and chemical disposal point. A children's play area, barbecue and picnic areas are added facilities. Ballymoney is a popular shopping town and the Riada Centre is a leading leisure establishment with a health suite which incorporates a high-tech fitness studio, sports hall, etc. Bicycle hire and golf 4 miles, riding 1 mile. There is much to see and do within this Borough and of interest is the Heritage Centre in Charlotte Street.

Directions: From A26/B62 Portrush - Ballymoney roundabout continue for approx. 1 mile on the A26 towards Coleraine. Site is clearly signed - follow International camping signs.

Charges 1998: Per unit incl. electricity £11.00 (7 days £66.00); unserviced £10.00 (£60.00). No credit cards.

Open: Easter - 1 October.

Reservations: Essential for peak periods and weekends. Address: 36 Glenstall Road, Ballymoney, Co. Antrim BT53 7QN. Tel: (012656) 66466. Ballymoney District Council: Tel: (012656) 62280; FAX: (012656) 67659.

B851 Blaney Caravan Park, Blaney

Quiet, family run park, beautifully maintained.

A park with a neat and tidy appearance and one that boasts quality rather than quantity, the 17 touring pitches, all with hardstanding and electric connections, are well spaced out around the perimeter and in the centre of the site. The roadways are wide and tarmac, with flower beds and shrubs adding detail and colour. A tent area is tucked into the bottom left hand corner and to the rear, at a higher level, are a small number of caravan holiday homes which blend unobtrusively. A modern toilet block houses showers (50p) with hot water, facilities for the disabled, and a laundry room with washing machine, dryer and ironing board. Waste and chemical disposal, a dog walk and night lighting. There is a small supermarket, post office and petrol station at the site entrance. For children there is a spacious and safe play area with sand pit, swings, etc. but the farm animals may be more appealing. Boules. Central barbecue area, or barbecues are permitted, with care, on the pitches. Blaney makes a good base for hill climbing, fishing, watersports or for seeking out local beauty spots such as nearby Lough Navar Forest which commands extensive views over Lough Erne.

Directions: From Enniskillen take the A46 road towards Belleek. The park is on the right after approx. 8 miles.

Charges 1999: Per unit £10.00 (high season); electricity £1.00; awning free (ventilated ground sheet); tent (2 person) £6.00.

Open: All year.

Reservations: Contact park. Address: Blaney, Co. Fermanagh BT93 7ER. Tel: (013656) 41634.

Useful Addresses

Northern Ireland Tourist Board

59 North Street, Belfast BT1 1NB.
Tel: (01232) 246609. Fax: (01232) 240960, Internet: http://www.ni-tourism.com

Ferry Services

P&O European Ferries	Sea Cat Scotland	Norse Irish Ferries
(01581) 200276	(0990) 523523	(01232) 779090
Cairnryan - Larne	Stranraer - Belfast	Liverpool - Belfast
Ferry (2¼ hours, 2 sailings daily each way) or Jet Liner (1 hour, 5 sailings daily each way)	(1½ hours, 4 daily each way)	(8½ hrs overnight, dail or 8½ hrs day service, up to 3 weekly)

Jersey

Jersey Tourism
Liberation Square, St. Helier, Jersey JE1 1BB
Tel: (01534) 500700 Fax: (01534) 500899

Guernsey and Herm

States of Guernsey Tourist Board
PO Box 13, White Rock, Guernsey
Tel: (014581) 26611

Sark

Sark Tourism Office
Sark (via Guernsey), Channel Islands.
Tel: (01481) 832345.

B977 Vaugrat Camping, St Sampson's, Guernsey

Neat, well tended site, close to beach, in northwest of island.

Vaugrat Camping is centred around attractive and interesting old granite farm buildings dating back to the 15th century, with a gravelled courtyard and colourful flower beds. Owned by the Laine family, Vaugrat provides 150 pitches on flat grassy meadows, which are mostly surrounded by trees, banks and hedges to provide shelter. Tents are arranged around the edges of the fields, giving open space in the centre, and while pitches are not marked, there is sufficient room. Cars may be parked next to tents. Only couples and families are accepted and the site is well run and welcoming. The site offers 25 fully equipped tents for hire. Housed in the old farmhouse, now a listed building, are the reception area, plus in the main season a shop (with ice pack hire) and upstairs 'Coffee Barn', with views to the sea, where breakfast is served. One can also sit here in the evenings. There is also a small games room with TV in the cider room complete with the ancient presses. The sanitary facilities are in two buildings, one of which is in the courtyard, with hot showers on payment, washbasins and hairdryers (on payment). There is a room here for disabled visitors with shower, basin and toilet (although there is a 6" step into the building). A laundry room here has a washing machine, dryer and iron. The other block is near the camping fields and provides toilets and washbasins in a row, set in a flat surface, plus one private cabin for ladies. Dishwashing facilities are housed in a room in this block with free hot water, with further sinks under cover outside. Chemical disposal. All these facilities are well kept and clean. There is a bus service within easy reach and car and bicycle hire are arranged. Fishing, riding and golf within 1½ miles. Hotel and bar nearby. No dogs are accepted. A torch may be useful.

Directions: On leaving St Peter Port, turn right onto coast road for 1½ miles. At filter turn left into Vale Road. Straight over at two sets of lights then first left turn by church. Follow to crossroads (garage opposite) turn right. Carry on past Peninsula Hotel, then second left, signed for site. Site on left after high stone wall (400 yds) with concealed entrance.

Charges 1999: Per adult £4.95; child (under 14 yrs) £3.95; car or boat £1.00. Families and couples only. Fully equipped tents to hire. Credit cards accepted.

Open: May - September incl.

Reservations: Made for independent campers for any length, with £10 deposit and balance on arrival. Hire details from site. Address: St Sampson's, Guernsey, Channel Islands GY2 4TA. Tel: (01481) 57468. FAX: (01481) 51841.

Camping in the Channel Islands

Full details on camping in the Channel Islands and a selection of parks can be found in the Alan Rogers' **BRITAIN and IRELAND** Guide. Camping holidays on the islands are limited to TENTS only. Caravans and motorcaravans are not permitted because of the narrow and sometimes crowded nature of the roads. Trailer tents (with canvas walls and roof) are allowed, but on Jersey advance booking must be made. Tents and camping equipment are often available for hire on site and car hire is easily arranged.

The British and Irish parks featured in this guide are only a small selection of those in our BRITAIN and IRELAND guide

DENMARK

Denmark is the easiest of the Scandinavian countries to visit, both in terms of cost and distance. The countryside is green and varied with flat plains, rolling hills, fertile farmland, many lakes and fjords, wild moors and long beaches, interrupted by pretty villages and towns. There are many small islands but the main land masses which make up this country are the islands of Zealand (Sjælland), Funen (Fyn) and the peninsula of Jutland (Jylland), which extends northwards from the German border at Flensburg. Copenhagen, the capital and Denmark's largest city, is on Zealand and is an exciting city with a beautiful old centre, a good array of museums and a boisterous night life. Camping in Denmark is a delight, with many sites now having facilities that rival, and sometimes even surpass, the best in other parts of Europe. Most sites now offer well designed facilities for disabled people and baby changing, and many now have private family bathrooms which generally include shower, WC and washbasin. You will find kitchens on most sites, many with hobs, ovens, microwaves and the occasional dishwasher. All these facilities are often free of extra charge. You will need either a valid International Camping Carnet, or a Danish Camping Pass (which can be purchased at the first camp you visit in Denmark). Denmark is an ideal destination for those who enjoy watersports of all types, cycling, fishing and sightseeing.

The Danish Tourist Board, 55 Sloane Street, London SW1X 9SY

Tel: 0171 259 5959 Fax: 0171 259 5955

Population
5,162,000 (1992), density 120 per sq.km.

Capital
Copenhagen (København).

Climate
The Danish climate can be changeable throughout the year. In general April-May is mild. June-Aug. is usually warm and sunny. Autumn is often sunny but can be unreliable and the winter months Dec-March tend to be cold, often with a little snow.

Language
The official language is Danish, but English is widely spoken.

Currency
The monetary unit is the Danish Krone (Dkr.) 1 Krone = 100 ore. Bank notes in circulation are: 1,000, 500, 100, and 50; coins are: 20, 10, 5, 2 and 1 krone, 50 and 25 ore.

Banks
In Copenhagen banks are open Mon-Wed & Fri 09.30-16.00. Thurs. to 18.00. Closed Sat. In the provinces opening hours vary from town to town. Note: Danish banks may refuse to exchange large foreign bank notes.
Eurocheques and other well known traveller's cheques are cashed by banks and many hotels, restaurants and shops, which also accept most international credit cards.

Post Offices
Open Mon-Fri 09.00/10.00-17.00/17.30, Sat 09.00/10.00-12.00 (some offices in Copenhagen are closed all day on Saturdays).

Telephone
The dialling code for Denmark is 0045. from Denmark to the UK dial 0044. Phone cards available from Telecom shops (Telebutik).

Time
GMT plus 1 (summer BST plus 1).

Shops
Hours may vary in the main cities. Regular openings are Mon-Thu 09.00-17.30. Fri 09.00-19.00/20.00. Sat 09.00-13.00/14.00. First Sat in every month most shops open 09.00-16.00/ 17.00.

Food and Restaurants
The cost of food is quite high and a stock of basic supplies is useful. However, supermarket prices are now fairly similar to London prices. The price of spirits is prohibitive but for wine and beer almost acceptable! Eating out can be expensive. Try sticking to 'Dagens Ret' - the day's speciality which is usually good value. The high point of Danish food culture is the cold table with a large variety of hot and cold fish and meat dishes in which 'smorrebrod' (open sandwiches), the great Danish speciality, play an important part.

Motoring
Driving is much easier than at home as roads are much quieter. Driving is on the right. Parking is much easier than ours, apart from main cities, often just off pedestrianised town centres. **Do not drink and drive** - any quantity is liable to immediate drastic action. Dipped headlights are compulsory at all times.
Speed limits: caravans and motorhomes (3.5 tons) 31 mph (50 kph) in built up areas, 44 mph (70 kph) for caravans on all other roads, for motorhomes 50 mph (80 kph) on other roads and 69 mph (110 kph) on motorways.
Parking: In Copenhagen parking discs are required where there are no meters. Meters take 1, 2, 5, 10 and 20 Kr. coins and discs are available from post offices, banks, petrol stations, and tourist offices.

Overnighting
Overnight stays outside camp sites is not permitted without the prior permission of the respective landowner. Camping in car parks and laybys is not permitted either. Strong measures are taken against unauthorised parking in dunes and on beaches - offenders being fined on the spot.

Useful Addresses
National Motoring Organisation:
Forenede Danske Motorejere,
FDM-Huset, PO Box 500, Firskovvej 32,
2800 Lyngby. Tel: 45930800.

2010 Hvidbjerg Strand Camping, Blåvand, nr Esbjerg (Jylland)

High quality, seaside, holiday site, with indoor pools and many activities.

A family owned, 'TopCamp' holiday site, Hvidbjerg Strand is on the west coast near Blåvands Huk, 43 km. from Esbjerg. All 650 pitches have electricity (6A) and 'comfort' pitches also have water, drain and satellite TV. Pitches are in rows on flat sandy grass, with areas divided by small trees and hedges. Four superb sanitary units provide WCs, washbasins (many in cubicles), roomy showers, spa baths, suites for the disabled, family bathrooms, kitchens and two blocks have laundry facilities. The latest unit is thatched in the traditional style with a central glass covered atrium. This includes a children's bathroom decorated with dinosaur characters, racing car baby baths, low height WCs, basins and showers, plus 10 high quality family bathrooms, a suite for the disabled and an excellent kitchen with eight double hobs and sinks, two ovens and adjacent dining area. All hot water and cooking facilities are free. Some family bathrooms may be rented for exclusive use. On-site leisure facilities include an impressive, tropical style indoor pool complex (free outside 1/7-10/8) with water slides, spa baths, Turkish bath and a sauna. A café/restaurant overlooks the pools. Elsewhere are TV rooms, solarium, outdoor barbecue areas with picnic tables, minigolf, horse riding, football, squash, badminton, fishing, many children's play areas, plus the latest indoor suite of supervised play-rooms designed for all ages with Lego, computers, video games, TV etc. (open 09.00-12.30 daily excl. Wed). A Blue Flag beach and windsurfing school are adjacent to the site and the town offers a full activity programme during the main season (mid June - mid Aug). Legoland is 70 km.

How to find it: From Varde take roads 181/431 to Blåvand. Site is signed left on entering the town. (Mind the speed bump on town boundary).

General Details: Open 21 March - 19 Oct. Supermarket. Café. Restaurant. Kitchen and laundry facilities. Pool complex. Comprehensive sporting and leisure facilities. Children's playgrounds. Sauna. Solarium. Bicycle hire. Dog showers. Car wash. Chemical disposal. Motorcaravan service point. Cabins for rent.

Charges guide: Per adult Dkr. 53; child (0-11 yrs) 38; pitch 28 - 38, payable high seasons and BHs only; electricity (6A) 19; 'comfort' pitch 35. Credit cards accepted.

Reservations: made without deposit. Address: Hvidbjerg Strandvej, 6857 Blåvand. Tel: 75.27.90.40. FAX: 75.27.80.28.

2030 Sandersvig Camping, Haderslev (Jylland)

Attractively laid out family site, in beautiful countryside 300 m. from beach.

This family run site offers the very best of modern facilities in a peaceful location and it is most attractively laid out. The 470 very large grassy pitches are divided up by hedges, shrubs and small trees into small enclosures, many housing only four units, all with electricity (6/10A). The site is well lit, very quiet at night and there are water taps close to most pitches. There are three sanitary blocks, one by reception, an older one (interior refitted) at the lower end of the site, and the newest at the upper end of the site. These offer British WCs, washbasins (some in private cubicles), and roomy showers (on payment). There are also suites for the disabled, six family bathrooms, baby rooms, excellent kitchens with ovens, electric hobs, dishwashing sinks, plus a very good laundry and a separate fish cleaning area. Cooking facilities and hot water in both kitchen and laundry are free of charge. The site also has a well stocked supermarket and fast food service with a TV lounge/dining room adjacent, an outdoor heated swimming pool which is free to campers, two artificial grass tennis courts, solarium, children's playground with trampolines and Denmark's largest bouncing cushion, games room with TV, pool table, arcade machines, telephones and tourist information. This site makes a very comfortable base for excursions. Visit the restored windmill at Sillerup 4 km. or nearby historic Kolding with its castle, museums and shops. The drive to the island of Fyn takes less than an hour, with miles of country lanes around the site for cycling and walking.

How to find it: Drive from Christianfeld through Fjelstrup and Knud village, turning right 1 km. east of the village from where site is signed.

General Details: Open Easter - 15 Sept. Supermarket (1/4-15/9). Takeaway (15/5-10/8). Swimming pool (15/5-1/9). Games/TV rooms. Solarium. Tennis. Beach. Fishing. Children's playground. Kitchen. Laundry. Chemical disposal. Motorcaravan service point.

Charges 1999: Per adult Dkr. 44; child (0-11 yrs) 25; pitch 10 - 25; electricity (10A) 20. No credit cards.

Reservations: Essential for high season (15/6-15/8). Write to site. Address: Espagervej 15-17, 6100 Haderslev. Tel: 74.56.62.25.

The sites in DENMARK featured in this guide

are shown on the map on page 371

DENMARK

2020 Møgeltønder Camping, Møgeltønder, Tønder (Jylland)

Pleasant family run site with excellent facilities, convenient for ports.

Only 5 minutes walk from one of Denmark's oldest villages and 10 minutes drive from Tønder with its well preserved old buildings and magnificent pedestrian shopping street. The old town of Ribe is just 43 km. A quiet family site, it has 250 large, level, numbered pitches on grass, most with electricity (6A), divided up by new plantings of shrubs and small hedges. Only 25 pitches are occupied by long stay units, the remainder solely for tourists, and there are 15 cabins for rent on site. Two superb, modern, sanitary units, one built in 1990 the other more recently, provide good roomy showers with divider and seat (on payment), washbasins with either divider/curtain or in private cubicles, British style WCs, plus excellent bathrooms for families and the disabled. In addition there are now two kitchens with hobs and dishwashing sinks (all free), plus a laundry with sink, two washing machines and a dryer. The site also has an excellent outdoor heated swimming pool and children's pool, a good children's playground with bouncing cushion and a range of trolleys, carts and tricycles. Small shop for essentials (fresh bread can be ordered daily), TV and games rooms, minigolf, telephone and tourist information. Golf course and bicycle hire in nearby Tønder.

How to find it: Turn left off the 419 Tønder - Højer road, 4 km. from Tønder. Drive through Møgeltønder village and past the church where site is signed. Note: the main street is cobbled so drive slowly.

General Details: Open all year. Shop. Swimming pool. Children's playground. Minigolf. Kitchen and laundry facilities. Car wash. Chemical disposal. Motorcaravan service point. Chalets for rent.

Charges 1998: Per adult Dkr. 45; child (0-12 yrs) 25; electricity 15.

Reservations: Not normally necessary. Address: Sønderstregsvej 2, Møgeltønder, 6270 Tønder. Tel: 74.73.84.60. FAX: 74.73.80.43.

2040 Riis Camping and Fritidscenter, Give (Jylland)

Quality, quiet touring site, 18 km. from Legoland and 3 km. from the Lion Park.

Riis is a friendly, family run 'TopCamp' site with 300 large touring pitches, on sheltered gently sloping well tended lawns surrounded by trees and shrubs. Electricity (6A) is available to 220 pitches, and there are 41 cabins and 5 apartments for rent. Two excellent sanitary units provide British WCs, washbasins with divider/curtain, and controllable showers with divider and seat (on payment). There are suites for babies and the disabled, family bathrooms (one with whirlpool bath), solarium, laundry, two excellent kitchens with hobs, ovens, dishwashing sinks, a large dining room/sitting room with TV, plus a covered barbecue grill area. Cooking facilities, family bathrooms and hot water are free, but the showers and whirlpool bath are extra. The outdoor heated pool and water-slide complex (charged for) and the adjacent small bar which serves beer, ice cream, soft drinks and snacks are only open in main season. There is also a small, well stocked shop next to reception for necessities. Other on site amenities include a comprehensive children's play area, outdoor bowling alley, table tennis, minigolf, TV lounge and bicycle hire. More comprehensive shopping and restaurants are in nearby Give. This is a top class site suitable for long or short stays in this very attractive part of Denmark.

How to find it: Turn onto Osterhovedvej southeast of Give town centre (near Shell Garage) at signpost to Riis and site. After 4 km. turn left into gravel drive which runs through the forest to the site. Alternatively, turn off the 442 Brande-Jelling road at Riis village north of Givskud.

General Details: Open 25 April - 7 Sept. Shop. Pool complex. Cafe/bar. Kitchen and laundry facilities. Dining room. Solarium. Table tennis. Minigolf. Bowling alley. Children's playground. TV lounge. Telephone. Tourist information. Car wash. Chemical disposal. Motorcaravan service point. Cabins and apartments to let.

Charges guide: Per adult Dkr. 49; child (under 12) 32; pitch 35 (23/6-4/8 only); electricity 18. Credit cards accepted.

Reservations: Site can become full in July/Aug. so reservations are advisable. Address: 7323 Give. Tel: 75.73.14.33. FAX: 75.73.58.66.

2060 Birkhede Camping, Ry (Jylland)

Well managed site, in beautiful quiet countryside on the edge of Lake Knudso.

Birkhede has 250 marked and numbered grassy pitches on two levels, divided by trees and shrubs, all with electricity (10A). Whilst the upper level is terraced, the lower is gently sloping but more suited to larger units. Although the entrance drive is gravel, on-site access is mainly tarmac with a card operated security barrier. The two sanitary units are of excellent quality, the main block behind reception has two complete sets of facilities, only one open outside main season. The other block serves the lower level of the site. These provide British WCs, washbasins in cubicles, controllable card operated showers with divider and seat, family bathrooms, baby room, kitchens with hobs, dishwashing and laundry sinks (hot water on payment), plus a fridge-freezer. Campers buy pre-charged cards (Dkr. 100) to obtain hot water in kitchen, laundry, and showers. The same card operates washing machines, telephones and the entrance barrier. Amenities include a takeaway and mini-market, free heated outdoor swimming pool (9 x 25 m) with water slide and children's pool (4 x 6 m), an adventure playground.   *continued overleaf*

60

2060 Birkhede Camping (continued)

The lake provides a bathing area, fishing (licences from reception) and a jetty. Good walks from the site include a climb to a viewpoint which looks out over Denmark's 'Lake District'.

How to find it: Turn off Silkeborg - Ry no. 15 road 4 km. southeast of Laven St. at Alling and follow signs to site.

General Details: Open 24 April - 15 Sept. Mini-market and takeaway (May-Sept). Swimming pool (1/6-1/9). Table tennis. Bicycle, boat and canoe hire. Fishing. Windsurfing. Golf 15 km. Children's playground. TV lounge. Kitchen. Laundry. Chemical disposal. Motorcaravan service point. Chalets and motel rooms for rent.

Charges 1999: Per adult Dkr. 51; child (0-11 yrs) 31; pitch mid June - mid Aug only 20 - 35; electricity 14 + 2.00 per kwh. No credit cards.

Reservations: Essential in high season - contact site. Address: Lyngvej 14, 8680 Ry. Tel: 86.89.13.55. FAX: 86.89.03.13. E-mail: birkhede@dk-camp.dk. Internet: www.dk-camp/birkhede.

2050 Terrassen Camping, Laven St, Silkeborg (Jylland)

Terraced, family run site, overlooking Lake Julso and the countryside.

Terrassen's 260 pitches are arranged on terraces with 6A electricity to most. A small additional tent area (without electricity) is at the top of the site where torches may be required. There are also 20 seasonal units, 9 tour operator units, 10 cabins, and 3 site owned caravans. The main sanitary unit is heated and modern and provides British WCs, washbasins (many in cubicles), controllable showers (on payment), 5 family bathrooms, children's bathroom, baby room, and facilities for the disabled. There is also a new kitchen with 10 hobs, 2 ovens and dishwashing sinks. An older re-furbished unit contains another kitchen, plus 4 more shower cubicles with external access - despite their outward appearance they are newly re-tiled and immaculate. Cooking facilities, family bathrooms, hot water and the swimming pool are free, only showers are extra. The solar heated swimming pool (8 x 16 m, open June-end August) has a paved terrace and is well fenced. Other amenities include an adventure playground and pets corner, ball games area with basket and volleyball, a well stocked shop is adjacent to the reception office, games and TV rooms, post box, telephone, tourist information, canoe hire, car wash and motorcaravan service point. A restaurant is just outside the site, and fishing and windsurfing on Lake Julso. This is a comfortable base from which to explore this area of Denmark where a warm welcome and good English will greet you. Don't forget to take a trip on Lake Julso on Hjejen, the world's oldest paddle steamer.

How to find it: From Silkeborg take the road no. 15 to Linas, turn right to Laven St. village, then right again towards Laven and follow signs to site.

General Details: Open 1 April - 15 Sept. Shop (1/5-15/9). Swimming pool (1/6-1/9). Kitchen. Laundry. Games/TV rooms. Children's playground. Pets corner. Canoe hire. Fishing and windsurfing on Lake Julso. Car wash. Chemical disposal. Motorcaravan service point. Cabins and caravans for hire.

Charges guide: Per adult: Dkr. 45; child (1-11 yrs) 25; pitch 10 - 20; electricity 20.

Reservations: Contact site - essential for high season. Address: Himmelbjergvej 9, Laven St, 8600 Silkeborg. Tel: 86.84.13.01. FAX: 84.84.16.55.

2080 Sølystgård Camping, Fuglsø, nr Ebeltoft (Jylland)

Seaside site with good views in attractive holiday location.

Located in a corner of the delightful Ebeltoft and Mols area, one of the best holiday spots in Denmark, this beach-side site is on Ebeltoft Bay, close to the Helgenæs peninsula, and surrounded by rolling countryside. The spacious site, originally a farm, is divided by hedges and trees into several well tended fields, which have varying slopes. The 280 pitches (200 for touring units) are unmarked but electricity (4/6A) is available in all areas and many places have sea views. The lovely old, thatched, white walled farm buildings form the central complex incorporating reception, a small shop and other facilities. There are two sanitary units, one a converted thatched barn solely for ladies, the other is more ordinary, with rooms for ladies and men. The former has a kitchen with hobs (on payment), dishwashing sinks (free hot water), baby room and an excellent whirlpool bathroom (on payment) at one end. Other facilities include British WCs, washbasins either in cubicles, with divider and curtain, or open, plus hot showers with divider and seat (on payment). There are facilities for disabled people, a sauna and solarium (on payment), laundry, telephone, ice pack service and tourist information. Leisure facilities include a centrally located tennis court and children's play area (with an amusing new swing), together with TV and games rooms. The beach offers good bathing with a water chute, and facilities for launching boats. Fishing is popular and the site has a boat to borrow without charge. Golf and riding are available near.

How to find it: Take road 15 from Århus to Rønde, turn right following signs to Fuglsø where you turn left towards the Helgenæs peninsula. Then left again at camp sign down a narrow lane to the site.

General Details: Open 1 April - 20 Sept. Shop. Sauna. Solarium. Whirlpool bathroom. Tennis. Billiards. Volleyball. Basketball. TV and games rooms. Children's playground. Fishing. Boat sliipway. Bicycle hire and golf 15 km. Riding 5 km. Kitchen. Laundry. Car wash. Chemical disposal. Cabins for rent.

Charges 1999: Per adult Dkr. 50 - 57; child (0-13 yrs) 26 - 30; electricity (4A) 20. No credit cards.

Reservations: Essential in high season - write to site. Address: Dragsmurvej 15, Fuglsø, 8420 Ebeltoft (Knebel). Tel: 86.35.12.39. FAX: as phone.

DENMARK

2090 Krakær Camping, Krakær, nr Ebeltoft (Jylland)

Sheltered, spacious forest site, with swimming pool and bistro.

Just north of Ebeltoft Bay in sheltered forest surroundings, but close to beaches and the port of Grenå. Krakær Camping's new family owners have carried out much modernisation and the 266 marked, but not separated, pitches are mostly on level terraces or in large clearings, together with 13 cabins for rent. Access roads are good and most pitches have electricity (10A) but long leads may be needed. Newer terraces are still maturing and could be muddy in wet weather. Two modern sanitary units, one below the reception complex, the other nearer the swimming pool, provide plenty of British style WCs and washbasins in cubicles, but rather fewer hot showers (on payment), which may be pressed in main season. Baby room, family bathrooms, a unit for disabled people, hand and hair dryers, two kitchens with dishwashing, plus a laundry with drying room. Hot water, cooking facilities and family bathrooms are free of charge, only showers are extra. A stylish refitted bistro and bar at the entrance (high season) also serves takeaway meals and has a pleasant terrace. Other amenities include a solar heated open-air swimming pool and toddlers' pool, supermarket, minigolf, TV and games room, telephone, post box and tourist information. Children have an excellent, imaginative adventure playground and pedal car track. There are glorious walks all around.

> **How to find it:** From road no. 15 at Ronde turn right to Femmøller Strand, then left towards Lyngsbæk. Site is clearly signed 2 km. along country lanes. Take care turning off main road - approach on a blind corner.
>
> **General Details:** Open all year. Shop (1/4-1/9). Bistro, bar and takeaway (15/6-15/8). TV/games room. Adventure play area. Minigolf. Swimming pool (1/4-1/9). Riding 200 m. Fishing and boat slipway 3 km. Golf and bicycle hire 8 km. Kitchen. Laundry. Chemical disposal. Motorcaravan service point. Cabins for hire.
>
> **Charges 1999:** Per adult Dkr. 57; child (0-11 yrs) 29; electricity 22. Less 12% outside 18/6-15/8. No credit cards.
>
> **Reservations:** Write to site. Address: GL Kærvej 18, Krakær, 8400 Ebeltoft. Tel: 86.36.21.18. FAX: 86.36.21.87.

2100 Blushøj Camping, Ebeltoft (Jylland)

Comfortable, family run touring site, with views over the Kattegat.

This is a traditional site where the owners are making a conscious effort to keep mainly to touring units - there are only 6 seasonal units and 4 cabins. The site has 230 pitches on level grass terraces surrounded by mature hedging and shrubs. Some have glorious views of the Kattegat and others overlook peaceful rural countryside. Most pitches have electricity (10A), but long leads may be required. One sanitary unit provides British style WCs, washbasins with dividers and showers (on payment). The other unit has a kitchen with a mini-oven and dishwashing sinks, dining/TV room, laundry and baby changing. A heated extension provides six smart family bathrooms, and additional WCs and washbasins, and is adjacent to the heated and fenced swimming pool (14 x 7 m) with a water-slide and terrace. Hot water, oven, family bathrooms and the swimming pool are free, only showers are extra. Good children's playground, minigolf, and well stocked shop. The beach provides for swimming, windsurfing and sea fishing. The owners also arrange traditional entertainment - folk dancing, local choirs, and accordion music some weekends in high season. This is a fine location for a relaxed family holiday, with numerous excursion possibilities including the fine old town of Ebeltoft (4 km), with its shops and restaurants, and the world's largest wooden sailing ship, the Frigate Jylland, now fully restored and open to the public.

> **How to find it:** From road 21 northwest of Ebeltoft turn off at junction where several sites are signed. Follow signs through the outskirts of Ebeltoft turning southeast to Elsegårde village. Turn left for Blushøj and follow camp signs.
>
> **General Details:** Open from 1 April - 15 Sept. Shop. Kitchen. Laundry. Swimming pool (June - Sept). Minigolf. Children's playground. Fishing. Riding 200 m. Bicycle hire, golf and boat slipway at Ebeltoft, 4 km. Chemical disposal. Cabins for rent.
>
> **Charges 1999:** Per adult Dkr. 48 - 55; child 24 - 27; electricity 15. No credit cards.
>
> **Reservations:** Advised for high season - contact site. Address: Elsegårdevej 53, 8400 Ebeltoft. Tel: 86.34.12.38.

2150 Sølyst Camping, Nibe (Jylland)

Family run site beside sheltered Limfjord, with swimming pool.

You will always be near to the water in Denmark, either open sea or, as here, alongside the more sheltered waters of a fjord. Sølyst provides 200 numbered pitches, most with electricity (6A), on gently sloping grass arranged in fairly narrow rows separated by hedges (140 for touring units). There are facilities for watersports and swimming in the fjord, the site also has a small heated swimming pool (8 x 16 m), with a children's pool and paved sunbathing area, and paddle boats can be rented. A little train provides rides for children and there is a good playground, minigolf, and TV room. The snack bar (open main season) provides takeaway meals and there are tables outside, under cover. The central sanitary unit provides British WCs, washbasins in cubicles, four family bathrooms, a baby room and facilities for disabled visitors. There is a kitchen with hobs, microwave, oven and dishwashing sinks, and a fully equipped laundry. A second unit provides two more family bathrooms and additional unisex WCs, basins and showers, and is located near the solarium. *continued overleaf*

2150 Sølyst Camping (continued)

Hot water (except in washbasins) is charged for. The mini-market at the site entrance is open daily. Good paths provide superb, easy walks in either direction, and indeed right into the nearby town of Nibe (1 km). This is a delightful old Danish town with picturesque cottages and 15th century church. Its harbour, once prosperous from local herring boats, is now more concerned with pleasure craft.

How to find it: Site is clearly signed from the no. 187 road west of Nibe town, with a wide entrance.

General Details: Open all year. Mini-market. Snack bar and takeaway. Swimming pool. Children's playground. TV room. Solarium. Fishing. Bicycle hire and riding1 km. Golf 4 km. Kitchen. Laundry. Motorcaravan service point. Chemical disposal. Cabins (12), rooms (3) and mobile homes (3) to rent.

Charges 1999: Per adult Dkr. 50 - 57; child (under 12 yrs) 26 - 30; pitch 20 (14/6-16/8 only); electricity 20. No credit cards.

Reservations: Contct site. Address: Løngstørvej 2, 9240 Nibe. Tel: 98.35.10.62. FAX: 98.35.34.88.

2140 Jesperhus Feriecenter, Nykøbing (Mørs)

Extensive, well run site with pool complex and many leisure activities, adjacent to Blomsterpark.

This large, busy and well organised 'TopCamp' site has 723 numbered pitches, mostly in rows, with some terracing, divided by shrubs and trees with shade in parts. Many pitches are taken by seasonal, tour operator or rental units, plus 70 chalets, so advance booking is advised for peak periods. Electricity (5A) is available on all pitches and water points are in all areas. Four first rate sanitary units are cleaned three times daily and the site operates a policy of regular maintenance and upgrading. Facilities include British WCs, washbasins in private cubicles or with divider/curtain, controllable showers with divider and seat, family and whirlpool bathrooms, plus suites for babies and the disabled. There are superb kitchens with full cookers and hoods, microwaves and dishwashing sinks, plus a fully equipped laundry. All hot water, cooking facilities, family bathrooms and sauna are free of charge, whirlpool bathroom and laundry are extra. The indoor and outdoor pool complex (daily charge) has three pools, diving boards, water slides with the 'Black Hole', spa pools, saunas, solarium, and a café and takeaway. Elsewhere is a separate restaurant/bar and a large supermarket. Activities include a 10 lane bowling centre, 'space laser' game, minigolf, volleyball, tennis, go-carts and other outdoor sports. An indoor hall includes badminton, table tennis, and children's 'play-world'. The latest addition is a 'Circus' every Wednesday in high season. Although it may appear to be just part of Jutland, Mors is an island in its own right surrounded by the lovely Limfjord. It is joined to the 'mainland' by a fine 2,000 m. bridge at the end of which are signs to Blomsterpark (Northern Europe's largest flower park which also houses a Bird Zoo, Butterfly World, Terrarium and Aquarium) and the camp site - both under the same ownership. The flower park, situated well to the north of Denmark, is an incredible sight from early spring to late autumn, attracting some 4,000 visitors a day to enjoy over half a million flowering plants and magnificent landscaped gardens. With all the activities at this site an entire holiday could be spent here regardless of weather, but Jesperhus is also an excellent centre for touring a lovely area of Denmark.

How to find it: From south or north, take road no. 26 to Salling Sund bridge, site is signed Jesperhus, just north of the bridge.

General Details: Open all year. Supermarket (1/4-1/11) with gas. Restaurant. Bar. Café. Takeaway. Pool complex. Very comprehensive leisure, sporting and entertainment facilities. Children's playgrounds. Pets corner. Golf. Fishing. Riding 2 km. Bicycle hire 6 km. Kitchens. Laundry. Chemical disposal. Chalets for rent.

Charges 1999: Per adult Dkr. 55; child (1-11 yrs) 40; pitch 50 (July, BHs. and w/ends only); electricity 25. Credit cards accepted.

Reservations: Recommended for holiday periods - write for details. Address: Jesperhus Feriecenter, Legindvej 30, 7900 Nykøbing, Mors. Tel: 97.72.37.01. FAX: 97.71.02.55.

DENMARK

2170 Klim Strand Camping, Klim, Fjerritslev (Jylland)

Large coastal, family holiday site, with quality facilities - a paradise for children.

This privately owned 'TopCamp' site has the full complement of quality facilities, including its own fire engine and trained staff. The site has 700 numbered pitches, all with electricity (10A), laid out in rows, many divided by trees and hedges and shade in parts. Some 300 of these are 'luxury' pitches, fully serviced with electricity, water, drainage and 18 channel TV hook-up. There are also 24 cabins to rent on site. The two main, centrally situated, heated sanitary buildings are very large, housing spacious showers, washbasins (some in cubicles) and British style WCs. A popular feature is the separate children's room with child size/height WCs, basins and half height shower cubicles. There are also baby rooms, bathrooms for families and disabled visitors, sauna, solariums, whirlpool bath, hairdressing rooms, fitness room, and even a dog bathroom. Two smaller sanitary units are located by reception and beach and there are well equipped kitchens and barbecue areas with dishwashing sinks, microwaves, gas hobs, and two TV lounges. All hot water, showers, cooking facilities and many family bathrooms are free of charge. On site activities include an outdoor water-slide complex, indoor heated swimming pool complex, tennis courts, pony riding (all free), numerous children's play areas, an adventure playground with aerial cable ride, roller skating area and ramp, a crèche, pizzeria and restaurant/bar (open 17.00 Mon-Fri, 12.00 Sat/Sun), supermarket, telephones and tourist information. There is live music and dancing twice a week in high season, bicycle and TV rental and an 18 hole golf course is nearby. Suggested excursions - trips to offshore islands, visits to local potteries, a brewery museum and bird watching on the Bygholm Vejle.

How to find it: Turn off the Thisted-Fjerritslev no. 11 road to Klim from where site is signed.

General Details: Open 15 March - 24 Oct. (incl. all amenities). Supermarket. Pizzeria. Restaurant. Bar. Solarium and sauna. Children's playgrounds. Bicycle and TV hire. Fishing. Riding. Golf 10 km. Comprehensive leisure, sporting and entertainment facilities. Laundry. Kitchens. Chemical disposal. Motorcaravan service point. Car wash. Chalets for rent.

Charges 1999: Per adult Dkr. 57; child (0-11 yrs) 40; pitch 40 (21/6-21/8 only); 'luxury' pitch 10 - 25 (according to season); electricity 25. Credit cards accepted.

Reservations: Essential for mid June - end August. Address: Havvejen 167, Klim, 9690 Fjerritslev. Tel: 98.22.53.40. FAX: 98.22.57.77. E-mail: ksc@klim-strand.dk. Internet: www.klim-strand.dk.

2130 Hobro Camping Gattenborg, Hobro (Jylland)

Imaginatively landscaped site with views over Hobro, Mariager Fjord and Vester Fjord.

This neat and very well tended site has 130 pitches on terraces arranged around a bowl shaped central activity area. Most pitches (100 for touring units) have electricity (5A) and there are many trees and shrubs. Footpaths connect the various terraces and activity areas. There are 30 seasonal units and 6 cabins for rent on site. The main heated sanitary building, towards the rear of the site, provides British style WCs, washbasins in cubicles, and controllable hot showers (on payment), plus two bathrooms, a kitchen and dishwashing sinks, and small laundry with a washing machine and two dryers. Facilities for disabled people and a baby room have been added. A tiny unit in the centre of the site has two unisex WCs and basins (cold water) and a small kitchen, whilst the reception building with a small shop and tourist information, has a covered picnic terrace behind, and also houses a large TV lounge and additional WC and basins. The small, heated swimming pool with water-slide is free and open in high season weather permitting. Well equipped children's playground, minigolf, basketball and football ground, table tennis, billiards, giant chess, and a woodland moon-buggy track. The site is 500 m. walk from the town, close to the Viking Castle of Fyrkat and the lovely old town of Mariager.

How to find it: From E45 exit 35, take road 579 towards Hobro Centrum. Site is well signed to the right, after railway bridge.

General Details: Open 26 March - 26 Sept. Shop. Swimming pool (high season). Children's play areas. Table tennis. Basketball. Football. Minigolf. Fishing 7 km. Bicycle hire near. TV lounge. Kitchen. Laundry. Chemical disposal. Motorcaravan service point. Car wash.

Charges 1998: Per adult Dkr. 48 - 55; child (2-11 yrs) 24 - 29; electricity 20. No credit cards.

Reservations: Contact site. Address: Skivevej 35, 9500 Hobro. Tel: 98.52.32.88. FAX: 98.52.56.61.

All the sites in this guide are regularly inspected by our team of experienced site assessors, but we welcome your opinion too.

See Readers Reports on page 367

Motorsport

A guide for campers, caravanners or motorcaravanners to some of Europe's foremost motor races.

In 1997 we decided to undertake a review, over a period of several seasons, of the most famous of Europe's motor races, including the formula 1 grand prix, and of course the Le Mans 24 hour race, particularly from the perspective of campers and caravanners.

During the past two years we have attended five Grand Prix (in France, Spain Monaco, Belgium and the UK) and the Le Mans 24 hour race, reports on all of which appear in this our second "Motorsports Feature" We have also competed in three International Historic Rallies, The Pyrenees, the Monte Carlo and the Tulip Rally

Of course there is a variety of specialist tour operators offering inclusive tour arrangements to many European motor races, but we really wanted to be wholly independent, and slot in attendance at some races alongside our Site Inspection Programme, and the sources of "tickets only" are fairly limited. We were therefore fortunate that, in every case, (apart from Le Mans where we were lucky enough to be given press passes courtesy of the Automobile Club de l'Ouest) we were able to obtain basic general admission tickets from "Just Tickets" who provide an excellent service, and whose advertisement appears in this guide.

Over the course of the next couple of years we hope to be able to fit in visits to more GPs and other races and thus to add to this Motorsports Feature to the point whereby it will provide a fairly comprehensive guide to European motor races for the independent camper, caravanner or motorcaravanner.

Belgian Grand Prix
Spa-Francorchamps

The Spa circuit is well-known as one of the most challenging of all the European Formula 1 venues. The circuit itself (which still uses some closed public roads) is longer than most, and covers quite a large area of countryside, including Francorchamps, Malmedy, Eau Rouge, and Stavelot, which happens to be the location of one of the sites featured in this guide

Le Mans – cars at the Dunlop Chicane.

(ACO Guy Beaulieu)

(074 Domaine de l'Eau Rouge) which is where we stayed during our visit to the 1997 Grand Prix

First of all it's worth mentioning that the circuit is not really based at Spa at all, but at Francorchamps, where there is direct access to the ticket office, main grandstands, pits and paddock, but it isn't by any means essential to base yourself here even if you can find a hotel or campsite with any space!

You can indeed camp at several places around the circuit, but judging from the fact that there was no camping/caravanning space left at all around the circuit when we arrived two days before the race, the fact that most of the camping areas are on a 45 degree slope and that there seem to be a total of about 10 portaloos for all the camping areas, you'll need to be pretty dedicated (and self-sufficient) to consider trying to "rough camp" Frankly we weren't that brave!

Our personal strategy was to book tickets (basic general admission only) in advance through our friends at Just Tickets (see advert on page xxx) and similarly to book at pitch in advance at Camping Eau Rouge (No 074 in our Guide) This proved to be a reasonably cost-effective and comfortable option, because it enables you to arrive on the Friday evening (or even on the Saturday evening) settle yourself onto your pitch and walk to the circuit either along the road or through the woods - its about 2km to the circuit at Stavelot, where you can get a pretty good close view over two corners and a short straight, and a more distant view of the following straight, but you must get in position early - I mean really early - the circuit actually opens at 1 am on race day, and if you're not in position by 6.30am don't bother trying! There are no stands at Stavelot, and you'll need to take your own chairs unless you're prepared to stand for ten hours. An umbrella and/or parasol is also pretty essential, as it's either very hot sunshine (34 degrees) or torrential rain. Spa is renowned for its unpredictable weather!

Our decision to camp at Eau Rouge, and to book in advance was fortuitous - we arrived on the Friday evening and apart from our reserved pitch there wasn't an inch of free space anywhere on the site, which was virtually taken over by GP enthusiasts - there was even a Ferrari goodies stand and a Lancia marquee! Given the sheer numbers the site coped pretty well, but expect long queues for the few hot showers!

You could of course drive to the circuit, either at Stavelot or at several other places, but beware of hefty parking charges (about £17) lack of space and a ruthless policy of towing-away illegally parked vehicles.. Frankly I doubt if its worth the hassle if you're staying at Eau Rouge, but on the other hand a 2km walk back after the race in a temperature of 34 degrees, carrying two chairs, an umbrella, camera, binoculars, VHF radio, thermos flasks etc isn't a lot of fun either, to say nothing of a similar, if much cooler, walk to the circuit in the dark at 5.30am

Was it worth it? I asked my 19 year old daughter who had never been to a Grand Prix before this question and her reply was "can you get tickets for next year, or could we try Monaco instead?" - as you'll see from our Monaco GP report, that's exactly what we did!

British Grand Prix
Silverstone

With general admission tickets, and a car-parking ticket provided by Just Tickets, we set off from Weymouth for Silverstone at 3.30am on race day, expecting heavy traffic, but in fact we didn't hit any serious traffic problems at all for the first two hours, and things only got bad when we were within six miles of the circuit.

With a bit of crafty map reading we managed to get our car into the car park by 6.30am, so all in all the journey had taken only three hours door to door, which wasn't as bad as we'd been led to believe, but I guess leaving home in the middle of the night wasn't such a bad idea after all, even though it seemed horrible at the time!

After spending an hour or so looking around the car displays, getting a hot cup of still early morning tea (it was freezing cold!) I tried to persuade my two friends that we ought to go straight to the track-side and grab a good spot, as I'd learned from my experience at Spa the previous year that people (the Germans in particular!) get into position very early indeed, and if you want a good view you must take up your position as early as possible. My friends were not too impressed by my arguments on this, as they were too interested in wandering around looking at the cars, so although we did end up with a reasonable view, near Abbey Curve, we were still a few rows back from the front - lesson 1 - if you want a front row spot, get there early and establish your territory!

At least we'd had the foresight to bring folding chairs, so we could sit down in reasonable comfort, rather than on a quagmire! The weather was absolutely terrible, pouring with rain, windy and very cold - this was supposed to be summer, but at least we were well prepared, wearing wellies, thick socks, two jumpers waterproof trousers and jackets, hats and umbrellas - after all this is England in July!

The long wait for the start of the GP was relieved by various interesting events, such as the Porsche Cup Race, a Formula 3000 Race, the first sight of the two-seater Maclaren, and the Red Arrows. Unfortunately we were right opposite the helicopter pad, which not only featured a military helicopter display, but was the arrival and departure point for all the VIPs, with helicopters arriving and leaving every ten seconds throughout most of the day - entertaining for five minutes, thoroughly annoying for the rest of the day! - it was chaos!

We were very glad there was a van nearby serving hot drinks and food - not great food mind you, but at least it kept you warm! There were also toilets close by, with long queues, but reasonably clean.

The race itself was exciting, especially as it was so wet, although I wasn't so impressed with the result as I'm a Villeneuve fan, and he only came 5th., but it was a good race, and everyone forgot about the rain and the cold.

The worst part of the day was getting out of the circuit after the race - we sat in my car for two and a half hours before we managed to get out of the field in which we'd parked! - the only redeeming feature being the sight of Eddie Jordan going by on a moped. We finally got away from the circuit at 7.30pm., and the drive home

was fairly tedious with heavy traffic most of the way. We got home just before 11pm. Was it worth it? Yes, it was cold. wet and tiring, but the race, and the day generally, were excellent, but its not cheap!

Clare Edwards

French Grand Prix
Circuit Nevers – Magny-Cours

The Magny-Cours circuit is situated literally in the heart of the French countryside! Arriving as we did, from the east, the approach to the circuit is via a myriad of tiny country lanes, which, in the days before the GP, are well signposted.

Given our previous experience at the Spanish GP in May, in addition to our admission tickets we had also obtained a car-parking ticket from Just Tickets. This ticket was for the East car park, which was easy enough to find, but on reflection we might have done better to have parked on the verge of the approach road (a country lane) as we would thus avoided at least some of the delay when leaving!

The Magny-Cours circuit is set in a natural bowl in the surrounding hills, and viewing from most parts is pretty good. We found "seats" on concrete terracing just before the Adelaide curve, and enjoyed a reasonable view of the straight, the curve itself and the straight beyond it.

Even so you get a still better view on TV, but of course what you don't get on TV is the atmosphere, which was wonderful. In contrast to Barcelona, the commentary, over a quite audible PA system (but also on FM radio if you prefer) was in French and English, so there was no problem keeping track of pit-stops etc. We were also opposite an electronic "scoreboard" which gave up-dated positions for the leading cars.

Only real problem was getting away afterwards - we actually sat in a queue of traffic that moved no more than ten metres in an hour! Once you do get out of the circuit the traffic is kept moving by a variety of police, gendarmes and other military personnel, but progress is still pretty slow.

So far as camping/caravanning is concerned, one option is simply to get a car-parking ticket and take your outfit into the East car park (a very large, reasonably flat, if rather muddy, field, where you can choose more or less any spot you like to pitch. There are sanitary facilities, in porta-cabins, close to the entrance from the car-park to the circuit itself, which seemed to be kept reasonably well cleaned, apart from mud - to be fair the weather had been terrible for several days prior to the race, so mud was an inevitability wherever you went.

Alternatively there are several two-star municipal campsites within about 10Km of the circuit, but the one-way system operated, and strictly controlled, by the police precluded our visiting these, although we did visit the four-star municipal "le Halles" at Decize, about 20Km from the circuit.

This is an attractive site, beside the river, with quite reasonably sized pitches, all with electricity, on level grass with ample shade. Unfortunately the sanitary facilities, although quite clean, were distinctly elderly, with mainly Turkish style WCs, and certainly not of a standard one would expect of more modern four-star campsite.

If you are prepared to travel further, the very comfortable Alan Rogers inspected/ selected site Des Bains, (No 5801) at St.Honore les Bains, is only about xx km away, and in normal conditions should be only about an hour or so's drive from the circuit - indeed it may well only take that long to get there on race day, but you'd probably best allow about three hours to get back

Le Mans – more than a place, more than a race

Think of Le Mans as a series of snapshots. Of Wolf Barnato's thunderous Bentley heading into the setting sun. Of the big cat Jaguars - disc brakes glowing in the dark - humbling the might of European engineering. Of Steve McQueen's heartbeat as he waits for the flag to drop in the classic movie Le Mans. Or the crescendo of sound as the first lap pack jostle for position on the run down to Mulsanne corner.

And above it all the gaudily lit ferris wheel slowly revolving in the night sky.

But Le Mans is more than that. It is an area of gently rolling hills and woods. An area without extremes. Of gentle summers and mild winters. Of Charolais beef cattle, and Guernseys kept for their creamy milk. Of cottage industries turning out traditional wooden furniture identical to the chairs and tables which have seen hundreds of years service in the village bars. An area never intentionally developed for commercial tourism, which annually attracts Parisians in their thousands, all of them seeking a reminder of their rural roots.
And central to it all is the city of Le Mans itself. Today a bustling mix of old and new,

Le Mans – grandstand night atmosphere.
A.C.O. Guy Beaulieu

Le Mans – refuelling a McLaren F1 GTR.

A.C.O. *Guy Beaulieu*

but once the scene of bloody religious wars, of tragedy and farce.

But despite the attractions of the surrounding countryside, the real magnet outside the city is the motor race circuit to the south. The first race was held in 1923 and that, like every other subsequent 24 hour race, was intended as a means of encouraging the development of road going cars.

At times the organising Automobile Club de l'Ouest may have seemed autocratic and dogmatic with their insistence on setting their own construction rules. At times the world rules governing what we should call *Grande Tourisme* cars seemed to be moving in a different direction to those applying to Le Mans. But such is the lure of the race that manufacturers will support it, even if it appears they put an entire year's effort and budget into a car which will be used once only. But invariably Le Mans has been proved right. Fans, many of whom support no other form of racing, still flock to the circuit for their annual dose of excitement. And lessons learned at Le Mans do find their way in to the cars we drive. Jaguar proved the durability and efficiency of disc brakes at Le Mans in the mid 1950s.

The practicality of turbochargers for small petrol engines was proved at Le Mans, and today it is complex re-inforced plastics and electronics which are proved

at Le Mans before finding their way in to mass production cars.

But that isn't why the fans flock there every year. They come for the atmosphere. Every June the circuit is alive and thriving like a great 24 hour family party. You could go through the entire race weekend without seeing a race car - if you wanted to. The fun fair stays open throughout the race and there are masses of stalls selling everything imaginable - and a few things you'll never understand - in the area from the Ford chicane and on towards Tetra Rouge.

Unlike many race circuits, at Le Mans you don't have to dine out exclusively on burgers and hot dogs. There are a number of good restaurants close to the track, but my favourites are La Boule d'Or, Hunaudieres and the Auberge - all of them adjacent to the Mulsanne straight.

Those with a sense of history will head for the main gate where the Le Mans museum has been moved. Cars on display are mute reminders of how far motor racing has come since the first 24 hour race in 1923.

But even if your trip to Le Mans isn't for the 24 hour race, you have to make a visit to the circuit. Much of it is on private land, but the famous Mulsanne straight is actually a public road. The N138.

The over four miles long Mulsanne straight was always the supreme test of a car's strength. Many a leading contender suffered engine failure on Mulsanne. By the late 1980's the organisers were becoming concerned about the speed of some of the competitors on Mulsanne. Cars like the WM team's Peugeots were getting close to 250mph. In an effort to reduce speeds, two chicanes were introduced. They have reduced speeds, but some of the leading competitors are still peaking at close to 200mph.

The public road avoids the chicanes, but unfortunately you can't speed. The speed limits are reinforced by wall to wall Gatso speed cameras. However the real thrill doesn't come from speeding down Mulsanne, but rather by parking and soaking up the atmosphere.
Within minutes the bustle of everyday traffic fades as your eyes follow the road down to a point on the horizon. It takes little imagination to bring to mind grainy black and white photos of Barnato's

Bentley, or the works Jaguars lining up to make a victorious statement as they crossed the finish in line astern.
Famous names, perhaps known only from history books, spring to mind. The names of those who have faced the toughest challenge in motor racing. Sir Henry Birkin, Earl Howe, Lord Selsdon, Mike Hawthorn, Phil Hill, Carroll Sheby, Roy Salvadori, Jacky Ickx, Henry Pescarolo, Derek Bell, Graham Hill, Mario Andretti. The list is as long as your memory and imagination.

That is Le Mans. It is more than a place. More than a race. It is an experience which everyone should enjoy at some time in their life.

Mike Cazalet

Camping at Le Mans

The Le Mans circuit itself offers racegoers several different `campsites' usually open from the Tuesday prior to the race until the Monday after it, but early booking, or early arrival, is essential if you are not to be disappointed.
These 'sites' include Camping Houx (or Nouveau) with numbered pitches and electrical connections, and a new sanitary block with showers and WCs. This site also has an annexe, Chemin aux

Le Mans Fact Sheet 1

Race weekend
Traditionally the third weekend of June every year. Scrutineering is held in the city, not at the track. There is also an annual 24 hour motorcycle race usually held on the first weekend in April.

Organisers
- L'Automobile Club de l'Ouest (ACO) for tickets and other information on 'phone (+00 33) 2.43.40.24.00 or fax (+00 33) 2.43.40.24.88.

Travelling times
All approximate, with caravan or motorhome:
- from Calais (via Paris 230 miles) 5½ hours
- from Calais (via Rouen 260 miles) 6 hours
- from Caen (94 miles) 3 hours
- from St. Malo (120 miles) 3 hours
- from Le Havre (138 miles) 3½ hours
- from Cherbourg (166 miles) 4 hours

Circuit length
8.45 miles.
There is also the shorter Bugatti circuit.

Le Mans Fact Sheet 2

Race tickets, and tickets for camping at the Circuit itself are obtainable from Just Tickets (see advertisement in this section) or direct from:

Automobile Club de l'Ouest,
Siege Social,
Circuit des 24 Heures,
72019 Le Mans Cedex.
Tel: 02.43.40.24.24.

Bear in mind that members of the ACO get a special discount on race tickets, access to their own 'club marquee' and other goodies, as well as the benefits of all-year-round breakdown cover throughout France, so you might like to consider actually joining the ACO - full details available from the address included here.

Boeufs, with good access to the starting straight.

La Chapelle camping is situated in the woods on the inside of the circuit near the Dunlop Bridge. Tertre Rouge is again close to the track, and to the funfair, whilst Camping Bleu is close to the main entrance/exit for a quick getaway. Camping Expo is also close to the entrance, and to the Museum, while Maison Blanche may allow you to get a view of the circuit from the roof of your motorhome or caravan.

Prices, in 1998, for these 'campsites' range from FFr. 180 - 450 for the whole period of the practice and the race itself, irrespective of how long you actually stay.

If you choose not to use the circuit's own camping facilities, and to stay at a 'proper' campsite, there are a fair number to choose from, including quite a few in the département of Sarthe (72) some of which are featured in the Alan Rogers Good Camps Guide to France, but bear in mind that all of these are likely to become very heavily booked-up over the weeks before during and after the race.

Amongst the several sites within about 30 miles of the circuit are:

Camping Municipal
Bresse-sur-Braye (about 45 km. SE of Le Mans). Unusual 4-star municipal with around 60 pitches.
Tel: 02.43.35.31.13.

Camping Municipal du Lac
St Calais (about 37 km. ESE of Le Mans). Fully described in the Alan Rogers Good Camps Guide for France (7202M)
Tel: 02.43.35.04.81

Camping Les Mollieres
Sille Guillaume (about 35 km. N of Le Mans). A well-shaded 3-star site with 130 pitches. Tel: 02.43.20.16.12

Camping Le Vieux Moulin
Neuville-sur-Sarthe (about 11 km. N of Le Mans). Pleasant 3-star site with about 100 pitches. Tel: 02.43.25.31.82

Camping Municipal La Route d'Or
La Fleche (about 40 km. SW of Le Mans). Fully described in the Alan Rogers Good Camps Guide for France (7201M).
Tel: 02.43.94.55.90

Castel Camping Chateau de Chanteloup
Savigne l'Eveque (15 km. NE of Le Mans). Fully described in the Alan Rogers Good Camps Guide (7203).
Tel: 02.43.27.51.07.

Monaco Grand Prix
Monte Carlo

One of the good things about banking with the Midland Bank is that they are part of the Hong Kong & Shanghai Bank Corporation, who are one of Stewart GPs principal sponsors. As we'd already arranged tickets for the Monaco GP, our local Midland manager Andy Lewis was persuaded that we were good enough customers for him to recommend that HSBC's Grand Prix Manager, Johnny Harrison, give us a tour of the paddock!

Although we were already reasonably familiar with the Monaco circuit and it's surroundings, the visit to the F1 paddock was a real eye-opener - first of all of course the paddock area is a long way from the temporary pits, which in any case are too small for anything other than routine servicing when the cars are out on the circuit, so everything else has to be done in the paddock, which involves a serious climb up lots of narrow stone steps - no wonder Monaco isn't the teams' favourite venue!

We were very lucky to have the paddock tour of course, which was absolutely brilliant, but there again the Monaco GP is a real "must" for any F1 enthusiast, and we were very pleasantly surprised how easy it is for the independent traveller to have a really good time here, with surprisingly little hassle.

Our original intention was to drive into Monte Carlo on the Friday prior to the race from our Alan Rogers campsite, La Vielle Ferme, at Villeneuve Loubet, suss out the situation, have our Paddock Tour, return to Villeneuve Loubet, leave our car there and use the train to travel in and out of Monte Carlo on the Saturday and Sunday.

We duly took the train on the Saturday morning - after a long queue for tickets we joined a packed, very slow, train which stopped for 20 minutes in Nice. The journey was said to take half an hour, but in fact took an hour. The return was even worse - we couldn't even get on the first two trains out of Monte Carlo, and this was only the qualifying day!

After some discussion we decided to risk the car on race day, although we were warned by some Germans on the campsite that we would need to leave really early, and to expect traffic jams, and they would be leaving Villeneuve Loubet at 5am!

We decided that a 5am start was not really on, so we left at 6.30 - to our amazement there was little traffic, and we drove straight into the first "parking for Grand Prix" car park we saw, walked about 400m to the centre of Monte Carlo and were sat down having breakfast at a local pavement bar in the Place d'Armes by 7.15am!

We'd managed to get some grandstand tickets near the Swimming Pool for the race, but quite frankly the extra cost of anything other than the very best stand tickets is arguably not really justified in terms of getting a good view - yes we were close to the track, but could only see a short stretch around the back of the swimming pool, and a more distant view down to the Rascasse and the Stars and Bars. If your main interest is getting a good view of the race, you need to buy the very best stand tickets, for which most us would need a second mortgage, or watch it on TV which is a lot cheaper

It's not the view, or lack of it, that we like to go to GPs for, it's the atmosphere of course, and in this respect Monaco is truly exceptional - where else (after 7pm) can you walk round most of the circuit, including the tunnel, drink in the history and the Campari, eat well and at surprisingly reasonable prices, spend an hour on the beach, gawk at the mega yachts, do some sightseeing, go to the Casino (no we didn't actually, but we could have) rub shoulders with former GP drivers to say nothing of watching the free practice, the qualifying and the race itself from a variety of situations?.

Perhaps we just got lucky (and yes we did so far as the Paddock visit went, and many thanks to Johnny Harrison for an excellent tour) but even without that particular bonus the Monaco GP looks like becoming an annual family pilgrimage from now on.

Spanish Grand Prix
Circuit de Cataluna – Barcelona

Our visit to the Spanish Formula 1 GP in May 1997 was something of an eye-opener!

Although we had acquired admission tickets in advance, from Just Tickets, whose advertisement appears on page xxx, we were unable to get to the Saturday qualifying, so getting into the circiut on the Sunday was a new experience. Our first mistake was to take the wrong exit off the Autoroute! You'd expect that Exit 13 would be the Exit immediately after Exit 12 wouldn't you? - well, it isn't - there's another unnumbered junction between 12 and 13, which we took by mistake, and ended up driving round a deserted suburb for about half and hour, until we eventually found someone who directed us to the circuit.

Once we found the circuit the problem was to find somewhare to park - there are plenty of numbered car-parks, but most are reserved or pre-booked, so unless you are able to attend the Saturday qualifying and buy a car parking ticket in advance, allow yourself plenty of time to find somewhere to park the car (like an hour or so!)

By chance we actually ended up in the car park next to the camping field, which involves a walk of about 10 minutes to the nearest circuit gate. The camping field is reasonably flat, but the access to it isn't, and it seemed to by used exclusively by motorhomes - I would n't have wanted to try to manouever a caravan into it, espcially in competition with several thousand cars using the entrance to the adjacent car-parking field!

The camping field had several WCs and showers in porta-cabins, which would probably have been fine if it wasn't for the fact that the car-park adjacent had no such facilities - this resulted in the WCs in the camping field being a tad pressed to put it mildly! All in all the the camping facilties at the circuit might best be described in one word - primitive!

In fact our advice would be to do the same as we did and to stay on one of the many excellent sites in the Costa Brava, and drive to the circuit by car - Bearing in mind that the circuit is north of Barcelona, and only about 1km off the autoroute (junction 13) it's actually within not much more than an hour or so's drive from a wide choice of good campsites.

The circuit itself is in a "bowl" in the surrounding hills, and there are good views from several vantage points - we found space on the grassy slope just above turns 1 and 2, which gave quite a good view, although not of the pits, so we tended to lose track of the situation after about 15 laps when cars started to pit - in retrospect a VHF/FM radio, preferably with headphones, would have been very useful to enable us to keep track of the pitstops etc via the (English language) commentary, because although we could see one of the many giant TV monitors their commentary was all in Spanish and the picture was very faint in the strong sunlight.

Frankly you get a better all round picture of a GP from the comfort of your armchair in front of the TV at home, but, crucially, what you miss is the incredible atmosphere - next time we'll know better, get there earlier, take a walkman type radio as well as binoculars, and more by way of a picnic, but even allowing for our mistakes, this is an event not to be missed if you enjoy motorsport!

Historic Rallies

Traditionally rallying was a sport that took place on public roads, and in its heyday attracted hundreds of thousands of spectators, particularly to the more famous international rallies such as the Monte Carlo, the Tulip Rally and the Alpine Rally.

Unfortunately as the sport became more and more professional, and cars became more and more unlike their normal road-going versions, and thus quicker and quicker the sport became the more or less exclusive preserve of the works teams, with fewer and fewer amateurs or other private entrants.

In recent years the World Rally Championship has become an increasingly popular TV spectacle, but this has meant that the modern versions of famous events such as "The Monte" bear little relation to the original concept, and nowadays most of the action takes place in daylight over closed roads (stages) with the start and finish in Monte Carlo, and no "concentration runs" from several starting points all over Europe, so the event has really changed out of all recognition. In 1998 the AC de Monaco decided to resurrect the Monte in its original format, and to run it once again as a traditional road rally for "period" cars – ie those of a type which competed in the old-style Monte Carlo Rally before 1975. To an extent they were following a lead set by the organisers of the Tulip Rally, the Alpine Rally and the Rally des Pyrenees, including a number of independent rally organisers who had been doing much the same thing for several years, with significant success. Having been a rally driver myself during the '60s, forced into retirement by the

The Rallye Monte Carlo Historique.

increasing cost and commercialism of "modern" rallying, I had been delighted to once more have had the opportunity to compete in International rallies on equal terms, and since 1995 we had used our 1971 Lancia Fulvia 1600HF coupé to compete on both the Rallye des Pyrenees and the Tulip Rally. When the AC de Monaco launched the 1st "Rallye Monte Carlo Historique" in 1998 we were therefore one of the first British entrants! - just as well as the event was well over-subscribed, although mainly with French, Belgian, Italian, German and Dutch competitors, so we were actually one of just seven British teams .

The Monte Carlo Rallye Historique is run on strictly traditional lines, as a regularity rally, with starts in Reims and Turin followed by Concentration Runs to Digne les Bains, a Communal Leg to Monte Carlo, followed by a night leg over closed roads in the mountains behind Monte Carlo, including the famous Col de Turini. Of course it is run in January when snow is inevitable, and timing is crucial as competitors are penalised for every second early or late at each control, and averaging exactly 50kph over tiny snow-covered roads in the Alps is no easy feat.

Starting from Reims at about 8.00pm on a

pouring wet January night we were astonished by the number of spectators, not just at the start but all along the route as well, even at 2.00am!

The following two days saw increasing numbers of spectators in every town and village through which we passed, and even more spectators lining the minor snow-covered roads through the Alps. Clearly Historic Rallying in the form of these major International events has caught the public's imagination, even though the event had little advance publicity.

In terms of results we would have been happy just to finish, so the fact that we actually came 14th overall, and third in class, was a real bonus, and yes, all being well we'll be back for the 1999 event, which, according to the much more prominent advance publicity looks like being even better. For those interested the Rally starts from Reims and Turin on the evening of Saturday 16th January, and finishes in Monte Carlo on Wednesday 20th January, and if any of our readers happen to be around, please give the black Lancia Fulvia coupé with the Alan Rogers logo a friendly wave!

Clive Edwards & Mervyn Brake

The authors in the Lancia Fulvia on the finishing ramp at Monte Carlo.

MOTORAIL
The Expressway into Europe

MOTORAIL the safe, comfortable, stress-free, time saving way to travel with your car to the South for your holiday.

For a brochure call our 24 hour Hotline
0990 02 4000

For bookings call
0990 848 848

Load the car onto the train in Calais

Settle down for a comfortable night's sleep

RE RailEurope

Grand Prix Racing

Just Tickets are the largest UK suppliers of spectator tickets to all Formula One events plus the le Mans 24 hours.

Our **Ticket only** service covers general admission, grandstand seats, also parking at most circuits.

At **Silverstone** and **Monaco** we also book helicopters as well as hospitality, including a new **Speciality Marquee** at Le Mans plus restaurant and private apartment both with viewing terrace at Monaco

Just Motoring offers inclusive self-drive arrangements with hotels, to all European Formula One events.

Brochure available in November
'Phone or fax for price lists

Just Tickets
1 Charter House
Camden Crescent
Dover, Kent
CT16 1LE
Tel: 01304 228866
Fax: 01304 242550

- -

Mr/Mrs/Ms

Address

Postcode

Event

Ref GCG/98

2160 Hirtshals Camping, Hirtshals (Jylland)

Traditional coastal site, close to ferry port for Norway and the North Sea Centre.

This tidy, family run site is well placed for touring the tip of Jutland, and is close to the ferry port (1 km.) from which there are regular crossings to Norway. On the edge of a residential area and facing the Skagerrak (it can be a little windy) it has direct access to the beach. The 155 numbered touring pitches, all with electricity (10A), are on open, flat, sandy grass and are separated into rows by low wooden rails, with more sheltered pitches for tents behind reception, together with 10 cabins for rent. All amenities, including reception, are in a neat modern block at the entrance. They include good sanitary facilities with modern, bright fittings, including controllable hot showers (on payment), washbasins in cubicles, facilities for babies and disabled people, and a laundry. In high season a small `portacabin' style block provides a further shower, washbasin and WC (for each sex) by the pitches furthest from the entrance. Dishwashing sinks with free hot water, gas rings and an oven are to be found in the campers' kitchen. There is a well stocked shop (with takeaway in season), a good children's' playground and a clubroom with TV. Restaurants, supermarkets and a swimming pool are to be found in the town. For the well protected or warm blooded, the main attraction of this site is the sea, with rewarding fishing and watersports. The coast from Hirtshals right up to the tip is almost one long beach with tide washed golden sand hard enough even to carry local buses - a quite memorable sight. Just north is Tversted, an ideal forest picnic spot, or 10 km. from Skagen is the fascinating buried church, or you might like to visit the remarkable Danish 'Sahara', the enormous dunes of Råbjerg Mile.

How to find it: Site is clearly signed from road nos. 13, 15 and 55. It is on the outskirts of the town.

General Details: Open 1 May - 12 Sept. Small shop, others and restaurants in the town. Club room and TV. Children's playground. Bicycle hire. Barbecue. Kitchen. Freezer. Laundry. Fish preparation sinks. Chemical disposal. Motorcaravan service point. Bus services. Cabins for hire.

Charges 1999: Per adult Dkr. 48 - 52; child (2-12 yrs) 20 - 25; electricity 20. No credit cards.

Reservations: Write to site for details. Address: Kystvejen 6, 9850 Hirtshals. Tel: 98.94.25.35. FAX: 98.94.33.43.

2180 Nordstrand Camping, Frederikshavn (Jylland)

Excellent site 2 km. from Frederikshavn and ferries to Sweden and Norway.

This is another `TopCamp' site and provides all the comforts one could possibly need with all the attractions of the nearby beach, town and port. The 430 large pitches are attractively arranged in small enclosures of 9-13 units surrounded by hedges and trees. Many of the hedges are of flowering shrubs and this makes for a very pleasant atmosphere. 250 pitches have electricity and drainage, a further 20 have water and there are 16 on hardstandings. There are 64 seasonal units, plus 23 cabins and 3 caravans for rent. The roads are all paved and the site is well lit and fenced with the barrier locked at night. Sanitary facilities are in two very large, centrally located, modern blocks and provide spacious showers (on payment), washbasins in cubicles and British style WCs, together with some family bathrooms, rooms for disabled people and babies, and laundry with free ironing. All are spotlessly clean. Good kitchens at each block provide mini-ovens, microwaves, hobs (free of charge) and dishwashing sinks with free hot water. Leisure activities include minigolf, tennis, table tennis, billiards, chess, and fishing. The reception complex also houses a café (open in high season), with a telephone pizza service available at other times. A supermarket, tourist information, telephone and post box also on site. The beach is a level, paved 200 m. walk. An indoor swimming pool complex is 2 km. There is much to see in this area of Denmark and this site would make a very comfortable holiday base.

How to find it: Turn off the main no. 40 road 2 km. north of Frederikshavn at roundabout just north of railway bridge. Site is signed.

General Details: Open 1 April - 15 Sept. Supermarket (all season). Café (15/6-15/8). Pizza service. Solarium. Beach. Fishing 200 m. Bicycle hire. Children's playgrounds. Laundry. Kitchens. Car wash. Chemical disposal. Motorcaravan service point. Chalets and caravans for rent.

Charges 1998: Per adult Dkr. 39 - 49; child (0-11 yrs) 25 - 32; pitch 27 - 30; electricity 6A 18, 10A 25. Credit cards accepted.

Reservations: Essential for high season and made with deposit (Dkr. 400). Address: Apholmenvej 40, 9900 Frederikshavn. Tel: 98.42.93.50 FAX: 98.43.47.85.

2215 DCU Camping Odense, Odense (Fyn)

Ideal base from which to explore this fairy-tale city.

Although within the confines of the city, this site is hidden away amongst mature trees and is therefore fairly quiet. The 225 pitches, of which 145 have electricity (10A), are on level grass with small hedges and shrubs dividing the area into bays. There are a number of seasonal units on site together with 14 cabins for rent. The large new (1997) sanitary unit provides up to the minute facilities including British style WCs, washbasins in cubicles, controllable hot showers, four family bathrooms, hand dryers and hairdryers, a baby room, and an excellent suite for disabled people. *continued overleaf*

DENMARK

2215 DCU Camping Odense (continued)

In addition there is a well equipped kitchen with gas hobs and dishwashing sinks, plus a laundry with washing machines and dryer. All hot water and cooking facilities are free. Shop, swimming pool complex, games marquee, TV room, large children's playground with bouncing cushion, table tennis, minigolf, ball games field and bicycle hire. A good network of cycle paths lead into the city. The Odense Adventure Pass (available at the site) allows free travel on public transport within the city limits, free admission to the swimming baths and a daily newspaper, with discounts on other attractions.

How to find it: From E20 exit 50, turn towards Odense Centrum, site entrance is 3 km. on left immediately beside the Texaco Garage.

General Details: Open 22 March - 20 October. Shop. Laundry. Kitchen. Swimming pool. Games marquee. Table tennis. TV. Children's playground. Minigolf. Bicycle hire. Tourist information. Telephone. Chemical disposal. Motorcaravan service point.

Charges guide: Per adult Dkr. 46 - 50; child 23 - 25; electricity 15 - 20.

Reservations: Contact site. Address: Odensevej 102, Odense S. Tel: 66.11.47.02. FAX: 65.91.73.43.

2200 Bøjden Strandcamping, nr Faaborg (Fyn)

Well equipped family site with beach, in the beautiful 'Garden of Denmark'.

Bøjden is located in one of the most beautiful corners of southwest Fyn (Funen in English) known as the 'Garden of Denmark'. Separated from the beach only by a hedge, many pitches have sea views as the site slopes gently down from the road. Arranged in rows on mainly level grassy terraces and divided into groups by hedges and some trees, the 270 pitches (180 for touring units) all have electricity (10A). Four special motorcaravan pitches also have water and waste points, and there is also a service point. The superb quality, centrally located sanitary building provides British style WCs, washbasins in cubicles, controllable showers with divider and seat (on payment), three family bathrooms, a baby room and excellent facilities for disabled people. Also in this building is a well appointed kitchen with hobs, oven and sinks, plus a laundry with washing machine and dryer. The older unit near reception provides more WCs, basins and showers, and a further kitchen. Cooking facilities and hot water are free, showers are extra. A swimming pool (13 x 9 m), and a paddling pool (8 x 5 m.) with a sun terrace, is open during suitable weather. Well equipped fenced toddlers playground, separate adventure playground, small aviary, games and TV rooms, solarium, fenced dog exercise area, bicycle and boat hire and a barbecue area. Restaurant and bar 100 m. Everyone will enjoy the beach (Blue Flag) for bathing, boating and water sports. The water is too shallow for shore fishing but boat trips can be arranged. Bøjden is a delightful site for an entire holiday, while remaining a very good centre for excursions.

How to find it: From Faaborg follow road 8 to Bøjden. Site on right 500 m. before ferry terminal (from Fynshav).

General Details: Open 1 April - 15 Sept. Shop. Takeaway. Swimming pool (15/5-25/8). Solarium. Children's adventure playgrounds. TV and games rooms. Bicycle and boat hire. Fishing. Riding. Minigolf. Golf 10 km. Kitchen. Laundry. Telephone. Tourist information. Chemical disposal. Motorcaravan service point. Cabins for rent.

Charges 1999: Per adult Dkr. 52; child (under 12); pitch (16/6-17/8 only) 25; electricity 20. Credit cards accepted.

Reservations: Recommended for high season - write for details. Address: Bøjden Landevej 12, 5600 Faaborg. Tel: 62.60.12.84. FAX: 62.60.12.94.

2205 Løgismosestrand Camping, Hårby (Fyn)

Countryside site with own beach and pool, surrounded by picturesque villages.

The owner of this site is the son of another Alan Rogers' site owner, and was the youngest campsite owner in Denmark when he purchased this site. Since that time he has refurbished the older sanitary unit, also built a new unit and, more recently, a new swimming pool (8 x 14 m) with a paddling pool (6 x 6 m), for which there will be small charge. The 200 pitches, some with a little shade, are arranged in rows and groups divided by hedges and small trees, 190 with electricity (10A). The sanitary units, kept very clean, have British style WCs, washbasins in cubicles, roomy showers (on payment), hairdressing and shaving areas, baby room, bathrooms for families and the disabled. The new unit also houses a very good laundry with sink, washing machine and dryer, plus an excellent fully fitted kitchen with stainless steel worktops, inset gas hobs, microwave and dishwashing sinks. Other on-site amenities include a large undercover games room, grassy playing field, adventure playground, minigolf, table tennis, bicycle and boat hire, pony riding. There is a large well stocked shop and a snack-bar (in season) with takeaway serving burgers, hot dogs, chicken, fish and chips at reasonable prices.

How to find it: Southeast of Hårby via Sarup and Nellemose to Løgismose Skov. Site is well signed. Lanes are narrow, large outfits should take care.

General Details: Open 27 March - 18 Sept. Shop. Snackbar/takeaway. Kitchen. Laundry. Swimming pool. Beach. Minigolf. Table tennis. Bicycle and boat hire. Pony riding. Children's playground. Telephone. Tourist information. Chemical disposal. Motorcaravan service point. Cabins for rent.

Charges guide: Per adult Dkr. 44; child 22; pitch 20 (23/6-10/8 only); electricity 18.

Reservations: Essential for high season - write for details. Address: Løgismoseskov 7, 5683 Hårby. Tel: 64.77.12.50. FAX: 64.77.12.51.

2220 Billevænge Camping, Spodsbjerg, nr Rudkøbing (Langeland)

Quiet, family run site in a woodland near beach on island of Langeland.

Billevænge is a family owned and managed site - not pretentious, but comfortable, attractive, sheltered, and very acceptable for a quiet relaxing holiday in lovely surroundings. The central point of the site is the duck pond, animal enclosure and children's play area. The 142 pitches are on sloping grass separated into groups by mature hedges and trees, with some pitches flatter than others. Most have electrical connections. A more open area, furthest from reception and the toilet facilities, is mainly reserved for tents. Site facilities are grouped together at the entrance. The original block, which has been refurbished, is kept clean and provides roomy showers (on payment), washbasins, some with partitions and curtain, a baby room, British style WCs, and power points. Family shower rooms include one large and one small toilet. Dishwashing facilities (metered hot water) are provided in the campers' kitchen (gas rings) and there is a laundry. Lovely walks may be had through the surrounding woods and the beach (shallow water, safe for children) is reached by path direct from the site (600 m). Boats can be hired for fishing and the site is proud of its record for really big catches. An excellent example of the Danes' outstanding expertise in bridge building can be seen here when one drives past Svendborg on Funen, across the bridge to Tasinge and then the longer, handsome structure to Langeland - the 'long island'. The island also has many old windmills and castles to visit.

How to find it: From Svendborg, cross bridges to Langeland and Rudkøbing on road 9. Cross island to Spodsbjerg and ferry terminal (bridge planned, but with toll). Turn right in town following signs 1.8 km. south to site.

General Details: Open 1 April - 31 Oct. Shop. Club room. TV room. Barbecue. Minigolf. Bicycle hire. Tourist information. Telephone. Post box. Children's playground and pets corner. Beach and watersports. Fishing 2 km. Laundry and cooking facilities. Chemical disposal. Motorcaravan service point. Cabins and caravans for rent.

Charges guide: Per person Dkr. 47; child (0-11 yrs) 25; pitch fee (21/6-3/8 only, not tents) 15; electricity 18.

Reservations: Recommended for high season. Write for details. Address: Spodsbjergvej 182, 5900 Rudkøbing. Tel: 62.50.10.06. FAX: 62.50.10.46. E-mail: billevng@post5.tele.dk.

2240 Lysabildskov Camping and Feriecenter, Lysabildskov, Sydals (Als)

Small, neat, attractive coastal site on island of Als, with excellent facilities and a warm welcome.

Located in the heart of the countryside, 600 m. from a small rocky beach, this well laid out, attractive site provides all the comforts one could need for a relaxed holiday or shorter stay. The site has 192 large grassy pitches all with electricity (10A) separated into small secluded areas by mature rose and flowering shrub hedges. The centrally located sanitary block is in the older style, but has been totally refurbished providing roomy showers, basins with dividers/curtains and British style WCs, plus family bathrooms, facilities for disabled people and a baby room with bath. Hot water is free. In addition there is a laundry and a campers' kitchen with dishwashing sinks and cooking hobs. These are supplemented by further facilities serving the swimming pool, apartments and reception complex and house further WCs and washbasins. Outdoor heated pool and children's pool (Dkr.6 per day), sauna, solarium, jacuzzi and a huge billiard room/TV lounge, tennis, ball games area, children's playground and playhouse. Fishing and windsurfing are possible from the beach. Well stocked shop with fast food service. The island of Als is connected to mainland Jutland by an excellent toll-free bridge.

How to find it: From Sønderborg drive towards Kegnæs on road no. 427, then towards Vibøge-Lysabild then follow the camp signs to Lysabildskov.

General Details: Open 1 April - 1 Oct. Shop. Takeaway (1/5-1/9). Swimming pool and children's pool (1/5-1/9). Sauna, solarium. and jacuzzi. Table tennis. Trampoline. Billiards. Boules. TV lounge. Barbecue area. Tennis. Ball games field. Children's playground. Fishing 600 m. Windsurfing. Telephones. Tourist information. Laundry. Cooking facilities. Chemical disposal. Motorcaravan service point. Apartments (11) and cabins (5) for rent.

Charges guide: Per person Dkr. 44 - 51; child 24 - 27; dog 5; electricity 17.

Reservations: Essential for high season (late June-mid Aug). Write to site. Address: Skovforten 4, Lysabildskov, 6470 Sydals. Tel: 74.40.43.98. FAX: 74.40.43.86.

2250 Hillerød Camping, Hillerød (Sjælland)

Neat, well run site well placed for touring Sjælland, Copenhagen and ferry to Sweden.

The northern-most corner of Sjælland is packed with interest, based not only on fascinating parts of Denmark's history but also its attractive scenery. Centrally situated, Hillerød is a hub of main roads, with this neat site clearly signed from the town. It has a park-like setting in a residential area with 5 acres of well kept grass divided up by attractive trees. There are 92 pitches of which 50 have electricity (10A). Amenities are centrally located in modern, well maintained buildings. The bright and airy toilet block is slightly older in style but provides very good facilities including curtained, free hot showers, washbasins with partitions and curtain and a laundry room. Facilities for babies and disabled people. Basic supplies are kept with reception, adjacent to a splendid, large, comfortable club room with sofas, tables and chairs, children's corner with video and books. A campers' kitchen adjoins the facilities for dishwashing (free hot water). Tennis, golf and an indoor pool are within 1 km. *continued overleaf*

DENMARK

2250 Hillerød Camping (continued)

Visit Frederiksborg Slot, a fine Renaissance Castle and home of the Museum of Danish national history. Excellent electric train service every 10 minutes (20 mins. walk) for visiting Copenhagen.

How to find it: Follow road no. 6 bypassing town to south until sign at junction (signed to Frederiksborg Slot). Turn towards town and site is signed to the right.

General Details: Open 10 April - 12 Sept. Small shop. Good club room with TV. Children's playground. Bicycle hire. Tennis and indoor pool near. Riding 2 km. Golf 3 km. Tourist information. Telephone. Laundry and cooking facilities. Motorcaravan service point. Chemical disposal. Cabins and tents to rent.

Charges 1999: Per person Dkr. 56; child (0-11 yrs) 28; electricity 20. Credit cards accepted.

Reservations: Recommended for high season - write for details. Address: Blytækkervej, 3400 Hillerød. Tel: 48.26.48.54. FAX: as phone. Internet: www.publicamp.dk/hilleroed.

2260 DCU - Camping, Nærum, nr Copenhagen (Sjælland)

Sheltered, friendly site with new enthusiastic management, well situated for visiting Copenhagen.

Obviously everyone arriving in Sjælland will want to visit "wonderful, wonderful Copenhagen", but like all capital cities, it draws crowds during the holiday season and traffic to match. The site is near enough to be convenient but distant enough to afford peace and quiet (apart from the noise of nearby traffic) and a chance of relaxing after sightseeing. Nærum, one of the Danish Camping Union sites, is only 15 km. and very near a suburban railway (400 m. on foot) that takes you to the city centre. The long narrow site covers a large area alongside the ancient royal hunting forests, adjacent to the small railway line and the main road. Power lines cross the site under which camping is not allowed so there is lots of grassy open space. The 275 touring pitches are in two areas - in wooded glades taking about 6 units each (mostly used by tents) or on more open meadows where electrical connections are available. There are two modern toilet blocks. The one in the meadow area has been refurbished and has free, controllable hot showers, partitioned washbasins with hot water and WCs. A new, very good block at reception can be heated and also provides a laundry, dishwashing and a campers' kitchen. Good facilities are provided for babies and the disabled, and four family bathrooms (free). General amenities include a shop, club room, TV, barbecue, playing field and playground. A full range of sporting facilities is within easy reach of the site and a café/restaurant within a few hundred metres. Nærum is useful for Copenhagen, but is also very near to the interesting friendly shopping complex of Rødøvre and the amusement park at Bakken.

How to find it: On E55/E47, take Nærum exit 15 km. north of Copenhagen. Turn away from village and, within a few hundred metres, turn left after bridge, where site is signed. Site is 1 km. (by road) from the station, signed.

General Details: Open early April - mid Sept. Shop. Café/restaurant near. Club room and TV. Laundry and cooking facilities. Barbecue. Minigolf. Children's play field and adventure playground. Bicycle hire. Tourist information. Telephone. Motorcaravan service point and car wash. Train service to Copenhagen.

Charges guide: Per adult high season Dkr. 47.50; child (0-12 yrs) 24; electricity 15; environmental charge 5; cabin 200. Copenhagen Card: 24 hrs 140 adult/70 child, 48 hrs 230 adult/115 child.

Reservations: Write to site for details. Address: Ravnebakken, 2850 Nærum. Tel: 42.80.19.57. FAX: 42.80.11.78.

FINLAND

Finland covers an area of 338,000 sq. km. (13,500 sq. miles) and consists of 10% water (forming 187,888 lakes), 69% forest and only 8% cultivated land. The maximum length is 1,160 km (721 miles), the maximum width is 540 km (336 miles). Being such a long country, there is a considerable difference in the type of landscape between north and south, with the gently rolling, rural landscape of the south giving way to the hills and vast forests of the north and treeless fells and peat-lands of Lapland. Forests of spruce, pine and birch are inhabited by hares, elks and occasional wolves and bears. It is well worth noting that, every few kilometres, signs depicting an elk warn motorists of the danger of these beasts dashing onto the road, with an average of 40 motorists per day being involved in accidents with this animal. If you are unfortunate enough to hit one, it must be reported to the police. International Camping Carnet or Finnish Camping Card required at many sites. We have deliberately chosen the beautiful Saimaa Lake District in the southeast of the country as an introduction, due to its popularity and easy access by excellent roads. Further information can be obtained from:

The Finnish Tourist Board, 30/35 Pall Mall, London SW1Y 5LP. Tel: 0171 839 4048. Fax: 0171 321 0696

Population
5,054,982 (1993); density 15 per sq. km.

Capital
Helsinki.

Climate
Summer is warm and bright due to the close proximity to the Gulf Stream, with average temperatures in Helsinki ranging from 13.7°C in May to 20.5°C in July; winter months -0.4°C in Dec (31°F) to 6.4°C (44°F) in April.

Language
Finnish - but most young people speak English.

Currency
The Markka or Finnmark, abbreviated to FIM, and divided into 100 pennies (p). Coins are 10p, 50p, 1, 5 and 10 FIM with notes of 20, 50, 100, 500 and 1,000 FIM.

Banks
Open 09.15 - 16.15 hrs Mon - Fri. Outside normal banking hours currency can be exchanged in most hotels or large department stores, or at harbours and railway stations.

Credit cards: are widely accepted in stores, petrol stations and on some campsites.

Post Offices
Open 09.00 - 17.00 hrs, Mon - Fri.

Time
GMT plus 2 hours.

Public Holidays
New Year; Epiphany; Good Fri; Easter Mon; May Day; 1st Sat after Ascension; Whit Sat; All Saints, 1st Sat in Nov; Independence Day, 6 Dec; Christmas, 25, 26 Dec. Other holidays are Vappu Night, 30 Apr, a spring festival and 'Midsummer', nearest Sat to 24 June.

Telephone
The dialling code for Finland is 00358. When calling the UK dial 99044 before the trunk number. Local calls can be made from telephone booths using 1, 5 or 10 FIM coins. Phone-card phones operate on cards purchased in advance (from Teleshops or some post offices).

Shops
Open 09.00 - 17.00 or 18.00 hrs on Mon - Fri and on Sat 09.00 - 14.00 or 15.00 hrs, although supermarkets are usually open to 20.00 hrs during the week. Department stores and shopping malls usually remain open to 18.00 hrs on Sat. The underground shopping arcade adjacent to the main railway station in Helsinki is open until 20.00 hrs every day. Butane is not available.

Motoring
Main roads in Finland are excellent and relatively uncrowded outside city limits; you can virtually have miles of dual-carriageway or motorway standard roads to yourself. The Finns are tolerant and cautious drivers and appear to adhere strictly to speed limits. You may encounter a few unsurfaced minor roads off the beaten track but these are usually quite safe for towing, providing you keep your speed down to about 30 mph. Do not drink and drive - penalties are severe (even jail sentences) if any alcohol is detected.

Speed limits: Caravans and motorhomes (3.5 tons) 31 mph (50 kph) in built up areas, caravans 50 mph (80 kph) all other roads, motorhomes 50 - 63 mph (80 - 100 kph) on other roads and 50 - 75 mph (80 - 120 kph) on motorways. Note: there are no emergency phones on the motorway network.

Tolls: There are no toll charges on motorways.

Overnighting
Not allowed outside campsites.

2900 Camping Kokonniemi, Porvoo

Delightful small campsite 50 km. east of Helsinki.

Convenient for the ferry if travelling along the southeast coast, the old town of Porvoo with its waterfront and old wooden houses warrants a stop. This site is 2 km. west of the town and has a garden-like appearance and a white timber reception area with hanging flower baskets. This building, the service buildings and cottages for hire are in an elevated position and backed by tall pines. At a lower level are 36 unmarked caravan pitches (32 with electricity) placed around the perimeter. These pitches are spacious and separated by a variety of shrubs and fruit bushes. Tents are pitched in the more open centre area. Sanitary facilities are kept very clean and include British style WCs, hot showers (free) with seat, hooks and mat, washbasins with soap, towels, mirror and shaving points. There is a laundry area and a campers' kitchen which doubles for dishwashing. *continued overleaf*

FINLAND

2900 Camping Kokonniemi (continued)

To the side of this building is the barbecue house with bench seating. Although beside the Kokonniemi sports centre and lake, on site there is a sauna, volleyball, badminton, bike hire and two children's play areas. Snacks and light meals are available at the café area adjoining reception and a small shop provides milk, bread, ice cream and confectionery.

How to find It: Leave road 7/E3 Helsinki - Porvoo at end of motorway and join road 55 for 4 km. Site ssigned.

General Details: Open 4 June - 22 August (limited services from 15 Aug). Small shop. Café. Sauna. Bicycle hire. Badminton. Volleyball. Sports centre and lake adjacent. Barbecue house. Chemical disposal. Cottages for hire.

Charges 1999: Per unit FIM 80 with Finnish camping card (90 without); every 3rd night 50% off; electricity 19. Some credit cards accepted, no Eurocheques.

Reservations: May be necessary for mid-summer/July: Address: 06100 Porvoo. Tel: (0)19 581 967 or (0)9 6138 3210. FAX: (0)9 713 713.

2903 Camping Kayralampi, Kouvola

Busy southern lakeside site 5 km. from Kouvola In the Province of Kymi.

This campsite appeals to families as it is located near an amusement park which, like the campsite, is run by the Children's Day Foundation. A footbridge leads from the site to the park which is across the road and well away from the site so that no noise carries. The site itself, which is under the control of a manager, is approached by way of a short country roadway leading to reception. Centrally positioned are the timbered service buildings and café. The adequate sanitary blocks with lemon, grey and white decor were very clean when we visited and include British style WCs, facilities for the disabled, washbasins, towels, spacious showers (free) and clothes lockers. There is also a laundry and drying room and a campers' kitchen and dishwashing area. There are 160 unmarked pitches, including the tent area, and 100 have electrical connections (16A). Many pitches are placed between trees and shrubs on level but rough ground, some are in a more open area towards the lake with tents alongside. There are also 35 wooden cottages for hire. Other on site facilities include a double tennis court, minigolf, boats for hire, children's play area, two barbecue houses, 1 smoke and 4 electric saunas. Entrance to the amusement park is free for campers (a pass is given), but amusement rides are charged. Basic food such as bread and milk is sold on site with a supermarket complex within 4 km.

How to find It: Site is at junction of roads 6 and 15, 5 km. east of Kouvola and is clearly signed.

General Details: Open all year. Basic food supplies available. Tennis. Minigolf. Boat hire. Children's play area. Saunas. Barbecue huts. Amusement park. Chemical disposal. Motorcaravan service point.

Charges guide: Per caravan or tent incl. 1 person FIM 45, 2-5 persons 70 (without Finnish camping card); with camping card 40 or 65; electricity 16.

Reservations: May be necessary for mid-summer/July: Address: Kanuunakuja 1, 45200 Kouvola. Tel: (0)5 321 1226. FAX: (0)5 321 1203.

2906 Taavetin Lomakeskus Ja Camping, Taavetti

Peaceful campsite on the shores of Lake Kivijärvi.

This campsite is situated in the commune of Luumäki, an area of natural beauty, Kivijärvi being the largest of 50 lakes. At the entrance to the site, just off road no. 6, stand red timbered buildings which house reception, shop, café and restaurant. Beyond this area a road follows the lake to the pitches, sanitary buildings and cottages for hire. There are 28 unmarked caravan pitches all with electrical connections (16A), some amongst the clearing in the trees, others nearer the lakeside. There are also 170 places for tents and 30 cottages for hire. The two sanitary blocks, one of an older design, were clean when we visited and have red decor with pine ceilings. Facilities include hot showers (free), washbasins, soap dispensers, towels, mirrors, electric points, single WCs, plus some in cabins with washbasins. Other facilities include a campers' kitchen and dishwashing area, washing machine and drying cabinet, chemical disposal and waste water point. The pleasant open style barbecue house, part of the kitchen area, has wooden bench seating. A second is at the beach. There is lake swimming, tennis court, volleyball, crazy golf, TV room, children's play area and 3 saunas. A small shop sells basic groceries such as bread and milk and soft drinks, coffee, snacks, breakfast or dinner can be ordered from the cafe/restaurant. The town of Taavetti is within 4 km, is historically interesting and has an assortment of shops, banks etc.

How to find It: Site is clearly signed, 500 m. from road no. 6 (towards Lappeenranta).

General Details: Open 4 June - 22 August. Small shop. Café (all season). Restaurant (1/6-14/8). Sports facilities as above. Fishing. Bicycle hire. Laundry facilities. Chemical disposal.

Charges 1999: Per unit FIM 60 with Finnish camping card (70 without); 1 person tent 35; electricity 16. Some credit cards accepted, no Eurocheques.

Reservations: are advisable for mid-summer/July. Address: 54510 Uro, Taavetti. Tel: (0)5 425 510 or (0)9 6138 3210. FAX: (0)9 713 713.

2909 Camping Ukonniemi, Imatra

Secluded site in South Karelia near one of the highest waterfalls in Finland.

This site offers a tranquil location within the Imatra Leisure Centre, 3 km. from the town centre where the incredible Imatra Falls can be seen during the summer season. The Leisure Centre covers an area of 600 hectares on the Salpausselka ridge and has a changing terrain to suit many activities. The site is under the control of a manager and is truly 'camping in the trees' with 37 unmarked level pitches, all with electricity (10A), many with water points, plus 84 tent places and 35 cottages. The reception and café are at the entrance with the sanitary block on the main avenue to the left. Kept clean and well maintained, this timber building includes free hot showers, washbasins and WCs. Facilities for disabled people, dishwashing in a campers' kitchen, and a laundry room. There is lake swimming, sauna, fishing, lake cruising, running tracks, a lakeside restaurant within the complex. Bread and milk sold at reception with shopping, banks, etc. in Imatra. Parts of this town are on the border zone with Russia.

How to find it: From Lappeenranta on road no. 6, site is clearly signed 1 km. after Imatra area sign.

General Details: Open 4 June - 15 August. Cafe. Lakeside restaurant. Bread and milk sold. Children's play areas. Lake swimming. Fishing, bicycle hire 1 km. Sauna. Chemical disposal.

Charges 1999: Per unit FIM 70 with Finnish Camping card (80 without); tent incl. 1 person 40; electricity 16. Some credit cards accepted, no Eurocheques.

Reservations: May be advisable for mid-summer/July. Address: Leiritie, 55420 Imatra. Tel: (0)5 472 4055 or (0)9 6138 3210. FAX: (0)9 713 713.

2912 Kultakivi Holiday Village, Punkaharju

Holiday village in forested countryside amid lakes and clearings.

This sprawling, 23 hectare holiday village offers a camping holiday to suit individual needs. You can get away from it all on a quiet secluded lakeside pitch, or participate in the many activities which suit all age groups. At the entrance and parking area stands a large elaborate building housing reception, restaurant and shop. Around this area is the tennis, minigolf, basketball and play area with water slide. The roadways lead into what is best described as a forest park environment with 135 cottages and cabins discreetly around the perimeter, mostly at the lakeside. There are 145 pitches with electricity (16A) in dry wooded or grassy terrain, with 500 tent places. The main sanitary block, which is well maintained, is towards the top of the site beside the TV room, with other WC and shower units at various points. Facilities include British style WCs, washbasins and free hot showers. There is a campers' kitchen and a dishwashing and laundry area (incl. in price). Amenities include a barbecue area, family saunas, several beaches and a naturist beach. For the more active there are jogging tracks and nature trails, fishing, boat and cycle hire. Evening entertainment can include wining, dining or dancing the night away. Although a more lively site, being placed well away from the pitches, the entertainment should not disturb campers.

How to find it: Site is clearly signed off road no. 14, approx. 9 km. south of Punkaharju.

General Details: Open 30 April - 31 Aug. Barbecue area. Jogging and nature trails. Fishing. Boat and bicycle hire. Entertainment. Chemical disposal.

Charges guide: Per unit FIM 70 without camping card, 60 with; electricity 20.

Reservations: Advised for mid-summer/July. Address: 58550 Putikko, Punkaharju. Tel: (0)15 645 151. FAX: (0)15 645 110.

AR Discount
Less 10%
on pitch fee

2915 Punkaharjun Lomakeskus Ja Camping, Punkaharju

Popular campsite in an area of outstanding beauty.

This site is part of a holiday centre located near the magnificent Punkaharju ridge. It stands next to the Kesamaa amusement park in a lakeside environment, making it one of the country's most popular sites. Past the entrance, which is marked by flags, is the reception area and to the right the fun park. There are 500 pitches including tent places, 130 with electricity, also many chalets and holiday homes for hire. Some pitches are placed back from the lake, and these are in avenues and separated by shrubs and hedges. Others are by the lakeside and unmarked. The main sanitary block is towards the lake and a smaller one sits further back. Modern, clean facilities include WCs, washbasins, spacious showers (free), and wash cubicles with WCs. Incorporated in the main building are campers' kitchens, dishwashing sinks and a laundry area. There is also a restaurant and shop with basic groceries, ice cream, etc. The fun park belongs to the campsite but a separate entrance fee is payable. Other on site facilities are netball, tennis, minigolf, lakeside beach, boats and bicycles for hire, barbecue area and 2 saunas. Local attractions are the Lusto Forest Museum, Retretti Art Centre and the oldest tourist hotel in Finland.

How to find it: Turn off at 'K' sign, 25 km. after Savonlinna on road no. 14 and site is 300 m.

General Details: Camping: 27 May - 26 August; fun park and other accommodation open all year. Restaurant. Small shop. Tennis. Netball. Minigolf. Boat and bicycle hire. Fishing. Riding 5 km. Golf 15 km. Fun park adjacent. Motorcaravan service point. Chemical disposal.

Charges 1999: Per unit FIM 80 - 85; tent for 1 person 40; electricity 19. Credit cards accepted.

Reservations: Advised mid-summer/July. Address: 58450 Punkaharju 2. Tel: (0)15 739 611. FAX: (0)15 441 784.

FINLAND

2918 Camping Vuohimaki, Savonlinna

Well managed site close to East Finland's most popular resort.

The resort of Savonlinna is built on a chain of islands and is unquestionably the jewel in East Finland's crown. This campsite, on the shores of Lake Pihlajavesi, is only minutes away from the town centre. Although lacking a landscaped appearance it is distinguished by a tall, elegant wooden building, dated late 1800s, which stands to the right of the security barrier and houses reception, restaurant, shop and offices. The camping area is approached by a one way system and there are 100 unmarked pitches for caravans, all with electrical hook-ups, space for 150 tents and 12 cottages for hire. The ground is part sloped, part terraced and the pitches rough but level. This is a more open site than usual, with most of the shade and trees around the perimeter, lakeside and tent area. The two modern sanitary blocks are kept spotlessly clean with grey and white decor and shiny chrome fittings. Facilities include WCs with paper, washbasins, soap and towels, free hot showers and facilities for disabled people. There is a campers' kitchen, dishwashing, barbecue and laundry area with washing machine, clothes line and free hot air dryer. Leisure amenities include volleyball, badminton, minigolf, watersports, boats and bicycle hire and two saunas. For children there are swings and slides. The restaurant serves pizzas, hamburgers, salads, etc. and the shop sells light groceries and confectionery.

How to find It: Site is signed off road no. 14, 3 km. west of Savonlinna.

General Details: Open 28 May - 29 August. Restaurant. Small shop. Volleyball. Badminton. Watersports. Boat and bicycle hire. Fishing. Children's play area. Saunas. Riding 200 m. Chemical disposal.

Charges 1999: Per unit FIM 80 with camping card (90 without); 1 person tent 45: electricity 19. Some credit cards accepted, no Eurocheques.

Reservations: Advisable for mid-summer/July. Address: 57600 Savonlinna. Tel: (0)15 537 353 or (0)9 6138 3210. FAX: (0)9 713 713.

2922 Camping Talpale, Varkaus

Well laid out family run site alongside a lake in North Savo.

The town of Varkaus, known for its paper industry, is surrounded by water and this campsite is located 3 km. from its centre in peaceful surroundings by the water's edge. Its well kept, orderly appearance gives it instant appeal. The reception and cafe area stand to the left at the entrance and to the right are avenues of individual hardstanding pitches separated by trees and shrubs. There is a total of 90 pitches, some grass and 52 with electrical hook-ups, a large tent area and 16 cottages to hire, placed away from the camping pitches. The grey wooden sanitary block is tastefully decorated with pine interior and grey and white units, all kept very clean. Facilities include hot showers (free) with curtains and clothes lockers, WCs with paper, washbasins, long bench mirror and shower for disabled people, etc. There is also a dishwashing area, laundry with drying cabinet, clothes lines, an excellent chemical disposal unit and campers kitchen. Snacks, soft drinks and beer are sold at the cafe, plus basic foodstuffs and souvenirs. On site is a barbecue house, sauna, lake swimming, beach ball, boat hire, bicycle hire, badminton. For children, wooden toys, slides, etc. are to the fore in a garden like space. To the rear of the site a gate leads to a parkland area and a bridge over the old canal, part of the Canal Museum in Varkaus.

How to find It: Site is signed from road no. 5 onto road no. 23, approx. 3 km. from Varkaus at Canal swing bridge.

General Details: Open 25 May - 31 August. Cafe. Sauna. Lake swimming. Boat and bicycle hire. Children's play area. Chemical disposal.

Charges guide: Per unit with camping card FIM 69 (without 86); family tent with card 76 (86); 1 person tent 45.

Reservations: Advised for mid-summer/July. Address: Leiritie, 78250 Varkaus. Tel: (0)17 552 6644. FAX: (0)17 552 6644.

2925 Camping Rauhalahtl, Kuoplo

Large site on the banks of Lake Kallavesl in North Savo.

This site comes highly recommended, with a reputation for being one of the country's finest campsites. It is consistently busy, which creates a constant buzz of activity. Tubs of coloured flowers garland the forecourt and when campers arrive the flag of their country is hoisted, a welcoming touch and a colourful display when all the nations visit. Reception, which offers a 24 hour service, stands close to the entrance and from here the site is laid out in neat avenues with tarmac roads. Pitches are clearly marked and all have hardstanding. The site is level and landscaped, the exception rather than the norm in Finland. This is a more open site than usual, but it still has adequate trees and shrubs with grass areas for awnings separating each of the 237 pitches which include special ones for larger motorcaravans, all with electrical hook-ups. There are also 300 places for tents and 90 cottages for hire. The two timber sanitary blocks were very clean with stainless steel washbasins, WCs, free hot showers and facilities for the disabled with a shower, WC, and washbasin. Baby room, large campers' kitchen and dishwashing, laundry service with free use of drying cabinet *continued overleaf*

2925 Camping Rauhalahti (continued)

'Ecopoints' for rubbish disposal. The restaurant offers a choice of menu serving Finnish lunch or snacks, pizzas, etc. and a mini-shop sells basic foodstuffs. This site forms part of the 80 hectare Rauhalahti recreational area and offers a beach and water sports, with equipment for hire and 3 saunas (2 electric and 1 smoke). For children there is a play room, puppet theatre, also a TV, swimming pool, tennis courts and much more. It is said Kuopio has three focal points, the Puijo Tower, Kuopio market and its harbour on the shores of the lake, all worth a visit.

How to find it: Site is clearly signed on road no. 5, 7 km. south of Kuopio.

General Details: Open 24 May - 31 Aug. Restaurant (all season). Mini-shop (11/6-14/8). Swimming pool (all season). Fishing. Bicycle hire. Riding. Golf 2 km. Leisure activities detailed above. Chemical disposal.

Charges 1999: Per unit FIM 95; family tent 85; electricity 20. Credit cards accepted.

Reservations: Advisable for mid-summer/July. Address: Kiviniementie, 70700 Kuopio. Tel: (0)17 361 2244. FAX: (0)17 262 4004. E-mail: rauhalahti.camping@kuopio.fi.

AR Discount
Every 5th night free

2928 Camping Visulahti, Mikkeli

Excellent campsite and holiday centre within 4 hours drive of Helsinki.

Mikkeli is capital of the Lake District, sitting at the cross-roads of a network of lakes and the labyrinth of Saimaa islands, with more than 3,000 km. of boating routes in its region. On the shores of a Saimaa lake stands this well equipped campsite which appeals to families and varying age groups. The staff are friendly, helpful and dressed in distinctive yellow T-shirts making them easily identified throughout the complex which comprises 30 hectares of landscaped park-land. From reception, immediately beside the security barrier, tarmac roadways lead past the 'Dinosauria' and water slides to the right and caravan pitches and tent places to the left. Alongside the camping area stand the restaurant, canteen, coffee pot, shop, vintage car exhibition and wax museum (the only one in Finland we are told). Beyond here the fun park continues with a motor-park and 'mini Finland'. Fitting into the layout are cottages and bungalows for hire. There are around 400 pitches for caravans and tents, 200 with electrical hook-ups (16A), unmarked and laid out in avenues. Although it is an open site, shrubs and flower beds divide it into bays in places. Sanitary facilities are housed in two blocks, one facing the caravan pitches and the other by the lakeside. They are kept very clean. There are adequate numbers of WCs, hot showers (free), washbasins and facilities for the disabled. There is also a campers' kitchen, dishwashing and laundry. Barbecue house, sauna and lake swimming. Despite the activity on site the noise level is low, with only slight road traffic during the night. Mikkeli market is worth a visit and a shopping complex with a choice of supermarkets is only minutes away.

How to find it: Site is clearly signed off road no. 5, 5 km. north of Mikkeli.

General Details: Open 18 May - 30 August (Dinosauria, etc. 18 May - 18 August). Fun park with many activities. Restaurant. Barbecue. Sauna. Lake swimming. Chemical disposal. Motorcaravan service point.

Charges guide: Per unit FIM 70 without camping card, 60 with card; 1 person tent 35; electricity 17 - 25.

Reservations: Advisable for mid-summer/July. Address: 50180 Mikkeli. Tel: (0)15 18 281. FAX: (0)15 176 209.

2930 Camping Koskenniemi, Hartola

Friendly, family run site in attractive riverside setting.

In the Eastern Hame region, 3 km. from the town of Hartola, this campsite is easily reached from Helsinki within a 2½ hour drive. It is in a delightful, quiet situation tucked in off the road and screened by trees, with a river winding its way through the 5.5 hectare site. Reception is incorporated into the attractive building which is the family home, guest house and restaurant. From here the road follows the river past 150 unmarked pitches for caravans and tents, 80 with electrical hook-ups (16A), sited mostly to the left with 10 wooden chalets spread along the river bank. The terrain is grassy, flat and open with trees interspersed and a pond towards the rear, giving it a garden-like appearance. The excellent sanitary block, adjacent to reception, is clean with modern units. A white wooden building, facilities include British style WCs, washbasins, free hot showers, and good facilities for the disabled with WC, shower and bench. There is a campers' kitchen, dishwashing sinks, laundry area with machines and free drying room. River fishing is available with a licence, and there are boats to hire, minigolf, sauna and conference room, and 2 barbecues, (one outside, one gas under cover). For children there is a play room, a small pool table, TV, books, toys and an outdoor playhouse with sand pit. The restaurant offers a varied menu. Bread and milk can be ordered from reception.

How to find it: Site is clearly signed on left off road no. 59, 3 km. south of Hartola.

General Details: Open all year. Restaurant. River fishing. Boats hire. Bicycle hire. Minigolf. Sauna. Barbecues. Play room. Golf 3 km. Chemical disposal. Motorcaravan service point. Rooms and cottagesto let.

Charges 1999: Per unit FIM 75 with camping card; 1 person tent 40; electricity 15. Credit cards accepted.

Reservations: May be necessary for mid-summer/July. Address: 19600 Hartola. Tel: (0)3 716 1135. FAX: (0)3 716 1086. E-mail: email@koskenniemi.com.

FINLAND

2932 Camping Sysmä, Sysmä

Family run site with lots of atmosphere, scenically situated on shores of Lake Päijänne.

This site is set on Finland's second largest lake, referred to as 'the pearl of the Finnish lakes' and 'the lake you can drink'. Here the air is pure with miles of countryside all around. Camping Sysmä, within walking distance of the village, has instant appeal. The reception and café area, with flower baskets and a smell of fresh coffee, stands by the entrance. The owner is friendly and smiling and the busy staff were getting the site fully operational for the season when we visited, the week after opening. There are 100 pitches for tents and 38 for caravans with electrical hook-ups (10A), plus 12 bungalows to hire. Pitches are placed amid many varieties of trees and by the water's edge, giving an overall attractive appearance. Although the various buildings of wooden construction that house all the sanitary and other site facilities look their age, even on the dilapidated side, everything inside was neat, tidy and clean. The facilities in the toilet area include British style WCs, washbasins with soap dispensers and towels, hair dryers, free hot showers with mats and bench seating. Plans are in hand to replace the buildings. There is a campers' kitchen, dishwashing sinks and laundry area. For leisure there is a TV room with comfortable chairs and log fire, table tennis, children's swimming pool and play area, water sports and boats and canoes for hire. Snacks are served at the café and there is a shop and garage at the gate, although all necessary shops, banks, etc. are to be found in Sysmä.

How to find it: Site is clearly signed 600 m. from the village of Sysmä on road no. 314.

General Details: Open 1 June - 31 Aug. Café. Shop at gate. TV room. Table tennis. Children's pool. Play area. Watersports. Boat hire. Chemical disposal. Motorcaravan service point.

Charges guide: Per unit FIM 70 (with camping card 60); electricity 15.

Reservations: May be necessary for mid-summer/July. Address: Huitilantie 3, 19700 Sysmä. Tel: (0)3/7171386 or (0)4/00809133. FAX: as phone. E-mail: anne.kurvinen@sci.fi.

The French sites featured in this guide are only a selection of those in our Good Camps Guide - FRANCE

FRANCE

France has such a variety of scenery from the mountain ranges of the Alps and the Pyrénées, the central massif, the river valleys of the Loire, Rhône and Dordogne, some 1,800 miles of coastline; and is so rich in history with its Gothic cathedrals of the north, the Romanesque churches of the centre and the west, the chateaux of the Loire, the prehistoric cave paintings of the Dordogne that it would take a life time to exhaust all the visit possibilities. Each area of the country looks different, feels different, has its own style of architecture and food, and often its own dialect giving a very strong sense of regional identity. Administratively, France is divided into Régions, which are then subdivided into Départements (95 in total) with an official number which forms the 'root' of the post code. The French Départements are roughly the equivalent of English counties (see page 138 for map). For further information contact:

The French Government Tourist Office (FGTO), 178 Piccadilly, London W1V 0AL

Tel: 0891 244123 (premium rate). Fax: 0171 493 6594

Population
57,800,000 (94), density 106 per sq.km.

Capital
Paris.

Climate
France has a temperate climate but it varies considerably, for example, Brittany has a climate similar to that of Devon and Cornwall, whilst the Mediterranean coast enjoys a subtropical climate.

Language
Obviously French is spoken throughout the country but there are many local dialects and variations so do not despair if you have greater problems understanding in some areas than in others. We notice an increase in the amount of English understood and spoken.

Currency
French currency is the Franc (subdivided into 100 centimes) in notes of Ffr. 500, 100, 50, and 20, and coins of Ffr. 10, 5, 2, 1 and 50c, 20c, 10c, 5c.

Banks
Open weekdays 09.00-1200 and 14.00-16.00. Some provincial banks are open Tues-Sat 09.00-12.00 and 14.00-16.00.

Credit Cards: Most major credit cards accepted in most outlets and for motorway tolls.

Post Offices
The French term for post office is either PTT or Bureau de Poste. They are generally open Mon-Fri 08.00-19.00 and Saturday 08.00-12.00 and can close for lunch 12.00-14.00. You can buy stamps with less queuing from Tabacs (tobacconists).

Time
GMT plus 1 (summer BST + 1) but there is a period of about three to four weeks in October when the times coincide.

Telephone
From the UK dial 00 33, followed by the 10 figure local number MINUS the initial "0" - in other words from the UK you will dial 0033 followed by the last NINE digits of the telephone number. To the UK from France dial 0044. Many public phone boxes now only take phone cards. (Telecarte) These can be purchased from post offices, tabacs, and some campsites.

Public Holidays
New Year; Easter Mon; Labour Day; VE Day, 8 May; Ascension; Whit Mon; Bastille Day, 14 July; Assumption, 15 Aug; All Saints, 1 Nov; Armistice Day, 11 Nov; Christmas, 25 Dec.

Shops
Often close on Mon, all or half day and for 2 hours daily for lunch. Food shops open on Sun morning.

Motoring
France has a comprehensive road system from motorways (Autoroutes), Routes Nationales (N roads), Routes Départmentales (D roads) down to purely local C class roads.

Tolls: Payable on the autoroute network which is extensive but expensive. Tolls are also payable on certain bridges such as the one from the Ile de Ré to the mainland and the Pont de St Nazaire.

Speed Restrictions: Built-up areas 31 mph (50 kph), on normal roads 56 mph (90 kph); on dual carriageways separated by a central reservation 69 mph (110 kph), on toll motorways 80 mph (130 kph). In wet weather, limits outside built-up areas are reduced to 50mph (80 kph), 62 mph (100 kph) and 69 mph (110 kph) on motorways. A minimum speed limit of 50 mph (80 kph) exists in the outside lane of motorways during daylight, on level ground and with good visibility.
These limits also apply to private cars towing a caravan, if the latter's weight does not exceed that of the car. Where it does by 30%, limit is 40 mph (65 kph) and if more than 30%, 28 mph (45 kph).

Fuel: Diesel sold at pumps marked 'gaz-oil'.

Parking: Usual restrictions as in UK. In Paris and larger cities, there is a Blue Zone where parking discs must be used, obtainable from police stations, tourist offices and some shops.

Overnighting
Allowed provided permission has been obtained, except near the water's edge or at a large seaside resort. Casual camping is prohibited in state forests, national parks in the Départmentes of the Landes and Gironde and also in the Camargue and also restricted in the south because of the danger of fire. However overnight stops on parking areas of a motorway are tolerated but not in a lay-by.

Useful Addresses
Automobile Club de France
FIA, 6-8 Place de la Concorde, 75008 Paris.
Tel: 01 43 12 43 12
Office hours Mon-Fri 0900-1800.
Automobile Club National
 (ACN), FIA & AIT, 5 ruee Auber, 75009 Paris.
Tel: 01 44 51 53 99.
Office hours Mon-Thu 0900-1800, Fri -1700

0200 Camping Caravaning du Vivier aux Carpes, Seraucourt-le-Grand

Small, quiet site, close to A26, two hours from Calais, ideal for overnight or longer stay.

This neat, purpose designed site is imaginatively set out taking full benefit of large ponds which are well stocked for fishing (Ffr. 35). There is also abundant wild life. The 60 well spaced pitches, all at least 100 sq.m. are on flat grass with dividing hedges. All have electricity (6A), some also with water points and there are special pitches for motorcaravans. The site has a comfortable feel, close to the village centre (with post office, doctor, chemist and small supermarket), but quiet. The spacious, clean sanitary block with British style WCs has separate, heated facilities for disabled visitors (also available to other campers in winter). Laundry facilities. Upstairs is a large TV/games room with table tennis and snooker. Small children's play area, bicycle hire and a petanque court. Riding 3 km, golf 11 km. The cathedral cities of St Quentin, Reims, Amiens and Laon are close, Disneyland is just over an hour, Compiegne and the WW1 battlefields are near and Paris easily reached by train. Day trips arranged to Paris (Ffr 160 p.p) or Disneyland with English speaking guide. The enthusiastic owners and the manager speak excellent English. No restaurant on site but good, reasonable hotels close. We were impressed by the ambience and recommend this site to those seeking tranquillity in an attractive setting. Gates close 10 pm, office open 10-11.30 am. and 5-7 pm. Motorcaravan services. Rallies welcome.

Directions: Leave A26 (Calais-Reims) at exit 11 and take D1 left towards Soissons. On entering Essigny-la-Grand (4 km.) turn sharp right on D72 signed Seraucourt-le-Grand (5 km). Site clearly signed (in centre of the village).

Charges 1999: Per unit incl. 2 persons and electricity Ffr. 90.00; extra person 15.00; child (under 10 yrs) 10.00; pet 5.00; use of motorcaravan service point 15.00. Discounts for students with tents. No credit cards.

Open: All year except Xmas - New Year.

Reservations: Recommended for peak season. Address: 10 Rue Charles Voyeux, 02790 Seraucourt-le-Grand. Tel: (0)3.23.60.50.10. FAX: (0)3.23.60.51.69.

0401 Hotel de Plein Air L'Hippocampe, Volonne, nr Sisteron

See colour advert between pages 96/97

Attractive, friendly site with good pool complex and sports opportunities.

Here is a site set in one of the most beautiful and unspoilt regions of France, the Haute-Provence. The air is clear and the smells of the thyme, lavender and other wild herbs have to be experienced to be believed. The site, started by Mme. Bravay and now in the hands of her sons, has a family feel to it. There are 447 pitches, 350 with 6A electricity, 334 with water also. Pitches are level, numbered and well marked by bushes, olive and cherry trees which not only make an attractive setting but also provide some welcome shade. The toilet blocks vary from quite old to very modern. All WCs are British style, hot water is free and washbasins are in cabins. Washing machines, chemical disposal and motorcaravan services. Reasonably priced bar, self service restaurant, takeaway and pizzeria (15/5-15/9). Small shop (July/Aug). The attractive pool complex (heated from 1/5) comprises a fairly deep swimming and diving pool, another large pool and a paddling pool for young children. Activities are organised in high season. Good sports facilities with some instruction include tennis (free outside 3/7-21/8), table tennis and archery. A disco is away from the pitches. Fishing on site, riding 600 m. The village is 600 m. The famous Gorge du Verdon is a sight not to miss and rafting and canoeing trips can be arranged. Many lesser known gorges wait to be explored and expeditions are organised. A very busy site, with lots going on for teenagers. Caravan storage. Mobile homes and bungalows to let.

Directions: Approaching from the north turn off N85 across river bridge to Volonne, then right to site. From the south right on D4 1 km. before Château Arnoux.

Charges 1998: Per unit with 2 persons Ffr. 58.00 - 117.00, with electricity 72.00 - 144.00, with water/drainage 100 sq.m. 72.00 - 155.00, 140 sq.m. 72.00 - 175.00; extra person (over 4 yrs) 15.00 - 25.00; extra car or m/cycle 10.00 - 12.00; dog free - 15.00; local tax 0.50 - 1.50. Special low season offers. Credit cards accepted.

Open: 27 March - 30 September.

AR Discount
Less 10%

Reservations: Made with deposit and fee (Ffr. 130). Address: Rte Napoléon, 04290 Volonne. Tel: (0)4.92.33.50.00. FAX: (0)4.92.33.50.49. Internet: www.l-hippocampe.com.

0301 Camping de la Filature, Ebreuil

Small peaceful riverside site with a difference.

Situated near the spa town of Vichy and bordering the Massif Central area, this site provides the opportunity to explore this lesser known and unspoilt area of France known as the Auvergne. Originally developed around a spinning mill (even today the hot water is provided by log burning - note the chimney), the site has an individuality not normally evident in French sites which is being perpetuated by its English owners with their artistic flair. Beside the River Sioule, there are 80 spacious, grassy pitches with some shade from mature fruit trees. All can be supplied with electricity (3 or 6A). The sanitary facilities, converted from original buildings, are all individual, opening into an alley with gaily painted arches. Well cleaned they provide free hot water, mostly British type toilets, showers and a bathroom, washcabins and hairdrying, plus chemical disposal. River bathing is said to be possible but it may be a little shallow at the height of the summer and there are fishing facilities on site. Bicycle hire - many tracks for mountain biking near. Riding, canoeing and tennis near. An area good for bird-watching and wild flowers (rare orchids). Washing machine and ironing facilities. Bread can be ordered. Excellent takeaway food - traditional French cooking or straightforward English (order 24 hrs in advance) and bar (both May - Oct). Weekly barbecue in high season. A site speciality is the sale of local wine. Minigolf. Table football. Children's play area. Table tennis. Barbecue facilities. Mobile homes for hire.

> **Directions:** Site signed at exit 12 of the A71 autoroute to Clermont Ferrand in the direction of Ebreuil. Site is west of Ebreuil beside the river, 6 km. from A71.
>
> **Charges 1999:** Per unit incl. 2 persons Ffr. 75.00 - 80.00; extra adult 25.00; child (under 16 yrs) 12.00; extra car 20.00; electricity 3A 10.00, 6A 18.00. Special low season reductions and meal arrangements. Credit cards accepted.
>
> **Open:** 31 March - 1 October.
>
> **Reservations:** Made with deposit (Ffr 200 per week of stay or full amount if stay costs less). Address: 03450 Ebreuil. Tel: (0)4.70.90.72.01. FAX: (0)4.70.90.79.48.

Don't wait to die to go to heaven, come to:

CAMPING DE LA FILATURE DE LA SIOULE

03450 EBREUIL, FRANCE

Tel: 0033 (0)4 70 90 72 01 Fax: 0033 (0)4 70 90 79 48

- Very clean facilities and a bathroom
- Really hot water • Excellent take away with pizza and barbecue evenings in high season
- Bar and terrace with Happy Hour
- Low season bargains for long stays
- Children up to 16 charged child rate
- Near to A71 for stopover or long stay

0402 Camp du Verdon, Castellane

Good site with swimming pool close to 'Route des Alpes' and Gorges du Verdon.

As you drive into Camp du Verdon, the neat and tidy air of the place is very striking. This is a very popular holiday area, the gorge, canoeing and rafting being the main attractions. Two heated swimming pools and numerous on-site activities help to keep non canoeists here. It is a large level site, part meadow, part wooded. The 500 pitches are numbered and separated by newly planted bushes. They vary in size (but mostly over the average) and 420 have 6A electricity, 120 with water and waste water points also. The site is lit and some lights are left on all night. The sanitary blocks are being refurbished. One is already finished with British style WCs and all the latest, easy to clean equipment and, as the rest are upgraded the Turkish style toilets will be replaced. Showers are pre-set and all facilities have hot water. One block has facilities for disabled visitors. Washing machines and irons, chemical disposal and motorcaravan services. Popular restaurant, takeaway opens twice daily and pizzeria/crêperie. Beside the retaurant is a terrace and a bar including a room with a log fire for cooler evenings. The two heated pools are open all season and a small fishing lake for children is restocked regularly. Playgrounds and minigolf. Archery, basketball, volleyball, bicycle hire, riding and table tennis. Games and competitions for all during July/Aug. Dances and discos suit all age groups (until 11 pm). With the facilities open all season, the site is very popular and is used by tour operators. Mobile homes to hire. Booking is advisable for July/Aug. The river Verdon runs along one edge of the site, so watch children.

> **Directions:** From Castellane take D952 west in direction of Gorges du Verdon and Moustiers. Site 1 km. on left.
>
> **Charges 1999:** Per unit with up to 3 persons Ffr. 90.00 - 185.00, acc. to season, size and facilities; extra person over 2 yrs 30.00 - 40.00; extra car, tent or caravan 20.00 - 30.00; dog 15.00; local tax 2.00, child (4-12) 1.00.
>
> **Open:** 15 May - 15 September.
>
> **Reservations:** Made for any length with booking fee (Ffr. 130) and deposit - details from site. Address: Domaine de la Salaou, 04120 Castellane. Tel: (0)4.92.83.61.29. FAX: (0)4.92.83.69.37.

0305 Camping-Caravaning La Petite Valette, Sazeret, Montmarault

Attractive, neat and tidy site with good facilities.

Originally a working farm, La Petite Valette has been transformed in three years by its hard working Dutch and German owners into a very attractive and peaceful campsite. The toilet facilities are housed in original outbuildings, each block having superb modern fittings, tiling, free hot water, chemical disposal and a large separate room with full facilities for disabled people. There are 50 level grassy pitches each with an electricity point (6A) and separated by new bushes and trees. There are only a few old trees so, as yet, there is little shade. Small fenced play area, table tennis, mountain bike hire and organised activities in July/Aug. A small lake in one of the lower fields is stocked for anglers. Ponies and small livestock keep the farm feeling alive. No shop but bread can be ordered. Meals and snacks are served all day in the farmhouse restaurant, also at outside tables in the garden which overflows with flowers. A small swimming pool has been added with a sunbathing area alongside. Two log cabins for hire. Montmarault is only 4 km. for shopping and you will find tennis, riding and sailing in the area.

Directions: From N145 Montmarault - Moulins, turn right at first roundabout on D46 signed St Pourcain. Turn left at next roundabout signed Deux-Chaises and La Valette. After 2.5 km. left at site sign and site is approx. 1 km.

Charges guide: Per adult Ffr. 19.50; child (0-8 yrs) 13.50; pitch 35.00; motorcaravan 15.00; dog 8.00; electricity (6A) 15.00. For one night stay 9/7-27/8, plus 10%.

Open: 1 April - 30 October.

Reservations: Contact site. Address: Sazeret, 03390 Montmarault. Tel: (0)4.70.07.64.57. FAX: (0)4.70.07.25.48.

0403 Camping Lac du Moulin de Ventre, Niozelles, Forcalquier

Small, peaceful lakeside site, close to the Luberon.

In the heart of Haute-Provence, near Forcalquier, a busy French town, this is an attractive site situated beside a small lake offering opportunities for swimming (supervised in season), canoeing or for hiring a pedalo and 28 acres of wooded, hilly land for walking. Trees and shrubs are labelled and the herbs of Provence can be found growing wild. A nature lover's delight - birds and butterflies abound. Some 80 of the 100 level, grassy pitches have electricity (6-10A) and there is some shade from the variety of trees. There is a bar/restaurant with waiter service, takeaway meals and themed evenings (high season). Pizzeria. Children's playground. Sanitary facilities are good, with hot showers, washbasins in cabins and some en-suite cubicles with showers and washbasins. Facilities for disabled people, baby bath, washing machines and fridges for hire. Shop for essentials; supermarket 5 km. Library. Organised activities in high season. Swimming pool (from 1/5). Fishing. Boules. Barbecues permitted in special area only. Well situated to visit Mont Ventoux, the Luberon National Park and Gorges du Verdon. Apartments, bungalows and caravans to let. A `Sites et Paysages' member. `Camping Cheque'

Directions: From A51 autoroute take exit for village of Brillanne and follow N100 east for 3 km. Site is signed near Forcalquier, 3 km. ESE of Niozelles.

Charges 1999: Per person incl. 2 persons Ffr. 105.00, with electricity 138.00; extra person 33.00; child (under 4 yrs) 18.00. Less 20% in low season, 20-60% for longer stays. No credit cards.

Open: 1 April - 20 October.

Reservations: Advisable for July/Aug. and made with deposit (30% of charge) and fee (Ffr. 100). Address: Niozelles, 04300 Forcalquier. Tel: (0)4.92.78.63.31. FAX: (0)4.92.79.86.92.

0500 Camping des Princes d'Orange, Orpierre

Attractive, terraced site within walking distance of charming medieval village.

This site, on a hillside above the village, has been gradually and thoughtfully developed over 20 years by its owners and their genuine, friendly welcome means many families return year upon year. On five terraces, its 120 generous pitches enjoy good shade from trees and canopies and have electricity (4A). Six sanitary blocks with mostly British style WCs, showers and washbasins in cubicles, dishwashing and laundry sinks, are very clean and accessible from all levels; laundry facilities are near reception. Swimming pool (20 x 10 m.) and paddling pool (1/6-20/9), play area, table tennis and games room. Bicycle hire 500 m. Reasonably priced takeaway service from the bar. No shop, but bread available each morning, and other basics from village (nearest shopping centre is Laragne, 12 km). Renowned for rock climbing, Orpierre also has an enchanting maze of medieval streets and houses. There is plenty of wonderful scenery to discover in the immediate vicinity, whilst not far away, some exhilarating hang gliding and parascending can be enjoyed. Whilst the steepness of the terrain and its somewhat remote location may not suit all, you will be made most welcome. Chalets and mobile homes for hire.

Directions: Turn off N75 road at Eyguians onto D30 - site signed at turning in centre of village of Orpierre.

Charges 1998: Per unit incl. 3 persons Ffr. 105.00, 2 persons 98.00; extra person 22.00; child (under 7 yrs) 14.00; electricity 14.00; local tax (over 16 yrs) 1.00. Less 25% in low season.

Open: 1 April - 1 November.

Reservations: Made with deposit (Ffr. 550) and fee (50). Address: 05700 Orpierre. Tel: (0)4.92.66.22.53. FAX: (0)4.92.66.31.08.

0603 Camping-Caravaning Domaine de la Bergerie, Vence, nr Nice

Large but quiet family type site attractively situated in hills near St Paul de Vence.

La Bergerie, a family owned site, is situated in the hills about 3 km. from Vence and 10 km. from the sea at Cagnes-sur-Mer. This extensive, lightly wooded site has been left very natural and is in a quiet, secluded position about 300 m. above sea level. Because of the trees most of the pitches are shaded and all are of a good size. It is a large site but, because it is so extensive does not give that impression. There are 450 pitches, 250 with 2/5A electricity) and 65 with water and drainage also. Both toilet blocks have been refurbished and provide hot water throughout, washbasins in cabins and excellent provision for disabled people (pitches near the block can be reserved). WCs are British style. Large swimming pool, paddling pool and spacious sunbathing area. Small bar/restaurant with takeaway and shop (all 1/5-30/9). No organised activities. Children's playground, bicycle hire, table tennis, tennis courts and 10 shaded boules pitches (lit at night) with competitions in season. Riding 6 km, fishing 10 km, golf 12 km. Two chalets to hire. Caravan storage. Hourly bus service (except Sundays) from site to Vence.

Directions: From autoroute A8 exit 47 take Cagnes-sur-Mer road in the direction of Vence. Site is west of Vence and it is necessary to follow `toutes directions' signs around the town to join the D2210 Grasse road. Follow this to roundabout (2 km.), turn left and follow site signs for 1 km. Site is on left in light woodland.

Charges 1998: Per unit incl. up to 3 persons in high season, 2 persons otherwise, simple pitch Ffr. 70.00 - 102.00; with electricity (2A) 89.00 - 121.00; special pitch with 3 services 109.00 - 141.00; extra person 32.00; child (under 5) 21.00; electricity (5A) 10.00; local tax 1.00. Less 5-10% for longer stays in low season. Credit cards accepted.

Open: 25 March - 15 October.

Reservations: Necessary only in July/Aug. for the special pitches and made with 25% deposit and Ffr. 85 fee. Address: Rte de la Sine, 06140 Vence. Tel: (0)4.93.58.09.36.

0605 Camping La Vieille Ferme, Villeneuve Loubet Plage, nr Antibes

Family owned site with good facilities, open all year, in popular resort area.

La Vieille Ferme is a family owned site with 135 level grass pitches, 106 with electricity (2-10A), water and waste water connections and the majority separated by hedges. Three toilet blocks (two heated for winter) provide mainly British style WCs, washbasins (in cabins) and pre-set showers. Unit for disabled people, chemical disposal and motorcaravan services. The blocks range from old to brand new, but they are all kept very clean. Dish and clothes washing sinks have hot water. Washing machines and a dryer. Shop in high season. Drinks, sweets and ices machine in TV room for all year use. The swimming pool (20 x 10 m.) is heated and covered for winter use (closed mid Nov-mid Dec) and beside it is a sunbathing area, children's pool (summer only) and jacuzzi. Table tennis, bicycle hire, basketball and a boule pitch are available and games and competitions are organised in July/Aug. Golf 2 km. Refrigerator hire and safety deposit boxes. The site aims to cater for all year caravanning and, even though the shop is closed in winter, gaz, bread and milk may be ordered. English is spoken at reception and the place has a very friendly feel. Chalets to let, for winter use as well.

Directions: From west take Antibes exit from Esterel autoroute and turn left towards Nice when joining the N7 outside Antibes. After 3½ km. on N7 turn left for site. From east take N7 towards Antibes and turn right after Villeneuve Loubet Plage. The turning off the N7, though signed, is not easy to see particularly at busy times but, coming from Antibes, it is on the left, more or less between the Bonne Auberge and the Parc de Vaugrenier. Site is 150 m. on right. (Note: avoid N98 Route du Bord de Mer.) Site has prepared its own small, yellow site signs.

Charges 1999: Per pitch incl. 2 persons: tent Ffr 82.00 - 127.00, caravan 92.00 - 155.00; extra person 22.00 - 28.00; child (under 5) 13.00 - 18.00; extra car 15.00 - 26.00; dog 10.00; electricity 2A 15.00, 6A 20.00, 10A 28.00; local tax 1.00. Less 10-30% for longer stays in low season. Credit cards accepted, but not Eurocheques.

Open: All year

Reservations: Advisable over a long season and made with 25% deposit and Ffr. 120 fee (high season only); (Sat.-Sat. only in July/Aug. and at Easter). Address: 296 Bvd. des Groules, 06270 Villeneuve Loubet Plage. Tel: (0)4.93.33.41.44. FAX: (0)4.93.33.37.28.

AR Discount
Third person free all year

France - Ardèche

0702 Camping-Caravaning L'Ardèchois, St Sauveur-de-Montagut

Well equipped site in spectacular setting.

This site is quite a way off the beaten track and the approach is winding and narrow in places. It is worth the effort, however, to find such an attractive hillside site with good amenities and a variety of pitches. All 85 touring pitches have electricity (6, 10 or 15A) and are said to be 100 sq.m. Some are alongside the small fast-flowing river, while the rest (60%) are on higher, sloping ground nearer the restaurant/bar. The access roads are tarmac but quite steep and larger units may find access difficult to some terraces. The main sanitary block, bar/restaurant, shop and soundproof 'salle de jeux' have been created by the careful conversion of old buildings and provide modern amenities in an attractive style (all 1/5-25/9). TV room, table tennis, bicycle hire and fishing. The swimming pool is heated from 1/5 (no shorts) and has an adjacent bar, snack bar and terrace. Sanitary facilities are good, with British toilets, hot showers, washbasins in cabins. etc. A block of equal quality is near the riverside pitches. Facilities for disabled people and babies, chemical disposal, dishwashing and laundry rooms, plus a motorcaravan service point. The owners have developed an extensive and unusual excursion programme for exploring this attractive area. Popular with the Dutch. Chalets and mobile homes for hire. `Camping Cheque'

Directions: From Valence take N86 south for 12 km, turn right onto D120 to St. Sauveur de Montagut, then take D102 towards Mézilhac for 8 km. to site.

Charges 1999: Per unit incl. 2 persons Ffr 88.00 - 106.00, with electricity 106.00 - 124.00; extra person (incl. children) 20.00; pet 10.00; electricity (6A) 18.00. Special rate for over 55s outside July/Aug. Credit cards accepted.

Open: 24 April - 25 September.

Reservations: Write with deposit (Ffr. 450) and fee (150). Address: 07190 St Sauveur-de-Montagut. Tel: (0)4.75.66.61.87. FAX: (0)4.75.66.63.67. E-mail: ardechois.camping@wanadoo.fr. Internet: http://www.ardechois-camping.fr.

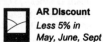

AR Discount
Less 5% in May, June, Sept

0703 Camping Soleil Vivarais, Sampzon, nr Ruoms

Large, quality site bordering the Ardèche river.

Beside the Ardèche river, with a sandy beach, Soleil Vivarais offers much, particularly for families with children. The 200 generously sized, level pitches (40 fully serviced) all have 10A electricity and many are shaded. Four modern, very clean sanitary blocks cope well with the demand. With a heated babies' and children's room (incorporating several delightful facilities at child height), four units for people with disabilities, ample areas for dishwashing (free hot water), washing machines and dryers, and chemical disposal, there is undoubtedly a full complement of facilities. During the day the proximity of the heated main and toddlers' pools (22.5 x 10.5 m and 100 sq. m, no bermuda style shorts) to the terraces of the bar and restaurant make it a pleasantly social area. In the evening the stage provides an ideal platform for varied entertainment. The disco adjacent to the bar (capacity 100-120) is popular with teenagers (well sound-proofed). The bar/restaurant complex is bright and modern. Takeaways and pizzas. Large shop. Extensive on-site 'animation' programme in June, July and Aug. offers water polo, aqua-aerobics, pool games and archery. Minigolf, tennis (both charged), fishing, basketball, petanque, table tennis and volleyball. Activities nearby, many with instruction and supervision, include mountain biking (bicycle hire from site), walking, canoeing, rafting, climbing and caving. Riding 500 m, golf 10 km. Used by tour operators (70 pitches). Chalets, mobile homes and tents for hire.

Directions: From Le Teil (on N86) take N102 westwards towards and through Villeneuve-de-Berg, disregarding first sign for Vallon-Pont-d'Arc. Continue on N102 before turning left on D103, toward Vogue and Ruoms, then left on D579 to Sampzon. Access to site is via bridge across the river, controlled by lights.

Charges 1999: Per unit incl. 2 persons and electricity Ffr. 111.00 - 184.00; extra person 25.00 - 38.00; child (under 10 yrs) free - 38.00; water and drainage free - 24.00; local tax 2.00 (over 10s). Credit cards accepted.

Open: 27 March - 20 September.

Reservations: Made by fax and credit card or write to site with deposit (Ffr 600) and fee (195). Address: Sampzon, 07120 Ruoms. Tel: (0)4.75.39.67.56. FAX: (0)4.75.93.97.10. E-mail: camping.soleil.vivarais@wanadoo.fr.

0704 Camping La Rouveyrolle, Casteljau, nr Les Vans

Attractive, family run site in peaceful surroundings beside the Chassezac river gorge.

Family run and aimed at families, this is a very tranquil site by the river in attractive countryside with vineyards and orchards. There are 100 good sized pitches here, all with electricity (4/5A) on flat grass, some with ample shade and others with less for those preferring the sun. The site has a relaxed atmosphere and provides good facilities for families, including an attractively shaped swimming pool, positioned to catch the sun all day. It was built by the site after the water level in the river dropped following the building of a dam upstream. The site offers a pleasant bar/restaurant (May - 15 Sept) serving a `dish of the day' and including takeaway, and animation (July/Aug). The sanitary facilities are in two modern blocks providing free hot showers in cubicles with separator, and some British style WCs although the majority are the Turkish type. There are part covered washing-up and laundry areas, including a washing machine. Shop (July/Aug.8-12.30 and 4.30-7.30) - the village is 500 m. Activities include tennis courts, bicycle hire and a new children's adventure playground, with the river beach (100 m.) providing swimming and canoeing in July/Aug. Fishing. The Cévennes and the Gorges of the Ardèche (20 km) are near. Riding, pot-holing and rock climbing (with guides) are available nearby and excursions can be arranged. Mobile homes (6 persons) for hire.

Directions: From A7 at Montélimar, take D102 west to Aubenas, then D104, south through Joyeuse and hamlet of Chandolas. Turn right just after bridge over the Chassezac onto D252. Turn right after 1.75 km. (site signed) then right at next crossroads. Site is 1 km. signed to right (do not turn into village La Rouveyrolle).

Charges 1999: Per unit incl. 2 persons Ffr 60.00 - 122.00; extra person 21.00 - 32.00; child under 7 yrs free, 7-16 yrs 16.00 - 26.00; electricity 20.00; local tax 1.00. Credit cards accepted.

Open: 1 April - 30 September.

Reservations: Write to site. Address: Casteljau, 07460 Berrias et Casteljau. Tel: (0)4.75.39.00.67. FAX: (0)4.75.39.07.28. E-mail: rouv@club-internet.fr. Internet: www.fr.vivarais.com.

AR Discount
Welcome drinks

0705 Camping-Caravaning Le Ranc Davaine, St Alban Auriolles, Ruoms

Family oriented site in southern Ardèche.

Situated between cliffs and rocks, this is quite a large site with 356 pitches, most of reasonable size. They are arranged on fairly flat, rather stony ground under a variety of trees giving shade and all are supplied with electricity (6 or 10A). An attractive large, irregularly shaped swimming pool (no bermuda-style shorts or shirts) is heated in low season and overlooked by terraces and the bar/restaurant which serves a good range of meals in pleasant surroundings, made more inviting in the evenings by lighting and floodlighting. The entertainment programme (July/August) is extensive and varied, with particular emphasis for younger children and teenagers (noisy discos!). The five sanitary blocks are adequate, with British style WCs, hot showers with dividers and many washbasins in private cabins. Washing machines, dryer and irons are provided. Besides the restaurant, other amenities include a pizzeria and takeaway, a large shop, children's play area, tennis, table tennis, minigolf and an extensive programme of water sports. Canoes are available to hire for excursions down the River Ardèche. There is a large tour operator presence. A Sites et Paysages member.

Directions: Continue south on D111 after Ruoms. Turn right just before Grospierres on D246, across bridge and then left on D208 towards Chandolas and site.

Charges 1999: Per unit incl. 2 persons Ffr. 85.00 - 145.00, with electricity 107.00 - 168.00; extra person over 2 yrs 24.00 - 34.00; plus local tax; animal free - 14.00. Credit cards accepted.

Open: 1 April - 15 September.

Reservations: Made with deposit (Ffr. 620) and fee (180). Address: St Alban Auriolles, 07120 Ruoms. Tel: (0)4.75.39.60.55. FAX: (0)4.75.39.38.50.

France - Ardèche

0706 Mondial Camping, Rivière Ardèche, Vallon Pont d'Arc

Attractive family run site beside the river, close to popular, busy resort.

Mondial is a good quality site catering for active families. It is close to the popular Ardèche resort of Vallon Pont d'Arc but is less frenetic than some of the other sites in the area. Shrubs are being planted to separate the pitches, and the majority have some shade from mature trees. Neatly arranged in short rows, all are of a good size and have access to electricity (6/10A). The site itself is quite long and narrow, with direct access at the far end to the river for bathing, fishing or canoeing (canoe hire from site) or just watching the activities. There is a modern restaurant and a bar where evening activities take place until midnight in high season. Some noisy activities may also be heard from nearby sites. Attractive heated pool (no Bermuda style shorts) with sunbathing areas (all these amenities 1/4-15/9). Tennis, volleyball, children's play area and archery beside the river. Shop (1/4-15/9). Three modern sanitary blocks are of a high standard, very clean when we visited and with unusually excellent facilities for disabled people. They provide comfortable hot showers, British and Turkish style WCs (no paper), washbasins in private cabins, washing machine and dishwashing facilities. Chemical disposal and motorcaravan services. Bicycle hire, golf 100 m, riding 300 m. The pretty village with shops, restaurants and bars is a short walk. The famous Pont d'Arc is 2 km. Used by tour operators (40 pitches). Mobile homes to rent.

Directions: From Vallon Pont d'Arc take D290 towards Pont St. Esprit - site is on right of this road. From A7 use Montelimar-Sud or Bolléne exit and D4 through Bourg St Andéol and St Reméze to Vallon Pont d'Arc.

Charges 1999: Per unit incl. 2 persons Ffr. 82.00 - 141.00; extra person 30.00 - 34.00; child under 5 yrs 20.00 - 28.00; extra small tent free - 15.00; dog 20.00; electricity 21.00; water and drainage 30.00; local tax 3.00 per person (over 10 yrs). Credit cards accepted.

Open: 15 March - 30 September.

Reservations: Made with deposit (Ffr. 600) and fee (100). Address: Route Touristiques des Gorges de l'Ardèche, 07150 Vallon-Pont-d'Arc. Tel: (0)4.75.88.00.44. FAX: (0)4.75.37.13.73.

0707 Camping Les Ranchisses, Chassiers, Largentière

Family site on the Route de Valgorge.

The Chevalier family (no relation to Maurice, as far as we know!) combine farming and wine-making with running a family campsite and an Auberge. In a somewhat lesser known area of the Ardèche at Chassiers, on the route de Valgorge, the site started life as 'camping à la ferme' but has now developed into a 130 pitch family campsite with an extensive range of facilities. These include a medium sized, heated pool (from 15/4, no shorts) with sunbathing areas and the Auberge, developed from the original 1824 building used to house silk-worms. Also open to the public, traditional dishes are served at lunch-time and in the evenings (1/4-15/9) both indoors and outside in very attractive surroundings. Shop in high season. The good sized, level, grassy pitches are in two main areas, one older (the original camping à la ferme) and well shaded, the other newer and with recently planted small trees. The great majority have 6A electricity, with 10 being fully serviced. There is frontage to a small lake which is connected to the river, providing opportunities for fishing or simple canoeing and at least one part of this appears safe for youngsters. Bicycle hire. There are two sanitary blocks, one excellent new one with the latest fittings, the other older, smaller one renovated to acceptable standards (including British style WCs). Chemical disposal. Washing machine. Both blocks were immaculate when seen in high season. Mobile homes to hire. The medieval village of Largentière (1 km.) is well worth a visit, with a Tuesday market and a medieval festival in July. `Camping Cheque' `FRENCH FLAVOUR'.

Directions: From Largentière take Route de Valgorge (D24) and Les Ranchisses is the first site on left.

Charges 1998: Per unit incl. 2 persons Ffr. 78.00 - 102.00, comfort pitch 105.00 - 135.00; extra person 16.00 - 25.00; child (under 10 yrs) 12.00 - 20.00; animal free - 6.00; electricity 17.00. Credit cards accepted.

Open: Easter - 27 September.

Reservations: Contact site for form; made with Ffr. 500 deposit. Address: Route de Valgorge, Chassiers, 07110 Largentière. Tel: (0)4.75.88.31.97. FAX: (0)4.75.88.32.73.

0709 Castel Camping Domaine des Plantas, Les Ollières-sur-Eyrieux

Good quality campsite in a spectacular setting on the banks of the Eyrieux river.

This site offers an attractive alternative to those in the more popular, and often crowded, southern parts of the Ardèche. The Eyrieux valley is less well known, but arguably just as attractive as those further south and a good deal less crowded, particularly in the main season. Perhaps the only drawback to this site is the narrow twisting 3 km. approach road which, although by no means frightening, may present something of a challenge to those with large outfits - no problem with a smaller caravan like ours and, in any case, the helpful owners have an ingenious system designed to assist campers on departure. With its own sandy beach beside the quite fast-flowing, but fairly shallow, river (used for bathing) the absence of a swimming pool should present no real deterrent (there are plans to add one). The bar, restaurant and disco are all housed in an original building which is quite impressive with its Protestant history and visible from the main road across the river long before you reach it. *continued overleaf*

0709 Castel Camping Domaine des Plantas (continued)

Many activities are possible - mountain biking, canoeing, canyoning, riding and walking. The pitches are terraced and shaded (some up and down walking) with 5A electricity (long leads may be needed). One large, central toilet block is in courtyard style, well equipped with washbasins in cubicles, showers, British style toilets and good provision for children. A smaller block is for the higher terraces. Washing up, laundry sinks (both H&C) and washing machine. Small shop open July/Aug, otherwise bread and milk to order. No barbecues allowed in July/Aug. Activities are arranged according to the campers' motivations, including excursions. Adventure play area beside the river. `Camping Cheque'

> **Directions:** South of Valence exit N86 at La Voulte and follow the D120 west for Les Ollières sur Eyrieux (20 km). After bridge in the village, take left turn and follow site signs - the road is single track and could be difficult for large units with bends and twists for 3 km. Vans leave the site in timed convoys, otherwise a site car goes in front of you.
>
> **Charges 1998:** Per unit incl. 2 persons Ffr. 110.00; extra person 22.00; child (under 8 yrs) 12.00; animal 10.00; electricity 20.00; local tax (over 10 yrs) 2.00. Less 30% outside 27/6-25/8.
>
> **Open:** 29 March - 15 September (all services from 1 June).
>
> **Reservations:** Made with deposit (Ffr. 400) and fee (120). Address: 07360 Les Ollières-sur-Eyrieux. Tel: (0)4.75.66.21.53. FAX: (0)4.75.66.23.65.

0902 Camping L'Arize, La Bastide-de-Sérou

Small, quality site in strategic location for touring this part of the Pyrénées.

You are assured of a warm welcome at this friendly little site nestling in a delightful, tranquil valley among the foothills of the Pyrénées beside the River Arize (good trout fishing) and just east of the interesting village of La Bastide de Sérou. The 70 large pitches are neatly laid out on level grass, all have 3/6A electricity (French type sockets) and are separated into bays by hedges and young trees. There is a small swimming pool with paved sunbathing area and a children's play area. The central sanitary block (unheated) offers spacious showers, a laundry room, dishwashing under cover and good facilities for disabled people and babies. The only omission is a chemical disposal point - the organic sewage system is incompatible with chemicals. Fishing, riding and bicycle hire on site. Restaurants and shops are a few minute's drive, plus interesting local activities including golf (5 km) and the national stud for the Merens horses. The owners who personally manage the site have negotiated discounts at local attractions. Bungalow tents for rent. A comfortable and relaxing base for touring this beautiful part of the Pyrénées with easy access to the medieval town of Foix and even Andorra for duty-free shopping.

> **Directions:** Site is southeast of La Bastide-de-Sérou. Take D15 towards Nescus. Site is right after approx. 1 km.
>
> **Charges 1999:** Per pitch incl. 2 persons and electricity 71.00 - 98.00; extra adult 20.00 - 29.00; child (2-7 yrs) 13.00 - 19.00. Credit cards accepted.
>
> **Open:** 1 March - 31 October.
>
> **Reservations:** Made with 25% deposit and fee (Ffr 55). Address: Lieu-dit Bourtol, 09240 La Bastide-de-Sérou. Tel: (0)5.61.65.81.51. FAX: (0)5.61.65.83.34. Internet: http://seronais.unisoft.fr.

1106 Camping Au Pin d'Arnauteille, Montclar, nr Carcassonne

Peaceful, spacious, developing site with superb views to the Corbières and beyond.

Enjoying some of the best and most varied views of any site, this rather unusual site is ideally situated for exploring, by foot or car, the little known Aude Dèpartement, the area of the Cathars and for visiting the walled city of Carcassonne (10 minutes drive). However, access could be difficult for large, twin axle vans. The site itself is set in 115 ha. of farmland on hilly ground with the original pitches on gently sloping, lightly wooded land and the new `grand-confort' ones semi-terraced with electricity (5/10A and lacking shade at present. A swimming pool (25 x 10 m.) with children's pool and paved sunbathing area is in a basin surrounded by green fields. Unisex sanitary facilities are modern, the main block part open, with another under the pool, one behind reception and a new small block in the developing area. British WCs, hot showers, basins in cabins, dishwashing under cover and laundry facilities. Facilities for disabled people and baby bath. Restaurant, takeaway (15/5-15/9) and a terrace. Small shop (15/5-15/9, out of season the site is a little out of the way). The reception building is vast; originally a farm building, subsequently a new top floor being added by former owners (to create a nursing home) but later converted to apartments. Table tennis and volleyball. Bicycle hire 10 km, fishing 2 km, rafting and canoeing near, plus marked walks. Chalets, mobile homes and bungalow tents to let. Used by tour operators (10 pitches). A developing site with enthusiastic owners for whom riding is the principle theme with stables on site (note: the French are more relaxed about hard hats, etc). `Camping Cheque'

> **Directions:** On D118 from Carcassonne, bypass village of Rouffiac d'Aude to small section of dual carriageway. Before end of this, turn right to Montclar up narrow road for 2.5 km. Site signed sharp left and up hill before village.
>
> **Charges 1998:** Per pitch incl. 2 persons Ffr. 73.00 - 90.00, pitch with electricity 90.00 - 107.00, pitch with water and drainage 105.00 - 127.00; extra person 18.00 - 23.00; child (under 7 yrs) 12.00 - 15.00. Credit cards accepted.
>
> **Open:** 1 April - 30 September.
>
> **Reservations:** Made with deposit of 25% of charges. Address: 11250 Montclar. Tel: (0)4.68.26.84.53. FAX: (0)4.68.26.91.10.

France - Aude / Aveyron

1107 Camping Club Les Mimosas, Narbonne

See colour advert opposite page 97

Lively site on Mediterranean Littoral, close to beaches at Narbonne Plage and Gruissac.

Being some 6 km. inland from the beaches of Narbonne and Gruissac, this site benefits from a somewhat less hectic situation than others in the popular seaside environs of Narbonne. The site itself is, however, quite lively with plenty to amuse and entertain the whole family. The 250 pitches (43 for tourers) are mainly of good size, most with electricity (6A), including a few 'grand confort', and have a reasonable amount of shade. Facilities include a large swimming pool (from mid May) and a smaller one (open earlier) with sunbathing areas, overlooked by a mezzanine level with a small lounge, amusements, etc. Three tennis courts, a sauna, gym, bicycle hire and minigolf, with riding nearby. A lagoon for boating and fishing is accessible via a footpath (about 200 m). The site also has the rather attractive Auberge Mandirac with a comfortable environment and interesting menu. Four sanitary buildings, two refurbished to a high standard with baby baths, etc, the other two of older design but well maintained, include showers, some British WCs, washbasins in cabins, laundry and dishwashing sinks, washing machines and chemical disposal. This could be a useful site meeting a variety of needs, on-site entertainment (including an evening on 'Cathare' history), and easy access to popular beaches and interesting towns such as Narbonne itself, Béziers or even Carcassonne. Chalets and bungalows to rent.

Directions: From A9 exit 38 (Narbonne Sud), go round roundabout to last exit taking you back over autoroute (site is signed from here). Follow signs to La Nautique and then Mandirac and site (total 6 km. from autoroute).

Charges 1998: Per basic pitch incl. 1 or 2 persons Ffr. 66.00 - 88.00, pitch with electricity 80.00 - 104.00, pitch with electricity, water and drainage extra. Credit cards accepted.

Open: 24 March - 31 October.

Reservations: Made with Ffr. 500 deposit (and 120 fee in July/Aug only). Address: Chaussée de Mandirac, 11100 Narbonne. Tel: (0)4.68.49.03.72. FAX: (0)4.68.49.39.45. Internet: www.agence-colibri.fr/camping-mimosas/

AR Discount
Outside 27/6-30/8
10 nights for price
of 9, 14 for 10

1202 Camping-Caravaning Les Rivages, Millau

Large site on town outskirts close to Tarn Gorges with good range of sporting facilities.

This site is well organised and is very popular, being close to the high limestone 'Causses' and the various river Gorges, particularly the Tarn, and their associated attractions, such as caves, remote villages, wildlife refuges, etc. Some 314 pitches occupy flat ground adjacent to the Dourbie river, close to its confluence with the Tarn. There is safe river bathing from the river beach. Pitches in the older part of the site are arranged in fours and tend to be a little crowded, with a bare 100 sq.m. space. In a newer, though less shaded part of the site, campers have more room. All pitches have electricity (6A), 98 have water and drainaway points also. Sanitary facilities are good, the four modern blocks providing washbasins in cabins, showers and toilets (British and Turkish style), dishwashing and laundry sinks, rooms for disabled people (not all blocks open in low seasons). A special block for children has baby baths, small showers, children's toilets and ironing - very nice for mothers, with a play area by it. The management provides a wide range of sporting and cultural options (there are said to be 26 different activities). On site are indoor and outdoor tennis courts, two badminton and two squash courts, football, volleyball, basketball and two swimming pools (from 10/5), table tennis, petanque and cyclo-cross track. River activities, walking, mountain biking, bird-watching, fishing and many more. Bicycle hire 500 m, riding 15 km. Children's play area and entertainment, with child minding (3-6 yrs). Shop (20/5-20/9), snack bar and restaurant/bar (all season). No discos.

Directions: Site is on the Nant (D991) road out of Millau.

Charges 1999: Per pitch incl. 2 persons Ffr. 76.00 - 111.00, with electricity 87.00 - 130.00; extra person (over 3 yrs) 18.00 - 21.00; pet 14.00 - 15.00; local tax (15/6-15/9) 2.00. Credit cards accepted.

Open: 1 May - 30 September.

Reservations: Advisable for Jul/Aug. with deposit (Ffr. 400) and fee (100). Address: Ave. de l'Aigoual, Rte. de Nant, 12100 Millau. Tel: (0)5.65.61.01.07. FAX: (0)5.65.59.03.56.

1200 Camping Peyrelade, nr Millau

Attractive site by a pebble beach in the Gorges du Tarn.

Situated at the foot of the Tarn gorges, on the banks of the river, this site is dominated by the ruins of the Château de Peyrelade. Bathing from the pebble beach is safe and the water is clean. The 140 touring pitches are terraced, level and shady with 6A electricity hook-ups (long leads may be required for riverside pitches) and nearby water points. One of the two toilet blocks has been refurbished. Young children are catered for, also people with disabilities and there are chemical disposal points, washing machines and a dryer. A children's paddling pool and the attractively designed swimming pool (proper swimming trunks, no shorts) are adjacent to the children's playground. Facilities in the adjacent leisure centre can be booked at reception at reduced charges. Amenities include a games room, mini-club and barbecue area. A bar, restaurant, pizzeria and takeaway services are housed near reception (all from 1/6). Fishing on site, bicycle hire 200 m, riding 1 km. Mobile homes to rent. *continued overleaf*

1200 Camping Peyrelade (continued)

Ideally placed for visiting the Tarn gorges, other attractions include Roquefort cheese, La Couvertriade (Knights Templar village) and the eastern Cevennes. Used by tour operators (40 pitches).

Directions: From N9 Sévérac - Millau road, turn east from Aguessac (follow Gorges du Tarn signs). Site is 2 km. past Rivière sur Tarn, on the right - the access road is quite steep.

Charges 1998: Per unit incl. 2 persons Ffr. 85.00 - 110.00; extra adult 16.00 - 20.00; child (under 5) 12.00 - 15.00; dog 7.00; electricity (6A) 18.00; local tax 1.00. Credit cards accepted.

Open: Easter - 15 September.

Reservations: Made with deposit (Ffr. 450) and fee (100). Address: 12640 Rivière-sur-Tarn. Tel: (0)5.65.62.62.54. FAX: (0)5.65.62.65.61.

1201 Castel Camping Val de Cantobre, Nant d'Aveyron, nr Millau

Attractive, terraced site in the valley of the Dourbie.

This site which has been imaginatively and tastefully developed by the Dupond family over a 25 year period, offers a bar, restaurant, pizzeria and takeaway facility. In particular, the magnificent carved features in the bar create a delightful ambience, complemented by a recently built terrace. True, the ground is hard in summer but staff supply robust nails if awning pegs prove a problem. Most of the pitches (all with electricity and water), are peaceful, generous in size and blessed with views of the valley. Three adjoining swimming pools have a new surround, bedecked by flowers and crowned by a large urn which dispenses water into the paddling pool. The shop, although small, offers a wide variety of provisions; including regional specialities. Tour operators use many of the pitches, but terrace design assures peace and privacy. The new sanitary block is impressive and is beautifully appointed, with British style WCs and a huge indoor dishwashing area. But it is the activity programme that is unique at Val de Cantobre. Adventurous visitors relish sports like river rafting, white water canoeing, rock climbing or jumps from Millau's hill tops on twin seater steerable parachutes. Around 15 such activities, all supervised by qualified instructors, are arranged by the owners. Passive recreationists appreciate the scenery, especially Cantobre, a medieval village that clings to a cliff in view of the site. Nature lovers will be delighted to see the vultures wheeling in the Tarn gorge alongside more humble rural residents. Butterflies in profusion, orchids, huge edible snails, glow worms, families of beavers and the natterjack toad all live here. It is easy to see why - the place is magnificent. Fishing. A warm welcome awaits from the Dupond family. Mobile homes and chalets for hire. `Camping Cheque' `FRENCH FLAVOUR'

Directions: Site is 4 km. north of Nant, on D991 road to Millau.

Charges 1998: Per unit incl. 2 persons and 4A electricity 120.00 - 145.00; extra person (4 yrs and over) 20.00 - 32.00; extra car or dog free - 10.00; electricity 10A 10.00. Credit cards accepted.

Open: 15 May - 15 September, with all facilities.

Reservations: Made for any length with deposit (Ffr. 82) and fee (18). Address: 12230 Nant d'Aveyron. Tel: (0)5.65.58.43.00. FAX: (0)5.65.62.10.36.

1208 Camping Club Les Genêts, Salles Curan (Lac de Pareloup)

Lakeside site in attractive area, with own swimming and spa pools.

This family run site is on the shores of Lac de Pareloup and offers both family holiday and watersports facilities. The main building houses reception, a restaurant, bar and a very well stocked shop. The 162 pitches include 102 grassy, mostly individual pitches for touring units. These are in two areas, one on each side of the entrance lane, and are divided by hedges, shrubs and trees. Most have electricity (6A) and many also have water and waste water drain. Two main sanitary units provide British style WCs, washbasins (many in cubicles), hot showers with small dividers and shelf, a suite for disabled people, chemical disposal, plus dishwashing and laundry sinks. Free hot water throughout. Refurbishment of the older unit is planned, whilst the other unit is new and modern. A building opposite reception contains the laundry, with washing machine and dryer, and a baby room with baths, changing mats, washbasin and WC. The terrace with the swimming pool and a spa pool (unsupervised and open June-Aug), has a snack bar adjacent (main season). The site slopes gently down to the beach and lake with facilities for all watersports including water skiing. Pedaloes, windsurfers and kayaks can be rented, and fishing licences are available. Minigolf, volleyball, boules, table tennis, bicycle hire. For children, there are Red Indian style tee-pees, pony riding and a children's playground. Full animation and activities programme in high season, and there is much to see and do in this very attractive corner of Aveyron. Mobile homes for rent (25). Used by tour operators (20 pitches). Caravan storage. A `Sites et Paysages' member.

Directions: From Salles-Curan take D577 for 4 km. approx., turning right into a narrow lane immediately after a sharp right hand bend. Site is signed at junction.

Charges 1998: Per unit incl. 2 or 3 persons and electricity Ffr. 89.00 - 149.00 acc. to season and location; extra adult 26.00; child (under 7 yrs) 18.00; extra tent, vehicle or animal 15.00; local tax 1.00. Credit cards accepted.

Open: 1 June - 15 September.

Reservations: Recommended for July/Aug - contact site. Address: 12410 Salles Curan. Tel: (0)5.65.46.35.34. FAX: (0)5.65.78.00.72.

AR Discount
Less 10% June/Sept
for min. 1 week

85

France - Calvados / Charente

1407 Camping de la Vallée, Houlgate

Fresh, well kept site, close to lively little resort of Houlgate.

Camping de la Vallée is an attractive site with good, well maintained facilities. Situated on a grassy hillside overlooking Houlgate, the 278 pitches (180 for touring units) are large and open, with hedging planted and all have electricity. Part of the site is sloping, the rest level, with gravel or tarmac roads. An old farmhouse has been converted to house a rustic bar and comfortable TV lounge and billiards room. Heated swimming pool (from 15/5) and tennis court. Shop. Small snack-bar with takeaway in season (from 15/5). A large grassy area has a children's playground, volleyball and a football field, there is tennis, bicycle hire, petanque and organised entertainment in Jul/Aug. There are three toilet blocks of a good standard with free hot water in the controllable, well fitted showers; washbasins in cabins; mainly British toilets, facilities for disabled people and baby bathroom. Dishwashing, laundry with machines, dryers and ironing boards (no lines allowed), chemical disposal and motorcaravan services. The beach is 1 km, the town 900 m. Fishing 1 km, riding 500 m. Championship golf course 2 km. English spoken in season. Mobile homes to rent. Used by tour operators (32 pitches). Very busy in high season, maintenance and cleaning could be variable at that time. Under new management.

Directions: Site is 1 km. from Houlgate, along D24A (route de Lisieux). Turn right onto D24, rue de la Vallée and look for site sign.

Charges 1999: Per person Ffr. 30.00; child (under 7) 20.00; pitch 45.00, with services 50.00; dog 15.00; electricity 2A 18.00, 4A 20.00, 6A 25.00; local tax 2.00. Less 10% outside main season. Credit cards accepted.

Open: 1 April - 30 September.

Reservations: Made with deposit (Ffr. 400) and fee (100) - write to site. Address: 88 rue de la Vallée, 14510 Houlgate. Tel: (0)2.31.24.40.69. FAX: (0)2.31.28.08.29.

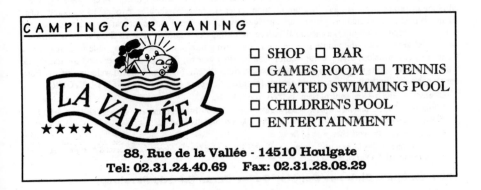

CAMPING CARAVANING

LA VALLÉE
★★★★

☐ SHOP ☐ BAR
☐ GAMES ROOM ☐ TENNIS
☐ HEATED SWIMMING POOL
☐ CHILDREN'S POOL
☐ ENTERTAINMENT

88, Rue de la Vallée - 14510 Houlgate
Tel: 02.31.24.40.69   Fax: 02.31.28.08.29

1602 Castel Camping Gorges du Chambon, Eymouthiers, nr Montbron

Family site in pretty, rolling Charente countryside.

Under British ownership, this site is arranged around a restored Charente farmhouse and its outbuildings. It provides an attractive, spacious setting with 120 large, marked pitches with electrical connections, on gently sloping grass and enjoying extensive views over the countryside. The pitches are arranged in two circular groups with a sanitary block at the centre of each. Built in a traditional style, the blocks provide British style WCs, hot showers and washbasins in private cabins. There are facilities for disabled people, a baby bath, chemical disposal, laundry facilities including tumble dryer, and good dishwashing rooms. To one side is a swimming pool (18 x 7 m) and minigolf. Converted from an old barn with an interesting gallery arrangement, are a bar and restaurant, plus takeaway which includes pizzas (1/6-31/8). Reception stocks some basic supplies (closes at 7 pm.) where bread can be ordered the day before. Games room, TV and table tennis, etc. Tennis. Bicycle hire. Children's play area. Fishing 400 m. Caravans and gite to let. No animals accepted in July/Aug. Used by tour operators (17 pitches).

Directions: From N141 Angoulême - Limoges road at Rochefoucauld take D6 to Montbron village. Follow D6 in direction of Piegut-Pluviers and site is signed down country road past holiday complex.

Charges 1998: Per pitch Ffr. 50.00; person 30.00; child (under 7 yrs) 15.00; car 12.00; electricity (6A) 20.00; local tax (adults) 1.00. Less 15% (not electricity) outside July/Aug. Credit cards accepted.

Open: 15 May - 15 September.

Reservations: Necessary for July/Aug. Write to site with min. Ffr. 200 deposit and fee (80). Address: Eymouthiers, 16220 Montbron. Tel: (0)5.45.70.71.70. FAX: (0)5.45.70.80.02.

1605M Camping Municipal de Cognac, Cognac

If you're a lover of brandy, this area is a must, with abundant vineyards and little roadside chalets offering tastings of Pineau (a Cognac based aperitif) and a vast range of Cognacs. This municipal site by the Charente river is convenient as a night stop or longer stay to visit the area, and for sleeping off the effects of the `tastings' - you probably won't even notice the slight noise from the nearby road! The 170 large pitches, all with electricity (5/6A), are neatly laid out and separated by shrubs and trees. Two modern toilet blocks have British and Turkish style WCs, including children's toilets and chemical disposal. Push-button showers with free hot water, washbasins in cabins, dishwashing and laundry sinks and a washing machine. A small swimming pool is on site (1/6-1/10) or the municipal pool is nearby. Restaurants, bars and shops may be found in the town centre, although the site offers a snack bar and entertainment (15/6-15/9). Other on-site amenities include volleyball, table tennis, a children's play area on grass and a sand pit. The famous Cognac Houses (Pineau, Martell, Remy Martin, etc.) and the Cognac Museum may be visited but there is no public transport to the centre (2.3 km). Riverside walks.

Directions: Site is signed from the N141 Saintes - Angoulême road following signs for the town centre. It is to the north of the town beside the river on the road to Ste-Sévère.

Charges guide: Per pitch incl. 4 persons Ffr. 100.00; extra person 16.00; child (0-7 yrs) 11.00. Less in low season. Less 10% for 4 days, 20% for 7 days.

Open: 1 May - 15 October.

Reservations: Recommended in high season. Write for more information to Office de Tourisme de Cognac, 16 Rue du 14 Juillet, 16100 Cognac. Tel: (0)5.45.82.10.71. FAX: (0)5.45.82.34.47. Address: Bvd. de Chatenay, Rte. de Ste-Sévère, 16100 Cognac. Tel: (0)5.45.32.13.32. FAX: (0)5.45.36.55.29.

VISIT THE `PAYS DU COGNAC'

On the banks of the Charente, just a few hundred metres from the prestigious Cognac Houses

we suggest *Camping de COGNAC* ★★★

Open 1 May - 15 October, in very attractive surroundings - 160 pitches, perfectly equipped, (snack - shop - swimming pool - volley-ball - entertainment, etc)

And only a few kilometres from the Gulf of Cognac at SAINT-BRICE, the Riding Centre at CHERVES-RICHEMONT, the Tennis Centre at SAINT-BRICE

For information and reservations contact:

Office de Tourisme, 16 rue du XIV Juillet, 16100 COGNAC. Tel: 05.45.82.10.71 Fax: 05.45.82.34.47 or Communauté de Communes de COGNAC, 16108 COGNAC-Cedex. Tel: 05.45.36.55.36. Fax: 05.45.36.55.29

1705 Camping L'Orée du Bois, La Fouasse, Les Mathes

Large, attractive site amidst beautiful pines and oaks of the Forêt de la Coubre.

L'Orée du Bois has 388 pitches of about 100 sq.m. in a very spacious, pinewood setting with 150 for touring units. These include 40 extra large pitches with hardstanding and individual sanitary facilities (built in small, neat blocks of four and containing your own shower, toilet, washbasin and washing up sink). Pitches are on flat, fairly sandy ground, separated by trees, shrubs and growing hedges and all have electrical connections (6A). The forest pines offer shade. The four main sanitary blocks are attractively designed with good modern fittings. They have British style WCs and free hot water to the controllable showers and the washbasins (in cabins). Three blocks have a laundry room, washing up under cover and fully equipped units for disabled people. The excellent bar, restaurant and crêperie have terraces overlooking the large pools,which include a water toboggan, and paddling pool (no shorts). A covered pool has been added. Takeaway and well stocked shop. Tennis court, boules, games room, TV lounge (with satellite), bicycle hire, two sand based children's play areas, volleyball, table tennis and new football and basketball areas. Twice weekly discos and free, all day children's entertainment are organised in July/Aug. Exchange facilities. Fairly near are sandy beaches (lifeguard in season), plus opportunities for walking, riding or cycling in the 10,000 hectare forest. Fishing 4 km, riding 300 m, golf 20 km. Rules are specific about silence 23.30 - 07.00 (except when entertainment is organised). Barbecues allowed in special areas. Caravans and mobile homes (45) for hire. Used by tour operators.

Directions: From the north follow D14 La Tremblade road. At Arvert turn onto D141 to Les Mathes and turn east, signed La Palmyre, to second roundabout where site signed. From the south, at Royan take D25 towards La Palmyre, then towards Les Mathes to roundabout where site is signed. Note: there is now a new roundabout with a boat on it - follow sign for La Tremblade. Site is signed from this road, and this way is said to be quicker.

Charges 1999: Per unit incl. 2 persons Ffr 90.00 - 160.00, with private sanitary facilities 130.00 - 210.00; extra person (over 3 yrs) 25.00; local tax 2.00 (child 4-10 yrs 1.00); animal 10.00. Less 10-15% for booked stays of 21 or 28 days. Min. 7 days in high season. No credit cards.

Open: 15 May - 15 September.

Reservations: Made with 30% deposit plus fee (Ffr 130). Address: 225 Rte. de la Bouverie, La Fouasse, 17570 Les Mathes. Tel: (0)5.46.22.42.43. FAX: (0)5.46.22.54.76. Internet: www.oree-du-bois.fr.

France - Charente-Maritime

1704 Camping International Bonne Anse Plage, La Palmyre

See colour advert between pages 96/97

Spacious, well organised, family run site amongst shady pine trees with large pool.

On the edge of the Forêt de la Coubre, just beyond the popular resort of La Palmyre, Bonne Anse has a lovely setting amongst pine trees, just a short stroll from the sweeping sands which almost surround an interesting inlet from the sea (now very tidal). It is a gently undulating site, designed to provide 860 level, marked pitches, of which 600 have electricity (6-8A). Most are shaded by the pines, the ones nearer the sea, less so (these are rather more sandy). Amenities are centred around the well designed entrance and reception building and include a restaurant (20/6-28/8) and bar with a spacious outdoor terrace which forms a social focus overlooking the boules area. Opposite is a lively pool complex with a heated pool (35 x 25m), two water toboggans and a splash pool with water slide. Shopping centre (all season) with supermarket, excellent delicatessen and takeaway, crêperie, shops for bread and pastries, holiday goods and papers, and a launderette, plus visiting traders' stalls (wines, seafood, etc) in high season. Children have a good playground, large video games room, TV (satellite), minigolf and table tennis. Entertainment and dancing in season. Fishing 1 km, riding 3 km, golf 5 km, plus watersports and tennis near. The site has direct access to cycle tracks (bicycle hire available) which avoid the main road and there are many supervised, safe beaches close, also a fitness track. Seven sanitary blocks (including two new ones and with further replacements planned) provide free hot water, washbasins in cabins, British style toilets with a few Turkish, hot (controllable in the new blocks) and cold showers and facilities for disabled visitors and babies. Washing up and laundry sinks under cover. English is spoken and rallies welcomed with visit programmes organised. Motorcaravan services. Exchange facilities. No dogs are accepted. Many (140) mobile homes for rent. Used by tour operators (150 pitches).

Directions: Leave A10 autoroute at Saintes and head for Royan (N150). In Royan take signs for La Palmyre (D25). At La Palmyre roundabout follow signs for Ronce-les-Bains and site is 1 km. on the left.

Charges 1998: Per unit incl. 3 persons Ffr. 157.00, 1 or 2 persons 131.00; local tax 2.00 or child (4-10 yrs) 1.00; extra person (over 1 yr) 38.00; electricity (6A) 25.00. Up to 40% discount on reservation. Credit cards accepted.

Open: 22 May - 5 September.

Reservations: Min. 5 days - phone, fax or write for details. Address: 17570 La Palmyre. Tel: (0)5.46.22.40.90. FAX: (0)5.46.22.42.30. E-mail: bonne-anse@wanadoo.fr. Internet: http://oda.fr/aa/bonne-anse-plage.

AR Discount
Less 15%
before 20/6

1713 Camping-Caravaning L'Ile Blanche, La Flotte, Ile de Ré

Good quality wooded site with covered pool.

In a popular holiday area, L'Ile Blanche is a good quality site. It provides 85 spacious touring pitches (120 sq.m.) all fully equipped with 10A electricity, water and drainage, together with 122 mobile homes (most privately owned). Under medium sized, mixed trees, it is a shady and pleasant environment with hard access roads. Two sanitary blocks, well designed and maintained, provide good facilities with free hot showers and washbasins mostly in cabins. Dishwashing and laundry sink in each block. Chemical disposal and motorcaravan service facilities. Smart, modern buildings by the entrance provide reception, shop (July/Aug) and a large restaurant/bar, open all season with takeaway. The restaurant overlooks the swimming pool, which is cleverly protected in poor weather by a sliding glass cover, and a children's pool, both with paved surrounds, plus a large, sandy children's play area. Entertainment is organised in season. Fishing, bicycle hire, riding 1 km, golf 10 km. The beaches and holiday villages of the Ile de Ré are within easy driving distance and there is a network of cycle paths in the area.

Directions: Cross bridge to Ile de Ré and follow La Flotte bypass on D735 signed St Martin de Ré. Site is approx. 1 km. after roundabout. Turning (to left) is quite narrow and sharp.

Charges 1999: Per pitch Ffr. 40.00 - 73.00; extra adult 27.00 - 39.00 (local tax incl.); child (under 16 yrs) 17.00 - 24.00; animal 8.00 - 12.00; electricity 19.00. Credit cards accepted.

Open: 1 April - 11 November.

Reservations: Contact site for details. Address: Déviation de La Flotte, 17630 La Flotte de Ré. Tel: (0)5.46.09.52.43. FAX: (0)5.46.09.36.94.

AR Discount
Welcome
refreshments

1714 Castel Camping Séquoia Parc, Saint Just-Luzac

New, top class site in the grounds of a château, with swimming pool.

A brand new campsite which opened in 1997, and has already been extended, Sequoia Park is set in the grounds of La Josephtrie, a very striking château, and offers high quality facilities. It has beautifully restored outbuildings and a spacious courtyard which is regally approached by a tree lined avenue. Reception is large, light and airy, with original beams and rough cast walls, and leads out to a courtyard housing shop, restaurant/bar (15/5-15/9) with takeaway. The site has been designed to a high specification to create an atmosphere that most will appreciate. The pitches are of 140 sq.m. and all have electricity (by '99 most will be fully serviced). They are separated by young shrubs but these have a way to go before they provide shade. The site is surrounded by mature trees and woodland. Three luxurious sanitary blocks have washbasins in cubicles and units with washbasin and shower. *continued overleaf*

1714 Castel Camping Séquoia Parc (continued)

Laundry, dishwashing, chemical disposal, facilities for disabled visitors and babies. The pool complex is impressive (and very popular) with a paddling pool and sunbathing terrace, shrubs and flower beds. Tennis, volleyball, a football field, games and TV room and bicycle hire, plus organised entertainment in July/Aug. Motorcaravan service point. Mobile homes to hire. Used by tour operators (23%). Already this is a popular site and reservation is necessary in July/Aug. 'Camping Cheque'

Directions: Site is 2.5 km. southeast of Marennes. From Rochefort take D733 south for 12 km. Turn west on D123 to Ile d'Oléron. Continue for 12 km. and turn southeast on D728 towards Saintes. Site clearly signed, 1 km. on left.

Charges 1998: Per unit incl. 2 persons and electricity Ffr. 90.00 - 150.00; extra person 20.00 - 27.00; child under 3 free, 3-7 yrs 12.00 - 17.00; local tax 2.00 (over 10 yrs).

Open: 1 May - 30 September.

Reservations: Made to site with Ffr. 120 deposit. Address: 17320 Saint Just-Luzac. Tel: (0)5.46.85.55.55. FAX: (0)5.46.85.55.56. For reservations from Ireland contact G and R Boyce, 6 Lynda Crescent, Jordanstown, Co. Antrim BT37 0NS. Tel/Fax: 01232/867988.

2001 Camping Arinella Bianca, Ghisonaccia

Very well designed, family run, beach side site on Corsica's east coast.

This site is a tribute to its owner's design and development skills as it appears to be in entirely natural 'glades' where, in fact, these have been created from former marshland with a fresh water lake. The 300 marked pitches, 164 for touring units and all with 6A electricity, are on flat grass among a variety of trees and shrubs, providing ample shade. They are irregularly arranged, but are all of a good size. The site is right beside a beach of soft sand which extends a long way either side of the attractive central complex of restaurant, shop, bar, amphitheatre, snack bar, etc. (all 15/5-15/9) which, together with the swimming pool, form the hub of this site. Four open plan sanitary blocks have free pre-set hot showers in large cubicles (some with dressing area), washbasins in cabins and mainly British style WCs. Open air dishwashing areas and a laundry with washing machines. Large range of sports and leisure facilities at, or adjacent to, the site, including windsurfing, canoeing, fishing, volleyball, bicycle hire, tennis, riding, children's mini-club and play area and a disco, plus an entertainment programme in the main season. Used by tour operators (71 pitches). Chalets and mobile homes for rent (60). 'Camping Cheque'

Directions: From N198 after entering Ghisonaccia look out for 'Route de la Mer' (D144) and site is on left (narrow turn) approaching south end of village (many other sites also signed at turn leading to site).

Charges 1998: Per unit incl. 2 adults Ffr. 99.00 - 129.00; 'grand confort' pitch plus 19.00; extra person 29.00 - 39.00; child (up to 7 yrs) free - 19.00; electricity (6A) 18.00; local tax 3.00 (child 1.00). Credit cards accepted.

Open: 1 April - 15 October.

Reservations: Write to site. Address: 20240 Ghisonaccia. Tel: (0)4.95.56.04.78 or (0)4.95.56.12.54.

N2004 Camping Naturiste de Riva Bella, Aleria

Relaxed, informal naturist site beside glorious beach.

Arguably this is camping and caravanning at its very best. Although offering a large number and variety of pitches, they are in such a huge area of varied and beautiful countryside and seaside that it is difficult to believe it could ever become overcrowded. The site is divided into several distinct areas - pitches and bungalows, alongside the sandy beach, in a wooded glade with ample shade, behind the beach, or beside the lake/lagoon which is a feature of this site. The ground is undulating, so getting an absolutely level pitch could be a problem in the main season. Electricity is available in most parts (but long cables needed). The sanitary facilities are in several blocks and are fairly typical of naturist sites, with British WCs, hot water to open plan washbasins and free hot showers in open plan cubicles. The new blocks have facilities for disabled people and babies. Fridge hire. Besides the beautiful beach, there is a variety of activities including volleyball, aerobics, sauna, table tennis, archery, fishing, mountain bike hire, half-court tennis, etc. You can even spend your time observing the llamas. Riding 5 km, golf 7 km. An excellent restaurant (all season) with reasonable prices overlooks the lagoon and a snack bar by the beach in main season (1/6-30/9). Large well stocked shop (15/5-4/10). There is an interesting evening entertainment programme. Noël Pasqual is fully proud of his site and the fairly unobtrusive rules are designed to ensure that everyone is able to relax, whilst preserving the beauty of the environment. There is, for example, a restriction on cars in certain areas (ample free parking). No barbecues. Generally the ambience is relaxed and informal with nudity only obligatory on the beach itself.

Directions: Site is approx. 8 km. north of Aleria on the N198 (Bastia) road. Watch for signs and unmade road to it and follow for 4 km.

Charges 1999: Per unit incl. 2 persons Ffr. 69.00 - 115.00; extra person 27.00 - 40.00; child (0-7 yrs) 15.00 - 22.00; extra tent 14.00 - 36.00; electricity 20.00; local tax 1.00. Various off season discounts. Credit cards accepted.

Open: 8 May - 15 October.

Reservations: Made with deposit (Ffr. 500) and fee/cancellation insurance (170). Address: 20270 Aleria. Tel: (0)4.95.38.81.10 or (0)4.95.38.85.97. FAX: (0)4.95.38.91.29. Internet: http://w3.teaser.fr/corsenet.

AR Discount
Less 5%

France - Côtes-d'Armor / Creuse \ Dordogne

2204 Camping Le Châtelet, St Cast le Guildo, nr St Malo

Pleasant site with views over the bay and steep path down to beach.

Carefully developed over the years from a former quarry, Le Châtelet is pleasantly and quietly situated with views over the estuary. It is well laid out, mainly in terraces, with 220 pitches of good size marked by hedges, all with electricity and 30 with water and drainage. A `green' walking area is a nice feature around the lower edge of the site. The narrow gravel access roads can make life awkward for larger units and make the site dusty in breezy weather. The two toilet blocks have mainly British style WCs, washbasins in cabins and pre-set free hot water in these and the showers. Small units for night use are at the extremities of the site. Parts of the blocks may be closed outside July/Aug. Chemical disposal and motorcaravan services. A little lake (unfenced) with some pitches around it can be used for fishing. An attractive, landscaped area has a heated pool and children's pool (from 15/5). Small children's play area. Shop for basics, takeaway (1/6-5/9), bar lounge and general room with satellite TV, pool table; dancing weekly in season. Games room with table tennis, amusement machines. Organised games and activities in season. A path leads down to a beach (about 150 m. but including steps). St Cast, 1 km. away to the centre, has a very long beach with many opportunities for sail-boarding and other watersports. Bicycle hire, riding and golf within 1.5 km. Used by tour operators (102 pitches). Mobile homes for hire.

Directions: Best approach is to turn off D786 road at Matignon towards St Cast; just inside St Cast limits turn left at sign for `campings' and follow camp signs on C90.

Charges 1999: Per person Ffr 25.00 - 30.00; child (under 7) 15.00 - 20.00; pitch 70.00 - 90.00, large pitch 77.00 - 103.00; electricity 6A 20.00, 10A 23.00; local tax 2.00 (high season only). No credit cards.

Open: 1 May - 1 September.

Reservations: Necessary for July/Aug. and made (min. 1 week) with deposit (Ffr. 250) and booking fee (130). Address: Rue des Nouettes, 22380 St Cast le Guildo. Tel: (0)2.96.41.96.33. FAX: (0)2.96.41.97.99.

AR Discount
Details
from site

2301 Castel Camping Le Château de Poinsouze, Boussac-Bourg

Well designed, high quality site, set in a beautiful château parkland.

Le Château de Poinsouze is a recently developed site with 102 pitches arranged on the open, gently sloping, grassy park to one side of the château's main drive - a beautiful oak tree avenue. The 94 touring pitches, some with lake frontage, all have electricity (6/10A), with water, waste water and sewage connections to many. A high quality sanitary unit is entered via a large utility area equipped with dishwashing and laundry sinks, sinks accessible for wheelchair users, a drinks machine, and two smaller rooms with washing machine, dryer and ironing. Four spacious rooms house British WCs, washbasins (some in cubicles), and roomy controllable showers. Baby baths, changing mats and child's WC, two suites for disabled people. Hot water is free. The children's playground has been designed with safety in mind. Behind reception is a good motorcaravan service point. The château (not open to the public) lies across the lake. Well restored outbuildings on the opposite side of the drive house a well stocked shop, takeaway, and a comfortable bar with games and TV and library room above. These surround the attractively designed, well fenced, swimming pool with waterslide, children's pool and terrace (all free), and are within an easy stroll of the camping area. Bicycle hire, free fishing in the lake (if you put the fish back); boats and lifejackets can be hired. Table tennis, pool table and table football games. A restaurant is planned. The site has a friendly family atmosphere, there are activities in main season including dances, children's games, triathlons, and marked walks. A large area is set aside for football, volleyball, basketball, badminton and other games. Dogs not accepted in high season. All facilities open all season, though times may vary. Mobile homes and tents for rent. Gîtes to rent all year. A top class site with a formula which should ensure a enjoyable family holiday. The massive 12th/15th century fortress, Château de Boussac, is open daily all year. `Camping Cheque'

Directions: Site entrance is 2.5 km north of Boussac on D917 (towards La Châtre).

Charges 1999: Per pitch incl. 2 persons Ffr. 80.00 - 100.00, `confort' pitch with electricity (6A), water, waste water 120.00 - 145.00, `grand confort' pitch with electricity (10A), water, waste, sewage 130.00 - 155.00; extra adult 20.00 - 30.00; child (2-7 yrs) 15.00 - 22.00; electricity (10A) for confort pitch 10.00 - 15.00. Credit cards accepted.

Open: 30 April - 19 September.

Reservations: Advisable during July/Aug; made with 30% deposit and Ffr 120 fee. Address: BP 12, Route de la Châtre, 23600 Boussac-Bourg. Tel: (0)5.55.65.02.21. FAX: (0)5.55.65.86.49.

AR Discount
Less 15% excl. high season - GC pitches

2401 Castel Camping Château Le Verdoyer, Champs Romain, nr St Pardoux

Dutch owned site developed in park of restored Château Le Verdoyer.

With beautiful buildings and lovely surroundings, Le Verdoyer is situated in this lesser known area of the Dordogne referred to as the Périgord Vert, with green forests and small lakes. The 37 acre estate has two such lakes, one in front of the Château for fishing and one with a sandy beach and swimming area where canoeing and windsurfing for beginners are also possible.

continued overleaf

2401 Castel Camping Château Le Verdoyer (continued)

There are 150 marked, level, terraced pitches (some a little rocky). Mostly of a good size (100-150 sq.m), all have electricity, with a choice of wooded area or open field, where hedges have grown well; 120 are 'confort' pitches with more planned. A swimming pool complex has two pools (25 x 10 m. and 10 x 7 m; the smaller one can be covered in low season) and a paddling pool. In high season activities are organised for children aged 5-13 years. There is definitely no disco! The modern toilet block in the old barn buildings is good, containing showers, washbasins in cabins and British WCs. There is another very well appointed block and both blocks have facilities for disabled people, baby baths and hot water also for dishwashing. Serviced launderette, motorcaravan service point and fridge rental. Multi-purpose shop. The courtyard area between reception and the bar is home to evening activities, and provides a pleasant place to enjoy drinks and snacks from the bar, with takeaway. A good value bistro serves meals in July/Aug. All-weather tennis court, volleyball, basketball and badminton, table tennis, minigolf and bicycle hire (tennis and bicycles are free in low season). Children's play areas. Small library. Bungalows and mobile homes to rent. The Château has rooms to let and its excellent lakeside restaurant is also open to the public. Used sparingly by a Dutch tour operator. *Camping Cheque'* `FRENCH FLAVOUR'

Directions: Site is 2 km. from Limoges-Chalus-Nontron road, 20 km. south of Chalus, well signed from main road.

Charges 1999: Per person Ffr. 25.00 - 35.00; child (2 -7 yrs) 18.00 - 25.00; pitch 32.00 - 46.00, `confort' 36.00 - 51.00, `grand confort' incl. electricity 73.00 - 97.00; electricity (5A) 17.00. Credit cards accepted.

Open: 1 May - 30 September.

Reservations: Write to site. Address: 24470 Champs Romain. Tel: (0)5.53.56.94.64. FAX: (0)5.53.56.38.70. E-mail: chateau@verdoyer.fr. Internet: www.verdoyer.fr.

2403 Camping Les Périères, Sarlat

Good quality small site with large pitches and swimming pool very close to town.

This little site is in a pleasant setting amid attractive trees on the edge of Sarlat. It has 100 pitches mainly on terraces on a semi-circle of a fairly steep hillside with shade in many parts. Of very good size, all are equipped with electricity, water connections and drainaway. It becomes full late June - late Aug. but a proportion of the site is not reserved, so space could be found if you are early. The five sanitary blocks, of varying size, are of good quality and should be sufficient, providing washbasins mostly in cabins, and free hot water. Washing machines and dryers. On the more level ground there is a small swimming pool, a paddling pool and two tennis courts. A recent addition is an indoor spa pool, open all season. The main buildings house a small shop, pleasant bar and just beyond these, is a terrace restaurant with takeaway (15/6-15/9). Interestingly, the owners have made space for a library, where visitors can read, study or play board games and Dutch billiards. Other activities include table tennis (indoors or out), football ground, sauna and a fitness track with exercise halts. Bicycle hire 1 km, fishing 5 km, riding or golf 7 km. Motorcaravan service point. Good quality bungalows to let. The site has a spacious air and is quite free from overcrowding, and is one of the most thoughtfully improved sites visited.

Directions: Site is east of the town on the D47 road in the direction of `Sous-Préfecture' and towards Croix d'Alon.

Charges 1998: Per unit in high season, incl. up to 3 persons Ffr. 158.00, with electricity 181.00, 2 persons 144.00 or 167.00. Per unit in low season incl. up to 2 persons 111.00, with electricity 133.50; extra person 34.00; child (under 7 yrs) 20.00; local tax 2.50. No credit cards.

Open: Easter - 30 September.

Reservations: Made for min. 1 week with deposit (Ffr. 550 per week) and fee (80). Address: Rte. Ste Nathalène, 24203 Sarlat Cedex. Tel: (0)5.53.59.05.84. FAX: (0)5.53.28.57.51.

AR Discount
Free tennis
excl. 21/6-7/9

Camping Les Périères

24200 SARLAT, DORDOGNE - PÉRIGORD

The 4-star site in a natural amphitheatre of woods and meadows.
A peaceful oasis in the heart of Black Périgord, yet only half a mile from the medieval town and gastronomic centre of Sarlat.

LARGE INDIVIDUAL PITCHES - EXCELLENT TOILET BLOCKS
SWIMMING POOLS, one covered and heated - SAUNA
TENNIS COURTS - VOLLEYBALL - TABLE TENNIS
LOUNGE BAR - SHOP - LIBRARY

France - Dordogne

2404 Castel Camping Le Moulin du Roch, Sarlat

Family managed site midway between Sarlat and Les Eyzies.

Most of the 195 separated pitches at Le Moulin du Roch are in rows backing onto fences but there are also many levelled places in natural woodland providing shade. All pitches have electrical connections and some have water and drainage. The toilet blocks are of very good quality with free hot water throughout and British style WCs. A well equipped washing area even includes a dishwasher. On the site is a medium sized swimming pool and children's paddling pool, both open from May if conditions permit, but not heated. Small shop and new large restaurant and extensive takeaway. Children's playground, table tennis, bicycle hire, tennis, fishing lake and forest trails for walking. Canoeing nearby. High season entertainment and sporting activities including canoe trips. Golf 15 km, bicycle hire 15 km. Mobile homes to let. The site becomes full for most of July/Aug. but only a few pitches are taken by tour operators. A friendly management makes visitors feel very welcome. `Camping Cheque'

Directions: Site is 10 km. from Sarlat on the D47 road to Les Eyzies.

Charges 1999: Per pitch incl. 2 persons Ffr 70.00 - 124.00, with electricity 88.00 - 142.00, with full services 107.00 - 161.00; extra person (over 9 yrs) 15.00 - 27.00; child (4-9 yrs) free - 10.00; extra car 5.00 - 12.00; local tax 1.00 per person. No credit cards.

Open: 1 May - 19 September.

Reservations: Accepted from 1/1 with deposit (and Ffr. 120 fee in July/Aug. only). Address: Rte. des Eyzies D47, 24200 Sarlat en Perigord. Tel: (0)5.53.59.20.27. FAX: (0)5.53.29.44.65. E-mail: moulin.du.roch@wanadoo.fr.

2409 Camping Soleil Plage, Vitrac, nr Sarlat

Spacious site with enviable location beside the Dordogne.

The site is in one of the most attractive sections of the Dordogne Valley, right on the riverside. It is divided into two sections - one section of 56 pitches has its own toilet block and lies adjacent to the reception, bar, shop and restaurant complex (all 15/5-18/9), which is housed in a renovated farmhouse. It is also close to a small sandy river bank and canoe station, from which canoes and kayaks can be hired for down-river trips or transport up-river for a paddle back to the site. Near the reception area is a swimming pool, paddling pool, tennis court and minigolf. The friendly bar provides extensive takeaway including interesting `plat du jour'. The attractive restaurant serves excellent Perigourdine menus. The larger section of the site (124 pitches) is about 250 m. from the reception area, and offers river bathing from a sizeable pebble bank. All pitches are bounded by hedges and are of good size, and in this section there are a few giant pitches for large families. Most have good shade. Open air table tennis, volleyball court and a children's playground occupy part of a large central recreation space. Fishing on site, bicycle hire 2 km, golf 1 km, riding 5 km. Sanitary facilities are provided by two modern blocks, with washing machines, chemical disposal and motorcaravan services. TV room. Various activities are organised including walks and sports tournaments. A weekly `soirée' usually involves a barbecue or paella, with band and lots of wine - worth catching! The site is increasingly popular, though in late August it begins to empty. Used by tour operators (80 pitches). A `Sites et Paysages' member.

Directions: Site is 8 km south of Sarlat. Take D704 and it is signed from Montfort castle. Coming from the west on D703, turn first right 1 or 2 km. after the bridge at Vitrac-Port, and follow the signs.

Charges 1999: Per person Ffr. 33.00; child (under 10 yrs) 20.00; pitch 53.00; local tax 1.00 (over 10s) in high season; dog 10.00; electricity (10A) 20.00. Less outside 20/6-1/9. Credit cards accepted.

Open: 1 May - 30 September.

Reservations: Essential July - early Aug. and made for exact dates: min. 1 week with deposit and fee; send for booking form. Address: Vitrac, 24200 Sarlat. Tel: (0)5.53.28.33.33. FAX: (0)5.53.29.36.87.

2415 Camping Les Deux Vallées, Beynac, Vézac

Developing woodland site in the heart of the Dordogne.

This site is enviably situated almost under the shadow of Beynac Castle. There are 110 flat, marked touring pitches, all of good size, and some generous, divided by trees and shrubs, all with electricity (6A). There is plenty of shade and the general feel is of unspoilt but well managed woodland. The main modern toilet block gives ample provision, with British style WCs, good access for disabled people and chemical disposal. A second smaller block is heated for off-season use. A good sized pool and children's pool provide on-site swimming from mid May, and it is a short distance to the Dordogne. A small lake, with island and tree-house, is for fishing or just sitting beside, and there are bicycle hire, volleyball, basketball, minigolf, boules, table tennis, table football and an intriguing outdoor pool game. Riding 4 km, golf 8 km. The owners run French courses (in low seasons) and quiz nights are a feature in the main season. Shop and bar/restaurant (both 1/4-30/9) which serves good value snacks and more ambitious meals to take away, eat inside or on the terrace. Another surprise is English breakfast! The site is being steadily upgraded by its British/Dutch owners who assure a very friendly welcome. Mobile homes and chalets to rent and some tour operator pitches (not mobile homes). A single track railway runs along the eastern boundary (trains are relatively infrequent). *continued overleaf*

2415 Camping Les Deux Vallées (continued)

Directions: Take D703 from Bergerac, go through Beynac and, just past village, left towards Sarlat on D57/D49. Shortly after, turn left and site is signed from here. This route involves a narrow railway bridge - to avoid continue on Sarlat road for a few hundred metres turning left at further site sign, cross unmanned level crossing and on to site.

Charges 1998: Per pitch Ffr. 18.00 - 36.00; adult 13.00 - 26.00; child (3-7 yrs) 8.00 - 16.00, free under 3; local tax (over 10 yrs) 2.00; first extra tent free, 2nd 5.00 - 10.00; electricity 6A 16.00, 10A 20.00; dog 3.00 - 6.00. Less 5-10% for stays over 14 days outside 15/7-15/8. No credit cards.

Open: All year.

Reservations: Advised for July/Aug. and made with deposit (Ffr 550) and fee (50). Address: 24220 Vézac. Tel: (0)5.53.29.53.55. FAX: (0)5.53.31.09.81. E-mail: les2vall@easynet.fr.

2408 Camping-Caravaning Le Moulin de David, Gaugeac, Monpazier

Secluded valley site with pool, on southwest of the Dordogne.

Owned and run by a French family who continually seek to improve it, this pleasant little site is one for those who enjoy peace, away from the hustle and bustle of larger sites closer to the main Dordogne attractions. Set in 14 ha. of wooded countryside, it has 131 pitches, 80 for touring units. Some are large, spacing is good and all have electricity. They are split into two sections; 35 below the central reception complex in a shaded situation, and 75 above on partly terraced ground with varying degrees of shade. The site has been attractively planted with a pleasing variety of shrubs and trees. Two well appointed sanitary blocks (one in each part) are well kept with British WCs and washbasins in cabins. Baby bath rooms and washrooms for disabled people in both blocks. Chemical disposal, dishwashing and laundry sinks, plus laundry. The reception block embraces a restaurant (doubles as games room), bar with shaded patio and takeaway. Good shop. A sun terrace abuts two swimming pools, one for small children. Children's play area and a small lake with water toboggan. Some events and games organised. Boules, half-court tennis, table tennis (own bats), volleyball, trampoline and bicycle hire. Canoe trips (with lunch). Riding 3 km, fishing 700 m. Library. Delightful wooded walk via long distance footpath (GR 36) to Château Biron, about 2-3 km distance. The Bastide town of Monpazier is also in walking distance. Tents, apartments, mobile homes and caravans for hire. Used minimally by a tour operator (15 pitches). A quiet, clean, well managed site. A 'Sites et Paysages' member.

Directions: Site is just south off the Monpazier - Villeréal road (D2), about 2 km. west of Monpazier.

Charges 1998: Per pitch Ffr. 24.50 - 45.00; person 20.00 - 33.50; child (under 2 yrs) free; extra child's tent 7.00 - 10.00; electricity 3A 19.00, 6A 23.00. Credit cards accepted.

Open: 13 May - 11 September.

Reservations: Advisable for Jul/Aug. with Ffr. 300 deposit plus fee (100). Address: Gaugeac, 24540 Monpazier. Tel: (0)5.53.22.65.25. FAX: (0)5.53.23.99.76. E-mail: moulin.de.david@wanadoo.fr.

2503 Camping du Bois de Reveuge, Huanne-Montmartin

New hill-side site with summer activities.

As du Bois de Reveuge was only opened in 1992 it still has a new look about it, in as much as there is little shade yet from the young trees. The enthusiastic owner has installed a good solar heated swimming pool with a lifeguard and swimming lessons. Being on a hillside, the pitches are on terraces with good views across the surrounding countryside and leading down to two lakes which may be used for fishing and canoeing. The site has private use of a 10 hectare lake set in a park 10 km. away where there is a watersport school and other boating opportunities. Tall trees have been left standing at the top of the hill where there are a few pitches, although most of these have been used for mobile homes for hire. The 200 pitches for tourists each have a water supply as well as electricity at 6A, and will eventually grass over. In high season there is a kiosk for basic food supplies and a restaurant with terrace. Four children's play areas are being developed. Three modern sanitary blocks, well spaced around the site, have British and Turkish style WCs and free hot water in showers, sinks and basins (mainly in cabins). High season `baby club', some entertainment for adults. Groups may request activities such as orienteering. A package deal includes use of canoes, boats and sailboards, as well as archery, fishing and pedaloes. For an extra charge, rock climbing, potholing and rowing on the river Ognon can be organised. Bicycle hire.

> **Directions:** The site is well signed from the D50 road. From the A36 autoroute south of the site, take exit for Baume-les-Dames and head north on D50 towards Villersexel for about 12 km. to camp signs.
>
> **Charges guide:** Per unit incl. 2 adults Ffr 100.00 - 160.00; extra person 15.00 - 30.00, 2-6 yrs 10.00 - 20.00.
>
> **Open:** 1 May - 30 September.
>
> **Reservations:** Made with Ffr. 70 deposit - contact site. Address: 25680 Huanne-Montmartin. Tel: (0)3.81.84.38.60. FAX: (0)3.81.84.44.04.

2602 Castel Camping du Château de Sénaud, Albon, nr Tournon

Pleasant site convenient for the autoroute or a longer stay.

Château du Sénaud, near the N7 south of Vienne, makes a useful stopover on the way south, but one could enjoy a longer stay to explore the surrounding villages and mountains. It is one of the original sites in the Castel chain and is still run with character and attention by Mme. Comtesse d'Armagnac. There are a fair number of permanent caravans used at weekends, but it also has some 85 pitches in tourist areas, some with shade, some with views across the Rhône valley. Electricity and water are available on all pitches. Swimming pool with water toboggan (1/5-15/9, depending on weather) and a tennis court. Four sanitary blocks have hot water in basins, showers and sinks, British and one Turkish style toilets, washbasins in cabins, some en-suite with shower in one block, and facilities for babies. Washing machine, chemical disposal and motorcaravan services. Shop (15/5-15/9). Bar, takeaway and good value small restaurant with simple menu (all 15/6-15/9). Fishing, bicycle hire, table tennis, a bowling alley and minigolf. Golf course adjacent and there are walks. Riding 6 km. Possibly some noise from the autoroute. Mobile homes and chalets to rent. Caravan storage. `Camping Cheque'

> **Directions:** Leave autoroute at Chanas exit, proceed south on N7 for 8 km. then east near Le Creux de la Thine to site. From south exit autoroute for Tain-Tournon and proceed north, approaching site on D122 through St Vallier then D172 towards Anneyron to site.
>
> **Charges 1998:** Per person Ffr. 26.00; child (under 7) 15.00; pitch 36.00; dog 10.00; visitor 10.00; electricity 6A 18.00, 10A 21.00. No credit cards.
>
> **Open:** 1 March - 31 October.
>
> **Reservations:** Made with deposit for min. 3 nights. Address: 26140 Albon. Tel: (0)4.75.03.11.31. FAX: (0)4.75.03.08.06.

AR Discount
Less 10% per week in late season; bike ride

2603 Camping Le Grand Lierne, Chabeuil, nr Valence

Conveniently and attractively situated family site on the route south.

In addition to its obvious attraction as an overnight stop, fairly convenient for the A7 autoroute, this site provides a pleasant base to explore this little known area between the Ardèche and the Vercors mountains and the Côte du Rhône wine area. It has 140 marked pitches, 76 for touring units. Mainly separated by developing hedges or oak trees, with good shade, some on flat grass, all have electricity (6/10A). A more open area exists for those who prefer less shade and a view of the mountains. A varied entertainment programme has a particular emphasis on activities for children, with excursions, both organised and informal. A disco for teenagers is organised by the owner's sons but is well managed to avoid noise. Two swimming pools, one covered and heated in low season (no bermuda shorts allowed in pool), a paddling pool and a 50 m. water slide. A bar/snack bar with terrace provides both `eating in' and takeaway (all season). Two modern sanitary blocks have hot showers, British style WCs and washbasins in cabins. Facilities for disabled people, small WC for children, chemical disposal, dishwashing area under cover (H&C) and washing machines and dryer (fairly expensive and no outdoor lines permitted, although some are provided). Shop, mini-tennis, children's playgrounds and trampoline, minigolf, table tennis, volleyball, a football field, small climbing wall and bicycle hire. Library. Bureau de change. Fridge rental. Motorcaravan service point. Fishing 3 km, riding 7 km, golf 3 km, archery and hang gliding near. No pets allowed in July/Aug. Barbecues provided in special areas. Used by tour operators (25 pitches). Bungalows, chalets and tents for hire. Caravan storage. The owners wish to keep a balance between nationalities and are also keen to encourage rallies and will arrange visit programmes. English spoken. A `Sites et Paysages' member. `Camping Cheque'

Directions: Site signed in Chabeuil about 11 km. east of Valence (18 km. from autoroute). It is best to approach Chabeuil from the south side of Valence via the Valence ring road, thence onto the D68 to Chabeuil itself.

Charges 1999: Per unit, incl. 2 adults Ffr 90.00 - 134.00; extra person 35.00; child (under 7 yrs) 28.00; electricity 6A 22.00, 10A 32.00; refrigerator rental 25.00; local tax 1.00. Credit cards accepted.

Open: 1 April - 30 September, with all services.

Reservations: Accepted with deposit (Ffr. 600) and fee (180). Address: BP.8, 26120 Chabeuil. Tel: (0)4.75.59.83.14. FAX: (0)4.75.59.87.95. Internet: www.grandlierne.com.

2604 Camping-Caravaning Le Couspeau, Poët Célard

Pleasant small site in picturesque area, near the village of Bourdeaux.

The approach is via a steep road, and with several hairpin bends to negotiate care is required. However, the views are reward enough, as a magnificent landscape of mountains and valleys unfolds. Developed from a hillside farm, with some buildings being 250 years old, the overall impression of beauty and tranquillity is reflected in the amiable attitude of the owners, who maintain a helpful, yet low profile, relaxed presence. Access to the 67 pitches (all with electricity) is reasonably easy; however, large motorcaravans or twin-axle caravans may experience some difficulty manoeuvring into position. Levelling blocks are also handy as some of the terraced pitches are slightly sloping. Mature trees provide shade and there are numerous water and rubbish points around the site. The two new sanitary blocks were spotless when seen. Laundry and dishwashing sinks are incorporated along with washing machines and a dryer in one block; this block also houses facilities for disabled campers. A small shop meets basic needs and a little restaurant/bar provides inexpensive meals and takeaway dishes (all 15/6-28/8), plus entertainment on two evenings per week. In addition to the main pool is another smaller, under cover one (heated in low season) plus a toddlers' pool. The cleanliness of all pools is exceptional whilst their proximity to the splendid children's play area means a watchful eye can be kept at all times. During high season an animation programme is arranged for young children, although teenagers may find the opportunities and location of the site rather restricting. Amenities include tennis and minigolf, supplemented by supervised family walking and cycling trips in the immediate area. Mountain bikes are for hire from the site, with guidance and advice on routes, should you wish to explore at your own pace. Rafting and canoeing available nearby, riding 15 km, fishing 5 km. Those who seek to unwind and relax should appreciate the delightful scenery and setting of this small site. Chalets, tents and mobile homes for hire. A `Sites et Paysages' member.

Directions: From Crest take D538 (signed Bourdeaux) and turn right onto D328B (signed Le Poët Célard). At T-junction turn right onto the D328 towards village then left onto D328A. The site is a short distance on the left.

Charges 1999:: Per unit incl. 2 persons Ffr 72.00 - 110.00; extra person 22.00 - 32.00; child 10.00 - 22.00; animal; free - 6.00; local tax 1.00; electricity 3A 15.00, 6A 18.00. No credit cards or Eurocheques.

Open: 1 May - 30 September.

Reservations: Advised for July/Aug. and made with deposit (Ffr 500) and fee (100). Address: 26460 Le Poët Célard. Tel: (0)4.75.53.30.14. FAX: (0)4.75.53.37.23.

AR Discount
Less 10% in low season

France - Finistère

2901 Castel Camping Ty Nadan, Arzano, nr Quimperlé

See colour advert opposite page 96

Country site beside the River Ellé, with swimming pools.

Ty Nadan is set deep in the countryside in the grounds of a country house 18 km. from the sea. It has 220 pitches, 160 with electricity, of good size on fairly flat grass, some on the banks of the river. The two toilet blocks are of an unusual design with access from different levels and are of fair quality. The blocks have British style WCs and free hot water in the washbasins (in cabins), sinks and showers. Access for disabled people may be a little difficult, though there are facilities in one block. Dishwashing facilities and laundry room. Heated swimming pool, pool with water slides and children's paddling pool (all 8/5-5/9), a small beach on the river, tennis, table tennis, pool tables, archery and trampolines. Riding is offered, bicycles, skateboards, roller skates and boats may be hired and there are facilities for fishing, canoeing and a small roller skating rink. Many activities are organised for children in season, particularly sports, excursions, etc. and including guided mountain bike tours and canoeing trips (daily in season to Quimperlé, returning by bus). Restaurant (w/ends only outside July/Aug), takeaway, bar and shop (all 23/5-5/9). Across the road, by the attractive house and garden in converted Breton outbuildings, a TV room, delightful crêperie and a disco. Tents, mobile homes and chalets for hire.

Directions: Make for Arzano which is northeast of Quimperlé on the Pontivy road and turn off D22 just west of village at camp sign.

Charges 1999: Per person Ffr. 30.00; child (under 7) 18.00; pitch 60.00; electricity (10A) 22.00; water/drainage 30.00; dog 12.00. Credit cards accepted.

Open: 8 May - 5 September.

Reservations: Made for exact dates with deposit (Ffr. 200) and fee (100). Address: Rte d'Arzano, 29310 Locunolé. Tel: (0)2.98.71.75.47. FAX: (0)2.98.71.77.31. E-mail: ty-nadan@wanadoo.fr. Internet: camping-ty-nadan.com.

AR Discount
Less 5% on pitch fee

2912 Camping Manoir de Kerlut, Plobannalec, nr Pont l'Abbé

See colour advert opposite page 96

Comfortable site in grounds of manor house on river estuary.

This site has neat, modern buildings and is laid out on flat grass in the grounds of the old 'manoir'. It provides 240 pitches, of which 165 are for touring units. All have electricity (5, 6 or 10A), many have water and drainage also and hardstanding is available on around ten pitches. One area is rather open with separating hedges planted, the other part being amongst mature bushes and some trees which provide shade. Sanitary facilities are in two good blocks, each with several rooms (not all open outside July/Aug). There are controllable hot showers, washbasins in cabins, British style WCs and chemical disposal, facilities for babies and disabled people and hot water is free. Amenities are good with a large modern bar with TV and entertainment in season, two heated swimming pools with children's pool, small shop, takeaway (all from 15/5), sauna, solarium and small gym. Tennis, volleyball, badminton, petanque, children's play area, games room and bicycle hire. Fishing 2 km, riding 3 km, golf 20 km. Exchange facilities. Laundry. Mobile homes and bungalows to rent. Used by tour operators (20 pitches).

Directions: From Pont l'Abbé, on D785, take D102 to Lesconil. Site is signed left, shortly after Plobannalec village.

Charges 1999: Per person 20.00 - 29.00; child (under 7 yrs) 10.00 - 15.00; pitch incl. car 50.00 - 96.00; electricity 2A 10.00, 5A 16.00, 10A 20.00. Credit cards accepted.

Open: 1 May - 15 September.

Reservations: Write to site with deposit (Ffr. 300) and fee (120). Address: 29740 Plobannalec-Lesconil. Tel: (0)2.98.82.23.89 FAX: (0)2.98.82.26.49.

AR Discount
Less 10% excl. 13/7-18/8

2904 Camping Le Vorlen, Beg-Meil, nr Quimper

Large, informal family site with pool, adjacent to sandy beach - family managed.

This spacious, unpretentious site is on 24 acres of level ground in a rural setting and caters for a wide variety of tastes with good sized pitches in a number of small 'bays' or meadows. Nature predominates creating an impression of tranquillity unusual in such a large site. The atmosphere is pleasantly laid-back and relaxed, with easy access (about 200 m.) to a long sandy south facing beach. Two thirds of the 600 pitches have electricity. Two modern toilet blocks have ample showers, free hot water, cabins, British toilets, and many sinks for washing up. In the two original blocks, in the older part of the site, the showers and washbasins have been modernised and baby baths provided (one unit for disabled people). British style WCs, all with external entry. Swimming pool (10/6-10/9) and paddling pool. Mini market and takeaway (27/6-1/9). Launderette. Torch useful. Children's play area. Bar in season just outside site entrance. Fishing, bicycle hire within 1 km. English is spoken. Mobile homes for hire.

Directions: Follow signs to Beg-Meil village; site is signed from there.

Charges 1998: Per unit incl. 2 adults Ffr. 103.00; extra person 24.00; child (under 7) 14.00; extra vehicle 8.00; electricity (6A) 15.00; local tax 1.80 (10-16 yrs 0.90). Less 20% outside 29/6-1/9. Credit cards accepted.

Open: 1 May - 20 September

Reservations: Write with deposit (Ffr. 200) and fee (50) by eurocheque or credit card. Address: 29170 Fouesnant, Beg-Meil. Tel: (0)2.98.96.97.36. FAX: (0)2.98.94.97.23.

Camping Le TY NADAN ★ ★ ★ ★

In the heart of the countryside, a stone's throw from the sea !

Southern Brittany

Route d'Arzano
29310 Locunolé

Tel. (33)2 98 71 75 47
Fax. (33)2 98 71 77 31

http:// www.camping-ty-nadan.fr

LES CASTELS
CAMPING & CARAVANING

Manoir de Kerlut

★ ★ ★ ★ Camp Site
in Southern Brittany

Camping L'Hippocampe **** NN

12km south of Sisteron, département Alpes de Haute Provence.
A very peaceful site 430m above sea level situated beside the lake with shade from olive and cherry trees. Only 600m from Volonne, a small provencal village.

2 SWIMMING POOLS with a surface area of 500m². Tennis, Archery, Organised Sports and Special Evening Shows. Guided activities: Rambling, Rafting, Mountain Biking, Canyoning (Gorges du Verdon)
Mobile Homes to hire, equipped with Satellite TV and telephones.
Bungalows and Trigano Tents to hire.
Heated Swimming Pool open from 1st May.

**L'Hippocampe
Route Napoléon
04290 VOLONNE**

**Tel: 04.92.33.50.00
Fax: 04.92.33.50.49**

Reservations advised

Bonne Anse
Plage

★ ★ ★ ★

Up to 40% discount on reservations

**Camping,
Caravanning
17570 Les Mathes
FRANCE**

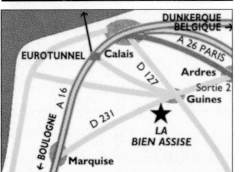

2905 Castel Camping L'Orangerie de Lanniron, Quimper

Beautiful, quiet site in mature grounds of riverside estate, 15 km. from the sea.

This is a peaceful, family site in 10 acres of a XVIIth century, 42 acre country estate on the banks of the Odet river. It is just to the south of Quimper and about 15 km. from the sea and beaches at Bénodet. The family have a five year programme to restore and rehabilitate the park, the original canal, fountains, ornamental Lake of Neptune, the boat-house and the gardens and avenues. The original outbuildings have been attractively converted around a walled courtyard which includes a heated swimming pool (144 sq.m.) with children's pool and a small play area. There are 200 grassy pitches, 149 for touring units, of three types (varying in size and services) on fairly flat ground laid out in rows alongside access roads. Most have electricity and 32 have all three services, with shrubs and bushes providing pleasant pitches. The original sanitary block, along one side of the courtyard, is good, with free hot water in all services. A second modern block serves the newer pitches at the top of the site. They have British toilets, washbasins in private cabins, showers and facilities for disabled people and babies. Shop. Bar, including Cyber café connected to the Web, snacks and takeaway, plus a restaurant in the beautiful XVIIth century Orangerie with very attractive views across the gardens (open daily to the public, reasonably priced and with children's menu). The Gardens are also open to the public and when we visited in May, rhododendrons and azaleas were magnificent, with lovely walks within the grounds. General reading, games and billiards rooms. Activities include tennis, minigolf, attractively set among mature trees, table tennis, fishing, archery and bicycle hire. Children's adventure playground and some farm animals. Karaoke. Animation is provided with a large room for indoor activities, also outdoor activities. TV/video room. Washing machines and dryers, motorcaravan services and chemical disposal. Five cottages in the park to let. The historic town of Quimper, which has some attractive old areas and a cathedral, is under 3 km. and two hypermarkets are 1 km. Used by tour operators. Mobile homes (9) for hire. All facilities available when site is open. Watch out for the 2-way bike! *'Camping Cheque'*

Directions: From Quimper follow `Quimper Sud' signs, then `Toutes Directions' and general camping signs, finally signs for Lanniron.

Charges 1999: Per person Ffr. 29.00; child (2-6 yrs) 19.00; vehicle 19.00; normal pitch (100 sq.m.) 49.00, with electricity (10A) 70.00, special pitch (120 sq.m. with water and electricity) 84.00, (140 sq.m. with electricity, water and drainage) 93.00. Less 10% outside July/Aug. Credit cards accepted.

Open: 15 May - 15 September.

Reservations: Contact site; made with deposit (Ffr. 400) and fee (100). Address: Château de Lanniron, 29336 Quimper Cedex. Tel: (0)2.98.90.62.02. FAX: (0)2.98.52.15.56. E-mail: lanniron@acdev.com. Internet: http://www.acdev.com/lanniron.

AR Discount
Welcome drink;
guided tour of park

2908 Camping Le Panoramic, Telgruc-sur-Mer, nr Châteaulin

Family site in west Brittany, quite close to a good beach.

This medium sized, 10 acre site is situated on quite a steep hillside, with fine views along the coast. It is well tended and personally run by M. Jacq and his family who all speak good English. The site is in two parts, divided by a fairly quiet road to the beach. The main upper site is where most of the facilities are located. The lower pitches are used only in July and August, but the heated swimming pool with terrace, children's pool and jacuzzi (all 15/5-7/9) and a children's playground are here. Some up-and-down walking is therefore necessary, but this is a small price to pay for such pleasant and comfortable surroundings. The 220 pitches are arranged on flat terraces, mostly in small groups with hedges and 20 pitches have services for motorcaravans. A good sandy beach is around 700 m. downhill by road, a bit less on foot. The main site has two well kept toilet blocks with another very good block opened for the main season, in the second part of the site. The three blocks have British and Turkish style WCs, washbasins in cubicles with free hot water and hot showers. Facilities for disabled people, baby baths, dishwashing, plus washing machines and dryers, chemical disposal and motorcaravan services. Small shop (1/6-7/9) and bar/restaurant with good value takeaway food also (1/7-31/8). Sports ground with free tennis, volleyball. Children's playground, games and TV rooms, children's club in season. Bicycle hire. Fishing 700 m, riding 6 km, golf 14 km. Sailing school nearby and lovely coastal footpaths. Barbecue area. Gites, houses and mobile homes for hire. Used by tour operators (20 pitches). A `Sites et Paysages' member.

Directions: From Telgruc town centre, take road with signs to camp and Trez-Bollec-Plage and continue to site on right. Stop at property no. 130 to read the Panoramic information boards.

Charges 1999: Per person Ffr. 25.00; child (under 7) 13.00; pitch 50.00; car 10.00; m/cycle 8.00; electricity 6A 20.00, 10A 28.00; water and drainage connection 15.00; dog 10.00; local tax (over 10 yrs) 2.00. Less 20% outside 5/7-24/8. No credit cards.

Open: 15 May - 15 September.

Reservations: Made for any period with deposit. Address: Rte de la Plage, 29560 Telgruc-sur-Mer. Tel: (0)2.98.27.78.41. FAX: (0)2.98.27.36.10.

2906 Camping Caravaning Le Pil Koad, Poullan-sur-Mer, nr Douarnenez

Family run, attractive site just back from the sea in Finistère.

Pil Koad has 110 pitches on fairly flat ground, marked out by separating hedges and of quite good, though varying, size and shape. Nearly all have electrical connections (10A) and original trees provide shade in some areas. There are two main toilet blocks in modern style with mainly British style WCs and washbasins, some in private cabins but mostly not. Free, pre-set hot water in these and in the showers. Laundry facilities and chemical disposal. There is a heated swimming pool and paddling pool, an attractive sunbathing patio and a tennis court. A large room, the 'Woodpecker Bar', is used for entertainment with discos and cabaret in July/Aug. Small shop for basics and takeaway (both 26/6-8/9, there are restaurants in the village). Children's playground. Table tennis, minigolf, volleyball and fishing. Weekly outings and clubs for children are arranged in season (30/6-30/8) with a charge included in the tariff. Bicycle hire or riding 4 km. Motorcaravan service point. Privately owned units or site owned mobile homes and chalets to rent occupy 39 pitches. Gates closed 10.30 - 7.30 in high season. The site is 6 km. from Douarnenez and 5 km. from the nearest sandy beach.

Directions: Site is 500 m. from centre of Poullan on road towards Douarnenez. From Douarnenez take circular bypass route towards Audierne; if you see road for Poullan sign at roundabout, take it, otherwise there is camping sign at turning to Poullan from the D765 road.

Charges 1999: Per pitch Ffr. 37.00 - 79.00, with water and drainage plus 15.00; person 20.00 - 29.00; child (under 7 yrs) 10.00 - 15.00; electricity (10A) 22.00; local tax (over 16 yrs, 1/6-30/9) 1.00. Credit cards accepted.

Open: 1 May - 15 September

Reservations: Made for min. 1 week with deposit (Ffr. 300) and fee (120). Address: Poullan, 29100 Douarnenez. Tel: (0)2.98.74.26.39. FAX: (0)2.98.74.55.97.

2909 Camping Le Raguenès Plage, Névez, nr Pont-Aven

Well regulated, attractive site in small seaside village, with beach access.

Personally run by the owner and her family who take great pride in the site, there are many attractive shrubs and trees and it is kept very clean and neat. A sandy beach can be reached by footpath (300 m.) and there is a sailing school and small fishing port adjacent to the site. The 287 pitches all have electrical connections and are of good size, on flat grass, arranged in rows on either side of asphalt access roads, separated by hedges and trees. It could be said that this site's best features are not discovered until you get past reception and the older sanitary block nearest the entrance; indeed the furthest sanitary unit is the most recently renovated and the quietest pitches are to the rear of the site. The sanitary facilities are in three well maintained blocks of different size, design and age. They provide British WCs, pre-set hot showers, washbasins in private cabins, plus free hairdryers and include good baby bathrooms, excellent facilities for disabled people and chemical disposal. Hot water is free throughout. Amenities include a sauna and a new, attractively designed, heated swimming pool with terrace (from 15/5). Table tennis, volleyball, games room, good play areas and animation are offered for children. A small bar and restaurant (from 1/6) have an outside terrace with lots of flowers; breakfast is served here. Takeaway. Small shop (from 15/5, supermarket 5 km.). Reading, TV rooms and films. Laundry. Exchange facilities. Fishing and watersports 300 m, riding 5 km. Bicycle hire can be arranged, with delivery. Motorcaravan service point. Used by tour operators (93 pitches). Mobile homes for hire.

Directions: From the D783 Concarneau - Pont-Aven road go south to Névez. Site is signed from there, 5 km. on the Raguenès-Plage road.

Charges 1998: Per unit incl. 2 persons Ffr. 130.00; extra person 30.00; child (under 7 yrs) 18.00; electricity 2A 15.00, 6A 20.00; dog 8.00; local tax (over 18 yrs) 2.00. Less 30% in April, May, June, 20% in Sept.

Open: 1 April - 30 September.

Reservations: Recommended in high season, min. 7 days preferred for July/Aug. Write with deposit (Ffr. 300). Address: 19 Rue des Iles, 29920 Névez. Tel: (0)2.98.06.80.69. FAX: (0)2.98.06.89.05.

2913 Camping des Abers, Landéda, nr Lannilis

Attractively situated, family run site in tranquil western Brittany.

This delightful 12 acre site is beautifully situated almost at the tip of the Ste Marguerite peninsula on the western shores of Brittany in a wide bay formed between the mouths (abers) of two rivers, L'Aber Wrac'h and L'Aber Bennoit. With soft, white sandy beaches and rocky outcrops and islands at high tide, the setting is ideal for those with younger children and the quiet, rural area provides a beautiful, tranquil escape from the busier areas of France, even in high season. Des Abers is set just back from the beach, the lower pitches sheltered from the wind by high hedges or with panoramic views of the bay from the higher places. There are 200 pitches arranged in distinct areas, partly shaded by hedges, trees and shrubs, all planted and carefully tended over 30 years by the Le Cuff family. Electricity is available to all (5A, long leads may be needed). Three toilet blocks (one part of the reception building and one of the others unisex) are kept very clean, providing washbasins in cubicles, British style WCs and showers (token from reception). Each has dishwashing sinks and chemical disposal. Facilities for disabled visitors and babies are at the reception block and a laundry and motorcaravan services are also here. Mini-market for essentials (15/6-30/8). Takeaway in high season. A pizzeria and a restaurant are next door, plus excellent restaurants nearby at the town of L'Aber Wrac'h, a well known yachting centre. The beach has good bathing (best at high tide), fishing, windsurfing and other watersports with miles of superb coastal walks. Canoes or windsurfers may be hired and instruction is available (July/Aug). Table tennis, good children's play area and indoor TV and games room. Live music, Breton dancing and French classes may be arranged in high season. Tennis and riding close. Mobile homes (8) for rent. Gates locked 22.30-07.00 hrs. Torch useful. The family owners who run the site with 'TLC', make you very welcome.

Directions: From Roscoff (D10, then D13), cross river bridge (L'Aber Wrac'h) to Lannilis. Go through town taking road to Landéda and from there signs for Dunes de Ste Marguerite, 'camping' and des Abers.

Charges 1999: Per person Ffr. 17.00; child (1-7 yrs) 9.00; pitch 26.00; car 6.00; electricity 12.00; dog 5.00. Less 20% outside July/Aug. Credit cards accepted.

Open: 1 May - 30 September.

Reservations: Write to site. Address: Dunes de Ste Marguerite, 29870 Landéda. Tel: (0)2.98.04.93.35. FAX: (0)2.98.04.84.35.

Le "CAMPING DES ABERS"
★ ★ ★

Situated in an exceptional tourist region
with marvellous views of the sea
10 terraced acres equipped with all
necessary facilities, next to safe sandy beach
Sea Angling — Walking — Swimming
Windsurfing — Horse Riding
Mobile homes to rent

2916 Camping Les Genets d'Or, Bannalec, nr Pont-Aven

Small, rural site in the heart of Finistère with English owners.

A jewel of a small site (52 pitches, 46 for touring units), Les Genets d'Or is situated in a tiny country hamlet at the end of a road from Bannalec, 12 km from Pont-Aven. The spacious surroundings offer a safe haven for young children and a rural, tranquil environment for adults. The gently sloping, grassy site is divided into hedged glades with trees providing shade. Most pitches have electricity (6A) and each glade has a water point. A toilet block of good quality provides the necessary amenities with British style toilets, free hot showers and adequate washing facilities. There is no bar or shop but there is an indoor room with snooker and table tennis, and bicycle hire. Riding 3 km, golf 20 km. The English owners ensure a warm friendly welcome and are justifiably proud of their renovated facilities which are kept in pristine condition. A flat (2 bed) and a cottage (4 bed) are also available for accompanying friends or relatives. Caravan storage available.

Directions: Take exit 4 from N165 towards Bannalec. In Bannalec turn right into Rue Lorec (signed Quimperlé) and follow camp signs.

Charges 1998: Per person Ffr. 12.00; child (under 6 yrs) 8.00; pitch 18.00; vehicle 8.00; m/cycle 5.00; dog 6.00; electricity (6A) 15.00. Less 10-15% outside July/Aug. No credit cards or Eurocheques.

Open: 1 April - 31 October.

Reservations: Contact site. Address: Kermerou, Pont Kereon, 29380 Bannalec. Tel/Fax: (0)2.98.39.54.35.

France - Gard

3005 Camping L'Eden, Le Grau-du-Roi, nr Montpelier

Good modern site close to beaches and Camargue, with swimming pool.

L'Eden is a good example of a modern, well run, purpose built 4-star site. It is on flat ground about 500 m. from a sandy beach, with 377 individual hedged pitches. The flowering shrubs and trees make it cool and very pretty. Shade is available on many of the pitches, electricity on most and some are fully serviced. Reservation is advisable for the main season. The five modern sanitary blocks are of unusual design, tiled blue or pink, and have free hot water everywhere. Toilets (some British style) as so often in France are in shorter supply than washbasins, which are in cubicles or private cabins; free pre-set hot showers, some en-suite with washbasins. Unit with baby bath, full facilities for disabled people and chemical disposal inside the blocks. Very attractive swimming pool with bridge, water toboggan and children's pool on site (from mid April) and a fitness centre next door. Supermarket, boutique, bar and restaurant with takeaway (all open all season). TV room and meeting room. Activities include half court tennis, minigolf, archery, bicycle hire, table tennis and a sports area with volleyball and basketball. All activities on site are free. High season organised events, sports, excursions and entertainment, a mini club for children (1/7-1/9) and a play area for 1-8 year olds. Marina with sailing lessons, fishing, riding and tennis nearby. Laundry facilities. Free bus service to beach in main season. Some tour operators.

Directions: There is now a road bypassing Le Grau-du-Roi from the west, easier if towing a caravan, as well as the approach from Aigues-Mortes. Turn left at sign to 'Port Camargue' and 'Campings' just northeast of Grau-du-Roi and follow signs for 'Phare de l'Espiguette' and after 200 m. right at second sign for l'Eden. **Note:** Not site with entrance at turn; for l'Eden go hard right onto access road and a further 200 m. around corner to site on left (busy access).

Charges 1999: Per pitch incl. 2 persons: simple (for small tents in July/Aug) Ffr. 125.00 - 175.00, with electricity and water 90.00 - 190.00, with electricity, water and drainage 90.00 - 201.00; extra person 10.00 - 30.00; local tax 1.00. Less 20% for a 2 week stay outside 1/7-26/8 or 5% for a 3 week stay in high season. Credit cards accepted.

Open: 27 March - 4 October.

Reservations: Made from Sat.-Sat. high season only with deposit and fee. Write to site between 1/1 and 15/5. Address: Port Camargue, 30240 Le Grau-du-Roi. Tel: (0)4.66.51.49.81. FAX: (0)4.66.53.13.20.

L'Eden is 500 m. from the beach at Port-Camargue (premier pleasure port of Europe).
We offer 5 ha. with 377 pitches, a commercial centre, snacks, bazaar, papers, bar/restaurant.
For your entertainment: swimming pool with water slide, table tennis, minigolf, halfcourt, archery, multi sports field, children's playground, sauna, sun-bed, gym, bicycle hire and day time and evening animation and miniclub in July/Aug.

3002 Camping-Caravaning La Petite Camargue, Aigues-Mortes
See colour advert between pages 96/97

Impressive site with large swimming pool on the edge of the Camargue.

This is a large site (605 pitches) with a huge swimming pool complex and other amenities to match, conveniently situated beside one of the main routes across the famous Camargue. Its position alongside this busy road is an advantage for access but could perhaps be a drawback in terms of traffic, although when we stayed overnight in season it was virtually silent. It offers a variety of good sized pitches, regularly laid out, with varying amounts of shade. There are, however, almost 200 mobile homes interspersed between the touring pitches, but most are set well back from the road. An attractive 'L' shaped pool complex and adjacent bar/restaurant with pizzeria and takeaway, range of shops, etc. are situated between the pitches and the road and are attractively designed, providing a wide range of facilities and activities. The four sanitary blocks provide very good, well maintained, modern facilities including many combined showers and washbasins with controllable hot water, British style WCs and chemical disposal. Motorcaravan service point. The site is conveniently situated for visiting the Camargue and not far from the sea, beaches and other sport facilities and activities, and it also provides a range of on site entertainment with a good activity programme and disco. Activities include riding at the adjoining large stables, a children's play area, tennis (charged July/Aug), table tennis and bicycle hire. Laundry facilities. Hairdresser and beauty centre. *continued overleaf*

3002 Camping-Caravaning La Petite Camargúe (continued)

The nearest beach is 3.5 km, with a free bus service in July/Aug. Fishing 3 km, golf 8 km. Caravan storage available. Mobile homes to let. Used by tour operators (57 pitches). A well run, busy site.

Directions: From autoroute A9 take exit 26 (Gallargues) towards Le Grau-du-Roi. Continue past Aigues-Mortes (18 km) on D62 and site is 2 km. on right, just before large roundabout for La Grand-Motte and Le Grau-du-Roi.

Charges 1999: Per unit with 1 or 2 persons: standard pitch Ffr. 73.00 - 152.00, with electricity 90.00 - 176.00; extra person (over 4 yrs) 26.00 - 33.00; local tax 1.00; second tent or car 18.00; animal 13.00. Credit cards accepted.

Open: 24 April - 19 September.

Reservations: Made with Ffr 480 deposit and 120 fee. Address: BP 21, 30220 Aigues-Mortes. Tel: (0)4.66.53.98.98. FAX: (0)4.66.53.98.80. E-mail: petite.camargue@wanadoo.fr.

3003 Camping Abri de Camargue, Le Grau-du-Roi, nr Montpellier

Pleasant site with both indoor and outdoor swimming pools.

This is an agreeable site, which has two swimming pools, one 250 sq.m. and a smaller, indoor heated one (12 x 6 m.) which is overlooked by the restaurant/bar (with heating and air conditioning) and sheltered terrace. The 277 flat pitches (147 for touring units) are said to average 100 sq.m., but there is some variation in size, and electricity and water are available on most. The site is well shaded, with trees and flowering bushes quite luxuriant in parts. The six toilet blocks have British WCs, washbasins with hot water in cabins, and free hot water also in adjustable showers and sinks. Facilities for dishwashing and laundry, chemical disposal and a motorcaravan service point. Maintenance may be variable - the site lacks a little 'TLC' at present. It is 800 m. from the nearest beach at Port Camargue and 2 km. from the one at L'Espiguette (in July and Aug. a free bus to L'Espiguette beach stops outside). There is a summer fair within walking distance can be noisy until late. Le Grau-du-Roi is 1½ km. and the old town of Aigues-Mortes 9. TV room. Bar, restaurant, takeaway and shop (all season). New children's playground. Petanque. Very good security. All facilities open when site is open. Tennis 800 m, riding or bicycle hire 2 km, fishing 3 km, golf 5 km. Mobile homes for let. English spoken. Telephones.

Directions: There is now a road bypassing Le Grau-du-Roi from west as well as the approach from Aigues-Mortes. Turn left at sign to `Port Camargue' and `Campings' just northeast of Grau-du-Roi. At next crossroads go left again towards `Phare de l'Espiguette/Rive Gauche' and after 200 m. you come to site on right. If approaching via the D979 from north, turn onto D62 and D62A towards La Grande Motte at junction north of Aigues-Mortes.

Charges 1999: Per unit incl. 1 or 2 persons and electricity Ffr 117.00 - 252.00; extra person or extra car 30.00 - 60.00; pet, boat or trailer 30.00. Credit cards accepted

Open: April - October.

Reservations: Only required for very high season (10/7-20/8) and made for min. 1 week. (Site will be happy to help with any length of stay - phone and talk to them). Address: 320 Rte. du Phare de l'Espiguette, Port Camargue, 30240 Le Grau-du-Roi. Tel: (0)4.66.51.54.83. FAX: (0)4.66.51.76.42.

France - Gard / Gers

3006 Domaine des Fumades, Les Fumades, Allègre, nr Alès

Attractive site near thermal springs, with friendly atmosphere and range of activities.

This site is an ideal base from which to explore the Gard region. Not only are its 200 grass pitches large and level with 4A electricity, but a variety of trees bestow privacy and shade to the majority of them. With three swimming pools, ample sunbathing space, tennis, volleyball, table tennis and boules, there is certainly plenty to do, whilst adjacent to the site a small river offers fishing and bicycle hire can be arranged. A lively animation and entertainment programme is designed to appeal to families with children but does mean the site can be rather boisterous at times. Two central sanitary blocks cope well with the pressures placed on them, providing plentiful free hot showers, washbasins in cabins, predominantly British style WCs (no paper), plus baby baths, facilities for disabled people, laundry and dishwashing, they are clean and well maintained. Two designated barbecue areas. Set in an attractive courtyard, the reception is particularly pleasant. Leading off this is a shop, bar, restaurant and takeaway. Large covered terrace, with games room, snack bar and a focus for evening entertainment. Bicycle hire and fishing on site, riding 2 km. It is a good area for walking, cycling, riding, climbing and fishing. Chalets, apartments and caravans for hire. A 'Sites et Paysages' member.

Directions: From Alès take D16 through Salindres, continue towards Allègre, until signs for Fumades (and thermal springs) on the right.

Charges 1999: Per standard pitch incl. 2 persons Ffr. 79.00 - 134.00, 'comfort' pitch incl. electricity 99.00 - 154.00; extra person 17.00 - 30.00; child (0-6 years) 10.00 - 13.00. local tax 1.00. No credit cards.

Open: 15 May - 15 September.

Reservations: Made with deposit (Ffr 800) and fee (150). Address: Les Fumades, 30500 Allègre. Tel: (0)4.66.24.80.78. FAX: (0)4.66.24.82.42. E-mail: domaine.des.fumades@wanadoo.fr.

3201 Le Camp de Florence, La Romieu

Attractive site on edge of historic village in pleasantly undulating Gers countryside.

Camp de Florence is run by a Dutch family who have sympathetically converted the old farmhouse buildings to provide facilities. There are 173 pitches of 100 sq.m. plus, all with electricity, three with hardstanding (these rather small) and terraced where necessary, arranged around a large field with rural views and a spacious feeling. Pitches near the main buildings have good shade but it gets progressively less the newer the pitch. However, 25 of these are fully serviced and shade will develop. There are two unisex toilet blocks with British style toilets, free hot water, showers and washbasins, some in cabins. These facilities may be under pressure at peak times. Washing machine and dryer, chemical disposal and motorcaravan services. Water points are limited. A restaurant, also open to the public, serves a range of food (15/5-15/9, closed Weds, with a barbecue instead). Swimming pool (15/5-15/9) with a beach effect so one can walk in on three sides, paddling pool (supervised July/Aug), children's play area, games area and a pets area typical of Dutch sites. Takeaway. Activities include a games room, tennis, table tennis, volleyball, petanque and bicycle hire. Clay pigeon shooting, video shows, discos, picnics, musical evenings and excursions are organised. Exchange facility. Shop in nearby village (bread available on site in season). The 13th century village of La Romieu is on the Santiago de Compostela pilgrim route and the collegiate church is well worth a visit (the views are magnificent from the top of the tower), as is the local arboretum, the biggest collection of trees in the Midi-Pyrénées. The Pyrénées are a two hour drive, the Atlantic coast a similar distance. Fishing 5 km, riding 10 km. The site arranges walking tours, etc. A few tour operator pitches (15). Mobile homes and chalets for hire (1 night stay possible outside July/Aug. with breakfast). 'Camping Cheque'

Directions: Site is signed from the D931 Agen - Condom road. Small units can turn left at Ligardes (signed) and follow D36 for 1 km. and take right turn for La Romieu (signed). Otherwise continue until outskirts of Condom and take D41 left to La Romieu and pass through village to site.

Charges 1999: Per unit incl. 2 persons Ffr. 65.00 - 112.00; extra person 21.00 - 35.00; child (4-9 yrs) 15.00 - 25.00; electricity 3A 15.00, 6A 20.00; water and drainage plus 12.00; dog 10.00; local tax 1.00 (child 4-9 yrs 0.50). Special prices for groups, rallies, etc. Credit cards accepted.

Open: 1 April - 31 October.

Reservations: Write or phone for information (English spoken). Address: 32480 La Romieu. Tel: (0)5.62.28.15.58. FAX: (0)5.62.28.20.04. E-mail: campdef@compuserve.com.

3206 Camping Lac des Trois Vallées, Lectoure

Large 40 hectare lively site with many facilities.

This site is situated in the Gers countryside in the heart of Gascony, a land of fortified village and 'foie gras', near the town of Lectoure which was once the main seat of the Counts of Armagnac and is now a spa town. Lac des Trois Vallées is popular with those who like activities and entertainment. It is, in fact, a large holiday complex and good for families with teenagers. There are three lakes for watersports, fishing, canoeing, surfing and swimming, with four water chutes (open to the public, from 15/5) and an impressive pool complex, hydro-massage facilities, plus sunbathing areas. *continued overleaf*

102

3206 Camping Lac des Trois Vallées (continued)

Lifeguards in season (1/6-10/9). Many activities include tennis, archery and mountain biking (with bicycle hire), with cabaret, shows and craft activities for all ages. Two restaurants, one beside the pool, the other by the lake (more a snack bar) which also provides takeaway. Three bars including 'The Pub' (hours according to season). Mini-market and launderette. The eight sanitary blocks have pre-set hot water, mixed style toilets, open air baby baths and chemical disposal. A busy site, they receive heavy use but when we visited all was in order (if some are a little dark inside) Motorcaravan service point. Some up and down walking is required as the site is in a valley situation. There are 450 pitches with 285 for independent units on shaded or open ground, all with electricity (10A). Used by tour operators (100 pitches). Mobile homes and tents for rent. Riding 4 km, golf 10 km. Caravan storage. 'Camping Cheque'

Directions: Site signed 2 km. outside Lectoure to the south, off the N21.

Charges 1999: Per unit incl. up to 3 persons Ffr. 114.00 - 163.00, with electricity 129.00 - 184.00, with water also 136.00 - 194.00; extra person 26.50 - 39.00. Special rates for couples, families, etc. Credit cards accepted.

Open: Easter - 11 September.

Reservations: Made with deposit (Ffr. 550) and non-refundable fee (150). Address: 32700 Lectoure. Tel: (0)5.62.68.82.33. FAX: (0)5.62.68.88.82.

3301 Camping de la Dune, Pyla-sur-Mer, nr Arcachon

Busy site with pool and other amenities separated from sea by famous giant dune.

La Dune is a good example of a busy French family site. It is informal, friendly and lively with a range of amenities. From its situation at the foot of the enormous dune you can reach the beach either by climbing over the dune (a ladder goes up nearly to the top) or driving round, or you can use the swimming pool at the far side of the site. The 325 marked pitches, some terraced but level, vary somewhat in size but all are hedged with shade from pine trees. Nearly half are caravan pitches with electricity, water and drainaway. Some of the roads on the site are quite narrow and parts are quite sandy. Three modern sanitary blocks including one small one and the original one which has been refurbished to make roomy showers and washbasins en-suite which can be heated in cool weather. It is a good provision with WCs of British and Turkish types, individual washbasins with many in cabins and pre-set hot showers. There are several small shops and a pleasant little bar and restaurant which can get busy and noisy at times (opens June, all other facilities are all season), with takeaway also. Purpose built barbecue (individual ones not allowed). Fridges for hire. Open-air theatre and organised sports and tournaments in eason. Children's playground with mini-club. Riding 2 km, fishing 3 km, golf 10 km. Motorcaravan services. Mobile homes and chalets for hire (39). English spoken in season.

Directions: There is a new road (D259) signed from N250 to Biscarrosse and Dune du Pilat, just before La Teste, avoiding Pyla-sur-Mer. At end of new road turn right at roundabout on D218 coast road. La Dune is 2nd site on right.

Charges 1998: Per unit incl. 2 persons: with tent Ffr 75.00 - 115.00; with caravan incl. electricity and water 95.00 - 135.00; extra person 20.00 - 35.00; extra child (under 7) 15.00 - 25.00; extra car 15.00 - 25.00; dog 5.00 - 15.00; local tax (over 18s) 1.10. Credit cards accepted.

Open: 1 May - 30 September.

Reservations: Made for min. 1 week with 25% deposit and fee (Ffr. 150) at least 1 month in advance. Address: Rte. de Biscarrosse, Pyla sur Mer, 33260 La Teste. Tel: (0)5.56.22.72.17. FAX: as phone.

3302 Camping de Fontaine-Vieille, Andernos-les-Bains, nr Arcachon

Large site on east side of Bassin d'Arcachon with pool and frontage to Bassin.

Fontaine-Vieille is a large well established site which celebrates its 50th anniversary in 1999, with many festivities planned. The site stretches along the edge of the Bassin d'Arcachon under light woodland in the residential area of the small town of Andernos. It has 840 pitches on flat grassy ground, some with views, marked by stones or newly planted trees; 540 have electricity. Several sanitary blocks, of rather unusual design provide adequate hot showers (perhaps on the small side), washbasins, some in cabins, British WCs, plus facilities for disabled people and children and washing machines. All blocks are being refurbished to a high standard and maintenance appears good. A beach runs along the Bassin which can be used for boating when the tide is in. When out, it is sand and mud but they claim that bathing in the channels is still possible. On site is an unheated swimming pool (30/5-10/9), plus paddling pool (Ffr. 80 leisure card for entire stay). Shop (1/6-10/9), bar with terrace and restaurant with takeaway (all 1/7-31/8, town shops, etc. near). Four tennis courts, TV room, children's play areas, adventure area and minigolf. Boat, sailboard and bicycle hire and sports are organised. Riding 5 km, golf 3 km. Communal barbecue. Caravan storage. Mobile homes, chalets and bungalows to rent.

Directions: Turn off D3 at southern end of Andernos towards Bassin at camp sign.

Charges 1999: Per unit with 2 persons Ffr. 60.00 - 85.00, with electricity (5A) 75.00 - 105.00; extra person 15.00 -20.00; child (2-7 yrs) 12.00 - 14.00; local tax 1.10. Credit cards accepted.

Open: 1 April - 30 September.

Reservations: Any length with deposit (Ffr. 500) and fee (120). Address: 4 Bvd. du Colonel Wurz, 33510 Andernos-les-Bains.Tel: (0)5.56.82.01.67. FAX: (0)5.56.82.09.81.

AR Discount
Low season & long stay - contact site

3306 Camping Le Palace, Soulac-sur-Mer, nr Royan

Large, traditional site close to beach, south of Royan across the estuary.

This large, flat site has good-sized individual pitches regularly laid out amongst a variety of trees including pines which provide good shade. On very sandy ground, pitches for caravans have hardened areas and electricity is available. Most pitches have water taps, some also have sewage connection. There are twelve separate toilet blocks, some smaller and more simple than others. All have British style WCs and free pre-set hot showers, some opening from the outside only. Washbasins in cabins are provided in some blocks, baby bathrooms (0-24 months) in four others and facilities for disabled people in one. A sandy beach is 400 m. and bathing is controlled by lifeguards. The site has a small swimming pool, also with lifeguards, attractively set in a raised, part grass, part tiled area. Around a lush green roundabout with a fountain at the centre of the site are various shops (mostly 1/6-5/9), restaurant (1/6-10/9) and bar with entertainment. Supervised children's playground with paddling pool. Bicycle hire. Programme of sports, entertainments and excursions in July/Aug. Tennis courts adjacent, riding 400 m. Washing machines. Mobile homes for hire. Caravan storage. English is spoken.

Directions: Site is 1 km. south of Soulac and well signed. Shortest and simplest way is via the ferry from Royan across the Gironde to Pointe de Grave, but this is quite expensive with a caravan. Alternatively go via Bordeaux.

Charges 1998: Per unit incl. 2 persons, 5A electricity and water Ffr. 88.00 - 118.00, plus drainage 90.00 - 120.00; extra person (over 10 yrs) 18.00 - 24.00; local tax 2.00. Prices higher without reservation. Credit cards accepted.

Open: 1 May - 15 September.

Reservations: Made for with deposit; contact site for details. Address: B.P. 33, Bd. Marsan de Montbrun, 33780 Soulac-sur-Mer. Tel: (0)5.56.09.80.22. FAX: (0)5.56.09.84.23. Internet: www.camping-palace.com.

3404 Camping Lou Village, Valras-Plage, nr Béziers

Family owned, good value site with direct access to beach.

Valras is perhaps smarter and is certainly larger than nearby Vias and it has a good number of campsites. Lou Village has direct access to a sandy beach and is a busy site with lots of facilities. Prices are quite competitive. However, it will become crowded in the high season in this popular area. The swimming pool, children's paddling pool, restaurant, bar and shops all form part of the 'village centre' where most of the site's activity takes place. There is a stage for entertainment, children's club, supermarket, bakery, takeaway (to 5/9), bazaar with daily papers and hairdressing salon. The bar has large screen TV and a terrace overlooking the pool. It is a busy area with a pleasant ambience. There are 600 pitches (including 200 mobile homes) of which 100 are 'grand confort' with electricity, water and waste water. Electricity (10A) throughout. Pitches further inland are of grass, partly separated by tall trees which provide good shade; nearer the beach pitches are smaller, sandy and separated by bushes and bamboo hedges. The four toilet blocks, one quite new, the older ones recently refurbished, are well situated with reasonable facilities. They provide a mixture of Turkish and British style WCs, free pre-set hot showers with no separator and washbasins, about half in cabins (H&C). Washing up and laundry sinks at each block, as are chemical disposal facilities. Considering their heavy use (this is a beach-side site), maintenance (in July) seemed quite satisfactory. Children's playground, football field, bicycle hire, minigolf, volleyball and tennis. There is lots to do off the site - sailing, windsurfing, riding (500 m), canoe kayak, river fishing (2 km), golf (12 km), bike rides and the history of the Languedoc to discover. Mobile homes and new chalets for rent. Used by tour operators (40 pitches). English spoken.

Directions: Site is south of Béziers. From autoroute, take Béziers-Ouest exit for Valras Plage and continue for 13-14 km. Follow 'Casino' signs and site is 1 km south of centre of Valras Plage in the direction of Vendres.

Charges 1999: Per unit incl. 2 persons Ffr. 80.00 - 130.00; extra person (over 7 yrs) 12.00 - 22.00; child under 7 free - 15.00; electricity (10A)18.00; local tax 1.90 (over 4 yrs). Credit cards accepted, but not Eurocheques.

Open: 25 April - 19 September.

Reservations: Made with deposit (Ffr. 700) and fee (150). Address: BP 30, 34350 Valras-Plage. Tel: (0)4.67.33.79. FAX: (0)4.67.37.53.56. Internet: www.aquaticamp.com/village.htm.

3402 Camping Le Garden, La Grande Motte, nr Montpellier

Useful site close to the sea in modern resort of La Grand Motte.

Le Garden is a mature site, situated 300 m. back from a fine sandy beach and with all the choice of sports, entertainment and other facilities of this popular holiday resort. With space for 117 caravans, 112 tents and 24 mobile homes, the 100 sq.m. pitches are hedged with good shade. All have 6A electricity, water and waste water facilities supplied. Three well situated toilet blocks provide British and Turkish style WCs, controllable hot showers, washbasins in cabins, plus baby bath and free hairdryers. Dishwashing and laundry sinks have hot water and there are washing machines. Unit for disabled people. A shopping complex is to one side of the site alongside a restaurant, bar and takeaway service. A swimming pool is on site with a children's paddling pool. Reception can exchange money and offers tourist information. Nearby are tennis courts, a riding club, casino and night club.

Directions: Entering La Grand Motte from the D62 dual-carriageway, keep right following signs for `campings'. Turn right at Centre Commercial on Ave de la Petite Motte and the site is the first on the right.

Charges guide: Per unit with 1-3 persons and electricity, water, drainage Ffr. 143.00, 4 persons 173.00; extra person 30.00; local tax 3.30. Reductions in low season.

Open: 1 March - 31 October.

Reservations: Not made. Address: 34280 La Grande Motte. Tel: (0)4.67.56.50.09. FAX: (0)4. 67.56.25.69.

3406 Hotel de Plein Air L'Oliveraie, Laurens

Site with many attractive features at the foot of the Cevennes, open all year.

This lively site has a lot to offer in terms of activities, particularly those for youngsters, including plenty of evening entertainment in the high season, but can be comfortable and quiet at other time. Most of the 116 pitches are large (up to 150 sq.m. in some parts). Arranged in rows on two levels, those on the higher level being older and with more shade from mature trees (mainly olives), all have electricity (6/10A). The ground is stony. The large leisure area is slightly apart from the pitches on the lower area, and includes a good sized pool and children's pool (open 1/6-30/9), with an attractive paved sunbathing area, a tennis court and tennis practice wall, volleyball, basketball, minigolf, bicycle hire, children's play area and adjoining riding stables. There are also good facilities for archery which is quite a feature of the site. Overlooking these is a large terrace with a bar/restaurant serving simple grills in high season. Indoor bar, also used as a lounge for films and activities for younger children. Small, well stocked shop (1/7-31/8, local shops at Laurens, 1 km). The main sanitary block on the higher terrace has been renovated to provide hot showers, washbasins in cabins, British WCs, covered dishwashing areas and a washing machine. A second block on the lower level is open in high season. Bureau de change and tourist information in reception. Caravan storage. A `Sites et Paysages' member.

Directions: Site is signed 2 km. north of Laurens off the D909 (Béziers-Bédarieux) road.

Charges 1998: Per unit incl. 1 or 2 persons Ffr. 36.00 - 100.00, with electricity 54.00 - 120.00, 3 or 4 persons 46.00 - 130.00, with electricity 64.00 - 150.00. Special rates for longer stays. Credit cards accepted.

Open: All year.

Reservations: Contact site. Address: 34480 Laurens. Tel: (0)4.67.90.24.36. FAX: (0)4.67.90.11.20.

3403 Camping Club International Le Napoleon, Vias Plage

Smaller family site in village bordering the Mediterranean at Vias Plage.

Vias is in the wine-growing area of the Midi, an area which includes the Camargue, Béziers and popular modern resorts such as Cap d'Agde. The single street that leads to Vias Plage is hectic to say the least in season, but once through the security barrier and entrance to Le Napoleon, the contrast is marked - tranquillity, yet still only a few yards from the beach and other attractions. Not that the site itself lacks vibrancy, with a new Californian-style, heated pool, bar, restaurant/pizzeria and extensive entertainment programme, but thoughtful planning and design ensure that the camping area is quiet, with good shade from many tall trees. The 250 partially hedged pitches (80 with hire units), most with electricity, vary in size (80-100 sq.m). Two of the three sanitary blocks have been refurbished to a high standard, including British WCs, washbasins in private cabins, baby bath, laundry and facilities for disabled people, all well maintained when seen in peak season. Chemical disposal and motorcaravan services. The site has its well stocked supermarket and there are plenty of other shops, restaurants, etc. all immediately adjacent. Activities include volleyball, bicycle hire, boules and TV, plus a wide range of entertainment (free). Fishing nearby. Chalets, mobile homes and apartments to let. Most facilities are available from May.

Directions: From Vias town, take the D137 towards Vias Plage. Site is on the right near the beach; watch carefully for turning between restaurant and shops.

Charges 1999: Per unit incl. 1 or 2 persons and electricity Ffr. 105.00 - 160.00; extra person 18.00 - 30.00; extra tent free - 15.00; extra car free - 18.00; local tax 2.00.

Open: Easter - 30 September.

Reservations: Taken from 1 Jan. with deposit (Ffr. 500) and fee (170). Address: Farinette Plage, 34450 Vias sur Mer. Tel: (0)4.67.01.07.80. FAX: (0)4.67.01.07.85. Internet: www.camping-online.com/ or www.aquaticamp.com.

France - Hérault

3407 Camping Village Le Sérignan Plage, Sérignan

Unusual, well equipped, family run site with indoor pool and direct access to sandy beach.

This is a large, but very comfortable site, built in a genuinely unique style. Here you will normally find room even in the high season, with around 500 touring pitches in several different areas and with the benefit of some of the most comprehensive amenities we have encountered. The touring pitches, mostly of a very good size with plenty of shade and virtually all with 5A electricity, are mainly on level grass, fairly separate from a similar number of seasonal pitches and rented accommodation. Perhaps the most remarkable aspect of this site is the cluster of attractive buildings which form the central amenity area, amongst which is a small indoor heated swimming pool of unusual design. This is not intended for use in high season, when the beach and sea offer a better alternative. The imaginative owners have also built an amazing new pool complex with interlinked pool areas with deep parts for swimmers, children's areas, slides, bridges, etc. attractively landscaped and surrounded by a large grass sunbathing area with loungers, and supervised - it is a very nice addition. These traditional style buildings are virtually a small village, with bar, restaurant (good value meals, with local specialities), takeaway (all 10/5-15/9), disco, small amphitheatre, supermarket, tabac, bureau de change, outdoor market and even a roof-top bar - all with an international, lively atmosphere (well used and perhaps showing some wear and tear). A range of entertainment is provided each evening in high season and daily sporting activities. There are nine unisex sanitary blocks. Six older ones of circular design provide roomy pre-set hot showers, open washbasins and British and Turkish style WCs. These are nearest the sea and central 'village' area, seasonal units and mobile homes and thus take the brunt of the wear and tear. The touring area furthest from the sea, but near the new pool complex, is peaceful with grass pitches well shaded by tall trees and has three modern toilet blocks of individual design. These are well thought out, excellent facilities with large controllable hot showers with washbasin (non-slip floor) and WC en-suite, well equipped baby rooms and facilities for disabled people. Dishwashing and laundry facilities are in all blocks, plus four washing machines. Remember, this is a seaside site in a natural coastal environment, so do not expect it to be neat and manicured; in parts nature still predominates. There ia direct access to a large sandy beach and to the adjoining naturist beach, both of which slope gently and offer safe bathing at most times (lifeguard in high season). Sailing and windsurfing school on the beach, bicycle hire on site, riding 2 km, golf 10 km. Used by tour operators. Ask for a 'Cucarracha' at the bar! *'Camping Cheque'*

Directions: From A9 take exit 35 (Béziers Est) and follow signs for Sérignan on the D64 (9 km.). Do not go into Sérignan, but take sign for Sérignan Plage for 4 km. At first camping sign turn right (one way) for approx. 500 m. Bear left past two naturist sites (one the sister to site to this).

Charges 1999: Per unit incl. 1 or 2 persons Ffr. 80.00 - 155.00; extra person 22.00; electricity (5A) 17.00; dog 15.00; plus local tax. Discounts in low season for children. No credit cards.

Open: 15 April - 15 September.

Reservations: Made from 1 Feb. with deposit (Ffr. 100 - 500, acc. to season) and fee (100). Address: 34410 Sérignan. Tel: (0)4.67.32.35.33. FAX: (0)4.67.32.26.36.

N3408 Camping Le Sérignan Plage Nature, Sérignan Plage

Very comfortable and distinctly characterful naturist site beside large sandy beaches.

Sérignan Plage Nature was for many years run as a private club but now has been largely refurbished as a straightforward naturist campsite under the same ownership as no. 3407 next door. Offering over 250 touring pitches (out of 500 including seasonal pitches and mobile homes) on level grass and all with 5A electricity, this is a very comfortable place to spend a holiday. The pitches vary in size, from 80 - 120 sq.m. The smaller ones are nearest the beach with less shade and sandy, whilst many of the larger grassy ones further back are comfortable with a proportion of shade from the variety of trees encouraged to grow to a good size by the use of waste water for irrigation. Amongst the several unusual features of this site which contribute to its character are the Romanesque architectural style of several of the buildings (one is called the 'Forum'), the friendly ambience of the bar and restaurant, the shops (open all season) and the range of entertainment, with several competing attractions on the same evening in season. In addition to a large supermarket, the site boasts a market for fruit and vegetables, along with a newsagent/souvenir shop and an ice cream kiosk. The several sanitary blocks, although of different design, all offer modern facilities with roomy hot showers, some washbasins in cabins and British and Turkish style WCs, all clean and well maintained when inspected in July. This is a comfortable, well equipped family oriented site, with many facilities and good quality entertainment in season, and with the additional benefit of direct access to a large, sandy naturist beach (lifeguard in high season).

Directions: From A9 exit 35 (Béziers Est) follow signs for Sérignan (9 km). Take road to Sérignan Plage (4 km) watching for camping signs and turn right (one way) for approx. 500 m. bearing left (note: it is second naturist site).

Charges 1998: Per unit incl. 1 or 2 persons Ffr. 75.00 - 140.00, 3 persons 95.00 - 160.00; extra person 15.00; electricity (5A) 15.00; dog 15.00; plus local tax. Discounts in low season for children. Credit cards accepted.

Open: 15 April - 15 September.

Reservations: Made from 1 Feb. with deposit (Ffr. 400), fee (100) and cancellation insurance (70). Address: 34410 Sérignan. Tel: (0)4.67.32.09.61. FAX: (0)4.67.32.26.36.

3500 Ferme-Camping Le Vieux Chêne, Dol-de-Bretagne

Attractive, family owned farm site between St Malo and Mont St Michel for families.

This site has been developed in the grounds of a farmhouse dating from 1638, with its lakes. It offers 200 good sized pitches, most with electricity, water tap and light, in spacious rural surroundings on gently sloping grass. They are separated by bushes and flowers, with mature trees for shade. A very attractive tent area (no electricity) is in the orchard. Three very good, unisex sanitary blocks have British style toilets, pre-set showers, washbasins in cabins, a baby room and facilities for disabled people. Two blocks have recently been totally refurbished, the third nearest reception is older but still in very good order. Small laundry with washing machine, dryer and iron, chemical disposal and motorcaravan services. Attractive pool complex with a medium sized, heated swimming pool, children's pool (from May, no shorts allowed), toboggans, slides, jacuzzi, etc. with lifeguard during July/Aug. TV room (satellite), table tennis and pool table. Other free facilities include a tennis court, trampolines (no safety mat), minigolf, giant chess and a children's play area. Riding July/Aug. Bicycle hire. There is also a bar, café with terrace overlooking the pools, takeaway, small shop (all 1/6-10/9). Supermarket in Dol (3 km). Fishing is possible in two of the three lakes. Some entertainment is provided in high season, free for children. Madame Trémorin opens the farmhouse to campers to look around on demand. Golf 12 km. Wooden chalets, mobile homes and gites for hire. Used by a Dutch tour operator (10 pitches).

Directions: Site is by the D576 Dol-de-Bretagne - Pontorson road, just east of Baguer-Pican. It can be reached from the new N176 taking exit for Dol-Est and Baguer-Pican.

Charges 1999: Per unit Ffr. 55.00 - 75.00; adult 22.00 - 28.00; child (under 7 yrs) 10.00 - 14.00; electricity (5/6A) 18.00 - 19.00. Credit cards accepted.

Open: 15 April - 15 September.

Reservations: Made with Ffr. 300 deposit (eurocheque preferred); contact site. Address: Baguer-Pican, 35120 Dol-de-Bretagne. Tel: (0)2.99.48.09.55. FAX: (0)2.99.48.13.37.

AR Discount
Less 5%

3504 Camping Le P'tit Bois, St Jouan des Guérêts, nr St Malo

Busy, very well kept site near ferry port and yachting centre of St Malo.

On the outskirts of St Malo, this neat, family oriented site is very popular with British visitors, being ideal for one night stops or for longer stays in this interesting area. Le P'tit Bois provides 274 large level pitches (approx. 140 for tourers) which are divided into groups by mature hedges and trees. Nearly all have electricity (6A) and over half have water. Two sanitary blocks, one in the newer area across the lane, are both of an unusual `open' design which may prove a little cool in poor weather. British style WCs, washbasins in cabins and free, pre-set showers. Chemical disposal in the men's sections, laundry facilities and baby baths in the ladies'. Simple facilities for disabled people. An attractive, sheltered area around the pools provides a focus for the site, containing a snack bar (15/5-1/9) with takeaway, small bar, TV/games rooms and outdoor chess. The complex includes a standard pool, two paddling pools and two water slides (from 1/5). At the far end are a tennis court and minigolf. To one side of the site is a children's playground (on hard sand) and volleyball. Small shop (from 15/5). At the entrance is a bar where entertainment is organised. Motorcaravan service point. No barbecues. Card operated security gates (Ffr 100 deposit). Fishing 1.5 km, bicycle hire or riding 5 km, golf 7 km. Many British tour operators (25%) and site-owned mobile homes and chalets to rent, but this does mean that facilities open over a long season (possibly limited hours).

Directions: St Jouan is west off N137 St Malo - Rennes, outside St Malo. Site signed from N137 (exit St Jouan).

Charges 1999: Per person Ffr. 29.00; child (under 7 yrs) 20.00; pitch and car 60.00 - 89.00; extra car 20.00; dog 25.00; electricity (6A) 20.00; water and drainage 15.00. Credit cards accepted.

Open: 1 May - 11 September.

Reservations: Made on receipt of 25% of total cost, plus fee (120) for July/Aug. Address: 35430 St Jouan-des-Guérêts. Tel: (0)2.99.21.14.30. FAX: (0)2.99.81.74.14. Internet: www.acdev.com/ptitbois.

3701 Camping de la Mignardière, Ballan-Miré, nr Tours

Pleasant little site quietly situated just southwest of Tours.

The situation of this little site may appeal to many - only 8 km. from the centre of the city of Tours, yet in a peaceful spot within easy reach of several of the Loire châteaux, notably Azay-le-Rideau, and with various sports amenities on or very close to the site. There are now 157 numbered pitches for touring units, all with electricity and 100 with drainage and water also. They are on flat grass and are of good size. Four modern sanitary blocks have British WCs, free hot water in the washbasins (in private cabins) and the sinks, and premixed hot water in the showers. There is a unit for disabled people, a baby bath in the heated block near to reception, chemical disposal and laundry facilities. Shop, two unheated, large swimming pools (15/5-15/9) with sunbathing terrace, a good tennis court, table tennis and bicycle hire. Bar, restaurant and crêperie with takeaway near (all 15/5-15/9). Just outside the site is a small 'parc de loisirs' with pony rides, minigolf, small cars, playground and other amusements. An attractive lake catering particularly for windsurfing is 300 m. (boards for hire or use your own) and there is a family fitness run. Fishing 500 m, riding 1 km, golf 2 km. Barrier gates with card (100 Ffr. deposit), closed 22.30 - 07.30 hrs. Reservation is essential for most of July/Aug. Mobile homes and chalets for hire.

Directions: From Chinon along A751, follow signs to site on entering Ballan-Miré. From Tours take D751 towards Chinon. Just after Joué-les-Tours look for and turn right at Campanile Hotel - follow signs to site.

Charges 1999: Per unit incl. 2 persons Ffr. 86.00 - 106.00, comfort pitch with 3 services 120.00 - 140.00; extra person 24.00 - 28.00; child (under 7) 16.00 - 18.00; electricity (6A) 18.00; dog 10.00. Credit cards accepted.

Open: 4 April - 4 October.

Reservations: Made for any length with deposit (Ffr. 260) and fee (90). Address: Ave des Aubépines, 37510 Ballan-Miré. Tel: (0)2.47.73.31.00. FAX: (0)2.47.73.31.01. E-mail: mign@france-campings.com. Internet: www.france-campings.com.mignardiere.

AR Discount
Less 10%
excl. July/Aug.

Camping ★ ★ ★ ★
DE LA MIGNARDIERE

37510 Ballan-Miré
Tel: 02 47 73 31 00 Fax: 02 47 73 31 01

All the comforts of a 4 star camp with a wide range of activities for enjoyment and relaxation of adults and children; swimming pool and tennis on site, water sports lake, ponies and minigolf very close, the Loire châteaux and all the attractions of Tours.

6 Mobile Homes and 8 Chalets for hire
From autoroute take exit for Chambray-les-Tours.

3801 Le Coin Tranquille, Les Abrets

Family run site with swimming pool and restaurant, in peaceful surroundings.

Le Coin Tranquille is set in the peaceful surroundings of the Dauphiny countryside, north of Grenoble and east of Lyon. It is well situated in relation to the Chartreuse Massif, the Savoy regions and the Alps. Developed originally by Martine's parents, who are still very active about the site, original trees such as walnuts now blend with many flowering shrubs to make a lovely environment doubly enhanced by the rural aspect and the marvellous views. Martine and Gilles have developed other aspects, one being the popular French Flavour Holidays emphasising the culture, gastronomy and nature of the area. It is a pleasant and friendly site with 182 comfortably sized pitches, 160 for tourers. All have electricity (2, 3 or 6A) on grass, separated by hedges. Swimming and paddling pools (15/5-30/9). Excellent restaurant (open all year, closed one day a week in low season) with a reasonably priced menu and takeaway. An excellent large sanitary block in the centre of the site has private cabins, British style WCs, controllable water, facilities for children and disabled people and a laundry. Two other refurbished blocks are on either edge of the site and all have dishwashing. Shop, two children's play areas on grass and a TV/video room, games room and quiet lounge. In high season children's games, slide shows and a programme for adults are arranged. Bicycle hire. Fishing 5 km. riding 6 km. A popular site where you may be tempted to remain enjoying the views and amenities or venture further to explore the interests of this region. Used by tour operators. A 'Sites et Paysages' member. `Camping Cheque' 'FRENCH FLAVOUR'

Directions: Site is northeast of Les Abrets. From the town take the N6 towards Chambery, turning left after about 2 km. where the camp is signed.

Charges 1999: Per pitch incl. 2 persons Ffr. 85.00 - 126.00; extra adult 24.00 - 33.00; child (2-7 yrs) 14.00 - 22.00; extra vehicle 13.00 - 21.00; electricity 2A 8.00, 3A 12.00 or 6A 19.00. Credit cards accepted.

Open: 1 April - 31 October.

Reservations: Write to site with deposit (Ffr. 600) and fee (100). Address: 38490 Les Abrets en Dauphine. Tel: (0)4.76.32.13.48. FAX: (0)4.76.37.40.67.

3711M Camping Municipal Au Bord du Cher, Veretz, nr Tours

Managed by the Barot family who provide a warm welcome and, in season, live on the site in their caravan, this is an inexpensive, well laid out site on the banks of the River Cher, with views through tall elm trees to the Château of Veretz. With 58 pitches, most divided by small hedges and all with at least 6A electricity, the site is just outside the town of Veretz where shops, restaurants, bars, etc. can be found. Baker 700 m. Outdoor swimming pool (July/Aug) 5 km. The large, modern, basic sanitary block includes free hot showers, British and Turkish style WCs, dishwashing under cover, chemical disposal, laundry and washing machine. Motorcaravan service point. Children's playground and table tennis. Fishing. Bicycle hire 5 km, riding 3 km. A new wooden chalet houses reception and plenty of tourist information, with notice boards giving weather forecasts, etc. Of particular interest is information for railway enthusiasts, there are restored steam trains and track in the area. River trips are possible on the river. Bus service from Tours station to Bleré passes site entrance. English spoken.

Directions: Site is at Veretz, via the N76 road, 10 km. southeast of Tours (much better than the municipal at St Avertin en-route).

Charges 1999: Per pitch Ffr. 11.00; adult 12.00; child (under 7 yrs) 6.00; vehicle 11.00; electricity 6A 13.00. No credit cards.

Open: end May - 19 September.

Reservations: Contact site. Address: 37270 Veretz. Tel: (0)2.47.50.50.48. FAX: (0)2.47.50.33.22 (Mairie). E-mail: mairie.veretz@wanadoo.fr.

AR Discount
Less 10%

3901 Camping-Caravaning La Plage Blanche, Ounans

Attractive riverside site with good amenities.

Situated in open countryside, along the banks of the River Loue, this site has 220 good sized, marked pitches on level ground, most with electricity (6A). Trees provide fully shaded and semi-shaded pitches. Approximately 1 km. of riverside and beach provide the ideal setting for children to swim and play safely in the gently flowing, shallow water. A canoe/kayak base is also on site. Modern, well kept sanitary facilities in three unusual blocks have hot showers with push-button controls, separate washing cabins, British style WCs and chemical disposal. Dishwashing facilities are provided in blocks of 8 sinks, there is a launderette and motorcaravan service point. Bar/restaurant with terrace (15/4-15/9), pizzeria and takeaway (all season). Activities include river fishing, table tennis, and bicycle hire. TV room. Children's play area. Riding 3 km, golf 10 km. Caravans for hire. Used by tour operators.

Directions: Ounans is 20 km southeast of Dole. From autoroute A39 from Dijon or autoroute 36 from Besançon, take Dole exit and then D405 to Parcey. After Parcey take N5 to Mont Sous Vaudrey (8 km) then D472 towards Pontarlier to Ounans from where site is signed.

Charges 1999: Per person Ffr. 25.00; child (under 7 yrs) 15.00; pitch 31.00; extra tent or car 12.00; dog 5.00; electricity (6A) 19.00; local tax (over 14 yrs) 2.00. Less 20% outside July/Aug. Credit cards accepted.

Open: 15 March - 31 October.

Reservations: Made with deposit (Ffr. 200) and fee (50) by Eurocheque. Address: 39380 Ounans. Tel: (0)3.84.37.69.63. FAX: (0)3.84.37.60.21.

AR Discount
Welcome drink.

3904 Camping La Pergola, Marigny, Lac de Chalain

Hillside, terraced site overlooking lake.

Bordering on Switzerland, overlooking the sparkling waters of Lac de Chalain, Le Pergola is set amidst the undulating, cultivated countryside of the Jura. Not on a main route, it is worth a detour for the restful peace of the country. It is a short distance from the magnificent Cascades du Herrison. This is a well appointed site with 200 level, mainly stony pitches, separated by small conifers and having some shade on numerous terraces with steep steps between, giving good views over the lake. All have electricity, water and drainage. A tall fence protects the site from the path which separates the camp from the lakeside beach but there are frequent gates. The entrance is nicely landscaped with flowers and a small waterfall next to the three pools (two heated) and entertainment area. An excellent new sanitary block is on the lowest level and there are four others on different terraces. Washing machines and dryers. Facilities for disabled people, who are advised to select a lower terrace. Good children's play area with children's club. The organised programme in high season includes cycle tours, keep fit sessions and evening entertainment with 2 discos weekly (until midnight). Table tennis and volleyball. Watersports include windsurfing, pedaloes and electric boats for hire. Shop and large restaurant at the entrance, which is also used by visitors to the lake. Used by British tour operators. `Camping Cheque'

Directions: Site is 2½ km. north of Doucier on Lake Chalain road D27.

Charges guide: Per unit incl. 2 persons, electricity and water: lake pitch Ffr. 90.00 - 207.50, plus supplement for lake-side 30.00; standard pitch 90.00 - 177.00; extra person 28.00; child (3-6 yrs) 20.00; baby (0-2 yrs) 10.00; extra car 15.00; dog 5.00; local tax 1.50. Credit cards accepted.

Open: 1 May - 30 September.

Reservations: Write to site with Ffr. 800 deposit and 170 fee. Address: 39130 Marigny. Tel: (0)3.84.25.70.03. FAX: (0)3.84.25.75.96.

France - Landes

4001 Airotel Le Boudigau, Labenne-Océan, nr Bayonne

Well shaded pinewood site 12 km. north of Bayonne.

This is a site which is well placed for either beach holidays or interesting excursions, being only 20 km. from Biarritz and 35 km. from the Spanish border. The beach 500 m. from the site (but plenty of free parking if a car is needed) has a supervised swimming area and is excellent for surfing. The terrain at Le Boudigau is basically sandy soil but it has become very hard and compressed. The pitches are all level, except for one small area with a very slight slope, all are a good size and are separated by a few young bushes. Of the 218 touring pitches, 200 have electricity (5A). One of the three sanitary blocks is devoted entirely to showers which are pre-set in cubicles with no shelf or divider. The other two identical blocks are in modern style with mainly British style WCs, washbasins in cabins and free hot water. New this season is a mother and baby room with bath and changing mat also an ironing room. Facilities for disabled people, chemical disposal and motorcaravan services. The redesigned pool area provides two large, irregularly shaped swimming pools and a paddling pool, with paved, sunbathing terraces and sun-beds, plus a solarium. The commercial aspects of the site are located just outside the entrance and are open to all. They include a large well stocked supermarket (all season), snack bar and bar/restaurant (June-Aug). Also provided are washing machines and dryers, TV room, table tennis, boule pitches, play area and volleyball. In high season a club is organised for children, with shows, folk groups and discos for adults. Bicycle hire and fishing on site, golf 7 km, riding 500 m. Mobile homes and chalets to let.

Directions: Turn off N10 at Labenne for Labenne-Océan and site is on right in village. From the north, join N10 via St Geours de Maremne.

Charges 1999: Per unit incl. 2 persons Ffr 60.00 - 145.00; extra adult 28.00; child 18.00; local tax: adult 3.30, child (1-18 yrs) 1.65; animal 15.00; extra car free - 20.00; electricity (5A) 20.00. Credit cards accepted.

Open: 15 May - 15 September.

Reservations: Made for any length with deposit (25%) and fee (Ffr. 140). Address: 40530 Labenne-Océan. Tel: (0)5.59.45.42.07. FAX: (0)5.59.45.77.76.

AIROTEL LE BOUDIGAU ★★★★

Camping International - 40530 LABENNE OCÉAN - ☎ 05.59.45.42.07
05.59.45.30.24
Fax: 05.59.45.77.76

★ Two swimming pools
★ Bar, Restaurant
★ Supermarket - Launderette
★ Entertainment

★ Chalets, Caravans and
  Mobile Homes for hire
★ Sandy Beach with naturist section
★ Nearby: Tennis, Mini golf
  Fishing and Horse Riding

On the South Coast of the Landes, under the pines, beside the sea

---

4010 Camping du Domaine de la Rive, Biscarrosse

Landes site in superb beach-side location on Lac de Sanguinet.

La Rive is set in pine woods and provides mostly level pitches of mixed size, numbered but not very clearly defined, and all with electricity (6A). There is good shade. Five modern toilet blocks are of good quality with washbasins in cabins and mainly British style toilets. Disabled people are catered for in three blocks and there are baby baths and chemical disposal. The bar, which also serves snacks and takeaway, has a games room adjoining and the restaurant provides reasonably priced meals (15/6-10/9). The swimming pool complex is wonderful, with various pools linked by water channels and bridges and four slides. There is also a jacuzzi and paddling pool, all surrounded by paved sunbathing areas and decorated with palm trees (proper swimming trunks). The beach is excellent, shelving gently to provide safe bathing for all ages. There are windsurfers and small craft can be launched from the site's slipway. Children's play area on sand, bicycle hire, fishing, two tennis courts, table tennis, boules, archery and football. Tournaments in various sports are arranged in July/Aug. Discos and karaoke evenings are organised outside the bar with a stage, plus a mini-club for children twice daily. Riding 10 km. A well stocked shop is at the site entrance (15/5-15/9). This is a friendly site with a good mix of nationalities. Used by tour operators (100 pitches). Mobile homes and cabins to hire. Caravan storage.

Directions: Take D652 from Sanguinet to Biscarrosse, and the site is signed on the right in about 6 km.

Charges 1999: Per pitch incl. 2 persons Ffr. 153.00; extra person 23.00; child (3-10 yrs) 15.00; boat 25.00. Less 30% outside July/Aug. Credit cards accepted.

Open: 1 April - 30 October.

Reservations: Advised for July/Aug. - write or fax site. Address: 40600 Biscarrosse. Tel: (0)5.58.78.12.33. FAX: (0)5.58.78.12.92. Internet: http://www.francecom.com/aft/camping/la.rive.

4004 Camping La Paillotte, Azur, nr Soustons

Very attractive, good lakeside site with an individual atmosphere.

La Paillotte, in the Landes area of southwest France, is a site with a character of its own. The camp buildings (reception, shop, restaurant, even sanitary blocks) are all Tahitian in style, circular and constructed from local woods with the typical straw roof (and layer of waterproof material underneath). Some are now being replaced but still in character. It lies right by the edge of the Soustons lake, 1½ km. from Azur village, with its own sandy beach. This is particularly suitable for young children because the lake is shallow and slopes extremely gradually, and there is a new water slide. For boating the site has a small private harbour where your own non-powered boat of shallow draught can be kept. Sailing, windsurfing (with lessons) and rowing boats and pedaloes for hire. The Atlantic beaches with their breakers are 10 km. Alternatively the site has two swimming pools (from 1/5). All 310 pitches at La Paillotte are marked, individual ones and are mostly shady with new shrubs and trees planted. The 125 pitches for touring units vary in price according to size, position and whether they are equipped with electricity, water, etc. The circular rustic-style sanitary blocks are rather different from the usual campsite installations, but are modern and fully tiled with British WCs and free hot showers in the central enclosed positions, then individual washbasins, partly enclosed with free hot water (some toilets and basins en-suite). Separate 'mini' facilities for children. Outside washing-up sinks with hot water, washing machines and dryers and chemical disposal. Other amenities include a shop (10/5-6/9), good restaurant with a very pleasant terrace overlooking the lake and a bar (all 1/6-10/9) and takeaway (high season). Sports, games and activities are organised for children and adults. 'Mini-club' room, again with 'mini' equipment. TV room. Activities include fishing, bicycle hire, table tennis, an amusement room with juke box. There is a library, treatment room and motorcaravan service points. Riding 5 km, golf 10 km. La Paillotte is an unusual site with its own atmosphere which appeals to many regular clients. Used by tour operators (45 pitches). Mobile homes and Polynesian style bungalows to rent. No dogs are accepted. Member 'Sites et Paysages' and 'Camping Qualité Plus'.

Directions: Coming from the north along N10, turn west on D150 at Magescq. From south go via Soustons. In Azur turn left before church (site signed).

Charges 1999: Per unit incl. 2 persons: standard pitch Ffr. 99.00 - 159.00; extra person (over 3 yrs) 20.00 - 32.00; electricity (10A) 28.00; water and electricity 30.00 - 40.00; pitch by lake plus 30.00 - 40.00; local tax (over 10) in July/Aug 1.65. Credit cards accepted.

Open: 21 May - 14 September.

Reservations: Advised for high season; made for Sat. to Sat. only 2/7- 27/8, with deposit (Ffr. 250 per week) and fee (160). Address: Azur, 40140 Soustons. Tel: (0)5.58.48.12.12. FAX: (0)5.58.48.10.73. Internet: www.francecom. com/aft/camping/la.paillotte.

4101 Le Parc du Val de Loire, Mesland, nr Blois

Family owned site with swimming pools, situated between Blois and Tours.

This site is quietly situated away from the main roads and towns, but is nevertheless centrally placed for visits to the châteaux; Chaumont, Amboise and Blois (21 km.) are the nearest in that order. It has 300 pitches of reasonable size, either in light woodland marked by trees or on open meadow with separators. Some 170 pitches have electricity, water and drainaway. The two original toilet blocks are of very fair quality with British WCs (external entry), washbasins in cabins, free hot showers at pre-set temperature, and hot water also in sinks. A third block has been added with modern facilities. There are units for disabled visitors, new baby bathrooms and laundry facilities. Three swimming pools are on site, the newest (200 sq.m.) with sunbathing area, and heated all season, plus a smaller pool with a very popular water slide, and a small children's pool. Other activities include a tennis court with floodlighting, good children's playgrounds with skate board facilities, bicycle hire, table tennis, minigolf, BMX track, tennis training wall, football practise pitch and basketball. Pony rides and some sports and competitions are organised in July/Aug. Barbecue area - some organised or DIY (free wood). There is a large shop with new bakery, a bar adjacent to the pools, with restaurant, snack service, TV room and large, new recreation room, plus pizzeria and takeaway. Wine tasting opportunities each Friday and a coach to Paris one day each week. Local walks on marked footpaths (maps Ffr.2). Fishing 2 km, riding 10 km, golf 9 or 25 km. Mobile homes and chalets for hire. Used by tour operators (100 pitches). Caravan storage available. Watch for the Rabbit family!

Directions: The village of Mesland is 5 km. northwest of Onzain, accessible from the Château-Renault/Amboise exit of A10 autoroute via D31 to Autrèche, continue 5 km. then left at La Hargardière at camp sign and 8 km. to site.

Charges 1999: Per unit incl. 2 persons: standard pitch (100 sq.m.) Ffr. 105.00 - 145.00, large pitch (150 sq.m.) with water and drainage 115.00 - 155.00; extra person 27.00 - 35.00; child (2-7 yrs) 16.00 - 20.00; electricity (6A) 16.00 - 20.00; animal 8.00 - 10.00. Credit cards accepted.

Open: 1 May - 15 September.

Reservations: Made for min. 4 days with deposit and fee (Ffr. 100). Address: Route de Fleuray, 41150 Mesland. Tel: (0)2.54.70.27.18. FAX: (0)2.54.70.21.71.

France - Loir-et-Cher

4103 Sologne Parc des Alicourts, Pierrefitte sur Sauldre

Secluded 21 hectare site in the heart of the forest with many sporting facilities.

This site is in a very secluded, forested area midway between Orléans and Bourges, about 20 km. to the east of the A10. There are 300 pitches, all with electricity connections (4/6A) and good provision for water. Most pitches are 150 sq.m. (min. 100) and vary from wooded to more open areas, thus giving a choice of amount of shade. There are three modern sanitary blocks with washbasins (open and in private cabins), razor points, hair dryers, controllable hot showers and baby/toddler bath rooms. Also provided are washing machines and drying facilities, chemical disposal and motorcaravan services. There is a restaurant using fresh produce and traditional cuisine plus a takeaway service in a pleasant bar with terrace. The shop has a good range of produce in addition to the basics (the nearest good sized town is some distance). All facilities are open all season. Leisure amenities are exceptional: an inviting pool complex (all season) with three pools (two heated), a spa and three water slides, a 7 hectare lake with fishing, bathing, canoes, pedaloes and children's play area, 5 hole golf course (very popular), football pitch, volleyball, tennis, minigolf, table tennis, boules, bicycle hire with cyclo-cross and mountain bikes and a way-marked path for walking and cycling. Competitions are organised for adults as well as children and, in high season, a club for children with an entertainer twice a day, a disco once a week and a dance for adults. A new animation room was added for '98. Used by tour operators.

Directions: From A71 take Lamotte-Beuvron exit (no. 3) onto D923 towards Aubigny. After 14 km. turn right at camp sign onto D24E. Site is clearly signed in 4 km.

Charges 1999: Per unit (incl. 2 persons) Ffr. 110.00 - 150.00; extra person over 18 yrs 35.00 - 45.00, 7-17 yrs 22.00 - 32.00, 1-6 yrs 17.00 - 23.00; electricity 4A 26.00, 6A 30.00; dog 28.00; local tax (1/6-13/9) 1.50, under 10 yrs 0.70. Reductions for low season longer stays. No credit cards.

Open: 12 May - 11 September.

Reservations: Made for min. 7 days for July/Aug. only, with 25% deposit and Ffr 100 fee. Address: Domaine des Alicourts, 41300 Pierrefitte sur Sauldre. Tel: (0)2.54.88.63.34. FAX: (0)2.54.88.58.40.

4104 Camping Château des Marais, Muides sur Loire, nr Chambord

Impressive site with excellent facilities, near famous royal château.

The château at Chambord, with its park, is certainly impressive and well worth a visit. The nearby Château des Marais campsite is also well situated to visit other châteaux in the 'Vallée des Rois'. The recently designed site, providing 199 large pitches, all with electricity (5A), water and drainage and with ample shade, is situated in the oak and hornbeam woods of its own small château (in which there are rooms to let all year round). It boasts a heated swimming pool and new water slide with its own pool, a pleasant bar/restaurant, bicycle hire, fishing lake, excursions by coach to Paris and an entertainment programme in high season. Riding 5 km, golf 12 km. The village of Muides sur Loire, with a variety of small shops, etc. is five minutes walk. Four modern, purpose built sanitary blocks have the latest facilities including some large showers and washbasins en-suite, British style WCs, chemical disposal, washing machine, etc. with hot water throughout. Motorcaravan service point. English is spoken and the reception from the enthusiastic owners and the staff is very welcoming. Used by tour operators (80 pitches). Bungalows and mobile homes to let, as well as the rooms in the château (breakfast included) - useful out of season.

Directions: From A10 autoroute take exit 7 to Mer, then cross the Loire to join the D951 and follow signs.

Charges 1999: Per pitch incl. vehicle and 2 persons Ffr. 140.00; extra person 33.00; child (under 5 yrs) 20.00; dog 10.00; electricity (5A) 20.00; local tax (over 16 yrs) 2.00. Credit cards accepted (for amounts over Ffr. 500).

Open: 15 May - 15 September, (rooms in château, etc: all year.)

Reservations: Advised July/Aug. and made with 30% deposit. Address: 41500 Muides sur Loire. Tel: (0)2.54.87.05.42. FAX: (0)2.54.87.05.43.

AR Discount
Aperitif in bar or restaurant

Château
des Marais
CAMPING-CARAVANING-HOTEL
★★★★ GRAND CONFORT

☆ waterslide ☆ canoe & kayak hire
☆ pony rides on site
☆ bungalow & mobile home to let

27, rue de Chambord
41500 MUIDES-SUR-LOIRE
Tél 02 54 87 05 42 Fax 02 54 87 05 43
J. BONVALLET

4403 Castel Camping Le Pré du Château, Guérande, nr La Baule

Select, small, quiet site for all units.

Rather different from the more usual Castel sites, this is much smaller. It has a quiet atmosphere, very popular with couples and retired people and is probably not for families with older children or teenagers. In the grounds of the 14th century Château de Careil, this small site, shaded by mature trees, has less than 50 good sized pitches, all with electricity (6/10A) and water, some with drainage also. Small swimming pool (10/6-5/9). Bread can be ordered (supermarket near). Children's playground, TV room, volleyball and table tennis. Sanitary facilities provide British style WCs with washbasins in cubicles, and are in the same building as reception. Four unisex shower and washbasin rooms have been added and the old external WCs have been re-tiled. En-suite facilities for disabled people, a baby room and a washing machine. Two restaurants are within walking distance. Tours of the Château are possible in the main season (Ffr. 25), also by candlelight in July/Aug (Ffr. 30). A market with fresh produce is held every Thursday with archery on Tuesday evenings - both in the Château courtyard.

> **Directions:** Take D92 from Guérande to La Baule and turn east to Careil before the town. From D99 Guérande - St Nazaire road, turn onto D92, following signs to `Intermarche' and for Château de Careil. Take care as site entrance gate is fairly narrow and located between two bends making access a little awkward.
>
> **Charges 1999:** Per unit incl. 2 persons and 6A electricity Ffr. 110.00 - 126.00; extra person 26.00; extra child (under 10 yrs) 16.00; 10A electricity 10.00; local tax 2.00. No credit cards.
>
> **Open:** 1 May - 30 September.
>
> **Reservations:** Possible with deposit (Ffr 450) and booking fee (50). Address: Careil, 44350 Guérande. Tel: (0)2.40.60.22.99. FAX: as phone. Internet: www.castels-campings.com.

4404 Castel Camping Parc Sainte-Brigitte, La Turballe, nr La Baule

Well established site in the grounds of a manor house, 3 km. from beaches.

A mature and spacious site, Ste Brigitte has 150 pitches, 106 with electricity (6A) and 25 with water and waste water also. Some are in a circular, park-like setting near the entrance, more are in the wooded areas under tall trees and others are on more open grass in an unmarked area near the pool. One can walk around much of the areas of the estate not used for camping, there are farm animals to see and a fishing lake is very popular. The main sanitary block has free hot water (takes time to come through) in all facilities and is of fair quality, supplemented by a second block next to it. They offer British style toilets, washbasins in cabins, with bidets for women, fully controllable showers, two bathrooms and sinks. Washing machines and dryer (lines provided), chemical disposal and motorcaravan services. Children's playground, bicycle hire, boules, volleyball, pool, `baby-foot' and table tennis. A TV room and `salle de reunion' are near the manor house. Heated swimming pool with children's pool. Small shop and a nice little restaurant/bar with takeaway (both 15/5-15/9). Bread is available (baker calls). A quiet place to stay outside the main season, with few facilities open; in high season it is mainly used by families and it can become very busy. Inland from the main road, it is a little under 3 km. from the nearest beach. Riding 6 km, golf 15 km. Used by a tour operator (20 pitches).

> **Directions:** Entrance is off the busy La Turballe-Guérande D99 road, 3 km. east of La Turballe. A one-way system operates - in one lane, out via another.
>
> **Charges 1998:** Per person Ffr 26.50 plus 1.00 tax; child (under 7) 19.00; pitch 28.50, with water and electricity 57.00; car 15.00; dog 9.50. No credit cards.
>
> **Open:** 1 April - 1 October.
>
> **Reservations:** Made for any length with exact dates and recommended for July/Aug, with deposit (Ffr. 400) plus fee (100). Address: 44420 La Turballe. Tel: (0)2.40.24.88.91. FAX: (0)2.40.23.30.42.

France - Loire-Atlantique

4409 Castel Camping Château du Deffay, Pontchâteau

Relaxed, family managed site, near the Côte Armor and Brière Regional National Park.

Château de Deffay is a refreshing departure from the usual Castel formula in that it is not over organised or supervised and has no tour operator units. The landscape is natural right down to the molehills, and the site blends well with the rural environment of the estate, lake and farmland which surround it. For these reasons it is enjoyed by many. However, with the temptation of free pedaloes (which are showing their age) and the fairly deep, unfenced lake, parents should ensure that children are supervised. The 120 good sized, fairly level pitches have pleasant views, either on open grass, on shallow terraces divided by hedges, or informally arranged in a central, semi-sloping wooded area. Most have 6A electricity. The main sanitary unit, housed in a converted barn, is well equipped with modern free controllable hot showers, British type toilets, washbasins in cabins with hooks and shelves. Provision for disabled people and a baby bathroom have been added and there are washing machines, a dryer and chemical disposal. Maintenance can be variable and, with the boiler located at one end of the block, hot water takes time to reach the other. Motorcaravan services. Extra facilities are available in the old courtyard area of the smaller château (which dates from before 1400) which is also where the bar and small restaurant with takeaway, well stocked shop and the solar heated swimming pool and paddling pool are located (all 15/5-15/9). The larger château (built 1880) and another lake stand away from this area providing pleasant walking. It is possible to book dinners in the château with a minimum of 20 persons. The reception has been built separately to contain the camping area. There is a play area for children on grass, a TV room below the bar and a separate room for table tennis. Animation in season. Tennis and swimming, pedaloes and fishing in the lake, all free, plus riding and bicycle hire. The Guérande Peninsula, La Baule Bay and the natural wilderness of the 'Grande Brière' are all near. Golf 5 km. Alpine type chalets (23) for letting have been built overlooking the lake and fit well with the environment. Torch useful. *'Camping Cheque'* 'FRENCH FLAVOUR'

Directions: Site signed from D33 Pontchâteau - Herbignac road near Ste. Reine. Also signed from D773 and N165.

Charges 1998: Per pitch simple Ffr. 39.00 - 55.00, with electricity (4A) 60.00 - 76.00; with 3 services 69.00 - 95.00; per adult 16.00 - 23.00; child (2-12 yrs) 11.00 - 15.00. Credit cards accepted.

Open: 1 May - 25 September.

Reservations: Accepted for a min. period of 6 nights with deposit (Ffr. 300) and fee (100). Address: BP 18, Ste. Reine, 44160 Pontchâteau. Tel: (0)2.40.88.00.57 (winter: (0)2.40.01.63.84). FAX: (0)2.40.01.66.55.

4410 Camping Caravaning International Le Patisseau, Pornic

Friendly, busy site near fishing port of Pornic with its own pool.

Le Patisseau is rurally situated 2½ km. from the sea. It is quite a relaxed site which can be very busy and even a little noisy in high season due to its popularity with young families and teenagers. The older part of the site has an attractive woodland setting, although the pitches are slightly smaller than in the newer 'field' section, but most have water and electrical connections (4, 6 or 10A). Hedges are growing well in the newer section marking individual pitches. A railway line runs along the bottom half of the site with trains two or three times a day, but they do finish at 10.30 pm. and the noise is minimal. The site has a small indoor restaurant and bar (both 26/6-28/8) on a terrace near the medium sized pool (all season). Two water slides have been added with their own pool. Games area with volleyball and table tennis and children's play areas, one large on sand. There are three sanitary blocks with the one behind reception most recently refurbished. The other two date from the late 80s and are beginning to show their age. These include free hot showers, washbasins in private cabins, British style WCs, child-size toilets, baby baths, fully equipped laundry rooms and dishwashing facilities. Chemical disposal. Shop (all season). Bicycle hire. Fishing 800 m, riding and golf 4 km. This a happy, busy site and the Morice family work very hard to maintain a friendly atmosphere, but do not expect it to be too neat and tidy with everything run like clockwork - they want people to enjoy themselves. Pornic itself is a delightful fishing village and the coastline is interesting with secluded sandy coves and inlets. Chalets and mobile homes for hire.

Directions: Site is signed at the roundabout junction of the D751 (Pornic - Nantes) road, and from the town centre.

Charges 1999: Per unit incl. 2 persons Ffr. 81.00 - 145.00; extra adult 26.00 - 28.00; child (under 7 yrs) 16.00 - 17.00; extra vehicle 20.00; electricity 4A 18.00, 6A 22.00 or 10A 30.00; local tax 1.65.

Open: 1 May - 11 September, with limited facilities outside July/Aug.

Reservations: Made with deposit (Ffr. 300) and fee (100); contact site by letter, phone or fax. Address: 29 Rue du Patisseau, 44210 Pornic. Tel: (0)2.40.82.10.39. FAX: (0)2.40.82.22.81.

4501 Les Bois du Bardelet, Gien

Attractive, lively family run site with lake and pool complex in eastern Loire.

This site, in a rural setting, is well situated for exploring the less well known eastern part of the Loire Valley. A lake and pools have been attractively landscaped in 20 acres of former farmland blending old and new with natural wooded areas and more open `field' areas with rural views. Bois du Bardelet provides almost 200 pitches for touring units, all more than 100 sq.m. with 80 electrical connections (15A) and some serviced (electricity, water and waste water). The communal areas are based on attractively converted former farm buildings and include two sanitary blocks with controllable hot showers, washbasins in private cabins, British type WCs, facilities for disabled people and for babies, free hairdryers and washing machines. The range of leisure facilities includes two swimming pools, one with a child's pool, the other indoor and heated, archery, a lake for canoeing and fishing, tennis, minigolf, boules, table tennis and bicycle hire (some activities high season only). A family club card can be purchased to make use of these activities on a daily basis. Shop for basics only (from 1/7, supermarket 5 km). Snack bar, takeaway and restaurant (15/5-15/9), pizzeria (1/7-30/8) (15/6-15/9), plus a pleasant terraced bar. Various excursions are organised, the most popular being to Paris on Wednesdays, which can be pre-booked. `Camping Cheque'

Directions: From Gien take D940 towards Bourges. After some 5 km. turn left just before Peugeot garage - follow signs to site for 1.5 km. (narrow road and turning from main road).

Charges 1999: Per unit incl. 2 persons Ffr 120.00, with electricity 145.00; extra person (over 2 yrs) 28.00 - 30.00; animal 8.00. Less 25% in low seasons (40% for over 60s). Credit cards accepted (amounts over Ffr 150).

Open: 1 April - 30 September.

Reservations: Made with deposit (Ffr. 350) and fee (100) - contact site for details. Address: Rte. de Bourges, Poilly, 45500 Gien. Tel: (0)2.38.67.47.39. FAX: (0)2.38.38.27.16.

4601 Castel Camping de la Paille Basse, Souillac, nr Sarlat

Site in high rural situation with panoramic views and good swimming pools.

Lying some 8 km. from Souillac, this family owned and managed site is easily accessible from the N20 and well placed to take advantage of excursions into the Dordogne. It is part of a large Domaine of 80 hectares, which is available to campers for walks and recreation. The site itself has a high location and there are excellent wide views over the surrounding countryside. The 250 pitches are in two main areas - one level in cleared woodland with good shade, the other on grass on open ground without shade. They are all minimum 100 sq.m., numbered and marked, with about 80 having electricity, water and drainaway; electricity is available near all the others. Good swimming pool complex, with a main pool (25 x 10 m.), a second one (10 x 6) and a paddling pool; not heated. Solarium and a crêperie adjacent to the pools. Shop. Restaurant, bar with terrace and takeaway. Disco room (twice weekly in season), TV rooms (with satellite) and cinema room. Archery (free) and tennis (charged). Children's playground and mini-club. Laundry facilities. Doctor calls. The main sanitary installations (there is also a small night unit at one end of site) are in three different sections, all centrally located close to reception. All have modern equipment including chemical disposal, and are kept very clean. Activities and entertainment organised in season. Golf 5 km, fishing or bicycle hire 10 km. Mobile homes for hire (15). The site can get very busy in main season, but there is space from mid Aug. `Camping Cheque'

Directions: From Souillac take D15 northwest towards Salignac-Eyvignes and after 6 km. turn right at camp sign on 2 km. approach road.

Charges 1998: Per person Ffr. 32.00; child (under 7) 20.00; pitch 52.00 or with 3 services 64.00; electricity 3A 19.00, 6A 32.00; local tax 1.00. Less 20% outside 15/6-1/9. Credit cards accepted.

Open: 12 May - 15 September.

Reservations: Made for min. 1 week with deposit and Ffr. 120 booking fee. Address: 46200 Souillac-sur-Dordogne. Tel: (0)5.65.37.85.48. FAX: (0)5.65.37.09.58. E-mail: paille-basse@wanadoo.fr.

France - Lot / Lot-et-Garonne

4605 Camping Le Rêve, Le Vigan

Very peaceful, clean site with pool far from the madding crowd.

Le Rêve is situated in the heart of rolling countryside where the Perigord runs into Quercy. Pitches are divided by shrubs, and a variety of attractive trees have grown well to provide some shade. There is plenty of space and some of the 60 pitches are very large. Most have access to electricity (6A) and there are now 9 pitches in the woods. The toilet block is modern, kept very clean and has been extended to include a heated enclosed area. There are free hot showers and washbasins in cabins, plus special cubicles for disabled people and a baby room. Washing machine and dryers, chemical disposal. The small swimming pool has a large children's paddling pool with 'mushroom' fountain. The reception area has been extended and houses a small shop, a pleasant bar and restaurant and takeaway. A small shaded children's playground, boules area, bicycle hire, table tennis and volleyball facilities complete the amenities. Fishing 5 km, riding 2 km. A few chalets for hire. Le Rêve continues to impress us with its tranquillity and the young Dutch owners are keen to develop the site in such a way that this will not be lost. A site particularly suitable for families with very young children. Caravan storage.

Directions: Follow N20 from Souillac towards Cahors. About 3 km. south of Payrac, turn right onto the D673 (signed Le Vigan and Gourdon). After about 2 km, Le Rêve is signed on the right down a small lane and the site is some 3 km. further on.

Charges 1999: Per adult Ffr. 23.00; child (under 7 yrs) 10.00; pitch 28.00; electricity (6A) 14.00. Less 20-35% outside July/Aug. No credit cards.

Open: 25 April - 23 September.

Reservations: Made for any length with deposit (Ffr. 300) and fee (20). Address: 46300 Le Vigan. Tel: (0)5.65.41.25.20. FAX: (0)5.65.41.68.52.

AR Discount
Less 15%
after 15 Aug.

4701 Moulin du Périé, Sauveterre-la-Lémance, Fumel

Immaculate, pretty little site tucked away in rolling wooded countryside.

This site has some 125 pitches, well spaced and marked on flat grass. Most have good shade, and pitches on a newer section are already benefiting from extensive planting of attractive trees and shrubs. Grass areas and access roads are kept very clean, as are the three modern, well appointed toilet blocks, which have facilities for babies and disabled people. Chemical disposal and motorcaravan service point. The attractive main buildings are converted from an old mill and its outhouses. Flanking the courtyard, as well as the restaurant (open air, but covered), are the bar/reception area in which people can meet and supervise younger children (there is even a Lego pit). A small shop sells essentials, with a good small supermarket in the village. Bar and new restaurant with snacks and takeaway. The site has a clean but rather small swimming pool, with a children's pool much the same size. A small lake next to the pool is used for inflatable boats and swimming. Next to this is a large games field for football, volleyball, etc. There is a 'boulodrome', two table tennis tables, bicycle hire, a trampoline and a children's playground. Fishing 3 km. The site organises a number of activities on and off site in season, including a weekly French meal and barbecues round the lake. Inclusive special interest holidays are centred on food and wine, or walking. Some tour operators and a few tents, a caravan and mobile homes for hire. Many clients return again and again, so book early. A 'Sites et Paysages' member. *'Camping Cheque'*

Directions: Sauveterre-la-Lémance lies by the Fumel - Périgueux (D710) road, midway between the Dordogne and Lot rivers. From the D710, cross the railway line, straight through the village and turn left (northeast) at the far end on to a minor road and past the Chateau. Site is 3 km. up this road.

Charges 1998: Per person Ffr. 34.00; child (under 7 yrs) 18.50; pitch and car 47.50; animal 21.00; electricity (6A) 20.50. Credit cards accepted.

Open: 4 April - 30 September.

Reservations: Advisable for July/Aug. Address: Sauveterre-la-Lémance, 47500 Fumel. Tel: (0)5.53.40.67.26. FAX: (0)5.53.40.62.46.

4703 Castel Camping Château de Fonrives, Rives, Villeréal

Neat, orderly site with swimming pool, in southwest of the Dordogne.

This is one of those very pleasant Dordogne sites set in pretty part-farmed, part-wooded countryside close to the delightful old town of Villeréal. The park is a mixture of hazelnut orchards, woodland with lake, château (mostly 16th century) and camping areas. Barns adjacent to the château have been tastefully converted - the restaurant particularly - to provide for the reception, the bar, B&B rooms, shop and games areas. The swimming pool is on the south side of this (10/5-20/9). There are 160 pitches, 116 for touring units. Of 100-150 sq.m, all have electricity and their own bin, 40 have taps also. Pitches near the woodland receive moderate shade, but elsewhere there is little to be gained from hedges and young trees. Some 'wild' camping is possible in one or two areas. The original sanitary block is clean and adequate with free hot water, push-button showers, washbasins in well appointed private cabins and British style WCs. There are two additional blocks with private bathrooms (weekly hire), facilities for children and laundry rooms. Chemical disposal and motorcaravan services. *continued overleaf*

4703 Castel Camping Château de Fonrives (continued)

The lake has a small beach and can be used for swimming, fishing or boating. A small field is set aside by the pool for volleyball and football. Newly renovated children's play area and new paddling pool. Reading room. Minigolf. Bicycle hire. Shop, restaurant, bar and snacks (all 10/6-10/9). Plenty of activities are organised for children and adults in season, including excursions and walks. Caravan storage available. Mobile homes, bungalows and chalets in the wood for hire.

Directions: Site is about 2 km. northwest of Villeréal, on the Bergerac road (D14/D207).

Charges 1999: Per unit incl. 2 adults Ffr. 81.00 - 120.00; extra person 25.00 - 33.00; child (under 7 yrs) 15.00 - 20.00; electricity 4A 18.00, 6A 20.00, 10A 25.00; dog 15.00; private bathroom 350 per week. Credit cards accepted.

Open: 8 May - 18 September.

Reservations: Advisable for July/Aug. Address: 47210 Rives. Tel: (0)5.53.36.63.38. FAX: (0)5.53.36.09.98.

4901 Castel Camping L'Etang de la Brèche, Varennes-sur-Loire, nr Saumur

Peaceful, spacious family site with swimming pool, adjacent to the Loire.

The Saint Cast family have developed L'Etang de la Brèche with loving care and attention over 25 years on a 25 ha. estate 4 km. west of Saumur on the edge of the Loire behind the dykes. It is a lovely base from which to explore the châteaux for which the region is famous and also its abbeys, wine cellars, mushroom caves and Troglodyte villages. It provides over 175 large, level pitches with shade from mixed tall trees and bushes, facing central grass areas with a nice spacious feel. Electricity to most pitches, water and drainaway on some. Three toilet blocks have been modernised to a high standard, providing showers and separate British WCs. Good hot water supply to washing up sinks, laundry, baby facilities and there are two units for disabled people. Chemical disposal and motorcaravan services. The good restaurant, also open to the public, blends well with the existing architecture and, together with the bar area and terrace, provides a social base and is probably one of the reasons why the site is popular with British visitors. A small lake (used for fishing) and wooded area ensuring a quiet, relaxed and rural atmosphere. The enlarged swimming pool complex provides three heated pools, plus a water slide and jacuzzi, for youngsters of all ages. A lovely new pool for little ones has safe miniature equipment (a prototype for the future?) Well organised, varied sporting and entertainment programme (July/Aug). Shop (butcher calls three times a week), epicerie, takeaway, pizzeria, general room, games and TV rooms. Tennis, basketball, football field and bicycle hire. Afternoon child minding. Low season excursions `Getting to know the area' and wine tastings. Torches needed at night. Used by tour operators. This is a comfortable holiday base for couples and families. `Camping Cheque'

Directions: Site is 100 m. north off the main N152, about 5 km. southeast of Saumur on the north bank of the Loire.

Charges 1998: Per unit incl. 2 persons Ffr. 85.00 - 135.00, 3 persons 105.00 - 150.00; extra adult 20.00 - 27.00; extra child (2-7 yrs) 10.00 - 15.00; electricity (10A) 16.00; water and drainage 13.00. Credit cards accepted.

Open: 15 May - 15 September.

Reservations: Made for min. 7 days with deposit and fee. Address: 49730 Varennes-sur-Loire. Tel: (0)2.41.51.22.92. FAX: (0)2.41.51.27.24. E-mail: etang.breche@wanadoo.fr.

4902 Camping de Chantepie, St Hilaire-St Florent, Saumur

Pleasant site with swimming pools, close to Saumur with lovely views over the Loire.

Your drive along the winding road bordered by apple orchards and vineyards is well rewarded on arriving at the floral entrance to Chantepie. The reception and shop are housed in the tastefully restored ancient farmhouse. The 150 level grass pitches are spacious, most with electricity (6A), and separated by low hedges of flowers and trees which offer some shade. Panoramic views over the Loire from the pitches on the terraced perimeter of the meadow are stunning, and there is a path leading to the river valley. Sanitary facilities are clean and adequate, although housed in separate buildings. There is hot water to all the private washbasins and pre-set showers. WCs are British style and there are facilities for disabled people. Two paddling pools and two heated swimming pools are surrounded by an attractive sitting area. Bar, terraced restaurant and separate takeaway (from 15/5). For those wanting to do their own cuisine, a well stocked herb garden is at their disposal. Leisure activities for all ages are catered for in July/Aug. by the `Chantepie Club'. Pony and donkey cart rides, bicycle and mountain bike hire (maps from reception), and there is a terraced minigolf course. New children's play area with wide variety of apparatus. Volleyball, TV, video games and table tennis. Fishing 200 m, riding 3 km, golf 2 km. Wine tasting evenings, excursions and canoeing expeditions are organised. Used by tour operators (30 pitches). Mobile homes (7) and Trigano tents for hire (10). `Camping Cheque'

Directions: Take D751 signed Gennes from Saumur. Turn left in Minerolle as signed and continue 4 km. to site.

Charges 1999: Per adult Ffr. 21.00 - 26.50; child (2-9 yrs) 11.60 - 14.50; pitch incl. car 50.50 - 63.00; electricity 14.00 - 17.50; local tax 2.00 (child 1.00). Credit cards accepted.

AR Discount
Less 10% in
June, 20% in
May or Sept.

Open: 1 May - 15 September.

Reservations: Contact site for details. Address: St Hilaire-St Florent, 49400 Saumur. Tel: (0)2.41.67.95.34. FAX: (0)2.41.67.95.85.

France - Maine-et-Loire / Manche

4906 Camping L'Européen de Montsabert, Coutures

Peaceful, spacious site, ideal for exploring the Saumur and Angers area.

Under management for the Commune of Gennes, this extensive campsite has a rural atmosphere in the shadow of Montsabert château, from where the visiting peacocks happily roam in the spacious surroundings. The 158 large pitches are mostly divided by hedges and provided with shade by the abundant mature trees. All pitches have water, waste water point and electricity (6A). The two modern toilet blocks with push-button showers, washbasins and bidets in cabins, British style toilets, outside dishwashing and laundry facilities, are more than adequate. Washing machine and dryer. Leisure facilities are generous and include a large gymnasium, minigolf, volley and basketball, table tennis, tennis, bicycle hire and a large 25 m. swimming pool. There is an expanse of grassed area for ball games. Picnic tables are provided in the shade near the entrance and a communal barbecue area is available. Activities such as windsurfing, canoeing, sailing and fishing are near, riding 15 km. There is a restaurant and takeaway (both 15/6-15/9) and a bar (1/6-15/9). This partially wooded site, fringed with impressive redwood trees, offers the peace of the countryside and yet easy access to Saumur and Angers. It is an ideal base for exploring, whether by foot, bicycle or car. Mobile homes and bungalows to rent. Used by tour operators (15 pitches).

Directions: From Saumur take D952 Angers road to Les Rosiers-sur-Loire, cross the river Loire to Gennes and take D751 signed Coutures. Follow camp signs in Coutures.

Charges 1999: Per pitch incl. 3 persons Ffr. 80.00 - 95.00, 2 persons in low season 70.00; extra person 20.00 - 25.00; electricity (6A) 15.00 - 18.00. Credit cards accepted.

Open: 1 May - 30 September.

Reservations: Contact site for details. Address: Montsabert, 49320 Coutures. Tel/Fax: (0)2.41.57.91.63.

AR Discount
Less 10% low
season (excl.
mobile homes)

Le Pays Gennois

CAMPING L'EUROPÉEN
★★★★

Montsabert - 49320 COUTURES - Tel/Fax: 02.41.57.91.63
Open from 01.05 until 30.09

Easy access, on the left border of the Loire (D751) between Angers and Saumur. Campsite L'Européen offers you restful and relaxing holidays on an exceptional site.

Mobile homes to let
Woodland park of 10 ha. - great comfort - heated swimming pool - sportsroom - tennis - swing golf - mini golf - basketball - French boules - canoe at 5 km - walking and cycling tours

BAR - SNACKS - RESTAURANT

5003 Castel Camping Lez Eaux, Granville

Family site with swimming pools just back from sea on Cotentin coast.

Set in the spacious grounds of a château, Lez Eaux lies in a rural situation just off the main route south, under 2 hours from Cherbourg. The nearest beach is 3 km, St Pair is 4 km. and Granville 7, and it is a very pleasant situation from which to explore this corner of the Cotentin peninsula. However, because of its location, Lez Eaux receives much 'en-route' trade, both from tour operator clients and independent campers on their way further south and at times this can put heavy pressure on the facilities (it is a good idea to book for peak season visits, or for single nights arrive early). There are 229 pitches, 50% of them taken by British and some Dutch tour operators with special places provided for late arrivals and early departures. Most pitches are of a very good size, semi- separated by trees and shrubs on either flat or very slightly sloping, grassy ground overlooking Normandy farmland and on either side of a small lake (with carp and other fish). All pitches have electricity (5/10A), some have drainage. Two modern toilet blocks have British WCs, washbasins in cabins, free hot showers and full provision for disabled people. They are cleaned three times daily. Small heated swimming pool (12 x 6 m.) and attractive fun pool with water slide (from 15/5). Shop. Small bar. Snacks and takeaway with set meal each night to order in advance (from 15/5). Activities include an adventure play area, good tennis court (Ffr. 40 per hour in high season), games room with table tennis, jacuzzi, bicycle hire, lake fishing and a TV room. Riding 5 km, golf 6 km. Torches required at night. Note: facilities not fully open until 15/5. 'Camping Cheque'

Directions: Site access is signed west about 7 km. southeast of Granville on main D973 road to Avranches.

Charges 1999: Per pitch incl. 2 persons Ffr. 105.00 - 125.00, pitch with 5A electricity 127.00 - 150.00, 10A electricity 136.00 - 160.00, with all services 140.00 - 170.00; extra person 32.00 - 38.00; child (under 7 yrs) 17.00 - 21.00. Credit cards accepted.

Open: 1 May - 15 September.

Reservations: Advisable for high season and made for min. 5 days with deposit (Ffr. 200) and fee (100). Address: 50380 St Pair-sur-Mer. Tel: (0)2.33.51.66.09. FAX: (0)2.33.51.92.02.

5000 Camping L'Etang des Haizes, La Haye-du-Puits

Attractive, informal site with small heated pool and pretty lake.

L'Etang des Haizes offers 98 good size pitches, of which 58 are for touring units, on fairly level ground, all with electricity (6A) and set in a mixture of conifers, orchard and shrubbery. Some very attractive slightly smaller pitches overlooking the lake and 40 mobile homes are inconspicuously sited. The two sanitary blocks are of modern construction, open plan and mixed, with British WCs, free controllable showers and washbasins in private cabins. Units for disabled people, washing up under cover, small laundry with two washing machines and a dryer, chemical disposal and motorcaravan services. The lake offers good coarse fishing for huge carp (we are told!), swimming (with a long slide), pedaloes, a small beach and now, believe it or not, a turtle can sometimes be seen on a fine day! Other facilities include a heated swimming pool, an attractive bar with terrace overlooking the lake and pool (both 15/5-10/9), two children's play areas, bicycle hire, table tennis, TV lounge, pool table, petanque, volleyball and archery, plus ducks and goats. Riding or golf 10 km. Only milk, bread and snacks (takeaway) on site, but supermarket in La Haye-du-Puits (1 km). Gate locked 22.00 - 07.00. The site is 8 km. from a sandy beach and a 25 km. drive from the Normandy landing beaches. Mobile homes to rent (18).

Directions: From Cherbourg follow N13 (Mont St Michel) road as far as Valognes, then the D2 to St Sauveur-le-Vicomte. Continue on the D900 for La Haye-du-Puits, go straight on at new roundabout on the outskirts of town and site is signed almost immediately on the right.

Charges 1999: Per unit incl. 2 adults Ffr 73.50 - 105.00; extra person 21.00 - 30.00; child (3-9 yrs) 11.20 - 16.00; electricity (6A) 17.50 - 25.00. Credit cards accepted.

Open: 1 April - 31 October.

Reservations: Made with 25% deposit. Address: 50250 St Symphorien-le-Valois. Tel: (0)2.33.46.01.16. FAX: (0)2.33.47.23.80.

 AR Discount
7 nights for cost of 6 excl. July/Aug.

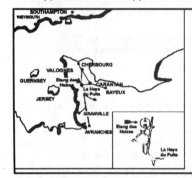

L'ETANG des HAIZES
★ ★ ★ ★
50250 La Haye du Puits

Ideal for an escapade

★ Chalet and Mobile Home to Hire

For your first night in France, relax and enjoy the comfort and atmosphere. During your stay visit Bayeux, Mont St Michel and enjoy typical Normandy meals with a bottle of real Calvados.

Tel: (0)2.33.46.01.16 Fax: (0)2.33.47.23.80.

5604 Camping de Penboch, Arradon, nr Vannes

Quietly situated site on the Golfe du Morbihan with good facilities.

Penboch is 200 m. by footpath from the shores of the Golfe du Morbihan with its many islands, where there is plenty to do including watersports, fishing and boat trips. There are also old towns with weekly markets near and it is 30 minutes walk to Arradon which has shops and restaurants. The site is in a peaceful, rural area and is divided into two parts - one in woodland with much shade and used mainly for mobile homes and youth groups (noisy at times) and the other main part, across a minor road on more open ground with hedges and young trees. Penboch offers 175 pitches on flat grass, mostly divided into groups; electricity is available on most pitches (6/10A). The three sanitary blocks, two on the main part of the site and one on the annex, provide showers with free hot water, washbasins in cabins and British style WCs. These blocks come under considerable pressure in peak season. Washing machines and dryers, chemical disposal and motorcaravan service point. There is a friendly bar with satellite TV, snacks and takeaway, where basic supplies are kept (all 22/5-12/9). A heated swimming pool with water slide toboggan and children's pool with mushroom fountain (15/5-13/9) are in the centre of the site and a good children's playground has interesting play equipment. Games room. Fishing 200 m, bicycle hire 6 km, golf or riding 10 km. Sailing and windsurfing 2 km. Washing machines and dryers. American motorhomes accepted in low season. Caravan storage. Mobile homes and bungalows for rent. Popular with British tour operators (40 pitches). A `Sites et Paysages' member.

Directions: From N165 at Auray or Vannes, take D101 road along the northern shores of the Golfe du Morbihan; or leave N165 at D127 signed Ploeren and Arradon. Take turn to Arradon, and site is signed.

Charges 1999: Per person Ffr. 25.00; child (under 7 yrs) 17.00; pitch incl. car 30.00 - 88.00; electricity 6A 17.00, 10A 20.00; water/drainage 12.00; dog free - 10.00; local tax (over 18 yrs) 3.00. Credit cards accepted.

Open: 3 April - 20 September.

Reservations: Recommended for high season and made for min. 7 days for the period 10/7-18/8. Address: 9 Chemin de Penboch, 56610 Arradon. Tel: (0)2.97.44.71.29. FAX: (0)2.97.44.79.10.

5601 Castel Camping La Grande Métairie, Carnac

Good quality site in southern Brittany with many facilities.

La Grande Métairie is quietly situated, a little back from the sea, close to impressive rows of the famous 'menhirs' (giant prehistoric standing stones). It has much to offer and is lively and busy over a long season. There is a feeling of spaciousness with a wide entrance and access road, with 575 pitches (223 for touring units), surrounded by hedges and trees. All have electricity (30 m. cables are needed in parts). Paddocks with ponds are home for ducks, goats and ponies to watch and feed and there is a large playing field with football posts. A heated swimming pool of 200 sq.m. is supplemented by two smaller pools and a children's paddling pool. An entertainment area includes an outside amphitheatre developed for musical evenings and barbecues. Three large toilet blocks are good and well maintained, with British toilets, washbasins in cabins, free pre-set showers and facilities for babies and disabled people, chemical disposal, and each with a laundry room. Shop, boutique, restaurant, good takeaway, bar lounge and terrace, and adjoining TV and games rooms. Occasional dances, etc. (pitches near these may be noisy late at night - the bar closes at midnight). Pony rides from site. Horse riding and golf near. Two tennis courts. Volleyball, basketball. Minigolf. Children's playgrounds. BMX track. Bicycle hire. Table tennis. Fishing (on permit). Organised events daytime and evening. Motorcaravan service points. Mobile homes for hire. Nearest beach 3 km. by road. Local market at Carnac on Sundays. Limited services before late May. American motorhomes accepted up to 30 ft. The site, although large and not cheap, is well known and popular. It has a large British contingent with about half of the pitches taken by several tour operators, plus many site owned mobile homes to rent and many British touring visitors.

> **Directions:** From N165 take Quiberon/Carnac exit onto the D768. After 5 km. turn left on D781 to Carnac and, following camp signs, turn left at traffic lights to the site.

> **Charges 1999:** Per person Ffr. 30.00; child (under 7 yrs) 20.00; pitch incl. car 128.00, with electricity (6A) 146.00 local tax (over 15) 2.20. Less 25% 29/5-2/7 and 28/8-18/9, 40% before 28/5. Credit cards accepted.

> **Open:** 27 March - 18 September (all services from 29/5).

> **Reservations:** Made (min. 1 week) with deposit (Ffr. 300 per week booked). Address: B.P. 85, 56342 Carnac-Cedex. Tel: (0)2.97.52.24.01. FAX: (0)2.97.52.83.58. E-mail: grande.metairie@wanadoo.fr.

5605 Camping Kervilor, La Trinité-sur-Mer, nr Carnac

Quieter, more spacious site, slightly inland from busy resort.

Kervilor may be a good alternative for those who find the beach-side sites in La Trinité too busy and lively. In a village on the outskirts of the town, it has 200 pitches on flat grass and is attractively landscaped with trees (silver birches) and flowers. The pitches, 180 with electricity (3 or 6A), are in groups divided by hedges, separated by shrubs and trees. Two modern sanitary blocks are good with further facilities in an older, less smart block by the entrance (the latter in need of refurbishment, but clean when seen). They offer pre-set, free hot showers, washbasins, many in cabins, British style WCs, chemical disposal and facilities for disabled people and babies. Dishwashing under cover and small laundry. Bar with terrace, a swimming pool, children's pool, water slide pool and sunbathing area (from 25/5). Play area on sand. Minigolf, pétanque, tennis, volleyball and table tennis outside and under cover. Bicycle hire. Fishing or riding 2 km, golf 12 km. Small shop for basics and takeaway food in season, but the facilities of the town are not far away by car (1½ km.). Sandy beach 2 km. Mobile homes for hire.

> **Directions:** Site is north of La Trinité-sur-Mer and is signed in the town centre. From Auray take the D186 Quiberon road; turn left at camp sign at Kergrioux on D186 to La Trinité-sur-Mer, and left again at outskirts of town.

> **Charges 1999:** Per person Ffr. 25.00; child (under 7 yrs) 16.00; local tax (over 10 yrs) 2.00; pitch 64.00; car 15.00; electricity 3A 13.00, 6A 16.00. Less 25% outside high season. No credit cards.

> **Open:** 15 May - 15 September.

> **Reservations:** Made with deposit (Ffr. 300) and fee (120). Address: 56470 La Trinité-sur-Mer. Tel: (0)2.97.55.76.75. FAX: (0)2.97.55.87.26.

5801 Camping Des Bains, St Honoré-les-Bains

Attractive family run site with pool, close to small spa-town.

With 130 large (100 sq.m.) separated pitches, 100 with 6A electricity, and many trees, this is an attractive site, owned and run by the Luneau family who are keen to welcome British visitors and it is well situated for exploring the Morvan area. However, the site is low-lying, pitches can be rather soft in wet weather and it can also be quite cold at night in early or late season. The site has its own small swimming pool (12 x 12 m) with a separate aqua slide (15/6-30/9), a children's play area, and two small streams for children to fish in, one of which is warm from the thermal springs. The actual thermal park is next door with added attractions for children. A traditional family bar (1/5-30/9) also provides food and a takeaway service (15/6-30/9). Table tennis, minigolf and entertainment weekly for children in July/Aug. The three sanitary units are of varying ages with mostly British WCs, washbasins in cabins and ample hot showers. Dishwashing sinks, baby bath, facilities for disabled people, chemical disposal and laundry facilities.
continued overleaf

5801 Camping Des Bains (continued)

Riding and fishing near, or `taking the waters' which, combined with the clean, pollution free environment, are said to be very good for asthma sufferers (cures run for three week periods). Bicycle hire 500 m. Modern gîtes for hire all year. Caravan storage. A `Sites et Paysages' member. ·

Directions: From the north approach via the D985 from Auxerre, through Clamecy and Corbigny to St Honoré-les-Bains, from where the site is signed `Village des Bains'.

Charges 1999: Per unit incl. 2 persons Ffr. 92.00; extra person 24.00; child (under 7 yrs) 14.00; dog 6.00; local tax extra; electricity (6A) 18.00. Less 20-30% outside 1/7-29/8. Credit cards accepted.

Open: 1 May - 30 September.

Reservations: Write to site with deposit (Ffr. 420) and fee (80). Address: BP 17, 15 Av. Jean Mermoz, 58360 St. Honoré-les-Bains. Tel: (0)3.86.30.73.44. FAX: (0)3.86.30.61.88.

5803 Castel Camping Manoir de Bezolle, St Péreuse-en-Morvan

Well situated site for exploring the Morvan Natural Park and the Nivernais area.

This site has been attractively landscaped to provide a number of different areas and terraces, giving some pleasant views over the countryside. Clearly separated pitches are on level grass with some terracing, the majority with electricity (6A or more). Several features are worthy of special mention including a large swimming pool and children's pool with terrace, a good restaurant with takeaway (main season), two small lakes and a Red Indian village with ponies. Sanitary facilities are in four units - a small older style unit by the pool and restaurant complex, and a new fibreglass unit containing two tiny family WC/basin/shower suites for rent. Two large units provide the main services with pre-set showers, baths, basins in cabins (many with cold water), mostly British WC's, provision for disabled people and a baby bath. Laundry, chemical disposal and motorcaravan services. Some sanitary facilities may be closed outside high season. Shop (15/5-15/9). Activities on site include riding, minigolf, a games room, bicycle hire for children (otherwise 8 km), table tennis and fishing. Mobile homes for rent, plus `yourtes' (fully equipped, Mongolian style tents). Caravan storage. `Camping Cheque'

Directions: Site is mid-way between Châtillon-en-Bazois and Château-Chinon, just north of the D978 by the small village of St Péreuse-en-Morvan.

Charges 1998: Per pitch incl. 2 persons Ffr. 80.00 - 115.00; extra person 20.00 - 30.00; child (under 7 yrs) 15.00 - 20.00; electricity (6A) 24.00 - 25.00, extra 4A 12.00; water and drainage connection 14.00; animal 10.00; visitor 15.00; extra car 10.00; local taxes 3.00. Credit cards accepted.

Open: 15 March - 15 October.

Reservations: Made with deposit (Ffr. 300) and fee (100); contact site for details. Address: 58110 Saint Péreuse en Morvan. Tel: (0)3.86.84.42.55. FAX: (0)3.86.84.43.77. Internet: www.lescastels.com/bezolle.

6001 Camping Campix, St Leu-d'Esserent, nr Chantilly

Unusual, peaceful, modern site in old sandstone quarry.

Opened in 1991, this informal site has been unusually developed in what used to be a sandstone quarry on the outskirts of the small town. The quarry walls provide very different boundaries to most of the site, giving a sheltered, peaceful environment. Trees have been grown to soften the slopes. Not a neat, manicured site, the 160 pitches are arranged in small groups on the different levels with stone and gravel access roads (some fairly steep and possibly muddy in poor weather). Torches are advised. Electricity (6A) is available to 150 pitches. There are many secluded corners mostly for smaller units and tents, and plenty of space for children to explore (parents must supervise - some areas, although fenced, could be dangerous). A path leads to the town where there are shops, restaurants and an outdoor pool (in season). At the entrance to the site, a large building houses reception and two clean sanitary units - one for tourers, the other unusually for groups. These have pre-mixed, free hot showers, washbasins in rows, some British style WCs, two suites for disabled people. Laundry facilities with washing machine and dryer. Because the facilities are divided into those for groups or individuals, facilities may be congested at peak times. Bread and milk delivered. A snack bar operates from a mobile unit (July/Aug). Chemical disposal. Bicycle hire. Fishing 1 km, riding or golf 6 km. This site is best suited to those wanting to get away from it all, who do not need sophisticated facilities, or to visit local places for interest providing you have your own transport. The friendly, English speaking owner will advise on these places of interest, which include Chantilly (5 km), the nearby Asterix Park and the Mer de Sable, a Western theme park. Disneyland is 70 km. It is possible to visit Paris by train, although a day return can be challenging.

Directions: St Leu d'Esserent is 11 km. west of Senlis, 5 km. west of Chantilly. From the north on the A1 autoroute take the Senlis exit, from Paris the Chantilly exit. Site is north of the town off the D12 towards Cramoisy, and is signed from the peripherique or in the town.

Charges 1998: Per unit Ffr. 20.00 - 30.00; small tent 5.00 - 25.00, acc. to location; person 15.00 - 25.00; child (under 10 yrs) 10.00 - 15.00; electricity 15.00 - 20.00. Credit cards accepted.

Open: 1 March - 30 November.

Reservations: Advised for July/Aug. Address: BP 37, 60340 St Leu-d'Esserent. Tel: (0)3.44.56.08.48 or (0)3.44.56.28.75. FAX: (0)3.44.56.28.75. E-mail: campixfr@aol.com.

AR Discount
Free ticket for La Mer de Sable for a min. 4 day stay.

France - Pas-de-Calais / Pyrénées-Atlantiques

6201 Castel Camping Caravaning La Bien-Assise, Guînes

See colour advert between pages 96/97

Mature, quality site with pools close to Calais and cross channel links.

The chequered history of `La Bien-Assise' goes back to the 1500s, but today the Château, farm and mill are all in the hands of the Boutoille family and they can provide you with a fascinating brief history. However, now the farm buildings house the shop, bar/grill, TV room and takeaway (from early May). The entrance to a more formal restaurant, `La Ferme Gourmande' (open all year, closed Mondays) is in the mellowed farmyard opposite the dovecote with the Auberge du Colombier next door. The pool complex (10/5-10/9) utilises a barn area to provide a partly covered, sheltered and heated pool (16 x 6), and fun pool with toboggan and paddling pool. There are 180 pitches mainly set among mature trees, apart from one new field. Of good size and connected by gravel roadways, shrubs and bushes make them `semi-delimité'. Three good toilet blocks are ample with many washbasins in cabins, controllable free showers, mostly British style WCs and provision for babies, clothes and dishwashing, and chemical disposal. Play areas, minigolf and a tennis court are sheltered by a garden wall, which together with the Château itself (Auberge and hotel rooms, all year), combine to give a comfortable, mature feel. Bicycle hire on site, fishing 8 km, riding 2 km. Its position 15 mins from Calais, the Channel Tunnel exit 6 km. and Boulogne 20 mins, make it a popular venue en-route north or south, but it is well worth a longer stay. The Boutoille family personally manage the site and reception opens long hours to meet the needs of those crossing the Channel. Local market. Used by tour operators (50 pitches). `Camping Cheque'

Directions: From ferry terminal follow A16 south (Boulogne) for junction 15, turning towards St Pierre de Calais to immediately pick up Guînes signs before going under autoroute following the D127. Continue beside canal to Guînes. Site is just southwest of village on D231 Marquise road. From Tunnel also follow A16 south (Boulogne) to immediately pick up Guînes signs at junction 11 and following D215 past St Tricat to Guînes. From south on autoroute A26, use exit 2 (Ardres, Guînes) onto N43 and D231 (15 km).

Charges 1998: Per pitch Ffr. 59.00; adult 25.00; child (under 8) 17.00; electricity (6A) 19.00. Less 7% in low season. Credit cards accepted (not Diners or Amex)

Open: 25 April - 20 September, (full facilities: 6/5-16/9).

Reservations: Advised for July/Aug; made with deposit (Ffr 250) and fee (50) for stays 5 days or more. Address: 62340 Guînes: Tel: (0)3.21.35.20.77. FAX: (0)3.21.36.79.20. E-mail: camping-bien-assise.fr. Internet: www.bien-assise.com.

AR Discount
Less 10% in low season.

6203 Camping Château de Gandspette, Eperlecques, nr St Omer

Family run site in grounds of château with swimming pools.

Conveniently situated for the channel ports and tunnel, this family run site provides useful overnight accommodation and has a range of facilities for a longer stay. It has the benefit of two swimming pools, one large and one smaller, with paved sheltered sunbathing area (15/5-30/9). There is also an attractive bar, grill restaurant and takeaway (all 15/6-15/9) situated in the 17th century building adjacent to the chateau. The circular gravel road gives access to a central open space and the 127 pitches (all 100 sq.m). Half are taken by semi-permanent French caravans, which intermix with some of the touring pitches, giving a real French ambience. All pitches have electricity (6A) and are delineated by trees and some hedging. Mature trees form the perimeter of the site, through which there is access to woodland walks, playing field and a children's play area. The partially renovated sanitary block provides satisfactory facilities with British style WCs and a mixture of open and cubicled washbasins. Push-button showers are in tiled cubicles. Covered dishwashing sinks with hot water, washing machines and dryers, and chemical disposal. Tennis, petanque, children's room with table tennis and electronic games. Riding 5 km. (ponies on site at weekends if reserved). Fishing 3 km, golf 5 km. Entertainment in season. Small supermarket in village 1 km. Rooms in the château (B&B). Used by tour operators (20 pitches). Market at Watten (Friday) and St Omer (Saturday). A `Sites et Paysages' member. `Camping Cheque'

Directions: From N43 St Omer - Calais southeast of Nordausques take D221 east. Follow camp signs for 5-6 km.

Charges 1999: Per unit incl. 2 persons Ffr. 100.00; extra person (over 4 yrs) 25.00, under 4 free; extra car 10.00; electricity (6A) 20.00; local tax 2.00 (child 4-10 yrs 1.00). Credit cards accepted.

Open: 1 April - 30 September.

Reservations: Needed for July/Aug. Address: 62910 Eperlecques. Tel: (0)3.21.93.43.93. FAX: (0)3.21.95.74.98.

6406 Camping du Pavillon Royal, Bidart, nr Biarritz

Comfortable, popular site by sandy beach, with excellent facilities and pool.

Le Pavillon Royal has an excellent situation on raised ground overlooking the sea, and with good views along the coast to the south and to the north coast of Spain beyond. Beneath the camp, and only a very short walk down, stretches a wide sandy beach. This is the Atlantic with its breakers and a central marked-out section of the beach is supervised by lifeguards. There is also a section with rocks and pools. If the sea is rough, there is a large swimming pool, paddling pool and sunbathing area on site. The site has 303 marked pitches, all with electricity. They include some for caravans with electricity, water and drainaway. Much of the camp is in full sun - shade in one part only.   *continued overleaf*

6406 Camping du Pavilion Royal (continued)

All sanitary blocks are of the highest quality with mainly British style WCs, washbasins in cabins, and free controllable showers; baby baths; good units for disabled people, all cleaned twice daily. Washing facilities closed at night except for night units. Washing machines and dryers, chemical disposal and motorcaravan services. Well stocked shop and restaurant with takeaway (all season). General room, TV room, games room with table tennis, also used for films, etc. Children's playground. Fishing and bicycle hire on site, riding 1 km. Sauna. No dogs are taken.

Directions: Do not go into Bidart as the site is on the Biarritz side. From the north, keep on main N10 bypassing Biarritz, then turn sharp back right on D911 (last possible road leading to Biarritz). After 600 m. turn left at camp sign (easy to miss). From A63 motorway take C4 exit.

Charges 1998: Per unit incl. 2 persons, electricity and water Ffr. 139.00 - 189.00; extra person (over 4 yrs) 30.00; extra car 25.00. Credit cards accepted.

Open: 15 May - 25 September.

Reservations: Advicsed in high season and made for exàct dates with deposit and fee. Address: Av. du Prince-de-Galles, 64210 Bidart. Tel: (0)5.59.23.00.54. FAX: (0)5.59.23.44.47.

6407 Castel Camping Le Ruisseau, Bidart, nr Biarritz

Pleasant, busy site with swimming pool, just back from sea, with reasonable charges.

This site, just behind the coast, is about 2 km. from Bidart and 2½ km. from a sandy beach but it does have two swimming pools on the site - one 1,100 sq.m. pool complex with slides on the main camp and one indoor heated pool with slide on the newer area opposite. There is also a little lake, where boating is possible, in the area at the bottom of the site which has a very pleasant open aspect and now includes a large play area. Pitches on the main camp are marked and of a good size, either on flat terraces or on a slight slope. The terrain is wooded so the great majority have some shade. There are 330 here with a further 110 on a second area where shade has developed and which has its own good toilet block. Electricity is available nearly everywhere. The unisex sanitary facilities consist of two main blocks and some extra smaller units. They have British style WCs, washbasins in cabins, free hot showers, nearly all pre-set, and are regularly refurbished and maintained. Washing machine. Shop. Large self-service restaurant with takeaway and separate bar with terraces, and TV. Two tennis courts (free outside July/Aug), volleyball, table tennis, fitness track, TV and games rooms, minigolf, fitness room, sauna, solarium and a large children's playground. `Animation' during main season: organised sports during day and evening entertainment twice weekly in season. Bicycle and surf board hire. Riding or golf 3 km. The site is very popular with tour operators (160 pitches). Mobile homes to rent. `Camping Cheque'

Directions: Site is east of Bidart on a minor road towards Arbonne. From autoroute take Biarritz exit, turn towards St Jean-de-Luz on N10, take first left at traffic lights and follow camp signs for 1.5 km. When travelling south on N10 the turning is the first after passing the autoroute entry point.

Charges 1999: Per unit incl. 2 persons Ffr. 96.00 - 120.00; extra adult 26.00 - 33.00; child (under 7) 14.00 - 18.00; electricity 21.00; dog 6.00; local tax (over 10) 2.20. Credit cards accepted.

Open: 8 May - 15 September, with all amenities.

Reservations: Made for exact dates, for min. a week or so in main season, with deposit (Ffr 350), .fee (62) and cancellation insurance (18). Total Ffr. 430. Address: 64210 Bidart. Tel: (0)5.59.41.94.50. FAX: (0)5.59.41.95.73.

6409 Airotel La Chêneraie, Bayonne

Good class site with swimming pool in pleasant situation 8 km. from sea.

A good quality site in a pleasant setting, La Chêneraie is only 8 km. from the coast at Anglet where there is a long beach and big car park. It also has a medium sized pool on site, open June-Aug, longer if the weather is fine, which makes it a comfortable base in this attractive region. Bayonne and Biarritz are near. There are distant mountain views from the site which consists of meadows, generally well shaded and divided partly into pitches and with some caravan plots with electricity, water and drainage. In the sloping part terraces give level pitches. Sanitary facilities consist of one very large central block of good quality with British toilets, washbasins in cabins and controllable, free hot showers, and three smaller units in other parts, all very clean. Baby baths, facilities for disabled people, chemical disposal, plus a washing machine and dryer. Shop, general kiosk and restaurant with all day snacks and takeaway. Tennis, a small pool for fishing, inflatables, etc, table tennis, children's playground and TV room. Bicycle hire or riding 5 km, golf 10 km. Tents, bungalows and mobile homes for hire. Used by tour operators (20 pitches). English spoken. A good site to know, it may have room if you arrive early.

Directions: Site is 4 km. northeast of Bayonne just off the main N117 road to Pau, signed at traffic lifgts. From new autoroute A63 take exit 6 marked `Bayonne St. Esprit'.

Charges 1998: Per pitch Ffr. 62.00 - 75.00, tent pitch 50.00 - 58.00; pitch with water and electricity 70.00 - 100.00; person 24.00 - 26.00; child (under 10 yrs) 14.00 - 16.00, local tax (over 18s) 1.10; electricity 18.00. Less 10-20% outside 1/6-1/9. No credit cards.

Open: Easter - 30 September, full services 1/6-15/9.

Reservations: Made for min. 1 week with deposit (Ffr. 400) and fee (100). Address: 64100 Bayonne. Tel: (0)5.59.55.01.31. FAX: (0)5.59.55.11.17.

France - Pyrénées-Atlantiques / Pyrénées-Orientales

6411 Camping du Col d'Ibardin, Urrugne

Family owned site with swimming pool at foot of Basque Pyrénées.

This site justly deserves praise. It is well run with emphasis on personal attention, the smiling Madame, her staff and family ensuring that all are made welcome and is attractively set in the middle of an oak wood. Behind the forecourt, with its brightly coloured shrubs and modern reception area, various roads lead to the 190 pitches. These are spacious and enjoy the benefit of the shade, but if preferred a more open aspect can be found. There are electric hook-ups and adequate water points. The two toilet blocks are kept very clean and house WCs (British style), a WC for disabled people, washbasins and free pre-set hot showers. The second block has been completely rebuilt to a high specification. Dishwashing facilities are in separate open areas close by and a laundry unit with washing machine and dryer is located to the rear of reception. Chemical disposal and motorcaravan service point. A small shop sells basic foodstuffs and bread orders are taken (1/6-15/9), but a large supermarket and shopping centre are 5 km. In July/Aug. there is catering and takeaway, also a bar and occasional evening entertainment which includes Flamenco dancing. Swimming pool and paddling pool, tennis courts, bicycle hire, boules, table tennis, video games and a children's playground and club with adult supervision. From this site you can enjoy the mountain scenery, be on the beach at Socoa within minutes or cross the border into Spain approximately 14 km. down the road. A few pitches used by tour operators.

Directions: Leave A63 autoroute at St Jean-de-Luz sud, exit no. 2 and join the RN10 in the direction of Urrugne. Turn left at roundabout (signed Col d'Ibardin) onto the D4 and site is on right after 5 km.

Charges 1998: Per unit incl. 2 persons Ffr. 65.00 - 100.00; extra adult 15.00 - 24.00; child (2-7 yrs) 10.00 - 14.00; electricity (4A) 16.00 - 18.00; animal free - 10.00; local tax 1.10 (high season). No credit cards.

Open: 1 April - 30 September.

Reservations: Accepted - contact site. Address: 64122 Urrugne. Tel: (0)5.59.54.31.21. FAX: (0)5.59.54.62.28. E-mail: camping-ibardin@wanadoo.fr.

AR Discount
Less 10%
min. 3 nights

6601 Camping-Caravaning California, Le Barcarès, Perpignan

Family owned, well cared for site with swimming pool, not far from beach.

Originally an orchard area, California has been developed with care and attention by Mr Benavail and his brother. Accessed directly off the main road in a popular area near Le Barcarès, it has 256 hedged pitches on level grass and is cool and shaded. The site now has a mature look with an attractive terraced pool bar area and an efficient reception area built in local materials. The 150 touring pitches, all with electricity and shade, vary a little in size and shape but average about 100 sq.m. Two modern toilet blocks have British style WCs, with free pre-mixed hot water in the washbasins, showers and sinks. Baby bath and small toilets. Chemical disposal and motorcaravan services. The site is about 900 m. from a sandy beach. It has a swimming pool of 200 sq.m. and children's pool, with free water slide (1/5-4/9) in a small separate pool. Restaurant and bar with takeaway and shop (all 21/6-31/8), wine store and pizzeria at entrance to site. Tennis, TV room, small multi-gym, mountain bike hire and BMX track on site and archery. River fishing 500 m. Washing machine. Car wash. Exchange facility. Children's animation in season and some evening entertainment. Only gas or electric barbecues on stands are allowed. Bungalows and mobile homes (100) to let.

Directions: Site is on the D90 coast road 2 km. southwest of Le Barcarès centre.

Charges 1999: Per unit with 2 persons Ffr. 109.00, with 10A electricity 126.00; extra person 28.00; child (under 7) 18.00; local tax (over 4) in Jul/Aug 1.00. Less 20-50% outside July/Aug. Credit cards accepted.

Open: 21 April - 24 September.

Reservations: Needed for high season; with deposit (Ffr. 500) and fee (80). Address: Route de St Laurent, 66420 Le Barcarès. Tel: (0)4.68.86.16.08. FAX: (0)4.68.86.18.20.

AR Discount
Free tennis in
high season

6603 Camping Cala Gogo, St Cyprien-Plage, nr Perpignan

Site by beach, with own swimming pool and varied amenities.

This large and well organised site (sister site to 6604 Le Soleil) is agreeably situated by a sandy beach where bathing is supervised and boats can be launched. Also on site is a good-size free swimming pool with children's pool and a pleasant terrace bar area adjoining. The 479 flat pitches for touring units are around 100 sq.m. They are now more fully marked with easier access and electricity everywhere and shade has developed. Some 20 pitches will be sacrificed to allow a large new swimming pool to be built in '99. Three of the five toilet blocks are basically good and provide British and Turkish style toilets, washbasins in cabins and free hot, controllable showers. The third and fourth blocks nearest the beach have been refurbished to a high standard. Maintenance may vary in high season. The large bar complex with disco and TV, becomes busy in season and could be noisy (popular with young people). Attractive small shopping mall, wine boutique and a very good supermarket. Full restaurant with excellent cuisine and service, plus a simple self-service restaurant with takeaway. A small bar by the beach opens in high season. A programme of events is organised in season: sports, etc. during the day, dancing or entertainment on a large stage recently built alongside the bar on some evenings.   *continued overleaf*

6603 Camping Cala Gogo (continued)

Tennis, table tennis and a children's playground. Fishing, riding, bicycle hire and golf within 5 km. Boat excursions and courses in skindiving, windsurfing or sailing nearby. Torches useful. Used by tour operators (135 pitches). Mobile homes to rent.

Directions: Site is south of St Cyprien and is well signed from roads around.

Charges 1999: Per person (any age) Ffr. 36.00, plus local tax 2.00 per adult, 1.00 per child; pitch (any unit) 57.00; electricity 17.00; dog 20.00. Less 20% outside July/Aug. Credit cards accepted.

Open: 29 May - 25 September with all services.

Reservations: Made for Sat. to Sat. and necessary for Jul/Aug, with deposit (Ffr 400) and fee (100). Address: La Vigie, 66750 St Cyprien-Plage. Tel: (0)4.68.21.07.12 (when closed (0)4.68.95.90.11). FAX: (0)4.68.21.02.19 (or (0)4.68.95.92.82).

AR Discount

Welcome drink

6604 Camping Le Soleil, Argelès-sur-Mer, nr Perpignan

Busy, family owned site with good size pitches and direct access to beach.

Le Soleil (sister site to 6603 Cala Gogo), with direct access to the beach, is popular and has grown in the last few years. A large site, more like a small village, it has 843 numbered pitches of ample size (722 for touring units), on sandy/grassy ground and with shade except, perhaps, in the newer extensions, and electricity (6A) in all areas. Access for caravans sometimes needs care on the narrow tree lined roads. It has a wide range of amenities and Spain and the Pyrénées are near enough for excursions. The seven sanitary blocks are of the type with external access to individual units and should give good coverage. They have plentiful pre-set hot showers and washbasins in cabins, some with only cold water. Chemical disposal and motorcaravan services. A large, impressive pool complex is to one side of the site with a tabac and bar nearby. A supermarket, general shop and restaurant for sit down or takeaway food is more centrally situated. Bar with disco (July/Aug) and beach bar. Activities on site include a children's adventure playground, TV room, tennis and bicycle hire, with riding in Jul/Aug (and nearby). Fishing on the adjacent river. Golf 6 km. Washing machines. Bureau de change and ATM machine. Doctor on site Jul/Aug. English is spoken and there is a comprehensive reservation system (advisable for most of July/Aug). No dogs are accepted. Used by tour operators (76 pitches). Mobile homes to rent.

Directions: Site is at north end of the beach about 1 km. from Argelès-Plage village.

Charges 1999: Per person (any age except babies) Ffr. 40.00; local tax (adults) 2.40; pitch 57.00; electricity 16.00. Less 20% in May, June and Sept. Swimming pool deposit Ffr. 100 per pitch. Credit cards accepted.

Open: 15 May - 30 September.

Reservations: Made from Sat or Wed (min. 1 week) with deposit (Ffr. 400) and booking fee (100). Address: Rte du Littoral, 66700 Argelès-sur-Mer. Tel: Season: (0)4.68.81.14.48. FAX: (0)4.68.81.44.34. Winter: (0)4.68.95.94.62. FAX: (0)4.68.95.92.81. Internet: campmed.com.

6607 Camping-Caravaning Le Brasilia, Canet Plage en Roussillon

Excellent, well run site beside beach with wide range of facilities.

La Brasilia is pretty and well kept with an amazingly wide range of facilities and activities. It is a large site, but does not seem so, with 826 hedged pitches all with 5A electricity. With a range of shade from mature pines and flowering shrubs, less on pitches near the beach, there are neat access roads (some narrow for large units). Nine modern sanitary blocks are well equipped and maintained, with British style WCs (some Turkish) and washbasins in cabins. One block is very modern and impressive with good facilities for children (as has one other block). All have washing up and laundry sinks with hot and cold water everywhere, chemical disposal, laundry room with washing machines and dryers, and facilities for disabled people. The sandy beach is busy, with a beach club (windsurfing board hire) and a naturist section to the west of the site. There is also a large California type pool (1/5-30/9, weekly charge in high season), with sunbathing areas and bar. Astroturf sports field beside the tennis courts and sporting activities such as aqua gym, aerobics, football, etc. Games and video room (club card in high season). Bicycle hire and fishing on site, riding 750 m, golf 12 km. The village area with shops, bars and restaurant is busy, providing meals, entertainment (including a night club) and a range of shops. In fact you do not need to stir from the site which is almost a resort in itself providing a cash dispenser, exchange facilities, telephone, post office and even weather forecasts. It has a nice, lively atmosphere but is orderly and well run - very good for a site with beach access. Torches useful. English is spoken. Bungalows, chalets and mobile homes to rent.

Directions: Site is north of Canet Port. From Canet Plage follow signs for Port, then `Campings', and then follow site signs (near the American Park).

Charges 1999: Per unit incl. 2 persons Ffr. 85.00 - 160.00; extra person (over 3 yrs) 16.00 - 30.00; child (under 3 yrs) free - 13.00; dog free - 15.00; electricity (5A) 16.00; local tax (over 3 yrs) 2.00. High season swimming pool entry (1 week) adult Ffr 60, child (4-10 yrs) 30. Low and mid seasons free. Credit cards accepted.

Open: 3 April - 2 October.

Reservations: Advised for July/Aug. Address: BP 204, 66141 Canet Plage en Roussillon. Tel: (0)4.68.80.23.82. FAX: (0)4.68.73.32.97. E-mail: brasilia@mnet.fr. Internet: www.francecom/aft/camping/brasilia.

6902M Camping Municipal La Grappe Fleurie, Fleurie-en-Beaujolais

With easy access from both the A6 autoroute and the N6, this site is ideally situated for night stops or indeed for longer stays to explore the vineyards and historic attractions of the Beaujolais region. Virtually surrounded by vineyards, but within walking distance (less them 1 km) of the pretty village of Fleurie, this is an immaculate small site, with 96 separated touring pitches. All are grassed and fairly level with the benefit of individual access to water, drainage and electrical connections (10A). Sanitary facilities are in two modern blocks with British and Turkish style WCs and very satisfactory shower and washing facilities. Two cold showers are provided for those wishing to cool down in summer. A small children's playground, table tennis, tennis and volleyball areas are on site. Restaurant and shopping facilities are available in the village, although the nearest swimming pool is 8 km. away.

Directions: From the N6 at Le Maison Blanche/Romanech-Thorins, take the D32 to the village of Fleurie from where site is signed.

Charges 1998: Per adult Ffr. 19.00; child under 5 yrs free, 5-10 yrs 10.00; caravan or motorcaravan 31.00; tent 18.00.

Open: 20 March - 25 October.

Reservations: Advised in high season. Address: 69820 Fleurie. Tel: (0)4.74.69.80.07 or the Mairie: (0)4. 74.04.10.44. FAX: (0)4.74.69.85.71.

7102M Le Village des Meuniers, Dompierre-les-Ormes, nr Mâcon

Opened in 1993, this site is a good example of current trends in French tourism development. The 120 neatly terraced, large pitches are on fairly level grass. All have electricity (15A), with water and drainage shared between 4 or 6 pitches in most parts. They enjoy some lovely views of the surrounding countryside - the Beaujolais, the Maconnais, the Charollais and the Clunysois. The site is 500 m. from Dompierre-les-Ormes, a small village of 850 people, with all services (banks, shops, etc. which are closed Sun/Mon). Sanitary facilities are mainly in an unusual, purpose designed hexagonal block, with most up-to-date furniture and fittings, all of a very high standard with British WCs. A smaller unit is in the lower area of the site, plus further WCs in the main reception building and in the minigolf complex. There is a café/bar, shop and takeaway, plus minigolf, bicycle hire and other recreational activities. An attractively designed, upmarket swimming pool complex has three pools with a toboggan run (open from end-June). Fishing 2 km. The site has its own high quality wooden gites, operated by Gites de France. This is one of the better municipals we have seen, and as the hedges and trees mature there should be more shade. Motorcaravan service point in the car park in front of the gites. This is an area well worth visiting, with attractive scenery, interesting history, excellent wines and good food. Used by tour operators.

Directions: Town is 35 km. west of Macon. Follow N79/E62 (Charolles/Paray/Digoin) road and turn south onto D41 to Dompierre-les-Ormes (3 km). Site is clearly signed through village.

Charges 1999: Per person Ffr. 22.00 - 35.00; child (under 7 yrs) 12.00 - 17.00; pitch 28.00 - 35.00; electricity 15.00. Special family rate (4 or more persons) Ffr. 100.00 - 120.00. Credit cards accepted.

Open: 7 May - 2 October.

Reservations: Contact site. Address: 71520 Dompierre-les-Ormes. Tel: (0)3.85.50.29.43. FAX: as phone in season (winter: (0)3.85.50.28.25).

Camping "La Grappe Fleurie" ***
F-69820 FLEURIE

Open 13.03 to 23.10
Tel: (0)4.74.69.80.07
Fax: (0)4.74.69.85.71

**Ten minutes from A6 exit
MACON Sud or BELLEVILLE**

Quiet campsite amidst the vineyards

7105 Camping Moulin de Collonge, Saint-Boil

Well run, family site in the heart of the Burgundy countryside.

This site offers an 'away from it all' situation. Surrounded by sloping vineyards and golden wheat fields, it has instant appeal for those seeking a quiet, relaxing environment. There are 50 pitches which are level and most have electrical hook-ups. Reception and sanitary facilities are housed in a converted barn which is tastefully decorated and well kept. White tiled floors and whitewashed walls give it a very clean appearance. There are British style WCs, curtained wash cubicles, shaving points and showers. Sinks for dishes and laundry are outside with washing machine and dryer inside. Hanging flower arrangements are in abundance and, like the shrubs and grounds, are constantly being attended to by the proprietor and his family (M. Gillot's other interest is the restoration of classic cars). Beyond the stream which borders the site are a swimming pool, patio and a pizzeria which is also open to the public all year. The pool is covered by a plastic dome - some of the walls can be opened in good weather. Ices and cool drinks can be purchased but there is no food shop - baguettes and croissants arrive at 8.30 each morning. Freezer for campers' use. Other on-site activities are bicycle hire, table tennis, fishing and pony trekking. The 'Voie Vert', a 40 km. track for cycling or walking starts near the site.

Directions: From Chalon-sur-Saône travel 9 km. west on the N80. Turn south onto the D981 through Buxy (6 km). Continue south for 7 km. to Saint-Boil and site is signed at south end of the village.

Charges 1998: Per unit Ffr. 26.00; adult 21.00; child (under 7 yrs) 11.00; electricity 16.00. Credit cards accepted.

Open: 15 May - 15 September.

Reservations: Accepted - contact site. Address: 71940 Saint-Boil. Tel: (0)3.85.44.00.40. FAX: as phone.

7107 Camping-Caravaning Château de l'Epervière, Gigny-sur-Saône

Enthusiastically run rural site in the grounds of a château.

Château de l'Epervière has undergone a transformation under its young owner Christophe Gay. Peacefully situated on the edge of the little village of Gigny-sur-Saône, yet within easy distance of the A6, it is in a natural woodland area, with red squirrels and deer, near the Saône river. With 100 pitches, most with 6A electricity, the site is in two fairly distinct areas - the original with semi-hedged pitches on reasonably level ground with plenty of shade from mature trees, close to the château and fishing lake, and a larger, more open area, still with good shade, with very big, hedged pitches on the far side of the lake. Smallish, unheated pool partly enclosed by old stone walls which protect it from the wind, plus an indoor heated pool with jacuzzi and sauna, children's play area and paddling pool. Bicycle hire. A good, recently refurbished restaurant in the château has a distinctly French menu and a takeaway. Shop for basics (from 1/5). The sanitary blocks, a large one by the château, a smaller one near the lake, provide modern facilities, with free hot showers, washbasins in cabins and British type WCs. Chemical disposal, dishwashing under cover and laundry areas, including a washing machine and dryer. Perhaps the most striking feature of this attractive site is the young owner's enthusiasm and the range of activities he lays on for visitors, which include wine tastings and regional tours. He is also the founder and driving force behind French Flavour Holidays, designed to provide an insight into French culture by special theme tours and activities (we arrived at the end of one of these and were amazed at the enthusiasm and enjoyment the two weeks had engendered). These weeks seem to appeal more to the British and other nationalities than to the French, however, a good French ambience has developed and Christophe's wine tastings in the cellars and château tours are not to be missed. Riding 12 km, golf 20 km. Used by tour operators (40 pitches). Apartments to let in the château. 'Camping Cheque' 'FRENCH FLAVOUR'

Directions: From N6 between Châlon-sur-Saône and Tournus, turn east on D18 (just north of Sennecey-le-Grand) and follow site signs for 6.5 km. From the A6, exit Châlon-Sud from the north, or Tournus from the south.

Charges 1999: Per adult Ffr. 26.00 - 32.00; child (under 7 yrs) 16.00 - 21.00; pitch 37.00 - 48.00; dog 10.00; electricity 18.00 - 21.00. Credit cards accepted.

Open: 4 April - 30 September.

Reservations: Contact site. Address: 71240 Gigny-sur-Saône. Tel: (0)3.85.94.16.90. FAX: (0)3.85.94.16.93.

7406 Camping La Colombière, Neydens, nr St Julien-en-Genevois

Good small site with pool, near Geneva.

La Colombière, on the edge of the small village of Neydens, is a few minutes from the A40 autoroute. It is a neat, tidy, rectangular site with four rows of pitches of grass on small stones between hard access roads with 107 places separated by fruit and other trees. With mountain ridges to both east and west and trees between, this is a peaceful site, well run by the Bussat family. Three good sanitary blocks have British style WCs and the usual amenities, plus a baby room, facilities for disabled people and chemical disposal. Motorcaravan services. Shop (1/6-1/10). An excellent bar restaurant has a terrace overlooking the heated pool (15/5-10/10). Guided cycle tours (to hire on site), mountain walks and music evenings arranged in high season. Fishing or riding 1 km, golf 5 km. Neydens makes a good base for visiting the Lac Leman region and is a very pleasant, friendly site. Chalets and rooms to let. `Camping Cheque'`

Directions: From A40 autoroute exit 13 south of Geneva, turn towards Annecy on D201 following camp signs.

Charges 1999: Per unit incl. 2 persons Ffr. 90.00; extra person 22.00; child (under 7 yrs) 17.00; dog 10.00; electricity (5/6A) 20.00. Less 10% outside July/Aug. Credit cards accepted.

Open: 20 March - 3 November.

Reservations: Write to site. Address: 74160 Neydens. Tel: (0)4.50.35.13.14. FAX: (0)4.50.35.13.40.

AR Discount
Less 15% in low season

8001 Castel Camping Domaine de Drancourt, St Valéry-sur-Somme

Popular site between Boulogne and Dieppe with swimming pools and other amenities.

A popular, lively holiday site within easy distance of Channel ports, Drancourt is in four sections. The original section has 100 numbered grassy pitches of good size with good shade; an extension taking 90 units is in light woodland and two newer touring sections on flat or gently sloping meadow, with little shade as yet and it can be dusty around reception buildings and château in dry weather. There are 326 pitches, of which 120 are occupied by tour operators. Electricity (6A) in all areas. Sanitary facilities consist of three blocks - the oldest (central) block which is now very tired and in need of refitting, a good modern one in the touring section, the third, recently refurbished and enlarged, near reception. All have British style WCs, washbasins in cubicles, roomy showers, and free pre-set hot water, some new family bathrooms and facilities for disabled visitors, plus laundry and dishwashing. Drainage difficulties can cause occasional problems around this refurbished block. Two free heated swimming pools (from 1/5), one inside and one open air, with water slide. Shop (from 1/5), takeaway and pizzeria (July/Aug) open until late and restaurant closing at 9 pm. A bar is in the château, a new large first floor bar and a pool-side bar with karaoke in season. TV rooms, one for children. Disco. Games room. Tennis court. Golf practice range and minigolf. Bicycle hire. Pony riding in season. Free fishing. Bicycle hire. Organised activities and excursions to Paris (June-Aug). Bureau de change. The pools and sanitary installations can become busy in peak season. Stony beach at Cayeux 8 km, or sandy beach 25 km. English is spoken. The site is run personally by the energetic owner and his staff. `Camping Cheque'`

Directions: Site is 2.5 km. south of St Valéry, near Estreboeuf, and is signed from the St Valéry road N40.

Charges 1999: Per person Ffr. 32.00 + local tax (over 10 yrs) 2.00; child (under 7) 25.00; caravan or tent 50.00; car 15.00; motorcaravan 65.00; electricity 4A 16.00, 6A 20.00. Credit cards accepted.

Open: Easter - 15 September.

Reservations: Advised for main season; contact site. Address: BP 22, 80230 Saint-Valery-sur-Somme. Tel: (0)3.22.26.93.45. FAX: (0)3.22.26.85.87.

AR Discount
Low season discounts

8006 Camping Le Val de Trie, Bouillancourt-sous-Miannay, Moyenneville

Natural countryside touring site, in a woodland location, near small village.

Le Val de Trie is a well managed little site with modern facilities and a small shop and snack bar which provides basic necessities, farm produce and takeaway dishes, plus a daily visit from the local baker. The 50 numbered pitches are grassy and of a good size, divided by small hedges with mature trees providing good shade in most areas. Electricity (6A) to all, water to 38. The original sanitary building provides British style WCs, showers, washbasins in cubicles and facilities for disabled people, babies and children, with free hot water. Small swimming pool (1/6-1/9), table tennis, boules and volleyball courts, fishing lake (free), bicycle hire, children's play areas and a small animal enclosure. Riding 5 km, golf 6 km. Shop (all season), snacks (1/6-1/9), with a bar and terrace. Good walks around the area. This site is very much off the beaten track and can be very quiet indeed in low seasons.

Directions: From A28 take Moyenneville exit turning right to Moyenneville. In town (site signed) take road towards Miannay. After 2 km. turn left to Bouillancourt sous Miannay and site is signed in village.

Charges 1999: Per unit incl. 2 persons without electricity Ffr. 69.00, with electricity 87.00; extra person 20.00; child (under 7 yrs) 13.00. Less outside July/Aug. No credit cards.

Open: 1 April - 1 November.

Reservations: Made with deposit; contact site. Address: Bouillancourt-sous- Miannay, 80870 Moyenneville. Tel: (0)3.22.31.48.88. FAX: (0)3.22.31.35.33.

AR Discount
No reservation fee charged

Camping Cheque

An exciting new way of taking your holiday abroad outside July and August.
Pay for your site fees with Camping Cheque vouchers.
Freedom and flexibility at very attractive prices.

98 Quality Sites

The majority feature in this Alan Rogers Guide (look for *Camping Cheque* in the text)
Many of the French sites are Castels sites or Sites et Paysages sites.
Key facilities open from 15 May to 15 September (minimum).

Easy to Book

One phone call books your Camping Cheques,
your ferry and your insurance.

Competitive Prices

Save between 10%-50% on public tariffs.

£231
*2 Adults with
car and caravan
10 nights site fees
Dover-Calais ferry*

Special Offers
7 nights for 6
14 nights for 11

£199
*2 Adults with
motorhome
10 nights site fees
Dover-Calais ferry*

Only **£8.50** *per night*
2 adults
pitch + electricity

Send in discount voucher F in this Guide for your
Free Catalogue

or Phone **01606 787655** to find out more

W elcome to a "different France".
If you have chosen France as your
holiday destination and dream of spending
your holiday in the countryside far from the crowds,
on a top-class campsite that stands out from the rest,
and if you consider tranquility, comfort and courtesy
an essential requirement, you won't be disappointed
when you stay with the Castels.

O n our
50 4-star
touring
sites, camping has
a completely diffe-
rent meaning. Why ?
Simply because we
have so much more
to offer you !

LES CASTELS

★ ★ ★ ★

CAMPING & CARAVANING

- Address   **LES CASTELS**
                   P I B S - C P 26
                   56038 VANNES CEDEX
- Telephone   **33 2 97 42 55 83**
- Fax   **33 2 97 47 50 72**
- See us on the web **http/www.les-castels.com**
                   http/www.castels-campings.com

STEP INTO THE FUTURE!

WITH A SPECIAL OFFER EXCLUSIVE TO ALAN ROGERS' GUIDE READERS

Step into the future at the European Park of the Moving Image, a unique experience in sound, images and sensations, amid a futuristic landscape. We invite you to journey through the history and future of film and image making. You'll find 22 breathtaking attractions located inside and outside including:

- a giant 600 m^2 screen in the Kinemax (equivalent to a seven storey building)
- the Dynamic Motion Simulators which thrust you forward in time
- the world exclusive Magic Carpet
- the Imax Solido; enter the heart of a film via liquid crystal glass
- a water symphony of lasers, music & fireworks
- the largest wall of images in the world

- located just off the A10 Paris/Bordeaux autoroute
- free translation headsets
- laser light show according to season
- open 365 days a year + free parking
- over 2000 hotel rooms on-site
- great restaurant facilities

FUTUROSCOPE
POITIERS   FRANCE

The European Park of the Moving Image

Reservations & Info (UK) 0171-499 8049
    (FR) 05.49.49.30.80

P&O Stena
LINE

at your service

quality

choice

working together

every **45** minutes

P&O Stena Line, the new independent ferry company operating from Dover and Newhaven.

With six superferries on our Dover to Calais route we now offer the biggest and best ships with the most sailings everyday. During daylight hours, there's a departure every 45 minutes.

Travel Newhaven to Dieppe and our Elite catamaran gives you the fastest option to the heart of France.

Whichever route you choose, naturally you can expect the very best quality of service.

At P&O Stena Line we take the time to make your journey special.

reservations
0990 980 980

Channel express.

Brittany · Jersey · Guernsey

If you're travelling to Brittany or the Channel Islands for your holiday next year, the first thing you need is your copy of the Condor 1999 Car Ferries Brochure.

With services, up to 3 times daily from Weymouth or Poole you can be in St. Malo* in as little as 5 hours, Guernsey 2 hours or Jersey from $3^1/4$ hours.

INFORMATION & RESERVATIONS: 01305 761551

CONDOR *Ferries*

UK · JERSEY · GUERNSEY · ST. MAL

*Service starts 30th April 1999

Dover-Ostend in just 2 hours

Caravaning
★★★★

l'Etoile d'Argens

TENNIS AND GOLF FREE LOW-SEASON

TEL: 04.94.81.01.41
83370 ST.AYGULF

8101 Camping Relais de l'Entre Deux Lacs, Teillet, nr Albi

Small, quiet, family run site between the Rassisse and Bancalié lakes.

This is a lovely little site, run by the Belgian family of Lily and Dion Heijde-Wouters. In part meadow, part semi-cleared woodland, with a small farm alongside, the site offers a range of modern amenities including a good sized pool (1/5-30/9) and an excellent bar/restaurant specialising in Belgian cuisine (also 1/5-30/9). It also serves a range of no less than 20 different Belgian beers, as well as French wine. Family orientated attractions include a weekly barbecue evening, children's activity programme and contests. A small library in reception includes some English books and games. The 54 pitches, all with electricity (3, 6, 10A), are on level terraces, mostly with ample shade and of varying size, up to 100 sq.m. The site is very well managed and the owners ensure that the generally tranquil atmosphere is not disrupted. Late arrivals or those wishing to leave before 8 am. are therefore sited in an adjacent meadow. Two sanitary blocks, with extra toilets at the lower part of the site. The main one is new with the latest fittings including free, pre-set hot showers, washbasins in cabins, British WCs and dishwashing sinks under cover. The older, smaller block, in the converted pigeon house, has similar, though older style fittings and is heated in winter when the new block is closed. It also has facilities for disabled people and washing machines. Bread to order, shop in the village. Volleyball, table tennis, boules, bicycle hire and a children's farm and playground. Riding 5 km, fishing 3 km. Canoes and kayaks for hire on the Rassisse lake. Caravans and chalets to rent. Caravan storage. This site is well situated for a variety of interesting excursions in an area not that well known to British visitors.

Directions: From the Albi ring-road, take the D81 going southeast to Teillet (approx. 20 km). Continue through the village on the D81 and site is on the right.

Charges 1999: Per unit incl. 2 adults Ffr. 78.00, with electricity 90.00 - 120.00, acc. to type; extra person 25.00; child (under 7 yrs) 12.00; extra tent 11.00. Less 20% outside July/Aug. for stays of min. 5 days. No credit cards.

Open: All year.

Reservations: Made with deposit (Ffr. 300) and fee (80). Address: BP 120, 81120 Teillet. Tel: (0)5.63.55.74.45. FAX: (0)5.63.55.75.65.

AR Discount
Free guided tours & walks

8301 Camping-Caravaning Les Pins Parasols, Fréjus

Family owned site with pool, 5 km. from beach; some pitches with individual sanitary units.

Not everyone likes very big sites, and Les Pins Parasols with its 189 pitches is of a size which is quite easy to walk around. Although on very slightly undulating ground, virtually all the plots are levelled or terraced and separated by hedges or bushes with pine trees for shade. They are of around 100 sq.m. and all with electricity. What is particularly interesting, is that 48 of the pitches are equipped with their own fully enclosed sanitary unit, consisting of British WC, washbasin, hot shower and washing up sink, all quite close together. The normal toilet blocks, in three different places, are of good average quality and give a plentiful supply with washbasins in cabins, free, pre-set hot showers and chemical disposal. Facilities available for disabled people. On site is a 200 sq.m. swimming pool with attractive rock backdrop and sunbathing terrace, a separate long slide with landing pool and a small children's pool. Small shop. Restaurant with takeaway (both 1/5-20/9). General room with TV. Half-court tennis. Tax free exchange facility. Bicycle hire 1 km, fishing 6 km, riding 2 km. There is a bus from the gate into Fréjus. The nearest beach is the once very long Fréjus-Plage, now reduced a little by the new marina, which is some 5½ km. away and adjoins St. Raphaël. Used by tour operators (20 pitches).

Directions: From autoroute A8 take exit 38 for Fréjus Est. Turn right immediately on leaving pay booths on a small road which leads across to D4, where right again and under 1 km. to site.

Charges 1998: Per normal pitch with electricity incl. 2 persons Ffr 125.00; pitch with sanitary unit incl. 2 persons 159.00; extra person 33.00; child (under 7) 22.00; car 9.00; dog 11.00. Less 10% outside 15/6-1/9. No credit cards.

Open: Easter - 30 September.

Reservations: Necessary for July/Aug. only and made for min. 10 days for exact dates with deposit (Ffr 600) but no fee. Address: Route de Bagnols, 83600 Fréjus. Tel: (0)4.94.40.88.43. FAX: (0)4.94.40.81.99.

8302 Esterel Caravaning, Agay, nr Fréjus

See colour advert
opposite page 97

Attractive, good site for caravans only, in hills east of St Raphaël, 3½ km. from sea.

Set among the hills at the back of Agay, in an attractive quiet situation with good views around, this site is 3½ km. from the sandy beach at Agay, where parking is perhaps a little easier than at most places on this coast. In addition to a section for permanent caravans, it has some 250 pitches for tourists, on which caravans of any type are taken but not tents. Pitches are on shallow terraces, attractively landscaped with good shade and a variety of flowering plants, giving a feeling of spaciousness and all with electricity connection and tap. There are 18 special ones which have their own individual washroom with WC, basin and shower (both with hot water) adjoining. Amenities include five heated, circular swimming pools, one large for adults, one smaller for children and three arranged as a waterfall. They are much used, attractively landscaped (floodlit at night) and are open all season. A pleasant courtyard area contains the shop, takeaway and the bar/restaurant and terrace which also overlooks the pools. Amenities and activities include a disco, archery, volleyball, minigolf, two tennis courts, bicycle hire, pony rides, petanque and - most unusual for France - a squash court. The two toilet blocks plus one smaller one adjacent to the tourist section are very satisfactory ones which can be heated and have British toilets, most basins in private cabins, and free hot water in all facilities, though the temperature varies a little at busy times. Facilities for disabled people. Cleaning of these blocks and dustbin emptying are very good. Laundry room. Motorcaravan service point and car wash. Organised events and entertainments in season. Children's playground. Good golf courses very close. Trekking by foot, bicycle or by pony in the surrounding natural environment of L'Esterel forest park. Wild boar come each evening to the perimeter fence to be fed by visitors. Mobile homes (245) with 2 bedrooms to let. A good site, well run and organised in a deservedly popular area.

Directions: You can approach from St Raphaël via Valescure but easiest way to find is to turn off coast road at Agay where there are good signs. From Fréjus exit from autoroute A8, follow signs for Valescure throughout, then for Agay, and site is on left. (Reader's comment: If in doubt, follow golf complex signs - or Le Clerc). The road from Agay is the easiest to follow.

Charges 1998: Per pitch incl. 2 persons: standard pitch Ffr. 135.00 - 160.00, de-luxe pitch 175.00 - 200.00; extra person 40.00; child (under 7) 25.00; animal 10.00; local tax 2.00. Less 10% in low seasons. Interactive CD 'Esterel 99' available from site.

Open: 20 March - 3 October.

Reservations: Necessary for high season and made for min. 1 week with deposit (Ffr. 500) and fee (100). Address: Rte. de Valescure, 83700 Agay-St Raphaël. Tel: (0)4.94.82.03.28. FAX: (0)4.94.82.87.37. (1 Jan- 15 March tel/fax: (0)1.42.81.96.23). Internet: www.esterel-caravaning.fr.

8307 Camping-Caravaning L'Etoile d'Argens, St Aygulf, nr Fréjus

See colour advert
opposite page 129

Large, well equipped yet peaceful site near beach, with good pool complex.

L'Etoile d'Argens is a large family site with 493 pitches, and the first impression on entering the gate is that it is spacious, neat, tidy and well cared for. It is family run and for all its size, it has a peaceful air. The swimming pool area has two adult pools and a children's paddling pool, with a large paved sunbathing area around it, and a bar, restaurant, pizzeria and takeaway near. The 493 pitches are in the typical French style, very formal with well clipped hedges and well cut grass. All are of a good size (some very large), 450 of them fully serviced with 10A electricity, water and waste water point. The older part of the site is more shaded with mature trees, but for early and late season the newer part is probably better, giving maximum sunshine. For each row of 25-30 pitches there is a small unisex toilet block with British WCs, washbasins (some in cabins) and controllable showers. These blocks are beginning to show their age, but improvements are continuing and they are kept very clean and well maintained. The site provides a small supermarket, four tennis courts (two flood-lit), minigolf (both free in low season), table tennis, football pitch and a children's playground. Free tennis coaching, aerobics, swimming games and dances are organised from mid June and there is a children's entertainer in July/Aug. New laundry and children's play area. Tour operators take some pitches but are not intrusive. The river runs along one side of the site and a free boat service (15/6-15/9) runs every 40 mins to the beach. It is also possible to moor a boat and fish from the river. Riding or golf 2 km, bicycle hire 4 km. the friendly staff at reception speak English (open 24 hrs).

Directions: Site is 4.5 km. NNW of St Aygulf, where camp signs are not easy to find. You can also approach by turning off the N98 coast road midway between St Aygulf and Fréjus, or from the N7 just outside Fréjus to west. At roundabout on the N7 take D8 signed Roquebrune, St Aygulf. After crossing river bridge with traffic lights site is signed on left (from roundabout 3.5 km).

Charges 1998: Per tent pitch (100 sq.m.) with electricity and 3 persons Ffr. 185.00; 'comfort' pitch (180 sq.m.), incl. 4 persons and services 212.00; 'luxury' pitch (c. 250 sq.m.) incl. 4 persons 280.00 - 300.00; extra person 40.00; child (under 7) 28.00. Less 25% in low seasons. Credit cards accepted.

Open: Easter - 30 September, with all services.

Reservations: Made for any period with substantial deposit and fee. Address: 83370 St Aygulf. Tel: (0)4.94.81.01.41. FAX: (0)4.94.81.21.45.

8316 Parc Camping-Caravaning Les Cigales, Le Muy

Family run site convenient for the attractions of this popular area.

In a natural, shady setting of 10 ha. this site is tucked in 1 km. from the busy N7, although unfortunately close to the A8 which could be noisy if the wind is in the wrong direction. The site itself offers the opportunity for a relaxing stay and it also makes an excellent base for exploring the coast or the hinterland and the Gorges du Verdon. Sand based, gravel roads lead to the numbered pitches which vary in size, with some terracing. The terrain is typical of the area with rough, sloped and stony, dry ground, but pitches are mostly level with shade given by trees which include cork, oak and umbrella pines, plus the sweet smelling mimosa and many shrubs that fill the air reminding us that this is Provence. Six modern sanitary blocks of varying size more than serve the 186 pitches, with showers, washbasins in cabins and facilities for disabled people. Dishwashing sinks outside but covered, laundry area with washing machine and chemical disposal. A pleasant feature is the swimming pool and sunbathing area, and also the patio at the restaurant/bar which is popular in the evening. Entertainment is organised in season, with a disco twice weekly and daytime activities. Restaurant (July/Aug) and shop (June - Sept). It is only 2 km. to Le Muy where a Sunday market is held. The N7 is on a bus route or take a train at Les Arcs (8 km). For sports enthusiasts, canoeing, riding and hang-gliding are organised. Fishing 2 km, riding 7 km, golf 10 km. Caravan storage available. Chalets to rent. A `Sites et Paysages' member.

Directions: Site is signed off approach to autoroute péage on A8 at Le Muy exit and is 2 km. west of Le Muy on N7. Cross dual-carriageway on approach to toll booth from Le Muy, site is 1 km. down road parallel to autoroute.

Charges 1999: Per unit incl. 2 persons Ffr. 65.00 - 120.00; extra person 18.00 - 30.00; child (under 7) 12.00 - 19.00; electricity 6A 15.00 - 21.00, 10A 20.00 - 29.00; plus local tax. Less 5% over 3 weeks. Credit cards accepted.

Open: 1 April - 30 October.

Reservations: Advisable for July/Aug. Address: 83490 Le Muy. Tel: (0)4.94.45.12.08. FAX: (0)4.94.45.92.80.

les **Cigales**
☆☆☆☆☆
ou vos vacances dans un Jardin *
* Or your holidays in a garden

CAMPINGS SITES & PAYSAGES FRANCE

721, chemin du Jas de la Paro - F 83490 LE MUY - Tél. 04 94 45 12 08 • Fax 04 94 45 92 80

8320 Camping-Caravaning Les Pecheurs en Provence, Roquebrune-Argens

Friendly, family run site beside river at the foot of the Roquebrune Rock.

Developed by the Simoncini family, this peaceful site, in over 4 ha. of mature countryside, will appeal to families who appreciate natural surroundings with many activities. The 150 touring pitches are of a good size with electricity (6/10A) and separated by trees or flowering bushes. Among the many features is an attractively paved, sheltered pool with paddling pool (lifeguard in season). The Provencal style buildings are delightful, especially the bar, restaurant and games room, with its terrace down to the river and the site's canoe station (access by locked gate). Beside the lake (path under road bridge) is another restaurant, also open to the public. This is near the sandy beach, minigolf and half-court tennis. Other than the beach area, the lake is used for water skiing. Sanitary facilities are variable, one block new in '97 being well equipped and with baby bath and facilities for disabled visitors, the other two blocks are less modern but well maintained with washbasins in cabins, dishwashing and laundry sinks, washing machine and chemical disposal. It is a good provision, opened as required. Activities include climbing the `Rock' with a guide. We became more and more intrigued with stories about the Rock. The `Holy Hole', `Three Crosses' and the Hermit all call for further exploration which Sabine is happy to arrange, likewise trips to Monte Carlo, Ventiniglia (Italy) and the Gorges du Verdon. The medieval village of Roquebrune is within walking distance. Animation is arranged in high season with visits to wine caves and rafting or diving schools. Used by tour operators. Mobile homes for hire. `Camping Cheque'

Directions: From A8 autoroute take Le Muy exit and follow N7 towards Frèjus for 13 km. bypassing Le Muy. After crossing over A8, right at roundabout towards Roquebrune sur Argens. Site on left in 2 km. before river bridge.

Charges 1998: Per unit incl. 2 persons Ffr 85.00 - 135.00, 3 persons 100.00 - 145.00; extra person 17.00 - 30.00; child (under 7 yrs) 11.00 - 20.00; electricity 6A 18.00, 10A 23.00; local tax (15/6-15/9) 2.00.

Open: Easter - 30 September.

Reservations: Made for touring pitches without fee; contact site. Address: 83520 Roquebrune sur Argens. Tel: (0)4.94.45.71.25. FAX: (0)4.94.81.65.13.

Between Fréjus and St Tropez, only 10 minutes from the sea, and in a natural wooded setting of 60 hectares:

VERY COMFORTABLE MOBILE HOMES TO RENT
with kitchen and 1, 2 or 3 bedrooms on large pitches with customised terrace

CAMPING: Quite large, separated pitches with water and electricity, in a green and well shaded environment; modern sanitary block with washbasins in private cabins, facilities for babies.

3 SWIMMING POOLS (600 m² +) ● 6 TENNIS COURTS ● FISHING
SNACK BAR ● RESTAURANT ● FITNESS ROOM ● SAUNA
JACUZZI ● SPORTS ● GYM ● MOUNTAIN BIKES ● MINI-CLUB
ARCHERY ● JAZZ ● ENTERTAINMENTS ● DISCOS ● SHOWS

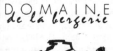

CAMPING CARAVANING ★★★★
Vallée du Fournel
83520 ROQUEBRUNE sur ARGENS
Tel: 33 4 94 82 90 11 Fax: 33 4 94 82 93 42

8317 Camping Domaine de la Bergerie, Roquebrune-sur-Argens

Well organised site with a holiday environment to suit all ages and tastes.

This is yet another excellent site near the Côte d'Azur which takes you away from all the bustle of the Mediterranean to total relaxation amongst the natural perfumes of Provence. Here, where cork oak, pine and mimosa flourish, is a 60 ha. campsite which varies from landscaped areas for mobile homes to flat, grassy terrain with avenues of 200 separated pitches for caravans and tents. All pitches average over 100 sq.m. and have electrical connections, with those in one area also having water and drainage. The four sanitary blocks are kept very clean and include hot showers, washbasins in private cubicles, British WCs, facilities for disabled people and for babies, chemical disposal points, plus dishwashing and laundry areas with washing machines. A well stocked supermarket is uphill behind the touring pitches. To the right of this, adjacent to the restaurant, are parking areas as being a spread out site, walking can be tough going. The restaurant/bar, a converted farm building, is surrounded by shady patios, whilst inside it oozes character with high beams and archways leading to intimate corners. Takeaway service. Alongside is an extravagantly designed complex with three swimming pools (15/5-30/9) and a keep fit centre (body building, sauna, gym). Five tennis courts, two half courts, volleyball, bicycle hire, mini football and more. Tournaments and programmes are organised daily and, in the evening, shows, cabarets, discos, cinema, karaoke and dancing at the amphitheatre prove popular (possibly until midnight). Fishing on site, riding, water skiing and rock climbing available nearby - in fact, few activities have been forgotten. When all that the site has to offer has been exhausted, either St Aygulf or Ste Maxime are 7 km, or drive inland and discover the delights of the hinterland. A good site for families with children and teenagers. Mobile homes for rent 15 Feb - 15 Nov.

Directions: Leave A8 at Le Muy exit on N7 towards Fréjus. Proceed for 9 km., then right onto D7 signed St Aygulf. Continue for 8 km. and then right at roundabout onto D8; site is on the right.

Charges 1998: Per unit incl. 2 adults and electricity (5A) Ffr. 95.00 - 130.00; 3 persons and electricity 120.00 - 178.00; 3 persons and electricity, water and drainage 140.00 - 200.00; extra adult 23.00 - 35.00; child (under 7 yrs) 17.00 - 24.00; electricity (10A) 12.00; local tax 2.00. No credit cards.

Open: 1 April - 30 September.

Reservations: With deposit (Ffr. 1,000 Eurocheque or bank draft). Address: Vallée du Fournel, 83520 Roquebrune-sur-Argens. Tel: (0)4.94.82.90.11. FAX: (0)4.94.82.93.42.

AR Discount
*Wecome drink
on Sundays*

8404 Camping Le Jantou, Le Thor, nr Avignon

Family run, attractive site beside River Sorgue.

The nicest feature of this attractive site is the 18th century Mas (Provencal farmhouse) and outbuildings which, together with a huge plane tree, form a centre-piece courtyard for the site facilities. The 160 pitches, around 90 for tourers, are somewhat unusually arranged in groups of mainly four pitches, the groups rather than the individual pitches being separated by tall hedges. They are mostly of a good size, on flat grass, with the majority having 3, 6 or 10A electricity and some including water and drainage. The site was originally designed and constructed in the late 70s (it has only been owned by the Tricart family for the last few years), but the two sanitary blocks which were previously of an older design and construction, have now been renovated and improved to provide modern facilities, including British style WCs, facilities for diabled people, chemical disposal, dishwashing and laundry sinks with hot water and washing machines and dryers. Snack bar and a little restaurant (July/Aug) and a shop for essentials (small supermarket a short walk). Some live entertainment is organised in season and stone built barbecues are under the plane tree. There is a swimming pool, bicycle hire and a new children's playground. A quite fast flowing river runs past the site which is suitable for fishing (licences from site), but not really for swimming due to the current. It is approached through a gate (unlocked). Riding 5 km, golf 10 km. Mobile homes for hire and some older long stay seasonal vans. Caravan storage.

Directions: Leave A7 autoroute at Avignon Nord exit on D942 towards Carpentras. Turn immediately south on D6 and proceed 8½ km. to join N100. Turn east for 3½ km. to Le Thor. Site is signed before entering the village.

Charges 1998: Per adult Ffr. 25.00; child (2-14 yrs) 13.00; pitch 30.50; electricity 3A 15.00, 6A 18.00, 10A 26.00; refrigerator 14.50; animal 6.00. 15th night free in high season, 8th in low season. Credit cards accepted.

Open: 28 March - 31 October.

Reservations: Advised for July/Aug; made with 20% deposit and Ffr. 50 fee. Address: 535 Ch. des Coudelières, 84250 Le Thor. Tel: (0)4.90.33.90.07. FAX: (0)4.90.33.79.84. E-mail: lejantou@avignon.pacwan.net. Internet: http://www.elansud.fr/lejantou/

AR Discount
*Less 5% high,
10% low season*

camping ★ ★ ★

J LE ANTOU

Au coeur de la Provence

All the comfort of a three star camp, with a calm and relaxing atmosphere.

For full details please contact us:

**M. & Mme. Tricart
84250 Le Thor
Tel: (0033) 4.90.33.90.07**

8502 Camping du Jard, La Tranche-sur-Mer

Well maintained, welcoming site, between La Rochelle and Les Sables d'Olonne.

First impressions at du Jard are good with a friendly welcome from M. and Mme. Besnard and each new arrival being personally shown to their pitch. The 350 pitches are level and grassy, hedged on two sides by bushes. The smallest are 100 sq.m. (the majority larger) and most are equipped with electricity, half with water and drainage also. It is a comparatively new site, but the variety of trees are beginning to provide a little shade. The site is 700 m. from a sandy beach but it also has its own heated swimming pool (from 25/5) with lifeguard, paddling pool and a new heated indoor pool with jacuzzi. Tennis court, minigolf, table tennis, bicycle hire, a play area, games room and TV room, also a sauna, solarium and fitness room with instructors. Three toilet blocks are well designed and maintained, light and airy, with excellent facilities for babies and disabled people. There is ample free hot water, mostly British style WCs, washbasins (most in cabins) and chemical disposal. In the same blocks are washing machines, dryers and dishwashing and laundry sinks. Restaurant, bar with terrace and a small shop for basics (all from 1/6), with many shops and restaurants near. Exchange facilities. Car wash. American motorhomes not accepted. Used by tour operators (100 pitches). An open, spacious site with a friendly atmosphere.

Directions: Site is east of La Tranche-sur-Mer, 3 km. from the D747/D46 roundabout, on the D46. From new bypass southeast of La Tranche, take exit for La Grière and then turn east to site.

Charges 1998: Per standard pitch incl. 2 persons Ffr. 125.00, with electricity (6 or 10A) 140.00 - 152.00, with electricity, water and drainage 155.00 - 165.00; extra person (over 5 yrs) 28.00; extra child (under 5) 19.00; extra small tent 20.00; tax (over 9 yrs) 1.10. Less 25% outside 1/7-25/8. Credit cards accepted.

Open: 25 May - 15 September.

Reservations: Advisable for July/Aug. (min. 1 week, Sat.- Sat.) with deposit (Ffr. 500). Address: 123, Route de la Faute, 85360 La Tranche-sur-Mer. Tel: (0)2.51 27 43 79. FAX: (0)2.51.27.42.92.

France - Vendée

8503 Camping La Loubine, Olonne-sur-Mer

Attractive, family site with friendly atmosphere and good facilities for teenagers.

The 365 pitches at La Loubine are level and grassy, with electricity, 245 with water and drainage also. The ones in the original part of the site have plenty of shade, the newer ones have not as yet. Around 110 are for touring units. The buildings around a pleasant courtyard overlooking the pool have been tastefully converted to provide an attractive bar, takeaway and shop (15/5-15/9). It is here that evening entertainment takes place. The restaurant is near reception (also 15/5-15/9). The swimming pool is large and there is also a paddling pool and water slide pool, all with sunbathing areas and sun-beds. An indoor pool has a jacuzzi and, nearby, is a sauna and fitness room (free). The four toilet blocks are modern and tiled throughout, with mainly British style WCs, washbasins in cabins and free, pre-set showers. Babies and disabled people are well catered for, there are washing machines, dryers, washing lines and irons, ample dishwashing and laundry sinks, chemical disposal and motorcaravan services. Activities and sports are organised with a daily club for children in August. Tennis, table tennis, minigolf, badminton, bicycle hire and a large children's play area (on grass and sand) are other activities. Riding 200 m, golf 3 km. The beach at Sauveterre is 1.8 km, Les Sables d'Olonne 5 km. No dogs are accepted. There is a night security barrier. Used by tour operators. Site owned mobile homes and chalets to hire.

> **Directions:** Site is west of Olonne beside the D80 road. Turn towards the coast at traffic lights, signed La Forêt d'Olonne and site (75 m).
>
> **Charges 1999:** Per pitch incl. 2 persons, with tent/caravan and car, without electricity Ffr. 121.00, with electricity (6A) 136.00, with all services 146.00; extra adult 25.00; extra child (under 7) 15.00; extra car 10.00. Less 30% outside 22/6-23/8. Credit cards accepted.
>
> **Open:** 3 April - 26 September, (full facilities from 15/5).
>
> **Reservations:** Made with deposit and Ffr 120 fee (min. 7 days in Jul/Aug.) Address: 1 Route de la Mer, 85340 Olonne-sur-Mer. Tel: (0)2.51.33.12.92. FAX: (0)2.51.33.12.71.

AR Discount
Welcome
refreshments

8504 Castel Camping La Garangeoire, St Julien-des-Landes

Rurally situated site in grounds of château, 15 km. from the Atlantic coast.

La Garangeoire is one of a relatively small number of seriously good sites in the Vendée, situated some 15 km. inland, near the village of St Julien des Landes. One of its more memorable qualities is the imaginative use which has been made of the old 'main road' to Noirmoutiers central to the site which now forms a delightful, quaint thoroughfare. Nicknamed the Champs Elysée, it is quite busy at times with most of the facilities opening directly off it and providing a village like atmosphere. The site is set in the 200 ha. of park-land which surrounds La Garangeoire, a small château. The peaceful fields and woods, where campers may walk, include three lakes, one of which may be used for fishing and boating (life jackets supplied from reception). The site has a spacious, relaxed atmosphere and many use it as a quiet base. There are two heated swimming pools (both 200 sq.m.) with water slides, fountains, etc. and a child's pool. The camping areas are arranged on either side of the old road, edged with mature trees. The 300 pitches, each with a name not a number and individually hedged, are especially large (most 150-200 sq.m.) and are well spaced. Most have electricity (6A), some water and drainage also. The ample sanitary facilities are of a good standard and well situated for all areas. A new excellent block has facilities for babies and disabled people. All have British style toilets, washasins in cabins and free controllable hot water. Good laundry facilities. Full restaurant, takeaway and new crêperie, with attractive courtyard exterior. Large playing field for children's activities, games room, 2 tennis courts, bicycle hire, table tennis, minigolf, archery and volleyball. Horse riding in July/Aug. Good shop and exchange facilities. Popular with tour operators (40%) and mobile homes to hire. `Camping Cheque'

> **Directions:** Site is signed from St Julien; the entrance is to the north off D21.
>
> **Charges 1998:** Per unit incl. 2 persons Ffr. 84.00 - 120.00, with electricity 101.50 - 145.00, with services 109.90 - 157.00; extra person 22.40 - 32.00; child (under 7) 11.20 - 16.00. Credit cards accepted.
>
> **Open:** 15 May - 15 September.
>
> **Reservations:** Made for min. 7 days with deposit (Ffr. 280) and fee (120). Address: St Julien-des-Landes, 85150 La Mothe-Achard. Tel: (0)2.51.46.65.39. FAX: (0)2.51.46.60.82.

8506 Airotel Domaine Le Pas Opton, Le Fenouiller, nr St Gilles-Croix

Well established site with good installations and swimming pool, 6 km. from sea.

Le Pas Opton is family managed and run and much work has been carried out to make it worth considering for a stay in this popular region. It is 6 km. back from the sea at St Gilles Croix de Vie and quietly situated. With a well established atmosphere, it is a select type of site but at the same time, offers on-site amenities such as a heated swimming pool (20/5-15/9) with water slide and children's pools and an attractive bar with a pleasant terrace looking across to the pool. There are 200 pitches, most of which have electricity and some hardstanding, water and drainage also. Those in the original part are well shaded by mature trees and tall hedges. The newer areas have less shade but are developing well with a more spacious feel. *continued overleaf*

8506 Airotel Domaine Le Pas Opton (continued)

The four toilet blocks are all of good quality. Kept very clean, they have British toilets, washbasins mainly in cabins for women, partly for men and free hot water in showers and sinks. Unit for disabled people, laundry facilities and chemical disposal, motorcaravan services. Shop, bar, café and takeaway (all 1/7-31/8), volleyball, basketball, table tennis, children's playground and car wash. Entertainment and some dancing is organised in season. The river Vie runs past the rear of the site (fishing possible, licences from village) and it is fenced and gated. Non-powered boats can be put on the river, but there can be a current. Riding, golf, bicycle hire within 7 km. and markets at St Gilles-Croix two or three times weekly. Chalet and large caravans for hire. Used by a tour operator (34 pitches).

Directions: Site is northeast of St Gilles, on N754 about 300 m. towards Le Fenouiller from junction with D32.

Charges 1998: Per unit incl. 2 persons Ffr. 71.50 - 94.50, with electricity (6A) 95.50 - 118.00, water and drainage also 111.50 - 134.00; extra adult 24.00; child (under 7) 14.00; local tax 2.20. Credit cards accepted.

Open: 20 May - 15 September.

Reservations: Advisable for main season and made from Jan. (min. 1 week) with deposit and fee. Address: Route de Nantes, Le Fenouiller, 85800 St Gilles Croix de Vie. Tel: (0)2.51.55.11.98. FAX: (0)2.51.55.44.94.

8508 Camping La Puerta del Sol, St Hilaire de Riez

Good quality site away from the busy coast, under new ownership.

La Puerta del Sol has been identified in the main French camping magazine as one of the European Top 30 sites and this is well deserved. For those seeking a quiet, peaceful and relaxing holiday this is certainly the site to head for. It has 184 individual pitches for touring units, mostly level and all separated by bushes, many in a sunny position. All are fully serviced with water, waste water point and electricity. When we visited in July it was a quiet haven away from the hectic coastal sites. Three toilet blocks of identical design and excellent quality have some British style WCs, washbasins in cabins and roomy adjustable showers, all with free hot water, baby baths, dishwashing and laundry sinks, a laundry and facilities for disabled visitors. The architectural style of the buildings gives the site its Spanish name. Reception is light and airy and the bar lounge, restaurant and takeaway have reasonably priced food (bar 15/5-15/9, restaurant and snacks 1/7-31/8). The bar terrace overlooks the heated swimming and paddling pools (15/5-15/9). Small shop (20/6-31/8). A mini-club is organised for children in July/Aug. with evening entertainment and dancing for adults. Children's play area on sand, tennis court, bicycle hire, volleyball, table tennis and video games. Riding, fishing and golf within 5 km. The nearest sandy beach is 5 km. and St Jean de Monts, 7 km. American motorhomes are accepted in limited numbers with reservation. Chalets (32) and caravans (4) for hire.

Directions: Site is 1 km. north of Le Pissot (which is 7 km. north of St Gilles Croix-de-Vie on D38) on the D59 road towards Le Perrier. Watch carefully for camp sign, you come on it quite suddenly.

Charges 1999: Per unit incl. up to 3 persons and 3 services Ffr 75.00 - 180.00, 2 persons 65.00 - 180.00; extra adult 18.00 - 35.00; child (under 7) 8.00 - 24.00; extra tent free - 30.00; animal 7.00 - 24.00. Credit cards accepted.

Open: 1 April - 30 September.

Reservations: Made for any period with deposit (Ffr. 900) and fee (200). Address: Les Borderies, 85270 St Hilaire de Riez. Tel: (0)2.51.49.10.10. FAX: (0)2.51.49.84.84.

AR Discount
*Welcome drink;
less for bikes*

8515 Camping La Yole, Orouet, St Jean de Monts

Attractive, popular, well run site, 1 km. from sandy beach.

La Yole offers 278 pitches, the majority under trees with ample shade and separated by bushes and the trees. All have electricity (6A), water and drainage and are of 100 sq.m. or more. Two of the sanitary blocks are of an older design but are nevertheless tiled and have British style WCs. There is free hot water to pre-set showers, washbasins in cabins and units for disabled people, all kept very clean. Outside, but under cover are large baby baths. The third block is in the newer part of the site and is very modern. It includes a hair care room and an indoor baby room. Laundry with washing machine, dryer and iron, and chemical disposal. The swimming pool is also quite new with a water slide, large pool, paddling pool, plus an indoor heated pool with jacuzzi. They are surrounded by a paved sunbathing area and overlooked by the bar and its terrace. There is also a restaurant, takeaway and a well stocked shop. Children have exceptional space with a play area on sand and a large field for ball games and picnics. Tennis, table tennis, pool and video games plus organised entertainment in high season. A pleasant walk through pine woods then by road leads to two sandy beaches. Fishing, golf and watersports are 6 km. at St Jean. The security barrier is closed at night. No dogs are accepted. Used by tour operators (45%). A Sites et Paysages member. This a friendly, popular site with welcoming owners. `Camping Cheque'

Directions: Signed off the D38, 6 km. south of St Jean de Monts in the village of Orouet.

Charges 1999: Per tent incl. 2 persons, electricity and water Ffr 90.00 - 135.00, caravan incl. drainage also 98.00 - 148.00; extra person 23.00 - 30.00; extra child (under 5) 13.00 - 19.00; local tax 2.20. Credit cards accepted.

Open: 1 May - 15 September.

Reservations: Advised, particularly for July/Aug. Address: Chemin des Bosses, Orouet, 85160 St Jean de Monts. Tel: (0)2.51.58.67.17. FAX: (0)2.51.59.05.35.

France - Vendée / Vienne

8519 Le Marais Braud, St Hilaire de Riez, nr St-Gilles-Croix

Small, unsophisticated site with swimming pool, near the sea.

Le Marais Braud occupies a peaceful wooded setting with level, grassy pitches, slightly inland from the busy coastal areas. The sandy beaches are within 7 km. by car. The facilities include a small heated swimming pool with a slide and a children's pool (from 15/6), tennis court and a small lake for fishing, which is also home to white and black swans, plus geese. The friendly bar and crêperie (with takeaway also) incorporate a games area with a skittle alley and there is a little shop for basics (all from 1/7). There are 150 pitches of 100 sq.m. with shade and some hedges, half with electrical connections (6A). One large and one smaller toilet block, both with free hot water, provide showers and wash cabins with shelves and hooks and mostly British style toilets, chemical disposal and a washing machine. Wooden chalets for rent. No tour operators. The site has a family atmosphere being managed by the owners, M. and Mme Besseau, but is only open for a very short season.

Directions: From St Hilaire de Riez, take the D38 north to Le Pissot, site is signed from the D59 road from Le Pissot to Le Perrier.

Charges guide: Per unit, incl. 2 persons Ffr. 75.00; extra adult 20.00; child 2-10 yrs 15.50, under 2 yrs 11.50; extra car 7.00; electricity (6A) 15.00; drainage 11.00. Less 15% in low seasons (June or Sept). Credit cards accepted.

Open: 1 June - 15 September.

Reservations: Write to site. Address: 298, Route du Perrier, 85270 St Hilaire de Riez. Tel: (0)2.51.68.33.71. FAX: (0)2.51.35.25.32.

8603 Camping Le Relais du Miel, Châtellerault

New site being developed in the grounds of country house, close to A10 autoroute.

With very easy access from the A10 and N10 roads, in the northern outskirts of Châtellerault, this family owned site is of very promising quality. The site is being developed in the 10 acre grounds of a rather grand house dating from Napoleonic times, beside the River Vienne and surrounded by majestic old trees. Twin barns form two sides of a courtyard behind the house, one of which has already been converted very stylishly into reception and a high ceilinged function and games room, plus a bar and restaurant which serves good value meals. Beyond are an orchard and stone gateposts leading onto ground, previously the home farm, which now forms 80 large, flat pitches. The grass is still rather rough but over 1,000 trees and bushes have been planted and all the 100-200 sq.m. pitches have electricity and water, 20 with drainage connections also. Tents are pitched in the orchard. Sanitary facilities of first class quality have been created from three sets of outbuildings with free controllable showers, washbasins in cabins, British style WCs, facilities for disabled people, chemical disposal, dishwashing sinks and a washing machine and dryer in one block. A swimming pool (15 x 7 m) with paved surrounds is beside a small snack bar with outdoor tables sheltered by a canopy and which is open in the evenings. You are welcome to stroll in the gardens and there is a gate in the walled grounds to the river bank where you may fish. Children's playground, bicycle hire, boules and games room with electronic games, pool and table tennis. Riding 5 km, golf 11 km. Basic essentials are kept, supermarket 400 m. Takeaway. Futuroscope is 16 km. Caravan storage available. Good English is spoken by M. and Mme. Mercier who have made a super start in developing their site.

Directions: Take exit no. 26 from the A10 autoroute (Châtellerault-Nord) and site is signed just off the roundabout. From the N10 follow signs for Antran north of the town.

Charges 1999: Per pitch incl. 2 persons, electricity and water Ffr. 130.00; extra person over 5 yrs 20.00; extra tent 20.00. Less 15% for 1 week, 20% for 2 weeks. Credit cards accepted.

Open: 1 May - 30 September.

AR Discount
Glass of local white winre

Reservations: Contact site for details. Address: Route d'Antran, 86100 Châtellerault. Tel: (0)5.49.02.06.27. FAX: (0)5.49.93.25.76. E-mail: lrdm.chat@wanadoo.fr.

8526 Camping La Guyonnière, St Julien-des-Landes

Unsophisticated site, away from the hectic coast.

La Guyonnière is a popular site for many reasons, the main ones being the free and easy atmosphere and its very competitive pricing. It is Dutch owned and the majority of its customers are Dutch, but English is spoken. It is a farm type site with a few different fields, each reasonably level and each having a toilet block. The pitches are very large (the few smaller ones are cheaper) and are separated by a tree and a few bushes, all having electricity (6A) although long leads may be required. The toilet blocks are very basic, but modern and functional. Some cubicles are quite small but they serve their purpose and were very clean when we visited. Hot water is free throughout, washbasins are in cubicles, showers pre-set and the WCs are British style. There is provision for babies and disabled visitors, with dishwashing and laundry sinks at each block. Reception sells bread. Bar with TV and pool table, plus tables outside. Off the bar is a pleasant restaurant (mid June - mid Sept). These are housed in farm buildings attractively converted. Entertainment is provided in the bar on high season evenings. Large play areas on sand and grass, table tennis, a sand pit and paddling pond, volleyball and football fields. The swimming pool is small and very plain, although there is a paddling pool and sunbathing areas. Being so far out in the country, this is a haven for cyclists and walkers, with many signed routes (bicycle hire available). A pleasant 500 m. walk takes you to Jaunay lake where fishing is possible (permits from village), canoeing (lifejackets from reception) and pedaloes to hire. Mobile homes and bungalow tents for hire.

Directions: From St Julien-des-Landes take the D12 west towards the coast. Site is signed after approx. 4 km. to the right and then 1 km.

Charges 1998: Per pitch Ffr. 25.00; adult 20.00; child (under 10 yrs) 12.50; car 10.00; electricity for caravan 12.50, tent 7.50; animal 10.00. Less 10-30% outside high season.

Open: 1 May - 1 October.

Reservations: Made with 25% deposit. Address: 85150 St Julien-des-Landes. Tel: (0)2.51.46.62.59. FAX: (0)2.51.46.62.89. E-mail: pierre.jaspers@wanadoo.fr. Internet: www.les-campings.com/guyonniere.

8702 Castel Camping du Château de Leychoisier, Bonnac la Côte

Elevated site in the grounds of a château, 10 km north of Limoges.

This large estate offers the opportunity to explore the château grounds and to walk down to the four hectare lake. It is ideally situated only 2 km. from the A20/N20 and 10 km. north of Limoges. There are 90 large grass pitches, some partly sloping with a mixture of sun and shade, and 76 having electrical connections (6A). The partially refurbished sanitary block is housed behind the bureau in an old building. There is ample supply of hot water throughout, the facilities are very clean but rather cramped. They include push-button showers, washbasins (some in private cabins) and British style WCs. There is provision for disabled visitors, a washing machine and chemical disposal. Adjacent to the toilet block is a restaurant (20/5-30/8) with a very pleasant terrace. The snack bar and bar are housed in an open-ended barn, partly protected by a canopy and attractive gazebo. An inviting sunbathing area surrounds the swimming pool (no shorts). Activities on site include bicycle hire, table tennis, tennis, volleyball, boules and bar billiards, and there is also a children's play area. The lake provides free fishing, boating, canoeing and a marked off area for swimming. Basic food provisions are obtainable from reception; bread and croissants must be ordered the night before. Mini-market 2 km, supermarket 5 km. Golf 15 km, riding 6 km. Torches are useful. Caravan storage. A quiet site where you have plenty of space.

Directions: From A20/N20 take exit no. 27 (west) signed Bonnac-La-Côte. Site is well signed from the village.

Charges 1998: Per pitch Ffr. 38.00 - 47.00; person 26.00 - 31.00; child (under 7) 17.00 - 20.00; electricity (4A) 18.00 - 21.00. No credit cards.

Open: 20 April - 15 September.

Reservations: Made with deposit (Ffr. 100) and fee (80), although short reservations without charge in low season. Address: 87270 Bonnac-La-Côte. Tel: (0)5.55.39.93.43. FAX: as phone. Internet: www.castels-campings.com.

CASTELS – CAMPING – CARAVANNING

Leychoisier

– For all information
– For reservations

Tel: 05 55 39 93 43
Fax: 05 55 39 93 43

CASTELS
& CAMPING
CARAVANING

CHÂTEAU
DE LEYCHOISIER

N° 24

COMFORT – CALME – COURTESY

France - Yonne

8901M Camping Municipal de Sous-Rôche, Avallon

This attractive site is in a low lying, sheltered, part wooded situation, 2 km. from the centre of Avallon. There is quite a choice of 109 pitches on the pleasant grassy terrain - on shady terraces, on flat open ground, or by a stream; 43 electrical connections (6, 8 or 14A). It may be very busy. The single toilet block is kept clean and has British style WCs, including one with basin and ramp for disabled visitors, individual washbasins (4 in cabins), showers, traditional sinks for clothes and dishes, all with free hot water. Chemical disposal and motorcaravan service point. Shop and takeaway (July/Aug). A children's playground is planned. Fishing on site, riding 4 km. Information and reading room with telephone. A very useful night stop on the way to or from Lyon and the south, worth a longer stay. Avallon is a picturesque town and good centre for visiting the wild valleys and lakes of the Morvan mountains.

Directions: From centre of Avallon take N944 to south towards Lormes. After 2 km. turn left at camp sign (a fairly steep, downhill road to site). From A6 take Avallon exit (8 km).

Charges 1998: Per person Ffr 18.00; child (under 7) 9.00; car 13.00; pitch 13.00; electricity 18.00. No credit cards or Eurocheques.

Open: 15 March - 15 October.

Reservations: Write to La Mairie. Address: Cousin La Roche, 89200 Avallon. Tel/Fax: (0)3.86.34.10.39.

The Départements of France

GERMANY

As a holiday destination it provides a rich variety of scenic and cultural interest. Although the German people are great travellers and can be found on holiday all over Europe, they nevertheless enjoy camping in their own country and good campsites can be discovered throughout the 16 'Länder'. Not only does the scenery provide great contrast - from the flat lands of the north to the mountains of the south and the forests of the west and east - but as it was only fully unified as one state in 1871, regional characteristics are a strong feature of German life and give a rich variety of folklore and customs. Medieval towns, ancient buildings and picturesque villages abound all over the country and add to the fascination of visiting Germany. Reunification may have provided many problems for politicians and people but has opened up a whole new area which was previously difficult to explore. Great strides are being made, particularly where investment has been attracted, to improve and modernise campsites. For further information contact:

German National Tourist Office, Nightingale House, 65 Curzon Street, London W1Y 8NE

Tel: 0891 600100   Fax: 0171 495 6129

Population
80,767,591 (1993); density 226 per sq.km.

Capital
Berlin. After unification in 1990, the German parliament chose Berlin as the national capital and voted to move the seat of government from Bonn to Berlin over a 12 year period.

Climate
In general winters are a little colder and summers a little warmer than in the UK.

Language
German. Most Germans speak some English, but it is appreciated if you try to use any knowledge of German that you have retained.

Currency
The unit of currency is the Deutschmark which comes in notes of 10, 20, 50, 100, 200, 500 and 1,000 deutschmark and coins of DM 0.01 (one Pfennig), 0.02, 0.05, 0.10, 0..20, 0.50, 1, 2 and 5. Exchange facilities in the former GDR may be difficult but there are banks in major towns.

Banks
Banking hours are Mon-Fri 08.30-12.30 and 14.00-16.00 with late opening on Thursdays until 18.00 hrs. Closed Sat.

Credit Cards: are becoming widely accepted but only the major cards are accepted in main department stores and restaurants in the large cities. Girocheques are widely accepted.

Post Offices
Open Mon-Fri 08.00-18.00 and Sat 08.00-12.00.

Time
GMT + 1, or BST + 1 in summer.

Telephone
The code to dial Germany from the UK is 0049.

Public Holidays
New Year; Good Fri; Easter Mon; Labour Day; Ascension; Whit Mon; Unification Day, 3 Oct; Christmas, 25, 26 Dec; plus, in some areas, Epiphany, Corpus Christi, Assumption, All Saints and Repentance days.

Shops
Open Mon-Fri 08.30/09.00 to 18.00/18.30, closed Saturday 14.00 (sometimes earlier).

Motoring
An excellent network of (toll-free) motorways (Autobahns) exists in the 'West' and the traffic moves fast. Remember in the 'East' a lot of road building is going on amongst other works so allow plenty of time when travelling and be prepared for poor road surfaces.

Speed limits: Caravans and motorhomes (2.8 tons) 31 mph (50 kph) or 19 mph (30 kph) in built up areas, 50 mph (80 kph) all other roads for caravans, 63 mph (100 kph) other roads and 81 mph (130 kph) motorways for motorhomes. Lower limits for heavier vehicles.

Parking: Don't park on roads with Priority Road signs. Meters and parking disc zones are in use.

Overnighting
If not forbidden by local regulations, then permitted at 'Rast platz' and on streets, but not open spaces.

Miscellaneous
Recycling: By law all sites must have 5 bins: 3 for glass, 1 for paper 1 for household waste.
Signs: 'Müll' - rubbish disposal; 'Einbahnstrasse' - one-way street.
'Mittagsruhe' - Virtually all campsite receptions shut completely for two hours, usually 13.00 - 15.00 hrs, with some slight variations. Barriers are locked, sometimes for pedestrians too.
Fishing: It is compulsory to pass a test (usually available at campsites providing fishing) on recognition of fish breeds, etc. before you fish.

Useful Addresses
National Motoring Organisations:
Automobil-Club von Deutschland (AVD) Lyoner Strasse 16, 60528 Frankfurt am Main Tel: 069 6606-0. Office hours 08.00-17.00
Allgemeiner Deutscher Automobil-Club (ADAC) Am Westpark 8, 81373 München. Tel: 089 76760.

**The sites in the GERMANY featured in this guide
are shown on the map on page 373**

GERMANY - North West

3000 Knaus Camping-Park Wingst, Wingst, nr Bremerhaven

Site in northwest near North Sea coast and River Elbe estuary.

With an impressive landscaped entrance, a shop and restaurant to one side and reception to the other and a barrier which is closed in the evening, this is a good quality site. It is a rural area with attractive villages, plenty of water and woodland, near to the interesting old port of Bremerhaven with its 29 km. of quays and maritime and fishing museums. The heart of this site is a deep set, small fishing lake and beach. Lightly wooded, pitches are accessed by circular roadways on differing levels and terraced where necessary. Because of the design you do not realise that there are 490 pitches, nearly all with electricity and clearly defined by shrubs and trees. There are two toilet blocks, one adjoining reception and one nearer the lake (access to this is by steps from the varying levels). The provision is good and well kept, with one block recently renovated. A swimming pool behind the hotel opposite the site is open to campers at a cost of 50 pf. per day, paid at reception. Zoo for small animals nearby and riding school with Icelandic horses which are small, quiet and very safe for children to learn to ride with good value inclusive daily rate, including lunch.

How to find it: Wingst is on the B73 Cuxhaven - Stade road, approx. 8 km. north of Henmoor.

General Details: Open all year except Nov. Restaurant. Children's playground. Minigolf. Table tennis. Fishing. Bicycle hire. Barbecue facility with roof. Riding and watersports near. Swimming pool opposite (see above). Chemical disposal. Caravans (10) to rent on site; contact site for details.

Charges 1998: Per person DM 8.50; child (3-14) 4.50; pitch 7.50 - 12.00; tent with m/cycle 7.50; electricity 3.50.

Reservations: Contact site. Address: Schwimmbadallee 13, 21789 Wingst. Tel: 04778/7604. FAX: 04778/7608.

3005 Camping Schnelsen Nord, Hamburg

Good quality site for visiting Hamburg.

Situated some 15 km. from the centre of Hamburg on the northern edge of the town, Schnelsen Nord is a suitable base either for visiting this famous German city, or as a night stop before catching the Harwich ferry or travelling to Denmark. This is a relatively new site but shade is now increasing. There is some traffic noise because the autobahn runs alongside (despite efforts to screen it out) and also some aircraft noise. However, the proximity of the A7 (E45) does make it easy to find. The 145 pitches are of good size (100 sq.m.), on grass with access from gravel roads. All have electric points (6A), are numbered and marked out with small trees and hedges. The single sanitary block is a well constructed modern building with good quality facilities and heated in cool weather. It has free hot water in basins (some in private cabins) and on payment for showers and washing up. Only very basic food supplies are stocked in reception as the site is only about 10 mins. walk from the restaurants and shops in town. There is a small children's playground, table tennis, swimming pool, tennis courts, golf and fishing within easy reach. Apart from some road traffic 'hum', as previously mentioned, this is a quiet, well laid out camp. They welcome tourists, but do not allow itinerant workers to stay.

How to find it: From the A7 autobahn take the Schnelsen Nord exit. Stay in outside lane as you will soon need to turn back left; follow signs for the Ikea store and site signs.

General Details: Open 1 April - 31 Oct. Shop (basics only). Children's playground. Facilities for the disabled. Washing machines and dryers. Sports facilities nearby.

Charges guide: Per adult DM 7.00; child (under 13 yrs) 4.00; caravan 12.00; car 4.50; motorcaravan 16.50 - 20.00; tent 10.00 - 12.00; electricity 4.00.

Reservations: Min.1 week without deposit. Address: Wunderbrunnen 2, 22457 Hamburg. Tel: 040/5594225.

3020 Campingplatz `Freie Hansestadt Bremen', Bremen

Small, good quality site in pleasant situation just outside the city.

Five kilometres from the city centre and in pleasant `green belt' surroundings, near to the university, a lake used for bathing and sailing, and an indoor swimming pool, this is a nice little site for visits to Bremen and district. Despite being so near the city, this site has a distinctly rural feel with quite an abundance of wildlife! There are good cycle rides and walks in the municpal woodland next door. It has 120 large pitches (90 for touring units) of at least 100 sq.m. on flat grass marked by stones on frontage, all with electricity and 12 with hardstanding for motorcaravans. The toilet block is of good quality, with British style WCs, free hot water in the washbasins (4 in private cabins) and sinks, and free fully controllable hot showers with seat and screen. Unit for disabled visitors.

How to find it: From the A27 autobahn northeast of Bremen take the exit for `Universität' and follow signs for University and then for camp.

General Details: Open all year. Shop (all year, fresh bread to order). Restaurant (all year). General room. Cooking facilities. Children's playground. Bicycle hire. Barbecue area. Washing machines and dryer. Chemical disposal.

Charges 1998: Per person DM 7.50; child (under 16) 4.50; caravan 11.00; tent 7.50 - 11.00; car on pitch 2.50; motorcaravan 15.50 - 18.00, acc. to size; m/cycle 1.00; dog 2.00. Some discount with camping carnet.

Reservations: made for any length, with deposit. Address: Am Stadtwaldsee 1, 28359 Bremen. Tel: 0421/212002. FAX: 0421/219857.

3010 Kur-Camping Röders' Park, Ebsmoor, Soltau

First-class, small, award winning site, close to many amenities.

Although near to Soltau centre (1.5 km), Ebsmoor is a peaceful location, ideal for visits to the famous Luneburg Heath or as a stop on the route to Denmark. Herr and Frau Röders are a happy and dedicated couple who make their visitors most welcome and Herr Röders speaks excellent English. The central feature of the wooded site is a small lake crossed by a wooden bridge. An abundance of trees and shrubs gives a secluded setting to an already well cared for appearance. Röders' Park only offers a tranquil stay - there is no entertainment. Two modern, very clean sanitary blocks (one with under-floor heating) contain all necessary facilities with a laundry room and an excellent, separate unit (including shower) for wheelchair users. There is an adequate children's play area, a basic shop, but no bar or restaurant except a breakfast service. Many sports activities are available locally. The site has 100 pitches (75 touring), all with electricity and water to hand, mostly with hardstanding and with reasonable privacy between positions. Some guest rooms are available in the main building.

How to find it: From Soltau take road no. B3 north and turning to site is on left after 1½ km. (opposite DCC camping sign) at yellow town boundary sign.

General Details: Open all year except 15 Jan -15 Feb. Electricity connections (6A). Small shop. Breakfast service. Children's play area. Bicycle hire. Fishing and riding 1.5 km. Golf 3 km. Chemical disposal. Motorcaravan services.

Charges 1999: Per pitch DM 17.00; person 8.50; child 7.50; dog 3.00; electricity (6A) 1.00 per stay plus 0.80/kw. No credit cards.

Reservations: Contact site. Address: Ebsmoor 8, 29614 Soltau. Tel: 05191/2141. FAX: 05191/17952.

3025 Campingpark Alfsee, Rieste, nr Osnabrück

Good modern site, 25 km. north of Osnabrück with many watersport facilities.

This is one of those inland sites which, being adjacent to lakes, has made the most of its situation to provide a wide range of watersports opportunities, and with good installations, to offer a base for enjoyable weekends or holidays. The Alfsee itself is a very large stretch of water for sailing, but even closer to the site, a short stroll from the entrance, is a small lake of 100,000 sq.m. where there is both a bathing section with sandy beach (free to campers) and a water-ski automatic tug, ski-lift style, on payment and open to all. The site has 340 pitches on flat grass (160 taken by permanent caravans). They are of irregular shape and size but mostly over 100 sq.m. with separators and there are many electrical connections. The three identical toilet blocks, heated in cool weather, are nice clean ones of good quality, with British style WCs, washbasins with free hot water, shelf, mirror (some in private cabins) and hot showers with screen and seat on payment. It is a good supply, with a unit for disabled visitors.

How to find it: From A1 autobahn north of Osnabrück take exit for Neuenkirchen and Vörden, turn left and follow signs for Alfsee and camp.

General Details: Open all year. Shop and restaurant (both April-Oct). Watersports (see above). Football practice field. Children's playground and entertainment. Grass tennis courts. Trampoline. Minigolf. Go-kart track. General room with amusement machines. Several washing machines and dryers. Cooking facilities.

Charges 1998: Per unit incl. 2 adults DM 22.75 - 32.50; extra adult 5.30 - 7.60; child or student 3.80 - 5.40; dog 3.00 - 5.00; electricity 3.00 (once only) plus meter. Overnight pitch (17.00 - 10.00 hrs) 18.00 - 25.00.

Reservations: made for any length without deposit. Address: 49597 Rieste. Tel: 05464/5166. FAX: 05464/5837.

3030 DCC Truma Campingpark, Leeden, Tecklenberg, nr Osnabrück

Large site with swimming pool and other amenities near Osnabrück.

This is a large site taking some 900 units and covers a wide area. Half the pitches (individual ones on mostly flat grassy areas but not separated) are for permanent caravans, leaving 450 for tourists and space is usually available. Many electrical connections. Sanitary installations consist of four good modern blocks (heated in cool weather) with British WCs, washbasins, some in private cabins, with shelf and mirror, controllable hot showers; free hot water in basins, on payment in showers and in sinks for clothes and dishes - it is a good supply. Facilities are provided for disabled visitors. On site is a new swimming pool complex and leisure area with heated two pools, children's pools and water slides. No English is spoken! Good walks from site - there is woodland not used for camping. Osnabrück is 15 km.

How to find it: Leave A1 autobahn at exit for Tecklenburg and Lengerich. Turn towards Lengerich, left at second traffic lights to `Leeden-Lotte' and follow camp signs. From N take exit for Lotte and follow Lengerich then Leeden.

General Details: Open all year. 300,000 sq.m. Shop (March - Oct). Restaurant/bar (March - Oct and Dec - Jan). Snacks (July/Aug). Swimming pools (mid May - mid Sept). Sports field. Minigolf. Children's playground. Dry ski in summer. Youth room with table tennis; occasional disco. Washing machine and dryer in each block. Cooking facilities. Riding nearby.

Charges 1998: Per person DM 7.50; child (4-13 yrs) 5.00; pitch 12.50 - 16.50; hiker's tent 11.50; electricity 3.00 + 0.75 per kw/h; dog 2.00. 10% off personal charges with camping carnet.

Reservations: Formal ones are complicated and probably unnecessary; send a card to site before arrival. Address: 49545 Tecklenburg-Leeden. Tel: 05405/1007. FAX: as phone.

GERMANY - North West

3035 DCC Kur Camping Park, Bad Gandersheim

Good site, easily reached from autobahn and well placed for visiting other Harz resorts.

Attractively situated between a tree-covered hill and the B64 road, this is a well run, formal site with a stream running through the middle. It has 460 pitches of which 300 are for touring units. They are all well marked and easily accessible, divided into long and short stay areas and a section for those with animals. Open all year, the site provides good amenities for both summer walkers and winter skiers. Although on the edge of the Harz area, the excellent security at the site allows one to leave the van, etc. whilst exploring the twisty and busy roads of the main resort towns or participating in one of the organised walks. The sanitary facilities are modern, with showers on payment (50 pf. coin), plus facilities for mother and baby, and child toilets. A restaurant serves snacks at lunch-time and evening meals (excl. Mondays). The pretty, old town is a 15 minute stroll.

How to find it: From autobahn A7 (E45), leave at Seesen, then route 64 to Bad Gandersheim. Site is on right, just before town and is well signed.

General Details: Open all year. Electricity throughout (10A). Bar/restaurant (Easter-31/10, 15/12-10/1, w/ends at other times). Shop (Easter-31/10 and 15/12-10/1). Minigolf. Table tennis. Children's play areas. Laundry facilities. Solarium. Dog shower. Tennis, riding, fishing, swimming, sailing, windsurfing all near. Motorcaravan service point.

Charges 1998: Per pitch DM 12.50 - 16.50; small tent 11.50; adult 7.50 plus local tax 1.00; child (under 13 yrs) 5.00 plus 0.50 tax; dog 2.00; electricity 0.50 plus meter. Credit cards accepted.

Reservations: Contact site. Address: Braunschweiger Str. 12, 37581 Bad Gandersheim. Tel: 05382/1595. FAX: 05382/1599.

3040 Camping Prahljust, Clausthal-Zellerfeld

Pleasant, large site in a good position to explore the Harz area.

This all year round site is well situated for both winter or summer holidays. It is a gently undulating site sloping down to a small lake. The receptionist/manager speaks good English and provides guests with an excellent information sheet in English. There are 1,000 pitches of which 350 are for permanent units, and three sanitary blocks with both private cabins and open troughs for washing. One block has a unit for wheelchair users. Amenities include a large, heated swimming pool (with a small charge) and a sauna. Fishing is allowed in the lake (licence essential). A bar, restaurant and a self service shop are close to reception and there is a good children's playground. Entertainment is organised in high season. Other attractions in the Harz include the highest point at Brocken (1,142 m.) with a narrow gauge steam railway and many walks.

How to find it: From autobahn A7 (E45) leave at Seesen and take route 242 for Clausthal Zellerfeld. Go through the town (direction Braunlage) and the site is 2 km. out of the town on the right, well signed. Coming from Braunlage, site is also signed `Rubezahl', on the left.

General Details: Open all year, as are bar, restaurant and shop. Electricity connections throughout (10A). Swimming pool . Sauna. Washing machines and dryers. Drying room. Children's playground. Fishing. Chemical disposal. Motorcaravan service point

Charges 1998: Per pitch DM 6.75 - 8.35; adult 6.55 - 8.15; child (under 14 yrs) 5.60 - 7.35; car 3.50 - 4.20; m/cycle 2.35; electricity 1.00 plus meter; dog 4.70 - 5.00; local tax 1.50.

Reservations: Write to site. Address: 38678 Clausthal-Zellerfeld. Tel: 05323/1300. FAX: 05323/78393.

3045 Knaus Camping Walkenried, Walkenried

Woodland site in the southern Harz with indoor pool.

The southern Harz area offers much for walkers and anglers and this site organises many outings ranging from free walks to coach trips to the highest mountain in the area at Brocken (1,142 m). It also has the benefit of an indoor pool, sauna and solarium. Outdoor activities available in the area include tennis, riding and watersports. There are about 150 touring pitches here of 80-100 sq.m. and arranged in well shaded groups on mainly slightly sloping grass and gravel. Most are separated by bushes or trees and have 4A, 2 pin electrical connections. There are some smaller hardstandings for motorhomes and a separate area for visitors with dogs. The tiled and heated sanitary facilities are satisfactory, with free hot water to the 12 showers and washbasins (private cabins for ladies) and a toilet for the disabled, and are all in the main building by the entrance. There is a large children's play area at the side of the site, also a barbecue and some seating here and by the small fishing lake. An indoor swimming pool is free for campers (open 9-12 and 3-6, all year except 1 Nov - 10 Dec).

How to find it: Walkenried is signed from the B4 Erfurt-Magdeburg road just north of Nordhausen and from the B243 Seesen-Nordhausen road. The site is signed in the town.

General Details: Open all year exc. Nov. Baker calls just after 8 am. Shop and restaurant (both all year). Indoor pool. Sauna and solarium. New children's play area. Small fishing lake. Bicycle hire. Laundry and cooking facilities. Chemical disposal. Caravans (10) and tents to rent on site; contact site for details.

Charges 1998: Per person DM 8.50; child (3-14) 4.50; pitch 7.50 - 12.00; tent with m/cycle 7.50; electricity 3.50.

Reservations: Contact site. Address: Ellricher Str. 7, 37445 Walkenried. Tel: 05525/778. FAX: 05525/2332.

3280 Camping und Ferienpark Teichmann, Vöhl-Herzhausen, Edersee

Well equipped site for active holidays on the shores of the Edersee.

By a 6 hectare lake with tree-covered hills all around, this well cared for site blends in attractively with its surroundings. There are facilities for windsurfing, row boats, pedaloes (no motor-boats), swimming and fishing, all in different areas and it is also suitable for a winter sports holiday (with ski runs near). There are many local walks and the opportunity exists for taking a pleasure boat trip and riding home by bicycle. Three good quality sanitary blocks for tourers can be heated and offer large, free hot showers, mother and baby rooms in two and for wheelchair users. Of the 460 pitches, half are for touring units. They are mainly on flat grass, all with electricity and with some hardstandings. There is a separate area for tents. Amenities include a mini-market and café. Good for families, there are many activities and a pitch can usually be found even for one night. A very large open air model railway is an attraction.

How to find it: From the A44 Oberhausen - Kassel autobahn, take exit for Korbach. Site is between Korbach and Frankenberg on the B252 road, 1 km. to the south of Herzhausen, about 45 km. from the A44.

General Details: Open all year. Electricity connections (6A). Café and shop (both summer only). Restaurant by entrance open all day (Feb-Dec). Watersports. Boat and bicycle hire. Lake swimming. Football. Fishing. Minigolf Beach volleyball (high season). Tennis. Table tennis. Children's playground. Large working model railway. Sauna and solarium. High season disco. Holiday homes to rent.

Charges 1998: Per unit with 2 persons, electricity, water and waste water, DM 19.90 - 45.90 according to size and season. Extra person (3 -16) 3.90 - 5.90; over 16, 7.20 - 9.90.

Reservations: Made with deposit (DM 100) and fee (10); write to site. Address: 34516 Vöhl-Herzhausen. Tel: 05635/245. FAX: 05635/8145.

3270 Campingplatz Lahnaue, Marburg an der Lahn

Satisfactory site adjacent to swimming pools and within walking distance of town.

This little municipal site should make a satisfactory stop on the B3 Frankfurt-Kassel road. Situated on a long, fairly narrow strip of land between the river Lahn and the road and railway (possibly some noise), there are pleasant walks from the site to the centre of the old university town. An adjoining sports complex includes large swimming pools, tennis, minigolf, a playground and general games area. The 76 touring pitches are on flat grass, some at the water's edge, numbered but not separated with electricity in most areas. The small sanitary block is modern and should be adequate. It has hot showers on payment, one washbasin with hot water per sex, the remainder cold, and first-class facilities for wheelchair users. Bread is ordered at reception the previous evening and there are many shops and restaurants in Marburg.

How to find it: Site is at the south end of the town adjoining the ring road. Turn off ring road at 'Marburg mitte' exit then follow camping signs.

General Details: Open 1 April - 31 Oct. Electricity connections (10A). Some provisions kept. Small restaurant with breakfast served. Table tennis. Minigolf. Fishing. Bicycle hire 1 km. Riding and golf 5 km. Cooking facilities. Washing machine and dryer. Chemical disposal. Motorcaravan service point.

Charges 1998: Per person DM 7.00; child (2-13 yrs) 3.00; caravan 6.00; tent 5.00; car 3.00; motorcaravan 9.00; electricity 2.00 plus 2.00 per day; waste 1.00. No credit cards.

Reservations: Usually unnecessary, but site address is 35037 Marburg. Tel: 06421/21331. FAX: as phone.

3210 Campingplatz Biggesee-Sondern, Olpe-Sondern

High quality leisure complex site, on shores of large lake in Südsauerland National Park.

In an attractive setting on the shores of the Biggesee lake, this site offers many leisure opportunities, as well as high quality camping facilities. It is therefore deservedly popular, and reservation is almost always essential. Well managed, the same company also operates two other sites on the shores of the lake, where space may be available, which is useful as it is also popular for a short stay, being quite near the A45 and A4 roads. There are 300 numbered pitches of 100 sq.m, of which about 250 are for tourists, either in rows or in circles, on terraces, with electricity and water points throughout. Sanitary facilities are in two blocks of excellent quality, heated when necessary. British style WCs (no paper), washbasins (many in cabins) and good showers, all with free hot water. Facilities for babies and laundry (keys from reception). Leisure activities are numerous. Watersports on the lake include sailing and windsurfing, with a school available. Skiing is possible and there are walks around the lake.

How to find it: From the A45 (Siegen-Hagen) autobahn, take the exit to Olpe, and turn towards Attendorn. After 6 km. turn to Bigge-Stausee. Site is signed.

General Details: Open all year. Electricity throughout (6A). Shop (closed Jan and Nov). Watersports and school. Swimming from beach. Football pitch. Table tennis. Roller-skating. Fishing. Bicycle hire. Tennis near. Riding 8 km. Golf 12 km. Children's playground and playroom. Solarium and sauna. Entertainment and excursions. Restaurant and snacks 300 m (Easter - 31/10). Cooking facilities. Laundry. Motorcaravan service points. Car wash area.

Charges 1999: Per unit incl. electricity DM 19.00 - 25.00; person 5.50 - 7.00; child (3-15 yrs) 3.00 - 4.00; dog 4.50. No credit cards.

Reservations: Probably essential for much of the year, but phone site. Address: Erholungsanlage Biggesee-Sondern, 57462 Olpe-Sondern, Am Sonderner Kopf 3. Tel: 02761/944111. FAX: 02761/944122.

GERMANY - West Central

3205 Campingplatz der Stadt Köln, Köln-Poll, Köln

Convenient site beside the Rhine, very close to motorway.

The ancient city of Cologne offers much for the visitor, with many museums, art galleries, opera and open-air concerts, as well as the famous Cathedral. The 'Phantasialand' theme park is close by at Brühl and the zoo and Rhine cruises are among other attractions. The site is pleasantly situated alongside the river, with wide grass areas either side of narrow tarmac access roads and low metal barriers separating it from the public park. Of 150 unmarked, level touring pitches, 50 have electricity and there is shade for some from various mature trees. The small toilet block has fairly basic facilities, with free hot water (06.00-12.00, 17.00-23.00 hrs) in the washing troughs and regularly in the token operated showers, above the large open-fronted room where you may cook, eat, and wash clothes and dishes. A small shop opens in the mornings for bread and offers basic supplies and snacks in the evenings.

How to find it: Leave autobahn A4 at exit no. 13 for Köln-Poll (just to west off intersection of A3 and A4). Turn left at first traffic lights and follow site signs through a sometimes fairly narrow one-way system to the riverside, back towards the motorway bridge.

General Details: Open Easter - 15 Oct. Electricity connections (10A). Kiosk (from 1/5). Café adjacent. Cooking facilities on payment. Fishing. Bicycle hire. Washing machine and dryer. Chemical disposal.

Charges 1998: Per adult DM 7.50; child (4-12 yrs) 4.50; caravan 6.00; motorcaravan 9 .00; tent 4.00 - 6.00; car 4.00; m/cycle 2.00; electricity 3.00.

Reservations: Write to site. Address: 51105 Köln 91 (Poll). Tel: 0221/831966. FAX: as phone.

 AR Discount
Less 10%

3215 Campingplatz Goldene Meile, Remagen, nr Bonn

Site on banks of Rhine between Bonn and Koblenz, adjacent to outdoor pool complex.

This site is beside the Rhine (boats of any type can be put onto the river) and adjacent to a large complex of open-air public swimming pools (campers pay the normal entrance). Although there is an emphasis on permanent caravans, there are about 250 pitches for tourists (from 500), 14 with water and waste water connections and 14 with waste water. They are either in the central, more mature area or in a newer area where the numbered pitches of 80-100 sq. m. are arranged around an attractively landscaped small fishing lake. They claim always to find space for odd nights, except perhaps at B.Hs. The main sanitary facilities are in the central block which is a good quality building, heated and kept clean, with British style toilets, washbasins (some in cabins), controllable hot showers with token from machine (1 DM) and new facilities for wheelchair users. The shower and wash rooms are locked at 10 pm. A smart toilet block serves the newer pitches near the lake. It also has dishwashing and laundry sinks, a washing machine and dryer, chemical disposal and cooking facilities. The central buildings also house a small bar/restaurant and a small shop for basic supplies (including bread to order). This site is in a popular area and, although busy in high season, appears to be well run.

How to find it: Remagen is 23 km. south of Bonn on the no. 9 road towards Koblenz. The site is on the road running close to the Rhine from Remagen to Kripp and is signed from the N9 south of Remagen, which avoids the congested town (signs also for 'Allwetterbad'). From A61 autobahn take Sinzig exit.

General Details: Open all year. Shop (Easter - Oct). Electricity connections in most areas (8A). Restaurant (closed Mon. low season). Children's playgrounds. Entertainment for children in July/Aug. Volleyball. Football. Bicycle hire. Riding 1 km. Chemical disposal. Motorcaravan services. Main gate locked at 10 pm. (also 1-3 pm.)

Charges 1999: Per person DM 9.00; child (6-16 yrs) 7.00, under 6 free; caravan pitch 12.50; tent 6.00 - 12.50 acc. to size; dog 2.00; electricity 4.00. No credit cards.

Reservations: can be made for at least a few days. Address: 53424 Remagen/Rhein. Tel: 02642/22222. FAX: 02642/1555.

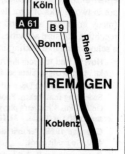

3212 Landal GreenParks Wirfttal, Stadtkyll

Site with pools and other facilities near the Belgian border between Cologne and Trier.

Peacefully set in a small valley in the heath and forest of the hills of the northern Eifel, Wirfttal has 250 pitches of which 150 are for tourists. Not fully separated, they mostly back onto fences, hedges etc. on fairly flat ground of different levels (steel pegs required for tents and awnings). About 80 sq.m, all have electricity and TV aerial points. Part of the site, but separate from the camping, is a holiday bungalow complex. A short walk up the hill is a swimming pool complex (free for campers) with three pools, one heated, and minigolf. At the site entrance is a small, free indoor pool, plus a sauna and solarium on payment, sports centre with two outdoor tennis courts (floodlit), adventure playground, volleyball, bowling and an indoor tennis and squash centre. All will be enchanted by the ducks and swans on the small lake. The main toilet block (heated and the only one open in low season) and two small units have free hot water in basins, showers and sinks; all ladies' washbasins and one for men are in cabins.

How to find it: Site is 1½ km. south of Stadtkyll on the road towards Schüller.

General Details: Open all year. Reception opens 9-12 am. and 2-5.30 pm (Sunday 10-12 only). Shop. Restaurant and snacks (high season). Tennis and 'platform' tennis. Riding. Fishing (free). Bicycle hire. Sports centre adjacent. Adventure playground. Winter sports. Bicycle and sledge hire. Animation in season. Chemical disposal.

Charges 1999: Per unit incl. up to 5 persons DM 29.00 - 52.00; extra person 4.50; dog 4.50; electricity 4.00.

Reservations: are made (Fri.- Fri. only in high season) with 50% deposit. Address: 54589 Stadtkyll/Eifel. Tel: 06597/92920. FAX: 06597/929250. Office open 7 days/week.

3265 Campingplatz Limburg, Limburg an der Lahn, nr Koblenz

Good municipal site by Cologne-Frankfurt autobahn.

Pleasantly situated on the bank of the river Lahn between autobahn and town - both the autobahn viaduct and the cathedral are visible - this is a useful overnight stop for travellers along the Köln - Frankfurt stretch. You may, however, be tempted to stay longer as there are other attractions here, notably a very fine swimming pool complex nearby and the attractive old town of medieval buildings a gentle stroll away. The site is on level grass with 200 touring pitches (out of 250 altogether) on either side of gravel tracks at right angles from the main tarmac road, which runs the length of the site. It is very popular with many nationalities and can become crowded at peak times, so arrive early. The main sanitary block near reception is rather old but improvements have been made (showers need a token). A new block at the other end of the site should be ready for '99. A bar/restaurant, open during the evenings, offers drinks, simple meals and takeaway. Kiosk for basic supplies. Some road and rail noise.

How to find it: Leave A3 autobahn at Limburg-Nord. Follow road into town, then signs for Camping-Swimming.

General Details: Open Easter - 30 Oct. Electricity connections (140, 6A) - some need long leads. Bar/restaurant. Kiosk. Swimming pool opposite. Shops and restaurants in town. Pleasure boat cruises. Fishing (permit on payment). Children's play area. Washing machines, dryers, cookers. Bicycle and motorcycle hire. Motorcaravan services.

Charges 1998: Per person DM 5.80; child (3 - 14) 3.00; car 3.00; m/cycle 2.50; caravan 5.50; motorcaravan 8.50; tent 3.50 - 5.00; boat 6.00; dog 2.00; electricity 3.30; shower token 1.50; waste fee 1.20.

Reservations: Contact site. Address: 65549 Limburg a.d. Lahn. Tel: 06431/22610. FAX: 06431/92013.

3225 Naturpark Camping Suleika, Lorch-bei-Rudesheim

Friendly, family run site on steep hillside in Rhine-Taunus Nature Park

Approached by a narrow and steep system of lanes through the vineyards, this situation is not for the faint hearted. Once you reach the site, it is steeply arranged in small terraces up the side of the wooded hill with a stream flowing through - the water supply is direct from springs. The surroundings are most attractive, with views over the vineyards to the river below. The Riesling Walk footpath passes above the site. Of the 100 pitches, 50 are for tourists, mostly on the lower terraces, in numbered groups of up to four units. There is a special area for younger campers. All have electricity and there are water points around. Cars are parked away from the pitches near the entrance. A central block contains a very pleasant restaurant and small shop for basics (bread to order), with sanitary facilities alongside. These are excellent, heated in cool weather and containing British style WCs, washbasins (some in cabins), free hot showers. Baby washroom, with WC, shower and bath. With steep walks from most pitches to the facilities, this is probably not a site for disabled visitors. This area is famous as it was briefly a 'Free State' (1919-23). You can taste and buy the owner's wine and other souvenirs. Good English spoken.

How to find it: Direct entrance is from B42 (cars only) between Rudesheim and Lorch, with height limit of 2.25 m. under a bridge. For higher vehicles site is signed on south side of Lorch. Follow signs on one-way system of lanes.

General Details: Open 1 March - 15 Nov. Site opens all day. Shade in most areas. Electricity connections (16A). Water from springs. Restaurant. Small shop. Children's playground. Some entertainment in season. Fishing. Bicycle hire. Riding 5 km. Laundry service. Toilet disposal but no chemicals. Motorcaravan services. 10 chalets for rent.

Charges 1998: Per adult DM 7.50; child 5.00; caravan 8.00; motorcaravan 10.00 - 12.00; tent 5.00 - 8.00; car 2.50; m/cycle 1.50; dog 3.00; electricity 2.00 plus meter. No credit cards.

AR Discount

Less 10% on person charge

Reservations: made with DM 50 deposit, so only worthwhile for a longer stay. Address: Lorch-bei-Rudesheim, 65382 Rudesheim 2 (Ass). Tel: 06726/9464. FAX: 06726/9440.

3230 Campingplatz Burgen, Burgen, nr Koblenz

Pleasantly situated site on banks of the Moselle between Koblenz and Cochem.

Burgen is between the road and the river on the flat grassy bank with attractive views and, like many sites alongside the Moselle, it may occasionally be flooded at very high tide. Most of the pitches on the river's edge are occupied by permanent caravans and attendant boats, but there are 120 individual numbered hardstanding pitches for tourists, with electricity, plus a meadow at one end. The site fills up for much of July/Aug. but a few pitches are kept for short stay visitors. The single central sanitary block is quite good, with British style toilets, washbasins with free hot water (5 in cabins), and 9 showers (on payment, token from reception or shop) which might be hard pressed in high season. With a railway across the water, the road and commercial boats, some noise may be expected. You can swim and fish in the Moselle, (small children's pool on site), or just use the site as a base for visiting local attractions.

How to find it: Site is on eastern edge of town, 30 km. from Koblenz (tight turn into site coming from Koblenz).

General Details: Open 1 April - 15 Oct. 35,000 sq.m. Electricity connections (10A). Shop (essentials only all season). General room with TV and games, drinks served. Small swimming pool (9.5 x 6.5 m. open Whitsun - 31 Aug.). Fishing and swimming in the Moselle. Slipway for boats. Table tennis. Children's playground. Bicycle hire 5 km. Boat trips. Restaurant 200 m. Washing machine and dryer. Chemical disposal. Motorcaravan services.

Charges 1998: Per person DM 7.00; child (1-13 yrs) 4.00; pitch 12.00; electricity 3.00. No credit cards.

Reservations: Any length with deposit. Address: 56332 Burgen/Mosel. Tel: 02605/2396. FAX: 02605/4919.

3470 AZUR Campingplatz Odenwald, Kirchzell, Eberbach, nr Heidelberg

Woodland site between the rivers Neckar and Main.

In the nature reserve of the Odenwald and only 7 km. from Amorbach with its 700 year old Benedictine Abbey, this site gives the impression of being deep in the forest and will appeal most to those who like the peaceful attractions of hills, trees and meadows. It is by a stream in a low lying valley, away from main through routes, although Heidelberg, Frankfurt and Würzburg are only an hour away. Just over half the pitches are taken by permanent caravans but there are 160 grassy and shaded tourist pitches around the site, with a separate area for tents. There is usually space but it can be full at Easter and Whitsun and in late July. Entertainment is organised at these times. Larger than usual, free, indoor pool with sauna. The sanitary facilities, in three main blocks, vary from satisfactory to above average quality and are kept clean, with heating in cool weather. They have British toilets, washbasins (some in cabins) and free hot water, plus a toilet and shower for the disabled in one. Reception is friendly and efficient.

How to find it: Site is 2 km. south of Kirchzell on the Eberbach - Amorbach road. Caravans approaching from Eberbach may choose to go on for 1 km. and turn back

General Details: Open all year. Many electrical connections (16A). Small shop (April - Sept). Restaurant. Children's playground. Table tennis. Indoor swimming pool, plus sauna and solarium. Bicycle hire. Barbecue. General room with TV (satellite). Washing machines and dryer. Mobile homes for hire. Motorcaravan service point.

Charges 1998: Per adult DM 8.00 - 10.00, acc. to season; child (2-12 yrs) 6.00 - 7.00; pitch 11.00 - 13.00; car or m/cycle 3.00 - 4.00; extra tent 3.00 - 4.00; dog 3.00 - 4.00; electricity 3.80.

Reservations: are made with deposit (DM 15) and fee (15); write for details. Address: 63931 Kirchzell-Eberbach. Tel: 09373/566. FAX: 09373/7375.

3235 Camping am Mühlenteich, Lingerhahn, Laudert, nr Koblenz

Friendly site to west of central Rhine and quite close to autobahn.

Set among trees and fields in the hills at the eastern end of the Hunsrück, this site is only 15 km. from the Rhine at Oberwesel. Bingen, Boppard and Koblenz are also reached easily via the A61 autobahn. With a new development of 50 pitches, many with electricity, water and waste water connections, there are now 100 for tourers in addition to the 250 for permanent caravans. Some are in the main part (for longer stays), others are in a more open situation opposite (caravans and tents are mixed together); space is usually available. The central sanitary block, in two sections, is large and of good quality. With a further building for high season, there is a satisfactory supply, with washbasins (some cabins for ladies in two blocks and for men in one), controllable hot showers on payment and British style WCs. On site is an unusual pool for swimming (free of charge) fashioned from a natural basin and fed by springs. A splendid new building houses reception, a shop and café and there is very good provision for children, including some popular children's play equipment and a video room, plus entertainment in July/Aug.

How to find it: From A61 autobahn take exit for Laudert. Follow signs through Lingerhahn village, between Laudert and Kastellaun. Site is just to the back of the village.

General Details: Open all year. Electrical connections (6/16A). Small shop. Café (Easter-Oct and holidays). Baker calls daily at 8.30 am. Cable/satellite TV. Youth disco room. Tennis. Basketball. Table tennis. Children's adventure playground. Football field. Wagon rides in season. Bicycle hire. Riding 6 km. Barbecue. Animation in high season. Chemical disposal. Motorcaravan services.

Charges 1999: Per person DM 7.00; child (under 14) 5.00; car 7.00; caravan or tent 7.00; motorcaravan 14.00; m/cycle 5.00; electricity 3.50; cable TV 2.00. No credit cards.

AR Discount
Less 10% on person fees.

Reservations: Contact site. Address: 56291 Lingerhahn. Tel: 06746/533. FAX: 06746/1566.

CAMPING PLATZ BURG LAHNECK

Lahnstein/Rhein, Orsteil Oberlahnstein
(Take 'Oberlahnstein' exit from B42 through road)

On the heights near the medieval castle Burg Lahneck and so free from possible Rhine flooding. Beside the public pool. The ideal base for those who want to explore the Rhineland with its wonderful scenery and historic buildings. Beautiful day excursions available in all directions (Rhine, Lahn, Moselle, Nahe, and Ahr valleys). Boarding point for Rhine steamers.

3220 Campingplatz Burg Lahneck, Lahnstein, nr Koblenz

Orderly, clean site with fine views over Rhine and swimming pool adjoining.

The location of this site is splendid, high up overlooking the Rhine valley and the town of Lahnstein - many of the pitches have their own super views. Adjacent is a good swimming pool with extensive grassy areas, and also the mediaeval castle Burg Lahneck (the home of the camp proprietor, which may be visited) with its smart restaurant. It is in the best part of the Rhine valley, and close to Koblenz and the Moselle. A `Kurcentrum', under 2 km. from the site, has a thermal bath from warm springs (reduced admission to campers) with sauna and solarium. The site consists partly of terraces and partly of open grassy areas, has a cared for look and all is very neat and clean. From early July to mid-Aug. it can become full. There are 115 touring pitches (out of 125) marked but not separated and mostly level, all with electricity. Sanitary facilities are in one central block and are of a good standard, well maintained and cleaned and heating has been installed. They have British style toilets and washbasins, with some cabins for both sexes. Hot water is free for washbasins and washing-up sinks, showers are on payment (DM 1). Reception staff are friendly and charges reasonable. There are a few Eurocamp pitches.

How to find it: From B42 road bypassing town, take Oberlahnstein exit and follow signs Kurcentrum and site.

General Details: Open Easter/1 April - 31 Oct. Electricity connections (10A). Small shop. Cafe/restaurant adjoining site, also Burg Lahneck restaurant. Swimming pool (reduced charges, 1/5-15/9). Children's playground. Tennis near. Riding 500 m. Fishing 3 km, Bicycle hire 2 km. Washing machine and dryer. Motorcaravan services.

Charges 1999: Per person DM 9.50; child (3-15 yrs) 4.50; car 6.00; tent 7.00 - 9.50, acc. to size; trailer tent or caravan 9.50; motorcaravan 13.00 - 15.50; m/cycle 2.50; dog 1.00; electricity 1.00 plus meter. No credit cards.

Reservations: made without deposit for exact dates. Address: 56112 Lahnstein/Rhein, (Ortsteil Oberlahnstein). Tel: 02621/2765. FAX: 02621/18290.

Camping "Am Mühlenteich" — 56291 Lingerhahn/Hunsrück

Proprietor: Willi Christ. Telephone (06746) 533. Winner of Gold Medal in national competition for outstanding camp blending with the landscape. Winner of A.D.A.C. Touristic Prize 1981.

6 km from Koblenz–Mainz autobahn – take exit for Laudert. A very well kept site with every comfort, open all year. Electrical connections for 400 pitches. Restaurant. Shop. Games Room. Youth Room and Adventure Playground. Tennis. Cable T.V. on all pitches.

GERMANY - West Central

3240 Eifel Ferienpark Waxweiler, Bitburg, nr Trier

Pleasant small site next to swimming pools, quietly situated close to town.

This small site in the western Eifel near Belgium and Luxembourg is rather away from main routes, but is easily accessible from the Prüm-Bitburg-Trier no. 51 road or the A60 autobahn. The 100 numbered tourist pitches, all with electricity, are in two flat sections, one alongside a river and open, the other in groups of four or five with hedges. Most are 80 sq.m. but 24 are 120 sq.m. with TV connection. There are also 86 well hidden, letting bungalows on sloping ground behind. Sanitary facilities in two blocks have free hot water to washbasins and showers. There is free admission to the municipal swimming pool complex nearby (two good sized pools, open June - Aug. and a smaller indoor pool open at other times).

How to find it: Site is north of Waxweiler off the road to Prüm - access is marked Ferienzentrum. Town is signed from the Prüm-Bitburg (51) fast road and the A60 autobahn.

General Details: Open 31 March - 5 Nov. Shop. Café. Kiosk for snacks. Table tennis. Children's playground. Fishing. No dogs July/Aug. Washing machines and dryers. Entertainment and activity programme in high season.

Charges 1998: Per pitch 35.00 - 51.00; person 4.00; electricity 3.50.

Reservations: are made (Fri.- Fri. only in high season) with deposit (DM 20). Address: 54649 Waxweiler (Eifel). Tel: 06554/427. FAX: 06554/1280.

3242 Country Camping Schinderhannes, Hausbay-Pfalzfeld

The editorial report for this site appears on page 160 next to its colour advertisement.

3245 Landal GreenParks Sonnenberg, Leiwen, nr Trier

Pleasant site of a high standard on hilltop above Moselle valley.

On top of a hill, this site has attractive views over the Moselle as you climb the approach road, 4 km. uphill from the wine village of Leiwen and the river. An outdoor public swimming pool complex is 1½ km. but the site has a splendid free indoor activity pool with child's paddling pool, whirlpool, cascade and slides. Also in this building are tenpin bowling, a sauna, solarium and fitness room, plus a snack bar. Minigolf, volleyball, a football pitch and good children's play equipment. Combining a bungalow complex (separate) with camping, the site has 146 large numbered pitches. All have electricity and TV connections. The single toilet block has under-floor heating and is of good quality, with British style toilets, washbasins in cabins (all for women, a couple for men) and free hot showers. Excursions and entertainment are organised in season. Two good restaurants and shop. Site is efficiently managed with helpful English speaking reception staff. Some tour operator pitches.

How to find it: From Trier-Koblenz motorway take exit for Schweich just north of Moselle bridge, turn towards Hetzerath on 49 road, right after 2 km. at Leiwen or Wittlich sign, into Leiwen. Follow signs for Ferienpark, Sonnenberg uphill 4 km. to site. From Koblenz on autobahn take Schweich exit and follow signs to Leiwen and site.

General Details: Open 20 Feb. - 6 Nov. 300,000 sq.m. Electrical connections (6A). Reception opens 9-12 am. and 2-5.30 pm (Sunday 10-12). Shop. Restaurant, bistro, bar and snacks (all season). Disco, entertainment and excursions at busy times. Indoor leisure centre with activity pool, 10 pin bowling. Volleyball. Football. Minigolf. Children's playground. Tennis near. Laundry. Chemical disposal. Motorcaravan services. Bungalows and apartments to let.

Charges 1999: Per unit incl. up to 5 persons DM 36.00 - 59.00; extra person 4.50; dog 4.50; electricity (6A) 4.00.

Reservations: Essential mid July - end August. Write with deposit (Fri. - Fri. only in high season). Address: Landal GreenParks Sonnenberg, 54340 Leiwen. Tel: 06507/93690. FAX: 06507/936936.

3250 Landal GreenParks Warsberg, Saarburg, nr Trier

Large, well organised site with comprehensive amenities including chair lift to town.

On top of a steep hill in an attractive location, this site and the long winding approach road both offer pleasant views over the town and surrounding area. A chair lift with a terminal near the site links it to the town and is free for campers - it is well worth a ride. There are 470 numbered tourist pitches of quite reasonable size on flat or slightly sloping ground, separated in small groups by trees and shrubs, with electricity (6A) available in most places.There are some tour operator pitches and a separate area of bungalows to rent. The three toilet blocks are of good quality, providing British style WCs, washbasins, (most in cabins for ladies, some for men), free hot showers and a unit for disabled persons. There are two good restaurants, a large shop and a free heated outdoor swimming pool close to a large children's play area. A site which should appeal to all age groups, with friendly, English speaking reception staff.

How to find it: From Trier on road 51 site is well signed in the northwest outskirts of Saarburg, also from all round town. Follow signs up hill for 3 km.

General Details: Open 26 March - 5 Nov. Reception opens 9 - 12 and 2 - 5.30 (Sunday 10-12 only). Shop. Restaurant and snacks, games rooms adjacent. Tennis and 'platform tennis'. Minigolf. Bicycle hire. Football field. Children's playground. Bowling. Entertainment in season for all ages. Riding and fishing 5 km. Washing machines and dryers. Chemical disposal. Motorcaravan service points. Bungalows (150) and large caravans for hire.

Charges 1999: Per unit incl. up to 5 persons DM 34.00 - 49.00; extra person 4.50; electricity 4.00.

Reservations: are made (Fri-Fri only in high season) with 50% deposit. Address: In den Urlaub, 54439 Saarburg. Tel: 06581/91460. FAX: 06581/2514.

3264 Campingplatz Büttelwoog, Dahn, Pirmasens, nr Saarbrücken

Convenient night stop en-route to Black Forest, in attractive countryside

Many visitors come here for an overnight stay and then stop for longer or return on their journey home, as it is both peaceful and in an attractive area close to the border with France. In a long, narrow valley with tall trees on either side, a hard access road leads from reception and shop and the bar/restaurant to flat, numbered, grassy pitches, all of which have electricity connections. Some 90 long stay pitches are situated further along and another section behind reception gives 130 touring pitches in all. The sanitary facilities, which are quite good, here and in another block in the main part, have free hot water to showers and washbasins, of which a few are in private cabins. Torch useful at night. This is a pleasant site in an interesting setting and the welcome is friendly.

How to find It: From Saarbrücken go towards Kaiserslauten on the A6/E50 or road no. 423. Take the Zweibrücken exit, then Pirmasens, finally turning to Dahn at Hinterweidenthal. Site is well signed in Dahn.

General Details: Open all year. Electricity connections (4A, mainly 2 pin). Small shop for essentials; café/bar for meals incl. breakfast (both March - Nov). Children's playground on sand. Minigolf. Bicycle hire. Riding. Swimming pools (indoor and outdoor) 300 m. Washing machine. Chemical disposal. Town 800 m.

Charges 1998: Per adult DM 9.00; child under 12 yrs 5.00, 12-16 yrs 7.00; pitch 11.00; electricity 3.50; small dog 5.00. Less 10% from 3rd night with camping carnet. No credit cards.

Reservations: Contact site. Address: 66994 Dahn/Pfalz. Tel: 06391/5622. FAX: 06391/5326.

3260 Knaus Camping-Park Bad Dürkheim, Bad Dürkheim, nr Ludwigshafen

Site with good amenities beside lake, on edge of town.

This large site is comfortable and has some 650 pitches (about half occupied by permanent caravans) but, being the best site at this well known wine town, it is very busy in main season. However, with some emergency areas they can usually find space. The site is long and narrow with individual pitches of fair size arranged on each side of the central road, which is decorated with arches of growing vines. A lake runs along one side and bathing is possible and non-powered boats can be launched. A new sports programme has been introduced offering guided tours, biking, canoeing and climbing. Three large sanitary blocks are spaced out along the central avenue and they should prove more than adequate. They have British toilets and free hot water in the individual basins, showers and sinks and are heated in cool weather. No dogs are taken. Some noise from light aircraft, especially at weekends.

How to find It: Bad Dürkheim is on the no. 37 road west of Ludwigshafen. Site is on the eastern outskirts, signed from the Ludwigshafen road.

General Details: Open all year except Nov. Some shade - trees are growing. Electrical connections everywhere. Shop (all year). Restaurant just outside gates. Sports programme. Tennis. Sports field. Children's playground. Garden chess. Sauna and solarium. Cooking facilities. Washing machine in each block. Chemical disposal. Motorcaravan services. Caravans (10) and tents to rent on site; contact site for details.

Charges 1998: Per person DM 8.50; child (3-14 yrs) 4.50; pitch 7.50 - 12.00; electricity 3.50.

Reservations: made for any length with deposit (DM 50). Address: In den Almen 3, 67098 Bad Dürkheim. Tel: 06322/61356. FAX: 06322/8161.

3402 Campingplatz Cannstatter Wasen, Stuttgart

Attractively modernised, well managed city site.

Situated on the outskirts of the city, but only a ten minute drive from the centre and with bus and train links just 500 m. away, this is a very convenient site. Completely fenced, it is beside the river Neckar, with a walkway into the city, and is surprisingly green, with pretty flower beds, bushes and trees. Even though all the 234 pitches are on hardstanding, they appear green, owing to the use of tiles with holes for grass. They are unmarked, have electricity hook-ups and 25 have water and waste water connections also. A separate grassy area for tents is in one corner. Attractively fenced water and waste units and an area of good quality children's play equipment on bark have been thoughtfully designed. Showers and washbasins (only a couple of private cabins at present) are of quite good quality in older buildings with heating, have free hot water, and are separate from the toilets. A chemical disposal room has a hand basin, soap and paper towels and there is a modern unit for disabled visitors. Opposite are dishwashing and laundry facilities (also heated) and a snack-bar/restaurant with terrace open daily 08.00-21.00. A small kiosk behind reception provides basic supplies and there is plenty of tourist information.

How to find It: Site is in Bad Cannstatt close to the Daimler Benz Stadium and a large car park. It is in the east of the city signed from the B10 which can be reached from A8 exit 55 via the B313, or A81 exit 17 via the B327.

General Details: Open all year (1 Nov - 31 March: barrier only open 08.00-10.00 and 17.00-19.00 unless prior arrangement made). Kiosk Easter - end Oct. (bread to order). Snack bar/restaurant (closed 20/12-15/1). Children's play area. Laundry. Chemical disposal. Motorcaravan service point (DM 5 charge for non-users of the site).

Charges 1998: Per person DM 8.00; child (2-14 yrs) 4.00; caravan 8.50; tent 6.00 - 8.00, acc. to size; car or m/cycle 4.00; motorcaravan 12.00; dog 4.00; electricity 3.00 for connection plus 1.00 per kw; water connection 0.50.

Reservations: Contact site. Address: Mercedesstrasse 40, 70372 Stuttgart. Tel: 0711/556696. FAX: 0711/557454.

3405 Camping Bad Liebenzell, Bad Liebenzell, nr Pforzheim

Good municipal site in northeast Black Forest, adjacent to modern swimming pool complex.

This good municipal site is attractively situated on the outskirts of the pleasant little spa town of Bad Liebenzell. It has direct access to an excellent, large, heated thermal swimming pool complex which is free to campers. Recently rebuilt, this includes swimming pools, wave pool and a long slide. There is also a children's pool and grassy sunbathing area and several tennis courts. The site is often full in high season when reservation is advisable (if not reserved arrive early). The 235 pitches (150 for tourists), 200 with electricity, are neatly arranged in rows on flat grass between hedges and trees and the good access roads. Three sanitary blocks are well maintained and have British toilets, individual basins with free hot water, shelf and mirror (in two blocks mostly in private cabins) and hot showers. There is provision for visitors with disabilities and babies, and enclosed washing-up sinks. Used by a British tour operator. This is a well run and orderly site.

How to find it: Site is just north of Bad Liebenzell, beside main 463 road; south of Pforzheim (25 km).

General Details: Open all year. 20,000 sq.m. Electricity connections (16A). Bar/restaurant. Small shop (all season but limited hours) - bread to order. Swimming pools (15/5-15/9). Cafe/bar by pool. Large room with TV and library. Tennis. Fishing. Bicycle hire. Children's playground. Cycle tracks, nature trails, cross country skiing 8 km. No dogs accepted. Washing machines and dryers. Cooking facilities. Chemical disposal. Motorcaravan services.

Charges 1999: Per person DM 10.00; child (4-16 yrs) 5.50; pitch 10.50; electricity on meter; local tax (per person, per night) 16/4-31/10 3.85, otherwise 2.85. Credit cards accepted.

Reservations: Write to site (no deposit). Address: 75378 Bad Liebenzell. Tel: 07052/40460. FAX: 07052/40475. E-mail: bad-liebenzell@cw-net.de. Internet: www.bad-liebenzell.de.

3415 Campingplatz Adam, Oberbruch, Bühl

Very good lakeside site by Karlsruhe-Basle autobahn near Baden-Baden.

This site is conveniently situated, only about 1.5 km. from the Bühl exit on the A5 autobahn and useful for outings to the Black Forest. There is a lake that is divided into separate areas for bathing or boating and windsurfing, with a long slide installed - the public are admitted to this on payment and it attracts many on fine weekends. All the touring pitches (220) have electricity connections, many with waste water outlets too and those for caravans are individual ones, with some special ones near the lake with water and drainage. Tents go along the lake surrounds and there are some places with hard paved centres to eliminate wet weather problems. At very busy times, units staying overnight only may be placed close together on a lakeside area of hardstanding. The two modern toilet blocks for tourers are well maintained and clean, offering individual washbasins with shelf and mirror (one block having mostly private washing cabins), hot showers on payment, facilities for babies and disabled people, laundry and dishwashing. The shop and restaurant/bar remain open virtually all year (not Mon. or Tues. in low season), so this is a useful site to use out of season. In general the site has a well tended look and good English is spoken by the pleasant staff.

How to find it: Take A5/E35-52, exit 52 (Bühl), turn towards Lichtenau, go through Oberbruch and left to site.

General Details: Open all year. 40,000 sq.m. Many electrical connections (10A). Limited shade. Shop (April - Sept). Restaurant (April - Nov). Football. Volleyball. Tennis. Minigolf. Bowling alley and games room with terrace. Children's playground. Bicycle hire. Fishing. Riding 5 km. Washing machine and dryer. Chemical disposal. Motorcaravan services.

AR Discount
Less 10% on person fees.

Charges 1998: Per person DM 7.50 - 11.00; young person (10-16 yrs) 5.50 - 6.50, child (3-10 yrs) 4.00 - 5.00; pitch 8.00 - 11.00, with services 12.00 - 15.00; electricity 3.00; dog 3.00. No credit cards.

Reservations: Write to site. Address: 77815 Bühl-Oberbruch. Tel: 07223/23194. FAX: 07223/8982.

3435 Terrassen-Camping Sandbank, Titisee

Pleasant, terraced lakeside site, in the Black Forest.

This is a satisfactory site overlooking Lake Titisee in this lovely area of the Black Forest. There are 200 marked pitches for tourists, on gravel with electricity and on terraces with good views over the lake. Trees provide good shade in some parts. The small town of Titisee is a pleasant 20 minute walk along the lakeside and with the attractions of this part of the Forest near - Freiburg, the Rhine Falls at Schaffausen, the source of the Danube at Donaueschingen, Basle in Switzerland - it is ideal for a long or short stay. The large sanitary block provides washbasins (many in cabins), hot showers on payment, baby room (key from management) and facilities for disabled people. There is a shop and a pleasant lakeside restaurant with terrace, which also provides takeaway food. Access to the lake is available for swimming, boating and carp fishing. Walks are organised and there is some music in high season. Reception staff are friendly and English is spoken.

How to find it: From Freiburg take road no. 31 to Titisee. From the centre follow camping signs then signs for Bankenhof, continuing on less well made up road past this site to Sandbank.

General Details: Open 1 April - 20 Oct. Shop. Electricity connections (16A). Bar/restaurant with takeaway. Children's playground. Fishing. Organised walks. Swimming in lake. Boat excursions from Titisee. Music in season. Washing machines and dryer. Chemical disposal. Motorcaravan services. English spoken.

Charges 1998: Per person: DM 6.00 - 8.00; child 4.00 - 5.00; pitch 9.50 - 12.00; electricity 2.50; dog 3.00 (2.00); local tax 1.80. Stay 14 days, pay for 10 outside July/Aug. Credit cards accepted.

Reservations: Not made. Address: 79822 Titisee. Tel: 07651/8243 or 8166. FAX: 07651/8286 or 88444.

3430 Schwarzwald-Camping Alisehof, Schapbach, nr Freudenstadt

Agreeable site in quiet central Black Forest situation.

This site, in a beautiful setting in a wooded valley, is for those who want to enjoy the activities of the Black Forest itself. Though very centrally situated in the Forest it is in a quiet position away from the main routes and big towns, with walks available from the camp. The 180 pitches are individual numbered ones of average size in rows on terraces on a slope, steep only at the top part; there are 120 on the lower slopes available for tourists. The three sanitary blocks, two on the lower terrace, one beside reception, are first class with free hot water in most washbasins, sinks and showers. Plans are in hand to provide eight family bathrooms (for hire). There are facilities for disabled visitors and baby rooms. In high season there is an entertainment programme for children and organised walks for adults. The friendly management speak English.

How to find it: Site is 1 km. northeast of Schapbach, which is southwest from Freudenstadt. From the A5 take the Appelweier/Oberkirch exit towards Freudenstadt turning right to Schapbach.

General Details: Open all year. Electrical connections (16A). Shop (all year). Pleasant bar lounge in old farmhouse, open late evening (all year except when very quiet). Restaurant near. Washing machine and dryers. Children's playground. Swimming pool at Schapbach (1 km). Fishing. Minigolf close. Riding 2 km. Chemical disposal. Motorcaravan service points.

Charges 1998: Per person DM 8.00 - 9.00; local tax 1.30; child (under 14) 4.00 - 5.50; pitch 8.00 - 9.00; tent 2.50 - 4.50; dog 3.00; TV connection 1.00; electricity 3.00 plus meter. Less 10% on person charge for stays over 7 days. No credit cards.

Reservations: Write to site before 31 May, with deposit (DM 10) and fee (10) by Eurocheque. Address: 77776 Bad Rippoldsau-Schapbach. Tel: 07839/203. FAX: 07839/1263.

151

GERMANY - South West

3420 Freizeitcenter Oberrhein, Rheinmünster, nr Baden-Baden

First-class, large holiday site near the Rhine.

This large site provides much to do and is also a good base for visiting the Black Forest. To the left of reception are a touring area and a section of hardstanding for motorhomes. The 250 touring pitches, all with electrical connections, includes 86 new ones with water and drainage also, beside one of the lakes which are a feature of the site. Two of the lakes are for swimming and non-powered boating (the water was very clean when we visited), the third, small one is for fishing. Seven modern sanitary buildings have free hot water and smart fittings, some with special rooms for children, babies and families. Other facilities include a restaurant, supermarket and snack bar. First-class children's play equipment is provided in several areas. This site is well worth considering for a holiday, especially for families with young and early teenage children. Separate large areas house long-term campers and chalets to let.

> **How to find it:** Site is signed from Rheinmünster, 16 km. southwest of Rastatt on B36. From north on A5/E35-52 take exit 51 (Baden-Baden) via Hügelsheim then south onto B36; from south take exit 52 (Bühl) and via Schwarzach and Rheinmünster or exit 52 to Rheinau then north on B36.

> **General Details:** Open all year. Electricity connections (mostly 16A, 3 pin, a few with 2 pin). Shop (1/4-30/9, local supermarket 3 km). Lakeside restaurant; snack bar (both 1/4-30/9). Modern children's play areas on sand. Tennis. Table tennis. Bicycle hire. Minigolf. Windsurf school. Swimming and boating lakes. Fishing. Riding 3 km. Golf 2 km. Family washcabins to rent. Chemical disposal. Motorcaravan services. Chalets for hire.

> **Charges 1998:** Per pitch with car DM 8.00 - 12.00; adult 8.00 - 13.00; child 7-15 yrs 5.00 - 9.00, under 6 yrs 4.00 - 6.00; dog 4.00 - 6.00; washcabin 10.00 - 14.00; electricity 3.50. Credit cards accepted.

> **Reservations:** Made for at least a week with deposit (DM 250) and fee (25). Address: 77836 Rheinmünster. Tel: 07227/2500. FAX: 07227/2400.

3450 Ferien-Campingplatz Münstertal, Münstertal, nr Freiburg

The editorial report for this site appears on page 160 next to its colour advertisement.

3440 Campingplatz Kirchzarten, Kirchzarten, nr Freiburg

Well equipped Black Forest site with excellent free swimming pools.

This municipal site is on the edge of the Black Forest, within easy reach by car of Titisee, Feldberg and Todnau, and 8 km. from the large town of Freiburg in Breisgau, and may be best suited for families. It is divided into 490 numbered pitches with electricity, 390 of which are for tourists. They have made the most of the ground available but most pitches, which are side by side on flat ground, are of quite reasonable size and marked out at the corners, though there is nothing to separate them. From about late June to mid-August it does become full, and it would be advisable to reserve in advance. The fine new swimming pool complex adjoining the site is free to campers and is a main attraction. The four pools include one of Olympic size which is heated and surrounded by spacious grassy sunbathing areas. The site's sanitary facilities are good, comprising four blocks, one for laundry and dishwashing only. Two blocks are modern with heating. They include British style toilets, individual washbasins with mirrors and shelves, free, fully controllable hot showers, facilities for disabled visitors and a baby bath. It is only a short stroll from the site to the village centre, which has supermarkets, restaurants, banks, etc.

> **How to find it:** From Freiburg take B31 (Donaueschingen) to Kirchzarten. Site is signed to the south of village.

> **General Details:** Open all year. 56,000 sq.m. Electricity connections (16A). Restaurant/bar. Shop. Swimming pool complex (15/5-15/9). Children's playground. Table tennis. Adventure playground, fitness track, tennis and minigolf near. Tennis (booked from site). Golf 3 km. Recreation programme in high season. No dogs accepted. Cooking stoves, washing machines, dryers, irons, sewing machines (all on meter). Chemical disposal. Caravans for hire.

> **Charges 1999:** Per person DM 7.50 - 13.50, incl. local tax; child (4-16 yrs) 5.50 - 7.50, third child and above 3.50 - 4.50; pitch 9.00 - 11.50; electricity 2.00 plus meter. Every 15th day free. Credit cards accepted.

> **Reservations:** made for min. 1 week without deposit. Address: Campingplatz, 79199 Kirchzarten. Tel: 07661/39375. FAX: 07661/61624.

CAMPING KIRCHZARTEN

A site in the southern Black Forest with every comfort for wonderful holidays. New heated outdoor swimming pool complex. Kurhaus with restaurant and reading room nearby. Riding, tennis, minigolf, children's playground in the wood. Fine walking country. Caravans for hire.

3445 Campingplatz Belchenblick, Staufen, nr Freiburg

Quality Black Forest site with good class facilities.

The site stands at the gateway, so to speak, to the Black Forest. Not very high up itself, it is just at the start of the long road climb which leads to the top of Belchen, one of the highest summits of the forest. It is well situated for excursions by car to the best areas of the forest, e.g. the Feldberg-Titisee-Höllental circuit, and many excellent walks are available nearby. Staufen is a pleasant little place with character. The three high quality sanitary blocks have free hot water in all washbasins and the fully controllable hot showers. With British toilets; individual washbasins with shelf and mirror (6 in private cabins), there are 21 family cabins with WC, basin and shower (some on payment per night for exclusive use). Of the 200 pitches, 50 have TV, water and waste water connections. On site is a small heated indoor swimming pool open all year and adjacent is a municipal sports complex building including an open-air pool and tennis courts. Reservation is necessary from early June to late August at this popular site, which is not a cheap one, but the charges include free hot water and the indoor pool.

How to find it: Take autobahn exit for Bad Krozingen, south of Freiburg, and continue to Staufen. Site is south of the town and signed.

General Details: Open all year. 18,000 sq.m. Numerous electrical connections (10-15A). Shop and general room where drinks and snacks served (both all year). Restaurant near. Indoor and outdoor pools. Tennis. Children's playground with barbecue section. Volleyball. Basketball. Skating. Hockey and football fields. Sauna and solarium. Bicycle hire. Washing machine. Chemical disposal. Motorcaravan services. Apartments for rent.

Charges 1998: Per person DM 10.50 - 13.50; child (2-12 yrs) 5.50; pitch 11.50; dog 3.00; electricity 1.00 p/kw hour; TV connection 1.50; drainage 2.00; washcabin 12.00.

Reservations: made without charge. Address: Münstertäler Str. 43, 79219 Staufen im Breisgau. Tel: 07633/7045. FAX: 07633/7908. E-mail: camping.belchenblick@t-online.de. Internet: http://members.aol.com/campbelche/camp_bel.htm.

Camping Belchenblick

Familie Wiesler • D-79219 Staufen
Südlicher Schwarzwald

We offer:
- Exemplary service
- Moderne sanitary facilities
- Family wash cubicles
- Indoor pool/sauna/solarium
- Fitness room
- Large barbecue area and children's playground
- tabletennis hall
- public open air swimming pool
- Tennis courts of the Staufen TC
- Bycicles for hire
- Shop and snacks
- Large sportsground with basketball, beachvolleyball
- Animation in July and August

E-Mail:camping.belchenblick@t-online.de   Tel. ++49 (0) 76 33 / 70 45
http://members.aol.com/campbelche/camp_bel.htm   Fax ++49 (0) 76 33 / 79 08

3442 Terrassen Campingplatz, Herbolzheim

Useful base for Europa Park and Black Forest, near the Rhine and A5.

This well equipped campsite is in a quiet location on a wooded slope to the north of Freiburg, close to the Black Forest. It is useful as a night stop when travelling between Frankfurt and Basel, and is just 10 km. from Europa Park, only a short way from the A5 autobahn. There are 73 caravan or motorcaravan grass pitches for tourists, all with electricity, on terraces linked by hard roads. A separate meadow for tents is at the top of the site (with three cabin toilets). The main toilet block has British style toilets, free hot water in washbasins, showers and sinks and there are new laundry and dishwashing facilities near reception. A WC for disabled visitors and a baby room are provided. The pleasant, small bar/restaurant offers a simple menu during the evenings, with restaurants and shops in the village (3 km). Activities include a small children's play area and table tennis, volleyball and football with the large open-air heated town swimming pool complex next door. The local market is held each Friday morning. This is good walking country and with only occasional entertainment, the site makes a very pleasant place in which to relax , the many trees, shrubs and plants giving a pleasant, peaceful atmosphere.

How to find it: From A5 Frankfurt - Basel autobahn take exit 57, 58 or 59 and follow signs to Herbolzheim. Site is signed in south side of village near swimming pool.

General Details: Open 1 week before Easter - 15 October. 2.5 ha.. Electrical connections (10A). Small bar/restaurant (Easter - 1/10). Shop for basics (order bread). Table tennis. Volleyball. Football. Heated swimming pool adjacent (1/4-15/9), other sports near. Bicycle hire 1 km. Riding 5 km. Washing machines. Chemical disposal. Motorcaravan services. Dogs not accepted 15/6-15/8.

Charges 1999: Per person DM 9.00; child (2-12 yrs) 5.00; pitch 10.00 (tents 9.00); electricity 2.00 + 1.00 p/kwh; dog (see above) 2.00. Credit cards accepted

Reservations: Contact site. Address: 79336 Herbolzheim. Tel: 07643/1460. FAX: 07643/913382. E-mail: s.hugoschmidt@t-online.de.

AR Discount
Less 10% on person fees, min. 14 days.

25.000 m², 360-380 m. above sea level, 12 terraces, 50 pitches 80-120 m².

Idyllic forrest setting in the very romantic Sulz valley. **Extremely peaceful.**

An oasis for genuine campers

Special award from Baden-Württemberg for a fine example of blending with the countryside and outstanding suitability for camping amid natu-

3455 Gugel-Drieländer Camping und Freizeitpark, Neuenburg

Good, large site in natural woodland close to the A5 Freiburg-Basel autobahn.

Neuenburg is ideally placed for night stops when travelling from Frankfurt to Basel on the A5 motorway and also for enjoying and exploring the south of the Black Forest. Set in natural heath and woodland, Gugel's is an attractive site where permanent caravans, away from the tourist area, with their well-tended gardens, enhance rather than detract from the natural beauty. There are 220 places for tourists either in small clearings in the tall trees which cover the site, in open areas or on hardstanding section used for single night stays. All have electricity. Opposite the entrance is a meadow where late arrivals and those who wish to depart before 7 am. may spend the night. Three good quality, heated, sanitary blocks have British style WCs and free hot water in washbasins (some in cabins), showers and sinks. Baby room and one for disabled visitors. There are two parallel heated indoor swimming pools, a sunbathing lawn, good children's play area and another with electric cars and motorcycles (on payment). A social room has been added with satellite TV where guests are welcomed with a glass of wine and a slide presentation of the attractions of the area. Opposite the entrance is a small lake where one can fish on daily permit or bathe. The Rhine is within walking distance. Being near the motorway, although this cannot be seen from the site, there is some road noise near the entrance. The excellent restaurant is popular with both campers and non-residents. An activity programme for both children and adults at Easter and July/Aug. includes sightseeing trips. The site may become crowded in high season but you should always find room. In general there is a good atmosphere and it can be recommended for both short and long stays.

How to find it: From autobahn A5 take Neuenburg exit, turn left at traffic lights, left at next junction and follow signs for 2 km. to site (called 'Neuenburg' on most signs).

General Details: Open all year. 130,000 sq.m. Electricity connections (6A). Small shop (Easter - end Oct). Restaurant (all year excl. Nov). Indoor pools. Boules pitch. Tennis courts with racquet and ball hire. Fishing. Minigolf. Table tennis. Bicycle hire. Community room with TV. Activity programme with organised walks, excursions, etc. and sports and competitions for children. Golf 5 km. Riding 1.5 km. Washing machines and dryers. Chemical disposal. Motorcaravan service point.

Charges 1999: Per person DM 8.90; child (2-15) 5.50; caravan/tent 9.60; small tent 6.60, car 7.60; motorcaravan 9.60 - 14.90, acc. to size; dog 3.60; electricity on meter. No credit cards.

Reservations: made for min 2 weeks in July/Aug. with deposit. Contact site.
Address: 79395 Neuenburg (Oberer Wald). Tel: 07631/7719. FAX: 07635/3393.

AR Discount
Discount after 10 nights, persons free

3452 Terrassen Camping Alte Sägemühle, Sulzburg

Pretty site beautifully situated in the southern Black Forest.

By a peaceful road leading only to a natural swimming pool and an hotel, beyond the picturesque old town of Sulzburg with its narrow streets, this attractive location is perfect for those seeking peace and quiet. In a tree-covered valley with a stream running through the centre, the site has been kept as natural as possible, Divided into terraced areas, the 50 pitches (up to 120 sq.m.) all have electrical connections, although long leads may be needed. The main building by the entrance houses reception, a small shop and the sanitary facilities which are of good quality, with showers and washbasins (two private cabins), dishwashing and a washing machine. Run by the Geuss family (Frau Geuss speaks reasonable English) the site has won an award from the state for having been kept natural, for example, no tarmac roads, no minigolf, no playgrounds, etc. Prior reservation is recommended in high season. There are opportunities for walking straight from the site into the forest, and many walks and cycle rides are shown on maps available at reception. Europa Park is less than an hour away. The tiny 500 year old Jewish Cemetery reached through the site has an interesting history. There are restaurants and other shops in Sulzburg just 1.5 km. away.

How to find it: Site is easily reached (25 minutes) from autobahn A5/E35. Take exit 64 for Bad Krozingen just south of Freiburg onto the B3 south to Heitersheim, then on through Sulzburg, or if coming from the south, exit 65 through Müllheim, Heitersheim and Sulzburg.

General Details: Open all year. Electrical connections (16A). Small shop for basics and local wines (all year). Natural, unheated swimming pool adjacent (June-Aug). Washing machine. Chemical disposal. Motorcaravan services. Bicycle hire in Sulzburg.

Charges 1999: Per person DM 8.00; child (1-15 yrs) 6.00; pitch 8.00 - 12.00; electricity 0.80 plus meter; dog 3.00; local tax (from 16 yrs) 1.00.

Reservations: Recommended - contact site. Address: 79295 Sulzburg. Tel: 07634/8550.

3410 Campingplatz Aichelberg, Aichelberg, Goppingen

Small, pleasant and friendly municipal site, near Stuttgart-München autobahn.

Being very near the Stuttgart-München autobahn (about midway between Stuttgart and Ulm) and a reasonable drive from the German border at Aachen, this small, shaded site makes an acceptable overnight stop. The pitches, on flat grass and hardstandings, are not marked out but adequate space is allowed and all have electrical connections. The main toilet block is well constructed and should be sufficient for the 90 static units and 36 tourist pitches. British WCs; free hot water in washbasins and sinks; one private cabin and two showers with free hot water, for each sex and a family washroom. On site are a small shop and bar, a restaurant is 250 m. away. There is a children's playground (on sand).

How to find it: Take autobahn exit Aichelberg in direction of Goppingen. If coming from München turn immediately left to site, if from Stuttgart follow signs.

General Details: Open all year. Electricity connections (10A). Well shaded. Shop for basic supplies (all year), village 4 km. Bar. Restaurant 250 m. Washing machine and dryer. Children's playground. Swimming pool 5 km.

Charges 1998: Per person DM 7.50; child (4-5 yrs) 3.00, (6-15 yrs) 4.00; pitch 8.00; electricity 3.00 + meter.

Reservations: Write to site (not necessary for overnight). Address: 73101 Aichelberg/Goppingen. Tel: 07164/2700. FAX: as phone.

3465 Camping Wirthshof, Markdorf, nr Friedrichshafen

Site with various sport and recreation facilities near the Bodensee.

Lying 7 km. back from the Bodensee, 12 km. from Friedrichshafen and with Markdorf near at hand to stroll into, this site could well be of interest to Britons with young children. Possible excursions include trips into Switzerland and Austria. The 324 individual touring pitches have electrical connections and are of about 80 sq.m. on well tended flat grass, joining access roads. On site is a pleasant heated swimming pool (25 x 12½ m.) with a grassy lying-out area; it is free to campers but is also open to outsiders on payment so can be busy in season (open perhaps mid-May to mid-Sept). Three well furnished toilet blocks give an ample total provision. Washbasins and showers have free hot water and there is a unit for disabled people. No dogs are accepted in July/Aug. and there is a special section for campers with dogs at other times. Many activities are organised over a long season.

How to find it: Site is on the eastern edge of Markdorf, on the B33 Ravensburg road.

General Details: Open 15 March - 30 Oct. Electricity connections (10A). Shop. Restaurant/bar. Swimming pool (10/5-10/9). Sports field with goal posts. Adventure playground. Bicycle hire. Normal minigolf; also `pit-pat', played at table height with billiard cues. Activity programme. Tennis near. Riding 8 km. Golf and fishing 10 km. Washing machines and dryers. Chemical disposal. New caravans for hire

Charges 1999: Per person DM 7.50 - 9.50; child (1-14 yrs) 4.50 - 6.50; pitch 13.00 - 15.00; dog 3.00; electricity 3.00. No credit cards.

Reservations: made with deposit (DM 80) and fee (20). Address: Steibensteg 12, 88677 Markdorf. Tel: 07544/2325. FAX: 07544/3982.

GERMANY - South East

3650 Camping Gitzenweiler Hof, Lindau, nr Friedrichshafen

Site with swimming pool in pleasant situation near Lindau.

Gitzenweiler Hof, which is some 3 km. from the Bodensee, is in a pleasant country setting. It is a very spacious site and although it has about 350 permanent caravans, it can still take about 350 tourist units (although it is advisable to book for July/Aug). In the tourist section most pitches are without markings with siting left to campers with the remainder in rows between access roads. There are some pitches with water, drainage, phone and TV connections. The swimming pool has attractive surrounds with seats, etc. There are four main, well maintained toilet blocks plus one small unit. They have British style toilets, washbasins, and free hot showers. A new block includes children's facilities and a shower/WC for disabled people. Lindau is an interesting town, especially by the harbour, and possible excursions include the whole of the Bodensee, the German Alpine Road, the Austrian Vorarlberg and Switzerland.

How to find it: Coming from the west on road no. 31, turn left 2 km. before Lindau; from München-Kempten (route 12) turn left 3 km. before Lindau. Camp signs at both places.

General Details: Open all year. 300 electrical connections (5A). Shop (limited in low season). Restaurant/bar (not Feb). Swimming pool (summer). Volleyball. Children's playground and playroom. Organised activities. Small zoo. Lake fishing. Table tennis. Minigolf. Washing machines, dryers and dishwasher. Motorcaravan service point.

Charges 1998: Per person DM 9.00; child under 10 yrs 3.00, 10-16 yrs 6.00; car 3.00; tent or caravan 6.00; motorcaravan 9.00 - 12.00, acc. to size; m/cycle 2.50; dog 2.00; electricity 3.00. Discounts for stays over 14 days and in winter. Single overnight hardstandings with electricity outside camp barrier at special price.

Reservations: made with deposit (DM 180.00) and fee (20.00). Address: 88131 Lindau-Oberreitnau. Tel: 08382/9494-0. FAX: 08382/9494-15.

3665 Ferien-Campingplatz Brunnen, Brunnen, Füssen, nr Kempten

Quietly situated lakeside site well placed for excursions.

Right by the Forggen-See, this site has a beach and jetty, although the water level of the lake can be low in early season and not reach up to the site. On slightly undulating ground, the 300 pitches (230 for touring units) are all individual ones with some terracing. Nearly all have hardstanding and they vary in size (60-100 sq.m). There is a separate meadow for tents in summer. Quietly situated, with views of high mountains, the site is excellently placed for excursions. Excellent sanitary facilities are housed in a tiled building with heating; there are several washrooms and toilet rooms (not all open in low seasons). Hot water is free. Facilities for disabled visitors and children.

How to find it: At Schwangau, 3 km. northeast of Füssen on the no. 17 Munich road, turn off at crossroads in village where there are signs to Brunnen and site.

General Details: Open all year except 5 Nov - 20 Dec. Electricity connections. Small shop. Restaurants 100 m. Children's playground. Fishing. Bicycle hire and riding 100 m. Boat slipway 2 km. Golf 2 km. Washing machines and dryers. Drying room. Cooking facilities. Dishwasher. Chemical disposal. Motorcaravan service point.

Charges 1998: Per person DM 10.00 – 12.00, incl. local tax; child (2-8) 5.00, (9-15) 8.00; pitch 8.00 - 10.00; electricity (overnight) 2.00 otherwise 1.00 per kw; dog 5.00 extra car 4.00.

Reservations: made for winter only, not summer, so arrive early especially when the weather is good. Address: Seestrasse 81, 87645 Schwangau-Brunnen. Tel: 08362/8273. FAX: 08362/8630.

3670 Internationaler Campingplatz Hopfensee, Füssen, nr Kempten

Luxury lakeside site, north of Füssen, for caravans and motorcaravans only.

Internationaler Camping is well placed to explore this region but is also an ideal holiday venue in its own right. At the centre of the site is a large building with an open village-like square, adorned with cascading flowers. It houses quite exceptional heated sanitary facilities with British style WCs, free hot water in washbasins (some in cabins), large showers and sinks, laundry and washing-up rooms, as well as children's wash rooms on the ground floor. On the upper floors are a heated swimming pool, treatment and physiotherapy suites, a cinema, fitness centre and children's play room. The excellent new restaurant and terrace face across the lake towards the setting sun. The 385 tourist pitches, most with shade, each have electricity, water, drain and cable TV connections. They are marked, numbered and of good size. Direct access to the lake for sailing, canoeing etc. and a place for parking boats. Charges are on the high side but the site has much to offer those looking for the best facilities in a beautiful area.

How to find it: Site is 4 km. north of Fussen. Turn off B16 to Hopfen and site is on left through a car park. From west on B310, turn towards Fussen at T-junction with B16 and immediately right again for the road to Hopfen.

General Details: Open all year except 1 Nov. - 17 Dec. 80,000 sq.m. Electricity connections (16A). Restaurant. Bar. Shop. Indoor pool and fitness centre. Supervised courses of remedial water treatments, massage, etc. Sauna, solarium and steam bath. Children's playground and kindergarten. Games room with table tennis, pool, etc. Bicycle hire. Tennis. Table tennis. Fishing. Riding 1 km. Ski school in winter. Motorcaravan service point. No tents taken.

Charges 1999: Per person DM 13.00 - 14.80; child 2-12 yrs 7.50 - 9.00, 12-18 yrs 10.00 - 13.50; local tax 2.40 - 3.00; pitch with cable TV & electricity 19.00 - 21.00 plus meter; private wash cabin 15.00. No credit cards.

Reservations: made without deposit; min. 14 days 16 June - 1 Sept (unless shorter time fits into charts). Address: 87629 Fussen - Hopfen am See. Tel: 08362/7431 or 917710. FAX: 08362/917720.

3675 Terrassen-Camping am Richterbichl, Rottenbuch, nr Peiting

Useful overnight site by the main Garmisch-Augsburg road.

This little site, beside the main B23 Garmisch-Augsburg road, has all the features required of a good transit site and might well be interesting for longer stays. About 110 pitches - 70 for tourists - are on flat terraces in rows on either side of access roads. They are not marked but about 80 sq.m. is allowed per unit and there is electricity in all parts. There could possibly be some road noise at front of site, so choose pitches in higher terraces if possible. The toilet block, within the main building and kept warm, is satisfactory with free hot water in washbasins (four in cabins) and sinks, on payment in the showers. A little lake on site can be used for bathing or boating. The pleasant bar has a TV and a children's room.

How to find it: Site is beside the B23 road on south side of Rottenbuch (12 km. south of Schongau).

General Details: Open all year. Electricity connections (10A). Basic provisions kept, bread to order (shops 5 mins). General room (drinks and breakfast served). Games room. Children's playground. Bicycle hire. Fishing 4 km. Washing machine and dryer. Chemical disposal. Motorcaravan service point. Caravans and apartments for hire.

Charges 1999: Per person DM 8.50; child (3-14) 5.00; pitch 8.00; electricity 2.00 + meter. Credit cards accepted.

Reservations: made for any period without deposit. Address: 82401 Rottenbuch. Tel: 08867/1500. FAX: 08867/8300. E-mail: christof.echtler@t-online.de.

AR Discount
Less 10% on per person fees in low seasons.

3680 Alpen-Caravanpark Tennsee, Krün, Garmisch-Partenkirchen

Attractive all year site for the active holiday, with excellent facilities.

This is an excellent site in beautiful surroundings, high up (3,000 m.) in the Bavarian Alps with views of the Zugspitze, etc. yet close to many famous places. Oberammergau (26 km) and Innsbruck (44 km) are two of many. Mountain walks are plentiful, with several lifts close by. The site has 139 serviced pitches with individual connections for electricity (up to 16A), gas, TV, radio, telephone, water and waste water disposal. The other 111 pitches all have electricity and some of these are available for overnight guests at a reduced rate. The first class sanitary block has under-floor heating, British style toilets, individual washbasins and hair dryers. Many private units have WC, shower, basin and bidet (for rent). Free hot water, a solarium, unit for disabled people, baby bath and also a dog bathroom! A heated room for ski equipment is well equipped. Another custom built block houses reception, restaurants (waiter, self service and takeaway), bar, cellar youth room and some apartments for rent. Well stocked shop. Many activities and excursions are organised. The Zick family run the site in a friendly and efficient manner.

How to find it: Site is just off Garmisch-Partenkirchen/Innsbruck road between Kleis and Krün (Garmisch 15 km).

General Details: Open all year except 13 Nov - 16 Dec. 30,000 sq.m. Shop. Restaurants with takeaway. Bar. Youth room with table tennis, amusements. Solarium. Bicycle hire. Children's playground. Organised activities and excursions. Cash dispenser for Euro cards. Dog bathroom. Cooking facilities. Washing machines and dryers. Chemical disposal. Motorcaravan service point. Apartments to rent. English is spoken

Charges 1999: Prices acc. to season (several price bands, winter charges highest): per person DM 12.50 - 13.00; 1-3 children (3-15 yrs) 6.50 - 7.50; local tax 1.75; pitch 14.90 - 24.00; summer tent pitches in adjacent meadow 10.50; dog 5.50; electricity, etc. on meter. Overnight rate on certain pitches 29.50 plus 10.00 for motorcaravan services. Easter family package 38.50. **Special senior citizens spring, early summer and autumn rates.**

Reservations: are made for exact dates: fee (DM 30 and deposit 20). Address: 82493 Klais/Krün (Bayern). Tel: 08825/17-0. FAX: 08825/17-236. E-mail: camping.tennsee@t-online.de. Internet: http://www.camping-tennsee.de.

3685 Camping Allweglehen, Berchtesgaden, nr Salzburg

Hilltop site with spectacular views.

Berchtesgaden, one of the best known districts of Germany and rightly so, has magnificent scenery and so much to do, see and explore. The spa town of Berchtesgaden began life as a salt mining town and indeed the salt mine is still in operation. Hitler built his 'Eagles Nest' on top of the Kehlstein (clearly visible from the site) and this is also open to the public (access by bus). Camping Allweglehen occupies a hilltop position with spectacular views across the pretty Ache valley to the town beyond and the distant sheer rock faces of the Watzmann mountain. The access road is steep (14%), particularly at the entrance, but the proprietor uses his tractor to tow for those of a nervous disposition! The 120 pitches, all for touring, are on a series of gravel terraces, separated by hedges or fir trees and all have good views and electricity. A separate sloping meadow is for tents. Delightful restaurant, with terrace and excellent menu at reasonable prices. Sanitary facilities are in two adjacent blocks near the restaurant, with British WCs, and free hot water to washbasins, showers and sinks. All in all, a splendid site where one could just sit and look at the views all day, although this would be a shame as the region has so much to offer.

How to find it: Site is 4 km. from town on B305 Berchtesgaden - Salzburg road. From autobahn take Salzburg Sud exit and follow B305 towards Berchtesgaden.

General Details: Open all year. Electricity connections (16A). Restaurant. Kiosk for essentials. Children's play area. Swimming pool (heated May-Oct). Solarium. Minigolf. Table tennis. Walks. Excursions. Laundry facilities.

Charges 1998: Per pitch DM 16.00; adult 7.80; child (4-16 yrs) 6.50; electricity 0.90 per kw. Eurocard accepted.

Reservations: Write to site (in German!). Address: 84171 Berchtesgaden. Tel: 08652/2396. FAX: 08652/63503.

157

3635 Camping München-Obermenzing, München

Useful site for visits to city or night stops.

On the northwest edge of Munich, this site makes a good stopover for those wishing to see the city or pass the night. The flat terrain is mostly covered by mature trees. Caravan owners are best off here as they have a special section of 130 individual plots, mainly separated from each other by high hedges and opening off the hard site roads with easy access. These have electricity and about 30 have water and waste water also. About 200 tents and motorcaravans are taken on quite large, level grass areas, with an overflow section so space is usually available. The single central sanitary block is large and it should be adequate. Cleaning appears satisfactory and there is heating in the low season. It provides British style toilets, individual washbasins, many in curtained cubicles and most with free hot water. Hot showers need tokens (DM 2) Shop and rest room with TV and drinks machine (including beer). Public transport is available to the city from very close by. By car the journey might take 20-30 minutes depending on the density of traffic. There is some road noise, but we spent a reasonably undisturbed night.

How to find it: Site is close to start of the A8 autobahn to Stuttgart and signed from there. From around the city follow signs `autobahn Stuttgart'. Be sure to turn right at final junction just before autobahn begins, keep left to site.

General Details: Open 15 March - 31 Oct. 50,000 sq.m. Electrical connections (10A). Shop (all season). TV room (April - Oct). Cooking facilities. Washing machine and dryers. Chemical disposal. Motorcaravan services.

Charges 1999: Per person DM 7.80; child (2-14 yrs) 4.00; car 6.00; tent 7.50; caravan 9.00; motorcaravan 12.00; m/cycle 4.00; electricity 2.00 plus meter; dog 2.00 (once only). Small per person surcharge (DM 2.50) for the Beer Festival (14/9-5/10). No credit cards.

Reservations: Not made and said not to be necessary. Address: Lochhausener Str. 59, 81247 München. Tel: 089/811 22 35. FAX: 089/814 48.07.

Camping
MÜNCHEN
Obermenzing

On your way through Munich follow always the direction sign `Autobahn Stuttgart' until the beginning of the Autobahn **except** when approaching from the Salzburg autobahn. In this case follow `Autobahn Lindau' signs to Gräfelfing; then take Pasing exit and follow `Autobahn Stuttgart'.

A modern camping site located at the beginning of the Autobahn Munich-Stuttgart in a 57,000 sq.m. park.

Open from 15 March to 31 October.

Resident Proprietor: Andreas Blenck
Lochhausener Str. 59, 81247 München
Tel: 0049 89-811 22 35
Fax: 0049 89-814 48 07

♦ Special plots for caravans.
♦ Electric supply for light and heating.
♦ First class sanitary accommodations.
♦ Hot showers, single cabins with basins.
♦ Washing machines.
♦ Dishwashing and cooking house.
♦ Self-service store for food and beverages.
♦ Tavern (Hofbräuhaus beer).
♦ Ca. 20 min. to the city by car.
♦ Good connections by bus, tram or S-train.

3690 Campingplatz Wagnerhof, Bergen, nr Rosenheim

Small but excellent site close to München - Salzburg autobahn near Chiemsee.

The pretty village of Bergen is 3 km. south of the A8 and about 10 km. from the Chiemsee, Germany's largest lake. Ringed by hills, with views of distant mountains and a large variety of different trees and plants, Wagnerhof is a well organised, pleasant site in a quiet location on the edge of Bergen. Owned by two brothers, one of whom speaks excellent English, there is always a welcome here. Most of the 140 tourist pitches are part hardstanding, part grass and have electricity. Two first class heated sanitary blocks have British style WCs, free hot water in washbasins (some in cabins) and sinks and on payment in showers. One block in the centre of the site is on the ground floor of a well constructed building and the smaller one is by reception. There is a tennis court and campers who stay for more than one night may use the town swimming pool next door free of charge. No entertainment is offered on site but the village is very near. *continued overleaf*

3690 Campingplatz Wagnerhof (continued)

Being so close to the A8, the site makes a good night stop between Munich and Salzburg but you may be tempted to stay longer to explore the Chiemsee, mountains, Salzburg and nearby attractions.

How to find it: From A8 autobahn, take exit for Bergen, follow signs to village; site signed on northern edge.

General Details: Open all year. 28,000 sq.m. Electricity connections (16A). Small shop (May - Oct). General room where drinks served. Shops and restaurants in village (a short walk). Swimming pool adjacent (May - Sept). Tennis. Children's playground. Bicycle hire 1 km. Fishing 8 km. Laundry facilities. Cooking facilities. Chemical disposal.

Charges 1999: Per person DM 7.00 - 9.50; + local tax 1.20; child (under 14 yrs) 4.50 - 5.50 + 0.60 tax; pitch 9.50 - 12.50, extra car or tent 4.75 - 6.25; electricity 4.00 (once only) + meter. No credit cards.

Reservations: made with deposit. Address: Campingstr. 11, 83346 Bergen. Tel: 08662/8557. FAX: 08662/5924.

3640 Campingplatz München-Thalkirchen, München

Reliable municipal site in river conservation area on the city outskirts.

This well run municipal site is quietly situated on the southern side of Munich in parkland formed by the River Isar conservation area, 4 km. from the city centre (there are subway and bus links). Pleasant walks may be taken in the park and the world famous Munich zoo is just 15 minutes walk along the river from the site. The large city of Munich has much to offer and the Thalkirchen site becomes very crowded during the season, when one may have much less space than one would like, particularly if only staying for one night. However, it is well equipped and clean, with a total of 550 pitches (150 for caravans, most with electricity, water and waste water; 100 for motorcaravans, mostly with electricity and a small area of hardstanding) of various sizes, marked by metal or wooden posts and rails. Like many city sites, groups are taken in one area. There are five toilet blocks, two of which can be heated, with seatless toilets, washbasins with shelf, mirror and cold water. Hot water for showers and sink is on payment. The facilities are hard pressed when the site is full. Out of the main season, when not all are open, there may be long walks from some parts. Facilities for disabled people are provided. The office, shop and snack bar open for long hours. The site is very busy (and probably noisy) during the Beer Festival (14 Sept - 5 Oct) when a daily per person surcharge of DM 7 applies.

How to find it: From autobahns follow 'Mittel' ring road to SSE of the city centre where site is signed; also follow signs for Thalkirchen or the Zoo and site is close. Well signed now from all over the City.

General Details: Open mid-March - end Oct. 40,000 sq.m. Electricity connections (10A). Some shade. Some pitches suitable for American motorhomes. Shop (7 am - 8.30 pm). Snack bar with covered terrace (7 am - 10 pm). Restaurant 200 m. Good children's playground. Tourist information, souvenirs and other services. Treatment room. Washing machines and dryers. Maximum stay 14 days. Office hours 7 am - 11 pm.

Charges 1998: Per person DM 7.90; child (2-14 yrs) 2.50; tent (acc. to size) 5.50 - 7.00; car 8.50; m/cycle 4.00; caravan incl. car 19.00; motorcaravan 11.00 - 13.00; electricity 3.50. Credit cards only accepted for souvenirs.

Reservations: not made except for groups - said to be room up to 4 pm. daily. Address: Zentralländstr. 49, 81379 München. Tel: 089/7231707. FAX: 089/7243177.

3630 Donau-Lech Camping, Eggelstetten, Donauwörth, nr Augsburg

Very pleasant, friendly site just off the `Romantische Strasse'.

The Haas family have developed this site well and run it very much as a family site, providing a useful information sheet in English. The lake provides swimming and wildlife for children and adults to enjoy. Alongside it are 50 marked touring pitches on flat grass arranged in rows either side of a tarred access road. With an average of 120 sq.m. per unit, electrical connections, and with water, waste water and TV connections on most pitches also, it is a comfortable site with an open feeling and developing shade. There are three separate pleasant, flat, grass areas near the entrance for people with tents (including youngsters, cyclists or motorcyclists) with unmarked pitches. Pitches for longer stay visitors are located beyond the tourers. All amenities are housed in the main building at the entrance with reception and a large bar area (with self-service machines for beer, soft drinks and microwave meals). Downstairs are a sauna and the sanitary facilities with eight controllable showers on payment (DM 1 for five minutes, slot in corridor - you can put two in and meter only runs when tap is on), toilets, washbasins with warm water and a dishwashing and laundry room, all of a satisfactory standard. Basic food supplies are kept. Suitable not only as a night stop on the way south, the site is also not far from Augsburg or Munich and the local area is very attractive; you may borrow bicycles from the proprietor.

How to find it: Turn off main B2 road about 5 km. south of Donauwörth at signs for Asbach-Bäumenheim Nord towards Eggelstetten, then follow camp signs for over 1 km. to site.

General Details: Open all year. Electricity connection (16A). Hardstanding area for winter. Shop (all year). Self service bar. General room. Youth room. Restaurants and other amenities a short drive. Table tennis. Lake for bathing on site (own risk); larger sailboarding lake 400 m. Sauna. Washing machine and dryer. Motorcaravan service point. Chemical disposal.

Charges 1998: Per person DM 8.00; child (4-12 yrs) 4.70; caravan 10.00; tent 6.00 - 10.00; car 2.50; motorcaravan 12.00; electricity 4.00 or on meter; dog 3.50.

Reservations: not needed - said always space. Address: 86698 Eggelstetten. Tel: 09002/4044. FAX: 09002/4046.

GERMANY - West Central / South West

3242 Country Camping Schinderhannes, Hausbay-Pfalzfeld

See colour advert opposite

Large countryside site with a lake in the Hunsrück.

Set in a 'bowl' of land which catches the sun all day long and with trees and parkland all around, this is a very peaceful and picturesque site, very close to, but rather different from, no. 3235. There are 250 permanent caravans which are in a separate area from 90 overnight pitches on hardstanding, which are on two areas near reception. For those staying longer, the site becomes visually more attractive as you drive down into the area around the lake to a further 160 numbered pitches. These are of over 80 sq.m. on grass, some with hardstanding and all with electrical connections and with water points around. You can position yourself for shade or sun. The lake is used for swimming and inflatable boats and for fishing. The sanitary buildings, which can be heated, are of a high standard with one section, in the reception/shop building, for the overnight pitches and the remainder close to the longer stay places. They have large, free, controllable showers for the short stay area, four private cabins in total, laundry and facilities for disabled people. A pleasant large restaurant features an open fire and includes a rest area with TV and a bowling alley downstairs. English is spoken by the helpful reception staff.

How to find it: From the A61 Koblenz - Ludwigshafen, take exit 43 Pfalzfeld (30 km. south of Koblenz) and on to Hausbay where site is signed.

General Details: Open all year. Electricity connections (10A). Barrier closed 10 pm - 7 am. Restaurant with TV and bowling alley. Shop (both 16/3-31/10 and maybe Xmas). Tennis (on payment). Basketball. Fishing. Bicycle hire 1 km. Children's play area and fort. Laundry facilities. Chemical disposal. Rallies welcome.

Charges 1999: Per adult DM 7.00; child 5.00; pitch 14.00; dog 3.00; electricity included. No credit cards.

Reservations: For groups only, contact site. Address: 56291 Hausbay-Pfalzfeld/Hünsrück. Tel: 06746/1674 or 8470. FAX: 06746/8214. Email: schinderhannes@mir-tours.de

This site is featured out of order - it is in West Central Germany and should be listed on page 148

3450 Ferien-Campingplatz Münstertal, Münstertal, nr Freiburg

See colour advert opposite

Very impressive site with indoor and outdoor pools, just on edge of Black Forest.

On the western edge of the Black Forest just before the road starts climbing up to Todnau and the Feldberg, this is a site of high quality well worth consideration for your stays in the region. It has some 260 individual pitches on flat gravel, their size varying from 80-100 sq.m. Marked by trees or other means, all have electricity and 180 have waste water drains, 40 with water, TV and radio connection. The site becomes full in season and reservations, especially in July, are necessary. There are' three sanitary blocks of truly first class quality in the section with the fully serviced (but slightly smaller) pitches. They have washbasins, half in private cabins, showers with glass doors and seat, a baby bath, a unit for visitors with disabilities and individual bathrooms for hire. All hot water is free. There is a large indoor swimming pool (14 x 7 m.) with sauna and solarium, and an outdoor pool on site.

How to find it: Münstertal is south of Freiburg. From A5 autobahn take Bad Krozingen and Colmar exit, turn southeast via Bad Krozingen and Staufen (bypassed) and continue 5 km. to the start of Münstertal, where camp is signed from the main road.

General Details: Open all year. 40,000 sq.m. Electricity connections (16A). Shop (all year). Restaurant, particularly good and well patronised (closed Nov). Indoor and outdoor swimming pools. Tennis. Minigolf. Children's playground. Games room with table tennis. Fishing. Bicycle hire. Tennis courses in summer, ski courses in winter - for children or adults. Riding 5 km. Golf 17 km. Chemical disposal. Motorcaravan services. Village amenities are near.

Charges 1998: Per person DM 10.90 - 13.50; child (2-10 yrs) 7.00 - 8.00; local tax 1.50 for over 16s; pitch 13.50 - 15.90; pitch with TV, water, drainage, radio, phone and electricity connections 20.00; electricity on meter; dog 5.00; private bathroom 15.00. No credit cards.

Reservations: are made without deposit. Address: 79244 Münstertal. Tel: 07636/7080. FAX: 07636/7448.

This site is featured out of order - it is in South West Germany and should be listed on page 152

Many continental camp sites, particularly in Germany, close for 2 or 3 hours at lunch time. There are usually parking areas outside where you can park and wait.

NORWAY

The Direct Sea Route to the Fjords

Color Line, with up to three sailings every week, provide the natural gateway to the magnificent fjord country.

The superb service and on board entertainment, for the one night crossing, makes the beginning and end to your holiday as enjoyable as your time in Norway.

Motoring in Norway is something quite special, a sightseeing tour in its own right. Here you can get away from the throng and enjoy the peace and serenity of fjord Norway. Numerous ferries plying the fjords provide an added opportunity to enjoy more of the beautiful scenery and the countless minor roads allow an insight into the true character of the Norwegian Countryside.

Our full colour 1995 brochure features an exciting selection of year round holiday options by car. From one and two centre self-catering chalets equipped with all the facilities one could wish for, to a range of pre-planned motoring tours including our ever popular Arctic Circle tour. Alternatively you may wish to plan your own tour of

Norway using our extensive hotel contacts. Our 'Go As You Please' option allows you total flexibility.

For those who simply fancy getting away from it all for a few days, our four day Sea Break to the delightful fjords of Norway is the answer. Wine and dine, dance the night away or simply relax and unwind - the choice is yours. A Sea Break offers unrivalled value **from just £54 per person** with children up to 16 receiving a 50% reduction when sharing with a minimum of 1 adult.

For a copy of our full colour brochure visit your local travel agent or telephone Color Line on 0191 296 1313.

ColorLine

INTERNATIONAL FERRY TERMINAL,
ROYAL QUAYS, NORTH SHIELDS,
TYNE & WEAR, NE29 6EE.

Sail away to the sites and delights of Denmark, Norway, Sweden & Holland.

Camping Holidays in Scandinavia and Holland are perfect for the outdoor life and great value when you sail away, in style, with Scandinavian Seaways.

One, all-inclusive price covers transportation for  you, your family and your car aboard one of our sleek white liners plus camping vouchers to any one of a large selection of superb sites all over Sweden, Norway, Denmark or Holland. You get a lot more than you imagine, for a lot less than you think.

See your travel agent or call our 24-hour Brochure Line on 0990 333 666 (quote reference 8B153) for a copy of our 1999 Motoring Holidays Brochure.

From £79 per person for 11 nights

SCANDINAVIAN SEAWAYS
A BETTER WAY OF TRAVELLING

Cruiseferries

Every night from Hull to the Continent

P&O North Sea Ferries sail each evening from Hull to Rotterdam and Zeebrugge saving you a tiring trek south.

Enjoy a great night out including a five course feast, live entertainment, casino, cinema, fantastic shops and fun for the kids. Plus a comfortable bed in a cosy cabin.

Wake up on the Continent with the whole day ahead of you and excellent road connections to all parts of Europe.

Get the full picture in our Cruiseferries Brochure – from your local Travel Agent or direct from us on 01482 377177 or for a range of holidays in Dutch cities, ask for the P&O North Sea Ferries Short Breaks Brochure, operated by Travelscene, on 0181 863 2787

P&O North Sea Ferries

3627 Azur Camping Ellwangen, Ellwangen

Good night stop or for a longer stay at developing site in an area of hills and lakes.

Situated in a quiet position on the edge of town, with the river Jagst along one side, this new six hectare site, from which you can see the large hilltop castle, has a park-like appearance with mature trees giving some shade. The 250 large, flat, grassy pitches (with one area of hardstanding to the right of the entrance) are off tarred access roads. Electricity is available for about half the pitches from central boxes. All the facilities are in one area to the left of the site entrance in modern units, with reception, the small shop for basic supplies and a bar/restaurant with terrace open all year. More sanitary facilities are being added as the site develops, with some private cabins now provided in addition to showers and washbasins, all with free hot water. There are dishwashing facilities, both inside and out, a small laundry, and rooms for chemical disposal, babies and disabled visitors, plus a motorcaravan service point. Some new play equipment for children is on sand and fishing is very popular here. Very close to the site is a heated indoor municipal wave-pool, with free access for campers and there are numerous other local attractions.

How to find it: From A7 Ulm - Würzburg autobahn take exit 113 and go into Ellwangen from where site is signed on road to Rotenbach village. It is next to the Hallenbad, with a fairly tight left turn into the entrance road.

General Details: Open all year, as are shop and restaurant/bar. Electricity connections (16A). Bicycle hire in town. Chemical disposal. Motorcaravan service point. Indoor pool 200 m. Fishing.

Charges 1998: Per person DM 7.00 - 10.00; child (2-12 yrs) 5.00 - 7.00; pitch 9.00 - 13.00; small tent 5.00 - 7.00; electricity 3.80.

Reservations: Contact site. Address: Rotenbacher Strasse, 73479 Ellwangen/Jagst. Tel: 07961/7921. FAX: 07961/562 330.

3610 Campingplatz im Volkspark Dutzendteich, Nürnberg

Satisfactory municipal site just outside the city.

A perfectly acceptable, if not luxurious, municipal site, this is at its best outside the main season when it is not so busy and the tall trees make it quite attractive as well as providing some shade. It is some 4 km. from the city centre (a 20 minute walk following signs takes you to the underground station) and 200 m. from the swimming pool and football stadium. Up to 200 units are taken on flat grass, 112 with electricity .The pitches are not marked out and the site does not like to turn people away so at the busiest times spacing might be close. The two fairly basic toilet blocks could be hard pressed in July and August. They have British style toilets, washing troughs (cold water), washbasins with hot water (some curtained cabins) and fairly small hot showers on payment (DM 2).

How to find it: From autobahns, take Nürnberg-Fischbach exit from A9 München-Bayreuth east of Nürnberg. Proceed 3 km. on dual carriageway towards city then left at camp sign. From city follow `Stadion-Messe' signs and site is well signed (near a large Grundig office block).

General Details: Open 1 May - 30 Sept. Electricity connections (10A). Café. Kiosk with basic supplies. General room with pool table, amusements, where drinks from shop can be consumed. Tennis (free). Children's play area in woodland. Washing machine and dryer. Chemical disposal. Motorcaravan services.

Charges 1998: Per person DM 9.00; child (3-13 yrs) 4.50; motorcaravan, caravan or tent + car 10.00; hiker or cyclist's tent 5.00; m/cycle 2.00; dog 2.00; electricity 1.00 p/kwh. No credit cards.

Reservations: not made and said to be unnecessary. Address: Hans Kalb Str. 56, 90471 Nürnberg 50. Tel: 0911/811122.

3620 DCC-Campingpark `Romantische Strasse', Dinkelsbühl, nr Ellwangen

Modern site, very close to well known town on Romantic Road.

Run by the German Camping Club (DCC), this site is by one of Germany's best known mediaeval towns, from which of course visits can be made to other places on the Romantic Road. There are 475 pitches (half of which are for touring) on broad grassy terraces overlooking a small lake. All are numbered and of about 80 sq.m., with electricity. A special area is kept for overnight stays. The lake can be used for bathing or one's own non-powered boat. The two large modern toilet blocks are of good quality and should satisfy all demands with British style toilets, washbasins with free hot water, some in private cabins, plentiful showers with hot water (DM 0.50 charge) and free hairdryers.

How to find it: Site is near road 25 and is signed in Dinkelsbühl towards Dürnwangen.

General Details: Open all year, also shop, (meals at least Easter, then May-end Sept.); 80,000 sq.m. Electrical connections (10A) and water points everywhere. Self-service shop. General/TV room. Children's playgrounds on sand and grass. Minigolf. Organised daytime activities in season. Bicycle hire. Washing machines, dryers and dishwashing. Cooking facilities.

Charges 1998: Per person DM 7.50; child (4-13) 5.00; (10% off these two with international camping carnet); local tax (over 4 yrs.) 1.25; pitch 16.50; dog 2.00; electricity 0.50 + meter.

Reservations: only through DCC and rather complex, costly, and usually unnecessary. Try phoning site shortly before arrival: 09851/7817. FAX: as phone.

GERMANY - South East

3605 Camping Rangau, Dechsendorf, nr Erlangen

Overnight halt close to A3 Würzburg - Nürnberg autobahn.

This site makes a convenient stopover, quickly and easily reached from the Würzburg - Nürnberg motorway and may be pleasant enough to stay a bit longer. It has 110 pitches which are mainly for tourists on flat ground, under trees, numbered and partly marked but only about 60-80 sq.m. There are also 60 permanent units. There is usually space and in peak season overnighters can often be put on adjacent football pitch. A reasonable sanitary block, heated when cold, has free hot water in well spaced washbasins and controllable showers. An older block provides WCs. A fair sized lake with direct access from the site can be used for sailing or windsurfing or for fishing on permit; boats are for hire. One can also swim here or in a swimming pool 200 m. away. The centre of Erlangen is 5 km.

How to find it: Take exit for Erlangen-West from A3 autobahn, turn towards Erlangen but after less than 1 km. at Dechsendorf turn left by camp signs and follow to site.

General Details: Open 1 April - 30 Sept. Restaurant for meals or drinks. Order bread from reception. Children's playground. Laundry facilities.

Charges 1998: Per person DM 6.50; child (under 12) 3.00; pitch 8.00; dog 2.50; electricity (6A) 4.00.

Reservations: are made without deposit and kept until 6 pm. Address: Campingstrasse 44, 91056 Erlangen-Dechsendorf. Tel: 09135/8866.

3615 Azur Camping Stadtsteinach, Stadtsteinach, nr Bayreuth

Friendly, well-managed site in the Franken Forest

Stadtsteinach is well placed for exploring this region with its interesting towns, forest walks and the Fichtel Mountains nearby and this is a comfortable base. Occupying a quiet position in gently undulating countryside with tree-clad hills rising to the east, there are 70 static caravans and space for 130 tourers. Brick main roads give way to hard access roads with pitches on either side, all of which have electricity. The site is on a gentle slope, pitches having been terraced where necessary and there are some hardstandings for motorcaravans. High hedges and trees separate pitches or groups of pitches in some areas giving the effect of camping in small clearings. There is a small restaurant with terrace and a shop. The two sanitary areas, one by the open field, the other part of the administration and restaurant building, are of good quality. They have British WCs and free hot water to the showers, sinks and washbasins (some in private cabins). There are facilities for people with disabilities. The solar heated swimming pool near the entrance is free to campers.

How to find it: Stadtsteinach is north of Bayreuth, off the A9/E51 Nürnberg-Berlin road, reached by the no. 303 road from this autobahn. The site is well signed.

General Details: Open all year. Electrical connections (16A). Restaurant and shop (Easter end Oct). Local shops 800 m. Children's play area. TV. Washing machines and dryers. Cooking rings on payment. Swimming pool (high season), bicycle hire and tennis nearby. Walking.

Charges 1998: Per adult DM 7.00 - 9.00, acc. to season; child (1-12 yrs) 5.00 - 6.00; pitch 10.00 - 12.00; car or m/cycle 3.00 - 4.00; extra tent 3.00 - 4.00; dog 3.00 - 4.00; electricity 3.80.

Reservations: Write to site with deposit (DM 20) by Eurocheque. Address: Badstrasse 5, 95346 Stadtsteinach. Tel: 09225/95401. FAX: 09225/95402.

3602 Azur Camping Romantische Strasse, Münster, nr Creglingen

Pleasant country site in good walking area.

The small village of Münster is on a scenic road just 3 km. from Creglingen and about 20 km. from the tourist town of Rothenburg which, although fascinating, is also extremely busy and commercialised. The AZUR site would, therefore, be much appreciated for its peaceful situation in a wooded valley just outside Münster, with 90 grass touring pitches, many with a small degree of slope. All the pitches have electricity, water and waste water connections, either side of a stream (fenced off from a weir at the top of the site), with about 40 long stay pitches and a tent area in different areas. Basic supplies are kept in a small shop and there is a pleasant bar/restaurant, a barbecue and covered sitting area and a heated indoor swimming pool and sauna. Just 100 m. away is a large lake for swimming and fishing. The main sanitary facilities have free hot water for the washbasins (two for each male/female in private cabins) and showers, and there is a small unit further into the site (but not of the same quality).

How to find it: From the Romantische Strasse between Rothenburg and Bad Mergentheim, exit at Creglingen for Münster (3 km) and site is just beyond this village.

General Details: Open 15 March - 15 Nov. Electrical connections (16A). Shop for basics, bar/restaurant and heated indoor pool (all April - Oct). Minigolf. Children's play area. Lake for swimming and fishing. Bicycle hire in town.

Charges 1998: Per adult DM 9.00; child (2-12 yrs) 6.00; pitch 12.00; dog 4.00; electricity 3.80.

Reservations: Advised in season. Address: 97993 Creglingen/Münster. Tel: 07933/20289. FAX: 07933/990019.

3625 Knaus Camping-Park Frickenhausen, Ochsenfurt, nr Würzburg

Pleasant riverside site just south of Würzburg.

Knaus continue to develop this site and it now has a small, heated, open-air swimming pool (for 'adults only' at specific times), whilst on an `island' surrounded by attractive trees alongside the gently flowing River Main is a large children's play area with modern equipment and a full size volleyball court on sand. Young trees are growing well on the site to replace the 300 lost in a violent storm a few years ago. There are 115 fair sized, numbered touring pitches on flat grass, arranged in sections leading from tarred access roads with flowers around. Most have electricity connections. About 80 long stay places are mostly separate nearer the river. All the amenities are in a long block opposite reception (Frau Hergeth speaks English). Sanitary facilities have free hot water in the quite large, fully controllable showers, the washbasins (some private cabins for women), and dishwashing sinks. Soap and paper towels are provided for the toilets. Upstairs is a small shop and a restaurant with a terrace for candle-lit meals, whilst downstairs is a small café/bar. The ducks are very friendly and will invite you to feed them.

How to find it: Take exit 71 (Ochsenfurt) from the A3 autobahn at Würzburg and continue on the B13. Do not cross the Main into town but follow Frickenhausen and site signs; the site is shortly on the right.

General Details: Open all year except Nov. Electricity connections (6A). Restaurant, cafe/wine bar and shop (weekends only in low season). Bread to order. Club room. Small swimming pool, public pool 300 m. Children's play area and beach volleyball on river island. Table tennis. Fishing. Boat marina. Cooking facilities. Washing machine and dryer. Chemical disposal. Caravans (10) and tents to rent; contact site for details.

Charges 1998: Per person DM 8.50; child (3-14 yrs) 4.50; pitch 7.50 - 12.00; small tent and m/cycle 7.50; electricity 3.50.

Reservations: Not made. Address: Ochsenfurter Str. 49, 97252 Frickenhausen. Tel: 09331/3171. FAX: 09331/5784.

3735 Spessart-Camping Schönrain, Gemünden-Hofstetten, nr Karlstadt

Site in attractive, peaceful woodland setting with swimming pool.

Situated a short distance from the town of Gemünden, with views of forested hills beside the river Main, this is a very friendly, family run site. Of the 200 pitches, 100 are for tourists with some of up to 150 sq.m. Most have electricity and some water and drainage also. A new area has been developed for tents. The site has an outdoor pool open from Whitsun to end Sept (weather permitting). A brand new sanitary building was under construction during our visit so facilities should be first class. A pleasant small restaurant and bar and a shop are on site with local full-bodied Franconian wine for sale. Frau Endres welcomes British guests and speaks a little English. There are opportunities for walking and riding in the adjacent woods, excursions are organised in the main season and it is possible to hire a bicycle, ride to Würzburg and catch the pleasure boat back, or take a combined bus and cycle ride. Fishing and boating are both very popular in the locality.

How to find it: From Frankfurt - Würzburg autobahn, take Weibersbrunn-Lohr exit and then B26 to Gemünden. Turn over the Main river bridge to Hofstetten. From Kassel - Wurzburg autobahn, leave at Hammelburg and take B27 to Gemünden, and as above.

General Details: Open 1 April - 30 Sept. Electrical connections (10A). Bar/restaurant (closed Tuesdays). Shop. Swimming pool. Children's playground. Table tennis. Bicycle hire. Excursions organised. Fishing or riding 400 m. Canoeing, cycling and walking near. Chemical disposal. Motorcaravan services. Caravans for hire.

Charges 1999: Per pitch 100 sq.m. DM 10.00, 150 sq.m. 15.00, small pitch for hikers or cyclists and small tent DM 8.00; person 8.00; child (under 14 yrs) 5.50; electricity 4.00. Less 10% for stays over 14 days. No credit cards.

AR Discount
Welcome drink

Reservations: Write to site. Address: 97737 Gemünden-Hofstetten. Tel: 09351/8645. FAX: 09351/8721.

GERMANY - South East

3730 Camping Park Bad Kissingen, Bad Kissingen

First class, family owned site adjacent to pretty spa town and its park.

Bad Kissingen is a very attractive town and was a favourite of Bavarian Kings, Austrian Emperors and Bismark, who lived here for a while. This quiet site is situated by the lakeside on the edge of town with direct access to the centre through the private entrance to the adjacent park. Herr Laudenbach, the friendly English-speaking owner, will greet you and personally conduct you to your pitch. A grassy, partially shaded site with a tarmac service road, there are only 99 pitches (80 with electricity, 40 with water and waste water connections), all well spaced out. Of these 20 are used by permanent units, so reservation is advisable. The exemplary sanitary block has a room for disabled people and it is kept very clean. Showers are on payment (DM 1). The laundry room has two washing machines and a dryer. A small, charming restaurant is open every evening and there is folk music to entertain you. Tennis, golf, minigolf and a swimming pool are all within easy reach and local excursions leave from the site. Gas barbecues are permitted. A large children's play area is in the adjacent park.

How to find it: Leave autobahn A7/E45 at Hammelburg. Take A287 for Bad Kissingen for 10 km. and site is on the right just before the town approach (and is signed).

General Details: Open 1 April - 15 Oct. Electrical connections (6A). Restaurant/bar (1/4-30/9). Children's play area. Aviary. Fishing. Bicycle hire and golf 1 km. Riding 3 km. Tennis, swimming pool and minigolf near. Washing machines and dryer. Chemical disposal. Motorcaravan services.

Charges 1999: Per person DM 9.50; child (under 12 yrs) 5.00; pitch for car/caravan or motorcaravan 11.00; tent 9.00; electricity 3.50; local tax 2.50; dog 2.50. No credit cards.

AR Discount
Less 10% on person fees

Reservations: Write to site. Address: Euerdorfer Str. 1, 97688 Bad Kissingen. Tel: 0971/5211. FAX: as phone.

3720 Campingplatz Naabtal, Pielenhofen bei Regensburg

Very pleasant, attractive riverside site in a beautiful tree-covered valley.

Regensburg is an ancient city on the Danube, near the 'Bavarian Forest' which, although not as well known as the Black Forest, is a lovely area of natural beauty. Naabtal makes an excellent night stop when travelling to or from Austria or Hungary and would also make a good base for exploring this interesting part of Germany. Two-thirds of the site is taken up by static caravans used for weekends and holidays. The 130 large pitches for tourists (all with electricity) are under willow trees by the riverside or in an open field, where a new sanitary building should be ready for the '99 season (to replace a small overnight unit). There is good shade in some parts and hills covered with trees rise all around - this is good walking and mountain biking country, with marked trails. The two original toilet blocks, part of larger buildings, are heated in cool weather. They have British style WCs and free hot water in the washbasins (some in private cabins), on payment in the showers. One of the buildings contains the shop and bar/restaurant and the other, a large meeting room with tables, catering facilities, a stage for festive occasions and a youth room with table tennis and video games. Sauna and solarium, and new, first class unit for disabled people. Alongside, under cover, are a skittle alley and next to this a tarmac curling rink. The children's playground has some imaginative fixed apparatus. Small boats can be launched on the placid river (where you may also swim at your own risk) and there are two good size tennis courts.

How to find it: Take exit 97 Nittendorf from the A3 Nürnberg - Passau , and follow road to Pielenhofen (Camping Naabtal is signed from exit). Cross river and turn right to site. Camp is about 11 km. from autobahn exit. From A93 exit 31 onto B8 towards Nittendorf, then B15 to Pielenhofen.

General Details: Open all year. Electricity connections (10A). Bar/restaurant (1/4-20/10 plus weekends and Xmas/New Year). Small shop (1/4-1/10, village shop 1.5 km). Tennis. Table tennis. Skittle alley. Football field. Volleyball. Curling rink. Sauna and solarium. Youth room with games. Bicycle hire. Fishing (permit required). Small boats on river. Riding 6 km. Golf 11 km. Reception will advise on local excursions, walks, cycle routes and sports. Washing machines, dryers and irons. Chemical disposal. Motorcaravan service point. Bungalows for hire.

Charges 1999: Per person DM 8.50; child 5.30; pitch 9.70; electricity 1.00 (once) + meter. No credit cards.

Reservations: Needed in high season; contact site. Address: 93188 Pielenhofen. Tel: 09409/373. FAX: 09409/723.

3715 Knaus Camping-Park Viechtach, nr Cham

Well managed site on the edge of the Bavarian Forest.

Although the Bavarian Forest is not as well known to the British as the Black Forest, it is an area of great natural beauty with rolling hills rising to over 1,500 m. at the highest point and ideal for those who enjoy wide open spaces. The National Park near Grafenau has a 200 km. network of footpaths and a unique collection of primeval flora and fauna. Camping-Park Viechtach, although reached via a small industrial area, is a relaxing place, well laid out in a woodland setting on the edge of the village. The various trees and shrubs give a 'garden' effect and there is good shade in most parts. A tarmac road winds between the grass pitches (most terraced) which are separated by rocks and trees and marked by plaques. There are 200 pitches (all with electricity), size varying from small for some motorcaravans to quite large for bigger units (120 sq.m.).   *continued overleaf*

3715 Knaus Camping-Park Viechtach (continued)

Two sanitary blocks are of fair quality, one central to the touring pitches, the other at the top end of the site on the ground floor of a larger building, with a drying room. Facilities are similar, with British style WCs and free hot water to washbasins (some in private cabins), sinks and showers. There is an attractive bar/restaurant with reasonable prices, a small shop for basic supplies and a camping shop. A heated indoor swimming pool has a sauna and solarium, the town swimming pool and tennis courts are nearby. Whether for a night stop or for a longer stay to visit the Bavarian Forest, this site is well worth considering. English is spoken by the friendly reception staff.

How to find it: Take the Viechtach exit from the B85 Weiden - Passau road, and follow the campsite signs.

General Details: Open all year except Nov. Electricity connections (4A). Restaurant. Shops (basics and camping equipment) Bread to order. Indoor swimming pool. Sauna and solarium. Large, renovated children's playground. Table tennis. Bicycle hire. Small games room. Several rooms for wet weather. Outdoor pool and tennis nearby. Washing machines, dryers and irons. Chemical disposal. Rooms in guest house, caravans (10) and tents to rent.

Charges 1998: Per person DM 8.50; child (3-14) 4.50; pitch 7.50 - 12.00; tent and m/cycle 7.50; electricity 3.50.

Reservations: Write to site. Address: Waldfrieden 22, 94234 Viechtach. Tel: 09942/1095. FAX: 09942/302222.

3725 Bavaria Sport Camping Park, Eging am See, nr Passau

Modern site with good facilities, near Passau.

Eging is a Kurbad village of the type found in many parts of Germany where warm and cold water baths are used in a variety of treatments. It is located in the southwest tip of the Bavarian Forest, in good walking country and occupies an open hilltop position amidst rolling forest countryside on slightly sloping ground about 600 m. from the small lake, treatment and sports centre. Mainly level numbered pitches on terraces of grass or fine gravel are divided by bushes and saplings on either side of tarmac roads. Water and electricity points are widely spaced (long cables may be needed). There is a small bar/restaurant with terrace and another larger one by the lake. A kiosk offers basic food supplies. The single sanitary block is of good quality with free hot water in washbasins (some in private cabins) and sinks, and on payment in the showers (by slot machine door locks). Facilities for disabled people are provided. Apart from the Kur facilities, there are opportunities for a wide variety of sports nearby - swimming, tennis, table tennis, minigolf, curling, fishing, pedaloes, volleyball, electric go-karts and small motorcycles, billiards, pool, amusement machines, walking and some winter sports.

How to find it: Take exit 113 (Garham) from A3 Regensburg - Passau autobahn. Pass turn to Eging, continuing to main road and turn right, then almost immediately left. Cross level crossing and site is on left by hotel. Site is also signed in Eging.

General Details: Open all year. Electricity connections (16A). Restaurant. Variety of sports (see above). Washing machines, dryers and irons.

Charges guide: Per adult DM 7.90 - 8.90; child (3 age bands from 3-18) 4.00 - 7.90; pitch 10.50 - 11.50; dog 4.50; electricity 4.80 (includes two shower tokens); local tax 0.60; rubbish tax 1.00. Credit cards not accepted.

Reservations: Write to site. Address: Grafenauer Strasse 31, 94535 Eging am See. Tel: 08544/8089. FAX: 08544/7964.

3695 Dreiflüsse Campingplatz, Irring bei Passau, Donautal

Good site overlooking the Danube near Passau.

Although the name of this site suggests an association with the three important rivers here, it is in fact some 9 km. from the confluence of the Danube, Inn and Ilz. Dreiflüsse Camping occupies a hillside position to the west of Passau with pitches on several rows of level terraces. The 180 places are not all numbered or marked, although electricity connection boxes determine where units pitch, and half have water and waste water connections. Trees and low banks separate the terraces which are of gravel with a thin covering of grass. The pleasant, modern Gasthof restaurant is at the entrance to the site, where the reception, shop and sanitary buildings are situated. The sanitary facilities include British type toilets and free hot water to the showers and washbasins (two cabins for women, one for men). There is a small heated indoor swimming pool (June-Oct, on payment), a play area and a place for dog walking. The energetic and very jolly owner is most popular with his regular visitors and he gives the site a very friendly air. This is a useful en-route stop or for a longer stay to explore the delights of Passau and the southern part of the Bavarian forest. The Zoo, breweries, walks and other attractions are near.

How to find it: From autobahn A3, take exit 115 (Passau-Nord) from where site is signed. Follow signs from Passau on road to west of city and north bank of Danube towards Winsdorf and Irring.

General Details: Open 1 April - 31 Oct. 40,000 sq.m. Some shade. Electricity connections (16A). Restaurant. Shop (both all season). Indoor pool (May - 15 Sept). Play area. Table tennis. Fishing. Bicycle hire. Riding. Bus service for Passau from outside site (a little erratic and finishes at 6 pm). Chemical disposal. Motorcaravan service point.

Charges 1998: Per person DM 7.50; child (4-12 yrs) 5.00; pitch 8.50 - 12.00; electricity 4.80 + kw. charge. Credit cards accepted.

Reservations: Write to site. Address: 94113 Irring am Sonnenhang 23, Passau/Donautal. Tel: 08546/633. FAX: 08546/2686.

AR Discount
Less 10% on pitch fees

GERMANY - South East / North East

3700 AZUR Ferienzentrum Bayerwald, Gottsdorf, nr Passau

Well run, quiet site with good sports facilities, in southeast Germany.

Attractively situated on high ground above, but not overlooking, the Danube (on which there is a regular boat service), this site has only 160 pitches, of which 40 are for permanent caravans. All are numbered, with electrical connections (11-16A), and stand mostly in rows of five or six with a high hedge backing each row. Reservations are advisable in season. The heated sanitary block provides British style WCs, free hot water in the individual washbasins (mainly in cubicles), showers and sinks. Public swimming pools - a heated indoor pool and outdoor one, heated with solar panels - are just below the site.

How to find it: Leave A3 (E56) Regensburg - Linz autobahn at Passau-Nord exit for the B388 towards Wegscheid. At Obernzell, turn left at Gottsdorf sign and follow to site - entrance is just before village on left.

General Details: Open 15 March - 15 Nov. 120,000 sq.m. Many electrical connections (11/16A). Self-service shop. TV room. Sports field with football pitch, volleyball, garden chess and extensive children's playground; also adventure playground and running track. Table tennis. Outdoor fitness facilities. Minigolf. Tennis. Swimming pools nearby. Washing machines and dryer. Cooking facilities. 40 bungalows or small houses for hire.

Charges guide: Per adult DM 7.00 - 9.00; child (1-12 yrs) 5.00 - 6.00; pitch 10.00 - 12.00; car or m/cycle 3.00 - 4.00; extra tent 3.00 - 4.00; dog 3.00 - 4.00; electricity 3.80.

Reservations: made with DM 20 deposit, write to site. Address: Mitterweg 11, 94107 Gottsdorf. Tel: 08593/880. FAX: 08593/88111.

3705 Knaus Camping-Park Lackenhäuser, Neureichenau, nr Passau

Pleasant site, offering walking, skiing, fishing and an indoor pool.

This extensive site is right at the southeast tip of Germany - the border with Austria runs through one side of the site and the Czech Republic is very close too. It is a very popular site and reservations may be advisable from mid-June to Sept. Mainly on sloping ground with good views from some parts, it has 500 pitches with terracing in some areas, nearly all available for tourists, and 40 chalets or caravans for hire. Electricity connections are available and water points are fed from pure springs. The many amenities (listed below) include a heated indoor pool (free) with child's pool, sauna and fitness room, and a new outdoor pool. The site is open all year and has much winter sports trade, with its own ski lift. The three sanitary buildings, all refurbished, are of good quality with free hot water in the washbasins (some in cabins), showers and sinks. They have under floor heating for cool weather. Rather off the beaten track for British campers, it is however a most pleasant site in a beautiful setting with 7 km. of walks available within the camp perimeters and an attractive, fishing lake. There is a friendly atmosphere here, with English spoken by reception staff.

How to find it: From Regensburg on the A3 take exit 115 into Passau, then road 12 towards Freyung, turning off just before Röhrnbach for Waldkirchen and on through Jandelsbrunn to Lackenhaüser.

General Details: Open all year except Nov. 146,000 sq.m. Electricity connections (4A). Supermarket. Restaurant/bar. General room for young. Caravan shop. Indoor and outdoor pools. Sauna, fitness room and massage facilities. Small lake (ice sports in winter). Fishing. Bowling alley. Church on site. Organised activities (July/Aug. and Xmas). Cooking facilities. Washing machines and dryers. Chemical disposal. Bungalows and caravans to rent.

Charges 1998: Per person DM 8.50; child (3-14 yrs) 4.50; pitch 7.50 - 12.00; electricity 3.50.

Reservations: made for any period without deposit. Address: Lackenhäuser 8, 94089 Neureichenau. Tel: 08583/311. FAX: 08583/91079.

3850 Campingplatz Strandbad Aga, nr Gera

Quiet site within reach of Dresden, Leipzig and Meissen.

Now that access has become easier there is much interest in seeing the historic cities of the east and Aga is within reach of Dresden, Leipzig, Meissen, Colditz and other interesting towns. Situated in open countryside on the edge of a small lake, with individual, fenced pitches for stays of more than a couple of days, overnighters are placed on an open area. All places have electricity. A new sanitary building is at one side of but near to all pitches, with free hot water to the washbasins, a few of which are in cabins and to the sinks; hot showers are on payment. These include a large (4 x 4 m.) room for wheelchair users. The restaurant/bar is also new and is open long hours. There is a small but well stocked shop and in high season a kiosk for drinks, ice creams, etc. The lake is used for swimming, boating and fishing and there is a small children's playground on one side (close to a deep part). Entertainment is organised in July and the friendly, enthusiastic owner is improving the facilities each year.

How to find it: From the A4 /E40 Chemnitz - Erfurt autobahn take the Gera exit (no. 58) then the B2 towards Zeitz, following Bad Köstritz signs at first then site signs.

General Details: Open 1 April - 1 Nov. Electrical connections (10A). Restaurant. Shop. Kiosk (June - Sept). Children's playground. Swimming and watersports in the lake. Entertainment in high season. Riding 1 km. Football 200 m. Washing machines and dryers. Motorcaravan service facilities. No English spoken.

Charges 1998: Per adult DM 7.00; child (3-13 yrs) 3.50; motorcaravan 12.00; caravan or tent 9.00; car 3.00; m/cycle 1.00; electricity 3.00 + 0.80 per kw/h; drainage 3.00.

Reservations: Write to site. Address: Reichenbacherstrasse 18, 07554 Aga. Tel: 036695/20209. FAX: as phone.

3847 Campingplatz Auensee, Leipzig

Impressive city site open all year.

It is unusual to find a first-class site in a city, but this large, neat and tidy site is one, with just 167 pitches of which about 140 are for short-term tourers. It is set in a mainly open area with tall trees and very attractive flower arrangements around, with some chalets and trekker huts for rent in the adjoining woodland, home to the shoe-stealing foxes. The individual, numbered, flat grassy pitches are large (100 sq.m.), all with electrical connections and five on hardstanding, arranged in several sections with a separate area for young people with tents. Three central points supply water and barbecue areas are provided. Children of all ages are well catered for with forts, an ultra-modern climbing frame all on sand, a 'super' swing and an enclosed court with tennis, football and basketball. Five sanitary buildings (all in one area), have differing mixtures of very modern equipment and offer free hot water to the washbasins (many in cabins), although tokens from reception are needed for the showers, which are smallish but have good dividers, and the hairdryers. You need a key for well equipped rooms for mother and baby and disabled visitors. Dishwashing facilities are both open air and inside and there is also a kitchen, a laundry room and two chemical disposal rooms. All the buildings can be heated. A modern restaurant and snack bar (breakfast, lunch and supper), plus a small shop are open all year round and there are rooms for television, billiards and children. Although public transport to the city centre goes every 10 minutes from just outside the site, it is far enough away from roads and the airport to be reasonably peaceful during the day and very quiet overnight. A popular site, it is best to arrive early.

> **How to find it:** Site is well signed 5 km. from Leipzig centre on the B6 to Halle. From the A9 Berlin - Nurnberg take exit 17 at Schkeuditz onto the B6 towards Leipzig.

> **General Details:** Open all year, as are shop, restaurant and snack bar. Electrical connections (10A). Entertainment rooms. Several children's play areas. Bicycle hire. Fishing close by. Barbecue with seating. Kitchen. Motorcaravan service point. Chemical disposal. English usually spoken.

> **Charges 1998:** Per person DM 8.00; child 6-13 yrs 4.00, 14-18 yrs 6.00; caravan 17.00; motorcaravan 15.00; tent 10.00; small tent (under 4 sq.m.) 6.00; car 5.00; electricity 0.75 per kwh.

> **Reservations:** Contact site. Address: Gustav-Esche Strasse 5. 04159 Leipzig. Tel: 0341/4651 600.

3833 Camping LuxOase, Kleinröhrsdorf, nr Dresden

Developing lakeside family site.

This is a pleasantly situated new park about half an hour from the centre of Dresden, in a very peaceful location with good facilities. It is owned and run by a progressive young family. On open grassland with views across the lake (access to which is through a gate in the site fence) to the woods and low hills beyond, this is a sun-trap with little shade at present. There are 150 large touring pitches (plus 50 seasonal in a separate area), marked by bushes or posts on generally flat or slightly sloping grass. All have electricity and 100 have water and waste water facilities. At the entrance is an area of hardstanding (with electricity) for late arrivals. A brand new sanitary building (with card entry) provides modern facilities with showers, washbasins and private cabins, all with free hot water, a large mother and child shower, baby changing room, units for disabled visitors and two units for hire. Also here are rooms for cooking, laundry, dishwashing and chemical disposal. More pitches are being developed and there are plans for minigolf, tennis, a sports field and another sanitary building. The main entrance building contains reception, where there is a large amount of tourist information, the shop (open am. all year, pm. in high season), the bar/restaurant (all year, in high season for lunch as well) and sauna. In front of the building is some very modern children's play equipment on bark and you may swim, fish or use inflatables in the lake. There are many interesting places to visit apart from Dresden and Meissen, with the fascinating Nationalpark Sächsische Schweiz (Saxon Switzerland) on the border with the Czech Republic offering some spectacular scenery.

> **How to find it:** From the A4 (Dresden-Bautzen) take exit 85 towards Radeberg, soon following signs to site via Leppersdorf and Kleinröhrsdorf.

> **General Details:** Open all year, as are shop, bar and restaurant. Electricity connections (10A). Bicycle hire. Lake swimming. Fishing. Children's play area. Sauna. Chemical disposal. Motorcaravan service point. Opera tickets organised at reception. Public transport to Dresden close by.

> **Charges 1998:** Per person DM 6.50 - 7.00; child (2-14 yrs) 4.00 - 4.50; motorhome or caravan and car 12.50 - 13.00; electricity 4.00 - 3.00; dog 3.50 - 4.00.

> **Reservations:** Contact site, also for details of offers. Address: Familie Lux, Arnsdorfer Strasse 1, 01900 Kleinröhrsdorf. Tel: 035952 56666. FAX: 035952 56024.

3842 Camping am Schlosspark, Lübbenau

Riverside site in delightful, woodland setting close to old town.

Situated about halfway between Berlin and Dresden, this is an attractive proposition for a short visit as well as a night stop, about 10 minutes walk from the centre of the much visited old town, on the banks of the Hauptspree. Taking 130 units (they may be rather close together at very busy times), 90 have electrical connections. Mainly on flat grass but with a central hardstanding area for motorcaravans and a long area for tents at the end. The refurbished sanitary facilities are quite good with free hot water for the washbasins (some private cabins), but the showers require tokens from reception. A kitchen is provided as well as dishwashing, laundry and chemical disposal. A small shop for basics is at reception, and there are more in the adjacent town, with a 'Tiergarten' café just 200 metres away and the Schloßpark hotel and restaurant through the woods. You can paddle your own boat, go for a trip in a gondola, explore the Spreewald or just look round the interesting old town from this pleasant site. A public path passes between the site and the river; insect repellent is advisable.

How to find it: From the A13 (Berlin - Dresden) take exit 9, turning right onto the B115 into Lübbenau then following site signs. At weekends the town is busy, requiring extra care and patience.

General Details: Open all year, as are the small shop and the café (200 m). Small children's play area. Boat and bicycle hire. Fishing. Motorcaravan service point. Huts and bungalows for hire.

Charges 1998: Per person DM 7.00; child (6-14 yrs) 3.50; caravan or motorhome 14.00; tent 5.00 - 8.00, acc. to size; dog 3.00; electricity 1.50 connection plus 2.50 per day.

Reservations: Essential probably only for May Day and Whitsun weekends. Address: 03222 Lübbenau. Tel: 03542/3533. FAX: as phone.

3827 Camping Sanssouci Gaisberg, Potsdam

Peaceful lakeside site for city visits to Potsdam and Berlin with excellent facilities.

The maturing site, about 2 km. from Sanssouci Park on the banks of the Templiner See in a quiet woodland setting, is looking very attractive, reflecting the effort which has been put into its development. A new reception, shop, takeaway, restaurant and bar have been added, and all pitches now have electricity, water and waste water connections. Tall trees mark out the 180 flat, grassy tourist pitches, and access is good for larger units. There is a separate area for tents by the lake. Sanitary facilities consist of one smallish toilet block of a good standard and, 50 m. further in, an excellent, very modern block containing free hot showers, washbasins in private cabins with hot water, and facilities for babies, dishwashing (1 DM) and laundry, plus a very good facility for wheelchair users. Reception staff are helpful with English spoken and a useful English language information pack is available for local attractions. The pool, sauna, solarium and skittle alley at the nearby Hotel Semiramis may be used by campers. Free transport in the mornings and evenings is operated by the site to the public transport stop, saving you the long walk.

How to find it: From A10 take Potsdam exit 7, follow B1 to within 4 km. of city centre then sign to right for camp. Or A10 exit 12 on the B2 into town and follow signs for Brandenburg/Werder. Site is southwest of Sanssouci Park on the banks of the Templiner See off Zeppelinstrasse 1,200 m. along a woodland drive.

General Details: Open 1 April - 4 Nov. Electricity connections (6A). New restaurant. Shop. Rowing boats, motorboats and pedaloes for hire. Fishing. Swimming in the lake. Children's play area in central woods. Bicycle hire. Washing machine and dryer. Chemical disposal. Site closed to vehicles 13.00-15.00 hrs.

Charges 1999: Per adult DM 11.40 - 13.10; child (2-15 yrs) 2.50; pitch 12.80 - 13.70; local tax 0.90; dog 6.90; electricity 3.50. Special low season offers. No credit cards.

Reservations: Not normally necessary. Address: An der Pirschheide/Templiner See 41, 14471 Potsdam. Tel: 0331/9510988. FAX: as phone. E-mail: recra@campingweb.com. Internet: http://www.campingweb.com.

3830 DCC Camping Am Krossinee, Schmockwitz, Berlin

Useful base for visiting Berlin.

The Deutcher Camping Club site here is efficiently run and there are daily coach tours (with tickets from reception) and public transport to the city both available from the site entrance, the journey by car to the city centre taking about 45 minutes. The Krossinsee is one of many clean lakes in the southeast of Berlin and is suitable for swimming, fishing and boating, with access by key through a gate from the woodland site. More than half the 450 pitches are for tourers. They are of varying but reasonable size, mainly on flat grass, most with electrical connections and a fair amount of shade. A separate area is set aside for tents. The sanitary facilities are of above average quality for a city site, situated in a modern building with plenty of private cabins, smallish showers (token from reception), hand and hair dryers, a baby room and a well equipped unit for disabled visitors. A kitchen and dishwashing room plus a separate laundry complete the provision. Near the entrance are a mini-market, a restaurant and a snack-bar which is open daily for breakfast, lunches and evening meals.   *continued overleaf*

3830 DCC Camping Am Krossinee (continued)

A small fenced area with children's play equipment (mainly climbing) is on sand and earth. For visits in high season you should try to arrive as early as possible as reservations are not taken.

How to find it: From southeast Berlin on the A10 ring road take exit 19 (Niederlehme) to Wernsdorf, then follow signs to Schmockwitz and site.

General Details: Open all year. Electricity connections (10A). Shop and snack bar (Apr - Oct). Restaurant. Lake swimming, fishing, boating (hire facilities) windsurfing school and woodland walks. Kitchen and dishwashing facilities. Laundry. Bicycle hire. Berlin coach trips (all year).

Charges 1998: Per adult DM 9.50; child (6-14 yrs) 4.50; pitch 12.50; hiker plus small tent 7.00; dog 3.00; electricity 2.50 plus 0.80 per kwh.

Reservations: Made for groups only. Address: Wernsdorfer Straße 45, 12527 Berlin. Tel: 030/675 8687. FAX: 030/675 9150.

3815 Azur Camping Ecktannen, Waren am Müritzsee

Large woodland site in German 'Lake District', midway between Berlin and Rostock.

Müritz is in the 'Land of 1000 Lakes' in one of Germany's 13 National Parks and has a surface area of 48 square miles. The site is at the northeast tip of the Müritzersee, although trees screen out a view of the lake, and slightly above it. There is direct access to the water with small jetties for boats, a bathing beach of sand and a lakeside restaurant. There are 330 touring pitches (all with 10A electricity) and further areas for tents. They are in undulating woodland, either under tall pines or in clearings where tree stumps have been left and small saplings are growing. The toilet arrangements are in two quite reasonable buildings with free hot water in the basins, the showers and for dishwashing. There is a small kiosk for basics in high season and a restaurant close by. If you are looking for a quiet (out of high season), simple site 'in the heart of nature', you may well enjoy a stay here.

How to find it: Follow the B192 southeast from Waren following Azur international signs.

General Details: Open 15 March - 15 Nov. Restaurant by lake just outside site. Town facilities 4km.

Charges 1998: Per adult DM 9.00; child (2-12 yrs) 6.00; pitch 12.00; dog 4.00; electricity 3.80.

Reservations: Not necessary. Address: 17192 Waren am Müritzsee. Tel: 03991/668513. FAX: 03991/664675.

Naturist Sites:

The naturist sites featured in this guide (the site numbers are prefixed with 'N') are:

N036 Rutar Lido (Austria), N2004 Camping Naturiste de Riva Bella and N3408 Camping Le Sérignan Plage Nature (France), N580 Flevo-Natuur Netherlands, N8537 Naturist Camping El Templo del Sol and 8752 Camping Naturista El Portus (Spain)

HUNGARY

There are many interesting areas of Hungary for the tourist apart from Budapest (for which you should allow at least a couple of days) and Lake Balaton (around 70% of the visitors here are German) and the British are warmly received. The Danube Bend in the northwest is justifiably popular, as is the northeast hills area (Eger and Miskolc), with the spectacular stalactites in the large cave system at the border with Slovakia in Aggtelek (north of Eger). The interesting towns of the Great Plain to the east of the Danube have a great Magyar tradition and there are many Thermal baths (often at campsites) to enjoy. There are also several notable wine areas and you can purchase quality wines at low prices. West of the Danube appears rather more advanced, while in the east and north it is still common to see agricultural workers with scythes and few tractors. There has been a rapid advance in the general standard of campsites, although the majority still have communal (single sex) changing for showers. All sites, however, have British style WCs. Most sites require payment in cash. It is advisable and convenient to use public transport when visiting Budapest. It is useful to know that the Hungarian tourist organisation (IBUSZ) has offices in most towns where you can also change money. Opening hours Mon-Sat 08.00-18.00/20.00 and 08.00-13.00 on Sundays. Hungarian National Tourist Information is handled in the UK by:

The Danube Travel Agency Ltd, 6 Conduit Street, London W1R 9TG. Tel: 0171 493 0263

Population
10,471,000 (1995); density 113 per sq. km.

Capital
Budapest.

Climate
There are four fairly distinct seasons - hot summer (June-Aug), mild spring and autumn very cold winter with snow.

Language
The official language is Magyar, but German is widely spoken, and English and French are also spoken particularly by those engaged in the tourist industry in the west of the country.

Currency
Hungarian forints (ft) come in notes of 10, 20, 50, 100 and 500 ft. When you change cash keep receipts - necessary to convert money at the end of your visit - it is illegal to export Hungarian currency. You can change money at any IBUSZ or regional tourist office, at most large hotels or campsites. Banks can be slow and exchange rates are the same everywhere.

Banks
Open Mon-Fri 09.00-14.00, Sat 09.00-12.00.

Post Offices
Usually open Mon-Fri 08.00-17.00/18.00, Sat. 12.00-14.00/18.00, but it is quicker to buy stamps at tobacconists.

Telephone
To call from the UK the code is 0036 followed by area code less initial 0, and number. From Hungary dial 06 followed by the area code. International calls from Hungary can be dialled direct from red or grey phone boxes but it may be easier through the international operator (09).

Public Holidays
New Year; 15 March; Easter Mon; Labour Day; Whitsun; Constitution Day, 20 Aug; Republic Day, 23 Oct; Christmas, 25, 26 Dec.

Time
GMT plus 1 (summer BST plus 1).

Shopping
Open Mon-Fri 10.00-18.00, Sat 10.00-14.00. Food shops open Mon-Fri 07.00-19.00, Sat 07.00-14.00. Home produced products, including food and restaurant meals are cheap by western standards. There appears to be no shortage of goods with articles being sold by the roadside and from garages and gardens. Traditionally Hungarians take their main meal at midday so there is a better range of dishes in the restaurants at midday. All eating places display signs indicating their class from I to IV which gives some guide to comparative prices. Set menus are good value.

Motoring
Main roads are very good, as is signposting. Dipped headlights are compulsory at all times. Most of the few motorways are single carriage, single lane and care is needed.
Fuel: On motorways and in large towns petrol stations open 24 hours otherwise 06.00-20.00. Eurocard accepted at some petrol stations.
Tolls: are payable on the M1 from the Austrian border to Györ and on the full length of the M5 (Budapest - Kiskunfelegyhaza); from '99 also on the M3 (Budapest - Fuzesabony) eastward.
Speed Restrictions: Caravans and motorhomes (3.5 tons) 31 mph (50 kph) in built up areas, caravans 44 mph (70 kph) and 50 mph (80 kph) on other roads and motorways respectively, motorhomes 50 mph (80 kph) and 75 mph (120 kph) respectively.
Parking: The centre of Budapest is closed to traffic. Do not park in places where you would not park in the UK.
Overnighting
Not allowed outside campsites.
Note: Camping Gaz can be difficult to obtain.

Useful Address:

National Motoring Organisation
Magyar Autoklub (MAK), FIA & AIT, Romer Floris utca 4a, Budapest 11. Tel: 1 212 2938.

510 Ózon Camping, Sopron

Peaceful and comfortable edge of town site close to the border.

Sopron was not over-run by the Turks or bombed in WW2, so 350 historic buildings and monuments have remained intact, making it the second major tourist centre after Budapest. It also has a music festival from mid-June to mid-July and is close to the Löverek hills. This surprisingly pleasant campsite is just over 4 km. from the centre, with the modern, chalet style reception at the entrance from where the oval site opens out into a little green valley surrounded by trees. There are also many trees within the site offering shade. The concrete access roads lead to 60 numbered grass pitches, all with electricity (6A). Some with water and waste water also are in the lower level on the left, where siting is more difficult for caravans. They are mostly flat, some with a slight slope, separated by hedges and vary from 40 sq.m. for tents up to 80 sq.m. for larger units. The sanitary facilities are in two buildings which are identical except that the one by reception has a laundry (free) whilst the other, near the swimming pool, has a sauna. They each have six fully controllable, curtained, hot showers (communal changing) close to the washbasins, so it could possibly be cramped here. British style WCs. Both blocks have free cookers, fridges and dishwashing. A small open air pool and paddling pool opens end May - Sept. There is a pleasant restaurant with good value meals above the friendly, helpful reception which also offers basic essentials, tourist information and money exchange. One member of staff spoke English on our last visit. Other shops at 50 and 500 m.

How to find it: From the A3 south of Wien, follow roads 16 (Kingenbach) and 84 to Sopron. Site is on road to Brennerberganya, well signed in Sopron.

General Details: Open 15 April - 15 Oct. Restaurant (all season). Essentials and money exchange at reception. Shops 150 m. Swimming pool (15/5-15/9). Sauna. Tennis 2 km. Fishing 1.5 km. Bicycle hire and riding 2 km. Bus service to town centre. Bungalows for hire.

Charges 1999: Per pitch incl. electricity DM 16.00; person 6.50; child (under 10) 4.50; dog 4.50. No credit cards.

Reservations: May be advisable in high season and are made if you write in German. Address: 9400 Sopron, Erdei Malomköz 3. Tel: 99/331-144. FAX: 99/331-145.

512 Camping-Gasthof Pihenö, Györ

Small friendly site on main Budapest - Vienna road.

This privately owned site makes an excellent night stop when travelling to and from Hungary as it lies beside the main no. 10 road, near to the end of the motorway to the east of Györ. It is set amidst pine trees with pitches which are not numbered, but marked out by small shrubs, in a small clearing or between the trees. With space for about 25 units, all with electrical connections (6A), there are also a dozen simple, one roomed bungalows and four en-suite rooms for hire. On one side of the camp, fronting the road, are two pleasant restaurants with terrace (menu in English) and the management offer a very reasonably priced package (if desired) which includes pitch and meals. The site has added a solar heated swimming pool, with a children's pool. The single, small toilet block has free hot water in washbasins. There are just two showers for each sex with pre-mixed hot water (10 ft for one minute) and curtained, communal dressing space. British style WCs. There is a room for washing clothes and dishes with a small cooking facility. A very friendly German speaking owner runs the site and a new restaurant with his wife who speaks a little English.

How to find it: Coming from Austria, continue through Györ following signs for Budapest. Continue on road no. 10 past start of motorway for 3 km. and site is on left. From Budapest, turn right onto road no. 10 at end of motorway, then as above.

General Details: Open 1 April - 30 Oct. Restaurant with good menu and reasonable prices. Swimming pool (10 x 5 m, open June -Sept). Bungalows and rooms for rent. Bread orders at reception previous evening.

Charges guide: Per pitch DM 4.00; person 2.00; electricity 1.00. Less 10% for stays over 4 days, 20% after 8.

Reservations: Write to site. Address: Oláh Ferenc, 9011 Györszentivan, Kertvaros 10. Tel/Fax: 96/316 461.

513 Panorama Camping, Pannonhalma, nr Györ

Very peaceful, pretty, hillside site.

In 1982 this became the first private enterprise campsite in Hungary and it offers a very pleasant outlook and peaceful stay at the start or end of your visit to this country. It is situated just 20 km. southeast of Györ, on a hillside with views across the valley to the Sokoro hills. On the edge of the village, it is just below the 1,000 year old Benedictine monastery, which has guided tours. The 75 numbered, hedged pitches (30 with 10A electricity) are on terraces, generally fairly level but reached by steepish concrete access roads, with many trees and plants around. The sanitary facilities are quite satisfactory with a small building near reception and a larger unit half-way up the site. They provide a total of 6 controllable, curtained, hot showers with curtained communal changing, 12 washbasins also with hot water and 8 British style WCs. Hot water is available for dishwashing and laundry.

continued overleaf

513 Panorama Camping (continued)

There are benches and a small, grass terrace below reception from where you can purchase beer, local wine and soft drinks, etc. Occasional big stews are cooked in high season, otherwise there is a good value restaurant 400 m. away in the village and a shop for essentials at 150 m. Hourly bus service to Györ.

How to find it: From no. 82 Györ - Veszprém road turn to Pannonhalma at Ecs. Site is well signed - the final approach road is fairly steep.

General Details: Open 1 May - 30 Sept. Bar and meals (1/6-15/9). Rest room with TV. Shops and restaurant close in village. Small children's play area. Table tennis. Fishing 4 km. Riding 3 km. Money exchange. Cooking facilities. Laundry. Chemical disposal. Rooms to let. No English spoken.

Charges 1998: Per adult Forints 400; child (2-14 yrs) 200; pitch 600; dog 150; electricity 300; local tax 100.

Reservations: Advisable for high season - write in German. Address: 9090 Pannonhalma, Fenyvesalza 4/A. Tel: 96/471 240.

511 Dömös Camping, Dömös, nr Esztergom

Pleasantly situated site on the Danube Bend between river and hills.

The area of the Danube Bend is a major tourist attraction and here at Dömös is a modern, friendly, peaceful site with large pitches and easy access. The Danube is just over 50 m. away and quite fast flowing. With Budapest just 45 km, Esztergom (the ancient capital of Hungary) 15 km. and the small town of Visegrad, with its impressive cliff fortress close by, this could make an ideal base from which to explore the whole area. There are about 100 quite large pitches, of which 80 have 6A electricity, in sections on flat grass, numbered and divided by small plants and some with shade from mature trees. Opposite the smart reception which has an under-cover terrace, is a small cafe, also with a terrace, and a little further along is the modern, long, brick built sanitary building. This is tiled and has sliding doors. Beyond the laundry are very satisfactory ample, large showers with individual changing and pre-mixed hot water, open washbasins and then toilets (British style). At the top of the site is an inviting open-air swimming pool with a grass lying out area and tiny children's pool. Alongside is a large bar with pool tables and table football, beside which is a dishwashing and cooking area (free). A small children's play area on grass is here, just before the 7 self-contained accommodation units for hire. Sightseeing tours are arranged and, for '98, horse-drawn carriage trips.

How to find it: Site is between the village and the Danube off road 11 Esztergom - Visegrad - Szentendre.

General Details: Open 1 May - 15 Sept, as is cafe. Bar (15/5-1/9). Shop (1/6-31/8). Swimming pool ((20 x 10 m, all season). Village facilities 300 m. Bicycle hire. Fishing 50 m. Tennis adjacent. Riding 1 km. Mountain walking tours. Laundry. Chemical disposal. English spoken.

Charges 1998: Per pitch, caravan and car Ft. 550; car 160; tent 450; adult 480; child (2-14 yrs) 350; electricity 300; local tax 200. Payment in cash only.

Reservations: Not normally made, but may for British visitors for period 15/7-15/8. Address: 2027 Dömös, Duna-Part (winter: Dömös Kft, 2500 Esztergom, Bottyán J. u. 11). Tel: 33/482-319 (winter tel/fax: 33/414-800).

516 Camping Zugligeti Niche, Budapest

Satisfactory, friendly site with easy access to Budapest.

Car parking is as difficult in Budapest as it is in any large town - Zugligeti Niche is the nearest camp to the tourist centre of the town with good public transport links. The site started life as a tram terminus and when this use was discontinued, it was turned into an acceptable camping site. The narrow entrance has an old tram car on either side, one used as the reception bureau, the other for snacks and basic food supplies. The entrance road, with hardstanding caravan places on either side, passes under a road bridge to similar pitches further up. Small terrace clearings have been made amidst the trees on the steep hill to one side of the caravan area which are only suitable for small tents with parking nearby for cars. The site has made clever use of the space available. The old tram station is now an attractive restaurant. The whole situation is a quiet one near the chair lift to the summit of the Janos mountain. Sightseeing tours are organised. This is a pleasant, friendly site although the sanitary arrangements are not quite up to our normal standards, although hot water is free and toilets are British style. The English speaking owner welcomes British guests.

How to find it: Take the Budakeszi exit from the Austria - Budapest M1 motorway, from where it is well signed at all junctions (look for squirrel logo). From the M0 ring road take M1 exit, then through Budakeszi.

General Details: Open all year. Restaurant (all year). Kiosk with basic supplies (1/5-1/10). Supermarket 500 m. Chemical disposal. Swimming pool and other entertainments at Margarit Island, 20 mins. by public transport.

Charges 1999: Per person Ft. 900; child 450; car or m/cycle 550; caravan or motorcaravan 1,900; tent 550; electricity 450; local tax 50. Payment in cash only.

Reservations: Necessary for August; write to site. Address: Camping Zugligeti Niche, Zugligeti ut. 101, 1121 Budapest. Tel: 01/200 83 46. FAX: as phone.

AR Discount
Less 10%;
welcome drink.

515 Fortuna Camping, Törökbálint, nr Budapest

Attractive site close to bus terminal for city centre.

This pretty site lies at the foot of a hill with views of the vineyards, but Budapest is only 25 minutes away by bus (stop 1 km). Surrounded by mature trees, the owner, Csaba Szücs, will proudly name all 150 varieties of bushes and shrubs which edge some of the pitches. A large, modern terraced restaurant with very reasonable prices saves the weary traveller from cooking. The open air swimming pool will help you to cool off in summer. Concrete and gravel access roads lead to the terraces where there are 120 individual pitches, all with electricity (16A, long leads may be needed), 14 with water, on slightly sloping ground. A field area provides for group bookings, with separate facilities. Four sanitary blocks have free hot water to washbasins and showers. There are extra toilets for disabled people. Washing up facilities, plus six cookers in a sheltered area. Herr Szücs and his family will endeavour to make your stay a comfortable one and his daughter will organise tours to Budapest or the surrounding countryside, and also explain the mysteries of public transport in Budapest.

How to find it: From the M1 Györ - Budapest, exit for Törökbálint following signs for town and then site. Fortuna is beyond and far better than the Flora site. Also accessible from the M7 Budapest - Balaton road.

General Details: Open all year. Restaurant and bar (1/5-30/10). Shop (15/6-31/8 or essentials from reception, order bread previous day). Swimming pool (15/6-31/8). Small children's play area. Excursions organised. Washing machine. Chemical disposal. Motorcaravan services. English spoken.

Charges 1998: Per person DM 6.00; child (4-14 yrs) 4.00; pitch 9.00; electricity 4.00.

Reservations: Advised for high season. Address: 2045 Törökbálint. Tel: 23/335 364. FAX: 23/339 697.

518 Jumbo Camping, Üröm, Budapest

Modern, thoughtfully developed site in northwest outskirts of Budapest.

On a hillside, with attractive views of the Buda hills and with public transport to the city from 500 m. away, this is a pleasant and comfortable, small site (despite the name). It is possible to park outside the short, steepish entrance which has a chain across. Reception, where you will be given a comprehensive English language information sheet, doubles as a cafe/bar area and bread orders are also taken here. The concrete and gravel access roads lead shortly to 55 terraced pitches of varying size, with hardstanding for cars and caravan wheels as well as large hardstandings for motorhomes. All pitches have 6A electricity (may need long leads) and some have water and waste water. They are mostly divided by small hedges and the whole area is fenced. The sanitary facilities are most satisfactory, with large, controllable free showers (communal changing). British style WCs. Dishwashing undercover and a terrace with chairs and tables. A small open-air swimming pool is beside the small children's play area.

How to find it: Site is signed on roads to Budapest - nos. 11 from Szentendre and 10 from Komaron. It is also approachable via Györ on M1/E60 and Lake Balaton on M7/E71.

General Details: Open 1 April - 31 Oct. Cafe where bread, milk and butter available. Shop and restaurant 500 m. Barbecue area. Swimming pool (10/6-10/9). Children's play area. Riding and tennis can be arranged. Bus to city 500 m. every 30 minutes. Washing machine, iron and cooking facilities on payment. Chemical disposal. English spoken and information sheet provided in English.

Charges 1999: Per pitch DM 2.50 - 8.00, acc. to size and season; adult 5.00; child (3-14 yrs) 3.00; electricity 2.00; dog 2.00; local tax 100 forints. Less 5% in low seasons. Payable in cash only (Forints). No credit cards.

Reservations: Write to site. Address: 2096 Üröm, Budakalászi ut 23-25. Tel: 26/351-251 or 60/310-901. FAX: 26/351-251.

522 Peisöczy Camping, Tokaj, nr Nyiregyhaza

Relaxing, shady, riverside site at small town.

From the middle of June to the middle of September, this site gets quite busy, but either side of these dates it is quiet and very relaxing. Set on the banks of the wide River Tisza, the level grass pitches, about 60 in number, are close together and narrow but quite long, off a hard circular access road so siting should be quite easy. All the pitches have electricity and there is much shade. The sanitary unit has external entry WCs (British style) and curtained showers with communal undressing. Clean but basic and looking a little tired now, they are located near the entrance, where there is also the high season reception, shop and restaurant. At other times, site yourself and a gentleman will call during the evening to collect the fee. Shops for basics outside the main season are in the town over the bridge, a 600 m. walk. There may well be some day-time noise from watersports on the river but it is very quiet by night. This is a useful base for visiting northeast Hungary, not far from the Ukraine and Romania. Tokai wine is produced in this area (similar to sherry, a strong desert wine).

How to find it: Tokaj is east of Miskolc and north of Debrecen. Site is just south of the river bridge on road no. 38. (Note: beware the noisy campsite signed on the other side of the road).

General Details: Open 15 April - 10 Oct. Shop and restaurant (15/6-15/9). Town 600 m. No English spoken.

Charges: Not available - probably modest.

Reservations: Advised for high season, but in German - otherwise arrive early. Address: 3910 Tokaj, Pf.36. Tel: 47/352-626.

HUNGARY

520 Autós Caraván Camping, Eger

Large, city site in attractive touring area of northern Hungary.

The city of Eger and its surroundings (including the very attractive Bukk mountain area between Eger and Miskolc) provide much for the tourist to see, indeed far too much to list here, but reception will provide lots of information for you. Most of the city attractions are quite close together, with good public transport from close to the site, which is just 2.5 km. from the centre. The site is large, with over 180 pitches, all with electricity (10A). They are on gently sloping hardstanding with much grass, lots of shade and tarred access roads and there is a separate tent area. The quietest part is at the reception end for, at the other side of the camping area, there are many bungalows and dormitory accommodation much used by young people. However, it is quiet at night thanks to 24 hour security patrols. The sanitary facilities are rather basic, with a couple of toilets behind reception, a `portacabin' style facility to the right (nearest for many pitches) with cold water washbasins and a large block at the end of the camping area which was in need of maintenance (used by the youngsters) with dishwashing and chemical disposal facilities. However, all facilities were clean when we visited in '98. At the far end of the park is an area with three outlets selling drinks (local wine), snacks and ices, beyond which is a large restaurant and another set in a cave. There are shops just outside the site entrance.

How to find it: Site is in the northern outskirts of the city on the west side of road no. 25. It is well signed (not usual camp signs at entrance) by a Shell station, just before the last high-rise flats.

General Details: Open 15 April - 15 October. Restaurant. Bar. Snacks. Money exchange (including travellers cheques). English spoken.

Charges guide: Per person DM 4.00, children under 6 free; caravan 8.00; motorcaravan 6.00; tent (2 person) 4.00; electricity incl. except for tents (2.00). Student card less 20%.

Reservations: Probably not necessary. Address: 3300 Eger, Rákóczi ut 79. Tel: 36/410 558. FAX: 36/411 768. E-mail: egertour@mailagria.hu. Internet: http://www.agria.hu./egertourist.

524 Dorcas Centre and Camping, Debrecen

Friendly, welcoming Christian `Aid Organisation' site.

Debrecen is an interesting old town, close to the Hortobagy National Park and convenient if you are looking for a break travelling to Romania or the Ukraine. Dorcas is a Dutch Christian organisation and the campsite provides holidays for special causes - indeed, while we were there, 40 children arrived from Chernobyl for their first trip abroad. The site is about 10 km. from Debrecen in a forest location, fenced and covered with trees. The 60 flat and grassy touring pitches are off tarmac access roads, arranged in four groups. Some pitches are divided by hedges, others marked out by trees and all have electricity available (6A). There is room in the large tenting area for more units, also with electricity, if necessary. The large sanitary building is tiled and of a rather open design. It is situated between the tenting area and the main pitch areas and is of reasonable quality with free hot water to the washbasins and controllable, large, curtained showers (external changing), British WCs; also facilities for dishwashing and laundry (key at reception). A very pleasant restaurant and terrace offers very good value meals (with menu in English) and a shop for basics. Small swimming pool (June - Aug.) and children's play equipment are next to it on grass. Through the site is an area for walks and a lake for fishing.

How to find it: From Debrecen take road no. 47 south for 4 km. then left towards Hosszupalyi for 6 km. Site is signed on the right.

General Details: Open 1 May - 30 Sept. Shop. Restaurant. Swimming pool (June-Aug). Lake and riding nearby. Good walks. Church services (in English) fortnightly or more often if requested. Bicycle hire. English spoken. Chalets and apartments for rent.

Charges 1998: Per unit incl. 2 adults US dollars 12.00; extra person 4.00; child (6-12 yrs) 2.00; local tax 0.50 (or HUF 120). Credit cards accepted.

Reservations: Probably unnecessary, but contact site. Address: 4002 Debrecen, Pf.146. Tel/Fax: 52/441-119.

526 Jonathermal Motel-Camping, Kiskunmajsa, nr Szeged

Large, well run site with marvellous indoor and outdoor pool complex.

Situated 3 km. to the north of the town of Kiskunmajsa, a few kilometres west of road no. 5 (E75) from Budapest (140 km.) to Szeged (35 km.) this is one of the best Hungarian campsites. The camping area is large, reached by tarred access roads and the unmarked pitches are located in several areas around the motel and sanitary buildings. Some shade is available and more trees are growing. All the 120 large pitches have 4A electricity and are set on flat grass where you place the pitch number allocated to you. Reception is part of the smart bar and rest room just to the right of the entrance. A brand new sanitary block provides first class facilities with free hot water for controllable showers and washbasins in private cabins and a unit for disabled visitors. Rubbish bins are provided and there is a separate chemical disposal facility, well marked. A kiosk sells bread (to order), fresh fruit and vegetables, groceries, stamps and postcards. *continued overleaf*

526 Jonathermal Motel-Camping (continued)

The pool complex is accessed via a path through the site fence which leads firstly to the entrance to the fishing lake, then past the restaurant. Entrance to the complex costs 300 forints for adults, 200 for children (weekly tickets available) which gives you a huge 100 x 70 m. open air pool with a beach along one side, the indoor pool, children's pool, thermal, sauna and cold dip. In addition there is an open air thermal pool, a children's playground with carved wooden animals, plus swings on grass, giant chess, volleyball, tennis and minigolf plus various places to eat and drink. Massage is available on payment. This professionally run site offers the chance of relaxation but is also well placed for visiting Szeged, Csongrad or Szolnok, as well as being close to the borders with Romania and the former Yugoslavia.

How to find it: From no. 5 (E75) Budapest - Szeged road take the Kiskunmajsa exit and site is well signed 3 km. north of the town.

General Details: Open all year. Kiosk on site for bread, etc. (shop opposite entrance, 120 m). Restaurant by pool complex, others near. Large swimming and thermal complex with other facilities (as above). Fishing (day permits available). Bicycle hire. Riding 300 m. Launderette. Chemical disposal. Motel rooms for rent. German spoken.

Charges 1999: Per person DM 4.00 - 5.00; child (6-14 yrs) 1.00 - 2.00; pitch 3.00 - 4.00; tent 1.50 - 2.00; electricity 4.00; dog 3.00; plus local tax.. Less 5-10% for longer stays. Credit cards accepted.

Reservations: Possibly necessary mid-July - mid-Aug. Address: 6120 Kiskunmajsa, Kokut 26. Tel: 77/481 855. FAX: 77/481 013.

530 Kék-Duna Camping, Dunaföldvár

Pleasant site on the banks of the Danube.

Dunaföldvár is a most attractive town of 10,000 people and you are in the heart of it in just two or three minutes by foot but, as a 'town site', Kék-Duna is remarkably peaceful and easily reached via the wide towpath on the west bank of the Danube. Apart from the obvious attractions of the river, with a large island opposite and pleasant walks available, the ancient town has a most interesting museum, the 'Burg', with a genuine dungeon and cells, Roman relics and with a panoramic view of the town and river from its top floor. There are too many places of interest within easy reach to list here, but we thoroughly endorse our reader's recommendation of this site. It is small, fenced all round and locked at night, with flat concrete access roads to 40 pitches. All have 3A electricity, the first half being open, the remainder well shaded. The modern, tiled sanitary building has a nicely decorated ladies' section and offers 10 curtained, controllable, free showers with communal changing. British style WCs. The rest of the facilities are also of above average standard. There is a small shop and café open from mid June (otherwise it is a short walk into the town), washing machine and dishwashing (outside with cold water). A thermal swimming pool is 200 m (under the same ownership).

How to find it: From no. 6 Budapest - Pecs road take exit at Dunaföldvár for Kecskemed road no. 52, and follow until slip road on right which leads on to the riverside towpath. Site is well signed.

General Details: Open 15 April - 15 Oct. Shop and café (from mid June), town shops close. Tennis 50 m. Riding 200 m. Washing machine. Excursion information. English speaking receptionist. Bungalows for hire.

Charges guide: Per adult Forints 200 - 340; child 150 - 180; pitch 480 - 580; tent 290 - 390; electricity 100.

Reservations: Advised for July/Aug. or arrive early. Address: 7020 Dunaföldvár, Hösök Tere 12. Tel: 75/341 529.

504 Autós 1 Camping, Zamárdi, nr Siófok

Large site with own direct access to Lake Balaton.

If you have young children or non-swimmers in your party, then the southern shores of the lake at this site are ideal as you can walk out for nearly 1 km. before the water rises to more than a metre in depth. It is a large site with 545 pitches, most with 6A electricity, and there must be the possibility of noise in high season, although it was peaceful during our visit in early June. There are many tall trees and the more attractive pitches are near the lakeside, some unshaded ones alongside the water. The rest, in a large central area which comprises the majority of the site, are flat, individual ones on grass. They are hedged and vary from small to quite large. A separate tent area is at the back of the site, adjacent to three very modern, tiled sanitary buildings (plus an old one on the right of the entrance). The facilities provide free hot water to push-button showers with private changing and warm to washbasins with single taps. British style WCs (no paper). Satisfactory dishwashing and laundry facilities (key from reception). Other amenities include a restaurant and a soft drinks and ice cream bar by the entrance and a bar further in, all with terraces. A shop is only 50 m. Plenty of children's wooden play equipment is on sandy grass by the lake. Next door is a large water slide area and boats for hire.

How to find it: Exit road no. 7/E71 between Balatonföldvár and Siófok towards Tihany, and the site is well signed.

General Details: Open 17 May - 8 Sept. Shop adjacent. Restaurant (from June). Lake swimming, fishing and non-powered boating. Money exchange. Bath (key from reception). Chemical disposal. Table tennis.

Charges guide: Per person DM 5.10 - 7.80; child 2.55 - 3.90; pitch 11.10 - 17.00; tent and car 7.40 - 11.40; electricity 1.50; dog 5.10 - 7.80; local tax (over 18 yrs) 1.00 - 1.50.

Reservations: Write to site. Address: 8261 Zamárdi. Tel: 84/348 863 FAX: 84/348 931. When closed write to Siotour AG Hauptbüro, 8600 Siófok, Szabadság tér 6. Tel: 84/310 900. FAX: 84/310 009.

503 Panorama Camping, Cserszegtomaj, nr Hévíz

Peaceful, hillside site near west end of Lake Balaton.

Camp sites around Lake Balaton generally have the disadvantage of being close to the main road and/or the railway, as well as being extremely busy in high season. Panorama is popular too, but is essentially a quiet site and also has the benefit of extensive views from the flat, grass terraces. Only the young or very fit are recommended to take the higher levels with the best views of all. There are just 50 pitches varying in size from fairly small to quite large (100 sq.m.), all with 10A electricity, with the lower terraces having fairly easy access. The site is a sun-trap and there is not much shade from the trees. Reception is to the left of the entrance and here also is a small shop and a delightful restaurant, with terrace, offering really good value meals at lunch-time and in the evenings. A little way up the site is the very satisfactory, tiled and heated sanitary building which has free hot water to large, curtained, controllable showers (communal changing), washbasins, dishwashing and British style toilets. At the right side of the building is a ladies' hairdresser and massage room. Local attractions include Lake Balaton (7 km.), whilst at Hévíz is the famous, large, warm water lake and there are castles to visit. The friendly proprietors speak no English but are keen to welcome British visitors and have a dictionary. As at many Hungarian sites, you will probably find German and or Dutch visitors who would assist if you speak no German at all.

How to find it: Site is about 2 km. north of Hévíz on the road signed to Sümeg. There is a long, hard access road with a large sign.

General Details: Open 1 April - 31 October. Shop (Mon - Sat, 07.30 - 10.00). Restaurant with bar. Washing machine. Ladies' hairdresser. Massage. Many walking and cycling opportunities. Riding and tennis 3 km.

Charges 1998: Per caravan incl. 2 persons DM 17.00, tent 13.00; electricity included.

Reservations: Advisable for May and Sept (the busiest months), and made in German. Address: 8372 Cserszegtomaj, Panorama Köz 1. Tel: 83/314 412.

508 Diana Camping, Aszófö, nr Balatonfüred

Large, quiet, friendly site in forest near Lake Balaton. ·

This very large site of about 12 hectares was developed many years ago as a retreat for the 'party faithful'. Now just 4 hectares are used by Mr and Mrs Keller-Toth, who have leased it from the Balatontourist organisation. There is, naturally, much woodland around which you may wander. There are 27 hedged pitches of 120 sq.m. (where two 60 sq.m. ones have been joined) on grass. Many have shade from trees, as have about 65 smaller individual ones. The remainder are amongst the trees which mark them out. There is no exact number of pitches, but about 200 units are taken in all, with 150 electrical connections (2 pin, 6 or 10A) on sloping ground. The toilet facilities are admittedly old but kept very clean with chemical disposal in the men's. The shower block across the path is open 6.30-10.30 am. and 4.30-10 pm. The very smart, new ladies' section has large, push-button showers with seat, divider and private dressing, whilst the facilities for men are older (with communal changing). Washbasins, for both men and women, are older with just two with hot water for each and many with cold only, shelf, mirror and razor points. At the back of the block is the entrance to a splendid, new children's washroom (key from reception), with 3 shower/baths 2 of which are designed for handicapped children. There is a well stocked shop, with the laundry just beyond with modern machines (key from reception). A large kitchen has 6 cookers but the cold water dishwashing is probably the least attractive area. The fair-sized restaurant, open all season, has tables, benches and flowers in troughs outside. In front of this area is under cover table tennis and the play area where animation is organised in high season. There are swings, a climbing frame on grass, a sand-pit and a slide into sand.

How to find it: From road 71 on the north side of the lake, turn towards Aszófö just west of Balatonfüred, through the village and follow the signs for about 1 km. along access road (bumpy in places).

General Details: Open 26 April - 28 Sept. Shop (open 08.00-17.00 low season or 22.00 high season) Restaurant (all season). Children's play area, with animation in high season. Volleyball. Tennis. Table tennis. Post box and telephones. Many walking opportunities. Lake 3 km.

Charges guide: Per caravan, car, electricity and incl. 3 persons DM 16.00 - 20.00, acc. to season; tent 2.70 - 3.00; motorcaravan 6.20 - 7.60; person 2.60 - 3.20; child (6-14 yrs) 1.30 - 1.60; dog 1.30 - 1.60. Local tax (over 18 yrs) 0.80. Special rates for disabled persons. Eurocheques up to 23,000 Forints accepted.

Reservations: are possible - write to site. Address: 8241 Aszófö. Tel: 87/445 013. FAX: as phone.

531 Sugovica Camping, Baja

Pleasant town site near Croatian and Yugoslavian borders.

If you are exploring Southern Transdanubia or en route south, then Baja is an acceptable stop, on the east banks of the Danube. The site is on a small island, quiet and relaxed, next to the hotel which owns it, where there is a small swimming pool on payment and a terraced restaurant. The 180 fair sized pitches (80 sq.m), all with 10A electricity and 7 with hardstanding, are on flat, grassy, firm ground, easily accessed from tarred roads and with some shade from the many trees. *continued overleaf*

531 Sugovica Camping (continued)

Behind reception are a small shop, TV room, laundry and a kitchen with fridge and freezer. The sanitary facilities are just about adequate, with British style WCs and free hot water to open washbasins and showers (communal changing), all clean when seen.

How to find it: Site is on Petoti island (sziget), well signed from just southwest of the junction of roads 51 from Budapest and 55 from Szeged, the bridge being close to a cobbled town square.

General Details: Open 1 May - 30 Sept. Shop. Restaurant 50 m. Swimming pool (8 x 15 m),large town pool 100 m. TV room. Tennis. Table tennis. Riverside walks. Fishing. Chemical disposal. No English spoken.

Charges 1999: Per adult DM 3.00; child (6-14) 1.50; pitch 6.00; tent 4.00; electricity included; local tax 1.00.

Reservations: not made. Address: 6500 Baja. Tel: 79 321 755. FAX: 79 323 155.

509 Balatontourist Camping Füred, Balatonfüred

Large, international camp on lake, with a wide range of facilities.

This is a holiday village rather than just a camping site, pleasantly decorated with flowers and shrubs, with a very wide range of shops, restaurants, fast food bars and sporting activities. Directly on the lake with 800 m. of access for boats and bathing, it has a large, grassy lying out area, a small beach area for children and various watersports are organised. Mature trees cover about two thirds of the site giving shade, with the remaining area being in the open. The 1,034 individual pitches of 60-120 sq.m. and all with electrical connections, are on either side of hard access roads on which pitch numbers are painted. Along the main road, which runs through the camp, are shops and kiosks, with the main bar/restaurant and terrace overlooking the lake. This building also has a 4-lane bowling alley and video games room. Close by is a street of fast food bars, about 10 in all, offering a variety of Hungarian and international dishes with attractive outdoor terraces under trees. There are other bars and restaurants dotted around the camp. There are five toilet blocks situated at various points around the site. The oldest are showing signs of age, while the two smart, modern blocks have free hot water in the showers (communal changing), with cold water only in washbasins, British style WCs and hot water for dishwashing and laundry. A range of sporting activities is available, the most spectacular of which is a water ski drag lift for which four towers have been erected in the lake with skiers pulled around the circuit. Windsurfing and sail boats permitted. A swimming pool was added in '98 and new sanitary facilities. Security is good. Many trips and pleasure cruises are organised. The site is part of the Balatontourist organisation.

How to find it: Site is just south of Balatonfüred, on the Balatonfüred - Tihany road and is well signed. Gates closed 1-3 pm. except Sat/Sun.

General Details: Open 2 April - 16 Oct. 270,000 sq.m. Electricity connections (4/10A). Numerous bars, restaurants, cafes and food bars (1/5-15/9). Supermarket. Stalls and kiosks with wide range of goods, souvenirs, photo processing. Money exchange. Duty free shop (hard currency). Hairdresser, etc. Sauna and solarium. Post office. Fishing. Water ski lift. Windsurf school. Children's play area on sand. `Bouncy castle'. Bicycle hire. Dodgem cars. Pedaloes. Tennis courts. Minigolf. Fitness centre. Video games room. Bowling alley. Riding 500 m. Washing machines. Chemical disposal. No dogs are accepted. Wide range of bungalows for rent.

Charges 1999: (Prices in DM, payable in Forints). Per caravan pitch incl. 3 persons and electricity 70 sq.m. 25.00 - 37.00, 100 sq.m. 28.00 - 44.00; tent pitch (60 sq.m.) incl. 3 persons 18.00 - 29.50; extra person (max. 6) 4.00 - 6.00; child (2-14 yrs) 2.00 - 4.00; local tax 1.60 per person over 18 yrs. Credit cards accepted.

Reservations: Write to site. Address: 8230 Balatonfüred. Tel: 87/342-872 or 343-823. FAX: 87/342-341. E-mail: cfured@balatontourist.hu.

507 Balatontourist Camping Kristóf, Balatonalmádi, Lake Balaton

Small site with excellent toilet facilities.

This is a delightfully small site with just 33 pitches and many tall trees. Square in shape, the generously sized pitches are on either side of hard roads, on level grass with some shade and 4A electricity. The site lies between the main road and railway line and the lake. There is no direct access to the lake, but a public lakeside area adjoins the camp, and site fees include the entry price. This is a neat little site with a kiosk for breakfast and dinner (steaks, etc) drinks, bread, milk and ice cream, with village shops and supermarket just 50 m. away. The excellent toilet facility is part of the reception building, with British WCs and free hot water in the washbasins and showers (more now built and all with own changing). Laundry room with hot water and a washing machine (small charge), a kitchen and sitting room with TV. Balatonalmádi is at the northern end of the lake and well placed for excursions around the lake or to Budapest, and suitable for anyone seeking a small, friendly site without the bustle of the larger sites.

How to find it: Site is on road no. 71 at Balatonalmádi, between the railway line and the lake and is signed.

General Details: Open 1 May - 13 Sept. 12,000 sq.m. Meals from kiosk. Children's playground. Tennis. Fishing. Bicycle hire 500 m. Riding 3 km. Laundry room. Chemical disposal. Bungalows for rent. Good English is spoken.

Charges 1999: (Prices in D.Marks, payable in Forints). Per pitch DM 12.00 - 20.00; adult 4.00 - 6.00; child 2.00 - 4.00; local tax 1.10 per person over 18 yrs. Credit cards accepted.

Reservations: Essential July - 20 Aug. Write to site for booking form. Address: 8220 Balatonalmádi. Tel: 88/438-902. FAX: 88/338-902. When closed contact: Balatontourist, 8201 Veszprém, POB 128. Tel: 88/426-277. FAX: 88/426-874. E-mail: ckristof@balatontourist.hu.

IRELAND

The Republic of Ireland, with its green, mist shrouded countryside, its loughs and wild indented coastline, must be explored slowly to enjoy the hospitality and savour the locals love of music - you can expect to find traditional music sessions in the pubs of all the towns of any size along the west coast. Indeed the west coast draws most visitors, be it to visit the mystical lakes and glens of Donegal, Galway and the Aran Islands or the dramatic peaks of the Ring of Kerry, but Dublin with its mix of youthfulness and tradition, the mountains and monastic ruins of County Wicklow, the cities of Cork and Waterford, are not to be missed. It is not only the landscape but 'the people' which brings visitors to Ireland.

Bord Failte (Irish Tourist Board), 105 New Bond Street, London W1Y OAQ

Tel: 0171 518 0800. Travel Enquiries: 0171 493 3201. Fax: 0171 493 9065

Population
3,500,000, density 50 per sq. km.

Climate
Similar to the UK but even wetter!

Language
English. The traditional tongue Gaelic (Gaeltacht) is spoken mainly in the southwest.

Currency
The Irish pound, known as the punt, divided into 100 pence. Denominations are 1, 2, 5, 10, 20, 50 pence and IR£1, notes of IR£5, 10, 20, 50 and 100.

Banks
Open Mon-Fri 10.00-12.30 and 13.30-15.00 (Thur 13.30-17.00), but note many small country towns are served by sub-offices open only certain days.

Post Offices
Main offices open Mon-Fri 09.00-17.30 and Sat 09.00-13.00. Stamps are sometimes available in shops selling postcards.

Telephone
To call the UK dial 00 44 followed by the local STD code omitting initial 0. From the UK dial 00 353 omitting the first 0 of the code plus number.

Public Holidays
New Year; St Patrick's Day, 17 Mar; Easter; 1st Mon in June; 1st Mon in Aug; last Mon in Oct; Christmas, 25 Dec.

Shops
Open Mon-Sat 09.00-17.30 or 18.00.

Motoring
Allow plenty of time when travelling in Ireland even though the roads are relatively uncongested. Poor road surfaces, unmarked junctions and poor weather conditions can delay. Signposting or the lack of them can be a problem. A good map is a necessity. Drive on the left as in the UK. A Green Card is advised as most policies provide only minimum coverage in the Republic of Ireland

Speed Limits: On certain roads, clearly marked, the speed limits are 40 mph (65 kph) or 50 mph (80 kph) - applying to a car and trailer as well.

Parking: As in the UK. Parking meters are in use - on the spot fines can be levied for offences.

Overnighting
It is possible to camp 'free' in areas where there is no registered site except in state forests (farmers will expect a pound or two).

1864 Knockalla Caravan and Camping Park, Portsalon

Family run park set amidst the breathtaking scenery of Donegal.

What adds to the popularity of this site is its location, nestling between the slopes of the Knockalla Mountains and Ballymastocker Bay. The fact that the beach here has been named 'the second most beautiful beach in the world' is not surprising. On entering this park, approached by an unclassified but short roadway, its elevated situation commands an immediate panoramic view of the famed Bay, Lough Swilly, Inishowen Peninsula and Dunree Head. The site is partly terraced giving an attractive, orderly layout with reception, shop and restaurant in a central position. The touring area is sited to the left of reception. All 50 pitches have electrical hook-ups and hardstanding, offering a choice of solely tarmac or with adjoining grass allowing for awnings. Tents are pitched on a lower level facing reception and to the far left of the tourers. Caravan holiday homes are placed around the right hand perimeter and to the rear of the park. The main sanitary block, a white, rough cast building, is situated in the touring section. Whilst not ultra modern in design, it is kept clean and fresh. There are washbasins, hand dryer, hair dryer, shaver points and showers (50p token) with hooks, soap dish, curtain divider and mat. Dishwashing area and campers' kitchen with hot water. An on site laundry service is operated by staff. There is a children's play area and TV/games room. Specialities at Knockalla are home made scones, apple cakes, jams, etc. plus a takeaway or table service (July/Aug). Full Irish breakfasts are served. Fishing and golf within 5 miles, riding and bicycle hire within 10 miles.

Directions: From Letterkenny take the R245 to Ramelton. Continue on R245 to Milford. Turn right onto R246 to Kerrykeel. In village turn left towards Portsalon and at second crossroads turn right onto Portsalon/Knockalla coast road. Turn right to park at sign.

Charges 1999: Per motorcaravan, caravan or family tent IR£10.00; awning IR£1.50; tent for 1 or 2 persons IR£7.00; extra person IR£2.00; electricity (5A) IR£1.00. No credit cards.

Open: 27 March - 17 September.

Reservations: Advised for July/Aug and B.H. w/ends. Address: Portsalon, Co. Donegal. Tel: 074/59108 or 53213.

1869 Greenlands Caravan and Camping Park, Rosses Point

Park with excellent facilities in the sand hills adjoining a championship golf course.

This is a well run park at Rosses Point, just off the N15 road, 8 km. from Sligo town. It is thoughtfully laid out with small tents placed to the front of reception and the hardstanding touring pitches separated from the trailer tent and caravan holiday home pitches which occupy the rear. The ground is undulating and adds interest to the overall appearance. Your view depends on where you are pitched - towards Coney Island and the Blackrock lighthouse, Benbulben Mountain or the seascape and the water lapping the resort's two bathing beaches. Sanitary and laundry facilities are modern and kept exceptionally clean, with WCs, washbasins, hot showers (50p token), razor and hairdryer points, mirrors and hand-dryers. Also dishwashing and laundry sinks, washing machine, dryer and iron. Electric hook-ups are available for touring units. Chemical disposal and motorcaravan service point. Night security. An information point and a TV room are located beside reception. There is a sand pit for children and a ground chess and draughts sets. A mini-market, restaurant and evening entertainment can be found in the village. Fishing and boat launching nearby (100 m.), bicycle hire 8 km. This is an excellent base from which to explore the `Yeats Country' and discover the beauty spots immortalised in his poems, such places as Lissadell, Dooney Rock, the Isle of Innisfree and the poet's burial place at Drumcliffe.

Directions: From Sligo city travel approx. 800 m. north on N15 road, turn left onto R291 signed Rosses Point. Continue for 6.5 km. and park is on right after village.

Charges 1998: Per unit high season: IR£7.50 plus 50p per person (family rate IR£10.00), low season IR£7.50, no per person charge; all season hiker/cyclist IR£5.00; electricity (5A) IR£1.00. Weekly rates available.

Open: Easter, then 21 May - 16 September.

Reservations: Contact park. Address: Rosses Point, Co. Sligo. Tel: (071) 77113 or 45618. FAX: (071) 45618.

1870 Gateway Caravan and Camping Park, Ballinode, Sligo

Family run park, convenient for the beauty spots immortalised by the poet W. B. Yeats.

This is the northwest's newest park and straight away it warrants the highest accolade for its excellent design and standards set. Its situation 1.2 km. from Sligo centre means this cultural city is easily accessible, yet Gateway's off-the-road location, screened by mature trees and fencing, offers a quiet relaxing environment. After the park entrance, past the family bungalow and to the left is parking space and the reception and services block which is fronted by columns and an overhanging roof with flower baskets and soft background music. Incorporated in this building are three separate rooms - one for TV, snooker and board games, the second for satellite TV and the third for selected video viewing. A passage divides the elongated building which also houses showers, WCs, washbasins and baby units in both the male and female areas. Showers, room for disabled visitors (WC and shower) are entered from the outside of this block which can be heated. In an adjacent building is a dishwashing area, laundry room, fully equipped campers' kitchen plus a large games room and a toddlers room with playhouses and fixed toys. A children's play area faces reception. There are 30 fully serviced touring pitches with hardstanding and satellite TV connection, 10 grass pitches with electrical hook-up for tents and 10 caravan holiday homes for hire. Touring pitches stand to the right and centre of the park, holiday homes to the left and rear, with tents at the top left. Evening relaxation could mean a 3 km. drive to romantic Half Moon Bay, or a drink in the fascinating surroundings of Farrells Brewery, which faces the park.

Directions: Site is 1.2 km. northeast of Sligo city, off the N16 Enniskillen - Belfast road. Approaching from the north on the N15, turn left at second traffic lights into Ash Lane, continue for 1.1 km. and turn left at traffic lights onto the N16 Sligo - Enniskillen road. Site entrance is on left in 50 m.

Charges 1998: Per unit incl. 2 persons IR£7.50; extra adult or child in July/Aug 50p; family rate IR£7.50 - 10.00; m/cyclist incl. tent IR£7.50; hiker or cyclist incl. tent IR£4.50; electricity (10A) IR£1.00.

Open: All year.

Reservations: Contact site. Address: Ballinode, Sligo, Co. Sligo. Tel: 071 45618. FAX: as phone.

IRELAND

1874 Cong Caravan and Camping Park, Cong, nr. Connemara

Family run touring park and hostel in a famous and scenic location.

It would be difficult to find a more idyllic and famous spot for a Caravan Park than Cong. Situated on the shores of Lough Corrib, Cong's scenic beauty was immortalised in the film 'The Quiet Man'. This park, which is immaculately kept, is 1.6 km. from the village of Cong, near the grounds of the magnificent and renowned Ashford Castle. The owner's house which incorporates reception, shop and the hostel, stands to the fore of the site. The 40 grass pitches, 36 with electricity, are placed at a higher level to the rear, with the tent area below and to the side - the policy on this site is for campers to 'choose a pitch' rather than have one allocated. Sanitary facilities and the hostel accommodation are entered from the courtyard area. These are tastefully decorated and kept clean. The campsite facilities include hot showers with curtains, hairdryers and washbasins. Also on site is a dishwashing area, launderette service, chemical disposal, central bin depot, barbecue, games room and extensive children's play area. Catering is also a feature. Full Irish or continental breakfast, dinner or packed lunch may be ordered, or home baked bread and scones purchased in the shop. When not spending time around the village of Cong with its picturesque river setting and Monastic relics, there is much to keep the active camper happy. Watersports, cycling, walking, climbing, caving and scenic drives can all be pursued. Riding or golf within 2 km, fishing and boat slipway 500 m. Bicycle hire on site. Not least of the 'on site' attractions at this park is a mini cinema showing 'The Quiet Man' film nightly all season.

Directions: Leave N84 road at Ballinrobe to join R334/345 signed Cong. Turn left at end of the R345 (opposite the entrance to Ashford Castle), take the next road on the right (approx. 300 m) and the park is on the right (200 m).

Charges 1999: Per adult IR£4.00; child IR£1.00; awning IR£1.50; electricity IR£1.50. Credit cards accepted

Open: All year.

Reservations: Contact park. Address: Lisloughrey, Lake Road, Cong, Connemara, Co. Mayo. Tel: (092) 46089. FAX: (092) 46448.

1878 Knock Caravan and Camping Park, Knock

Clean, friendly park with many local attractions including religious shrine.

This park is immediately south of the world famous shrine, which receives many visitors. Comfortable and clean, the square shaped campsite is kept very neat with tarmac roads and surrounded by clipped trees. The pitches are of a decent size accommodating 38 caravans or motorcaravans, 20 tents and 14 holiday caravans (for hire). All pitches have hardstandings (5 doubles) and 52 have electricity (13A), with an adequate number of water points. There is also an overflow field. The modern sanitary block, with good facilities for disabled visitors and a nice sized rest room attached, has 4 controllable hot showers (on payment) and adequate washing and toilet facilities. A laundry and dishwashing room is also part of this building. A children's playground is provided in the centre of the site. Because of the religious connections of the area, the site is very busy in August and indeed there are unlikely to be any vacancies at all for 14 -16 August. Besides visiting the shrine and Knock Folk Museum, local activities include golf, riding and fishing. This is also a good centre for exploring scenic Co. Mayo.

Directions: Take the N17 to the Knock site which is just south of the village. Camp site is well signed.

Charges 1998: Per unit IR£5.50 - 6.00, plus 25p per person (weekly IR£36 plus IR£1 per person); hiker or cyclist and tent IR£3.50 - 4.00; electricity IR£1.50.

Open: 1 March - 31 October.

Reservations: Taken for any length, no deposit, but see editorial for August. Address: Claremorris Road, Knock, Co. Mayo. Tel: (094) 88100 or 88223. FAX: (094) 88295.

1896 Lough Ree (East) Caravan and Camping Park, Ballykeeran, Athlone

Touring park alongside a river, screened by trees and reaching the water's edge.

Drive into the small village of Ballykeeran and this park is discretely located behind the main street. The top half of the site is in a woodland situation and after the reception and sanitary block, Lough Ree comes into view and the remaining pitches run down to the shoreline. There are 40 pitches, 20 with hardstanding and 35 with electricity. The toilet block, with partly tiled walls, is clean without being luxurious. It houses WCs, washbasins, razor and hairdryer points, mirrors and hot showers (50p). Chemical disposal. Dishwashing sinks are outside and a new laundry room has been added. A wooden chalet with accommodation and campers' kitchen is available for the use of campers and fishermen. A restaurant and singing pub are close. With fishing right on the doorstep there are boats for hire and the site has its own private mooring buoys, plus a dinghy slip and harbour. Golf or riding 4 km.

Directions: From Athlone take N55 towards Longford for 4.8 km. Park is in village of Ballykeeran, clearly signed.

Charges 1999: Per adult IR£2.50; child (under 14 yrs) IR£1.00; caravan and car IR£4.00; motorcaravan IR£3.00; family tent IR£2.00; hiker/cyclist and tent IR£3.00; awning IR£2.00; electricity IR£1.00. No credit cards.

Open: 1 April - 2 October.

Reservations: Contact park for details. Address: Ballykeeran, Athlone, Co. Westmeath. Tel: (0902) 78561 or 74414. FAX: (0902) 77017. E-mail: athlonecamping@tinet.ie.

1910 Camac Valley Tourist Caravan and Camping Park, Dublin

See colour advert opposite page 33

New touring park with top class facilities convenient for ferry ports and Dublin city.

This new campsite, opened in '96, is not only well placed for Dublin, but also offers a welcome stopover if travelling to the more southern counties from the north of the country, or vice versa. Despite its close proximity to the city, being located in the 300 acre Corkagh Park gives it a country atmosphere. The site entrance and sign are distinctive and can be spotted in adequate time when approaching on the busy N7. Beyond the entrance gate and forecourt stands an attractive timber fronted building. Its design includes various roof levels and spacious interior layout, with large windows offering views of the site and an exit to what will be a patio area. Housed here is reception, information, reading, TV and locker rooms plus sanitary facilities which include WCs, good sized showers (50p token) and central floor units with washbasins. There are also facilities for disabled people, baby room, laundry, washing up and chemical disposal. A second well designed sanitary block is now operational, also a children's playground with wooden construction play frames and safety base. A shop and coffee bar are open in June, July and August. There are 163 pitches, 50 for tents placed to the fore and the hardstandings for caravans laid out in bays and avenues with electricity, drainage and water points. Young trees separate pitches and roads are tarmac. Dogs not accepted in July/Aug. Fishing 8 km, bicycle hire 1.5 km,, riding 9 km, golf 6 km. After a day of sightseeing in Dublin, which can be reached by bus from the site, Camac Valley offers relaxation with woodland and river walks or a number of first class restaurants and pubs nearby.

> **Directions:** From north follow signs for West Link and M50 motorway. Exit M50 at junction 9 onto N7 Cork road. Site is on right of dual carriageway (by Green Isle Hotel) after 2 km. Clearly signed on N7 and from ferry ports.
>
> **Charges 1999:** Per unit incl. 2 persons IR£7.00 - 9.00, incl. up to 4 children IR£8.00 - 11.00; extra person IR£1.00; child (under 7 yrs) 50p; motorcyclist, cyclist or hiker with tent IR£3.00 - 4.00 per person; awning IR£1.00; extra small tent IR£3.00; electricity (10A) IR£1.00. Credit cards accepted.
>
> **Open:** All year
>
> **Reservations:** Advance bookings necessary. (max. stay operates at certain times). Address: Corkagh Park, Naas Road, Clondalkin, Dublin 22. Tel: (01) 464 0644. FAX: (01) 464 0643. E-mail: camacmorriscastle@tinet.ie.

1914 Valley Stopover and Caravan Park, Kilmacanogue

Small, family run park located in quiet, idyllic setting and convenient for Dublin ferries.

This neat and attractive ¾ acre park situated in the picturesque Rocky Valley could be used either as a transit site or for a longer stay. It has instant appeal for those who prefer the more basic 'CL' type site. There are 15 grassy pitches, 11 with electricity, 3 hardstandings, 2 water points, night lighting and a security gate. Toilet facilities, which were very clean when we visited, are housed in one unit and consist of 2 WCs with washbasins and a shower (50p). Dishwashing/laundry sink, a spin dryer, chemical disposal point, a campers' kitchen and hot water is available. A cooked Irish breakfast is available in the family guest house. Dairy products are available and bread can be ordered. Fishing 10 miles, bicycle hire 4 miles (can be delivered), riding 2 miles, golf 4 miles. Staying put here you are only minutes from Enniskerry which lies in the glen of the Glencullen river. Here you can enjoy a delight of forest walks, or visit Powerscourt, one of the loveliest gardens in Ireland. If wanting to be at the sea, travel 6 km. to Bray and you are in one of the oldest seaside resorts in the country. Small caravan to hire.

> **Directions:** Turn off Dublin-Wexford N11 road at Kilmacanogue - follow signs for Glendalough. Continue for 1.6 km and take right fork signed 'Waterfall'. Park is first opening on the left in approx. 200 m.
>
> **Charges 1999:** Per caravan or tent with car IR£7.00; motorcaravan IR£6.00; tent with bike IR£3.00; electricity £IR1.00; awning IR£1.00. No credit cards.
>
> **Open:** Easter - 31 October.
>
> **Reservations:** Advised for July/Aug; contact park. Address: Valleyview, Killough, Kilmacanogue, Co. Wicklow. Tel: 01 2829565.

AR Discount

Less 25% Easter - June or 7 nights for price of 6

1916 Moat Farm Caravan and Camping Park, Donard

Heart of the country experience within easy driving distance of Dublin or Rosslare.

Camping at its most idyllic is what can be enjoyed at this campsite. Here a true feel of the countryside abounds for it is part of a working farm environment and offers incredible vistas across a scenic landscape. Driving into the village of Donard in West Wicklow you little suspect that alongside the main street lies this tranquil 5 acre site. The entrance is approached by way of a short road where the ruins of a Medieval church overlook the forecourt and reception. Facing down the site is the sanitary block which is kept clean and includes WCs, large showers and washbasins. Facilities for visitors with disabilities, a well equipped laundry room with sink, washing machine, dryer and ironing board. Next to this is a TV room with easy chairs and a long window giving a panoramic view over the site and beyond. Chemical disposal facilities are at the end of this building and a campers' kitchen with sinks, fridge and freezer with ice pack facilities is beside the farmyard buildings. Three large barbecues and a patio area are provided. There are 40 pitches for caravans and tents. The pitches with hardstanding to the right, some sheltered by tall trees, occupy both sides of a broad avenue.   *continued overleaf*

IRELAND

1916 Moat Farm Caravan and Camping Park (continued)

These are spacious and incorporate awning and car space, and all have electricity and drainage points. Tents are pitched on the grass area to the centre and left. This site makes a good base for touring or going on foot, for this is a walker's paradise with a 30 minute circular walkway around the perimeter of the site. Riding on site. There is fishing (3 km), mountain climbing or sites of archaeological interest nearby. Bicycle hire 15 km, golf 13 km. Caravan storage available.

Directions: From south on N81 turn off 14 km. north of Baltinglass at old Tollhouse pub. Site is clearly signed.

Charges 1999: Per unit IR£8.00; adult IR£1.00; child 50p; tent (1 or 2 persons) IR£6.00; m/cyclist incl. tent IR£4.00; hiker or cyclist incl. tent IR£3.50; awning free; electricity (10A) IR£1.50. No credit cards.

Open: All year.

Reservations: Contact site. Address: Donard, Co.Wicklow. Tel: 045 404727. FAX: as phone.

1915 River Valley Caravan and Camping Park, Redcross Village

Friendly, family run park in small village in the heart of Co. Wicklow.

This well run park is in the small country village of Redcross. Although only 58 km. from Dublin, being based here you are in the heart of the countryside with beauty spots such as the Vale of Avoca, Glendalough and Powerscourt within driving distance, plus the safe beach of Brittas Bay 6 km. Although there are 80 caravan holiday homes, the 100 touring pitches are together in a separate area. There are 80 with electricity (6A) and, with a choice of hardstanding or grass. A luxurious new, central sanitary block with a modern, well designed appearance is a special feature. Hot water is available for dishwashing and there is a laundry area, chemical disposal and motorcaravan service points. Within this 12 acre site children can find day long amusement, whether it be `Fort Apache' the children's adventure playground, the new `tiny-tots' playground, or at the natural mountain stream where it is safe to paddle. They may, however, prefer to get to know the farm animals and birds in the pets corner. Other amenities include TV, games room, a tennis court, par-3 golf course and bowling green, plus a new sports complex with badminton courts and indoor football and basketball. An attractive wine and coffee bar with a conservatory is an inviting asset (1/6-31/8). Try `Ballykissangel' punch and get in the mood for a sing-a-long. An alternative may be the cosy atmosphere of the restaurant with many home made, traditional dishes. A late arrivals area has electric hook-ups, water and night lighting. Rally area and caravan storage. No dogs accepted in July/Aug. Fishing 4 miles, riding 2 miles, bicycle hire 9 miles.

Directions: From Dublin follow N11 Wexford road. Turn right in Rathnew, then left (under railway bridge) onto Wexlow-Arklow road. Continue for 11 km. and turn right at Doyle's Pub. Park is in Redcross Village, under 5 km.

Charges 1999: Per caravan or tent IR£6.00 - 8.00; person (over 2 yrs) IR£1.00; m/cycle, cyclist or hiker and tent IR£4.00 - 5.00; motorcaravan incl. 2 persons IR£8.00 - 9.00; electricity IR£1.00. No credit cards.

Open: 15 March - 23 September.

Reservations: Made with IR£10 deposit. Address: Redcross Village, Co. Wicklow. Tel/Fax: (0404) 41647.

930 Morriscastle Strand Caravan and Camping Park, Kilmuckridge

Family run park with direct access to sandy beach and convenient for Rosslare Port.

Whether you use this park as a stopover, or choose it as a longer stay destination, you will find it to be in a quiet relaxing location. Situated minutes from the pretty village of Kilmuckridge it offers well maintained and clean facilities. There are 145 privately owned caravan holiday homes on site but these are kept separate by high hedging. The entrance to the touring park is to the right of reception by way of a tarmac drive. This leads to the secluded, gently sloping, grass pitches which enjoy an open aspect overlooking marshland which attracts wild geese and ducks, whilst the sea brings in crabs, eels and fish. To the right of the site lie the sand-hills and paths to the beach. The 105 pitches are numbered and marked by concrete slabs, each has electricity (6A) and drainage point. Two sanitary blocks house all toilet facilities which include spacious WCs, washbasins and unisex showers (on payment). There is provision for disabled people, a baby bath, campers' kitchen, dishwashing area, launderette, chemical disposal and outside cold showers. Shop, snacks and takeaway in high season, also a games room, two tennis courts, football field and children's play area. The beach has a lifeguard in season. Kilmuckridge is approximately 3 km. with an assortment of shops, pubs offering nightly entertainment and top class restaurants, such as The Rafters, a picturesque spot which helps characterise this charming village. Golf 9 km, riding 16 km. Dogs are accepted only in certain areas (not with tents).

Directions: Site is 25 km. east of Enniscorthy. Travelling south on N11 Dublin/Wexford road branch onto R741 at Gorey. Continue for 19 km. to Ballyedmund. Turn left at petrol station and follow signs for Kilmuckridge and site.

Charges 1998: Per unit incl. 2 persons IR£7.00 - 10.00, incl. up to 4 children IR£9.00 - 11.00; extra person IR£3.00; child (under 7 yrs) IR£1.00; motorcyclist, cyclist or hiker with tent IR£3.00 - 4.00 per person; awning IR£1.00; extra small tent IR£3.00; electricity (5A) IR£1.00.

Open: 3 May - 28 September.

Reservations: Made with IR£10 deposit; contact site by phone or letter (use off season numbers Oct - April). Address: Kilmuckridge, Co. Wexford. Tel: (053) 30124/30212; off season (01) 453 5355. FAX: (053) 30365; off season (01) 454 5916. E-mail: camacmorriscastle@tinet.ie.

I933 Casey's Caravan Park, Clonea, Dungarvan

Family run site with direct access to the beach.

Set on 20 acres of flat grass, edged by mature trees, this park offers 284 pitches which include 118 touring pitches, all with electrical hook-ups and 30 with hardstanding. The remainder are occupied by caravan holiday homes. The central sanitary block, which is operated on a key system, has good facilities kept spotlessly clean, a top priority for the owner. There are showers on payment (50p), free hot water to open style basins and washing up sinks (10p). Also housed in this block is a small laundry with machine and dryer. A further luxurious and modern block has been added with an excellent campers' kitchen, laundry room and toilet for the disabled. There is direct access from the park to a sandy, blue flag beach with a resident lifeguard during July/Aug. Facilities on the site include a large children's adventure play area with bark surface, situated in its own field, (not supervised by camp staff). Near the site entrance is a games room with pool table, table tennis and amusements, crazy golf and TV lounge. A good leisure centre is adjacent should the weather be inclement. There is no shop, but two village stores are near the beach. The park is 5½ km. from Dungarvan, popular for deep sea angling, from which charter boats can be hired and three 18 hole golf courses are within easy distance.

> **Directions:** From Dungarvan centre follow R675 east for 3.5 km. Look for signs on the right to Clonea Bay and site. Site is approx. 1.5 km.
>
> **Charges 1998:** Per unit IR£10.50 - 11.00; hiker or cyclist IR£4.00; electricity IR£1.00.
>
> **Open:** 2 May - 7 September.
>
> **Reservations:** Are made, but not between 9 July - 15 Aug; contact park. Address: Clonea, Dungarvan, Co. Waterford. Tel: (058) 41919.

 # Casey's Caravan & Camping Park

Clonea, Dungarvan, Co Waterford Tel: 058 41919

Top class facilities	Two ablution blocks with laundry & kitchen
Playground	Games room and TV room
Electric sites for tents & tourers (5A)	EU Blue Flag beach
Dungarvan town 3½ miles	Two nearby shops with takeaway
Choice of scenic views to visit	Deep sea and river angling
18 hole golf course in easy reach	Adjacent hotel with 19 metre pool and leisure centre with bowling alley

---

I957 Creveen Lodge Caravan and Camping Park, Healy Pass

Immaculately run, small hill farm park, overlooking Kenmare Bay.

The address of this park is rather confusing, but Healy Pass is the well known scenic summit of the road (R574) crossing the Beara Peninsula, which lies between Kenmare Bay to the north and Bantry Bay to the south. Several kilometres inland from the north coast road (R571), the R574 starts to climb steeply southward towards the Healy Pass. Here, on the mountain foothills, is Creveen Lodge, a working hill farm. Although not so famed as the Iveragh Peninsula, around which runs the Ring of Kerry, the northern Beara is a scenically striking area of County Kerry. Creveen Lodge, which commands views across Kenmare Bay, is divided among three gently sloping fields separated by trees. Reception is to be found in the farmhouse which also offers guests a comfortable sitting room. A small separate block, which is well appointed and immaculately maintained, has toilets and showers, plus a communal room with a fridge, freezer, TV, ironing board, fireplace, tables and chairs. Full Irish breakfast is served on request. This park is carefully tended with neat rubbish bins and rustic picnic tables informally placed, plus a children's play area with slides and swings. To allow easy access, the steep farm track is divided into a simple one-way system. There are 20 pitches in total, 16 for tents and 4 for caravans with an area of hardstanding for motorcaravans. Electrical connections are available. This is walking and climbing countryside or, of interest close by, is Derreen Gardens. Fishing 2 km, bicycle hire 9 km, boat launching 9 km. Also available in the area are water sports, horse riding, 'Seafari' cruises, shops and a restaurant.

> **Directions:** Park is on the Healy Pass road (R574) 1½ km. southeast of Lauragh.
>
> **Charges 1999:** Per unit IR£6.00; person IR£1.00; hiker or cyclist incl. tent IR£3.50 per person; electricity £1.00.
>
> **Open:** Easter - 31 October.
>
> **Reservations:** Write to site with an S.A.E. Address: Healy Pass, Lauragh, Co. Kerry. Tel: (064) 83131.

IRELAND

1958 Waterville Caravan and Camping Park, Waterville, Ring of Kerry

Family run park in scenic location overlooking Ballinskelligs Bay.

Drive into Waterville and immediately feel welcome - the Horgan family place emphasis on being hospitable and attentive to their guests. The 60 touring pitches, many with hardstanding, are located in three areas. Some are convenient for reception, whilst others are pitched to the middle and rear. There is also a sheltered corner allocated to campers, with 21 caravan holiday homes (15 for hire), unobtrusively placed around the perimeter and centre, giving the park a spacious, neatly laid out appearance. Sitting high above the bay, the view in all directions is magnificent and the well tended grounds with plants, shrubs and cordyline trees gives a tropical appearance, especially on a fine sunny day. Three sanitary blocks are well maintained and clean. There are hot showers (50p token), facilities for disabled people, washing up and laundry areas, drying room, chemical disposal and motorcaravan service point. Campers' kitchen, shop (June-Aug) and TV room. Waterville is on the 'Ring of Kerry', convenient for all the scenic attractions for which the area is famed. Fishing, golf and bicycle hire within 3 km.

Directions: Travelling south on the N70, park is 1 km. north of Waterville, 270 m. off the main road.

Charges 1998: Per unit IR£7.00 - 7.50, incl. 2 persons IR£9.00 - 9.50 or family incl. IR£10.00 - 10.50; small tent (1 or 2 persons) IR£6.00 - 6.50; extra adult IR£1.00; child 50p; hiker or cyclist incl. tent IR£3.50; m/cyclist incl. tent IR£3.50 - 4.00; electricity (6A) IR£1.00; awning IR£1.50; hardstanding or extra car IR£1.00. No credit cards.

Open: Easter - 18 September.

Reservations: Made with fee IR£5 plus IR£15 deposit. Address: Waterville, Ring of Kerry, Co. Kerry. Tel: (066) 9474191. FAX: (066) 9474538.

1959 Fossa Caravan and Camping Park, Killarney

Mature, well equipped park in scenic location, 5½ km. from Killarney.

A 10 minute drive from the town centre brings you to this well laid out park which is instantly recognisable by its forecourt on which stands a distinctive building housing a Roof Top restaurant, reception area, shop and petrol pumps. The park is divided in two - the touring area lies to the right, tucked behind the main building, and to the left is an open grass area mainly for campers. Touring pitches, with electricity and drainage, have hardstanding and are angled between shrubs and trees in a tranquil, well cared for garden setting. To the rear at a higher level and discreetly placed are 45 caravan holiday homes. The toilet facilities are modern and kept very clean. A second amenities block is placed to the far left of the grass area beside the tennis courts. Other facilities, apart from a shop (April - Sept), takeaway and restaurant (June, July and Aug), include a TV lounge, campers' kitchen, laundry room, washing up area, children's play area, picnic area, games room, bicycle hire, night lighting and security patrol. Fishing 2 km, golf 1 km, riding 3 km. Not only is Fossa convenient for Killarney, it is on route for the famed 'Ring of Kerry', and makes an ideal base for walkers and golfers.

Directions: Park is to the right on the R562/N72, 5½ km. west of Killarney on the road to Killorglin.

Charges 1999: Per unit IR£3.00 - 3.50; adult IR£3.00; child 75p; electricity IR£1.00; m/cycle and tent per person IR£4.25 - 4.50; hiker or cyclist per person IR£3.50 - 4.00; awning IR£1.50; extra car IR£1.50. Credit cards accepted.

Open: 15 March - 31 October.

Reservations: Advisable in high season and made for min. 3 nights with IR£10 deposit. Address: Fossa, Killarney, Co. Kerry. Tel: (064) 31497. FAX: (064) 34459.

Useful Addresses - Ferry Services to Ireland

Irish Ferries	Stena Line	Swansea-Cork Ferries
0990 171717	0990 707070	01792 456116
Holyhead - Dublin *(3¼ hrs)*	Fishguard - Rosslare *(3½ hrs)*	Swansea - Cork *(10 hrs)*
Pembroke - Rosslare *(3¾ hrs)*	Holyhead - Dun Laoghaire	
	(99 mins - 3½ hours acc. to vessel)	

1961 Mannix Point Camping and Caravan Park, Cahirciveen

Quiet and peaceful, beautifully located seashore park.

It is no exaggeration to describe Mannix Point as a nature lovers' paradise. It is situated in one of the most spectacular parts of the Ring of Kerry, overlooking the Portmagee Channel towards Valentia Island. Whilst the park is flat and open, it commands splendid views in all directions, it is right on marshland which teems with wildlife (2 acre nature reserve) and it has immediate access to the beach and seashore. The owner has now planted around 500 plants with plans for around 1,000 more trees and shrubs. There are 42 pitches, 15 for tourers and 27 for tents, with electrical connections (6A) available. A charming old fisherman's cottage has been converted to provide reception. A cosy sitting room with turf fire, and emergency dormitory for campers, is a feature. Toilet facilities, now upgraded and immaculate, have well designed showers and free hot water. There is a modern campers' kitchen, laundry facilities, chemical disposal and motorcaravan service facilities. There is no television, but compensation comes in the form of a knowledgeable, hospitable owner who is a Bord Fáilte registered local tour guide. This park retains a wonderful air of Irish charm aided by occasional impromptu musical evenings. Watersports, bird watching, walking and photography can all be pursued here, but note that dogs are not allowed on site in June, July and August. Bicycle hire 800 m. riding 3 km, golf 14 km. Local cruises to Skelligs Rock with free transport to and from the port for walkers and cyclists. This is also an ideal resting place for people walking the Kerry Way.

Directions: Park is 250 m. off the N70 Ring of Kerry road, 800 m. southwest of Cahirciveen (or Cahersiveen) on the road towards Waterville.

Charges 1999: Per adult IR£3.25 - 3.40; child IR£1.50 - 2.00; caravan or motorcaravan IR£1.00 - 2.00; tent no charge; electricity IR£1.00; hiker/cyclist, incl. tent IR£3.25 - 3.40; m/cyclist IR£3.50 - 3.90. Book 7 nights, pay 6. Reductions for groups if pre-paid.

Open: 15 March - 15 October, the rest of the year also, if you write first.

Reservations: Made with deposit of one night's fee. Address: Cahirciveen, Co. Kerry. Tel/Fax: 066/9472806.

1964 The Flesk Muckross Caravan and Camping Park, Killarney

Seven acre park at gateway to National Park and Lakes, near Killarney town.

This family run park has undergone extensive development and offers high quality standards. Housed in one of Europe's most modern toilet blocks are well designed shower and toilet areas, decorated in co-ordinating colours. Every detail has been added, including soap dispensers, hand dryers, vanity area with mirror and hair dryer, also a baby bath/changing room. Pitches are well spaced out and have electricity (10A), water, and drainage connections; 21 also have hardstanding with a grass area for awnings. Other on site facilities include petrol pumps, supermarket (all year), delicatessen and café (March - Oct) with extra seating on the sun terrace. Laundry room, campers' kitchen with dishwashing sinks, a comfortable games room and chemical disposal point, plus night lighting and night time security checks. The grounds have been well cultivated with further shrubs, plants and an attractive barbecue and patio area. This is left of the sanitary block and is paved and sunk beneath the level roadway. Surrounded by a garden border, it has tables and chairs, making a pleasant communal meeting place which commands excellent views of Killarny's mountains. Fishing 300 m, boat launching 2 km.

Directions: From Killarney town centre follow the N71 and signs for Killarney National Park. Site is 1½ km on the left beside the Gleneagle Hotel.

Charges 1998: Per unit IR£3.00 - 3.50; adult IR£3.00; child 50p; extra car 50p; tent incl. 1 or 2 persons IR£2.50 - 3.00; m/cylist incl. tent IR£3.75 - 4.00; hiker or cyclist incl. tent IR£3.50 - 3.75; awning IR£1.50; electricity IR£1.00.

Open: 12 March - 31 October.

Reservations: Advisable in peak periods, write to park. Address: Muckross Road, Killarney, Co. Kerry. Tel: (064) 31704. FAX: (064) 34681. E-mail: killarneylakes@tinet.ie.

ITALY

Italy only became a unified state in 1861, hence the regional nature of the country today. There are 20 distinct regions and each one retains its own relics of an artistic tradition generally acknowledged to be the world's richest. However, the sharpest division is between north and south. The north is an advanced industrial area, relatively wealthy, whereas the south is one of the economically less developed areas of Europe. Central Italy probably represents the most commonly perceived image of the country and Tuscany, with its classic rolling countryside and the historical towns of Florence, Siena and Pisa, is one of the most visited areas. Venice is unique and as beautiful as its reputation suggests. Rome, Italy's capital, on its seven hills with its Roman legacy, is independent of both north and south. Naples, the natural heart of the south, is close to some of Italy's ancient sites such as Pompei.

Italian State Tourist Board, 1, Princes Street, London W1R 8AY Tel: 0171 408 1254 Fax: 0171 493 6695

Population
58,000,000, density 191.7 per sq. km.

Climate
Varying considerably between north and south; the south enjoys extremely hot summers and relatively mild and fairly dry winters, whilst the mountainous regions of the north are much cooler with heavy snowfalls in winter.

Language
The language is Italian derived directly from Latin. There are several dialect forms and some German is spoken near the Austrian border.

Currency
The unit of currency is the Lira (plural Lire). Notes are 1000, 2000, 5000, 10,000, 50,000 and 100,000; coins: 50, 100, 200 and 500.

Banks
Open Mon-Fri 08.30-13.30 and 15.00-16.00.

Post Offices
Open Mon-Sat 08.00-17.00/18.30. Smaller towns may not have a service on a Saturday. Stamps can also be bought in 'tabacchi'.

Time
GMT plus 1 (summer BST +1).

Public Holidays
New Year; Easter Mon; Liberation Day, 25 Apr; Labour Day; Assumption, 15 Aug; All Saints, 1 Nov; Immaculate Conception, 8 Dec; Christmas, 25, 26 Dec; plus some special local feast days.

Shops
Open Mon-Sat 08.30/09.00-13.00 and 16.00-19.30/20.00, with some variations in the north where the break is shorter and closing is earlier.
Food: Pizza must be sampled in Italy - thin and flat and cooked in traditional wood fired ovens. Also the ice-cream (gelato).

Telephone
To call Italy the code is 0039. From 19 June 98, you do need to include the `0' in the area code. To phone the UK dial 00 44 followed by the UK code minus the initial 0. As well as coins, tokens (gettone) from Tabacchi, bars and some news stands are used for calls; phone cards are available.

Motoring
Driving Licence: A valid EC (pink) UK driving licence is acceptable. The older green UK licence must be accompanied by an official Italian translation (from the Italian Tourist Office or the AA). However, DVLA will exchange licences for the pink EC version with the appropriate fee.
Tolls: Payable on the extensive and expensive Autostrada network. If travelling distances, save time by purchasing a `Viacard' from pay booths or service areas.
Speed limits: Caravans and motorhomes (3.5 tons) 31 mph (50 kph) in built up areas, 44 mph (70 kph) and 50 mph (80 kph) for caravans on other roads and motorways respectively, 56 mph (90 kph) and 80 mph (130 kph) for motorhomes.
Fuel: Petrol stations on the Autostrada open 24 hours. Elsewhere times are 07.00-13.00 and 16.00-19.30; only 25% open on Sundays. Most motorway service stations accept credit cards, apart from American Express and Diners.
Parking: There are 'Blue Zones' in all major towns. Discs can be obtained from tourist and motoring organisations or petrol stations. In Venice use the special car parks on the mainland, linked by ferry and bus to Venice.

Overnighting
Not generally allowed on open land. May be

6410 Camping Genova Est, Bogliasco, nr Genoa

Attractive, wooded site above Bogliasco just south of Genoa.

This site of 12,000 sq.m. is close to the Genoa motorways coming from the north or west and although it has limited facilities, it is near the town and the sea. The Buteros who run and own the site both speak good English and are very enthusiastic and anxious to please. The approach from the main road twists and climbs but should present no problem. There are 54 touring pitches. The two modern sanitary blocks are well maintained with free hot showers and a washing machine. New facilities include units with WC, washbasin and shower en suite. Small shop, a bar and restaurant. Free bus service to beach.

How to find it: From autostrada A10 take Nervi exit and turn left (south) on the SS1 towards La Spezia. In Bogliasco look for a sharp left turn with a large sign for the site. Follow narrow winding road for 2 km. to site.

General Details: Open 1 March - 30 Oct. Electricty (3/5A). Shop and bar/restaurant (Easter - 30 Sept). Fishing 1.5 km. Chemical disposal. Motorcaravan services. Mobile home and 3 caravans to let. Not suitable for disabled people.

Charges 1998: Per person L. 9,000; small tent 7,500; large tent or caravan 9,000; motorcaravan 12,000; car 4,500; m/cycle 3,500; electricity 2,500. Credit cards accepted.

Reservations: Contact site. Address: Via Marconi-loc Cassa, 16031 Bogliasco (GE). Tel/Fax: 010/3472053.

6400 Camping de Wijnstok, Imperia, nr San Remo

Pleasant, clean site on the Italian Riviera, where good ones are rare.

The Italian Riviera between Genoa and Ventimiglia has few campsites, and most become overcrowded. At de Wijnstok, however, you are at least assured of two important things: sufficient space (pitches are marked out) and a decent toilet block. This has been recently renovated with full tiling in all sections and 3 private washing cabins each for men and women with free hot water in them; mainly British style WCs; hot showers on payment. The site is on grassy soil with a number of trees and shade is also provided in the hot season by overhead matting screens; there is some shade on all pitches. Most pitches have 3A electrical connections. Reservation is advisable for July to mid-Aug., but as part of the site is not subject to reservation there is always a chance of finding space. De Wijnstok is only some 100 yards from the sea, which is reached via a tunnel under the road. The local beach is not one of the most attractive but it has been much improved. Open all year, there are, however, few facilities available outside the main season.

How to find it: Site lies on the western boundary of Imperia very close to the SS1 coast road. From autostrada A10 take exit for Imperia-Ouest and turn right on coast road (SS1).

General Details: Open all year. Approx. 10,000 sq.m. Pizzeria and shop (high season). Supermarket close, on main road. Bar. Toddler's paddling pool. Washing machines. Chemical disposal. Bungalows and caravans for hire.

Charges guide: Per person L. 7,900 - 8,200; child (0-8 yrs) 6,900 - 7,200; pitch 14,000 - 15,000; extra car or tent 8,000; electricity 3,000.

Reservations: made with L. 90,000 deposit and L 10,000 fee. Address: Via Poggi.2, 18100 Imperia. Tel: 0183/64986.

6405 Camping C'era una Volta, Villanova d'Albenga, Albenga, nr Alassio

Well situated site, back from sea, with swimming pools and other amenities.

A slightly unusual site, this one is about 8 km. back from the sea, situated on a hillside with some panoramic views, and with pitches on terraces in different sections of the site. The pitches - about 100 each for caravans (mainly on hardstandings) and tents - are not very large, perhaps 50 sq.m. and careful siting may be needed, although cars can park in different areas at busy times. In two parts, pitches are equipped with electricity (6A), water and drainaway. The toilet block has been modernised and provides WCs mainly of British style, washbasins with cold water, some with shelves, and free hot showers. The site has a good atmosphere and amenities include a swimming pool of 200 sq.m. and two children's pools in a pleasant setting, open all main season. There is a small section on its own, on the hilltop and fenced off, specially for naturists. Charges are high in season but the site is well organised and maintained. Private beach (4 miles) - reduced cost to campers.

How to find it: Leave autostrada A10 at Albenga, turn left and left again at roundabout for SS453 for Villanova. Follow Villanova signs to T-junction, turn left towards Garlenda, turn right in 200 m. and follow signs to site.

General Details: Open 1 April - 30 Sept. Shade in parts, but trees mostly small. Shop. Bar, pizzeria (April - Sept). Attractive restaurant. Takeaway (high season). Disco (July/Aug). Swimming pool complex (July/Aug). 2 saunas. Tennis. Large adventure playground. Fitness track with exercise points. Small but excellent gymnasium. Riding 500 m. Golf 2 km. Programme of organised sports and other events in season, also dancing or entertainment some nights. Chemical disposal. Bungalows for hire.

Charges guide: Per pitch incl. up to 3 persons L.30,000 - 64,000, acc. to season and type of pitch; extra person 10,000 - 16,000; VAT and electricity included. Discounts for longer stays in low season.

Reservations: are made for min. of a few days with 30% advance payment. Address: 17038 Villanova d'Albenga (SV). Tel: 0182/580461 or 582871. FAX: 0182/582871.

The holiday village 'C'era una Volta' extends over a tree- and bush-covered area of 100,000 sq.m. It is a unique park, where the green trees and the colour and fragrance of the flowers are an essential part of the holiday. The terraced site has small Villas, Bungalows, Apartments and Pitches for Caravans and Tents. Our Sport and Recreation Centre has **4 Swimming Pools,** Tennis, Mini-Tennis, Keep-fit-Trail, Children's play area, Dancing and Musical events, Fitness-room, **Tecnogym,** Naturist Solarium, Miniclub and Animation.

★★★★

C'ERA UNA VOLTA

CAMPING BUNGALOW CARAVAN
CENTRO TURISTICO

Camping Bungalow Caravan - Centro Turistico
C'ERA UNA VOLTA
I-17038 VILLANOVA D'ALBENGA (SV)
Riviera dei Fiori
Tel. 0039/0182580461 • Fax 0039/0182582871

ITALY - North West

6220 Camping Mombarone, Torre Daniele

Pleasant, small all year site suitable for en-route stop.

Mombarone is a pleasant, all year meadow site immediately off the SS26 and close to the small village of Torre Daniele and provides a useful transit stop. It could also offer a base to explore the Ivrea area with many good ski-ing areas close by. A small site, 80 of the 120 pitches are for permanent units. Electricity (2A) is available. Toilet facilities are provided in one block with British and Turkish style WCs and showers on payment. There is a small bar but shops and restaurants are a few minutes away.

How to find it: Take the Quincinetto exit from the A5 (north of Ivrea) and turn right on the SS26. Site is by the 45 km. stone, within 30 m. of the town.

General Details: Open all year. Bar. Shops and restaurants close. Fishing. Riding 5 km. Chemical disposal.

Charges 1998: Per person L. 5,000; child (under 10 yrs) 4,000; caravan 5,000; car 2,000; motorcaravan 7,000; electricity 2,000. No credit cards.

Reservations: Write to site. Address: Settimo Vittone Reg. Torre Daniele (TO). Tel: 0125/757907. FAX: 0125/757396.

6240 Camping Valle Romantica, Cannobio, Lake Maggiore

Attractive site with good facilities in scenic situation.

The pretty little town of Cannobio is situated between Verbania and Locarno on the western shore of Lake Maggiore. It could make a base for exploring the Lake and its islands, although progress along the winding lake-side road, hemmed in by mountains, is slow. Serious mountain walkers are well catered for, and the Swiss resort of Locarno is not far. Steamers cross the Lake, but the only car ferry across is between Verbania and Laveno. This lovely site was established about 40 years ago by the present owner's father, who planted some 20,000 plants, trees and shrubs, and there is much to interest botanists in this tree-clad mountain valley. The site has a swimming pool in a sunny position, and there is a pool in the river, where, except after heavy rain, children can play. The 130 pitches are on flat grass among the trees, which provide good shade and serve to separate the numbered pitches (but mean some narrow site roads). The three sanitary blocks have British style WCs, free hot water in the basins and showers, controlled by taps. Electricity (4A) is available on most pitches, although long cables are needed in some parts. The small supermarket is well stocked, and there is a pleasant bar/restaurant with waiter service and takeaway. Entertainment (folk music) is provided one night per week in the high season. The owner takes a keen and active personal interest in the site, and English is spoken.

How to find it: From the centre of Cannobio (from where site is signed) take the valley road towards Malesco; site is 1 km. on the right.

General Details: Open 19 March - 26 Sept. 30,000 sq.m. Shop. Bar/restaurant. Swimming pool (15/5-15/9). Table tennis. Children's playground. Fishing (licence required). Bicycle hire 1 km. Fridge boxes to hire. Washing machine. Chemical disposal. Motorcaravan services.

Charges 1999: Per person L. 10,000 - 11,000; child (1-12 yrs) 6,500 - 7,500; pitch 16,000 - 20,000; extra tent 5,000; electricity 5,000. No credit cards.

AR Discount
Less 10% in low season.

Reservations: Made for min. 11 nights with deposit (L. 120,000) and fee (80,000). Address: 28822 Cannobio (Verbania). Tel: 0323/71249. FAX: 0323/71360.

6245 Camping Riviera, Cannobio, Lake Maggiore

Good lakeside site near northern end of Lake Maggiore, with access for watersports.

Under the same active ownership as Valle Romantica, this site is directly on the lake with scenic views across the water and surrounding mountains. Over 280 numbered pitches, 220 with 4A electricity (long cables may be needed) are on flat grass either side of hard surfaced access roads, and are divided by trees and shrubs. The whole site has a well cared for appearance, and is certainly one of the best lakeside sites in the area. The five sanitary blocks, one new and two with facilities for the disabled, are of good quality with British style WCs and controllable hot water to basins and showers. The site shop is well stocked and the town is only a short distance. A pleasant bar/restaurant with covered terrace, provides waiter service and takeaway. Being situated between the main road and the lake, pitches near the entrance may suffer from traffic noise. There is a small jetty and easy access to the lake for boats, swimming and other watersports. Sailing and windsurfing regattas are organised. The site could make a suitable base for exploring the area, although progress on the busy winding road may be slow!

How to find it: Site is by the lake side, just north of the town of Cannobio. There are several sites nearby, and care should be taken not to overshoot Riviera as turning round could be difficult!

General Details: Open 19 March - 17 Oct. 22,000 sq.m. Shop. Bar/restaurant with takeaway. Pizzeria. Fridge boxes for hire. Fishing (licence required). Boat slipway. Sailing and windsurfing schools. Bicycle hire 500 m. Washing machines. Chemical disposal. Motorcaravan service point.

Charges 1999: Per person L. 10,000 - 11,000; child (1-12 yrs) 6,500 - 7,500; pitch 16,000 - 20,000; extra tent 5,000; electricity 5,000. No credit cards.

AR Discount
Less 10% in low season.

Reservations: Made for min. 11 nights with deposit (L.120,000) and fee (80,000). Address: 28822 Cannobio (Verbania). Tel: 0323/71360. FAX: as phone.

6250 Camping Au Lac du Como, Sorico This site appears out of order on page 192.

6259 Camping Punta d'Oro, Lake Iseo

Pleasant. small site on Lake Iseo.

Lago d'Iseo is the fifth largest of the northern lakes and one of the least known outside Italy. However, it is a popular tourist spot for Italians so has not escaped exploitation. Camping Punta d'Oro, at the town of Iseo in the southeast corner of the lake, is a small, delightful campsite. It slopes gently down to the lake from the railway line (they say, an infrequent local service) and there could be some road noise. The very pretty site, adorned with trees and plants, has 55 grass pitches (with just 15 static caravans) on either side of decorative brick roads. Electricity (5A) is available and trees at the corners define the places. There are good views across the lake to wooded mountains on the opposite shore where small villages shelter down by the water and further mountains rise behind the site. It has a small bar/shop/restaurant with a terrace. Two small sanitary blocks, refurbished to a high standard, have a mix of British and Turkish style WCs and free hot water in washbasins, sinks and showers. There are two narrow slip-ways for launching boats onto the lake which is also used for swimming. It is a good centre for exploring the lake, Monte Isola (Italy's largest lake island) by ferry from Iseo or to ascend Monte Gugliemo (1,949 m) which is reported to take about 3½ hours. With no entertainment programme, this could well suit those who are looking for a very pleasant base without the activity of a larger site.

How to find it: Leave A4 (Milan-Venice) autostrada at Ospitaletto exit, go north to Rodengo and then take SS510 to Iseo. Punta d'Oro is at northern end of town - cross the railway line and turn right at corner where site is signed.

General Details: Open 1 April - 31 October. 6,000 sq.m. Shop. Bar/restaurant. Access to lake. Fishing. Games room. Bicycle hire 500 m. Riding 4 km. Golf 7 km. Washing machine. Chemical disposal. Motorcaravan services.

Charges 1998: Per person L. 6,500 - 9,000; child 5,000 - 6,500; pitch 14,000 - 23,000, acc. to size; electricity included. Credit cards accepted.

AR Discount

Welcome drink

Reservations: Write to site. Address: via Antonioli 51, 25049 Iseo (BS). Tel: 030/980084. FAX: as phone. E-mail: punta@franciacorta.it.

6285 Camping Zocco, Manerba del Garda, Lake Garda

Good lakeside site with access for watersports.

Lake Garda is a very popular holiday area with a good number of sites well placed to explore the many attractions nearby. Camping Zocco is in a quiet, scenic location sloping gently down to the lake where there is a small jetty and good access to the water from a shingle beach. The 200 pitches for tourists, all with electricity (4A), and from 60-80 sq.m. in size, are either on slightly sloping ground from gravel roads, on terraces or around the perimeters of two open meadows. A variety of trees, including olives which provide oil for the owners, give shade, in parts and the camp has a well cared for appearance. There is a bar with terrace, a new restaurant/pizzeria and a shop. Entertainment is provided for children during July/August, there are two hard tennis courts and a football pitch. Water sports can be enjoyed on the lake. Three tiled sanitary blocks, one of which has been rebuilt, are well spread around the site. They have mainly British style WCs, free hot water in the washbasins, sinks and showers, and facilities for disabled people. The brothers who run this site welcome British visitors and English is spoken.

How to find it: From Desenzano head north on road 572 towards Salo. Take road to Manerba where site signed.

General Details: Open 1 April - 26 September. 50,000 sq m. Bar. Restuarant/pizzeria. Bar on the beach. Shop (from May). Watersports. Fishing. Tennis. Football. Children's play area. Bicycle hire 1.5 km. Riding and golf 3 km. Washing machines. Chemical disposal. Motorcaravan service point. Apartments and caravans for hire.

Charges 1998: Per person L. 7,000 - 9,000; child (3-11 yrs) 5,900 - 8.000; pitch incl. electricity 15,000 - 19,000; small boat 3,800 - 6,500. Credit cards accepted.

AR Discount

Less 10% in low season on person fee; min 7 days.

Reservations: Made for min. 7 days with deposit (L. 150,000) deducted from final bill. Address: via del Zocco 43, 25080 Manerba (BS). Tel: 0365/551605. FAX: 0365/552053 (winter tel/fax: 0365/551036).

See colour advert between pages 192/193

6252 Camping San Francesco, Rivoltella, Lake Garda

This highly-rated site has been recommended by our Italian Agent, but his recommendation arrived too late for us to arrange an inspection during '98. This brief preliminary description is based on our agent's comments, pending our inspection. The site is situated at the beginning of the peninsula of Sirmione on Lake Garda, with natural shade and a private 400 m. beach. Sanitary facilities are said to be excellent, and the site has its own sports centre, with swimming pools, tennis, archery, etc. Windsurfing and sailing are possible on the lake. There are 300 pitches for touring units (60-70 sq.m), all with electricity and 25 with water and drainage. Tents, caravans and mobile homes to rent.

How to find it: From A4, between Brescia and Verona, exit towards Sirmione. Take S11 to Rivoltella; site signed.

General Details: Open May - Sept. Shop. Restaurant. Snacks. Tennis. Children's playground. Chemical disposal.

Charges 1998: Per person L. 11,500; child (under 6) 10,500; pitch incl. electricity 24,500. Credit cards accepted.

Reservations: Address: Strada Vic, S. Francesco, 25010 Rivoltella (BS). Tel: 030/9110245. FAX: 030/9119464.

ITALY - North West

6253 Camping Piani di Clodia, Lazise, nr Verona

See colour advert between pages 192/193

New site on Lake Garda.

As might be expected in a popular area like Lake Garda, there are many camping sites and this new one is a welcome addition. Piani di Clodia, located between Lazise and Peschiera in the southeast corner of the lake, has lovely views across the water to Sirmione's peninsula and the opposite shore. The rectangular site slopes down to the water's edge and has over 1,000 pitches, all with 5A electricity, terraced where necessary and back to back from hard access roads. As yet there is little shade - some mature trees remain but most are young at present. A really good swimming pool complex at the top of the site has three semi-circular pools covering 1,700 sq.m. One can be heated and two have a variety of slides and hydro-massage. The area is fenced with lifeguards in attendance (open 10.00-13.00 and 15.00-18.00 hrs) with a good sunbathing area and a bar. The shopping area is in the centre of the site with an entertainment arena in the open and another on the roof, which is covered. The self-service restaurant with takeaway (lunch time and evening) and bar (open 07.00-24.00) have a large terrace, part of which is covered. Animation staff provide a variety of entertainment for both children and adults and there are facilities for many sports and pastimes (see below). Although there is a fence between the site and the lake, there are access points to a private beach and opportunities for watersports. Seven modern, good quality sanitary blocks are well spaced around the site, with a mix of British and Turkish style WCs and free hot water in washbasins, sinks and showers. All have facilities for the disabled and one has a baby room. Many tour suggestions by foot or bicycle and a wealth of tourist information are available from the reception office where English is spoken. Small British tour operator presence.

How to find it: Site is south of Lazise on road SS249 before Peschiera.

General Details: Open 20 March - 5 October. 220,000 sq.m. Shopping complex with supermarket, general shops for clothes etc. Two bars. Self-service restaurant with takeaway. Swimming pools. Tennis. Table tennis. Gymnastics. Bicycle hire. Riding near. Large grass space for volleyball and other ball games. Good children's playground. Outdoor theatre. Animation programme. Golf 12 km. Caneva acqua park, Gardaland (one of the biggest funfairs in Europe) close. Washing machines, dryers and laundry service. Motorcaravan service point. Chemical disposal.

Charges guide: Per person L. 7,000 - 12,500; child (under 9 yrs) 4,500 - 8,500; pitch with electricity 16,000 - 27.000, with water also 18,000 - 30,000.

Reservations: Write to site. Address: Localita Bagatta, 37017 Lazise (VR). Tel: 045/7590456. FAX: 045/7590939.

6255 Camping La Quercia, Lazise sul Garda, nr Verona

Large, popular site with very good recreational facilities and excellent beach on Lake Garda.

An extensive, popular site on a slight slope leading down to Lake Garda, La Quercia can accommodate around 1,000 units when full. Pitches are in regular double rows between access roads and are mostly marked by trees. Most pitches are shady, though those furthest from the lake are more open to the sun. Although siting is not always easy, staff do help in high season. The six toilet blocks are sufficient and are of a very high standard. La Quercia has a fine sandy beach on the lake, with diving jetties and a roped-off section for launching boats or windsurfing. The water is very clear compared to some lake beaches. Much of the site activity centres around the Olympic sized swimming pool and terrace bar, restaurant and pizzeria. There is also a children's pool and a large, landscaped spa pool (small charge). Sports facilities are exceptional, with a floodlit table tennis area, floodlit football field, multi-gym, archery, volleyball and tennis. A second café/restaurant nearer the beach also houses a large screen TV and a top quality ice-cream bar. Several shops cater for all needs, with slightly cheaper supermarkets en route to Verona. The evening entertainment is a little daunting at first, with the young team working hard to involve everyone. The site is a short distance from the exquisite lakeside town of Lazise and is a short drive from Verona, one of Italy's finest cultural centres (the open-air Opera in the Roman Amphitheatre is a unique, and affordable, experience). La Quercia has always been a popular site as, although its prices have been quite high, it does offer a great deal for your money, including a wide choice of organised activities and amenities, most of which are free (see below). Many of the courses require enrolment on a Sunday. A reader reports that on Saturday nights in high season there may be some late night noise from a disco outside the site. English spoken. Used by tour operators.

How to find it: Site is on south side of Lazise. From north on Trento - Verona A22 autostrada take Affi exit then follow signs for Lazise and site. From south take Peschiera exit and site is 7 km. towards Garda and Lazise.

General Details: Open 10 days before Easter - 30 Sept. 200,000 sq.m. Shade in parts. Electrical connections (4/6A) to each pitch. Supermarket. General shop. Bar and self-service restaurant. Tennis court. Table tennis. Riding stables. Football. Aerobics and yoga. Facilities for boats on the lake. Supervised children's playground. Minigolf. Organised events (sports competitions, games, etc.) and free courses in swimming, surfboard. canoeing, tennis, archery, climbing, judo. Evening entertainment or dancing. Baby sitting service. Free weekly excursion. Medical service. Laundry. Chemical disposal. Over 100 bungalows with own facilities; details from site. English spoken.

Charges guide: Per person L. 10,100; child (under 5) 6,500; pitch 22,250; reserved pitch 25,600. Low season discount for pensioners and rainy days.

Reservations: are made Sat - Sat for certain pitches. Address: 37017 Lazise sul Garda (Verona). Tel: 045/6470577. FAX: 045/6470243.

6280 Camping Week End, Cisano, San Felice del Benaco

Modern well equipped site with superb views over the lake.

Created among the olive groves and terraced vineyards of the Chateau Villa Louisa, which overlooks it, this site enjoys some superb views over the small bay which forms this part of Lake Garda. Although it is some 400 m. (along a private path/road direct from the site) from the lake itself, for many the views resulting from its situation on higher ground will be ample compensation for it not being an actual 'lakeside site'. Being situated above the lake, in quiet countryside, it provides an unusually tranquil environment, although even here it can become very busy in the high season. The site has one good sized swimming pool and a children's pool which compensate for its not actually having frontage onto the lake, and some visitors, particularly families with children, will doubtless prefer this. There are some 220 pitches, all with electricity (from 3A), of which about 30% are taken by tour operators and statics. The touring pitches are in several different areas, mainly on flat grass and many enjoying superb views. The three sanitary blocks are modern and well maintained with free hot water to showers, washbasins and washing-up areas. Mainly British style WCs, large showers, a few washbasins in cabins and facilities for disabled people. There is a large restaurant, with terrace and lawn from which again there are lovely views, providing waiter and takeaway meals at reasonable prices, and a well stocked shop.

How to find it: Approach from Salo (easier when towing) and follow site signs.

General Details: Open 26 April - 21 Sept. Bar/restaurant. Shop. Swimming pools. Entertainment programme in season. Children's playground. Windsurfing, water skiing, golf and tennis near. First aid room. Washing machines and dryer. Chemical disposal. Bungalows and caravans for hire. English spoken.

Charges guide: Per unit incl. electricity L. 15,000 - 22,000; adult 7,500 - 10,000; child (3-10) 6,500 - 8,500.

Reservations: Contact site. Address: Via Vallone della Selva 10, 25010 San Felice del Benaco (Brescia). Tel: 0365/43712. FAX: 0365/42196.

...so unique!! ★★★★
camping 〔villaggio〕

WEEKEND

Quiet family site, well maintained. Modern toilet facilities. Free hot water in the showers and basins. Washing machine, bar, restaurant, pizzeria, small shop. Very scenic. 2 swimming pools, children's playing area, volleyball, table tennis, music and dancing in the evenings. Send for our brochure. Reservations accepted. Caravan, tent and bungalow for hire. New 6 person mobile-homes. Individual washing cubicles. Internet: http://www.weekend.it. e-mail: cweekend@tin.it

Via Vallone della Selva, 10 - 25010 SAN FELICE DEL BENACO (BS) ITALIA - Tel. 0039/0365 43712 Fax 0365 42196

6276 Villagio Turistico Camping Eden, Portese, nr Salo

Terraced hill-side camp overlooking Lake Garda.

The southwest corner of Lake Garda, a very popular tourist area, has an abundance of campsites of varying character, mainly depending on the nature of the terrain. At the small port of Portese the ground rises steeply from the lake and Camping Eden occupies part of this, rising some 60 m. from the entrance to the highest point. A one-way system of narrow roads, quite steep in places, links the terraces, most with shade from olive trees. There are said to be 180 pitches for tourists which are fairly small (50-60 sq.m). All have electricity (3A) but most of those with views over the lake are occupied by the site's own accommodation or by a tour operator. The attractive entrance has reception, a good swimming pool and children's pool, a shop and a restaurant which has a terrace where dancing and entertainment take place. The site has its own small beach area on the lake on the opposite side to the entrance road. Two small children's playgrounds, one by the pools and one at the top of the site. Video games, satellite TV, cinema and disco, with entertainment in July/Aug. Two sanitary blocks, one behind the restaurant, the other in the centre with quite a walk and steps from the furthest parts have some British type WCs, but the majority are Turkish. Hot water is free for washbasins, sinks and small showers (no changing space).

How to find it: From Desenzano exit on A4 Milan-Venice motorway go north on SS572 towards Salo. Turn towards lake to Portese and follow yellow camp sign – very acute turn into site. Easiest approach is from Salo with site on your right just before village.

General Details: Open 1 April - 30 Sept. 44,000 sq.m. Good shade some parts. Shop. Restaurant. Swimming pools. Children's playgrounds. Table tennis. Entertainment. Disco. Games room. Small private beach. Boating and watersports. Washing machines and dryers. Bungalows and caravans to hire.

Charges 1998: Per person L. 7,500 - 11,000; child (2-9 yrs) 6,000 - 9,300; pitch 14,500 - 20,700; extra car 5,000 - 7,500; boat 5,500 - 7,800; dog 8,000 - 10,500.

Reservations: Write to site: Address: Via Preone 45, 25010 Portese di San Felice del Benaco (BS). Tel: 0365/62093. FAX: 0365/559311.

6020 Camping Union Lido Vacanze, Cavallino, nr Venice/Venezia

See colour advert opposite

Superb, well organised seaside site with aqua-park and excellent facilities.

This well known site is extremely large but has first class organisation and it has been said that it sets the standard that others follow. It lies right by the sea with direct access to a long and broad beach of fine sand which fronts the camp. Shelving very gradually, the beach, which is well cleaned by the site, provides very safe bathing. The site is laid out regularly with parallel access roads under a covering of poplars and pine trees which serve also to mark out numbered pitches of adequate size (2,600 for touring units). There are separate parts for caravans, tents and motorcaravans, plus one mixed part. All have 5A electricity and 1,096 have water and drainaway also. The redesigned entrance now provides a large off-road overnight parking area with electrical connections, toilets and showers for those arriving after 9 pm. An aqua-park includes a swimming pool, lagoon pool for children, heated whirlpool and a slow flowing 160 m. long 'river' for paddling or swimming. Covering 5,000 sq.m. this is under lifeguard supervision and is open mornings and afternoons. There is also a heated pool for hotel and apartment guests, available to others on payment. The 16 sanitary blocks, which open and close progressively during the season, have free hot water in all facilities and are kept very clean. They have British style WCs, washbasins with shelf and mirror (many in cabins), hot showers, footbaths and deep sinks for washing dishes and clothes. Six blocks have facilities for disabled people. A comprehensive main shopping area set around a pleasant piazza has a wide range of shops including a large supermarket. There are seven restaurants and several pleasant and lively bars. A selection of sports is offered in the annexe across the road and fitness programmes under qualified staff are available in season. The golf 'academy' with professional in attendance, has a driving range, pitching green, putting green and practice bunker. There are regular entertainment and activity programmes for both adults and children. Union Lido is above all an orderly and clean site and this is achieved partly by strict adherence to regulations suiting those who like comfortable camping undisturbed by others and good management.

How to find it: From Venice-Trieste Autostrada leave at exit for airport or Quarto d'Altino and follow signs first for Jesolo and then Punta Sabbiono, and camp will be seen just after Cavallino, on the left.

General Details: Open 1 May - 30 Sept. 600,000 sq.m. Good shade. Many shops, open till late. Restaurants, bars, pizzerias. Aqua-park (from 15/5). Tennis. Riding. Windsurfing school in season. Table tennis. Minigolf. Skating rink. Two fitness tracks in 4 ha. natural park with children's play area and supervised play. Boat excursions. Bicycle hire. Recreational events for adults and children, day and evening. Italian language lessons. Golf academy. Church service in English in Jul/Aug. Exchange facilities and cash machine. Ladies' and gent's hairdressers. Launderette. First aid centre, doctor's surgery with treatment room and ambulance. Motorcaravan service points. Chemical disposal. Luxury apartments, bungalows, caravans and mobile homes for hire and site owned hotel by entrance.

Charges 1999: Three different rates: (i) high season 26/6-28/8; (ii) mid-season 22/5-26/6 and 28/8-11/9, and (iii) off-season, outside these dates. Per person L. 9,500, 11,700 or 13,500; child under 3 yrs 5,700, 7,600 or 9,500, under 12 yrs 8,000, 10,000 or 12,000; pitch incl. electricity 17,000, 20,500 or 30,500; with water and drainage 22,000, 25,000 or 35,000. VAT included. Min. stay in high season 1 week. Credit cards accepted.

Reservations: made for the letting units only, but site provides 'priority cards' for previous visitors. Address: 30013 Cavallino (Venezia). Tel: 041/968080 or 2575111. FAX: 041/5370355. Internet: www.unionlido.com. UK contact: G. Ovenden, 29 Meadow Way, Heathfield, Sussex TN21 8AJ.

6250 Camping Au Lac du Como, Sorico, Lake Como

See advert in colour section opposite

Small site in scenic position on Lake Como.

Au Lac du Como is in a most pleasant location at the head of Lake Como in the centre of the village of Sorico facing south down the water and surrounded by wooded mountains. There is direct access to the lake for swimming, boating and other watersports with windsurfing appearing to be the most popular pasttime. Static units predominate but the camping area is directly by the lake where there is said to be room for 74 touring units. However, as pitches are not marked out, pitching can be a little haphazard and the area may become crowded, particularly in high season when reservation is advised. Cars are parked just away from tents and caravans. The owner speaks good English and insists on respect for other residents so ball games, barbecues and loud music are not allowed. There is one good sanitary block in the centre of the static part and two smaller basic ones. These have mainly British WCs. Hot water in the larger block is on payment but free in the other two except for washing up and laundry. There is a hotel/restaurant at the entrance with the bar open all day, an excellent breakfast service and evening meals. Well situated for exploring the area and nearby Switzerland, there are marked paths and trails for walking and biking in the mountains with an interesting nature park close. Most guests are German and Dutch but British find their way here and are welcome.

How to find it: Easiest route is north on SS36 from Lecco to Nuovo Olonio and west on SS402 (signed Gravelona) to Sorico; site is then on the left in centre of village. Can be approached on SS340 from Como on lake-side road which is quite narrow in places but an interesting drive.

General Details: Open all year. 20,000 sq.m. Electricity connections (3A). Supermarket. Hotel bar and restaurant. Sauna and solarium. Fishing. Canoes, kayaks, bicycle hire. Washing machine and dryer. Chemical disposal. Motorcaravan service point. Bungalows, rooms and apartments to rent.

continued overleaf

The pleasant holiday park with quality, style and atmosphere in a friendly environment right on to the Venetian Cavallino coast.
Open from 1st May to 30th September.

Camping - Caravan - Bungalow

Spacious, fitted pitches on grass under pines and poplars, for tents, caravans and motorcaravans. Many caravan pitches have water and drainage points. Caravans and mobile homes for hire, with shower and WC.
Bungalow "Lido" with kitchen-living room, 2 double bedrooms (twin beds), shower and separate WC and terrace including some for disabled guests.

Fitness - Sport - Play Park

Spacious area with games and keep-fit equipment, with trained staff, Multi-use sportsground for roller blading and other activities, volley ball, swimming instruction, wind surfing school, diving centre with school and diving excursions at sea, table tennis, minigolf, tennis and riding school. Archery and football competition. Golf Academy.
The Happy Place! Children's play area with much equipment. Climbing games, supervised play.

Animation - Entertainment - Activities

Amphitheatre for concerts and music shows.
Organised activities: Painting courses, artistic activities, games & recreation by trained staff.

UNION LIDO
Vacanze
★ ★ ★ ★

I - 30013 CAVALLINO - VENEZIA
Tel. Camping (041) 968080, 2575111
Tel. Hotel (041) 968043, 968884
Telefax (041) 5370355

e-mail: unionlid@tin.it
http://www.omninets.com/union/

UNITER
UNI EN ISO 9002   CAVALLINO

NEW: the first campsite in Europe to be granted UNI EN ISO 9002 certification.

Park Hotel Union Lido

3 Star hotel with modern airy rooms, some of which have been completely refurbished. Self-catering complex with 24 two-storey flatlets.
Heated swimming pool, with splash and whirlpool also available in the early and late season for our Hotel and self-catering guests.

Aqua Park

An experience! 5000 sq metres of water landscape with a gentle river, a lagoon for the children, swimming pool, whirlpools and a waterfall (15.5 - 30.9).

Scout camp for 8-12 yr olds on holiday with their parents in July-August.

camping
SanFrancesco
★★★★

New swimming pool and water games. New, first-class toilet and shower block

The camping ground is situated right at the beginning of the beautiful Sirmione peninsula, known as the 'pearl of Lake Garda'. The restaurant, pizza parlour, supermarket, two bars and sanitary facilities have just been renovated. The ground covers 100,000 m² of shady terrain reaching right down to the lake and a 300 m long beach. Our sports facilities on 35,000 m² include a big swimming pool (1,400 m²) with a lagoon for children and water games. Furthermore there is the possibility to engage in more than 10 different sports. Leaving the Milan to Venice motorway at the Sirmione exit, this ground is easy to access: and it is an ideal base for visiting the theme parks of Gardaland and Caneva nearby.

Strada Vic. S. Francesco - 25015 Desenzano del Garda (BS) - Tel. 030/9110245 - Fax 030/9119464
http://www.camping.it/garda/sanfrancesco - E.mail: sanfrancesco.garda@camping.it

NORCENNI GIRASOLE CLUB
CAMPING LE MARZE
CAMPING SAN FRANCESCO

Camping Villaggio Hotel Ristorante
Au Lac de Como

1-22010 SORICO
Tel. 0039/034484035
Fax 0039/034484802
Mobile 0039/335/216421
Internet: http://www.misterbyte.it/aulacdecomo
E-mail: aulacdecomo@misterbyte.it

The Hotel Au Lac de Como, surrounded by the green of the Berlinghera, the natural oasis "Pian di Spagna" and the bright blue Lake, offers comfortable, modern rooms and apartments. Next to the Hotel is the Campsite with its own private beach. There are bungalows and splendid Mobile Homes for hire. In a peaceful setting, you can spend a novel and refreshing holiday and have a go at the various exciting sporting activities such as Paragliding, Hang-gliding and Outings in the surrounding forest.

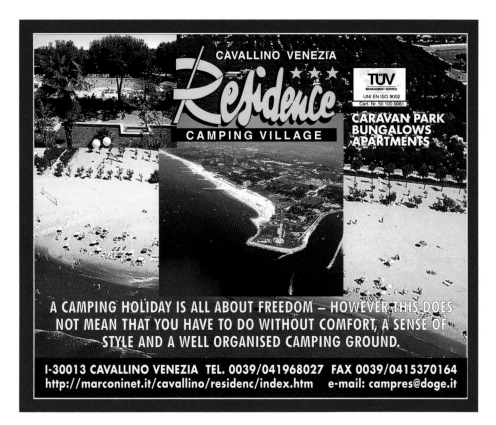

★ ★ ★ ★

PARCO CAMPEGGIO
DELLE PISCINE

I-53047 SARTEANO (SIENA)
Tel. 0039/057826971
Fax 0039/0578265889
E-mail: bagnosanto@krenet.it
http://www.evols.it/bagnosanto

A special feature of our site is the three good-sized swimming pools, fed by the thermo-mineral spring water for which our spa is famous and maintained at a temperature of 24°C, in a green park-like setting. They are all free to those staying at the camp. Our comfortable amenities include very modern sanitary blocks, restaurant, bar and tennis. The surroundings are rich in art, history and gastronomy. Indeed the 'Delle Piscine' camp is the perfect base for visits to the important historical sites of central Italy.

Camping Naturista
El Portus
Cartagena SPAIN

Editorial Entry for this site see Spanish section Page 308

ELECTROLUX –
FOR THE LIFE OF LEISURE

With the life we lead today leisure is of increasing importance, so is the need to have cool fresh food and drinks to hand wherever you are.

Electrolux have the most comprehensive range of portable refrigerators and coolers in the industry. They have a product for every conceivable use and application.

The mobilLife range of portable refrigerators is ideal for use either at home or away. There are models suitable for use on outings with the kids, or just in the garden for barbecues.

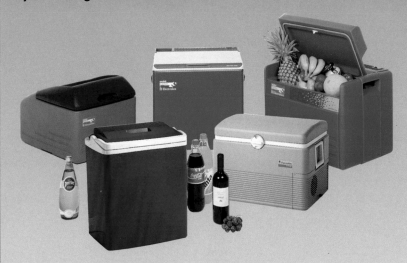

HOLIDAY

Stocking up for the holiday? Taking the children or grandchildren with you? Where to store the left-over Christmas turkey?

Electrolux has the answer. Their top of the range mobilLifes are portable top-opening absorption refrigerators. There is a choice of models and they are all three-way just like the model fitted in a caravan. You can run from gas or 230v while stationary, or plug into the cigar lighter 12v socket whilst on the move. They are ideal when you are camping, or useful as an additional refrigerator at home. Whatever the occasion Electrolux can help solve the problem.

Sitting in your car in long summer traffic jams in the sweltering heat, wouldn't it be great to just reach into the back of your car and take out a long cool drink?

Electrolux mobilLife thermoelectric coolers work on the Peltier system from a 12v supply, so you can plug them directly into the cigarette lighter of the car, and have cool drinks to hand at any time. No more do you need to search for a roadside café, or queue in busy motorway service stations. Refreshment is to hand at any time of day or night. With the aid of an adaptor, you can run your mobilLife cooler on the 24v system on a truck or boat. A 230v adaptor means you can use it at home as well. Some of the products even allow you to reverse the plug and use your mobilLife as a food warmer, ideal for an outing on colder days, or for keeping the takeaway warm.

Reasonably priced, these coolers are also ideal for day trips and excursions. Whatever the application Electrolux has a portable product to suit.

SAIL TO FRANCE OR SPAIN ON THE CREST OF A WAVE.

Get your French or Spanish trip off to the best possible start with P&O European Ferries from Portsmouth, the UK's best connected ferryport.

With superb 'Les Routiers' approved restaurants, excellent onboard shopping, great facilities for children and a choice of entertainment, you'll arrive relaxed and in great shape to continue your journey.

We also offer day trips to Cherbourg or Le Havre as well as three night MiniCruises to Northern Spain on Britain's largest and most luxurious Cruiseferry, Pride of Bilbao.

And if you're in a real hurry to get away, you can always take advantage of our 'SuperStar Express' which will whisk you across to Cherbourg in just

2 hrs 45 minutes during the summer.

For more information, call 0990 980 555 or visit your local travel agent.

For the latest brochure, call our Hotline on 0870 9000 212.

PORTSMOUTH TO BILBAO, CHERBOURG & LE HAVRE

Altogether more civilised. **P&O** European Ferries **PORTSMOUTH**

Spring, summer and autumn.

Agenzia Verdonia

● ● ● ● ● ● ● ● ● ● ● ● ● ● ● ● ●

A four-star vacation in three seasons.

*I*magine an oasis with all the comforts of a 4-star holiday park: 24 hectares of countryside close to the lake, panoramic view, bungalows with from 2 to 5 beds, ample, well-equipped camping spaces, every type of service, 3 splendid swimming pools with waterslides and hydromassage... And then tennis, basketball, volleyball, bicycles, exercise walk, windsurfing, canoeing, courses, championships and organised activities directed especially at children. At Piani di Clodia the daytime is spent enjoying yourself, whereas the evenings are even better, with shows, entertainment, music and dancing. Piani di Clodia: this is a real holiday!

OPEN FROM MARCH TO OCTOBER.

ACTIVITIES

SWIMMING POOLS

RELAXATION

SPORTING ACTIVITIES

HOME COMFORTS

PIANI DI CLODIA
★ ★ ★ ★

Loc. Bagatta, 37017 Lazise - (Verona - Italy)
Tel. ++39.045.7590456 - Fax ++39.045.7590939 - www.pianidiclodia.it

CAMPING
CAPALONGA
NATURE AT THE SEASIDE

★ PITCHES WITH MOORINGS ALONGSIDE
★ FULLY EQUIPPED CARAVANS AND MAXI-CARAVANS TO BE RENTED
★ NEW WOODEN CHALETS WITH AIR CONDITIONING. TWO WCS, ONE IN
SHOWER ROOM AND THE SECOND IN THE BEDROOM WITH KING-SIZED BED

CAMPING CAPALONGA
I 30020 BIBIONE PINEDA (VENICE)
CALL: 0039-0431-438351

CAMPING RESIDENCE IL TRIDENTE
I 30020 BIBIONE PINEDA (VENICE) Tel: 0039-0431-439600

Camping in natural
surroundings

Like an English park

High class rooms and chalets
to rent

Fully equipped

SEA VIEWS

6250 Camping Au Lac du Como (continued)

Charges 1999: Per person L. 5,000 - 10,000; child 3,500 - 7,000; pitch 7,000 - 20,000; car 6,000; m/cycle 5,000; dog or boat 3,500 - 7,000. Credit cards accepted.

Reservations: Advised for high season; write to site. Address: Via Cesare Battisti 18, 22010 Sorico (CO). Tel: 0344 84035 or 84716. FAX: 0344/84802.

6010 Camping Capalonga, Bibione Pineda, nr Venice/Venezia

See colour advert opposite

Quality site with a very good beach and excellent sanitary blocks.

Capalonga is a large, well developed and cared for site, right beside the sea. The pitches are of variable size (70-90 sq.m.) and nearly all marked out; some can be reserved. All have electrical connections (4A) and there is good shade almost everywhere. The site is pleasantly laid out - roads run in arcs which avoids the 'square box' effect. Some pitches where trees define the pitch area may be tricky for large units. The beach is a very wide sandy one which is cleaned by the site and never becomes too crowded; a concrete path leads out towards sea to avoid too much sand-walking. The sea bed shelves extremely gently and is very safe for children and the water is much cleaner here than at most places along this coast. Along the other side of the site runs a large lagoon, where boating (motor or sail) can be practised. The site provides a landing stage and moorings. There is also a swimming pool (25 x 12½ m.). The site has seven toilet blocks with hot water throughout; they are well and frequently cleaned. Two newer blocks built side by side have special facilities for disabled people and very fine children's rooms with washbasins and showers at the right height. British and some Turkish style toilets, individual basins, some in private cabins, and a whole wall of mirrors. Large new playing field with exercise stations, football pitch and general area for ball games. Capalonga is an excellent site, with comprehensive facilities.

How to find it: Bibione is about 80 km. east of Venice, well signed from afar on approach roads. 1 km. before Bibione turn right towards Bibione Pineda and follow camp signs.

General Details: Open 1 May - 30 Sept, with main shop and restaurant. 250,000 sq.m. Electrical connections (4A). Large supermarket. General shop for campers and beach goods, cards, papers, etc. Self-service restaurant and separate bar. Swimming pool. Boating. Fishing. Launderette. Children's playground. Sports field. First-aid room. Car wash. Chemical disposal. Motorcaravan services. Caravans and bungalows for hire.

Charges 1998: Four charging seasons. Per person L. 10,000 - 16,000; child 1-4 yrs free - 8,000, 5-8 yrs free - 12,000; pitch with electricity 19,000 - 32,000; pitch with water and drainage also 21,000 - 34,000; extra car 4,000 - 8,000; boat 12,000 - 22,000 acc. to season and size.

Reservations: Recommended for July/August and made from Sat. to Sat. only, with large deposit and fee. Address: Viale della Laguna 16, 30020 Bibione Pineda (VE). Tel: 0431/438351.

6015 Camping Residence Il Tridente, Bibione Pineda, Bibione

Natural woodland site on Adriatic, with Residence and excellent facilities.

This is an unusual site as only half the area is used for camping. Formerly a holiday centre for deprived children, it occupies a strip of woodland 200 m. wide and 400 m. long stretching from the main road to the sea. It is divided into two parts by an apartment block of first class rooms with air conditioning and full cooking and bathroom facilities which are for hire. The 230 tourist pitches are located amongst tall pines in the area between the entrance and the Residence. Pitch sizes vary according to the positions of the trees, but they are of sufficient size and have 4A electrical connections. The ground slopes gently from the main building to the beach of fine sand and this is used as the recreational area with two swimming pools - one 25 x 12½ m. and a smaller children's pool - tennis courts, table tennis and sitting and play places. The three sanitary blocks, two in the main camping area and one near the sea, are of excellent quality. All have similar facilities with mixed British and Turkish style WCs in cabins with washbasins, good showers, free hot water throughout and facilities for disabled people. The Residence includes an excellent restaurant, bar and well stocked supermarket. An animation programme includes activities for children in high season. Boats may be kept at the quay on the sister site, Capalonga (no. 6010), about 1 km. away. With thick woodland on both sides, Il Tridente is a quiet, restful site with excellent facilities.

How to find it: From A4 Venice - Trieste autostrada, take Latisana exit and follow signs to Bibione and then Bibione Pineda and camp signs.

General Details: Open Easter - 30 Sept. 54,500 sq.m. Restaurant. Bar. Supermarket. Swimming pools. Children's playground. Tennis. Table tennis. Mini-football. Volleyball. Animation. Washing machines and dryers. Chemical disposal. Motorcaravan services. Caravans and wooden chalets for hire.

Charges 1998: Per person L.10,000 - 16,000; child 1-4 yrs free - 8,000, 5-10 yrs free - 10,000; pitch 19,000 - 30,000; extra car 4,000 - 8,000; VAT included.

Reservations: are made; contact site for details. Address: via Baseleghe 12, 30020 Bibione Pineda. Tel: 0431/439600 (winter: 0431/438351).

6260 Camping Europa Silvella, San Felice del Benaco, Salo, nr Brescia

Site beside Lake Garda with various amenities.

This lakeside site was formed from the merger of two sites with the result that the 300-plus pitches (about 220 for tourists) are spread among a number of sections of varying type. The chief difference between them is that the marked pitches close to the lake are in smaller groups and closer together so that one has less space, whereas in the larger, very slightly sloping or terraced grassy meadows further back one can have 80 sq. m. or more instead of 50. With shade in many parts and electricity available, 40 new pitches have water and drainage. Some areas contain bungalows. The site has frontage to the lake in two places (with some other property in between), with beach and jetty. Windsurfing can be practised with a school in season. Large new swimming pool complex with 'hydro massage' (jacuzzi) plus a children's pool. Recently completed sanitary blocks include washbasins in private cabins, facilities for the disabled and a children's room with small showers, British WCs and basins. All blocks have free hot water. There is a supermarket and restaurant complex and a new children's playground. A leisure card (costing L. 10,000 for adults, 7,000 for children) is required to participate in the activities.

How to find it: From Desenzano at southerly end of Lake Garda follow S572 north towards Salo. Following signs for San Felice turn off towards lake. Then follow yellow tourist signs bearing camp name.

General Details: Open 1 April - 30 Sept. Shop. Bazaar. Restaurant/bar. Laundry. Swimming pools. Tennis. Table tennis. Children's playground. Bowling. Surf boards, canoes and bicycles for hire. Entertainment (nightly in season). Disco. Swimming, surfing and tennis lessons. First aid room. Chemical disposal. Bungalows and caravans to let.

Charges guide: Per person L. 6,500 - 10,000; child (2-9 yrs) 5,500 - 8,500; pitch with car, electricity, water and drainage 17,000 - 25,000; pitch with electricity only 15,000 - 22,000; small tent pitch, no electricity 14,000; extra car 8,000 - 12,000; trailer 8,000 - 15,000. Rates include VAT.

Reservations: not usually necessary for caravans and tents, but will be made for min. 7 days with 30% deposit and L.25,000 fee. Address: Via Silvella 10, 25010 S. Felice del Benaco (Brescia). Tel: 0365/651095. FAX: 0365/654395.

6235 Camping Monte Brione, Riva del Garda

New municipal site at northern end of Lake Garda.

The small resort of Riva at the head of Lake Garda shelters under a rocky escarpment and from ancient times has been an important communication and trading centre on the route between Verona and the Alps. Today it is a picturesque centre for enjoying the lake and nearby attractions. Monte Brione is quietly situated on the edge of town at the foot of an olive covered hill, 250 m. from the lake. There are 116 pitches on flat grass, marked by trees and posts in groups of 4 around a water and electricity (6A) service point. Unmarked terraces on the hillside take 15 tents. Good tarmac roads dissect the site which has a neat, well tended air. Although near a small residential development, there are good views of the mountains. Two modern sanitary blocks, one at either end of the site, have mixed Turkish and British style WCs and free hot water in washbasins (private cabins), good sized showers and sinks. Facilities for disabled people. Shop for basic supplies, snack bar, bar and covered terrace. Good sized swimming pool with a sunbathing area. Limited entertainment and animation in high season and two children's play areas. The town is within walking distance by a lakeside path and has many shops and restaurants.

How to find it: Leave A22 at Garda-Nord exit for Torbole and Riva. Just before Riva, through short tunnel, then turn right at camp signs.

General Details: Open Easter - early Oct. 33,000 sq.m. Bar with terrace. Shop for basics. Snack bar. Swimming pool (1/6-30/9). Minigolf. Table tennis. Bowls. TV/video. Bicycle hire. Organised activities. Fishing 1 km. Riding 3 km. Sailing, boating and tennis near (reduced rates for campers). Chemical disposal. Motorcaravan services.

Charges 1999: Per person L. 12,500; child (3-12 yrs) 8,300; pitch 18,500; dog 6,200. Credit cards accepted.

Reservations: Write to site with 20% deposit (refundable) of anticipated bill. Address: Via Brione 32, 38066 Riva del Garda (TN). Tel: 0464/520885 or 520890. FAX: 0464/553178.

6225 Camping Due Laghi, Levico Terme, nr Trento

Good modern site with swimming pool and mountain views, close to lake and spa town.

This modern site is close to the main road but is quiet and only 5 minutes walk from the Levico lake where it has a small attractive private beach where one can put boats. There are 420 numbered pitches on flat grass, in rows marked by slabs. Most are said to be approx. 80 sq.m. but there are now 60 larger pitches (90 sq.m) with electricity, water, TV and phone connections. On site is a good swimming pool of over 300 sq.m. with a children's pool. It is therefore suitable for a stay as well as overnight. It is said to become full 15/7 - 15/8 but there is always a chance of finding space. The central toilet block is of good quality and very large, with British and Turkish type WCs, washbasins with free hot water (some in cubicles), free showers with pre-set hot water and a unit for disabled people. Some private WCs may be hired. This is a most attractive site with a variety of trees and flowers. The site supplies a comprehensive descriptive guide to the attractions of the region. English is spoken.

How to find it: Site is 20 km. southeast of Trento just off the S47 road towards Padova (camp sign at turning).

continued overleaf

6225 Camping Due Laghi (continued)

General Details: Open 25 May - 30 Sept. Electrical connections (3/6A) in all parts. Shop. Sauna. Restaurant, pizzeria and cafe/bar, with takeaway. Music weekly in high season. Children's playground. Tennis. Bicycle hire. Fishing and riding 1 km. Golf 5 km. Laundry. Chemical disposal. Motorcaravan service points. Walks from site.

Charges 1999: Per person L. 10,000 - 12,500; child 2-5 yrs 6,000 - 8,000, 6-11 yrs 7,000 - 10,000; pitch 14,000 - 21,000 acc. to size and facilities. Club card for entertainment, activities, etc. obligatory in July/Aug. L. 10,000 per pitch/family. Discounts for longer stays in low season. No credit cards.

Reservations: min. 1 week in peak season, with deposit and fee. Address: Loc. Costa 3, 38056 Levico Terme (Trento). Tel: 0461/706290. FAX: 0461/707381.

AR Discount
Two bikes free for one day.

6265 Villagio Turistico Camping Ideal Molino, San Felice, Salô, nr Brescia

Small Garda lakeside site with a garden-like atmosphere.

Ideal Molino, directly on the shore of Lake Garda, is one of the smaller sites in this area and occupies a very pleasant, mainly level position, with a hill rising quite steeply behind and views across the water. It might well appeal to those who prefer a quiet place without organised entertainment and the friendly atmosphere of a family owned and run camp. There is a slip-way for powered boats with moorings (at extra cost), opportunities for windsurfing and swimming in the lake from the small stony beach or jetty (unsupervised). Some of the 70 pitches are in rows under flower covered pergolas where the ground is hard, with others on grass in the open right by the lake on the other side of the central building. They are small by some standards (60-80 sq.m) and most cars are parked away from the pitches. There is a slight slope down to the water and a few terraced pitches for tents below the bungalows. All have electricity (4A), some water and drainage. There are three small sanitary blocks, one at each end and one in the central building housing the shop and restaurant. Although old, they are tiled and very clean with British WCs and free hot water in washbasins, sinks and showers. It is one of the few sites in the area where one can reserve and this is advised for high season in this popular area. Small children's playground with table tennis, a boules court and two volleyball courts. It makes a good base for exploring the many nearby attractions, the Dolomites to the north as well as day visits to Verona and Venice. English is spoken and the site does not like the playing of radios or TV's or any noise after 11 p.m.

How to find it: From A4 Milan-Venice motorway take exit for Desenzano, follow north on SS572 towards Salo, turn towards the lake following signs for San Felice and then yellow tourist signs bearing the camp name.

General Details: Open Easter - 30 Sept. 17,000 sq m. Well shaded in parts. Shop. Restaurant/bar with terrace. Table tennis. Boules. Volleyball. Fishing. Boating. windsurfing and water-skiing. Bicycle hire 4 km. Riding and golf 3 km. Laundry service. Chemical disposal. Well-equipped bungalows for hire. No pets.

Charges 1998: Per person L. 7,200 - 11,300; child (2-9 yrs) 5,900 - 8,800; pitch 14,500 - 22,000. No credit cards.

Reservations: made for min 7 days from February onwards with fee and deposit; write to site. Address: via Gardiola 1, 25010 San Felice del Benaco (Brescia). Tel: 0365/62023. FAX: 0365/559395.

ITALY - North West

6230 Camping San Christoforo, Pergine Valsugana, nr Trento

Quiet, mountain site near lake, with views and swimming pool.

This part of Italy is becoming better known by those wishing to spend time by a lake in splendid countryside, but away from the more crowded, better known resorts. Lake Caldonazzo is one of the smaller lakes, but is excellent for watersports, with some twenty lifeguards on duty in the season. Camping San Christoforo is a new site which lies on the edge of the small town of the same name and is separated from the lake by a minor road, but with easy access to it. The site has 160 pitches on flat grass on either side of hard surfaced access roads. The pitches are of a good size, numbered in front and separated by trees with 3A electricity available. The modern sanitary block has British style WCs, free hot water in the basins (some in cabins) and showers controlled by a single tap; there are footbaths, sinks with free hot water for washing up and laundry and facilities for disabled people. There is a swimming pool (20 x 20 m.) with sunbathing area and small children's pool. The village shops are close, and the site has a quiet and well cared for air; English is spoken. Used by a tour operator.

How to find it: Site is southeast of Trento, just off the SS47 road; well signed from the village of S. Christoforo.

General Details: Open 25 May - 15 Sept. Electrical connections throughout. Small well stocked shop. Bar/restaurant (all year) with waiter service and takeaway. Swimming pool and child's pool. Bicycle hire. Minigolf. Fishing and boating 200 m. Riding 5 km. Golf 2 km. Washing machine and dryer. Chemical disposal.

Charges 1999: Per person L. 10,000 - 12,500; child 2-5 yrs 6,000 - 8,000, 6-11 yrs 7,000 - 10,000; pitch 16,000 - 17,000; extra car free - 6,000; dog 6,000. Discounts for longer stays in low season.

Reservations: Not accepted. Address: Loc. San Christoforo, 38057 Pergine Valsugana (TN). Tel: 0461/706290. FAX: 0461/707381.

AR Discount
Two bikes free for one day.

6210 Camping Steiner, Leifers/Laives, nr Bozen/Bolzano

Site with swimming pools and good facilities in central Dolomites, south of Bolzano.

Being on the main S12 which now has a motorway alternative, Camping Steiner is very central for touring with the whole of the Dolomite region within easy reach, as well as Bolzano, Merano and other attractive places. It has its share of overnight trade but is also a camp with much on site activity where one can spend an enjoyable holiday. It is a smallish site with part taken up by bungalows and the tourist pitches, mostly with good shade, are in rows on either side of access roads. They are all individual ones and most are on hardstandings. The two sanitary blocks, one new, can be heated in cool weather and have free hot water in washbasins, sinks and showers and British style WCs. Full in season, the site is run personally by the proprietor's family and one has a friendly reception, with good English spoken. Two free swimming pools, an open air one, 20 x 10 m. (open May-Sept. and heated in spring), and a 12 x 6 m. enclosed pool (all season, except July/Aug. and heated to about 25°). The site has an excellent small restaurant and takeaway service, with good choice. An 18 hole golf course is 30 minutes away.

How to find it: Site is on S12 in northern part of Leifers, 8 km. south of Bolzano. From motorway if approaching from north, take Bolzano-Süd exit and follow Trento signs for 7 km; from south take Ora exit and proceed for 14 km. towards Bolzano.

General Details: Open 28 March - 7 Nov. 20,000 sq.m. Electrical connections (6A) everywhere. Shop. Meals in hotel. Small restaurant and takeaway. Cellar bar with taped music, dancing at times. Swimming pools. General room. Sauna. Children's playground and paddling pool. Table tennis. Chemical disposal. Bungalows and hotel rooms to let.

Charges guide: Per person L. 7,000 - 9,000; child (0-6 yrs) 4,500 - 6,000; pitch incl. car and 6A electricity 18,000 - 22,000; dog 8,000; extra car 6,000. Less 5-10% after 2 weeks stay.

Reservations: are made for minimum one week with reasonable deposit. Address: 39055 Leifers bei Bozen (Südtirol). Tel: 0471/950105. FAX: 0471/951572.

6205 International Camping Dolomiti, Cortina d'Ampezzo

Family run site in mountain setting beside famous resort.

The Cortina region boasts several good sites and this is one of the nearest to the town. It is a grassy site beside a fast flowing river in a broad flat area which is surrounded by mountain scenery - a quiet situation 3 km. from the town centre. The good sized pitches are marked out by white stones on either sides of access roads and most have electricity (4A). Half the site is well shaded. There is a heated swimming pool on site. It makes a good centre for touring the Dolomites or for more active pursuits such as mountain walking. The main toilet block is a large one and the installations, which should be adequate, include mainly Turkish style WCs, with some British, washbasins with hot water sprinkler taps, and free controllable hot showers. A heated block has been added which has facilities for disabled visitors. With no reservations made, arrive early in the day in the first three weeks of August.

How to find it: Site is south of Cortina, to west of main S51. There are signs from the road.

General Details: Open 15 May - 20 Sept. Small shop (open long hours) and coffee bar. Swimming pool (1/7-31/8). Restaurant 600 m. Basic children's playground (hard base). Chemical disposal. Washing machines and ironing.

Charges 1998: Per person L.7,000 - 13,000; child (under 6) 5,000 - 8,000; pitch 9,000 - 17,000. No credit cards.

Reservations: Not made. Address: 32043 Cortina d'Ampezzo. Tel: 0436/2485. FAX: 0436/5403.

6200 Camping Olympia, Toblach/Dobbiaco

Dolomite Mountains site on main route with excellent facilities.

Olympia, always good, has now been given a face-lift by the redesigning of the camping area and the refurbishment of the already excellent sanitary accommodation. Tall trees at each end of the site have been left, but most of those in the centre have been removed and pitches have been re-laid in a regular pattern. They include 12 fully serviced with electricity, water, waste, gas and TV and phone points. The static caravans are together at one end leaving the centre for tourists and with a grass area at the other end for tents. An attractive centre piece has a fountain surrounded by flowers. The excellent sanitary provision is in the main building which also has reception, restaurant, shop and apartments. Of a very high standard, there are 7 special cabins with WC, washbasin and shower to rent. British style WCs and free hot water in washbasins (not in cabins but separated) showers and sinks. There are also two small blocks at each end of the camp with WCs and showers. The attractive restaurant is open all day, all year, and opposite is a snack bar. On the far side of the site, where campers can walk amidst the woods, is a little children's play area and a few animals. Small swimming pool, open when weather permits.

How to find it: Site is between Villabassa and Toblach/Dobbiaco. From A22 Innsbruck-Bolzano, take Bressanone/ Brixen exit and east on SS49 for about 60 km. From Cortina take SS48 and SS51 northwards then west on SS49.

General Details: Open all year. 45,000 sq.m. Restaurant. Shop. Snack bar (not April/May or Oct/Nov). Tennis. Swimming pool. Sauna, solarium, steam bath and whirl pools. Table tennis. Minigolf. Fishing (on payment). Bicycle hire. Children's play area. Animation programme in high season for children and adults. Horse riding near.

Charges guide: Per person L. 11,000; child (3-10) 9,000; pitch 18,000; car 6,000; small tent 9,000.

Reservations: Write to site. Address: 39034 Toblach (Sudtirol). Tel: 0474/972147. FAX: 0474/972713.

6201 Camping Antholz, Antholz-Obertal

All year campsite in the heart of the Dolomites.

Appearances can be deceptive and this is the case with Camping Antholz. At first sight the 130 pitches (with 4A electricity), numbered, but only roughly marked, make this a very ordinary looking campsite. Just inside the entrance is a pleasant looking building with reception and a smart restaurant. It is when one investigates the sanitary accommodation that one realises that this is no ordinary site, as the provision is quite superb, with under-floor heating, hair salon, cosmetics room, baby room, British WCs and free hot water in washbasins, sinks and showers. High up in the Anterselva valley, there are splendid views of near and distant peaks. The shop has limited basic supplies (village 500 m), the bar is open all day and the restaurant, with terrace, opens 18-22.00 hrs. This is good skiing country in winter (ski bus, ski school, ski lifts) and, with a new National Park near, provides good walking in summer.

How to find it: From Bressanone exit on A22, go east on SS49 through Brunico and turn north (signed Antholz) for about 12 km. Pass Antholz village and site is on right.

General Details: Open all year. 25,000 sq.m. Restaurant (all year). Small shop. Children's playground. TV room. Table tennis. Bicycle hire. Tennis near. Washing machine and dryer. Motorcaravan service point.

Charges guide: Per unit incl. 2 persons and electricity L. 31,500 - 34,500; child (2-12 yrs) 5,500 - 6,500.

Reservations: Write to site. Address: 39030 Antholz-Obertal (BZ). Tel: 0474/492204. FAX: 0474/492444.

6000 Camping Marepineta, Sistiana, nr Trieste

Site 18 km. west of Trieste with good swimming pool and sea views over Baia di Sistiana.

This site is on raised ground near the sea, with views over the Sistiana Bay, Miramare Castle and the Gulf of Trieste. A pebbly beach, with a car park, lies just beyond the site, a drive of about 1 km. (free bus from camp every 40 mins 9 am.-7 pm). Alternatively there is a large swimming pool (unheated), on site with a new terrace. The development of this site continues with modern reception buildings and improved sanitary facilities. Over 350 of the 500 pitches are for tourists. On gravel hardstanding (awnings possible) in light woodland, all have electricity (from 3A) with water near. Space is nearly always available (1-15 Aug. busiest). Animals are allowed in a designated area. Six toilet blocks of varying quality have hot water in washbasins, including some in cabins, free showers and British and Turkish style WCs. Facilities for disabled people. Sinks for laundry and dishes, most with hot water. Late arrivals area with water and toilet facilities. The Rilke footpath runs along the seaside border.

How to find it: From west on A4 take Duino exit, turn left and camp is 1 km. on right; from east approach on S14.

General Details: Open 1 May - 30 Sept. Shop (15/5-15/9). Bars. New pizzeria with terrace. Disco. Swimming pool (1/6-15/9) with lessons. Children's playground. Football, volleyball and mini-basket. Tennis. Table tennis. Games room. Organised entertainment in season. Fishing 1 km. Bicycle hire 500 m. Riding 2 km. Golf 10 km.. First aid post. Laundry with dryer and ironing. Chemical disposal. Motorcaravan service point. New mobile homes for hire.

Charges 1998: Per pitch incl. electricity and water L. 10,000, 15,000 or 23,000, pitch with view of the bay 15,000, 19,000, 29,000; person 5,500, 7,500, 10,000; child (3-12) 4,000, 6,000, 8,000. No credit cards.

Reservations: Will be made with 40% deposit and L 30.000 fee. Address: 34019 Sistiana 60/D, Duino-Aurisina (TS). Tel: 040/299264. FAX: 040/299265.

AR Discount
Less 10% on person fees in low season (min. 3 days).

ITALY - North East

6005 Villaggio Turistico Camping Europa, Grado, nr Trieste

Large seaside site with swimming pools and other amenities.

This large flat site on the edge of the sea can take over 600 units. All pitches are marked, nearly all with good shade and electricity (4A) in all parts. The terrain is sandy in the areas nearer the sea, where cars are left in parking places, not by your pitch. Dogs are taken only in a special section in limited numbers. There is direct access to the beach but the water is shallow up to 200 m. from beach, with growing seaweed. However, there is a narrow wooden jetty which one can walk along to deeper water. For those who prefer, there is a new swimming pool near the sea and, on the site, a medium sized heated pool and smaller children's pool. The four main toilet blocks have free hot water, half British WCs and hot showers. Facilities for disabled people. The site reports two new blocks. Not a super site perhaps, but a good honest one which is probably the best in the area. Reservation for high season may be advisable.

How to find it: Site lies 4 km. east of Grado on road to Monfalcone. If road 35L is taken to Grado from West, continue through the town to Grado Pineta.

General Details: Open 10 April - 20 Sept. Supermarket; small general shop (May - Sept). Bar and self-service restaurant, with takeaway (all season). Swimming pools (May - Sept). Tennis courts. Football pitch. Table tennis. Fishing. Bicycle hire. Children's playground. Dancing, at times, in season; some organised activities July/Aug. Washing machines. Chemical disposal. Motorcaravan services. Good quality bungalows for hire, also some caravans.

Charges 1998: Per person L. 8,000, 9,500 or 13,000; child (3-10 yrs) free, 5,500 or 8,000; pitch incl. electricity 14,000, 15,000 or 23,000. Less 10% for longer stays out of season.

Reservations: made for min. 1 week from Sat. to Sat., with deposit in high season (50% of total). Address: PO Box 129, 34073 Grado (Gorizia). Tel: 0431/80877. FAX: 0431/82284.

6037 Campeggio Giuliana Bungalow, Ca'Ballarin, Cavallino

Small site, open all year.

This camp is unique in this area in two respects, firstly it is open all year and, secondly it is 500 m. from the sea and not directly by the shore. 40 bungalows and 4 caravans (for hire) are situated along each side of the square shaped camp with space in the centre, under vines, for 20 units. Pitches, mainly on sand, are not marked or numbered but some order is given as the owner tells campers where to stay. Flowers and the overhead vines make a pleasant, garden like atmosphere. The small sanitary units have British style WCs and free hot water. The restaurant `Anna` is open for the summer season but, being in the village, shops and other restaurants are very close. Musical entertainment in the restaurant twice weekly. Venice is a 40 minute bus/boat ride away, Lido di Jesolo 25 minutes. The beach is 500 m. and involves crossing a main road. The friendly owner speaks good English and will help with local information.

How to find it: From A4 Venice-Trieste autostrada take airport exit. At airport continue on SS14, follow signs for Jesolo, then Punta Sabbioni and camp will be found at the restaurant Anna in the village of Ca'Ballarin.

General Details: Open all year. Shade most parts. Restaurant (summer only), others and shops near. Small children's play area. Bicycle hire. Riding, golf 1 km. Fishing 5 km. Motorcaravan service point. Bungalows for hire.

Charges 1998: Per person L. 9,000 - 12,500; tent 12,000 - 15,000; caravan 14,000 - 18,000. No credit cards.

Reservations: Write to site. Address: via Rialto 13, Ca'Ballarin, 30013 Cavallino (VE). Tel: 041/968039. FAX: 041/5370443. E-mail: campgiul@iol.it. Internet: www.camping.it/veneto/camping.

 AR Discount *Less 10%*

6040 Camping Village Garden Paradiso, Cavallino, nr Venice

Very good medium size, seaside site with swimming pools.

There are many sites in this area and there is much competition in providing a range of facilities. Garden Paradiso has built three excellent swimming pools in the centre of the site near the restaurant and shopping complex. Compared with other sites here, this one is of medium size with 835 pitches. Most have electricity (from 4A), water and drainage points and all are marked and numbered with hard access roads, under a good cover of trees. Flowers and shrubs abound giving a pleasant and peaceful appearance. The site is directly on the sea with a beach of fine sand. There are four brick, tiled sanitary blocks around the site with a mix of British and Turkish style WCs, free hot water in the basins, showers and sinks, and facilities for babies. The restaurant, with self-service at lunch time and waiter service at night, is near the beach with a bar/snack bar in the centre of the site. Entertainment, animation and excursions are organised.

How to find it: Leave Venice-Trieste autostrada either by taking the airport or Quarto d'Altino exits; follow signs to Jesolo Punta Sabbioni. Take the first road on the left after Cavallino and site is a little way along on the right.

General Details: Open 1 May - 30 Sept. 13,000 sq.m. Restaurant. Snack bar. Shops. Tennis. Table tennis. Minigolf. Swimming pools. Organised entertainment and excursions. Bicycle hire. Fishing 2 km. Riding 1 km. Children's play area. Washing machines and dryers. Chemical disposal. Motorcaravan services. Caravans for hire.

Charges 1998: Per person L. 5,500 - 12,900; junior (1-6 yrs) or senior (over 60 yrs) 3,800 - 10,100; pitch 12,000 - 31,000. Less 10% for stays over 30 days (early) 20 days (late) season. Credit cards accepted.

Reservations: Made with deposit (L. 250,000 - 300,000) - write to site for details. Address: 30013 Cavallino (VE). Tel: 041/968075. FAX: 041/5370382. E-mail: garden@vacanze-natura.com.

6020 Camping Union Lido Vacanze, Cavallino, Jesolo, nr Venice/Venezia

6010 Camping Capalonga, Bibione Pineda, Bibione, nr Venice/Venezia

6015 Camping Residence Il Tridente, Bibione Pineda, Bibione

The editorial reports for these sites appear on pages 192/3 opposite their colour advertisements

6035 Camping Mediterraneo, Treporti, Jesolo, nr Venice/Venezia

Large site with a wide range of amenities including large swimming pools.

This big site has been considerably improved in recent years and is near Punta Sabbioni from where boats go to Venice. Mediterraneo is directly on the Adriatic Sea with a 480 m. long beach of fine sand which shelves gently and also two large pools (one for adults, the other for children) and a whirlpool. Sporting, fitness and entertainment programmes are arranged and sea swimming is supervised at designated hours by qualified lifeguards. The 750 touring pitches, of which 500 have electricity (from 4A), water and drainaway, are partly in boxes with artificial shade, some larger without shade, with others in unmarked zones under natural woodland equipped with electric hook ups where tents must go. The eight modern sanitary blocks are good quality with British type WCs and free hot water in the washbasins, showers and sinks. The commercial centre near reception has a supermarket and other shops with a restaurant, bars and a pizzeria near the pools. This is an organised and efficient site.

How to find it: Site is well signed from Jesolo-Punta Sabbioni road near its end after Ca' Ballerin and before Ca' Savio. Follow camp signs, not those for Treporti as this village is some way from the site.

General Details: Open 1 May - 30 Sept. 170,000 sq.m. Shop. Large bar and snack bar by pool; full restaurant elsewhere. Tennis. Minigolf. Table tennis. Bicycle hire. Surf and swimming school. Regular monthly programme of sports, organised games, excursions etc; dancing or shows 3 times weekly in main season. Fitness programme. Riding and golf 3 km. Refrigerator hire. Washing machines. Chemical disposal. Motorcaravan service point.

Charges 1999: Four rates. Per person L. 5,600 - 13,200; child (3-5 yrs) 4,000 - 10,500; pitch with electricity 11,300 - 26,700; pitch with 3 services 12,500 - 32,000; tent pitch with electricity 8,700 - 24,100. Credit cards accepted.

Reservations: made with large deposit. Address: 30010 Ca'Vio-Treporti (VE). Tel: 041/966721 or 22. FAX: 041/966944.

6030 Camping dei Fiori, Treporti, Lido del Cavallino, nr Venice

Excellent small site with swimming pools and special hydromassage pools.

The peninsula Lido del Cavallino, stretching from the outskirts of Lido del Jessolo to Punta Sabbioni, has almost 40 good camps directly on the Adriactic sea and convenient for visiting Venice and other interesting places in northeast Italy. Dei Fiori stands out amongst the other small camps in the area. As its name implies, it is aflame with colourful flowers and shrubs in summer and presents a neat and tidy appearance whilst providing a quiet atmosphere. About a quarter of the pitches are taken by static units, many for hire. The 400 pitches, with 5A electricity, are either in woodland where space varies according to the trees which have been left in their natural state, or under artificial shade where regular shaped pitches are of reasonable size. Well built bungalows for hire enhance the site and are in no way intrusive, giving a village-like effect. Shops and a restaurant are in the centre next to the swimming pools. Nearby is the hydro-massage bath which is splendidly appointed and reputed to be the largest in Italy. This is under the supervision of qualified staff, as is the fitness centre. A charge is made during middle and high seasons but not in low season. The long beach is of fine sand and shelves gently into the sea. The resident animation team offer a daily programme for children and activities for adults which includes games, tournaments and entertainment. Regulations ensure the site is quiet between 11 pm. - 7.30 am. and during the afternoon siesta period. Three sanitary blocks are conveniently situated around the site and are of exceptional quality with British style WCs, well equipped baby rooms, good facilities for disabled people, washing machines and dryers and free hot water in all facilities. Venice is about 40 minutes away by bus and boat and excursions are arranged from the site. The site is well maintained by friendly, English speaking management.

How to find it: Leave A4 Venice-Trieste autostrada either by taking the airport or Quarto d'Altino exits and follow signs for Jesolo and then Punta Sabbioni and camp signs just after Ca'Ballarin.

General Details: Open 27 April - 4 Oct. 10,000 sq.m. Restaurant. Snack bar (1/5-30/9). Shops. Tennis. Table tennis. Minigolf. Basketball. Entertainment and excursions. Swimming pools. Children's play area. Children's club. Windsurfing. Fitness centre, hydro-massage bath and programmes (1/5-30/9). Bicycle hire 1 km. Riding, fishing and golf 3 km. Washing machines and dryers. Chemical disposal. Motorcaravan service point. Bungalows and caravans for rent.

Charges 1999: Four seasons. Per person L. 7,000 - 13,600; child (1-5 yrs) 5,200 - 10,700; pitch with 3 services 14,500 - 32,200, pinewood pitch with electricity 13,400 - 28,500; tent pitch in pinewood with electricity 11,000 - 26,000. Credit cards accepted. Min. stay 7 days in high season (4/7-29/8).

Reservations: Advised for high season (incl. Whitsun) and made for min. 7 days. Write for application form as early as possible. Address: 30010 Treporti (VE). Tel: 041/966448. FAX: 041/966724.

6025 Camping Residence, Cavallino, nr Venice/Venezia

See colour advert between pages 192/193

Pleasant, well run site by beach with first class, clean installations.

The Litorale del Cavallino has a large number of excellent sites, giving a good choice for those wishing to visit and stay in this area near Venice. Camping Residence is a very good site with a sandy beach directly on the Adriatic and is well kept, with many floral displays. Pitches are marked out with small fences or pines, which give good shade, and are laid out in regular rows on level sand. These boxes vary in size with those for caravans larger than those for tents and all have electricity connections (6A). A medium size site (for this region) of 300 tourist pitches, it is smaller than 6020 (page 192) but has the same strict rules regarding noise (no radios or dogs, quiet periods and no unaccompanied under 18s) but is less formal and more personal. The beach fronting has been enlarged and improved and the sea bed shelves gradually making it safe for children. Excellent swimming pools and sunbathing areas have been added and there is a good animation programme in high season for both children and adults. Venice can be easily reached by bus to Punta Sabbioni and ferry across the lagoon and there are organised excursions to places of interest. The three large sanitary blocks are very clean with full facilities including free hot water in basins, sinks and showers with British style WCs. Although good, they are being refurbished.

How to find it: From A4 Venice-Trieste autostrada take exit for Airport or Quarto D'Altino, follow signs for Jesolo and then Punta Sabbioni. Take first left after Cavallino and camp is about 800 m. on right hand side (well signed).

General Details: Open 24 March - 15 Sept. 70,000 sq m. Supermarket, separate shops for fruit and other goods. Well appointed restaurant with separate bar. Takeaway. Children's playground. swimming pool. Dancing or disco by beach until 11 pm three times weekly June-August and entertainment programme. Fitness programme. Boat moorings for hire at nearby marina. Ladies hairdresser. Car wash. Table tennis. Small tennis court. Video games room. Post office. Bureau de change. Minigolf. Doctor will call. Chemical disposal. Modern apartments for four, bungalows and maxi-caravans for hire.

Charges guide: Per person L. 5,500 - 10,500; child (under 5 yrs) 3,800 - 8,200; pitch 12,000 - 24,000; extra car 3,000 - 6,000.

Reservations: Made for min. 1 week with L. 150,000 deposit. Address: via F.Baracca 47, 30013 Cavallino (Venezia). Tel: 041/968027 or 968127. FAX: 041/5370164.

6050 Camping Caravanning della Serenissima, Oriago, nr Venice/Venezia

Convenient site for overnight stay or for visiting Venice and other places in this region.

This is a delightful little site of 150 pitches (all with 16A electricity) where one could stay for a number of days whilst visiting Venice (12 km), Padova (24), Verona (24), Lake Garda (135) or the Dolomites. There is a good service by bus and boat to Venice and the site is situated on the Riviera del Brenta, a section of a river with some very large old villas. The site is used mainly by Dutch and British with some Germans, and is calm and quiet. It is long, narrow and flat with numbered pitches on each side of a central road. There is good shade in most parts with many trees, plants and grass. The single sanitary block is just adequate, has been and still is being improved, with free hot water in washbasins, showers and sinks. Mainly Turkish style WCs. The management is very friendly and good English is spoken.

How to find it: From east take road S11 at the roundabout SSW of Mestre towards Padova and site is 2 km. on your right. From west, leave autostrada A4 at Dolo exit, follow signs to Dolo, continue on main road through this small village and turn left at T-junction (traffic lights). Continue towards Venice on S11 for site about 6 km on your left.

General Details: Open Easter - 10 Nov. Shop (all season). Restaurant and bar (June - Oct). Children's play area. Fishing. Bicycle hire.Golf 6 km. Reduced price bus/boat ticket to Venice if staying for 3 days. No organised entertainment but local markets etc. well publicised. Chemical disposal. Motorcaravan services. Bungalows and mobile homes to rent.

Charges 1998: Per unit L. 16,000 - 18,000; adult 10,000; child (3-12 yrs) 8,000. Credit cards accepted.

Reservations: are made. Address: 30030 Oriago (Venezia). Tel: 041/921850. FAX: 041/920286. E-mail: camping.serenissima@shineline.it.

6055 Villagio Turistico Isamar, Sa. Anna di Chioggia, nr Venice/Venezia

Seaside site south of Venice with six good swimming pools.

Many improvements have been made here over the years and these continue. Although directly by the sea, with its own beach of fine sand, it is a fair way from the entrance to the sea. The largest camping area, which may be cramped at times, is under pines, grouped around the pool, large modern sanitary block, shops, etc. near reception. A smaller area is under artificial shade near the beach with an Olympic size, salt-water swimming pool, children's pool and four new pools. Here also are an entertainment area, bar/restaurant, pizzeria and small toilet block. Between these sections are well constructed bungalows for rent and a third area has been developed mainly for the site's own accommodation. The pitches, on either side of access roads, vary in size and all have electricity. The site may become crowded in high season. The main toilet blocks are of good quality with British WCs (small block has only Turkish style), and free hot water in washbasins, showers and sinks. An extensive entertainment and fitness programme is offered and there is supervised play for children over 4, a disco and a games room. High proportion of Italian holidaymakers and also popular with the Germans and Dutch.

How to find it: Turn off 309 road towards sea just south of Adige river 10 km. south of Chioggia, and 5 km. to site.

General Details: Open 13 May - 24 Sept. Supermarket. Large bar/pizzeria and self-service restaurant. Tennis. Hairdresser. Swimming pools. Children's playground. Fridge hire. Disco. Entertainment programme. No dogs.

Charges 1998: Four rates acc. to season (highest 22/7-19/8): Per person L. 5,000 - 14,500; child (2-5 yrs) 4,000 - 12,500, ; pitch with full facilities 7,000 - 34,000; tent pitch 5,000 - 15,000. Less 10% for stays over 3 weeks.

Reservations: made for min. 7 days with deposit (L. 30,000) from Sat. or Thurs. Address: Isolaverde, 30010 Sa. Anna di Chioggia (VE). Tel: 041/498100. FAX: 041/490440.

6065 Camping Tahiti, Lido delle Nazioni, nr Ravenna

Excellent site with swimming pools and other amenities north of Ravenna.

Tahiti is a very pleasant, well run site less than a mile from the sea (with small fun train link). Flowers and shrubs enhance its appearance and, unlike many sites of this size, it is still family owned and run. As well as the swimming pool, there is a Caribbean style water-play fun area surrounded by palms and with a bar. Good children's playground with `mini-club' where staff organise activities, a small outdoor theatre for summer entertainment, a tennis court and good minigolf. Needs are well catered for with a self-service restaurant, bar, pizzeria, supermarket and shops. The 400 pitches are of varying size, back to back from hard roads and defined by trees with shade in most areas. There are 38 pitches with a private unit containing a WC and washbasin. Electricity (3A) is available throughout. One sanitary block has been rebuilt to a very high standard and the two other smaller ones refurbished. They have a mix of British and Turkish style WCs and free hot water for washbasins, sinks and showers. The new block has a baby room and make-up/hairdressing room. English is spoken by the friendly management, although the British have not yet really discovered this site which is popular with Italians and Germans.

How to find it: Turn off SS309 35 km. north of Ravenna to Lido delle Nazioni and follow camp signs.

General Details: Open 18 May - 21 Sept. Self service restaurant. Pizzeria. Bar. Supermarket and shops. Swimming pools. Children's playgrounds. Tennis. Table tennis. Minigolf. Volleyball. Football. Organised entertainment and excursions in high season. Daily medical service. Chemical disposal. Chalets and bungalows for hire.

Charges guide: Per person L. 6,800 - 10,900; child (under 8) 7,800 - 9,900; pitch incl. electricity 16,800 - 20,900, with water 18,000 - 23,500; private WC plus 6,000 - 12,000.

Reservations: Min. 1 week (2 weeks in high season) with deposit. Address: 44020 Lido delle Nazioni (Ferrara). Tel: 0533/399699 or 379500. FAX: 0533/379700. E-mail: info@tahiti.com. Internet: http://www.campingtahiti.com.

6075 Camping Cesenatico, Cesenatico, nr Ravenna

Large, edge of town site with access to private beach.

The northern Adriatic coast of Italy is popular with British visitors and this is a well appointed site about midway between Rimini and Ravenna. It is a large site under trees on flat grass at the northern end of Cesenatico. Apart from the nearby attractions of San Marino, Ravenna and Rimini, Florence and Venice are within easy reach for day visits. However the site also provides many attractions of its own, with access to a private beach, sports and entertainment for children. There are 800 pitches, half for tourers, marked by trees so size varies, all with 4A electricity. An unusual feature is the 37 small toilet blocks around the site. Of mixed construction and quality, but acceptable with mainly Turkish style WCs, free hot water to some basins, showers and dishwashing points, plus washrooms for disabled people.

How to find it: Site is on the SS16 on north edge of Cesenatico, and is well signed.

General Details: Open 1 April - 25 Sept. Bar/restaurant and takeaway. Supermarket. Hairdresser. Bazaar. Tennis. Minigolf. Table tennis. Watersports. Disco. Washing machines and dryers. Motorcaravan service point.

Charges guide: Per adult L. 6,000 - 10,500; child (3-8) 5,000 - 8,500; pitch 13,500 - 18,000, with electricity 16,500 - 24,500; small tent incl. 2 persons 21,000 - 30,000. Minimum price per pitch 28,000 - 42,000.

Reservations: Write to site. Address: Via Mazzini 182, 47042 Cesenatico (FO). Tel: 0547/81344. FAX: 0547/672452. E-mail: gesturist@linknet.it.

ITALY - Central

6060 Camping Comunale Estense, Ferrara

Very useful municipal site, on outskirts of city.

Ferrara is an interesting and historic city, well worth a short visit. The old city, surrounded by ancient walls, is attractive and mainly pedestrianised, with several museums, a cathedral and a wealth of architectural interest, but as a result of an apparent lack of publicity, has relatively few foreign visitors. The recently established municipal campsite, on the northern outskirts offers comfortable facilities for all types of unit and includes 50 fairly large pitches, with numerous electrical connections, and two adjacent well fitted sanitary blocks (one heated) with large free hot showers, British and Turkish style WCs, etc. The showers have no separated dressing area, the hooks are on outside walls and the tiled floors become very slippery. In summer the two blocks seem to open on alternate days, presumably to save on cleaning and one suspects this may be a bit variable. However, despite the somewhat uncared for overall appearance, it proved to be perfectly adequate and comfortable, with a friendly reception and reasonable prices. No on-site facilities other than those described above, but there is an excellent trattoria within walking distance (1 km.) and a wide choice of other eating places in the city itself.

How to find It: Site is well signed from the city and is on the northern side of the ring road.

General Details: Open all year. Restayrant adjacent. Bicycle hire. Fishing 500 m. Golf 100 m. Riding 3 km. Chemical disposal.

Charges 1999: Per person (over 8 yrs) L. 7,000; pitch 12,000; dog 3,000. No credit cards.

Reservations: Policy not known - contact site. Address: Via Gramicia, 76, 44100 Ferrara. Tel: 0532/752396. FAX: as phone. Tourist information office: Tel: 0532/209370. FAX: 0532/212266. E-mail: infotur.comfe@fe.nettuno.it.

6602 Camping-Hotel Citta' di Bologna, Bologna

Good quality site in historic city.

This site was established as recently as '93 on the edge of the Trade Fair Centre of this ancient and historic city. Although near enough to the motorway to be aware of traffic `hum', the site is surrounded by fields and trees giving a peaceful atmosphere. The intention was not only to make a camp site, but to provide high quality motel-type rooms for use by those visiting trade fairs. Although the bungalows are self-contained, a fine sanitary block for campers' use has been constructed in the centre of the camping area. Hot water is free in washbasins and sinks and on meter in the showers. There is excellent provision for the disabled (with British WCs and free showers) with alarms which ring in reception. WCs, except for two in each section are Turkish style. The 150 pitches are numbered and marked out by young trees (60-75 sq.m.) on level grass with hardstandings (open fretwork of concrete through which grass can grow) in two areas. A restaurant is planned but there is no date for completion. The site is excellent for an overnight stop or for longer stays to explore Emilia-Romagna.

How to find it: Site is well signed from `Fiera' exit on the autostrada on the northeast of the city.

General Details: Open all year (except 10 days at Christmas). 63,000 sq.m. Electrical connections (6A) in all areas. Excellent facilities for the disabled. Bar. Soft drinks and snacks available from machine. Small children's play area. Table tennis. Football. Minigolf. Volleyball. Shops and restaurant 500 m. Medical room - doctor will call. Washing machines. Chemical disposal. Motorcaravan services. Bus service to city centre from site.

Charges 1999: Per person L. 6,500 - 9.000; child (3-8 yrs) 5,000 - 6,500; pitch 14,000 - 18,000; electricity included. Credit cards accepted.

Reservations: Write to site. Address: Campeggio Citta' di Bologna, Via Romita 12/4a, 40127 Bologna. Tel: 051/325016. FAX: 051/325318. E-mail: campinghotelbologna@iol.it.

AR Discount
Less 5% on tarrif.

6608 Camping Torre Pendente, Pisa

Pisa's most central site.

Torre Pendente is a friendly site, well run by the Signorini family who speak good English and make everyone feel welcome. It is within walking distance of the famous leaning tower (but via a dimly lit underpass). Obviously its position means it is busy throughout the main season. A medium sized site, it is on level, grassy ground with tarmac or gravel access roads and some shade. There are 220 touring pitches, 160 with 5A electricity. The sanitary facilities are very adequate with hot showers and mainly British style toilets (cleaning may be variable). A swimming pool is planned, but meanwhile the municipal pool is near. The shop, bar and restaurant cater for all pockets. Consider a visit in mid-June to coincide with the town fiesta - the candle-lit river banks and leaning tower are something to behold.

How to find It: From autostrada A12, exit at Pisa Nord and follow signs for 5 km. to Pisa. The site is well signed at a left turn into the town centre (Viale delle Cascine) and is then a short distance on the left hand side.

General Details: Open week before Easter - 15 October. 24,000 sq.m. Shop. Bar. Restaurant. Children's playground. Bicycle hire. Riding 3 km. Chemical disposal. Motorcaravan services. Caravans and bungalows for hire.

Charges 1999: Per adult L. 10,000 - 11,000; child (3-10 yrs) 6,000; car 6,000; tent 10,000; 1 person tent 7,000; caravan 11,000; motorcaravan 15,000; m/cycle 3,000. No credit cards.

Reservations: Contact site. Address: Viale delle Cascine 86, 56122 Pisa. Tel: 050/561704. FAX: 050/561734. E-mail: leda@mailbox.iunet.it. Internet: www.codekard.it/torrependente.

AR Discount
Welcome drink

6600 Camping Barco Reale, San Baronto, nr Pistoia

Beautiful site in Tuscany hills, with fine views.

Just 40 minutes from Florence and an hour from Pisa, this site is beautifully situated high in the hills with fine views. Part of an old, walled estate, there are pleasant walks available in the grounds. A quiet site, now of 10 ha, and with good shade from mature pines and oaks, there are 175 numbered pitches, all for tourists but not all easily accessible for towed units. All have electrical connections (3, 5 or 10A) and 50 pitches now have water and waste water drainage also. The two modern sanitary blocks are centrally positioned and are kept very clean with British and Turkish type WCs, free hot water throughout, two toilets for disabled people and a baby room. Bathrooms are planned. The site has an attractive bar, a very smart restaurant with terrace and a good sized swimming pool. Live music and other entertainments, including games for children, are arranged in high season. There is a small shop on site and others in the village 1 km. away. Outside the site itself but part of the estate are other leisure facilities listed below. A lake for fishing, a disco and an indoor pool are 5 km. away. This is an attractive site which will appeal to those who prefer a quiet site but with plenty to do for all age groups. No fires are permitted.

How to find it: From Pistoia take the Vinci - Empoli - Lamporecchio signs to San Baronto. From Empoli follow signs to Vinci and San Baronto. Final approach is around a sharp bend and up a steep slope.

General Details: Open 1 April - 30 Sept. Restaurant. Bar. Disco. Small shop. Swimming pool. Children's playground. Table tennis. Volleyball. Football. Chess. Bowls. Bicycle hire. Golf 7 km. Fishing 3.5 km. Indoor pool near. Entertainment. Excursions on foot and by bus (all season). Laundry. Chemical disposal. Motorcaravan services.

Charges 1999: Three charging periods. Per person L. 9,500 - 12,000; child 0-3 yrs 5,000 - 6,500, 3-12 yrs 6,000 - 8,000; tent 7,800 - 9,500; trailer tent or caravan 10,000 - 12,500; motorcaravan 14,500 - 17,500; car 5,000 - 6,800; m/cycle 3,500 - 5,000; electricity 2,500. Tax included. Credit cards accepted.

Reservations: Contact site. Address: Via Nardini 11/13, 51030 San Baronto-Lamporecchio (PT). Tel: 0573/88332. FAX: as phone.

CAMPING BARCO REALE

via Nardini, 11/13 • I-51030 S. Baronto (PT)
Tel. and fax 0039/057388332

Swimming pool -
Volleyball -
Outdoor draughts -
Skittle alley - Trekking -
Football field - "Boccia" -
Children's playground -
Supermarket -
Restaurant -
Tennis (3 Km)

The Campsite lies on a hill in a pine and oak wood with a lovely panorama. The house where Leonardo da Vinci was born and the famous town of Tuscany are not far away; excursions by bus are organised. Barco Reale is an ideal site for a pleasant holiday from April to September owing to guided walks among the olive groves and wine country, the wonderful scenery, the local culture and the climate.

IN THE HEART OF TUSCANY

6635 Camping Le Pianacce, Castagneto Carducci, nr Donoratico

Terraced site in Tuscan hills 6 km. back from sea with pleasant pool; south of Livorno.

In a quiet situation 6 km. back from sea at Donoratico, this site has an attractive medium-sized swimming pool and a new children's pool with water games which are overlooked by a terrace leading from the bar. Said to be suitable for tents and caravans the site is, however, on steeply rising ground. The 113 pitches for tourists, all with 3A electricity, are in tiered rows on fairly narrow terraces. Access to most is not easy because the limited space between the small dividing hedges and the high bank of the next terrace restricts manoeuvring so installation is now made by the site's tractor. All pitches are shady. There are now three toilet blocks, including a newer small one at the top of the site. They have all been refurbished to a high standard; British style WCs, individual washbasins with hot water; free hot showers. The site is almost entirely for tourists, with very few seasonal units, but it is likely to be full from about mid-July to 20 Aug. It is a quiet site and peaceful at night. There is a nature reserve adjacent and the sandy beach is 20 km. long so there are no restrictions.

How to find it: Turn off the main S1 just north of Donoratico in hamlet of Il Bambolo at signpost to Castagneto Carducci. After 3 km. turn left signs to Bolgheri and site, then follow camp signs. Single track final approach.

General Details: Open 20 March - 15 Oct. 80,000 sq.m. Shop. Restaurant/bar. Swimming pool and children's pool with water games (from 22/5). Tennis. Minigolf. Bicycle hire. Children's playground. Fishing 6 km. Riding 5 km. Motorcaravan service point. Chemical disposal. New mobile homes for hire.

Charges 1999: Four charging seasons. Per person L. 7,200 - 13,000; child (0-10 yrs) 5,100 - 10,000; motorcaravan or caravan/tent, incl. car 12,500 - 22,000; 2 man tent incl. m/cycle 9,200 - 16,000; extra car 3,000 - 7,000; dog 5,100 - 10,000. Some special offers in low season.

Reservations: made with deposit; contact site. Address: Via Bolgherese, 57022 Castagneto Carducci (LI). Tel: 0565/763667. FAX: 0565/766085.

6630 Camping Montescudaio, Montescudaio, nr Cecina

Well developed site, with swimming pool, south of Livorno.

This site has been fashioned out of a very extensive area of natural undulating woodland (with low trees) and has its own character. There are 300 pitches for touring units plus 170 seasonal units, bungalows or large caravans, in separate clearings. The pitches vary in size, some quite small, and there is varying shade. Electrical connections (3A) are available in all parts. With installations of good quality and a comprehensive range of amenities, this is an attractive site which has almost arrived at the end of its development. It is 4 km. from the sea at the nearest point but there is a large free swimming pool on the site with separate children's pool. The modern sanitary blocks are well appointed with hot water in the two main blocks. The facilities are comprehensive and should provide a good supply, with British style toilets, individual washbasins with shelves, free warm water (premixed) in some basins and showers and baby baths. Used by tour operators (25 pitches). The site reports a new botanical garden and further gardens around the centre and pool areas. There should usually be space.

How to find it: From new autostrada (Livorno-Grosseto) take Cecina, Guardistallo, Montescudaio exit. Follow signs to Guardistallo, <u>not signs to Montescudaio</u>. The site is on the Cecina-Guardistallo road, 2 km. from Cecina.

General Details: Open 7 May - 19 Sept. 250,000 sq.m. Shops. Bar. Restaurant in main season. Open-air pizzeria at one end of site with bar, many tables and small dance floor for nightly family disco from mid-June. Swimming pool. Tennis. Minigolf. Bicycle hire. Good children's playground. Table tennis. Organised events programme in main season. Medical service. Chemical disposal. Motorcaravan services. Bungalows (13) and caravans (71) for hire.

Charges 1999: Per person (any age) 8,200 - 10,500; pitch (any unit) incl. electricity 17,800 - 24,000; electricity included. No credit cards.

Reservations: Write to site with L. 100,000 deposit (Euro 51.54). Address: Casella Postale no. 4, 56040 Montescudaio (Pisa). Tel: 0586/683477. FAX: 0568/630932. E-mail: mocamp@luda.livorno.it. Internet: www.campingmontescudaio.com.

AR Discount
Less 5%

During 1998 changes were made in respect of dialling codes for some European countries. These changes affect only calls made to those countries from abroad.

To call an Italian telephone number from the UK, it is now necessary to dial the International code (00 39 for Italy), followed by the local Area code IN FULL, then the Area code then the telephone number of the person being called.

For example: 00 39 2 555555 becomes 00 39 02 555555.

6637 Camping Il Gineprino, Marina di Bibbona

New, small site near Mediterranean coast in Tuscany.

This is a pleasant part of Tuscany with many interesting places within visiting distance. Il Gineprino is on the edge of Bibbona but not directly on the coast. As the site was only opened in 1995, the ground is a bit bare in parts and the young trees not grown enough yet to provide shade. It is small (15,000 sq.m) when compared with most sites in this area with 100 pitches, but it does have a swimming pool and an excellent restaurant. Cars have to be parked in a separate place opposite the site entrance. The 70 touring pitches are numbered and marked by saplings at the corners and all have a water tap and electricity (4A). There is entertainment provided on two or three evenings each week in high season and excursions can be arranged. The beach is about 400 m. and can be reached on foot through a pine wood. The two sanitary blocks, one at each end, have British and Turkish style WCs and free hot water in washbasins and showers, with cold for dish and clothes washing. Family room (on payment) with WC, washbasin and shower and facilities for disabled people. The site reports a new area for motorcaravans. The friendly owner, who speaks some English, is keen to welcome British guests.

How to find it: Site signed on approach from main SS1 coast road between La California and Marina di Bibbona.

General Details: Open April - end Sept. 15,000 sq.m. Shop, restaurant with terrace (both 1/5-15/9). Swimming pool (1/5-15/9). Games room. TV room. Table tennis. Bicycle hire. Football pitch. Volleyball. Fishing 500 m. Riding 1 km. Some entertainment in high season. Excursions. Chemical disposal. Motorcaravan service point. Caravans (8) and new bungalows (9) to rent.

Charges 1998: Per person L. 8,000 - 14,000; child (under 8 yrs) 6,500 - 10,000; tent, caravan or motorcaravan with electricity 14,000 - 20,000; small tent, no electricity 14,000 - 17,000. No credit cards.

Reservations: Write to site. Address: Via del Platani, 57020 Marina di Bibbona. Tel/Fax: 0586/600550. (Winter: c/o Arch. Roberto Valori, via F.lli Rosselli 7, 57023 Cecina (LI). Tel/Fax: 0586/683500).

6610 Camping Panoramico, Fiesole, Florence/Firenze

Hilltop site with fine views on the outskirts of Florence.

This is a good site in a fine hilltop situation, appreciably fresher and quieter than near the town, and with good installations. However, it can become overcrowded in main season with too many pushed in and a steep final access on which it is difficult for caravans to restart when halted by parked cars. The site will assist with a jeep if required and we still rate it one of the best sites around Florence if you want to stay a while, though further from the centre (7 km.) than some of the others. There is a bus service from Fiesole to the centre of Florence (tickets from site office) but it is a long uphill walk back to the camp. The 120 pitches are on terraces and steep walks to and from the various facilities could cause problems for people with mobility or breathing problems. The sanitary installations are not too large but of quite good quality, with mainly British style WCs, and free hot water in washbasins and showers. If you only want a quick overnight stop for a rapid tour round Florence, you could try Camping Internazionale Firenze, on southwest side of, and quite close to the city, and quickly reached from the Certosa exit of autostrada A1.

How to find it: From A1 take Firenze-Sud exit and follow signs to Fiesole (which lies NNE of central Firenze). From Fiesole centre follow `Camping Fiesole' - not `Panoramico' which is only on site entrance - 1 km.

General Details: Open all year. 25,000 sq.m. Shade in many parts. Electrical connections throughout (3A). Shop (30/3-30/10). Bar (30/3-30/10). Snack bar (15/7-15/9). Motorbike rental. Fridges, irons and little cookers for campers' use. Washing machines. Chemical disposal. Bungalows and caravans for hire.

Charges 1999: Per person L. 13,000, incl. local tax; child (3-12 yrs) 9,000; pitch 22,000. Credit cards accepted.

Reservations: Not taken and said to be unnecessary if you arrive by early afternoon. Address: Via Peramonda 1, 50014 Fiesole (Firenze). Tel: 055/599069. FAX: 055/59186.

6611 Camping Il Poggetto, Troghi, nr Firenze

Small family run site near Firenze.

This new site, only 15 minutes from Firenze, has a lot to offer. It benefits from a very nice panorama and on one side, a few acres of the Zocchi family vineyards add to its charm. The owners have a wine producing business background and you can purchase their wines at the site's shop. All pitches have electricity and range in size (80-100 sq.m). There are two sanitary blocks which were very clean during our visit, with a mix of British and Turkish style WCs and washbasins and showers with free hot water. Washing machines and dryers are available.. The restaurant offers mainly pizzas and pasta, as you would expect in Italy, and a large terrace for both the restaurant and bar overlooks the two good sized swimming pools. A regular bus service runs directly from the site for visiting Firenze. Tennis 100 m.

How to find it: Leave A1 at `Incisa Valdarno' exit. Turn left, then right towards Firenze. Site is 5 km, well signed.

General Details: Open 1 March - 31 Oct. Volleyball. Games room. Table tennis. Bicycle and scooter hire.

Charges 1998: Per person L. 10,500 - 12,000; child (0-12 yrs) 7,000 - 7,500; pitch 18,500 - 20,000.

Reservations: Contact site. Address: Via Il Poggetto 143, 50010 Troghi (Firenze). Tel: 055/07323. FAX: as phone. E-mail: poggetto@tin.it. Internet: www.codekard.it/ilpoggetto

6612 Camping Villagio Norcenni Girasole Club, Figline Valdarno, nr Firenze

Secluded haven for campers in the heart of Tuscany.

A busy, well run site in a picturesque, hilly situation 32 km. south of Florence, the Norcenni Girasole Club has been efficiently run by the Cardini family since 1982. An excellent swimming pool with water slide, a heated covered pool, fitness centre and an attractive bar and restaurant, grouped together, are of particular note.There are now over 200 places for touring units, all with 4A electricity, many occupied by tour operators. Although on a fairly steep hillside, pitches are on level terraces accessed from good, hard roads. Sanitary facilities are good with mixed British and Turkish style WCs. Free warm water is dispensed through a single push-button tap. There are five family bathrooms for hire but, being very popular, these need to be booked in advance. An animation programme includes music evenings and activities for children. Excursions are arranged, courses in Italian or Tuscan cooking. English is spoken.

How to find it: From Florence take Rome AI/E35 autostrada and take Incisa exit. Turn south on route 69 towards Arezzo. In Figline turn right for Greve and watch for Norcenni signs - site is about 4 km up a twisting, climbing road.

General Details: Open 1 March - 31 Oct. 110,000 sq.m. Supermarket and gift shop. Bar and restaurant. Pizzeria. Washing machines and dryers. Flood-lit tennis. Swimming pools. Fitness centre with jacuzzi and Turkish bath. Chemical disposal. Riding. Excursions. Bungalows to rent.

Charges guide: Per person L. 11,200 - 12,500; child (under 12 yrs) 6,500 - 7,200; car 6,200 - 6,900; m/cycle 5,200 - 5,800; caravan 9,700 - 10,700; tent 8,900 - 9,800; motorcaravan 15,600 - 17,200; electricity 2,100 - 2,300.

Reservations: Contact site. Address: Via Norcenni 7, 50063 Figline Valdarno Tel: 055/959666. FAX: 055/959337.

6623 Centro Turistico San Marino, San Marino

Good modern site with swimming pool.

According to one guide book, the Republic of San Marino is "an unashamed tourist trap which trades on its falsely preserved autonomy". It has its own mint, produces its own postage stamps, issues its own car registration plates and has a small army, but in all other respects, is part of Italy. However, tourists do seem to find it interesting, particularly those with patience to climb to the battlemented castles on the three highest ridges. Centro Turistico San Marino is a good 4 km. below this, at 400 m. above sea level and spreading gently down a hillside, with lovely views across to the Adriatic. It has a good variety of trees but, as most of these are young, not much shade as yet. Caravan pitches are on level terraces with hardstanding, accessed from hard roads, separated by hedges with water and electricity (5A). Smaller pitches on lower terraces are for tents. Four good sanitary blocks are spread around the site with British and Turkish style WCs and free hot water in washbasins, sinks and showers. The attractive, almost circular, swimming pool has hydro-massage and solarium. Shop with limited supplies. Restaurant with terrace overlooking the pool with good views. In high season, staff organise activities for children and adults. Used by a tour operator (15 pitches). Good English is spoken and British campers are welcomed.

How to find it: Leave autostrada A14 at exit Rimini-Sud (or SS16 where signed), follow SS72 west to San Marino. Site is signed from about 15 km.

General Details: Open all year. 100,000 sq.m. Shop (all year, closed Tues. in winter). Restaurant (all year). Swimming pool (1/6-10/9). Hydro-massage. Solarium. Children's play area. Table tennis. Volleyball. Football. Archery. Boules. Tennis. Bicycle hire. Riding 5 km. Golf 10 km. Fishing 7 km. Small amphitheatre. Animation programme (high season). Washing machines. Motorcaravan service point. Chemical disposal. Bungalows for hire.

Charges guide: Per person L. 7,000 - 12,000; child (4-10 yrs) 3,500 - 10,000; tent 6,000 - 11,000; caravan 6,000 - 16,000; car 2,500 - 7,000; motorcaravan 7,000 - 21,000; TV connection 1,000 - 5,000. Credit cards accepted.

AR Discount
Less 5%
all year

Reservations: Write to camp. Address: Strada San Michele 50, 47031 Cailungo, R.S.M. Tel: 0549/903964. FAX: 0549/907120. E Mail: cturistico@omniway.sm.

See colour advert
between pages 192/193

6624 Camping Villaggio Rubicone, Savignano Mare

This site has been recommended by our Italian Agent and will be inspected by us during '99. Rubicone covers over 30 acres of landscaped, level ground by the sea and has its own 170 m. long and 40 m wide beach. There is shade from poplar trees for some of the 630 touring pitches which vary in size (up to 90 sq.m). The majority have electricity (5A), 40 with water and waste water, and 20 with their own sanitary facilities. For the remainder, there are modern facilities with free hot water for showers and washbasins (half in private cabins), mainly British style toilets and a good unit for disabled visitors. Hot water for dishwashing and laundry (washing machines also). There are many sporting opportunities and, across the railway line (via an underpass), are swimming pools for adults and children.

How to find it: Site is 15 km. northwest of Rimini. From Bologna exit the A14 at Rimini north and head for the S16 to Bellaria and San Mauro a Mare; site is well signed.

General Details: Open 1 May - 30 Sept. Restaurant, snack bar and shop (all season). Swimming pool. Children's play equipment. Tennis. Beach showers. Boat launching. Sailing and windsurfing schools. No dogs accepted.

Charges 1998: Per person L. 13,000; child (2-8) 11,500; pitch 16,500 - 23,000; electricity 3,500.

Reservations: Contact site. Address: Via Matrice Destra 1, 47039 Savignano Mare (FO). Tel: 0541/346377. FAX: 0541/346999. E-mail: info@campingrubicone.com. Internet: http://www.campingrubicone.com.

6620 Campo Norina, Pesaro

Small, seaside site with own private beach on Adriatic Riviera.

This small, rectangular site is sandwiched between mountain, road and railway and the coast. The private beach of fine sand runs the 320 m. length of the site and as the shore is said to slope gently, could make a base for a family holiday as well as for visiting the attractions nearby, both inland and along the northern Adriatic coast. The main access road runs near the railway line, with pitches arranged either side of smaller roads at right angles to the shore. The places are marked by numbered stones and backed by hedges, all having electrical connections (3A). There is a children's play area and a small platform for dancing during the high season. Stone groynes, running parallel to the shore, some 70 m. from it, should make for calm water. The site has a family atmosphere. The pleasant bar/restaurant has a pizzeria as well as specialising in local sea food. The three toilet blocks, although showing signs of age, are tiled and clean with a mixture of British and Turkish style WCs. Cold water only in washbasins and dishwashing sinks, with hot water on payment in showers. English spoken by the friendly management.

How to find it: Site is mid-way between Pesaro and Fano. From autostrada, take Fano exit and follow signs on the SS16 for Pesaro and Rimini. The access road goes under the railway (high enough for motorcaravans), which it shares with Camping Marinella, and care is needed to enter Norina rather than its rival.

General Details: Open 7 April - 15 Oct, as is bar/restaurant. 25,000 sq.m. Shade in some parts. Shop and bazaar (open during season). Washing machine. Chemical disposal. Electricity in all parts. Small children's playground. Dancing (July/Aug). Tennis 400 m. Riding 1 km. San Marino 40 km. and other attractions near.

Charges guide: Per adult L.7,500 - 12,000; child (0-6 yrs) 4,500 - 7,500; pitch incl. electricity 15,000 - 22,000, small pitch for tent 8,000 - 10,000; dog 3,000 - 5,000; boat 5,000 - 7,500. VAT included.

Reservations: Necessary for August, with deposit and fee - write to site. Address: Marina Ardizia 181, 61100 Pesaro. Tel: 0721/55792. FAX: 0721/55165.

6625 Camping La Montagnola, Sovicille, nr Siena

Quiet, clean site close to Siena, Volterra and San Gimignano.

An agreeable alternative to sites closer to the centre of Siena, La Montagnola is set in secluded woodland to the north of the village of Sovicille. The owners have worked hard to provide a good basic standard of amenities. The 66 pitches are of good size (80 sq.m), clearly marked and have reasonably good shade. All are suitable for caravans and motorcaravans with electricity (5A). Water points are plentiful and the pitches furthest up the hill are arranged in a circle around a central barbecue area. There is an overflow field for tents with no shade and another for sports. A single toilet block provides free hot showers and sufficient washbasins (cold water) and mainly British style toilets - not luxurious, but adequate and clean. A friendly bar/shop area offers snacks and basic provisions; a large supermarket is 6 km. (San Rocco a Philli or Rosia), a small one 6 km. (Sovicille). Two restaurants are in the village. This site could make an excellent touring base for central Tuscany and is not too far from the motorway for short stays, perhaps including a visit to Siena (10 km. with an hourly bus service from the site)

How to find it: From north on the Firenze - Siena motorway take Siena Ovest exit onto SS73 Ponente road from where site is signed. From south (Grosseto) take SS223 turning at crossroads to Rosia from where site is signed.

General Details: Open Easter - 30 Sept. Small shop. Bar. Restaurants and supermarkets near. Chemical disposal.

Charges guide: Per person L. 9,000; child (4-12 yrs) 5,000; pitch 8,000; electricity 2,000.

Reservations: not really necessary. Address: 53018 Sovicille (Siena). Tel: 0577/314473. FAX: as phone. (Winter address: SS73 Ponente 190, Siena. Tel and fax: 0577/349286).

6640 Camping Pappasole, Vignale Riotorto, nr Follonica

Large, well run site on coast with many sporting activities.

This lively site offers plenty of sporting activities and is located 250 m. from its own sandy beach, facing the island of Elba. It is a large site on flat, fairly open ground offering 450 pitches of 90 sq.m. many with electricity (3A) and water, others with electricity, water and waste water connections. Some 344 of the pitches have their own individual sanitary facility with WC, shower and washbasin, and next to these a compartment with 4-burner gas stove, fridge, sink with H&C and drainer, and 5 cupboards (extra cost for this about £5 per night). Pitches are separated by bushes with some shade from medium sized trees and artificial shade in other areas. There may be some road or rail noise in certain areas. There are three modern sanitary blocks with free hot water for the washbasins and showers and mainly Turkish but with some British style WCs. These facilities may be a fair walk from some of the pitches. Laundry facilities are provided. The central focus of the site is a covered area (a very tall, open marquee type structure, floodlit at night) for dancing, music and entertainment which is surrounded by the main camp buildings. There are many sporting opportunities including archery, windsurfing and sailing, tennis, excellent swimming pools and activities and excursions are organised.

How to find it: Site is north of Follonica just off the 'new' SS1 and well signed.

continued overleaf

6640 Camping Pappasole (continued)

General Details: Open 27 March - 16 Oct. Restaurant. Snacks. Bar. Shop. Swimming pools (15/5-26/9). Children's play area. Tennis. Table tennis. Bowls. Archery. Handball. Watersports. Minigolf. Bicycle hire. Fishing. Riding 100 m. Activity and excursion programmes (15/5-5/9). Fridge hire. Medical services. Safety deposit boxes. Laundry facilities. Chemical disposal. Motorcaravan services. Bungalows for rent.

Charges 1999: Per person L. 6,000 - 16,000; child (3-10) 4,500 - 8,500; pitch 15,500 - 37,000, electricity incl; individual sanitary facility 8,500 - 23,000. Credit cards accepted.

Reservations: made for whole weeks, Sat. - Sat. Address: Loc. Carbonifera, 57020 Vignale Riotorto (LI). Tel: 0565/20420. FAX: 0565/20346. Internet: www.pappasole.li.it.

AR Discount
Less 10% in low season

6645 Parco-Campeggio Delle Piscine, Sarteano

See colour advert between pages 192/193

Site with three thermal pools, 6 km. from A1 autostrada southeast of Siena.

Sarteano is a spa and the main feature of this site is the three swimming pools fed by the natural thermo-mineral springs and held at a temerature of 24°. Two of these (one large with whirlpool), set in a park-like ground with picnic tables, are free to those staying on the site; a third, also good sized, on the site itself, is opened in main season for exclusive use of campers. Even apart from the pools, the site is a good one which is worth considering, either as a sightseeing base or as an overnight stop from the Florence - Rome motorway (site is 6 km. from exit). The 450 flat pitches, many occupied by long-stay clients, are fully marked with hedges. They claim they will always find space and reservations are not usually made. Two toilet blocks, one new and of excellent quality, provide very reasonable provision. Mainly British style WCs; washbasins with hot water; free hot showers of different types; particularly numerous sinks for clothes and dishes, with hot water. A friendly welcome. Used by a tour operator.

How to find it: From autostrada A1 take exit for Chiusi and Chianciano. Sarteano (6 km.) and site are signed.

General Details: Open 1 April - 30 Sept. Electrical connections (6A) all parts. Shop (town 200 m). Restaurant/bar. Takeaway. Newspaper kiosk. Swimming pools (one all season). TV room and videos. Tennis. Table tennis. Volleyball. Exchange facilities. Free guided cultural tours. Local market on Fridays. Chemical disposal. Motorcaravan services. Dogs are not taken.

Charges 1999: Per adult L. 13,000 - 17,000; child (3-10 yrs) 9,500 - 11,000; car 5,000 - 7,000; tent or caravan 13,000 - 17,000; motorcaravan 18,000 - 24,000; electricity 4,000. Less 10% for stays over 25 days.

Reservations: May be possible if you write, but probably not necessary (see above). Address: 53047 Sarteano (Siena). Tel: 0578/26971. FAX: 0578/265889. E-mail: bagnosanto@kranet.it. Internet: www.evols.it/bagnosanto.

6653 Camping Listro, Castiglione del Lago

Small, unpretentious site on the western edge of Lake Trasimeno.

A simple, pleasant, flat site right on the shore of the lake, Camping Listro is a few hundred yards north of the historic town of Castiglione. It provides 100 pitches all with electricity. The sanitary facilities are clean and adequate, although most of the WC's are of the Turkish type. Facilities on the site are fairly limited with only a small shop and snack bar, but there are bars and restaurants close by, as are sporting facilities, including a good swimming pool and tennis courts. There is a small children's play area and a private beach on the lake shore. Dogs are accepted in the low season only. Barbecues are permitted but there is no organised entertainment. English is spoken and British guests are particularly welcome.

How to find it: From A1/E35 Florence-Rome autostrada take Val di Chiana exit and join the Perugia (75 bis) superstrada. After 24 km. take Castiglione exit and follow town signs. Signs to site are just before the town.

General Details: Open 1 April - 30 Sept. Bar. Shop. Snack bar. Children's play area. Table tennis. Volleyball. Private beach. Tourist information. Motorcaravan services.

Charges guide: Per person (over 3 yrs) L. 6,000 - 7,000; caravan or motorcaravan 6,000 - 7,000; tent 5,000 - 7,000, acc. to season and size; car 2,000 - 2,500; m/cycle 1,500; electricity incl. Less 10% for stays over 8 days.

Reservations: Contact site. Address: Via Lungolago, 06061 Castiglione del Lago (PG). Tel: 075/951193 (winter: 075/9658235). FAX: 075/9658200.

6650 Camping Kursaal Hotel, Passignano sul Trasimeno

Well located, orderly site on north east edge of Lake Trasimeno, 1 km. from town.

Anna Posta, the charming manager of this pretty, well run site speaks some English and would give a real welcome to British guests. The lake is checked for water quality every week and the site has its own small beach. All water sports are available. The attractive bar and restaurant are complemented by a small well stocked shop, all of which are open from 8 am.-11 pm. daily. Part of the site is very shady with coniferous trees and part is open with flowering trees giving a total of 160 pitches, each of 80 sq.m. but not all marked. There are plentiful electrical connections (15A) and no static pitches. Two sanitary blocks, well arranged and spotless, provide mainly British type toilets, free hot showers and facilities for disabled people and babies. A family atmosphere is encouraged on the site but this is not a place for the more uninhibited. There is a 16 room hotel on site on the site which could be of interest, for example to families who have elderly parents with them.

How to find it: Take exit 'Passignano est' from the Perugia spur of the Florence-Rome autostrada; the site is well signed from there.

General Details: Open 25 March - 30 Oct. Bar/restaurant (live music in bar in high season). Shop - supermarket 500 m. Good swimming pool (free). Small play area for children. Fishing. Bicycle hire 500 m. Riding 2 km. Chemical disposal. Motorcaravan services. Hotel and bungalow accommodation.

Charges 1999: Per adult L. 9,000 - 10,000; child 0-3 yrs 3,000, 4-10 yrs 7,000 - 8,000; caravan or tent 11,000 - 15,000; car 3,000; motorcaravan 14,000 - 18,000; dog 2,000; electricity 2,500. Credit cards accepted.

AR Discount
Less 10% on person fee excl. July/Aug.

Reservations: Accepted with 30% deposit (by Eurocheque payable to Camping Kursaal). Address: 06065 Passignano sul Trasimeno. Tel: 075/828085. FAX: 075/827182.

6654 Camping Badiaccia, Castiglione del Lago

Lakeside camp with on-site activity and excursion possibilities.

Lake Trasimeno is not Italy's most beautiful lake, as the immediate environs are rather flat, although within sight of distant mountains. However, it does provide a base from which to visit interesting places in this part of central Italy or as a night stop when travelling to Rome, being near the A1 autostrada. Camping Badiaccia, being directly on the lake, gives an almost seaside atmosphere and it has a good selection of sporting opportunities with four special staff in high season to organise activities for children and adults. Being well tended and maintained, it has a pleasant appearance enhanced by a variety of plants and flowers and, although some pitches are smaller than average, there is good shade in most parts. The 195 pitches for touring are numbered and separated by trees and bushes in rows from hard access roads. As well as swimming in the lake, there is a good sized swimming pool (20 x 10 m) and small one for children. A large area by the lake has access from the site. Guided excursions to Rome and Florence are organised in high season and a list detailing local markets is displayed. Open all season are a pleasant restaurant, snack bar and a shop. The two centrally positioned sanitary blocks have a mix of Turkish and British style WCs and free hot water in washbasins, sinks and showers. At the time of our visit, good English was spoken by the Dutch receptionist. Accommodation to rent.

How to find it: From the A11 Milan-Rome autostrada take Val di Chiana exit and turn east towards Perugia on the SS75bis. Leave this at Castiglione exit and go south on SS71 to Castiglione where site is well signed.

General Details: Open 1 April - 30 Sept. 55,000 sq.m. Restaurant. Shop. Snack bar. Electricity (4A). Swimming pool and children's pool (1/6-30/9). Play area. Tennis. Table tennis. Boules. Minigolf. Volleyball. Football. Beach volleyball. Windsurfing. Watersports. Fishing. Boats for hire. Riding 7 km. Golf 15 km. Entertainment and excursions in high season. Washing machines. Chemical disposal.

Charges 1998: Per person L. 8,000 - 9,500; child (3-10 yrs) 6,000 - 8,500; tent 8,000 - 9,000; caravan 9,000 - 10,000; motorcaravan 10,000 - 11,500; car 3,000; electricity incl.

AR Discount
Less 10% for 7 days, 15% for 14 days excl July/Aug

Reservations: Write to site. Address: Via Trasimeno 1 - Voc. Badiaccia 91, 06061 Castiglione del Lago (PG). Tel: 075/9659097. FAX: 075/9659019.

During 1998 changes were made in respect of dialling codes for some European countries. These changes affect only calls made to those countries from abroad.

To call an Italian telephone number from the UK, it is now necessary to dial the International code (00 39 for Italy), followed by the local Area code IN FULL, then the Area code then the telephone number of the person being called.

For example: 00 39 2 555555 becomes 00 39 02 555555.

6665 Camping Le Soline, Casciano di Murlo, nr Siena

Small, terraced site with most facilities, some 20 km. south of Siena.

A country hillside site, 800 m. from the village of Casciano, Le Soline has room for 100 caravans and 40 tents set on seven terraces beneath the main buildings. They range in size from 36-80 sq.m. and all caravan pitches have electricity (6A). In high season cars must be parked away from the pitches. The site has its own power supply, and occupying an area of 70,000 sq.m, there are many olive and other small trees which do not, however, provide much shade for the pitches. There are also a few bungalows for hire. The restaurant, pizzeria (all season), shop (closes Oct) and heated swimming pools are by the entrance, which has a large visitors car park. Riding is possible from the site. A good quality sanitary block is on the third terrace, providing mixed British and Turkish style WCs, washbasins (most with hot water) and hot showers on payment, dishwashing (cold water only) and a toilet for the disabled. The site reports a new block with facilities for babies. There are excellent panoramic views of the surrounding countryside and the site is well positioned to visit the many historic and cultural places in the area.

How to find it: From Siena, turn off the SS223 Siena - Grosseto road to the left to Fontazzi (about 20 km.) and keep right for Casciano, following signs.

General Details: Open all year. Restaurant, pizzeria and shop (15/3-15/10). Swimming pools (15/3-15/10). Volleyball. Children's playground. Mini-football field. Bicycle hire. Barbecue area (not allowed on pitches). Riding 600 m. Fishing 3 km. Golf 10 km. Laundry. Car wash. Chemical disposal. Motorcaravan services. Bungalows for rent (3).

Charges 1999: Per person L.10,000; child (2-12 yrs) 7,000; car 3,000; m/cycle 2,000; caravan 10,500; tent 8,000 - 9,500; motorcaravan 11,500; electricity 2,000. Credit cards accepted.

Reservations: Write to site. Address: 53010 Casciano di Murlo (Siena). Tel: 0577/817410. FAX: 0577/817415. E-mail: casoline@amiata.net.

6660 Camping Maremma-Sans-Souci, Castiglióne della Pescaia, nr Grosseto

Seaside site on Mediterranean coast between Livorno and Rome.

Family owned and run, this seaside site is in natural woodland, in which the minimum amount of undergrowth has been cleared to provide 430 individually marked and hedged, flat pitches for tourists. They are mostly small and cars must go to a numbered, shaded and secure car park near the entrance - an inconvenience to those who rely on the car for lighting, though it does mean less vehicle movement on the site. Roads are mostly narrow and bordered by trees (this is a protected area, and they cannot fell the trees) so access to some parts is difficult for caravans, and each pitch is earmarked either for caravans or for tents. A good sandy beach is less than 100 m. from one end of the camp (say 400 m. from the other) and is normally used only by campers. There are five small, acceptable toilet blocks strategically situated around the site. Three have large private cabins each with WC, basin and shower; this has considerably increased the supply of hot showers, which are on payment. Mainly British, some Turkish style toilets. Maremma is a friendly site right by the sea which should appeal to many people who like its style of relaxed camping. This particular region enjoys a very sunny climate with minimum rainfall, and there are occasional water problems. The sea was clean when we visited in May.

How to find it: Site is 2½ km. northwest of Castiglione on road to Follonica.

General Details: Open 1 April - 31 Oct. 100,000 sq.m. overall. Access not easy inside site. Electrical connections (3A) for all caravan pitches. Shop. Excellent restaurant (self service in season) serving a range of local fish and fresh pasta. Bar with pizzas and other snacks. Volleyball. Washing machines. Car wash. Chemical disposal. Excursions organised to Elba and Rome. Sailing school. Caravans for hire. Good English spoken. No dogs taken 16/6-31/8.

Charges guide: Per person L. 7,000 - 12,000; child (under 6 yrs) 5,500 - 7,500; pitch and car 10,000 - 18,000.

Reservations: necessary for July/Aug. and will be made for min. 1 week with deposit (L. 5,000). Address: 58043 Castiglione della Pescaia (Grosseto). Tel: 0564/933765. FAX: 0564/935759.

6663 Camping Amiata, Castel del Piano

Mountain campsite in Tuscany, open all year.

Mount Amiata, the highest point in Tuscany, is accessible by car and becomes very crowded in the height of summer. However, there are splendid views and, away from the summit, the woods and pathways of the lower slopes are beautiful with forests of chestnut and beech inhabited by deer and wild boar. The lush vegetation and fresh mountain air make for superb walking. On a hill-top some 8 km. from Mt Amiata, Camping Amiata is in a nice situation. The site is heavily wooded which provides good shade and pitches, on slightly sloping ground, are separated by hedges which, in parts, offer more privacy than most sites. A narrow road leads to a small square which has reception, shop and pleasant bar/restaurant. From here a hard road leads to side roads with pitches on either side on slightly sloping ground. There are games and TV rooms and a platform with good views which can be used for picnics and where limited musical entertainment is offered in high season. The sanitary accommodation has been, or is, being refurbished and in the main block (heated) behind the restaurant, is mainly in cabins with British style WCs, washbasins and showers, all with free hot water.   *continued overleaf*

6663 Camping Amiata (continued)

In some parts the blocks are unisex. More a base from which to explore than one to remain on all day as the dense tree cover restricts the views.

How to find it: From SS223 (Grosseto-Siena), turn east at Paganico and signs to Castel del Piano or, from SS2 (Siena-Rome) turn west to Abbadia San Salvatore and signs for Castel del Piano.

General Details: Open all year. 42,000 sq.m. Electrical connections (6/10A). Shop. Restaurant. Snacks. Playing field. Bicycle hire 1 km. Riding 3 km. Fishing 15 km. Limited entertainment in high season. Washing machine. Chemical disposal. Motorcaravan service point. Flats for rent.

Charges guide: Per person L. 6,800 - 10,200; child (1-6 yrs) 5.600 - 7,000; pitch 6,800 - 15,000. Credit cards accepted.

AR Discount
Less 5%

Reservations: Write to site. Address: via Roma 15, 58033 Castel del Piano (GR). Tel: 0564/956260. FAX: 0564/955107. Internet: www.codecard.it/campingtoscana.

6656 Camping Il Collaccio, Castelvecchio di Preci

Unusual campsite with good amenities in rural Umbria.

Tuscany has grabbed the imagination and publicity, but parts of nearby Umbria are just as beautiful and deserve to be better known. Preci is tucked away in the tranquil depths of the Umbrian countryside. The natural beauty of Monti Sibillini National Park is near and there are many marked paths and guided excursions. Historic Assisi and Perugia and the walled market town of Norcia are worth exploring and distinctive Umbrian cuisine to be enjoyed. Il Collaccio is owned and run by the Baldoni family who bought the farm over 30 years ago, rebuilt the derelict farmhouse in its original style and then decided to share it by developing a campsite and accommodation to rent. The farming aspect was kept and its products can be bought in the shop and sampled in the excellent restaurant. The camping area has been carved out of the hill-side which forms a natural amphitheatre with splendid views. At first sight the narrow steep entrance seems daunting (the owner will assist nervous 'towers'). The 100 pitches are on level terraces but the thousands of trees, planted to replace those cut down by the previous owner, are not yet mature enough to provide much shade. An interesting feature is a tree plantation on a lower slope where they are experimenting with cultivating truffles - patience is needed as the results will not be known for ten years! Three modern sanitary blocks have British and Turkish style WCs, cold water in washbasins and hot, pre-mixed water in showers and sinks. Excellent, heated swimming pool and children's pool, tennis court, volleyball, basketball, small football pitch, boules and mountain biking. With sparsely populated villages across the valley on the mountain slopes and surrounded by stunning scenery, this site is unusual and different with peace and quiet, activities for those who wish it, good excursions and some entertainment in high season. Small, but not intrusive, tour operator presence.

How to find it: From SS77 Foligno-Civitonova Marche, turn south at Muccia for Visso from where Preci is signed.

General Details: Open 7 April - 15 Oct. 100,000 sq.m. Electrical connections (6A) - long lead useful. Restaurant (all season). Shop (basics, 1/7-31/8). Swimming pool and children's pool (15/5-30/9). Play area. Tennis. Volley and basket ball. Football. Table tennis. Boules. Cycling and walking. Canoeing 2 km. Fishing 10 km. Washing machine. Motorcaravan service point. Chemical disposal. Dormitories for groups and chalets and rooms for hire.

Charges 1998: Per person 9,000 - 11,000; child (3-12 yrs) 4,500 - 5,500; tent 9,000 - 11,000; caravan or motorcaravan 11,000 - 13,000; car 3,000 - 5,000; electricity included. Credit cards accepted..

Reservations: Write to site. Address: Azienda Agricola Il Collaccio, 06047 Castelvecchio di Preci (PG). Tel: 0743/939005. FAX: 0743/939094. E-mail: collaccio@mail.caribusiness.it.

6655 Camping Internazionale, Assisi

Modern, well equipped site with good restaurant and a fine view of the city.

Camping Internazionale is on the west side of Assisi and has new facilities which provide tourers with a good base to visit both St. Francis' city and nearby Perugia and Lake Trasimeno. The toilet block is well appointed and clean, with free hot showers, plenty of washbasins, mainly Turkish style WCs (4 British) and facilities for disabled people. The restaurant has a large garden, and the city is lit up in the evenings to provide a beautiful backdrop to a reasonably priced meal, pizzas to local Umbrian dishes (closed Tues). The 175 pitches are large and clearly marked, on flat grass, and all have electricity (16A). As yet, there is little shade - the trees will take a while to reach full maturity, and it can be very hot in this part of Italy (a swimming pool is planned). However, Assisi boasts one of the finest cathedrals in Christendom, among many other attractions, and a stay in this area should not be cut too short.

How to find it: Site lies on the south side of the SS147, which branches left, off the SS75 Perugia - Foligno road. Follow Assisi signs, and it is clearly signed just over 1 km. from the city.

General Details: Open Easter - October. Restaurant/pizzeria with self-service section. Bar with snacks. Shop. Kitchen for campers. Table tennis. Video games. Bicycle hire. Tennis. Volleyball. Roller skating area. Riding 2 km. Excursions. Bus service to city. Washing machine. Chemical disposal. Motorcaravan services.

Charges 1998: Per adult L. 8,000; child (3-10 yrs) 6,000; tent 7,000; caravan or motorcaravan 9,000; car 3,000; m/cycle 2,000; electricity included. Credit cards accepted.

Reservations: made for 1 week stays in high season, but not really necessary. Address: San Giovanni in Campiglione 110, 06081 Assisi (Perugia). Tel: 075/813710 or 816816. FAX: 075/812335.

6800 Camping Europe Garden, Silvi Marina, nr Pescara

Site with swimming pool and views to the sea, 13 km. northwest of Pescara.

Although not many Britons seem to visit these parts, this is somewhere decent to stay on the south east Italian coast. It lies just back from the coast (2 km) on raised ground with views over the sea. The 250 pitches, all with 10A electricity, are nearly all on terraces - if installation of caravans is difficult a tractor is always available to help. Cars stand by units on about half the pitches, in nearby parking spaces for the remainder. A fair amount of shade is available. There is a good swimming pool of 300 sq.m. on site, plus small children's pool, and a private sandy beach at Silvi about 2 km. away to which there is a bus service provided in July and August. There are two good toilet blocks which are well cleaned and provide mixed British and Turkish style WCs, washbasins with free hot water, not fully enclosed, and free hot showers. Free weekly coach excursions to different parts of the Province (10/7-30/8).

How to find it: Turn off inland S16 coast road at km. 433 stone for Silvi Alta and follow camp signs. From autostrada A14 take Pineto exit from north and Montesilvano exit from south. Signing is very good.

General Details: Open 1 May - 20 Sept. Electrical connections in all parts. Self-service shop. Restaurant. Bar. Tennis. Children's playground. 30 good bungalows for hire.

Charges guide: Three charging seasons. Per person L.6,500 - 10,500; child (3-8 yrs) 5,000 - 7,500; pitch 15,000 - 22,500; m/cycle and 2-man tent 10,500 - 19,500; hiker and 2-man tent 9,000 - 19,500; electricity 2,500. Discounts for longer stays outside high season.

Reservations: made with L.150.000 deposit for first 2 weeks of August (min 2 weeks), at other times without deposit. Address: 64028 Silvi (Teramo). Tel: 085/930137 or 932844-5 (winter 085/75035). FAX: 085/932846. E-mail: nsantare@tin.it.

6805 Camping Heliopolis, Pineto

Attractive site with individual sanitary arrangements and with direct access to beach.

Heliopolis is an attractive, well run site with a friendly English speaking lady owner. We just had to include this site - it is so spacious, although orderly, with an individual shower, WC and kitchen for 140 of the 250 touring pitches. Electrical connections (4A) are available on 16 places and cars are parked near the entrance. The site opens directly onto a wide sand and shingle beach which is very safe for children. Like most Adriatic sites, it is close to the railway, and there is some noise from passing trains. There are two excellent toilet blocks for campers, one for men and one for women. A pleasant bar, a games room, a sizeable, attractive pool and children's pool, plus a good restaurant, plus various beach facilities are all available. Like most Italian sites, this one is very full in July/August.

How to find it: Site is to the north of the town, clearly signed from A14 road (exit Pineto) and SS16 (in town centre). If coming from the north, it is worth the extra money to take the A14; the SS16 is busy and boring.

General Details: Open 1 April - 30 Sept. Bar/restaurant. Shops. Laundry facilities. Swimming pool (from June). Tennis and play pitches. Children's playground. Entertainment organised in high season. Doctor attends 2 hrs daily. A good site for disabled people. Chemical disposal. Caravans and tents for hire.

Charges guide: Three charging seasons. Per standard pitch L.18,000, 22,000 or 32,000; pitch with private facilities 32,000, 35,000 or 45,000; small tent pitch 8,000, 10,000 or 13,000; person 6,000, 8,000, 10,000; child (3-12 yrs) 5,000, 7,000, 9,000; electricity included.

Reservations: Write to site for details. Address: Contrada Villa Fumosa 1, 64025 Pineto (TE). Tel: 085/9492720 -30 or -50. FAX: 085/9492171.

6812 Happy Camping, Rome

A 'proper' camping site with no bungalows or static caravans.

This site, just 10 km. north of Rome, is well situated to visit the glories of the Eternal City. The 36,000 sq.m. are set in a sloping country area in two sections and it is surprising how remote it seems. There are 166 pitches arranged on terraces and trees provide shade in most parts. The two sanitary blocks are well positioned and hot water is free in the shower, washbasins and dishwashing sinks. There is a good shop, pleasant bar, a very acceptable restaurant and a new pizzeria. The large swimming pool and children's pool have safety attendants. There is a bus service every 30 minutes to the metro station. Sig. Bordini and his staff speak English.

How to find it: From the Rome ring road (GRA) take exit 5 on Cassia Bis. Black on white 'Happy' signs are well sited all the way (about 1 km).

General Details: Open April - 31 Oct. 36,000 sq.m. Shop. Bar. Restaurant. Pizzeria. Swimming pool. Washing machine and dryer. Chemical disposal. Motorcaravan service point.

Charges 1998: Per person L. 9,500 - 11,500; child (3-14 yrs) 3,000 - 3,500; tent 5,100 - 5,800; caravan 7,500 - 9,000; motorcaravan 9,500 - 11,500; car 5,100 - 5,800; m/cycle 1,500 - 1,600; electricity included. Credit cards accepted.

Reservations: Contact site. Address: Via Prato delle Corte 1915, 00123 Roma. Tel: 06/33626401 or 3320270. FAX: 06/33613800. Internet: www.webeco.it/happycamping.

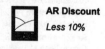

AR Discount

Less 10%

6810 Camping Seven Hills, Rome

Excellent, busy, hillside site with easy access to Rome.

A number of sites are available for visiting the 'Eternal City' and campers needs and preferences will vary. If you are looking for a site away from the centre, Seven Hills makes an excellent base. Situated in a delightful valley, surrounded by two of the seven hills of Rome, just off the Autostrada ring road to the north of the city 4 km. from the city centre. The site runs a bus shuttle service to the city with the frequency dictated by demand. Arranged in two sections, the top half, near the entrance, restaurant and shop, consists of small, flat, grass terraces with 2-4 pitches on each, with smaller terraces for tents, all from hard access roads. Access to some pitches may be tricky. The flat section at the lower part of the site is reserved for ready erected tents used by British (and one Dutch) tour operators who bring guests by coach. These tend to be younger people, but they have their own disco near the swimming pool and are not too obtrusive. The site is a profusion of colour with flowering trees, plants and shrubs and a good covering of trees provides shade. A feature of the site is a 'mini-zoo' - a few small animals are enclosed and peacocks strut around the terraces. The 80 pitches for tourers are not marked out, but the management supervise in busy periods and all should have sufficient space. The excellent central buildings house the well stocked shop and attractive restaurant and bar terrace. Excellent English is spoken and many notices are in English. The three soundly constructed sanitary blocks are well situated around the site, with open plan washbasins, free hot water in the average sized showers and British style WCs. Dishwashing under cover with cold water. All cash transactions on the site are now made with a plastic card (similar to a BT phone card) available at reception. As with all city sites, it can be busy and perhaps a little noisy. There are bungalows to hire but they are of average standard.

How to find it: Take exit 3 from the autostrada ring-road on to Via Cassia (signed SS2 Viterbo - NOT Via Cassia Bis) and look for camp signs. Turn right after 1 km (13 km. stone) and follow small road for about 1 km. to site.

General Details: Open mid-March - mid-Oct. 50,000 sq.m. Shade in most parts. Electrical connections (3A) to some pitches. Shop. Bar/restaurant and terrace. Money exchange. Bus service to Rome. Table tennis. Volleyball. Swimming pool (salt water). Disco. Horse riding. Golf (good course 4 km). Washing machines and irons. Chemical disposal. Excursions and cruises arranged.

Charges guide: Per person (over 4 yrs) L.12,000; tent 6,000 - 9,000; caravan 11,000; car 6,000; motorcaravan 15,000; m/cycle 3,000.

Reservations: Write to site. Address: Via Cassia 1216, 00191 Rome. Tel: 06/30310826. FAX: 06/30362751.

6808 Camping La Genziana, Barrea

Unsophisticated campsite high in the Abruzzi mountains.

This is the place to get away from it all. At night you can almost hear the flowers grow. Situated in the middle of Italy, it is well away from towns, yet only an hour or so from Rome or Pescara. This is a simple site with adequate facilities but Sig. Pasetta makes everyone so welcome. There are 110 pitches, of which 100 have 3A electrical connections, with 50 more for tents. Mountain walking tracks start from the site and facilities for swimming, riding and fishing are all nearby. Not suitable for disabled people.

How to find it: From autostrada A25, either take route 83 from Celano and site is signed 4 km. before Barrea, or take route 17 from Pratola/Sulmona to Castel di Sangro, then route 83 through Barrea to site.

General Details: Open all year. Bar and small shop but Barrea has most things just 500m down the road. Motorcaravan service point.

Charges guide: Per person L. 8,000; child (under 9 yrs) 5,000; caravan 12,000; tent 11,000 - 12,000; motorcaravan 12,000; car 5,000; pet 5,000; electricity 2,000. No credit cards.

Reservations: Contact site. Address: Loc. Tre Croci, Parco Nazionale d'Abruzzo, 67030 Barrea (AQ). Tel: 0864/88101. FAX: as phone.

ITALY - South

6815 Fondi Holiday Camp, Salto di Fondi, nr Sperlonga

Picturesque seaside site with unusual cultural activity, midway between Rome and Naples.

Fondi is a big but peaceful site, midway between Rome and Naples, 300 m. off the main road. Largely covered by a pinewood, carefully tended flowers and trees and the white painted buildings make it a very pleasant site. Sand dunes protect from offshore breezes and during high season there are cultural and sporting activities. A troop of ballet dancers entertain and teach, plays and shows are staged in the open-air theatre and a mini judo festival is held. Films are shown and there is a wardrobe of over 400 costumes for the children. The management also sponsor theatre activity in the town. As well as the beach of fine sand, there are two swimming pools in the entertainment area near the restaurant, just back from the sea. With tennis courts, table tennis and a disco, there appears to be always something going on during the main season. The 100 pitches for tourists are at the back of the site. They have some shade and are on flat grass, all with 3/5A electricity. One large and five smaller toilet blocks are modern and have mainly Turkish, but some British type WCs. Hot howers are on payment, with cold water for washbasins and dishwashing; two family washrooms (hot water) and facilities for disabled people. The large restaurant offers self service at lunch times with waiter service during the evenings. The private beach is 250 m. wide. Signora Banotti, the owner speaks excellent English. All in all, an excellent site.

How to find it: Sperlonga is on the coast road SS213 between Gaeta and Terracina, 7 km. from Terracina. It is reached from the Rome - Naples autostrada, depending on approach, from several exits between Frosinone and Ceprana. Site is signed from Sperlonga and Terracina.

General Details: Open 1 April - 28 Sept. 40,000 sq.m. Bar/restaurant, pizzeria, snack bar (all June- Sept). Supermarket. Greengrocer. Hairdresser. Chemical disposal. Swimming pools. Tennis. Table tennis. Handball. Disco. TV. Live theatre and ballet. Organised excursions. Washing machines and dryers. Dogs not permitted.

Charges guide: Per pitch incl. 2 persons L.30,000 - 65,000; extra person 9,000 - 20,000.

Reservations: Write to site. Address: Via Flacca km 6,800, 04020 Salto di Fondi (LT). Tel: 0771/555029 or 556282. FAX: 0771/555009.

6820 Camping Baia Domizia, Baia Domizia, Mondragone, nr Napoli

Large, formal seaside site north of Naples with many amenities.

This very large site, about 70 km. north west of Naples, is largely covered by a pinewood, much of which has been left in its natural state. There are 1,200 touring pitches, often in clearings on ground which may be grassy, a bit sandy, or on hardstanding. Finding a good pitch may take time, but staff help in season and there are many pitches numbered for reservation purposes. Many varieties of bushes, roses and other flowers have been added to the natural surroundings. The site is run on strict lines, with various regulations (eg. no dogs or radios) but it is not a regimented site, and the general atmosphere is quiet but easy-going. Although the site is so big, there is never very far to walk to the beach, though from the ends it may be some 300 m. to the central shops and restaurant. Near these is a good sized swimming pool, a pleasant alternative to the sea on windier days, with a smaller children's pool. Seven good toilet blocks all have British style WCs, hot water in all washbasins (many in cabins) and showers, and facilities for disabled people. A wide range of sports and other amenities is available.

How to find it: Turning to Baia Domizia leads off Formia-Naples road 23 km. from Formia. From Rome-Naples autostrada, take Cassino exit to Formia. Site is to the north of Baia Domizia itself.

General Details: Open 1 May - 30 Sept. 450,000 sq.m. Many parts well shaded, but full sun near beach. Electrical connections (3A). Supermarket and general shop. Bar. Self-service restaurant with pizzeria. Ice cream parlour. Sports ground. Children's playground. Bicycle hire. Windsurfing hire and school. Fishing and riding 3 km. Tennis near. Excursions. Bureau de change. Doctor on site daily. Washing machines, spin dryers. Chemical disposal. No dogs.

Charges 1998: Per person L. 5,900 - 14,000; child charged as adult; car or m/cycle 3,500 - 6,000; tent or caravan 9,000 - 19,500; motorcaravan 10,400 - 22,700; electricity included. Less 10% outside 24/5-4/9. No credit cards.

Reservations: none, but min. 1 week stay in high season.(July/Aug). Address: 81030 Baia Domizia (Caserta). Tel: 0823/930164 or 930126. FAX: 0823/930375.

6835 Camping Riposo, Piano di Sorrento, nr Napoli

Small site with few facilities but reasonable charges.

Just 300 m. from the picturesque port of Piano di Sorrento is the tiny site of Camping Riposo. Simple, pretty and clean, this is only for those who just want a secluded place to park their ˋvan whilst they explore this famous area. There are no entertainments and no pool - just a tiny bar and shop. The Scalici family offer a courteous and helpful service. The site is shaded by citrus trees and there are three excellent food shops nearby. Electrical connections are available and there is free hot water.

How to find it: From Meta follow plentiful directions for either Riposo or Costa Alta (no. 6830) off main road SS145 (to Sorrento from autostrada at Castellamare). Access could be tricky for large units but gates open wide.

General Details: Open 1 June - 30 Sept. Small bar and shop. Caravans for hire.

Charges guide: Per person L. 7,000; child (1-6 yrs) 5,000; tent 6,000 - 8,500, acc. to size; caravan 8,500; motorcaravan 11,000; car 5,500; m/cycle 3,000; electricity and tax included.

Reservations: Write to site. Address: Via Cassano 12/14, 80063 Piano di Sorrento (NA). Tel: 081/8787374.

6830 Villagio Turistico Costa Alta, Piano di Sorrento, nr Napoli

Pleasant, shady site on headland above the sea.

Although sites like Camping Pini and Giardino delle Esperidi (San Agnello) are of a similar standard and price, Costa Alta is better located. We do not recommend any sites beyond Sorrento town centre because of the daily, chaotic congestion on the only main road. Costa Alta has 118 pitches, 50 of which are permanently reserved, and there are also 60 bungalows. The site is on a gentle slope. The toilet blocks have free hot water, but only one small block is suitable for disabled people. The swimming pool (25 x 12 m.) charges on a daily rate (L 5,000) and is open from 15 June. Facilities include a snack bar and a well run restaurant. A supermarket and other shops are just 100 m. away. There is tennis and table tennis and evening entertainment in July and August. Lift access to the small area of so called beach.

How to find it: Piano di Sorrento is 2 km. before Sorrento centre approaching on the SS145 from Castellamare. Site is well signed, but Camping Riposo nearby has clearer signs to follow.

General Details: Open 15 March - 31 Oct, as are restaurant and bar. Shade in most parts, not all. Electrical connections. Tennis. Table tennis. Dancing and video shows July/Aug. Bungalows and chalets for hire.

Charges guide: Per person L. 10,000 - 14,000; child (2-6 yrs) 5,500 - 8,000; caravan 9,000 - 13,500; tent 7,500 - 13,000; car 4,000 - 6,500; motorcaravan 13,000 - 16,000; electricity 4,000.

Reservations: are made for any period, with 10% deposit. Address: Via Madonna di Roselle 20/A, 80063 Piano di Sorrento (NA). Tel: 081/5321832. FAX: 081/8788368.

6845 Centro Turistico San Nicola, Peschici, Gargano Peninsula

Busy, top class site on most attractive, sandy cove (but 80 km. from the autostrada).

This is a really splendid site occupying a hill side, sloping down to a cove with a 500 m. beach of fine sand, protected by cliffs at each end. Surrounded by tree clad mountains, it is a quiet, well regulated site which is part of, but separate from, a tourist holiday complex. Hard roads lead to well constructed, grassy terraces, under shade from mature trees. By the beach is another camping area on grass, but with little shade and minimal space. There are 750 pitches of varying size, all with 5A electrical connections. Cars may have to be parked away from the pitches in high season. There are no static caravans but bungalows are available for rent. Six excellent, modern toilet blocks, two in the beach part, the others around the site, are of superb quality with British and Turkish style toilets and free hot water in washbasins (some with toilets in cabins), showers and dishwashing facilities. The shopping complex (open during busiest seasons) has a supermarket, greengrocer, fish stall, hairdresser and bazaar for holiday items. The large bar/restaurant with another small shop and two small bars are by the beach. Entertainment for young and old by the restaurant in high season. The site is fairly remote with some tortuous roads towards the end of the 80 km. trip from the autostrada. With a neat, tidy appearance, flower beds provide a garden atmosphere of calm serenity. Popular with German campers (tannoy announcements and most notices in German only!)

How to find it: Leave the Autostrada A14 at exit for Poggio Imperiale, and proceed towards Peschici and Vieste. When signs for Peschici and Vieste diverge, follow Vieste signs keeping a sharp lookout for San Nicola. Then follow black signs for Centro Turistico San Nicola and pass Camping Baia San Nicola (on your left) just before site. It will take at least 1½ hrs from the motorway. Note: There is also a San Nicola Varano en-route which must be ignored.

General Details: Open 1 April - 15 Oct. 120,000 sq.m. Supermarket, fruit and fish shops, bazaar. Beach bars (from 1/5). Bar/restaurant. Tennis. Watersports. Children's playground. Organised activity July/Aug. Cash point. Excursions. Washing machines and dryers. Chemical disposal. Bungalows for rent. No dogs July/Aug.

Charges guide: Per adult L. 6,500 - 14,000; child (1-8 yrs) 4,500 - 10,000; tent 6,500 - 14,000; caravan or trailer tent 8,500 - 17,000; car 5,000 - 8,500; motorcaravan 12,000 - 21,000. Min. stay 7 days 18/6-3/9.

Reservations: Only made for site's own accommodation (min. 1 week). Address: 71010 Peschici (Foggia), Gargano. Tel: 0884/964024. FAX: 0884/964025.

6803 Camping Villagio Athena, Paestum

Compact, well run site by the sea and 1 mile from the Greek temples.

This level site, which has direct access to the beach, has most facilities to hand. Some of the site is in woodland, but sun worshippers will have no problem here. The access is easy and the staff are friendly. There are 150 pitches, of which only 20 are used for static units and these are unobtrusive. Sanitary facilities are in two blocks with mixed British and Turkish style WCs, washbasins (cold water) and hot showers on payment. Dishwashing and laundry sinks, and toilets for disabled people. Cabaret shows provided in July/Aug. The management, the Prearo brothers, aim for a pleasant and happy environment.

How to find it: Take the SS18 through Paestum and, at southern end of town, turn right and follow road straight down to sea. Site is well signed.

General Details: Open 1 April - 30 Sept. 20,000 sq.m. Shop and bar. Restaurant (all day June - mid Sept). Riding. Tennis 1 km. Watersports. Chemical disposal. Hourly bus service. Bungalows for hire. No dogs. No barbecues.

Charges guide: Per person L. 7,000 - 9,000; pitch 15,000 - 23,000.

Reservations: Contact site. Address: Via Ponte di Ferro, 84063 Paestum (SA). Tel: 0828/851105 (winter 0828/724725).

ITALY - South

6842 Camping Sant' Antonio, Seiano, Vico Equense

Peaceful base from which to explore Pompei, Herculaneum and Sorrento.

This pretty little site, just across the road from Seiano beach, would suit caravanners who like a peaceful (for Italy) location. There are only 150 pitches which are in shade offered by orange, lemon and walnut trees. The single sanitary block provides hot and cold showers, washbasins and British style WCs. Hot water is on payment. There is a regular 15 minute bus service to the Circumvesuviana railway which runs frequently to Sorrento, Pompei, Herculaneum and Naples - the only sensible way to travel for non-party sightseeing.

How to find it: Take route SS163 from Castellamare to Sorrento. Just after the tunnel by-pass around Vico Equense, watch for the hard right turn for Seiano beach and follow the signs down the narrow road.

General Details: Open 15 March - 15 Oct. 10, 000 sq.m. of flat, shady ground with easy access. Electricity to all pitches (3A). Small shop, bar and restaurant. Fishing and boat slipway 100 m. Barbecues allowed. Caravans for rent.

Charges guide: Per person L. 9,000 - 10,500; caravan 9,000 - 10,500; motorcaravan 11,000 - 13,500. Credit cards accepted.

Reservations: Contact site. Address: Via Marina d'Equa, Seiano, 80069 Vico Equense (NA). Tel: 081/8028570 (when closed 081/8028576). FAX: as phone.

AR Discount
Less 10%

6850 Sea World Village, San Giorgio, Bari

Seaside site in the far south of Italy, with new name and management.

There are few good sites in this part of Italy but Sea World Village (formerly Camping Internazionale San Giorgio) is acceptable as a transit stop or short stay. The new owners are livening up the old, rather neglected site. Bari is a busy city, but Sea World Village is on the southern edge. There are 20 tourist pitches, all with electricity, well separated from the static pitches. Access to the sea is via rocks and concrete platforms, with a small swimming pool at the water's edge, plus a separate, man-made, sandy beach which is cleaned daily. The large car park and many changing cabins means the site is crowded at weekends with day visitors. The sanitary block is of modern construction with mainly British style WCs and free hot showers. There are 42 bungalows, several of which are built in the local `Trulli' style, for hire on a weekly basis.

How to find it: Take the Bari exit from autostrada A14 and follow signs for Brindisi on the dual carriageway ring road (Tangenziole). After exit 14 watch carefully for the San Giorgio exit. Turn left and site is signed 200 m. ahead, across traffic lights.

General Details: Open all year. 50,000 sq.m. Bar/restaurant, pizzeria and market open during season. Writing room. Doctor calls. Roller skating, hockey, football and tennis areas. Bowling. Disco. Watersports.

Charges guide: Per person L.10,000; car 7,000; m/cycle 3,000; tent 6,000 - 8,000; caravan, motorcaravan or large tent 10,000; electricity 2,000.

Reservations: Only made for site bungalows. Address: San Giorgio, ss Adriatica 78, 70126 Bari. Tel: 080/5491202.

6852 Village Camping Marina di Rossano, Rossano

Excellent site in the far south.

This is the most welcoming site we have visited in this area. Most of the staff in reception, the shops, bar and restaurant speak English with a smile. The location is not so far as it seems - it can be reached by either the west or east autostrada, without the final tortuous or very busy roads to some nearer coastal sites. It took us over 4 hours from Naples and it is approximately 2 hours from Bari. There are about 200 pitches, all under tall, shady poplar trees. It is entirely secluded and leads directly to a large stretch of private beach. There are several toilet blocks mostly with free hot water. Dogs are only accepted with medical clearance and payment. Very suitable for disabled people, their own facilities are provided. There are many apartments and bungalows to rent. The site has an excellent swimming pool and sporting facilities, with attentive entertainment staff, at reasonable prices.

How to find it: From the north take the east coast highway (route 106 - Ionica). Leave at Rossano exit and a football stadium is immediately opposite with a site sign to its left. Follow signs for 1 km. to site. From the south, at Rossano exit turn left under road bridge. Turn left immediately before football stadium.

General Details: Open 1 April - 30 Sept. Shops. Bars. Restaurants. Swimming pools. Private beach. Basketball. Volleyball. Bicycle hire. Apartments and bungalows for hire.

Charges guide: Per pitch L. 32,000 - 38,000; adult 6,000 - 10,000; child (3-5 yrs) 6,000 - 7,000; second car 2,000 - 3,200; dog 2,500 - 4,000; electricity incl. Credit Cards accepted.

Reservations: Contact site. Address: C. da Leuca, CP98, 87069 Rossano (Cosenza). Tel: 0983/516054. FAX: 0983/512069. Internet: www.masternet.it/itwg/itw01997.htm.

Sardinia

The rugged coastline of Sardinia, rising from the sea of varying colour, including the incredible green of the Costa Smerelda, will amaze you. With some beaches of fine white sand, others surrounded by cliffs or rocky coves, much of the 1,300 km. of coastline is seldom visited by tourists. There are no motorways but the roads are generally quite good, apart from in the really remote areas. Petrol stations are few and far between, and close early, some even before noon. The capital, Cagliari, lies in the south of the island and has interesting architecture with some charming small resorts in the vicinity. There are regular car ferries to the islands of the north coast and to Corsica. Lobster is a speciality and the best local wine is Vernaccia, a strong amber coloured wine with a definite orange flavour. The weather is hot, dry and sunny from May to September, with a sea breeze to cool you on the beaches. We include two sites on the island. For ferry information contact:

Southern Ferries Ltd, 179 Piccadilly, London W1V 9DB. Tel: 0171 491 4968

6860 Camping Capo d'Orso, Palau, Sardinia

Pretty seaside site on northern edge of Costa Smerelda.

This is a well established and decidedly pretty site on a hillside sloping down to the sea and facing Caprera Island and several beaches, some 4½ km. from the village of Palau. The terrain is fairly rocky but the 450 pitches are on level, sparsely grassed terraces, with quite good access roads. Most have 3A electricity and are of a fair size (40-80 sq.m). Cars are parked away from the pitches in July/Aug. This side of the island seems generally to be hotter and more sheltered from the wind, but there is not a lot of shade. Although the site is open from April - Sept, the restaurant, bar, pizzeria, takeaway and shop are only open from 1 June, and other facilities, including the scuba-diving, sailing school and boat excursions to the nearby small islands only operate in the main season. Other facilities include caravans and bungalows for hire, tennis, an underground disco, children's and adults entertainment programme (in high season). There are also pontoon moorings for boats and boat hire arrangements in high season. Sanitary facilities, in three blocks, are adequate, with hot showers (on payment in season, free at other times), open plan washbasins, washing-up and laundry sinks (cold water) and mainly Turkish, but with some British, type WCs. They seemed to be well maintained when we visited in late May, although not all the blocks were open at that time. This site could be a useful alternative to our other site on Sardinia, being somewhat cheaper, smaller and less formally organised, but with significantly less shade.

How to find it: Site is 5 km. from Palau, in northeast Sardinia, on coast opposite (southwest of) Caprera Island.

General Details: Open 1 April - 30 Sept. Bar/restaurant. Pizzeria. Takeaway. Shop (all from 1/6). Disco. Chemical disposal. Entertainment programmes and excursions. Scuba diving, windsurfing, sailing (all main season). Boat hire and moorings. Tennis. Bungalows and caravans for hire.

Charges guide: Per pitch L. 9,000 - 16,000; tent pitch for 2 persons 6,000 - 11,000; adult 6,000 - 11,000; child 4,000 - 8,000; car or m/cycle 2,000 - 6,000; extra tent 3,000 - 7,000; electricity 3,000.

Reservations: Contact site for details. Address: 07020 Palau (SS). Tel: 0789/702007. FAX: 0789/702006.

6855 Camping Baia Blu La Tortuga, Aglientu, nr S. Teresa di Gallura

Aptly named, large site situated on a bay of startling blue sea and golden sand.

La Tortuga is in one of the nicest corners of this island, enjoying welcome breezes and convenient for the ferry at St Teresa di Gallura (for Corsica). The site is under the same ownership as Marepineta (no. 6000) and has excellent facilities including some very modern sanitary units. The four blocks of a similarly unusual design provide an exceptionally good ratio of facilities to pitches. The most unusual feature is the combined shower/washbasin cabins, with controllable hot showers (on payment) and free hot water to the basins. Apart from the large number of showers, British and Turkish style WCs and washbasins, there are numerous footbaths, basins for children, sinks for dishes and laundry (hot water am. clothes, pm. dishes) and facilities for the disabled. Washing machines, dryers and irons. The 700 pitches, all with 3A electricity, are arranged in rows between tall pines, eucalyptus and shrubs with good access avenues and plenty of shade. Catering facilities include an attractive restaurant, pizzeria and takeaway and a small, pleasant bar. A large and still developing site with direct access to the beach and an extensive range of amenities, both on site and nearby. Used by tour operators.

How to find it: Site is on the north coast between the towns of Costa Paradiso and S. Teresa di Gallura (18 km.) at Pineta di Vignola Mare.

General Details: Open 6 April - 3 Oct. Bar. Restaurant, pizzeria, snack bar and takeaway (May-Sept). Supermarket. Children's playground. Tennis. Volleyball. Football. Table tennis. Games and TV rooms. Disco 50 m. Barbecue area. Chemical disposal. Wind surfing school. Facilities and school for divers. Entertainment and sports activities organised in season. Riding near. Excursions. 50 mobile homes and 37 caravans for hire.

Charges 1998: Four charging seasons. Per person L. 7,500 - 16,500; junior (under 10 yrs) or senior (over 60 yrs) 5,500 - 13,000; pitch 10,500 - 26,500; electricity 3,500.

Reservations: made with L. 30,000 deposit. Address: Pineta di Vignola Mare, 07020 Aglientu (SS), Sardegna. Tel: 079/602060 (winter: 0365/520018). FAX: 079/602040. (winter: 0365/520690).

LUXEMBOURG

The Grand Duchy of Luxembourg is an independent sovereign state, 999 square miles in area lying between Belgium, France and Germany. Geographically, the Grand Duchy is divided into two sections: in the north the uplands of the Ardennes, a hilly and scenic region, in the south mainly rolling farmlands and woods, bordered on the east by the wine growing area of the Moselle Valley. Luxembourg City is one of the most spectacularly sited capitals in Europe and home to about one fifth of the population. Luxembourg is essentially a Roman Catholic country. For further information contact:

Luxembourg Tourist Office, 122, Regent Street, London W1R 5FE

Tel: 0171 434 2800 Fax: 0171 734 1205

Population
389,800; density 151 per sq. km.

Capital
Luxembourg City.

Climate
A temperate climate prevails, the summer often extending from May to late October.

Language
Letzeburgesch is the national language, with French and German also being official languages.

Currency
Luxembourg Franc interchangeable with the Belgium Franc. Divides into 100 centimes and comes in coins worth 5, 10, 20 and 50 francs and notes worth 100, 500, 1000 and 5000 francs.

Banks
Open 08.30/09.00-12.00 and 13.30-16.30.
Credit Cards: are widely accepted.

Post Offices
Open 08.00-12.00 and 14.00-17.00 (but those in villages often operate more restricted hours).

Time
GMT plus 1 (summer BST +1).

Telephone
For calls from Luxembourg to the UK the code is 0044 followed by the STD code omitting initial 0. To call Luxembourg from the UK the code is 00 352 followed by the number (no area codes).

Public Holidays
New Year; Carnival Day, mid-Feb; Easter Mon; May Day; Ascension; Whit Mon; National Day, 23 June; Assumption, 15 Aug; All Saints; All Souls; Christmas, 25, 26 Dec.

Shops
Open Mon 14.00-18.30. Tues to Sat 08.30-12.00 and 14.00-18.30, (grocers and butchers close at 15.00 on Sat).

Motoring
Speed Limits: Caravans and motorhomes (3.5 tons) 31 mph (50 kph) in built up areas, caravans 46 mph (75 kph) and 56 mph (90 kph) on other roads and motorways respectively, motorhomes 56 mph (90 kph) and 75 mph (120 kph). Fuel: Visa and Eurocard are accepted.
Parking: A Blue Zone area exists in Luxembourg City (discs from ACL, police stations, tourist offices) but parking meters are also available.

Overnighting
Generally only allowed on camp sites.

Useful Addresses
Motoring Organisation:
Automobile Club du Grand-Duche de Luxembourg (ACL)
54 route de Longwy, 8007 Bertrange. Tel: 450045. Offices hours ; Mon-Fri 08.30-12.00 and 13.30-18.00

Tourist Information:
Tourist Information Societies (Syndicat d'Initiative) with offices in most towns. Closed lunch time - times vary. The National Tourist Office in London is very helpful.

770 Camping Gaalgebierg, Esch-sur-Alzette

Good quality site near French border

Occupying an elevated position on the edge of town, this pleasant site is run by the local camping and caravan club. Although surrounded by hills and with a good variety of trees, not all pitches have shade. There are 150 pitches (100 for tourists) 100 sq.m., on grass, marked out by trees, some on a slight slope. All have 16A electricity and TV points. There is a small bar (on demand) with terrace, a shop for basics, plus table tennis and a children's playground. The site has an entertainment and activities programme in peak season. The sanitary units, which can be heated, provide British WCs, washbasins with free hot water (some in cubicles), hot showers on payment, excellent facilities for disabled people and babies, and dishwashing and laundry sinks. All have been recently re-furbished and have a key-card entry system. The site now operates its own minibus for visits to Luxembourg city and other excursions, free to campers. The site also provides the Luxembourg card.

How to find it: Site is well signed from the centre of Esch, but a sharp look out is needed as there are two acute right-handers on the approach to the site.

General Details: Open all year. Shop. Bar. Restaurant near. Children's playground. Volleyball. Table tennis. Boules. Badminton. Swimming pool and tennis nearby. Entertainment in season. Laundry. Chemical disposal.

Charges 1999: Per pitch LFr. 130; adult 130; child (3-12 yrs) 65; electricity (16A) 50; local tax per person 20. Less 10% for stays of 7 days, 20% for 30 days excl. July/Aug. No credit cards.

Reservations: Write to site with deposit. Address: 4001 Esch-sur-Alzette. Tel: 541069. FAX: 549630.

776 Camping Europe, Remich

Useful touring site by River Moselle, close to town activities.

This municipal site is the best we could find on the road which runs alongside the Moselle. Its facilities are acceptable and clean, but not luxurious, it is convenient for the town centre and is good value. We recommend that you arrive early in season as the site fills up quickly. The 110 marked pitches, all with 10A electricity, are on level grass with no static or long stay units. The municipal swimming pool and ice skating complex is at one end of the site (no direct access). The sanitary building contains British WCs, washbasins with cold water only and free hot showers. The town is a picturesque and popular resort with a tree shaded promenade along the river bank, wine cellars and facilities for wine tasting, many sporting facilities, entertainment and restaurants.

How to find it: From Rue de Moselle (running alongside river) just south of the river bridge, turn (by large car park) into Rue de Camping, and site is on left.

General Details: Open 5 April - 16 September. Chemical disposal. Within walking distance of services and attractions.

Charges 1998: Per pitch LFr. 130; adult 120; child (under 15 yrs) 60; electricity 35.

Reservations: Write to site for details. Address: Rue de Camping, 5550 Remich. Tel: 698018.

775 Camping Bettembourg, Bettembourg

Small municipal site, exclusively for tourists with immaculate modern facilities.

This small site on the southern outskirts of Bettembourg is beautifully maintained. The 25 pitches, accessed from a central paved roadway, have some neatly trimmed dividing hedges and all have 16A electricity. The sanitary facilities are exceptional with British WCs, washbasins in cubicles, spacious showers with dividers, seat and hooks, a superb suite for disabled visitors, fully equipped baby room, dishwashing and laundry facilities, all with free hot water. The warden is justifiably proud of them. A cosy club room with TV and coffee bar is available should the weather be inclement. Brochures showing the local cycle path network and other tourist information may be obtained from reception. A good value site.

How to find it: From the town centre follow camping signs, site lies to the south of the town, near the railway station and marshalling yard (not noticeably noisy at time of visit).

General Details: Open 15 April - 30 September. Clubroom with coffee bar and TV. Laundry. Chemical disposal. Reception closed 12.00-14.00; barrier closed 23.00-07.00. Only French spoken.

Charges 1998: Per pitch incl. electricity LFr. 150; adult 150; child (3-14 yrs) 70.

Reservations: Write to site for details. Address: Parc Jacquinot, 3241 Bettembourg. Tel: 513646. FAX: 520357.

781 Caravaning-Parc Martbusch, Berdorf

Relaxing, well tended site on edge of small town, with excellent facilities.

A municipal site adjacent to the sports facilities of an elegant small town, this site is kept neat and tidy by the parks department. The touring section is well screened from the long stay area and shaded by mature trees. The 110 grassy touring pitches (plus 50 for seasonal units) are divided by hedges, all with electricity (10A) and accessed from tarmac roadways. The sanitary facilities are housed in two good quality modern buildings which provide British WCs, washbasins (some in cubicles), spacious showers with dividers, seats and hooks (07.00-11.00 and 17.00-22.00 only), dishwashing and laundry facilities, units for babies and disabled visitors. Hot water is free throughout. There is a shop and snack bar, TV and games rooms and a `salle de séjour'. Adjoining the site is a recreation complex which includes minigolf, tennis, indoor swimming pool (adults LFr 70; child 40; open during July/Aug), fitness centre, playgrounds, marked walks and rock climbing in the surrounding area.

How to find it: Site and recreation centre are well signed from the Consdorf - Echternach road in Berdorf centre. Follow signs to `piscine' towards Beaufort and Grundhof.

General Details: Open all year. Shop and snack bar (1/4-31/10). Children's playground. TV and games room. Fishing, bicycle hire 6 km. Riding 8 km. Golf 15 km. Bottle bank. Laundry. Chemical disposal. Recreation centre adjacent.

Charges 1998: Per pitch LFr. 160; adult 160; child (3-14 yrs) 100; electricity 60. No credit cards.

Reservations: Write for details to: Tourist Info-Service CR, 7 an der Laach, 6550 Berdorf. Tel: 790643. Site address: 3 Bäim Maartbēsch, 6552 Berdorf. Tel: 790545. FAX: 799182.

**The sites in LUXEMBOURG featured in this guide
are shown on the BENELUX map on page 369**

LUXEMBOURG

764 Camping `Auf Kengert', Larochette

Agreeable site with good shop and restaurant, northeast of Luxembourg city.

A friendly welcome awaits you at this peacefully situated, family run site, 2 km. from Larochette, with 180 individual pitches, all with electricity (4/16A). Some are in a very shaded woodland setting, on a slight slope with fairly narrow access roads. There are six hardened pitches for motorcaravans on a flat area of grass, complete with motorcaravan service facilities. Further pitches are in an adjacent and more open meadow area. The well maintained sanitary installations are in two parts with free hot water throughout; the modern unit has British WCs, washbasins (some in cubicles), and excellent, fully equipped, dedicated cubicles for disabled visitors. The showers (older in style) and a laundry room are located below the central building which houses the restaurant, large well stocked shop, etc. There is a good swimming pool for the summer months. This site is popular in season, so early arrival is advisable, or you can reserve.

How to find it: From Larochette take the CR118 (towards Mersch) and just outside town turn right on CR119 towards Schrondweiler, site is 2 km. on right.

General Details: Open 12 Feb - 8 Nov. Shop. Bar. Restaurant. Children's playground. Swimming pool (Easter - end Sept). Paddling pool. Fishing, bicycle hire, golf 8 km. Riding 4 km. Laundry. Chemical disposal. Motorcaravan services. Bottle bank. Good English spoken.

Charges 1999: Per person LFr. 320 - 400; child (2-18 yrs) 160 - 240; electricity 80; walkers and cyclists less 10%.

AR Discount
*Welcome drink,
bottle of wine,
Luxembourg card*

Reservations: Write to site. Address: 7633 Larochette/Medernach. Tel: 837186. FAX: 878323. E-mail: kengert@club.innet.lu. Internet: www.come.to/kengert.

765 Camping de la Sûre, Reisdorf

Riverside site, with pleasant atmosphere, popular with fishermen.

Located on the edge of this small town, this site has 160 numbered pitches, most with electricity (16A) and arranged around a tarmac access road. Some are on the river bank (heaven for a keen fisherman - advance booking advised). They are not separated but are marked with small trees. There are some static units, but these are nearest the road in their own fenced area, leaving the prime pitches for tourists. The town centre is within easy walking distance, and cycle ways abound. The sanitary facilities are modern and clean, having been recently refitted and extended, with British WCs, some washbasins in cubicles, showers with dividers and seats, and free hot water throughout. Other services include a small shop, a café/bar with takeaway meals, a playground, minigolf and fishing.

continued overleaf

765 Camping de la Sûre (continued)

How to find it: From river bridge in Reisdorf, take road to Echternach, de la Sûre is the **second** campsite on the left.

General Details: Open 1 April - 30 October. Small shop. Café/bar. Takeaway. Laundry. Chemical disposal. Children's playground. Minigolf. Sports field. Canoeing. Fishing.

Charges 1998: Per pitch LFr. 200; adult 180; child (under 14 yrs) 80; electricity 80. Discounts for long stays and off season.

Reservations: Write to site. Address: 23 Rue de la Sûre, 9390 Reisdorf. Tel: 836246 or 836509. FAX: 869237.

763 Camping La Pinède, Consdorf

Pleasant municipal site in the Mullerthal region.

La Pinède is situated adjacent to the municipal sports field, with the main sanitary facilities located under the stand. These provide British style WCs, washbasins (cold water only) and controllable hot showers in a building which can be heated in cool weather. A further small, modern unit at the far end of the site is opened in July/Aug. and there are more refurbished facilities to the rear of the café/bar beside the site entrance. The site provides 107 individual, hedged, grassy spaces for tourists all with electricity (10A), plus 42 pitches housing static units. Other amenities include a small adventure-style children's playground, minigolf, football field, volleyball and tennis courts. There is no shop on site but all necessary shops and services are in the town within walking distance. The immediate area is popular for cycling and hiking and the river Moselle and vineyards are an easy day trip by car.

How to find it: Consdorf is southwest of Echternach. Site is well signed from the centre of Consdorf.

General Detail: Open 15 March - 15 November. Electricity connections (10A). Café/bar. Children's playground. Minigolf. Tennis.

Charges 1998: Per pitch LFr. 150; adult 140; child (under 14 yrs) 70; electricity 60.

Reservations: Write to site for details. Address: 33 Rue Burkapp, 6211 Consdorf. Tel: 790271. FAX: 799001.

791 Camping Kalkesdelt, Ettelbruck

Agreeable, good value site on a hilltop overlooking the town.

Quietly located about 1 km. from the centre of Ettelbruck, this municipal site has a nice atmosphere with well tended gardens and grass. The modern main building includes reception, a 'salle de séjour' (with library and TV), some excellent new WCs and washbasins, a room for disabled people and a laundry. An older sanitary unit provides British style WCs, washbasins (cold water) and free hot showers with divider, shelf and hooks. It can be heated in cool weather. The 150 marked pitches are generally slightly sloping, some on terraces backed by banks and trees, others on an open area at the top of the site. All are accessed from tarmac roadways and have electricity available (16A). The restaurant, snack bar and takeaway are open each evening in season. A baker calls daily at 7.30 am. (order day before). Breakfasts can also be served. Reception has good tourist information and English is spoken. There is a small playground, table tennis and children's entertainment in high season.

How to find it: Site signed on western outskirts of Ettelbruck off N15 and approached via a short one-way system.

General Details: Open 1 April - 31 Oct. Restaurant. Snack bar and takeaway. Bicycle hire. Playground. Table tennis. Entertainment in season. Laundry. Chemical disposal. Bottle bank.

Charges 1998: Per pitch LFr. 130; adult 120; child (3-14 yrs) 50; electricity 80; local 'Eco' tax 20. No credit cards.

Reservations: Contact site for details Address: Rue de Camping, 9022 Ettelbruck. Tel: 812185. FAX: 819839.

767 Camping des Ardennes, Hosingen

Good value site in a very attractive small town, noted for its floral displays.

This small municipal site is located on the edge of this most attractive town with an easy level walk to all amenities and parks and floral arrangements to admire during the summer season. The 50 level, open, grassy pitches all have electricity (10A) and are arranged on either side of surfaced roadways, with a few trees providing a little shade in places. The single sanitary unit, which can be heated in winter, is well appointed, modern and very clean, with British WCs, large shower cubicles (with full screens), and open washbasins in separate men's and women's facilities. Hot water is free throughout. Dishwashing and laundry facilities with washing machine and dryer (instructions in English), also clothes lines. The site has a tiny inflatable swimming pool principally for children, a small playground, barbecue, café/bar and boule pitch. Skis and winter sports equipment for hire. English is spoken by the Dutch wardens.

How to find it: Site is off the main N7 road north of Diekirch and is signed from the centre of the town, with the sports complex.

General Details: Open all year. Café/bar (hours variable). Laundry. Children's pool and playground. Boule. Winter sports equipment for hire. Rooms for rent (B&B). Adjacent sports complex with tennis and football, etc.

Charges 1999: Per pitch LFr. 150; adult 150; child (3-12 yrs) 75; electricity 75.

Reservations: Write to site for details. Address: 9809 Hosingen. Tel: 91911.

NETHERLANDS

The Netherlands offers a warm welcome to British visitors, and the general standard of campsites has improved considerably during the last few years. It is a country partly reclaimed from the sea (one-fifth of the country lies below sea level). A flat fertile landscape is punctured by dykes, windmills, church spires and marvellously ornate gabled terraces flanking peaceful canals, broken by the forests of Arnhem, the bulb fields in the west, the Ijsselmer and unique and independent Friesland (with its own language) in the north. Amsterdam is the liberal, sometimes irreverent, capital with its horseshoe of 17th century canals, tall elegant houses and 62 museums. The Hague is the seat of government as well as a royal city home to Queen Beatrix and Rotterdam is the world's greatest port. Cycling is extremely popular - an estimated 14 million bicycles, that is one per man, woman and child of the population, so take care when driving or take your own with you and join them!

For further information contact:

Netherlands Board of Tourism, PO Box 523, London SW1E 6NT

Tel: 0891 200277. Fax: 0171 828 7941.

Population
15,200,000, density 447 p/sq. km.

Climate
The sea has a great affect on the climate of the Netherlands. The average winter is mild - although a sudden cold snap in January or February will have the skaters out with a vengeance on the water- ways. Summers are warm with temperatures averaging 16-17°C centigrade in July and August. In the east and southeast winters are colder and summers warmer. Spring is the driest season.

Language
Dutch is the native tongue. English is very widely spoken, so is German and to some extent French. In Friesland a Germanic language, Frisian is spoken. The Dutch are very language- conscious partly because they are great travellers, to be found in all parts of the world - often running camp sites!

Time
GMT + 1 (summer BST + 1).

Currency
Dutch currency is the Guilder or Florin written as Dfl. or Nfl. and made up of 100 cents. Notes are 10, 25, 50, 100 and 250, coins are 5, 10, and 25 cents pieces and 1, 2.50, and 5 Nfl.

Banks
Open Mon-Fri 09.00-16.00/1700. Exchange offices (GWK) are often open longer hours.

Post Offices
Open Mon-Fri 08.30-17.00. Some offices open Sat 08.30-12.00.

Telephone
To call the Netherlands from the UK the code is 00 31, the UK from the Netherlands, 00 44.

Public Holidays
New Year; Good Fri; Easter Mon; Queen's Birthday, 30 Apr; Liberation Day, 5 May; Ascension; Whit Mon; Christmas, 25, 26 Dec.

Shops
Shops open Mon-Fri 09.00/ 09.30 -17.30/18.00. Sat. closing 16.00/ 17.00. In big cities, stores have late opening Thurs. or Fri. and close Mon. morning. The Dutch are early diners - restaurants open 17.30-22.00/23.00.

Motoring
There is a comprehensive motorway system but, due to the high density of population, all main roads can become very busy, particularly in the morning and evening rush hours. There are many bridges which can cause congestion.

Tolls: There are no toll roads but there are a few toll bridges and tunnels notably the Zeeland Bridge, Europe's longest across the Oosterschelde. Speed Limits: Built up areas 31 mph (50 kph), other roads 50 mph (80 kph) and motorways 62 mph (100 kph) or 75 mph (120 kph). Cars towing a caravan or trailer are limited to 50 mph (80 kph) outside built-up areas.

Parking: Blue Zones exist in most towns and free parking discs are available from police stations.

Overnighting:
Prohibited outside campsites.

Useful Addresses
Motoring Organisations:
Koninklijke Nederlandsche Automobiel Club (KNAC), Westvlietweg 118, Leidschendam. Tel: (070) 399 7451. Offices hours Mon-Fri 09.00-17.00.
Koninklijke Nederlandsche Toeristenbond (ANWB), Wassenaarsweg 220, The Hague. Tel: (070) 3141420 Offices hours Mon-Fri 08.00-17.30
Tourist Information:
The Netherlands has 440 Tourist Information Offices (VVV) throughout the country which claim to be able to deal with any enquiry.

Four Seasons Touring organise and escort themed holidays and short breaks for caravan owners tailored to your group's requirements (minimum 10 units) to France, Holland, Belgium and UK. We are experienced caravanners and well-known contributors to caravanning magazines; for further details please ring Dave and Liz King - 01494 580058, fax 01494 583123.

NETHERLANDS

593 Camping De Dousberg, Maastricht

Spacious site in leisure park on outskirts of historic city.

Founded by the Romans, Maastricht is the Netherlands' oldest and most southern city. Situated in South Limburg, the Belgian and German borders are very close. Dousberg Parc, 4 km. from the city centre, incorporates a wide range of sporting facilities including very large outdoor and indoor swimming pools, partly `subtropical' (free for campers), a tennis centre with indoor and outdoor courts, cycling training track, climbing wall and artificial ski slope. Camping de Dousberg, situated 300 m. up a gentle hill from the park entrance, forms part of this centre. It has 300 large pitches, most with electricity and TV connections and easy access to water, arranged in hedged bays which radiate outward from the centre. Three similar toilet blocks, situated around the site, offer functional facilities of a good standard. Hot water is on payment for showers but free for dishwashing. British style WCs. There is a small shop at the centre and a cafe/bar at the entrance. It is quite a busy site, with visitors of many nationalities, some groups of youngsters, but it is well run and well situated for visiting a lively, interesting city.

How to find it: From the north on the Eindhoven - Liège motorway (A2/E25) take Maastricht/Hasselt exit and follow signs for Hasselt and then municipal signs for `Dousberg'. From the Liège direction follow signs for `Centrum' and then `Dousberg'.

General Details: Open 26 March - 1 Nov. Small shop (5/4-15/9). Bar/restaurant (5/4-15/9). Tennis centre. Large outdoor and indoor pools (1/3-1/11). Climbing wall. Artificial ski slope, Cycling track. Children's play areas. Laundry facilities.

Charges guide: Per person Nfl. 7.00; child (under 12 yrs) 5.50; tent or caravan 7.50; motorcaravan 10.00; car 4.00; m/cycle 2.75; electricity 4.00; local tax 1.50.

Reservations: Write to site. Address: PO 2860, 6201 MB Maastricht. Tel: 043/343 21 71. FAX: 043/343 05 56.

592 Vakantiecentrum De Zwarte Bergen, Luyksgestel, nr Eindhoven

Large woodland site with swimming pools, south of Eindhoven.

In a pleasant woodland setting, De Zwarte Bergen is a holiday type of site with many permanent caravans and bungalows (some to let) but there are also plenty of touring spaces. These are mainly situated in a newly cleared area near the swimming pools which has 250 numbered pitches of up to 120 sq.m. arranged in circles of 8-10, with car parking adjacent. Water, electricity and TV connections are available. It is an attractive setting with quite a few tall pines left standing and young bushes and trees planted to separate the groups. Towards the centre is a central complex with a large entertainment, bar and restaurant, a snack bar and supermarket. Three sanitary blocks, two close to the main touring area supplemented by a small portacabin style unit, provide small, close together washbasins with some in cabins with cold water and free hot showers and, whilst very clean and tidy, are becoming slightly dated. This is an area with easy access to a number of tourist attractions and, taking account also of the range of amenities listed below, it is a site which does offer something for longer stays.

How to find it: Site is near the Belgian border south of Eindhoven, northwest of Luyksgestel. From A21/E34 motorway (Antwerpen - Eindhoven) near Eersal take Luyksgestel exit. Turn left at traffic lights to Luyksgestel; site is signed before Weebosch.

General Details: Open all year. Complex of heated open air swimming pools (1/5-10/9), free to campers but open to others on payment. Supermarket (1/4-31/10). Restaurant and bar, disco, snack bar (weekends and holidays). Recreation programme July/Aug. Playgrounds, animals and birds. Minigolf. Petanque courts. Basketball. Football field. Two all-weather tennis courts. Launderette. Motorcaravan services. Tourist information. Bungalows for hire.

Charges guide: Per unit incl. 2 persons with all services Nfl 31.95; person (over 3 yrs) 4.80; local tax 0.60; extra person (over 3 yrs) 4.80; hiker or cyclist pitch incl. 2 persons 25.00. Credit cards accepted.

Reservations: are made with 50% payment in advance, Sat.- Sat. only in July/Aug, any period at other times. Address: P.B. 50, 5575 ZH Luyksgestel. Tel: 0497/541373. FAX: 0497/542673.

"Heritage Classic European Rescueline"

If your car breaks down or you are involved in an accident, a free phone call to Green Flag National Breakdown's European Control Centre will bring rapid assistance. Their English speaking controllers will be able to pinpoint your position and brief the nearest approved garage or agent so you will soon be on your way.

Not only does Heritage Classic European Rescueline provide an excellent breakdown assistance service, but it also provides comprehensive insurance cover for you and your passengers.

Summary of Vehicle Breakdown Cover			Summary of Personal Insurance Cover		
Cover Before Commencement of Travel	To provide a replacement vehicle if your vehicle is lost through breakdown or accident up to 7 days prior to departure	Up to £750	Cancellation and Curtailment	Provides insurance cover for holiday cancellations from the moment the premium is paid and for unused travel and accommodation not used if you have to curtail your holiday	Up to £3,000*
Roadside Assistance and Towing	Most breakdowns can be repaired quickly at the roadside although occasionally the vehicle may need to be towed to a garage	No financial limit	Medical and Other Expenses	Cover includes medical and hospital fees and additional accommodation charges. In the event of a medical emergency the National Breakdown Controller will contact Assistance International who will contact the relevant hospital and guarantee its charges. They will also arrange repatriation to the UK (including Air Ambulance) when necessary	Up to £2 million*
Emergency Labour Costs	Should your vehicle need repairs to enable you to continue your journey	Up to £100	Additional Hospital Benefits	This is an addition to any amount payable under "Medical and Other Expenses"	Up to £600 (£20 per day)
Location and Despatch of Any Necessary Spare Parts	Where these are not available locally (excluding their actual cost)	No financial limit	Personal Accident	To provide compensation following an accidental bodily injury	Up to £15,000
Alternative Travel Expenses Following Loss of Use of Vehicle	The cost of transporting your party to their original destination, or repatriation to the UK, or the cost of a hire car to allow you to continue your journey	No financial limit, except £750 overall if car hire is provided	Baggage	"New for Old" cover for items less than 2 years old	Up to £1,500*
Extra Accommodation Costs	While awaiting completion of local vehicle repairs	£45 per person per day	Money and Documents	Cover for loss of travel documents and money from 72 hours prior to departure	Up to £500
Vehicle Repatriation	Cost of transporting vehicle and passengers to the UK	No financial limit	Loss of Passport	Additional travel expenses incurred in replacing lost/stolen passport	Up to £250
Vehicle Collection	The additional travelling expenses for one person to collect vehicle (once overseas repairs have been completed)	Up to £600	Additional Expenses	To cover cost of travel and accommodation if your ferry or rail transporter is delayed	Up to £200
Alternative Driver	Cost of chauffeur and additional accommodation costs should only driver become incapacitated	No financial limit	Additional Accommodation	Or tent hire costs if tent becomes uninhabitable during your holiday	Up to £100
Theft	To pay for damage to your vehicle as a result of break in	Up to £175	Delay	Compensation if your ferry crossing is delayed of £20 per 12 hours	Up to £60
Legal Expenses	To cover costs of providing legal defence or in pursuing claims against third parties following a road traffic accident	Up to £25,000	Personal Liability	If you are held to be legally liable for injury or damage to other people or their property, cover is provided to pay for damages and claimants costs and expenses	Up to £1 million
Advance of Funds/Customs Duty	An advance of funds to act as security for bail or to overcome any Customs Duty claim	Up to £4,000	Legal Expenses	To cover cost of pursuing a claim against a third party whilst on holiday	Up to £25,000
				*Excesses: The first £25 of each and every claim per insured is excluded	

Great Value Vehicle Breakdown & Recovery
plus Personal Insurance Cover

Period of Cover	Vehicle Breakdown	Personal Insurance Adult	Personal Insurance Child*
	Cost of Heritage Classic European Rescueline		
1 Day	£19.00	£6.00	£4.00
2 Days	£20.00	£7.00	£4.50
3 Days	£21.00	£8.00	£5.00
4 Days	£22.00	£9.00	£6.00
5 Days	£24.00	£10.00	£6.50
6 Days	£26.00	£12.00	£7.00
7 Days	£28.00	£13.00	£7.50
8 Days	£30.00	£14.00	£8.00
9 Days	£32.00	£15.00	£8.50
10 Days	£33.00	£16.00	£9.00
11 Days	£34.00	£17.00	£9.50
12 Days	£35.00	£18.00	£10.00
13 Days	£36.00	£19.00	£11.00
14 Days	£37.00	£21.00	£11.50
15 Days	£38.00	£22.00	£12.00
16 Days	£39.00	£23.00	£12.50
17 Days	£40.00	£24.00	£13.00
18 Days	£41.00	£25.00	£13.50
19 Days	£43.00	£26.00	£14.00
20 Days	£44.00	£27.00	£15.00
21 Days	£45.00	£28.00	£15.50
22 Days	£46.00	£29.00	£16.00
23 Days	£48.00	£30.00	£17.00
24 Days	£49.00	£31.00	£17.50
25 Days	£50.00	£32.00	£18.00
26-32 Days	£59.00	£39.00	£23.00
33-39 Days	£68.00	£46.00	£27.00
40-46 Days	£77.00	£52.00	£32.00
47-53 Days	£86.00	£59.00	£36.00
54-60 Days	£95.00	£66.00	£41.00
61-67 Days	£104.00	£72.00	£45.00
Additional Week or part	£9.00	£6.00	£4.00
Caravan/TrailerSupp.	£13.00	-	-

Children from 4 up to 14 years. Children under 4 Free. Premiums include Insurance Premium Tax.

HERITAGE CLASSIC EUROPEAN RESCUELINE DEPARTURE PACK - Available free to all Heritage Classic European Rescueline policyholders - containing a GB sticker, useful tips on preparing your vehicle for the journey, details of documentation required for both vehicle and travellers, and a country guide to motoring abroad.

Please Note:
1. LIMITS OF COVER: Each Section of the insurance has an overall limit per Insured Person, but please note that other limits within the section may apply. For example, the overall limit under the Baggage Section is £1,500 but there is a single item limit of £250, and in respect of valuables as defined under this section a limit of £300 applies.
2. Heritage Classic European Rescueline contains a "7 DAY REFUND GUARANTEE". If the insurance does not meet your needs please return it to the issuing agent within 7 days (and before your date of departure) and the premium will be refunded in full.
3. This insurance is designed to cover most hazards which may affect your holiday, but it does contain certain conditions and exclusions. These are detailed in the full policy wording.

IMPORTANT: This leaflet only gives a summary of the cover provided by Heritage Classic European Rescueline. You are strongly advised to read the full wording of this insurance as it constitutes your "contract of insurance". Full details of the policy wording are available on request but in any event will be provided when you purchase the insurance.

HOW TO APPLY

FOR IMMEDIATE COVER - TELEPHONE 01308 897809 OR FAX 013 08 89 80 17 -VISA, VISA DELTA, MASTERCARD, SWITCH AND SOLO ACCEPTED OR COMPLETE AND RETURN THE APPLICATION FORM OVERLEAF AND SEND IT WITH YOUR CHEQUE TO:

DENEWAY GUIDES & TRAVEL LTD
CHESIL LODGE, WEST BEXINGTON, DORCHESTER, DORSET, DT2 9DG.
TELEPHONE: 01308 897809   FACSIMILE: 013 08 89 80 17

Bishopsgate

HERITAGE CLASSIC EUROPEAN RESCUELINE

APPLICATION FORM

NAME OF APPLICANT (Mr/Mrs/Miss/Ms) ....

ADDRESS...

.... Post Code ....

TEL. NO .... WORK ....

PERIOD OF TRAVEL........................... DAYS COMMENCING ON ....
NAMES OF ALL PASSENGERS IN VEHICLE (State Mr/Mrs/Miss/Ms)

AGE
(if under 16)

1 APPLICANT...   ....

2 ....

3 ....

4 ....

5 ....

6 ....

VEHICLE DETAILS

MAKE & MODEL...

REG. NO...............................EST. VALUE...YEAR......................

MOTOR INSURERS..EXPIRY DATE...........................

ARE YOU A MEMBER OF A CAR CLUB ....

CARAVAN/TRAILER DETAILS

MAKE & MODEL ....

VALUE .... YEAR ....

COUNTRIES TO BE VISITED

....

....

COVER REQUIRED

PERSONAL TRAVEL INSURANCE   PREMIUM

.... Adults @ .... each   £ ....

.... Children @ .... each   £ ....

Vehicle Breakdown Insurance   £ ....

Caravan/Trailer (if applicable)   £ ....

                                                              Total £ ....

Less 10% Alan Rogers Guide Readers Discount

Amount Payable   Total £ ....

- Please make cheques payable to: **Deneway Guides & Travel Ltd.**
- Please debit my Visa ❑   Visa Delta ❑   Mastercard ❑   Switch ❑   Solo ❑ card (please tick)

Name that appears on card ....

Expiry date...........................Card No..Signature...

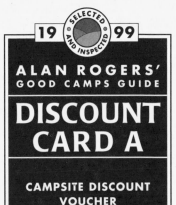

This voucher entitles the holder to the relevant discounts or special offers at those campsites featured in this guide which have a small Alan Rogers logo beneath their Site Report. This section of the voucher should be retained by the holder, but made available for inspection at the campsite for the purpose of verifying your entitlement to the relevant discount or offer.

VOUCHER NUMBER

06219

E99/

Save Money!

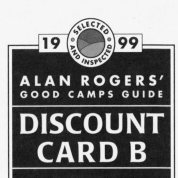

This voucher entitles the holder to a discount of 10% on Travel & Breakdown Insurance arrangements made via this Guide, as advertised between pages 256/7. To arrange cover please complete the proposal and send this, together with the appropriate premium and this voucher to: Deneway Guides & Travel Ltd., Chesil Lodge, West Bexington, Dorchester, DT2 9DG - Tel 01308 897809, Fax 01308 898017. A proposal form and the discount voucher will need to be completed and sent to Deneway Guides & Travel along with payment for the relevant premium in all circumstances **except in very urgent cases (ie those within seven days of departure) when we can arrange cover via telephone or (preferably) fax.**

VOUCHER NUMBER

06219

E99/

Save Money!

This voucher entitles the holder to a 5% discount on caravan or motorcaravan insurance arranged through Bakers of Cheltenham. Please complete the enquiry form on page 234/5 and send it, together with this voucher, to Bakers of Cheltenham, Freepost GR1604, The Quadrangle, Imperial Square, Cheltenham, Gloucestershire, GL50 1BR.

VOUCHER NUMBER

06219

E99/

Save Money!

CARD A CAMPSITE DISCOUNT VOUCHER

Valid 01 Jan - 31 Dec 1999

NAME:

ADDRESS:

SIGNATURE:

Save Money

CARD B TRAVEL & BREAKDOWN INSURANCE DISCOUNT VOUCHER

Valid 01 Jan - 31 December 1999

NAME:

ADDRESS:

SIGNATURE:

Save Money

CARD C
CARAVAN OR MOTORCARAVAN INSURANCE DISCOUNT VOUCHER

Valid 01 Jan - 31 December 1999

NAME:

ADDRESS:

SIGNATURE:

Save Money

This voucher entitles the holder to reclaim the cover price of this Alan Rogers Good Camps Guide Europe 1999 when making a booking with Sites Abroad Programme (see details facing page 257). Please send the completed voucher to Sites Abroad, Hartford Manor, Greenbank Lane, Northwich, Cheshire CW8 1HW, when making your booking.

VOUCHER NUMBER

06219

E99/

Save Money!

This voucher entitles the holder to reclaim the full cover price of this Guide (£9.99) when booking a travel inclusive holiday arrangement with The Caravan & Camping Service, whose advertisement appears on page 377. To claim your refund this voucher should be sent to The Caravan & Camping Service, 69 Westbourne Grove, London W2 4UJ when making your booking with them.

VOUCHER NUMBER

06219

E99/

Save Money!

This card entitles the holder to a FREE COPY of the 1999 Camping Cheques Catalogue (see page 128). Please send the completed card to Camping Cheques, Hartford Manor, Greenbank Lane, Northwich, Cheshire CW8 1HW.

VOUCHER NUMBER

06219

E99/

Save Money!

This voucher entitles the holder to the following discounts: **Musée Condé** - a FFr5 reduction for adults and those aged 12-17 years, or FFr2 for children under 12. **Musée Vivant du Cheval (The Living Horse Museum)** a FFr10 reduction for adults and a FFr3 reduction for children 4-16 years. **The Aérophile Balloon** - A FFr5 reduction for adults and a FFr2 reduction for children.

VOUCHER NUMBER

06219

E99/

Save Money!

CARD D SITES ABROAD DISCOUNT VOUCHER

Valid 01 Jan -31 Dec 1999

NAME:

ADDRESS:

SIGNATURE:

Save Money

CARD E CARAVAN & CAMPING SERVICE DISCOUNT VOUCHER

Valid 01 Jan -31 Dec 1999

NAME:

ADDRESS:

SIGNATURE:

Save Money

CARD F CAMPING CHEQUES DISCOUNT VOUCHER

Valid 01 Jan -31 Dec 1999

NAME:

ADDRESS:

SIGNATURE:

Save Money

Haynes
THE BOOK ®

CARD G CHANTILLY DISCOUNT VOUCHER

Valid 01 Jan -31 Dec 1999

NAME:

ADDRESS:

SIGNATURE:

Save Money

597 Camping De Paal, Bergeyk, nr Eindhoven

First class campsite, especially suitable for families with young children.

A lot of money has been invested in this touring site (no static mobile homes) in recent years, and the excellent facilities now provided mean that reservation in July/Aug. is essential. Situated in 34 hectares of woodland, there are 544 touring pitches (plus 70 seasonal pitches) offering a choice of sunshine or shade (the site map shows the choice for each pitch). All have 6A electricity, water, waste water and a bin (daily collection) and range in size up to 150 sq.m. on flat grass. Numbered and generally separated by trees in shaded areas, there is also a choice of area for parking, either on the pitch or in special car parks, affording extra safety for the children whose importance here is paramount. Each group of pitches is provided with a play area for children (31 in all) with additional facilities comprising a very large open sand-based area with adventure play equipment (with safety inspection certificate) and a large 'barn' for wet weather (also on sand). In high season an animation team of ten provide further entertainment. The high quality indoor heated swimming pool is open all season and consists of play pools for babies, children and a smaller, deeper one for parents, supervised in high season. The heated outdoor and toddlers pools are also shallow. Two ultra modern sanitary buildings, specifically designed with families in mind, have magnificent facilities. Toilets are separate at either side of the buildings. Dishwashing and laundry sinks plus a spin dryer just inside the main entrance, then wash-cabins and showers with family rooms (bath, shower, washbasin), baby bathrooms, and standard showers, all with lots of space, plus 2 children's toilets. Rooms for wheelchair users are at the back. Two other older buildings are also very well fitted out. A well equipped modern laundry is just past the quite large shop (open all season, varying hours). A new bar, reception and restaurant complex is planned for '98. Currently these are quite satisfactory, but in older buildings (the old schoolhouse). Maps can be purchased in reception showing some of the many walking and cycling opportunities in this attractive area, whilst a short walk from the camp entrance brings you to a tennis complex with 6 indoor courts (Sept-May) with 10 outdoor all weather courts (all equipment available for hire) and a pleasant lounge bar in which to relax. Whilst catering splendidly for children, outside the high season there are many regular adult visitors to this comfortable, friendly site, very capably run by the Martens family and staff.

How to find it: From E34 Antwerpen - Eindhoven road, take exit 32 (Eersel) and follow signs for Bergeyk and site (2 km from town).

General Details: Open Easter/1 April - 31 Oct. Shop, bar and snacks (all season). Restaurant (high season). Indoor pool (all season). Outdoor pool (May - Sept). Bicycle hire. Tennis. Children's play areas. Theatre. Bicycle storage room. Laundrette. Chemical disposal. Motorcaravan services. Trekkers' huts for rent.

Charges guide: Per pitch incl. 2 persons and services Nfl 51.00; extra person (over 1 yr) 6.00; cyclist 13.50; dog 6.00. Discounts outside 5/7-16/8 daily 30%, over 7 days 35%, (over 55's 40% for more than 7 days).

Reservations: Essential for July/Aug. and made for min. 1 week Sat to Sat. Address: De Paaldreef 14, 5571 TN Bergeyk. Tel: 0497/571977. FAX: 0497/577164.

594 Vryetydspark Elfenmeer, Herkenbosch, nr Roermond

Large professionally managed site with swimming pools and other amenities.

In the southern part of the country between the borders with Germany and Belgium (both quite close), this is a big site with amenities on holiday camp scale. Situated in the Meinweg National Park, it is very popular for weekend breaks, even out of season, and the facilities are also offered on a daily basis. These include two very good outdoor heated swimming pools, both 25 x 15 m. one deep, one shallow, and a small children's pool (open about 7/5-7/9). Sunbathing areas extend down to the grassy surrounds of a lake used for boating and swimming. These are free to campers except for initial fee for identity pass. There are many permanent large caravans or seasonal tourers, but around half of the 800 pitches are available for touring units, with electricity (4A) in most areas. Also many bungalows for rent in a separate area. Pitches average about 90 sq. m. and are mostly in separate enclosures of 10 or so pitches, backing on to hedges, etc. Part is light woodland, part open grass. The new or refurbished toilet blocks were clean and probably an adequate provision. They provide WCs, washbasins with cold water, pre-set free hot showers, babies' room and toilets for disabled people. Launderette. Fishing lake. Minigolf. Bowling alley. Organised sports in season. Supermarket. Restaurant/bar (April-Oct) and seasonal takeaway facilities. Large, efficient reception, with English spoken.

How to find it: From Roermond take Wassenberg road to southeast (to find this exit you can follow white signs to `Roerstreek' industrial estate); pass turning to right to Herkenbosch after 6 km. and turn left to site 1 km. further on.

General Details: Open 28 March - 25 Oct. Supermarket. Restaurant/bar (April-Oct). Takeaway. Organised sports programme. Fishing lake. Large children's playground on grass and sand. Riding and sailing and windsurfing courses arranged nearby. Minigolf. Bowling alley.

Charges guide: Per person (from 2 yrs) Nfl 4.75 - 5.75; pitch (any unit) 8.00 - 14.00; electricity (4A) 5.25.

Reservations: made only Sat. to Sat. and recommended in peak weeks, perhaps from 7/7-10/8, with full payment in advance. Address: Meinweg 1, 6075 NA Herkenbosch (L). Tel: 0475/53 16 89. FAX: 0475/53 47 75.

NETHERLANDS

591 Vakantiecentrum De Hertenwei, Lage Mierde, nr Tilburg

Large, spacious site in southern Netherlands with swimming pools.

Set in the southwest corner of the country quite close to the Belgian border, this relaxed site covers a large area. In addition to 100 quite substantial bungalows with their own gardens (some residential, 30 to let), the site has some 350 touring pitches. These are in four different areas on oblong meadows surrounded by hedges and trees, with the numbered pitches around the perimeters. There is a choice of pitch size (150, 100 or 64 sq.m.) and all have 4A electrical connections, many with water and drainage as well. The most pleasant area is probably the small one near the entrance and main buildings - these are a long walk from some of the furthest pitches. Amenities includes a small indoor heated swimming pool (12 x 6 m.) open all year (with admission charge), sauna, jacuzzi and solarium. Three outdoor pools, the largest 25 x 10 m. are open late May to early Sept. A modern building houses a restaurant, canteen and snack bar with a disco in the basement. Four toilet blocks of slightly differing types but all of quite good quality are well spaced around the site, with British style WCs, virtually all washbasins in private cabins, good, controllable showers and can be heated in cool weather. Hot water for all facilities is free. Some blocks have units for disabled people, hair washing cabins and baby baths.

How to find it: Site is by the N269 Tilburg - Reusel road, 2 km. north of Lage Mierde and 16 km. south of Tilburg.

General Details: Open all year. Supermarket (Easter - end Oct, nearest 2 km). Bar by indoor pool. Outdoor pool (May - Aug). Restaurant, cafeteria with snack bar (all year). Disco. Two tennis courts. Children's playgrounds and play meadows. Sauna, solarium and jacuzzi. Bicycle hire. Fishing 4 km. Golf 18 km. In season recreation programme with films, dances or disco, sports, bingo, etc. Bus service to Tilburg or Eindhoven with stop at entrance. Launderette. Chemical disposal. Motorcaravan services.

Charges 1998: Per unit incl. 2 persons and electricity Nfl. 38.50 - 48.50, acc. to type; extra person 5.75; local tax 0.60; extra car 5.75. Less 25-40% in low seasons. No credit cards.

Reservations: are made for min. 1 week, in summer Sat to Sat. only, with deposit. Address: Wellenseind 7-9, 5094 EG Lage Mierde. Tel: 013/509 12 95.

590 Camping Hilvarenberg & Safari Camping, Beekse Bergen, Hilvarenbeek

Large, impressive lakeside leisure complex, with many amenities, near Tilburg.

Beekse Bergen is an impressive leisure park set around a very large, attractive lake. The park offers a range of amusements which should keep the most demanding of families happy! These include not only water based activities such as windsurfing, canoeing, jetski, rowing and fishing, but also a small amusement park, a cinema, tennis courts, minigolf and many more. The lake is bordered by sandy beaches, children's playgrounds, open-air swimming areas and water slides. Transport around and across the lake is provided by a little `train' or a sightseeing boat. These and most of the amenities are free to campers. Part of the resort is the Beekse Bergen Safari Park with reduced entry for campers, where you can see the many wild animals from either your own car, a safari bus or two safari boats, the Stanley and the Livingstone. On the far side of the lake, as well as bungalows and tents for hire, there are two distinct campsites - one on flat meadows surrounded by hedges and trees near the lake, the other in a more secluded wooded area reached by a tunnel under the nearby main road. The 600 numbered pitches are about 100 sq.m, and all have electrical connections. The lakeside area has a very good waterside restaurant, a cafe and takeaway, supermarket and indoor children's swimming pool, as well as the best sanitary facilities. The Safari Campsite has a `typical safari environment' and a viewpoint over the Safari Park (with free, unlimited entry for campers staying here). There is an independent central complex with catering, playground and launderette, plus an entertainment team. In general, the sanitary facilities are quite adequate in terms of numbers and cleanliness and include British WCs and free hot showers and some washbasins in private cabins. This is an area with many other recreational activities, including the award winning Effteling amusement park.

How to find it: From A58/E312 Tilburg - Eindhoven motorway, take exit to Hilvarenbeek on the N269 road. Park and campsite are signed Beekse Bergen.

General Details: Open 3 April - 7 Nov. Leisure park 24 April - 5 Sept. Restaurants, cafes and takeaway (weekends only in low seasons). Supermarket. Children's playgrounds and indoor pool. Beaches and lake swimming. Watersports including rowing boats (free) and canoe hire. Amusements. Tennis. Minigolf. Fishing. Recreation programme. Bicycle hire. Riding. Golf 5 km. Launderettes. Chemical disposal. Bungalows, cabins and equipped tents to rent. Twin axle caravans not accepted.

Charges 1998: Per person (from 2 yrs) Nfl 6.80; pitch 19.00 - 31.00; electricity included; local tax 1.10 per person. Discounts for weekly stays, camping packages available. Credit cards accepted.

Reservations: Necessary for high season and B.Hs. Address: Leisurepark Hilvarenberg, Beekse Bergen 1, 5081 NJ Hilvarenbeek. Tel: 013/536 00 32. FAX: 013/536 67 16.

595 Camping-Caravanning Heumens Bos, Heumen, nr Nijmegen

Friendly site, family run for families.

The area around Nijmegen, the oldest city in the Netherlands, has large forests for walking or cycling, nature reserves and old towns to explore, as well as being quite close to Arnhem. A warm welcome from the Grol family awaits you at this well run site. It covers 30 acres and is open over a long season for touring families (no groups of youngsters allowed) and all year for bungalows. It offers 165 level, grass touring pitches (all with 6A hook-ups), numbered but not separated, in glades of 10 and one large field, all with easy access. Cars are parked away from the caravans. One small section for motorcaravans has some hardstandings. The main, high quality sanitary building plus another new block are modern and heated, providing showers on payment, British style WCs, rooms for families and disabled people and free hot water to the private cabins and other washbasins. External, covered dishwashing facilities. Another smaller building has acceptable facilities and there is a smart, new launderette. The restaurant, which offers a quality menu (the owners are former restaurateurs) and a new terrace, is close to the comfortable bar and there is a snack bar too as well as a large shop. An open air swimming pool with a small children's pool is maintained at 25°C by a unique system of heat transfer from the air. For children there is a separate glade with play equipment on sand and grass, table-tennis, entertainment in July/Aug. and a large wet weather room. A founder member of the Holland Tulip Parc group.

How to find it: From the A73 Nijmegen - Venlo take exit 3 (4 km. south of Nijmegen) and follow site signs.

General Details: Open 1 April - 1 Nov. (bungalows all year). Shop (1/4-13/9). Bar, restaurant and snack bar (all season). Heated swimming pool (1/5-1/10). Bicycle hire. New all weather tennis courts. Boules. Table tennis. Activity and excursion programme (high season). Fishing 2 km. Golf and riding 8 km. Launderette. Chemical disposal. Motorcaravan service point. Modern bungalows, caravans and tents for hire.

Charges 1999: Per pitch incl. 2 persons, caravan or tent Nfl. 32.00 - 42.00, motorcaravan 38.00 - 47.00; extra person (over 4 yrs) 6.00; electricity 4.50; dog (max 1) 6.00. Special low season weekends (incl. restaurant meal) - contact park. Credit cards accepted.

Reservations: Made without charge and advisable for July/Aug. Address: Vosseneindseweg 46, 6582 BR Heumen. Tel: 024 358 1481. FAX: 024 358 3862.

NETHERLANDS

588 Vrijetijdspark Vinkeloord, Vinkel, nr s'Hertogenbosch

Large, pleasant holiday site with many amenities.

Run by the same group as Beekse Bergen (no 590), Vinkeloord is a large site with a bungalow park and motel accommodation in addition to 500 camping pitches. These are divided into several grassy areas, many in an attractive wooded setting, and 350 with electrical connections. There are also some new fully serviced pitches. Open all year, the site is a popular holiday choice with activities organised in the main seasons. The varied amenities are located in and around a modern, central complex. They include heated outdoor swimming pools, an indoor leisure pool with slide, fitness room, 10 pin bowling alley, minigolf and tennis courts. There is also a small, landscaped lake with sandy beaches suitable for swimming and inflatable boats, overlooked by a large children's play area. Some of the touring pitches also overlook the water. Campers have free entry to the adjacent `Autotron' attraction. The eight toilet blocks are well situated for all parts of the site. The clean and simple facilities are a bit of a mixture (some unisex) with some warm water for washing, some individual washbasins and pre-set showers.

How to find it: Site is signed from the N50/A50 road between s'Hertogenbosch and Nijmegen, approx. 10 km. east of s'Hertogenbosch at Vinkel.

General Details: Open all year. Supermarket. Bar. Modern, up-market restaurant. Snack bar/takeaway (high season only). Free outdoor heated swimming pools (May - early Sept). Indoor leisure pool (on payment). Sauna, solarium and fitness room. 10 pin bowling alley. Tennis courts. Minigolf. Table tennis. Sports field. Bicycle hire. Fishing. Barbecue area. Children's play areas on sand. Many organised activities in season. Conference facilities, motel bedrooms and bungalows for hire.

Charges guide: Per person (from 2 yrs) Nfl 4.65 - 8.20; pitch simple: 7.70 - 14.10, serviced (water and TV connections) 13.35 - 17.95, with waste water 16.00 - 20.00, fully serviced with own sanitary facility 40.00; electricity 5.90 - 7.50. Special camping packages available. Credit cards accepted.

Reservations: Recommended for high season - write for details. Address: Vinkeloord 1, 5382 JX Vinkel (North Brabant). Tel: 073/532 29 66. FAX: 073/532 16 98.

see advertisement on page 246

587 Camping De Vergarde, Erichem, nr Tiel

Family oriented site in a quiet setting.

Situated north of s'Hertogenbosch and west of Nijmegen and Arnhem, De Vergarde has two sections on either side of a lake. Static holiday caravans are on the left, with 220 touring pitches in named sections on the right (about one third seasonal). With good access, pitches are numbered on flat grass and include 30 new ones with electricity (6A) and TV connections. There are trees all round the perimeter (but no shade on the pitches) and the site has a spacious, open feeling with the lake adding to its attractiveness. Sanitary facilities are in three blocks of an excellent standard, with British style WCs, family showers, washing machines and baby bathrooms. Most, but not all, hot water is on payment. The shop opens daily and the restaurant/bar in high season plus weekends in low season. There is a heated pool each for adults and children, the latter also being catered for with minigolf, pony riding, pets corner, horse drawn wagons, large play area, volleyball and a large indoor games room for wet days. Two tennis courts. Lots of ducks and geese gather around the lake, which can be used for fishing (but not swimming).

How to find it: From the A15 Dordrecht/Nijmegen road exit at Tiel West (also MacDonald's) and follow signs to Erichem village.

General Details: Open 1 March - 30 Oct. Swimming pools (1/5-1/9). Shop (1/5-1/10). Restaurant (1/5-1/10). Minigolf. Pony riding. Pets corner. Bicycle hire. Children's play area. Volleyball. Basketball. Games room. Tennis courts. Fishing. Chemical disposal. Motorcaravan services.

Charges 1999: Per unit incl. 2 adults and services (electricity, water and drainage) Nfl. 34.00 - 39.00; extra person 6.00; dog 5.00. Special weekly rates. Low season less 20%.

Reservations: Contact site. Address: Erichemseweg 84, 4117 GL Erichem. Tel: 0344/57 20 17. FAX: 0344/57 22 29. E-mail: info@devergarde.nl. Internet: www.devergarde.nl.

589 Kampeercentrum Klein Canada, Afferden, nr Nijmegen

Pretty site with good facilities in the Maas valley, close to German border.

Following the war, the family who own this site wanted to emigrate to Canada - they didn't go, but created this attractive site with the maple leaf theme decorating buildings, pool and play equipment. Buildings adorned with flowers house the main amenities near the entrance and the site has a sheltered atmosphere with many ornamental trees. There are two touring areas, one on an island surrounded by a landscaped moat used for fishing, the other on flat ground on the other side of the entrance. They provide 120 large pitches, all with 4A electricity, water, drainage and TV. Some 190 seasonal pitches form other areas to the back of the site. The island pitches have excellent, unisex sanitary facilities with free hot water, private cabins, controllable showers and family facilities in heated rooms alongside the bar. The other pitches are served by a good block with push-button showers. Small indoor pool, sauna and solarium and an outdoor pool (with slide) and children's pool with a sunbathing area. A traditional bar with a pool table has takeaway facilities tucked away behind and there is a small shop (bread to order). This is a good quality site with a lot to offer for a comfortable stay in charming surroundings.

How to find it: Site is signed off N271 Nijmegen - Venlo road, just south of the A52/E31 motorway into Germany.

General Details: Open all year. Bar, restaurant, snack bar, takeaway and shop (all April - Oct). Outdoor pool (May - Sept). Indoor pool (all year). Sauna and solarium. Tennis. Fishing. Children's playground. Bicycle hire.

Charges guide: Per unit: high season incl. up to 4 persons Nfl. 49.50, low season incl. 2 persons 37.00; extra person 6.25; dog 4.00; local tax 1.25 per person.

Reservations: made with Nfl. 10 deposit Address: Dorpsstraat 1, 5851 AG Afferden (Limburg). Tel: 0485/53 12 23. FAX: 0485/53 22 18.

586 Camping Betuwestrand, Beesd, nr Utrecht

Pleasant, conveniently situated site for night stop or longer stay.

Just off the A2/E25 motorway, this is a large site with 200 places for tourers (all with 10A electricity, most with drainage) in addition to its 500 well established permanent units. The touring pitches are in four distinct areas with many around the edges of an attractive lake with a large sandy beach. For families with young children there is another area away from the water. The toilet blocks are of a good standard and include British WCs, family rooms and facilities for disabled people. Hot water is on payment in both showers and washbasins in cabins. Smart reception block and also a restaurant (open to the public), shop, bar, TV room and children's play area. An area of the lake is cordoned off for swimming with a slide and boards and it is also suitable for windsurfing.

How to find it: Site is 25 km. SSE of Utrecht, clearly signed from both directions on the A2/E25 road between Utrecht and s'Hertogenbosch. Take the exit 14 (Beesd) and site is 200 m.

General Details: Open 1 April - 30 Sept. Shop. Restaurant. Bar/TV room. Playground. Good lake fishing. Bicycle hire. Launderette. Tennis. Mobile homes for hire. No dogs accepted.

Charges guide: Per unit incl. up to 2 persons, electricity and tourist tax Nfl 31.00; extra person 6.00

Reservations: Necessary in high season - contact site. Address: A. Kraalweg 40, 4153 XC Beesd. Tel: 0345/68 15 03. FAX: 0345/68 16 86.

569 SVR Camping De Victorie, Meerkerk

Nature at its best on a family run site convenient to North Sea ports.

Within an hour's drive from the port of Rotterdam you can be pitched on this delightful site in the `green heart of Holland'. De Victorie, a working farm and a member of a club of small, `green' sites, offers an alternative to bustling seaside sites. Everything about it is surprising and contrary to any preconceived ideas. To the left of the entrance stands a modern building which houses reception, open plan office and space with tables and chairs, where the friendly owners may well invite you to have a cup of coffee. Adjoining is the main sanitary block which is kept spotlessly clean with British style WCs, washbasins, mirrors, etc. and showers (on payment). There is a dishwashing area and laundry room, plus additional sanitary facilities situated around the spacious site. The 70 grass pitches are level and generous in size with 4A electricity supply. You can choose to be pitched in the shade of one of the orchards, or in the more open meadow area. The freedom of the farmland is especially enjoyed by children. Apart from the farm animals, wildlife and tractor rides, there is a trampoline, table tennis, fishing, bicycle hire and a play field for football. The farm shop sells milk, eggs, cheese and ice cream.

How to find it: From Rotterdam follow A15 to junction with A27. Proceed 6 km. north on A27 to Noordeloos exit (no. 25) and join N214. Site is signed approx. 200 m. after roundabout at Noordeloos (do not enter vilage).

General Details: Open 15 March - 31 Oct. Farm shop. Children's play area. Bicycle hire. Fishing. Riding. Chemical disposal.

Charges 1999: Special price for SVR Club and AR readers: Per person Nfl. 2.50; caravan, tent or motorcaravan 2.50; car 1.00; large motorcaravan 3.50; electricity (4A) 2.50; local tax 0.35. No credit cards.

AR Discount

See text

Reservations: Contact site. Address: Broekseweg 75-77 4231 VD Meerkerk. Tel: 0183/352741 or 351516. FAX: 0183/351234.

NETHERLANDS

584 Camping De Pampel, Hoenderloo, nr Arnhem/Apeldoorn

Tranquil forest site in De Hooge Veluwe National Park.

A site with no static holiday caravans is rare in the Netherlands and this adds to the congenial atmosphere at De Pampel, which is enhanced by its situation deep in the forest, with 9 ha. of its own woods to explore. This peaceful park offers many opportunities for interesting outings with the two National Parks in the vicinity, the Kroller-Muller museum and the city of Arnhem. The area has excellent cycle paths which can be joined from a gate at the back of the site. Therre are 180 pitches (20 seasonal). You can choose to site yourself around the edge of a large open field with volleyball, etc. in the middle, or pick one of the individual places which are numbered, divided by trees and generally quite spacious. All have 4A electricity (no heaters allowed) but the furthest pitches are some distance from the sanitary facilities. The swimming pool and child's pool, heated by solar panels, are open Easter - Oct. Modern play equipment has special safety surfaces. There is just one building which houses reception, a restaurant, bar, snack bar, laundry and dishwashing, and the sanitary facilities, which are modern and a very good new addition at the end (showers on payment, British style WCs). Full catering facilities are provided in high season (6 weeks of July/Aug), otherwise at weekends only. Barbecues by permission only, no open fires.

How to find it: From the A50 Arnhem-Apeldoorn road exit for Hoenderloo and follow signs.

General Details: Open all year. Swimming pool (Easter - Oct). Restaurant. Bar. Snack bar. Shop (1/4-31/10). Children's play area. Pets corner. Sports area. Chemical disposal.

Charges 1999: Per unit incl. 2 persons Nfl. 35.00, without car 30.00; extra person 8.00; child (under 11 yrs) 6.00; dog 7.50; electricity (4A) 5.00. Less 10% 1/9-25/3.

Reservations: Made with deposit (Nfl. 100). Address: Woeste Hoefweg 33-35, 7351 TN Hoenderloo. Tel: 055/378 1760. FAX: 055/378 1992.

582 Camping de Hertshoorn, Garderen

Attractive, good quality site with woodland pitches.

Although this is quite a large site, this is not immediately apparent with its woodland location. Careful design has allowed both single pitches in little glades and groups on cleared grassy areas with plenty of gentle shade. Around 300 of the pitches are for tourists with some seasonal units placed around the edges of the site. All have 4A electrical connections, over 200 with water and drainage also. Cars must be parked on the entrance car park. Three excellent toilet blocks provide comprehensive facilities with a variety of cabins and showers with free hot water (showers electronically timed), British style WCs, dishwashing facilities and freezers. An older block houses a well equipped laundry. The very smart reception (more like a hotel than a camp site!) provides information packs in English, with a pleasant restaurant at the rear which the owners, the Selderijk family, call `a living room for guests'. Well kept, small animal paddocks and stables entertain the children and there is a variety of play equipment around the site. There are indoor heated swimming and paddling pools and outdoor paddling pools. Garderen is a pretty village, 1 km. away, and the area is very suitable for cycling.

How to find it: From A1/E30 between Amersfoort and Apeldoorn, take Garderen exit. Cross the N344, through village and site is signed on Putten road.

General Details: Open 31 March - 30 Oct. Supermarket. Restaurant (closed Mondays). Snacks. Swimming and paddling pools. Minigolf. Children's farm. Play areas. Bicycle hire. Entertainment for children in high season. Baby equipment hire. Laundry facilities.

Charges 1998: Per unit incl. electricity and 2 persons Nfl. 25.00 - 50.00; extra person 5.00; local tax 0.92 per person. Weekly family packages - details from site.

Reservations: Recommended for high season. Address: Putterweg 68-70, 3886 PG Garderen. Tel: 0577/461529. FAX: 0577/461556.

585 Camping de Hooge Veluwe, Arnhem

This site has been recommended by our Dutch agent, although we have yet to make a formal inspection ourselves. It is said to be of excellent quality (5 stars) and is situated opposite the National park De Hooge Veluwe and the Kroller Muller museum. It is also near the Burgers Zoo and Safari Park and Burgers Park, all of which make interesting visits. The site itself is quite large with a swimming pool, bar/restaurant, shop and other facilities, although it has a fairly high proportion of static units. A full report will be included in the next edition of our guide once we have had the opportunity to inspect the site at first hand.

How to find it: Leave the A12 motorway at exit 25 (Oosterbeck) and follow signs for Hooge Veluwe. Site is on right after about 4 km.

General Details: Open Late March - early October.

Reservations: Contact site. Address: Koningsweg 14, 6816 TC Arnhem. Tel: 026/4432272. FAX: 026/4436809.

KAMPEERCENTRUM ★ ★ ★ ★ ★

DE HOOGE VELUWE

Kampeercentrum De Hooge Veluwe is a campsite where many campers from different countries come to spend their holiday, because of its unique location in the green heart of the Netherlands, right in front of the entrance to the national park "De Hooge Veluwe".

Camping de Hooge Veluwe
Koningsweg 14 • 6816 TC ARNHEM
Phone (+31)- 26-443 2272 • Fax: (+31)- 26-443 68 09

N580 Flevo-Natuur, Zeewolde

Large, well equipped naturist site in quiet forest location.

This large naturist site, set amongst the densely wooded area of the southern Flevoland polder, is well equipped and well organised. The central feature of the site is an island recreation area with a sandy beach, sunbathing lawns, children's animal enclosure, volleyball and boules areas. There are two large swimming pools, outdoor and indoor (the indoor one is open all year), and a small children's pool directly linked to the main pool. Adjacent are a sauna and solarium. A daily events programme is organised with activities for children and adults, including bingo, dancing, etc. Other amenities include tennis courts, a restaurant/bar, small snack bar with takeaway and supermarket (1/4-31/10). The 750 pitches, about half available for tourists, are mainly in groups separated by hedges. Cars must be parked on the car park at the entrance, which gives a quiet, spacious atmosphere. Visitors with motorcaravans are at a disadvantage as they are placed in a more remote area away from the centre (with inferior portacabin style sanitary facilities). The main sanitary facilities consist of three blocks, one of which can be heated for winter use. They have British style WCs, free hot showers (communal) and facilities for the disabled. This is a friendly site where naturist cards are unnecessary - entrance is open to all and day visits are possible. Nudity is obligatory in all areas when the temperature reaches 20° C.

How to find it: From the A28/E232 motorway (Amersfoort-Zwolle) take the Nijkerk exit, and turn towards Zeewolde. After 500 m. cross lifting bridge onto Flevoland then follow signs for Flevo-Natuur. From the opposite direction (ie. Almere) follow signs to Nijkerk, and then site.

General Details: Open all year. Supermarket. Bar. Restaurant (closed Oct - Dec). Swimming pools. Sauna and solarium. Table tennis. Minigolf. Boules. Volleyball. Entertainment programme. Launderette. Bungalows for rent.

Charges guide: Per tent or caravan Nfl 12.50, with electricity 16.00; person 13.50; child (4-14 yrs) 7.00. Less outside high season. Credit cards accepted. Arrival after 15.00 hrs.

Reservations: Recommended for July - mid-Aug. and school holidays especially for electricity. Address: Wielseweg 3, 3896 LA Zeewolde. Tel: 036/552 82 41.

**The sites in the NETHERLANDS featured in this guide
are shown on the BENELUX map on page 369**

NETHERLANDS

583 Camping Kerkendel, Kootwijk, nr Arnhem

Friendly, family site with high quality amenities.

Kerkendel is a good quality touring site, small enough to allow friendly, personal attention from the owners, the Van Asselt family. Very suitable for families with young children, the 170 pitches are arranged in small groups with play equipment in many of the central open spaces. Cars are parked on car parks at the entrance. Hedges and attractive trees provide shade and electricity (3A) is available on all pitches. A super new sanitary block has under-floor heating and a room with a wide range of washing and shower facilities with the emphasis on families (baby rooms, family shower rooms, low washbasins, etc). Another excellent new building with no children's facilities, is for those who prefer a quieter environment. Hot water is free and entry controlled by a card system. The adjacent fully equipped dishwashing (dishwasher!) and laundry room is of the same high standard. Two small blocks with WCs (British style) only will be replaced within the next few years which will ensure that there are adequate facilities when the site is busy. Activities include a small indoor and a heated outdoor swimming pool, tennis (small charge), volleyball and table tennis. Children's playground, TV room, a good restaurant and snack bar, and a small supermarket. Plenty of tourist information and advice are available from reception and bicycles are for hire to try out the network of cycle paths in the area. The site is surrounded by woodland and sandy open spaces (this is the largest sand 'dune' in Western Europe) and is very close to two National Parks and the city of Arnhem with its Burger Zoo and Open Air Museum.

> **How to find it:** Kootwijk is 10 km. west of Apeldoorn. From A1/E30 motorway, take Kootwijk exit and site signed.
>
> **General Details:** Open 1 April - 1 Nov. Shop. Restaurant. Snack bar with takeaway. TV room. Indoor and outdoor swimming pools. Tennis. Bicycle hire. Volleyball. Children's playground. Laundry facilities. Chalets to rent.
>
> **Charges 1998:** Per unit incl. 2 persons NLG 27.00 - 49.50; extra person 5.00; dog 8.50; local tax 0.92 per person; electricity included. Credit cards accepted.
>
> **Reservations:** Made free of charge - write for details. Address: Kerkendelweg 49, 3775 KM Kootwijk. Tel: 0577/45 62 24. FAX: 0577/45 65 45. E-mail: kerkendel@tref.nl. Internet: http://www.kerkendel.nl.

598 Camping De Roos, Beerze-Ommen

Family run site in a area of outstanding natural beauty.

This is a nature lovers campsite, in an atmosphere of tranquillity. It is in Overijssel's Vecht Valley, a unique region set in a river dune landscape on the River Vecht. The river and its tributary wends its way unhurriedly around and through this spacious site, in a natural setting which the owners of De Roos have carefully preserved. Conserving the environment is paramount here and pitches and necessary amenities have been blended into the landscape with great care. Pitches, many with electric hook-up, are naturally sited, some behind blackthorn thickets, in the shadow of an old oak, or in a clearing scattered with wild flowers. De Roos is also a car-free campsite during peak periods. Vehicles must be parked at the car park. Torches are necessary for night time. Facilities include a health food shop and tea room. Four well maintained sanitary blocks are kept fresh and clean. The two larger blocks are heated and contain good sized showers, baby bath/shower and wash cabins, all with free hot water, and WCs (no paper). There are washing-up sinks and a launderette adjacent to shop. For children, a number of small playgrounds and a kite flying field. Swimming, fishing and boating is possible in the Vecht and there is a children's pool and beach area, also landing stages with steps. The owners have compiled walking and cycling routes (in English) and follow the ever changing countryside of the Vecht Valley.

> **How to find it:** Leave A28 at Ommen exit no. 21 and join N340 for 19 km. to Ommen. Turn right at traffic lights over bridge and immediately left on local road towards Beerze. Site on left after 8 km just after Reeze village sign.
>
> **General Details:** Open 28 March - 1 November. Health food shop. Tea room. Bicycle hire. River swimming. Volleyball. Basketball. Boules. Table tennis. Launderette. Chalets for hire.
>
> **Charges 1998:** Per unit incl. 2 persons Nfl. 23.25; electricity 3.60; local tax 0.80. Discounts in low season.
>
> **Reservations:** Contact site; reservations made with Nfl. 10 fee. Address: Beerzeweg 10, 7736 PJ Beerze-Ommen (Overijssel). Tel: 0523/251234. FAX: 0523/251903.

599 Camping De Vechtstreek, Rheeze-Hardenberg

Quality site with a fairy-tale theme.

It would be difficult for any child (or adult) to pass this site and not be curiously drawn to the oversized open story book which marks its entrance. From here young children turn the pages and enter the exciting world of Hannah and Bumpie, two of the nine characters around which this site's fairy-tale theme has been created. The young owners of De Vechtstreek have given their park a special identity by creating this fairy-tale. The colourful characters appear on finger boards and signs throughout the site. Not only is the story acted out in the restaurant at the Saturday children's buffet, the story continues in the indoor water play park which is dominated by Hannah's Castle. This is also a campsite which offers top class facilities. These include three modern heated sanitary blocks with free hot showers, baby room, family shower and outside washing-up area. Excellent laundry room, well stocked supermarket and restaurant. The snack bar and takeaway overlooks the water play area. There are 200 touring pitches mostly laid out in bays which accommodate around 12 units. In the centre of each is a small children's play area. There are many water points and pitches have electricity (4A). Although there are numerous static vans these are unobtrusive and placed away from the touring area. The site has a mature appearance with many trees and shrubs. There is access at the rear of the site to a fishing, swimming and boating recreation area. Additional facilities include a children's theatre and daily activity club.

How to find it: From Ommen take N34 Hardenberg road for 9 km. Turn right on N36 and proceed south for approx. 3.5 km. Turn left at first crossroads and immediately left again on local road. Site clearly signed on left in 2 km.

General Details: Open 1 April - 25 October. Supermarket. Restaurant, snacks and takeaway. Fairy-tale water play park. Activity club. Football field. Theatre. Launderette.

Charges 1998: Per unit incl. 2 persons Nfl. 29.90 - 42.70, 3 persons 32.80 - 46.85, 4 persons 35.70 - 51.00; electricity 5.00; local tax 0.60.

Reservations: Contact site: Address: Grote Beltenweg 17, 7794 RA Rheeze-Hardenberg. Tel: 0523/261369. FAX: 0523/265942.

581 Rekreatiepark De Luttenberg, Luttenberg, nr Zwolle

Large, peacefully set park with many facilities.

This woodland site is near the Sallandse Heuvelrug nature reserve in a hilly location and is well placed for relaxing walking and cycling tours. It is a large park with 125 seasonal pitches around the perimeter and 225 touring pitches (all with 4A electricity) in a central area off tarred access roads. The individual, numbered and separated, large pitches are in rows divided by hedges and trees, with easy access, on mainly gently sloping or undulating grass. A separate cluster is for dog owners. A new heated sanitary block gives a satisfactory overall provision with two other facilities each offering 4 pre-set hot showers on payment, 12 open washbasins (4 with free hot water) and 8 British style WCs. Outside are under cover dishwashing points. Small shop for essentials with fresh bread. Large bar and eating area with terrace and small, separate restaurant (low season: Tues. and Fri-Sun). Barbecue with seating. The fair-sized swimming pool and a small one for children, plus boules, football, tennis, table tennis, minigolf, volleyball and an animal enclosure provide plenty to keep younger visitors happy. Member of the Holland Tulip Parc group.

How to find it: From N35 Zwolle - Almelo turn onto N348 Ommen road east of Raalte, then turn to Luttenberg and follow signs. From A1 (Amsterdam - Hengelo) take exit 23 at Deventer onto N348 then as above.

General Details: Open 28 March - 4 Oct. Shop. Bar. Restaurant. Swimming pool (15/5-15/9). Tennis. Table tennis. Volleyball. Boules. Bicycle hire. Minigolf. Riding 4 km. Chemical disposal. Bungalows for hire.

Charges 1998: Per pitch incl. 2 persons and electricity Nfl. 30.00, 3 persons 35.00, 4 persons 40.00; car or m/cycle 5.00; cyclists, 2 persons 25.00; extra person (over 3 yrs) 6.00; dog 7.00.

Reservations: Contact site. Address: Heuvelweg 9, 8105 SZ Luttenberg. Tel: 572 30 14 05. FAX 572 30 17 57.

NETHERLANDS

578 Recreatiecentrum D'Olde Lantschap, Wateren, nr Meppel

Family site with swimming pool, in pretty countryside.

This site is situated in the historic and beautiful area of Drente, on the borders of Friesland amid small lakes and pretty villages, and is set well away from main roads. The 290 pitches, all with electricity (4A) are of ample size, sited around the perimeter of about ten small or partitioned level fields. The hedges are mature and there are many tall trees surrounding and sheltering the site. One large sanitary block and another smaller block which services the furthest fields provide British WCs and free hot showers, but they are both a fair walk from some of the pitches. The site amenities are all near the entrance and include a thatched bar and a shop for provisions. Popular with Dutch families, entertainment is organised for young children and adults in the season. There is a sports field, a heated indoor pool, a lake for fishing and another larger lake for swimming with a beach.

How to find it: Site is about 24 km. north of Meppel. When approaching from the south (Zwolle) on the A28 turn onto the N32 to Meppel and then Diever. From Diever follow road to Wateren, from where the site is signed.

General Details: Open 1 April - 1 Nov. Indoor swimming pool. Bar. Snack bar (all season). Restaurant 500 m. Children's play areas. Fishing. Bicycle hire. Riding 1 km. Entertainment at times. Laundry facilities. Chemical disposal.

Charges 1999: Per person (over 2 yrs) Nfl 4.05; pitch 15.35; cyclist or hiker's tent pitch 12.05; electricity 3.75; dog 3.95; local taxes 2.55. No credit cards (but electronic payment accepted).

Reservations: Made without deposit. Address: Schurerslaan 4, 8438 SC Wateren. Tel: 0521/38 72 44. FAX: 0521/38 75 93.

579 Camping 't Kuierpadtien, Wezuperbrug, nr Emmen

Large, friendly site in northeast with its own dry-ski slope.

This all year round site is suitable as a night stop, or for longer if you wish to participate in all the activities offered in July and August (on payment). These encompass canoeing, windsurfing, water shutes and the dry-ski slope, which is also open during the winter so that the locals can practise before going en masse to Austria. There are three opportunities for swimming with an indoor pool supplemented by a heated outdoor pool (June-Aug) and the lake itself. Sauna, solarium, whirlpool and tennis also. Children's play areas, volleyball and basketball. There are plenty of local attractions and brochures for these are available at reception. Restaurant (all year), supermarket (May-Aug, bread all year). The site itself is in a woodland setting on the edge of the village. The pitches, all with electricity, are of reasonable size and are flat and grassy. There are eight quite acceptable sanitary blocks with British style WCs and free hot showers (17.30 - 10.00 in July/Aug).

How to find it: From N34 Groningen-Emmen road exit near Emmen onto N31 towards Beilen. Turn right into Schoonord where left to Wezuperbrug. Site is at beginning of village on the right.

General Details: Open all year. Electricity connections (4A). Supermarket. Restaurant. Indoor and outdoor pools. Sauna. Solarium. Tennis. Volleyball. Basketball. Dry ski slope. Children's play areas. Chemical disposal. Motorcaravan services.

Charges 1998: Per person (over 1 yr) Nfl. 7.60; pitch 15.75, 22.75 or 31.50, acc. to season; car 5.00.

Reservations: Recommended for July/Aug. and made with deposit. Address: Oranjekanaal NZ 10, 7853 TA Wezuperbrug. Tel: 0591/38 14 15. FAX: 0591/38 22 35. E-mail: kuierpad@icns.nl. Internet: www.kuierpad.nl.

577 Camping Stadspark, Groningen

Woodland site for city visits or passing through night halt.

The Stadspark is a large park to the southwest of the city, well signed and with easy access. The campsite is within the park with many trees and surrounded by water. It has 200 pitches (50 seasonal), of which 130 have 4A electricity. The separate tent area is supervised directly by the manager. There are two sanitary blocks, one of which is being refurbished for '99. Hot water for showers and dishwashing is on payment. Shop daily, cafe April - mid-Sept. Leisure facilities include bicycle hire, fishing and canoeing. The Paterswoldse Lake is near for windsurfing, swimming or sailing. Buses to the city leave from outside and timetables, etc. are provided by Mrs Swieter, the helpful, English speaking manager.

How to find it: From Assen on the A28 turn left onto A7. Turn onto N370 and follow signs (Stadspark, quite close).

General Details: Open 15 March - 15 Oct. Shop. Café (1/5-15/9). Bicycle hire. Fishing. Canoeing. Riding and golf 10 km. Chemical disposal. Motorcaravan service point.

Charges 1999: Per adult Nfl. 4.75; child (2-12 yrs) 3.25; caravan or tent 7.00; car 4.50; motorcaravan 8.00 - 10.00; electricity 3.50. No credit cards.

Reservations: Contact site. Address: Campinglaan 6, 9727 KH Groningen. Tel: 050/525 1624. FAX: 050/525 0099.

575 Camping De Kleine Wielen, Leeuwarden

Lakeside site in wooded park near historic town of Leeuwarden.

Situated 5 km. from the historic town of Leeuwarden, this site is set in the attractive Groene Ster recreation park in an area of woods, small canals, lakes and fields. Most of the 200 touring pitches are on an island in the lake which has a cove for swimming and sunbathing. Other pitches are either in wooded clearings or on open fields in separate areas from the 130 seasonal and permanent units. There are two new sanitary buildings on the island which provide in total; 10 hot showers on payment, 14 private cabins and 8 washbasins with free hot water and 18 British style WCs. Dishwashing at both (separate building for one). Very pleasant grassy areas for relaxation surround the lake which can be used for swimming, fishing and small boats. Amenities within walking distance include a heated swimming pool, minigolf and a jogging track of 1,800 m. for the more energetic camper! An Otter Park has been opened next to the site where fresh water animals (otters, beavers, polecats, etc.) can be seen in a natural environment. Evening entertainment is a bus ride away in Leeuwarden.

How to find it: Site is 5 km. east of Leeuwarden on the N355 road to Hurdegaryp and Groningen and is signed.

General Details: Open 1 April - 30 Sept. Shop (limited hours). Launderette. Chemical disposal. Licensed canteen for snack meals. Youth room. Watersports and swimming in lake. Good children's play equipment on sand. Swimming pool/minigolf near. Bus stop 200 m. Caravans/chalets to rent.

Charges guide: Per caravan/tent Nfl 5.00; motorcaravan 11.00; person 5.25; child (2-12 yrs) 3.00; car 5.00; m/cycle 3.75; dog 3.00; electricity 3.50; shower 1.00.

Reservations: Necessary for high season. Address: Groene Ster 14, 8926 XE Leeuwarden. Tel: 0511/43 16 60. FAX: 0511/43 25 84.

576 Recreatioord-Watersportcentrum De Kuilart, Koudum

Well run, modern site by Friesland's largest lake, ideal for watersports.

With its own marina and private boating facilities, De Kuilart attracts many watersports enthusiasts. The marina provides windsurfing and sailing lessons and boat hire, and there are special rates at the site for groups and sailing clubs. However, the site has an excellent indoor swimming pool as well as an area for lake swimming and on land there are sports facilities including tennis, a sauna and solarium, and woods for cycling and walking. It may also therefore appeal for a relaxing break in a pleasant area not much visited by British campers. Pitches at De Kuilart (some with electricity, water, waste water and TV connections) are set in groups of 10 to 16 on areas of grass surrounded by well established hedges. Four modern sanitary blocks are well spaced around the site and are of above average quality, although showers are on payment and most washbasins (half in private cabins) have only cold water. British style WCs. The restaurant provides good views of the lake and woodland. Dogs are not accepted. A member of the Holland Tulip Parks group.

How to find it: Site is southeast of Koudum, on the Fluessen lake. Follow the camping sign off the N359 Bolsward - Lemmer road.

General Details: Open 21 March - 31 Oct. Restaurant/bar. Supermarket (May - 1 Sept). Launderette. Sauna and solarium. Sports field. Indoor pool (3 sessions daily, 1 swim free). Lake swimming area. Children's playground. Recreation team (high season). 400 berth marina with windsurfing, boat hire and boat shop. Garage at harbour.

Charges guide: Prices outside 2/7-20/8 in brackets. Per unit incl. 2 persons Nfl 31.00 (25.00), with electricity 34.50 (28.50); all service plus 3.00; extra person 6.00; extra car 3.25; boat on trailer 3.50; tourist tax and babies under 1 year included. Special weekend rates at B.Hs.

Reservations: Recommended as site is very popular; made from Sat. - Sat. only in peak season. Address: Kuilart 1, 8723 CG Koudum. Tel: 0514 52 22 21. FAX: 0514 52 30 10.

NETHERLANDS

574 Camping Sint Maartenszee, Sint Maartenszee, nr Den Helder

Excellent family site with good facilities in North Holland.

Situated within easy travelling distance of the attractive and interesting towns of North Holland, especially Alkmaar, this family site is separated from the sea by 900 m. of grassy dunes. With the dune environment, the ground is basically sandy but grass has grown well and hedges are now established. Specialising in family holidays, unusually for the Netherlands only touring units are taken (with a bungalow park adjacent). The 300 pitches are arranged in lines backed by high hedging; 200 have electricity and 150 are fully serviced with water, drainage and cable TV connections. In low, neat buildings, all facilities are of a high standard, particularly both first class, modern sanitary blocks. Hot water for showers is free (with a fascinating panel demonstrating how solar power helps to heat the water!), and it includes wash-cabins, family shower rooms and baby bathrooms. Raised level showers for children are a nice special feature. A dishwashing and laundry room has hot water on payment with a microwave provided. Each block has a couple resident on site to clean and maintain standards throughout the day. A good restaurant/bar, with attractive terrace overlooking the minigolf, has a sitting area with open fire and board games provided. This is a pretty and interesting area of the Netherlands and Sint Maartenszee is quite near the fascinating man-made barrier built to form the Ijsselmeer which allowed the reclamation of so much land.

How to find it: From Alkmaar, take the N9 northwards towards Den Helder. Site is signed after approx. 18 km. towards the sea at St-Maartensvlotbrug.

General Details: Open 21 March - 21 Sept. Restaurant/bar (all season). Supermarket (all season). Minigolf. Volleyball. Basketball. Children's play areas. Bicycle hire. Bus service from village to Alkmaar (cheese market on Fridays April - Sept). No dogs or transistors accepted.

Charges guide: Per unit: 60 sq.m. pitch Nfl. 16.00 - 21.00, with electricity 22.50 - 27.50; 90 sq.m. pitch 25.50 - 34.00, fully serviced 28.50 - 40.50; person 5.50, plus local tax 1.10.

Reservations: Made for approx. 100 pitches (all with electricity) with deposit (details from site) but 40% are kept free from reservation for any length of stay. Address: Westerduinweg 30, 1753 BA Sint Maartenszee. Tel: 0224 56 14 01. FAX: 0224 56 19 01.

572 Camping-Jachthaven Uitdam, Uitdam, nr Monickendam

Large waterside site for sailing and windsurfing enthusiasts, northeast of Amsterdam.

Situated beside the Markermeer which is used extensively for watersports, this large site has its own private yachting marina (320 yachts and boats). It has 350 seasonal and permanent pitches, many used by watersports enthusiasts, but also offers marked pitches on open, grassy ground overlooking the water for tourers. Electrical connections are available and amenities include a shop, TV room, tennis, children's playground and a bar/cafe. Sanitary facilities are rather basic in fairly open buildings with hot showers on payment and British style WCs. There is a special area for campers with bicycles. Very much dominated by the marina, this site will appeal to watersports enthusiasts, with sailing, windsurfing and swimming opportunities, but it is also on a pretty stretch of coast, only 15 km. from Amsterdam.

How to find it: From the A10, take the N247 towards Volendam then the Monnickendam exit south in the direction of Marken, then Uitdam.

General Details: Open 1 April - 1 Nov. Shop. TV room. Tennis. Children's playground. Bar/restaurant (weekends and high season). Yacht marina (with fuel) and slipway. Watersports facilities. Entertainment in high season.

Charges guide: Per unit incl. 2 persons Nfl 35.00 (tent 27.50, without car 21.50); extra person 7.50; dog 5.00; boat on land 7.50, in marina 2.00 - 2.50 per metre. Less 20% outside July/Aug. excl. B.Hs.

Reservations: Contact site. Address: Zeedijk 2, 1154 PP Uitdam. Tel: 020/4031433. FAX: 020/4033692.

570 Molengroet Recreatieverblijven, Noord-Sharwoude, nr Alkmaar

Pleasant site close to lake for watersports.

Whether you wish to stop over on the way to the Afsluitdijk across the top of the Ijsselmeer or partake in watersports, this is a modern site, just 40 km from Amsterdam. The enthusiastic manager, Tom van den Ham, believes you must cater for all ages (`young people are our future') and he provides a range of facilities to meet the varying needs. Therefore, the 300 touring pitches are grouped according to services provided, ranging from simple pitches with no services, to those with 10A electricity, TV, water and waste water 'comfort pitches'. These pitches also have the best sanitary facilities in a modern heated building with free, pre-set hot showers. The two other buildings were renewed in '98. A large shop is open April to October, but bread and milk may be obtained at other times from reception. The restaurant opens during the same period and there is a snack bar in high season - order snacks from the restaurant otherwise. Bicycles, surfboards and small boats may be hired and there are opportunities for tennis, squash, sauna, riding and swimming near. The nearby lake with surf school is attractive, particularly for teenagers. A site bus can take you to the local pool or the beach. Friendly multi-lingual reception staff provide local information and a range of on-site entertainment is carefully controlled by Tom.

How to find it: From Haarlem on A9 to Alkmaar take the N245 towards Schagen. Site is southwest of Noord Sharwoude, signed to west on road to Geestermerambacht.

General Details: Open all year. Shop (April - Oct). Restaurant (April - Oct, not Mon/Tues. in low season). Snack bar (high season). Fishing. Bicycle hire. Watersports close. Riding 5 km. Golf 6 km. Entertainment (high season and weekends. Chemical disposal. Motorcaravan services. Hotel (catering more for groups). Camping cottages to rent.

Charges 1999: Per unit incl. 2 persons Nfl. 33.50, with private sanitary facility 60.00. Reductions in low season and for longer stays. Credit cards accepted.

Reservations: Made with 50% deposit on booking, balance 3 weeks before arrival. Write to site. Address: Molengroet 1, Postbus 200, 1723 ZL Noord-Scharwoude. Tel: 0226/39 34 44. FAX: 0226/39 14 26. E-mail: info@molengroet.nl.

565 Camping Club Soleil, Noordwijk, nr Den Haag

Quality site not far from Amsterdam.

The facilities here are first class, including an indoor heated swimming pool with 'massage water' and watershute, a plunge bath for children, tennis court and sun-trap terrace all free of charge. The children's play equipment is very satisfactory and they also have a play/activity room and an animal enclosure. The shop (open in high season), launderette and restaurant (Indian speciality and Dutch meal of the day) plus takeaway are all of a high standard. A 1,500 m. dune beach is 1.5 km. The site provides just over 100 pitches of 80 sq.m. plus on flat grass, mainly individual ones separated by small trees or hedges and all having (or with close access to) electricity, TV and water connections. There are some hardstandings for motorhomes. The main sanitary building is modern and has free hot water to the showers (some with external entry), washbasins, some in private cabins, baby room and dishwashing facilities. There is a secondary 'portacabin' style facility of an excellent standard (open in high season) and a chemical disposal point. Much thought has gone into the design of this park and the cars for the seasonal pitches and bungalows are parked outside the camping area. Visitors at the site during our visit were very impressed with all the facilities. There was little noise apparent from aircraft (Schipol airport).

How to find it: From Amsterdam to Den Haag A4/A44 take exit 3 towards Noordwijk and follow ANWB camping signs (not frequent, just keep going). Take turning to right (small sign) shortly after Camping De Wijde Blick.

General Details: Open 1 April - 31 Oct. Shop (summer). Restaurant. Takeaway. Indoor pool and tennis (both free). Launderette. Animal enclosure. Bungalows and mobile homes for hire.

Charges guide: Per family pitch incl. TV connection, electricity and water Nfl 65.00 plus local tax 1.32 per person. Low season discounts 10-30%.

Reservations: Made for Sun.-Sun. only in high season. Write to site. Address: Kraaierslaan 7, 2204 AN Noordwijk. Tel: 0252 37 42 25. FAX: 0252 37 64 50.

NETHERLANDS

560 Recreatiecentrum Delftse Hout, Delft

Well run, modern site within easy reach of Delft.

Pleasantly situated in Delft's park and forest area on the eastern edge of the city, this site is part of the Koningshof group. It has 200 tourist pitches quite formally arranged in groups of 4 to 6 and surrounded by attractive young trees and hedges. All have sufficient space and electrical connections. Modern buildings near the entrance house the site amenities. These include modern toilet facilities with free hot showers and a spacious family room. A good sized first floor restaurant serves snacks or full meals and has an outdoor terrace overlooking the swimming pool and pitches. There is also a bar and recreation room. Reception provides friendly service and tourist information and also houses a shop for basic food and camping items. A small outdoor pool, volleyball, basketball and an adventure playground are in one corner. Walking and cycling tours are organised and there is a recreation programme in high season. A special package deal can be arranged including tickets to local `royal' attractions and a visit to the Royal Delftware factory.

How to find it: Site is 1 km. east of Delft; take the Delft/Pijnacker exit no. 9 from the A13 motorway, turn towards Pijnacker and then right at first traffic lights, following camping signs through suburbs and park to site.

General Details: Open all year. Restaurant, bar and shop (all 1/4-1/10). Outdoor swimming pool (1/5-15/9). New children's playground. Table tennis. Recreation room. Bicycle hire. Fishing 500 m. Riding 10 km. Golf 5 km. Regular bus service to Delft. Laundry. Motorcaravan service point. Chemical disposal. Chalets and caravans to let.

Charges 1999: Per caravan or tent plus car incl. 2 persons Nfl 41.50; motorcaravan 39.50; fully serviced pitch 47.00; extra person (over 3 yrs) 2.50; local tax 1.00; electricity (10A) 6.00; cable TV connection 2.00; dog (1 per pitch) 4.00. Low season discounts and for senior citizens (over 55). Special packages. Credit cards accepted.

Reservations: Essential for high season (not made by telephone). Address: Korftlaan 5, 2616 LJ Delft. Tel: 015/213 00 40. FAX: 015/213 12 93. E-mail: info-delftsehout@tours.nl. Internet: www.tours.nl/delftsehout.

566 Camping Het Amsterdamse Bos, Aalsmeer, nr Amsterdam

Neat municipal site in large park area quite close to city.

Het Amsterdamse Bos is a very large park to the southwest of Amsterdam, one corner of which has been specially laid out as the city's municipal site. Close to Schiphol Airport (we noticed little noise), it is about 12 km. from central Amsterdam. A high season bus service runs from the site every 35 mins. during the day to the city (local service at other times 300 m.). The site is well laid out alongside a canal, with unmarked pitches on separate flat lawns mostly backing onto pleasant hedges and trees, with several areas of hardstanding. It takes 400 tourist units, with 150 electrical connections. An additional area is available for tents and groups. The four older style sanitary blocks were clean when we visited but rather let the site down, appearing somewhat small and well used. Hot water is on payment to the washbasins but there are free pre-set hot showers; British style WCs. Near the entrance are laundry and snack bar facilities.

How to find it: Amsterdamse Bos and site are west of Amstelveen. From the A9 motorway exit for either Amstelveen or Aalsmeer (easier), turn towards Aalsmeer and look out carefully for camp signs.

General Details: Open 1 April - 15 Oct. 50,000 sq.m. for camping. Small shop. Cafe/bar and snack bar. Children's sand pit. Fishing. Fishing, boating, pancake restaurant in park. Laundry facilities. Chemical disposal. Motorcaravan services. Camping huts to rent.

Charges 1998: Per person Nfl 8.50; child (4-12 yrs) 4.25; car 4.25; motorcaravan 10.75; tent 5.50; caravan 6.50; m/cycle 2.25; dog 2.25; electricity 4A 3.50. Group reductions. No credit cards.

Reservations: A limited number only will be made for `serious enquirers'. Address: Kleine Noorddijk 1, 1432 CC Aalsmeer. Tel: 020/641 68 68. FAX: 020/640 23 78.

567 Gaasper Camping Amsterdam, Amsterdam

Well laid out site near Metro station, southeast of Amsterdam.

As Amsterdam is probably the most popular destination for visits in the Netherlands, a second site here may be useful. Gaasper is on the southeast side, a short walk from a Metro station with a direct 20 minute service to the centre. Situated on the edge of a large park with nature areas and a lake (with sailing facilities and new swimming beaches), there are also opportunities for relaxation. The site is well kept and neatly laid out on flat grass with attractive trees and shrubs. There are 410 pitches in two main areas - one more open and grassy, mainly kept for tents, the other more formal with numbered pitches mainly divided by shallow ditches or good hedges. Areas of hardstanding are available and all caravan pitches have 4/10A electrical connections (20 tent pitches have 4A connections). Some 60 seasonal and permanent units have their own area. In high season the site becomes very crowded and it is necessary to arrive early to find space, especially since reservations are not taken (see below). The three modern, clean toilet blocks for the tourist sections should be an adequate provision. Unisex in some sections, they have washbasins (cold water), some in private cabins and pre-set hot showers with push-button. Hot water for showers and some washing-up sinks is on payment. British style WCs. Facilities for handicapped. Although this is a typical, busy city site, it is better than many and there is a friendly welcome, with good English spoken.

How to find It: Take the exit for Gaasperplas from the section of A9 motorway which is on the east side of the A2. Note: do not take the Gaasperdam exit which comes first if approaching from the west.

General Details: Open all year except 1/1-14/3..Small shop (15/3-15/10). Cafe/bar plus takeaway (1/4-15/10). Shopping centre and restaurant nearby. Children's play area on grass. Fishing and riding 200 m. Golf 2 km. Washing machine and dryer. Chemical disposal. Motorcaravan service points.

Charges 1998: Per person Nfl. 6.50; child (4-12 yrs) 3.50; car 6.00; m/cycle 3.00; caravan 9.00; motorcaravan 11.00; tent 7.00 - 9.00, acc. to size; electricity 4.50; dog 3.75. No credit cards.

Reservations: are not made for Easter, Whitsun, July or August. Address: Loosdrechtdreef 7, 1108 AZ Amsterdam. Tel: 020/696 73 26. FAX: 020/696 93 69.

561 Camping De Oude Maas, Barendrecht, by Rotterdam

Peaceful riverside site convenient for Rotterdam.

The entrance is the least inspiring part here and you have to drive right up to the barrier in order to activate the intercom. Once through this, you pass a long strip of mixed seasonal and touring pitches. There are two more attractive touring areas, one for 12 units with electricity, water and waste water connections in a hedged group near to the reception, shop, restaurant and river. They have their own small, mediocre sanitary building, but there is a more modern one a short walk away. This has free hot water to the showers, private cabins and washbasins, British style WCs, facilities for the disabled, baby room and dishwashing. The third section is in a woodland setting, well back from the river on flat grass. It has a small `portacabin' type facility but again it is not far from the main sanitary building. The site is easily accessed from the A15 southern Rotterdam ring road and is situated right by the river, so it is well worth considering if you are visiting the city or want a peaceful stop.

How to find It: From the Rotterdam ring road south take exit 20 (Barendrecht) and follow signs to Achterzeedijk and Oude Maas.

General Details: Open all year. Restaurant, bar and snacks (all year). Shop (1/6-31/8, town 3 km). Fishing. Bicycle hire. Swimming pool and golf near. Launderette. Chemical disposal.

Charges guide: Per adult Nfl 5.90; child (under 15 yrs) 2.90; car 5.90; motorcaravan 7.70; caravan or tent 5.90; electricity (10A) 3.20; dog 3.20. Credit cards accepted.

Reservations: May be advisable high season. Write to site. Address: Achterzeedijk 1a, 2991 SB Barendrecht. Tel: 0786 77 24 45. FAX: 0786 77 30 13.

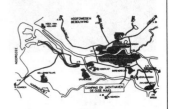

562 Camping Duinrell, Wassenaar, nr Den Haag (The Hague)

Very large site adjoining pleasure park and impressive tropical pool complex.

Duinrell means 'well in the dunes' and the water theme is continued in the adjoining amusement park and in the extensive indoor pool complex which are Duinrell's main attractions. Entry to the popular pleasure park is free for campers - indeed the camping areas surround and open out from the park. The 'Tiki' tropical pool complex has many attractions which include slides ranging from quite exciting to terrifying (according to your age!), whirlpools, saunas and many other features. There are also free outdoor pools and the centre has its own bar and cafe. Entry to the 'Tiki' complex is at a reduced rate for campers. Duinrell is open all year and a ski school (langlauf and Alpine) with 12 artificial runs, is a winter attraction. The campsite itself is very large with 1,300 tourist places on several flat grassy areas and it can become very busy in high season. As part of a continuing improvement programme, 700 pitches are now marked and have electricity, cable TV, water and drainage connections. Six toilet blocks, including two very good new ones, serve the tourist areas. They have British WCs, washbasins with warm water, free hot showers and can be heated in cool weather. The amenities shared with the park include restaurants, a pizzeria and pancake house, supermarket and a theatre (shows in high season). The original 900 permanent units have been reduced to around 400, gradually being replaced with smartly furnished 'Duingalows', self catering bungalows available to rent all year. Accommodation in family rooms is also provided in the estate's old coach house.

How to find it: Site is signed from the N44/A44 Den Haag-Amsterdam road, but from the south the turning is about 5 km. after you pass the sign for the start of Wassenaar town - then follow camp signs.

General Details: Open all year. Amusement park and Tiki tropical pool complex as detailed above. Restaurant, cafes, pizzeria and takeaways (weekends only in winter). Supermarket. Entertainment and shows in season. Bicycle hire. Bowling. Winter ski school. Fishing. Laundry facilities.

Charges 1998: Per unit on 'comfort' pitch incl. electricity Nfl. 20.00, with cable TV 25.00; 'nature' pitch 17.50; person (over 3 yrs) 18.50, over 65 13.50; extra car 7.50; m/cycle 2.50; dog 10.00. Overnight stays between 17.00-10.00 hrs (when amusement park closed) less 25%. Credit cards accepted.

Reservations: Recommended in high season, Easter and Whitsun (min. 1 week), 50% payment required 6 weeks in advance plus fee (15.00). Address: Duinrell 1. 2242 JP Wassenaar. Tel. 070/515 52 57. Fax: 070/515 53 71. E-mail: info@duinrell/nl. Internet: www.duinrell.nl.

For a list of sites which are open all year - see page 366.

£189

563 Camping Koningshof, Rijnsburg, nr Leiden

Relaxed, well run site between Den Haag and Amsterdam.

Koningshof is not far from site no. 562 but is of an entirely different type. Much smaller, it is run in a personal and friendly way with 175 numbered pitches for touring units divided into separate small groups of 4-12 by hedges and trees. Electrical connections (4/10A) are available in all areas. Cars are parked in areas around the perimeter. There are 135 static caravans, some for hire. Sanitary facilities are provided in three good blocks, one of which is new, with under floor heating. They have British WCs, washbasins (some in private cabins with hot water) or in general washrooms (cold water only), free controllable hot showers and facilities for the disabled. The reception, a pleasant restaurant, bar and snack bar are grouped around a courtyard style entrance decorated with seasonal flowers. On site is a small heated swimming pool (13½ x 7 m.), with separate paddling pool (open May - Sept) and imaginative children's play equipment. It is 5 km. to a sandy beach, 15 km. to Den Haag and 30 km. to Amsterdam. The site has a number of regular British visitors from club connections and the welcome is friendly, with English spoken. A very useful local information booklet (in English) is provided.

How to find it: From N44/A44 Den Haag - Amsterdam motor road, take exit 7 for Oegstgeest and Rijnsburg. Turn towards Rijnsburg and follow camp signs.

General Details: Open all year. Shop (1/4-15/9). Restaurant and bar with snacks and takeaway (1/4-25/10). Small swimming pool (unsupervised, 1/5-1/10). Solarium. Adventure playground and sports area. Tennis courts. Fishing pond (free). Bicycle hire. Entertainment in high season. Room for shows. Riding and golf 5 km. Washing machines and dryers. Chemical disposal. Motorcaravan service point. Chalets for hire.

Charges 1999: Per pitch incl. 2 persons Nfl 41.50; extra person (over 3 yrs) 2.50; second car (in car park) 4.00; electricity (10A) 6.00; local tax per person 1.00. Low season and senior citizen discounts; special group rates. Security barrier key deposit 25.00 (refundable). Credit cards accepted.

Reservations: Necessary for July/Aug. and made for any length with deposit and fee (payable by credit card). Address: Elsgeesterweg 8, 2231 NW Rijnsburg. Tel: 071/402 60 51. FAX: 071/402 13 36. E-mail: koningshof@tours.nl.

Some sites have supplied us with copies of their brochures

which we are pleased to forward to readers.

See our Brochure Service on page 366

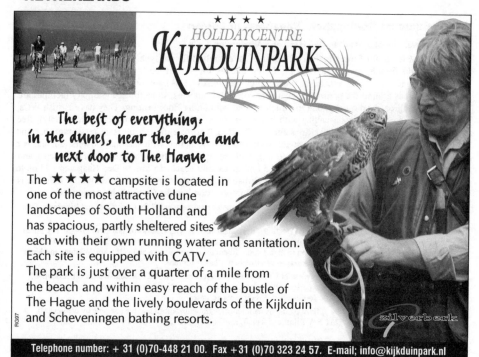
564 Recreatiecentrum Kijkduinpark, Den Haag

Rapidly developing park close to long beach.

This used to be a site with 1,700 touring pitches plus further statics, but its transformation into an ultra-modern, all year round centre is well under way, with many huts, villas and bungalows built along with a brand new reception. The new, wooded, touring area is immediately to the left of the entrance, with 450 pitches in shady glades of bark covered sand. There are simple ones for tents, some pitches with electricity only and many with electricity (6A), water, waste water and cable TV connections. The sanitary facilities have been replaced with brand new facilities since our last visit, also the supermarket, snack bar, shop and restaurant. The main attraction here is the Meeresstrand, 500 m. from the site entrance, which is a long, wide, sandy beach with flags to denote suitability for swimming and popular with windsurfers.

How to find it: Site is southwest of Den Haag on the coast and Kijkduin is well signed as an area from all round Den Haag.

General Details: Open all year. Snack bar and shop. Restaurant. Supermarket (all April-Sept at present). Bicycle hire. Riding 5 km. Fishing 500 m. Special golfing breaks. Entertainment and activities organised in summer. Launderette. Accommodation to rent.

Charges 1998: Per simple pitch incl. car Nfl 25.00, with electricity 33.00; motorcaravan pitch 35.00; adult 6.50; child (under 15) 3.50; dog (max 1) 6.00; tourist tax 2.50. Less 10-30% in low seasons. Credit cards accepted.

Reservations: Advisable for high season, write to site. Address: Machiel Vrijenhoeklaan 450, 2555 NW Den Haag. Tel: 070/448 21 00. FAX: 070/323 24 57. E-mail: info@kijkduinpark.nl.

557 Camping de Molenhoek, Kamperland, nr Middelburg

Quietly situated Zeeland site near watersports centre.

This family run site makes a pleasant contrast to the livelier coastal sites in this popular holiday area. It is rurally situated 3 km. from the Veerse Meer which is very popular for all sorts of watersports. Catering both for 300 permanent or seasonal holiday caravans and for 100 touring units, it is neat, tidy and relatively spacious. The marked touring pitches are divided into small groups with surrounding hedges and trees giving privacy and some shade, and electrical connections are available. Sanitary facilities, in one old (partly refurbished) and one newer block, include some washbasins in private cabins with free hot water and showers, dishwashing and clothes sinks with hot water on payment, British style WCs, plus toilet and shower facilities for the disabled and provision for babies. Other amenities, grouped in front of a pleasant, open, grassy area with a children's paddling pool and playground, include a shop and a simple bar/restaurant with terrace and TV room. Entertainment is organised in season (dance evenings, bingo, etc.) as well as a disco for youngsters. An indoor pool and tennis courts are nearby. Although the site is quietly situated, there are many excursion possibilities in the area including the towns of Middelburg, Veere and Goes and the Delta Expo exhibition.

How to find it: Site is west of the village of Kamperland on the `island' of Noord Beveland. From the N256 Goes - Zierikzee road, exit west onto the N255 Kamperland road. Site is signed south of this road.

General Details: Open 29 March - 25 Oct. Restaurant/bar (high season only). Well stocked shop (all season). Entertainment in high season. Children's playground, pool and animals. TV room. Bicycle hire. Riding 1 km. Fishing 2.5 km. Indoor pool, tennis and watersports close. Chemical disposal. Motorcaravan service point. Caravans for hire.

Charges guide: Per unit, incl. 2 persons and electricity Nfl. 40.75, 6 persons 45.75; dog 5.00. Less 25% outside high season.

Reservations: Are made - details from site. Address: Molenweg 69a, 4493 NC Kamperland. Tel: 0113/37 12 02.

Kampeer- en recreatiecentrum

DE MOLENHOEK

Only five minutes from the beach and Veerse Meer.
Quiet campsite with small fields separated by hedges.
Good restaurant and snackbar. Activity programme. Young
people's room and disco. Playground and swimming pool for children.
A good campsite for the whole family for a short or long stay.
Close to the "Oosterchelde" works and the "Pÿlerdam".

A CAMPSITE WHERE EVERYONE IS HAPPY!

Molenweg 69A-4493 NC Kamperland Tel: (+31) 113 371202

559 Camping Rondeweibos, Rockanje

Holiday site near North Sea coastal resort.

This site is situated near the pleasant seaside resort of Rockanje, quite convenient for the North Sea ferry ports. Very much a holiday caravan site (privately owned or to let), it is large, with lines of static units separated by semi-wild hedges and trees. Of nearly 1,000 pitches, just 85 are available for tourers. However, these have their own pleasant area, separated from the rest of the site by the main access road. The pitches here are on grassy/sandy ground and divided into groups by more formal hedges. All have electricity and cable TV connections available with water points near. Sanitary facilities are in two blocks, one near the touring area, and which be heated. They provide neat, clean, acceptable facilities with hot showers on payment and British style WCs. A good range of amenities (listed below) includes a popular medium sized outdoor swimming pool with a slide and whirlpool. Rockanje is situated on Voorne (which used to be an island), an area of beaches, dunes, woods and lakes. A popular area with Dutch holidaymakers, beach activities and watersports opportunities are plentiful. Rockanje's beach is a 10 minute walk.

How to find it: From the N15/A15 motorway towards `Europoort' take exit marked Brielle-Hellevoetsluis onto the N57 and over the bridge. After 7 km. take the Rockanje exit and site is signed at next junction and in Rockanje itself.

General Details: Open: mid-March - late-Oct. Supermarket (limited hours in low seasons). Cafe, restaurant and bar (weekends only in low seasons). Tennis. Boules. Good children's playground. Swimming pool (15/5-15/9). Children's games room and organised activities in high season. Launderette. Bus service 100 m.

Charges guide: Per person Nfl 6.00; caravan or tent 9.00; motorcaravan 15.00; car 4.00; m/cycle 1.00; electricity 4.00; dog/cat 3.50.

Reservations: Essential in high season - contact site. Address: Schapengorsedijk 19, 3235 LA Rockanje. Tel: 0181/40 19 44. FAX: 0181/40 23 80.

556 Zeeland Camping de Wijde Blick, Renesse, nr Zierikzee

Neat, well kept site in popular North Sea coast holiday area.

This site is run in a friendly and personal way by the owners, the van Oost family. Within walking distance of the village of Renesse, it is in a quiet, rural location. Laid out in a fairly formal way, with attractive trees and hedges, the site has 170 numbered tourist pitches arranged in groups of 4 to 8, all with electrical (4A) and TV connections. Cars are parked away from the pitches by the access roadways. Sanitary facilities in two blocks are very modern with first class, clean facilities including washbasins in cabins, controllable showers, facilities for disabled people and a new washroom for children under 6 years old. A bath is on payment. Dishwashing sinks all have free hot water and are arranged around glass roofed courtyards with seating, plants and music. The main amenities at the entrance to the site include an outdoor swimming pool with sunbathing terrace, an informal, timber clad bar/restaurant, a supermarket and a laundry (with cartoons for the children to watch). Many activities are organised for children - the campsite mascot, Billy Blick, is amusing as he welcomes the children. Very much a busy holiday area, there are restaurants and shops in the village (market on Wednesdays) and the sandy beach is 2 km. from the site.

How to find it: Renesse is on the near 'island' of Schouwen on the Haamstede - Zierikzee R106 road and site is signed to the east of the village.

General Details: Open all year. Swimming pool (1/5-15/9). Shop. Restaurant/bar (both Easter - Oct). Good children's play area on sand. Table tennis. Bicycle hire. Tennis and minigolf close. Riding 2 km. Golf 5 km. Fishing 1.5 km. Motorcaravan service point. Chemical disposal. No dogs are accepted. Cabins to rent.

Charges 1998: Per unit incl. 2 persons Nfl. 28.50 - 32.50, with electricity 38.00 - 42.00; extra person 6.50; local tax included. No credit cards.

Reservations: Recommended for high season - contact site. Address: Hogezoom 112, 4325 CK Renesse, (Zeeland). Tel: 0111/468888. FAX: 0111/468889. E-mail: dewijdeblick@zeelandnet.nl.

558 Camping de Veerhoeve, Wolphaartsdijk, nr Goes

Family run site, near the shores of the Veerse Meer, ideal for families.

Situated in a popular area for watersports, this is a site well suited for sailing, windsurfing or fishing enthusiasts. As with most sites in this area there are many mature static and seasonal pitches. However, part of the friendly, relaxed site is reserved for touring units with 150 marked pitches on grassy ground, 100 with electrical connections. Sanitary facilities, in three blocks, have been well modernised with full tiling and include British style WCs and hot showers on payment. Other amenities include a good shop, TV, sports field and a children's playground. Slipway for launching boats and horse riding nearby.

How to find it: From N256 Goes-Zierikzee road take Wolphaartsdijk exit. Follow through village and signs to site.

General Details: Open: 3 April - 30 October. Shop (all season). Restaurant and snack bar (July/Aug. otherwise at weekends). Tennis court. Children's playground. Bicycle hire. Fishing. Watersports and boat launching 1 km. Riding 1 km. Golf 7 km. Laundry facilities. Motorcaravan service point. Chemical disposal. Accommodation for groups. Mobile homes, chalets and tents for hire.

Charges 1999: Per pitch incl. 2 persons Nfl. 31.00 - 36.00; electricity 5.00; dog 5.00. Tax included. Credit cards accepted.

Reservations: Write to site. Address: Veerweg 48, 4471 NC Wolphaartsdijk. Tel: 0113/581155. FAX: 0113/581944.

552 Vakantiepark Zeebad, Breskens

Large, friendly site near beach and ferry port.

Under the same ownership as no. 550 Pannenschuur, Camping Zeebad is just along the coast road. It is partially surrounded by small lakes and is adjacent to the beach. The established areas are well shaded but these are mainly reserved for seasonal units. However, there are 120 numbered touring pitches of 80 - 100 sq.m. with growing hedges. Cars are not allowed beside the pitches but alternative parking is provided. One tiled sanitary block near the entrance (some distance from the touring pitches) is supplemented by two rather cramped mobile units. Hot water is on payment and facilities at the main block include separate wash cabins, a family room and laundry facilities. British style WCs. There is an organised activity programme for children in high season. Swimming pools and minigolf are nearby and the town of Breskens is within walking distance (15 mins). An indoor pool and sports complex were planned.

How to find it: From Breskens take the coast road west and site is less than 1½ km. on the left.

General Details: Open all year. Electricity available in all parts. Restaurant with outdoor terrace. Bar. Snack bar. Supermarket. Games room. Children's playground. Activity programme for children. Weekly disco. Bicycle hire. Mobile homes for hire.

Charges guide: Per person (over 2 yrs) Nfl 5.00; pitch 25.00; dog 5.00; local tax 1.00. Less in low seasons.

Reservations: Contact site for details. The site is very busy 20/7-15/8, but some pitches are normally kept for short stays. Address: Nieuwesluisweg 5, 4510 RG Breskens. Tel: 0117/38 13 38. FAX: 0117/38 31 51.

551 Camping Groede, Groede, nr Breskens

Friendly, family run site two minutes from dunes and sandy beach.

Camping Groede is a friendly, fair sized site on the same stretch of sandy beach as no. 550. Family run, it aims to cater for the individual needs of visitors and to provide a good all-round holiday. Campers are sited as far as possible according to taste - in family areas, in larger groups or on more private pitches for those who prefer peace and quiet. In total, there are 560 pitches for tourists (with 400 seasonal units also), 275 with electrical connections (4A) and 260 with water and drainage connections also. Sanitary facilities are good with a high standard of cleanliness, British style WCs, free hot showers and some washing cabins also with hot water. A restaurant/bar provides a friendly service and there is also a snack bar (both weekends only in low season). Visitors are invited to join locals in archery and card games. Other activities include football, volleyball and plenty of activities for children in peak season. Groede is ideally sited for ferry stopovers and short stay visitors including hikers are very welcome, as well as long stay holiday makers. Run by the family van Damme who ask visitors to complete a confidential questionnaire to ensure that their site offers the best possible service and provide you with a comprehensive information booklet (in English).

How to find it: From Breskens take the coast road for 5 km. to site. Alternatively, the site is signed from Groede village on the more inland Breskens - Sluis road.

General Details: Open 27 March - 31 Oct. Shop, restaurant and snack bar (all weekends only in low seasons). Recreation room. Sports area. Several children's play areas (bark base). Bicycle hire. Fishing. Riding 1 km. Golf 12 km. Chemical disposal. Motorcaravan service point.

Charges 1998: Per pitch incl. 2 persons Nfl 21.50 - 31.50, with 4A electricity 25.00 - 35.00, with water and drainage also 28.00 - 38.00; extra person 4.00 (incl. taxes). No credit cards.

Reservations: Will be made (with Nfl 25 fee) but half the pitches are kept unreserved. Address: Zeeweg 1, 4503 PA Groede. Tel: 0117/37 13 84. FAX: 0117/37 22 77.

Holiday fun all the year round

'Recreatiecentrum Pannenschuur' is in Zeeuws Vlaanderen within walking distance of the beach and sea. You can be sure of a friendly welcome at the comfortable chalets and caravans. The indoor swimming pool, Turkish bath, sauna and various sports facilities will provide lots of fun for families and groups. Our programme of activities and the nearby tourist attractions will make this a memorable holiday.

RECREATIECENTRUM PANNENSCHUUR

Zeedijk 19, 4504 PP Nieuwvliet-Bad, Tel.: +31 117 37 23 00, Fax: +31 117 37 14 15
E-mail: info@pannenschuur.nl - Internet: www.pannenschuur.nl

A MEMBER OF
zilverberk

550 Recreatiecentrum Pannenschuur, Nieuwvliet, nr Breskens

Seaside site near Belgian border with new indoor pool complex.

This is one of several coastal sites on the narrow strip of the Netherlands between the Belgian frontier near Knokke and the Breskens ferry. Quickly reached from the ports of Ostend, Zeebrugge and Vlissingen, it is useful for overnight stops or for a few days to enjoy the seaside. A short walk across the quiet coast road and steps over the dike bring you to the open, sandy beach. Quite a large site, most of the 600 pitches are taken by permanent or seasonal holiday caravans but there are also 160 pitches for tourists mostly in their own areas. In short rows backing onto hedges all have electricity (6A), water and drainage connections. A new sanitary building provides first class facilities including a children's washroom, baby room and some private cabins (shower tokens from the supermarket). The other star attraction is the recently completed complex which provides a super indoor heated swimming pool with baby and children's sections, jacuzzi, sauna, Turkish bath and solarium. Also leading off the central café style area are a restaurant, snack bar and launderette. Overall, a very good site.

How to find it: At Nieuwvliet, on the Breskens - Sluis minor road, 8 km. southwest of Breskens, turn towards the sea at sign for Nieuwvliet-Bad and follow signs to site.

General Details: Open all year. Supermarket (all year except 5/1-14/2, restricted hours in low seasons). Restaurant (all year except 4/1-7/1). Snack bar and takeaway (1/3-1/11). Swimming pool (all year). Sauna and solarium. Large games room for young with snooker, pool tables, amusement machines, soft drinks bar. Children's playground and play field. Bicycle hire. Fishing 500 m. Riding 2 km. Golf 4 km. Organised activities during season. Launderette. Chemical disposal. Motorcaravan service point. Bungalows and caravans for hire.

Charges 1999: Per person (over 2 yrs) Nfl. 6.50, plus tax 2.10; pitch incl. electricity 32.50; dog 7.50. Rates available for weekly stays. Credit cards accepted.

Reservations: Recommended (high season Sat.- Sat. only) and made with deposit and fee. Address: Zeedijk 19, 4504 PP Nieuwvliet-Bad (Zeeland). Tel: 0117/37 23 00. FAX: 0117/37 14 15. E-mail: info@pannenschuur.nl.

AR Discount
Less 10% for person & pitch if over 55 yrs.

See report on page 228

NORWAY

Norway has the lowest population density in Europe, which is not surprising when one realises that about one quarter of its land is above the Arctic Circle. It is a land of contrasts, from magnificent snow capped mountains, dramatic fjords, vast plateaux with wild untamed tracts, huge lakes and rich green countryside. Oslo is the oldest of the Scandinavian capitals and one of the most prettily sited, whilst Bergen is the fjord capital, Trondheim is an atmospheric city with its medieval heart intact, and Tromsø, with its stunning 'Arctic Cathedral', likes to think of itself as the capital of the North. You can see the Northern Lights (Aurora Borealis) between November and February, north of the Arctic Circle, which lies between Mo i Rana and Bodø. During certain freak weather conditions it may be seen further south. The Midnight Sun is visible north of the Arctic Circle in summer - at Bodø between early June and early July, at Tromsø from late May to mid July, and at Nordkapp from mid May until late July. However you can never guarantee these experiences - it depends on meteorological conditions. Midsummer night's eve is celebrated all over the country, with thousands of bonfires along the fjords. Conservation of the environment was a practical reality in Norway long before it became a fashionable International issue. This, and the more recent improvements in the infrastructure, with many new tunnels and upgraded roads replacing some of the older more tortuous sections, explains why tourism is increasing rapidly. With main roads throughout the country now perfectly adequate for average sized caravan and motorcaravans, the most popular regions and routes do become busy during the short summer season (June - Aug). Road numbers are being upgraded to the new E-road status. Further information from:

Norwegian Tourist Board, Charles House, 5-11 Lower Regent Street SW1Y 4LR

Tel: 0171 839 6255 Fax: 0171 839 6014

Population
4,300,000 (1997); density 13 per sq. km.

Capital
Oslo.

Climate
The Gulf Stream follows the coast and the weather is less extreme on the west coast. Generally weather in summer and winter is unpredictable (it can be very wet). Average temperatures 18.2° in Oslo, 14.5° in Bergen, 12.7° in Tromso in July. In Jan. -3.7° in Oslo, 1.5° in Bergen, and -4.7° in Tromso. Daylight hours in Oslo are 6 hrs 3 mins in Jan. and 18 hrs 41 mins in July whilst Tromso in Jan. has no daylight and in July, 24 hours

Language
Norwegian, but English is widely spoken, particularly by the young.

Currency
The Norwegian krone, divided into 100 ore. Denominations are 10, 50, 100, 500, and 1000 kr.

Banks
Open Mon-Fri 09.00-15.00. Every largish village and town in Norway has a bank, although rural branches may have restricted opening hours.

Post Offices
Opening hours vary but are generally 08.00/08.30- 16.00/ 17.00 Mon-Fri, 08.00-13.00 on Saturdays.

Time
GMT plus 1 (BST plus 1 in summer).

Telephone
To phone from the UK, the code is 0047 plus the number. From Norway to the UK, the code is 095 44, plus the number (omitting the initial 0).

Shops
Normal hours: Mon-Fri 09.00-16.00/17.00, Thu 09.00-18.00/20.00 and Sat 09.00-13.00 /15.00. There are 2,600 tax-free shops in Norway. If you buy goods for more than 308 kr make sure you get a tax refund. After deduction of a handling charge you'll get 11-18% of the buying price back in cash, at ports or major border crossings.

Food
more expensive than in the UK, except for very good vegetables, fruit and some fish. Smoked and fresh salmon are excellent and reindeer steak very tender. A small beer in a cafe can cost £3.

Camping Gaz
Not readily available, though some larger sites stock 904 and 907 refills. You can buy camping gaz from Statoil and AGA Progas, which have outlets throughout Norway.

Motoring
Roads are generally uncrowded around Oslo and Bergen but be prepared for tunnels and hairpin bends. Certain roads are forbidden to caravans or best avoided (advisory leaflet from the Norwegian Tourist Office). Vehicles must have sufficient road grip and in the winter it may be necessary to use winter tyres with or without studs or chains. Towed caravans up to 2.3 m. wide are permitted; if between 2.3 and 2.5 m. (max permitted width) the car towing it must be at least as wide as the caravan. Drink driving laws are extremely strict.

Tolls:
Vehicles entering Bergen on weekdays must pay a toll. Vehicles up to 3.5 tonnes entering Oslo pay a toll. Tolls are also levied on certain roads.

Speed Limits:
Caravans and motorhomes (3.5 tons) 31 mph (50 kph) in built up areas, caravans 50 mph (80 kph) on all other roads, motorhomes 50 mph (80 kph) on other roads and 56 mph (90 kph) on motorways.

Fuel:
Mon-Fri petrol stations are closed between 19.00 and 05.00. At weekends stations are closed other than in closely populated areas. Major credit cards accepted in larger petrol stations.

Parking:
Parking regulations in towns are very strict and subject to fines. Yellow parking meters give 1 hour, Grey -2 and Brown - 3 hours.

Overnighting
You can camp in open areas provided you are at least 150 m away from houses or cabins. Caravans may not park on laybys or picnic sites. Open fires forbidden 15 April - 15 September.

Note: Mosquitoes can be a problem in summer (from June) - go prepared.

NORWAY

Camping in Norway

There are more than 1,000 campsites in Norway and you have the option to take your own tent, caravan or motorcaravan, or to use cabin (Hytte) accommodation. Camping costs for a unit incl. two persons with electricity is Nkr. 80-150 per night, whilst a cabin will cost Nkr. 200-600 per night depending on size and level of facilities. The Norwegian Public Roads Administration (Statens Vegvesen), in conjunction with local authorities, has started creating roadside campsites with basic facilities (Bobil parks). These are primarily designed for motorcaravans to overnight, some are free, others operate an honesty box system. With an ever increasing number of 'wild-campers', and these new facilities, it is not surprising that in certain areas commercial campsites are reluctant to spend money on expensive refurbishment, opting instead to increase their cabin accommodation to supplement reducing income.

So few British were going to Norway in the early 'nineties that it was an act of faith on our part to extend our guide north of Denmark. We must admit to have been heavily influenced by the arrival on the scene of Color Line who adopted a positive approach to the British camping market. More recently, the Scandinavian Seaways service to Göteborg in Sweden, has become equally popular as a entry route to Norway, for those who live closer to Harwich. In our first year entries were heavily concentrated around Bergen, this being the area traditionally favoured by British visitors, but since then we have steadily expanded our coverage. To enable the more adventurous to reach the Arctic Circle and Nordkapp, we have expanded north with a small selection of sites including the most northerly campsite in the world. The main E6 'Arctic Highway' is a good tarmac surfaced road, running some 2,000 km. from Oslo until it joins the E69 north of Alta, which then takes you the final 100 km. on to Nordkapp itself. During '98 the ferry linking Kåfjord to Honningsvåg is due to be replaced by a new tunnel and road section, the charges being similar to the existing ferry service.

We continue to give low priority to the coast to the south of Stavanger/Oslo or to the valleys to the east of Oslo/Trondheim, although these are deservedly popular among Norwegian campers, they are of least interest to British campers. Norway is primarily touring country, very few campers spend more than two nights in any one camp, preferring to move on in search of wonderful scenery just around the corner. To fit in with this we have arranged our sites in a loose circuit starting at Stavanger and Haugesund, moving north via Bergen through fjordland to Trondheim. From here one can either travel north to the Arctic Circle or Nordkapp (returning through Norway or via our sites in Sweden), or turn south and continue the circuit via the eastern valleys and Oslo. Such is the attraction of the dramatic rural scenery that few campers will wish to linger long in Norway's urban gateways; we have accordingly resorted to the unusual practice of describing briefly the camping situation in each of the main gateways rather than restricting our information to one or more key sites.

There are several negatives which deserve mention. Norway can be very expensive. With few exceptions most things cost double what they cost in Britain (dependant on the exchange rate). Although it is not good normal practice, campers should buy as much food and drink as possible before leaving Britain. Norway's west coast and central mountains and fells can also be very wet; only the well equipped should consider relying entirely on tented accommodation.

Camping at the Gateways

Traditionally, British campers view Bergen as the usual gateway to Norway. If the visitor expects to tour only in the fjord country to the north and immediately inland then it makes sense to return to Bergen, However, looking further afield, beyond the three main fjords, there is much to be said for considering the two other west coast gateways of Stavanger and Haugesund, both well served by Color Line from Newcastle. Along the south coast there are several gateways served by cross-Baltic ferries from Denmark and Germany. For the long distance driver prepared to drive via Sweden, Oslo will be the obvious entry point. The following notes provide a quick guide to camping at the four main gateways.

Bergen

Unless there is little choice, we do not recommend camping in built-up Bergen. There are four sites within 10 km. of the focal old harbour:

Camping Sandviken - a congested overnight camping site for motorcaravans in the industrial harbour within walking distance of the Color Line quay.

Bergenshallen Camping - a small tract set aside for camping in a suburban shopping complex at Landas, 5 km. south of the town centre.

Paradis Caravan Camping - a van parking site at a suburban sports complex 7 km. south of the centre.

Midttun Motel - adjacent to a small motel in Nesttun, 9 km. south of the town centre, near the airport.

Further out of town, going inland on the main 580 highway which leads to Hardangerfjord from Nesttun, are three more attractive sites which until now we have been hesitant to recommend but which have been steadily upgraded to the point where they deserve consideration.

The first to be reached is **Grimen Camping,** a very small site just off the 580 on the shore of an attractive lake. At weekends and during the school holidays it is usually fully occupied by knowing Norwegians visiting Bergen. The owner runs a nice general store next door. He also offers a good choice of small lake-side huts at prices which are unusually low by Norwegian standards. Only a few hundred metres further on the opposite side of the 580 is another lakeside site, **Bratland Camping,** which is larger but which also tends to be fully occupied at popular times. A few miles further down the 580 is an even larger lakeside site, **Lone Camping,** which has been very sensibly developed in recent years to the point where it deserves recommendation, despite its distance (nearly 20 km) from central Bergen.

Fredrikstad

For those arriving in Norway via Gothenburg, Fredikstad is not only the obvious gateway but it is one of Norway's most interesting cities and certainly deserves at least a day or two. It has a delightful waterfront, bubbling with cheerful nautical activity. Its historic old town, across the river from the newer town, is one of the best preserved in Europe and is also bustling with life. There are many other attractions, including a choice of two good camps sites. Within walking distance of the old town, from where the new town can be reached by frequent foot ferry, is a small greenfield municipal site, **Fredrikstad Motel and Camping.** Further south, along route 107, at Torsnes is a very different proposition, **Bevo Camping,** which occupies woodland on the fjord shore, commanding a wonderful view of this very attractive stretch of coast. Although Bevo attracts many statics, there is usually space for tourers - the friendly manager likes to guide visitors to a suitable site on his bike!

Haugesund

Now served by Color Line, Haugesund is well worth considering as a departure port. It is a well preserved small town, with traditional wood buildings predominant, and a lively marine atmosphere and it has a better choice of campsites than any other major Norwegian town. About ten miles east of the town centre, just off the main route 11 leading to Oslo, there is the very large, very well equipped and imaginatively designed **Grindafjord Naturcamping** (named after its entertaining animal life!). Along the coast of the unspoilt southern half of neighbouring Karmoy island (reached by bridge) there are several rather basic but spectacularly sited waterfront sites (Karmoy deserves a visit to wander around the picturesque old fishing port of Skenshaven) but our favourite is the municipal site on the northern outskirts of the town, but only a mile from the town centre! Named **Haraldshaugen** after the neighbouring monumental obelisk - a national shrine honouring the Viking hero Harald the Fairhaired - this site is formed by a boulder strewn meadow on the shore of Haugesundfjord. It has an excellent sanitary block and a small shop.Unlike Grindafjord where statics predominate, no statics are permitted at Haraldshaugen. Another plus is the friendly atmosphere; the site is managed by the local Red Cross, run by volunteers, and all profits go into charitable medical services in the community.

> **Grindafjord Naturcamping:**　　5570 Aksdal. Tel: 47 52 77 57 40.
> **Haraldshaugen Camping:**　　Post boks 1309, Gard, 5501 Haugesund. Tel: 52 72 80 77.

Oslo

In general, the sites in Oslo (like most major city sites) are large and very crowded. If you do need to stay in Oslo, the following sites are available, although we have received poor reports:

> **Ekeberg Camping** is on a hilltop with panoramic views across the city. Very busy in high season, the undulating grassy areas are unmarked. Only open 1 June - 31 Aug, it accepts about 700 units (including groups). When full the sanitary facilities are fully stretched. Site is well signed (Ekeberg) from E18 running southeast to Sweden in a suburb. Address: Ekebergvein 65, 1181 Oslo 11.
>
> **Bogstad Camp and Turistsenter** Open all year. Follow signs from the E18 through suburbs. Also signed from 120 ring-road. Address: Ankervn 117, 0757 Oslo 7.
>
> **Stubljan Camping** Open all year, On Oslo's southern boundary.

Stavanger

Although most British tourists head for Bergen, Stavanger is also well worth considering as a gateway. Despite its reputation as an 'oil town', Stavanger is very attractive and compact and in no sense inferior to Bergen. It is well served by Color Line - indeed Color's late night departure schedules in effect offer the motorist an extra half day in Norway compared with Bergen. It is a most convenient gateway for exploring south Norway and, unlike Bergen, has a site which we can highly recommend. **Mosvangen Camping** (Henrik Ibsens grt 21, 4021 Stavanger) is only 2 km. from the centre and only just off the E18 road as it enters the town from the south. It is on the shore of the lake from which it takes its name. Gently undulating. well shaded and divided by trees, it has 200 pitches and is very well equipped.

NORWAY

2315 Ringoy Camping, Ringoy (Hordaland)

Simple site by Upper Hardangerfjord.

Although the village of Ringoy is quiet and peaceful, it occupies a pivotal position, lying not only midway between two principal ferry ports of Upper Hardangerfjord (Kinsarvik and Brimnes), but also by the junction of two key roads (routes 7 and 13). There are several sites at the popular nearby resort town of Kinsarvik, but none compares for situation or atmosphere with the small, simple Ringoy site. This site is basically a steeply sloping field running down from the road to the tree-lined fjord, with flat areas for camping along the top and the bottom of the field. The toilet block is small and simple (with metered showers and British style WCs), but well designed, constructed and maintained by the Raunsgard family who are particularly proud of the site's remarkable shore-side barbecue facilities. On arrival you find a place as there is no reception - someone will call between 8 and 9 pm.

How to find it: Site is on route 13, midway between Kinsarvik and Brimnes.

General Details: Open all year. Simple facilities, possibly inadequate during peak holiday weeks in July. No shop but village mini-market and garage within a minute's walk. Rowing boat available (free).

Charges guide: Per unit Nkr. 80; electricity (10A) 15.

Reservations: Write to site. Address: 5782 Ringoy. Tel: 53.66.39.17.

2325 Sundal Camping, Mauranger (Hordaland)

Excellent gateway site for fjordland, from either Stavanger or Bergen.

Maurangerfjord is a steep-sided arm leading off the eastern shore of the middle reaches of the Hardangerfjord. The village of Mauranger commands magnificent views across the waters. Cutting through the village is a turbulent stream, popular with those in search of trout. Its waters are ice-cold, for they descend from the nearby Folgafonn ice-cap and its renowned glacier, an hour's brisk walk from the village. Sundal Camping is divided into two sections: a wooded, waterfront site between the local road and the fjord, which combines camping with a small marina; and an open meadow site uphill of the local road. Both are served by separate well equipped toilet blocks. Sundal is not only ideally situated for Folgafonn; it is also the nearest good site to the charming small town of Rosendal, famous for the stately home of the celebrated Rosenkrantz family.

How to find it: Route 48 crosses Hardangerfjord by ferry from Gjermundshavn to Lofallstrand from where a clearly marked local road runs northeast for 16 km. along the fjord waterfront to Mauranger.

General Details: Well equipped with most facilities. Stream and lake fishing. Canoe and rowing boat hire. Small shop. Pleasant small hotel adjacent with attractive restaurant and bar.

Charges: not available.

Reservations: Contact site. address: P.O. Box 5476, Mauranger, (Hordaland). Tel: 53.48.41.86.

2320 Odda Camping, Odda (Hordaland)

Neat, lakeside municipal site, just within walking distance of Buar glacier and the Vidfoss Falls.

Bordered by the Folgefonna glacier to the west and the Hardangervidda plateau to the east and south, Odda is an industrial town with electro-chemical enterprises based on zinc mining and hydro-electric power. At the turn of the century Odda was one of the most popular destinations for the European upper classes - the magnificent and dramatic scenery is still there, together with the added interest of the industrial impact which is well recorded at the industrial museum at Tyssedal. This municipal site has been attractively developed on the town's southern outskirts, just over a kilometre from the centre on the shores of the Sandvin lake (good salmon and trout fishing) and on the minor road leading up the Buar Valley to the Buar glacier and Folgefonna ice-cap. It is possible to walk to the ice face but in the later stages this is quite hard-going! The site is spread over 2½ acres of flat, mature woodland, which is divided into small clearings by massive boulders deposited long ago by the departing glacier. Access is by well tended tarmac roads which wind their way among the trees and boulders. There are 50 tourist pitches including many with electrical connections. A single timber building at the entrance houses the reception office (often unattended) and the simple, but clean sanitary facilities which provide, for each sex, 2 WCs, one hot shower (on payment) and 3 open washbasins. There is also a small kitchen with dishwashing facilities and a washing machine and dryer in the ladies washroom. The site fills up in the evenings and can be crowded with facilities stretched from the end of June to early August.

How to find it: Site is on the southern outskirts of Odda, signed off road to Buar, with a well marked access.

General Details: Open 1 June - 31 Aug. Town facilities close. Washing machine and dryer. Kitchen.

Charges guide: Per tent and car Nkr. 75; caravan and car 90; m/cycle 65; electricity 20.

Reservations: write to site. Address: Borsta, 5750 Odda (Hordaland). Tel: 53.64.34.10.

2330 Eikhamrane Camping, Nå, Sorfjord (Hordaland)

Small, neat site among orchards on western shore of Sorfjord.

Sorfjord, well known for its fruit growing, has long been on a popular route for travellers across Norway via Utne (where Norway's oldest hotel is a tourist attraction in its own right) and a short ferry crossing across Hardangerfjord. Travellers are also attracted by the Folgefonn ice cap, the most accessible of the great glaciers, which lies at the head of Sorfjord. About halfway along the western shore of Sorfjord is Eikhamrane Camping. Arranged on a well landscaped and partly terraced field which slopes alongside the road to a pebbly lakeside beach, it was formerly part of an orchard which still extends on both sides of the site and uphill across the road. There is room for 50 units (about 20 caravans or motorcaravans and 30 tents) on unmarked, well kept grass with 20 electrical hook ups. There are attractive trees and good gravel roads, with areas of gravel hardstanding for poor weather. Many pitches overlook the fjord where there are also thoughtfully positioned picnic benches. Two small timber sanitary blocks, one for toilets with external access, the other for washbasins (open) and showers (on payment) are simple but very well kept. There is a small kitchen with dishwashing facilities (hot water on payment) and 2 laundry sinks outside, under cover. The office (bread to order and home-grown fruits available) is in the old farmhouse, home of the owners, the Mage family. The site is well situated for watersports (sailing, canoeing and rowing), fishing and the nearby Digranes nature reserve (birdwatching).

How to find it: Site on road no. 550 just outside the village of Nå, on the western shore of Sorfjord, 32 km. south of Utne and 16 km. north of Odda.

General Details: Open 1 June - 31 August only. Some supplies kept at reception office - bread and milk to order. Watersports and fishing in lake. 5 cabins to let (Nkr. 180 - 250).

Charges guide: Per person Nkr. 10; child (4-12 yrs) 5; pitch 50; extra tent 30; awning 20; electricity 10.

Reservations: write to site. Address: 5776 Nå (Hordaland). Tel: 53.66.22.48.

2370 Botnen Camping, Brekke (Sogn og Fjordane)

Good first stop for those going north from Bergen.

For those setting forth north on route 1 from Bergen there are suprisingly few attractive sites until one reaches the southern shore of mighty Sognefjord. At Brekke is a well known tourist landmark, the remarkable Breekstranda Fjord Hotel, a traditional turf-roofed complex which tourist coaches are unable to resist. A mile or two beyond the hotel, also on the shore of the fjord, is the family run Botnen Camping. An isolated, simple (2-star) site which slopes steeply, it is well maintained. It has its own jetty and harbour, complete with rowing boats and canoes for hire and commands a splendid view across the fjord to distant mountains.

How to find it: Site is 2 km off the coast road running west from Brekke.

General Details: Open 1 May - 1 Sept. Children's play area. Swimming, fishing and boating in fjord. Boats and canoes for hire.

Charges guide: Per person Nkr. 10; child 5; caravan 40; tent 30; electricity 15.

Reservations: Contact site. Address: 5950 Brekke. Tel: 57.78.54.71.

2340 Mo Camping, Norheimsund (Hordaland)

Simple, well kept family site in scenic location with friendly welcome.

The main road leading inland from Bergen (route 7) is pleasant but perhaps unexciting until it reaches Norheimsund where is joins Hardangerfjord, one of the `Big Three' of Norway's spectacular fjords. Mo Camping is an attractive site on what appears to be a small lake but is actually an arm of the main fjord. At the head of this arm (within walking distance of the site, but along the side of the road) are the spectacular Steinsdals Falls which draw half a million visitors annually to view the falls from behind! This little site is part of a small working farm run by the Mo family. It has some 40 unmarked touring places, with 25 electrical connections possible, on a curve of flat, well kept grass. There are also two small areas of hardstanding for poor weather. The camping area is divided from the working part of the farm by a line of charming, traditional, wooden farm buildings which include the family home, the office and the sanitary facilities (in a converted barn). Rather cramped, these include for each sex a shower (on payment) and 2 WCs with washbasins opposite. They are hard-pressed when the site is full. A laundry, plus dishwashing and drying facilities are to be added. General shop at nearby filling station (200 m.). Although offering only basic facilities, this site is well looked after and is ideally situated with many good walks in the area, free fishing from the site and a 2-seater canoe for hire.

How to find it: Site is by the no. 7 road just over 1 km. west of Norheimsund.

General Details: Open 1 June - 31 August only - minimal facilities, but town 1 km. and shop 200 m. Fishing. Chemical disposal. Motorcaravan services.

Charges guide: Per person Nkr. 5; child (under 12 yrs) 3; caravan, motorcaravan or tent with car 60; tent without car 35; m/cycle 35; local tax 40; electricity (16A) 20.

Reservations: Write to site. Address: 5600 Norheimsund, Hardaland.

NORWAY

2350 Espelandsdalen Camping, nr Ulvik (Hordaland)

Basic, farm campsite, but `a glimpse of untamed Norway'.

If one follows Hardangerfjord on the map and considers the mighty glacier which once scooped away the land along its path, it is easy to imagine that it started life in Espelandsdalen. Here is the textbook upper glacial valley. Espelandsdalen runs from Granvin to Ulvik, both of which lie at the heads of their respective arms of Hardangerfjord. A minor road (route 572) links the two small towns with sharp climbs at either end (tricky for caravans). The valley bed here is occupied by a series of connected lakes. For generations farmers have struggled to make a living out of the narrow strip of land between water and rock. One farmer has converted a narrow, sloping field bisected by the road into a modest campsite taking about 40 units. Above the road is a small office, a sanitary block (washing trough with hot water, a shower on payment and WCs) and a neat row of chalets for hire. Looking down on these is the family farmstead. The grassy meadow pitches below the road run down to the lake-shore. Campers come for fishing, walking or skiing, or just to marvel at the views of the valley and its towering mountain sides.

> **How to find it:** The northern loop of the 572 road follows Espelandsdalen and the campsite is on this road, about 6 km. from its junction with route 13 at Granvin (steep gradients - see above).

> **General Details:** Open all year. Some electricity connections (8/10A). Basic foodstuffs kept in office. Swimming, fishing and boating in lake. Boat hire. Ski track 2 km. Ten cabins to let.

> **Charges guide:** Per unit Nkr. 50; person 10; child (4-12 yrs) 5; hikers tent 20; electricity 20.

> **Reservations:** Contact site. Address: 5736 Granvin (Hordaland). Tel: 56.52.51.67. FAX: 56.52.51.67.

2360 Ulvik Fjord Camping, Ulvik (Hordaland)

Small, quiet, orchard site on outskirts of Ulvik, on the fjord.

Ulvik was discovered by tourists 150 years ago when the first liners started operating to the head of Hardangerfjord, and to this day, a regular stream of cruise liners work their way into the very heartland of Norway. A century and a half of visitors has meant that Ulvik is now a well-established tourist destination, describing itself as `the pearl of Hardanger' but, with only just over 1,000 inhabitants, it still manages to retain an unspoilt village atmosphere. Access is by narrow, winding roads, either along the side of the fjord or up a steep road behind the town - probably not to be recommended for caravans (see How to find it). This pretty little site is 500 m. from the town centre occupying what must once have been a small orchard running down to the lake beside a small stream. There is room for about 30 units on undulating ground which slopes towards the fjord, with some flat areas and a few electrical connections. There are no facilities other than a small wooden building which houses reception, a small kitchen (with a cooker and sink) and the sanitary facilities. These are well kept and comprise, for each sex, 2 open washbasins, WCs and 2 modern showers on payment. Swimming or fishing is possible in the fjord. Meals may be taken at the hotel opposite and the town shops, etc. are close.

> **How to find it:** Ulvik is reached by road no. 572; the site is on the southern side of town, opposite the Ulvikfjord Pension. There is a ferry from road 7 at Brimnes. Cars and caravans can now connect with road 7 via a new tunnel.

> **General Details:** Open 20 May - 31 Aug. Kitchen. Boat slipway, fishing and swimming in fjord. Hotel opposite, shops and restaurants in town. 10 cabins for hire.

> **Charges guide:** Per unit 65; hiker's or cyclist's tent 35; person 15; child (4-12 yrs) 10; electricity 20.

> **Reservations:** write to site. Address: 5730 Ulvik. Tel: 56.52.65.77.

2380 Tveit Camping, Vik/Vangsnes (Sogn og Fjordane)

Charming, neat, family run site, ideally placed for exploring the Balestrand area.

Located in the district of Vik on the south shore of Sognefjord, 4 km. from the small port of Vangsnes, Tveit Camping is part of a small working farm. Reception and a kiosk open most of the day in high season, with a phone to summon assistance at any time. Four terraces provide 45 pitches with 30 electricity connections (10A). Modern heated sanitary facilities provide British style WCs, washbasins (one per sex in cubicle), controllable hot showers (on payment), a unit for disabled visitors, kitchens with facilities for dishwashing and cooking, and a laundry with washing machine, dryer and iron (hot water on payment). Other facilities include TV rooms, a fenced playground and a slipway. A shop, café, pub and post office are by the ferry terminal in Vangsnes 4 km. away. On the campsite you will find a restored Iron Age burial mound dating from 350-550AD, whilst the statue of Fritjov `The Intrepid' towers over the landscape at Vangsnes. Visit the Kristianhus Boat and Engine Museum or see traditional Gamalost cheese making in Vik, and in Fjærland across the fjord is the Norwegian Glacier Museum.

> **How to find it:** Site is by the Rv 13 between Vik and Vangsnes, 4 km. south of Vangsnes.

> **General Details:** Open 15 April - 15 Oct. Kiosk (15/6-15/8). TV rooms. Children's playground. Slipway and boat hire. Fishing. Bicycle hire. Riding 15 km. Laundry. Kitchen. Motorcaravan service point. Car wash. Cabins for rent.

> **Charges 1998:** Per unit incl. 2 persons Nkr. 80 - 100; extra person (over 5 yrs) 10; electricity 20.

> **Reservations:** Write to site. Address: 5865 Vangsnes, Sogn og Fjordane. Tel: 57.69.66.00. FAX: 57.69.66.70.

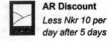

AR Discount
Less Nkr 10 per day after 5 days

2385 Sandvik Camping, Gaupne (Sogn og Fjordane)

Compact, popular, small site on edge of town and close to the Nigardsbreen Glacier.

This small site has 60 touring pitches, 32 with electrical connections (8/16A), arranged on fairly level grassy terrain either side of a gravel access road, on the edge of this small town. A large supermarket, post office, banks, etc. are all within a level 500 m. stroll. The single central sanitary unit provides British style WCs, washbasins with dividers, and two hot showers per sex (on payment). In addition there is a multi-purpose unit serving the needs of families or the disabled with facilities for baby changing and a further WC, basin and shower with ramp for access. A small campers' kitchen provides dishwashing facilities, hot-plates, oven and fridge (all free of charge) together with tables, chairs and TV. The separate laundry has sinks with free hot water and a washing machine and dryer. The owner tells us that these facilities are scheduled for refurbishment, so campers can look forward to even better standards. A café in the reception building is open mid June-August for drinks and meals. The small shop sells ices, soft drinks, sweets, crisps, etc. This is a useful site for those using the spectacular Rv 55 high mountain road from Lom to Sogndal or for visiting the Nigardsbreen Glacier and Jostedalsbreen area of Norway.

How to find it: Signed just off the Rv 55 Lom-Sogndal road on the eastern outskirts of Gaupne.

General Details: Open May - Sept. Shop. Cafeteria (mid June-Aug). Kitchen. Laundry. TV. Children's playground. Cabins for rent.

Charges guide: Per pitch Nkr. 50; tent, caravan or motorcaravan 30; adult 20; child (4-14 yrs) 10; electricity 20. Credit cards accepted.

Reservations: Write to site. Address: 5820, Gaupne. Tel: 57.68.11.53. FAX: 57.68.16.71.

2390 Kjornes Camping, Sogndal (Sogn og Fjordane)

Simple farm site in a prime fjordside location, ideal for those on a budget.

Occupying a long open meadow which slopes down to the tree lined waterside this site is ideal for those who prefer the simple life, just enjoying the peace and quiet, the lovely scenery or a spot of fishing. Access is via a narrow lane with passing places, which drops down towards the fjord 3 km. from Sogndal. The site takes 100 touring units, but there are only 36 electrical connections (16A). There are also 8 cabins for rent but no static caravans. The sanitary unit is basic but clean, providing British style WCs, mostly open washbasins, and 2 hot showers per sex (on payment). A small kitchen has a dishwashing sink with free hot water, plus a double hot-plate and fridge (also free). The laundry is 'al fresco' with a small roof covering the sink, washing machine and dryer. A chemical disposal point completes the facilities. A scenic route (Rv 55) runs along the entire north shore of Sognefjord and the Sogndalfjord to Sogndal and then continues across the Jotunheimen mountain plateau towards Lom.

How to find it: Site is off the Rv 5, 3 km. east of Sogndal, 8 km. west of Kaupanger.

General Details: Open 1 June - end Aug. Kitchen. Laundry. Cabins for rent.

Charges guide: Per unit Nkr. 45; adult 15; child 5; small tent 30; electricity 20.

Reservations: Write to site. Address: 5800 Sogndal, Sogn og Fjordane. Tel: 57.67.45.80.

2400 Camping Jolstraholmen, Vassenden (Sogn og Fjordane)

Well presented, family run site on the E39 between Sognefjord and Nordfjord.

This attractive site is located between the road and the fast-flowing Jolstra River (renowned for its trout fishing), 1.5 km. from the lakeside village of Vassenden, and behind the Statoil filling station, restaurant and supermarket complex which is also owned and run by the site owner and his family. The 60 pitches (some marked) are on grass or gravel hardstanding all with electricity (10A) and some have water and waste points. A river tributary runs through the site and forms an island on which some additional tent pitches are located, and there are also 19 cabins. The main heated sanitary facilities, in rooms below the complex, provide British style WCs, open washbasins, controllable hot showers with divider and seat (on payment), plus one family bathroom per sex. These are supplemented by a small unit located on the island. Two small kitchens provide dishwashing and cooking facilities (free) and the laundry has sinks, washing machine and dryer. Other amenities include a children's playground, 50 m. waterchute (open summer, weather permitting), minigolf, covered barbecue area, and boat hire. Ski-slopes are within 1 km., guided walking tours are organised, and a recently created riverside and woodland walk follows a 1.5 km. circular route from the site and has fishing platforms and picnic tables along the way.

How to find it: Site is beside the E39 road, 1.5 km. west of Vassenden, 18 km. east of Førde.

General Details: Open all year. Supermarket. Restaurant. Garage. Laundry. Kitchens. Barbecue area. Children's playground. Minigolf. Waterchute. Rafting. Fishing. Guided walks. Boat hire. Cabins for rent.

Charges guide: Per unit Nkr. 30 - 40; small tent 20 - 30; adult 15 - 20; child (5-15 yrs) 5 - 10; electricity 30. Credit cards accepted.

Reservations: Write to site. Address: 6840 Vassenden, Sogn og Fjordane. Tel: 57.72.71.35. FAX: 57.72.75.05.

NORWAY

2436 Byrkjelo Camping, Byrkjelo, nr Sandane (Sogn og Fjordane)

Pretty, good value site, in village location, ideal base for Nordfjord and Jostedalsbreen.

This neatly laid out and well equipped small site offers 50 large marked and numbered touring pitches, 40 with electricity (10A) and 15 with gravel hardstanding. The neatly mown grass, attractive trees and shrubs and the warm welcome from the young and enthusiastic owners make this a very pleasant place to stay. The good heated sanitary unit provides British style WCs, washbasins, and 5 shower rooms each with washbasin, changing space and seats (on payment). In addition, a multi-purpose unit serves families and disabled people, with facilities for babies and incorporating a further WC, basin and shower with handrails, etc. The campers' kitchen has dishwashing sinks, hot-plates and dining area, all free. A separate laundry provides a sink, washing machine, dryer and airing rack. Fishing is available in the river adjacent to the site and a riding stables is 5 km. Reception and a small kiosk selling ices, sweets and soft drinks, is in an attractive cabin and there is a bell to summon the owners should they not be on site when you arrive. Garage, mini-market and cafe 100 m. and the lively town of Sandane is 19 km.

How to find it: Site is beside the Rv 1 in the village of Byrkjelo, 19 km. east of Sandane.

General Details: Open 20 May - 1 Sept. Kiosk. TV room. Minigolf. Small children's playground. Fishing. Riding 5 km. Laundry. Kitchen. Motorcaravan service point. Chemical disposal. Cabins for rent.

Charges 1999: Per unit Nkr. 60; adult 10; child 5, electricity 20.

Reservations: Advisable in peak season. Address: 6867 Byrkjelo. Tel: 57.86.74.30. FAX: 57.86.71.54.

2480 Bjorkedal Camping, Volda (Møre og Romsdal)

Interesting, excellent value, boat builder's campsite in outstanding location.

On the Rv 1 north of the Nordfjord, in Møre og Romsdal, is a lovely bowl shaped valley famous throughout Norway for traditional boat building. Bjorkedal Camping is situated on a grassy open plateau about 300 m. off the main road and overlooking the farmland and mountains around the lake. There is space for 25 units with 10 electricity connections (16A) and 5 nicely designed cabins for rent. The small, modern and spotlessly clean sanitary unit provides British style WCs, washbasins with dividers and curtains, one controllable hot shower per sex (on payment), plus a WC and washbasin unit with ramped access for disabled people. A kitchen with dishwashing sink and a full cooker (free of charge), a laundry with sinks and washing machine, plus a cosy TV lounge completes the facilities. For a thousand years boats have been hand built in this valley by the Bjorkedal family. Site owner, Jakob Bjorkedal, will show you the old water powered saw mill which he has reconstructed, and there are usually some examples of his boat building craft in the magnificent workshop with a most spectacular `cathedral' style timber roof. There is an extensive network of footpaths both in the valley and leading up into the surrounding circle of mountains where you can see the old cabins of the herdsmen, one dating back to the 17th century. Other activities are small game hunting and freshwater fishing.

How to find it: Signed off the Rv 1, midway along western side of Bjorkedal lake, 21 km. north of Nordfjordeid.

General Details: Open all year. Laundry. Kitchen. TV lounge. Small game hunting. Freshwater fishing.

Charges guide: Per unit Nkr. 40; adult 10; child 5; electricity 15.

Reservations: Write to site. Address: 6120 Folkestadbgd. Tel: 70.05.20.43.

2460 Prinsen Strandcamping, Alesund (Møre og Romsdal)

Lively, fjordside site, just outside the attractive small town of Alesund.

Although 5 km. from the town centre, this is a more attractive option to the more crowded sites closer to town, even so, this is mainly a transit and short-stay site. Divided by trees and shrubs, and sloping gently to a small sandy beach with views down Borgundfjord, the site has 125 grassy pitches, 25 cabins and 7 rooms, 110 electricity connections (16A) and 75 cable TV hook-ups. The main heated sanitary unit, in the reception building, has British style WCs, mostly open washbasins, controllable hot showers (on payment), plus a sauna for each sex. A small kitchen has cooking facilities but only 2 dishwashing sinks, and the laundry has a sink, 2 washing machines and a dryer. Further older facilities mainly serving rooms and cabins, include a multi-purpose bathroom for the disabled people and families (key from reception). A hatch beside the central access road serves as the only chemical disposal point and a motorcaravan service point (not drive over type - difficult for some units). Reception shares space with the small shop, bread can be ordered daily, and English papers are also usually available. Small children's playground, barbecue areas, slipway and boat hire, and a TV room. Alesund has lovely Art Nouveau architecture, Sunnmøre Folk Museum has 50 old houses, a boat collection and medieval and Viking artefacts, and on the island of Giske we recommend a visit to the `Marble Church'.

How to find it: Turn off the E136 at roundabout signed to Hatlane and site. Follow signs to site.

General Details: Open all year. Shop (1/6-1/9). Restaurant 800 m. Sauna. TV room. Children's playground. Slipway. Boat hire. Fishing. Bicycle hire. Kitchen. Laundry. Chemical disposal. Cabins and rooms for rent.

Charges 1999: Per unit incl. up to 6 persons Nkr. 130.00; electricity 20.00. Credit cards accepted.

Reservations: Write to site. Address: Ratvika, 6015 Alesund. Tel: 70.15.52.04. FAX: 70.15.49.96.

2470 Åndalsnes Camping and Motel, Åndalsnes (Møre og Romsdal)

Leafy, sheltered site, close to town and the spectacular Trollstigen Mountain Road.

This attractive, popular site is situated in mature woodland beside the Rauma river 1 km. from the town centre, and close to Romsdalfjord and the breath-taking Trollstigen mountain road with its 11 giant hairpins that scale the sheer rock face. The reception, well stocked shop and cafeteria complex are on the opposite side of the road to the main touring area. The 213 grassy pitches are arranged informally between the many trees and shrubs, with 180 electric hook-ups (16A, long leads may be required). Two heated sanitary units provide British style WCs, washbasins (some in cubicles), controllable hot showers with divider and seat (tokens on payment), hairdryers, plus facilities for the disabled. Kitchens and laundries have facilities for cooking, dining, dishwashing, ironing plus token operated washing machines and dryers. The cafeteria, which doubles as a function room/TV lounge, serves breakfast and dinner and is open daily though times vary according to demand.

> **How to find it:** Turn off the Rv 1 by the bridge to the south west of the town, towards Trollstigen and Romsdalfjord. Site is signed.
>
> **General Details:** Open 1 May - 15 September. Shop and cafeteria (15/5-30/8). Kitchen. Laundry. Minigolf. Bicycle hire. Canoe and boat hire. Fishing. Children's playground. Chemical disposal. Motorcaravan services. Chalets and cabins to rent.
>
> **Charges 1998:** Per caravan or motorcaravan Nkr. 70; cyclist or m/cyclist and tent 50; extra tent 45; adult 15; child (4-12 yrs) 7.00; electricity 22. Credit cards accepted.
>
> **Reservations:** Write to site. Address: 6300 Åndalsnes. Tel: 71.22.16.29. FAX: 71.22.62.16.

2450 Bjølstad Camping, Malmefjorden (Møre og Romsdal)

Delightful rural retreat on Malmefjorden, close to the Atlantic Highway.

This small site, which slopes down to Malmefjorden, a sheltered arm of Fraenfjorden, has space for just 40 touring units on grassy, fairly level, terraces either side of the tarmac central access road. A basic, clean sanitary unit provides British style WCs, one controllable hot shower with divider and shelf per sex (token on payment), plus washbasins with dividers, but one in cubicle (for ladies). A small campers' kitchen has two dishwashing sinks and a hot-plate, whilst the laundry has a washing machine and dryer. A delight for children is a large, old masted boat which provides hours of fun playing at pirates or Vikings, plus the more conventional swings, etc. At the foot of the camp is a waterside barbecue site, a special shallow paddling area for children and a jetty. Both rowing and motorboats (with lifejackets) can be hired, one can swim or fish in the fjord, and there are 10 cabins for rent. No dogs accepted on site. This site is an ideal base for visiting Molde International Jazz Festival (annually mid-July), or the famous Varden viewpoint with its magnificent views over this 'Town of Roses', the fjord and 222 mountain peaks, both only 15 minutes drive from the site. Further afield, the small town of Bud is famous for its WW2 German coastal fortress, or one can drive the fantastic and scenic Atlantic Highway (toll road) as it threads its way across the many islands and bridges to the west of Kristiansund.

> **How to find it:** Turn off Rv 64 on northern edge of Malmefjorden village towards the village of Lindset (lane is oil bound gravel). Site is 1 km.
>
> **General Details:** Open 20 May - 1 Oct (maybe earlier if pre-booked). Children's playground. Boat hire. Fjord fishing and swimming. Laundry. Kitchen. Cabins for rent.
>
> **Charges 1999:** Per unit Nkr. 70 - 80; small tent 40; adult 10; child 5; electricity 15. Credit cards accepted, but not Eurocheques.
>
> **Reservations:** Write to site. Address: 6445 Malmefjorden, More og Romsdal. Tel: 71.26.56.56. FAX: 71.26.56.56.

2495 Vegset Camping, Snåsa (Nord-Trøndelag)

Pleasant site north of Snåsa, beside the E6 road.

Only 7 km. from Snåsa on the banks of Lake Snåsavatn, this site consists of 10 chalets and an extensive area for touring units, mainly on quite a slope. A new, well equipped sanitary block provides showers (Nkr. 5), plus a shower with toilet suitable for disabled people. There is a kitchen, TV room and a kiosk selling groceries. Snåsa is a centre for the South Lapp people who have their own boarding school, museum and information centre there. The Bergasen Nature Reservation is close to the village and is famous for its rare flora, especially orchids. The Gressamoen National Park is also near.

> **How to find it:** Site is just off the E6 road, 7 km. from Snåsa.
>
> **General Details:** Open Easter - 10 Oct. Kiosk. Kitchen. TV room. Swimming, fishing and boat hire.
>
> **Charges guide:** Per unit Nkr. 80.
>
> **Reservations:** Contact site. Address: 7760 Snåsa. Tel: 74.15.29.50.

NORWAY

2490 Skjerneset Camping, Averoy (Møre og Romsdal)

Extraordinary island site with fishery museum near Kristiansund.

The tiny island of Ekkilsøya lies off the larger island of Averoy and is reached via a side road and bridge (no toll) from the Rv 64 just south of Bremsnes from where the ferry crosses to Kristiansund. Although the fishing industry here is not what it used to be it is still the dominant activity and Skjerneset Camping has been developed by the Otterlei family to give visitors an insight into this industry and its history. Most of the old `Klippfisk' warehouse is now a fascinating 'fisherimuseum' and aquarium, with the remainder housing the sanitary installations, 3 small 4-bed apartments, a kitchen, laundry and lounges. There is space for 20 caravans or motorcaravans on gravel hardstandings around a rocky bluff and along the harbour's rocky frontage and all have electricity (16A). A small grassy area for 10 tents is under pine trees in a hollow on the top of the bluff together with the children's swings and 5 fully equipped cabins. Sanitary facilities are heated but basic, unisex, and perhaps a little quirky in their layout, but they provide British WCs, washbasins in cubicles and controllable hot showers. Free hot water throughout. The kitchen provides 2 full cookers plus a hot-plate and dishwashing sinks, and the small laundry has a sink and washing machine. All were free of charge at the time of inspection. A new small sanitary unit together with a motorcaravan service point were planned. The small reception kiosk also has small stocks of basic foods. Motor or rowing boat hire, organised sea-fishing or sightseeing trips in the owner's new sea-going boat. For non-anglers who want a fish supper, fresh fish are always available. Please note: this is a working harbour with deep unfenced water very close to pitches.

> **How to find it:** Site is on the little island of Ekkilsøya which is reached via a side road running west from the main Rv 64 road, 1.5 km. south of Bremsnes.
>
> **General Details:** Open all year. Kiosk. Kitchen. Laundry. TV. Boat hire. Fishing.
>
> **Charges guide:** Per unit Nkr. 90 (Less 20% outside 20/6-20/8); electricity 20.
>
> **Reservations:** Write to site. Address: Ekkilsoya, 6553 Bremsnes, More og Romsdal. Tel: 71.51.18.94. FAX: 71.51.18.15.

2485 Krokstrand Camping, nr Storforshei (Nordland)

Cosmopolitan and popular riverside site only 18 km. from the Arctic Circle.

Attractively arranged amongst the birch trees, with a fast flowing river and waterfall alongside, and views of snow covered mountains, this site is a popular resting place for all nationalities on the long trek to Nordkapp. There are 60 unmarked pitches and electrical connections (16A) for 20 units. The well maintained, spotlessly clean, small sanitary unit provides British style WCs, open washbasins and 2 controllable hot showers per sex, with curtain and seat (on payment). The laundry has a washing machine and dryer, and the small kitchen a double hot-plate and dishwashing sink. There is also a chemical toilet emptying facility and a conveniently located water tap and hose for motorcaravan tank filling. The small reception kiosk is only open for a short time mornings and evenings, but campers are invited to find a pitch and pay later. Directions in English are given to the owner's house (within walking distance) for emergencies. An excellently maintained and brightly painted children's playground includes a trampoline, and families can enjoy a game of minigolf on the equally well tended course. Being only 18 km. drive from the Arctic Circle with its Visitor Centre, this site is in an ideal location. The small village just outside the camp entrance has a hotel with restaurant, a souvenir shop, and those interested in WW2 history will find the neatly tended grave of a Russian soldier by the site gate. The nearest town for shopping is Mo-i-Rana (60 km).

> **How to find it:** Entrance is off the E6 at Krokstrand village opposite the hotel, 18 km. south of Arctic Circle.
>
> **General Details:** Open 1 June - 20 Sept. Children's playground. Minigolf. Restaurant and souvenir shop nearby. Kitchen. Laundry.
>
> **Charges 1999:** Per unit Nkr. 70; adult 10; child 5; extra tent/hiker's tent 45; electricity 20. No credit cards.
>
> **Reservations:** Write to site. Address: Krokstrand, 8630 Storforshei. Tel: 75.16.60.74.

2465 Lyngvær Lofoten Bobilcamping, Lyngvær, Lofoten Islands (Nordland)

Superbly positioned site by the sea on the Lofoten Islands.

This well laid out site, built in '91/92, has room for 200 units, half with access to electrical connections. The facilities are new, clean and good, although there are rather few of them. Showers, a little cramped, are on payment (Nkr. 10). There are extra unisex showers and toilets beside reception. A communal kitchen has cooking and washing up facilities and a large sitting area with satellite TV. There are several play areas and boat hire (rowing and motor boats, canoes and pedaloes). The site has its own salmon and sea trout fishing. It is a good area for walking, both by the sea and in the mountains.

> **How to find it:** Site is signed from the ferry terminal.
>
> **General Details:** Open 15 March - 31 Aug. Kitchen. TV lounge. Children's play areas. Boat hire. Fishing.
>
> **Charges guide:** Per unit Nkr. 80; electricity 20. Fifth night free.
>
> **Reservations:** Write to site. Address: Postboks 30, 8310 Kabelvåg. Tel: 76.07.87.81.

Taking your own tent, caravan or motorhome abroad?

Eurocamp Independent
FREEPOST ALM 1584
Hartford Manor
NORTHWICH
Cheshire
CW8 1BF

Book from over 90 sites in:

Ireland
France
Holland
Belgium
Germany
Switzerland
Austria
Italy
Spain
Portugal

sites ABROAD

THE LOW COST PITCH AND FERRY RESERVATION SERVICE

No Stamp Required

Sites Abroad
FREEPOST ALM1584
Hartford Manor
Northwich
Cheshire
CW8 1BF

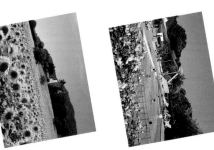

sites ABROAD

TAKING YOUR OWN TENT, CARAVAN OR MOTORHOME ABROAD?

Booking Made Easy

One phone call will book your whole holiday - sites, channel ferry or shuttle crossings and insurance.

Variety of Sites

From 4 star sites with a full range of facilities to well-run municipal sites.

Quality and Service

All sites meet rigorous standards for safety and cleanliness.

Value for Money

A competitive package at a price you will find hard to beat.

For a brochure call now on:

01606 787667

ABTA

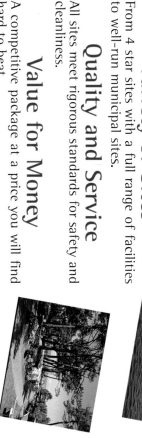

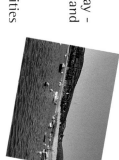

Mr/Mrs/Miss _____ Initials _____

Surname _____

Address _____

Postcode _____

How many adults are in your party? _____

If applicable what are the ages of your children? _____

Do you have a:

tent ☐ trailer tent ☐ caravan ☐ motorhome ☐

How many times have you taken your own equipment abroad? _____

Tick if you do not wish to receive direct mail from other carefully screened companies whose products or services we feel may be of interest ☐

sites ABROAD

SAAR

2475 Saltstraumen Camping, Saltstraumen (Nordland)

All weather site on `coastal route', close to the largest Maelstrom in the world.

The site is rather ordinary but it is conveniently located within walking distance of an outstanding phenomenon, the strongest tidal current in the world, where in the course of 6 hours between 33,800 and 82,700 billion gallons of water are pressed through a narrow strait, at a rate of about 20 knots. The effect is greatest at new or full moons, check tide tables to determine the best time to visit. The 60 touring pitches are mostly level gravel hardstandings in rows, with electricity (10A) to all, but a few `softer' pitches are available for tents. The heated sanitary facilities are basic but clean, and provide British style WCs, open washbasins and free hot showers. The latter are just shower heads with dividers between and communal changing, although in the ladies' room with some shower curtains. Kitchen with two full cookers, laundry with washing machine and dryer. Adjacent to the site is a filling station with shop, hairdressers and nearby are a hotel and cafeteria. The site is 33 km. from Bodø and 50 km. from Fauske.

> **How to find it:** From the Rv 80 (Fauske -Bodø) turn south on to the Rv 17, site is 12 km. at Saltstraumen adjacent to the Statoil station.
>
> **General Details:** Open all year. Kitchen. Laundry. TV room. Children's playground. Minigolf. Fishing. Motorcaravan service point, Chemical disposal.
>
> **Charges guide:** Per caravan Nkr. 100; motorcaravan 85; tent 75; electricity 25. Visa cards accepted.
>
> **Reservations:** Write to site. Address: Boks 85, 8056 Saltstraumen. Tel: 75.58.75.60. FAX: 75.58.75.40.

2455 Ballangen Camping, Ballangen (Nordland)

Pleasant, lively site with small pool and waterslide, on the E6 outside of town.

This conveniently located site is on the edge of a fjord with a small rocky beach, with direct access off the main E6 road. Reception shares space with the extremely well stocked shop and takeaway (main season). The 150 marked pitches are mostly on sandy grass, with electricity (10/16A) available to 120. There are a few hardstandings, also 50 rental cabins on site. The sanitary facilities are housed in an older style building, but the fittings are more modern and provide British style WCs, washbasins (some in cubicles), and controllable hot showers (on payment). The kitchen with dishwashing sinks, a full cooker, hot-plates and a covered seating area, plus a laundry are also in the same building. Facilities for the disabled, sauna and solarium are in a much older building which the owner intends to replace in the near future. TV room with tourist information, coffee and games machines, small outdoor pool and waterslide (charged for), tennis court, minigolf, children's playground, free fjord fishing and boat and bicycle hire. A supermarket and other services are in Ballangen 4 km. from the site. An interesting excursion is to the nearby Martinstollen Mine where visitors are guided through the dimly lit Olav Shaft 500 m. into the mountain. Narvik with it's wartime connections and museums is 40 km.

> **How to find it:** Access is off the E6, 4 km. north of Ballangen, 40 km. south of Narvik
>
> **General Details:** Open all year. Shop. Takeaway. Kitchen. Laundry. Sauna and solarium. TV/games room. Swimming pool and waterslide. Tennis. Minigolf. Fishing. Boat and bicycle hire. Car wash. Cabins for rent.
>
> **Charges guide:** Per unit, incl. 4 persons Nkr. 100; electricity 20; small tent 80; m/cycle or cycle and tent 60. Credit cards accepted.
>
> **Reservations:** Contact site. Address: 8540 Ballangen. Tel: 76.92.82.97. FAX: 76.92.81.50.

2435 Solvang Camping, Alta (Finnmark)

Old-style site, with relaxed, welcoming atmosphere, on the Altafjord.

This restful little site is set well back from the main road, so there is no road noise. It overlooks the tidal marshes of the Altafjord, which are home to a wide variety of bird-life, providing ornithologists with a grandstand view during the long summer evenings bathed by the Midnight Sun. The 30 pitches are on undulating grass amongst pine trees and shrubs, and are not marked, but there are 12 electric hook-ups (16A). The site also has 7 cabins and some rooms for rent. The heated sanitary facilities are basic and in a fairly old building, but provide British style WCs, mostly open washbasins and free controllable hot showers, together with a kitchen containing two full cookers and dishwashing sinks, plus a small laundry. In its own little kiosk outside is the modern chemical disposal point and outside a waste water drain which, with a little ingenuity, is possible to use for draining a motorcaravan tank. The site is run by a church mission organisation, with only limited funds available for repairs and refurbishment. However, all facilities are clean and in good order (out of season, the site provides holidays for needy children and carers). Small football pitch and children's playground, also a large lounge with TV. Places of interest in the area are Alta Museum with its ancient rock-carvings, and the Savco Canyon, the largest in Europe, with the controversial Alta Power Station and 100 m. dam at its upper end.

> **How to find it:** Site is signed off the E6, 10 km. north of Alta.
>
> **General Details:** Open 1 June - 10 Aug. Kitchen. Laundry. TV lounge. Children's playground. Cabins for rent.
>
> **Charges guide:** Per unit Nkr. 90; cyclist tent 70; electricity 30. Credit cards not accepted.
>
> **Reservations:** Write to site. Address: Transfarelv, 9500 Alta. Tel: 78.43.04.77.

NORWAY

2445 Slettnes Fjordcamp, Oteren (Finnmark)

Useful stopover southeast of Tromso beside the E6 road.

Beside a narrow fjord and surrounded by snowy capped mountains, this is a large site mainly for permanent caravans but with room for 20 touring units. A very well kept site, there are neat flower beds outside reception. Sanitary facilities consist of two toilets each for male and female with washbasins with mirror, etc. There are three showers each, communal but with no charge and good hot water. A kitchen houses a sink unit, full size cooker and microwave.

> **How to find it:** Site is beside the E6 road near Oteren.
>
> **Charges guide:** Per unit Nkr. 100.
>
> **Reservations:** Contact site. Address: 9047 Oteren. Tel: 77.71.45.08.

2425 Kirkeporten Camping, Skarsvåg, Nordkapp (Finnmark)

The most northerly campsite in the world (71° 06' 50").

This is a superb site with the most modern sanitary installations. In two under-floor heated buildings, linked by a covered timber walkway they provide British style WCs, open washbasins and free controllable hot showers with divider and seat, sauna, plus two family bathrooms, a baby room, and an excellent unit for disabled visitors. A laundry with washing machine and dryer, and a kitchen, with hot-plates, sinks and a dining area complete the facilities. All have quality fittings, excellent tiling and beautiful woodwork - the owner is a carpenter by profession. Considering the climate and the wild unspoilt location this has to be one of the best sites in Scandinavia, and also rivals the best in Europe. An added bonus is that the reindeer often come right into the campsite to graze. The 30 pitches, 22 with electricity (16A), are on grass or gravel hardstanding in natural 'tundra' terrain beside a small lake, together with 10 rental cabins and 5 rooms. The reception/cafeteria at the entrance is open daily. Sea fishing and photographic trips by boat can be arranged and buses run 4 times a day to Honningsvåg or the Nordkapp Centre. We suggest you follow the marked footpath over the hillside behind the campsite, from where you can photograph 'Nordkapp' at midnight if the weather is favourable. We also advise you pack warm clothing, bedding and maybe propane for this location.

Note: Although overnighting at Nordkapp Centre is permitted, it is on the very exposed gravel car-park with no electric hook-ups or showers.

> **How to find it:** On the island of Magerøya, from Honningsvåg take the E69 for 20 km. then fork right signed Skarsvåg. Site is on left after 3 km. just as you approach Skarsvåg.
>
> **General Details:** Open 10 May - 10 Sept. Cafeteria. Kitchen. Laundry. Sauna. Good motorcaravan service point. Cabins and rooms for rent.
>
> **Charges guide:** Per unit Nkr. 110; person 20; small tent 80; electricity 20. Credit cards not accepted.
>
> **Reservations:** Not usually necessary. Address: 9763 Skarsvåg, Nordkapp. Tel: 78.47.52.33. FAX: 78.47.52.47.

2415 Kautokeino Fritidssenter & Camping, Suohpatjávri (Finnmark)

Newly developed, friendly, lakeside site, 8 km. south of Kautokeino.

The 30 pitches here are not marked and are generally on a firm sandy base, amongst low growing birch trees, with 20 electric hook-ups (10A) available. There are also 8 cabins and 7 motel rooms for rent and these are very attractively designed and furnished. Although the grass is trying to grow, the ground is frozen from September until May so it takes many years to establish. The sanitary building is modern, heated and well maintained, with 2 British style WCs, 2 open washbasins and 2 controllable hot showers (on payment) per sex. A small kitchen has a full cooker, dishwashing sinks and refrigerator, the laundry has washing machine, dryer and ironing facilities. A separate bathroom for the disabled also contains baby changing facilities. The site rents canoes, boats and pedalos and free fishing is available in the lake. During the season when there are enough guests, the owner arranges an evening campfire around two Sami tents, with 'lectures' about the Sami people. There are good walks in the area to some special Sami sites, shops and other services are in Kautokeino just 8 km. away, and the site is 35 km. north of the Finnish Border.

> **How to find it:** Site is 8 km. south of Kautokeino on the Rv 93. (Do not confuse with another site of similar name in the town)
>
> **General Details:** Open 1 June - 30 Sept. Kitchen. Laundry. Chemical disposal point. Football. Volleyball. Boat hire. Fishing.
>
> **Charges guide:** Per unit Nkr. 65-75; adult 10; child 5; hikers tent 45; electricity 25. Visa card accepted.
>
> **Reservations:** Write to site. Address; Suohpatjávri, 9520 Kautokeino. Tel: 78.48.57.33. FAX: as phone.

2500 Trasavika Camping, Viggja, nr Orkanger (Sør Trøndelag)

Terraced site with glorious views and sandy beach, 40 km. from Trondheim.

On a headland jutting into the Trondheimfjord and some 40 km. from Trondheim, Trasavika occupies such an attractive position that the extra distance into town is bearable. The 65 pitches are on an open grassy field at the top of the site, or on a series of terraces below which run right down to the small sandy beach, easily accessed via a well designed gravel road. There are 40 electricity hook-ups (10A). To one side, on a wooded bluff at the top of the site, are 14 cabins and the neat, sanitary unit. British style WCs, open washbasins and two controllable hot showers per sex (on payment). Hot water also on payment in the kitchen and laundry which have a hot-plate, dish and clothes washing sinks, washing machine and dryer. The reception complex also houses the small shop, licensed café (20 June-end Aug. only), and a TV/sitting room. Nobody travelling as far as mid-Norway would dream of not visiting the unusually interesting and attractive historic city of Trondheim, for long the capital of Norway.

How to find it: Site is on the edge of Viggja on the Rv 65 between Orkanger and Buvik, 17 km. from the E6 and 40 km. west of Trondheim.

General Details: Open 1 May - 30 Sept. Shop. Café. Kitchen. Laundry. TV/sitting room. Children's playground. Jetty and boat hire. Free fishing. Cabins and apartments for rent.

Charges guide: Per caravan or motorcaravan Nkr. 100; tent 90; small tent 70; electricity 25. Credit cards accepted.

Reservations: Write to site. Address: 7354 Viggja, Sør Trondelag. Tel: 72.86.78.22.

2505 Magalaupe Camping, Oppdal (Sør Trøndelag)

Rural, good value, riverside site, close to Dovrefjell National Park.

Lying in a sheltered position with easy access from the E6, this site offers fairly simple facilities but a host of unusual activities in the surrounding area, including caving, canyoning, rafting, gold panning, mineral hunting, and musk oxen, reindeer and elk safaris. In winter the more adventurous can also go snow-mobiling or skiing in the high Dovrefjell National Park. The 70 unmarked and grassy touring pitches, 36 with electricity (10/16A), are in natural surroundings amongst birch trees and rocks on several different levels and served by gravel access roads. There are also 8 attractive cabins for rent. The small, but very clean, heated sanitary unit provides a British style WC, 3 washbasins (1 cubicle) and two hot showers (on payment) per sex. This is supplemented by two further WC/washbasin units in the building which also houses the reception and kiosk for ices, soft drinks, etc., the TV lounge, plus a bar open mid June - Aug. As the site rarely fills up, these simple facilities should be adequate at most times. Other amenities include a small kitchen with dishwashing facilities, hot-plate and freezer, plus a combined washing/drying machine. Supermarkets and other services can be found in Oppdal (11 km.).

How to find it: Site is signed to the western side of the E6, 11 km. south of Oppdal.

General Details: Open all year. Kiosk. Bar (mid June - Aug). TV lounge. Fishing. Kitchen. Laundry. Motorcaravan service point. Car wash. Cabins for rent.

Charges 1999: Per unit incl. 4 persons and electricity Nkr. 90; small tent without electricity 50; extra person 10. No credit cards or Eurocheques.

Reservations: Write to site. Address: Rute 5, 7340 Oppdal. Tel: 47.72.42.46.84. FAX: as phone.

2510 Håneset Camping, Roros (Sør Trøndelag)

Acceptable, high plateau site, close to the UNESCO World Heritage town of Roros.

At first sight Håneset Camping it is not promising, lying between the main road and the railway, and nor is the gritty sloping ground of the site very imaginatively landscaped - for grass, when it grows up here, is rather coarse and lumpy. However, as we soon discovered, it is the best equipped campsite in the town, and ideal to cope with the often cold, wet weather of this bleak 1,000m. high plateau. The 50 unmarked touring pitches all have electricity (10/16A), and most facilities are housed in the main building. These include reception, shop and cafeteria (mid June-Aug), a huge sitting/TV room and two well equipped kitchens which the owners, the Moen family, share with their guests, plus 9 rooms for rent. The heated sanitary installations provide three separate rooms for each sex with British WCs, open washbasins and controllable hot showers (on payment). A washing machine and two laundry sinks are in one of the ladies' rooms. Outside, the only other amenities are 13 rental cabins, a children's playground, and a chemical disposal point. People flock from all over Europe to visit this remarkably well preserved mining town. For over 300 years it was one of Europe's leading copper mines, and during all that time it never suffered serious fire. As a result it occupies a special place on UNESCO's world heritage list for its unique concentration of historic wooden houses. The walk to the town takes around 20 minutes.

How to find it: Site is on the Rv 30 leading south from Roros to Os, 3 km. from Roros.

General Details: Open all year. Shop and cafeteria (mid June-August). Children's playground. Kitchen. Laundry. Chemical disposal. Cabins and rooms to let.

Charges 1999: Per caravan or motorcaravan Nkr. 110 - 135; tent 90; electricity 20. No credit cards.

Reservations: Write to site. Address: 7460 Roros, Sør Trondelag. Tel: 72.41.13.72. FAX: 72.41.06.01.

NORWAY

2515 Gjelten Bru Camping, Alvdal (Hedmark)

Cosy, village site in wooded riverside location, close to the small town of Alvdal.

Located just a few kilometres west of Alvdal, this peaceful little site with its traditional turf roof buildings, makes an excellent base from which to explore the area. The 48 touring pitches are on level neatly trimmed grass, served by gravel access roads, and with electricity (10A) available to 37. Some pitches are in the open and others under tall pine trees spread along the river bank. The heated sanitary facilities are housed in two buildings which provide a good supply of British style WCs, a mix of conventional washbasins and stainless steel washing troughs, and controllable hot showers on payment. A separate unit with WC, basin, shower and handrails to serve disabled campers. Two small kitchens, one at each block, provide dishwashing facilities, hot-plates and an oven, all free. Across the bridge on the other side of the river and main road, the site owners also operate the local, well stocked mini-market. The UNESCO World Heritage town of Roros is 75 km. to the northeast of this charming little site, and the Dovrefjell National Park is also within comfortable driving distance.

> **How to find it:** On the Rv 29 at Gjelten 3.5 km. west of Alvdal. Turn over the river bridge opposite the village store and post office, and site is immediately on the right.

> **General Details:** Open all year. Kitchen. Fishing. Supermarket, post office and public telephone nearby. Children's swings. Chemical disposal. Cabins to rent.

> **Charges 1999:** Per unit Nkr. 110; electricity 15. No credit cards.

> **Reservations:** Write to site. Address: 2560 Alvdal. Tel: 62.48.74.44. FAX: 62.78.70.20.

2555 Lom Motell and Camping, Lom (Oppland)

Mountain resort site, 500 m. from town and Stave Church.

This small site provides pitches for 60 touring units on slightly sloping grass on either side of a modern motel only 500 m. from the centre of this famous town and its beautiful medieval wooden Stave Church. There are 52 electrical connections (10A), and the large heated sanitary unit provides a good supply of British style WCs, washbasins in cubicles, but only two hot showers per sex (on payment). A further free hot shower is for those using the sauna/solarium (Nkr 30), or the very comprehensive, free gym facilities, plus a unit for families or disabled visitors (key from reception). The small kitchen provides two dishwashing sinks with free hot water, and hot-plates for cooking (also free). A separate laundry houses washing machines, dryers and sinks. Also on site is a ski room, plus 16 cabins, 4 apartments and 8 motel rooms for rent. Reception shares space with the small shop, and the licensed motel serves both dinners and breakfasts (times according to demand). Besides the lovely mountain views from the site and the attractions of Lóm, the site is a good base from which to explore the mountains, take a trip to see the Briksdal Glacier or visit the Norwegian Mountain Museum and Fossheim Mineral Centre.

> **How to find it:** Site is 500 m. from roundabout in centre of Lom, beside the Rv 55 towards Sogndal.

> **General Details:** Open all year. Kiosk. Cafeteria. Kitchen. Laundry. Sauna and solarium. Gymnasium. Motorcaravan service point. Children's playground. Ski preparation room. Cabins and motel rooms for rent.

> **Charges guide:** Per unit incl. 5 persons Nkr. 125; small motorcaravan + 2 persons 110; m/cycle and tent 90; bicycle and tent 70; electricity 25. Visa cards accepted.

> **Reservations:** Write to site. Address: Postboks 88, 2686 Lom. Tel: 61.21.12.20. FAX: 61.12.12.23.

2545 Rustberg Hytteulerie & Camping, Øyer, nr Lillehammer (Oppland)

Traditional family site, convenient for visiting the 'Olympic area' of Norway.

Conveniently located beside the E6 and just 20 km. from Lillehammer, this attractive terraced site provides a comfortable base for exploring the area. Like all sites along this route it does suffer from road noise at times, but the site facilities and nearby attractions more than compensate for this. There are 90 pitches with 60 for touring units, most reasonably level and with some gravel hardstandings available for motorcaravans. There are 50 electrical connections (10A). Heated sanitary facilities provide British style WCs, washbasins (mostly in cubicles), and hot showers (on payment), two luxurious family bathrooms and a unit for disabled visitors. The campers' kitchen and dining room provides facilities for dishwashing together with a microwave and hob (all free). A separate laundry provides sinks, washing machine, dryer and drying cupboard. Also on site is a very good children's playground, an unusual billiard golf game, and a small open air swimming pool with water-slide which is open June-Aug. (weather permitting). The small reception building also houses a kiosk stocking basic foods. The Maihaugen Folkmuseum and Lillehammer town are 20 km, Hunderfossen (5 km.) has the Norwegian Road Museum and the more adventurous can ride the Olympic bobsleigh track.

> **How to find it:** Site is well signed from the E6, 20 km. north of Lillehammer.

> **General Details:** Open all year. Kiosk. Kitchen. Laundry. Swimming pool and water-slide. Billiard golf. Children's playground. Motorcaravan services.

> **Charges guide:** Per unit Nkr. 125; small tent 110; electricity 20. Visa cards accepted.

> **Reservations:** Write to site. Address: 2636 Øyer. Tel: 61.27.81.84. FAX: 61.27.87.05.

2550 Strandefjord Camping, Leira, nr Fagernes, Valdres (Oppland)

Mature, wooded, lakeside site in the Valdres district just outside Fagernes.

Fagernes lies on the north shore of an impressive glacial lake - Strandefjorden, and just 4 km. to the southeast at Leira, on a corner of this lake, is Strandefjord Camping. This undulating, woodland site behind a light industrial estate, has 70 touring pitches, but can take up to 250 units in scattered clearings amongst the trees and beside the lake. Many pitches are only suitable for tents and only 75 have electricity (10A). Also 30 seasonal units, 31 cabins and rooms on site. The main heated, but rather basic, sanitary unit could be hard pressed in high season. It has British WCs, washbasins (some in cubicles), but only two hot showers per sex (on payment). Separate rooms house a small kitchen with dishwashing and cooking facilities (free of charge), and a laundry. More showers and WC's can be found together with saunas (which are equipped with TV!) under the main site complex which also houses reception, a licensed restaurant, and conference room. Other on-site facilities include a fitness track, tennis and beach volleyball courts, children's play areas, minigolf, boat hire. Fishing and swimming in the lake are possible. It is a two minute walk to the village mini-market.

How to find it: Turn off E16 Oslo road on Rv 51 at Leira village 4 km. east of Fagernes. Site is 50m.

General Details: Open all year. Restaurant (June-Aug). Laundry. Kitchen. Sauna. Children's play areas. Conference room. Lake swimming. Fitness track. Tennis. Beach volleyball. Minigolf. Boat hire. Chemical disposal.

Charges guide: Caravan or motorcaravan Nkr. 120; tent and car 100; cycle or m/cycle and tent 85; electricity 25. Credit cards accepted.

Reservations: Write to site. Address: 2920 Leira. Tel: 61.36.23.65. FAX: 61.36.24.80.

2570 Fossheim Hytte and Camping, nr Gol, Hallingdal (Buskerud)

Idyllic touring site beside the Hallingdal river on the 'Adventure Road'.

Centred on the country town of Gol is one of Norway's favourite camping areas, Hallingdal. This small touring site lies just 4 km. west of the town, on the river bank, and is shaded by elegant tall birch trees. Despite being just below the main road and with a railway in the trees on the opposite side of the river, surprisingly little noise penetrates this idyllic setting. There are 50 grassy touring pitches, with electricity (10/16A) available to 40, and most overlook the river. In addition there are 13 cabins and 4 rooms for rent, but no static caravans are permitted. The site is well equipped, with a modern heated sanitary unit providing British style WCs, washbasins (some in cubicles), free controllable hot showers with dividers and seats, a separate unit for disabled people and a sauna. Small kitchen and laundry rooms provide cramped facilities for dishwashing and cooking (free of charge), plus sinks for clothes washing and a washing machine and dryer. Other facilities include a large, very comfortable TV lounge, a children's play area, canoe hire, and trout fishing with a specially constructed wooden walkway and platform for disabled anglers. A small shop is open in season with bread to order. (Note: there is another site of similar name in the adjoining Hemsedal).

How to find it: Site is 4 km. west of Gol on route Rv 7 leading to Geilo.

General Details: Open all year. Shop (1/6-31/8). TV lounge. Sauna. Children's play area. Bicycle hire. Trout fishing and canoeing. Laundry. Kitchen. Chemical disposal. Motorcaravan service point. Cabins and rooms for rent.

Charges 1999: Per unit incl. 2 persons and electricity Nkr. 120 - 160. Credit cards accepted.

Reservations: Write to site. Address: 3550 Gol. Tel: 32.02.95.86. FAX: 32.02.95.85. E-mail: foshytte@online.no. Internet: www.flyshop.no/fossheim.

2590 Camping Sandviken, Tinnsjo (Telemark)

Remote, lakeside site, in scenic location, suitable for exploring Hardangervidda.

With its own shingle beach, at the head of Tinnsjo Lake, Camping Sandviken provides 130 grassy, mostly level, pitches. In addition to the 30 seasonal units and 13 cabins, there are 80 numbered tourist pitches with electricity (5A), plus an area for tents, under trees along the waterfront. The tidy heated sanitary unit has British WCs, washbasins (some in cubicles), hot showers with dividers and seats (on payment), a sauna, solarium and a dual purpose disabled/family bathroom with ramped access and baby changing mat. Kitchen and laundry rooms provide facilities for cooking, dish and clothes washing (hot water on payment). The office/reception kiosk also sells sweets, soft drinks, ices etc. and a baker calls daily in July. A 1 km. stroll takes you to the tiny village of Tinn Austbygde which has a mini-market, bakery, café, bank, garage and post office. On-site leisure facilities include minigolf, TV and games rooms, a children's play area, watersports and fishing.

How to find it: Easiest access is via the Rv 37 from Gransherad along the western side of the lake.

General Details: Open all year. Kiosk (May-15 Sept). Kitchen. Laundry. Sauna. Solarium. Minigolf. Children's playground. Fishing. Boat hire. TV and games room. Motorcaravan service point. Chemical disposal. Cabins for rent.

Charges guide: Per person Nkr. 15; child (4-18 yrs) 10; caravan or motorcaravan 70 - 85, acc. to season; tent 60 - 75; m/cycle 40 - 50; electricity 20. `Quickstop' (8 pm-9 am) 65 - 80.

Reservations: Write to site. Address: 3650 Tinn Austbygd. Tel: 35.09.81.73.

NORWAY

2600 Rysstad Feriesenter, Setesdal (Aust-Agder)

High quality site in spectacular setting within easy reach of Stavanger and Kristiansand.

Setesdal is on the upper reaches of the Otra river which runs north from the port of Kristiansand right up to the southern slopes of Hardangervidda. It offers a wide range of scenery, often spectacular where the valley cuts through high, steep sided mountains. It is an area famous for its colourful mining history (silver) and for its vibrant art (especially music) and folklore. Thanks to a major new hydro-electric project, a spectacular mountain road has now opened linking Setesdal with Sirdal to the west, bringing Setesdal within easy and pleasant driving range of Stavanger. At the junction of this new road and Setesdal is the small village of Rysstad, named after the family who have developed camping in this area. The site occupies a wide tract of woodland between the road and the river towards which it shelves gently, affording a splendid view of the valley and the towering mountains opposite. The site is in effect divided into two sections; one is divided by trees and hedges into numbered pitches, some occupied by chalets to hire, the other is an adjacent open field. Good modern sanitary facilities are found under the reception block with showers on payment, washbasins in cubicles, washing up sinks and cooker. There is an attractive area on the river's edge for barbecues and entertainment with an arena type setting. The little village is within walking distance.

How to find it: Site is about 1 km. south of the junction between route 39 (from Kristiansand) and the newly extended route 45 (from Stravanger).

General Details: Open 1 May - 1 Oct. Electrical connections (20). Children's play area and amusement hut. Sports field. Fishing, swimming and boating (boats for hire). Fitness track. Bicycle hire. TV room. Laundry facilities with washing machine. Campers' kitchen. Centre includes café, shop, bank, garage and restaurant.

Charges guide: Per person Nkr. 10; caravan or tent 100; hiker's tent 35; electricity 25. Credit cards accepted.

Reservations: Write to site. Address: Midt i Setesdal, 4692 Rysstad. Tel: 37.93.61.30. FAX: 37.93.63.45.

2610 Neset Camping, Byglandsfjord (Aust-Agder)

Modern site by lake in Otra valley, good for activity holidays in south Norway.

On a semi-promontory on the shores of the 40 km. long Byglandsfjord, Neset is a good centre for activities or as a stop en route north from the ferry port of Kristiansand (from Denmark). Byglandsfjord offers good fishing (mainly trout) and the area has marked trails for cycling, riding or walking in an area famous for its minerals. The site has a stone workshop where your finds can be identified and courses in stone polishing are arranged. Climbing, rafting and canoe courses (including trips to see beavers) are organised and there are bicycles, canoes and pedaloes for hire. Ski-ing is possible in the area in winter. Neset is situated on well kept grassy meadows by the lake shore with the water on three sides and provides 180 unmarked pitches, most with electricity available. The main building houses reception, a small shop and a restaurant with fine views over the water. There are three modern sanitary blocks which can be heated, two with comfortable hot showers on payment, washing up facilities (metered hot water) and a kitchen. Chalets and three caravans available to hire. Barbecue area and children's play equipment around the site. This is a well run, friendly site where one could spend an active few days.

How to find it: Site is on route 39, 2½ km. north of the town of Byglandsfjord on the eastern shores of the lake.

General Details: Open all year. Restaurant. Shop. Campers' kitchen. Children's playground. Lake swimming, boating and fishing. Bicycle, canoe and pedalo hire. Courses in stone polishing. Climbing, rafting and canoeing.

Charges guide: Per unit Nkr. 105; tent and m/cycle 70; adult 10; child (5-12 yrs) 5; electricity 20.

Reservations: Write to site (also for details of courses). Address: 4680 Byglandsfjord. Tel: 37.93.42.55.

2612 Holt Camping, Tvedestrand (Aust-Agder)

Useful little site on outskirts of popular small Norwegian resort.

Tvedestrand is an attractive small resort with a pretty harbour, which is very popular with the Norwegians for their own holidays. Holt Camping is quite pleasantly situated beside the main E18 road, some 3 km. from the town - there is a little noise from the road during the day but we were not disturbed when staying overnight. The campsite is part level, part sloping grassland and about half of the pitches have 16A electrical connections. There are the usual cabins for hire. The single small sanitary block has excellent, well maintained facilities including hot showers on payment (1 per sex), washbasins (H&C) and provision for dishwashing and laundry (washing machine and dryer). Serving both the touring pitches and the cabins, the facilities may well be under pressure during busy times. There is a shop and café immediately outside the site entrance. This site could be very useful for those seeking a break in a part of Norway frequented more by the Norwegians themselves than by visitors from abroad.

How to find it: Site is beside the main E18 coast road (which actually bypasses the town), about 1 km. south of the turn off to the town itself.

General Details: Open 1 June - 31 Aug (huts all year). Shop/café outside. Laundry facilities. Children's play area.

Charges guide: Per unit incl. 2 persons and electricity Nkr. 100.00, without electricity 80.00.

Reservations: Contact site. Address: 4900 Tvedestrand. Tel: 37.16.02.65.

2615 Olberg Camping, Trøgstad (Østfold)

Peaceful, village farm site, close to Lake Øyeren within easy reach of Oslo.

A newly developed, delightful small site, Olberg Camping is located on neatly tended grassy meadow with newly planted trees and shrubs. There are 35 large, level pitches and electricity connections (10A) are available for 12 units. The excellent heated sanitary facilities are housed in a purpose built unit, created in the end of a magnificent large, modern barn and have a ramp for wheelchair access. They provide controllable hot showers, British style WCs and washbasins, with one bathroom for families or disabled people. Laundry and dishwashing share the same facilities at present, with a sink, washing machine and ironing board provided. A small kitchenette provides a full size cooker and food preparation area. Free hot water throughout. The reception building also houses a small gallery with paintings, glasswork and other crafts. A short drive down the adjacent lane takes you to the beach on Lake Øyeren, and there are many woodland walks in the surrounding area. Oslo is only 30 km, the old church and museum at Trøgstad, and Båstad church are all worth visiting. Bicycles can be hired and the local tennis court is also available. Children will love the ducks, rabbits, cats, sheep and hens, as well as the small playground with its sand-pit, trampoline, swings and climbers, but please bear in mind that this is a working farm, with the attendant potential dangers for small children.

> **How to find it:** Site is signed on Rv 22, 20 km. north of Mysen on the southern edge of Båstad village.
>
> **General Details:** Open all year. Kiosk. Craft gallery. Laundry and cooking facilities. Children's playground. Bicycle hire. Tennis and riding nearby. Cabins for rent.
>
> **Charges guide:** Per unit incl. 2 adults Nkr. 110; extra adult 10; extra child 5; electricity 20.
>
> **Reservations:** Write to site. Address: 1860 Trøgstad. Tel: 47.69.82.86.10. FAX: 47.69.82.85.55.

The Good ArctiCamps Guide

Very few British campers are to be seen in North Norway, beyond the Arctic Circle. Except for a few enthusiasts with several weeks to spare, it is too far to drive. Yet it has much to offer.

The best way to get to North Norway is to take advantage of the special promotional fares offered by Braathens via Bergen or Oslo and then travel on by road or by ferry from Trondheim or Bodo. Car hire in North Norway is hideously expensive. However, there is an alternative: public transport. To the annoyance of taxpayers in South Norway the Norwegian government pours subsidy into North Norway and much of this goes into a remarkable network of transport services by ferry, coach and bus. These services are operated with modern vehicles to regular published timetables and all carefully interconnect. Full details are provided in a comprehensive timetable available from the Norway Tourist Board in London. This includes the amazing Hurtigruten - the 100 year old coastal 'steamer' - which links all the main coastal towns on a daily basis in each direction and which can be used for hopping from town to town starting from Bergen. Backpackers use their youth rail passes to travel by train from Oslo or Stockholm to the Arctic rail gateways of Bodo and Narvik and then explore North Norway by bicycle or public transport. However, for those who are not into lightweight camping there are two forms of camping which are unique to the Arctic and which require virtually no equipment whatsoever: rorbu camping and sjohus camping.

Arctic Norway happens to be the world's most important cod fishing coast. Every spring thousands of fishing folk pour into the coastal towns and villages to catch and process cod. Over several centuries two forms of accommodation have developed to serve this massive migration; small huts on the waterfront, like boathouses, for the fishing crew, known as rorbu, and large sheds on the quayside for the workers in the fishery, known as sjohus (sea house). The rorbu traditionally has only one or two bunk-bedrooms, plus sitting room, kitchen and washroom. The sjohus usually has three floors with cod processing on the ground floor, ample public rooms on the second floor and bunk-bedrooms on the second and third floors. In effect the rorbu is a fisherman's flat while the sjohus is a fishery hostel. Over the past twenty years, the rorbu and sjohus have been adapted for use by campers during the summer when the cod have fled elsewhere. Most are spartan, offering what might be described as bunk-house accommodation. However, some conversions (and modern versions) are in the de luxe category and charge over £100 per room per night. The normal charges range between £10 and £20 per person per night.

Although this might seem expensive by most camping standards it is very cheap by Norwegian standards and it does provide a form of camping which is highly appropriate to Arctic Norway. As a result the rorbu and sjohus tend to be heavily booked by Scandinavian visitors during the peak holiday month of July but in the months on either side of July there is usually plenty of available space (look for the sign 'ledig' for vacancy) and off-season bargains are often on offer.

The Good ArctiCamps Guide (continued)

For the first time camper to this area we recommend three basic options: the immediate area around Tromsø; the neighbouring island of Senja; and the offshore islands of Lofoten. These offer convenient local transport; a wide range of rorbu and sjohus accommodation; and - last but not least - a fascinating landscape which combines one of the world's most spectacular coastal mountain ranges with a thriving and picturesque fishing and sea faring community.

Tromsø Environs   There is one rather unexciting conventional campsite on the outskirts of Tromsø. If an overnight stay in the town is needed, we would recommend the central Skipperhuset, the last remaining guest house for sea captains. There is a large conventional site with a spectacular view across the fjord about 15 miles north of Tromsø; this site, **Skittnelv**, has a range of small plank huts for hire by the night. About 20 miles south of Tromsø there is a most unconventional site, **Straumhella**, where rooms are available in an outdoor museum of part-restored historic rural buildings, again in a spectacular location overlooking the turbulent sound, but to get the feel of authentic rorbu and sjohus camping one should venture forth by local Tromsbuss and ferry to either of two small islands, 35 miles north of Tromsø, **Sandoy** and **Vannoy**, each of which has one traditional fishery converted into simple camping facilities.

Senja   Easily reached either by Hurtigruten or by the faster and more frequent express ferry, Senja can be explored by bus. Scattered around the island, mostly on the wilder western shore, are almost a dozen rorbu/sjohus campsites. The tiny islet of Husoy, on the northern tip of Senja, has a particularly enchanting sjohus, famed for its fresh fish cafe. Expensive, but worth a visit just to witness the location, is Hamn, an isolated fishery now being transformed into a sjohus resort. Other good centres for Arcticamping are Mefjordvaer, Gryllerfjord and Torsken, with Hamn all on the north-west coast.

Lofoten   Separated from the mainland by the wide (and often wild) Vestfjord, the Lofoten group of islands can be reached easily by air or ferry from Tromsø, Senja or Bodo, or by road via the neighbouring Vesteralen island group. Even more dramatic than Senja, the jagged mountain backbone - long known to sailors as the Lofoten Wall - provides what must be one of the world's most spectacular camping scenes. Hugging the protected eastern shore is a series of fishing villages, where the fishing industry is still alive and well, and which offer several score sites providing rorbu and sjohus accommodation. See our selected site, no. 2465, on page 256. We were particularly impressed by the following (going down the coast from northeast to southwest):

Lofoten Rorbuferies at Kabelvag (only a few miles from the island capital of Svolvaer);
Henningsvaer Rorbuer and Giavers Sjohus at Henningsvaer;
Nusfjord Rorbu at the UNESCO - recognised village of Nusfjord;
The abundant choice of rorbu/sjohus accommodation at the picturesque adjacent villages of Reine and Hamnoy (among the best is Captain Nyboen's little establishment);
The youth hostels (Vandrerhjem) in Stamsund and Å, both in sjohus and both welcoming adults (although now both so popular among backpackers that many visitors have to be turned away).

There are also several good conventional campsites on Lofoten, one of which is outstanding both for its location and its management (its toilets are serviced three times a day). So impressive is the view from this site, **Fredvang**, that people travel from elsewhere in Lofoten just to stand and stare. The owners have installed several cabins for hire.

Information   There are three levels for provision of tourist information. At the national level the Norway Tourist Board (NORTRA) has offices in Britain at Charles House, Lower Regent Street, London SW1Y 4LR. At the regional level - corresponding to counties - Nordland Reiseliv, Storgaten 4A, PO Box 434, N-8001 Bodo, includes Lofoten in its territory; Troms Reiser, Storgaten 63, PO Box 1077, N 9001 Tromsø covers Tromsø, the surrounding area and Senja; and Finnmark Opplevelser, PO Box 1223, N-9501 Alta, covers the area to the north of Troms, including North Cape. Each of the three areas highlighted in this report has its own local tourist board and these can usually provide material of a much more detailed nature, including local bus timetables, large-scale local maps and accommodation guides; these are:

Tromsø Arrangements, 61/63/3 Storgaten, PO Box 312, N-9001 Tromsø;
Senja Tour, Radhusveien 1, PO Box 326, N-9301 Finnsnes and
Destination Lofoten, PO Box 210, N-8301 Svolvaer.

PORTUGAL

Portugal occupies the southwest corner of the Iberian peninsula and is a relatively small country, bordered by Spain in the north and east and the Atlantic coast in the south and west. However, for a small country it has tremendous variety both in its way of life and traditions. The Portuguese consider the Minho area in northern Portugal to be the most beautiful part of their country with its wooded mountain slopes and wild coast line, a rural and conservative region with picturesque towns. Central Portugal (the Estremadura region) with its monuments, evidence of its role in the country's history, has fertile rolling hills and adjoins the bull-breeding lands of Ribatejo (banks of the Tagus). The huge, sparsely populated plains south east of Lisbon, the cosmopolitan yet traditional capital, are dominated by vast cork plantations supplying nearly half the world's cork, but it is an impoverished area, and visitors usually head for Evora. The Algarve compensates for the dull plains south of Evora and has attracted more tourist development than the rest of the country. Portugal is therefore a land of contrasts - the sophisticated development of the Algarve as against the underdeveloped rural areas where time has stood still. There is a more liberal constitution now but the country is still poor and the cost of living generally low, although there has been a marked increase in prices in the Algarve. For British visitors, with large distances to travel, longer stays out of season are particularly attractive and most camp sites are actively encouraging this type of visitor. For further information contact:

ICEP Portuguese Trade & Tourism Office, 22/22a Sackville Street, London W1X 1DE
Tel: 0171 494 1441. Fax: 0171 494 1868.

Population
9,900,000, density 106.6 per sq.km.

Capital
Lisbon (Lisboa)

Climate
The country enjoys a maritime climate with hot summers (sub-tropical in the South) and mild winters with comparatively low rainfall in the South, heavy rain in the North.

Language
Portuguese, but English is widely spoken in cities, towns and larger resorts. French can be useful.

Currency
The currency unit is the escudo, divided into 100 centavos and its symbol - the dollar sign - is written between the escudo and centavo units. Notes are issued for 5,000$00, 1,000$00, 500$00, and 50$00. Coins are issued for 50$00, 25$)), 20$00, 10$00, 5$00, 2$50, 1$00, and $50. One thousand escudos is a 'conto'.

Banks
Open Mon-Fri 08.30-11.45 and 13.00-14.45. Some large city banks operate a currency exchange service for tourists 18.30-23.00

Post Offices
Offices (Correios) normally open Mon-Fri 09.00-18.00, some larger ones on Saturday mornings.

Time
From the last Sunday in Sept to the last Sunday in March, the time in Portugal is GMT. During summer it is GMT + 1 hr (as the UK).

Telephone
To telephone Portugal from the UK dial 00 351. To the UK from Portugal dial 00 44. You need to be patient to get a line. Phone cards available (500 /1200 esc) from post offices, and tobacconists.

Public Holidays
New Year; Carnival (Shrove Tues); Good Fri; Liberty Day, 25 Apr; Labour Day; Corpus Christi; National Day, 10 June; Saints Days: Lisbon 13 June, Porto 24 June; Aassumption, 15 Aug; Republic Day 5 Oct; All Saints, 1 Nov; Immaculate Conception, 8 Dec; Christmas, 24/25 or 25/26 Dec.

Shops
Open Mon-Fri 0900-1300 and 1500-1900. Sat 0900-1300. Shopping centres are open much longer hours.

Food: Along the Atlantic coast fresh fish and shellfish are to be found on every menu - Caldeirada is a piquant mixed stew. However, Portugal is perhaps best known for Port and Maderia but don't forget the Vinho verde - marvellous with freshly caught sardines!

Motoring
The standard of roads is very variable - even some of the main roads can be very uneven. The authorities are making great efforts to improve matters, but other than on motorways or major highway routes (IP's) you should be prepared to make slow progress. Watch Portuguese drivers, as they tend to overtake when they feel like it.

Tolls: Tolls are levied on certain motorways (auto-estradas) out of Lisbon, and upon southbound traffic at the Lisbon end of the giant 25th Abril bridge over the River Tagus.

Speed Limits: Car - Built-up areas 31 mph (50 kph), other roads 56 mph (90 kph), Motorways min. 25mph (40 kph) Max. 75mph (120 kph). For towing vehicles in built-up areas 31 mph (50 kph), other roads 43/50 mph (70/80 kph) and Motorways min. 25 mph (40 kph) max. 62mph (100 kph)

Fuel: Petrol stations are open from 0700-2200/2400 and some 24 hours. Credit cards are accepted but Visa is preferred. Use of a credit card incurs a surcharge of 100 esc.

Parking: Parked vehicles must face the same direction as moving traffic. Some towns have 'Blue Zones', discs available from ACP or the police.

Overnighting
Generally not allowed and fines may be imposed.

Useful Addresses
National Motoring Organisation
Automovel Club de Portugal (ACP)
Rua Rosa Araujo 24-26, 1200 Lisbon.
Tel: 563931.
Office hours Mon-Fri 09.00-13.00, 14.00-17.00.

PORTUGAL - West Coast

801 Orbitur Camping Mata do Camarido, Caminha, nr Viana do Castelo

Pleasant site in northern Portugal close to the Spanish border.

This site is managed by a friendly couple and is a short 200 m. walk from the beach. It has an attractive and peaceful setting in woods alongside the river estuary that marks the border with Spain. With a pleasant, open feel, fishing is possible in the estuary and bathing from the rather open, sandy beach. The site is partly shaded by tall pines with other small trees planted to mark the large sandy pitches. The roads throughout the site have recently been resurfaced and the water, electrical supply and lighting have been updated. The clean, well maintained toilet block is centrally located with British style toilets, washbasins (cold water) and free hot showers, extra dishwashing and laundry sinks (cold water).

How to find it: Turn off main coast road (N13-E50) along estuary 3 km south of Caminha at sign to site.

General Details: Open 16 Jan - 30 Nov. Restaurant, snacks and supermarket (all May - Sept). Tennis. Children's playground. Laundry. Motorcaravan service point. Bus service 800 m. English spoken. Gates locked 11 pm.

Charges 1998: (to 31 May 99) Per person esc. 600; child (5-10 yrs) 300; car 510; tent 500 - 840; caravan 610 - 700; motorcaravan 740 - 1,000; electricity 360. Off season discounts (up to 70%). Credit cards accepted.

Reservations: Contact Orbitur - Central de Reservas, Rua Diogo do Couto, 1-8°, 1100 Lisboa. Tel: (0)1/811 70 00 or 811 70 70. FAX: (0)1/814 80 45. E-mail: info@orbitur.pt. Internet: http://www.orbitur.pt.

802 Orbitur Camping Viana do Castelo, Viana do Castelo

Site in northern Portugal with direct access to sandy beach.

This site is worth considering as it has the advantage of direct access, through a gate in the fence (locked at night), to an excellent sandy beach, very popular for windsurfing. There are around 187 pitches on slightly undulating, sandy ground - most with good shade. As usual with Orbitur sites, pitches are not marked and it could be crowded in July/Aug. There are some hardstandings for caravans and electricity (16A) in all parts. Some pitches are very sandy. The clean, well kept sanitary facilities are in two blocks one of which has been recently refurbished incorporating facilities for disabled campers. Both blocks have mostly British style WCs, washbasins with cold water, but to date the second block has only cold water. Small children's play area and a solid table tennis table. A pleasant restaurant terrace overlooks the site and a ferry crosses the river to the town centre. The site is also convenient for visiting the medieval town of Ponte de Lima (24 km), with its whitewashed houses, towers and Roman bridge, and Viana do Castelo is famous for its beautiful embroideries and festival processions.

How to find it: On the N13 coast road driving north to south drive through Viana do Castelo and over estuary bridge, turn immediately right off N13 towards Cabedelo and the sea. Site is the second camp signed

General Details: Open 16 Jan - 30 Nov. Supermarket, restaurant with terrace and bar (all April - Oct). Room with TV, video and fireplace. Children's playground. Adjacent swimming pool (from 15/6). Tennis. Telephone and post box. Medical post. Laundry. Motorcaravan service point. Bus service 200 m. English spoken. Bungalows for hire.

Charges 1998: (to 31 May 99) Per person esc. 600; child (5-10 yrs) 300; car 510; tent 500 - 840; caravan 610 -930; motorcaravan 740 - 1,000, all acc. to size; electricity 380. Off season discounts (up to 70%). No credit cards.

Reservations: Contact Orbitur - Central de Reservas, Rua Diogo do Couto, 1-8°, 1100 Lisboa. Tel: (0)1/811 70 00 or 811 70 70. FAX: (0)1/814 80 45. E-mail: info@orbitur.pt. Internet: http://www.orbitur.pt.

803 Orbitur Camping Rio Alto, Estela, nr Povoa de Varzim

Well managed site with good facilities adjacent to beach and golf course.

This site, which has recently been aquired by the Orbitur group, makes an excellent base for visiting Porto (by car), which is some 35 km. south of Estela. It takes around 600 units on sandy terrain, and is adjacent to what is virtually a private beach (access via a tunnel under dunes) and also to an 18 hole golf course. It has some hardstandings and electricity (5A) to most pitches. The area for tents is furthest from the beach and windswept, stunted pines give some shade. There are special (cheaper) arrangements for car parking - away from camping area with safety in mind. Four well equipped sanitary blocks have large free hot showers, British type WCs. Brown floors and decor give a very dark impression, also there are strange, ill fitting drain covers in the showers. Washbasins, dishwashing and laundry sinks under cover. Washing machines and ironing, plus units for disabled people. There is a restaurant, snack bar and, unusually for a seaside site, a swimming pool across the road from reception where tennis courts are also located. The tunnel is open 9 am.-7 pm. and the beach has a lifeguard from 15 June.

How to find it: Site is reached via a cobbled road leading directly off EN13 coast road towards the sea (just north of Estela), 12 km. north of Póvoa de Varzim. Travel 2.6 km. along the narrow cobbled road and look to the right for an Orbitur sign which lays well back from the road. Take this indicated right for 0.8 km. to site (speed bumps).

General Details: Open all year. Restaurant (1/5-30/9) Bar and snack bar (all year). Mini-market (1/5-30/9, w/ends other times). Laundry. Swimming pool (1/6-30/9). Tennis. Children's playground. Games room. TV. Golf (reduced for campers). Fishing. Bicycle hire. Chemical disposal. Motorcaravan service point. Entertainment in season.

Charges 1998: Per adult esc. 520 - 635; child (4-11) 230 - 270; car 600 - 690, in car park 250 -360; m/cycle 350 - 500; tent 310 - 900, caravan 760 - 1,280; motorcaravan 960 - 1,100; electricity 335 - 360. Credit cards accepted.

Reservations: Contact Orbitur - Central de Reservas, Rua Diogo do Couto, 1-8°, 1100 Lisboa. Tel: (0)1/811 70 00 or 811 70 70. FAX: (0)1/814 80 45. E-mail: info@orbitur.pt. Internet: http://www.orbitur.pt.

805 Orbitur Camping São Jacinto

Small site in attractive location on a peninsula between sea and lagoon.

This site is in the Sao Jacinto nature reserve, on a peninsula between the Atlantic and the Barrinha, with views to the mountains beyond. The area is a weekend resort for locals and can be crowded in high season; therefore it may be difficult to find space in Jul/Aug, particularly for larger units. Swimming and fishing are both possible in the adjacent Ria, or the sea, 20 minutes walk from a guarded back gate. There is a private jetty for boats and the manager will organise hire of the decorative 'Molericas' boats which are beautifully decorated and were used in days gone by to harvest seaweed for the land. It is not a large site, taking roughly 200 units on unmarked pitches, but in most places trees help provide natural limits and shade. Two toilet blocks were very clean when inspected, and contain free hot showers, dishwashing, laundry sinks, and a washing machine and ironing board in a separate part of the sanitary block. A new deeper bore-hole now supplies drinking water. Small shop, restaurant offering local food at reasonable prices and bar. The children's playground has also been recently refurbished.

How to find it: Turn off N109 at Estarreja to Torreira and São Jacinto; bypassing Murtosa. Turn left over bridge and Sao Jacinto is further down the road on the right.

General Details: Open all year except Dec/Jan. Shop (May-Sept). Restaurant/bar (June-Oct). Children's playground. Table tennis. Telephone and post box. Laundry. Motorcaravan services. Bus service 20 m. Tourist information English spoken. Orbitur bungalows for hire.

Charges 1998: (to 31 May 99) Per person esc. 590; child (5-10 yrs) 290; car 480; m/cycle 330; tent 480 - 820; caravan 590 - 920; motorcaravan 710 - 1,000, all acc. to size; boat 380; electricity (6A) 380. Off season discounts (up to 70%). Credit cards not accepted.

Reservations: Contact Orbitur - Central de Reservas, Rua Diogo do Couto, 1-8°, 1100 Lisboa. Tel: (0)1/811 70 00 or 811 70 70. FAX: (0)1/814 80 45. E-mail: info@orbitur.pt. Internet: http://www.orbitur.pt.

807 Orbitur Camping Praia de Mira

Small well kept site on quiet inlet close to beach.

A seaside site set in pinewoods, Praia de Mira is situated to the south of Aveiro and Vagos, in a quieter and less crowded area. It fronts onto a lake at the head of the Ria de Mira, which eventually runs into the Aveiro Ria. A back gate leads directly to the sea and a wide quiet beach 300 m. away. The site has around 350 pitches which are not marked but with trees creating natural divisions. Electricity (5A) and water points are plentiful. The refurbished toilet blocks are clean, and include British style WCs, 14 free hot showers and washing machines. The site provides an inexpensive restaurant, snack bar, lounge bar and TV lounge, and a well stocked supermarket. The Mira Ria is fascinating - brightly painted boats known as "Moliceros" with a distinctly Norse look about them collect seaweed which is used to enrich the soil for growing fresh vegetables. This is a rapidly diminishing occupation.

How to find it: Turn off N109 at Mira, about 27 km. south of Aveiro towards Praia de Mira. A small sign after about 5 km. shows a left turn leads direct to the site. If you miss it, the site is signed from the beach resort.

General Details: Open 1 Feb - 30 Nov. Shop and restaurant/bar (May-Sept). Snack bar. TV room. Laundry. Children's playground. Telephone and post box. Motorcaravan services. Bus service 150 m. English spoken.

Charges 1998: (to 31 May 99) Per person esc. 600 child (5-10 yrs) 300; car 510; m/cycle 350; tent 500 - 840; caravan 610 - 930; motorcaravan 740 - 1,000, all acc. to size; boat 370; electricity 380. Off season discounts (up to 70%). Credit cards accepted.

Reservations: Contact Orbitur - Central de Reservas, Rua Diogo do Couto, 1-8°, 1100 Lisboa. Tel: (0)1/811 70 00 or 811 70 70. FAX: (0)1/814 80 45. E-mail: info@orbitur.pt. Internet: http://www.orbitur.pt.

809 Orbitur Camping Gala, Figueira da Foz, nr Coimbra

Large site close to resort and with path to nearby private beach.

This site, for around 1,500 units, is on sandy terrain in a pinewood. Some pitches near the road may be rather noisy. One can drive or walk the 300 m. from the back of the site to a private beach; bathing needs caution when windy - the warden will advise. The site fills quickly in July/August and units may be very close together, but there should be plenty of room at other times. There are a few individual pitches with electricity and water (only 50 sq.m), the majority (70 sq.m) are unmarked with electricity (15A). The three toilet blocks have British and Turkish style toilets, individual basins (some with hot water) and 16 free hot showers. All were clean at time of inspection despite obviously heavy usage.

How to find it: Site is 4 km. south of Figueira beyond the two rivers; turn off main road over 1 km. from bridge on southern edge of Gala, then 600 m. to site.

General Details: Open all year. Supermarket, restaurant/bar (all May-Sept). Lounge. Children's playground. Tennis. Laundry. Motorcaravan service point. Orbitur bungalows for hire. No dogs permitted. English spoken.

Charges 1998: (to 31 May 99) Per person esc. 600; child (5-10 yrs) 300; car 510; m/cycle 350; tent 500 - 840; caravan 610 - 700; motorcaravan 740 - 1,000, all acc. to size; boat 370; electricity 360. Off season discounts (up to 70%). Credit cards accepted.

Reservations: Contact Orbitur - Central de Reservas, Rua Diogo do Couto, 1-8°, 1100 Lisboa. Tel: (0)1/811 70 00 or 811 70 70. FAX: (0)1/814 80 45. E-mail: info@orbitur.pt. Internet: http://www.orbitur.pt.

PORTUGAL - West Coast

840 Campismo O Tamanco, nr Louriçal

Peaceful countryside site, with homely atmosphere, flowers and fruit trees.

The new young Dutch owners, Irene and Hans, are sure to give you a warm welcome at this delightful little touring site. They have great plans for '99 which include a swimming pool, children's play area, restaurant and bar, and courses in flower arranging and gold and silversmithing. There will also be entertainment for the children during the day. The site has been very popular with mature couples and winter campers. The 100 good sized pitches are separated by cordons of fruit trees, ornamental trees and flowering shrubs, on level grassy ground. There is electricity (16A) to 72 pitches and 5 pitches are suitable for large motorhomes. The site is lit and there is nearly always space. The single sanitary block, just behind the owners house at the front of the site, provides spotlessly clean and generously sized facilities. These include British style WCs, pre-set showers and washbasins in cabins - with easy access for disabled people. Dishwashing and laundry sinks outside under cover. Hot water is free. The owners keep a range of provisions and local produce with bread and milk deliveries daily. The site is within walking distance of local shops. Market in Louriçal every Sunday. One can fish or swim in a nearby lake, and the resort beaches are a short drive. Possibly some road noise on pitches at the front of the site.

How to find it: From N109/IC1 (Leira-Figuera de Foz) road, 25 km. south of Figuera in Matos de Carriço, turn on to N342 road (signed Louriçal 6 km). Site is 1.5 km. on left.

General Details: Open all year. TV room/lounge. Supermarket 800 m. Washing machine. Milk and bread deliveries daily. Bicycle hire. Chemical disposal. Bungalows and a large house (4 double bedrooms) for rent.

Charges 1998: Per adult Esc 350 - 400; child (up to 5 yrs) 150; tent, caravan or trailer 300; car 200; m/cycle 100; motorcaravan 500; dog 80; electricity 340. Less 30-60% for 7/14 days and longer off season. Credit cards accepted.

AR Discount
Welcome drink;
bottle of wine

Reservations: Contact site. Address: O Tamanco Lda, Casas Brancas, 3100 Louriçal. Tel/Fax: 036-952551.

846 Camping-Caravanning Vale Paraiso, Nazaré

Well managed, shady site near the coast, open all year.

This pleasant campsite is by the main N242 road in 8 ha. of undulating pine woods and provides over 600 pitches, many of which are on sandy ground only suitable for tents. For other units there are around 250 individual pitches of varying size on harder ground with electrical connections (4/6/10A) available. Sanitary facilities are good, with free hot water for washbasins, showers, laundry and dishwashing sinks. Nearly all WCs are British style and there are facilities for disabled people. A range of sporting and leisure activities includes a good outdoor swimming pool with sunbathing areas and a children's adventure playground. Supermarket selling a large selection of goods, a bar/snack bar, takeaway and a restaurant with regional cuisine. Picnic basket service. Several long beaches of white sand are within 2-15 km. allowing windsurfing, sailing, surfing or body-boarding,. Animation for children, adult social events and evening entertainment are organised in season. Specific group entertainment is available on request. Nazaré is an old fishing village with narrow streets, a harbour and many outdoor bars and cafés, with a lift to Sitio. There is much of historical interest in the area although the mild Atlantic climate is also conducive to just relaxing. The owners are keen to welcome British visitors and English is spoken.

How to find it: Site is 2 km. north of Nazaré, on the EN242 Marinha Grande road.

General Details: Open all year. Shop. Restaurant (March - Sept). Café/bar with TV. Tabac. Takeaway. Café (all year). Swimming pool (March - Sept). Volleyball. Basketball. Football. Badminton. Amusement hall. Bicycle hire. Washing machine and dryers. Chemical disposal. Motorcaravan service point. Bungalows and tents for rent.

Charges 1998: Per person esc.370 - 595; child (3-10 yrs) 170 - 265; tent 305 - 650; caravan 365 - 790; car 305 - 490; motorcaravan 425 - 910; m/cycle 205- 330; electricity 295 - 485. Every fifth night free. Credit cards accepted.

Reservations: Contact site. Address: EN 242, 2450 Nazaré. Tel: 062/561800. FAX: 062/561900. E-mail: camping.vp.nz@mail.telepac.pt.

CAMPING CARAVANING ***
VALE PARAISO

NATURE·SEASIDE·BEACH·TRADITION·CULTURE·ENTERTAINMENT·QUIET·CLEANLINESS·SECURITY

NAZARÉ - Portugal

810 Orbitur Camping Sao Pedro de Moel, nr Leira

Large and pleasant, seaside site close to small resort in central Portugal.

A quiet and attractive site is situated under tall pines, on the edge of the rather select small resort of São Pedro de Moel. The attractive, sandy beach, about 500 m. walk downhill from the site, (you can take the car, although parking may be difficult in the town) is sheltered from the wind by low cliffs. The site has four clean toilet blocks with mainly British style toilets (some with bidets), individual basins (some with hot water) and free hot showers mostly in one block. The shady site can be crowded in July/Aug, when units might be rather too close for comfort, as the pitches are in blocks and unmarked. There are 500 pitches (50 sq.m), of which 250 have electrical connections (15A) and water, a few used for permanent units. Although there are areas of soft sand, there should be no problem in finding a firm pitch. A large modern restaurant and bar are open all year.

How to find it: Site is 9 km. west of Marinha Grande, on the right as you enter São Pedro de Moel. The busy road from Marinha Grande is a combination of cobbles and very rough and badly patched surfaces - take it slowly!

General Details: Open all year. 75,000 sq.m. Supermarket, large restaurant and bar with terrace. TV and games room. Children's playground. Tennis. Telephone and post box. Medical post. Laundry. Car wash. Motorcaravan services. Bus service 100 m. Mobile homes and Orbitur bungalows for hire.

Charges 1998: (to 31 May 99) Per person esc. 600; child (5-10 yrs) 300; car 510; m/cycle 350; tent 500 - 840; caravan 610 - 930; motorcaravan 740 - 1,000, all acc. to size; boat 370; electricity 380. Off season discounts (up to 70%). Credit cards accepted.

Reservations: Contact Orbitur - Central de Reservas, Rua Diogo do Couto, 1-8°, 1100 Lisboa. Tel: (0)1/811 70 00 or 811 70 70. FAX: (0)1/814 80 45. E-mail: info@orbitur.pt. Internet: http://www.orbitur.pt.

845 Parque de Campismo Colina do Sol, S. Martinho do Porto

Well appointed touring site, near to beach, with own swimming pool.

Only 1 km. from the small town of S. Martinho do Porto, Colina do Sol has around 350 pitches marked by fruit and ornamental trees on grassy terraces. Electricity (6 or 10A) is available to all, although some may need long leads. The attractive entrance with its beds of bright flowers, is wide enough for even the largest of units and newly surfaced roads are pleasant for manoeuvring. There is a warm welcome from the receptionist and good English is spoken. Two large, clean and modern sanitary blocks provide British style WCs (some with bidets), washbasins - some with hot water, and free hot showers. Dishwashing and laundry sinks are outside. A well stocked supermarket and a restaurant, cafeteria, and bar are open May - Sept, with a delightful paved terrace beside the large clean swimming pools, one for children. New children's play area and a motorcaravan service area. The beach is at the rear of the camp, with access via a gate which is locked at night (22.00-08.00). The site is a convenient base for exploring the Costa de Prata and for excursions to old town of Leiria, with its crenellated walls towering high above the rock faces, and to the famous shrine of Fátima. Market in S. Martinho do Porto on Sunday.

How to find it: Turn from EN 242 (Caldas-Nazaré) road northeast of San Martinho do Porto. Site is clearly signed.

General Details: Open all year except 15/12-15/1. Supermarket. Restaurant/cafe with bar (high season). Swimming pool. Lounge. Children's playground. Telephone and post box. Medical post. Motorcaravan service point. Car wash.

Charges 1998: Per adult esc. 575; child (4-10 yrs) 275; small tent 495, large 585; caravan or motorcaravan 715 - 880; car 475; m/cycle 320; electricity 320.

Reservations: Contact site. Address: 2465 S. Martinho do Porto. Tel: 062/989764. FAX: 062/989763.

811 Orbitur Camping Valado, Nazaré

Popular site close to busy resort on central west coast.

This site is on the edge of the old, traditional fishing port of Nazaré which has now become something of a holiday resort and popular with coach parties. The large beach in the town, about 2 km. downhill (steeply) from the site, is sheltered by headlands and provides good bathing. The site is on undulating ground under tall pine trees, takes around 500 units and, although some smallish individual pitches with electricity and water are for reservation, most of the site is not marked and units could be close together especially in July/Aug. About 420 have electricity. The restaurant, bar and supermarket are in one block. Three toilet blocks, very clean when inspected, have British and Turkish style WCs, washbasins and showers (cold water), and 17 free hot showers, plus dishwashing and laundry sinks under cover.

How to find it: Site is on the Nazaré - Alcobaca road - 2 km. east of Nazaré.

General Details: Open 1 Feb - 30 Nov. Supermarket. Bar, snack bar and restaurant with terrace (May - Sep). TV/general room. Children's playground. Tennis. Telephone and post box. Medical post. Laundry. Car wash. Motorcaravan services. English spoken. Bus service 20 m. Bungalows and mobile homes for hire.

Charges 1998: (to 31 May 99) Per person esc. 590; child (5-10 yrs) 290; car 480; m/cycle 350; tent 480 - 820; caravan 590 - 920; motorcaravan 710 - 1,000, all acc. to size; boat 380; electricity 380. Off season discounts (up to 70%). Credit cards accepted.

Reservations: Contact Orbitur - Central de Reservas, Rua Diogo do Couto, 1-8°, 1100 Lisboa. Tel: (0)1/811 70 00 or 811 70 70. FAX: (0)1/814 80 45. E-mail: info@orbitur.pt. Internet: http://www.orbitur.pt.

PORTUGAL - West Coast

813 Orbitur Camping Guincho, Areia, nr Cascais

Large site convenient for visiting Lisbon, with nearby beach.

Although this is a popular site for permanent or long stay caravans with 1,295 pitches, it is nevertheless quite attractively laid out among low pine trees and with the A5 autostrada to Lisbon (30 km), it provides a useful alternative to sites nearer the city. Located behind sand dunes and a wide, sandy, but somewhat windswept beach, the site offers a bar/restaurant, supermarket, general lounge with pool tables, games, TV room and laundry. There is a choice of pitches (mainly about 50 sq.m.) most with electricity (15A), although siting amongst the trees may be tricky, particularly when the site is full. The three sanitary blocks are in the older style but are clean and tidy with British type WCs, washbasins with cold water, free hot showers, dishwashing, washing machines, dryer and facilities for disabled people.

How to find it: Approach from either direction on N247. Turn inland 6½ km. west of Cascais at camp sign. Travelling direct from Lisbon site is signed at the end of the A5 autopista.

General Details: Open all year. 70,000 sq.m. Supermarket, Restaurant, bar and terrace (open March-Oct). General room with TV. Tennis. Children's playground. Entertainment in summer. Excursions. Telephone and post box. Medical post. Laundry. Car wash. Motorcaravan services. Bungalows for hire.

Charges 1998: (to 31 May 99) Per person esc. 700; child (5-10 yrs) 350; car 620; m/cycle 430; tent 630 - 980; caravan 740 - 1,030; motorcaravan 880 - 1,160, all acc. to size; boat 570; electricity 400. Off season discounts (up to 70%). Credit cards accepted.

Reservations: Contact Orbitur - Central de Reservas, Rua Diogo do Couto, 1-8°, 1100 Lisboa. Tel: (0)1/811 70 00 or 811 70 70. FAX: (0)1/814 80 45. E-mail: info@orbitur.pt. Internet: http://www.orbitur.pt.

814 Lisboa Camping, Parque Municipal de Campismo de Monsanto, Lisbon

Excellent new site outside the city with outstanding amenities.

This site was rebuilt completely for Expo 98 and is without doubt the finest in Portugal. It is quite expensive but you get a lot for your money. The wide entrance, with ponds, fountains is impressive, with trees, lawns and flowering shrubs leading up to the swimming pool, is probably this site's most attractive feature. The site is on sloping ground with many modern terraces and is well shaded by trees and shrubs. The 170 motorcaravan pitches are on concrete hardstanding, each with its own services which include a large wooden picnic table and chairs! There is a separate area for tents. The eight immaculate solar powered sanitary blocks are superb. They contain all facilities that campers, including disabled people, could wish for. The whole site is designed to be accessible to disabled campers. The two pools with a snack bar are excellent, as is the on site Roman theatre which functions in season. There are 70 new chalet style bungalows for hire. There is a small supermarket on site but also a Jumbo shopping centre 5 mins walking distance. The site is 8 km. from central Lisbon with two bus routes giving a regular service, and 10 km. from a decent beach. It is the closest site for visiting Lisbon

How to find it: From Lisbon take the motorway towards Estoril, the camp is signed from junction 4 onto the 1C17, the site has huge signs off this road at the first exit to Buraca. The site is immediately on the right.

General Details: Open all year. 340,000 sq.m. Electrical connections. Shops and restaurants. Hairdressers. Tennis. Minigolf. Sports field. 2 Playgrounds Two swimming pools. Roman theatre General and TV rooms. Launderette. Post office. Bank. Medical post. Car wash. Organised excursions. No chemical disposal.

Charges 1999: Per adult esc. 560 - 800; child under 6 yrs free, 6-11 yrs 420 - 600; tent 560 - 1,000; caravan 840 - 1,200; car 350 - 500; motorcaravan 840 - 1,200; m/cycle 280 - 400.

See colour advert between pages 320/1

Reservations: not made. Address: Estrada da Circunvalacao, 1400 Lisboa. Tel: 01/7609620/22. FAX: 01/7609633

815 Orbitur Camping Costa da Caparica, Costa da Caparica, nr Lisbon

Site with many permanent pitches and small touring section at coastal resort 20 km. from Lisbon.

This is very much a site for 600 permanent caravans but it has very easy access to Lisbon (10 km.) via the motorway, by bus or even by bus and ferry. It is in a small resort, favoured by the Portuguese themselves, which has all the usual amenities plus a good sandy beach (200 m) and promenade walks. There is a small area for touring units which includes some special pitches for motorcaravans. Two of the three toilet blocks have mostly British style toilets, washbasins with cold water and free hot showers. The third is older and has cold water. Facilities are provided for disabled campers.

How to find it: After crossing the Tagus bridge (toll) on A2 motorway going south, immediately take turning for Caparica and Trafaria. At the 7 km. marker on IC120 turn right (at Orbitur sign); site is at second roundabout.

General Details: Open all year. Supermarket. Large bar/restaurant (Feb-Nov). Children's playground. Some organised activities and shows in season - outdoor disco/entertainment area. Excursions. Washing machine. Treatment room; doctor calls daily in season. Motorcaravan services. Bungalows and mobile homes for hire.

Charges 1998: (to 31 May 99) Per person esc. 690; child (5-10 yrs) 345; car 620; m/cycle 430; tent 620 - 980; caravan 730 - 1,030; motorcaravan 870 - 1,170, all acc. to size; boat 560; electricity 420. Off season discounts (up to 70%). Credit cards accepted.

Reservations: Contact Orbitur - Central de Reservas, Rua Diogo do Couto, 1-8°, 1100 Lisboa. Tel: (0)1/811 70 00 or 811 70 70. FAX: (0)1/814 80 45. E-mail: info@orbitur.pt. Internet: http://www.orbitur.pt.

816 Parque de Campismo de Porto Covo, Porto Covo, nr Sines

Site close to fine beaches of the Costa Azul, with own pools.

This is a site in a popular seaside resort where a fairly large proportion of the pitches are occupied by Portuguese units. However, it has a sense of space as you pass the security barrier to reception which is part of an uncluttered and attractively designed square area. The pitches are somewhat small but are reasonably level, all have electricity (5/10A), some with limited shade from young trees. The sanitary blocks are clean and have free hot showers and the usual amenities plus cold outside showers, foot baths and ironing facilities. A mini market stocks essentials and souvenirs or a short walk to the village gives access to shops, bars and restaurants. Recreation room with games and TV, and children's playground off the main square. Swimming pools have areas for sunbathing. Dedicated barbecue areas are close to the pools. A jolly bar and restaurant with terrace offers a Portuguese menu (popular with the locals) at reasonable prices. The beaches are a short walk and feature steep cliffs and pleasant sandy shores.

How to find it: From E201-1 Cercal - Sines road (note: the road changes from the E201 at Tanganheira). Take left turn (southwest) to Porto Covo and site is well signed on the left.

General Details: Open all year. Restaurant/bar. Mini-market in season. Children's play area. Swimming pools. Barbecue areas. Telephones. Bungalows and flats for rent. Bus service to Porto Covo and Lisbon from site.

Charges 1998: Per adult esc. 470; child 235; tent 455 - 595; car 365; m/cycle 255; caravan 495 - 700; boat 350 - 410. All plus 7% VAT. Credit cards accepted.

Reservations: Write to site. Address: Porto Covo, 7520 Sines. Tel: 069/95136. FAX: 069/95239.

818 Parque de Campismo de Milfontes, Vila Nova de Milfontes

Pleasant site with good facilities, within walking distance of town and beach.

This popular site is within walking distance of the town and beach. Well lit and fenced, it has around 500 shady pitches on sandy terrain, which are marked out and divided by hedges and nicely paved paths. Some pitches may be too small for caravan and car and cars may have to be parked in an internal car park. Electricity (6A) is in all parts. The four toilet blocks (one new) are clean and well maintained and two blocks have suites for disabled people with ramped entrances. There is a good supply of mainly British style WCs, bidets, washbasins (some with hot water), hot and cold showers and some children's facilities, in a mix of combinations and styles. Hot water is free. Also dishwashing and laundry sinks with cold water outside under cover. The site has a restaurant and bar complex. Well stocked supermarket. Watersports, fishing, canoeing and swimming are possible from the resort beaches.

How to find it: From N120 coast road at Cercal, turn on E390 and continue into Vila Nova de Milfontes. Turn right in town and follow camp signs. Site is on right at end of no through road.

General Details: Open all year. Supermarket (1/4-30/9). Bar and snacks (1/4-30/9). Restaurant (June-Sept). TV room. Children's playground. Fishing and bicycle hire 1 km. Telephone. Laundry. Car wash. Chemical disposal. Motorcaravan services. Mobile homes and cabins for hire. English spoken. Dogs not permitted.

Charges 1998: Per person esc 300 - 540; child (5-10) 150 - 270; tent 220 - 450; caravan or motorcaravan 285 - 550; car 180 - 370; m/cycle 160 - 285; electricity 300. Credit cards accepted.

Reservations: Contact site. Address: 7645 Vila Nova de Milfontes. Tel: 083/96140 or 96693. FAX: 083/96104.

AR Discount
Less 10%
(excl. rental uints)

819 Camping Sintana, Vila Nova de Milfontes

Large site with beach access, shaded by pines.

This is a large site with a huge entrance off the road and then a 500 m. drive through a pine forest to reception. It has good sized, level pitches, although the numerous tall pines concentrate the mind when manoeuvring. There are two large, cheerful sanitary blocks with an array of equipment catering for every need. This includes British style WCs and free hot showers. Another large building houses reception, a bar with terrace and restaurant with an unusual internal terrace. Also a TV room games area with darts, pool and electronic games. A hundred metres away into the site is a fountain in a circle of lawn and a covered walkway supporting blooms of vivid colours if you wish to just sit and relax. Further into the site there is another bar and snack bar with a first floor terrace and a well stocked supermarket. Unusually the children's playground and other sports facilities such as tennis courts are just outside the boundary of the site opposite reception. The beaches (600 m. through a rear entrance) are excellent, gently shelving, with rocks and cliffs surrounding a fine sandy bay. Torches useful.

How to find it: From E201-1 Cercal - Sines road (note: road changes from the E201 at Tanganheira), take the left (southwest) to Porto Covo and follow signs (south) to Vila Nova de Milfontes. Site is well signed on the left.

General Details: Open all year. Restaurant/bar with snacks (all year). Large restaurant (summer only). Shop. Large children's play area. Table tennis. TV lounge. 5 a side soccer pitches. Tennis courts. Barbecue area. Telephone. First aid area. Car wash. Buses to local village and Lisbon (3 hrs journey).

Charges 1998: Per adult ptas 520; child 260; tent 500 - 620; car 300; caravan 620; motorcaravan 640; electricity 330. Plus 7% VAT. Credit cards accepted.

Reservations: Contact site. Address: Sitava Turismo, SA Brejo da Zimbreira, 7645 Vila Nova de Milfontes. Tel: 083/899343, 899 569, 899 or 570. FAX: 083/899571. E-mail: sitava@mail.telepac.pt.

PORTUGAL - Algarve

841 Parque de Campismo de Armação de Pêra

Modern, attractive site with excellent facilities and own pool.

This site has a wide attractive entrance with a large external parking area. The 1,200 pitches are on level grassy sand, marked by trees which provide some shade, and are easily accessed from tarmac and gravel roads. Electricity (10A) is available for most pitches. Three modern, clean and well maintained sanitary blocks, provide British and Turkish style WCs, some with bidets, washbasins, and showers with hot water on payment. There is a suite for disabled campers. The restaurant, café and bar, and well stocked supermarket should cater for most needs, and you can relax around the swimming pools, one for children (lifeguard in summer). The disco near to the entrance and café complex is soundproofed which should ensure a peaceful night for non-revellers. The well maintained children's play area has a safe, sandy base. The site is within easy reach of Albufeira, Portimão and makes an excellent base for stays in this region and for winter sun-seekers. Fishing, hunting and watersports nearby.

How to find it: Turn off EN125/ IC4 road in Alcantarilha, taking the EN269-1 towards the coast. Site is on left side before Armação de Pêra. There are other sites in the area, so be sure to find the right one.

General Details: Open all year. Supermarket. Restaurant (1/5 - 30/9). Self service café. Three bars (1/5-30/9). Kiosk. Games and TV rooms. Tennis. Children's playground. Swimming pool (all year; entrance fee July - Sept). Disco. Medical centre. Telephone and post box. Car wash. Laundry. Bungalows for hire.

Charges 1998: Per adult esc. 550; child (4-10 yrs) 275; tent or awning 500 - 650, acc. to size; caravan or motorcaravan 550 - 700; m/cycle 400; electricity 400. Less 50% in low season for 3 day stay or more

Reservations: Contact site. Address: 8365 Armação de Pêra. Tel: 082/312296 or 312260. FAX 082/315379.

843 Parque de Campismo de Sagres, Sagres

Pleasant and extremely well maintained site at western tip of the Algarve.

Not very far from the lighthouse in the unspoilt southwest corner of Portugal, this site has 960 pitches for tents and 120 for tourers. They are sandy pitches located amongst pine trees which give good shade. There are some hardstandings and electricity (5A) throughout. The three modern, spacious sanitary blocks are excellently maintained and cleaned, providing hot and cold showers (hot showers are free), British style WCs, bidets, washbasins with cold water and footbaths. Dishwashing and laundry sinks are under cover outside the blocks, with washing machines and ironing boards provided. The restaurant, bar and cafe/grill provide a range of reasonably priced meals including breakfast, and there is a well stocked supermarket. This is a good site for those seeking winter sun, or as a base for exploring this `Land's End' region of Portugal, and is away from the hustle and bustle of the more crowded resorts. The beaches and the town of Sagres (the departure point of the Portuguese navigators) with its fort, are a short drive.

How to find it: Turn off road EN268, approx 2 km before Sagres, site is signed.

General Details: Open all year. Supermarket (1/4-1/11). Restaurant/bar and cafe/grill (all 1/4-30/9). TV room. Bicycle hire. Barbecue area. Children's playground. Fishing. Golf 12 km. Medical post. Laundry. Car wash. Chemical disposal. Motorcaravan service point. English spoken.

Charges 1999: Per adult esc. 500 - 700; child (4-10 yrs) 250 - 350; small tent or awning 400 - 600, medium 500 - 750, large 600 - 850; caravan small 500 - 750, large 600 - 850; car 250 - 450; m/cycle 150 - 250; motorcaravan small 600 - 800, large 600 - 950; electricity 250 - 350. Less 40-60% for 3 days or more 1/10 - 31/5.

Reservations: Write to site. Address: 8650 Vila do Bispo (Algarve). Tel: 082/624371. FAX: 082/624445.

820 Orbitur Camping Valverde, Praia da Luz, nr Lagos

Large, well run site with many individual pitches and good range of amenities.

A little over 1 km. from the village of Praia da Luz and its beach and about 5 km. from Lagos, this site is certainly worth considering for your stay in the Algarve. Taking around 1,000 units, it has 600 numbered pitches, mostly 40-60 sq.m., some larger - up to 100 sq.m. which are enclosed by hedges. All are on flat ground or broad terraces with good shade in most parts from established trees and shrubs. Six large, clean, toilet blocks, have British style WCs, washbasins and sinks, some with cold water only, free hot showers and units for disabled people. On site is a swimming pool with slide (200 sq.m), children's pool (adults charged, under 10's free). This is an excellent, well maintained site with good security. It attracts a good number of long-term winter visitors who are actively encouraged by Orbitur, and the site is extremely well managed by Senhor Pinto and his wife, who are helpful and friendly.

How to find it: Fork left on N125 road 3 km. west of Lagos to Praia da Luz and site is under 1 km.

General Details: Open all year. 100,000 sq.m. Supermarket, shops, restaurant and bar complex (April - Oct). Takeaway. Coffee shop. Swimming pool with slide (June-Sept). Children's pool. Playground. Tennis court. General room with TV. Excursions. Laundry. Motorcaravan service point. Bungalows, apartments and caravans to let.

Charges 1998: (to 31 May 98) Per person esc. 730; child (5-10 yrs) 365; car 620; m/cycle 430; tent 630 - 960; caravan 630 - 970; motorcaravan 930 - 1,160, all acc. to size; boat 570; electricity (6A) 420. Off season discounts (up to 70%). Credit cards accepted.

Reservations: Contact Orbitur - Central de Reservas, Rua Diogo do Couto, 1-8°, 1100 Lisboa. Tel: (0)1/811 70 00 or 811 70 70. FAX: (0)1/814 80 45. E-mail: info@orbitur.pt. Internet: http://www.orbitur.pt.

821 Camping Albufeira, Albufeira, nr Faro

Attractive, high quality site, with many amenities, close to town and beaches.

The spacious entrance to this site will accommodate the largest of units (watch for severe speed bumps at the barrier!). One of the better sites on the Algarve, with installations and amenities well above the usual standard, and of which the English speaking staff are justifiably proud. The 1,500 pitches are on fairly flat ground with some terracing, trees and shrubs give reasonable shade in most parts. There are some marked and numbered pitches of 50-80 sq.m. Winter stays are encouraged, with many facilities remaining open including a heated pool. An attractively designed complex of traditional Portuguese style buildings on the hill forms the central area of the site, has pleasant views and is surrounded by a variety of flowers, shrubs, well watered lawns and there is a fountain. The waiter and self-service restaurants, a pizzeria, bars and a sound proofed disco, have views across the three swimming pools and a waterslide pool. There are five clean toilet blocks, some a little tired.and all have British style toilets, washbasins, controllable showers, laundry and dishwashing sinks with free hot water throughout. They may be hard pressed when the site is full (July/Aug) and are distant from some pitches.

How to find it: From N125 coast road or N264 (from Lisbon) at new junctions follow signs to `Albufeira'. Site is approx. 1 km. from junctions, on left.

General Details: Open all year. Supermarket and shops. Restaurants. Bars. Disco. Swimming pool complex. Tabac. Laundry. TV room. Hairdresser. Safe deposit. ATM service. Car rental office on site. Children's playground. Excursions and organised entertainment. Bicycles/motorbikes for hire. Tennis. Minigolf. Sports park. Telephone and post box. Medical post. Car wash. Camp bus service to Albufeira (2 km). Caravans and apartments for rent.

Charges 1998: Per adult Esc 795; child (4-10) 395; car 795; caravan or tent 795 - 895, acc. to size; motorcaravan 1170 - 1,790; m/cycle 530; electricity 450. (50% discount winter season).

Reservations: are made to give individual pitch, no deposit or fee. Address: 8200 Albufeira (Algarve). Tel: 089/587629. FAX: 089/587633.

823 Camping Olhão, Pinheiros de Marim, nr Olhão

Large, well laid out and acceptable site in eastern Algarve.

This site, taking around 1,000 units and open all year, has mature trees to provide reasonable shade. The pitches are marked, numbered and in rows divided by shrubs with electricity and water to all parts. Permanent and long stay units take 20% of the pitches and the tourist pitches fill up quickly June and August - so arrive early. Amenities include very pleasant swimming pools and tennis courts (fees for both), a very good restaurant/ bar (open all year, very popular with local Portugese and it accepts credit cards) and a café/bar with TV and games room. The eleven sanitary blocks, which were clean when seen with facilities for disabled campers in one block, are specifically sited to be a maximum of 50 m. from any pitch. Each has British toilets, bidets and a free hot showers. There is some noise nuisance from an adjacent railway. Mobile homes for rent. The large, sandy beaches in this area are on offshore islands reached by ferry and are, as a result, relatively quiet; some are reserved for naturists. There is a bus service to the nearest ferry at Olhao.

How to find it: Just over 1 km. east of Olhão, on EN125, take turn to Pinheiros de Marim. Site is 300 m. on left.

General Details: Open all year, as are all facilities. Supermarket. Kiosk. Restaurant. Bar. Laundry. Children's playgrounds. Swimming pool (all year). Tennis. Volleyball. Bicycle hire. Café and general room with TV. Medical post. Car wash area. Chemical disposal. Bus service 50 m. Mobile homes and caravans to hire.

Charges 1998: Per adult esc. 300 - 600; child (5-12 yrs) 150 - 300; car 250 - 500; tent 200 - 420, 300 - 600 or 500 - 1,000, acc. to size; caravan or motorcaravan 400 - 800 or 600 - 1,200; m/cycle 125 - 250; car 250 - 500; electricity 210. Less for longer winter stays.

Reservations: Contact site. Address: 8700 Olhao (Algarve). Tel: 089/700 1300. FAX 089/700 1390. E-mail: sbsicamping@mail.telepac.pt. Internet: http://www.sbsi.pt/camping.

822 Orbitur Camping, Quarteira, nr Faro

Algarve site near the sea on the outskirts of Quarteira.

This is a large attractive site on undulating ground with some terracing, taking 795 units. On the outskirts of the popular Algarve resort of Quarteira, it is 600 m. from a sandy beach which stretches for 1 km. to the town centre. Many of the unmarked pitches have shade from tall trees and there are a few small individual pitches of 50 sq.m. with electricity and water for reservation. There are 680 electrical connections (15A). The five sanitary blocks provide British and Turkish style toilets, individual basins mainly with cold water, shelves and mirrors, and free hot showers plus new facilities for disabled visitors. Like others along this coast, the site encourages long winter stays. The swimming pools are excellent, featuring adult, children's and a further small pool at the bottom of the water chute (open in high season). There is a large restaurant and supermarket which have a separate entrance for local trade.

How to find it: Turn off N125 south towards Quarteira in Almancil (8 km. west of Faro). Site is 5 km.

General Details: Open all year. 10.6 ha. Supermarket, self-service restaurant (Feb - Nov). Separate takeaway (from late May). General room with bar and TV. Tennis. Kiosk. Open air disco. Medical treatment room. Doctor on call. Washing machines. Car wash area. Motorcaravan services. Orbitur bungalows for hire.

Charges 1998: (to 31 May 99 Per person esc. 740; child (5-10 yrs) 370; car 610; m/cycle 420; tent 620 - 960; caravan 750 - 1,020; motorcaravan 930 - 1,150, all acc. to size; boat 560; electricity 420. Off season discounts (up to 70%). Credit cards accepted.

Reservations: Contact Orbitur - Central de Reservas, Rua Diogo do Couto, 1-8°, 1100 Lisboa. Tel: (0)1/811 70 00 or 811 70 70. FAX: (0)1/814 80 45. E-mail: info@orbitur.pt. Internet: http://www.orbitur.pt.

844 Parque de Campismo Quintos dos Carriços, Praia de Salema

Attractive, peaceful, valley site with dedicated naturist area, in unspoilt western Algarve.

A traditional tiled Portugese style entrance leads you down a steep incline into this excellent and well maintained site which has a village atmosphere. The site has been developed over the years by the Dutch owner and his family. It is spread over two valleys (which are real sun-traps), with the partially terraced pitches marked and divided by trees and shrubs (oleanders and roses). A small stream (dry when seen) meanders through the site. The more remote part of this site which is 250 m. from the main site is dedicated to naturists. Although the site is lit torches may be required in more remote areas. The four sanitary blocks are modern, spacious, well tiled with quality fittings, and are clean. These provide British style WCs, washbasins with cold water, and hot showers on payment. Dishwashing and laundry sinks and a washing machine plus an excellent facility for disabled people. Well stocked mini-market. The restaurant and bar open daily in season. A very popular site for summer and winter sun-worshippers, within easy driving distance of resorts, the many fine beaches provide ample opportunities for diving, swimming and fishing. Nearby are tennis, squash, riding and golf and there are excellent walks.

How to find it: Turn off RN125 (Lagos-Sagres) road at junction to Salema (17 km. from Lagos); site is signed.

General Details: Open all year. Mini-market (all year). Restaurant (daily 1/3-15/10). Bar (once a week only 15/10-1/3). TV room. Telephone and post box. Bicycles, scooters, mopeds and m/cycles for hire. Fishing and golf 1 km. Riding 8 km. Safety deposit. Money exchange. Laundry. Car wash. Chemical disposal. Apartments for rent.

Charges 1999: Per adult esc. 660; child 330; tent 660 - 850; caravan 910; car 660; m/cycle 475; motorcaravan 1,000 - 1,150; electricity 215. Discounts for long winter stays. Credit cards accepted.

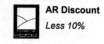

AR Discount
Less 10%

Reservations: Contact site. Address: Praia de Salema, 8650 Vila de Bispo (Algarve). Tel: 082/695201, 695400 or 695401. FAX: 082/695122.

834 Orbitur Camping Evora, Evora

Well equipped site with swimming pool, close to historic walled town.

Situated some 1½ km. from the historic former provincial capital, this is one of the most modern and well equipped sites in the Orbitur chain with the benefit of a good sized, new swimming pool and one for children (separate charge). There is also a pleasant small restaurant, popular also with locals. The manager organises special menus and entertainment for groups if requested. Two refurbished sanitary blocks have free hot showers and modern British style WCs. Most of the 500 good sized pitches have 15A electricity and those in the older part of the site (some 250) have well developed shade. There is a children's play area and tennis court. A small market sells essentials and a range of local specialities. A useful site from which to explore the town and surrounding area with its megalithic monuments.

How to find it: Site is 1½ km. southwest of the town on the N380 road to Alcacovas.

General Details: Open all year. Restaurant, bar, snack bar and shop (April-Oct). Swimming pool (May - Sept). Tennis court. Children's play area. Shop. Laundry. Motorcaravan services. Mobile homes for rent

Charges 1998: (to 31 May 99) Per person esc. 600; child (5-10 yrs) 300; car 510; m/cycle 350; tent 500 - 840; caravan 610 - 930; motorcaravan 740 - 1,000, all acc. to size; boat 370; electricity 380. Off season discounts (up to 70%). Credit cards accepted.

Reservations: Contact Orbitur - Central de Reservas, Rua Diogo do Couto, 1-8°, 1100 Lisboa. Tel: (0)1/811 70 00 or 811 70 70. FAX: (0)1/814 80 45. E-mail: info@orbitur.pt. Internet: http://www.orbitur.pt.

835 Camping Markadia, Barragem de Odivelas, nr Alvito

Superb, lakeside touring site, in unspoilt setting.

This site will appeal most to those nature lovers who want to 'get away from it all' and who enjoy pursuits such as walking, fishing or riding. The lake is in fact a 2,500 ha. reservoir, and more than 120 species of birds can be found in the area. The open countryside and lake provide excellent views and a very pleasant environment, albeit somewhat remote. This is an outstanding site by any standards. The stellar views in the very low ambient lighting are wonderful at night, the site is lit but a torch is required. There are 130 unmarked pitches on undulating grassy ground with ample 16A electrical connections. The friendly Dutch owner has carefully planted the site so each pitch has its own oak tree to provide shade. Four very modern, clean, and superbly equipped sanitary blocks, are built in traditional Portuguese style. They have controllable showers, British style WCs and bidets, washbasins, dishwashing and laundry sinks (open air); free hot water throughout. The bar/ restaurant with terrace is open daily in season but weekends only in winter. One can swim in the reservoir and rowing boats, pedaloes and windsurfers may be hired. You may bring boats, although power boats are discouraged on environmental grounds. Facilities and amenities may be reduced outside the main season.

How to find it: From the N2 between Torrao and Ferreira do Alentejo, take the E257 2 km. north of Odivelas for 3.5 km. Turn right towards Barragam, site is 3 km. on left after crossing head of reservoir, follow wide dirt track.

General Details: Open all year. Bar. Restaurant (Oct - March weekends only or on request). Shop (all year). Lounge. Children's playground. Telephone. Medical post. Fishing. Boat hire. Bicycle hire. Tennis. Riding. Laundry. Car wash. Chemical disposal. Motorcaravan service point. Apartments for rent. Dogs not permitted July/Aug.

Charges 1998: Per adult esc.720; child (5-10 yrs) 360; tent or caravan 720; car or m/cycle 720; motorcaravan 1,440; electricity 360. Less up to 60% acc. to season. No credit cards.

AR Discount
Less 10%

Reservations: are made - write to site for details. Address: Aptdo 17, Barragem de Odivelas, 7920 Alvito. Tel: 084/763141. FAX: 084/763102.

836 Parque Municipal de Campismo, Barragem de Idanha-a-Nova

Smart, good value site, with pool and quality installations, in attractive location. near Castelo Branco

This very attractive, well laid out site is unlike most municipal sites with its high level of sophistication. It is located in quiet, unspoilt countryside close to a reservoir, near the small town of Idanha-a-Nova. The site has around 500 spacious unmarked pitches on wide grassy terraces and there is a little shade from young trees. Electricity (16A) is included in the price. The four large sanitary blocks, built in the traditional Portuguese style, provide plentiful British style WCs (some with bidets), washbasins, some in private cabins, free hot showers, foot baths and facilities for disabled visitors. Dishwashing and laundry sinks (cold water). Amenities include tennis courts with stadium-style spectator seating and a medium sized swimming pool with child's pool, together with several children's playgrounds. Good supermarket, restaurant, bar and terrace complex is located centrally on site, open in high season.

How to find it: Approach from the south using the N240. Turn off at Ladoeiro on to N354 and follow signs to Barragem and site. Do not approach via the town of Idanha-a-Nova.

General Details: Open all year. Supermarket (1/7-30/9). Cafe, bar and restaurant (1/7-30/9). Swimming pool. Tennis. TV room. Washing machines. Medical post. Car wash. Canoe hire. Bungalows for hire.

Charges 1998: Per adult esc. 250; child (4-10 yrs) 125; tent (small) 125, (large) 375; caravan 500; car 250; m/cycle 125; motorcaravan 500; electricity 120. Discounts for long stay off season.

Reservations: Write to site. Address: Barragem de Idanha-a-Nova, Castelo Branco. Tel: 077/22793.

832 Orbitur Camping Guarda, Guarda

Small inland site perched on a hill-top, with a good panoramic view.

This site takes around 135 units and is just 50 km. from the Spanish frontier, on perhaps the most popular route for entering Portugal, so it makes a good transit site. Mostly covered by mature pine trees, it is on sloping, and in places terraced, ground partially surrounding a public park. There are some level pitches for caravans and the site is well lit at night. The two sanitary blocks are an adequate supply with British and Turkish style toilets, washbasins with cold water and three free hot showers per sex. Electrical connections (long leads may be required). The service provided by the restaurant/bar tends to be tailored to demand. Guarda has some interesting historic buildings and the region is also noted for its colourful markets, Serra cheese, handicrafts of all descriptions, religious festivals and winter sports.

How to find it: Site is 5 km. from the new bypass road on a hill-top on western side of town. Follow signs for the centre of Guarda then camp signs.

General Details: Open 1 March - 30 Oct. Mini-market, restaurant, bar (May - Sept). General room with TV. Telephone and post box. First aid. Laundry. Motorcaravan service point. Bus service 50 m.

Charges 1998: (to 31 May 99) Per person esc. 590; child (5-10 yrs) 290; car 500; m/cycle 340; tent 480 - 820; caravan 590 - 920; motorcaravan 710 - 1,000, all acc. to size; boat 380; electricity 380. Off season discounts (up to 70%). Credit cards accepted.

Reservations: Contact Orbitur - Central de Reservas, Rua Diogo do Couto, 1-8°, 1100 Lisboa. Tel: (0)1/811 70 00 or 811 70 70. FAX: (0)1/814 80 45. E-mail: info@orbitur.pt. Internet: http://www.orbitur.pt.

PORTUGAL - Inland

831 Orbitur Camping Castro Daire, Castro Daire

Traditional small touring site beside the Carvalhal spa.

Situated in the mountains in the Dao Lafões tourist region, between Castro Daire and Visieu, only the main road (somewhat noisy but quite well screened) separates the site from the sulphur spa and hotel complex. This has a swimming pool and tennis court (open from June). The site is small, very attractive with a garden-like atmosphere, and has two modern and clean sanitary blocks. These have free hot showers, British toilets and washbasins with cold water. There are sinks for clothes and washing up at various points through the site. The pitches are on level grass, terraced in places, with some shade from pine and oak trees. There are 60 electrical connections (15A). A small purpose built building has an open fire to barbecue food and there is a snack bar. This is a comfortable base from which one can explore the historic old spa towns and villages of this most beautiful and unspoilt mountain region.

How to find it: Site is 5 km. south of Castro Daire beside the A2 road to Visieu.

General Details: Open 1 June - 30 Sept. Bar (July/Aug). Barbecue house. Children's playground. Telephone and post box. Laundry. Tourist information.

Charges 1998: (to 31 May 99) Per person esc. 490; child (5-10 yrs) 245; car 440; m/cycle 310; tent 410 - 710; caravan 510 - 780; motorcaravan 620 - 960, all acc. to size; boat 360; electricity 380. Off season discounts (up to 70%). Credit cards not accepted.

Reservations: Contact Orbitur - Central de Reservas, Rua Diogo do Couto, 1-8°, 1100 Lisboa. Tel: (0)1/811 70 00 or 811 70 70. FAX: (0)1/814 80 45. E-mail: info@orbitur.pt. Internet: http://www.orbitur.pt.

833 Orbitur Camping Arganil, Sarzedo, nr Arganil

Quiet, inland site attractively situated on the hillside above the river Alva.

The site is located in the hamlet of Sarzedo, some 2 km. from the town of Arganil. A spacious and well planned site, delightfully situated among pine trees above the River Alva where one can swim, fish, canoe and windsurf. The 150 pitches, most with electricity (15A), are of a reasonable size and are mainly on flat sandy grass terraces shaded by tall trees. The site is kept beautifully clean and neat. Access roads are tarmac. There is an excellent restaurant serving local food and an attached bar with terrace, plus a shop (closed Tuesdays) and a children's play area. Sanitary facilities are clean and well maintained, with mainly British WCs, controllable free hot showers, washbasins in semi-private partitioned cabins and hairdressing area. Ramped entrances make it suitable for disabled visitors.

How to find it: From EN17 Guarda-Coimbra road, take EN342 towards Arganil. Site is signed in the village of Sarzedo, about 2 km. northwest of Arganil.

General Details: Open all year. Restaurant. Bar (July/Aug). Children's play area. TV room. Tennis. Telephone and post box. Laundry. Car wash. Swimming pool in Arganil. Bus service 50 m. Bungalows for hire.

Charges 1998: (to 31 May 99) Per person esc. 490; child (5-10 yrs) 245; car 440; m/cycle 310; tent 410 - 710; caravan 510 -780; motorcaravan 620 - 960, all acc. to size; boat 360; electricity 380. Off season discounts (up to 70%). Credit cards not accepted.

Reservations: Contact Orbitur - Central de Reservas, Rua Diogo do Couto, 1-8°, 1100 Lisboa. Tel: (0)1/811 70 00 or 811 70 70. FAX: (0)1/814 80 45. E-mail: info@orbitur.pt. Internet: http://www.orbitur.pt.

837 Parque Campismo de Cerdeira, Campo do Gerês

Impressive, quiet, 'away from it all' site with excellent facilities, in National Park.

Placed in the National Park of Peneda Gerês, amidst spectacular mountain scenery, this excellent modern site offers modern facilities in a truly natural area. The National Park is home to all manner of flora, fauna and wildlife, including the roebuck, weasel, badger, wolf and wild boar. The well fenced, quiet, site has some 350 good sized unmarked, mostly level, grassy pitches in a shady woodland setting. Electricity (5 or 10A) is available for most pitches, though some long leads may be required. Although the site is lit, a torch would be useful. There are three very clean sanitary blocks with mixed style WCs, washbasins and controllable showers. Hot water is free throughout. Dishwashing and laundry sinks under cover. A very large timber, lodge style complex which is tastefully designed and decorated near the site entrance provides a restaurant serving a full range of good value meals (including breakfasts). The restaurant is being extended for '99. There is a bar and terrace, mini-market and a small playground for children. Fishing, riding, swimming, canoeing, mountain biking and climbing in the area.

How to find it: From N103 (Braga-Chaves road), turn left at the 101 signed Vilaverde. Turn right to Terras de Bouro (road 308 and 205-3). From Terras de Bouro take the 307 to Covied, turn left at site sign, site is 5 km.

General Details: Open all year. Mini-market. Restaurant/bar (1/4-15/10, but open at weekend and holidays). Children's playground. Bicycle hire. TV room. Telephone and post box. Medical post. Laundry. Motorcaravan services. Tourist information. Bungalows for hire. Good English spoken.

Charges 1999: Per adult esc. 600 - 700; child (5-11 yrs) 350 - 450; tent 600 - 900; small tent 500 - 600; caravan 700 - 1,000; car 550 - 650; m/cycle 350 - 450 ; motorcaravan: 800 - 1,100; electricity 4A 350, 10A 750. Credit cards accepted.

Reservations: Contact site. Address: Campo do Gerês, 4840 Terras de Bouro. Tel: 053/351005 or 357065. FAX: 053/357065.

AR Discount

Less 10% in high season, 20% low

838 Parque Natural de Vilar de Mouros, nr Seixas

Traditional, small and friendly site, in quiet country location, with own pool.

Located some 15 minutes walk (downhill) from the village of Vilar de Mouros and very close to the Spanish border, this small site is ideal for those looking for a more traditional campsite. The 45 marked pitches for caravans and motorcaravans, all with electricity (2 or 5A), are on slightly sloping, grassy terraces, with a separate unmarked area for tents, all set amongst trees and vines on a hillside. There are two toilet blocks, very much in the quainter, older Portuguese style, providing British style WCs (some with bidets), washbasins (cold water), and free hot showers, they also had soap and paper towel dispensers. Dishwashing and laundry sinks (cold water) under cover also a washing machine and dryer in a separate building. The site has a good range of other amenities which include a tennis court, unusual small stone swimming pool, children's pool (free to campers), and a small children's play area. There is a good cafe/bar (open 8 am.-11 pm), takeaway service, a self-service restaurant with shady terrace, and a mini-market. By far the most popular attraction is the regular Saturday evening organised gastronomic and folklore trips (with free mini-bus transport) to the site owners own hotel 2 km. away. There are mobile homes and hotel rooms for hire. French and a little English spoken.

How to find it: Site is signed from the N13, just north of Seixas, turn towards Vilar de Mouros. Site is on right just before village.

General Details: Open all year. Mini-market. Cafe/bar. Self-service restaurant. Swimming pool. Tennis court. TV room. Washing machine. Children's pool and playground. Telephone and post box. Medical post. Bicycle hire. Local folklore entertainment trips. Hotel rooms and mobile homes for rent.

Charges 1999: Per adult esc. 550; child 270; tent (small) 500, (large) 500; caravan 500 - 600; car 450; m/cycle 300; motorcaravan 500 - 600; electricity 400

Reservations: Contact site. Address: Vilar de Mouros, 4910 Caminha. Tel: 058/727472. FAX: as phone.

THE ORBITUR CHAIN OF CAMPS

Orbitur is the largest Portugese campsite chain which has sites all over Portugal and boasts a central booking agency and E mail service which may be used to avoid disappointment at peak season. There are 22 sites which have prime camping pitches and supporting facilities along with bungalows and mobile homes for rent. The following sites have not been inspected for this guide:

Orbitur Camping Visieu   **Orbitur Camping Angeiras**

Orbitur Camping Montargil   **Orbitur Camping Portalegre**

Orbitur Camping Madalena-Gaia

Reservations for any of the sites should be made through the central office (not to individual sites); write to Orbitur at:

Orbitur - Central de Reservas,

Rua Diogo do Couto, 1-8°, 1100 Lisboa.

Tel: (0)1/811 70 00 or 811 70 70. FAX: (0)1/814 80 45.

E-mail: info@orbitur.pt. Internet: http://www.orbitur.pt.

See colour advert
between pages 320/1

Membership of the Orbitur Camping Club, taken either with your booking or at any site (free for pensioners) grants a 10% discount on site charges. Camp charges are reasonable and there is a general reduction of 40% to 70% (depending on length of stay) from October to March inclusive.

"Orbitur has been offering a quality camping service for over 30 years, always concentrating on quality of service. The Orbitur sites are well maintained and are in good locations. All sites strive to satisfy the needs of all campers, including handicapped people. Children's needs and playgrounds are common to all sites and entertainment is becoming the norm at all sites in summer. Orbitur also offers a vast range of sports facilities along with a programme of providing swimming pools for most sites. Health and safety is of prime importance with first aid centres being provided along with efficient and effective safety systems which comply with local control authorities."

Colin Samms

SPAIN

Spain, which occupies the larger part of the Iberian peninsula, is the fourth largest country in Europe, with extremes of climate, widely contrasting geographical features and diversity of language, culture and artistic traditions. The peninsula's dominant feature is the Meseta, the immense plateau at its centre, where the summer heat is intense and the winters long and rigorous. The area to the north, with the mountains of the Pyrenees and the Asturian Picos de Europa, is the exact opposite with no extremes of temperature - green and lush. The east and south coast, protected by the Sierra ranges, enjoy a typically Mediterranean climate and in the extreme south there is virtually no winter season. In Almeria and Murcia, lack of rain as on the Meseta, gives rise to an almost desert landscape, however, the coastline has become a Mecca for those seeking sun all the year. Great monuments survive from a history affected by the Romans, Moors and the Renaissance, but modern Spain is breaking out as the '90s develop. Already Spain has hosted the Olympics, the World Fair and Madrid has been the Cultural Capital of Europe; a long cry from the 33 year dictatorship of Franco. There is a vitality about Spain now and in the cities there is always something happening - in politics, in fashion, in the clubs, on the streets, not forgetting the more traditional fiestas. Tourism is important to Spain, as the 'Costas' have proved, but there is a new awareness of the needs of the more discerning independent traveller, a new, albeit long overdue, concern for the environment and generally a more welcoming attitude.

Spain's capital is, of course, Madrid, but the country is divided, like the USA or Germany, Austria or Switzerland, into 17 different federal states called `autonomias', each with its own capital. For example the capital of Catalunya is Barcelona, that of Galicia is Santiago de Compostela; each federal state has its own government and parliament, and its own prime minister. The central government in Madrid retains power over the national economy and foreign affairs, for example, but other matters such as tourism are the exclusive preserve of the autonomias, which explains why there are different regulations for camping, caravanning and campsites in the various different autonomias. These differences extend to matters such as `wild camping', `overnighting' and even the classification (grading) of campsites.

So far as campsites are concerned, Spain has much to offer in terms of some of the best large sites in Europe, such as Playa Montroig, but it also has many attractive smaller sites which will appeal to many of our readers. There are quite a lot of sites which claim to be open all year, but services on most may well be limited to a minimum (eg. only one sanitary block operating and the shop open at weekends only). Even though all the sites featured in this guide have indicated positively that they will be open during the periods stated, we would still advise anyone contemplating a visit out of season to check first rather than rely entirely on information provided so far in advance! Readers should also bear in mind that a pitch of 80 sq.m. is considered to be large in Spain (worth remembering if you have a large outfit), although many sites, particularly in Catalunya, are now increasing pitch size to 100 sq.m. Finally we should mention that there has been a growing tendency in recent years for what we call `Spanish weekenders' - domestic tourism, whereby the Spanish themselves take pitches for an extended period to use as a weekend `holiday home' - this tends to give some sites a rather strange appearance during the week when many pitches are occupied by caravans, tents, etc. but not a soul is to be seen.

Spanish National Tourist Office, 57/58 St James's Street, London, SW1A 1LD

Tel: 0171 499 0901. Fax: 0171 629 4257

Population
39,000,000, density 77 per sq. km.

Capital
Madrid

Climate
Spain has a very varied climate depending where you are and the time of year. Temperate in the north, which also has most of the rainfall, dry and very hot in the centre, subtropical along the Mediterranean coast . The average winter temperature in Malaga is 57°F.

Language
Castilian Spanish is spoken by most people with Catalan (northeast), Basque (north) and Galician (northwest) also used in their respective areas.

Currency
Spanish peseta which circulates in coins of 1, 5, 10, 25, 50, 100, 200 and 500 ptas, and notes of 1000, 2000, 5000 and 10,000 ptas.

Banks
Open Mon-Fri 09.00-14.00 Sat 09.00-13.00 (only certain towns). In tourist areas you will also find 'cases de cambio' with more convenient hours.

Post Offices
Offices (Correos) open Mon-Sat 08.00-12..00. Some open late afternoon, while some in the large cities open 08.00-15.00. Queues can be long and stamps can be bought at tobacconists (tabac).

Time
GMT plus 1 (summer BST + 1).

Telephone
From the UK, the code is 00 34 followed by the internal area code, *including* the initial 9, and exchange number. To call the UK dial 07 44. Make international calls from 'telefone internacional' boxes or from 'Telefonica' offices.

Public Holidays
New Year; Epiphany; Saint's Day, 19 Mar; Maundy Thurs; Good Fri; Easter Mon; Labour Day; Saint's Day, 25 July; Assumption, 15 Aug; National Day, 12 Oct; All Saints Day, 1 Nov; Constitution Day, 6 Dec; Immaculate Conception, 8 Dec; Christmas, 25 Dec.

Shops
Open Mon-Sat 09.00-13.00/14.00, afternoons 15.00/16.00-19.30/20.00. Many open longer.

Food: The Spanish in general eat much later than we do. Lunches start at 13.00 or 14.00 and evening meals 21.00-22.00, so the streets remain lively until late. You can go to a 'restaurante' for a full meal or to a 'bar' where you have a succession of 'tapas' (small snacks) or 'raciones' (larger ones). Fish stews (zarzuelas) and rice based 'paellas' are often memorable.

Motoring

The surface of the main roads is on the whole good, although secondary roads in some rural areas can be rough and winding and have slow, horse drawn traffic. In Catalan and Basque areas you will find alternative names on the signposts, for example, Gerona - Girona and San Sebastian - Donostia.

Tolls: Payable on certain roads - A1, 2, 4, 6, 7, 8, 9, 15, 18, 19, 66, 68 and for the Cadi Tunnel , the Vallvidrera Tunnel (nr. Barcelona) and the Tunnel de Garraf on the A16.

Fuel: Petrol stations on motorways often open 24 hrs. Credit cards are accepted at most stations. **Speed Limits:** Built-up areas 31 mph (50 kph) or less for both car and car towing. Other roads 56/62 mph (90/100 kph). On motorways, 75 mph (120 kph). For cars towing: other roads 43/50 mph (70/80 kph), on motorways 50 mph (80 kph). **Parking:** 'Blue' parking zones (zone azul) are indicated by signs and discs are available from hotels, the town hall and travel agencies. In the centre of some large towns there is a zone 'ora' where parking is allowed only against tickets bought in tobacconists.

Overnighting

There are different regulations in the various different autonomias (see introduction).

Useful Addresses

Real Automovil Club de Espana (RACE), José Abascal 10, 28003 Madrid 3 . Tel: 4773200.

Costa Brava

The Costa Brava was the archetype Spanish destination in the early years of mass tourism and the tower blocks in some of the resorts are a dubious testimony to the days of the £50 package holiday. Fortunately package holiday trends changed before the developers could wreak total havoc and many villages and resorts remain very attractive and retain their charm, helped enormously by the towering cliffs and sheltered coves which give this coast its name - the 'Wild Coast'. There are of course some distinctly lively resorts, such as Lloret, Tossa and Calella in the province of Barcelona, but also several quieter ones. The coastal scenery is often spectacular and the climate pleasant - somewhat less hot than further south - making this one of the most attractive areas for the British, particularly for those who drive through France, since it is possible to reach the Costa Brava with only one night stop en-route.

8005 Camping Cadaqués, Cadaqués

Small site with large pool and mountain views overlooking Port Lligat.

Picturesque Cadaqués is accessible by a winding road over the hills behind Roses and has an air of isolation. The attractive promenade is lined with restaurants and you can sit and watch the fishermen land their catches. The site is on the outskirts of Port Lligat where Salvador Dali constructed his famous home which has recently been opened to the public. This site is ideal as a stopover point to see this magnificent house in a most unusual setting or to enjoy the local cuisine, beaches and watersports. There are 200 pitches of 60-70 sq.m, some with a slight slope, and a separate area for tents. This is used by transit campers who are mainly staying short periods to visit the Dali attraction rather than to stay for extended periods. The large swimming pool is adjacent to the bar and restaurant with a large terrace giving stunning views of the mountains, the Port of Lligat, Dali's house and the nature reserve. The site has an extremely large well stocked supermarket, which produces its own bread and there are in-house laundry facilities. There are few activities other than the pool and we stress that this is more a site to be used strategically rather than for holidays - there is no other site nearby to facilitate access to this area. The Port of Lligat is slowly being changed to accommodate the visitors to what is anticipated to become one of the most popular historic destinations in Spain.

How to find it: Leave autopista A7 (Figueres - Girona) at exit 4 and take C260 to Roses and on to Cadaqués.

General Details: Open Easter - 15 Sept. Electricity connections (5/10A). Restaurant/bar. Supermarket. Swimming pool (high season). Dogs not accepted. Laundry service and ironing. Chemical disposal.

Charges 1998: Per adult ptas 535; child 410; tent 675; caravan 675; car 535; m/cycle 430; motorcaravan 980; electricity 385. Plus 7% VAT. Credit cards accepted.

Reservations: not generally necessary. Address: Ctra. de Port Lligat 17, 17488 Cadaqués (Costa Brava). Tel: 972/258126. FAX: 972/159383.

SPAIN - Costa Brava

Camping-Caravaning Castell Mar and Camping Castell Montgri

Due to popular demand we have re-instated these two campsites which, although seen recently by our Spanish agent, we have not visited since 1996. These are, theredore, brief `interim' reports:

8010 Camping-Caravaning Castell Mar, Castelló d'Empúries, nr Figueres

With around 70% of the pitches here occupied by tour operators, readers may be surprised that we should include this site in a guide aimed primarily at independent campers and caravanners. The reason is that those areas of the site which do cater for independent visitors are very attractive and the site generally offers a wide range of good quality facilities and activities.

How to find it: Site is on main Torroella de Montgri - L'Estartit GE641 road, clearly signed.

Open: Early May - mid-October.

8071 Camping Castell Montgri, L'Estartit, nr Gerona/Girona

This is a modern seaside holiday site with only about 300 pitches and quite suitable for families. Situated just behind the sand-dunes and beach, it is close to the famous Empuria Brava complex.

How to find it: Site is adjacent to the PK405 coast road between L'Escala and Roses.

Open: Early May - late September.

8015 Camping-Caravanning La Laguna, Empuria Brava

Unusually relaxed spacious site on isthmus, with direct access to beach and estuary.

La Laguna is aptly named, the site actually being spilt into two halves joined by a bridge over the lagoon. The approach to the site is by a long (4 km.), more or less, private road. This is quite an unusual site for this area, being laid out very informally among mature pine trees, in contrast to other large more formally designed sites nearby. More trees have been planted in newer areas on the other side of the lagoon. There are 750 pitches clearly marked on grass and sand, all with 6A electricity (a long lead may be useful). The facilities, particularly the sanitary installations, are quite elderly and the site's attraction is much more in terms of its informality, friendliness and value for money (particularly for long stays) than its amenities. Four toilets blocks, placed to avoid long walks, are simple in design but adequate, with free hot water, plenty of dishwashing sinks, well equipped laundry room and chemical disposal. An attractive bar restaurant overlooks the lagoon and a swimming pool and riding school are on site (May-Sept), likewise a bar and shop. There is beach frontage with a sailing school. It is said to be possible to cross over to Empuria Brava when the tide is out. The river is hidden by a high bank with a path along the top.

continued overleaf

8015 Camping-Caravanning La Laguna (continued)

How to find it: Site is signed from the Castello d'Empuries bypass at the junction with the road for Sant Pere Pescador. Follow approach road for approx. 4 km.

Charges guide: Per person ptas. 470 - 730; child (5-10 yrs) 400 - 600; tent or caravan 470 - 730; car 470 - 730; motorcaravan 830 - 1,280; m/cycle 400 - 600; electricity 400. Less for longer stays and OAPs. Credit cards accepted.

General Details: Open 27 March - 24 Oct. Bar. Restaurant. Shop. Swimming pool (15/5-15/9). Tennis (free in low season). Minigolf. Sailing school. Fishing. Bicycle hire. Riding. Chemical disposal. Mobile homes to let.

Reservations: Contact site for details. Address: 17486 Castello d'Empuries (Girona). Tel: 972/45.05.53 (when closed 972/20.86.67). FAX: 972/45.07.99 (when closed 972/20.86.67). E-mail: info@campinglaguna.com. Internet: www.campinglaguna.com.

AR Discount
Less 5% for over 21 days

8020 Camping-Caravaning Int. Amberes, Empuria Brava

Large, friendly site 50 m. from wide, sandy beach.

Situated in the 'Venice of Spain', Empuria Brava is interlaced with inland waterways and canals, where many residents and holiday-makers moor their boats directly outside their homes on the canal banks. Internacional Amberes is 50 m. from the wide, sandy beach, which is bordered on the east and west by the waterway canals (no access into them from the beach, only by car on the main road). The site can arrange temporary moorings for boats at Empuria Brava on request. The sea breeze here appears regularly during the afternoon so watersports are very good and hire facilities are available. Amberes is a surprisingly pretty and hospitable site where people seem to make friends easily and get to know the staff, who organise the sports and children's programmes. The site has 650 hedged pitches with light shade from many smallish trees, 550 with electricity and water, and there are pleasant views from some parts. Sanitary facilities are in four blocks, all recently renovated and with hot showers, British style WCs and vanity style washbasins. The restaurant and bar are located on entry to the site rather than around the pool area. The small, pleasant restaurant adjoining the bar area serves excellent food in copious quantities and tables outside add to the atmosphere. The swimming pool is on an elevated terrace, raised out of view of most onlookers, with a small children's pool adjoining. Football and volleyball are organised and a 'secret garden' style minigolf is special. Rented accommodation includes mobile homes, bungalows and apartments in a complex opposite the pool.

How to find it: Site is signed from the main roundabout leading into Empuria Brava from the Roses - Castello d'Empuries road (4 km. from Roses).

General Details: Open 15 May - 30 Sept. Supermarket. Restaurant/bar. Disco bar and restaurant. Takeaway. Watersports - windsurfing school. Boat moorings. Organised activities and entertainment. Swimming pool. Football. Table tennis. Tennis. Bicycle hire. Riding. Fishing. Volleyball. Minigolf. Golf 15 km. Children's play- grounds (one new). Washing machines. Chemical disposal. Motorcaravan service point. Accommodation for rent.

Charges 1999: Per adult ptas. 430 - 600; child (2-12 yrs) 310 - 500; tent or caravan 760 - 1,580; car 430 - 600; m/cycle 390 - 550; motorcaravan 990 - 1,990; electricity 420. Less 20% for pensioners for stays of 15 days or over in low seasons. Credit cards accepted.

Reservations: Contact site for booking form. Address: 17487 Empuriabrava (Girona). Tel: 972/45.05.07 (1/5-30/9). FAX: 972/67.12.86 (all year).

8035 Camping Caravaning L'Amfora, Sant Pere Pescador

See colour advert opposite page 288

Spacious, medium sized site with direct access to the beach.

This is a friendly, colourful site with a Greek theme to its appearance. There are 525 pitches, all with electrical connections and most with water tap, on level grass with small trees and shrubs. Of these, 64 pitches are large (180 sq.m.) and have their own, individual sanitary facilities. This rare feature consists of small blocks of four units (toilet, shower and washbasin), each unit 'owned' by one pitch for their stay - virtually 'en-suite' camping. The other main sanitary blocks offer free hot water, washbasins in cabins, hairdryers and baby rooms. Further separated pitches of 95 sq.m. have been developed with limited shade as yet. Access is good for disabled visitors. An inviting terraced bar and self-service restaurant overlook two large swimming pools (one for children), which are divided by an attractive arch and fountain. A restaurant, takeaway, pizza service and supermarket are available. Sports facilities include two tennis courts, basketball and horse riding (in season). Evening entertainment (pub, disco, shows) and children's animation are organised in season and watersports activities available on the beach.

How to find it: From A7 motorway take exit 3 (N-11) towards Girona/Barcelona. Exit for Figueres/Roses towards Roses on the C260 and, 9 km. before Roses turn right to Sant Pere Pescador.

General Details: Open Easter, then 15 May - 30 Sept. Bar. Self service and waiter service restaurants. Takeaway. Pizza service. Swimming pools. Table tennis. Tennis. Windsurfing. Sailing. Bicycle hire. Minigolf. Football. Volleyball. Children's playground. Entertainment and organised activities for children. Supermarket. Exchange facilities. Car wash. Laundry facilities. Bungalows and mobile homes to rent.

Charges 1999: Per person ptas. 450 - 500; child (2-9 yrs) 350 - 400; pitch 1,600 - 3,500, with individual sanitary 2,200 - 4,800, large pitch (180 sq.m.) with sanitary 2,600 - 5,600; electricity (5A) incl. Plus 7% VAT. Discounts for pensioners for long stays. No credit cards.

AR Discount
Less 10% on pitch in low season

Reservations: With deposit (ptas. 10,000) and fee (2,500). Address: Av. Josep Tarradellas 2, 17470 Sant Pere Pescador (Girona). Tel: 972/52.05.40 or 52.05.42. FAX: 972/52.05.39.

SPAIN - Costa Brava

8030 Camping Nautic Almata, Castelló d'Empúries, nr Figueres

Seaside site with swimming pool, boat moorings, watersports and entertainment.

Situated in the middle of the Bay of Roses, south of Empuria Brava and beside the Parc Natural dels Aiguamolls de l'Empordà, this is a site of particular interest for nature lovers (especially bird watchers). A beautifully laid out site, it is arranged around the river and waterways, so will suit those who like to camp close to water. It is worth visiting because of its unusual aspects and the feeling of being on the canals, as well as being at a high grade beach-side site. A big site with 1,300 fairly similar, large, individual, numbered pitches, all with electricity and on flat ground. Its name no doubt derives from the fact that boats can be tied up at a small marina within a lagoon in the site. A slipway also gives access to a river and thence to the sea, giving good opportunities for watersports. There is also direct access from one end of the site to a long sandy beach and on site there is a swimming pool of 300 sq.m. with much grassy sunbathing space. A good bar/restaurant, rotisserie and pizzeria are near the pool, with shade. The sanitary blocks are all of a high standard and recently renovated, with a new one added. They have British style toilets, washbasins with shelf or flat surface, free hot showers, fully controllable with two taps, some en-suite showers and basins and also baby baths. Taps to draw hot water for washing-up and laundry sinks. Good facilities for disabled visitors. There is an impressive entertainment programme for both children and adults all season. The facilities on this site are impressive.

How to find it: Site is signed off the C252 between Castello d'Empuries and Vildemat at end of 1 km access road.

General Details: Open 10 May - 27 Sept. including all facilities. Excellent supermarket. Restaurant and bar. Also two separate bars by beach where discos held in main season. Water-ski and windsurfing schools. Tennis, squash, volleyball, `fronton' all provided free. Minigolf. Games room with pool and table tennis. Extensive riding tuition with own stables and stud. Children's play park (near river). Hairdresser. Car, motorcycle and bicycle hire. Free car wash. Washing machines. Chemical disposal. 10 bungalows and 50 self-contained rooms for hire. One tour operator.

Charges 1998: Per pitch ptas 1,665, 3,275 or 3,900; person (over 3 yrs) 305 - 350; boat 740 - 900; dog 355 - 435. All plus 7% VAT. No credit cards.

Reservations: Write to site. Address: 17486 Castelló d'Empúries (Girona). Tel: 972/454477. FAX: 972/454686. E-mail: almata@lix.intercom.es.

8050 Camping Aquarius, Sant Pere Pescador, nr Figueres

Well run family site in quiet seaside situation suited to families and sun-lovers.

Aquarius has direct access to a quiet sandy beach with a gentle slope and good bathing, and is a site for those who really like sun and sea, with a quiet situation. One third of the site has good shade with a park-like atmosphere. An extension with less shade provided an opportunity to enlarge the pitches and they are now all at least 70-100 sq.m. which is good for Spain. A total of 430 are all numbered with 400 6A electrical connections. The main sanitary facilities are in attractive, large tiled blocks with British toilets, washbasins set in flat surfaces, all with hot water (some in private cabins for each sex) and free hot showers, fully controllable. Facilities for disabled people are provided plus baths for children and there is also hot water in the sinks. An excellent new block has under-floor heating, so is open all season, features family cabins with showers and basins. A large terrace area outside the bar/restaurant is unusually designed with split level terraces and attractive flower and water arrangements by the German owner who not only has an architectural background, but also has a wealth of knowledge on the whole Catalan area and culture. He has written a booklet of suggested tours (available from reception). The whole family are justifiably proud of the site, which is strictly and efficiently run, and they continue to make improvements (eg. a good new tarmac access road completed recently). There is a 50 sq.m. `play centre', open all season and with a qualified attendant and a playground near the beach. The sea here is shallow for quite a long way out. The beach bar complex with shaded terraces and minigolf has marvellous views over the Bay of Roses. The `Surf Center' with rentals, school and shop is ideal for enthusiasts and beginners alike.

How to find it: Turn off main road by bridge south of Sant Pere Pescador and follow camp signs; the site reports that the access road has now been resurfaced.

General Details: Open Easter - 16 Oct. Supermarket with butcher. Pleasant restaurant and bar with terrace. Restaurant and bar by beach. `Surf Center'. Takeaway. Children's playground and games hall. Play centre. Table tennis. Volleyball. Minigolf. Bicycle hire. Football field. Boules. Riding 5 km. Golf 12 km. Barbecue and dance once weekly when numbers justify. Special animation for children. Dogs allowed in one section. Laundry facilities. Car wash. Chemical disposal. Motorcaravan service point. Site is run by a German family who speak good English.

Charges 1999: Per adult 425 - 550 ptas; child (1-10 yrs) 275 - 400; car 425 - 550; m/cycle 325 - 475; tent or caravan 900 - 2,300; motorcaravan (up to 3.6 tons) 1,325 - 2,850; animal 235 - 425; electricity 400. All plus 7% VAT. Discounts for pensioners on longer stays. No credit cards.

Reservations: are made for any length with £50 deposit and £15 fee. Address: 17470 Sant Pere Pescador (Girona). Tel: 972/52.00.03. FAX: 972/55.02.16. E-mail: camping@aquarius.es. Internet: www.aquarius.es.

AR Discount
Stay 10 days,
1 dayfree.

8040 Camping Las Dunas, Sant Pere Pescador, nr Figueres

Large, well organised site beside sandy beach, with pool and many activities.

Las Dunas is right by a sandy beach (with direct access) which stretches along the site for nearly 1 km. with a windsurfing school and beach bar. There is also a much used swimming pool (30 x 14 m.) with small children's pool. Las Dunas is a very large site with 1,500 individual pitches, now increased in size to 100 sq.m. which is good for Spain. They are laid out on flat ground in long regular parallel rows, hedged and with shade available in the older parts of the site. Space is usually available even in the main season. A special area is set aside for campers with dogs. Five excellent large sanitary blocks with resident cleaners (7-9) have British style toilets (no paper - a policy of the management), mostly controllable hot showers and washbasins in cabins. There are facilities for babies and disabled people. There is a large bar with terrace and also a pleasant, more secluded pub-type bar with slightly higher prices. A magnificent disco club, in a soundproof building is reputedly the biggest on the Costa Brava! With free entertainment in season and good security arrangements, this site is good for families with teenagers. Used by British tour operators.

How to find it: Use autostrada exit no. 5 towards Escala and turn north 2 km. before reaching La Escala at sign to St Martin de Ampurias.

General Details: Open 9 May - 25 Sept. Electrical connections in most parts. Large supermarket and other shops. Large self-service restaurant. Takeaways. Large bar with terrace. Disco club. Beach bar in main season. Children's playgrounds. Tennis. Minigolf. Football and rugby pitches. Basketball. Volleyball. Sailing/windsurfing school and other watersports. Organised programme of events 15/6-31/8 - sports, children's games, evening shows, music and entertainment, partly in English. Laundry facilities. Motorcaravan services. Exchange facilities. Large caravans for hire. Dogs taken in only one section mid June-mid Sept.

Charges 1998: Per pitch (any unit) incl. electricity 1,700, 2,200, 3,300 or 3,900 ptas; adult 350; child (2-9 yrs) 300. All plus 7% VAT.

Reservations: made for numbered pitches with deposit and fee. Address: Apdo. de Correus 23, 17130 La Escala, Costa Brava (Girona). Tel: 972/520400 or 520401. FAX: 972/550046.

See colour advert between pages 288/9

8060 Camping La Ballena Alegre 2, Sant Pere Pescador, nr Figueres

Very large site in quiet position by long beach, with own swimming pool.

La Ballena Alegre 2, sister site to the Ballena Alegre south of Barcelona, is a big, relaxed site taking 1,744 units, part in a lightly wooded setting, part open, and with some 1,600 m. of frontage directly onto a sandy beach. The grass pitches are individually numbered and of adequate size (over 200 are 100 sq.m.) with pitching informally arranged. Electrical connections (5A) are available in all parts and there are 48 fully serviced pitches. The site is under new management and all five of the toilet blocks have been refurbished to a very high standard. These feature large pivoting doors for showers, wash cabins, etc, special low facilities for children, baby baths and unusual floors of slatted wood aid drainage. All looks and feels good and seems very functional. A unit for disabled people is in the block nearest reception. There are restaurant and bar areas beside the terraced swimming pool complex (four pools including a children's pool) and there is a good shop and bakery on site (with bread delivered by bike). A little train ferries people along the length of the site. Plenty of entertainment and activities are offered, including a large shop for watersports, with a centre for hire and lessons, and a new open air fitness centre beside the beach bar!

How to find it: Best approach is from the Figueres-La Escala road, turning to the north 2 km. west of La Escala at sign to San Martin d'Empúries and following camp signs. Access has now been entirely asphalted.

General Details: Open 15 May - 27 Sept. 250,000 sq.m. Supermarket. Bar. Self-service restaurant (23/6-28/8). Takeaway (22/5-27/8). `Croissanterie' (15/6-28/8). Full restaurant (evenings all season) and beach bar in high season. Swimming pool complex (all season). Three tennis courts. Table tennis. Watersports centre. Fishing 300 m. Bicycle hire. Fitness centre. Children's playgrounds. Sound proofed disco. Dancing twice weekly and organised activities, sports, entertainments, etc. in season (23/6-24/8) but generally a quiet day. Go-karting nearby with bus service. Safe deposit. Cash point. Resident doctor and site ambulance. Car wash. Dog showers. Launderette. Chemical disposal. Motorcaravan service point. New bungalows to rent (11).

Charges 1998: Per pitch incl. electricity (5A) ptas. 1,700, 3,300 or 3,650, acc. to season; pitch with drainage plus 200; person 350; child (3-9 yrs) 275. All plus 7% VAT. Discount of 10% on pitch charge for pensioners all season. No credit cards.

Reservations: made with deposit (ptas. 12,000), min. 10 days 10/7-10/8; contact site for details. Address: 17470 Sant Pere Pescador (Girona). Tel: 972/53.03.02 or 52.03.26. FAX: 972/52.03.32. E-mail: infb2@ballena-alegre.es. Internet: http://www.ballena-alegre.es. Winter address: Ave. Roma 12, 08015 Barcelona. Tel: 93/226.13.02. FAX: 93/226.65.28.

See colour advert between pages 288/9

SPAIN - Costa Brava

8070 Camping La Escala, La Escala

Neat and tidy, small site within walking distance of beach and town.

Under the same ownership as Las Dunas (no. 8040), but a complete contrast, this is one of those sites where you can walk both to the beach and to the centre of a modest sized but lively, yet historical, popular holiday resort. It is therefore not very large, but the pitches are level, marked and well shaded. They have managed to carve over 200 out of the area so they are small - just room for the car and caravan or tent - but all pitches have electricity, water and drainage. The central toilet block is basic but clean, with British style toilets (no paper), washbasins, two in cabins for ladies, free hot water and 25 free showers. Dishwashing and laundry sinks with hot water. In season there is a supermarket and small bar with terrace. The site has 12 modern 2-tier bungalows to let at reasonable charges.

How to find it: On entry to La Escala at first roundabout turn right, at second roundabout turn left and then continue 1 km. to site on right. Watch for gate in high wall.

General Details: Open Easter - 25 Sept. Most well shaded. Shop. Bar (open in high season). Restaurant. Good value English restaurant (Angela's) at the port area. Bungalows for hire.

Charges guide: Per person 350 ptas; child (2-9 yrs) 275; pitch incl. electricity 1,375 - 2,125; dog 350 - 450. All plus 7% VAT.

Reservations: Not necessary. Address: Apdo. Correus 23, 17130 La Escala, Costa Brava (Gerona). Tel: 972/77.00.08 or 77.00.84. FAX: 972/55.00.46.8103.

8103 Camping El Maset, Sa Riera, Begur, nr Gerona/Girona

Little gem of a site in lovely surroundings, close to beaches.

This is a delightful, tiny site with 109 pitches, of which just 14 are for caravans or motorcaravans, the remainder suitable only for tents. The site entrance is steep and access to the caravan pitches can be quite tricky. All these pitches have electricity, water and drainage with some shade. Access to the tent pitches, which are more shaded on terraces on the mountainside (more of a hill really!) seems quite straightforward, with parking for cars not too far away - of necessity the pitches are fairly small. There are also seven traditional Catalan style `bungalows' to rent (4-6 persons, fully equipped and with sun terraces). For such a small site the amenities are quite extensive and there is a swimming pool. The facilities include a bar/restaurant, with terrace and takeaway, children's games room and play area on sand and a supermarket. Sanitary facilities, in three small blocks, were clean and include free hot showers, British style WCs, soap and hot-air dryers, hot water to washbasins in two blocks and a baby bath. Under cover washing up area (H&C) and washing machine. This small site provides the standard of service normally associated with the best of the larger sites. It is situated in the tiny resort of Sa Riera with access to beaches (300 m), including a naturist beach (via a longer uphill path). Begur, with its beautiful, small, quite unspoilt bay and beach, is 10 minutes by car.

How to find it: Site is 2 km. north of Begur (Bagur). Follow signs for Playa de Sa Riera and site (steep entrance).

General Details: Open 26 March - 25 Sept. Bar/restaurant, takeaway (all season). Shop (from May). Children's play area. Area for football and basketball. New games room. Swimming pool (all season). Solarium. Fishing 300 m. Golf, bicycle hire 1 km. Chemical disposal. No dogs allowed. Bungalows to rent (4-6 persons, fully equipped).

Charges 1999: Per person 560 - 710 ptas; child (1-10 yrs) 420 - 550; car 550 - 700; m/cycle 390 - 490; tent 590 - 760; caravan 690 - 890; motorcaravan 750 - 950; electricity 400 (tent) or 550 (caravan). Credit cards accepted.

AR Discount
Less 10% in low season, min. 1 week.

Reservations: Write to site. Address: Playa de Sa Riera, 17255 Begur (Gerona). Tel: 972/623023. FAX: 972/623901.

8074 Camping Paradis, nr Escala

Modern site with three pools and access to the beach.

If you prefer a quieter site out of the very busy resort of L'Escala, then this site is an excellent option. A large, friendly, family run site which is divided by the quiet beach access road, the site itself has a private access to the very safe and unspoilt beach contained in a charming bay with soft sand and offering all manner of watersports. There are 308 pitches all with electricity, some on sloping ground but the pitches themselves tend to be flat. Established pine trees provide shade for most pitches with more coverage on the western side of the site. Non-stop maintenance ensures that all facilities are always of a high standard. The site has modern sanitary blocks which are clean with free hot showers and facilities for disabled people. There are three swimming pools, the largest, completed in '98, has an idyllic setting on the top of a cliff overlooking Montgó Bay and offering fabulous views as you relax amongst the magnificent pool bars, restaurants and other facilities provided for this large pool. The site operates its own sub-aqua diving school and campers can experience diving in the pool or more adventurous coastal diving where appropriate. A children's play area is provided and many other recreational facilities including organised activities for children in high season. A 'road train' service runs to the local town and there are many interesting items of historic interest in the area. An extensive modern complex of restaurants, bars and takeaways is at the site entrance, supplemented by many local bars and restaurants all within walking distance.

How to find it: Leave autopista A7 at exit 5 for Viladimat, then L'Escala. Site well signed from town centre.

General Details: Open 1 March - 31 Oct. Bars. restaurants and takeaway. Shop. Swimming pools (3). Pool bar. Beach 100 m. Children's play areas. Animation for children (high season). Basketball, volleyball and badminton. Kayak hire. Sub aqua school. Washing machines and dryers. Chemical disposal. Bungalows and chalets for hire.

Charges 1998: Per adult ptas 350 - 475; child 250 - 325; pitch 1,350 - 2,250; electricity 450. Plus 7% VAT. No credit cards (site has an ATM facility at entrance).

Reservations: advisable in high season. Address: Av. de Montgó, 260, Apdo Correus 216, 17130 L'Escala (Costa Brava). Tel: 972/770200 or 771795. FAX: 972/772031.

AR Discount
*Less 10% in
low season*

8072 Camping Les Medes, L'Estartit, nr Gerona/Girona

See colour advert
opposite page 288

Immaculate, friendly, family site with pool, open all year.

Les Medes is a refreshing change from some of the 'all singing, all dancing' sites so popular along this coast. The friendly owners are justifiably proud of their neat, well equipped and well run site. Set back from busy L'Estartit itself, it is a peaceful and pretty oasis and a little train runs from near the site (June-Sept) to the town, The nearest beach is 800 m. With just 186 pitches, the site is small enough for the owners to know their visitors and being campers themselves, they have been careful in planning their facilities and keep the site immaculate. The level, grassy pitches range in size from 60-80 sq.m. depending on your unit. All have electricity (10A) and the larger ones (around half) also have water and drainage. All are clearly marked in rows, but with no separation other than by the deciduous trees which provide summer shade. The two modern, spacious sanitary blocks are very clean and well maintained, providing British toilets, hot and cold water in washbasins (in private cabins), good sized showers with dividers and shelves, very good facilities for disabled people and baby baths. Washing machines are provided in each block and there is hot and cold water for dishes and clothes washing. The pool area is attractively landscaped in front of the old Catalan farmhouse buildings which house reception and the small, air conditioned bar and restaurant, providing a grassy sunbathing area and an open air dance floor for twice weekly music evenings (in season). The site has well equipped apartments with central heating and TV to rent. A small indoor pool (heated) with sauna and solarium and good access for disabled people is a new addition.

How to find it: Site is signed from the main Torroella de Montgri - L'Estartit road GE641. Turn right after Camping Castel Montgri, at 'Joc's' hamburger/pizzeria and follow signs.

General Details: Open all year. Bar and snacks (all year). Restaurant (1/4-30/9). Shop (all year, limited in winter). Outdoor swimming pool (15/6-15/9). Indoor pool with sauna, solarium and masseur (15/9-15/6). Children's play area with small hut for games. Converted stables for indoor children's area and TV room, from where animation and excursions are organised in July/Aug. Large chess. Table tennis. Volleyball. Boules. Bicycle hire. Fishing 800 m. Riding 300 m. Golf 5 km. Car wash. Chemical disposal. Motorcaravan services. No dogs allowed. Apartments to let.

Charges 1998: Per person ptas 420 - 600; child (0-10 yrs) 265 - 435; pitch 900 - 1,350; electricity 430. All plus 7% VAT. Special offers for longer stays in low seasons. No credit cards.

Reservations: Recommended for July/Aug. Write to site with 5,000 ptas. deposit. Address: 17258 L'Estartit (Catalunya). Tel: 972/75.18.05. FAX: 972/75.04.13. E-mail: campingslesmedes@cambrescat.es. Internet: http://www.info3.es/campingslesmedes.

SPAIN - Costa Brava

8080 Camping El Delfin Verde, Torroella de Montgri, nr Gerona/Girona

Large, good quality, friendly site with own beach and extremely large swimming pool.

A popular, busy site in a quiet location El Delfin Verde has its own long beach, which campers have to themselves, stretching along its frontage. An attractive large pool in the shape of a dolphin is a feature of the site with a total area of 1,800 sq.m. with lifeguard (no bermuda shorts). A large bar, full restaurant and separate takeaway are open in the main season and overlook the pool area. There is a further restaurant with slightly cheaper, good value food in the main complex with an open air arena. This is a large site with nearly 6,000 persons at peak times. Level grass pitches nearer the beach are marked by indicators and there are now many separated by small fences and newly planted hedging. All have electrical connections and access to water points. There is shade in some of the older parts and a particularly pleasant area of pine trees in the centre with pitches marked but not separated, sandy and not so level. There are five excellent large sanitary blocks and a further new sixth smaller block, all with resident cleaners. In this new block and the second newest, half the washbasins are in private cabins. All blocks have free hot water in the washbasins, fully controllable showers (2 taps) of good, comfortable size with seat, plus British style toilets. El Delfin Verde is a large and cheerful holiday site with many good facilities, sports and free entertainments and is well worth considering for your Costa Brava holidays. Used by a number of British tour operators. Dogs not allowed 9/7-9/8.

How to find it: A very long camp approach road leads off the road from Torroella de Montgri to Palafrugell (watch carefully for the sign, particularly if coming from Palafrugell); there is a signpost to site at the end of it.

General Details: Open 27 March - 26 Sept, incl. shops, one restaurant and one bar. 290,000 sq.m. Supermarket (very well stocked and priced) and other shops. Two restaurants, grills and pizzerias. Three bars - one on site closes 11 pm, pool bar open until 1 am; small bar by beach open in season. `La Vela' barbecue and party area. Sports area (football, volley, etc.), 8 tennis courts. 2 km. exercise track. Dancing and floor shows weekly in season. Disco. Excursions organised. General room with TV. Video room. Bicycle hire. Minigolf. Children's playground. Trampolines. Badminton. Fishing 1 km. Golf 4 km. Hairdresser. Laundry facilities. Car repairs, servicing, and washing. Chemical disposal. Apartments, mobile homes and bungalows (with own pool) to let.

Charges 1999: Per pitch, incl. electricity 1,700, 2,600, 3,500 or 4,100 ptas; per person 375; child (2-9 yrs) 325; dog (low season only) 375; extra car 1,000 - 2,000; boat free - 375. All plus 7% VAT. No credit cards.

Reservations: Only a guarantee to admit - no specific pitch allocated. Write (all year) with deposit of ptas. 10,000. Address: Apdo Correos 43, 17257 Torroella de Montgri (Gerona). Tel: 972/75.84.50. FAX: 972/76.00.70. E-mail: eldelfinverde@dracnet.es. Internet: www.eldelfinverde.com. For bungalows and apartments, from 1/10-30/6, write to 08021 Barcelona, c/Muntaner 415 or from 1/7-30/9 to site.

See colour advert between pages 288/9

8090 Camping Caravaning Cypsela, Platja de Pals, nr Gerona/Girona

Impressive, de-luxe site, 2 km. from the sea, with many amenities.

The most striking feature of this site is its rather sumptuous complex of sport facilities and amenities near the entrance. This consists of a fine swimming pool, a good children's pool and playground, two excellent squash courts, tennis court, volleyball and table tennis, a restaurant and bar with terrace and other entertainment rooms. These include a children's playroom with entertainment (with video screen), amusements room with pool, football tables and video games, and a lounge for adults entertainment, with piano for twice weekly concerts. The bar/restaurant is very pleasant, with set course meals at low cost, as well as a full menu and takeaway service. The main part of the camping area is pinewood, with 1,146, clearly marked pitches of sandy gravel of a good size for Spain. The newer extensions at the rear of the site have more grass and pitches are hedged with a mixture of trees. The four sanitary `houses' are of excellent quality with comprehensive cleaning schedules, providing British style toilets, three with washbasins in private cabins, free hot water and adjustable showers. Three of the four have children's rooms with baby baths and larger ones for older children. There is also good provision for disabled people and many sinks with hot water. Cypsela is a busy, well organised site which can be thoroughly recommended, especially for families, very efficiently run, with fittings of good quality and everything clean and maintained to a high standard. The gates are closed at night. Several tour operators.

How to find it: Cypsela is on the road running from the Torroella de Montgri to Bagur down to Platja de Pals.

General Details: Open 15 May - 26 Sept. 200,000 sq.m. Access easy but care needed with trees in places. Electrical connections in all parts. Supermarket and other shops. Well appointed restaurant: or cheaper meals served in cafeteria. Bar. Lounge with drinks/snacks. Hairdressers. Swimming pools. Tennis. Squash. Table tennis. Football field. Minigolf. Social room/TV. Dancing weekly in season. Organised sports and games activities in daytime. Bicycle hire, riding 150 m. Golf 6 km. Fishing 7 km. Barbecue and party area. Children's playroom with organised activities. Games room with pool tables, etc. Free hourly bus service to beach. Serviced launderette. Ironing. Chemical disposal. Own sewage disposal plant. Car wash. Doctor always on site; well equipped treatment room. Air conditioned telephone parlour! No dogs are taken.

Charges 1998: Per person ptas. 600 - 750; child (2-10 yrs) 460 - 575; tent, caravan or motorcaravan incl. 1 vehicle 2,000 - 2,500; extra vehicle 760 - 950; extra tent 300; electricity 450; water and drainage 325. All plus 7% VAT. Less 5-10% for longer stays in low season.

Reservations: Write to site for details. Address: Ctra. Pals-Playa de Pals, km. 3, 17256 Pals (Girona). Tel: 972/66.76.96. FAX: 972/66.73.00.

Dreams can not be put into picture.

If you have ever dreamed about enjoying a deserved holiday, in a privileged surrounding, near the sea, in the middle of nature, with all the comfort,... ask for our brochure and discover how your dreams can come true*

✉ CAMPING CYPSELA - 17256 PALS (Girona) SPAIN
☎ +34 972 667 696 - Fax +34 972 667 300
e-mail: info@cypsela.com http://www.cypsela.com

*Our special offers will make it even more easy for you.

SPAIN - Costa Brava

8075 Camping Estartit, Estartit

Friendly, Belgian run site with small swimming pool, 300 m. from Estartit town.

Although facilities at this site are fairly limited, a short walk down the hill brings you into the heart of the extremely popular Estartit with its authentic tapas bars and street entertainment. Set in tall pine trees in a valley situation, this is a peaceful site with 160 pitches, all with electrical connections (2/6A), terraced and mostly suitable for tents (with some steep drops between terraces). However there are two long sand/gravel areas for motorhomes and caravans, separated by a canal. The site itself is surprisingly quiet, considering its proximity to the town - there is no need to use a vehicle once on site. One modern, fully tiled sanitary block provides hot and cold showers (small fee for hot water), small laundry with washing machines and a separate baby area. On site facilities include a bar/restaurant and shop (high season). There is a small swimming pool with a children's section, with a play area next to it, plus an attractive shaded area beside the bar. Access around the site could be difficult for disabled people.

How to find it: Site is signed from Estartit town centre.

General Details: Open Easter/1 April - 1 Oct. Bar/restaurant and shop (1/6-15/9). Swimming pool (all season). Children's play area. Children's activities and adult social events arranged (barbecue, bingo, etc). Fishing, bicycle hire, riding and golf within 1 km. Laundry facilities. Chemical disposal. Apartments for rent. Site is guarded day and night. No dogs 20/6-20/8.

Charges 1998: Per person 560 ptas; child (2-10 yrs) 400; car 550; caravan or family tent 595; small tent 495; motorcaravan 950; m/cycle 425; electricity 2A 350, 6A 425. Plus 7% VAT. Less 10-30% outside high season (10/6-31/8). No credit cards.

Reservations: Contact site for details. Address: 17258 Estartit (Girona). Tel: 972/75.89.09 or 75.19.09. FAX: 972/75.09.91. Winter address (15/10-15/3) Vrancken Joss, Plantenstraat 74, 3500 Hasselt, Belgium.

AR Discount
Further 10% on normal discount

8120 Kim's Camping, Llafranc, nr Palafrugell

Pleasant, attractive, terraced site near the sea. with swimming pool.

Situated on the wooded slopes of a narrow valley leading to the sea, this steep site provides 325 grassy and partly shaded, terraced pitches, with many larger pitches on a plateau with the pool and shop. They are connected by winding driveways, narrow in places, and most have electrical connections (6A). There is adequate sanitary provision including free warm showers, British style WCs and laundry facilities. Amenities include a children's playground, an excellent pool area with adult and small children's pools, a bar, restaurant and 'al fresco' eating. All amenities are offered at a high standard of cleanliness and efficiency. The site is under 1 km. from the beach at Llafranc. This is a good place for holidays to enjoy the bustling atmosphere of Llafranc town and beach, but staying in a quieter environment. There is an outstanding view along the coastline and of the Pyrenees from Cap Sebastian close by. English is spoken by the very friendly management and staff.

How to find it: Turn off for Llafranc from the Palafrugell - Tamariu road at turning signed `Llafranc, Caella, Club Tenis'. Site is 1 km. on, next to the El Paraiso hotel.

General Details: Open Easter - 30 Sept. Shop. Bar. Cafe/restaurant (15/6-15/9). TV room. Swimming pools (1/6-30/9). Children's play area. Fishing, bicycle hire 500 m. Golf 14 km. Car wash. Chemical disposal. Bungalows and mobile homes for hire.

Charges 1999: Three charging seasons. Per person 450 - 750 ptas; child (3-11 yrs) 365 - 475; car 450 - 775; m/cycle 400 - 500; tent 550 - 875; caravan 550 - 950; motorcaravan 650 - 1,300; electricity 475. Plus 7% VAT. Credit cards accepted.

Reservations: Made with deposit (ptas. 10,000). Address: 17211 Llafranc-Palafrugell (Girona). Tel: 972/30 11 56 or 61 16 75. FAX: 972/61 08 94. E-mail: info@campingkims.com. Internet: www.campingkims.com.

AR Discount
Welcome drink

la ballena alegre 2

SANT PERE PESCADOR
GIRONA

Access: A-7, exit (sortida) 5, direction L'Escala. Road (Gi-623) Km 18,5 and turn of at St. Marti d'Empuries.

ADAC 1

erkende camping ANWB

ESPAÑA

GRAN CONFORT

In English I am called the **"Happy WHALE"**. Situated next to the natural park of "The Aiguamolls de l'Empordà" and the Roman remains of Empuries, you will find the ideal spot to spend a good time with your family. The camp is situated along a 1.700 m long, large, sandy beach (where by the way, you won't find any whales). We offer a fantastic animation program and all facilities you need for a restful holiday.

LA BALLENA ALEGRE 2
Inf.B2-AR
E-17470 Sant Pere Pescador (Girona) Spain
Tel. 34 / 972 52 03 02
Fax 34 / 972 52 03 32

Internet: http://www.ballena-alegre.es
E-mail: infb2@ballena-alegre.es

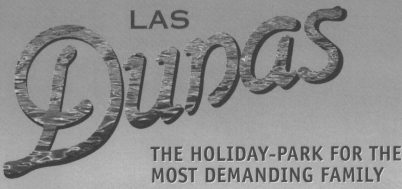

Camping Caravaning

el delfin verde

Apartat de correus 43 - E-17257 TORROELLA DE MONTGRI
Tel. (34) 972 758 454 - Fax (34) 972 760 070
URL: http://www.eldelfinverde.com
E-mail: eldelfinverde@drac.com

One of the best and most beautiful holiday sites on the COSTA BRAVA

In quiet surroundings, by a magnificent wide and miles-long sand beach and with the largest fresh-water swimmpingpool of the Costa Brava. By the way, we also have the most generously-sized pitches of the region. Many green areas and groups of trees. Commercial centre. Fresh water plant.

GASTRONOMY: 3 bars, 2 restaurants, 2 grills, pizzeria, 2 snackbars and beach bar.

SPORTS: large sports area for hand-, volley-, basket- and football and badminton. 8 tennis courts, minigolf (3000 m2 - 18 holes), windsurfing school.

ACTIVITIES: Organised 'fiestas', disco 'light', dancing. Excursions, organised sports competitions and movie/video shows.

7 Modern ablution blocks with hot water everywhere, money exchange, safe, medical service, tel.

BUNGALOWS AND APPARTMENTS FOR HIRE.

Open: 22.3 - 21.9.

HOLIDAY ON THE BEACH...

Hugo Heusch s.a. |comunicació

...AND IN THE POOL

Waiting for you at EL PINAR BEACH CAMP:
300 metres of fine soft sand beach,
pine woods, easy motorway access
and organised events for everybody,
every day. And that is not all!
There is also a superb freshwater
swimming pool in a carefully landscaped
garden, a snack bar, a supermarket,
organised activities, etc...

Now at EL PINAR BEACH CAMP-more of everything! Discover us.

elPinar
BEACH CAMP
COSTA BRAVA

C/ Villa de Madrid
E-17300 - Blanes (Girona)
Tel. (34) 972 331 083

CAMPING VILANOVA PARK

Apartado (postbus 64)
Tel. (34) 93 893 34 02 • Fax (34) 93 893 55 28
E-08800 Vilanova i la Geltrú (Barcelona)

*An elegant site
with country club
atmosphere!*

50 km South of Barcelona, in
the wine and champagne
centre of Catalonia with
more than 600 palm trees.
Quiet situation. Very modern
sanit. install. w. hot water
everywhere. Swimming pool
of 1.000 sqm and children's
pool with big colour
fountain (lighted in the
evenings). Excellent
restaurant "Chaine de
Rôtisseurs" in old catalan
mansion. Superm., shops,
English press, children's
progr., activities. Large
pitches w. electr. conn.
Private, large ecological park
of 50.000 sqm. f. beautiful
walks and picnics.
Access: Motorway A-7,
coming fr. Barcelona: exit 29;
coming fr. Tarragona:
exits 30 & 31; follow indic.
Vilanova i la Geltrú/Sitges.

**Open throughout the year.
We speak English.**

Your Holiday Park

PARC DE VACANCES
Sanguli Salou
CAMPING & BUNGALOW PARK

CAMPING & BUNGALOW PARK SANGULÍ, situated in Salou in the heart of the Costa Daurada and only 50 m from the beach, offers all amenities only a high-class camping site can offer.

"This one I can recommend"

- An animation programme for young and old; daily entertainment in an exceptional amphitheatre with a capacity of 2000 seats.
- 6 swimming pools, 2 supermarkets, 4 bars, 2 children's playgrounds, gift-shop, restaurant, take-away-meals, launderette, etc.
- Sports facilities, such as tennis, mini-golf, squash, indoor football, basketball, petanque, volleyball, etc.
- 6 modern ablution blocks, offering the highest level of hygiene and comfort (facilities for the disabled and babies etc.).

All this, surrounded by a unique nature and precious gardens, makes CAMPING & BUNGALOW PARK SANGULÍ your ideal holiday destination.

SPECIAL PRICES IN LOW SEASON
AWARDED "CAMP SITE OF THE YEAR 1988" BY THE CATALAN GOVERNMENT, "CAMP SITE OF THE YEAR 1992" BY THE ROYAL DUTCH TOURING CLUB ANWB, "CAMP SITE OF THE YEAR 1994" BY THE FRENCH MAGAZINE "CARAVANIER".

Prolongació carrer E, s/n. - Apartado de Correos 123.
43840 SALOU (Tarragona) España
Tels.: 977 38 16 41 - 977 38 16 98 - Fax: 977 38 46 16
http://www. sangulí.es e-mail: mail@sangulí.es

Please send further information
Name ....
Street ....
Town ....
Country ....

ALAN
ROGERS

Cala Llevadó
camping

Cala Llevadó
camping ★★★

First-class Camping and
Caravanning site. **Fabulous situation**
in he most beautiful part of
the **Costa Brava**. Isolated and quiet.
4 beaches. Swimming pool, children's
playground, bar, restaurant,
supermarket, laundry service,
hairdressing, medical service.
**Exceptional and luxurious sanitary
facilities**, with free hot water.
Numbered pitches.
Open 1.5 - 30.9
Internet: http://www.calallevado.com

Sport and animation:
swimming-pool, tennis, windsurfing,
diving, compressed air, excursions,
minigolf, basket, mountain-bike.

Reservation service. Caravans and
bungalows for hire. Write to:

Camping **Cala Llevadó**
Post Box 34, 17320 **Tossa de Mar**
Costa Brava - Spain
Tel (34) 972 340 314
Fax (34) 972 341 187
E-mail: calallev@grn.es

8200 Camping Cala Llevadó, Tossa de Mar, nr Gerona/Girona

See colour
advert opposite

Beautifully situated cliff-side site with excellent facilities.

For splendour of position Cala Llevadó can compare with almost any in this book. Situated on high ground, it has fine views of the sea and coast below and is shaped something like half a bowl. There are flat terraced areas for caravans and tents on top of the two hills at the sides and a great many individual levelled pitches for tents along the slopes leading down to the sea. There is usually a car access (may be narrow) not far from these. Many electrical connections cover all caravan sectors and one tent area. High up in the centre with a good aspect is the attractive restaurant/bar with a large terrace overlooking the high quality children's play area and the free swimming pool (20 x 10 m.), which is much frequented, plus paddling pool. There is a rather steep road leading right down to one of the four sandy or pebbly coves (one naturist) with a car park at the foot. Some other pleasant little coves can also be reached by climbing down on foot. Some up-and-down walking must clearly be expected on this site and should be considered if older or disabled people are included in your party. There are four very well equipped sanitary blocks well spaced around the site and built in an attractive style, with fully controllable, free hot water in washbasins (some in cabins) and in well equipped showers, baby baths and British style toilets. Water points around. The reception area has post office/telephone facilities. Cala Llevadó is luxurious and has character, with many regular clients and the atmosphere is informal and friendly. Only 150 of the 650 pitches are accessible for caravans, so reservation in season is vital. It is peacefully situated but only five minutes away from the busy resort of Tossa. Torches needed at night. There are lots of watersports activities locally.

How to find it: Cala Llevadó leads off the new Tossa-Lloret road about 3 km. from Tossa; the approach from either direction now presents no problems.

General Details: Open 1 May - 30 Sept, including all amenities. Large supermarket. New restaurant/bar with terrace. Swimming pools. Tennis. Three children's play areas. Entertainment for children (4-12 yrs). Sailing, water ski and windsurfing school. Fishing. Scuba diving. Post office/telephone. Washing machines and dryer. Laundry service. Chemical disposal. Motorcaravan service point. Tents (7) and caravans (7) for hire.

Charges 1998: Per person 580 - 850; child (3-14 yrs) 360 - 475; car or m/cycle 580 - 850; tent 580 - 850; caravan 660 - 920; motorcaravan 950 - 1,320; electricity 450. Plus 7% VAT. Credit cards accepted.

Reservations: accepted with deposit and fee. Address: Ctra. de Tossa - Lloret km. 3, 17320 Tossa de Mar (Girona). Tel: 972/340314. FAX: 972/341187. E-mail: calalleva@grn.es. Internet: www.calallevado.com.

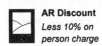

AR Discount
Less 10% on person charge

8101 Camping Playa Brava, Platja de Pals, nr Gerona/Girona

Surprisingly 'green' and quiet, beach-side site with good facilities.

As well as having direct access to a large beach and to watersports facilities on both beach and river, this is a very grassy, level site. Shade is provided by a mixture of fir and broad-leaf trees for most of the 500 pitches. These all have electricity (10A), a third with water and drainage also, and are of a good size ranging from 75-100 sq.m, with many large ones. There is an air of spaciousness and general tidiness. The 4 modern sanitary blocks have British WCs, controllable hot showers, with dressing area and hooks, washbasins with hot water, undercover dishwashing facilities and 6 washing machines. Facilities are provided for the disabled. Amenities include a medium sized pool and children's pool, with a large grass sunbathing area, two tennis courts, volleyball, children's play area on grass and an entertainment programme during July and August. There is a good golf course close by. The bar/restaurant, with terrace, provides both waiter service and takeaway meals, and there is a supermarket.

How to find it: Site is 3 km. north of the village of Pals, in the direction of Platja de Pals. Follow road for 3 km. past golf course to beach; well signed.

General Details: Open 16 May - 20 Sept. Bar/restaurant. Takeaway. Supermarket. Swimming pool (from 1/6), with large, grassy sunbathing area. Tennis. Volleyball. Minigolf. New children's play area. Fishing. Watersports on river and beach, including sheltered lagoon for windsurfing learners. Chemical disposal.

Charges 1998: Per person ptas. 300; child (2-9 yrs) 250; pitch incl. electricity 3,400. Less in low seasons. All plus 7% VAT. Discount for longer stays in low season.

Reservations: Write to site. Address: 17256 Platja de Pals (Gerona). Tel: 972/636894. FAX: 972/636952.

During 1998 changes were made in respect of dialling codes for some European countries. These changes affect only calls made to those countries from abroad.

To call a Spanish telephone number from the UK, it is now necessary to dial the International code (00 34 for Spain), followed by the local Area code IN FULL, then the Area code then the telephone number of the person being called.

For example: 00 34 555555 becomes 00 34 92 555555.

8150 Camping Internacional de Palamós, Palamós, nr Gerona/Girona

Site with good swimming pool quite close to town.

This site has a large swimming pool, surrounded by a grass sunbathing area and with its own bar/terrace. It is 1 km. from the town and only 400 m. to the nearest beach. It might have space when others are full and has over 500 level, terraced pitches on a gentle slope, of moderate size, with variable shade. Electrical connections (6A) are available in most parts. Three toilet blocks, one of which is large and modern providing good facilities with free hot water in washbasins, pre-set showers with push-button and facilities for disabled people. The two more elderly, smaller blocks are somewhat basic, with mostly Turkish, but some British WCs and cold showers. There are some tour operator pitches and mobile homes and bungalows to rent.

How to find it: Cars can approach site from central Palamós, but town streets are too narrow for caravans which should turn off C255 road just outside Palamós to north by Renault garage, signed to Kings Camping and La Fosca, turn right just before Kings and from there follow Internacional signs.

General Details: Open 26 March - 9 Oct. Swimming pool (36 x 16 m.), with paddling pool. Self-service shop. Restaurant and bar. Laundry room with washing machines etc. Hourly bus services to town.

Charges guide: Per person 325 ptas; child (under 10) 250; pitch for car and tent/caravan 1,635, 1,850 or 2,150, acc. to season; tent (m/cycle but no car) 1,100, 700 or 540; electricity 400; water/drainage 200. All plus 7% VAT.

Reservations: Write to site with 5,000 ptas deposit. Address: Apdo Correos 100, 17230 Palamos (Girona). Tel: 972/31.47.36. Office tel: 972/31.49.48 or 31.49.48. FAX: 972/31.85.11.

Camping - Caravaning INTERNATIONAL PALAMOS

E-17230 PALAMOS (COSTA BRAVA)
Postal address: Apartado Correus 100.
Tel. (34) 972 314736. Fax. (34) 972 318511
Access: Take exit towards Palamós-Norte and continue towards Playa La Fosca.
Modern, quiet, family site, very near to the beautiful PLAYA DE FOSCA (La Fosca beach) and in the centre of the COSTA BRAVA, with lots of shade from trees, and many flowers which gives you an idea of being in a garden!
3,000 sqm. of green area with swimming pools (33 x 16m & 10 x 5m), solarium and all installations of a good holiday site, incl. free hot water 24 hours a day.
"Bungalow tents Trigano" (4 pers), mobile homes (6 pers) and wooden bungalows "Campitel" for rent. Open: Easter-Sept.

8140 Camping Caravaning Treumal, Calonge, Platja d'Aro, nr Girona

Very attractive terraced site on hillside with direct access to small beaches.

This pretty site has been developed in the attractive gardens of a large private house (used for some of the main facilities), creating the effect of a private, personal place that has adapted itself beautifully to camping with a tranquil atmosphere. It is in a quiet situation (although some noise may be expected from the busy coast road on pitches nearer the entrance) on a pine-wooded hillside leading down to the sea, with 579 pitches on well shaded terraces. Because of trees and difficult access, only perhaps 300 are accessible to caravans; also, cars may not park by tents or caravans in high season, but must be left on car parks or roads. This is not a site for large units. Electrical connections are available in all parts. The three well maintained sanitary blocks have British toilets and free hot water in both the washbasins (with some in private cabins) and the controllable showers, and a tap to draw from for the sinks. Drinking water may be salty. There is access from different parts of the site to the main beach of coarse sand, with good bathing, and direct access to two smaller pretty coves.

How to find it: Access to site is signed from the C253 coast road 3 km. south of Palamos.

General Details: Open Easter/1 April - 12 Oct. Supermarket. Bar. Takeaway. Good restaurant with attractive shaded terrace (15/5-15/9). Table tennis. Fishing. Children's play area and sports area. Bicycle hire 2 km. Riding, golf 5 km. Washing machines. Chemical disposal. Motorcaravan service point. Traditional Spanish-style rooms and small mobile homes to let.

Charges 1999: Per person ptas 780; child (4-10 yrs) 430; caravan, car and electricity 2,760; motorcaravan and electricity 2,760; tent, car and electricity 2,620, extra car, m/cycle or boat 870. Plus 7% VAT. No credit cards.

Reservations: are made to guarantee admission (needed more for caravans than for tents) with deposit. Address: Aptdo Correos 348, 17250 Playa de Aro (Girona). Tel: 972/65 10 95. FAX: 972/651671.

8102 Camping Mas Patoxas, Pals, nr Gerona/Girona

Unpretentious site with satisfactory facilities in main season, set back from the coastal resorts.

This is a useful site for those who prefer to be apart from but within easy travelling distance of the beaches (5 km) and town (1 km) in high season. It has very easy access, being set on a slight slope with level terraces providing 500 grassy pitches of a minimum 72 sq.m. All have electricity (5A) and water, 150 have drainage also. There are some pleasant views but not a lot of shade. Although there are some 70 static units, there is the impression of more as they are sited together near the entrance and pool. No tour operators. The three sanitary blocks are modern with controllable hot showers, some washbasins with hot water, British style WCs, baby bath and three children's cabins with washbasin and shower. Dishwashing facilities are under cover (H&C) and five washing machines. A restaurant/bar provides both waiter service meals and takeaway food to order (all open all season). Shop. Activities include a medium sized swimming pool with sunbathing area and entertainment during the main season. Although there are no specific facilities for disabled people, access throughout the site looks to be relatively easy.

How to find it: Site is approx. 1½ km. south of Pals on the left hand side going towards Palafrugell on the GE650.

General Details: Open all year except 19 Dec - 14 Jan. Restaurant/bar. Pizzeria. Takeaway. Shop (1/6-30/9). Swimming pool (1/6-30/9). Tennis. Table tennis. Volleyball. Football field. Entertainment in high season. Fishing, golf 4 km. Bicycle hire, riding 2 km. Laundry facilities. Chemical disposal. Bungalows and mobile homes to rent.

Charges 1999: Per person 400 - 700 ptas; child (1-10) 300 - 450; caravan 1,300 - 2,150, tent with car 1,100 - 1,700. Plus VAT @ 7%. Low season offers. Credit cards accepted.

AR Discount
Welcome drink

Reservations: Write to site. Address: Ctra. Palafrugell-Torroella km.5, 17256 Pals (Girona). Tel: 972/636928 or 636361. FAX: 972/667349.

Calonge - Costa Brava - Girona

Cala GOGO

CAMPING • BUNGALOW PARK CALA GOGO

E-17250 **PLATJA D'ARO**
GIRONA
APARTAT CORREUS, 80
Tel. (34) 972.65.15.64
     (34) 972.65.15.43
Fax (34) 972.65.05.53
E-Mail: calagogo@calagogo.es
Web: www.calagogo.es

1st. Category site, directly at the sea. Bungalows, mobile homes and 'Trigano' tents for hire. Organised activities for children and adults in high season. Medical service. OFF- SEASON
Open: 27.3 - 26.9. **-35%**

8160 Camping Cala Gogo, Platja d'Aro, nr Gerona/Girona

Large, successful and vibrant site by sea with swimming pool and many amenities.

One of the best known campsites in Spain, its situation on a wooded hillside leading down to a small cove with a sandy beach is one of considerable natural beauty. In a high central position there are two good sized pools (25 x 12 m.) and children's pool - an excellent provision. Close by are shops, restaurant and a bar with adjoining terrace with views over the pools down to the beach, all open for the whole season. A second floodlit restaurant and bar are down by the beach (reached via a tunnel under the main road - possibly some road noise) and is open from June. The resort of Platja d'Aro is 2 km. Cala Gogo is divided into over 1,000 individual pitches, some shaded, others with artificial shade. These range in size from 50-100 sq.m. without the car, which stands in front of or near your unit (there are now many more of the larger pitches and some have water connection). The site is active and bustling, with over 3,000 campers when full. The distance from the busy beach with good bathing, depends on your pitch. Some are right by the beach, others up to 800 m. uphill, but two `Gua gua' (South American Spanish for bus) tractor trains, operating all season, take people up and down and add to the sense of fun and energy. A programme of animation which includes sports, tournaments, entertainment, etc. for children and adults is arranged free of charge (7 nights a week), as are the sports centre facilities of tennis, volleyball, basketball, etc. and the minigolf, plus a `mini-club' and crèche for small ones. Also fairly close is a new aqua-park offering waterslides, wave simulation etc. with a bus from the camp. There is another quieter beach adjacent. The seven sanitary blocks are quite satisfactory and are continuously cleaned. The newest one, in a section at the top of the site, is fully tiled with British WCs, free hot water in the washbasins set in flat surfaces (some private cabins), and free hot showers. The gates are closed to cars at midnight and the site is well supervised. Small number of tour operators pitches.

How to find it: Site is on the main road between Palamos and Platja d'Aro, 4.5 km. south of Palamos.

General Details: Open 27 March - 26 Sept, including amenities. 160,000 sq.m. Artificial or natural shade on most pitches. Electrical connections. Large supermarket. General shop. Tobacconist. Restaurants and bars in two places. Swimming pools and paddling pool. Children's playground and crèche. Sports centre. Table tennis. Sailboards and pedaloes for hire. Fishing. TV/video room. Grass minigolf. Bicycle hire 3 km. Riding 10 km. Golf 5 km. Bureau de change. Telephones. Medical service. Good 24 hr security service. Laundry. Chemical disposal. Motorcaravan service point. No dogs are accepted in July/Aug. Bungalows, Trigano tents and mobile homes to rent.

Charges 1999: Three charging seasons. Per person 475 - 800 ptas; child (2-9) 245 - 400; tent 550 - 1,075; caravan or trailer tent 640 - 1,215; car 490 - 850; motorcaravan 800 - 1,350; electricity (5A) 495. All plus 7% VAT. No credit cards.

Reservations: are made for min. 1 week with deposit (10,000 ptas.), no fee. Address: Apdo 80, 17250 Platja d'Aro (Girona). Tel: 972/651564. FAX: 972/650553. E-mail: calagogo@calagogo.es. Internet: www.calagogo.es.

AR Discount
Less 10%
excl. 21/6-31/8

CAMPING **BLANES**

E-17300 **BLANES - COSTA BRAVA**
Postal address: P.O. box 72
Tel. (34) 972 33 15 91 - Fax (34) 972 33 70 63

Right by a sandy beach on flat ground within a pine-tree forest. Only for touring campers - no residential camping! Quiet location with a pleasant and international atmosphere. Among other things equipped with excellent ablution blocks with warm water in showers; washing maschine, supermarket, snackbar, solarium; all pitches with electr. conn.; daily medical service; windsurfing, etc. We speak English.

25% from 1.5 till 15.6 **DISCOUNT** and in September.

10% With ICC card **MORE** (off-season)

8130 Camping Internacional de Calonge, Platja d'Aro, nr Gerona/Girona

Smart, spacious site with wide range of amenities, open all year.

This spacious, well laid out site has access by a footbridge over the coast road to a pretty beach. It is a family site with a good pool, plus large sunbathing area and a range of amenities which include a comfortable restaurant serving good food at reasonable prices. The site is set on sloping ground and is quite large with 800 pitches, all with 5A electricity, of which some 400 are suitable for caravans, the remainder being set on attractively landscaped terraces. Access to some pitches may be a little difficult. There is good shade from the tall pine trees. Some sites which are nominally 'open all year' offer nothing but a pitch during winter, but Calonge has a heated sanitary block and the bar/restaurant is fully open April - Oct. inclusive and open in the evenings even during the winter months with a log fire. The generous sanitary installations in the new and renovated blocks include British style WCs, free hot showers and some washbasins in private cabins, and can be heated. Used by tour operators, mainly in their own separate areas and some mobile homes similarly situated. Good security. The site reports recent developments including a new pool, new pitches and a little train for use within the site.

How to find it: Site is on inland side of coast road between Palamos and Platja d'Aro, just south of Sa. Calonge and 4 km. south of Palamos.

General Details: Open all year. Electrical connections throughout (5A). Shop (Easter-30/10, supermarket 500 m). Bar/restaurant (all year). Swimming pool (1/4-30/10). Children's playground on sand. Fishing 300 m.. Bicycle hire. Table tennis. Tennis. Volleyball. Riding 10 km. Golf 4 km. Cash machine. Exchange. Hairdresser. Laundry facilities. Chemical disposal. Motorcaravan service point. Trigano tents and mobile homes to let.

Charges 1998: Per adult 425 - 715; child (2-10 yrs) 220 - 385; tent 550 - 855; caravan 580 - 855; car 570 - 800; motorcaravan 850 - 1,195; m/cycle 405 - 570; electricity 475. All plus 7% VAT. Discounts for retired people for longer stays Oct - end May. No credit cards.

Reservations: Write to site with deposit (6,000 ptas). Address: Aptdo. Correos 272, 17251 Calonge (Girona). Tel: 972/65 12 33. or 65 14 64. FAX: 972/65 25 07. Internet: http://www.abaforum.es/cic. E-mail: zubarosi@abaforum.es. UK contact: Mr J Worthington, 0161-799-1274.

8235 Camping Blanes, Blanes

This site has been recommended by our Spanish Agent, but has not yet been inspected by our site assessors. It is a 206 pitch site situated in 2 hectares in a pine wood at S'Abanell beach, about 1 km. from the centre of Blanes. There is a bus service to and from the town which stops outside the campsite. It is said to be a quiet family-orientated site, and to have 'all facilities'.

How to find it: From A7 autopista, take exit 10, or the A19 and follow signs to Palafolls.

Charges 1999: Per pitch, including caravan, car and electricity ptas. 1,850; adult 630; child 525. Credit cards accepted.

General Details: Open: 1 April - 20 September.

Reservations: Contact site. Address: Avenida Villa de Madrid 33, 17300 Blanes (when closed: Apdo 72, 17300 Blanes). Tel: 972/331591 (or 972/858021 when site is closed). FAX: 972/337063 (all year)

During 1998 changes were made in respect of dialling codes for some European countries. These changes affect only calls made to those countries from abroad.

To call a Spanish telephone number from the UK, it is now necessary to dial the International code (00 34 for Spain), followed by the local Area code IN FULL, then the Area code then the telephone number of the person being called.

For example: 00 34 2 555555 becomes 00 34 92 555555.

SPAIN - Costa Brava

8230 Beach Camp El Pinar, Blanes, nr Gerona/Girona

See colour advert between pages 288/9

Pleasant, family orientated, smallish site adjoining good beach.

Previously named Camping El Pinar, this is a family site without tour operators or mobile homes. The new name sums up the direction in which the owners are developing the site, with an emphasis on a more participatory approach with an increase in the amount of activities and facilities - mostly directed towards sports. At the southern edge of Blanes beach, with direct access, it is about 2 km. from the town. The 495 pitches, all with electricity and a min. of 60 sq.m. are mostly shaded by pine or broad leaf trees. The site is in two sections, the second across the road, with its own sanitary block only being used in July and August. The modern sanitary facilities are tiled, have British styleWCs and controllable hot showers. There are baby baths and open plan washbasins (mostly cold water only). Dishwashing facilities are under cover. A café and takeaway are amongst the facilities, plus an aerobic centre with professional instructor (but no real gym equipment when we visited). Beach activities and games are organised. Other facilities include a small supermarket and a well enclosed, secure children's play area on grass. A swimming pool has been added. This site will appeal particularly to families seeking easy access to a long beach (shelves quite steeply) and the attractions of a major resort. Regular bus service into Blanes.

How to find it: Site is the last going south from Blanes centre. Follow camp signs in Blanes until El Pinar sign.

General Details: Open Easter - 30 Sept. Bar/restaurant with takeaway. Small supermarket. New swimming pool. Volleyball. Table tennis. Children's playground. Programme of activities for adults and children organised in season (2/5-16/9), including Spanish classes, dancing, bicycle excursions, aerobics. Excursions. Watersports near. Bungalows and mobile homes to let. Chemical disposal. Motorcaravan service point.

Charges 1999: Per person 475 - 630 ptas; child 425 - 525; pitch incl. electricity 1,500 - 1,850; plus 7% VAT. Credit cards accepted.

Reservations: Write or phone site (no deposit). Address: Villa de Madrid s/n, 17300 Blanes (Girona). Tel: 972/33.10.83. FAX: 972/33.11.00. E-mail: elpinar@mx3.redestb.es.

AR Discount
Less 25% for over 7 nights excl. 15/6-1/9

8240 Camping Botànic Bona Vista (Kim), Calella de la Costa, nr Barcelona

Delightfully attractive, small site on hillside south of Calella de la Costa.

While Calella itself may conjure up visions of mass tourism, this site is set on a steep hillside some 3 km. out of the town. Apart from perhaps some noise from the nearby coast road and railway, it is a quite delightful setting, with an abundance of flowers, shrubs and roses (1,700), the design successfully marrying the beautiful botanic surrounds with the attractive views of the bay. The 160 pitches, all with electricity, are 60-80 sq.m. or more, on terraces with some shade. Access roads are steep and many of the pitches enjoy lovely views. There are quite good beaches, including a naturist beach, just across the road and railway, accessible via a tunnel and crossing. The standard of the sanitary installations in three blocks is quite outstanding for a small site (indeed for any site). They include controllable, free hot showers, with dressing area, British WCs and (in the newest block) some washbasins (H&C) in cabins, a bidet in the ladies' and a baby room. Dishwashing facilities with hot water, are under cover and there are washing machines. The bar/restaurant is unusual in having a circular, central open-hearth fire/cooker, and serves both eat-in and takeaway meals, with roof top terrace. Amenities for children include a playground, satellite TV, with 2 pool tables in a separate room and a new recreation park (2,000 sq.m.) with table tennis, football, petanque, etc. A barbecue and picnic area has been added. On arrival, park at the restaurant and choose a pitch - the owner is most helpful with siting your van.

How to find it: From the N11 coast road site is signed travelling south of Calella (at km. 665), and is on right hand side of road - care is needed as road is busy and sign is almost on top of turning (next to Camping Roca Grossa). Entrance is very steep. From Barcelona, after passing through Sant Pol de Mar, go into outside lane shortly after 'Camping 800 m.' sign and keep signalling left. Site entrance is just before the two lanes merge.

General Details: Open all year. Electricity throughout. Bar/restaurant, takeaway and shop (all w/ends then 1/5-31/10). Sauna, solarium and jacuzzi. Large children's playground. Recreation park. Satellite TV. Games room. Barbecue and picnic area. Fishing 100 m. Bicycle hire 1 km. Riding, golf 3 km. Watersports near. Chemical disposal.

Charges 1999: Per person ptas. 550; child (3-10 yrs) 475; car 550; tent or caravan 550; motorcaravan 1,100; m/cycle 475; electricity (6A) 475. All plus 7% VAT. No credit cards.

Reservations: Write to site. Address: Ctra. N-ll, Km.665, PO Box 38, 08370 Calella (Catalunya). Tel: 93/7692488. FAX: 93/7695804. E-mail: bonavista@redestb.es. Internet: http://www.datum.es/bonavis.htm.

AR Discount
Less 50% for over 30 days 1/10-31/3

Costa Daurada

The 'Golden Coast' is aptly named with a fine band of pale yellow sand stretching almost continuously along its length. It covers the shores of Barcelona and Tarragona provinces, from the Rio Tordera to Vinaros. The section south of Barcelona includes the well known resorts of Sitges, Tarragona and Salou and is backed by pine-covered hills. The northern section includes Arenys and Calella, and is flatter country, with a fair penetration of industry. The area is famed for its fresh vegetables and fish and in Barcelona boasts one of the most exciting cities in the world.

8310 Camping La Ballena Alegre, Castelldefels, nr Barcelona

Spacious, well laid out site on beach, with comprehensive shops and restaurant/bars.

La Ballena Alegre is one of the best known sites in Spain. About 16 km. from the centre of Barcelona, it has a super sandy beach more than a kilometre long and 100 m. wide, although some may prefer the 25 x 13 m. swimming pool (and small children's pool). It is a very large site, most of which is covered by a pinewood and divided into 1,450 pitches of about 70 sq.m. with 1,000 for touring units going on the left hand side. Space is not usually a problem, certainly outside July/Aug. The sanitary blocks have been much improved and are all good, although they still vary in size and type, two being new ones. All have free warm water in washbasins and the new blocks have some private cabins, There are free controllable hot showers, mostly British style WCs, units for disabled people, plus dog showers. Cleaning is good - a cleaner is on duty at each block during the day. Attractive bar/restaurant and pool terrace with entertainment in season. Although not a quiet site, with a lively atmosphere in high season and some aircraft noise, this is nevertheless a well run one, with personal supervision.

How to find it: From Barcelona on the N11 you can turn off on to the C245 road to Gava and Castelldefels or take the motorway A2 spur towards Castelldefels - El Prat de Llobregat and continue to Castelldefels. Entrance leads directly off C246 dual carriageway `Autovia Castelldefels' on coast side of the road, by a service station.

General Details: Open 1 April - 30 Sept. Probably about 260,000 sq.m. Mostly well shaded. Electrical connections of 220v. everywhere. Large supermarket and other shops. Restaurants (self and waitress service), and adjoining bar and snack bar. Hairdressers. Soundproofed disco. Organised sports activities: aerobics, squash, roller skating, bicycle track, swimming, football etc., and evening entertainment twice weekly in season. Sports area with football. Children's playground. Tennis. Fishing. Riding 1 km. Golf 6 km. Garage (petrol and servicing) by entrance. Washing machines. Bureau de change. Good treatment room with nurse; doctor calls daily. Roman amphitheatre where folk dances, shows etc. are staged. Chemical disposal. Motorcaravan service point. Chalets and bungalows to rent.

Charges 1998: Per person ptas. 575; child (under 10) 260; pitch incl. car and electricity 1,425 - 2,650, with tent 1,100 - 1;600. All plus 7% VAT. Credit cards accepted.

Reservations: only made in the sense of guaranteeing admission. Site address: Autovia Castelldefels km.12.5, 08840 Viladecans (Barcelona). Tel: 93/658.05.04. FAX: 93/658.05.75. E-mail: ballena1@ballena-alegre.es. Internet: www.ballena-alegre.es. Winter: Aptdo de Correos 438, 08080 Barcelona. Tel: 93/226.13.02. FAX: 93/226.65.28.

AR Discount
Less 10% for over 30 days

8390 Camping Vilanova Park, Vilanova i la Geltru, Sitges, nr Barcelona

Hillside site with views to sea, good quality installations and large pool complex.

This large modern site has been equipped with costly installations of good quality. The most remarkable feature is the swimming pool complex with one very large pool where water jets and a coloured floodlit fountain can be turned on. Together with a smaller children's pool, this covers an area of some 1,000 sq.m. In the same area is the shopping centre and the large bar and restaurant, set around old Catalan farm buildings where dancing or entertainment takes place when numbers permit. The site is 4 km. from Vilanova town and beach (with local bus service), and 11 km. from Sitges. At present there are 1,260 pitches on the site with a very significant proportion occupied by a variety of well screened static units, but with 460 for touring units which are located in the lower part of the site. They are divided by markers at the front and mostly of good average size, say 70 sq.m. for caravans and a bit less for tents. Some larger pitches (100 sq.m.) have electricity, water and drainage. The terrain, hard surfaced and mostly on very gently sloping ground, has many trees and considerable shade. A new sanitary block is to be added and the existing two large, well maintained blocks are to be renovated. Already of excellent quality, they can be heated and have British style WCs, washbasins (over half in cabins) with free hot water, and others of standard type with cold water. Free controllable hot showers and hot water for washing dishes, cold for clothes; also serviced laundry. A new attraction is a Wildlife Park, inhabited by deer and bird-life. Very pleasant, it has picnic areas and footpaths. Barcelona is easily accessible - buses every hour in the main season or electric train from Vilanova i la Geltru every 20 minutes.

How to find it: Site lies 4 km. northwest of Vilanova i la Geltru towards L'Arboc. From Barcelona-Tarragona autopista take exit 29 and turn towards Vilanova. There is no exit at no. 29 from Tarragona direction; from here you must take exit 30, go into Vilafranca and turn right for Vilanova. The Vilanova bypass is now open so that one need not go into the town. Alternatively from the N340 from L'Arboc directly on attractive but very winding road for 11 km. signed Vilanova i la Geltru.

General Details: Open all year. Electrical connections throughout (6A). Supermarket (Easter - 30 Sept), souvenir shop. Full restaurant and larger bar with many tables where simpler meals served (both all year). Swimming pools (Easter - 15 Oct). Bicycle hire. Tennis. Riding adjacent. Golf 5 km. Fishing 3 km. Launderette. Chemical disposal. Chalets, bungalows, caravans and cabins for rent.

Charges 1999: Per person 560 - 890 ptas; child (4-10 yrs) 350 - 560; car 560 - 890; tent or caravan 560 - 890; motorcaravan 925 - 1,550; m/cycle 230 - 670; electricity (6A) 560; water connection 350 - 560. All plus 7% VAT.

Reservations: are made in sense of guaranteeing to admit, with deposit. Address: Aptdo 64, 08800 Vilanova i la Geltru (Barcelona). Tel: 93/893 34 02. FAX: 93/893 55 28.

See colour advert between pages 288/9

8410 Park Playa Bara, Roda de Bara, nr Tarragona

See colour advert
between pages 288/9

Excellent, well maintained site near beach, with comprehensive amenities.

This is an impressive site which is family owned and has been carefully developed over the years. On entry you find yourself in a beautifully sculptured, tree lined drive with an accompanying aroma of pine and woodlands. Considering its size, with over 850 pitches, it is still a very green and relaxing site with an immense range of activities. It is well situated with a direct access to a long sandy beach (via a tunnel under the railway and 50 m. walk). An important feature is the attractive, medium sized heated swimming pool of irregular shape in the centre of the site, with separate small pool for children, landscaped with grass and trees surrounding and additional terraced sunbathing areas. A new heated pool has been added with toboggan slides, jacuzzi and spa bath. There is an adjacent bar when the pool is open. Pitches vary in size but are larger than the Spanish average, the older ones terraced and well shaded with pine trees, the newer ones more open, with a variety of trees and bushes forming separators between them and with electricity (5A) and water. Arrive early to find space in peak weeks (see Reservations). The toilet blocks are of different sizes and types, but all very good, with British style WCs, free hot water in washbasins and showers and in many of the sinks. There are some private cabins for both sexes in some blocks, children's baths, basins and toilets and facilities for disabled. The water is rather salty here but spring water is available from special taps. The site is well laid out with an attractive central roadway. Much care with planning and in the use of natural stone and flowering plants gives a pleasing appearance, which particularly shows in the Roman-style amphitheatre, part of the comprehensive amenity complex at the front of the site. Extensive animation programme in main season. Modern fitness suite with up-to-date equipment and instructor. Used by British tour operators.

How to find it: Site entrance is off the main N340 just opposite the Arco de Bara. From autopista A7, take exit 31.

General Details: Open 10 March - 30 Sept. with all amenities. Electrical connections (5A) in all parts. Supermarket and other shops. Full restaurant and larger bar where simpler meals and takeaway served, bars also in 3 other places, and self-service restaurant on beach. Swimming pools. 'Frontennis' ground and tennis courts (both floodlit). Roller skating. Football. Sports area. Windsurf school. Volleyball. Basketball. Gymnasium. Petanque. Minigolf, arranged on a map of Europe. Fishing. Bicycle hire 2 km. Riding 3 km. Golf 4 km. Entertainments centre: amphitheatre with stage and dance floor, large busy games room with pool, football, table tennis, electronic machines; bar, video room with screen and seating, satellite TV, disco room 11 to 4 am. (weekends only outside high season). Exchange facilities and cash point machine. Hairdresser. Washing machines. Chemical disposal. Motorcaravan service point.

Charges guide: Per person 430 - 860 ptas; child (1-9 yrs) 310 - 620; car 860; large tent or caravan 860; motorcaravan 1,500; small tent 620; m/cycle 620; electricity 495. All plus 7% VAT. In low season reductions for pensioners in low season and for sports. No credit cards.

Reservations: Contact site for details. Address: 43883 Roda de Bara (Tarragona). Tel: 977/80 27 01. FAX: 977/80 04 56. E-mail: barapark@lix.intercom.es. Internet: http://www.barapark.es.

8520 Camping Caravaning Marius, Montroig, nr Tarragona

Agreeable site with family atmosphere and personal touch, by a sandy beach.

A quiet, well tended site which is not too huge, Marius has a pleasant atmosphere. It is right beside a good sandy beach, with direct access and no roads to cross - you can almost fall out of bed and on to the beach! The site is divided into 350 individual pitches of adequate size so it does not become too overcrowded. They are quite shady, 300 with electricity and 8 with water and drainage also. Dog owners go on one half of the site. Two sanitary blocks have free hot water in both showers and half the washbasins, plus the 21 private cabins, British style WCs, plus an excellent new shower block. The site is near nos. 8540 and 8530, and the lively fishing port of Cambrils is about 7 km. Some train noise.

How to find it: Entrance is 28 km. from Tarragona on the Valencia road (N340).

General Details: Open 1 April - 15 Oct. 4 ha. Bar and restaurant (June-Sept). Supermarket (May - 15 Oct). Children's playground. Fishing. Windsurfing. Table tennis. Water ski and pedaloes nearby. Bicycle hire 4 km. Golf 6 km. Washing machine. Chemical disposal. TV sets and bicycles not permitted.

Charges 1999: Three charging seasons. Per person 500, 600 or 800 ptas; child (under 10) 200, 300 or 400; pitch 1,400, 1,800 or 2,300. Plus 7% VAT. Credit cards accepted.

Reservations: Contact site. Address: 43892 Miami-Playa (Tarragona). Tel: 977/810684. FAX: 977/179658. E-mail: cmpmarius@seric.es.

8483 Camping Caravaning Tamarit-Park, Tamarit, Tarragona

See colour advert between pages 320/1

Well cared for, modern site with direct access to beach.

This is a well designed, attractive site, beautifully situated at the foot of Tamarit castle (church service Sunday, 10 am), at one end of a 1 km. long beach of fine sand. It is only 9 km. from Tarragona and 16 km. from Port Aventura. The 550 pitches, some with sea views, are marked out on hard sand and grass and most are attractively separated by a variety of Mediterranean shrubs, pines and palm trees. All have electricity (6A) and are 70, 90 or 100 sq.m. in area (long electric leads and metal awning pegs needed in places). Wide internal roads give good access for even the largest of units. Sanitary blocks are modern and tiled, providing excellent facilities with British style WCs and some large shower cabins with free, controllable hot water, washbasins and dressing area. Some private bathrooms may be rented. Dishwashing facilities are under cover with hot water and laundry facilities are provided. Catering includes a beach-side restaurant, terrace and takeaway. There is an animation programme in season. A vast, attractively designed, lagoon-type swimming pool with bar and solarium has been added. The site is approached by a long access road, rather narrow but with passing places, reached across a new bridge (6 m.) over the railway line (little or no train noise on the site). This is a well designed and maintained site, with good facilities and security. The early morning sun shining on the blue sea and the golden stone of Tamarit castle is a memorable sight!

How to find it: Site is 8 km. north of Tarragona, signed from the N340 (km. 1172). Continue on narrow road for 1 km. to site entrance, on the left side at the end of the road.

General Details: Open all year with one heated sanitary block, otherwise from 25 March. Bar, restaurant, takeaway (March - Dec). Supermarket (April - Sept). Swimming pool (May - Oct). Tennis. Volleyball. Petanque. Minigolf. Table tennis. Children's playground. Fishing. Bicycle hire 9 km. Riding 3 km. Golf 6 km. Washing machines. Car wash. Exchange facilities. Car wash. Chemical disposal. Motorcaravan services. Chalets and Trigano tents to let.

Charges 1998: Per person 600 - 800 ptas; child (1-9) 400 - 600; pitch incl. car 2,200 - 2,500; electricity 500. Plus 7% VAT. Discounts for students, pensioners, large families and long stays in low season. Credit cards accepted.

Reservations: Write to site. Address: Platja Tamarit, 43893 Tarragona (Catalunya). Tel: 977/650128. FAX: 977/650451. E-mail: tamaritpark@tamarit.com.

8484 Camping-Caravaning Gavina, Creixell de Mar

Modern, friendly site with direct access to 400 m. beach.

Sister site to Camping Tamarit (8483), Gavina is a modern, friendly beach site. It has 400 pitches (60 sq.m.), 220 with electricity (6A), set on flat grass and sand, separated by tall hedges which provide adequate shade. The wide, sandy beach is adjacent to the site with opportunities for a wide range of watersports including sailing, windsurfing and water skiing. There are two sanitary buildings, the second being of good quality, tiled with free hot water to the showers and some washbasins. In the first block, the showers have no dividers and hooks outside. No facilities for disabled visitors. The attractive restaurant/bar has a terrace overlooking the sea and entertainment is arranged in high season. Well stocked supermarket. There is a children's play area, a tennis court and a sports area.

How to find it: Take exit 32 from A7 Barcelona - Tarragona autopista and follow N340 towards Tarragona until km. 1181 sign. Take road for Creixell Platja and follow well signed road to site (by the sea).

General Details: Open Easter/1 April - 30 Sept. Bar/restaurant. Supermarket. Children's play area. Tennis. Table tennis. Telephones. Exchange facilities. Safe deposit boxes. Laundry facilities. Sports area. Bungalows for rent.

Charges 1998: Per person ptas 500 - 600; child (under 10 yrs) 350 - 450; pitch (any unit) 1,700 - 2,000; electricity 500. Plus 7% VAT.

Reservations: Contact site. Address: 43839 Creixell de Mar (Tarragona). Tel: 977/801503. FAX: 977/800527.

SPAIN - Costa Daurada

8482 Camping La Pineda de Salou, La Pineda

Useful site for Port Aventura and Acquapark.

La Pineda is just outside Salou towards Tarragona and this site is just 300 m. from the Acquapark and 2.5 km. from Port Aventura, to which there is an hourly bus service from outside the camp entrance. On site there is a medium sized swimming pool and children's pool, open from mid June, with a large lying out terrace with sun loungers, as well as various entertainments aimed at young people. The shop, restaurant and bar are open all season and there are acceptable sanitary facilities. These include British style WCs, free hot water to the washbasins, showers, baby bath, dishwashing and laundry sinks. There are two washing machines in each block. The second building is opened in high season only. The 336 flat pitches (280 for touring) are mostly shaded and of about 70 sq.m. All have 5A electricity. The beach is only about 400 m. away. This is a friendly and convenient site, without being outstanding.

How to find it: From A7 just southwest of Tarragona take exit 35 and follow signs to Port Aventura then site.

General Details: Open 15 March - 15 Oct. Restaurant, bar, snacks and shop all season. Swimming pools (from mid-June). Small TV room. Bicycle hire. Games room with videos and drink/snack machines. Chemical disposal.

Charges 1998: Per person ptas. 430 - 590; child (1-10 yrs) 310 - 460; car 415 - 650; caravan 530 - 800; motorhome 810 - 1,100, electricity 395 - 425. Credit cards accepted.

Reservations: Made for high season (min. 7 nights) contact site. Address Ctra de la Costa Tarragona a Salou, km 5, 43480 La Pineda (Tarragona). Tel: 977/37 21 76. FAX: 977/37 06 20.

8470 Camping La Siesta, Salou, nr Tarragona

See colour advert between pages 320/1

Lively site in centre of Salou with swimming pool.

La Siesta is only 250 m. from the sandy beach and not very much more from all the life of Salou, which is very popular with the British and has just about all that a highly developed Spanish resort can offer. For those who do not want to walk this distance, there is a swimming pool of 300 sq.m., free of charge and open all season, on the camp itself, with filtered water. The site is divided into 400 individual pitches which are large enough and have electricity connections (10A), with smaller ones for tents. There is one box for the tent or caravan and a shared one for the car, with some shade from the trees and shrubs that are part of the site's atmosphere. In July/Aug. siting of campers is carried out by the management, who are friendly and helpful. There are three satisfactory sanitary blocks, the best of which is on the left in the quieter area of the site. There are 48 free hot showers. Young campers are sited to the rear of the restaurant.

How to find it: Both new roads from Tarragona and Reus end at a large roundabout from where the camp is only about 200 m. and signed through a one way system in the town.

continued overleaf

8470 Camping La Siesta (continued)

General Details: Open Easter - 31 Oct. (shop and restaurant all season to 15 Oct.). 50,000 sq.m. Electrical connections (10A). Large supermarket. Swimming pool (all season). Self-service restaurant and bar with terrace overlooking pool; also cooked dishes to take away. Dancing some evenings till 11 pm. Many other shops, restaurant and dancing near. Children's playground. Medical service daily in season.

Charges 1999: Per person 695 ptas; child (4-9 yrs) 515; car 695; tent or caravan 695; motorcaravan 1,000; electricity 400. Less in low season. All plus 7% VAT.

Reservations: Advised 1/7-20/8 and made in sense of guaranteeing a shady place, with electricity if required. Deposit asked for. Address: 43840 Salou (Tarragona). Tel: 977/38.08.52. FAX: 977/38.31.91. E-mail: siesta@tinet.fut.es. Internet: http.www.fut-es/nsiesta.

8481 **Camping Cambrils Park, Salou, nr Tarragona**

See colour advert between pages 320/1

Modern site with first-class facilities.

An impressive entrance drive, lined with palm trees and flowers, leads from the large reception building at the entrance of this site to the pitches and facilities. It is set some way back from the beach in a generally quiet setting. The 611 slightly sloping, grassy pitches of around 90 sq.m. are numbered and separated by trees. All have 10A electricity, 50 also with water and waste water connections. They are served by three excellent sanitary buildings which have free hot water to the washbasins (half in cabins), showers, units for disabled people, dishwashing, laundry and baby bath sections. Hand and hairdryers are provided and there is also a serviced laundry. The large supermarket, souvenir shop and `panaderia' (fresh-baked bread and croissants) are open daily. The takeaway and restaurant offer a wide selection and from 10/6 there is a very large bar between the pool and games area. Another bar is on the central island in the 1,000 sq.m. swimming pool, which has a slide and a grass lying out area. There are many sporting opportunities, with a football pitch (on sand), multi-games court, tennis, basketball, volleyball and petanque. Children have a large adventure fortress on sand, daily animation, pool, table football and other games. In high season there is a daily show on the 'island' in the pool. A small number of tour operator pitches at present. It is a walk of about 500 m. to the beach and 4 km. to Port Aventura.

How to find it: Site entrance is signed off the coast road from Salou, in Cambrils.

General Details: Open 1 May - 30 Sept. Restaurant. Takeaway. Supermarket. Souvenir shop. Swimming pools. Minigolf. Football. Basketball. Volleyball. Animation and entertainment (from 10/6). Fishing, bicycle hire 500 m. Riding 1 km. Golf 15 km. Doctor on site July/Aug. Chemical disposal. Motorcaravan service point. No dogs.

Charges 1999: Per person ptas. 630; child (3-12 yrs) free - 420; pitch incl. electricity 3,300, with water and waste water 3,700; all plus 7% VAT. Less 40% outside 21/6-31/8. Credit cards accepted.

Reservations: Contact site. Address: Apdo de Correos 123, 43840 Salou (Tarragona). Tel: 977/35 10 31. FAX: 977/35 22 10. E-mail: mail@cambrilspark.es. Internet: www.cambrilspark.es.

8540 *Camping Caravaning Club La Torre del Sol, Montroig, nr Tarragona*

Large, pleasant site beside beach with good amenities and pools complex.

A member of the French Airotel chain, Torre del Sol occupies a good position with direct access to the beach and has many on site activities. It can offer good shade on a high proportion of the 1,500 individual numbered pitches, which are mostly of about 70-80 sq.m. There is usually space for odd nights but for good places between 10/7-16/8 it is advisable to reserve. Dog owners go to a special section. The site has the sort of very comprehensive amenities (listed below) found at some of the good large Spanish sites and there is always plenty to do. There is a complex of three swimming pools, two heated (fully open May - Sep/Oct) with a pizzeria, bar and ice cream service adjoining. The site offers much animation with a programme of events, for children and adults, in high season. The tiled, sanitary facilities consist of four well maintained blocks giving a good provision with hot water and with some nice tiled units added on to three blocks comprising private cabins with washbasins and hot showers. British style toilets, units for disabled people and babies. Radios and TVs are banned. Part of the site is between the railway and the sea so there may be occasional train noise.

How to find it: The entrance is off the main N340 road about 30 km. from Tarragona towards Valencia. From motorway take Cambrils exit and turn west on N340.

General Details: Open 15 March - 15 Oct, amenities from 1 April. 24 ha. Electrical connections in all parts. Large supermarket and other shops at entrance. Restaurant. Takeaway. Bar with large terrace where shows and dancing held in high season. Beach bar. Pizzeria. Cinema; 3 TV lounges (satellite); separate room for films or videos on TV screen. Well-soundproofed disco. Hairdressers. Swimming pools. Solarium. Sauna. Tennis. Table tennis. Squash. Minigolf. Bicycle hire. Fishing. Windsurfing school; sailboards and pedaloes for hire. Children's playground and crèche. Riding 3 km. Golf 4 km. Fridge hire. Medical service. Safe deposit. Bureau de change. Car repair and wash service. Washing machines. Chemical disposal. Bungalows, mobile homes and Trigano tents for hire.

Charges 1998: Per person ptas. 400 - 950; child (under 10 yrs) 300 - 800; pitch with car, tent, caravan 1,800 - 2,800; motorcaravan and electricity 1,850 - 2,900; extra car 400 - 1,000. All plus 7% VAT. Discounts in low season for longer stays. Credit cards accepted.

Reservations: Made only for Jul/Aug. before 15 June, in sense of guaranteeing admission, with fee (3,000 ptas). Address: 43892 Miami Playa (Tarragona). Tel: 977/810486. FAX: 977/811306.

See colour advert between pages 320/1

8530 Camping Caravaning Playa Montroig, Montroig, nr Tarragona

One of Europe's top sites with excellent facilities and pool complex, beside sandy beach.

Playa Montroig is about 30 km. beyond Tarragona set in its own tropical gardens with direct access to what amounts to a private section of a very long sandy beach. This offers good bathing, windsurfing, surfboarding and a diving raft in the sea. The main part of the site lies between the sea and the railway (there is an underpass). The whole site is divided into individual pitches of acceptable size, mainly marked out at front and back and with good shade provided by a variety of lush vegetation including very impressive palms set in wide avenues. There are now over 2,000 pitches, all with electricity and 330 with water and drainage connections also.

The site has two outstanding features. There is an excellent swimming pool complex near the entrance with two heated pools (one for children) and a larger unheated one adjoining. The other feature is the 15 sanitary buildings, many of them small but of very good quality with toilets and washbasins, plus really excellent, air conditioned larger buildings housing large showers, washbasins (many in private cabins) and separate WCs. There are several launderettes and special facilities for the disabled and for babies. A 24 hour cleaning service operates. Water points around site (water said to be very pure from the site's own wells). There are two restaurants (500 places in each) and four bars. One in the camp itself has video and activity room upstairs and an adjoining bar and small dance floor, air conditioned, for more traditional dancing in a club atmosphere. The one by the main road at the entrance has a smart restaurant and a separate open-air dance floor for livelier dancing till late. Two takeaways also. Multi-purpose hall, the `Eurocentre', with 250 person capacity and specially equipped for entertainment and activities, large screen videos, films, shows and meetings (air conditioned). Fitness suite. Children's day care centre (multi-lingual staff). Camp theatre `La Carpa', a spectacular open air theatre, an ideal setting for shows and beach parties. New `Tam-Tam Eco Park, a 20,000 sq.m. forest zone where an expert will introduce you to the natural life of the area. This is an excellent site for those who like sunshine and sea and can be recommended without hesitation. No dogs are taken and TVs, sometimes very obtrusive on Spanish sites, are not allowed. Mid-day rest period 13.00-16.00 hrs. A range of bungalow accommodation is available for rent.

How to find it: The entrance is off the main N340 nearly 30 km. southwest from Tarragona. From the motorway take Cambrils exit and turn west on N340.

General Details: Open 1 March - 31 Oct. About 150,000 sq.m. Good shopping centre with supermarket, greengrocer, butcher, fishmonger, tobacconist and souvenir shops. Restaurants and bars. Dancing, shows, films and videos (see Eurocentre and La Carpa above). Eco-park (see above). TV lounges (3) incl. satellite. Also beach bar. Children's playground. Free kindergarten with multi-lingual staff. Junior and teenage clubs. Fitness centre. Skate-boarding. Jogging track. Activities centre with tourist information. Sports area for volleyball, football and basketball. Tennis. Minigolf. Table tennis. Organised activities for children and adults including pottery and gardening classes. Windsurfing and water skiing courses. Surfboards and pedaloes for hire. Boat mooring. Launderettes. Ladies' and men's hairdressers. Car wash. Bicycle hire. Bureau de change. Safety deposit boxes. Special telephone service. Doctor always available. Mobile homes, bungalows to rent - details from site.

Charges guide: Per person 450 - 800 ptas; child (under 10) 350 - 700; standard pitch B with electricity 1,900 - 3,200, standard pitch A with electricity 2,100 - 3,900, premium pitch with water also 2,300 - 4,200; extra car or boat 350 - 700. All plus 7% VAT. Discounts for longer stays and for pensioners.

Reservations: are possible and made with refundable booking fee (4,000 ptas). Address: Dept. de Reservas, Apdo 3, 43300 Montroig (Tarragona). Tel: 77/81.06.37. FAX: 77/81.14.11.

See colour advert
opposite page 320

N8537 Naturist Camping El Templo del Sol, L'Hospitalet de L'Infant

Although we have yet to make a formal inspection of this site our Spanish Agent has, and we have also seen it ourselves from the outside when inspecting Camping Cala d'Oques (no. 8535) which is adjacent to it, and which has access to the same beaches. Unlike Cala d'Oques, which is at beach level, El Templo del Sol is a terraced site perched high on the cliffs overlooking this superb beach, which is reached via a staircase. The site's luxurious buildings are in Moorish style, with facilities, including de-luxe sanitary installations, a cinema, bar/restaurant and supermarket, which are said to be among the best in Europe. There is, as yet, not a lot of shade and the swimming pool will not be fully open until summer '99. Under the same French management as 8540 Torre del Sol.

How to find it: From N340 south of Tarragona, exit at km. 1123 towards L'Hopitalet and follow signs.

General Details: Open 15 May - 15 October. English spoken.

Charges guide: Per person ptas. 550; child (under 10 yrs) 450; caravan or tent incl. car 2,550; motorcaravan 2,850. Credit cards accepted.

Reservations: Contact site. Address: 43890 L'Hospitalet de l'Infant (Tarragona).Tel: 977/823434. FAX: 977/811306.

8480 Camping Sanguli, Salou, nr Tarragona

Large, spacious site close to beach and within town area with pools and much entertainment.

Owned, developed and managed by a local Spanish family, this large site lies little more than 100 m. from the good sandy beach, across the coast road and a small, manned railway level crossing (some train noise at times). Although large, Sanguli manages to convey the intimacy of smaller, family run sites. There are three attractive, good sized pools (with children's pools), one with grassy lying-out area partly shaded near the entrance, and a second deep one as part of the sports complex with tennis court, two squash courts, a `fronton', minigolf and football practice area. The third is part of the new amphitheatre area at the top of the site. This will allow over 2,000 campers to sample the free nightly entertainment and enjoy the attractively designed new pool. All the pools have adjacent amenity areas, bars, etc. and from mid-June to mid-Sept. there is a comprehensive programme of entertainment. Excellent sports facilities. The site is also fortunate to be placed near the centre of Salou and so can offer the attractions of a busy resort while still being private. It is only 3 km. from Port Aventura. The sanitary facilities have been comprehensively updated and improved including a further new block in '98. They provide mostly hot water in showers and basins, including many individual cabins with `en suite' facilities. The new blocks provide excellent facilities - the showers mostly with dividers, shelves and hooks. British style WCs. All are kept very clean. The general appearance of the site has greatly improved over the years, with trees growing well, which serve to indicate the boundaries of the pitches. There is provision for 1,1,80 places, with pitch size being increased to 90 sq.m. and all with electricity connections (10A). The trees now provide natural shade. This is a large, busy site providing something for all the family, but still big enough to give peace and quiet for those looking for it. The management are friendly and very efficient. Used by some British tour operators.

How to find it: On west side of Salou about 1 km. from centre, site is well signed from the coast road to Cambrils and from the other town approaches.

General Details: Open 19 March - 31 Oct, with shop, meals and facilities available all season. 150,000 sq.m. Many electrical connections. Two supermarkets. Bars and restaurant with takeaway. Swimming pools. Sport complex with tennis, squash, football practice ground, etc. Children's playground. Minigolf. Fishing 800 m. Bicycle hire 100 m. Riding 3 km. Golf 8 km. First-aid room. Launderette with service. Chemical disposal. Motorcaravan service point.

Charges 1999: Three charging seasons. Per adult 630; child (3-12 yrs) 400 - 420; standard pitch (70-75 sq.m.) 2,100 - 3,400, `special' pitch (90 sq.m.) 2,100 - 3,800, `master' pitch (90 sq.m.) incl. water 2,300 - 4,200; extra car or m/cycle 640 - 840; electricity included. All plus 7% VAT. Less 25-35% outside high season for longer stays. Special long stay offers for senior citizens. Credit cards accepted.

Reservations: made up to 1 March with sizeable booking fee; write to site. Address: Prolongacion Calle E s/n, Apdo de Corrreos 123, 43840 Salou (Tarragona). Tel: 977 381641 or 381698. FAX: 977 384616. E-mail: mail@sanguli.es. Internet: www.sanguli.es.

See colour advert
between pages 288/289

8536 Camping-Caravanning L'Ametlla Village, L'Ametlla de Mar

One of a small number of new campsites recommended by our Spanish Agent during the autumn, which will be visited by our inspectors during '99, this is a small site in an idyllic situation. Near the picturesque fishing village of L'Ametlla de Mar, famous for its fish restaurants, and close to the Ebro Delta nature reserve, it is only about 20 minutes from Europe's second largest theme park, Port Aventura. The new site has a good range of facilities, including a bar/restaurant, swimming pool, electrical connections and modern sanitary facilities, which are said to be excellent. Being new there is, as yet, little shade. Bungalows for rent. English is spoken.

How to find it: From A7 Barcelona - Valencia, take exit 39 for L'Ametlla de Mar. Follow coast and site is 2.5 km. south of the village.

General Details: Open all year. Supermarket. Bar/restaurant. Swimming pool. Bungalows to rent.

Charges 1999: Per person ptas. 650 - 700; child (under 10 yrs) 480 - 510; car 650 - 700; tent or caravan 700 - 750; motorcaravan 1,225 - 1,300; m/cycle 480 - 510; electriciy 575. All plus 7% VAT. Less for longer stays, especially during low season.

Reservations: Contact site. Address: Apdo. Correus 240, Paraje Santes Creus, 43860 L'Ametlla de Mar (Tarragona). Tel: 977/267784 or 910/435781. FAX: 977/267868.

All the sites in this guide are regularly inspected by our team
of experienced site assessors, but we welcome your opinion too.

See Readers' Reports on page 367

8535 Camping-Pension Cala d'Oques, Hospitalet del Infante

Peaceful, simple site right beside the sea.

Cala d'Oques, or Goose Bay - this was where the migrant geese landed on return from wintering in South Africa. Hence the geese featured on the camp logo and the two guard geese who watch the entrance. The site itself has been developed with care and dedication by Elisa Roller over 20 years or so. Part of its appeal lies in its situation beside the sea with a wide beach of sand and pebbles, its amazing mountain backdrop and the views across the bay to the town and part by the atmosphere created by Elisa, her family and staff - friendly, relaxed and comfortable. The restaurant has a reputation which extends well outside the site (the cook has been there for 15 years) and the family type entertainment is in contrast to that provided at the larger, more fashionable sites of the Costa Daurada. In total there are 235 pitches, mostly level and laid out beside the beach, with more behind on wide, informal terracing. Odd pine and olive trees are an attractive feature but do not provide much shade. Electricity is available (10A, long leads may be needed). Gates provide access to the beach with cold showers to wash the sand away. The main sanitary facilities are a rather haphazard development in part of the main building which houses the restaurant, reception, the apartments to let and the family's home. They are simple but well kept with hot water to showers (a little small and no divider; shower heads from reception) and to just some of the washbasins. British style WCs. The far end of the site has a small block with toilets and washbasins. For those interested, a naturist beach is around the little headland just south of the site.

How to find it: Hospitalet del Infante is south of Tarragona, accessed from the A7 (exit 38) or from the N340. From the south take first exit to Hospitalet del Infante. Follow signs in the village, site is 2 km. south, by the sea.

General Details: Open all year. Restaurant/bar and shop (both Easter - 30 Sept). Village facilities, incl. shop and restaurant 1½ km. Fishing. Bicycle hire 2 km. Riding 3 km. Chemical disposal. Rooms to let.

Charges 1999: Per person ptas. 595 - 765; child (under 10 yrs) free; tent or caravan 595 - 765; car or m/cycle 595 - 765; motorcaravan 845 - 1,065; dog 350 - 395; electricity 435 - 495. No credit cards.

Reservations: Contact site. Address: Via Augusta, 43890 Hospitalet del Infante (Tarragona). Tel: 977/82.32.54. FAX: 977/82.06.91. E-mail: eroller@tinet.fut.es. Internet: www.fut.es/~eroller/

AR Discount
Less 5%

Costa del Azahar

The `Orange Blossom' Coast runs down the east coast from Vinaros to Almanzora, with the great port of Valencia in the middle. Orange groves grow right down to the coast, particularly in the northern section and the area is rich in fresh food from land and sea. Wine, fruit and flowers play large parts in the local economy and Paella and Zarzuela are said to have originated here. Most of the best beaches are found in the area of Peñiscola or to the south of Valencia and the area is very, very sunny.

8580 Camping Bonterra, Benicasim, nr Castellón/Castelló

Appealing, Mediterranean style site by the main road but with surprisingly little noise.

If you are looking for a site which is not too crowded and has good facilities, you will be welcomed here. It is not right by the edge of the sea but it is near enough to a good, shady beach to walk - say 300 m. - and parking is not too difficult if you want to take the car. Good beach for scuba or underwater swimmers - hire facilities available at Benicasim. There is also a small, free swimming pool on the camp itself if you prefer, with a children's pool, attractively laid out with bar, restaurant and terrace overlooking. The camp has been extended, with extra toilet blocks, giving a total of nearly 400 pitches at peak times which are marked out at their corners giving a minimum of 70 sq.m. Around half of the pitches are opened up from July. Bonterra has a clean and neat appearance with reddish soil mixed with some grass and quite a number of trees which are gradually giving good shade. Some rail noise (20 trains per day). There are four quite attractive, well maintained sanitary blocks which are sensibly laid out. They have British style toilets, some private cabins and washbasins with hot water, others with cold, 56 free hot showers with solar heating. There are showers and WCs for the disabled. No dogs are accepted in Juy/Aug. A well run site.

How to find it: Site is east of Benicasim village, with entrance off the old main N340 road running a little back from the coast. Coming from the north, turn left at sign `Benicasim por la costa'. On the A7 from the north use exit 45, from the south exit 46.

General Details: Open Easter - 30 Sept. 5.5 ha. Reasonable shade. All pitches have electrical connections. Restaurant. Bar. Snacks all season. Children's playground (some concrete bases). Disco. Adjacent supermarket. Bicycle hire. Laundry service. Chemical disposal. Motorcaravan services. Mobile homes and new chalet style bungalows to let (details from site).

Charges 1998: Per adult ptas. 240 - 440; child (3-9 yrs) 220 - 400; car 280 - 500; m/cycle 190 - 345; caravan or tent 660 - 1,200; motorcaravan 940 - 1,710; pitch Easter, July/Aug 1,850 - 2,300; electricity 6A 400, 10A 735. All plus 7% VAT. Special long stay rates excl. July/Aug. Credit cards accepted.

Reservations: made if you write at least a month in advance. Address: Avda. de Barcelona, Aptdo 77, 12560 Benicasim (Castelló). Tel: 964/30.00.07. FAX: 964/30.00.60. When closed: 964/30.02.00.

8755 Camping-Caravanning Moraira, Moraira

Interesting smaller site with swimming pool, overlooking the town.

Quietly situated in an urban area but amongst old pine trees and just 400 m. from a sheltered bay, this little site has been terraced to provide shaded pitches of varying size (access to the pitches is difficult for larger units). Some pitches have been provided with water and waste water facilities and a few have sea views. A high quality sanitary block with polished granite floors and marble fittings has recently been built to a unique and ultra-modern design. It provides extra large free hot showers and British style WCs. An attractive swimming pool with paved sunbathing terrace is another recent addition, which is also used for sub-aqua instruction. A sandy beach is 1.5 km. and shops, bars and restaurants are within walking distance.

How to find it: Site is best approached from Teulada. From A7 take exit 63 onto N332. In 3.5 km. turn right signed Teulada and Moraira. In Teulada fork right to Moraira. At junction at town entrance turn right signed Calpe and in 1 km. turn right into road to site on bend immediately after Res. Don Julio.

General Details: Open all year. Electricity connections (6/10A). Bar/restaurant and shop (main season). Swimming pool. Sub-aqua with site boat and instruction available. Tennis. Washing machine. Motorcaravan service point.

Charges 1998: Per person ptas. 575; child (4-9 yrs) 425; caravan 700; tent 575; motorcaravan 900; pitch incl. car and unit 1,600. All plus 7% VAT. Less 15-60% in low seasons.

Reservations: Write to site for details. Address: Camino Paellero 50, 03724 Moraira-Teulada (Alicante). Tel: 96/574.52.49. FAX: 96/574.53.15.

SPAIN - Costa del Azahar

8615 Camping-Caravaning Kiko, Playa de Oliva

Efficient, comfortable site beside Blue Flag beach and marina.

This site is located with direct access onto a spectacular, white, fine sandy beach that runs for miles - Kiko is towards the northwest end, which leads into a beautifully situated small marina and yacht club. Unfortunately the beach is not visible from the campsite itself, which is set at a lower level, behind a grassy bank. There are 220 pitches with hard surfaces, of variable size but access to them from the rather narrow internal roads could be difficult fot larger units. All pitches have 16A electricity (long leads may be needed) and shade and privacy is provided by deciduous trees and tall hedges. Four modern sanitary blocks are very clean and fully tiled with free hot water, large showers, washbasins (a few in cabins), British style WCs and excellent facilities for disabled visitors (who will find this site flat and convenient). There is a small bird sanctuary at the entrance, opposite the bar and supermarket. A larger beach bar is on the beach itself, which is good for swimming. The site's restaurant is also here and specialises in Valencian rice dishes and fresh fish (winning a Michelin award in '98) with entertainment in season. The footpath to the marina leads into the town - about a 10 minute walk. This is an excellent site for water sports enthusiasts and medium sized boats can be trolleyed onto the beach. Windsurfing is reputed to be good (details from reception) and there is a diving school from mid-June.

How to find it: From A7 north of Benidorm take exit 61 to the town and then the beach; site is at the northwest end.

General Details: Open all year. Bar. Beach-side bar and restaurant (all year). Supermarket (open all year, excl. Sundays). Children's playground. Watersports facilities. Entertainment for children from mid-June. Telephones. Exchange facilities. Laundry facilities. Petanque. Bicycle hire. Beach volleyball. Bungalows and apartments for rent.

Charges 1998: Per person 640 ptas; child 490; pitch 1,600 - 2,175; electricity (16A) 230 plus meter. Plus 7% VAT. Low season discounts (10-60%) for longer stays and for pensioners. Credit cards accepted.

Reservations: Contact site. Address: Apdo. 70, 46780 Playa de Oliva. Tel: 96/2850905. FAX: 96/2854320.

8560 Camping Playa Tropicana, Alcossebre, nr Castellón/Castelló

Upmarket, pleasant site with pool in quiet seaside situation beside a good beach.

Playa Tropicana has a beautiful position away from the main hub of tourism, right by a good sandy beach which shelves only gently for bathing. There is a shingle beach for fishing nearby and a promenade in front of the site. It is a quiet position and it is a drive rather than a walk to the centre of the village resort. The site takes 300 units on individual, marked pitches separated by lines of flowering bushes. The larger pitches (up to 100 sq.m.) are in the newer area where shade has developed. The original ones have been enlarged to 80 sq.m. with good shade. There are 50 places for motorcaravans with water and drainage. Movement of cars may need care when the site is full. An excellent, fully tiled toilet block has been added to the improved original one to give a good supply. British WCs, and free hot water in well spaced washbasins, including 16 in cabins, in the fully controllable showers (with screen) and the sinks. Baby baths. Some units with WC, basin and shower, and facilities for disabled people. A swimming pool (18 x 11 m.) and terrace with an individual style and a children's pool (8 x 4 m.) have been added to the restaurant complex. A site which would appeal to discerning campers.

How to find it: Alcoceber (or Alcossebre) is between Peniscola and Oropesa. Turn off N340 at campsite sign towards the town and follow signs along coast road to south of town, to site.

General Details: Open 15 March - 31 Oct. 31,000 sq.m. Electrical connections everywhere. Large supermarket (all season). Large restaurant (Easter - 30/9). Drinks served on terrace. Swimming pool. Children's playground. Volleyball. Table tennis. Fishing. Riding 3 km. Treatment room. Washing machine. Chemical disposal. Motorcaravan service point. Apartments and villa to let. No dogs are taken. No TVs allowed in July/Aug.

Charges 1999: Per person 905 ptas; child (1-10 yrs) 715; per unit incl. electricity (4A) 3,135. All plus 7% VAT. Special promotion in July - less 20% for min. 14 days. Credit cards accepted.

Reservations: made for min. 15 days with substantial deposit (5,000 ptas) and fee (5,000). Address: 12579 Alcossebre (Castellón). Tel: 964/412463 or 412448. FAX: 964/412805. Internet: www.tropicanabeach.es.

AR Discount
Less 20-45%
excl. July/Aug

Costa Blanca

The Costa Blanca (the White Coast) derives its name from its 170 miles or so of silvery-white beaches along the central section of the Spanish Mediterranean coastline. There are many sheltered bays and most beaches shelve quite gently. The countryside behind the coast remains largely untouched by mass tourism and is well worth exploring, as are places such as Alicante, Cartegena and Valencia. The most popular resort is Benidorm, which has very much shed its 'lager lout' image. Large sums of money have been spent building a beautifully paved promenade stretching the whole length of the beach, with palm trees at regular intervals. The beach itself is cleaned every night and the whole town presents a very well cared for image with plenty of police patrols in evidence. However, don't be too complacent as petty pilfering does occur. In the winter the town is filled with older people who never pose a problem, whilst in summer it is noisier and more boisterous with families and younger people on holiday.

8680 Camping Armanello, Benidorm

Friendly site with swimming pool just behind the town.

About 1 km. back from the eastern Benidorm beach (the one on the other side of the town is less crowded), Armanello is quietly situated just far enough away from the main coast road to avoid excessive noise. It is a natural, 'green' site, with pitches marked out in bays of 10 or 12 in former citrus and olive groves. There is a small and much-used swimming pool (summer only). About 103 units are taken on flat ground with 10A electricity. Two toilet blocks (arranged back to back) have washing and shower facilities with hot and cold water, British toilets, some washbasins in cabins, hot showers and baths. Hot water also for laundry and dishwashing. New facilities near reception include a washroom, shower and WC for disabled people. The site is popular with long stay Spanish units in winter.

How to find it: From new bypass (N332) take Levante Beach road into Benidorm; watch for site signs after 1 km.

General Details: Open all year. 25,000 sq.m. Shop (all year). Bar. Restaurants near. Swimming pool (summer). Fishing, bicycle hire, riding 1 km. Golf 5 km. Laundry facilities. Chemical disposal. Motorcaravan service point.

Charges 1999: Per caravan/car incl. 2 persons 900 ptas; adult 550; child (under 10) 450; motorcaravan 1,600. Plus 7% VAT. Credit cards accepted.

AR Discount
Less 10%

Reservations: contact site (much winter trade when reservation is advised). Address: Ave de la Comunidad Valenciana, 03500 Benidorm. Tel: 95/853190. FAX: 065/583100.

8681 Camping Villasol, Benidorm

Excellent, modern site with large swimming pool and views, close to town and beach.

Villasol is a genuinely excellent, modern site. There is a small indoor pool, heated for winter use and a very attractive, large outdoor pool complex featuring a lovely, sheltered pool in a beautifully landscaped, grassy sunbathing area where palm trees, shrubs and flowers create a colourful and exotic atmosphere. The pool is overlooked by the bar/restaurant and restaurant terrace. The modern, well fitted sanitary blocks provide free, controllable hot water to the showers and washbasins and British WCs. The site is terraced, with tarmac roads and gravel pitches (80-85 sq.m.). All 314 have electricity and TV connections. Shade is mainly artificial as yet. The town and Levante beach are 1.3 km. within easy walking distance leaving your car on site. Evening entertainment programme. For first class amenities in pleasant and fairly quiet surroundings, this is an excellent choice. Reservation is advised even in winter.

How to find it: From autopista take Benidorm exit (no. 65) and turn left at second set of traffic lights. After 1 km. at more lights turn right, then right again at next lights. Site is on right in 400 m. From northern end of N332 bypass follow signs for Playa Levante. In 500 m. at traffic lights turn left, then right at next lights. Site on right after 400 m.

General Details: Open all year. Electricity throughout (5A). Restaurant. Bar. Shop. Swimming pools, outdoor and indoor. Children's playground. Satellite TV. Laundry facilities. No dogs are accepted. Mobile homes to rent.

Charges 1999: Per person ptas. 575 - 790; child (1-9 yrs) 450 - 575; car 575 - 790; small tent 600 - 850; caravan 600 - 1,350; motorcaravan 1,175 - 2,140; electricity 450. All plus 7% VAT. Discounts for longer stays in winter.

Reservations: Write to site. Address: Avda. Bernat de Sarriá, s/n, 03500 Benidorm (Alicante). Tel: 96/585.04.22 or 680.08.98. FAX: 96/680.64.20.

SPAIN - Costa Blanca

8683 Camping Benisol, Benidorm

Mature `green' site with golf practice facilities.

Camping Benisol is older than the other three sites we feature in Benidorm. It is run by Jean and Brigitte Picard who provide a friendly atmosphere with a range of languages being spoken. The site is mature with well developed hedging and trees giving a good degree of privacy to each pitch. The trees are severely pruned in the winter but make tremendous growth by the summer enhanced by extra artificial shade. There are 230 touring pitches (60-80 sq.m.), all with electricity and 75 with drainage. Connecting roads are not all tarmac. The modern sanitary facilities, heated in winter and kept very clean, have free hot water to the washbasins, but by token (50 ptas) to the showers and for clothes and dish washing. Amenities include a pool with small slides (summer) and facilitiés listed below. The golf practice range is free to campers, although a charge is made for balls. Some day-time road noise should be expected.

How to find it: From autopista take Benidorm exit (no. 65), At second set of traffic lights turn left. In 1 km. at next lights continue straight on and site is on right after 500 m. From N332 at northern end of bypass follow sign for Benidorm Playa Levante and site is on left in 100 m.

General Details: Open all year. Electrical connections (4/6A). Free satellite TV link. Restaurant with terrace and bar (summer only). Shop (only 1 hour per day in winter, for essentials). Swimming pool (summer, nearest 2.5 km). Small children's play area. Minigolf. Table tennis. Jogging track. Tennis. Golf driving range. Bicycle hire 2.6 km. Fishing 3 km. Golf 12 km. Laundry. Bus route. Bungalows, caravans and rooms to let. Caravan storage adjacent.

Charges 1998: Per unit ptas. 1,600 - 1,800 for 60 sq.m. pitch, 1,800 - 2,200 for 70 sq.m; person 500 - 550; child (1-10 yrs) 400 - 450; extra tent or car 500 - 550; m/cycle 400 - 450; electricity (220v) 375 per kw/hr. All plus 7% VAT. Less 15-60% in low seasons.

Reservations: Contact site for details. Address: Avda. de la Comunidad Valenciana, s/n, 03500 Benidorm. Tel: 96/5851673. FAX: 96/5860895.

8685 Camping Caravaning El Raco, Benidorm

Quality site with indoor and outdoor pools and views.

This purpose built site with excellent facilities and very competitive prices, originally opened in '96, has now been extended to provide 343 pitches. There is wide access from the Runcon de Loix road (no problem with access for large RVs but check pitch availability before arrival). The site is fairly quietly situated 1.5 km. from the town, Levante beach and promenade. The road has both footpaths and a cycle track, making the site a good choice for motorcaravanners who may prefer to leave their unit on site. Wide tarmac roads lead to pitches of 80 sq.m. or more, surfaced in rolled grit and separated by low, cypress hedging; there is not much shade as yet. Free satellite TV connections are provided to each pitch and there are 94 with all services. The whole site is on a slight downward slope away from the entrance and affords excellent views of the rugged mountains, although this open aspect could be a disadvantage in windy weather. The facilities are excellent. The two toilet blocks are large and well provided with showers, washbasins, laundry and dishwashing sinks (all with free hot water) and facilities for disabled people. The shop is well stocked and the prices reasonable. The swimming pool is a lovely feature surrounded by a grass sunbathing area. No slides or diving boards - and no shade, except perhaps parasols. A new indoor pool has been opened for winter use. A clean, tidy and good quality site.

How to find it: From the autopista take Benidorm exit (no. 65) and turn left at the second set of traffic lights. After 1 km. at another set of lights turn right, then straight on at next lights for 300 m. to site on right. From northern end of N332 bypass follow signs for Benidorm Playa Levante. In 500 m. at traffic lights turn left, then straight on at next lights for 300 m. to site on right.

General Details: Open all year. Electricity (5, 6, 10A) and satellite TV connections. Restaurant (good value). Bar (also open to public). Outdoor swimming pool (1/4-31/10). Indoor heated pool (1/11-31/3). Shop. Exchange facilities. Children's playground. Bicycle hire, fishing 1.5 km. Golf 8 km. Beach 1 km. Laundry facilities. Caravan storage.

Charges 1998: Per person ptas. 575 - 625; child (1-9 yrs) 375 - 440; car 525 - 625; tent 525 - 625; caravan 630 - 715; motorcaravan 850 - 1,025; m/cycle 400 - 475; electricity (220v) 395 - 445. Less for longer stays. VAT incl.

Reservations: Not accepted. Address: Avda. Doctor Severo Ochoa, s/n, 03500 Benidorm (Alicante). Tel: 96/5868552. FAX: 96/5868544.

8741 Camping Florantilles, Torrevieja, nr Alicante

Modern site with good views, some 4 km. behind the coast, open all year.

Florantilles is a very well laid out, attractive site with good views over the top of the neighbouring citrus groves to a distant salt lake. In winter and spring the delicious scent of orange blossom fills the air, a quiet haven away from the bustle of the nearby coastal resorts. Mimosa trees provide shade for the 271 good-sized pitches (around 90 sq.m.) which are laid out on wide terraces; some very large pitches are available at extra cost. Electricity connections (10A) are provided for each pitch, together with water and a raised drain. The two main sanitary blocks provide British style WCs, controllable hot showers and laundry facilities .Several smaller blocks dotted around the site with toilets and showers but no hot water. The attractive site entrance has a large parking area with car wash facilities, with the entrance to the camping area protected by a barrier (key).

continued overleaf

8741 Camping Florantilles (continued)

Good size swimming pool (supervised in season), plus children's pool, restaurant, bar and shop (limited opening in low season). Keep fit , barbecues arranged in season. Walking clubs are popular, also bird watching, cycling and golf (discounts available). Swiss owned and British managed.

How to find it: Leave A7 autopista at exit 77 on to recently upgraded and renumbered CV90 (formerly C3321). 1 km. south of Torrevieja turn inland (northwest) onto the C3323 signed San Miguel. In 4 km. turn right at sign `Los Montesinos' and campsite sign. Site is on left after 200 m.

General Details: Open all year. Bar/restaurant. Shop (limited hours in low seasons). Swimming pool (closed winter). Tennis. Boules. Children's playground. Golf 4 km. Watersports near. Laundry facilities. Caravan storage.

Charges 1998: Per person ptas 300 - 600; child (1-12 yrs) 250 - 500; caravan/car or motorcaravan 700 - 1,400; electricity 400. All plus 7% VAT. Special low season discounts. No credit cards.

Reservations: Contact site. Address: 03193 S. Miguel de Salinas (Alicante). Tel: 96/5720456. FAX: 96/6723250.

8742 Camping Internacional La Marina, La Marina, nr Elche

Busy, well managed holiday site close to beach, with good facilities.

Run by a Belgian family, this site is nevertheless very popular with the Spanish themselves, with around half of the 394 pitches taken by seasonal units. For touring units, there are four different type and size of pitch ranging from 50 sq.m. for tents to 100 sq.m. with electricity (5A), TV, water and drainage. Shade is available and the pitches are well maintained on fairly level, gravel ground. An area for tents is in a small orchard. The site has a good sized swimming pool, paddling pool and `plunge' pool and beside the pools .is a bar/restaurant with terrace (Spanish menu). These are very busy in season and tickets are required for the pool. A fitness centre and covered, heated pool (14 x 7 m. 300 ptas. charge) have been added. An elegant new central sanitary block has been built with the best of modern facilities. Heated in winter, it has free controllable hot water to large showers and wash cabins and facilities for disabled visitors. Two other blocks are still to be renovated, these having only cold water to washbasins. A gate has been added to give access to the long sandy beach, just 500 m. away through the coastal pine forest.

How to find it: Site is 2 km. west of La Marina on seaward side of N332 Guardamara de Segura - Santa Pola road.

General Details: Open all year. Bar/restaurant and supermarket (all year also). Swimming pools (Easter - Oct). Indoor pool (heated Oct - Easter). Fitness centre. Sauna. Tennis. Table tennis. Children's playground. Fishing 500 m. Bicycle hire 8 km. Golf 15 km. Hairdresser. Laundry facilities incl. irons. Exchange facilities. Car wash. Chemical disposal. Motorcaravan service point. Chalets (5 persons) to rent.

Charges 1999: Per person ptas. 600; child (under 10 yrs) 400; pitch 1,200 (50-70 sq.m.), 1,900 (70-90 sq.m.) or 2,400 (100 sq.m.); pitch with water, sewerage 2,400; electricity 350. Plus 7% VAT. Less in low season, plus good discounts for longer stays 16/9-14/6, excluding Easter. Credit cards accepted.

Reservations: Made with deposit (ptas 500); min. 5 days Easter and Aug). Address: Ctra N-332 km.76, 03194 La Marina (Alicante). Tel: 96/541.90.51. FAX: 96/541.91.10. E-mail: lamarina@apdo.com.

AR Discount
Gift of local pottery

SPAIN - Costa Blanca

N8752 Camping Naturista El Portus, Cartagena

See colour advert between pages 192/3

Attractive, very friendly naturist site right beside the Mediterranean, open all year.

Set in a secluded, mountain fringed, south facing bay, El Portus is a fairly large site with direct access to a sandy beach and enjoying magnificent views. With its own micro-climate, this part of Spain enjoys all year round sunshine. Mid-day temperatures which seldom drop below 20°C and water almost always warm enough for swimming makes this an ideal site for hibernating! There are some 400 numbered pitches, ranging from 60-100 sq.m, all but a few having electricity (5/10A), mostly on fairly level, if somewhat stony, ground with a reasonable amount of shade which is gradually increasing as more trees are planted making parts very attractive. The sanitary facilities are housed in five blocks of varying style which are opened as required and are gradually being refurbished. The standard of provision and maintenance is generally good, with British style WCs, open plan hot showers, dishwashing and laundry facilities, but with only cold water to open plan washbasins. However, we suspect they may be a little hard-pressed in peak season (mid July - mid Aug). Unit for disabled visitors, key from reception. Three drinking water points are clearly marked near the steps to the restaurant and non-drinking water points are well spaced around the site. There is large, supervised swimming pool and paddling pool in a sheltered, landscaped situation with grass areas for sunbathing close to the beach and a beach bar/snack bar open mid June - mid Sept. At other times there is a smaller heated pool located above the camping area, near the restaurant and close to a hillside area (known as `Beverley Hills') with a fair number of quite luxurious mobile homes. New children's play area. The restaurant with a nice relaxed atmosphere is open all year with an adjacent TV room/library, bar and shop. It enjoys superb views across the bay and of the surrounding mountains and provides a good choice of meals including a `Menu del Dia' which is also available on a half-board arrangement, including breakfast. This is a very comfortable site with welcoming, English speaking reception staff.

How to find it: Site is on the coast, 10 km. west of Cartagena, via Canteras. Follow signs to Pryca commercial centre, then turn right to Canteras. After passing through village take left turn (signed) down to El Portus.

General Details: Open all year. Restaurant. Shop. Swimming pools. Tennis. Volleyball. Table tennis. Petanque. Yoga. Scuba-diving club (July/Aug). Windsurfing. Spanish lessons. Small boat moorings. Disco and entertainment (high season). Golf near. Chemical disposal. Motorcaravan services. Mobile homes and chalets to rent.

Charges 1999: Per person ptas. 775; child (3-7 yrs) 570; pitch 1,630, with electricity 2,300; extra tent 400; extra car or m/cycle 475; dog 525. Discounts for longer stays in low season (over 7, 14 or 21 days). Credit cards accepted.

Reservations: made with large deposit. Address: 30393 Cartagena. Tel: 968/55.30.52. FAX: 968/55.30.53. E-mail: portus@hipocom.es. Internet: www.hipocom.es/portus/.

Barry Westwood is the UK co-ordinator for Camping Naturiste El Portus and La Manga. Both sites are open all year and Epsol can advise and arrange ferry tickets plus site fees, transport or car hire from Alicante or Murcia airports. Mobile homes also available to rent

EPSOL Tours, 22 Cromhamstone, Stone, Aylesbury HP17 8NH Tel: 01296 747260 Fax: 01296 747430

8753 Camping-Caravaning La Manga, La Manga, nr Cartagena

Impressively large, well equipped, `holiday style' campsite with own beach and pool.

On arrival at this site, one's first impressions of the efficient reception area, etc. are very favourable, but you could easily be put off by the large number of semi-permanent mobile homes, many of which are situated beneath ugly tin roofs (for shade) which seem to dominate that part of the site which adjoins the main access road. This would be a pity, as this site has many excellent features which outweigh any negative impressions created by these rather unsightly residential units. La Manga itself seems to be largely undiscovered by the British (although our World Cup squad stayed at La Manga Club here in '98) and it is certainly an area which will appeal to those who like busy and quite smart holiday resorts. La Manga is a 22 km. long narrow strip of land, bordered by the Mediterranean on one side and by the Mar Menor on the other. There are sandy bathing beaches on both sides and considerable development in terms of hotels, apartments, restaurants, night clubs, etc. in between - shades of Miami Beach in fact! The campsite is fairly quietly situated on the approach to `the strip' and enjoys the benefit of its own semi-private beach alongside the Mar Menor, with a sailing, canoeing and windsurfing school and the site's own, good restaurant and bar right beside the beach. The beach is dotted with impressive tall palm trees and the sea is very shallow and warm, so it is ideal for families with small children. There are some 1,000 touring pitches of two sizes (84 or 110 sq m), regularly laid out in rows on level gravel. They are separated and shaded by high hedges and all have electricity and water connections. Seven toilet blocks of standard design are well spaced around the site. They provide cold water to washbasins, controllable hot showers and covered cold water sinks (three with hot water) for washing up and laundry. Large, supervised pool complex, with bar/snack bar alongside, a well stocked supermarket and a wide range of activities. This site's excellent facilities are ideally suited for holidays in the winter, when the weather is said to be similar to an English summer (that could mean anything, we know, but hopefully you'll catch the drift) - November daytime temperatures, for example, are usually above 20°C. Note: the snack bar, pool complex, open air cinema and medical centre are only available in season. *continued overleaf*

8753 Camping-Caravaning La Manga (continued)

How to find it: Use exit 15 from MU312 dual-carriageway towards Cabo de Palos, signed Playa Honda (site signed also). Cross bridge and double back on yourself. Site entrance is visible beside dual-carriageway with flags flying.

General Details: Open all year. Electricity connections (10A). Supermarket. Restaurant. Bar. Snack bar. Swimming pool complex. Tennis courts. Petanque. Open air cinema. Minigolf. Basketball. Volleyball. Football area. Children's play area. Sailing school. Golf at La Manga Club (1 km). Public phone. Safe deposit. Medical service. Laundry service. Mobile homes and chalets to rent.

Charges 1998: Per 84 sq.m. pitch incl. 2 persons ptas 2,550 - 3,350, 3 persons 2,850 - 3,775, 4 persons 3.150 - 4,200; per 110 sq.m. pitch incl. 2 persons 3,000 - 4,000, 3 persons 3.300 - 4.400, 4 persons 3,725 - 4,900; prices for up to 8 persons available; child under 6 yrs free; electricity included. All plus 7% VAT. Less 10, 20 or 25% for stays of more than 7, 14 or 21 days in low season. Special prices for long winter stays.

Reservations: are made. Address: 30370 La Manga del Mar Menor, Cartagena (Murcia). Tel: 968/563014. FAX: 968/563426. E-mail: caravaning@interxen,com. Internet: www.arrakis.es/ -caravaning.

8751 Camping Cuevas Mar, Palomares, Cuevas del Almanzora

Pleasant, good quality new site in popular area, open all year.

Only opened in '95 but already gaining a reputation for excellent, comfortable facilities, Cuevas Mar is a welcome addition in a region very popular with British visitors who appreciate its year-round dry, sunny climate. Quietly situated just back from the coast road (little or no road noise on site) and 500 m. across the road from the beach, the site offers 136 exceptionally large pitches for Spain (80-100 sq.m), all with electricity connections (6A) and firm surfaces. The pitches are screened by hedges and young trees which afford a degree of shade and have easy access from wide roads. The sheltered, tiled, oval-shaped pool (14 x 9 m) is surrounded by a grassy sunbathing area and has a thoughtfully provided long ramp to help the elderly or infirm (other than access ramps, there are no other facilities for disabled people at present). Although unheated, the pool is kept open all year. Beside the pool is a free jacuzzi, petanque and a small, shaded outdoor bar area. The central sanitary block is well designed, generous in size and adequate, providing large tiled shower cubicles, British style WCs and (rare and much appreciated) full length mirrors! Good laundry and dishwashing facilities are under cover with free hot water everywhere. Two drinking water points (in common with many other sites in this very dry area, drinking water is supplied from tanks refilled by tanker delivery and the remainder of the water on site is non-potable).

How to find it: Site is on the landward side of the Villaricos - Garrucha road, 4 km. from Villaricos, 6 km. from Garrucha. From the N340 use exit for Cuevas del Almanzora (km. 537), and follow signs for Palomares, then site.

General Details: Open all year. Shop. Outdoor bar by pool. Restaurant 200 m.

Charges 1998: Per person ptas. 600; child 500; car 600; caravan or tent 600; motorcaravan 1,200; m/cycle 500; dog 200; electricty 500. Discounts for longer winter stays.

Reservations: Contact site. Address: 04618 Palomares, Cuevas del Almanzora (Almeria). Tel: 950/46 73 82.

8750 Camping Los Gallardos, Los Gallardos

Friendly, English owned and managed site with all year round facilities.

Since 1991 Anthony and Shirley Jackson and their family have built this site up from barren land into the comfortable, homely site one finds today. Set in open country with views of the distinctive mountains of the region in the distance, Los Gallardos is a green oasis in which to enjoy some of the sunniest and driest winter weather to be found in mainland Europe and very many British campers do just that! There are 114 good sized, flat pitches marked by flowering trees with easy access and firm surfaces. The majority have 5/10A electricity and a few have all services with 15A electricity if required, although these new pitches have no shade as yet. The central sanitary block has good-sized showers, British style WCs and free hot water for showers and washbasins, with one hot tap to draw water for dishwashing and laundry. The Jacksons are keen to help visitors get the best out of their stay and organise plenty of activities all year round. The swimming pool (unheated), with sunbathing area, sunbeds and keep fit sessions, is open all year, as is the adjacent bar/restaurant (daily 9-4, 7-late) where special dish evenings, Sunday roasts, bridge mornings and games evenings are organised regularly. Excursions to Granada, local restaurants and places of interest are arranged. A good area for walking and beaches are within 10 km. Two full sized grass lawn bowling greens have been created (temporary membership for campers). Reception and small shop with English foodstuffs and fresh bread each day. Although the site itself is quiet, some road noise from the busy nearby N340 should be expected.

How to find it: Leave the CN340 at km. 525, signed Los Gallardos and follow camp signs.

General Details: Open all year, as are shop, bar, restaurant and swimming pool. Spit roast chicken to order. English breakfasts. Swimming pool. Bowling greens. Animal farm. Boules. Bridge mornings. Spanish lessons. Exchange library, video and jigsaw puzzle hire. Golf 8 km. Riding 3 km. Excursions. Information sheets. Hairdresser calls weekly. Washing machines and dryer. Chemical disposal. Motorcaravan service point. Caravan storage.

Charges 1998/9: Per person ptas. 475; child 325; car 475; caravan or tent 475; motorcaravan 950; m/cycle 375; electricity 325. Discounts for longer stays and up to 65% in winter. Credit cards accepted.

Reservations: Write to site. Address: 04280 Los Gallardos (Almeria). Tel: 950/52.83.24. FAX: as phone. E-mail: campgall@lander.es. Internet: www.lander.es/~campgall.

Costa del Sol

The Costa del Sol stretches from Gibraltar north-eastward along the Mediterranean coast for some 250 miles and, even in April and October, averages 7-8 hours of sunshine daily, with average temperatures of around 20°C. The most popular (and most commercialised) resorts are Torremolinos and Marbella, both of which have much to offer, but there are several quieter and more tranquil resorts such as Fuengirola and Nerja. For sightseeing, there are many historic towns and cities within range, including Seville, Granada, and Cordoba, as well as a host of Andalucian villages.

8760 Camping Mar Azul, El Ejido, nr Almeria

Sea-front site, on its own by beach, with good sized pitches and many sporting activities.

Right beside the sea, on flat ground and with direct access to a sandy beach, Mar Azul is in a dry and sunny area of Spain where there are not many other camping sites. The landscape is dominated by the Sierra Nevada (but is rendered somewhat unsightly behind the site by local farmers' use of acres of plastic cloches, as along most of this coast). The site normally has space as it has not yet become widely known. About 450 individual, numbered pitches are quite attractively laid out with palm trees between them and at 90 sq.m. are larger than most in Spain. Artificial shade is provided on most pitches. The four toilet blocks are of good quality with British style toilets, washbasins and free hot showers. A circular, unheated swimming pool with child's pool and a terrace and sun-beds, is near the beach, a further pool is in the centre of the site, where there is a large area set aside for many sports, a third pool has been added. The site lies out on its own, but the large development of Almerimar with golf course, large hotel, restaurant, some shops, etc. is little over 1 km. along the beach. El Ejido is 8 km.

How to find it: Turn off main N340/E15 road at km. 409 (El Ejido-Almerimar) exit. Site is on east side of El Ejido, from where it is signed.

General Details: Open all year. Supermarket (1/4-15/10). Bar (1/4-15/10 and winter weekends). Restaurant (1/4-15/10). Swimming pools and child's pool (1/4-15/10). Tennis. Fronton. Squash. Table tennis. Fitness centre. Boules. Volleyball. Badminton. Basketball. Riding. Archery. Bicycle hire and circuit. Roller skating. Minigolf. Football practice area. Fishing. Windsurfing school and equipment for hire. Activities organised for children. Golf 1.5 km. Washing machines. Treatment room; doctor visits in season. Chemical disposal. Motorcaravan service point. Bungalows to rent (details from site). Caravan storage.

Charges 1998: Per person 300 - 625 ptas.; child (2-10 yrs) 200 - 550; tent or caravan 300 - 625; car 300 - 625; motorcaravan 600 - 990; electricity 300 - 450. All plus 7% VAT. Credit cards accepted.

Reservations: are made for any length. Address: Apdo. Correos 39, 04700 El Ejido (Almeria). Tel: 950/497585 or 497505. FAX: 950/497294. E-mail: cmazul@a2000.es.

AR Discount
Less 10% on person charge

8770 Camping El Paraiso, Almuñecar

Smaller, attractive, family run site on beach with excellent restaurant.

This is a well maintained site of 80 pitches on the beach at Almuñecar Costa Tropical. It is open all year and is a useful stopping point when moving to the south coast from Granada. It is quiet and tucked away, unlike the larger sites along the coast. The owner has a penchant for blue tiles and this is evident in the various facilities on site. Imaginative use of patterned tiles brings the site to life and is most attractive under the canopy of huge trees which provide plentiful shade to most pitches. There is a variety of sanitary blocks which have been added over the years. All are clean and well maintained. A strong feature of the site is the restaurant/bar complex which has been cleverly designed and the patio area is very pretty indeed. A step out of the rear entrance past the supermarket takes you to the beach with sand of varying textures. The esplanade is attractive with many restaurants and bars. Again this is relatively peaceful, unlike the major holiday beaches on the Costas. Part of the site is on a gentle slope but the pitches are level and all are supplied with electricity. There is a free car wash and lots of covered parking on site. The site is well managed and good security is in place day and night. There are generous discounts for extended off season stays. Bus service from directly outside the site to La Herradura, a fishing resort suburb of Almuñecar. Buses also run to Granada, Nerja and Motril.

How to find it: Access from N 340 at 317.5 km. marker; follow site markers down towards beach - site is on left.

General Details: Open all year. Electricity connections (4A). Very good bar/restaurant. Supermarket. Laundry facilities. Car wash. Beach. Tennis club 500 m. Walks from site.

Charges 1998: Per adult 650 ptas; child 550; tent 650 - 1025; caravan 890; car 650; motorcaravan 1,025; m/cycle 450; electricity 250. All plus 7% VAT. Less 30-65% for extended stays.

Reservations: Contact site. Address: Ctra N340 km.317.5, Almuñecar (Granada). Tel/Fax: 958/632370.

Some sites have supplied us with copies of their brochures
which we are pleased to forward to readers.
See our Brochure Service on page 366

8711 Nerja Camping, Maro-Nerja

Spectacularly situated small site with swimming pool and glorious views.

So many Spanish camp sites seem to look like local authority car parks that it is nice to be able to report on one that is about as unlike a car park as you could possibly get! Set on the lower slopes of the Sierra Almijara, some 5 km. from Nerja and 2 km. from the nearest beach, Nerja Camping is a delightful small site of 60 pitches (30 with 15A electricity) with impressive views of the surrounding mountains and nearby Mediterranean. Being situated slightly above but alongside the main coast road, it is easy to find - the price you pay is some traffic noise but this seems hardly to detract from the relaxing and almost idyllic ambience. The pitches are of reasonable size on flat terraces with mainly artificial shade, whilst the roads, although quite steep, are newly surfaced and should present little problem except perhaps to drivers of really huge motorhomes. The site also boasts a small swimming pool, a bar/restaurant serving simple fresh dishes and even large breakfasts, all cooked and served by the Irish owner Peter Kemp and his Spanish wife Make on the terrace beside their magnificent carob tree. The single sanitary block is of modern design and construction with British type WCs, some free hot showers, washbasins (1 only with hot water), dishwashing sinks (cold water) under cover and laundry facilities.

How to find it: Site signed from N340 5 km. north of Nerja (from Nerja, go 50 m. past site to cross main road).

General Details: Open all year except Oct. Swimming pool (excl. Feb/March). Bar/restaurant (March - Sept). Essentials from the bar. Pool table. Mountain bike hire. Washing machines. Chemical disposal. Bus service nearby.

Charges 1999: Per person ptas. 550; child (2-10 yrs) 450; tent 550 - 700; caravan 700; car 550; motorcaravan 800; m/cycle 400; electricity 450. All plus 7% VAT. Less 20-40% outside 1/6-30/9. Long stay rates. No credit cards.

Reservations: Write to site for details. Address: Ctra. N340 - km. 297, 28787 Maro - Nerja (Malaga). Tel: 95/2529714. FAX: 95/2529696.

8782 Camping-Caravaning Laguna Playa, Torre del Mar

Beach-side family run site with own swimming pool.

Laguna Playa is a modern site with very friendly staff who give a personal service. Alongside one of the Costa del Sol beaches, the site is well placed for visits to Malaga and Nerja with a regular bus service 700 m. away. The site organises weekly trips to the famous Alhambra Mosque in Granada. Pitches are flat, of average size and with good artificial shade supplementing that provided by the established trees on site. All pitches have electricity. Attractive adults and children's swimming pools open in high season. The two modern, well equipped sanitary blocks have free showers. The site runs a busy restaurant offering value for money, plus a bar and supermarket. There is a children's play area and the site organises various competitions including `petan' in the summer. A unique feature is that the owners will exchange English gas cylinders for a Spanish version and the reverse if you are headed for home.

How to find it: Site is on the sea front Paseo Maritimo, at Torre del Mar on the main N340 Malaga - Nerja road.

General Details: Open all year. Electricity connections (5/10A). Bar/restaurant and supermarket (all year). Swimming pools. Children's play area. Laundry facilities. Car wash. Bungalows to rent.

Charges 1998: Per adult 565 ptas; child 445; tent 565; caravan 625; car 565; motorcaravan 1150; m/cycle 445; electricity 350 (metered in winter). All plus 7% VAT. Less 10-50% longer stays in low/mid seasons.

Reservations: Write to site. Address: Prolongación Paseo Marítimo, s/n 29740 Torre del Mar (Malaga). Tel: 95/2540631. FAX: 95/2540484.

8801 Camping La Rosaleda, Los Boliches, nr Fuengirola

Smaller family site with pool, 1 km. north of Fuengirola.

This is a small friendly site of 112 pitches tucked in the hills to the north of the fashionable resort of Fuengirola. It is convenient for visiting Torremolinos and the numerous major theme parks close by. The site enjoys some good views towards the mountains and over the town towards the sea, the beach is approximately 1 km. south of the site. There is an attractive, medium sized swimming pool with paved surround and a grass sunbathing area. The pitches are of about 60 sq.m. and on flattish, grassy/sandy ground with a good proportion having electricity (5A). Many are separated by chain link fencing, some with hedges and established trees giving natural shade for most pitches. The two sanitary blocks are dated but clean and appear to be adequate. There are free hot showers, British type WCs, dishwashing and washing sinks under cover and three washing machines. The site is very busy in July/August.

How to find it: For some reason the camping signs at 211.5 km. on the eastern N 340 at Fuengirola autopista direct you into the busy town centre before recrossing the autopista to gain access to the site at the end of a gravel road. However, it is a straightforward approach from the west.

General Details: Open all year. Bar/restaurant (1/6-30/9) serving mainly pizzas (to takeaway) and pastas. Small supermarket (1/7-30/9). Swimming pool (15/3-30/10) with pool-side bar in main season. Fishing 800 m. Bicycle hire 500 m. Riding 2 km. Golf 5 km. Washing machines. Chemical disposal.

Charges 1999: Per adult ptas. 650; child 325; caravan 850; motorcaravan 1,000; tent 750; car or m/cycle included; electricity 300. No credit cards.

Reservations: Write to site. Address: N-340 km. 211.5, Los Boliches, 29640 Fuengirola (Malaga). Tel: 952/460191. FAX: 952/581966.

AR Discount
Less 10%
if no other
discounts taken

311

SPAIN - Costa del Sol

8805 Camping Los Jarales, Mijas-Costa

Spacious, medium sized site with pool and close to attractive beaches.

This is a well maintained site on the Costa del Sol which is open all year. The site is on a slope but the pitches are level, and all are supplied with water, waste water drainage, electricity, terrestrial and satellite TV connections. Larger motorhomes are capable of 'plumbing in' if required. The central sanitary block is clean and well equipped offering free showers and hot water at the sinks. There is a good size swimming pool (high season), along with a pleasant restaurant and bar which open all year. The beaches are a few minutes walk on the far side of the N 340. Most pitches have natural shade from established, attractive trees. A children's play area is near the restaurant. The site is ideal for visiting Ronda, Marbella and the numerous theme parks close by. The staff are very friendly and will assist with bookings if required. A supermarket on site opens in the summer but there are many supermarkets nearby, along with a myriad of bars and restaurants. Bus service from outside site to town.

How to find it: Site is well signed off the main N340 at the 197 km. marker between Fuengirola and Marbella.

General Details: Open all year. Electricity connections (5, 10 or 15A). Serviced pitches with TV. Bar/restaurant near beach. Supermarket. Swimming pool. Children's play area. Basketball/tennis court. Laundry. Car wash.

Charges 1999: Per adult 400 - 600 ptas; child 350 - 500; tent 350 - 650; caravan 450 - 800; car 350 - 500; motorcaravan incl. 2 persons 1,450 - 2,500; m/cycle 300 - 400; electricity 350 (metered in winter). All plus 7% VAT.

AR Discount
Less 10%
excl. July/Aug.

Reservations: Write to site. Address: Ctra. N340 km.197, Mijas-Costa (Malaga). Tel/Fax: 952/930003.

8803 Camping La Buganvilla, nr Marbella

Large site 7 km. from Marbella with footbridge access to beach.

This site takes its name from the display of flowers native to Spain which can be seen on the restaurant/bar complex. It is large, (300 pitches) with three large sanitary blocks attractively painted powder blue. The facilities provided are more than adequate and were spotlessly clean when seen. Some of the main pitches are shaded by trees, and there are other areas for tents in heavily wooded areas (electricity provided). All other pitches have electricity and there are 20 fully serviced pitches for larger motorhomes. The site has a large bar and restaurant area, the patio of which overlooks the swimming pools. The adult pool is well maintained and free, as is the children's version. The northern part of the site is terraced with some large, additional separate pitches specifically for tour operators. There is a supermarket and modern car wash (at a cost of 200 ptas). A footbridge connects the site directly with the golden sands of the Costa del Sol beaches and, although the site is close to the N340 traffic, noise seems to be absorbed by the abundant trees on its southern edge. The resort of Fuengirola is 19 km. east.

How to find it: Access is between Marbella and Fuengirola off the N340 at the 188.8 km. marker. It is advisable to gain access to the site travelling from Fuengirola to Marbella otherwise you will be obliged to tackle a rough track around the rear of the site (the U-turn over the road bridge to achieve this is worthwhile!). Follow campsite signs.

General Details: Open all year. Electricity connections (10A). Large bar/restaurant complex. Supermarket. Swimming pools. Children's play areas. Basketball and tennis in season. Laundry facilities. Car wash. Footbridge to beach. Regular bus service available from outside site. Good security at all times.

Charges 1998: Per adult 525 ptas; child 425; tent 750; caravan 800; car 525; motorcaravan 975; m/cycle 425; electricity 350. All plus 7% VAT.

Reservations: Contact site. Address: Ctra N340 km.188.8, 29600 Marbella (Malaga). Tel: 952/831973 or 4. FAX: 952/831974. E-mail:buganvilla@spar.es. Internet: http:www.costadelsol.spa.es/camping/buganvilla.

AR Discount
Less 10%
excl. July/Aug.

8809 Camping El Sur, Ronda

Small and interesting family owned site close to Ronda.

The generous manoeuvring area and delightfully decorated entrance to this site are a promise of something different which is fulfilled in all respects. The very friendly family who run the site have worked hard for ten years combining innovative thinking with excellent service. The single sanitary block is immaculate and the free hot showers a real treat. The average size pitches are partially shaded by carefully planted olive and almond trees. Most pitches have relaxing views of the surrounding mountains but at an elevation of 850 m. the upper pitches allow a clear view of the fascinating town of Ronda which should be visited. Most pitches have electricity and water and are terraced on sand/grass. The restaurant is in three large sections and is a delight, serving excellent food at reasonable prices (the owners eat there). The bar and restaurant are bedecked with very tasteful local artistry which may be purchased as a quality memento of the area and the views from the complex are enjoyable, especially at sunset. The various leisure facilities are very clean, well maintained and the personal touches of the owners are obvious which make the experience of using them more enjoyable. The kidney shaped pool is most welcome in summer as temperatures soar. Two children's play areas with safe activities and minigolf. This peaceful site also offers some attractive cabins and chalets for hire. *continued overleaf*

8809 Camping El Sur (continued)

How to find it: Site is well signed from town centre and is off no. 341 Algeciras road, 1.5 km. south of Ronda.

General Details: Open all year. Electricity connections (5A). Bar and very large, high quality restaurant. Swimming pool. Children's playground and adventure play area. Off road bicycle hire. Laundry facilities. First aid room and doctor on call. Bungalows and chalets for hire.

Charges 1998: Per person 425 ptas; child 300; tent 400; caravan 400; car 400; m/cycle 300; motorcaravan 800; electricity 300. Plus 7% VAT

Reservations: Recommended for July/Aug. Address: Ctra Ronda - Algeciras, km. 1.5 Apartado de Correos 127, 29400 Ronda. Tel: 95/2875939. FAX: 95/2877054.

8800 Camping-Caravaning Marbella Playa, Marbella

Large modern site on northern outskirts of Marbella, with good pool.

This site is on the outskirts of the internationally famous resort of Marbella with public transport to the town centre. A sandy beach is about 150 m. with direct access. There are 430 pitches of up to 70 sq.m. with natural shade (additional artificial shade provided), with electricity throughout. A large swimming pool complex with a restaurant/bar and palm trees provides a very attractive feature. The three sanitary blocks are modern with free hot showers, 2 small baths, 2 private cabins and 16 washbasins in each. Two fully equipped units for disabled visitors and all facilities are kept very clean. Laundry and washing up areas are modern and in good order. The supermarket is very large. The site is busy in high season but the high staff/customer ratio and the friendly staff approach ensures a comfortable stay.

How to find it: Site is 12 km. east of Marbella with access close to the 193 km. point on the main N340 road.

General Details: Open all year, as are supermarket, bar, restaurant and café. Electricity connections (16/20A). Swimming pool (April-Sept). First aid centre. Children's playground (on gritty sand). Bureau de change.

Charges 1998: Per person 300 - 550 ptas; child (1-10 yrs) 260 - 475; car 300 - 555; caravan/tent 500 - 935; m/cycle 280 - 500; motorcaravan 1,310 - 1,700; electricity 385; minimum pitch fee 1,400 - 2,600. All plus 7% VAT. Reductions for long stays and senior citizens outside 16/6-31/8.

Reservations: Write to site. Address: Ctra N-340, Km. 192,800, 29600 Marbella, Costa del Sol (Malaga). Tel: 95/2833998. FAX: 95/2833999.

AR Discount
Less 10% excl. July/Aug

Costa de la Luz

This is the stretch of coast running from Gibraltar in the east to the Portuguese border in the west. Despite being even further south, it does not enjoy quite the same climate as the Costa del Sol as it borders the Atlantic rather than the Mediterranean - but this may be an advantage during high summer. The eastern end of this coast is quite attractive with many wonderful views across to Africa and we feature several sites in this area. However, the western end, apart from the Donana National Park and some large beaches, is rather different. We searched this coast, running from La Rocia up to Huelva, looking for a site and, so far, have found just one at this end up to guide standards (at Isla Cristina).

8850 Camping Paloma, Tarifa, nr Algeciras

Attractively situated site with beaches nearby, 12 km. northwest of Tarifa.

A spacious, neat and tidy, family orientated site, Paloma is 700 m. from the nearest beach which has good facilities for bathing and windsurfing. The site has some 380 pitches on mostly flat ground, although the westerly pitches are sloping. The pitches are of a reasonable size, separated by hedges and some are shaded by mature trees; approximately 200 pitches have electrical connections. There are two modern sanitary blocks, one of a good size, though a long walk from the southern end of the site. The other is smaller and open plan, serving the sloping areas of the site. They have mostly Turkish style WCs, some British, washbasins with cold water, (some in cubicles and with bidets for women) and 12 free controllable hot showers. Dedicated facilities for disabled visitors are provided in the smaller sanitary block with access from sloping ground, also a babies room. All sanitary facilities were very clean when seen. There is a small (free) swimming pool with a paved sunbathing area and an attractive thatched, stone bar. Paloma has a small children's play area on sand and several modern. Fully equipped bungalows to rent.

How to find it: Site is signed off the N340 Cadiz road at Punta Paloma, about 10 km. northwest of Tarifa, just west of the km 74 marker. Watch carefully for the site sign - no advance notice. Follow the signs down a sandy road for 300 m, the site is on the right.

General Details: Open all year (no electricity from Nov.- March). Electricity connections (10A), Shop. Busy bar and good restaurant. Swimming pool with adjacent bar (high season only). Children's playground. TV in bar. Excursions. Washing machine. Bungalows to rent.

Charges 1998: Per person 580 ptas; child 550; car 450; m/cycle 375; tent or caravan 450; motorcaravan 800; electricity 425. Plus 7% VAT. Discount of 40% from 1/11-31/3 (no electricity).

Reservations: made for one part of site, for any length and without deposit. Address: Ctra. Cadiz-Malaga Km. 70, 11380 Tarifa (Cadiz). Tel: 956/68.42.03.

8855 Camping Tarifa, Tarifa

Attractive, family run site adjacent to 5 km. of golden beach.

The long, golden sandy beach is a good feature of this site being ideal for windsurfing. It is clean and safe for swimming, the beach being adjacent to the site with a private access. The site has a pleasant, open feel and is reasonably sheltered from any road noise. It has been thoughtfully landscaped and planted out and is remarkably clean. The 288 level pitches are of varying sizes and are surrounded by pine trees which provide shade. All have electricity and there are adequate water connections. Two modern sanitary blocks have British WCs and free, controllable hot showers. There are facilities for campers with disabilities and a baby room. All sanitary facilities were spotless when seen. The site's excellent bar/restaurant is open all year, as is the well stocked supermarket which produces its own hot bread. There is a large children's play area with safe, modern activities. At the time of inspection the bar was being extended to include a very large patio and entertainment area. Also a well designed swimming pool complex including a pool bar was nearing completion, on target for the summer of '98.

How to find it: Site is on main N340 Cadiz road at the 78.87 km. marker, 7.5 km. northwest of Tarifa. There are large modern signs well ahead of the site with a deceleration lane if approaching from the Tarifa direction, large gaily coloured signs mark the approach to the site.

General Details: Open all year. Electricity connections (5/10A). Bar/restaurant. Supermarket (all year). New swimming pool complex with bar. Car wash. Good security with CCTV.

Charges 1998: Per person 600 ptas; child 500; tent 450; caravan 475; car 450; m/cycle 400; motorcaravan 775; electricity 425.

Reservations: Recommended for July/Aug. Address: Ctra. N340 km. 78.87, 11380 Tarifa (Cadiz). Tel: 956/684778. FAX: as phone. E-mail: camping-tarifa@globalmail-net.

8860 Camping Fuente del Gallo, Conil de la Frontera, nr Cadiz

Small site on a sloping, grassy position with excellent pool and two beaches nearby.

Fuente del Gallo is a clean friendly site with two nearby beaches which are suitable for bathing and watersports. Although good beaches, access to them is down fairly steep, stony paths and may not be suitable for older or disabled persons, particularly when attempting to return to the camp site at the end of the day. The long approach roads from the village pass through a very pretty avenue of palm trees at one point. The attractive bar and restaurant facilities are of a high standard with very reasonable prices (breakfasts served). The 200 marked and numbered pitches are somewhat cramped. Nearly all have electricity and there are some trees and bushes separating them. One of the sanitary blocks has recently been modernised and it is clean and well looked after, with hot water on payment. There is also a new integral section with excellent facilities for disabled people and babies. The second sanitary block is more mature. A strong feature of this site is the new, well designed swimming pool area, sporting a superb adult pool, a toddlers pool, children's play area, TV room, games room and pool bar. This area is also the focus of floodlit Spanish entertainment evenings in season. The helpful staff are equipped to book discounted trips to local attractions or short tours to Africa.

How to find it: From the Cadiz-Algeciras road (N340) at km. 21.9, follow signs to Conil de la Frontera town centre, then shortly right to Fuente del Gallo and `playas' following signs.

General Details: Open week before Easter - 1 Oct, with all amenities. Electricity connections (10A). Restaurant/bar. Shop. Swimming pool (1/6-1/10). Children's playground. Watersports on beach. Fishing 300 m. Bicycle hire, riding 1.5 km. Golf 5 km. Excursions. Car wash area. Laundry room with 2 washing machines. Chemical disposal. Caravan storage..

Charges 1999: Per person 545 ptas; child 455; tent 455; caravan 530; car 455; motorcaravan 910; electricity 455. All plus 7% VAT. Less 11-30% for longer stays. Credit cards accepted.

Reservations: Write to site. Address: Apto. 48, 11140 Conil de la Frontera. (Cadiz). Tel: 956/440137 or 442036. FAX: 956/442036.

AR Discount
Less 10% in low season, 5% in high

8871 Camping Giralda , Isla Cristina

Large, attractive family run site close to beach and river.

The fountains at the entrance and the circular `thatched' reception building set the tone for this very large, well managed and pleasant site which is just four years old. The 700 pitches are spacious on sand/grass and most benefit from the attractive mature trees which abound on the site. Most pitches have electricity (there are around 700 pitches (142 for tents). Access to the excellent beach is gained by a short stroll, crossing the minor road alongside the site and passing through attractive pine trees. The four large, modern, semi-circular `thatched' sanitary blocks are very clean and have British WCs and very good free, controllable hot showers. The site's excellent glassed bar/restaurant overlooks the river, which provides the northern site boundary and pleasant views whilst relaxing, especially at sunset. Two circular free swimming pools, one for children, are also near the restaurant, as is a resident windsurfing, canoeing and sailing school. There is also a large children's play area with safe modern activities. The many additional activities include those listed below. There is a separate area within this huge site where organised groups of children come to enjoy the activities offered within a dedicated adventure area. The accommodation and sanitary arrangements for these activities are totally separate to those provided for campers and thus there is little impingement.

How to find it: Site is off N431 Portugal - Huelva road, 10 km. east of Ayamonte. Take the Isla Cristina road, (C4117) off to the left, pass through Isla Cristina then onto La Antilla and site is 600 m. on the left - well signed.

General Details: Open all year. Electricity connections. Shop. Restaurant/bar. Snacks. Swimming pools. Basketball. Archery. Volleyball. Petan. Soccer. Mountain biking. Beach games. Table tennis. Watersports school. Children's play area. Organised activity area for children. Laundry service. Site contract security all year.

Charges 1998: Per person 625 ptas; child 500; tent 625; caravan 725; car 625; m/cycle 475; motorcaravan 1,200; electricity 500. Plus 7% VAT. Winter discounts.

Reservations: Recommended for July/Aug. Address: Ctra. Provincial 4117, Isla Cristina-La Antilla km 1.5, 21410 Isla Cristina (Huelva). Tel: 959/343318. FAX: 959/343284.

AR Discount
Less 10% excl. July/Aug.

Central

This area comprises the whole of inland Spain, south of a line just south of Burgos (Lat. 42°) excluding the coastal strip - see map on page 375.

9280 Camping-Motel Sierra Nevada, Granada

Good site with swimming pool, useful for visiting Granada.

This is a good site either for a night stop or for a stay of a few days while visiting Granada. Quite a large site with an open feeling and, to encourage you to stay a little longer, a medium sized swimming pool of irregular shape with a smaller child's pool (admission charge 200 ptas) is open in the main season. Granada has much to offer for sightseeing, including the Alhambra; it also has some interesting shops and there are usually one or two excellent shows. The site fills up considerably each evening in the season, so the earlier you arrive, the better your chances of securing a good pitch. The site is in two connected parts with more mature trees and facilities to the northern end. There is less shade to the south but more modern facilities (less than a year old in '98). Electrical connections are available. There are two main toilet blocks, one with a separate new unit with free hot showers and facilities for disabled people and babies. Extensive facilities by the pool which can be made available at peak times. Mostly British style toilets some with bidets, individual basins with mirrors and free hot showers.

How to find it: Site is just outside the town to the north, on the road to Jaén and Madrid. From the autopista, take Granada North - Almanjayar exit 126 (close to the central bus station). Follow road back towards Granada and site is shortly on the right, well signed.

General Details: Open 1 March - 31 Oct, as are the café, bar and restaurant. About 10,000 sq.m. Electricity connections (5A). Shop (15/3-15/10). Swimming pool (15/6-15/9). Bar/café by pool. Rather expensive restaurant. Tennis courts. Children's playground (with hard surface). Fishing 10 km. Bicycle hire 3 km Riding 6 km. Doctor lives on site. Washing machine. Car wash. Chemical disposal. Motorcaravan sevice point. Frequent bus service to city centre from outside site. Motel apartments.

Charges 1999: Per person 600 ptas; child (3-10 yrs) 500; car 600; tent 500 - 600; caravan 600; motorcaravan 1,400; electricity (5A) 400. All plus 7% VAT. Credit cards accepted, but not Eurocheques.

Reservations: Contact site. Address: Avd. Madrid 107, 18014 Granada. Tel: 958/150062. FAX: 958/150954.

AR Discount
Less 10% for over 1 week

CAMPING - MOTEL
SIERRA NEVADA

1st. Categorie

Ideal situation to visit beautiful Granada, at only 3 km of the centre, well comunicated by bus (every 15 min.). Two swimming pools, tennis, table tennis, lots of shade. Access: Leave the ringroad at exit 126.

Avda. Madrid, 107 • E-18014 GRANADA
Telf. (34) 958 15 00 62 • Fax (34) 958 15 09 54

9270 Camping Suspiro Del Moro, nr Granada

Impressive site in Sierra Nevada mountain range, useful for sightseeing.

Suspiro Del Moro is 11 km. south of Granada on the N323 Motril road or, alternatively, can be approached on the scenic mountain road from Almunecar (lots of bends this way). Many places of interest are within reasonable distance of the site, including La Alhambra, Granada and the Parador of La San Francisco. Based high in the Sierra Nevada mountain range, the area offers spectacular views from just outside the site, with trees and fences inhibiting the views inside. The site is cool and peaceful, family run and is beautifully kept, with gravel paths leading to 72 flat, grass pitches. The one main sanitary block is modern with British WCs, free hot showers and washbasins with hot water. The laundry and washing up facilities are also of a high standard. Three small toilet blocks are situated around the camping area. A very attractive Olympic sized swimming pool, together with a restaurant with bar tables, umbrellas and waiter service, covers a large area behind the main camping site. The restaurant offers a large, varied menu and, like the site itself, displays a professional image. A smaller bar and TV lounge is available, and a well stocked supermarket. This is an impressive site all round.

How to find it: On the N323 road, 11 km. from Granada on the road to Motril.

General Details: Open all year. Supermarket, restaurant/bar (both all year, depending upon occupancy). Bar. TV lounge. Swimming pool, with children's end (high season only). Small children's play area on gravel. Table tennis. Table football. Riding 2 km. Golf 5 km. Bicycle hire 15 km. Regular bus service from outside site to Granada. Chemical disposal. Bungalows to rent. Caravan storage.

Charges 1998: Per person 475 ptas; child 375; pitch 900; electricity 275. Major credit cards accepted.

Reservations: May be made for high season. Write to site. Address: N323, km. 145 (Cruce Ctra. Almunecar), 18630 Granada. Tel: 958/555411. FAX: 958/555105.

AR Discount
Less 15% in low season, 5 % in high

9080 Campamento Municipal El Brillante, Cordoba

Very busy site with shaded pitches.

Cordoba is one of the hottest places in Europe - the 'frying pan' of Spain - and the pool here is more than welcome, being large and bordered by pleasant terraced gardens. If you really want to stay in the city, then this site is a good choice. It has 125 neat pitches which are attractively spaced alongside the canal which runs through the centre of the site. Most pitches are now covered by artificial and natural shade but, to get the best ones, it is essential to arrive early in any season as the site becomes very crowded. The entrance is narrow and may be congested so care must be exercised. There is a colourful aviary close to the entrance. The blocks have been renovated and an impressive new block added with facilities for babies and disabled people. The bar/restaurant has also been renovated, air conditioned and has plenty of shade. Cordoba is a fascinating town and the Mosque/Cathedral is one of the great buildings of Europe and not to be missed.

How to find it: Entering Cordoba by the NIV/E25 road from Madrid, drive into the city centre. After passing the Mosque/Cathedral, turn right onto the main avenue, continue and take the right fork where the road splits, and follow signs for the campsite and/or the district of El Brillante. Keep a sharp eye out for camp signs as they are partially hidden behind foliage.

General Details: Open 1 May - 30 Sept. Bar, restaurant, shop, swimming pool, all high season only. Large supermarket 300 m. Children's play area. Aviary. Bus service to city centre from outside site. Chemical disposal.

Charges 1998: Per adult ptas. 560; child 400; car 560; tent 400 - 560, acc. to size; caravan 560; motorcaravan 875; m/cycle 300; electricity 365.

Reservations: are not made. It is essential to arrive early in high season. Address: Avda. del Brillante 50 (Centro), 14012 Cordoba. Tel: 957/278481. FAX: 957/282165.

9085 Camping Carlos III, La Carlota, nr Cordoba

Good alternative site for Cordoba, 25 km. from the city.

This is a very large, busy site especially at weekends, but it has many supporting facilities including a good swimming pool for adults and separate children's pool. With the bar and catering services open all year, the site has an more open feel than the bustling municipal site in Cordoba. Unusually the site has its own hairdressing salon. The touring areas offer considerable shade for the 300 pitches which are separated, and canopied by trees on level, sandy ground. Around two thirds have 5A electrical connections. Sanitary facilities, in two modern blocks, have mixed British (40%) and Turkish WCs and hot showers in the block near reception. Permanent units, mobile homes and bungalows (to rent) are in a separate area, where there are sporting facilities. There may be some slight road noise.

How to find it: From N-IV Cordoba-Seville motorway take La Carlota exit at km. 429 point; site is well signed..

General Details: Open all year. Bar/restaurant, shop (all year). Swimming pools (high season). Aviary. Table tennis. Boules. Minigolf, Children's play area. Volleyball. Football. Chemical disposal. Motorcaravan services. Bus service outside site. Village 2 km.

Charges 1998: Per person ptas. 475; child (under 12 yrs) 375; car 475; m/cycle 400; tent 475; caravan 500; motorcaravan 725; electricity (5A) 350. Plus 7% VAT. Discounts (10-20%) for longer stays and outside high season. Credit cards accepted.

Reservations: Probably necessary in July/Aug. Address: Ctra. Madrid-Cadiz km. 430.5, 14100 La Carlota (Cordoba). Tel: 957/300697 or 957/300526. FAX: as phone.

9081 Camping Villsom, Dos Hermanas, nr Seville

Clean, fairly shady site with attractive pool and bar area.

This is a fine city site with an excellent new sanitary block supplementing the recently modernised existing facilities and consisting of a peaceful and attractive restaurant, bar and reception area. This, together with a new minigolf and table tennis area, has resulted in the number of pitches being reduced slightly to around 180. We are told that the oranges from the trees, which almost enclose a very pretty outdoor bar area, are sold to Britain for marmalade. The site has a small shop and a most inviting small pool. Temperatures can be hotter here than almost anywhere in Spain and the pool seems essential, as are the orange trees. There is satellite TV in the bar/café. Restaurant 80 m, supermarket 400 m. Bus service from outside site to city. It is essential to book if intending to visit this site in peak weeks.

How to find it: There are many signs for Dos Hermanas - you need to be about 10 km. from Seville on the NIV to Cadiz. Look for 'Continente' store and sign on left and very soon afterwards turn right onto the second road marked Salida dos Hermanas - Isla Menor once you have passed under a road bridge; site is immediately on the right.

General Details: Open all year. Bar/café with satellite TV (open for breakfast and evening meals July/Aug). Swimming pool (June-Sept). Minigolf. Table tennis. Small shop (at reception). Laundry facilities. Children's playground. Restaurant and supermarket close.

Charges 1998: Per adult 495 ptas; child 425; tent 425 - 485; caravan 540; car 510; motorcaravan 635; m/cycle 425; electricity 315 All plus 7% VAT.

Reservations: Write to site. Address: Ctra. Sevilla-Cadiz, km. 554.8, 41700 Sevilla. Tel/Fax: 95/472.08.28.

SPAIN - Central

9083 Camping Monesterio, Monesterio

Attractive, recently constructed and conveniently located new site.

This modern site, located on the Ruta de la Plata in the Sierra de Tudia, is ideal for those travelling to or from Seville or the eastern Algarve. It has an easy access from the road and bags of space to manoeuvre for large rigs. The traditionally styled, modern sanitary installations include WCs, washbasins and showers with facilities for disabled people and children, plus dishwashing and laundry sinks. Hot water is free throughout. The pitches, which are spacious, all have electrical connections (16A). Also on site is a good swimming pool, launderette, supermarket and horse riding facilities. This well laid out site has shade in parts and is well fenced and lit. We have read a poor report in MMM (Sept) but when our inspector visited later in the season, all was in good order and he recommended the site.

How to find it: From Merida to Seville CN 630 turn right after the km. 760 marker approx 5 km. south of Monesterio. Site is well signed directly off the road

General Details: Open Easter - 15 Sept. Supermarket. Launderette. Swimming pool. Horse riding.

Charges 1998: Per pitch ptas. 1,500; adult 450; child 400; tent 425 - 500; caravan 450 - 500; motorcaravan 800 - 1,500; m/cycle 350; electricity 400. All plus 7% VAT.

Reservations: Contact site. Address: CN 630, km. 726, Monesterio, Badajoz. Tel: 924/516352. FAX: 924/516316.

9087 Camping Mérida, Mérida

Attractive well maintained site, close to architecturally interesting town.

Camping Mérida is ideally located to serve both as a base to tour the local area and as an overnight stop en route when travelling either north/south or east/west. The site lies behind the restaurant, café and pool complex, beside the main road to Madrid but there is considerable noise from the busy road directly alongside the site. There are 130 good sized pitches, most with some shade and on sloping ground, with ample electricity connections (long leads may be needed). The central sanitary facilitiy provides showers (some hot, some cold) with hooks and seat outside in a changing area, British WCs, and washbasins. Free hot water throughout. Dishwashing (H&C) and laundry sinks (cold only) are at the end of the block under cover. There is a clean medium sized swimming pool and a children's pool (with lifeguard), and a small shop for essentials. No English is spoken, but try out your Spanish. Reception is open until midnight, torches are necessary on this site. Mérida is an interesting town with a Roman amphitheatre and other ruins, a classical Theatre Festival, and a National Museum of Roman Art.

How to find it: Site is alongside road NV (Madrid-Lisbon), 5 km. east of Mérida, at km. 336.6 point.

General Details: Open all year. Shop. Restaurant/cafeteria. Bar. Swimming pool. Children's playground. Safe deposit. Money exchange. Medical post. Chemical disposal. Bungalows and group accommodation to rent. Caravan storage.

Charges 1998: Per adult ptas.475; child 425; tent or caravan 475; car 475; motorcaravan 675; electricity 375. All plus VAT. Credit cards accepted.

AR Discount

Welcome drink

Reservations: Write to site. Address Ctra. N-V Madrid-Portugal km 336, Mérida (Extremadura). Tel: 924/303453. FAX: 924/300398.

9088 Camping de Fuencaliente, Fuencaliente, nr Cuidad Real

Quiet site between Sierra Modrona and Sierra Morena with large pool.

This site nestles in an attractive valley between the Sierra Modrona and the Sierra Morena. It is ideal as a stopover if crossing Spain coast to coast, if you wish to visit the fascinating historic town of Toledo or finally if you desire a quiet `away from it all' break. There are very few other desirable sites in this region of Castilla - la Mancha, this one is open all year round and is very peaceful with good views through pined slopes. There is a large pool with a separate children's area, which is most is welcome in summer as this part of Spain gets very hot. The site is spacious with some shade from young trees but most shade is provided by artificial means. There are dedicated barbecue facilities and areas allocated for tents. The site has a good restaurant overlooking the pools. The large sanitary block is modern with excellent facilities and unusually there is no charge for electricity or use of the pool. The 91 pitches are generous at over 100 sq.m. and all have electrical connections and water. They are well maintained, as is the children's play area. Prices are very reasonable and the food was excellent when we visited. The local village of Fuencaliente is 5 km. south and provides the usual village facilities including some very good Spanish restaurants and bars.

How to find it: Site is on N420 road at 105 km. marker approx. 5 km. north of Fuencaliente.

General Details: Open all year. Electrical connections (6A). Swimming pool (1/6-15/9, free). Restaurant/bar (all year). Supermarket. Children's playground. Shaded barbecue areas and dedicated seating. Laundry sinks. Chemical disposal.

Charges 1998: Per person 550 ptas; child 500; tent 475 - 550; caravan 550; car 300; m/cycle 250; motorcaravan 900; pitch incl. electricity 400. Plus 7% VAT.

Reservations: Recommended for July/Aug. Address: Km 105, N420, Cordoba - Tarragona, C/Quintanilla, 23. 1º B Fuencaliente (C. Real). Tel: 926/698170 or 470381.

9089 Camping Despeñaperros, Santa Elena (Jaén), nr Linares

New site in a strategic position with excellent facilities.

Despeñaperros is a very smart site in the heartland of La Mancha, run by a co-operative of five very friendly people who employ helpful staff. This site is an ideal break point for those travelling from Madrid towards the Costa del Sol, or those wishing to explore the local attractions including the narrow mountain Gorge of Despeñaperros (literally 'the throwing over of the dogs'); also Valdepeñas, acknowledged as the centre of the most prolific wine centre in Spain. The site is located in a 30 year old pine grove which is part of the Despeñaperros nature reserve. All 116 pitches are of a good size, have natural shade from the mature pine trees and unusually have their own electricity, water, TV connections and waste water drainage. The two central sanitary blocks are of a high standard and the charming restaurant and bar are excellent, sharing wonderful views of the mountains with the swimming pools.

How to find it: On the N1V- E5 'Autovia de Andalucia' between Bailen and Madrid at km. 257, at the village of Santa Elena, the site is well signed.

General Details: Open all year. Electricity connections (10A). Restaurant/bar and shop (high season). Swimming pools (in season). Tennis. Washing machines. First aid room. Chemical disposal. Good sevurity. Caravan storage.

Charges 1999: Per adult 410 - 460 ptas; child 325 - 380; tent 435 - 485; car 410 - 460; caravan 435 - 475; motorcaravan 650 - 815; m/cycle 245 - 295; electricity 435. Credit cards accepted.

Reservations: Contact site. Address: 23213 Santa Elena (Jaén). Tel: 953/66 41 92.
Internet: www.arrakis.es/~hermanos/camping.

AR Discount
Less 5% in low season

9090 Camping El Greco, Toledo

Quiet, spacious site with attractive pool.

Toledo was the home of the painter and the site that bears his name boasts a beautiful view of the city from the restaurant, bar and pool. The friendly, family owners make you welcome and are proud of their site. Ivy clad pergolas run down each side of the swimming pool (charged) with tables in the shade - it can be very hot here. There is an hourly air conditioned bus service to the city centre from the gates, which tours the outside of the walls first. There is always plenty of space and reservation is said not to be necessary. There are 150 pitches of 80 sq.m. with electrical connections and shade from strategically planted trees. Access to some pitches may be tricky for caravans (narrow and at an angle). A new sanitary block was built in '98 including modern facilities for disabled campers and all the facilities are modern and kept clean. The site stretches along the river Tagus but fishing in it is a better bet than swimming. This site is worth a few days for the amazing sights of the old city of Toledo and the pool is a good feature, but it is only an hour's drive from Madrid and thus makes a good base for a longer stay.

How to find it: Site is on the C502 road on the edge of town, signed towards Puebla de Montelban; site signs also in city centre. From Madrid on N401, turn off right towards Toledo city centre but right again at gates to the old city. Site signed from next right turn. Don't follow 'Camping' signs on road into Toledo from Madrid (an inferior site).

General Details: Open all year. Swimming pool (1/6-5/9; adults 375 ptas, child 275). Restaurant/bar (all year) with good menu and fair prices. Shop in reception (all year). Volleyball. Children's playgrounds. Laundry facilities.

Charges 1998: Per person ptas. 550; child (3-10 yrs) 475; car 550; m/cycle 480; caravan or trailer tent 625; tent 590; motorcaravan 1,140; electricity (6A) 475. Plus 7% VAT.

Reservations: unnecessary and not made. Address: Ctra. Comarcal 502, 45004 Toledo. Tel/Fax: 925/220090..

9091 Camping Soto del Castillo, Aranjuez, nr Madrid

Useful stop-over municipal site with good facilities, south of Madrid.

Situated near the centre of the royal town of Aranjuez, worthy of a visit with its beautiful palaces, leafy avenues and gardens, and 47 km. south of Madrid, this is a useful en-route site. A little tourist train runs from the site daily. The site is close to the River Tajo in a park-like situation amid mature trees. The 225 touring pitches, all with electricity, are set on flat grass, unmarked amid tall trees. Siting is informal but places are of moderate size. Good facilities include a pool, small supermarket and restaurant (also open to the public) with takeaway, TV room, children's play area and volleyball. The largest sanitary block is heated in winter and well equipped with roomy hot showers, some washbasins in cabins and British WCs. Two smaller blocks, of more open design, have been refurbished. Washing up facilities have cold water.

How to find it: Site is just north of the town centre (from where it is signed) Aranjuez is bypassed by the old NIV, so ensure you follow the signs for the town, some 47 km. south of Madrid. Watch for sign to site - a sharp left turn off the main road with little notice, at the end of a small archway of trees.

General Details: Open all year. Electricity throughout. Bar. Restaurant. Takeaway. Small shop. Swimming pool (June-Sept). Children's play area. Volleyball. TV room. Bicycle hire. Laundry facilities. Chemical disposal. Walking distance of palace, gardens and museums, etc. Apartments for rent.

Charges 1998: Per person ptas. 450 - 600; child (3-10 yrs) 375 - 475; car 375 - 500; caravan 525 - 675; motorcaravan 575 - 750; tent 400 - 650; electricity 500. Discounts for groups or long stays. Credit cards accepted.

AR Discount
Less 10% excl. July/Aug.

Reservations: Write to site. Address: Soto del Rebollo s/n, 28300 Aranjuez (Madrid). Tel: 91/8911395. FAX: 91/8914197.

SPAIN - Central

9095 Camping Ciudad de Albarracin, nr Teruel

Satisfactory site for visiting interesting, historic town in southern Aragon.

Albarracin is a much frequented, fascinating town with a Moorish castle and other antiquities to see, set in the 'Reserva Nacional de los Montes Universales', with some wonderful scenery around. The site is set on a hillside at the back of the town, with views of it and a walk of perhaps 500 m. to the centre. It is modern and long, set on fairly flat ground, sloping for the last third. There are 70 pitches (to be increased to 130), all with electrical connections, separated by trees and ranging in size up to 70 sq.m. The modern sanitary building has British style WCs for ladies and mixed British and Turkish for men. The vanity style washbasins have free hot water, as do the showers, which are quite large but have no divider. There is a baby bath in the ladies' and provision in between for dishwashing and laundry with one machine. No shop but essentials available from the bar. The bar/restaurant, with terrace and TV, is said to be open all season, but there are shops, bars and restaurants in the town as well. A municipal swimming pool, just 100 m. away, is open in high season and there is a small children's play area. No English spoken yet, until the owner's children gain in confidence!

How to find it: From Teruel north on N330 for about 8 km. then west on A1512 for 37 km. Well signed in town.

General Details: Open 1 April - 31 Oct, as is bar/restaurant. Essentials from bar. Town shops 500 m. Special room for barbecues with fire and wood provided.

Charges guide: Per person ptas. 350; child (under 14) 250; car, caravan and tent 700; motorhome 600; electricity 300. Credit cards accepted.

Reservations: No English spoken; policy not known but probably not necessary. Address: Ciudad de Albarracin, Amparo Hernandez Lozano, 44100 Albarracin, (Teruel). Tel: 978/71 01 97 or 07.

9210 Camping Pico de la Miel, La Cabrera, nr Madrid

Useful site north of Madrid, close to N1/E.

Pico de la Miel is well signed and easy to find, 2-3 km. southwest off the main road, with an amazing mountain backdrop. Whilst mainly a long-stay site for Madrid, with a variety and number of very well established, fairly old mobile homes, there is a separate area with its own toilet block for touring units. Over 60 pitches on rather poor, sandy grass, some with artificial shade, are clearly marked; others, not so level, under the odd pine tree are not marked, plus more for tents (the ground could be hard for pegs). Electricity connections are available. The tiled toilet block is good, light and airy with some washbasins in cabins and free hot water to laundry and washing up sinks. An en-suite unit with ramp is provided for people with disabilities. An excellent pool complex is supervised. The bar/restaurant and shop have a terrace overlooking a good, modern children's playground. Tennis court. Chalets to hire.

How to find it: Site is well signed from the N1. Going south use exit 57 or 58, going north exit 59 or 60, and follow site signs.

General Details: Open all year. Electricity connections. Shop. Restaurant. Bar. Swimming pool, Tennis. Note: amenities may not be available all year.

Charges 1998: Per person ptas. 610; child 505; car 560; tent or caravan 610; motorcaravan 915; electricity 375. All plus 7% VAT. Less 10-25% for longer stays.

Reservations: Contact site. Address: Ctra. N1, km. 58, 28751 La Cabrera (Madrid). Tel: 918/688082 or 698541. FAX: 918/688082.

9025 Camping Regio, Salamanca

Convenient, touring site, next to hotel complex with good pool.

Salamanca is one of Europe's oldest university cities, and the old town has much to commend it. It is also a useful staging post en route to the south of Spain or central Portugal. The site is some 4 km. outside the town on the road to Madrid. It is behind the Hôtel Regio and shares with it a quality restaurant, somewhat cheaper cafeteria and a very good swimming pool and children's pool (small charge). Other facilities include tennis and basketball courts, and a children's playground. The 200 pitches are on slightly sloping ground, with some shade in parts and very sparse grass, the site was dusty when we visited. The pitches are marked out but not too formally, with electricity points (15A) in little red-roofed towers and enough for all; water points are plentiful. The two large toilet blocks in the older style, one for women and one for men, provide British WCs, washbasins and free hot showers - all reasonably clean when seen but in need of some refurbishment.

How to find it: Take the N501 route from Salamanca towards Avila and Madrid. Hôtel Regio is on the right after about 4 km.

General Details: Open all year. Restaurant, cafe and swimming pool at adjoining hotel. Shop. Laundry. Telephone and post box. Safe deposit. Money exchange. Medical post. Car wash. Tennis and basketball courts. English spoken.

Charges guide: Per adult ptas. 425; child 375; tent (small) 375, (large) 425; car 425; caravan 425; m/cycle 375; motorcaravan 675; electricity 425. Credit cards accepted.

Reservations: Write to site. Address: Ctra. de Madrid, km 4, 37900 Santa Maria de Tormes. Tel: 923/130888. FAX: 923/130044.

PLAYA MONTROIG
CAMPING & BUNGALOW PARK

vacaciones
VIVAS

A family holiday park equipped to the highest standards, surrounded by large tropical gardens and with a spectacular swimming pool. Situated in front of a wonderful sandy beach; PLAYA MONTROIG is a very safe and clean holiday park, that offers, among other things, the following services and installations: wide variety of leisure activities (including tournaments, shows, excursions, etc...), Hobby Centre (workshop), Sport Club (tournaments and sport activities), Junior Club & Teenager Club. Sport area with basketball and football fields, skateboard track, archery, jogging track. Fitness, tennis, minigolf, a large shopping centre, restaurants, bars and discotheques.

LC & CP

Dream Holidays

COSTA DAURADA - MONT-ROIG - TARRAGONA
CATALUNYA · ESPAÑA

*Splendid Holidays
in contact with Nature*

Take notice of our special offers!

For further information & reservation:
Apartado de Correos 3
E-43300 Mont-roig [Tarragona] · ESPAÑA
Tel.: 34/977/81.06.37 · Fax: 34/977/81.14.11

http://www.playamontroig.com
E-mail: info@playamontroig.com

E-43840 SALOU
(Tarragona)
C/ Norte, 37
Tel. (34) 977 38 08 52
Fax (34) 977 38 31 91
Internet: http://www.fut.es/~siesta
E-mail: siesta@tinet.fut.es

LA SIESTA
CARAVANING
CAMPING

A real holiday site, situated in the centre of the elegant, intern. holiday resort of SALOU, in the always sunny prov. of Tarragona. Excellent installations as swimming pool and paddling pool, free hot water, electr. conn. f. tent and caravan, supermarket, restaurant, bar, cafeteria, etc. At only 100m from a large, magnificent beach and at 900m from the theme-leisure park "PORT AVENTURA".

BUNGALOWS AND MOBILE HOMES FOR HIRE OPEN 14.3 - 3.11.

Very reasonable of-season fees and 10% P/N reduction from 14.3 till 15.6 and in Sept. and Oct.

Only 40 km from Santander (ferry) and 70 km from Bilbao (ferry), easily and quickly reached along the magnificent, new, toll-free autovia and the coast roads.

A 25 ha. holiday site with a large (4 ha) recreation and sports area and a precious, 8 ha natural park with animals in semiliberty.

Modern, first category installations. Beautifull surroundings with direct access to wide, clean beaches. Surrounded by meadows and woods.

Service and comfort for the most exacting guests. Properly marked pitches.

English spoken. Open from Easter to 30th September.

Your beautiful holiday destination in SPAIN

CAMPING
PLAYA JOYEL

E-39180 NOJA
(SANTANDER, CANTABRIA)
SPAIN
Tel. (34) 942 63 00 81
Fax (34) 942 63 12 94

COSTA DAURADA –SPAIN–

An ideal camp site to enjoy nature, the sun, a shallow beach and aquatic sports. The mild climate permits you to swim in the sea from April to October. Good location for visits to the numerous important Roman ruins in and around Tarragona - Tarraco was the provincial capital of the ancient empire. Also nearby are the old monasteries of Poblet, Santes Creus, Montserrat and other places of cultural interest.

THEME PARK "PORT AVENTURA" AT 14 KM.

Unusually beautiful, quiet and isolated location (1km distance from the N-340 road and the railway line). Over 350-metre-long front to the beach. Restaurant-bar directly on the beach. Original CHILDREN' S programmes. 2 play grounds, ping-pong, we organize games constantly. Sports area with floodlit tennis courts, sports fields, etc. Now also swimming-pool of 500 m2.

OPEN THROUGH-OUT THE YEAR. Off-season special prices and discounts of 35% for pensioners and students with students card. We speak English.

Access: A-7, exit (salida) no. 32, then take the N-340 towards Tarragona, at km. 1172 towards to the beach and turn left at the end of the road.

NATURE • SUN BEACH • AQUATIC SPORTS

Tel. (34) 977 650 128
Fax (34) 977 650 451
E-43893 **TARRAGONA**
TAMARIT- **COSTA DAURADA**
Internet: http://www.tamarit.com
E-Mail: tamaritpark@tamarit.com

erkende camping
ANWB

BUNGALOWS

Cambrils-Park
CAMPING

Ctra. Salou - Cambrils, Km. 1   43850 CAMBRILS (TARRAGONA) - España
✉ Apartado de Correos 123   43840 SALOU (Tarragona) - España
☎ 977 35 10 31 - Fax 977 35 22 10
e-mail : mail@cambrilspark.es
http://www.cambrilspark.es

The only de luxe site on the Costa Dorada.

CAMBRILS-PARK, a real holiday camping park, which you will find all types
of installations and services even for the most pretentious guests.
SWIMMING POOLS, BARS, RESTAURANT, SPORTS, SHOWS,
MINI-CLUB... and a wide and varied ANIMATION programme for young
and old. Enjoy your holidays with us, more than anywhere else.
Come to Cambrils-Park, where your dreams will come true.

Please send further information

Name ....
Street ....
Town ....
Country ....

ALAN
ROGERS

No other city has its lungs as close to its heart as Lisbon.

900 hectares of green
just a stone's throw away
from the city centre.

800 camping
accommodation units

170 equipped lots

A forest site - totally
refurbished and open
all the year round.

Swimming pool,
restaurant, outdoor cafés,
2 multi-purpose sport
centres, mini golf,
shoppingarea,
and games rooms.

70 bungalows

Swimming pool

For further information
please contact us at:
Estrada da Circunvalação
1500 - 171 - LISBOA
Tel: 351-1-7609620
Fax: 351-1-7609633

LISBOACAMP I N G

Turismo
de
Lisboa

Portugal

ORBITUR

The name to remember for camping in Portugal

The most beautiful chain of 23 camping sites.

302 BUNGALOWS

SEA, SUN, WOODLAND and a MILD CLIMATE.

THE WARMEST WELCOME FROM NORTH TO SOUTH OF PORTUGAL

NEW: MADALENA★★★★ **(Gaia)**
LUSO (Mealhada)
RIO ALTO (Póvoa de Varzim)

MOTORHOMES SANI STATIONS
FULLY EQUIPPED BUNGALOWS

DISCOUNTS from 10 to 70%
for Orbitur Camping Club Members.

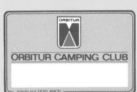

ORBITUR CAMPING CLUB

i ORBITUR
CENTRAL DE RESERVAS
Rua Diogo do Couto 1-8º
1100 LISBOA (Portugal)
Tel. 351.1.811 70 00 / 811 70 70
Fax. 351.1.814 80 45
Internet: http://www.orbitur.pt.
E-Mail: info @ orbitur.pt.

OUR FRANCE & SPAIN *Direct*

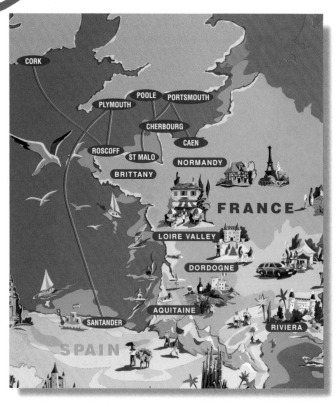

Travelling to Holiday France or Spain?
Why drive the long way round when you can sail direct?
We land you closer to where you'd like to be.

Brittany Ferries
The Holiday Fleet

BROCHURES 0990 143 554 (24HRS) RESERVATIONS 0990 360 360
OR SEE YOUR TRAVEL AGENT

9200 Camping Caravaning El Escorial, El Escorial, nr Madrid

Site with swimming pools and other amenities 50 km. northwest of Madrid.

There is a shortage of good sites in the central regions of Spain, but this is one, well situated for sightseeing visits with the El Escorial monastery, the enormous civil war monument of the Valle de los Caidos is very close and Madrid and Segovia both 50 km. There are 1,358 individual pitches (some marked), of which 750 are occupied by permanent caravans. Another 250 `wild' spaces for tourists are on open fields, with improving shade (long cables may be needed for electricity) and there should usually be space. There are three large new or refurbished toilet blocks, plus two smart, new small toilet blocks for the `wild' camping area. British style WCs, some without seats; washbasins with free hot water (some in cabins), hot showers with push-button but controllable temperature, baby baths and facilities for disabled campers. The blocks can be heated in cool weather. The general amenities on site are good and include three swimming pools (unheated), plus a children's pool in a central area with a bar/restaurant with terrace and plenty of grassy sitting out areas. A large range of smart sports activities are available. Very large supermarket selling fresh meat, vegetables and fresh baked bread daily.

How to find it: From the south go through the town of El Escorial, follow the M 600 - Guadarrama road - the site is near the 8 km. marker, 3.5 km north of town on the right. If approaching from the north use the A6 autopista take exit 47 and the M600 towards El Escorial town. Site is on the left.

General Details: Open all year. Large supermarket (1/3-31/10) and souvenir shop. Restaurant/bar and snack bar (1/3-31/10). Disco-bar. Swimming pools. Three tennis courts. Two football pitches. Basketball. `Fronton'. Two well equipped children's playgrounds on sand. Riding, golf 7 km. Chemical disposal. Caravan storage.

Charges 1998: Per person 650 ptas; child (3-9 yrs) 625; caravan or tent 650; car 650; motorcaravan 1,150; electricity 400. VAT included. Credit cards accepted.

Reservations: to guarantee admission made if you write but considered unnecessary. Address: Apdo. Correos 8, 28280 El Escoril (Madrid). Tel: 91/890.24.12.

AR Discount
Less 10%
15/9-15/6 excl.
Easter week

E-28280 EL ESCORIAL (Prov. MADRID) • Tel. (34) 91 890 24 12 • Fax (34) 91 896 10 62

Situated in the most beautiful part of Castille, 3 km from the impressive National Monument VALLE DE LOS CAIDOS (Valley of the Fallen, a memorial to the dead in the Spanish Civil War, where Francisco Franco is also buried) and 8 km from the famous Monastery of SAN LORENZO DE EL ESCORIAL, pantheon of the Spanish kings since Charles I.

Restaurant • Cafeteria • Supermarket
• hot water in showers and washbasins
• disco-pub • 90 m2 pitches with electr.conn.

• 3 swimming pools • 3 tennis courts
• 2 fronton (basque ball game, similar to squash) courts, basket ball.
Bungalows for hire

9250 Camping Costajan, Aranda de Duero

Good night stop en route to or from ferries, 75 km. south of Burgos.

This site has 225 pitches (with electricity) with around 100 available for all types of tourer. Large units may find access to the variably sized pitches a bit tricky among mixed olive and pine trees and on the slightly undulating sandy ground. Ignore the few unsightly static caravans, as this is a shady, clean and friendly spot for an overnight stop. A swimming pool complex is also open to the public (under the same management). The good, modern sanitary facilities have hot and cold water, dishwashing and laundry sinks and just one water point. New bungalows to rent - details from site. Reception opens 8 am. - 2 pm. and 6 pm. - 10 pm.

continued overleaf

9250 Camping Costajan (continued)

How to find it: Turn off N1 at junction 144 signed Aranda de Duero north. Follow signs to site (under 1 km).

General Details: Open all year. Shop (all year). Cafe, swimming pool and bar (all 15/5-15/9). Tennis. Football. Minigolf. Fishing 3 km. Riding 2 km. Exchange facilities. Washing machine. Chemical disposal. Bungalows for rent.

Charges 1998: Per person ptas. 465 - 575; child 435 - 490; caravan 517 - 655; small tent 435 - 490, large tent 465 - 575; car 465 - 515; motorcaravan 710 - 760; m/cycle 360 - 410; electricity 425. Credit cards accepted.

Reservations: Said to be unnecessary. Address: Ctra. no.1, km. 162, 09400 Aranda de Duero (Burgos). Tel: 947/502070. FAX: 947/511354.

9023 Camping Camino de Santiago, Castrojeriz, nr Burgos

Small countryside site with outstanding views, slightly remote with a superb location.

This site lies to the west of Burgos on the outskirts of Castrojeriz, an unspoilt original small Spanish rural town. In a superb location, almost in the shadow of the ruined castle high on the adjacent hillside, it will appeal to those who like peace and a true touring campsite without all the modern trimmings, at a reasonable cost. The 50 marked pitches are level, grassy, divided by hedges and shaded by trees, with electricity available to all. Sanitary facilities are adequate, with showers (two free hot showers each sex, heated by solar panels), British and Turkish style WCs, and washbasins with cold water only. All of these are in the older style, but were well maintained and clean when we visited. A further small sanitary block is next to the barbecue area. A small shop with basic necessities shares space with the bar/coffee shop and reception and there are two shady terraces outside. A games room with table football, a pool table and table tennis, and two tennis courts complete the facilities.

How to find it: From N120 (Osorno-Burgos) road, turn onto BV404 for Villasandino and Castrojeriz. Turn left at crossroads on southwest side of town and then left at campsite sign.

General Details: Open 1 May - 30 Sept. Shop (1/6-30/8). Bar, café/coffee shop with terrace (1/6-30/8). Games room. Tennis courts. Barbecue area. Mountain bike hire. Washing machines. Fishing 2 km. Riding 15 km. Safe deposit. Medical post. Chemical disposal. Caravans and tents for hire.

Charges 1998: Per person ptas. 350; child 300; tent small 300 large 350; caravan 350; car 300; m/cycle 150-250; motorcaravan 575; electricity 300. All plus 7% VAT. Credit cards accepted.

Reservations: Write or fax site for details. Address: C/.Virgen del Manzano, s/m , 09110 Castrojeriz (Burgos). Tel: 947/377255. FAX: 983/359549.

9021 Camping Municipal Fuentes Blancas, Burgos

Comfortable, municipal site, within easy reach of Santander ferries.

Burgos is an attractive city, ideally placed for overnight stop en route to the south of Spain. The old part of the city around the cathedral is quite beautiful and there are pleasant walks along the river banks. Fuentes Blancas is a municipal site with clean, modern, sanitary facilities in five blocks, although some may not be open outside July/Aug. These include British WCs, vanity style washbasins, free hot showers and facilities for babies. There are around 350 marked pitches of 70 sq.m. on flat ground, 112 with electrical connections and there is good shade in parts. A small shop caters for most needs and the terraced snack bar is friendly without being noisy. A swimming pool is open in main season only. The site has a fair amount of transit trade and reservations are not possible for August, so arrive early. Bus service to city or a fairly shaded walk.

How to find it: From the north (Santander) follow signs for E5/N1 (E80/N620) Valladolid/Madrid on the main through road (dual-carriageway). Immediately after crossing river turn left at small camp sign and follow river east in direction of Cartuja de Miraflores. Site is approx. 3 km. on left.

General Details: Open 1 March - 30 Sept. Electricity connections (6A). Small shop (1/4-30/9). Bar/snack bar (all season). Swimming pool (15/5-15/9). Children's playground. Table tennis. Basketball. Football. Fishing 150 m. Bicycle hire 2 km. Safe deposit. Medical post. Money exchange. Washing machine. Chemical disposal. Motorcaravan service point. Information service. English spoken.

Charges 1998: Per pitch incl. caravan and electricity ptas 1,625 (package); adult 525; child (2-10 yrs) 375. Plus 7% VAT. Credit cards accepted.

Reservations: Not made. Address: Ctra. Cartuja Miraflores, 09193 Burgos. Tel: 947/48 60 16. FAX: as phone.

Northern Spain

This area includes the Costa Verde, the Basque Coast, the Pyrenees and inland Spain north of a line between Valladolid and just north of Burgos (lat. 42°). The Costa Verde is largely unspoiled, with clean water, sandy beaches and rocky coves against a backdrop of mountains including the magnificent Picos de Europa. The beaches and countryside on the Basque Coast are rather more developed in terms of tourism and industry and tend to be very popular, particularly during July and August. Both these areas are easily accessible from the ports of Santander or Bilbao. The Pyrenees stretch from the Bay of Biscay in the west (with the highest peaks) to the Mediterranean in the east, and include two spectacular natural parks, the Ordesa in Aragon and Aigues Tortes in Catalonia. The mountain gorges and valleys remain largely unspoiled. Visitors will find much of 'Old Spain' in gastronomy and the way of life generally.

9024 Camping As Cancelas, Santiago de Compostela

Hillside site, with quality facilities, overlooking the pilgrims' city.

As Cancelas currently has 156 marked pitches (30-70 sq.m), arranged in terraces and divided by trees and shrubs, on a hillside overlooking the city. The site has a steep approach road which extends into most pitch accesses which can be difficult for large units. Electrical hook-ups (5A) are available, the site is lit at night and a security guard patrols. There is a regular bus service into the city from the bottom of the hill outside the site, and a small mini market (open late and handy for off season use) is just 5 minutes level walk away. The site has a well kept, unsupervised, swimming pool and children's pool which are free to campers. The two modern, luxurious toilet blocks provide British WCs, washbasins in marble tops, hand dryers and sockets, spacious controllable showers with dividers, hooks and marble seats and a suite for the disabled with ramped access. The quality and cleanliness of the fittings is outstanding as is the standard of cleanliness throuhout the day. In addition, there are dishwashing, laundry and chemical disposal facilities. Free hot water throughout. Lounge bar with TV (open all year), restaurant and mini market (open July/Aug) together with a small children's playground. No English is spoken. Santiago, with its legendary festivals and processions, is the destination for Christians, who find their way to the city across the centuries old pilgrims' routes.

How to find it: From the N550 La Coruna - Santiago road, at large roundabout (near petrol station, Repsol), take exit to Lugo (C547)/La Coruna (A9), and immediately turn left into Rua das Cancelas (site is signed), turn right at stadium, site is 800 m. on left.

General Details: Open all year. Mini market. Restaurant. Bar. Laundry. Swimming pools. Children's playground. Telephone and post box. Safe deposit. Medical post.

Charges 1999: Per adult ptas. 550 - 600; child 400 - 475; car 400 - 645; tent 550 - 645; caravan 550 - 665; m/cycle 400 - 500; motorhome 1,100 - 1,290; electricity 450. Plus VAT.

Reservations: Write to site. Address: Rue do 25 de Xulio 35, 15704 Santiago de Compostela. Tel: 981/58.04.76 or 58.02.66. FAX: 981/57.55.53.

AR Discount
Less 5% for over 7 days

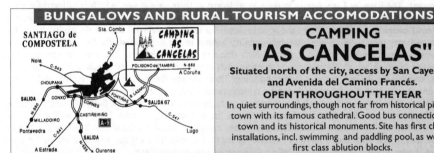

8942 Camping Los Manzanos, Santa Cruz, nr La Coruña

Large clean site with good pool well placed for visiting La Coruña.

This site is to the east of the historic port of La Coruña, not far from some ria (lagoon) beaches and with good communications to both central and north Galicia - it is only an hour and a half drive from Santiago de la Compostela, for example. The site has a steep sloping access and is divided by a stream into two main sections, linked by a wooden bridge. Some interesting sculptures create focal points and conversation pieces. The lower section is on a gentle slope. Pitches for larger units are marked and numbered, all with electricity (10A) and, in one section, there is a fairly large, unmarked field for tents. Two good toilet blocks have modern installations and free hot showers. The site impressed us as being very clean, even when full, which it tends to be in high season. The swimming pool was clean, with a lifeguard, free to campers, and stays open most of the day and evening. Small shop with fresh produce daily, and restaurant/bar serving good food and a range of wines at reasonable prices. Señor Sanjurjo speaks good English and visitors are assured of a friendly welcome. Some aircraft noise.

How to find it: From E50 motorway, do not go right into Coruña, but take the N-VI link road across the bridge, following signs towards Meiras and Lugo. Just over the bridge turn left towards Santa Cruz. Turn right at the centre of Santa Cruz and the site is signed from there.

General Details: Open Easter - 15 Sept. Swimming pool. Shop. Restaurant/bar. Children's playground. Barbecue area. Telephone and post box. Medical post.

Charges 1998: Per adult ptas 590; child 490; tent 590; car 590; caravan 600; motorcaravan 1,180; electricity 450. All plus 7% VAT.

Reservations: Write to site. Address: Ctra. Sta Cruz - Meiras, km. 0.7, La Coruña. Tel: 981/61.48.25.

SPAIN - North

8941 Camping Valdovino, Valdovino, nr Ferrol

Friendly site with top class facilities close to supervised beach.

This site is on the edge of the village, about 300 m. from the beach. The sea here can be lively but at the back of the beach is a calm ria (lagoon) suitable for younger children. The camping area is divided into small enclosures with space for four to six large units each and takes about 150 units in all. They are well shaded by trees and surrounded by hedges of blue hydrangeas. All have access to electricity (16 or 25A), with some lighting at night. The large, central toilet block is clean and luxurious, with baby baths, facilities for disabled people, pre-set warm showers, British WCs, a good supply of washbasins, and is pleasantly decorated. An excellent restaurant and bar offer attractive food via waiter service, cafeteria or takeaway. The owner speaks good English and can provide information about excursions.

How to find it: From Pontedueme on the N-VI, drive north, but at Fene branch towards Cedeira rather than Ferrol. The road meets the C646 at the coast in Valdovino itself, and the site is almost opposite, down the road to the beach.

General Details: Open all year. Supermarket. Restaurant/bar. Café. Takeaway and ice-cream parlour. Children's playground. Basketball. Fronton courts. Bicycle hire, fishing 500 m. Golf, riding 15 km. Safe deposit. Laundry. Medical post. Chemical disposal. Apartments for rent. Caravan storage.

Charges 1999: Per adult ptas 600; child 475; tent 645; car 645; caravan 665; m/cycle 500; motorcaravan 1,290; electricity 450. Plus 7% VAT. Credit cards accepted.

AR Discount
Less 5%
for 5 days

Reservations: Write to site. Address: Apdo 104 (Ferrol), Valdovino (La Coruña). Tel: 981/48.70.76 98187012 (out of season). FAX: 981/486131

8945 Camping Lagos de Somiedo, Somiedo

Most unusual small site in the towering mountainous Asturias Natural Park.

Thirty-five kilometres of winding narrow roads with rock overhangs, hairpin bends and breathtaking views finally bring you to the lake and campsite at 1,600 m. A site for powerful small campervans, cars, backpackers and walkers of endurance, it is **not** recommended for medium or large motorhomes and caravans. The friendly Lana family make you welcome at their unique site, which is tailored for those who wish to explore the natural and cultural values of the Somiedo National Park without the support of 'normal' campsite amenities. There are separate areas for tents and vehicles and no electricity, but in this extraordinary glacial valley you can leave reality behind in the exploration for the marvels of nature including bears, wolves and wild goats which frequent these mountains. The site has one charming wooden building which functions as reception, bar, restaurant, library and sanitary block. Stringent conservation regulations prohibit further building. There are hot showers, sinks and British style toilets within the thoughtfully decorated building, which contains many items of natural interest. A very small village within 500 m. has a small bar/restaurant set tight into the vertical rock face, offering traditional food but be careful of the wooden clogs scattered in the entrance as you enter. Here you will witness the cultural heritage of men and women living in harsh, though beautiful, surroundings. There is a cool wind here most of the time and a torch is essential at night. The owner's daughter will instruct on the local flora, fauna, wildlife and history and take you for excursions on horseback.

How to find it: From N634 via Oviedo turn left on A515 at Cornellana for 9 km. At Longona turn left on AS227; at 38 km marker, Pol de Somiedo, turn left for 3.38 km. and at Urma left again for 5.29 km. Site signed at village.

General Details: Open Easter - 15 Oct. Combined reception, small restaurant, bar. Essentials sold in the bar. Horse trekking. Barbecue area. Group tent area. Small children's play area. Two small village houses for rent.

Charges 1998: Per adult ptas. 500; child 450; tent incl. 2 persons 500; tent with 3 or more persons 550; car 450; m/cycle 375. All plus 7% VAT. Credit cards accepted.

Reservations: not necessary. Address: Valle de Lago, 33840 Somiedo (Asturias). Tel: 98/5763776 or 52280279.

8940 Camping Los Cantiles, Luarca, nr Oviedo

Well maintained cliff-top site to west of Gijón and Oviedo.

Luarca is a picturesque little place with an inner harbour and two sandy beaches adjoining. Los Cantiles is 2 km. east of town on a cliff top jutting out into the sea, with good views. The site has no permanent units and is a pleasant place to stop along this under-developed coastline. The 230 pitches, 83 with electricity (3A) are mostly on level grass, divided by shrubs. You can take the car to the Laurca beaches and the small town is within walking distance downhill. There is a friendly welcome from the Dutch owner. Two modern, clean sanitary blocks have mainly British toilets; washbasins with hot water and free hot showers. Units for disabled people and baby bathroom. The site is 300 m. from an indoor pool, sauna and fitness centre. A disco pub and restaurants are in the town (1.4 km). English spoken.

How to find it: Turn off main N634 road at Km 502.7 point east of Laurca; site is signed

General Details: Open all year. Small shop (all year). Bar with hot snacks (main season). Lounge/reading room. Bicycle hire. Fishing 70 m. Laundry. Chemical disposal. Caravans and chalets to rent. Caravan storage.

Charges 1998: Per adult ptas. 450; child (4-10 yrs) 400; tent 450 - 525; caravan 550; motorcaravan 800; car 450; m/cycle 300; electricity 300. Plus 7% VAT.

AR Discount
Less 10% after 3 days, 15/9-15/6

Reservations: Contact site. Address: Ctra. N-634 km. 502.7, 33700 Luarca (Asturias). Tel/Fax: 98/5640 938.

8950 Camping Costa Verde, Colunga

Busy but acceptable site by a good beach.

This site is some 1½ km. from the town of Colunga and has adequate rather than luxurious facilities which are beginning to show signs of heavy usage. The most attractive feature is a spacious, supervised beach with a low tide lagoon which is ideal for younger children. The 160 regularly laid out pitches which cater for some 630 campers will all be full in high season and, indeed, were fairly full when we visited in June. Electricity is available throughout. A new sports and play area, plus barbecues, is at the end of the site across a bridge which, although mainly fenced off, could allow mischievous children to fall into the river is so minded! The single toilet block has a mixture of British and Turkish style toilets (all British for ladies). Showers are large (without separators) but you do need a token from the camp shop for hot water. The shop is well stocked and the bar is friendly. The owner makes his own cider!

How to find it: From Santander take the N634 to Ribadesella, and continue for 21 km. along the N632 coast road towards Gijón. Take the right turn towards Lastres from the centre of Colunga.

General Details: Open Easter - early Oct. Shop. Electricity connections (6A). Bar/cafe. Sports field. Children's playground. Telephone and post box. Safe deposit. Laundry. Little English spoken.

Charges 1998: Per adult ptas 475; child (over 5 yrs) 425; tent 425 - 475; caravan 525; car 425; m/cycle 350; motorcaravan 800; electricity 325. VAT included. Credit cards accepted.

Reservations: essential for peak weeks and made for exact dates with deposit. Send for booking form. Address: 33320 Colunga (Asturias). Tel: 98/5856373.

8955 Camping Arenal de Moris, Caravia Alta, Prado

Peaceful, rural site, very close to sea and mountains.

This site is close to three fine sandy beaches and is surrounded by mountains in the natural reservation area known as the Sueve. A hunting reserve, this is important for a breed of short Asturian horses, the `Asturcone'. The Picos de Europa are only 35 km, Covadonga and its lakes is near and Ribadesella is 12 km. It is an ideal area for sea and mountain sports, horse riding, walking, birdwatching and cycling. Camping Arenal's 350 grass pitches are of 40-70 sq.m. Some are terraced with little shade, others on an open, slightly sloping field with views of the sea. Three sanitary blocks have comfortable, controllable showers (no dividers) and vanity style washbasins, laundry facilities and external dishwashing (cold water). The restaurant with terrace serves local dishes and overlooks the pool across to hills and woods. There is a supermarket, tennis court and a play area in a lemon orchard. The beach is a short walk.

How to find it: Site is signed from the N632 Ribadesella - Gijón road at km. 14 point.

General Details: Open 1 June - 31 Aug. plus weekends April, May and Sept. Electricity (5A). Supermarket. Restaurant. Swimming pool. Tennis. Children's play area. Laundry. Chemical disposal. Little English spoken.

Charges 1998: Per person ptas. 510; child 485; car 495; m/cycle 395; caravan 625; tent 510; motorcaravan 857; electricity 340.

Reservations: Contact site. Address: Ctra. 632, 33344 Caravia Alta. Tel: 985/85 30 97. FAX: 985/85 30 97.

8965 Camping Picos de Europa, Avin-Onis, Cangas de Onis

New site in ideal situation to explore western end of the Picos de Europa.

It is said that, due to their proximity to the sea, the Picos (peaks) are called `Europa' as early navigators, on sighting them, knew they were again near the continent of Europe. Indeed, it is probably best to follow the coast to reach Cangas de Onis, the gate to the Picos, when first locating the site. Once settled you can explore these dramatic limestone mountains on foot, by bicycle, by horse, etc. Covadonga with its lakes and national park is only 13 km. On the other hand, the coast at Llanes is only 25 km. The site itself is newly developed with direct access off the AS114 in a valley beside a fast flowing river. Local stone has been used for the L-shaped building at the entrance which houses reception, a restaurant and the main sanitary facilities. The bar has an unusual circular window and small terrace overlooking the river. The 140 marked, smallish pitches have been developed in three avenues, on level grass backing on to hedging and with electricity to most. The tent area is over the bridge past the fairly small, round swimming and paddling pool. Extra toilet facilities, showers, baby bath, etc are also here. Laundry and dishwashing facilities and chemical toilet disposal are under cover in a separate round building. Extra pitches are being developed. Excursions can be arranged in the mountains, on horseback if wished. Canoes can be hired and the site also runs a Speleology school and has a hostel nearby with 100 beds.

How to find it: Site is 15 km. east of Cangas on AS114 road.

General Details: Open all year. Bar, restaurant and shop (open main season). Swimming pool. Excursions. Canoeing, riding and caving. Washing machine. Chemical disposal. Hostel accommodation.

Charges 1998: Per adult ptas. 500; child (under 14 yrs) 450; small tent 500; large tent or caravan 600; car 450; m/cycle 350; motorcaravan 700; electricity 350. All plus 7% VAT.

Reservations: not needed outside July/Aug. Address: 33556 Avin-Onis. Tel :98/5844070. FAX: 98/5844267.

SPAIN - North

8962 Camping La Isla - Picos de Europa, Potes

Relaxed and friendly family site, with good shade and mountain views.

La Isla is beside the road from Potes to Fuente Dé, with mountain views and good shade. A warm welcome awaits from the lady owner, who speaks good English. The 160 unmarked pitches are arranged around an oval gravel track (one-way system), under fruit and ornamental trees. Electricity is available, though some may require long leads. The single sanitary block is clean and in the older style, but is steadily being up-graded. It provides British WCs, washbasins with cold water, and free hot showers. Laundry and dishwashing sinks (cold water). A small bar/cafe is by the (very clean) small river, serving good value meals, local dishes and takeaway and overlooking a barbecue and picnic area under the trees. Small heated swimming pool (caps compulsory, unsupervised). Potes with its Monday market is 4 km, whilst the monastery at Toribio is also within easy reach. There are opportunities for riding and 4x4 safaris, together with mountain sports and active outdoor pursuits. Chalets and tents to let on site, also very attractive chalets to hire 2/3 km. further up the valley (owned by the same family).

How to find it: Site is on the right hand side, 4 km. outside Potes, on N621 Potes to Espinama/Fuente Dé road.

General Details: Open 1 April - 31 Oct. Electricity connections (3A). Small shop. Cafe/bar and terrace. Takeaway service. Small swimming pool. Children's playground. Barbecue and picnic area. Telephone and post box. Safe deposit. Washing machine. Freezer service. Apartments to let (phone/fax 942/73.30.73).

Charges 1998: Per adult ptas. 435 - 460; child (0-10 yrs) 350 - 375; pitch in July/Aug. incl. car and unit 1,250, other times: large tent 435, small 400; caravan or trailer tent 460; car 435; m/cycle 270; motorcaravan 1,000 - 1,100; electricity 300 - 315. All plus VAT. Credit cards accepted.

Reservations: Write to site. Address: Potes - Turieno (Cantabria). Tel: 942/73.08.96. FAX: as phone.

8963 Camping La Viorna, Potes

Well appointed terraced site, with magnificent mountain views in heart of Picos de Europa.

The wonderful views from the open terraces of this site make it an ideal base for a stay in this region and it is especially popular with mature couples and motorcaravanners. The 110 pitches of around 70 sq.m. are marked by newly planted trees which will, in time, provide shade - but not for a few years yet (the site is only a few years old). There is good access for all sizes of unit and electricity to all pitches. In high season tents may be placed on less accessible, steep areas. The single sanitary block is good and is surrounded by beds of flowers. Its interior is clean and modern with British WCs, washbasins (cold water) and hot showers. Facilities for disabled visitors double as a baby unit (key from reception). Laundry room with washing machine and dishwashing room (cold water). Restaurant/bar (in season) with terrace overlooking the excellent swimming pool (23 x 13 m.) and children's pool (bathing caps compulsory). The pools are unsupervised but heated and free. Well stocked shop. The site is 2 km. from Potes, capital of the Picos (Monday market), close to the Toribio Monastery and a short, but spectacular, drive from Fuente Dé. Many sporting activities can be arranged (rafting, canoeing, etc).

How to find it: Take N621 from Unquera to Potes. After town left fork signed Toribio de Liebana and site is 800 m.

General Details: Open Easter/1 April - 30 Oct. Electricity connections (3 or 6A). Shop. Restaurant/bar with terrace (in season). Swimming pools. Children's playground. Games room. Telephone and post box. Medical post. Laundry. Tourist information. Some English spoken.

Charges 1998: Per pitch ptas. 1,250 - 1,350; adult 450 - 475; child 375 - 400; car 450 - 475; m/cycle 375 - 400; electricity 3A 275, 6A 350. All plus VAT.

Reservations: Contact site. Address: Ctra Santo Toribio, Potes (Cantabria). Tel: 942/732021. FAX: 942/732019.

8964 Camping El Molino de Cabuérniga, Sopeña

Rural `alpine meadow' location, close to old Spanish village.

Located in a peaceful valley with views of the mountains, beside the river Saja and only a short walk from the old and attractive village, this site is on an open, level, grassy meadow with few trees. There are 102 marked pitches, all with electricity (3A, may need long leads). A single, modern sanitary block provides free hot showers in curtained cubicles, British WCs and washbasins (cold water). Dishwashing (H&C) and laundry sinks are outside the block. The site also has a small shop for basic needs, café, bar and barbecue area (open in main season). There is a small, but very simple, children's playground. This comfortable site is very good value and ideal for a few nights whilst you explore the Cabuérniga Valley which forms part of the Reserva Nacional del Saja. The area is great for indulging in active pursuits with opportunities for mountain biking, climbing, walking, swimming or fishing in the river, horse riding, hunting, paragliding and 4x4 safaris. Sopeña Fiesta is in mid-July.

How to find it: From N634 at Cabezon de la Sal turn on C625 for approx. 10 km. to km. 42 where site is signed before Valle de Cabuérniga. Turn into village (watch for low eave, bearing right. Watch for small green site signs.

General Details: Open all year. Shop. Café. Bar. Barbecue. Terrace. Children's playground. Safe deposit. Money exchange. Laundry. Tourist information. New, attractive apartments to rent. No English spoken.

Charges 1998: Per adult ptas. 425; child 350; tent 425; caravan 450; car 425; m/cycle 350; motorcaravan 650; electricity 275. All plus VAT. Credit cards accepted.

Reservations: Write to or fax site. Address: 39515 Sopeña de Cabuérniga (Cantabria). Tel/Fax: 942/706259.

8960 Camping La Paz, Vidiago, nr Llanes

Superb and unusual terraced site, by the sea, with spectacular views.

La Paz is arranged on several terraces with sea views, with a lower area in a valley. The way down to the beach is steep but the views, both to the Picos de Europa and to seaward, from the upper terraces are impressive. There are 434 pitches of between 30-70 sq.m, quite a few only suitable for tents, and electricity (3 or 5A) is available. Because of the steep access, units are positioned on upper terraces by site staff with Landrovers. The area at beach level is more suitable for very large units. The four, first class sanitary blocks, with some interesting and unusual design features, are modern, well equipped and spotlessly clean. These have British WCs, washbasins, hot showers (tokens from reception), and baby bath. There are also full laundry and dishwashing facilities. Spring water is available from a number of taps throughout the site. There is a cliff-top café/restaurant and bar overlooking the beach, and a mini-market. It is best to book in high season since the site is deservedly popular and one of the best managed along this coast with a policy of respecting the maximum capacity. La Paz is above Vidiago beach where there are opportunities for swimming, windsurfing and fishing. It is also well placed for excursions to the eastern end of the Picos de Europa. Llanes 10 km. to the west, will appeal to shoppers.

How to find it: From Santander take N634 towards Llanes. Site signed from main road at km.292, before Vidiago.

General Details: Open 1 June - 20 Sept. Cafe/restaurant and bar. Mini market. Laundry. Lounge. Watersports. Table tennis. Games room. Fishing. Telephone and post box. Safe deposit. Medical post. Chemical disposal. Motorcaravan services. Tourist information. English spoken.

Charges 1998: Per adult ptas 555; child 495; car 545; m/cycle 450; tent 555; caravan 715; motorcaravan 950; electricity 375. All plus VAT @ 7%. Credit cards accepted.

Reservations: Recommended for peak weeks. Address: Km.292 C.N.634 Irun-Coruna, Playa de Vidiago, 33597 Vidiago-Llanes (Asturias). Tel: 985/41.10.12. FAX: 985/41.12.35.

Camping - Caravaning

LA PAZ

E-33597 Vidiago - LLANES (ASTURIAS)
Road N-634 (E-70), km 292.
Tel. (34) 985 41 10 12 • Tel. & fax (34) 985 41 12 35

In extraordinary quiet, very beautiful surroundings and directly at the fantastic, very clean beach. 170.000 sqm. surface with very good installations. At only 45 km from the famous mountain chain **"PICOS DE EUROPA"**. The country side is really very beautiful; a "must" for all nature lovers.

8971 Camping Caravaning Playa de Oyambre, San Vicente de la Barquera

Excellent quality modern site with own swimming pool, near good beaches.

This exceptionally well managed site is ideally positioned to use as a base to visit the spectacular Picos de Europa or one of the many sandy beaches along this northern coast. The site is in lovely countryside (good walking and cycling country), with views of the Picos , 5 km. from San Vicente de la Barquera. The 200 marked pitches are mostly of a good size (average 80 sq.m. with the largest ones often taken by seasonal units). They are arranged on gentle wide terraces with little shade and with electricity in most places. The excellent sanitary facilities, in one central main block, are spotless with cleaners on duty all day and evening. The showers are spacious with a divider and hooks; British WCs, a good supply of washbasins and facilities for babies and the disabled. Free hot water throughout. Dishwashing (H&C) and laundry sinks (cold only) and washing machines (tokens from reception) are also provided. The site is lit and a guard patrols at night. A well stocked supermarket is open until 10 pm. and there are fresh fish deliveries 3 days a week. Good, clean and homely restaurant, and a large bar with TV and games machines. The fair sized swimming pool and a children's pool have a lifeguard on duty, and there is also a basketball and football court. The site gets busy in season and there can be some noise.

How to find it: Site is signed at the junction to Comillas, at km. 265 on the E70, 5 km. east of San Vicente de la Barquera. The entrance is quite steep (take care with caravans).

General Details: Open Easter - 30 Sept. Electricity connections (5A). Supermarket (15/6-15/9). Restaurant. Bar/TV lounge. Games room with machines. Swimming pools (1/6-15/9). Children's playground. Basketball. Football. Fishing 1 km. Riding 5 km. Safe deposit. Medical post, doctor visits daily. Laundry. Chemical disposal. Motorcaravan service point. Hotel rooms and chalets for rent. English spoken.

Charges 1999: Per adult ptas. 500; child 450; pitch 1,050; electricity 350. All plus VAT. Credit cards accepted.

Reservations: Advised, particularly if you have a large unit. Write to site. Address: San Vicente de la Barquera, 39547 Los Llaos (Cantabria). Tel: 942/711461. FAX: 942/711530. E-mail: oyambre@ctv.es.

AR Discount
Less 10%
in low season

8970 Camping Las Arenas, Pechon

Pleasant, green and spacious touring site, with mountain views and beach access.

This campsite is in a very quiet, but rather spectacular location bordering the sea and the Tina Mayor estuary, with views to the mountains and access to a small beach. It is a very green, 10 ha. site with lots of shade from acacias, oak and poplar trees, and is good value for your holiday budget. Taking 337 units, half of the site is divided into marked, grassy pitches (60 sq.m) in various bays or on terraces with sea and mountain views, but some up and down walking. Electrical connections are available and the roads are asphalted. The clean, and well tiled sanitary facilities are in the older style. The various blocks provide a good supply of British WCs and washbasins, with hot showers (no divider, token on 100 ptas payment), plus dishwashing, laundry sinks and washing machines. There is a well stocked supermarket, restaurant and snack bar (open when site is open) and there are opportunities for fishing, swimming, diving, windsurfing or cycling from the site. For older teenagers a disco/bar is only a kilometre away.

How to find it: Turn off N634 Santander - Coruna road, just east of Unquera onto road to Pechon. Site is 2 km.

General Details: Open 1 June - 30 Sept. Electricity connections (5A). Restaurant. Snack bar. Supermarket. Children's playground. Fishing. Windsurfer and bicycle hire. Telephone and post box. Safe deposit. Medical post. Money exchange. Laundry. English spoken. Apartments to let.

Charges 1998: Per adult ptas 550; child 450; tent 550; car 550; caravan 675; motorcaravan 900; m/cycle 390; electricity 325; All plus 7% VAT. Credit cards accepted.

Reservations: Contact site. Address: 39594 Pechon. Tel: 942/717188. FAX: as phone.

8961 Camping El Helguero, Ruiloba, nr Santillana del Mar

Well designed site with pool, good facilities for the disabled, close to good beaches.

Although this site is surrounded by tall trees, there is little shade for the pitches. It caters for around 240 units on slightly sloping ground, with many marked out pitches on different levels, all with access to electricity. There are also attractive tent and small camper sections amongst interesting rock formations. Two toilet blocks, although showing signs of age, are clean and cared for, with free hot water in all installations. These include British style WCs, washbasins and soap dispensers, showers with curtains, plus facilities for disabled visitors and children, dishwashing, laundry sinks and washing machine. There is a good, clean swimming pool and children's pool (bathing caps compulsory - sold on site). We were pleased to see the pool also had an access lift for visitors with disabilities. In high season a well stocked shop provides fresh food and other goods, and the bar and restaurant complex is busy and friendly - you can have a typical Spanish meal for £8. This is a good site for disabled people, in a peaceful location, and is excellent value out of main season. One can generally find space here even in high season, but arrive early. The site is used by tour operators. Santillana del Mar is 12 km.

How to find it: From the C6316 road from Santillana del Mar to Comillas, turn left at Sierra. Site is signed as 'Camping Ruiloba'.

General Details: Open Easter - 30 Sept. Electricity connections (6A). Shop (July/Aug. 9 am - 1 pm). Restaurant/bar, other restaurants in village. Swimming pool with lifeguard. Children's playground. Games machines. Activities for children and entertainment for adults. Bicycle hire. Fishing 3 km. Tourist information. Medical post. Laundry. Chemical disposal. Motorcaravan service point. Chalets to let. Caravan storage.

Charges 1999: Per adult ptas 400 - 500; child (4-10) 375 - 400; caravan/tent 400 - 500; car 400 - 500; m/cycle 250; motorcaravan 800 - 1,000; electricity 350. Credit cards accepted.

Reservations: Write to site. Address: 39527 Ruiloba (Cantabria). Tel: 942/722124. FAX: 942/721020.

AR Discount
Less 5%
in July, min
5 days

8980 Camping Municipal Bella Vista, Santander

Municipal site on approach to Cabo Mayor lighthouse.

An agreeable site, with a well cared for look, Bella Vista is on raised ground in a quiet location. There are good views and walks and the site is about 300 m. from a sandy cove which is approached by flight of steps down the cliff. The long, narrow site is grassy with a tarred access road but without too much shade, providing 207 marked pitches. An area under pine trees at one side, gives a degree of shelter for small tents. Electricity (6/10A) is available and some pitches with water and drainage also. A restaurant, shop and laundry are on site. The six toilet blocks (3 men's and 3 women's in separate buildings) have been refurbished to a good standard and are well maintained. They have British style WCs, washbasins, controllable, free hot showers with sloped dressing area, but no divider, plus dishwashing and laundry sinks. This is primarily a transit site, very popular with British and Dutch visitors, and space is usually available. An excellent stop-over for those arriving at, or departing from, the port of Santander.

> **How to find it:** Site is to the northeast of the town on the road to Cabo Mayor lighthouse. On leaving ferry terminal turn right - follow coast road for approx. 5 km.
>
> **General Details:** Open all year, including amenities. Shop. Café. Children's playground. Basketball and football. Minigolf. Petanque. Fishing, golf 200 m. Riding 2 km. Safe deposit. Medical post. Money exchange. Laundrette and ironing. Chemical disposal. Bus service. Tourist information. English spoken. Bungalows for hire. Caravan storage.
>
> **Charges 1998:** Per adult ptas. 615; child 460; pitch 1,540, with services 2,050; small tent 460 - 665, acc. to size; car 615; m/cycle 410; electricity 385. Credit cards accepted.
>
> **Reservations:** No stated policy, but site address is Carretera del Faro S/Nº, 39012 Santander. Tel: 942/39.15.30 or 39.15.36. FAX: 942/39.15.36.

AR Discount
Less 20-50%
in low season,
over 3 days

8990 Camping Los Molinos de Cantabria, Bareyo

Peaceful site with excellent views close to Cantabrian coast.

Camping Los Molinos at Bareyo is ideal for those who wish to enjoy a tranquil setting with excellent views after or before the trials of a channel crossing and for touring the local area. There is a sister site 8 km. away (8995). Divided into two main areas, the lower established area has many permanent units and southern mountain views. The newer, upper areas are terraced and planted with young trees. The higher the terrace the better the inland views (long electrical leads). The very top level is for tents at present and offers wonderful views of the mountains inland and the sea to the north. There are 500 average sized, level touring pitches with little shade. A large separate area is for tents. Modern sanitary buildings with British style WCs and free, controllable showers are kept very clean. Dishwashing (H&C) and laundry sinks are at the end of the blocks under cover. Facilities for disabled campers with ramps. First floor restaurant and bar with pleasant terrace, two heart shaped swimming pools, one for children (with lifeguard), and a mini-market. In high season there is free bus twice daily to the beach and town. The owners hope to offer more facilities in '99 as the upper levels of the site are developed.

> **How to find it:** From Autovia E70-A8 Bilbao -Santander road, take exit 185, N634 to Noja take first right S403, turn onto SP 4141 for approximately 5 km. site is signed to the left on local road.
>
> **General Details:** Open Easter - Sept. Shop. Restaurant/bar. Children's playground. Telephone and post box. Safe deposit. Laundry. Medical post. Chemical disposal. Bungalows for hire.
>
> **Charges 1998:** Per adult ptas 500; child 350; tent 600; car 300; caravan or motorcaravan 1,000; m/cycle 300; electricity 375. Plus 7% VAT. Credit cards not accepted.
>
> **Reservations:** Write to site. Address: 39190 Bareyo (Cantabria). Tel: 942/670569. FAX: as phone.

8995 Camping Los Molinos, Noja

Site with good facilities close to an excellent beach.

Los Molinos at Noja is ideally located for touring the local area and as an overnight stop en route when travelling by ferry via Bilbao or Santander. It is 300 m. from the Playa del Ris beach which has fine sand and clear water. The site is divided into two main areas both with a large number of permanent units. There are 500 average sized touring pitches, on level ground, but with little shade; all have electricity. Modern sanitary buildings with British style WCs and free hot showers are central and clean. Dishwashing (H&C) and laundry sinks are at the end of the blocks under cover. Facilities for disabled campers. Also on site are two bars (disco in season), a first floor restaurant with a pleasant terrace with reasonabe prices, café for snacks, a pizzeria, tapas and takeaway. Two swimming pools, one for children (with lifeguard), and a well stocked supermarket. Unusually the site has its own karting complex.

> **How to find it:** From Autovia E70-A8 Bilbao -Santander road, take exit 185, N634 to Noja take first right S403. It is approximately 10 km. to Noja. Follow signs to Playa del Ris where the site is signed..
>
> **General Details:** Open 12 Feb - 15 Nov. Supermarket. Restaurant/bars. Cafés. Takeaway and ice-cream parlour. Children's playground. Basketball. Safe deposit. ATM cash machine. Laundry. Medical post. Chemical disposal. Car wash. Bus service to beach and town (high season). Mobile homes for rent.
>
> **Charges 1998:** Per adult ptas. 450 - 600; child 450 - 475; tent 550 - 700; car 300 - 350; caravan or motorcaravan 900 - 1,300; m/cycle 300 - 400; electricity 375. Plus 7% VAT. Credit cards not accepted.
>
> **Reservations:** Write to site. Address: Playa del Ris, 39180 Noja (Cantabria). Tel: 942/630426. FAX: 942/630425.

9000 Camping Playa Joyel, Noja, nr Santander

See colour advert
between pages 320/1

High quality, comprehensively equipped busy site with pool, by superb beach.

This very attractive holiday and touring site is some 40 km. from Santander and 70 km. from Bilbao, with 1,000 well shaded, marked and numbered pitches (70-80 sq.m.). Electricity is available (3A with new blue Euro-sockets). Six spacious toilet blocks have British WCs, vanity style washbasins, large shower cubicles, baby baths (free hot water throughout) and dishwashing facilities plus a large laundry. The swimming pool complex with lifeguard is free (caps compulsory). Other facilities include a superb restaurant and bar, well stocked supermarket, good value takeaway, hairdresser, kiosk, and a general shop with souvenirs, camping gaz, etc. There is no shortage of entertainment on site with a soundproof pub/disco (July-Aug), large indoor games hall with minigolf, video and table games, plus tennis courts, riding, an animal park, children's playgrounds, recreation area and the superb beach (cleaned daily 15/6-20/9). 'No cycling on site' rule in July/Aug. Although prices are higher, this well managed site has a lot to offer families with much going on in high season when it gets very busy. Used by tour operators.

How to find it: From A8 at Beranga km.185 take N634 then, almost immediately, S403. Follow signs to site.

General Details: Open Easter - 30 Sept. Restaurant (July/Aug). Bar, café and snacks (all season). Takeaway (July/Aug). Supermarket (all season). General shop. Kiosk. Swimming pools (15/5-15/9). Tennis. Pub/disco (July/Aug). Games hall. Gym park. Children's playground. Pharmacy - doctors visit daily in season. Riding. Fishing. Animal park. Barbecue area. Bicycle hire 1.5 km. Golf 20 km. Laundry. Hairdresser (July/Aug). Safe deposit. Money exchange. Freezer service. Car wash. Security patrols at night. Motorcaravan service point. English spoken.

Charges 1999: Per adult ptas. 500 - 750; child (under 10) 350 - 600; pitch 1,500 - 1,600; electricity 375 - 400. All plus 7% VAT. No credit cards.

Reservations: made for 1 week or more. Early arrival or reservation is essential in high season. Address: 39108 Noja (Santander-Cantabria). Tel: 942/630081. FAX: 942/631294.

9035 Camping Portuondo, Mundaka

Attractive terraced site suitable only for tents or small units.

This site is a good base from which to explore the local area and the old Spanish town. However, the entry to this well cared for site is steep (18%) and at an oblique angle to the road (best approached from the Bermeo direction) and the 135 pitches are not suitable for large outfits. In fact, caravans are not accepted at all 15 July - 20 Aug. The site is partly terraced, with pitches marked and numbered and there is some shade. Most pitches are very slightly sloped and all have electricity (5A, some need long leads). The good quality sanitary facilities include controllable hot showers, washbasins, mostly British WCs and a heated baby room. Dishwashing and laundry sinks are outside under cover. Hot water is free. The owner also runs a restaurant (at site entrance) with a full range of meals and a takeaway. Small shop. There is a large covered patio with tables and benches above the shower block and a barbecue area.

How to find it: From N634 or autopista (S. Sebastian-Bilbao), turn at Amorebieta onto the C6315 road to Gernika/Bermeo. Approach site from Bermeo direction due to oblique access.

General Details: Open all year. Shop (15/6-15/9). Restaurant and takeaway (1/3-30/11). Bar. Table tennis. Barbecue area. Fishing 100 m. Safe deposit. Washing machines and dryers. Chemical disposal. New bungalows for rent. English spoken. Caravan storage.

Charges 1999: Per adult ptas. 575; child 500; pitch 1,250; pitch with electricity 1,650; small tent pitch 575. All plus 7% VAT. Less 5-10% for longer stays. Credit cards accepted.

Reservations: Write to site. Address: 48630 Mundaka (Bizkaia). Tel: 94/687.77.01. FAX: as phone. E-mail: recepcion@campingportuondo.com.

AR Discount
Less 15%
excl. 16/6-14/9

9038 Camping Orio, Orio

Typical seaside site, suitable for first/last night of tour.

This site has 400 pitches, with many long stay units and privately owned statics, but there should be space for tourers. Only 50 m. from the beach, there is no shade. The pitches are in rows divided by tarmac roads and hedges, all with electricity (5A). The main sanitary block provides showers (pre-set) with large changing rooms, washbasins, British WCs and baby baths. Hot water is free. Good facilities for wheelchairs. Two smaller, older sanitary blocks are opened in high season. Small swimming pool, children's pool (unsupervised), squash and tennis courts, with fishing in the nearby river and the sea. A cafe/bar and mini market are open in July/Aug. This site is fairly expensive in high season, with the cheaper pitches furthest from the beach, but closer to the sanitary blocks.

How to find it: Turn off N634 road at km. 12.5 in centre of Orio (sign is easy to miss), and follow signs to site. Take care, the streets in Orio town centre are not wide.

General Details: Open 1 Jan - 31 Oct. Cafe. Bar. Mini market. Money exchange. Swimming pools. Barbecue area. Children's playground. Squash and tennis courts. Fishing. Telephone and post box. Safe deposit. Medical post. Mobile homes for rent. Dogs not accepted. No English spoken.

Charges guide: Per unit incl. 2 persons ptas. 1,655 - 3,300 (area A - nearest beach), 1,585 - 3,175 or 1,530 - 3,055; extra adult 270 - 540; child (2-10 yrs) 225 - 445. VAT included. Credit cards accepted.

Reservations: Write to site. Address: 20810 Orio (Gipuzkoa). Tel: 943/83.48.01. FAX: 943/13.34.33.

9030 Camping Igueldo, San Sebastian

Site on high ground just outside the town.

Igueldo has an imposing situation on top of a hill, by the side of San Sebastian, with a fine panoramic view on the land side. It is also quite a pleasant site in a part of Spain where Britons may want to find a camp and where there are not many available. Although not a luxurious one, it is a friendly place. The sanitary blocks have been extended and improved to give a much more satisfactory provision. The terrain has been divided into 289 individual pitches, though they are not very large - 70 sq.m. They are of two types, 191 with electricity (5A) and water. There are also some tiny tent pitches of 20 sq.m. San Sebastian is a large, pleasant and quite fashionable town which has all the shops, restaurants, entertainment and night life that one could want, as well as some sandy beaches, which are usually busy in the season. The nearest beach is about 5 km. from the site.

How to find it: The turning to Igueldo is on the west side of the town and is well signed from the main road.

General Details: Open all year. 33,000 sq.m. Little shade. Shop. Bar. Restaurant with takeaway food.

Charges 1999: Per unit, incl. car, 3 persons, and with services ptas. 3,100, without services 2,750; extra adult 450; child (3-10 yrs) 325; small tent pitch, incl. car, 2 adults 1,500; electricity 350. All plus 7% VAT. Special winter prices available.

Reservations: none made. Address: 20190 Igueldo. Tel: 943/214502. FAX: 943/280411.

9070 Camping Pirineos, Santa Cilia de Jaca, nr Jaca

Pretty site with attractive swimming pool, convenient for touring in the Pyrenees.

This all year site has a quite mild climate, being near the River Aragon and not too high. Unusually for Spain the trees are mainly oak and provide reasonable shade. Although there is space for caravans, it is possibly more suited for motorcaravans, owing to the kerbs and trees to be negotiated. The large number of permanent units detracts a little from the overall impression and there is some daytime road noise along one side. However, there is an attractive swimming pool and children's pool with bar and terrace which is open from mid-June to end of August, as is the supermarket. The restaurant and bar are open all year lunch-times and evenings. One heated sanitary block is open all year, providing a quite satisfactory supply, with hot water for the showers, washbasins, dishwashing and laundry sinks. A second, very modern block is open June to August only. Both have British WCs. It is a friendly site which is also useful for off-season camping on the all-electric(6A), mostly level and quite large pitches.

How to find it: Site is 15 km. west of Jaca on the N240 (65 km. northwest of Huesca).

General Details: Open all year. Shade in parts. Restaurant and bar (open all year). Supermarket (high season, otherwise essentials kept in bar). Swimming pools (July/Aug). 2 tennis courts. Table tennis. Children's playground. Fishing. Petanque. Launderette. Chemical disposal. No dogs accepted in high season. Small hotel recently added and accommodation to let.

Charges 1998: Per adult 650; child (2-9 yrs) 625; car 650; caravan or tent 650; motorhome 1,150; electricity 575; all plus 7% VAT: Credit cards accepted.

Reservations: Contact site. Address: Centro de Vacaciones, Ctra N240 km 300, 22791 Santa Cilia de Jaca (Huesca). Tel: 974/377351. FAX: as phone. Internet: http://www.pirinet.com/pirineos/

9100 Camping Casablanca, Zaragoza

Typical small city site suitable for overnight stop.

Although not a perfect site, Casablanca is reasonable for overnight or for a short stay. On flat meadow (with little grass) there are 180 pitches with 10A electricity. It does lack shade, and it can be hot here. It has a medium sized swimming pool on site, although this is only open July/Aug. The sanitary block is basic with little hot water and could be hard-pressed at busiest times. British style WCs.

How to find it: Site is just outside town to southwest in the Val de Fierro district; access roads lead off N11 Madrid road (km. 316) or N330 Valencia road and are well signed, if a little difficult to follow.

General Details: Open 1 April - 15 Oct. Shop and restaurant/bar (from 1 June). Town shop 200 m. Many electrical connections.

Charges guide: Per adult ptas. 565; child 460; car 565; tent/caravan 565; motorcaravan 900; electricity 420.

Reservations: can be made to Campings Betsa, C/Nov. 139, 17600 Figueras (Gerona). Tel: 976/753870. FAX: 976/753875.

9105 Camping Lago Park, Nuevalos, nr Zaragoza

Attractively situated site with many visitors for the Monasterio de Piedra.

The drawbacks here are the rather steep access, possible up and down treks to the sanitary block (which might not cope with a full site) and possible noise from the disco (although soundproofed), which doubtless gets very busy with the many tent pitches. If you can accept all this or visit out of the main season, you will be rewarded with a site which is positioned just outside the ancient village, between lake and mountains, and which is very suitable as a base for exploring this really attractive area. On a steep hillside, the 250 pitches are on terraces. With only a few pitches suitable for large caravans, just over 50% have electricity (10A). They are numbered and marked by trees. The single sanitary block has British style WCs (some Turkish for men), washbasins with cold water and some controllable hot showers (no dividers). If you are placed on the left side of the site, the pool toilets are more easily accessible. Facilities on site include the swimming pool and a restaurant/bar and shop. A bull-ring is now apparently used as children's play area, although brochures show young bulls in action.

> **How to find it:** From Zaragoza (120 km.) take A2/N11/E90 road. Turn on C202 beyond Calatayud to Nuevalos (25 km). From Madrid exit A2 at Alhama de Aragon (13 km). From all directions take signs for Monasterio de Piedra.
>
> **General Details:** Open 1 April - 30 Sept. Restaurant/bar (open June-Sept). Shop (all season). Swimming pool (late June-Sept). Chalets (4 persons) to rent.
>
> **Charges guide:** Per person ptas. 600; child (3-10 yrs) 575; car 530; m/cycle 525; caravan or tent 650; motorcaravan 1,250; electricity 550. Credit cards accepted.
>
> **Reservations:** Contact site. Address: 50210 Nuevalos. Tel: 976/8490.38, 84.90.48 or 84.90.57.

9125 Camping Lago de Barasona, La Puebla de Castro, nr Huesca

Hillside site by lake in the pre-Pyrenees.

This site is beautifully positioned in terraces by the shores of the Lago de Barasona (a large reservoir), with views of hills and the distant Pyrenees. The local administration has put together some excellent tourist information (in English) and a brochure detailing the local way-marked walks and the owner has matched this with his own quality brochure. The recently discovered Roman town of Labitolosa, just 1.5 km. away on foot, direct from the site, is best seen in high summer when further excavations take place. The site has its own canoes for hire and waterskiing is available also in July and August. You may also swim and fish in the lake which has a very shallow area extending for 20 m. or so. If you prefer, the site offers its own outdoor pool, open from as early as April when the weather is often quite warm. The very friendly, English speaking owner would welcome more British visitors, especially in the spring, when the area is very attractive. The grassy, fairly level pitches are up to 100 sq.m. in size for larger units and all have 6A electricity connections. Many are well shaded and views of the lake and/or hills are available. Some up and down walking is necessary to the shop (July/Aug) and restaurant, swimming pool and the two sanitary units. The lower, recently modernised building is nicely presented, although hot water is only available in the cabins (3 for ladies, 1 for men) and the smallish showers (no divider), and some dishwashing and laundry sinks. Volleyball, football and a new children's play area were all under construction. A pleasant and peaceful site in a lovely area.

> **How to find it:** Site is on the west bank of the lake, close to km. 25 on the N123, 4.5 km. south of Graus (approx. 80 km. north of Lleida/Lerida).
>
> **General Details:** Open 1 April - 30 Sept. Bar/snack bar and restaurant (all season). Shop (15/5-15/9). Swimming pool (15/5-15/9). Tennis. Table tennis. Mountain bike hire. Canoe, motor boat and pedaloes for hire, fishing, canoeing etc. Walking (maps provided). Riding 4 km. Money exchange. Mobile homes and bungalows to let.
>
> **Charges 1999:** Per person ptas. 590; child (2-10 yrs) 485; car 675; caravan or tent 675; motorcaravan 1,100; electricity 485. Credit cards accepted.
>
> **Reservations:** Not needed outside mid-July - mid-August. Address: Ctra N-123a, km. 25, 22435 La Puebla de Castro (Huesca). Tel: 974/54 51 48. FAX: as phone. E-mail: camping-lago-barasona@spicom.es.

9142 Camping Solana del Segre, Bellver de Cerdanya, nr Puigcerda

Rustic site with mountain views in scenic area, for outdoor sports enthusiasts.

The Sierra del Cadi offers some spectacular scenery and the Reserva Cerdanya is very popular with Spanish skiers. This site is situated in an open sunny lower valley beside the River Segré where the trout fishing is reputed to be good (permits from Bellver village). The immediate area is ideal for walkers and offers many opportunities for outdoor sports enthusiasts; riding, golf, hang-gliding, canoeing and rock climbing can be arranged with reception. The superb Olympic watersports facility in the interesting old town of Le Seu (25 km, market day Tues), boasts an impressive man-made white water canoeing course where tuition is provided for the brave-hearted. The site is in two sections, the lower one nearer the river being the main tourist one, mainly flat and grassy with pitches of 70 sq.m. or more, mostly marked by trees and all with 6A electricity and quite easy access. There are 300 pitches in total. Sanitary facilities are in three sections and are of satisfactory quality, with free hot water. The showers are of fair size with seats outside.

continued overleaf

9142 Camping Solana del Segre (continued)

The shop and bar/restaurant open Easter - mid Sept. and Christmas, otherwise at weekends only, but the town is very close. Fair-sized swimming pool, children's play area, games room/disco, volleyball and petanque. There is a large number of seasonal units in the summer and the site is very busy at weekends.

How to find it: On the N260 from Puigcerda, the site is just beyond Bellver de Cerdanya towards La Seu (Seo).

General Details: Open all year except 14 Sept - 10 Oct. Shop, Bar/restaurant (see text). Children's play area. Games room. Swimming pool (from June). Many sports in area. Motorcaravan service point. Chemical disposal.

Charges guide: Per person 630; child (under 10) 550; tent, caravan, car all 630; motorcaravan 1,300; electricity 600. Credit cards accepted.

Reservations: Generally only necessary at weekends in high season. Address: Ctra N-260, Km 198. 25720 Bellver de Cerdanya (Lleida). Tel: 973/510310. FAX: 973/510698.

9060 Camping Peña Montañesa, Labuerda, nr Ainsa

Large, riverside site by the Ordesa National Park in the Pyrenees.

Although situated quite high up in the Pyrenees, Pena Montanesa is easily accessible from Ainsa or from France via the Bielsa Tunnel, and is ideally situated for exploring the beautiful Pyrenees. The site is essentially divided into three sections opening progressively throughout the season and providing progressively less shade as the trees in the newer section grow. The 525 pitches on fairly level grass are of approximately 75 sq.m. and 10A electricity is available on virtually all of them. The newer pitches (open in the main season) have the benefit of a new sanitary block, heated when necessary. It has free hot water for the showers, cold for the open plan washbasins, facilities for the disabled, a small baby bathroom and British style WCs. The older pitches are served by an older sanitary block of nevertheless satisfactory standard, with similar provision. This is quite a large site which has grown very quickly and as such may at times be a little hard pressed. Near the entrance are grouped the facilities that make the site so attractive. Apart from a fair sized outdoor pool and children's pool, there is a heated indoor pool with jacuzzi and sauna (open all year) and an attractive bar, restaurant (with open fire) and terrace. The supermarket and takeaway are opposite. Used by tour operators and 58 bungalows for rent.

How to find it: Site is 2 km. from Ainsa, on the road from Ainsa to France.

General Details: Open all year. Bar. Restaurant. Takeaway. Supermarket. Outdoor pools (March - Oct). Indoor pool, jacuzzi and sauna (all year). Children's playground. Boules. Minigolf. Table tennis. Bicycle hire. Riding. Fishing 100 m. Canoeing near. Washing machine. Chemical disposal. Caravans and bungalows to rent.

Charges 1999: Per person ptas. 660; child (1-9 yrs) 560; pitch 1,950; dog 300; electricity 560. All plus 7% VAT. Credit cards accepted.

Reservations: are made for camping with ptas. 10,000 deposit by visa, giro or eurocheque (25,000 ptas. for a bungalow). Address: Ctra. Ainsa-Bielsa, km.2, 22360 Labuerda-Ainsa (Huesca). Tel: 974/50.00.32. FAX: as phone. E-mail: penemontanesa@pirineo.com. Internet: http://pirineo.com/pena_montanesa.

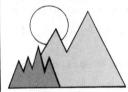
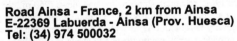

9123 Camping El Solsones, Solsona

Useful nightstop in a peaceful situation.

Situated on a hillside, 2 km. from Solsona with pleasant views of the hills on three sides and an open feeling, this all year site would make for a pleasant short stop, with all facilities open. There are many weekend units, but still room for 100 caravans and 100 tents out of the 312 pitches. These are slightly sloping, with some shade available and 4, 6 or 10A electricity. The modern sanitary facilities are in two buildings, with free hot water to the showers, washbasins, laundry and dishwashing sinks. There is a swimming pool for the high season, a small aviary and children's play equipment. For winter visitors, the 'Ski Port del Conte' is 18 km. and there are facilities for riding, golf and walking in the vicinity. A friendly welcome is provided by the owner who has no English, but good French.

How to find it: Solsona is at the junction of the L301, C1410 and C149 in Lleida, 45 km. northwest of Manresa. The site is 2 km out of town on the LV4241 signed to Sant Llorenc de Morunys and Ski Port del Comte.

General Details: Open all year as are shop, restaurant and bar. Bicycle hire. Children's play area. Petanque. Fronton. Aviary. Swimming pools. Golf, riding and skiing nearby. Motorcaravan service point. Chemical disposal.

Charges guide: Per person ptas. 560; child (2-10 yrs) 490; car and caravan or tent 1,120; motorcaravan 900; electricity (4A) 300: Plus 7% VAT. Credit cards accepted.

Reservations: Contact site for high season (in French). Address: Ctra Sant Llorenc, Km 2. 25280 Solsona. (Lleida). Tel: 973/482861. FAX: 973/481300.

9121 Camping de la Vall d'Ager, Ager, nr Lleida

Very peaceful all year round site in lovely setting.

Ager is not on a through-route to anywhere, so if you are coming here it is for a specific reason, hence the peaceful situation. One of the main reasons for being here is that it is a hang glider's paradise, the Montsec mountain (1,677 m.) overlooking the site in the Catalan pre-Pyrenees, being the launch point. When you also consider that climbing, walking, mountain biking, canoeing and other water sports are all available in the vicinity, you may well wish to visit this pleasant site. There are 180 touring pitches on slightly sloping ground, marked out by trees and with some shade. Electricity (10A) is available to all. The central sanitary building provides good facilities, with soap and paper towels in the toilet sections and free hot water in the washbasins and large showers (with divider and lots of room to change). The building also houses separate rooms for disabled people, dishwashing (hot) and laundry (cold) facilities, plus a washing machine and dryer downstairs. There is a large bar with snack area and a restaurant which opens all year. The village is only 3-400 m.

How to find it: Site is on edge of the village, which is on L904, either direct from Balaguer (28 km. NNE of Lleida) or from C147 Balaguer/Tremp road. Either way, the L904 has old, narrow sections requiring caution.

General Details: Open all year, as are the bar, snack bar and restaurant. Shop (main season only). Bicycle hire. Delta-wing store. Swimming pools. Children's play equipment. Chemical disposal. Accommodation to let.

Charges guide: Per person ptas. 550; child (under 10 yrs) 500; tent, caravan, motorcaravan all 550; electricity (10A) 600. Credit cards accepted.

Reservations: Unlikely to be needed. Address: 25691 Ager, La Noguera (Lleida). Tel: 973/455200/1/9. FAX: 973/455202.

8506 Camping-Caravaning Serra de Prades, Vilanova de Prades, nr Reus

Tranquil site on edge of village, nestling in granite foothills.

On the edge of the village of Vilanova, on the lower mountain slopes with good views (950 m), this is a welcoming and peaceful site. The 215 pitches are on terraces formed with natural stone and with good access from resurfaced roads; 90% have electricity (176 with 6A, 13 with 10A). The planting of hedges and trees continues, to separate pitches and provide a green environment and shade. All facilities are at the entrance to the site and include a modern, very well maintained sanitary block with British style WCs and are heated. Solar power is used to ecologically supplement the hot water supply and there are recycling bins for rubbish. The bar/restaurant offers a wide range of meals. There is plenty to do in the area and the site has facilities for riding (with guided treks) and for the hire of 4x4 vehicles. The helpful staff will give you many leaflets and brochures to guide you to interesting visits, including the attractive, old village itself. The village swimming pool is 100 m. and is free for campers.

How to find it: From autopista A2 take exit 8 (L'Albi) and follow signs to El Vilosell, Vallclara, then Vilanova de Prades. Alternatively from exit 9 (Montblanc) and turn right on N-240 towards Vimbodi, turn left on T-7004 to Vallclara, Vilanova de Prades and site.

General Details: Open all year. Shop. Bar/restaurant. Satellite TV. Archery. Basketball. Volleyball. Tennis. Riding with guided treks. 4x4 vehicle hire. Entertainment organised in season. Swimming pool 100 m. Laundry facilities. Safety deposit. Exchange facilities. Chemical disposal. Motorcravan service point. New bungalows (5) to rent.

Charges 1999: Per person ptas. 595; child (under 10 yrs) 495; tent 595; caravan 595; car 595; m/cycle 495; motorcaravan 1,190; m/cycle 495; electricity 495. Plus 7% VAT. Credit cards accepted.

Reservations: Write to site. Address: c/Sant Antoni s/n, 43439 Vilanova de Prades. Tel/Fax: 977/86.90.50. E-mail: serraprades@svt.es. Internet: www.svt.es/serraprades.

AR Discount
Less 10% on person charge

SWEDEN

Sweden covers an area almost twice that of the UK but has a population only one seventh of ours, with over half the land surface covered by forests and lakes. Stretching from north of the Arctic circle for 1,000 miles to a southern limit about level with Glasgow, inevitably the roads are quiet and almost traffic free with a range of scenery varying from the vast, wild open spaces of Lapland to the rich forests of the south and a choice of climate to match. The very beautiful southwest region, the 'Swedish Lake and Glass country', makes a perfect introduction to this fascinating land. It is easily reached, either by a wide choice of ferries or overland from Norway. The area is dominated by the two great lakes, Vänern (2,000 sq. miles) and Vättern (750 sq. miles), Europe's second and third largest lakes. Stockholm, the capital, is a delightful place built on a series of fourteen small islands, housing monumental architecture and fine museums giving it an ageing, lived-in atmosphere and providing the country's most active culture and night life. Today Sweden enjoys one of the highest standards of living in the world and a quality of life to go with it. For further information contact:

Swedish Travel and Tourism Council, 73 Welbeck Street, London W1M 8AN

Tel: 0171 487 3135. Fax: 0171 935 5853.

Population
8,700,000, density 19.3 per sq. km.

Capital
Stockholm

Climate
Sweden enjoys a temperate climate thanks to the Gulf Stream. The weather is similar to Britain's, apart from the fact that there is generally less rain and more sunshine in the summer.

Language
English is fairly widely spoken but a phrase book is advised.

Currency
Swedish currency is the Krona (plural Kronor) made up of 100 öre. It comes in coins of 50 öre, 1 kr, 5 kr and 10 kr, and notes of 20, 50, 100, 500, 1,000 and 10,000 kr.

Banks
Open Mon-Fri 09.30-15.00. Some city banks stay open til 17.30/18.00. All are closed on Sats.

Post Offices
Open 09.00-18.00 on weekdays and 09.00/10.00 - 13.00 on Saturdays. You can also buy stamps at stationers and tobacconists.

Telephone
To dial Sweden from the UK, dial 00 46 followed by the area code (omitting the initial zero) followed by number. For Britain dial 009 44.

Time
GMT plus 1 (summer BST +1).

Public Holidays
New Year; Epiphany; Good Fri; Easter Mon; Labour Day; Ascension; Whit Sun/Mon; Midsummer, Sat between 20-26 June; All Saints, Sat between 31 Oct-6 Nov; Christmas, 24-26 Dec.

Shops
Open Mon-Fri 09.00-18.00. Sat 09.00-13.00/16.00. In some large towns department stores remain open until 20.00/22.00.
Food: The Swedes generally eat fairly early. Lunch can start at 11.00, the evening meal at 18.00. A typical Swedish 'Smorgasbord' can be enjoyed all over the country.

Motoring
Roads are much quieter than in the UK. Secondary roads may be gravel surfaced but are still good. Dipped headlights are obligatory.
Speed Limits: Caravans and motorhomes (3.5 tons) 31 mph (50 kph) in built up areas; 50 mph (80 kph) on other roads for caravans. Motorhomes 44 - 56 mph (70 - 90 kph) on other roads and 56 - 69 mph (90 - 110 kph) on motorways.
Fuel: Away from large towns, petrol stations rarely open 24 hrs. Buy diesel during working hours, it is rarely available at self service pumps. Credit cards generally accepted except in some 24 hr stations where payment must be made in 20/100 kr notes.
Parking: Meters are in use in several larger towns.

Overnighting
Allowed in most areas, with the permission of the landowner.
Note: Mosquitos can be a problem in summer (from June) - go prepared.

Useful Addresses
National Motoring Organisations:
Motormannens Riksforbund (M),AIT, Sturegatan 32, Stockholm. Tel: 08 7823800.
Kungl Automobil Klubben (KAK)FIA, Gyllenstiernsgatan 4, 11526, Stockholm. Tel: 0860 0055.

The Gothenberg Gateway

Gothenberg is unusually well served for visiting campers with no fewer than five sites, four of which are run by leisure giant Liseberg (operator of the city's renowned theme park). Most central is Liseberg's **Karralund** site in a pleasant suburb only 2 miles east of the town centre; this is magnificently equipped but rather regimented and likely to be congested. Close by, in a lovely small nature park, is **Delsjo Camping**. Also run by Liseberg as a Karralund overflow, this site is basic and only open during peak summer holiday weeks. On the southern outskirts of the town are two sites: the small but friendly independent **Krono Camping**, located in a convenient but uninteresting suburb and Liseberg's leisure beach complex, **Askim Strand**, where tourers tend to be dominated by holiday villas, chalets, huts and statics. Although further out of town, Liseberg's latest acquisition, **Lilleby Havsbad**, is closest to Scandinavian Seaways Terminal.   *continued overleaf*

The Gothenberg Gateway (continued)

The **Lilleby Havsbad** campsite is easily accessible for the town centre by car or bus and is delightfully located in a rustic coast setting. With only 123 pitches it is also the smallest and there are no huts or statics. All the usual facilities are provided and serviced to a high standard. Details are as follows:

How to find it: Turn off E6 going north from Gothenberg on to Torslanda side road and then follow campsite signs.

General Details: Open May - September. Modern block with all facilities, including cooking. Small shop.

Charges guide: Per unit Skr. 125 - 140.

Reservations: Contact site. Address: Lillebyvagen, 42353 Torslanda. Tel: 031/560 867. FAX: 031/561 605.

2645 Råå Vallar Camping, Råå, Helsingborg (Skåne)

Large, privately managed, seaside site with good facilities and swimming pool complex.

Convenient for the ferry terminal at Helsingborg, this is a very busy site and there is no doubt that it can become very crowded in high season and periods of good weather. Nevertheless, it provides a good stop over for those using the ferry port of Helsingborg on journeys to and from Denmark. The site has 450 marked and numbered pitches separated by tarmac roads and small hedges and shrubs, 218 of these have electricity (10A). The site also has 17 statics, 7 cottages and 5 caravans for hire. There are 5 sets of sanitary facilities (including those in the pool complex) which should be sufficient even when site is full. These have a good mix of showers (some without dividers and all without curtains) all have communal undressing and hot water on payment, washbasins (free hot water) and British style WCs. Although they are clean, the proximity to the beach means that sand and water is walked in all the time. Large laundry and three well equipped campers' kitchens, together with facilities for the disabled and babies. Other facilities include a new restaurant and bar complex, serving reasonably priced meals until 11 pm. Takeaway, small well stocked supermarket, video games arcade, TV room, children's playgrounds and bicycle hire service. The excellent outdoor swimming pool complex is heated, with swimming instructors on hand daily and a lifeguard at all times. There are separate pools for children, beginners, and experienced swimmers. The pool complex is charged for but campers have 50% discount. Although some facilities are open very late, the site was fairly quiet at night when inspected.

How to find it: Turn off E6 motorway 5 km. south of Helsingborg Centrum onto road no 111 for Råå, drive towards the coast and follow campsite signs to site.

General Details: Open all year. Supermarket (24/5-31/8). Restaurant. Bar. Takeaway (all 30/4-31/8). Laundry. Cooking facilities. Swimming pool complex (1/6-18/8). Beach and promenade. Video games arcade. TV room. Children's playgrounds. Bicycle hire. Telephone. Caravans and cottages for hire.

Charges 1998: Per unit Skr. 130 - 160; electricity 6A 30, 10A 40.

Reservations: Essential in high season. Write to site for details. Address: Kustgatan, 252 70 Råå. Tel: 042/10.76.80. FAX: 042/26.10.10.

2640 Krono Camping Båstad-Torekov, Torekov, nr Båstad (Skåne)

Good quality site in natural woodland edging the sea on western Swedish coast north of Helsingborg.

This Krono camp is 500 m. from the fishing village of Torekov, 14 km. west of the home of the Swedish tennis WCT Open at Båstad on the stretch of coastline between Malmö and Göteborg. Useful en route from the most southerly ports, it is a very good site and worthy of a longer stay for relaxation. It has 510 large pitches (390 for touring units), all numbered and marked, mainly in attractive natural woodland (mostly pine and birch) with some on more open ground close to the shore. Of these, 350 have electricity and cable TV, 77 also having water and drainage. Three very good sanitary blocks include a modern one of high quality and two older blocks. Hot water is free and there are facilities in each block for cooking, dishwashing, babies and disabled visitors. A laundry is at the reception complex. This modern complex is professionally run and is also home for a good shop, two small boutiques, a snack bar with takeaway, restaurant, minigolf, and a fishermen's style bar (Zorba's), open until 1 am. The spacious site covers quite a large area and there is a cycle track along the shore to the beach with bathing. Several good children's play areas (games organised in high season) and an outdoor stage for musical entertainment and dancing (also in high season). This well run site is a pleasant place to stay.

How to find it: From E6 Malmö - Göteborg road take Torekov/Båstad exit and follow signs for 20 km. towards Torekov. Site is signed 1 km. before village on right.

General Details: Open 1 April - 12 Sept. Restaurant, snack bar with takeaway (7/6-15/8). Bar. Shop and kiosk. Minigolf. Sports fields. Children's play areas. Bicycle hire. TV room. Beach. Fishing. Tennis close. Golf 1 km. Riding 3 km. Games, music and entertainment in high season. Laundry. Cooking facilities. Chemical disposal. Motorcaravan service point. Bungalows, tents and cabins for hire.

Charges 1999: Per unit Skr. 135 -175; electricity/TV connection 40. Credit cards accepted, but not Eurocheques.

Reservations: Write to site for details. Address: 260 93 Torekov. Tel: 0431/364525. FAX: 0431/364625. E-mail: info@kronocamping.se.

2650 Skånes Djurparks Camping, Jularp, Höör (Skåne)

Unique, small, friendly, family run site in conservation area with unusual features and attractions.

This site is probably one of the most unusual we feature. It is adjacent to the Skånes Djurpark, a zoo park with Scandinavian species, and has on site a reconstructed Stone Age Village. The site is in a sheltered valley and has 90 large, level grassy pitches all with 10A electricity, a few with waste water drain, and a separate area for tents. A small, heated, family swimming pool is behind reception, a mini shop and a children's playground. A restaurant is just outside the entrance. The most unusual feature is the sanitary block - it is underground! The air-conditioned building houses superb and ample facilities including roomy showers in private cubicles, washbasins and British style WCs, 2 fully equipped kitchens, laundry and separate drying room and an enormous dining/TV room. Facilities for disabled people and baby changing. Free hot water. The site has a number of underground, caveman style, 8 bed (dormitory type) holiday units for families or groups. They open onto a circular courtyard with barbecue area and have access to the kitchens and dining room in the sanitary block. There are good walks through the nature park and around the lakes, where one can see deer, birds and other wildlife.

How to find it: Turn off no.23 road 2 km. north of Höör (at roundabout) and follow signs for Skånes Djurpark. Camp entrance is off the Djurpark car park.

General Details: Open all year. Mini-shop (April - Oct). Café (June - Aug). Swimming pool (June - Aug). Restaurant nearby. Children's playground. Stone Age Village. Fishing 1.8 km. Riding and golf 8 km. Bicycle hire 3 km. Telephone. Tourist information. Cooking facilities. Laundry. Chemical disposal. Holiday apartments for hire.

Charges 1999: Per unit Skr. 115; electricity 25 (summer) - 35 (winter). Credit cards accepted, but not Eurocheques.

Reservations: Recommended for high season (July/Aug). Address: Jularp, 243 93 Höör. Tel: 0413/553270. FAX: 0413/200 61. E-mail: grottbyn@hoor.mail.telia.com.

2655 Tingsryds Camping, Tingsryd (Småland)

Pleasant, well managed municipal site by Lake Tiken, well placed for Sweden's Glass District.

Tingsryds' 129 large pitches are arranged in rows divided by trees and shrubs, with some along the edge of a lakeside path (public have access). All have electricity (10A) and there is shade in parts. Access is from a tarmac perimeter road and the facilities are housed in buildings near the site entrance, with the reception building having the restaurant, cafe, bar and a small shop. The sanitary installations are in two buildings, one with showers with curtains (on payment, communal undressing), washbasins and British style WCs, the other a campers' kitchen with hobs and dishwashing sinks and further sinks outside under cover (hot water from separate tap), laundry with ironing, facilities for disabled people, and changing rooms, lockers and showers for the sports activities. Although these facilities are in the older style, all are well maintained and very clean. The site is well lit at night. Adjacent to the site is a small beach, grassy lying out area, playground and lake swimming area and three tennis courts. Hire of canoes, fishing and minigolf on site (public access also). Supermarkets, a heated indoor `Waterworld', bowling alley and restaurants in the town (1½ km), which can be reached via a level path/cycle track directly from the site. An ideal place from which to explore the factories and shops of the `Kingdom of Crystal'.

How to find it: Site is 1½ km. from Tingsryd off road no. 120, well signed around the town.

General Details: Open 1 April - 20 Oct. Shop (1/5-15/9). Restaurant, cafe, bar (1/5-15/9). Tennis. Minigolf. Children's playground. Boules. Lake swimming. Beach volleyball. Canoe hire. Fishing. Bicycle hire 1 km. Golf 15 km. Tourist information. Laundry. Cooking facilities. Chemical disposal. Motorcaravan services. Cabins for rent.

Charges 1999: Per unit incl. electricity Skr. 110 - 130. Credit cards accepted, but not Eurocheques.

Reservations: Recommended for high season. Write to site. Address: 362 32 Tingsryd. Tel: 0477/10554 (season) or 0477/11825 (off-season). FAX: 0477/11825. Internet: www.camping.se.

2660 Ågårds Lantgårdscamping, Hillerstorp (Småland)

Small, tranquil site with simple facilities, home cooking and a warm welcome.

On an old Swedish farm, this site is adjacent to the Store Mosse National Park and close to the High Chaparral Western Theme Park (!) and Smålands Motor Museum. The most delightful thing about this family run site, apart from its quiet location, is the wonderful home cooking available straight from the farmhouse kitchen. Fresh bread is available every morning and you can also sample traditional meals and barbecues (order in advance). The site has 80 large pitches set on open meadows near the farmhouse and facilities, 50 with electricity (10A). The simple sanitary block houses hot showers, washbasins and British style WCs, facilities for babies and the disabled, with dishwashing sinks at one end (free hot water throughout). The site is not lit. Children will love the farm animals and birds. Swimming and fishing are possible in local lakes and the Store Mosse National Park provides walking or cycling.

How to find it: Site is 4 km. south of Hillerstorp on road no.152. Turn at sign to Ågårds and site.

General Details: Open all year. Shop, home cooking and meals (both 30/4-30/9). Telephone. Tourist information. Farm animals. Children's playground. Walking, swimming, cycling and fishing near. 3 or 4 mobile homes to rent.

Charges guide: Per unit Skr. 100; electricity 25. Credit cards accepted.

Reservations: Nearly always space. Address: 330 33 Hillerstorp. Tel: 0370/22007. FAX: 0370/22270.

SWEDEN - South

2665 SweCamp Rosenlund, Jönköping (Småland)

Town site overlooking Lake Vättern, ideal for visiting the important city of Jönköping.

Rosenlunds is a good site, useful as a break in the journey across Sweden or visiting the city during a tour of the Lakes. It is on raised ground overlooking the lake, with some shelter in parts. There are 280 pitches on well kept grass which, on one side, slopes away from reception. Some pitches on the other side of reception are flat and have hardstandings and there are 200 electrical (10A), 100 cable TV and 40 water connections. The owners have refurbished and extended the sanitary facilities which include hot showers (some in cubicles), washbasins and British style WCs, plus provision for the disabled and babies. There is a laundry, dishwashing facilities, a well stocked shop and a TV room. Jönköping is one of Sweden's oldest trading centres with a Charter dating back to 1284 and several outstanding attractions. These must include the Calle Ornemark wood carving centre at Riddersberg Manor, the museums of the `Safety match', ceramics and weaponry and the superb troll artistry of John Bauer.

How to find it: Site is well signed from E4 on eastern side of Jönköping. Watch carefully for exit on this fast road.

General Details: Open all year. Shop. Restaurant (May - Sept). Playground. TV room. Bicycle hire. Minigolf. Fishing 500 m. Riding 7 km. Telephone. Tourist information. Laundry facilities. Chemical disposal. Motorcaravan service point. Caravans, rooms and cottages for hire.

Charges 1999: Per unit incl. all persons Skr. 135; electricity/TV 35. No credit cards or Eurocheques.

Reservations: Recommended for July - write to site for details. Address: Villa Bjorkhagen, 55454 Jönköping. Tel: 036/122863. FAX: 036/126687. E-mail: villabjorkhagen@surpnet.se.

2670 Grännastrandens Familjecamp, Gränna (Småland)

Large, lakeside site with modern facilities and busy continental feel, below the old city of Gränna.

Flat fields separate Gränna from the shore, one of which is occupied by the 25 acres of Grännastrandens where there are 500 numbered pitches, including a tent area and some pitches which are seasonally reserved. The site is flat, spacious and very regularly laid out on open ground with only a row of poplars by the lake to provide shelter, so a windbreak may prove useful against any onshore breeze. About 260 pitches have electrical connections and there is a good internal road system. There is one large, sanitary block in the centre of the site with modern, well kept facilities which include British style WCs, some with external access, washbasins and hot showers in private cubicles (on payment). There are dish and clothes washing sinks, laundry facilities and provision for disabled people, with a further small, older block by reception. Part of the lake is walled off to form an attractive swimming area with sandy beaches, slides and islands. Obviously the great attraction here is the lake. It offers beaches, bathing, fishing, sailing and superb coastal walks. Outstanding, however, is the 30 minute ferry crossing from the tiny harbour next to the site to Visingsö, the beautiful island reputedly inhabited for over 6,000 years. It is this excursion, complete with its gentle tour by horse drawn `remmalag' which alone warrants Grännastrandens as your base. Gränna is also the home of the famous peppermint rock which you can watch being made before you sample. In the Hallska Gården in the old city centre you will also find potteries, paper makers, basket weavers and goldsmiths. Gränna is also the centre of hot air ballooning and on 11 July each year there are ascents from Sweden's only `balloon airport'.

How to find it: Take Gränna exit from E4 road (no camping sign) 40 km. north of Jönköping. Site is signed in the centre of the town, towards the harbour and ferry.

General Details: Open 1 May - 30 Sept. Shop. Café outside site (1/5-31/8) or town restaurants close. TV room. Children's playground. Lake swimming area. Boating and fishing. Telephone. Laundry and drying. Cooking facilities. Chemical disposal. Cabins and rooms to let.

Charges 1998: Per unit Skr. 120, with electricity 150. Credit cards accepted.

Reservations: Write to site for details. Address: Grännastrandens Familjecamp, Box 14, 563 21 Gränna, Småland. Tel: 0390/10706. FAX: 0390/30059.

2675 Lysingsbadet Camping, Västervik (Småland)

Large site with unrivalled views of the `Pearl of the East Coast' - Västervik and its fjords and islands.

One of the largest sites in Scandinavia, Lysingsbadet has around 1,000 large, mostly marked and numbered pitches, spread over a vast area of rocky promontory and set on different plateau, terraces, in valleys and woodland, or beside the water. It is a very attractive site, and one which never really looks or feels crowded even when busy. There are 83 full service pitches with TV, water and electricity, 163 with TV and electricity and 540 with electricity only, the remainder for tents. Reception is smart, efficient and friendly with good English spoken. The 10 modern sanitary blocks of various ages and designs house a comprehensive mix of showers, basins and WCs. All contain good quality fittings and are kept very clean. There are several campers' kitchens with dishwashing sinks, cookers and hoods, and laundry rooms. Free hot water throughout and all facilities free of charge. Campers are issued with `key cards' which operate the entrance barriers and are used to gain access to sanitary blocks, swimming pool complex and other facilities. An hourly bus service to Västervik runs from the site entrance May-Sept.

continued overleaf

2675 Lysingsbadet Camping (continued)

On site are a full golf course, minigolf, heated outdoor swimming pool complex, children's playgrounds, boat hire, tennis, basketball, volleyball and fishing. A licensed restaurant is supplemented by a café/takeaway and a range of shops. For children, Astrid Lindgren's World theme park at Vimmerby is an easy day trip and for adults the delights of the old town of Västervik and its shopping.

How to find it: Turn off the E22 for Västervik and keep straight on at all junctions until you see the first campsite sign. Follow signs to site.

General Details: Open all year. Supermarket and shops, restaurant and café/takeaway (all 1/6-31/8). Swimming pool complex (1/6-31/8). Golf. Minigolf. Tennis. Basketball. Volleyball. Boat hire. Fishing. Entertainment and dances in high season. Children's playgrounds. Quick Stop service. Telephones. Laundries. Hairdresser. Tourist information. Bus service. Cooking facilities. Motorcaravan service point. Hotel rooms, cabins and caravans for rent.

Charges 1998: Per unit Skr. 120 - 170; electricity 35. Credit cards accepted.

Reservations: Advisable for peak season (July/Aug). Write to site for details. Address: 593 53 Västervik. Tel: 0490/36795. FAX: 0490/36175.

2680 Krono Camping Saxnäs, Färjestaden (Öland)

Large site well placed for touring Sweden's Riviera - fascinating and beautiful island of Öland.

This family owned site, part of the Krono group, has 420 marked and numbered touring pitches arranged in rows on open, well kept grassland dotted with a few trees, all with electricity (10A). A further unmarked area without electricity can accommodate around 60 tents. 320 of these pitches also have TV connections and a further 116 also have water connections. The site has about 130 long stay units and cabins for rent. Reception is efficient and friendly with good English spoken. Three sanitary blocks provide a good supply of roomy private showers, washbasins, some washbasin/WC suites and WCs. There are facilities for babies and disabled visitors. Good, well equipped laundry room and campers' kitchen facilities with cookers, microwaves and dishwasher (free) together with dishwashing sinks. Hot water is free throughout. The site has a licensed restaurant, pizzeria, café, shop, minigolf, volleyball and football field together with a good children's playground. In high season a crèche and children's organised games also operate. Dances are held on Wed/Sat in season with other activities on other evenings. The beach is sandy, slopes very gently and is very safe for children. Nearby attractions include the 7 km. long Öland road bridge, Kalmar and its castle, museums and old town on the mainland, Eketorp prehistoric fortified village, Öland Djurpark and many old windmills.

How to find it: Cross the Öland road bridge from Kalmar on road no. 137. Take exit for Öland Djurpark/Saxnäs, then follow campsite signs. Site is just north of the end of the bridge.

General Details: Open 17 April - 18 Sept. Shop (17/5-22/8). Pizzeria, licensed restaurant and café (all 17/5-22/8). Children's playground and crèche. Boules. Beach with volleyball. Fishing. Bicycle hire. Minigolf. Football. Riding 2 km. Family entertainment and activities organised. Telephones. Tourist information. Laundry. Cooking facilities. Chemical disposal. Motorcaravan services. Cabins for rent.

Charges 1998: Per unit Skr. 125 - 170, with electricity 155 - 200, with TV also 165 - 215. Weekend and weekly rates available. Credit cards accepted, but not Eurocheques.

Reservations: Essential for high season (July/Aug). Address: 386 95 Färjestaden, Öland. Tel: 0485/35700. FAX: 0485/35664. E-mail: kronocamping.saxnas@saxnasturism.se.

AR Discount
Less 10%
(not cabins)

2700 Borås Camping, Borås (Västergotland)

Pleasant municipal site in a park setting 2 km. north of the city centre.

Borås Camping is within easy walking distance of a swimming pool complex, Djurpark and shopping centre, and is convenient for ferries to and from Göthenberg. Located on the outskirts of Borås, this tidy, well managed site provides 490 large, numbered, level pitches, carefully arranged in rows on well kept grass with good tarmac perimeter roads. There is some shade in parts. Seven good, clean sanitary blocks provide hot showers, washbasins, WCs and facilities for babies and the disabled, in various combinations, most opening directly from outside. Good campers' kitchens with hobs, extractor hoods, and dishwashing sinks (free of charge) and laundry facilities are provided. Many activities are available both on the site and nearby, many free to campers; the excellent outdoor heated swimming pool complex, Alidebergsbadet, is only 400 m. away. Canoes and pedaloes are available on the small canal running through the site. Small shop for necessities and fast food service. Also on site is a Youth Hostel and many cabins for rent. The shopping precinct at Knalleland is only 500 m. away, the Zoo (Djurpark) is 400 m. The site can issue the `Boråscard' which gives free and discounted access to city car parks, transport, museums and attractions during your stay.

How to find it: Exit road no. 40 from Göthenberg for Borås Centrum and follow signs to Djurpark and road no. 42 to Trollhåtten through the town. Turn left to site.

General Details: Open all year. Shop. Takeaway. Several children's playgrounds. Minigolf. Swimming, tennis, frisbee, badminton, football, croquet, table tennis, jogging tracks, basketball all nearby. Telephones. Laundry. Cooking facilities. Motorcaravan service point. Tourist information. Cabins for rent.

Charges 1998: Per unit Skr. 105 - 135; electricity 25.

Reservations: One should always find room here. Address: 500 04 Borås. Tel: 033/121434. FAX: 033/140582.

SWEDEN - West

2710 Krono Camping Lidköping, Lidköping - Lake Vänern (Västergotland)

High quality, attractive site with lake and leisure facilities.

This attractive site provides about 430 pitches on flat, well kept grass. It is surrounded by some mature trees, with the lake shore as one boundary and a number of tall pines have been left to provide shade and shelter. There are 274 pitches with electricity (10A) and TV connections and 91 with water and drainage also, together with 60 cabins for rent. A tour operator takes a few pitches. Excellent, modern sanitary facilities are provided in two identical blocks with under-floor heating, attractive decor and lighting (and music), and there is free hot water throughout. They have controllable hot showers (in roomy private cubicles), partitioned washbasins, British style WCs, make up and hairdressing areas with mirrors, electric points and shelves, baby room and facilities for the disabled. Dishwashing sinks are available outside each block. Good kitchens with cookers and microwaves are also provided. There is a laundry, a small shop (a shopping centre is very close) and a coffee bar with conservatory seating area in the reception complex. Very good playgrounds are provided for the children, together with a play field, TV room (cartoon videos shown) and an amusement and games room. Solarium, bicycle hire, minigolf and volleyball. The lake is available for watersports, boating and fishing with bathing from the sandy beach or there is a swimming pool complex (free for campers) adjacent to the site.

> **How to find it:** From Lidköping town junctions follow signs towards Läckö then pick up camping signs turning right at second roundabout. Continue to site on left (½-1 km).
>
> **General Details:** Open 13 April - 15 Sept (full services 13/6-14/8). Small shop. Coffee bar with snacks. Minigolf. Volleyball. Solarium. Children's playgrounds. TV room. Games and amusements room. Bicycle hire. Play field. Swimming pool adjacent. Lake swimming, fishing and watersports. Telephone. Tourist information. Laundry facilities. Cooking room. Motorcaravan service point.
>
> **Charges 1998:** Per unit Skr. 125 -155; electricity/TV connection 40.
>
> **Reservations:** Write to site. Address: Läckögatan, 531 54 Lidköping. Tel: 0510/26804. FAX: 0510/21135.

2720 Hökensås Holiday Village and Camp Site, Tidaholm (Västergotland)

Well run site and holiday complex in wild, unspoiled national park.

This good site is part of a holiday complex including wooden cabins for rent. It is relaxed and informal, with over 200 pitches either under trees or on a more open area at the far end, divided into rows by wooden rails. These are numbered and electricity is available on 130. Tents can go on the large grassy open areas by reception. The original, recently refurbished, sanitary block near reception has been supplemented by a newer one in the wooded area. These provide free hot showers with communal undressing and curtained cubicles, open washbasins with hooks and mirrors, and WCs. There are separate saunas for each sex and facilities for the disabled and babies. A campers' kitchen is provided at each block with cooking, dishwashing and laundry facilities. A children's playground, tennis court and minigolf are near the entrance and there is a small, but well stocked shop with a comprehensive angling section. A café with tables on a terrace outside also serves takeaway snacks. Hökensås is located just west of Lake Vättern and south of Tidaholm, in a beautiful national park of wild, unspoiled scenery. The park is based on a 100 km. ridge, a glacier area with many impressive boulders and ice age debris but now thickly forested with majestic pines and silver birches, with a small, brilliant lake at every corner. The forests and lakes provide wonderful opportunities for walking, cycling (gravel tracks and marked walks) angling, swimming and when the snow falls, winter sports.

> **How to find it:** Approach site from no. 195 western lake coast road. at Brandstorp, about 40 km. north of Jönköping, turn west at petrol station and camp sign signed Hökensås. Site is about 9 km. up this road.
>
> **General Details:** Open all year. Shop. Café with takeaway. Children's playground. Tennis. Minigolf. Sauna. Lake swimming. Fishing. Telephone. Tourist information. Laundry. Cooking facilities. Cabins for hire.
>
> **Charges 1998:** Per unit Skr. 110 (more for Midsummer celebrations); electricity 30 - 35.
>
> **Reservations:** Write to site for details. Address: Blåhult, 522 91 Tidaholm. Tel: 0502/23053.

2730 Ekudden Camping, Mariestad - Lake Vänern (Västergotland)

Well established site on the eastern shore of Lake Vänern with swimming pools adjacent.

Ekudden occupies a long stretch of the lake shore to the south of the town, in a mixed woodland setting, and next door to the municipal complex of heated outdoor pools and sauna. The lake, of course, is also available for swimming or boating and there are bicycles, tandems and canoes for hire. The spacious site can take 425 units and there are about 160 electrical hook-ups (10A). Most pitches are under the trees but some at the far end of the site are on more open ground (without electricity) with good views over the lake but some distance from the facilities. Sanitary facilities are provided in three low wooden cabins all of which have been recently refurbished or renewed. These have hot showers (on payment with token from reception) some with curtains and communal undressing, some in private cubicles, and both open and cubicled washbasins. In addition there are facilities for the disabled with good access ramps and baby changing rooms. All are clean and well maintained.

continued overleaf

2730 Ekudden Camping (continued)

There are two kitchens with dishwashing (free hot water) and other covered sinks, outside in groups of four (cold water only) around the site. The site becomes very busy in high season.

How to find it: Site is south of the town and well signed at junctions on the ring road and from E20 motorway.

General Details: Open 1 May - 15 Sept. (full services 15/6-16/8). Shop. Takeaway (in high season). Swimming pools adjacent. Canoes, bicycles and tandems for hire. Children's playground and bouncy castle. Minigolf. TV room. Lake swimming, boating and fishing. Telephone. Tourist information. Laundry facilities. Cooking facilities. Mobile homes for hire.

Charges 1998: Per unit Skr. 100 - 130; electricity 30.

Reservations: Essential in high season. Write to site. Address: 542 01 Mariestad. Tel 0501/10637.

2740 Laxsjöns Camping Och Friluftsgård, Dals Långed (Dalsland)

Lakeside site with swimming pool in beautiful Dalsland region.

Laxsjöns is an all year round site, catering for winter sports enthusiasts as well as summer tourists. On the shores of the lake, the site is in two main areas - one flat, near the entrance, with hardstandings and the other on an attractive, sloping, grassy area adjoining. In total there are 300 places available for caravans or motorcaravans, all with electricity, plus more for tents. Rooms and cabins are also available for rent. A good, modern toilet block has hot showers on payment (communal undressing), open washbasins, WCs and a hairdressing cubicle with free dryer. With a further small block at the top of the site, the provision should be adequate. Other services include a shop, laundry, clothes drying rooms for bad weather, cooking rooms for tenters and provision for the disabled. Outside there is a good swimming pool (1.9 m, open 10 am - 9 pm.) with paddling pool, minigolf, unusual table top minigolf, tennis, trampoline and a playground. There is a restaurant at the top of the site with a good range of dishes in high season, and a lake for swimming, fishing and canoeing (boats available). The site is located in the centre of Dalsland, west of Lake Vänern, in an area of deep forests, endless lakes and river valleys, and is one of the loveliest and most interesting regions in this always peaceful and scenic country.

How to find it: From Åmål take road no. 164 to Bengtfors, then the 172 towards Dals Långed. Site is signed about 5 km. south of the town 1 km. down a good road.

General Details: Open all year. Restaurant (high season). Shop. Tennis. Minigolf. Sauna. Children's playground. Swimming pool. Lake for swimming, Fishing and boating. Laundry and drying facilities. Cooking facilities.

Charges 1998: Per unit Skr. 110 - 125; electricity 20.

Reservations: Advisable in peak season. Write to site for details. Address: 660 10 Dals Långed, Dalsland. Tel: 0531/30010. FAX: 0531/30555.

2750 Sommarvik Fritidscenter, Årjäng (West Värmland)

Good quality site in beautiful surroundings beside lake Västra Silen, for family holidays.

Sommarvik has some 250 large, separated and numbered pitches arranged in terraces on a pine wooded hillside, some overlooking the lake; 100 of these have electrical connections and 30 are all service pitches. It offers much in the way of outdoor pursuits and peaceful countryside. The site is served by five sanitary blocks which house a good mix of private shower cubicles (hot water on payment), washbasins (free hot water), WCs, family bathrooms, and facilities for disabled people and baby changing. All are kept clean. In addition there are good campers' kitchens with cookers and sinks, and laundry facilities. The site has 43 cabins for rent, 40 long stay units, with a youth hostel and conference centre also on site. A very large and smart restaurant offers a full range of meals, soft drinks, beers and wines, and takeaway meals. On site activities include swimming in the lake from a sandy beach (safe for children), canoe hire, windsurfing, rowing boats, fishing, sauna, tennis courts, football field, organised Elk safaris, minigolf, quizzes, guided walks, and there are good children's playgrounds. The site also organises local folk music during the main season. You can ride trolleys around the area on disused railway tracks or take a day trip to go gold panning. The site is within easy reach of the Norwegian border and Oslo. Skiing is also available (when there is snow) and there is an indoor swimming pool complex 3 km. away in Årjäng. This is a very scenic region and one which makes an ideal base for a family holiday with lots of activities and sightseeing trips available.

How to find it: Site is signed from roads nos. 172 and E18. It is 3 km. south of Årjäng Centrum.

General Details: Open all year. Restaurant and takeaway (1/6-30/8). Shop (all year). Minigolf. Lake swimming. Canoe, row boat and windsurfer hire. Bicycle hire. Fishing. Tennis. Sauna. Football field. Children's playgrounds. Range of organised activities. Riding 5 km. Golf 9 km. Telephone. Tourist information. Cooking facilities. Laundry. Chemical disposal. Motorcaravan service point. 'Quick stop' pitches for overnight stays. Cabins for hire.

Charges 1998: Per tent Skr. 90 - 140; caravan or motorcaravan 110 - 200; electricity included. Credit cards accepted, but not Eurocheques.

Reservations: Recommended for peak seasons (summer and winter). Write to site for details. Address: 672 00 Årjäng. Tel: 0573/12060. FAX: 0573/12048. E-mail: swecamp@sommarvik.se. Internet: www.sommarvik.se.

AR Discount
Less 20%
on canoe hire

SWEDEN - West / Central

2760 Frykenbaden Camping, Kil (Värmland)

Quiet, friendly site on the shores of Lake Fryken.

Frykenbaden Camping is in a wooded area and takes 250 units on grassy meadows surrounded by trees. One area nearer the lake is gently sloping, the other is flat with numbered pitches arranged in rows. There are 125 pitches with electricity, satellite TV and phone connections and a further 25 with electricity only. Reception, a small shop and takeaway are located in a traditional Swedish house surrounded by lawns sloping down to the shore, with minigolf, a children's play barn and playground, with pet area, also close by. The main sanitary block is also here. It is of good quality and heated in cool weather with showers on payment, open washbasins, a laundry room and room for families or disabled people. With a further small block with equally good facilities, the overall supply is better than average for Swedish sites. Well equipped camper's kitchen with ovens, hobs and sinks together with tables and benches and separate fish cleaning sinks near the lake. Swimming and canoeing are possible in the lake as well as fishing in the sites' own area (payment per kg. caught). There is a good value restaurant at the adjacent golf club which can be reached by a pleasant walk. Fryken is a long, narrow lake, said to be one of the deepest in Sweden, and it is a centre for angling. Frykenbadens is on the southern shore, and is a quiet, relaxing place to stay away from the busier, more famous lakes. There are plenty of other activities in the area (golf, riding, ski-ing in winter) and Kil is not too far from the Norwegian border.

How to find it: Site is signed from the no. 61 Karlstad - Arvika road, then 4 km. towards lake following signs.

General Details: Open 15 May - 15 Sept. (full service 15/6-16/8). Small shop. Snack bar and takeaway. Minigolf. Children's play barn and playground. Fishing from site with rods for hire. Lake swimming. Canoes and bicycles for hire. Telephone. Tourist information. Campers' kitchen. Cabins for rent.

Charges 1998: Per unit Skr. 110 - 120, electricity 35.

Reservations: Write to site. Address: Frykenbaden PL. 1405, 665 00 Kil. Tel: 0554/40940.

2800 Glyttinge Camping, Linköping (Östergötland)

Top quality site with enthusiastic and friendly management.

Only 5 minutes by car from the Ikea Shopping Mall and adjacent to a good swimming pool complex, Glyttinge is a most attractive site with a mix of terrain - some flat, some sloping and some woodland. It is maintained to a very high standard and there are flowers, trees and shrubs everywhere giving it a cosy garden like atmosphere. There are 239 good size, mostly level pitches of which 125 have electricity (10A). The main centrally located sanitary block (supplemented by additional smaller facilities at reception) is modern, well constructed and exceptionally well equipped and maintained. It provides showers in private cubicles with dividers, hooks and seat, washbasins, and WC suites with basins, soap dispensers, hand dryers, and soothing music! There are excellent separate facilities for the disabled, a solarium, laundry and baby changing rooms. The superb kitchen and dining/TV room is fully equipped with everything you could possibly need to prepare and enjoy a meal. Hot water is free throughout. Children are well catered for - the manager has laid out a wonderful, fenced and very safe children's play area and, in addition, parents can rent (minimal charge) tricycles, pedal cars, scooters and carts. There is also a wet weather playroom for children, shop with gifts, fresh bread, milk, soft drinks and ices are sold. Takeaway snacks include burgers, pizzas and chips. Also on site - minigolf, football field, and bicycle hire. Adjacent to the site is a heated outdoor swimming pool complex with 3 pools (charged). There is a bus stop at the camp gate. Attractions nearby include the town of Linköping, Aviation Museum, Land Museum and the new Ikea Shopping Mall.

How to find it: Exit the E4 Helsingborg - Stockholm road north of Linköping at signs for Ikea and site. Turn right at traffic lights and camp sign and follow signs to site.

General Details: Open 28 April - 3 Oct. Shop and takeaway (28/6-15/8). Swimming pool complex adjacent (1/5-25/8). Minigolf. Football. Bicycle hire. Children's playground. Fishing 5 km. Riding and golf 3 km. Telephones. Tourist information. Cooking facilities and dining/TV room. Laundry. Motorcaravan services. Cabins for hire.

Charges 1998: Per unit Skr. 115 - 140; electricity 30. Credit cards accepted, but not Eurocheques.

Reservations: Recommended for July/Aug. Write to site for details. Address: Berggardsvagen, 582 49 Linköping. Tel: 013/174928. FAX: 013/175923. E-mail: glyttinge@swipnet.se. Internet: www.camping.se/plats/e28.

2810 Vätterviksbadet Camping, Vadstena, Östergötland (Lake Vättern)

Large and busy, municipal site on the shore of Lake Vättern.

This is an acceptable site for overnighters or short stays on one of the main north south routes. The site has some 550 mostly marked and numbered pitches separated by low wooden rails on flat grass between the road and lake. Of these, 292 have electricity (10A). Some shade in parts and although the main areas of the site are lit, torches may be required at the furthest extremities. The site is very long and narrow and it is quite a walk to facilities from the distant ends of the site. There is some road noise and many long stay units on site. The site is fenced and the barrier is locked promptly at 10 pm. The three sanitary blocks are of varying ages and designs, the oldest at the northern end of the site. All contain a mix of cold water and free hot water facilities.

continued overleaf

2810 Vätterviksbadet Camping (continued)

Some private shower cubicles, some with divider, seat and curtain and some with communal undressing. There is a good supply of washbasins, but rather fewer WCs and hand dryers. In addition there are limited facilities for the disabled and a baby changing room. Two small kitchens have basic facilities, and there is a small laundry at each of the two newer blocks - mostly cold water. The site has a good shop and takeaway service, a waterslide pool and one can swim from the safe sandy beach at the lake.

How to find it: Site is alongside the no. 50 Jönköping - Örebro road, 3 km. north of Vadstena.

General Details: Open 30 April -13 Sept. Shop. Takeaway. Lake swimming. Waterslide pool. Minigolf. Volleyball. Children's playground. Telephone. Laundry. Cooking facilities. Car wash. Tourist information.

Charges 1998: Per unit Skr. 125; electricity 25.

Reservations: Essential for peak season (July/Aug). Write to site for details. Address: 592 80 Vadstena. Tel: 0143/12730. FAX: 0143/15190.

2820 Skantzö Bad Camping, Hallstahammar (Västmanland)

Attractive, well maintained municipal site beside Strömsholms Kanal between Örebro and Stockholm.

A very comfortable and pleasant site just off the main E18 motorway from Oslo to Stockholm, this has 180 large marked and numbered pitches, 156 of these with electricity (10A). The terrain is flat and grassy, there is good shade in parts and the site is well fenced and locked at night. There are 22 new alpine style cabins for rent with window boxes of colourful flowers. Reception is very friendly. The sanitary block serving the camping area is located in the reception area and is maintained and equipped to a high standard, providing free hot showers (now in private cubicles with washbasin), basins (free hot water) and WCs, facilities for disabled people and baby changing. In addition there are good campers' kitchen facilities, a good laundry with drying room/lines, washing machine and dryer. Barbecue grill area. Cafeteria, fresh bread and milk, etc sold. Very large, fenced, outdoor, heated swimming pool and waterslide, children's playground, tennis courts, minigolf and games area complex (free to campers). Direct access to the towpath of the Stromsholms Kanal and nearby is the Kanal Museum. The site provides hire and transportation of canoes for longer canal tours.

How to find it: Turn off E18 at Hallstahammar and follow road no. 252 to north of town centre and signs to site.

General Details: Open 1 May - 31 August. Cafeteria and shop (7/5-29/8). Swimming pool and waterslide (21/5-22/8). Minigolf. Tennis. Children's playground. Bicycle hire. Fishing. Canoe hire. Golf 8 km. Telephone. Conference room. Tourist information. Cooking facilities. Laundry. Chemical disposal. Motorcaravan service point. Cabins for hire.

Charges 1999: Per unit Skr. 100; electricity 30. Credit cards accepted.

Reservations: Write to site for details. Address: Box 506, 734 27 Hallstahammar. Tel: 0220/24305. FAX: 0220/24187. Internet: www.camping.se/plats/u05.

2830 Ängby Camping, Bromma (Stockholm North)

Good short stay or transit site on the edge of Lake Mälaren, close to central Stockholm.

Of all the sites close to central Stockholm, this appears to be the best option, being only some 500 m. walk from the Metro that takes you to the heart of the city in 15 minutes. The site also sells the famous `Stockholm Card' which gives unlimited access to transport and most attractions throughout the city. The site can accommodate around 160 units with easy access. Some level pitches are behind reception, others on the wooded hillside area nearer the lake - all with electricity (10A), satellite TV to around half. There is a separate area for tents. Reception is friendly with good English spoken. Two recently refurbished and heated sanitary blocks, one serving the camping area, the other the cabins provide hot showers on payment with divider and curtain (communal undressing), washbasins, and WC/hand basin units (cold water). Campers' kitchens have sinks, ovens and hobs and a laundry (hot water on payment). Facilities for disabled visitors. There is a sauna and a cafeteria which serves coffee, pastries, beer, soft drinks and takeaway snacks. Breakfasts served in main season. There is some road noise and campers do leave early and return very late, as one would expect in this situation. There is a guard in reception all night, the owner lives opposite and the police visit regularly - it all adds to the feeling of security. The site is adjacent to a small park with a water slide and pool, minigolf, children's playground, café and bathing beach. There are some fine lakeside walks on good paths and a jogging track from the site. Fishing and canoe hire. It is possible to hike or cycle to Drottningholm Palace and gardens from the site.

How to find it: Leave E18 at exit for road no.275 and drive towards Vallingby/Brommaplan; then turn right off the 275 for S. Angby and site.

General Details: Open all year. Cafeteria and takeaway (15/5-31/8). Small shop (15/5-31/8). Sauna. Fishing. Minigolf. Water slide. Children's playground. Games room. Jogging track. Canoe hire. Tennis courts, supermarket and restaurant 400 m. Indoor swimming pool 1 km. Bicycle hire 10 km. Golf 5 km. Telephone. Tourist information. Cooking facilities. Laundry. Chemical disposal. Cabins for rent.

Charges 1999: Per unit Skr. 145 - 155, acc. to unit type; electricity 25. No credit cards or Eurocheques.

Reservations: Essential in peak season. Address: Blackebergstr. 27, 16850 Bromma. Tel: 08/370420. FAX: 08/378226.

2840 Stockholm SweCamp Flottsbro, Huddinge

Neat, quiet lakeside site with ski slope and good security 18 km. south of Stockholm.

Flottsbro is a small site with good quality facilities and very good security, located some 18 km. south of Stockholm. There are 74 large numbered pitches for caravans and motorhomes and a separate unmarked area for tents. Pitches are arranged on level terraces, but the site itself is sloping and the reception and restaurant are at the bottom with all the ski facilities and further good sanitary facilities with sauna. The main site road is tarmac. At the time of inspection, there was only one sanitary block on the camping area but an additional one has been opened to serve the tenting area. The modern facilities include free private hot showers, WCs and washbasins, a suite for disabled people, baby changing facilities and a family bathroom. An excellent campers' kitchen has electric cookers and sinks with hot water, all free of charge. Small laundry with washing machine, dryer (charged for) and sink. The reception area is remote from the entrance but a very good security system is in place, campers have keys to the barrier and sanitary installations, there is a night guard and an entry phone/camera surveillance system on the entrance for good measure. Once you have negotiated the entry phone you will find a friendly and more personal service at reception. Do not be tempted to walk to reception from the gate, it is a long way down and a steep climb back. Other facilities on site include the ski slope and lift, restaurant which serves a selection of simple meals and snacks, beer, tea, coffee and soft drinks. The site has a small lakeside beach and grassy lying out area with children's playground and plenty of room for ball games. There is also minigolf, volleyball, frisbee, jogging track, canoe hire. A large supermarket and the local rail station are 10 minutes by car from the site. The area is also good for walking, cycling and cross-country skiing.

How to find it: Turn off the E4 at Vårby/Huddinge and turn left on road no.259. After 2 km. turn right and follow signs to Flottsbro.

General Details: Open all year. Restaurant. Sauna. Minigolf. Volleyball. Frisbee. Jogging track. Canoe hire. Children's playground. Telephone. Tourist information. Cooking facilities. Laundry. Chemical disposal. Motorcaravan services. Cabins for rent.

Charges 1998: Per caravan or motorcaravan Skr. 130; tent 110; electricity 30 plus 0.70 per kwh. Credit cards accepted.

Reservations: Advisable for both summer and winter peak times. Write to site for details. Address: Box 1216, 141 25 Huddinge. Tel: 08/7785860. FAX: 08/7785755.

2835 Orsa Grönklitt Camping, Orsa (Dalarna)

Quiet, budget priced site, adjacent to the Grönklitt Bear Park.

Primarily designed for winter, with a ski slope adjacent, the site is a rather large and featureless, gravel hardstanding, providing room for more than 50 units with electricity (10A) for all, but particularly good for larger motorcaravans. In summer, this quietly located site rarely has more than a dozen occupants, yet it is half the price of the crowded, often noisy sites in Orsa town 14 km. away. The excellent, very modern, small sanitary unit is heated. It has one unisex WC with external access and, inside for each sex, there is one WC and washbasin cubicle, and two hot showers with curtains and communal changing area. Suite for disabled visitors, drying room and chemical disposal point. A well equipped kitchen has two hobs and two dishwashing sinks. All showers, hairdryers, hot water, drying and kitchen facilities are free. Reception is at the holiday centre with its rental cabins, inn, tourist information and other services, about 1 km. below the camping area, and one should book in here and obtain a key for the sanitary unit before proceeding to the site. The Grönklitt Bear Park, with bears, wolves, and lynx is within a short scramble up the hillside from the site and there are magnificent views over this scenic lakeland area.

How to find it: From Orsa town centre follow the signs to Grönklitt and `Björn Park'. Site is 14 km.

General Details: Open all year. Kitchen. Drying room.

Charges guide: Per unit, incl. all persons Skr. 75.00; electricity 30. Credit cards accepted.

Reservations: Not necessary. Address: Box 23, 794 21 Orsa. Tel: 0250/462 00. FAX: 0250/461 11. E-mail: fritid@orsa-gronklitt.se. Internet: www.orsa-gronklitt.se.

2845 Svegs Camping, Sveg (Jamtland)

Neat, riverside municipal site, on the `Inlandsvagen' route through Sweden.

The town centre is only a short walk from this friendly municipal site, with two supermarkets, café and tourist information office adjacent. The 160 pitches are in rows, on level grass, divided into bays by tall hedges, and with electricity (10/16A) available to 70. The sanitary facilities provide British style WCs, stainless steel washing troughs, controllable hot showers with communal changing areas, and a unit for the disabled. These are in the older style, functional rather than luxurious, and although a little short on numbers will probably suffice at most times as the site is rarely full. The kitchen and dining room with TV, has four full cookers and sinks, plus more dishwashing sinks outside under cover. Free hot water throughout. Laundry facilities include a washing machine and dryers, and an ironing board.

continued overleaf

2845 Svegs Camping (continued)

The site has boats, canoes, cycles and rickshaws for hire, and the river frontage has a barbecue area and fishing platforms. Alongside the river with its fountain, and running through the site is a pleasant well lit riverside walk. Places to visit include the town with its lovely church and adjacent gardens, some interesting old churches in the surrounding villages, and 16th Century Remsgården, 14 km. to the west.

How to find it: Site is off road 45 behind the tourist information office in Sveg.

General Details: Open all year. Children's play area. TV room. Minigolf. Canoe, boat, rickshaw and bicycle hire. Fishing. Kitchen. Laundry. Chemical disposal.

Charges 1998: Per unit Skr. 110; tent and car 90; cyclist or m/cyclist and tent 90; electricity 25 - 30. Credit cards accepted.

Reservations: Contact site. Address: Kyrkogränd 1, 842 32 Sveg. Tel: 0680/107 75 FAX: 0680/103 37.

2850 Östersunds Camping, Östersund (Jamtland)

Extensive, modern, woodland site, a good base for exploring central Sweden

Östersund lies on Lake Storsjön, which is Sweden's Loch Ness, with 200 sightings of the monster dating back to 1635, and more recently captured on video in 1996. Also worthy of a visit is the island of Frösön where settlements can be traced back to pre-historic times. This large site has 300 pitches, electricity (10A) and TV socket available on 120, all served by tarmac roadways. There are also 41 tarmac hardstandings available, and over 200 cottages, cabins and rooms for rent. The sanitary facilities are in three units, two providing British style WCs, washbasins and controllable hot showers (on payment) with communal changing areas, plus suites for the disabled and baby changing; the third has four family bathrooms each containing WC, basin and shower. There are two kitchens, each with full cookers, hobs, fridge/freezers and double sinks (all free of charge), and excellent dining rooms. Laundry facilities include three washing machines (charged) and dryers and drying cabinet (free). Also on site is a very good motorhome service point suitable for all types of unit including American RVs, and a children's playground. Adjacent to the site are the municipal swimming pool complex with cafeteria (indoor and outdoor pools), a Scandic hotel with restaurant, minigolf, and a Statoil filling station. A large supermarket and bank are just 500 m. from the site, and Ostersund town centre is 3 km.

How to find it: Site is to the south of the town off road 605 towards Torvalla, turn by Statoil station and site entrance is immediately on right. (well signed from around the town).

General Details: Open all year. Children's playground. Kitchen. Laundry. Motorcaravan service point. Cottages, cabins and rooms for rent.

Charges 1998: Per unit Skr. 125 - 150 (incl. electricity/TV), 90 - 150 (without). Credit cards accepted (not Amex).

Reservations: Contact site. Address: Krondikesvagen 95, 831 46 Östersund. Tel: 063/14.46.15. FAX: 063/14.43.23.

2855 Flogsta Camping, Kramfors (Västernorrland)

Delightful small municipal site, a good base to explore the `High Coast'.

Kramfors lies just to the west of the E4, and travellers may well pass by over the new Höga Kusten bridge (one of the largest in Europe), and miss this friendly little site. The area of Ådalen and the High Coast, which reaches as far as Örnsköldsvik, is well worth a couple of days of your time, also Skuleskogen National Park, and Norfallsvikens, an old fishing village with many original buildings. The attractive garden-like campsite has around 50 pitches, 21 with electrical connections (10A), which are arranged on level grassy terraces, separated by shrubs and trees into bays of 2-4 units. All overlook the municipal swimming pool complex (one day free admission to campers), and attractive minigolf course. The non-electric pitches are on an open terrace nearer reception, and there are 16 rental cabins on site. Excellent sanitary facilities consist of nine well equipped family bathrooms, each with British style WC, basin with soap dispenser and hand dryer, shower (on payment), plus a laundry with washing machine and dryer. These are supplemented by more WCs and showers in the reception building with a free sauna facility. A separate building houses the kitchen, with hot-plates, fridge/freezer and TV/dining room (all free of charge). Also on-site is a small children's play area on a sandy base. The reception building has a small shop and snack-bar and is staffed 07.00-23.00 hours from 9/6-11/8. Outside these dates a warden calls daily. The town centre with supermarkets and restaurants is a 20 minute easy walk through a housing estate, and do use the excellent covered and elevated walkway to cross the main road and railway to the pedestrian shopping precinct with its floral arrangements and fountain.

How to find it: Well signed from road 90 in the centre of Kramfors, the site lies to the west in a rural location beyond a housing estate and by the Flogsta Bad, municipal swimming pool complex.

General Details: Open May - end Sept. Shop. Snack-bar. TV. Children's playground. Laundry. Kitchen. Cabins for rent.

Charges 1998: Per unit Skr. 85 - 95; cyclist/hiker and tent 55; electricity 25.

Reservations: Contact site. Address: 872 80 Kramfors. Tel: 0612/100 05. FAX: 0612/71.13.13.

SWEDEN - North

2860 Umeå Camping, Umeå (Västerbotten)

Good quality municipal site, on outskirts of university city.

An ideal stop-over for those travelling the E4 coastal route, or a good base from which to explore the area, this site is 6 km. from the town centre, almost adjacent to the Nydalsjön lake, ideal for fishing, windsurfing and bathing. There are 320 grassy pitches arranged in bays of 10-20 units, divided by shrubs and small trees, all with electricity (10A), and some fully serviced (electricity, water, waste water). The large, heated, central sanitary unit is modern and well equipped with British style WCs, open washbasins, controllable hot showers with communal changing areas, and a sauna. Well equipped kitchen with a large dining room adjacent, and a laundry with washing machines, dryers and ironing. The showers, kitchen facilities, hot water and dryers are all free of charge. These facilities are supplemented in high season by a basic smaller unit, plus a `portacabin' style unit both with WCs and handbasins only. Outside the site adjacent to the lake, but with direct access, are football pitches, a small open-air swimming pool with waterslide, minigolf, mini-car driving school, skateboard ramp, beach volleyball, a mini-farm and there are cycle and footpaths around the area. Umeå is also a port for ferries to Vasa in Finland (4 hrs).

How to find it: From the E4 on the northern outskirts of the town, turn at traffic lights, where site is signed.

General Details: Open all year. Shop and snack-bar (summer only). Volleyball. Children's playgrounds. Bicycle hire. Boat hire. Fishing. Riding 10 km. Golf 18 km. Kitchen. Laundry. Car wash. Chemical disposal. Cabins for rent.

Charges 1999: Per unit Skr. 135; electricity 30; serviced pitch 170. Credit cards accepted, but not Eurocheques.

Reservations: Contact site. Address: Nydala Fritidsområde, 901 84 Umeå. Tel: 090/16.16.60. FAX: 090/12.57.20.

2865 Camp Gielas, Arvidsjaur (Norrbotten)

Modern site with excellent sporting facilities on outskirts of town.

This site is well shielded on all sides by trees, providing a very peaceful atmosphere. The 150 pitches, 80 with electricity (16A) and satellite TV connections, are level on sparse grass and accessed by tarmac roadways. There are two modern heated sanitary units with British style WCs, open washbasins and controllable hot showers with divider and seat (on payment), a unit for the disabled, well equipped kitchens (free of charge), also a laundry with washing machine and dryer. The unit by the tent area also has facilities for disabled people and baby changing. The sauna at the sports hall is free to campers, who may also use all the indoor sporting, gymnasium and solarium facilities at the usual rates. Also on site is a snack-bar. The lake on the site is suitable for boating, bathing and fishing and other amenities include tennis courts, minigolf, canoe and boat hire and children's playgrounds, There is a swimming pool and a 9-hole golf course nearby, and hunting trips can be arranged.

How to find it: Site is well signed from road 95 in the town.

General Details: Open all year. Snack bar. Minigolf. Children's playgrounds. Sauna. Solarium. Sporting facilities. Boat and canoe hire. Lake swimming. Kitchen. Laundry. Car wash. Motorcaravan service point. Chemical disposal. Cottages, cabins and apartments (65) for rent.

Charges 1998: Per unit Skr. 100; hiker's tent 70; electricity 20. Credit cards accepted.

Reservations: Contact site. Address: Järnvägsgatan 111, 933 22 Arvidsjaur. Tel: 0960/556 00 FAX: 0960/106 15.

2870 Jokkmokks Turistcenter, Jokkmokk (Norrbotten)

Attractive municipal site in a popular tourist area, 8 km. from Arctic Circle.

Large and well organised, this site is bordered on one side by the river and with woodland on the other, just 3 km. from the town centre. It has 170 level, grassy pitches, with an area for tents, plus 59 cabins and 26 rooms for rent. Electricity (10A) is available to all touring pitches. The heated sanitary buildings provide British style WCs, mostly open washbasins and controllable showers - some are curtained with a communal changing area, a few are in cubicles. A unit (by reception) has a baby bathroom, a fully equipped suite for disabled visitors, games room, plus a very well appointed kitchen and launderette. A further unit with WCs, basins, showers plus a sauna, is adjacent to the heated open-air swimming pool complex. All facilities, hot water and the pools are free. There is a very smart restaurant and bar, plus a takeaway. Free river fishing. There are opportunities for snow-mobiling, cross-country skiing in spring, or ice fishing in winter. Nearby attractions include the first hydro-electric power station at Porjus, built 1910-15 (free tours between 15/6-15/8), Vuollerim (40 km.) reconstructed 6,000 year old settlement, with excavations of the best preserved ice-age village, or try visiting for the famous Jokkmokk Winter Market (first Thurs-Sat February) or the less chilly Autumn Market (end of August).

How to find it: Site is 3 km. from the centre of Jokkmokk on road 97.

General Details: Open all year. Shop, restaurant and bar (in summer). Takeaway (high season). Swimming pools (summer). Sauna. Bicycle hire. New children's playground. Minigolf. Football field. Games machines. Fishing (licences sold). Riding 2 km. Kitchen. Laundrette. Chemical disposal.

Charges 1998: Per unit Skr. 110 - 140; small tent 70 - 90; electricity 30. Credit cards accepted (not Amex).

Reservations: Contact site. Address: Box 75, 962 22 Jokkmokk. Tel: 0971/123 70. FAX: 0971 124 76.

AR Discount
Low season offers

SWITZERLAND

This land locked country, with 22 independent Cantons sharing languages with its four neighbours, has some of the most outstanding scenery in Europe which, coupled with its cleanliness and commitment to the tourism industry, makes it a very attractive proposition. The Swiss are well known for their punctuality and hard work and have the highest standard of living of any country in Europe, which makes Switzerland one of the most expensive yet problem free countries to visit. The Berner Oberland is probably the most visited area with a concentration of picturesque peaks and mountain villages, though the highest Alps are those of Valais in the southwest with the small busy resort of Zermatt giving access to the Matterhorn. Zurich in the north is a German speaking city with a wealth of sightseeing. Geneva, Montreux and Lausanne on the northern shores of Lake Geneva make up the bulk of French Switzerland, whilst the southernmost canton, Ticino, is home to the Italian speaking Swiss, with the resorts of Lugano and Locarno. For further information contact:

Swiss National Tourist Office, Swiss Centre, Swiss Court, London W1V 8EE
Tel: 0171 734 1921 Fax: 0171 734 4577

Population
6,800,000, density 165.5 per sq.km.

Capital
Bern.

Climate
No country in Europe combines within so small an area such marked climatic contrasts. In the northern plateau surrounded by mountains the climate is mild and refreshing. South of the Alps it is warmer, coming under the influence of the Mediterranean. The Valais is noted for its dryness.

Language
The national languages of Switzerland are German 65% (central and east), French 18% (west), Italian 10% (south), Romansh - a derivative of Latin 1% (south east), and others 6%. Many Swiss, especially those involved in the tourism industry speak English.

Currency
The unit of currency is the Swiss franc, divided into 100 centimes, coming in coins of 5, 10, and 20 centimes and Sfr 0.5, 1, 2, 5. Notes are Sfr 10, 20, 50, 100, 500, 1000.

Banks
Open Mon-Fri 08.30-16.30. Closed for lunch in Lausanne and Lucerne 12.30-13.30/14.00

Post Offices
Open Mon-Fri 07.30-12.00 and 13.45-18.30. Sat 07.30-11.00 or later in some major city offices.

Time
GMT plus 1 (summer BST +1).

Telephone
From the UK, the code is 00 41 followed by the area code (omitting the initial zero) followed by number. Phone cards are available.

Public Holidays
New Year; Good Fri; Easter Mon; Ascension; Whit Mon; Christmas, 25 Dec; Other holidays are observed in individual Cantons.

Shops
Generally open Mon-Fri 08.00- 12.00 and 14.00- 18.00. Sat 08.00-16.00. Often closed Monday mornings.

Food: The cost of food in shops and restaurants can be expensive; it may be worthwhile to consider 'stocking-up' on basic food necessities purchased in the UK, or elsewhere in Europe. Note that, officially,only 2.5 kgs per head of foodstuffs may be imported into the country The local specialities to try if there is money in the budget are 'Fondue' or 'Raclette' in French speaking Switzerland and 'Rösti' in German speaking Switzerland.

Motoring
The road network is comprehensive and well planned. If the roads are narrow and circuitous in parts, it is worth it for the views. An annual road tax is levied on all cars using Swiss motorways and the 'Vignette' windscreen sticker must be purchased at the border (credit cards not accepted), or in advance from the Swiss National Tourist Office, plus a separate one for a towed caravan or trailer .

Fuel: On motorways, service stations are usually open from 0600- 2200/2400. On other roads it varies 0600/0800-1800/2000. Outside these hours petrol is widely available from 24 hr automatic pumps - Sfr 10/20. Credit cards generally accepted.

Speed Limits: Cars in built-up areas 31 mph (50 kph), other roads 50 mph (80 kph), and motorways 75 mph (120 kph). For towing vehicles on motorways 50 mph (80 kph).

Parking: Blue Zones are in operation in certain cities, discs obtainable from most petrol stations, restaurants and police stations.

Overnighting
Only permitted at a few motorway rest areas.

900 Camping Waldhort, Reinach, Basel/Basle

Satisfactory site for night halts or visits to Basel.

Although there are almost twice as many static caravans as spaces for tourists, this is a quiet site on the edge of a residential district, within easy reach of Basel. The site is flat, with 220 level pitches on grass with access from the tarmac road which circles round inside the site. Trees are now maturing to give some shade. All pitches have electricity (6A) and are situated near the good quality, central sanitary block. This has British WCs, free hot water (except in the sinks where it is on payment) and facilities for disabled people. *continued overleaf*

SWITZERLAND

900 Camping Waldhort (continued)

Owned and run by the Camping and Caravanning Club of Basel, it is a neat, tidy and orderly site and there is usually space available. An extra, separate camping area has been added behind the tennis club which has pleasant pitches and good sanitary facilities. Reinach is within walking distance from where there is a tram service into Basel.

How to find it: Take Basel - Delémont motorway spur, exit at 'Reinach-Nord' and follow camp signs.

General Details: Open 13 March - 16 Oct. 23,000 sq.m. Small shop with terrace for drinks. Children's playground with 2 small pools. Table tennis. Swimming pool and tennis next to site. Washing machine and dryer. Chemical disposal. Motorcaravan services.

Charges 1999: Per person Sfr. 7.00; child (6-14 yrs) 4.50; car 3.50; tent 4.00 - 6.00; caravan 6.00 - 8.00; motorcaravan 8.50 - 14.50; m/cycle 2.80; electricity included. Credit cards accepted.

Reservations: made for main season; advance payment asked for single nights, otherwise no deposit. Address: Heideweg 16, 4153 Reinach bei Basel. Tel: 061/711 64 29. Fax: 061/711 48 33.

905 Camping Bois du Couvent, La Chaux-de-Fonds

Hill-top site at 1,060 m. in the Swiss Jura.

The road from Lake Neuchatel to Chaux-de-Fonds, which stands just inside the Swiss border with France in the northwest of Switzerland, has been greatly improved with parts to motorway standard. La Chaux-de-Fonds is the biggest watch and clock making centre in Switzerland and one of the largest agricultural centres. Completely destroyed by fire in 1794, it was rebuilt to a geometric plan. Postage stamps for Switzerland and many foreign countries are printed here. Camping Bois du Couvent is situated at the southern end of the town on a hill-top with splendid views. More than half the pitches are taken by static caravans but the 70 places for tourists, with 10A electrical connections, although not marked, are obvious, with an open lawn for tents. The camp has a pleasant appearance and tarmac and gravel roads link the terraces, some of which have shade from tall trees. There is a nice restaurant, but no shop as there is a supermarket 1 km. away in town. Very little English is spoken but the warden has good tourist information available. Two sanitary blocks have British style WCs, free hot water in washbasins and on payment in sinks and showers.

How to find it: Site is signed and is at the south end of La Chaux-de-Fonds. Coming from Neuchatel, turn left at 2nd roundabout after tunnel.

General Details: Open all year. 60,000 sq.m. Restaurant (open all year except Tues, 08.00 - midnight). Shop 1 km. Children's playground. Some entertainment for children in summer. Minigolf 300 m. Bicycle hire and tennis 100 m. Clock museum 1 km. Heated pool 500 m. Washing machine and dryer. Chemical disposal.

Charges 1999: Per person Sfr. 3.50; child (4-16 yrs) 1.20; caravan 9.50; motorcaravan 14.00; family tent 8.00; car 3.00; m/cycle 2.00; electricity 3.00. Chalets, bungalows and caravans for hire.

Reservations: Write to site. Address: 2301 La Chaux-de-Fonds. Tel: 079/240 50 39. FAX: 032/914 48 77.

903 Camping Paradis Plage, Colombier, nr Neuchatel

Pleasant lakeside site with good facilities, near French border.

This area of Switzerland deserves to be better known as there is much of interest here near the French border. Paradis Plage is nicely situated on the shores of Lake Neuchatel, with access to the lake. The 160 pitches available to tourists are numbered and marked out on flat grass under a covering of tall, mature trees. All have electricity (10A) and some have gravel hardstanding for caravans and motorcaravans. There are separate areas of grass where pitches are not marked, including a small overflow section for individuals or groups. The 200 static pitches are occupied mainly at weekends and high season and are neatly set out together in rows. Although a motorway runs over the site near the entrance, we did not notice any undue noise as this seemed to be screened out by the trees. Access to the site is rather narrow but adequate. A very pleasant restaurant with a large terrace, well stocked shop and takeaway (all to end Sept) form the focal point in the centre with views through the trees to the lake. Three sanitary blocks, well sited around the site, have been refurbished and make a good provision with British style WCs. Laundry rooms have electric rings for free use. Friendly, English speaking management. Well placed for walking in the Jura or touring the Bernese Oberland.

How to find it: Leave the short stretch of motorway at Colombier from where the site is signed.

General Details: Open 1 March - 31 Oct. 40,000 sq.m. Restaurant and shop (1/3-30/9). Small children's pool (20/6-20/8). New children's play area. Table tennis. Bicycle hire. Fishing. Boating. Sports complex nearby with indoor and outdoor tennis courts, squash, bowls and football. Riding 5 km. Golf 12 km. Washing machines and dryers. Chemical disposal. Motorcaravan service point.

Charges 1999: Per person Sfr. 6.00; child (6-15 yrs) 3.00; tent or caravan 8.00 - 15.00; motorcaravan 9.00 - 15.00; car 1.00 - 2.00; electricity 3.50; local tax 2.00 per pitch. Discounts for stays over 17 days (10%) up to 30 days (23%). Credit cards accepted.

Reservations: Write to site. Address: 2013 Colombier. Tel: 032/841 24 46. FAX: as phone.

906 TCS Camping Caravaning Kappelenbrücke, Bern

Fairly new site for overnight or longer stay, near city.

This relatively new site, being just outside the Federal Capital, is conveniently placed either for an overnight stop, or for exploring the city and surrounds. A frequent bus service to the city passes the entrance. The 305 pitches (230 for touring) are numbered but not marked out and you choose your own place; cars are parked away from the pitches. All have electricity (4A or more). There are some static units but there should always be room. The two new toilet blocks of exceptional quality, have British WCs, enclosed washbasins with free hot water; also in the showers. One block is heated in cool weather. The sinks for washing clothes and dishes have free hot water and are under cover. There is a good children's playground, and the shop also serves drinks which can be taken to a pleasant rest room nearby or consumed on the terrace. This pleasant, well cared for site is near a small lake which is unsuitable for bathing, although there is now, however, a swimming pool and children's pool on site. It is probably the best site for visiting Bern.

How to find it: Take the 'Bethlehem' exit from N1 motorway on western side of Bern, towards Aarberg, and site will be seen on right before river.

General Details: Open all year except 6-18 Feb. 35,000 sq.m. Electrical connections throughout. Special pitches for motorcaravans. Shop/bar. TV room. Day room. Children's playground. Table tennis. Fishing. Baby room. Washing machines and dryers. Chemical disposal.

Charges guide: Per person Sfr. 4.40 - 6.00; child (6-16 yrs) 2.20 - 3.00; tent or caravan 5.20 - 17.00, acc. to type; motorcaravan 18.00; electricity 2.50 or 4.00; local tax 1.40.

Reservations: Write to site. Address: Wohlenstrasse 62c, 3032 Hinterkappelen (BE). Tel: 031/901 10 07. FAX: 031/901 25 91.

909 Camping Avenches Port-Plage, Avenches

Large site with good boating possibilities on Lake Murten.

This is a large site by Swiss standards, located in a quiet, open situation directly on Lake Murten with its own marina and excellent access to the water. The camp is well cared for, with 200 out of the 700 pitches available for tourists. These are of reasonable size (80 sq.m.) with shade in parts from tall trees and electrical connections are available (6A). It is, above all, a site for those interested in watersports. At the centre of the site is a large building which houses a general shop, butcher, baker and the main sanitary facilities. A separate restaurant is nearer the lake shore. There are three toilet blocks, all of excellent quality with British style WCs.

How to find it: Site is signed near Avenches on the Bern - Lausanne road no.1 (**not** the motorway).

General Details: Open 1 April - 30 Sept. 80,000 sq.m. Electrical connections most pitches. Restaurant. Shop, butcher and baker. First aid room. Children's playground. Pedaloes. Chemical disposal. Motorcaravan service point.

Charges 1998: Per person Sfr. 7.00; child (4-16 yrs) 4.00; car 4.00; caravan 10.00; tent 6.50 - 10.00, acc. to size; motorcaravan 14.00; electricity 3.50; local tax 1.00.

Reservations: Write to site with Sfr. 20 fee. Address: Camping-Port-Plage, 1580 Avenches. Tel: 026/675 17 50. FAX: 026/675 44 69.

912 Camping Lido Luzern, Lucerne/Luzern

Site in good touring area popular with the British.

Luzern is a traditional holiday resort of the British and this site has many British visitors. It lies near the shore of Lake Luzern, just outside the town itself. Next to the site (but not associated with it so you have to pay for entrance) is the Lido proper, which has a large sandy beach, bathing in the lake and sports fields. The town of Luzern has excellent shopping and sightseeing; one could walk there along the lake in about 20 minutes, or nearby buses run into town up to midnight. The site is divided into separate sections for caravans, motorcaravans and tents; the first two have hardstandings which, in effect, provide rather formal and small individual pitches. There are about 80 electrical connections (10A). Quiet in early season, from late June to late August it usually becomes full and, especially in the tent section, can at times seem rather crowded. The sanitary installations are in three sections, two being close to the reception area. A large and very modern block incorporates toilets, basins, showers, washing facilities, a rest room and cooking area with electric rings (pre-payment). British WCs: mostly individual basins, some in cabins for women, with hot water; hot water for showers and sinks is on payment. The blocks can be heated. Good English is spoken and the charges are reasonable.

How to find it: Follow Lido signs out of Luzern and a large sign to Lido will be seen on right just outside of town.

General Details: Open 15 March - 31 Oct. 23,000 sq.m. Shade in parts. Smallish shop. Takeaway. Community room. Organised excursions. Doctor on call. Chemical disposal. Caravans to rent.

Charges 1999: Per person Sfr. 6.50; child (6-14 yrs) 3.25; local tax (over 11s) 1.20; car 5.00; tent 3.00; caravan 6.00 - 10.00; motorcaravan 12.00 - 17.00; m/cycle 3.00; dog 3.00; electricity by meter.

Reservations: Write to site. Address: Lidostr. 6, 6006 Luzern. Tel: 041/370 21 46. FaAX: 041/370 21 45.

SWITZERLAND

913 Terrassencamping Vitznau, Vitznau, nr Lucerne/Luzern

Quiet site scenically positioned on shores of Lake Luzern.

Camping Vitznau is situated in the small village of the same name, above and overlooking the lake, with splendid views across the water to the mountains on the other side. It is a small, neat and tidy site very close to the delightful village on the narrow, winding, lakeside road. The 120 pitches for caravans or motorhomes (max length 7 m.) have 15A electricity available to most. They are on level, grassy terraces with hard wheel tracks for motorcaravans and separated by tarmac roads, and although of sufficient rather than large size, with single rows on each terrace, all places have unobstructed views. However, larger units might have difficulty manoeuvring onto the pitches. There are separate places for tents. The single, well constructed sanitary block has British WCs, washbasins in flat vanity tops and free hot showers. Dish and clothes washing is under cover with metered hot water. There is a general room for wet weather, a games room and a well stocked shop but no restaurant as the village ones are about 5 minutes walk away. Trees provide shade in parts and this delightful camp makes an excellent base for exploring around the lake, the town of Luzern and the nearby mountains.

How to find it: Site is signed from the centre of Vitznau.

General Details: Open 1 April - 5 Oct. 20,000 sq.m. 1,446 feet above sea level. Shop. Swimming pool and children's splash pool. Fishing. Bicycle hire. Golf 10 km. Watersports near. Washing machines and dryers. Chemical disposal. Motorcaravan service point.

Charges 1999: Per person Sfr. 7.50 - 9.00; child under 6 yrs 2.50, 6-16 yrs 5.00; pitch 13.00 - 17.00; local tax 1.60; electricity 4.00. Credit cards accepted.

Reservations: Write with deposit (Sfr 20). Address: 6354 Vitznau. Tel: 041/397 12 80. FAX: 041/397 24 57.

915 Camping Seebucht, Zürich

Busy lakeside site quite close to the city.

Being a smallish site only 4½ km. from the centre of the important town of Zürich and in a pleasant situation with well kept lawns, Seebucht has more demands on space than it can meet. With 300 touring pitches (136 with 6/10A electricity), it may well pack units rather closely in season but there is much transit trade so there are usually vacancies each day if you are early (no reservations). Caravans go on flat hardstandings (cars cannot always stand by them); tents, for which space may be easier to find, go on lawns. The grassy strip alongside the lake is kept free for recreation. The site reports new sanitary facilities including more showers. The original block provided British style toilets, with some Turkish style for men, washbasins (cubicles for women) with cold water and hot showers on payment.

How to find it: Site is on the southern side of the town and the western side of the lake, at Wollishofen; well signed from most parts of town and at motorway exit.

General Details: Open 1 May - 30 Sept. 20,000 sq.m. Shop. Café for meals or drinks. Bathing possible into fairly deep water. Fishing. Jetty where small boats can be launched. Chemical disposal. Motorcaravan service point.

Charges 1999: Per person Ffr. 7.00; child (4-16 yrs) 4.00; small tent (max. 3 persons) 12.00; large tent or caravan 14.00; motorcaravan 16.00 (plus 5.00 if over 6 m); car 3.00; electricity 3.00; plus local tax 1.20.

Reservations: not made; for information only: Address: Seestrasse 559, 8038 Zürich-Wollishofen. Tel: 01/482 16 12. FAX: 01/482 16 60.

921 TCS Camping Pointe à la Bise, Vésenaz, nr Geneve/Geneva

Busy lakeside site within easy reach of Geneva.

Although the majority only stop for a few nights at this site whilst visiting Geneva (it is well placed for this), TCS have refurbished the sanitary block to a high standard and rebuilt the reception, shop, and restaurant building giving the site a new appearance which may well tempt for a longer stay. Pointe a la Bise is directly on the lake and has superb views of the lake and surrounding mountains. The 200 pitches, 70 with electricity are not marked so, although electricity boxes roughly determine where each unit goes, you do not have an exactly defined place, which might make for crowding in high season. Tall trees provide some shade. It is possible to swim in the lake or at the lido 5 km. away and there is a large children's pool. Windsurfing and small boats under 10 hp may be used from the camp. Being away from the main road, this is a quiet site with a relaxed atmosphere - no disco, but occasional light, live music entertainment during high season and a programme of activities for children and adults in July/Aug. The pleasant bar/restaurant is open all day and there is a takeaway. Community room which has tables, chairs and TV, with a baby room next door. The raised restaurant terrace overlooks the pool and small children's playground. The improvements have lifted this from a reasonable site to a good one and the friendly, English speaking manager will be pleased to advise on nearby attractions. He also organises and leads a bicycle ride weekly in high season which includes lunch in a French restaurant. The single sanitary block has British style WCs, free hot water in washbasins, sinks and showers and a baby room. There are a number of static caravans but these are grouped to one side of the tourist area.

How to find it: Follow lakeside road from city centre towards Thonon (lake on left) for 6.5 km. and site is signed.

continued overleaf

921 TCS Camping Pointe à la Bise (continued)

General Details: Open Easter - 25 October. 32.000 sq.m. Electricity connections (4/10A). Shop. Bar/restaurant with takeaway (until late Sept). Children's pool (15/5-15/9). Playground. Lake swimming and watersports. Fishing. Bicycle hire. Golf 3 km. Washing machines and dryers. Chemical disposal. Motorcaravan service point.

Charges guide: Per person Sfr. 4.80 - 5.80; child (6-15 yrs) less 50%; pitch 6.50 - 19.00 acc. to size and season; motorcaravan 22.00; electricity 3.00; local tax 0.50. Credit cards accepted.

Reservations: Write to site, Address: 1222 Vésenaz. Tel: 022/752 12 96. FAX: 022/752 37 67.

918 Campingplatz Buchhorn, Arbon

Small, well ordered site on Lake Bodensee in northeast Switzerland.

This small but clean and pleasant site is directly on Lake Bodensee and situated in the town's parkland. There is access for boats from the camp but powered craft must be under a certain h.p. and advice on this should be sought from the management. There are splendid views across this large inland sea and interesting boats ply up and down between Constance and Lindau and Bregenz. The town swimming lido in the lake, with a restaurant, is here, quite close to the camp. The site is well shaded with pitches for tourists by the water's edge and an overflow field for tents next door. There are a number of static caravans but said to be room for 100 tourists, pitches being on a mixture of gravel and grass, flat areas on either side of access roads, most with 6A electricity. A railway line runs directly along one side but one gets used to the noise from passing trains (ask for a pitch near the lake). A single, well constructed set of buildings comprise reception, shop (small terrace for drinks) and sanitary facilities. These should just about suffice in high season, are clean and modern with free hot water in basins, showers and sinks. British WCs. This is a beautiful area and the site is well placed for touring around Lake Bodensee, the Austrian Vorarlberg, Liechtenstein and northeast Switzerland. Watersports and steamer trips are available on the lake, walks and marked cycle tracks around it and a nature reserve is near.

How to find it: On Arbon-Konstanz road 13, signed 'Strandbad' and 'Strandbad Camping' on leaving Arbon.

General Details: Open 28 March - 17 Oct. Well shaded. Shop (basic supplies, drinks and snacks - all season). General room. Children's playground. Town swimming lido 400 m. Tennis 150 m. Watersports and excursions on lake. Washing machine, dryer and drying area. Fridge. Chemical disposal. Gates closed 12-14.00 hrs daily.

Charges 1999: Per person Sfr. 6.65; child (6-16 yrs) 3.10; small tent 5.65; large tent, caravan or motorcaravan 11.35; car 3.10; m/cycle 1.05; electricity 2.05.

Reservations: Write to site. Address: 9320 Arbon. Tel: 071/446 65 45. FAX: 071/446 48 34.

Arbon *Camping Buchhorn*

One of the finest camping sites on the shores of Lake Constance
❖ 100 yards of own sandy beach
❖ idyllic site under old, high trees
❖ perfect, new sanitation equipment
❖ shop with Camping-Gaz
❖ free entrance to the Lido, 200 yds
❖ closed daily from 12 am to 2 pm
Edi+Lotty Hurter, CH-9320 Arbon
071 446 6545 Fax 071 446 4839

924 TCS Camping Le Petit Bois, Morges

Pleasant site by Lake Geneva near Lausanne, with swimming pool adjacent.

This site is most attractively situated amid a complex of municipal sports fields, by the shore of Lake Geneva, with a view of the mountain across the lake. Almost next door is an excellent, heated swimming pool which is free to campers (better here than bathing in the lake). It is an easy walk into Morges. The terrain is divided up regularly into pitches, 170 for tourists, which are said to be all 80 sq.m. There are 140 electricity connections (4A) and 8 large pitches for motorhomes with water, electricity and drainage. Sanitary installations, recently renovated, are now good and have free hot water in the washbasins, controllable showers and washing-up sinks. British WCs. Unit for disabled people.

How to find it: Coming from Lausanne leave the Lausanne - Geneva autoroute at the exit for `Morges-ouest', from Geneva exit at `Morges'. Proceed towards the town and turn left at T-junction and then sharp right to reach site.

General Details: Open Easter - 19 Oct. 36,000 sq.m. Well stocked shop. Bar/restaurant (with service) and takeaway. Washing machines, dryers and irons. Baby room. Small general room. Children's playground. Treatment room; doctors will call. A little `animation' in season. Sports area. Chemical disposal. Motorcaravan services.

Charges guide: Per person Sfr 4.80 - 6.00; child (6-16) less 50%; pitch 6.30 - 19.00 acc. to facilities and season; dog 1.00; car 2.00; m/cycle 1.00; local tax 0.80.

Reservations: Made for min. 1 week with deposit (Sfr 80) and fee (20). Address: 1110 Morges (Vaud); Tel: 021/801 12 70. FAX: 021/803 38 69.

SWITZERLAND

942 Camping Manor Farm, Interlaken

See colour advert opposite

Lakeside site in the Bernese Oberland popular with the British.

Manor Farm has, for some years, had a large proportion of Britons among its guests, for whom this is one of the traditional touring areas. The site lies outside the town on the northern side of the Thuner See, with most of the site between road and lake but with one part on the far side of the road. Interlaken is rather a tourist town but the area is rich in scenery, with innumerable mountain excursions and walks available and the lakes and Jungfrau railway near at hand. The flat terrain is divided entirely into individual, numbered pitches which vary considerably both in size (from 40-100 sq.m.) and price; 450 are now equipped with electricity, water, drainage and cable TV connections. Reservations are made, although you should find space except perhaps in late July/early August, but the best places may then be taken. The ground becomes a little muddy when wet. Around 30% permanent or letting units. There are seven separate toilet blocks which are practical and soundly constructed but mostly fairly small, although they have been much improved recently. They have British toilets, washbasins and showers, with free hot water in all blocks for washbasins, showers and baths. Twenty private units are available for rent. Bathing is possible in the lake at two points and boats can be brought if a permit obtained. The area is good for cycling and walking. The site is efficiently and quite formally run, with good English spoken. The site is used by tour operators.

How to find it: Site is about 3 km. west of Interlaken along the road running north of the Thuner See towards Thun. Follow signs for 'Camp 1'. From the motor road bypassing Interlaken (A8) take exit marked 'Gunten, Beatenberg', which is a spur road bringing you out close to site.

General Details: Open all year. 70,000 sq.m. Electricity connections (10A). Shade in some places. Shop (1/4-15/10). Site-owned restaurant adjoining (1/3-30/11). Snack bar with takeaway on site (1/6-31/8). TV room. Football field. Children's playground and paddling pool. Minigolf. Bicycle hire. Table tennis. Sailing and windsurfing school. Boat hire. Fishing. Riding 3 km. Golf 500 m (handicap card). Daily activity and entertainment programme in high season. Excursions. Bureau de change. Tourist information. Washing machine, dryer, ironing. Car wash. Chemical disposal. Motorcaravan service point. Bungalows, caravans and tents to let.

Charges 1999: Per person Sfr. 5.70 - 9.10; local tax 1.60; child (6-15 yrs) 2.60 - 4.30 (under 6 free); pitch 7.00 - 33.00, acc. to season and type (see description above); boat 2.00 - 6.00; electricity 0.80 - 4.00. acc. to amperage. (0.5, 4 or 6A). Various discounts for longer stays. Credit cards accepted.

Reservations: Taken for high season (min. 3 days) with booking fee (Sfr. 20). Address: 3800 Interlaken-Thunersee. Tel: 033/822 22 64. FAX: 033/823 29 91.

927 Camping de Vidy, Lausanne

Friendly site in popular city on Lake Geneva.

The interesting and ancient city of Lausanne - its first cathedral was built in the 6th century - spills down the hillside towards Lake Geneva until it meets the peaceful park in which this site is situated. The present owners took the site over from the City council in 1987 and have enhanced its appearance by planting many flowers and shrubs. Although only minutes from the city centre, only a gentle hum of traffic can be heard and the site exudes peace and tranquillity. A public footpath separates the site from the lakeside, but there is good access. The World HQ of the Olympic movement is adjacent in the pleasant park, which is also available for games and walking. Hard access roads separate the site into sections for tents, caravans and motorcaravans, with 10A electrical connections in all parts, except the tent areas. Pitches are on flat grass, numbered but not marked out, with 245 (of 350) available for tourists. A few apartments for hire. Two excellent sanitary blocks, one near reception (heated) and one on the opposite side of the site, have mostly British, some Turkish style WCs, free hot water in washbasins, sinks and showers with warm, pre-mixed water. Facilities for disabled people. A third small block of the same standard has been added. The lakeside bar/restaurant (also open to the public) provides entertainment in season in the various rooms so that the young and not so young can enjoy themselves without impinging on each other. The keen young couple who manage the site speak good English, whom they welcome. The site has a neat and tidy appearance. There is a frequent bus service into Lausanne and boat excursions on the lake.

How to find it: Left of the road to Geneva, 500 m. west of La Maladière. Take autobahn Lausanne-Süd, exit La Maladière, and follow signs to camp (very near). Care needed at motorway exit roundabout.

General Details: Open all year. Well stocked shop (1/5-30/9). Self-service bar/restaurant with takeaway during season. Children's playground. Evening entertainment mid-June - Aug. Swimming in lake. Fishing. Chemical disposal. Motorcaravan service point.

Charges 1999: Per person Sfr. 6.50; student 6.00; child (6-16 yrs) 5.00; car 2.50; m/cycle 1.50; tent, caravan or motorcaravan 10.00 - 12.00; 2 person tent 7.00; local tax 1.40 (caravan) 1.20 (tent). No credit cards.

Reservations: Write to site. Address: 1007 Lausanne-Vidy (Vaud). Tel: 021/624 20 31. FAX: 021/624 41 60. Internet: http://www.campinglausannevidy.ch.

Touring Britain, France and Europe

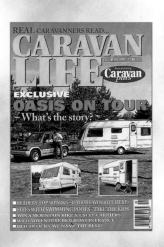

For tests and touring features 12 months of the year choose Britain's premier caravan and motorhome magazines.

THE CAMPING AND CARAVANNING CLUB

Carefree

TRAVEL SERVICE

The Club's own overseas travel service, Carefree, operates in 15 European countries and can offer everything from simple ferry bookings to all-inclusive holidays.

Offering a complete menu of holiday options, the Club can give substantial savings on every aspect of your holiday, including:

- **Ferry bookings**
- **Campsites abroad**
- **All-inclusive holidays**
- **Guided Tours**
- **French Flavour Holidays**
- **Club Holiday Rallies**
- **Theme Parks**
- **Travel insurance**

Carefree Travel Service is an exclusive service to Camping and Caravanning Club members. Club membership also offers the opportunity to stay at discounted rates on the Club's 90 UK sites; excellent free sites guides; monthly magazine and access to tailor made insurance, breakdown and financial services.

It's well worth joining!

For further details on Club membership and Carefree Travel Service, telephone **01203 422024** quoting ref no. 9545

or write to:

Carefree Travel Service,
Camping and Caravanning Club,
Greenfields House,
Westwood Way,
Coventry
CV4 8JH

The Camping and Caravanning Club

946 Camping Jungfrau, Lauterbrunnen, nr Interlaken

See colour
advert opposite

Friendly site with good quality installations, in attractive mountain surroundings.

This site has a very imposing situation in a steep valley with a fine view of the Jungfrau at the end. You can laze here amid real mountain scenery, though it does lose the sun a little early. There are naturally many more active things to do - mountain walks or climbing, trips up the Jungfrau railway or one of the mountain lifts or excursions by car. The site is quite extensive and is grassy with hard surfaced access roads. It is popular and, although you should usually find space, in season do not arrive too late. All 391 pitches (250 for touring) have electricity (10-15A) and 50 have water and drainage also. There are three sanitary blocks, the new one at the far end being a good modern one with hot water in all basins and showers, and the others having been thoroughly renewed and modernised. All have British toilets and free hot showers. Hot water for washing-up. New facilities for disabled visitors and baby baths. It is also open for winter camping and the buidings are heated in cool weather. The site is owned and run by the von Allmen family who provide a warm welcome (English spoken). Improvements over recent years have made this an excellent site. About 30% of the pitches are taken by seasonal caravans. The site is used by a tour operator and by groups of youngsters from many different countries - pitches at the top of the site may be quieter. Hostel accommodation in winter only. Free bus to ski station (winter only).

How to find it: Go through Lauterbrunnen and fork right at far end before road bends left, 100 m. before church. The final approach is not very wide.

General Details: Open all year, including shop. 50,000 sq.m. Good shade in parts. Supermarket. New self-service restaurant with takeaway. Good general rooms with tables and chairs, TV, jukebox, drink machines, amusements, with second one elsewhere. Well equipped and cared for children's playgrounds and covered area for children also. Washing machine, spin dryer and ironing. Hair dryer. Excursions and some entertainment in high season. Mountain bike hire. Doctor will call. Chemical disposal. Motorcaravan service point. Bungalows and caravans to let.

Charges 1999: Per person Sfr. 6.20 - 7.60, plus local tax 2.40; child (6-15 yrs) 3.10 - 3.80, plus 1.00; car 3.50; caravan or motorcaravan 12.00 - 18.00; tent 6.00 - 15.00; hiker's tent 4.00; electricity 2.50 + meter. Discounts for camping carnet and for stays over 3 nights outside high season.

Reservations: made for any period with deposit; write for details. Address: 3822 Lauterbrunnen. Tel: 033/856 20 10. FAX: 033/856 20 20.

957 Camping Eienwäldli, Engelberg, nr Lucerne/Luzern

See colour
advert opposite

All year quality site with indoor pool in scenic location.

This super site has facilities which must make it one of the best in Switzerland. It is situated in a beautiful location 3,500 feet above sea level and surrounded by mountains on the edge of the delightful village of Engelberg. Being about 35 km. from Luzern by road and with a rail link, it makes a quiet, peaceful base from which to explore the Vierwaldstattersee region, walk in the mountains or just enjoy the scenery. The area is famous as a winter sports region and summer tourist resort and Eienwaldli is open most of the year. The indoor pool has been most imaginatively rebuilt as a Felsenbad spa bath with adventure pool, steam and relaxing grottoes, Kneipp's cure, children's pool with water slides, solarium, Finnish sauna and eucalyptus steam bath. There is an extra charge to use this. Half of the site is taken up by static caravans but these are grouped together at one side. The camping area is in two parts - nearest the entrance there are 57 hardstandings for caravans and motorcaravans, all with electricity (10A) and beyond this is a flat meadow for about 70 tents. The reception building, as well as housing the pool complex, has a shop, a café/bar where simple meals are served, and rooms and apartments to rent. There is also a Gasthof/restaurant opposite the entrance. The excellent toilet block, heated in cool weather, has British style WCs, free hot water in washbasins (in cabins) and sinks and on payment in the showers.

How to find it: From the N2 Gotthard motorway, leave at exit `Stans-Sud' and follow signs to Engelberg. Turn right at T-junction on edge of town and follow signs to `Wasserfall' and site.

General Details: Open all year exc. Nov. 40,000 sq m. Electrical connections (10A). Shop. Restaurant. Café/bar. Small lounge. Indoor pool complex. Ski facilities. Children's playground. Golf driving range and 9-hole course near. Washing machines and dryers. Chemical disposal.

Charges 1999: Per person Sfr 6.50; child (6-15 yrs) 3.50; local tax 1.90; caravan 11.00; car or m/cycle 2.00; motorcaravan 13.00; tent 7.00 - 11.00; electricity 2.00 + meter; cable TV 2.50. Credit cards accepted.

Reservations: necessary summer and winter high seasons. Made with Sfr 50 deposit. Address: 6390 Engelberg. Tel: 041/6371949. FAX: 041/6374423. Internet: www.eienwaeldii.ch.

930 Camping Le Bivouac, Les Paccots, Châtel St Denis, nr Lausanne

Pleasant, small site with swimming pool, in mountains north of Montreux.

A nice little mountain site, Le Bivouac has its own small swimming pool and children's pool. Most of the best places are taken by seasonal caravans (130) and there are now only 30 pitches for tourists. Electricity (10A) is available. The site is also open for winter sports caravanning and all the sanitary facilities are heated. The good provision has British style toilets, pre-set free hot water in washbasins, showers and sinks, for clothes and dishes, and a baby room, and new facilities have been added in the main building with more showers, free hot water and laundry facilities. *contined overleaf*

SWITZERLAND

930 Camping Le Bivouac (continued)

Entertainment is organised in high season. This is a good centre for walking and excursions.

How to find it: From N12/A12 Bern-Vevey motorway take Châtel St Denis exit, turn towards Les Paccots (1 km).

General Details: Open all year. Shop (15/5-15/9). General room. Café with takeaway (15/5-15/9). Swimming pool (1/6-15/9). Table tennis. Fishing. Bicycle hire 2 km. Riding 4 km. Laundry facilities. Chemical disposal.

Charges 1999: Per person Sfr. 6.00 plus local tax (adults) 1.20; child (6-16 yrs) 4.00; pitch incl. car 15.00; electricity (10A) 4.00. 10% off with camping carnet. No credit cards.

Reservations: Advised for July/Aug. and made for 1 week with deposit (Sfr. 50) and fee (10). Address: 1618 Châtel St Denis. Tel: 021/948 78 49. FAX: as phone.

AR Discount
Less 10%
excl. taxes

933 Camping Bettlereiche, Gwatt-Thun

Small, lakeside site with good facilities, in popular area.

Bettlereiche is an ideal site for those who wish to explore this part of the Bernese Oberland and who would enjoy staying on a small site in a quiet area, away from the larger sites and town atmosphere of Interlaken. There are 90 numbered, but unmarked pitches for tourists, most with 4A electricity, and about the same number of static units, with hard access roads. Cars must be parked away from the pitches. Although there are some trees, there is little shade in the main camping area. Direct access to the lake is available for swimming and boating. The single sanitary block is well constructed and modern with British WCs. Free hot water is provided for the washbasins in cabins (cold otherwise) and in the showers and facilities should be just adequate in high season. The friendly management speak good English. Part of the restaurant is reserved for young people. Some animation in high season.

How to find it: From Berne-Interlaken autoroute, exit Thun-Süd for Gwatt and follow signs for Gwatt and site.

General Details: Open Easter - 5 Oct. 15,000 sq.m. Shop. Restaurant (no alcohol). Room for disabled. Washing machine and dryer. Lake swimming. and boating. Chemical disposal. Motorcaravan services.

Charges guide: Per person Sfr. 4.60 - 6.20; child 50%; pitch 6.30 - 19.00; local tax 2.40.

Reservations: Write to site. Address: 3645 Gwatt. Tel: 033/336 40 67. FAX: 033/336 40 17.

939 Camping Vermeille, Zweisimmen, nr Gstaad

Attractive, small mountain site with good facilities, for families.

This small, well run camp is about 1,000 m. above sea level, on a road followed by many tourists and can serve either as a night stop or as a holiday base for those who like a mountain site with many attractive excursion possibilities. In summer there are 40 pitches for tourists, in winter 25 (the remainder of the 125 total being seasonal lets), with 130 electrical connections (from 6A) available. There is a small free swimming pool which can be heated, open mid-May to late September if weather permits. The site is equipped for winter sports camping and a fair proportion of the available space, therefore, consists of hardstandings for caravans on stony ground. However, there are also lawns for tents. The sanitary installations have been upgraded and now include a baby room and facilities for disabled people. In the main building, they are fully enclosed and heated in winter. The facilities are kept extremely clean and include British WCs, troughs and washbasins for washing with a few private cabins, and hot water for washing up (new facilities) and showers on payment.

How to find it: Site is north of town on no. 11 road. Turn off where signed and go past a different site on left of access road. From N6 motorway take exit for Wimmis/Spiez (From Spiez before town, from Saanen after town).

General Details: Open all year. 9,000 sq.m. Limited shade. Shop for food and sports goods. Restaurant 100 m. on main road and in Zweisimmen. Two rooms for general use, one with sink and cooking facilities. Children's play area and trampoline. Mountain bike hire. Washing machine. Chemical disposal. Motorcaravan service point.

Charges 1999: Per person Sfr. 6.90; child 6-12 yrs 3.80, under 6 yrs 2.20; local tax 0.80 (0.40); pitch 8.00 - 13.50; m/cycle 3.00; car 4.00; electricity 2.00 (winter 2.00 - 9.00). Less 10% on person charge outside July/Aug.

Reservations: Made for min. 5 nights with deposit (Sfr. 40) and small fee (10). Address: 3770 Zweisimmen. Tel: 033/722 19 40. FAX: 033/722 36 25. E-mail: camping.vermeille@spectraweb.ch.

944 Camping Jungfraublick, Interlaken

Pleasant site on edge of town with splendid mountain views.

Interlaken is a very popular holiday town and we offer a second site here which contrasts with the larger one on the opposite side of the town. Situated in the district of Matten, within walking distance of the centre and handy for excursions to Grindelwald, Lauterbrunnen and the Jungfrau, Jungfraublick faces up the Lauterbrunnen valley towards the majestic Jungfrau mountain. The Interlaken by-pass motorway runs along one side of the camp but, being in a deep cutting, the noise of traffic is screened out. There is some noise from the access road but an earth bank has been constructed to cut this down. The 135 marked pitches are on flat grass with hard access roads and 80 have electricity (2-6A). Although there are trees, there is not too much shade. It is a pleasant site with friendly, English speaking management and a neat appearance. The sanitary facilities are divided between two buildings near the entrance and there is a small swimming pool. Small shop for basics, with shops and restaurants near (1 km).

How to find it: Take Lauterbrunnen/Grindelwald motorway exit, turn towards Interlaken and site is on the left.

General Details: Open 1 May - 25 Sept. 13,000 sq.m. Shop (from 20/5). Children's play area. Small swimming pool (mid June - end Aug). Heated rest room with TV. Bicycle hire. Golf 4 km. Washing machines and dryers. Chemical disposal. Motorcaravan service point.

Charges 1999: Per person Sfr. 5.60 - 6.50; child 3.30 - 4.00; pitch 14.00 - 28.00; + local tax. Credit cards accepted.

Reservations: Write to site with deposit (Sfr 30) and fee (10). Camping Jungfraublick (7), Gsteigsttr. 80, 3800 Matten, Interlaken. Tel: 033/822 44 14. FAX: 033/822 16 19.

948 Camping Gletscherdorf, Grindelwald, nr Interlaken

Small site with good toilet block quite close to town.

On flat ground in a valley with mountains around, this site has a scenic situation with views to the Eiger. It has 120 pitches (80 for touring units), most of which are individual, marked ones in the main section, with an unmarked overflow field. Electrical connections are available (10A). The sanitary block is tiled and of excellent quality with free hot water. However, it is only small and might be barely adequate in peak weeks. However, it is kept very clean and has British WCs, washbasins with shelf and mirror and controllable, free hot showers. There are good walking opportunities in the area and a mountain climbing school in the village. Reservation is essential for July/August.

How to find it: To reach site, go into town and turn right at camp sign after town centre; approach is quite narrow and steep down hill but there is an easier departure road.

General Details: Open 1 May - 20 Oct. for tourists (in winter, seasonal lets only). Small shop. Bicycle hire 1 km. Golf 500 m. Washing machines and tumble dryer. Chemical disposal. Motorcaravan service point. No dogs accepted.

Charges 1999: Per person Sfr. 6.90 plus local tax 2.30; child (6-16 yrs) 3.00; pitch 5.00 - 15.00, acc. to size and season; electricity 3.00 - 3.50. No credit cards.

Reservations: Contact site. Address: 3818 Grindelwald. Tel: 033/853 14 29. FAX: 033/853 31 29.

951 Camping Aaregg, Brienz, nr Interlaken

Lakeside site east of Interlaken.

A very good site in a delightful lakeside setting, Aaregg is suitable for overnight or longer stays. At the eastern end of Brienzersee with splendid views of lake and mountains, there is room for 213 units. The pitches are on flat grass and include 15 of 100 sq.m. with hardstanding, water and drainage. There are some permanent units and the site could become full in high season. Pitches fronting the lake cost more. There is electricity (10A) in most parts and good shade in some. *continued overleaf*

951 Camping Aaregg (continued)

Good sanitary blocks have British style WCs, washbasins (some in cabins), hot showers (on payment) and facilities for disabled people. The site is owned and run by Frau Zysset and her sons.

How to find it: Site is on road no. 6 on east side of Brienz with entrance road between two petrol stations, well signed. From new Interlaken-Luzern motorway take Brienz exit and turn towards Brienz, site then on left.

General Details: Open 1 April - 31 Oct. Shop. Café with terrace. Takeaway in season. Children's play area. Laundry facilities. Chemical disposal. Motorcaravan services. English is spoken.

Charges 1999: Per person Sfr. 6.60 - 7.60; child (6-16 yrs) 3.00 - 3.50, (1-6 yrs) 1.00; local tax 1.60 (child 0.80); tent or caravan 10.00 - 13.00; car 3.00; motorcaravan 12.00 - 15.00; small tent pitch 6.00 - 7.00; m/cycle 2.00; dog 2.00; electricity 3.00; extra small tent 3.00 - 4.00; pitch with services plus 8.00; lakeside pitch (in season) plus 10.00.

Reservations: Made for any period (except Jul/Aug when min. is 14 days) with deposit (Sfr 20). Address: 3855 Brienz. Tel: 033/951 18 43. FAX: 033/951 43 24. E-mail: camping_aaregg@bluewin.ch.

936 Camping Grassi, Frutigen, nr Spiez

Small, quiet site on the road to Kandersteg.

This is a small site with about half the pitches occupied by static caravans, used by their owners for weekends and holidays. The 70 or so places available for tourists are not marked out but it is said that the site is not allowed to become overcrowded. Most places are on level grass with two small terraces at the end of the site. There is little shade but the site is set in a river valley with trees on the hills which enclose the area. It would make a useful overnight stop en-route for Kandersteg and the railway station where cars can join the train for transportation through the Lotschberg Tunnel to the Rhône Valley and Simplon Pass, or for a longer stay to explore the Bernese Oberland. Electricity (6 or 8A) is available for all pitches but long leads may be required in parts. The well constructed sanitary block has good quality installations including British style WCs and also a rest room with TV. There is a kiosk for basic supplies, but shops and restaurants are only a 10 minute walk away in the village.

How to find it: Take the Kandersteg road from Spiez and leave at 'Frutigen Dorf' from where the camp is signed.

General Details: Open all year. 15,000 sq.m. Kiosk. Children's play area. Mountain bike hire. Outdoor and indoor pools, tennis and minigolf in Frutigen. Ski-ing and walking. Washing machine and dryer. Chemical disposal.

Charges 1999: Per person Sfr. 6.20; child 1-6 yrs 1.00, 6-16 3.00; pitch 6.00 - 12.00; electricity 1.50; + local tax

Reservations: Write to site. Address: 3714 Frutigen. Tel: 033/671 11 49 or 671 37 98. FAX: 033/671 11 49.

Camping Grassi Frutigen

Located off the road, alongside the Engstligen Stream, this is the location for the quiet and well-equipped site in the summer holiday resort of Frutigen, about 15km from Spiez, Adelboden and Kandersteg.

- Inexhaustible choice of excursions
- Free loan of bicycles, guided mountainbike tours

Winter camping: to skiing resorts of Adelboden, Kandersteg, Elsigenalp, Swiss ski-school, only 10-12km.

Infos: W. Glausen, CH-3714 Frutigen
Tel. 0041-33-671 11 49/671 37 98

949 Camping Eigernordwand, Grindelwald

Mountain site at the foot of the Eiger.

Grindelwald is a very popular summer and winter resort and Eigernordwand, at 950 m. above sea level, is dramatically situated very close to the north face of the famous mountain in a delightful situation. The slightly sloping pitches have gravel access roads but are not marked out. There are some trees around but little shade, although there are splendid views of surrounding mountain peaks. Being so high it can become cool when the sun goes down. Excursions to the Jungfrau and climbing or walking tours are organised. Some static caravans remain during the winter with about 140 places for tourists in summer. Electrical connections (10A) are available. There is a good quality restaurant and hotel at the entrance. The new sanitary block, heated in cool weather, is of excellent quality and has British style WCs, a drying room and facilities for disabled people.

How to find it: 800 m. before entering Grindelwald bear right past Grund railway station. Turn right over bridge, follow railway line for 500 m. and cross stream to camp on right.

General Details: Open all year. 12,000 sq.m. Restaurant. Hotel. Kiosk for basic supplies. Children's playground. Barbecue hut. Ski lifts, cable cars near. Washing machines. Drying room. Chemical disposal. Motorcaravan services.

Charges 1999: Per person Sfr. 8.00; child (3-12 yrs) 4.00; tent 7.00 - 10.00; caravan 9.00 - 11.00; motorcaravan 9.00 - 12.00; car 3.00; m/cycle 2.00; electricity 3.00 (summer); dog 4.00; local tax 2.70. After 10 days, 1 day free.

Reservations: Write to site. Address: 3818 Grindelwald. Tel: 033/853 42 27.

954 Camping Lido Sarnen, Sarnen, nr Luzern

Good lakeside site in a popular area.

Sarnen is about 20 km. south of Luzern on the main road to Interlaken and is, therefore, ideally placed for ski-ing in winter and sightseeing in summer. The summit of the well known Mt. Pilatus can be reached by mountain railway (the steepest of its type in the world) from Stansstad, or steamer trips on Lake Luzern. The site is on flat ground directly on the lake with lovely views of near and distant mountains. Suitable for long or short stays, it makes an ideal base for this part of Switzerland or for a night stop if passing through. The 220 pitches, 80 for tourists with electricity, are of 80-90 sq.m. on grass with hard access roads (some narrow). There is shade in parts and the location is quiet on the edge of the small town. The exceptionally good sanitary arrangements, heated in cool weather and including a baby room, are in the main reception building at the entrance to the site. Hot water is free to washbasins, on payment in the showers and sinks. British style WCs. The site is part of the town Lido complex with a large, heated swimming pool and child's pool and facilities for non-powered boats. There is a pleasant walk along the lakeside. The restaurant, with large terrace, is self-service at lunch, waiter service at night.

How to find it: Follow signs from southern junction where town road meets the main road from Interlaken.

General Details: Open all year. 20,000 sq.m. Electricity connections (10A). Shop. Restaurant. Tennis. Table tennis. Watersports. Swimming pools. Good children's playground. Room for the disabled. Washing machines and dryers. Chemical disposal. Motorcaravan services.

Charges 1999: Per person Sfr. 6.00 - 7.50; child (6-11 yrs) 3.00 - 4.00, under 6 free; local tax 1.20; lakeside pitch 9.00 - 12.00; inner pitch 7.00 - 9.00; car by pitch 3.00; m/cycle 2.00; electricity 3.00.

Reservations: advised for high season and made with Sfr. 30 deposit. Address: 6060 Sarnen. Tel: 041/660 18 66. FAX: 041/662 08 66. E-mail: camping.sarnen@bluewin.ch.

963 Camping Sémiramis, Leysin

High level mountain site in well known winter and summer resort.

Leysin came to fame at the end of the last century when it was found that the pure mountain air was conducive to the cure of turberculosis. The discovery of antibiotic drugs in 1955 made the lengthy natural treatment redundant and Leysin turned to tourism as a summer and winter resort. At 4,500 feet above sea level in the Vaudois Alps, there are spectacular views over the Rhône valley. Reputably enjoying more hours of sunshine than anywhere in Switzerland, Leysin has become a well equipped resort with ski-ing facilities including a new cable way to a revolving restaurant. The village straggles up the mountain side and Sémiramis is at the start of this. With 125 pitches and on a slight slope with static caravans on the upper level, the meadow at the entrance provides 70 places for touring visitors. No places are marked out and long leads may be required for the 6 or 15A hook ups. There is little shade but the views are breathtaking and mountains protect the camp to the north. There are two sanitary blocks, heated in cool weather, one on the ground floor of the hotel and one next to the snack bar, shop and reception. British style WCs. Free hot water is dispensed through a single tap in washbasins, showers and sinks. Tennis courts and the town's large ice rink (open all year) are next to the camp with restaurants and shops nearby. This neat, compact site has very friendly, English speaking management and provides an excellent base to enjoy the amenities of the region.

How to find it: Take the Leysin road at Le Sepey on the Aigle-les Diablerets road and turn left immediately after the town sign (just past the Subaru garage).

General Details: Open all year. 12,000 sq.m. Shop. Snack bar. Children's play area. TV room in bar. Boules. Table tennis. Badminton. Washing machine and dryer. Chemical disposal. Motorcaravan services. Caravans for hire.

Charges 1999: Per person Sfr. 5.80 - 6.20; child (6-16 yrs) 3.00 - 4.70; tent 3.00 - 4.00; caravan 7.00 - 7.20; car 4.00 - 5.50; m/cycle 2.00; motorcaravan 12.00 - 15.00 or 12.50 - 15.50, acc. to size and season; electricity 2.70 plus meter; local tax 3.25 (child 1.70). Higher prices in winter.

Reservations: Write to site with deposit (Sfr. 50). Address: 1854 Leysin. Tel: 024/494 18 29. FAX: 024/494 20 29.

SWITZERLAND

960 Camping Rive-Bleue, Le Bouveret, nr Lausanne

Site by Lake Geneva with good swimming pool and lakeside installations.

At the eastern end of Lac Léman, the main feature of this site is the very pleasant lakeside lido only a short walk of 300 m. from the site and with free entry for campers. It has a swimming pool (25 x 15 m.), with a water toboggan and plenty of grassy lying-out areas, a bathing area in lake, boating facilities with storage for sailboards, canoes, inflatables etc, sailing school, pedaloes for hire. Also here and, like the lido, under same ownership as the camp, is a quality hotel which at the rear has a cafe for food and drinks with access from the lido. The camp itself has 200 marked pitches on well kept flat grass, half in the centre with 6A electricity, the other half round the perimeter. Two decent toilet blocks with British WCs, washbasins with shelf, mirror and cold water in the old block, hot in the new, pre-set free hot showers with seat and screen, push-button operated but water runs on well.

How to find it: Approach site on Martigny-Evian road no. 21 and turn to Bouveret-Plage south of Le Bouveret.

General Details: Open 1 April - 30 Sept. Shop, restaurant by beach (both all season). Bicycle hire. Fishing. Covered area for cooking with electric rings and barbecue. Drying room. Chemical disposal. Euro-relais station for motorcaravans (Sfr. 12).

Charges 1999: Per person Sfr. 7.20 - 8.70, plus local tax 0.60; child (6-16 yrs) 5.00 - 6.00, plus local tax 0.30; car 1.70; tent 6.10 - 9.70, acc. to season and size; caravan 7.80 - 10.60; motorcaravan 9.50 - 12.20; electricity 3.10.

Reservations: are recommended and made for any length with Sfr. 20 non-refundable reservation fee. Address: Bouveret-Plage, 1897 Le Bouveret. Tel: 024/482 42 42 (reservation 481 21 61). FAX: 024/481 21 08.

971 TCS Camping Les Iles, Sion

Pleasant, well organised campsite in the Rhône Valley.

Sion is an ancient and interesting town on the main route from Martigny to Brig and the Simplon Pass into Italy. Les Iles is an excellent, well organised and pretty site, useful for a night stop when passing through or for a longer stay to explore the region or relax in a pleasant area. Although it is near a small airport, it is understood that no planes fly at night. The rectangular site has 440 level pitches for tourists, 340 with 4A electricity and 22 serviced with water and waste water also. Well laid out, a profusion of flowers, shrubs and trees lead to a lake which supplements the pool for swimming and may be used by inflatable boats. There is a good area of grass for sunbathing and two playgrounds for children. Six good sanitary blocks are spaced around the site with British style WCs, free hot water in washbasins, showers and sinks, as well as baby rooms and provision for disabled people. The site has a popular restaurant with terrace and a well stocked shop (both all year) with others in the town (4 km). A very varied entertainment programme for children and adults is offered in July/Aug. with organised excursions and a wealth of interesting activities near including watersports, mountain biking, para-gliding, etc from Swissraft. English is spoken and the warden is pleased to advise on places to visit.

How to find it: Site is about 4 km. west of Sion and is signed from road 9 and the motorway exit.

General Details: Open all year exc. 1 Nov - 19 Dec. 80,000 sq.m. Electrical connections (4A). Shop. Restaurant. Swimming pool (12 x 10 m. mid May - mid Sept). Children's play areas. Football field. Table tennis. Tennis 100 m. Golf and horse riding 6 km. Good animation programme in July/Aug. and many sporting opportunities nearby. Bicycle hire. Washing machines and dryers. Baby rooms. Motorcaravan service point. Chemical disposal.

Charges guide: Per person Sfr. 5.20 - 6.60; child (6-16) 50%; pitch 6.20 - 22.00; electricity 4.00; local tax 0.80.

Reservations: Write to site. Address: 1951 Sion. Tel:027/346 43 47. FAX: 027/346 68 47.

966 Camping des Glaciers, La Fouly, nr Martigny

Mountain site with first-class facilities and spectacular views.

Situated at 1,600 m. above sea level, Des Glaciers is set amidst magnificent mountain scenery in a very quiet, peaceful location in the beautiful Ferret Valley. Being just off the main Martigny - Grand St Bernard route, it could make a night stopalong this road but as this would entail a 13 km. detour along a minor road, it is more convenient for a longer stay. Those seeking peace, quiet and fresh mountain air or an opportunity for mountain walking would be well suited here. Marked tracks bring Grand St Bernard and the path around Mont Blanc within range, among many other possibilities with an abundance of flora and fauna for added interest. Guides are available if required. The camp offers two types of pitches - about half in an open, undulating meadow with campers choosing where to go and the proprietor advising if numbers require this and the rest being level, individual plots of varying size in small clearings either between bushes and shrubs or under tall pines. Equally suitable for all units from small tents to large caravans. A small stream runs through the site. Of the 170 places, 150 have 15A electricity so a small heater can be used if evenings become chilly. There are three sanitary units, all of exceptional quality and heated when necessary. The oldest and smallest is under reception, there is another in the centre of the open area and a new block in the centre of the site. Hot water is free in all basins (some in cabins), showers and sinks. British style WCs. Each block has washing machines and dryers and the older block a drying room. A special baby room has been incorporated in the new block.

continued overleaf

966 Camping des Glaciers (continued)

An interesting feature of the site is a large, half-oval tent structure with beds and kitchen facilities for the use of those who wish to pack the evening before departure and a new wet weather room has been added for campers. There are sports facilities and swimming pools at 18 and 25 km. but this is, above all, a camp for those who wish to enjoy the mountain atmosphere, get close to nature or walk in the mountains where there are refreshment stops at mountain huts. The charming lady owner, fluent in six languages, is always ready to welcome you and to give information on the locality.

How to find it: Leave the Martigny-Gd St Bernard road (no. 21) at Orsieres and follow signs to La Fouly. Site is signed on right at end of La Fouly village.

General Details: Open 15 May - 30 Sept. 70,000 sq.m. Shade in parts. Small shop. Other shops and restaurant 500 m. Children's playground. Bicycle hire 500 m. Riding 8 km. Washing machines and dryers. Baby room. Chemical disposal. Motorcaravan service point.

Charges 1999: Per person Sfr. 6.00; child (2-12 yrs) 3.50; pitch 10.00 -.16.00; electricity 3.00; dog 1.00. Less 10% in June and Sept. Credit cards accepted.

Reservations: Made without deposit. Address: 1944 La Fouly (VS). Tel: 027/783 17 35. FAX: 027/783 36 05.

AR Discount
Less 5% in high season, 10% in June/Sept.

973 Camping Gemmi, Susten, nr Sion

Small, friendly, family site in Rhône Valley.

The Rhône Valley is a popular through route to Italy via the Simplon Pass and a holiday region in its own right. Enjoying some of the best climatic conditions in Switzerland, this valley, between two mountain regions, has less rainfall and more hours of sunshine than most of the country. It is an area of vines and fruit trees with mountain walks and the majestic Matterhorn nearby. Gemmi is a delightful small camp in a scenic location with 65 level pitches, all with 16A electricity, on well tended grass amidst a variety of trees, some of which offer shade. Some pitches for motorcaravans with water and drainage. The modern, central sanitary block, part of which is heated, is of excellent quality and kept very clean. It has British WCs and free hot water in washbasins (some in private cabins), showers and sinks. Private bathrooms are available for hire on a weekly basis. The pleasant, friendly owner speaks fluent English, maintains high standards and has bucked current trends by establishing a camp for tourists with no resident static units. An attractive wooden building at the entrance includes a well stocked shop and small bar/restaurant where snacks and a limited range of local specialities are served.

How to find it: From east (Visp), turn left 1 km. after sign for Agarn Feithieren. From west (Sierre), turn right 2 km. after Susten by Hotel Millius, then after 300 m. right at sign for Camping Torrent.

General Details: Open 23 April - 9 Oct. 10,000 sq.m. Shop. Terrace bar and snack restaurant. Children's playground. Tennis, swimming and walking near. Fishing 10 km. Riding 2 km. Washing machines and dryers. Chemical disposal. Motorcaravan services.

Charges 1999: Per adult Sfr 6.00 - 7.00; child 1-6 yrs 3.50 - 4.50, 6-16 yrs 4.50 - 5.50; pitch 10.00 - 14.00; pitch with drainage 14.00 - 18.00; electricity 3.00; private sanitary facility 150.00 per week; local tax 0.80 (0.40, under 16); dog 2.00. Credit cards accepted.

AR Discount
Welcome drink.

Reservations: Necessary for high season - no charge. Address: Briannenstrasse, 3952 Susten-Leuk. Tel: 027/473 11 54. FAX: 027/473 42 95.

972 Camping Bella Tola, Susten, nr Sion

Site with good facilities, swimming pool and individual pitches.

An attractive site with good standards, Bella Tola is on the hillside above Susten (east of Sierre) with good views over the Rhône valley. It boasts a good sized heated swimming pool and children's pool (both free to campers) which, like the restaurant and bar overlooking them, are also open to non-campers and so more crowded at weekends and holidays. In the low rain climate of the Valais the pool is naturally much used. Pitches are nearly all on sloping ground which varies in steepness, but extensive terracing is being carried out. Some 200 of the 260 individually numbered pitches have 16A electrical connections. The fullest season is 10/7-10/8, but they say that there is usually room somewhere. The three good quality modern sanitary blocks should provide quite sufficient coverage and have British style toilets, individual basins (some in cabins), with free hot water in some ladies' basins, showers and sinks for clothes and dishes. Torches advised. Further improvements are underway including facilities for the disabled. Very pleasant management. Used by tour operators (20%). Guests are requested to comply with environmental rules by sorting rubbish as directed.

How to find it: Turn south from main road at Susten where camp is signed.

General Details: Open 12 May - 30 Sept. 200 electrical connections - long leads may be needed. Shop. Restaurant. Swimming pool (22/5-19/9). Tennis courts. General room with TV. Baby room. Films, organised sports, activities, guided walks etc. in July/Aug. Riding near. Washing machines, dryers and irons. Car wash. Motorcaravan services.

Charges 1999: Per person Sfr 7.50 - 9.50, plus local tax 0.80; child 2-6 yrs 2.50 - 4.50, 6-16 yrs 5.00 - 6.50, plus 0.40; pitch 10.00 - 25.00, acc. to type and season; electricity 3.50; dog 2.50. Credit cards accepted.

Reservations: will be made with deposit and fee (Sfr. 25). Address: 3952 Susten. Tel: 027/473 14 91. FAX: 027/473 36 41. E-mail: bellatolla@rhone.ch. Internet: www.rhone.ch/bellatola.

SWITZERLAND

969 Camping Swiss-Plage, Salgesch, Sierre

Large, well run site with natural lake, in the Rhône Valley.

This is a good site and is well run by its English speaking owner and, although about half is occupied by static caravans, there are still 250 pitches for visiting tourists. The site is also slightly unusual in that much of the terrain has been deliberately left in its natural state. The wooded section gives good shade and trees and roads determine where units go. There is a central open meadow and some quiet spots are a little further from the amenities. Most pitches, although unmarked, have 10A electricity available. Some new, marked pitches have electricity, water and drainage. One part of the site may be reserved but some space is usually available. The centre of the site has a natural lake which is kept clean and is suitable for small boats (not windsurfers) and bathing - they say the water is tested weekly. It is possible to stroll along the banks of the Rhône. The main sanitary block in the centre has been refurbished to a high standard and can be heated in cool weather. Although the two other blocks are showing signs of age, the total provision should be sufficient. British style WCs, free hot water in basins in the new block, cold in some of the others, and hot showers on payment. Outside the excellent restaurant is a snack bar which offers good grill meals and 30 different pizzas which can also be taken away.

How to find it: From either direction on road no. 9 or more recent bypasses, follow signs for Salgesch which brings you past site entrance 3 km. northeast of Sierre. Care is required to spot first sign in Sierre at multi-road junction.

General Details: Open Easter - 3 Nov. 11,000 sq.m. Self-service shop. Bar/restaurant with terrace. Takeaway food. Lake. Paddling pool. Children's playground. Table tennis. Fishing (on payment). Volleyball. Badminton. Some entertainment in high season. Washing machine and dryer. Chemical disposal. Motorcaravan service point.

Charges 1999: Per person Sfr. 6.30, plus local tax 0.60; child (4-14 yrs) 3.00 plus tax 0.30; pitch 14.00; electricity 2.50; dog 2.00. Less 10% in low season. Credit cards not accepted.

Reservations: necessary and made for any length with deposit. Address: 3960 Sierre-Salgesch (Valais). Tel: 027/455 66 08 or 481 60 23. FAX: 027/481 32 15.

Camping Swiss-Plage, Sierre-Salgesch (Valais) Switzerland

The only camp in the Valais region with its own natural bathing lake (entry free for campers), with temperature around 18°C. Part sunny, part shaded pitches. Well maintained sanitary facilities. Restaurant. Self-service shop. Starting point for innumerable excursions (Val d'Anniviers, etc). Sports centre (tennis, badminton, beach volleyball, sauna, climbing wall, fitness centre, etc) 800 m.

967 Camping de Molignon, Les Haudéres-Evoline

Mountain site with stunning views in the Herens Valley.

The uphill drive from Sion in the Rhône Valley is enhanced by the Pyramids of Eusegeine, through which the road passes via a short tunnel. These unusual structures, cut out by erosion from masses of morainic debris, have been saved from destruction by their unstable rocky crowns. De Molignon, surrounded by mountains, is a quiet, peaceful place where, although there may be some road noise, the rushing stream and the sound of cow bells are likely to be the only disturbing factor in summer. The 100 pitches for tourists are on well tended, level terraces leading down to the river. Some 72 have electricity and are marked by numbered posts. Small shop for basic supplies (mid-July to mid-Sept) and a pleasant restaurant (open all year) with a good menu at reasonable prices. Although this is essentially a place for mountain walking (guided tours available), climbing and relaxing, there is a geological museum in Les Haudéres, which has links with a British University, cheese making and interesting flora and fauna. Skiing and langlauf in winter. The two sanitary blocks, heated in cool weather, have British style WCs, free hot water in sinks and washbasins and on payment in the showers. Good English is spoken by the owner's son who is now running the site, who will be pleased to provide information.

How to find it: Follow signs southwards from Sion for the Val d'Herens through Evoline to Les Haudéres where the site is signed on the right of the road.

General Details: Open all year. 15,000 sq.m. 1,450 m above sea level. Electrical connections (10A). Basic food supplies (1/7-10/9). Restaurant. Small playground. Guided walks, climbing, winter skiing. Fishing. Bicycle hire 3 km. Riding 15 km. Tennis and hang-gliding near. Washing machines and dryer. Motorcaravan service point.

Charges 1999: Per person Sfr. 4.50 - 4.80; child (4-16 yrs) 2.00 - 2.50; pitch 8.00 - 13.00; electricity 2.00; local tax 1.10 (child 0.55). Credit cards accepted.

Reservations: Write to site. Address: 1984 Les Haudéres-Evoline. Tel: 027/283 12 40. FAX: 027/283 13 31. E-mail: camping.molignan@bluewin.ch.

977 Camping Santa Monica, Raron

Neat and compact all year campsite in the Rhône Valley.

We offer several different styles of campsite in the Rhône Valley and now add this pleasant, well tended site which stays open all year. The Simplon Pass is the only main route from Switzerland to Italy which avoids motorways and the need to buy the Swiss motorway vignette. It is also an easy pass for caravans which is only closed occasionally in winter and, even then, this way is possible by using the Brig-Iselle train ferry through the mountain. About half the site is occupied by static caravans and the site's own accommodation, but these are to one side leaving two flat, open meadows, bisected by the hard access road, so do not intrude on the tourist camping area. The 140 level pitches, all with 16A electricity, are roughly defined by saplings and electrical connection boxes. There is a small (12 x 4 m) swimming pool with another smaller one for children and a shop/bar/restaurant (open in high season) in the reception building, with other shops and restaurants near. Being right beside the main road 9, one does not have to deviate to find a night stop but it would also make a good base for exploring the area. It has an air of peace although, being so near the road, there is some traffic noise. Mountain views, close on south side, distant across interesting valley. The single, heated sanitary block is towards the entrance, has British style WCs and free hot water in washbasins and sinks and on payment in the showers. There are facilities for the disabled. Table tennis on site and tennis courts next door. Two cable ways start near the site entrance for winter skiers and summer mountain walkers.

How to find it: On the south side of road 9 between Visp and Susten, signed.

General Details: Open all year. 40,000 sq.m. Electricity (16A). Bar, restaurant and shop (May - Oct). Small pool and child's pool. Children's playground. Table tennis. Bicycle hire. Walking country, cable cars near. Riding 10 km. Motorcaravan service point (Euro-Relais). Chemical disposal.

Charges 1999: Per person Sfr. 5.00 - 6.00; child (6-16 yrs) 3.00 - 4.00; tent (max 3 persons) 7.00 - 8.50; caravan 9.50 - 12.00; electricity 3.00 (winter 5.00); local tax 0.50 (child 0.25). Special offer outside 1/7-15/8: 2 persons (caravan) for 1 week Sfr. 115.00, extra person 25.00, plus electricity. Credit cards accepted.

Reservations: Write to site. Address: 3942 Raron (VS). Tel: 027/934 24 24. FAX: 027/934 24 50.

987 Camping Piccolo Paradiso, Avegno, nr Locarno

Pleasant, popular site in mountain valley setting.

Locarno, in the most southern of Swiss cantons, Ticino, is a very popular holiday area with activities associated with lakes and mountains. Being on the south of Locarno, Avegno is also a good base from which to visit Lake Maggiori and this part of northern Italy. There are a number of very good camps around to which we add this one to give as much choice as possible. During our stay we were impressed with the friendly, happy atmosphere, much of which is engendered by the owner who appears to know visitors who return year after year and greets them enthusiastically. The lively social life revolves around the central bar/restaurant and terrace. However, all noise has to cease at 11 pm. The 300 tourist pitches are on two level terraces in a river valley, marked by numbered stones set into the ground. Spaces are not over-large but seem to suffice. There are 200 electrical connections, in all areas except the areas set aside for small tents. Three sanitary blocks are well spaced around the site and, although not too large, should be enough. Hot showers are on payment. British style WCs. The owner has a hut in the mountains in which campers can spend the night if climbing. Children are welcomed and catered for with two playgrounds, a small pool and organised games in high season making this an ideal family site.

How to find it: From Locarno follow signs for 'Valle Maggia' and then camp signs to site (6 km.).

General Details: Open 1 March - 31 Oct. 4.5 ha. Self-service bar/restaurant (mainly Italian type fast food) with terrace. Children's pool. 2 children's play areas. River bathing. Boating. Table tennis. Volleyball. Mountain bike hire. Entertainment in high season. Washing machines and dryers. Chemical disposal. Motorcaravan services.

Charges 1999: Per person Sfr. 7.00 - 8.00; child (4-14 yrs) 5.00 - 6.00; caravan, motorcaravan or large tent 12.00 - 18.00, acc. to unit and season; medium tent 11.00 - 15.00; dog 3.00; electricity (10A) 4.00.

Reservations: Write to site with Sfr. 50 deposit. Address: 6670 Avegno, v. Maggia. Tel: 091/796 15 81. FAX: 091/796 31 70.

Some sites have supplied us with copies of their brochures

which we are pleased to forward to readers.

See our Brochure Service on page 366

SWITZERLAND

988 Camping Lido Mappo, Tenero, nr Locarno

Orderly but friendly site with good installations on Lake Maggiore.

Lido Mappo lies on the lakeside at the northeast tip of Lake Maggiore, about 5 km. from Locarno, and has views of the surrounding mountains and hills across the lake. A variety of trips can be made from here by car, steamer or mountain lift. The site has its own narrow beach with a frontage of some 400 m., mainly sandy, but the lake, shelving very gradually, has a stony floor. Boats can be brought and left on the shore or at moorings. The site is attractively laid out in rows of numbered pitches, half for tents and half for caravans and mostly split up by access roads or hedges. The pitches (428 for touring) vary in size, those by the lake costing more and most are well shaded. Electricity (10A) is available on all pitches. Although reservations are only made for longer stays, there is a fair chance of finding a place. Five toilet blocks, which can be heated, are always well kept but some are newer than others. They have washbasins, all in cabins for women and some for men, free hot water and British WCs. Facilities for disabled people and a new baby room. With helpful staff who speak good English, it is a quiet site.

How to find it: On the Locarno side of Tenero, a road with sign to camp will be seen leading off the Bellinzona - Locarno road to the south.

General Details: Open 19 March - 24 Oct. Supermarket. Restaurant/bar. Takeaway (high season). Large children's playground. Bathing raft in lake. Fishing. Bicycle hire. Riding and golf 5 km. Washing machines and dryers. Cooking facilities. Refrigerated compartments for hire. Chemical disposal. Motorcaravan service point. No dogs accepted.

Charges 1999: Per unit incl. 2 persons Sfr. 32.00 - 46.00, on lakeside 42.00 - 70.00, acc. to season; extra person (over 3 yrs) 6.00 - 7.00; extra car 5.00 - 6.00; m/cycle 3.00 - 4.00; trailer 4.00 - 5.00; electricity included. Less 5% for stays over 10 days. Credit cards accepted.

Reservations: Min. 1 week (2 weeks lakeside) July/August, or 2 weeks at other times. Large deposit and smaller fee. Address: 6598 Tenero (Ticino). Tel: 091/745 14 37. FAX: 091/745 48 08. E-mail: lidomappo@bluewin.ch.

990 Camping Delta, Locarno

Good lakeside site within walking distance of central Locarno.

Camping Delta is actually within the Locarno town limits, only some 800 m. from the centre, and it has a prime position right by the lake, with bathing direct from the site, and adjacent to the municipal lido and sports field. Boats can be put on the lake and the site also has moorings on an estuary at one side. It has 300 flat pitches of 80-100 sq.m.; they are marked out at the rear but have nothing between them. There are also 30 smaller `student pitches' for those without a car. The single central toilet block is kept very clean and should be about large enough though it could be hard pressed at the busiest times. Hot water is free in the washbasins (some in cabins for women), fully controllable showers and sinks; WCs are British type. Delta is a well run and well situated site. No dogs are accepted.

How to find it: From central Locarno follow signs to Camping Delta, Lido or Stadio along the lake. Beware that approaching from south there are also Delta signs which lead you to Albergo Delta in quite the wrong place.

General Details: Open 1 March - 31 Oct. 65,000 sq.m. Partly shaded. Electrical connections (10A) all parts. Small supermarket. Restaurant/bar with limited menu. Fitness room. Sauna. Children's playground. Table tennis, amusements. Fishing. Bicycle hire. Golf 200 m. Riding 4 km. Washing machine and dryer. Chemical disposal. Motorcaravan service point. Caravans for hire.

Charges 1998: Per person Sfr. 10.00 - 15.00; child (3-18 yrs) 5.00; normal pitch 20.00 - 30.00; lakeside pitch 30.00 - 40.00; electricity 5.00; local tax 1.00. Credit cards accepted.

Reservations: made for any length with booking fee (Sfr. 100). Address: Via G. Respini 7, 6600 Locarno. Tel: 091/751 60 81. FAX: 091/751 22 43. E-mail: info@campingdelta.com.

991 Park-Camping Riarena, Cugnasco, nr Bellinzona

Site with swimming pool between Bellinzona and Locarno.

An agreeable site close to the route from the St. Gotthard to the south, Riarena may appeal both to those who are looking for a convenient night stop and to those seeking a holiday site, as it has a medium sized swimming pool and children's pool. Most of the site is covered by tall trees and it is in a peaceful setting, far enough from the main road to be away from noise. The sanitary block is of good quality and has British toilets, individual basins with shelf and mirror (a few in private cabins) and free hot water in all facilities. It is however small for the size of the site, though showers have been increased to 16 and facilities for disabled visitors added. The 210 pitches (170 for touring units) are now all individually marked with 10A electrical connections available. July is busiest; there is usually space at other times.

How to find it: From motorway exit Bellinzona south in the direction of Locarno. After 10 km. at large roundabout turn to Gudo-Bellinzona for 2.5 km. and follow signs for Cugnasco from where site is well signed.

General Details: Open 1 April - 20 Oct. 38,000 sq.m. Well shaded. Electrical connections available. Shop (15/5-15/9). Restaurant. Takeaway. Play area. Swimming pools (25/5-15/9). Mountain bike hire. Fishing 1 km. Riding 2 km. Golf 10 km. Siesta time 12.00-14.00 hrs. Washing machines and dryers. Chemical disposal.

Charges 1999: Per unit incl. 2 persons and tax 27.00 - 35.00; extra adult 7.00 - 8.00; child under 6 yrs 3.00 - 4.00, 6-14 yrs 4.00 - 5.00; dog 3.00; electricity 3.50. Credit cards accepted.

Reservations: Made without charge. Tel: 091/859 16 88. FAX: 091/859 28 85.

993 Camping Al Censo, Claro, nr Bellinzona

Tranquil site on old Gotthard - Bellinzona road.

A most agreeable, pretty site on the old Gotthard - Bellinzona road, Al Censo is suitable for those wanting a peaceful night away from the motorway. There is a number of permanent caravans, but room for 90 touring pitches, 52 with electricity (6A) on both sides of reception but not marked out. The site is on a very gentle slope amidst mainly mature trees. The two small sanitary blocks are well appointed and should be sufficient even in high season. British type toilets. Warm water is supplied through a single tap into washbasins. Free hot showers. The site is well maintained and regularly cleaned.

How to find it: Well signed at northern end of Claro on old St Gotthard-Bellinzona road. From motorway exit Bellinzona Nord and head north on old pass road. From the north, take Biascon exit and go south on old pass road.

General Details: Open 20 March - 30 Oct. 20 ha. Good shade in most parts. Self-service shop (limited supplies), drinks served. Play area. Unheated swimming pool. Sauna and whirlpool (in season). Games room (3 pin ball tables). Table tennis. Washing machines and dryers. Chemical disposal. No entry to site 12-14.00 hrs.

Charges 1999: Per person Sfr. 7.00; child (1-12 yrs) 5.20; pitch 9.00 - 18.00; tax 1.30; dog 1.00; electricity 3.00.

Reservations: made without charge. Address: 6702 Claro. Tel: 091/863 17 53.

995 TCS Camping Piodella, Muzzano, nr Lugano

Excellent lakeside site with sandy beach.

This modernised site, on the edge of Lake Lugano facing south down the lake must rank as one of the best in Switzerland. There are 210 numbered tourist pitches of good size, with shade in the older part nearest the lake and young trees in the new area. Cars must be parked in the car park, not by your pitch. Roads have been relaid and a marina has been added. The former sanitary block has been refurbished and a splendid new one has been built. This includes a baby room, bathroom for the disabled, British style WCs and free hot water in the washbasins, sinks and good sized showers. As the site is now open all year, these facilities are heated in cool weather. A good, large swimming pool and a child's pool have been added and one can also bathe from the sandy beach. There is a children's playground on a safe base with good, fixed apparatus and two new tennis courts. The site is a short way from the end of Lugano's airport but there appears to be no night flying or movements by large aircraft. There is a new bar/restaurant with a pleasant terrace. Although the site is well placed for exploring Lugano, southern Switzerland and northern Italy, many will be content to stay put and enjoy the facilities of the site.

How to find it: Piodella is on the Bellinzona-Ponte Tresa road; take motorway exit for Ponte Tresa and turn left at T-junction in Agno. Follow signs for Piodella or TCS. Site is at south end of the airport.

General Details: Open all year except 3-14 March and 3-28 Nov. Electricity connections in all areas (4, 6 or 10A). Shop. Bar/restaurant. Swimming pools. Tennis. Day and TV rooms. Children's playground. Washing machines and dryers. Chemical disposal. Motorcaravan services.

Charges guide: Per person Sfr. 5.50 - 7.00; child (6-16 yrs) 50%; pitch 9.00 - 28.00, acc. to season and type; motorcaravan 23.50 - 28.00; local tax 1.25; electricity 2.40 - 4.00, acc. to amps.

Reservations: Write to site. Address: 6933 Muzzano. Tel: 091/994 77 88. FAX: 091/994 67 08.

981 Camp Au, Chur

Satisfactory site on through route in attractive part of country.

This modern site has some 120 individual pitches, not very big (say 60 sq.m.) but all with electricity (10A), and about an equal number of unmarked ones on an open meadow, all on flat grass. The toilet block is also modern and of good quality but would frankly be too small if the site were full. It has British style toilets, washbasins with free hot water, shelf and mirror, hot showers on payment and is heated in cool weather. There are no water points outside the block. Despite this drawback Camp Au is a good site for a night stop or a few days exploring this attractive mountain region. It is rarely full and with much short-stay trade, usually has vacancies. About 400 m. walk away is a sports centre including both an indoor and outdoor swimming pool, and the centre of Chur, said to be the oldest town in Switzerland. is about 3 km. The main entrance to the camp is reached by passing under a bridge with only 3.05 m. clearance - there is an alternative but with only 3.30 m.

How to find it: Site is on south side of town; from motor road take `Chur N' exit from north and continue on main road - signs eventually appear. From south `Chur S' exit and follow camp signs. See above for height limit.

General Details: Open all year. Small shop. Both swimming and tennis centre (next to camp) have restaurants. General room where drinks served. Children's playground. Table tennis. Washing machine and dryer. Chemical disposal. Motorcaravan services.

Charges 1998: Per person Sfr. 6.00; child (6-12 yrs) 3.00; local tax (over 12s) 0.80; 1 or 2 person tent 6.0, 3 or 4 person 8.00, family tent 12.00; caravan 12.00; motorcaravan 14.00; car 4.00; m/cycle 2.00; electricity 3.30 (p/kw. in winter); dog 1.50; local tax (over 12) 0.30.

Reservations: Write to site. Address: Felsenaustrasse 61, 7000 Chur. Tel: 081/284 22 83. FAX: 081/284 56 83.

SWITZERLAND

982 Campingplatz Pradafenz, Churwalden

Mountain site with excellent facilities and services.

In the heart of the village of Churwalden on the Chur - St Moritz road, Pradafenz makes a convenient night stop and being amidst the mountains, is also an excellent base for walking and exploring this scenic area. There are 38 ski lifts serving the district with one starting from the camp entrance both for winter ski-ing and summer walking. Being at 1,200 m. above sea level and surrounded by pine clad mountains, the views are breathtaking and the air fresh and clean. The absence of entertainment on site makes this a quiet, peaceful place although a variety of entertainment is offered in the region. At first sight, this appears to be a site for static holiday caravans but the owner has made a large rectangular terrace at the rear for 50 touring units. This area has a hardstanding of concrete frets with grass growing through and 'super-pitch' facilities of electricity (10A), water, drainage, gas and TV sockets. Cars must be parked in a separate park. A flat meadow is also available for tents or as an over-flow for caravans. Although the gravel road which leads to the tourers' terrace is not very steep, the friendly German speaking owner will tow caravans there with his tractor if this is required. The single sanitary block is half underground and is very well appointed with free hot water in all washbasins (some in private cabins) and sinks, with showers on payment. British style WCs. There is a baby room and another with hair dryers. A warm temperature is maintained all year. Because of its nearness to a ski lift, campers are provided with a key for the block during their stay. The site reports a new restaurant. In high seasons a kiosk at the entrance provides basic food items (village supermarket 300 m. along with other shops and restaurants).

How to find it: Site is 300 m. from the main road, signed in the centre of the village.

General Details: Open all year except 30/4-1/6. 13,000 sq.m. New restaurant. Snacks. General room. Washing machines. Kiosk for basic foods. Restaurants and shops 300 m. Walking. Skiing. Fishing or golf 4 km. Bicycle hire 200 m. Washing machines, dryers and separate drying room. Chemical disposal.

Charges 1999: Per person Sfr. 6.00 - 6.50; child (up to 12) 4.00 - 4.50; local tax 1.80 (child 0.80); caravan 10.00 - 13.00; car 3.00; tent small 4.00, large 8.00; motorcaravan 12.00 - 15.00; electricity 2.00 (meter in winter). Prices higher in winter. No credit cards.

Reservations: Advisable for winter; write to site. Address: 7075 Churwalden. Tel: 081/382 19 39. FAX: 081/382 19 21.

AR Discount
Less 25% in May, June, Sept & Oct excl. tax & electricity

983 Camping Sur-En, Sur-En/Sent, nr Scuol

All year campsite with excellent facilities.

Sur-En is at the eastern end of the Engadine valley, about 10 km. from the Italian and Austrian borders. The area is, perhaps, better known as a skiing region, but has summer attractions as well. At nearby Scoul there is an ice-rink and thermal baths, plus a wide range of activities including mountain biking, white water rafting and excursion possibilities. As you approach on the road 27 and spot the site way below under the shadow of a steeply rising, wooded mountain, the drop down may appear daunting. However, as you drive it becomes reasonable, although the site owner will provide assistance for nervous towers. A level site, it is in an open valley with little shade. They say there is room for 120 touring units on the meadows where pitches are neither marked nor numbered; there are 80 electrical connections. The modern, heated sanitary block near the restaurant, shop and reception building is of a high standard and there is a further small provision in the main building when required. British WCs and free hot water in washbasins and showers. The good restaurant with a covered terrace overlooks the children's play area so that adults can enjoy a drink and keep watch on their children whilst enjoying the mountain views. Entertainment for both adults and children is arranged in July/Aug. and a symposium for sculptors is held during the second week in July. Excursions are also arranged in high season. The friendly, English speaking owner seems to have created a very pleasant atmosphere and although the camp might be used for a night stay during transit, it could well attract for a longer period.

How to find it: Site is clearly visible and also signed from main road 27 to the east of Scuol.

General Details: Open all year. 20,000 sq.m. Electrical connections (6A). Shop (all year). Restaurant (closed Nov. and April and on Tues. and Wed. in low season). Takeaway (high season). Swimming pool. Good children's playground. Bicycle hire. Animation in high season. Golf 8 km. Activities near - see text above. Washing machine and dryer. Motorcaravan service point. Chemical disposal. Bus service to Scuol for train to St Moritz.

Charges 1999: Per person Sfr. 5.80; child (6-16 yrs) 2.90; caravan 13.40 - 15.00; tent 9.90 - 13.40; motorcaravan 13.40 - 15.00. Credit cards accepted.

Reservations: not made. Address: 7554 Sur-En/Sent. Tel: 081/866 35 44. FAX: 081/866 32 37.

985 TCS Camping Farich, Davos

Small, pleasant site on road to the Fluela Pass.

Davos extends for about 4 km. between Davos-Dorf and Davos-Platz between the Fluela Pass and Klosters. A ski centre in winter, Davos has the largest ice rink in Europe and cable cars to nearby peaks. Farich is situated on the edge of Davos-Dorf, at the start of the Pass road and, as the road rises as it passes the campsite, there is some road noise particularly at weekends and public holidays when hoards of motorcyclists race round two passes - Fluela and Julier - with scant regard for other road users. The 90 pitches, mainly under tall pines, are on either side of a fenced river with bridges between. These are not marked or numbered but the centre road and the 50 electricity points roughly determine where units go. A small shop provides basic food and a pleasant bar serves good grill meals. There is a small children's play area, table tennis and bicycle hire, with a swimming pool 1 km. The single sanitary block is at the rear of reception with British style WCs and free hot water in washbasins, sinks and showers.

How to find it: On the main road at eastern end of Davos-Dorf at the start of the Fluela Pass.

General Details: Open 16 May - 28 Sept. 13,000 sq.m. Electrical connections (4A). Shop, Grill meals. Children's playground. Bicycle hire. Table tennis. Swimming pool 1 km. Chemical disposal. Motorcaravan services.

Charges guide: Per person Sfr. 5.80; child 6-15 yrs) 2.90; pitch 5.20 - 13.50; electricity 4.00.

Reservations: Write to site. Address: 7260 Davos-Dorf. Tel: 081/416 10 43.

984 Camping St Cassian, Lenz, nr Lenzerheide

Mountain site with good facilities in scenic area.

Although St Cassian caters mainly for static holiday caravans, it has room for 40 touring units and is suitable for a night stop travelling to or from St Moritz, or for a longer stay. The site is on a gentle slope but the touring pitches (out of 200) are terraced between the statics under a cover of tall pines. Being 1,415 m. above sea level in a north-south valley, this is a peaceful location surrounded by scenic views and abundant sunshine; 140 signed walking paths of various degrees of difficulty start from the site. Although there is no organised entertainment on the site, there are many opportunities at the holiday resort of Lenzerheide Valbella 3 km. Tennis, 18 hole golf course, bars and discos, heated swimming pool and a lake for fishing and watersports are near. Good bus services (with a stop outside the entrance) serve the region and many places of interest are accessible by car. The small, heated, good quality sanitary facility is in the main block which also houses reception and an excellent restaurant. It has free hot water in washing troughs and sinks and on payment in the showers, and British style WCs.

How to find it: Site is 20 km. from Chur on the no. 3 Chur-St Moritz road, between Lenzerheide and Lantsch/Lenz.

General Details: Open all year. Restaurant. Shop for basics. Fishing 3 km. Bicycle hire and riding 1 km. Golf 200 m. Washing machine and dryer. Chemical disposal.

Charges 1999: Per person Sfr. 6.50 - 7.00; child (6-16 yrs) 4.00 - 4.50; car 2.50; m/cycle 1.50; caravan 8.50; motorcaravan 11.00; tent large 8.50, small 5.50; electricity (10A) 2.50 - 3.00.

Reservations: Made with Sfr. 20 deposit. Address: 7083 Lenz bei Lenzerheide. Tel: 081/384 24 72. FAX: 081/384 24 89.

980 Camping Silvaplana, Silvaplana, nr St Moritz

Family run site on edge of lake in the Engadine region.

Silvaplana is situated at the junction of the road from Italy over the Malojapass, the road from northern Switzerland via the Julierpass, and the road which continues through St Moritz to Austria. Camping Silvaplana, therefore, might be useful for a night stop if travelling this way. Although the surrounding scenery across the lake is very pleasant, there is nothing remarkable about the site except that it was reported that a wind blows along the lake most afternoons which is used by wind surfing enthusiasts. However, it is probably the best campsite in the area, with facilities next to the site for volleyball and football and good walking possibilities. There is a shop for basic supplies and a restaurant just away from the entrance which is open all day June-Oct. The site is mainly level and the 200 pitches for tourists are numbered and marked by posts or tapes, with 120 electical connections (10A). To be fair, our visit was the day after they had opened and the brother and sister who had taken over the running from their parents, seemed keen and enthusiastic to make changes. The sanitary accommodation is old, but acceptable, with British style WCs and free hot water in washing troughs, sinks and showers. There are no washing machines for campers but staff provide a laundry service. A fenced river runs through but the lake shore is unprotected (with access for boats to the lake).

How to find it: Look for camp signs on main road to the west of town, entrance to site is by underpass.

General Details: Open 15 May - 15 Oct. 50,000 sq m. Restaurant outside site (June-Oct). Shop. Watersports, climbing, walking, sports centre near, swimming in lake - pool 4 km. in St Moritz. Small children's play area. Fishing, tennis near. Laundry service. Chemical disposal. Motorcaravan services.

Charges 1999: Per person Sfr. 8.00; child 5-12 yrs 4.50, 12-16 yrs 6.50; tent 5.00 - 7.00; caravan 9.00; motorcaravan 12.00; car 8.00; m/cycle 3.00; electricity 2.80.

Reservations: Write to site. Address: 7513 Silvaplana. Tel: 081/828 84 92.

The following sites are understood to accept caravanners and campers all year round, although the list *also includes some sites open for at least 10 months*. For sites marked * please check our report for dates and other restrictions. In any case, it is always wise to phone as, for example, facilities available may be reduced.

Austria	Britain	3045*	Hungary	562	809	8711*	2650
003*	B035	3210	515	563	810	8741	2660
004	B080	3212	516	564	811*	8742	2665
005	B089*	3215	526	567*	813	8750	2675
006*	B091	3235	Ireland	570	814	8751	2700
007	B203	3242	I870	579	815	8752N	2720
009	B303	3245*	I874	580N	818	8755	2740
010	B385*	3260*	I910	584	820	8760	2750
011	B407	3264	I916	588	821	8761N	2830
012*	B557	3280	I964*	589	822	8800	2835
013	B595	3405*	Italy	591	823	8801	2840
014	B851	3410	6037	592	833	8850	2845
015*		3415	6060	Norway	834	8940	2850
016	Denmark	3420	6200	2315	835	8941	2860
017	2020	3430	6201	2350	836	8964	2865
018	2090	3440	6220	2400	837	8980	2870
019	2140	3445	6250	2455	838	9024	
020	2150	3450	6400	2460	840	9025	Switzerland
022		3452	6602*	2475	841	9030	905
023	Finland	3455	6605	2480	843	9035	906*
026*	2903	3470	6610	2490	844	9038*	927
036N	2930	3615	6623	2505	845*	9060	930
044		3620	6663	2510	846	9070	936
048	France	3625*	6665	2513		9081	939
	0200*	3630	6808	2545	Spain	9085	942
Belgium	0605	3650	Luxembourg	2550	8072	9087	946
053	2415	3665*	767	2555	8102*	9089	949
054	3406	3670*	770	2570	8130	9090	954*
056	8101	3675	781	2590	8240	9091	957*
058		3680*		2610	8390	9121	963
059	Germany	3685	Netherlands	2615	8506	9123	967
066	3000*	3690	550		8535	9142*	971*
067	3010*	3705*	552	Portugal	8536	9200	977
072	3020	3710	556	801*	8615	9250	981
074*	3025	3715*	560	802*	8680	9270	982*
	3030	3720	561	803	8681		983
	3035	3725		805*	8683	Sweden	984*
	3040	3850		807*	8685	2645	995*

SITE BROCHURE SERVICE

The following sites have undertaken to supply us with a quantity of their brochures. These leaflets are interesting and useful supplements to our reports and most contain colour photographs or illustrations of the site. If you would like any of these simply cut out or photocopy this page, tick the relevant boxes and post it to us. Please enclose a large, stamped, self addressed envelope (at least 9" x 6", on average, 5 brochures will weigh 100 gms, =31p 2nd class post). Please note that we cannot accept requests over the phone and that our supplies are normally exhausted by the end of August. Send your requests to: **Deneway Guides Ltd, Chesil Lodge, West Bexington, Dorchester, Dorset DT2 9DG**

Austria
- 017 Kranebitten ☐

France
- 0401 Hippocampe ☐
- 0403 Lac Moulin de Ventre ☐
- 0603 La Bergerie ☐
- 1107 Les Mimosas ☐
- 1202 Les Rivages ☐
- 1407 La Vallée ☐
- 1713 L'Ile Blanche ☐
- 2004N Riva Bella ☐
- 2301 Poinsuze ☐
- 2403 Les Périères ☐
- 2409 Soleil Plage ☐
- 2901 Ty Nadan ☐
- 2906 Pil Koad ☐
- 2909 Raguenes Plage ☐
- 3006 Des Fumades ☐
- 3403 Napoleon ☐
- 4409 Chateau de Deffay ☐
- 4501 Bois de Bardelet ☐
- 5801 Des Bains ☐
- 6001 Campix ☐
- 6203 Gandespette ☐
- 6411 Col d'Ibardin ☐
- 8101 Entre deux Lacs ☐
- 8404 Le Jantou ☐
- 8508 Puerta del Sol ☐
- 8603 Relais de Miel ☐

Germany
- 3735 Schonrain ☐

Italy
- 6020 Union Lido ☐

Portugal
- Orbitur Group ☐

Spain
- 8010 Castels Montgri/Mar ☐
- 8035 Amfora ☐
- 8040 Las Dunas ☐
- 8060 La Ballena 2 ☐
- 8072 Les Medes ☐
- 8080 El Delfin Verde ☐
- 8090 Cypsela ☐
- 8102 Mas Patoxas ☐
- 8103 El Maset ☐
- 8120 Kim's ☐
- 8130 Calonge ☐
- 8150 Palamos ☐
- 8160 Cala Gogo ☐
- 8200 Cala Llevedo ☐
- 8230 Beach Camp El Pinar ☐
- 8235 Blanes ☐
- 8390 Vilanova Park ☐
- 8410 Playa Bara ☐
- 8470 La Siesta ☐
- 8480 Sanguli ☐
- 8481 Cambrils Park ☐
- 8482 La Pineda De Salou ☐
- 8483 Tamarit Park ☐
- 8484 Gavina ☐
- 8530 Playa Montroig ☐
- 8535 Cala d'Oques ☐
- 8536 Ametlla Village ☐
- 8540 La Torre del Sol ☐
- 8560 Playa Tropicana ☐
- 8580 Bonterra ☐
- 8615 Kiko ☐
- 8742 La Marina ☐
- 8752 El Portus ☐
- 8753 La Manga ☐
- 8755 Moraira ☐
- 8800 Marbella Playa ☐
- 8960 La Paz ☐
- 8970 Arenas-Pechon ☐
- 9000 Playa Joyel ☐
- 9024 As Cancelas ☐
- 9060 Pena Montanesa ☐
- 9200 El Escorial ☐
- 9280 Sierra Nevada ☐
- Garoa Campings ☐

PLEASE NOTE: These are the sites' own brochures, the contents of which we have no control over. We cannot therefore accept any responsibilities for errors, omissions, inaccuracies or misleading information contained therein. We make every effort to fulfill requests as promptly as possible, but this offer is subject to stocks being supplied to us and still being available at the time of receiving your request.

REPORTS BY READERS

We always welcome reports from readers concerning sites which they have visited. Generally reports provide us with invaluable feedback on sites already featured in the Guide or, in the case of those not featured in our Guide, they provide information which we can follow up with a view to adding them in future editions. However, *if you have a complaint about a site, this should be addressed to the campsite owner, preferably in person before you leave.* When contacting us, please make your comments either on this form or on plain paper. It would be appreciated if you would indicate the approximate dates when you visited the park and, in the case of potential new sites, provide the correct name and address and, if possible, include a site brochure. Send your reports to:

Deneway Guides & Travel Ltd, Chesil Lodge, West Bexington, Dorchester DT2 9DG

Name of Park and Ref. No. (or address for new recommendations):

....

....

Dates of Visit: ....

Comments:

Reader's Name and Address: ....

....

....

....

REQUESTS FOR INFORMATION

For your convenience, we have printed below some slips which you may cut out and fill in your name and address to obtain further information from any of the sites in the guide in which you are interested. Send the slip *to the site concerned* at the address given in the site report, not to us.

ALAN ROGERS' GOOD CAMPS GUIDE - 1999
ENQUIRY FORM

To (name of site): ....

Please send me a copy of your brochure and details of your conditions for making reservations.

We have our own trailer caravan / motor caravan / tent / trailer tent (delete as appropriate).

Name: ....

Address: ....

....

MAP - Austria

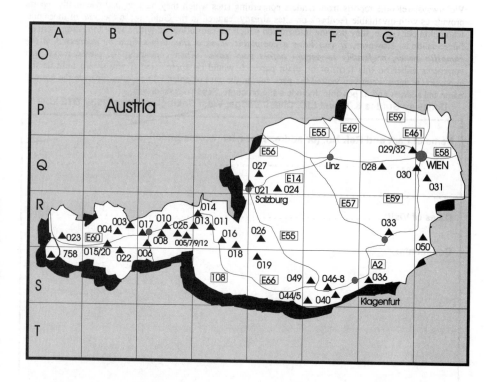

MAP - Hungary

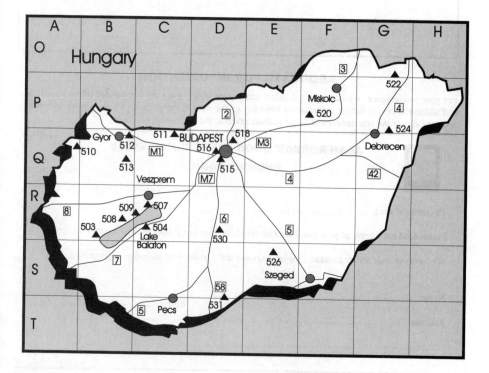

MAP - The BENELUX Countries
Belgium, Luxembourg and the Netherlands

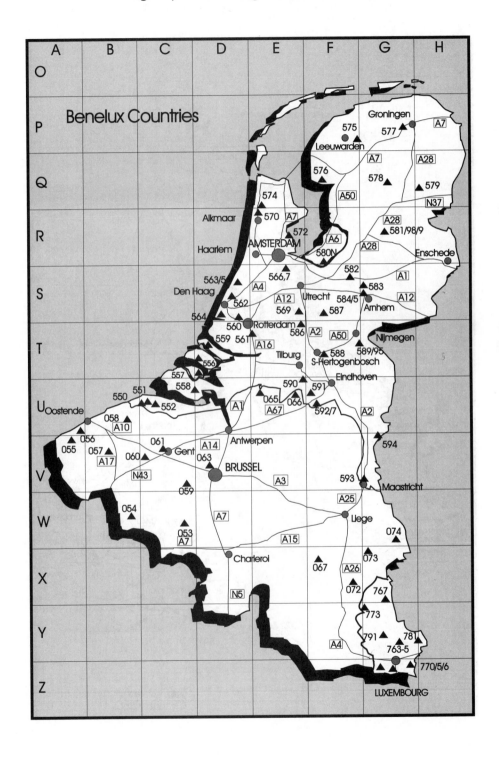

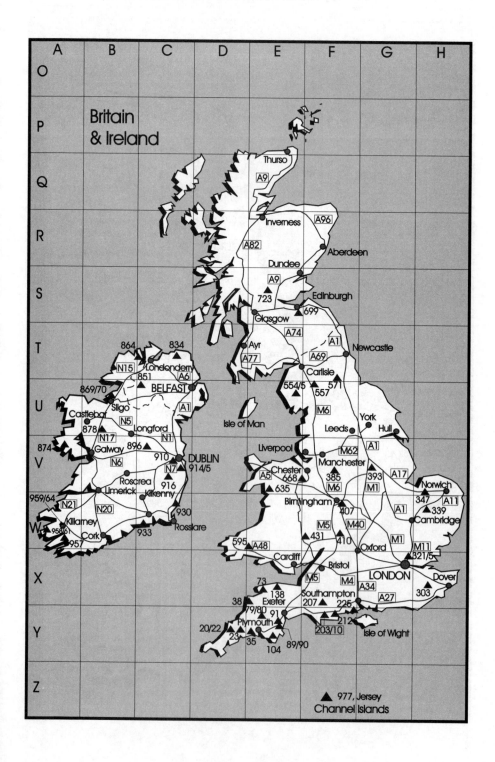

MAP - Denmark

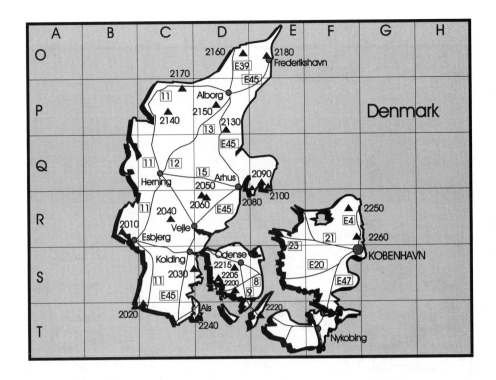

MAP - Finland

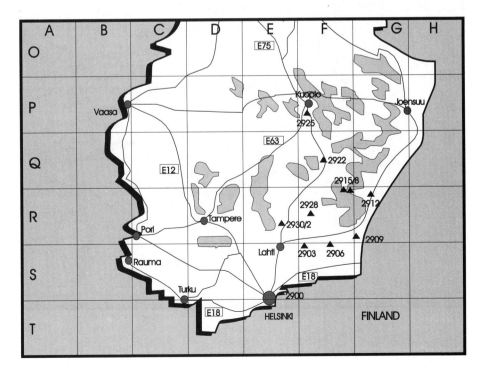

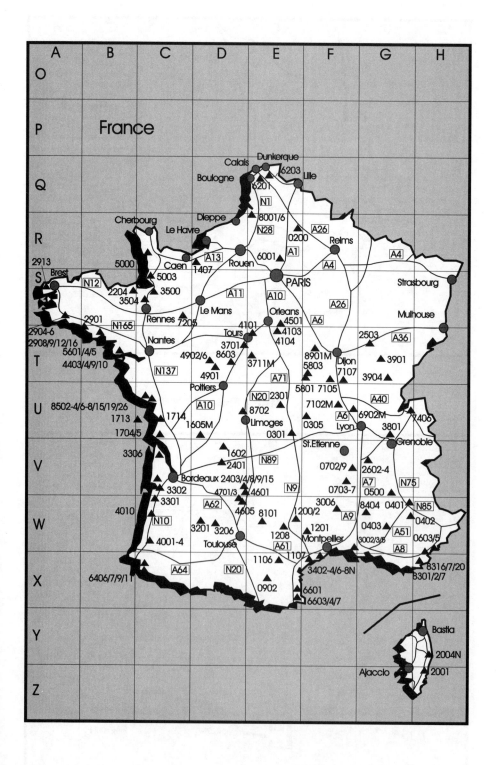

France

Calais — Dunkerque — 6203 — Lille
Boulogne — 6201
N1
Cherbourg — Dieppe — 8001/6 — A26 — Reims
Le Havre — N28 — 0200 — A4
2913 — 5000 — Caen — A13 — 6001 — A1 — A4
Brest — 5003 — Rouen
N12 — 3500 — PARIS — Strasbourg
2204 — A11 — A10
3504 — Le Mans — A26 — Mulhouse
2901 — N165 — Rennes — 7205 — Orleans — A6 — A36
2904-6 — Nantes — 4101 — 4501 — 2503
2908/9/12/16 — N137 — 4103 — 8901M — 3901
5601/4/5 — 4902/6 — 8603 — 4104 — 5803 — Dijon
4403/4/9/10 — 4901 — 3701 — 7107 — 3904
— 3711M — A71 — 5801 7105
Poitiers — N20 — 2301 — 7102M — A40
8502-4/6-8/15/19/26 — A10 — 8702 — 6902M — 7406
1713 — 1714 — Limoges — 0305 — Lyon — 3801
1704/5 — 1605M — 0301 — St.Etienne — Grenoble
3306 — 1602 — N89 — 0702/9 — 2602-4 — N75
2401 — 0703-7 — A7 — N85
Bordeaux 2403/4/8/9/15 — N9 — 0500 — 0401
3302 — 4701/3 — 4601 — 3006 — 8404 — 0402
3301 — A62 — 4605 — 8101 — 1200/2 — A9 — 0403 — A51 — 0603/5
4010 — N10 — 3201 3206 — 1208 — 1201 — Montpellier — 3002/3/5 — A8
4001-4 — Toulouse — A61 — 1107
1106 — 3402-4/6-8N — 8316/7/20
A64 — N20 — 6601 — 8301/2/7
6406/7/9/11 — 0902 — 6603/4/7

Bastia
2004N
Ajaccio — 2001

MAP - Germany

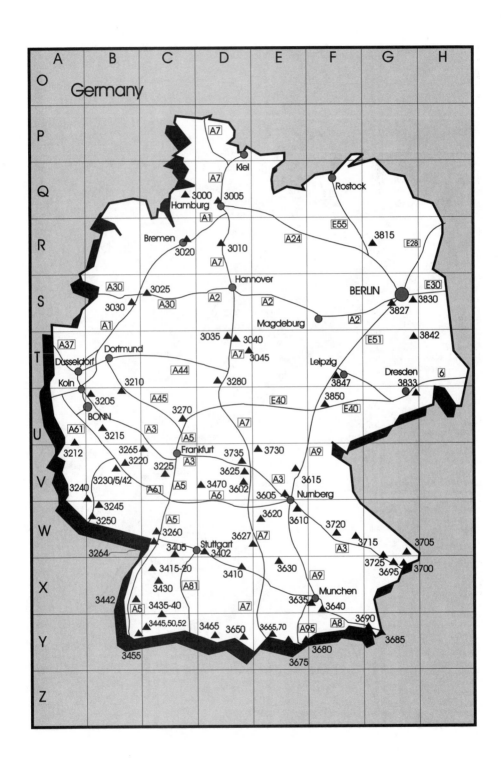

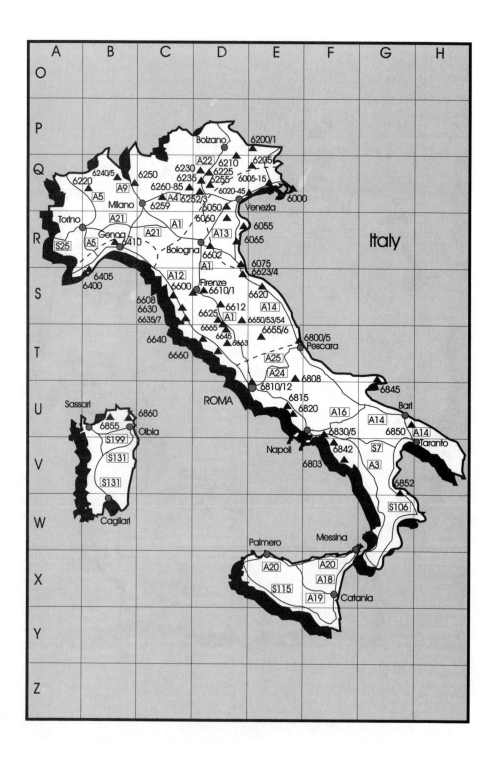

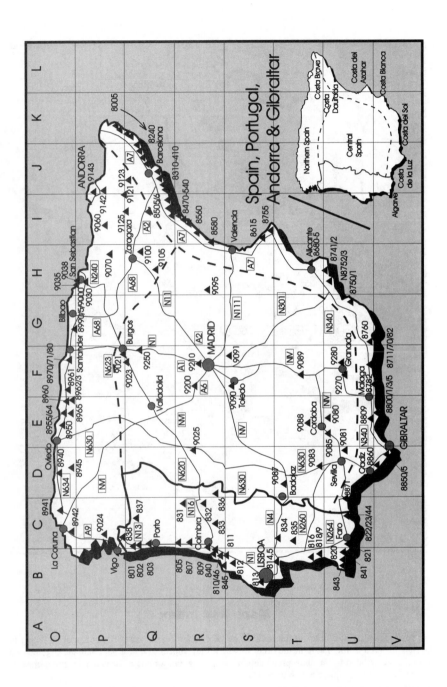

Spain, Portugal, Andorra & Gibraltar

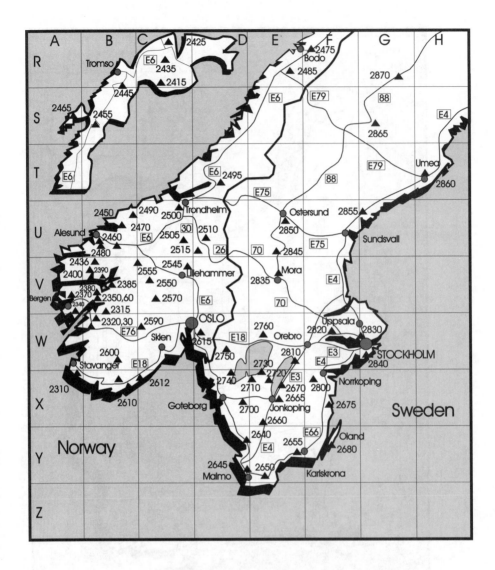

Maps and Index

The Site Index: The Site Index at the back of the guide (starting on page 381) comprises a listing of all the sites featured in this guide in the order in which they appear giving a page number together with a grid reference related to the appropriate country map - e.g. taking Spain for example, site number 9250 is to be found in grid square FQ on page 321.

New sites: Sites that are new to the guide this year are highlighted n bold text in the index.

The Town Index: Comprises an alphabetical town name index to each country giving the names of all the towns where sites are featured.

The Maps: The maps are on pages 368 - 377. These may be used to identify the approximate location of sites; each site is identified on the appropriate map by reference to an individual site number and we include a grid system for each map. One can therefore identify the grid square (e.g. square BY) in which a particular site is situated.

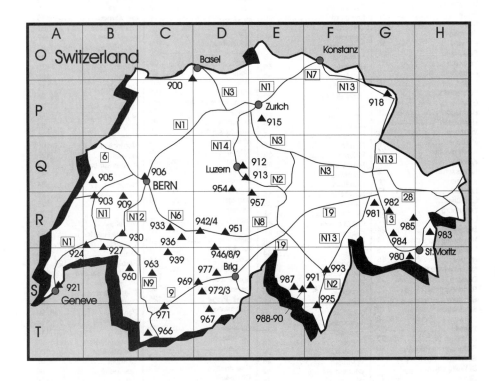

Planning a holiday in Europe ?
Take it easy !

With just one call to Caravan & Camping Service

☎ 0171 792 1944
FOR COLOUR BROCHURE

Caravan & Camping Service specialises in Pitch and Ferry Reservations on carefully selected sites in 8 European countries.

With just one phone call you can book your ferry and make confirmed reservations on any number of top quality sites for your own tent, motorcaravan or touring caravan.

All at great value prices you will find hard to match.

Holidays are tailor made to *your own* requirements and include a complete personal travel pack, with information on driving abroad, maps and guides.

Caravan & Camping Service is a member of A.I.T.O. and all holidays are fully bonded.

or write to Caravan & Camping Service, FREEPOST, 69 Westbourne Grove, London W2 4BR

TOWN and VILLAGE INDEX

379

Index of Campsites

383

8540	La Torre del Sol	IR	..299
8530	Playa Montroig·	IR	..300
N8537	*El Templo del Sol*	*IR*	*..300*
8480	Sanguli	IR	..301
8536	*Ametlla Village*	*IR*	*..301*
8535	Cala d'Oques	IR	..302

Costa del Azahar

8580	Bonterra	IR	..303
8755	Moraira	IS	...303
8615	Kiko	IS	...304
8560	Playa Tropicana	IR	..304

Costa Blanca

8680	Armanello	HT	..305
8681	Villasol	HT	..305
8683	Benisol	HT	..306
8685	El Raco	HT	..306
8741	Florantilles	HU	..306
8742	Int. La Marina	HU	..307
N8752	El Portus	GU	..308
8753	*La Manga*	*HU*	*.308*
8751	*Cuevas Mar*	*HU*	*.309*
8750	Los Gallardos	HU	.309

Costa del Sol

8760	Mar Azul	GU	..310
8770	*El Paraiso*	*FU*	*..310*
8711	Nerja	FU	..311
8782	*Laguna Playa*	*FU*	*..311*
8801	Rosaleda	EV	..311
8805	*Los Jarales*	*EV*	*..312*
8803	*La Buganvilla*	*EV*	*..312*
8800	Marbella Playa	EV	..313
8809	*El Sur*	*EV*	*..312*

Costa de la Luz

8850	Paloma	DV	..314
8855	*Tarifa*	*DV*	*.314*
8860	Fuente del Gallo	DV	.315
8871	*Giralda*	*CU*	*.315*

Central

9280	Sierra Nevada	FU	..316
9270	Suspiro Del Moro	FU	..316
9080	El Brillante	EU	..317
9085	Carlos III	EU	..317
9081	Villsom	DU	..317
9083	Monesterio	DT	..318
9087	Mérida	DT	..318
9088	*Fuencaliente*	*ET*	*.318*
9089	Despeñaperros	FT	..319
9090	El Greco	FS	..319
9091	Soto del Castillo	FS	..319
9095	Albarracin	HR	.320
9210	*Pico de la Miel*	*FR*	*..320*
9025	Regio	DR	.320
9200	El Escorial	FR	..321
9250	Costajan	FQ	..321
9023	De Santiago	FQ	..322

9021	Fuentes Blancas	FP	..322

North

9024	As Cancelas	CP	..323
8942	Los Manzanos	CO	.323
8941	Valdovino	CO	.324
8940	Los Cantiles	DO	.324
8945	*Lagos de Somiedo*	*DO*	*.324*
8950	Costa Verde	EO	..325
8955	Arenal de Moris	EO	..325
8965	*Picos de Europa*	*EO*	*..325*
8962	La Isla	EO	..326
8963	La Viorna	EO	..326
8964	El Molino	EO	..326
8960	La Paz	EO	..327
8971	Oyambre	FO	..327
8970	Las Arenas	FO	..328
8961	El Helguero	FO	..328
8980	Bella Vista	FO	..329
8990	*Molinos Cantabria*	*GO*	*.329*
8995	*Molinos*	*GO*	*.329*
9000	Playa Joyel	GO	..330
9035	Portuondo	HP	.330
9038	Orio	HP	..330
9030	Igueldo	HP	..331
9070	Pirineos	HP	..331
9100	Casablanca	HQ	.331
9105	Lago Park	HQ	.332
9125	Lago de Barasona	IQ	..332
9142	Solana del Segre	JP	...332
9060	Peña Montañesa	IP	...333
9123	El Solsones	JQ	..334
9121	Vall d'Ager	IQ	..334
8506	Serra de Prades	IQ	..334

SWEDEN

	Gothenberg Gateway		335
2645	Råå Vallar	DY	..336
2640	Båstad-Torekov	DY	..336
2650	Skånes Djurparks	EY	..337
2655	Tingsryds	EY	..337
2660	Ågårds	EX	..337
2665	Rosenlund	EX	..338
2670	Grännastrandens	EX	..338
2675	Lysingsbadet	FX	..338
2680	Saxnäs	FY	..339
2700	Borås	DX	.339
2710	Lidköping	EX	..340
2720	Hökensås	EX	..340
2730	Ekudden	EX	..340
2740	Laxsjöns	DX	.341
2750	Sommarvik	DW	.341
2760	Frykenbaden	EW	.342
2800	Glyttinge	FX	..342
2810	Vätterviksbadet	EW	..342
2820	Skantzö Bad	FW	.343
2830	Ängby	GW	.343

2840	Flottsbro	GW	.344
2835	Orsa Grönklitt	EV	..344
2845	Svegs	EU	.344
2850	Östersunds	EU	..345
2855	Flogsta	GU	.345
2860	Umeå	HT	..346
2865	Geilas	GS	.346
2870	Jokkmokks	GR	.346

SWITZERLAND

900	Waldhort	CO	.347
905	Bois du Couvent	BQ	.348
903	Paradis Plage	BR	..348
906	Kappelenbrücke	CQ	.349
909	Avenches	BR	..349
912	Lido Luzern	CQ	.349
913	Vitznau	DQ	.350
915	Seebucht	EP	.350
921	Pointe à la Bise	AS	.350
918	Buchhorn	GP	..351
924	Le Petit Bois	BR	..351
942	Manor Farm	DR	.352
927	De Vidy	BR	..352
946	Jungfrau	DS	..353
957	Eienwäldli	ER	..353
930	Le Bivouac	BR	..353
933	Bettlereiche	CR	..354
939	Vermeille	CS	..354
944	Jungfraublick	DR	.355
948	Gletscherdorf	DS	..355
936	Grassi	CR	..356
951	Aaregg	DR	.355
949	Eigernordwand	DS	..356
954	Lido Sarnen	DQ	.357
963	Sémiramis	CS	.357
960	Rive-Bleue	CS	.358
971	Les Iles	CT	..358
966	Des Glaciers	CT	..358
973	Gemmi	DS	.359
972	Bella Tola	DS	.359
969	Swiss-Plage	DS	.360
967	De Molignon	DT	..360
977	Santa Monica	DS	..361
987	Piccolo Paradiso	ES	.361
988	Lido Mappo	ES	..362
990	Delta	ES	.362
991	Riarena	FS	.362
981	Camp Au	CR	.363
993	Al Censo	FS	..363
995	Piodella	FT	..363
982	Pradafenz	GR	.364
983	Sur-En	HR	.364
985	Farich	GR	.365
984	St Cassian	GR	.365
980	Silvaplana	GS	..365

Maps and Index

The Site Index: The Site Index at the back of the guide (starting on page 381) comprises a listing of all the sites featured in this guide in the order in which they appear giving a page number together with a grid reference related to the appropriate country map - e.g. taking Spain for example, site number 9250 is to be found in grid square FQ on page 321.

New sites: Sites that are new to the guide this year are highlighted n bold text in the index.

The Town Index: Comprises an alphabetical town name index to each country giving the names of all the towns where sites are featured.

The Maps: The maps are on pages 368 - 377. These may be used to identify the approximate location of sites; each site is identified on the appropriate map by reference to an individual site number and we include a grid system for each map. One can therefore identify the grid square (e.g. square BY) in which a particular site is situated.